SPANISH
LAW
DICTIONARY

DICCIONARIO DE TÉRMINOS JURÍDICOS

Spanish-English
English-Spanish

español-inglés
inglés-español

SPANISH
LAW
DICTIONARY

DICCIONARIO DE TÉRMINOS JURÍDICOS

Spanish-English
English-Spanish

español-inglés
inglés-español

PETER COLLIN PUBLISHING

Editorial Team
P.H. Collin
Lourdes Melcion
Roehampton Institute London

Fernanda Chicharro Bernat
Elena Martínez Caro
Universidad Complutense Madrid

Reader
Jorge Díaz-Cintas
Roehampton Institute London

Adviser
Jeroni Sureda
Universitat Autònoma de Barcelona

First published in Great Britain 1999
Reprinted 2003
Peter Collin Publishing is an imprint of Bloomsbury Publishing Plc,
38 Soho Square, London W1D 3HB

British Library Cataloguing-in-Publication Data
A catalogue record for this book is available from the British Library

ISBN 1-901659-09-7

Text typeset by PCP
Printed by WS Bookwell, Finland

PREFACE

This dictionary provides the user with the basic vocabulary used in British, American and Spanish law with translations in the other language.

The subject matter covers criminal, civil, commercial and international law, dealing with situations as different as the solicitor's office, the courtroom, and the prison. The level of languages range from the very formal (including many Latin terms) to prison slang.

The dictionary covers current usage in Britain, the USA and Spain and includes very many examples to show how the words and phrases are used in context and how they can be translated. Comments are also included in both languages to clarify entries that relate to specific legal terms, institutions and organizations of a country where either English or Spanish is spoken and which have no equivalent in the other language.

PREFACIO

El objetivo de este diccionario es ofrecer al usuario el vocabulario esencial del lenguaje jurídico anglosajón y español con sus correspondientes traducciones en la otra lengua.

El vocabulario cubre la terminología relacionada con el derecho civil, penal, comercial e internacional y recoge expresiones utilizadas en una gran variedad de situaciones y escritos jurídicos. El diccionario, sin embargo, no sólo se limita al registro formal sino que también recoge una amplia gama de expresiones y palabras coloquiales de uso frecuente en ámbitos estrechamente relacionados con el mundo legal.

Una innovación importante en este diccionario es la introducción de ejemplos de uso contextualizados que vienen acompañados de sus traducciones correspondientes. Además, se introducen comentarios en las dos lenguas para facilitar la comprensión de ciertos términos específicos que hacen referencia a la legislación, las instituciones y los organismos propios de los distintos países de habla inglesa o castellana cuando no existen traducciones equivalentes en el otro idioma.

USING THE DICTIONARY

The Dictionary aims to provide a clear layout which will help the user find the required translation as easily as possible.

Each entry is formed of a headword in bold type, with clearly numbered divisions showing different parts of speech, or lettered divisions showing differences of meaning.

Words which are derived from the main entry word are listed under that word, each time preceded by a lozenge.

In the English-Spanish section, the headword is followed by the phonetic transcription to illustrate pronunciation.

As far as is possible, abbreviations are not used in the dictionary, apart from the following:

abrev	abreviatura	abbreviation
adj	adjetivo	adjective
adv	adverbio	adverb
EE UU	Estados Unidos	United States
f	femenino	feminine
GB	Gran Bretaña	Great Britain
inv	invariable	invariable
m	masculino	masculine
n	nombre	noun
nf	nombre femenino	feminine noun
nfpl	nombre femenino plural	plural feminine noun
nm	nombre masculino	masculine noun
nmf	nombre masculino o femenino	masculine or feminine noun
nmfpl	nombre masculino o femenino plural	plural masculine or feminine noun
nmpl	nombre masculino plural	plural masculine noun
pl	plural	plural
pp	participio pasado	past participle
vi	verbo intransitivo	intransitive verb
vr	verbo reflexivo	reflexive verb
vt	verbo transitivo	transitive verb
vt/i	verbo transitivo o intransitivo	transitive or intransitive verb
US	Estados Unidos	United States

CÓMO USAR ESTE DICCIONARIO

El diccionario presenta una estructura clara y fácil de manejar. Está dividido en dos partes: español-inglés, inglés-español.

Las palabras principales aparecen en negrita y siguen un orden alfabético.

Las palabras derivadas vienen precedidas de un rombo.

En la segunda parte, los vocablos ingleses que encabezan la entrada van acompañados de su transcripción fonética.

Las funciones gramaticales se introducen mediante números: 1, 2, etc.

Las letras (a), (b), etc. introducen una división semántica seguida de una explicación en cursiva y entre paréntesis.

Las abreviaciones se han mantenido a un mínimo y a continuación se ofrece una lista de las que aparecen:

abrev	abreviatura	abbreviation
adj	adjetivo	adjective
adv	adverbio	adverb
EE UU	Estados Unidos	United States
f	femenino	feminine
GB	Gran Bretaña	Great Britain
inv	invariable	invariable
m	masculino	masculine
n	nombre	noun
nf	nombre femenino	feminine noun
nfpl	nombre femenino plural	plural feminine noun
nm	nombre masculino	masculine noun
nmf	nombre masculino o femenino	masculine or feminine noun
nmfpl	nombre masculino o femenino plural	plural masculine or feminine noun
nmpl	nombre masculino plural	plural masculine noun
pl	plural	plural
pp	participio pasado	past participle
vi	verbo intransitivo	intransitive verb
vr	verbo reflexivo	reflexive verb
vt	verbo transitivo	transitive verb
vt/i	verbo transitivo o intransitivo	transitive or intransitive verb
US	Estados Unidos	United States

DICCIONARIO ESPAÑOL-INGLÉS
SPANISH-ENGLISH DICTIONARY

Aa

abajo *adv* down; **abajo firmante** = undersigned; **nosotros, los abajo firmantes** = we, the undersigned; **hacia abajo** = down; **más abajo** = hereunder *o* thereinafter *o* hereinafter

abandonado, -da *adj* abandoned *o* neglected; *(edificio)* derelict; **las autoridades locales solicitaron una orden de retirada de la patria potestad para la familia de los niños abandonados** = the local authority applied for a care order for the family of neglected children

abandonar 1 *vt (dejar)* to abandon *o* to leave *o* to desert *o (en protesta)* to walk out; **abandonar un caso** = to abandon an action; **abandonó a su familia y se marchó al extranjero** = he abandoned his family and went abroad; **los dos niños han sido abandonados por su padre** = the two children have been deserted by their father; **se divorció de su mujer porque ésta abandonó el hogar** he divorced his wife because of her desertion; **la tripulación abandonó el barco que se hundía** = the crew abandoned the sinking ship **2** *vi (retirarse)* to retire

abandono *nm* **(a)** *(desamparo)* abandonment; **abandono conyugal** *o* **de hogar** = desertion **(b)** *(renuncia)* surrender; *(negativa a aceptar una responsabilidad)* disclaimer **(c)** *(negligencia)* neglect; **los niños habían sufrido abandono** = the children had suffered from neglect

abarcar *vt* **(a)** *(abastecer)* to cater for **(b)** *(informar sobre)* to cover *o* to include

abastecedor, -ra *n* supplier

abastecer *vt (suministrar)* to supply *o* to furnish *o* to cater for; *(atender a un cliente)* to serve a customer

abastecimiento *nm (suministro)* supply

abdicar *vt* to renounce; **abdicar de un derecho** = to waive one's right

abierto, -ta *adj* open *o (sin límites fijos)* open-ended *o* US open-end; *(evidente)* overt; **billete abierto** = open ticket; **cheque abierto** = open cheque; **crédito abierto** = open credit; **cuenta abierta** = open account; **mercado abierto** = open market; **prisión abierta** = open prison

◊ **abiertamente** *adv* openly; **admitió abiertamente que había vendido drogas** = he openly admitted that he had sold drugs

abigeato *nm (robo de ganado)* rustling

abigeo *nm (ladrón de ganado)* rustler *o* cattle thief

abjuración *nf* abjuration

abjurar *vi* to abjure

abogacía *nf* the legal profession *o* the Bar

abogado, -da *n* **(a)** *(asesor jurídico)* lawyer *o* solicitor; *(que actúa en un juicio)* barrister *o* counsel *o* attorney; **abogado criminalista** *o* **penalista** = criminal lawyer; **abogado del Estado** = Treasury counsel *o* lawyer acting as counsel for the State; **abogado de guardia** *o* **de oficio** *o* **de servicio** = duty solicitor; **abogado de turno** = legal aid lawyer; **abogado defensor** *o* **de la parte demandada** = defence counsel; **abogado especialista en derecho internacional** = international lawyer; **abogado especialista en derecho marítimo** = maritime lawyer; **abogado especialista en derecho mercantil** *o* **de empresa** = commercial lawyer *o* company lawyer; **abogado especializado en derecho político** = constitutional lawyer; **abogado principal** = leading counsel *o* leader; **contratar** *o* **dar instrucciones a un abogado** = to instruct a solicitor; **informe de un abogado sobre un caso** = counsel's advice *o* opinion **(b)** **el cuerpo de abogados** = the Bar; **abogado en ejercicio** = member of the Bar; **comenzar a ejercer como abogado ante los tribunales** = to be called to the bar

> El abogado del Estado es un funcionario público que ostenta la representación y defensa de los intereses del Estado

abogar *vi (defender)* to plead

abolición *nf* abolition; **hacer campaña por la abolición de la pena de muerte** = to campaign for the abolition of the death penalty

abolir *vt* **(a)** *(suprimir)* to abolish; **el Senado votó para abolir la pena de muerte** = the Senate voted to abolish the death penalty **(b)** *(abrogar)* to repeal

abonable *adj (adeudable)* debitable

abonado, -da *n* subscriber

abonar *vt (pagar)* to pay; **abonar en cuenta** = to credit; **abonar al contado** = to pay cash ◊ **abonarse** *vr (suscribirse)* to subscribe

abono *nm* payment *o* credit

abordaje *nm* **(a)** *(choque)* collision (of ships) **(b)** *(incitación al sexo)* soliciting

abordar *vt* **(a)** *(arrimarse)* to collide; *(subir a bordo)* to board **(b) (acometer)** = to approach *o* to tackle **(c)** *(incitar al sexo)* to solicit

abortar *vt* to abort *o* to terminate a pregnancy

aborto *nm (interrupción del embarazo)* abortion *o* child destruction; **aborto despenalizado** = legal abortion; **aborto no provocado** = miscarriage; **el aborto ilegal es un delito grave** = illegal abortion is a notifiable offence

abreviado, -da *adj* short *o* abridged *o* brief; **título abreviado de una ley** = short title

abrir 1 *vt* to open; **abrir la sesión** = to call a meeting to order; **abrir un expediente** = to start disciplinary proceedings *o* to open a file; **abrir un proceso** *o* **una acción judicial** = to take legal action; **abrir una cuenta bancaria** = to open a bank account; **abrir una línea de crédito** = to open a line of credit; **volver a abrir** = to reopen; **después de recibir nuevas pruebas, la policía ha vuelto a abrir la investigación sobre el asesinato** = after receiving new evidence, the police have reopened the murder inquiry; **la vista se volvió a abrir el lunes por la tarde** = the hearing reopened on Monday afternoon; **hemos abierto una oficina en Londres** = we have opened an office in London **2** *vi* to open; **abrimos al público los domingos** = we open for business on Sundays; **la oficina abre a las 9 de la mañana** = the office opens at 9 a.m.; **nuestras oficinas abren de 9 a 6** = our offices are open from 9 to 6

abrogable *adj* repealable

abrogación *nf (revocación)* repeal *o (anulación de algún contrato)* defeasance

abrogar *vt (revocar)* to repeal; **los diputados están presionando para que se abrogue la Ley de Extranjería** = MPs are pressing for the repeal of the Immigration Act

abrogatorio *adj* **cláusula abrogatoria** = annulling clause

absentismo *nm* absenteeism

absolución *nf* acquittal; **libre absolución** *o* **absolución incondicionada** = absolute discharge *o* full pardon; **absolución condicional** = conditional pardon

absoluto, -ta *adj* absolute; **dominio absoluto de una propiedad** = freehold property; **monopolio**
absoluto = absolute monopoly; **privilegio absoluto** = absolute privilege; **propiedad absoluta** = freehold; **propiedad absoluta de un inmueble** = fee simple; **propietario absoluto** = freeholder *o* ground landlord; **tener la propiedad absoluta de un inmueble** = to hold an estate in fee simple; **título no absoluto** = qualified title; **interés absoluto** = overriding interest; **filial en propiedad absoluta** = wholly-owned subsidiary

absolutorio, -ria *adj* acquitting; **fallo absolutorio** = verdict of not guilty

absolver *vt* **(a)** *(exculpar)* to clear *o* to acquit; **tras haber sido absuelto, salió del juzgado sonriendo** = after his acquittal he left the court smiling; **el tribunal absolvió a dos de los acusados** = the court acquitted two of the accused; **se le absolvió del delito** = he was acquitted of the crime **(b)** *(liberar)* to discharge; **los acusados fueron absueltos por el juez** = the prisoners were discharged by the judge

absorber *vt* to absorb *o* to take over; **la empresa fue absorbida por una gran multinacional** = the company was taken over by a large international corporation

abstención *nf* abstention *o* forbearance; **la moción se aprobó por 200 votos contra 150, con 60 abstenciones** = the motion was carried by 200 votes to 150, with 60 abstentions

abstenerse *vr* to abstain *o* to hold back; **abstenerse de algo** = to refrain from (doing) something *o* to abstain from something *o* to forbear; **se abstuvo de emprender otra acción judicial** = he forbore from taking any further action; **se abstuvo de firmar el contrato de arrendamiento hasta que hubo comprobado los detalles** = he held back from signing the lease until he had checked the details; **sesenta diputados se abstuvieron de votar sobre la pena capital** = sixty MPs abstained in the vote on capital punishment; **le pidieron que prometiera abstenerse de toda actividad política** = he was asked to give an undertaking to refrain from political activity

abundante *adj (importante)* substantial

abusar *vi (aprovecharse)* to abuse; **abusar de la autoridad de uno** = to abuse one's authority **(b)** *(violar)* **abusar de** = to abuse; **había abusado de menores** = he had abused small children

abuso *nm* **(a)** *(uso indebido)* abuse *o* misuse; **abuso de confianza** = breach of trust *o* betrayal of trust *o* breach of confidence; **abuso de derecho** = abuse of process; **abuso de poder** = abuse of power **(b)** *(delito sexual)* **abusos deshonestos** = indecent assault *o* molestation; **abusos deshonestos de menores** = child abuse *o* sexual abuse of children; **cometer abusos deshonestos** = to molest; **condenado por abusos deshonestos a niños** = a convicted child molester; **se le acusó de cometer abusos deshonestos con niños en el parque** = he was accused of molesting children in the park

acabar *vt (terminar)* to complete; **acabar con** = to break up; **acabar algo a tiempo** *o* **en el plazo previsto** = to meet a deadline
◊ **acabarse** *vr* to break up *o* to come to an end; **la reunión se acabó a las 12.30** = the meeting broke up at 12.30

académico, -ca *adj* academic; **discusión académica (de un caso práctico)** = moot case; **títulos académicos** = professional qualifications

acaparador, -ra *n* hoarder *o* monopolist *o (estraperlista)* profiteer

acaparamiento *nm (atesoramiento)* hoarding *o* monopolizing

acaparar *vt (capturar)* to capture *o* to monopolize

acatamiento *nm* respect *o* observance

acatar *vt* to respect *o* to observe; **acatar la ley** = to abide by the law

acceder *vi* **(a)** *(tener acceso)* to access; **acceder a algo** = to gain access to something **(b)** *(conceder)* to agree; **acceder a una petición** = to grant a request; **se ha accedido a que el contrato de arrendamiento tenga una validez de veinticinco años** = it has been agreed that the lease will run for twenty-five years

accesión *nf* accession

acceso *nm (entrada)* entry; **acceso de paso** = access; **tener acceso a algo** = to have access to something *o* to access something; **se quejó de que se le negaba acceso de paso a la carretera principal** = he complained that he was being denied access to the main road

accesorio, -ria 1 *adj (secundario)* incidental **2** *nm (complementario)* accessory

accidental *adj* accidental; **muerte accidental** = death by misadventure; **un caso de muerte accidental** = a case of accidental death; **el forense dictaminó muerte accidental** = the coroner's verdict was death by misadventure

accidente *nm* accident; **accidente de circulación** = road accident; **accidente laboral** = industrial accident; **accidente mortal** = fatal accident; **seguro contra accidentes** = accident insurance

acción *nf* **(a)** *(acto)* action; **acción colusoria** = collusive action; **acción delictiva** = unlawful act; **acción secreta** = covert action; **acción u omisión** = act or default; **acción u omisión culposa** = actus reus **(b)** *(proceso)* action *o* case; **acción de lesión jurídica** action in tort; **acción civil** = civil action; **acción contra la cosa** = action in rem; **acción**

innegable = estoppel; **acción judicial** = court action *o* court case *o* proceedings; **acción penal** = criminal action; **acción personal** = personal action *o* action in personam; **acción popular** = class action; **acción por daños y perjuicios** = action for damages; **acción por libelo** = action for libel *o* libel action; **acción procesal** = lawsuit *o* legal action; **derecho de acción** = chose in action **(c)** *(participación)* share; **acciones** = stocks and shares; **acciones con garantía** = qualifying shares; **acciones en empresas americanas** = dollar stocks; **acciones liberadas** *o* **cubiertas** = fully paid-up shares; **acciones no redimibles** = debenture stock; **acciones ordinarias** = ordinary shares *o* equities *o* US common stock; **acciones preferentes** = preference shares; **capital en acciones** = share capital; **capital en acciones diferidas** = deferred shares; **capital en acciones ordinarias** = shareholders' equity *o* equity capital; **certificado de acciones** *o* **título de acción** = share certificate *o* stock certificate; **emisión de acciones** = share issue; **número de acciones en propiedad** = stockholding; **sociedad por acciones** = joint-stock company; **tenedor de acciones** = holder of stock *o* of shares in a company; **la empresa ofreció 1,8 millones de acciones en la bolsa** = the company offered 1.8m shares on the market; **compró una serie de acciones de Marks and Spencer** = he bought a block of shares in Marks and Spencer; **las acciones bajaron en la bolsa londinense** = shares fell on the London market

accionario *adj (capital en acciones)* **capital accionario** = share capital

accionista *nmf* shareholder *o* stockholder *o* holder of stock *o* of shares in a company; **accionista mayoritario** *o* **accionista minoritario** = majority *o* minority shareholder; **capital de los accionistas** = shareholders' equity; **el abogado que actúa en nombre de los accionistas minoritarios** = the solicitor acting on behalf of the minority shareholders

acelerar *vt* to hurry *o* to speed up; **los líderes del grupo parlamentario están tratando de acelerar el proyecto de ley a su paso por la comisión** = the government whips are trying to hurry the bill through the committee stages

aceptable *adj* acceptable *o* admissible; **la oferta no es aceptable para ambas partes** = the offer is not acceptable to both parties

aceptación *nf* acceptance; **aceptación de comparecencia por causa de la defensa** = entry of appearance; **aceptación de dinero** *o* **de bienes a modo de satisfacción** = satisfaction; **aceptación de la defensa** = acknowledgement of service; **aceptación de una oferta** *o* **de una propuesta** = acceptance of an offer; **casa de aceptación** = accepting house; **no aceptación de una letra de cambio** = non-acceptance; **no aceptación de una**

solicitud de patente = notice of opposition; **oferta y aceptación de modificación** = accord and satisfaction

aceptante *nmf* acceptor

aceptar *vt* **(a)** *(admitir)* to accept *o* to allow; *(un cheque, una letra)* to honour; **aceptar como prueba** = to admit as evidence; **aceptar la comparecencia del acusado** = to enter appearance; **aceptar una demanda** *o* **una apelación** = to allow a claim *o* an appeal; **aceptar una oferta condicionalmente** *o* **con reserva** = to accept an offer conditionally; **aceptar sobornos** = to take bribes; **aceptó la oferta de un trabajo en Argentina** = she accepted the offer of a job in Argentina; **aceptó 200.000 ptas por el coche** = he accepted 200,000 ptas for the car; **aceptar una firma** = to honour a signature **(b)** *(mostrarse conforme)* to agree; **aceptar hacer algo** = to agree to do something; **después de discutirlo un poco, aceptó nuestro plan** = after some discussion he agreed to our plan

acercarse a *vr* to approach

acertado, -da *adj* **comentario acertado** = fair comment

achacar *vt* *(imputar)* to impute; **achacar la culpa** = to lay the blame

aclaración *nf* **(a)** *(clarificación)* clarification; **el inspector del IVA pidió una aclaración de las facturas** = the VAT inspector asked for an explanation of the invoices **(b)** *(explicación)* explanation; **el texto de la cláusula es ambiguo y necesita una aclaración** = the wording of the clause is ambiguous and needs clarification **(c)** *(glosa)* gloss

aclarar *vt* **(a)** *(clarificar)* to clarify; **la oposición pidió al ministro que aclarase su afirmación** = the Opposition asked the minister to clarify his statement **(b)** *(resolver)* to clear up

aclaratorio, -ria *adj* *(explicativo)* explanatory; **lea las notas aclaratorias antes de rellenar el formulario** = read the explanatory notes before filling in the form

acoger *vt* to receive; **acoger en una familia** = to foster
◊ **acogerse** *vr* to take refuge; **acogerse a** = to pray in aid; **me acojo a la ley más favorable** = I pray in aid of the most favourable rule; **todo el personal se ha acogido al plan de pensiones de la empresa** = all the staff have joined the company pension plan

acometer *vt* to attack *o* to assault

acometimiento *nm* aggression *o* simple assault; **acometimiento y agresión** = assault and battery

acomodamiento *nm* *(acuerdo)* agreement *o* settlement; **acomodamiento entre acreedor y deudor** = composition; **firmante por acomodamiento** = accommodation maker

acomodar *vt* to adjust *o* to accommodate

acomodo *nm* arrangement *o* settlement

acompañar *vt* to accompany *o* to enclose; **acompañar a alguien** = to accompany *o* to go with; **enviaron una carta formal de queja acompañada de una factura** = they sent a formal letter of complaint, accompanied by an invoice

aconsejar *vt* to advise; *(recomendar)* to recommend; **aconsejar en contra** = to advise against; **el asesor jurídico aconsejó solicitar un requerimiento contra los directores de la empresa** = the legal adviser recommended applying for an injunction against the directors of the company; **el director del banco aconsejó no cerrar** *o* **saldar la cuenta** = the bank manager advised against closing the account; **nos han aconsejado llevar a la compañía naviera a los tribunales** = we are advised to take the shipping company to court; **nuestros abogados han aconsejado no demandar al propietario** = our lawyers have advised against suing the landlord

acontecimiento *nm* event; **adelantarse a los acontecimientos para impedir algo** = to pre-empt

acorazado, -da *adj* armoured; **cámara acorazada de un banco** = strongroom *o* vault

acordado, -da *adj* agreed; **según los términos acordados** = on agreed terms *o* on terms which have been agreed upon; **sentencia acordada entre la defensa y la acusación con respecto a los cargos** = plea bargaining

acordar *vt* to agree; **acordar una moratoria** = to grant a delay; **se acordaron las cifras entre las dos partes** = the figures were agreed between the two parties; **se tienen que acordar todavía los términos del contrato** = terms of the contract are still to be agreed
◊ **acordarse de** *vr* *(recordar)* to remember; **¿se acordó de firmar la declaración?** = did you remember to sign the statement?

acorde *adj* in agreement; **acorde a razón** = reasonable

acordonar *vt* *(aislar)* to cordon off *o* to seal off; **la calle fue acordonada después de que se descubrió la bomba** = the street was cordoned off after the bomb was discovered

acosar *vt* *(hostigar)* to harass

acoso *nm* *(hostigamiento)* harassment; **acoso sexual** = sexual harassment; **se quejó de acoso policial** = he complained of police harassment *o* of harassment by the police

acostumbrado, -da *adj* customary

acotación *nf* *(límite)* limit

acreditado, -da *adj* **(a)** *(reconocido)* accredited; **agente acreditado** = recognized agent **(b)** *(de confianza)* reputable; **una firma acreditada de asesores contables** = a reputable firm of accountants; **únicamente utilizamos transportistas acreditados** = we use only reputable carriers

acreditar *vt* to credit *o (certificar)* to certify

acreedor, -ra 1 *adj* **saldo acreedor** = credit balance **2** *n* creditor; **acreedor con garantía** *o* **acreedor asegurado** *o* **pignoraticio** = secured creditor; **acreedor diferido** = deferred creditor; **acreedor hipotecario** = mortgagee; **acreedor no asegurado** *o* **acreedor sin garantía** = secured *o* unsecured creditor; **acreedor preferente** = preferential creditor; **acreedor por sentencia firme** *o* **acreedor judicial** = judgment creditor; **acreedor testamentario** = legatee; **junta de acreedores** = creditors' meeting

acta *nf* **(a)** *(informe judicial)* record *o* proceedings; **acta de acusación** = bill of indictment; **acta notarial** = affidavit; **actas de un tribunal** = record; **actas del proceso** = record of the proceedings **(b)** *(memorial)* **actas** = minutes; **actas de un congreso** = conference proceedings; **libro de actas** = minutebook; **redactar las actas** *o* **levantar acta** = to take the minutes *o* to minute; **el presidente firmó el acta como expresión fiel de la última reunión** = the chairman signed the minutes as a true record of the last meeting; **el presidente firmó las actas de la última junta** = the chairman signed the minutes of the last meeting; **esto no constará en las actas de la junta** = this will not appear in the minutes of the meeting; **los comentarios del presidente sobre los auditores quedaron reflejados en el acta** = the chairman's remarks about the auditors were minuted; **no quiero que esto conste en acta** = I do not want that to be minuted *o* I want that not to be minuted **(c)** *(en un contrato)* **acta adicional** = rider; **acta constitutiva de sociedad** = memorandum of association **(d)** *(certificado)* certificate; **acta de defunción** = death certificate; **acta matrimonial** *o* **de matrimonio** = marriage certificate; **acta de nacimiento** = birth certificate

activamente *adv* actively

actividad *nf* activity; **cambio de actividad** = change of use; **empresa en plena actividad** = going concern; **extender las actividades de un negocio** = to branch out

activista *nmf* militant; **activistas del sindicato hicieron callar a la persona que hablaba** = the speaker was shouted down by militant union members

activo, -va 1 *adj* active; **socio activo** = active partner **2** *nm* asset; **activo circulante** = current assets; **activo congelado** = frozen assets; **activo de caja** = bank reserves; **activo ficticio** = fictitious assets; **activo fijo** = capital assets *o* fixed assets; **activo intangible** = intangible assets; **activo líquido** *o* **disponible** = liquid assets; **activo tangible** = tangible assets; **valor de activo** = asset value; **su activo supera el pasivo** = he has an excess of assets over liabilities

acto *nm* act *o* action; **acto criminal** = actus reus; **acto de rebeldía** = rebellion; **acto delictivo** = offence; **acto ilegal** = malfeasance; **acto ilícito civil** = tort *o* wrong; **acto impugnado** = contested act; **acto jurídico** = legal act; **acto legal realizado con un fin ilegal** = misfeasance; **acto público** = public function; **acto seguido** = immediately afterwards *o* whereupon; **en acto de servicio** = in the course of duty; **en el acto** = forthwith; **hacer acto de presencia** = to attend *o* to put in an appearance

actuación *nf (funcionamiento)* action *o* performance; **carta previa a una actuación judicial** = letter before action; **delito de actuación temeraria** = common assault; **la compañía tuvo una mala actuación** = the company performed badly

actual *adj (vigente)* current *o* present *o* ruling; **trabajo actual** = work in hand; **valor actual** = present value; **¿cuál es la dirección actual de la empresa?** = what is the present address of the company?; **las acciones son demasiado caras al precio actual** = the shares are too expensive at their present price; **extenderemos la factura a los precios actuales** = we will invoice at ruling prices **(b)** *(del presente mes)* **del actual** = instant; **nuestra carta del seis del actual** = our letter of the 6th instant; **su carta del seis del actual** = your letter of the 6th inst
◊ **actualmente** *adv* at present *o* currently; **seis asesinatos que están actualmente bajo investigación** = six murders which are currently being investigated

actualidad *nf* **en la actualidad** = currently

actuar *vi* to act *o* to perform; **actuar como representante de una empresa americana** = to act as an agent for an American company; **actuar de buena fe** = to act in good faith; **actuar en nombre de alguien** = to act for someone *o* to act on someone's behalf; **actuar para la acusación** = to prosecute; **el Sr López actúa para la acusación y el Sr Anglada para la defensa** = Mr López is prosecuting, and Mr Anglada is appearing for the defence

actuarial *adj* actuarial; **cuadros** *o* **tablas actuariales** = actuarial tables; **las primas se calculan por métodos actuariales** = the premiums are worked out according to actuarial calculations

actuario *nm* actuary

acuchillar *vt* to slab *o* to knife

acudir *vi* to come *o* to go; **acudir a las urnas** = to go to the polls; **acudir a los tribunales** = to go to court; **acudir a una cita** = to keep an appointment; **acudir a una llamada** = to come to the rescue

acuerdo *nm* **(a)** *(pacto)* arrangement *o* agreement; *(entre acreedor y deudor)* composition *o* settlement; *(entre dos compañías de seguros)* knock-for-knock agreement; **acuerdo amistoso** = amicable settlement; **acuerdo comercial** *o* **de comercialización** = marketing agreement; **acuerdo de arbitraje** = arbitration agreement; **acuerdo de pago** = accord and satisfaction; **acuerdo entre caballeros** = gentlemen's agreement *o* US gentleman's agreement; *acuerdo entre naciones* = treaty *o* comity (of nations); **acuerdo escrito** = written agreement; **acuerdo no escrito** = unwritten agreement; **Acuerdo General sobre Aranceles Aduaneros y Comercio** = General Agreement on Tariffs and Trade (GATT); **acuerdo privado** = understanding; **acuerdo salarial** = pay settlement; **acuerdo verbal** unwritten *o* verbal agreement; **escritura de acuerdo** = deed of arrangement; **proyecto de acuerdo** = scheme of arrangement; **llegar a un acuerdo sobre los precios** *o* **salarios** to reach an agreement *o* to come to an agreement on prices *o* salaries; **llegar a un acuerdo con los acreedores** to come to an arrangement with the creditors *o* to reach an accommodation with creditors; **llevar a un acuerdo a las dos partes** = to effect a settlement between two parties; **romper un acuerdo** = to break an agreement; **vender (una casa) por acuerdo privado** = to sell (a house) by private treaty; **se ha llegado a un acuerdo** = an agreement has been reached *o* concluded *o* come to; **se llegó a un acuerdo amistoso entre las partes** *o* **se llegó a un acuerdo para no ir a juicio** = a settlement was reached out of court; **las dos partes llegaron a un acuerdo al margen de los tribunales** *o* llegaron a un acuerdo amistoso = two parties settled out of court; **confían en llegar a un acuerdo amistoso** *o* **a un acuerdo para no ir a juicio** = they are hoping to reach an out-of-court settlement; **las dos partes llegaron a un acuerdo sobre la partición de la propiedad** = the two parties came to an understanding about the division of the estate; **retirarse de un acuerdo con el permiso escrito de la otra parte** = to contract out of an agreement; **el acuerdo no es conforme con la anterior sentencia del tribunal** = the settlement is not compliant with the earlier order of the court; **se redactó el contrato con el acuerdo de todas las partes interesadas** the contract was drawn up with the agreement of all parties concerned **(b)** *(negocio)* deal; **acuerdo global** *o* **general** package deal *o* blanket agreement; **cancelar** *o* **anular un acuerdo** = to call off a deal; **fijar un acuerdo** *o* **negociar un acuerdo** = to arrange a deal *o* to set up a deal *o* to do a deal; **firmar un acuerdo** = to sign a deal *o* to sign an agreement **(c)** *(conformidad)* compliance *o* connivance *o* compromise; **de acuerdo** *o* **en**

acuerdo = consistent *o* ad idem; **de acuerdo con** = compliant *o* accordingly *o* in accordance with *o* *(según)* as per; **actuar de acuerdo con** = to follow; **estar de acuerdo** = to concur *o* to conform; **estar de acuerdo con** = to agree with; **no estar de acuerdo** = to disagree *o* to differ; **siento no estar de acuerdo** = I beg to differ; **uno de los magistrados no estaba de acuerdo con el resto** = one of the judges differed from the others; **no hubo acuerdo entre los miembros del jurado y no pudieron dar un veredicto** = the jury disagreed and were not able to return a verdict; **los documentos han sido redactados de acuerdo con las disposiciones de la Ley** = the documents have been drawn up in compliance with the provisions of the Act; **el tribunal ha actuado de acuerdo con el precedente establecido por la sentencia del Tribunal Supremo** = the court has followed the precedent set in the sentence of the Supreme Court; **presento la demanda por daños y perjuicios de acuerdo con las instrucciones de nuestros asesores legales** = I am submitting the claim for damages in accordance with the advice of our legal advisers

acumulación *nf* consolidation *o* accrual; **acumulación de acciones** = joinder; **acumulación de** *o* **del interés** = accrual of interest; **acumulación de provisiones** = hoarding of supplies

acumular *vt* to accumulate *o* to hoard *o* to consolidate; *(interés)* to accrue ◊ **acumularse** *vr* to accumulate; **el juez ordenó que las acciones se acumularan** = the judge ordered the actions to be consolidated

acuñación *nf (de monedas)* coinage

acusable *adj (imputable)* chargeable

acusación *nf* **(a)** *(denuncia)* accusation *o* complaint *o* information *o* imputation; **acusación falsa** = slander; **hacer una acusación** = to lay (an) information; **se ordenó al juez que volviera a oir la acusación** = the justice was ordered to rehear the information **(b)** *(cargo)* charge *o* indictment; **acusación formal en un juicio** = arraignment; **acusación por delito penal** = preferment of charges; **acta de acusación** = bill of indictment; **jurado de acusación** = grand jury; **el secretario del juzgado leyó en voz alta la acusación** = the clerk to the justices read out the indictment **(c)** *(parte demandante)* prosecution; **abogado de la acusación** = prosecution counsel *o* counsel for the prosecution; **negociación** *o* **trato con la acusación** = plea bargaining; **actuar para la acusación** = to prosecute; **el Sr Solana actúa para la acusación, y el Sr Pereda para la defensa** = Mr Solana is prosecuting, and Mr Pereda is appearing for the defence; **las costas del caso correrán a cargo de la acusación** = the costs of the case will be borne by the prosecution

acusado, -da 1 *adj* **(a)** *(pronunciado)* sharp; **caída acusada de los precios** = sharp drop in prices **(b)** *(procesado)* accused; **compareció ante el tribunal acusado de malversación de fondos** = he appeared in court on a charge of embezzling *o* on an embezzlement charge 2 *n* the accused; **acusado, -da ante un tribunal** = prisoner at the bar; **banquillo de los acusados** = dock; **el acusado es una bellísima persona** = the accused is a person of excellent character; **la policía condujo al acusado al juzgado** = the police brought the accused into the court; **todos los acusados se declararon inocentes** = all the accused pleaded not guilty

acusador, -ra 1 *adj* **abogado acusador** = prosecution counsel *o* counsel for the prosecution 2 *n* prosecutor; **acusador fiscal** *o* **acusador público** = public prosecutor; **acusador particular** = private prosecutor

acusar *vt* **(a)** *(presentar cargos)* to accuse *o* to charge *o* to indict; **acusar de un delito** = to prefer charges; **¿de qué se le ha acusado?** = of what has she been accused? *o* what has she been accused of?; **fue acusado de asesinato** = he was accused of murder *o* he was indicted for murder; **se les acusó de asesinato** = they were charged with murder; **se le acusó de conducir por el lado contrario de la carretera** = he was booked for driving on the wrong side of the road; **se le acusó de malversar el dinero de sus clientes** = he was charged with embezzling his clients' money **(b)** *(por escrito)* **acusar recibo de** = to acknowledge receipt of

acuse *nm* **acuse de recibo** = acknowledgement of receipt; **carta de acuse de recibo** = letter of acknowledgement; **servicio de correos con acuse de recibo** = recorded delivery

adecuación *nf* **adecuación a la finalidad que poseen** = fitness for purpose

adecuado, -da *adj* suitable *o* proper *o* appropriate; *(competente)* competent; **lo más adecuado** = best

adelantado, -da *adj* advance; *(en fecha futura)* forward; **ir adelantado** = to be ahead of schedule; **por adelantado** = in advance; **compras por adelantado** = forward buying *o* buying forward; **pagar por adelantado** = to pay in advance; **flete a pagar por adelantado** = freight payable in advance

adelantar *vt* to bring forward *o* to advance; **adelantar la fecha del reembolso** = to bring forward the date of repayment; **adelantar a un vehículo** = to overtake; **han adelantado la fecha de la vista a marzo** = the date of the hearing has been brought forward to March
◊ **adelantarse** *vr* **adelantarse a alguien** *o* **adelantarse a los acontecimientos para impedir** *o* **prevenir algo** = to pre-empt someone; **la fecha de la vista se ha adelantado al 10 de mayo** = the date of the hearing has been advanced to May 10th

adelante *adv* forward; **de ahora en adelante** *o* **más adelante** = hereafter *o* henceforth; **más adelante** = hereunder *o* thereinafter *o* hereinafter; **de ahora en adelante será más difícil evitar registros aduaneros** = henceforth it will be more difficult to avoid customs examinations

adelanto *nm* advance; **un adelanto** = a cash advance

adeudable *adj* *(abonable)* debitable

adeudar *vt* to charge; *(cargar en cuenta)* to debit an account

adeudo *nm* *(asiento del débito)* debit entry; **nota de adeudo** = debit note

adhesión *nf* accession; **contrato de adhesión** = standard form contract; **Tratado de Adhesión** = Treaty of Accession

adición *nf* addendum; **adición a una póliza** = endorsement

adicional *adj* additional; **cuestión** *o* **tema adicional** = collateral issue; **solicitar un seguro** *o* **cobertura adicional** = to ask for additional cover

adicto, -ta *nmf* addict; **adicto al trabajo** = workaholic

adiestramiento *nm* training

adjudicación nf **adjudicación de acciones** = allotment

adjudicar *vt* **(a)** *(conceder)* to award; **adjudicar los daños** = to award damages; **adjudicar un contrato a una empresa** = to award a contract to a company *o* to place a contract with a company; **el juez adjudicó las costas al acusado** = the judge awarded costs to the defendant **(b)** *(asignar)* to allot; **adjudicar algo en una subasta** = to knock something down to a bidder; **se le adjudicó la mercancía por 1 millón** = the stock was knocked down to him for 1 million

adjuntar *vt* to enclose *o* to attach *o* to annex; **adjuntar una factura a una carta** = to enclose an invoice with a letter; **adjunto copia del contrato** = I am enclosing a copy of the contract; **le adjunto una copia de mi carta anterior** = I am attaching a copy of my previous letter

adjunto, -ta *adj* herein *o* herewith; **carta adjunta** = covering letter *o* note; **documento adjunto** = enclosure *o* annexe; **remitir adjunto** = to enclose; **una carta con dos cheques adjuntos** = a letter enclosing two cheques; **de acuerdo con el sistema de pago adjunto** = according to the schedule of payments attached hereto; **adjunto le enviamos el cheque** = please find the cheque enclosed herewith; **le envío adjunta una copia de mi carta del 24 de junio** = attached is a copy of my letter of June 24th; **le envío adjunto el cheque** = please find the cheque enclosed herewith

administración *nf* **(a)** *(gerencia)* administration; *(dirección)* management; **administración pública** = civil service; **consejo de administración** = board of directors; **mala administración** = maladministration *o* mismanagement; **la empresa fracasó a causa de la mala administración de su director** = the company failed because of the director's mismanagement; **trabaja en la administración pública** = he has a job in the civil service **(b)** *(intervención judicial)* receivership; **administración de justicia** = dispensation of justice; **administración fiduciaria** = trusteeship; **fianza de administración** = administration bond; **sentencia de administración** = administration order **(c)** *(el Estado)* **la Administración** = government *o* central government; **Administración local** = local government

administrador, -ra 1 *n* **(a)** *(director o gerente)* administrator *o* manager; *(de tierras)* = land agent; **administrador único** = sole agent **(b)** *(fideicomisario)* **administrador, -ra de una empresa** = trustee; **los administradores del fondo de pensiones** = the trustees of the pension fund; **actuaba de administrador** = he was acting in a fiduciary capacity; **administrador público** = Public Trustee **(c)** *(síndico de quiebra)* **Administrador Judicial** = Official Receiver; **nombramiento de Administrador Judicial** = letters of administration 2 *nf* administratrix

administrar *vt* **(a)** *(gestionar)* to administer *o* to manage; **administrar justicia** = to administer justice *o* to dispense justice; **administrar propiedad** = to manage property; **administrar mal** = to mismanage; **administra grandes fondos de pensiones** = she administers a large pension fund **(b)** *(hacer tomar)* to administer; **se le acusó de administrar un veneno a la anciana** = she was accused of administering a poison to the old lady ◊ **administrarse** *vr:* **la empresa pasó a administrarse judicialmente** = the company went into receivership

administrativo, -va 1 *adj* administrative; *(gerencial)* managerial; **auxiliar administrativo** = office junior; **derecho administrativo** = administrative law; **lenguaje administrativo** = officialese; **personal administrativo** = office staff; **trabajo administrativo** = paperwork; **tribunal administrativo** = administrative tribunal 2 *n* clerk; **administrativo de primera** = junior clerk

admisibilidad *nf* admissibility; **el tribunal decidirá sobre la admisibilidad de la evidencia** = the court will decide on the admissibility of the evidence

admisible *adj* admissible; **los documentos no se consideraron relevantes al caso y por consiguiente no fueron admisibles** = the documents were not considered relevant to the case and were therefore not admissible

admisión *nf* admission; **admisión de culpa** = admission *o* confession; **principio de admisión de pruebas** = rule of evidence

admitir *vt* to admit *o* to accept *o* to recognize; **admitir a trámite** = to allow; **admitir como abogado** = to admit; **admitir la derrota** = to concede defeat; **admitir una firma** = to acknowledge a signature; **no admitir** = to exclude *o* to refuse; **se admiten ofertas** = open to offers; **la empresa admite ofertas por la fábrica vacía** = the company is open to offers for the empty factory; **admitió haber robado el coche** = she admitted having stolen the car; **el tribunal admitió las fotografías como prueba** = the court agreed to admit the photographs as evidence; **se le admitió en el Colegio de Abogados** *o* **como abogado en 1980** = he was called (to the bar) *o* he was admitted in 1980; **la dirección no admite responsabilidad por objetos personales de los clientes** *o* **por objetos de valor de su clientela** = the management disclaims all responsibility for customers' property; **el acusado se negó a admitir la jurisdicción del tribunal** = the prisoner refused to recognize the jurisdiction of the court; **el abogado admitió que su cliente debía el dinero** = counsel conceded that his client owed the money; **el testigo admitió durante el interrogatorio que nunca había estado cerca de la casa** = the witness conceded under questioning that he had never been near the house

adopción *nf* adoption; **hogar de adopción** = foster home; **procedimientos de adopción** = adoption proceedings; **sentencia de adopción** = adoption order

adoptar *vt* **(a)** *(aprobar)* to adopt *o* to pass; **adoptar un acuerdo** = to pass a resolution; **adoptar una medida judicial** = to adopt a legal measure **(b)** (prohijar) to adopt *o* to foster

adoptivo, -va *adj* adoptive *o* adopted; **hijo adoptivo** *o* **hija adoptiva** = adoptive child *o* foster child; **hogar adoptivo** = foster home; **padre adoptivo** *o* **madre adoptiva** = foster father *o* foster mother; **padres adoptivos** = adoptive parents *o* foster parents

adquirido, -da *adj* **interés adquirido** = vested interest; **mal adquirido** = ill-gotten

adquiriente *nmf* purchaser *o* taker

adquirir *vt* to acquire *o* to get *o* to gain; **adquirir una compañía** = to take over a company; **¿cómo lo adquirió?** = how did it come into his possession *o* how did he get possession of it?; **adquirió una experiencia práctica trabajando en un banco** = he gained some useful experience working in a bank; **nuestros productos se pueden adquirir en**

todas las tiendas de material informático = our products are obtainable in all computer shops

adquisición *nf* acquisition *o* purchase *o* takeover; **adquisición forzosa** = compulsory purchase; **adquisición no aceptada por la junta directiva de la empresa** = contested takeover; **oferta pública de adquisición (OPA)** = takeover bid *o* offer; **orden de adquisición forzosa** = compulsory purchase order; **hacer una oferta de adquisición de una empresa** = to make a takeover bid for a company; **retirar una oferta de adquisición** = to withdraw a takeover bid; **la adquisición de García y Hnos por Solá S.A** = the acquisition of García y Hnos by Solá Ltd; **la empresa rechazó la oferta de adquisición** = the company rejected the takeover bid; **la revelación de la oferta de adquisición hizo subir el precio de las acciones** = the disclosure of the takeover bid raised share prices; **la adquisición resultó en 250 despidos** *o* **en 250 empleados sin trabajo** the takeover caused 250 redundancies

adquisitivo, -va *adj* **poder adquisitivo** = purchasing power; **prescripción adquisitiva** = adverse possession

adscribir *vt* to base; **el director de la sección europea está adscrito a nuestra oficina de Londres** = the European manager is based in our London office

aduana *nf* customs *o* Customs and Excise; **artículos sujetos a derechos de aduana** = dutiable goods *o* dutiable items; **declaración de aduana** = customs declaration; **despacho de aduanas** = customs clearance; **oficial de aduanas** = revenue officer; **pasar por la aduana** = to go through customs; **le registraron el coche en la aduana** = her car was searched by customs; **se le detuvo en la aduana** = he was stopped by customs

aduanero, -ra 1 *adj* **depósito aduanero** = bonded warehouse; **registro aduanero** = customs examination; **unión aduanera** = customs union; **mercancías bajo precinto aduanero** = goods (held) in bond; **entrada de mercancías bajo precinto aduanero** = entry of goods under bond **2** *n; (oficial de aduanas)* customs officer *o* customs official

aducir *vt* to adduce; **aducir pruebas** = to adduce evidence

adulterar *vt* to adulterate *o* to falsify; **adulterar la verdad** = to adulterate the truth; **adulterar pruebas** = to falsify evidence

adulterio *nm* adultery; **su mujer le acusó de cometer adulterio con la secretaria** = his wife accused him of committing adultery with the secretary

adúltero, -ra *adj* adulterous; **tuvo una relación adúltera con la Srta. X** = he had an adulterous relationship with Miss X

adulto, -ta *adj y n* adult

adversario, -ria *n* adversary *o* opponent

adverso, -sa *adj* adverse; *(contrario)* perverse

advertencia *nf* **(a)** *(aviso)* caveat; **hacer una advertencia** = to enter a caveat **(b)** *(amonestación)* caution *o* warning; **se colocaron carteles** *o* **letreros de advertencia por toda la obra** = warning notices were put up around the construction site

advertir *vt* **(a)** *(prevenir)* to warn; **advertir al público de la existencia de carteristas** = to issue a warning about pickpockets; **advirtió a los accionistas que los dividendos podían verse reducidos** = he warned the shareholders that the dividend might be cut; **el gobierno advirtió que podrían aplicarse aranceles a la importación** = the government warned of possible import duties; **el juez advirtió al jurado que el juicio sería largo y complicado** = the judge warned the jury that the trial would be long and complicated; **el policía advirtió al conductor que no excediese el límite de velocidad** = the policeman warned the motorist not to exceed the speed limit **(b)** *(aconsejar)* to advise **(c)** *(amonestar)* to caution

aerograma *nm* air letter

afectar *vt* **(a)** *(influir)* to affect *o* to apply to; **las nuevas regulaciones** *o* **reglamentaciones oficiales no nos afectan** = the new government regulations do not affect us; **la decisión del tribunal afectará futuros casos referentes a los trámites de inmigración** = the decision of the court bears on *o* has a bearing on future cases where immigration procedures are disputed; **las ventas de la compañía en el Extremo Oriente se vieron seriamente afectadas por el embargo** = the company's sales in the Far East were seriously affected by the embargo **(b)** *(implicar)* to involve *o* to encumber; **hay un aumento de delitos que afectan a chicas jóvenes** = there is an increase of crimes involving young girls **(c)** *(dañar)* to hurt; **la crítica por parte de la prensa no afectó a nuestras ventas** = the criticism in the newspapers did not hurt our sales **(d)** *(adscribir)* to earmark; **afectar fondos** = to earmark funds **(e)** **en lo que afecta a** = with reference to

afecto, -ta 1 *adj* liable for *o* subject to **2** *nm* affection

afianzado *nm* **(persona que recibe una garantía)** warrantee

afianzamiento *nm (garantía)* guarantee

afidávit *nm (declaración)* affidavit

afiliación *nf* affiliation; **afiliación sindical** = union membership

afiliado, -da *adj* associated; **compañía afiliada** *o* **empresa afiliada** = associate company *o* related company; **las compañías afiliadas a una asociación comercial** = the member companies of a trade association

afiliarse *vr (unirse)* to join

afín 1 *adj (relacionado)* related **2** *nm* relative

afirmación *nf* assertion; *(declaración)* statement

afirmar *vt* **(a)** *(declarar)* to claim *o* to allege *o* to assert *o* to state; **afirma que las acciones son de su propiedad** = she claims that the shares are her property **(b)** *(consolidar)* to firm
◊ **afirmarse** *vr (consolidarse)* to firm

afirmativo, -va *adj* affirmative *o* positive; **la junta dio una respuesta afirmativa** = the board gave a positive reply; **la respuesta fue afirmativa** = the answer was in the affirmative

aflicción *nf* grief *o* bereavement

aforado, -da *adj* privileged; **persona aforada** = privileged person

> Se entiende por aforado la persona que por su cargo tiene derecho a un tratamiento especial ante los tribunales

afrenta *nf* affront *o* insult

afrontar *vt* to confront *o* to face; **afrontar una acusación** = to face a charge

agarrar *vt* to pinch

agencia *nf* agency *o* bureau; **agencia de cobro de morosos** = debt collection agency *o* collecting agency; **agencia de colocación** = employment office *o* bureau *o* agency; **agencia de detectives** = detective agency; **agencia de informes comerciales** = credit agency *o* credit bureau; **agencia exclusiva** = concession; **agencia inmobiliaria** = estate agency; **agencia paralela** = bucket shop; **montó una agencia de seguros** = he set up in business as an insurance broker; **una agencia de contraespionaje** = a counter-intelligence agency

agenda *nf* diary *o* appointments book *o* schedule; **tienen una agenda muy apretada esta mañana** = they have a tight schedule this morning

agente *nm* **(a)** *(intermediario)* agent *o* dealer; *(en finanzas)* broker; **agente autorizado** = authorized dealer; **agente comprador de deudas** = debt factor; **agente de bolsa** = stockbroker *o* accounts clerk; **agente de negocios** = middleman; **agente de seguros** = insurance broker; **agente de viajes** = travel agent; **agente del crédere** = del credere agent; **agente electoral** = canvasser; **agente fiduciario** = trustee; **agente inmobiliario** = estate agent; **agente provocador** = agent provocateur; **agente publicitario** *o* **de publicidad** = advertising agent; **agente secreto** = secret agent; **se estableció como agente libre de seguros** = he set up in business as an insurance broker **(b)** *(funcionario)* officer; **agente de aduanas** = customs officer; **agente de policía** = police officer; **agente judicial** = bailiff *o* process-server

agio *nm* speculation
◊ **agiotista** *nmf* speculator *o* profiteer

agitar *vt* to stir up

agotar *vt* to exhaust; **el apelante ha agotado todas las vías de apelación** = the appellant has exhausted all channels of appeal; **la compañía ha agotado todo el presupuesto dedicado a la expansión** = the company has exhausted all its development budget

agravado, -da *adj* aggravated

agravante 1 *adj* **circunstancia agravante** = aggravation; **hurto con circunstancias agravantes** = aggravated burglary; **daños con agravante** *o* **agravantes** = aggravated damages **2** *nm* aggravation

agraviado, -da *adj* aggrieved; **parte agraviada** = injured party

agravio *nm* **(a)** *(injuria, daño)* tortious act; **agravio indemnizable en juicio civil** = tort; **acción legal por agravios** *o* **acción de agravio** = action in tort; **proceso judicial por agravio** = proceedings in tort; **responsables conjuntos de un agravio** = joint tortfeasors **(b)** *(queja)* grievance

agredir *vt* to attack; **tres hombres armados agredieron al guardia de seguridad** = the security guard was attacked by three men carrying guns

agregado, -da *n* attaché; **agregado cultural** *o* **militar** = cultural *o* military attaché

agresión *nf* assault *o* attack *o* battery *o* aggression; **agresión grave** = aggravated assault; **agresión sexual** = sexual assault; **acometimiento y agresión** = assault and battery; **persona que comete una agresión** = tortfeasor; **los actos de agresión contra la policía van en aumento** = there has been an increase in attacks on police

agresivo, -va *adj* aggressive *o* violent; **conducta agresiva** = aggressive behaviour

agresor, -ra *nmf* attacker; *(persona que comete una agresión)* tortfeasor; **reconoció a su agresor y dio su descripción a la policía** = she recognized her attacker and gave his description to the police

agrupación *nf* association

agrupar *vt* to group together *o* to bracket together; **los delitos de agresión, abuso y acoso sexual están agrupados bajo el título 'delitos contra la libertad sexual'** = the offences of assault, abuse and sexual harassment are grouped together under the heading 'offences against sexual freedom'

◊ **agruparse** *vr* to group together

aguantar *vt (apoyar)* to support; **el mercado no aguantará otra subida de precios** = the market will not support another price increase

aguardar *vt* to await

aguas jurisdiccionales *nfpl* exclusion zone

ahí *adv* there; **de ahí** = therefrom

ahora *adv* now; **hasta ahora** = heretofore; **de ahora en adelante** = hereafter *o* henceforth; **de ahora en adelante será más difícil evitar registros aduaneros** = henceforth it will be more difficult to avoid customs examinations

ahorcamiento nm *(ejecución)* hanging

ahorcar *vt* to hang; **les ahorcaron delante de la prisión** = the hangings took place in front of the prison

ahorrar *vt (economizar)* to save; **el gobierno está alentando a las empresas a ahorrar energía** = the government is encouraging companies to save energy; **está ahorrando para comprar una casa** = she is saving to buy a house; **intenta ahorrar dinero y va al trabajo a pie** = he is trying to save money by walking to work; **para ahorrar tiempo, sigamos con la discusión en el taxi mientras nos lleva al aeropuerto** = to save time, let us continue the discussion in the taxi to the airport

ahorro *nm* saving; **Caja Postal de Ahorros** = National Savings

aislacionismo *nm* isolationism

aislacionista *nmf* isolationist

aisladamente *adv (sin nadie más)* in isolation

aislamiento *nm* isolation; **política de aislamiento** = splendid isolation

aislar *vt* **(a)** *(separar)* to isolate; *(acordonar)* to seal off; **la policía aisló todas las carreteras que conducían a la ciudad** = police sealed off all roads leading to the town **(b)** *(boicotear)* to boycott

ajeno, -na *adj* **(a)** *(de otro)* somebody else's **(b)** *(impropio)* **ajeno al caso** = immaterial

ajustar *vt* to adjust; *(regular)* to regulate; **ajustar cuentas** = to get even

◊ **ajustarse** *vr (estar de acuerdo)* to conform; *(atenerse a)* **ajustarse a** = to hold to; **el proyecto de ley propuesto se ajusta a las recomendaciones de la Asociación de Consumidores** = the proposed Bill conforms to the recommendations of the Consumers' Association; **se le criticó por no ajustarse a las normas** = he was criticized for non-conformance with the regulations; **trataremos de que se ajuste al contrato** = we will try to hold him to the contract

ajuste *nm (acuerdo)* adjustment *o* arrangement; **ajuste de cuentas** = settlement; *(uso figurativo)* **todos los indicios apuntan a que se trata de un ajuste de cuentas** = the indications are that it is an underworld killing; **ajuste de los precios** = price fixing

ajusticiar *vt* to execute

alarma *nf* alarm; **alarma antirrobo** = burglar alarm; **alarma contra incendios** = fire alarm; **al introducir la mano por la ventana, activó la alarma antirrobo** = as he put his hand through the window he set off the burglar alarm

albacea *nmf* personal representative; **albacea testamentario** = administrator *o* executor *o (ejecutora testamentaria)* executrix; **albacea universal** = general executor; **le nombraron albacea testamentario de su hermano** = he was named executor of his brother's will; **se comunicó al albacea la legalidad del testamento** = the executor was granted probate *o* obtained a grant of probate

albaceazgo *nm (fideicomiso)* trust; **establecieron un albaceazgo familiar para sus nietos** = they set up a family trust for their grandchildren

albarán *nm* delivery note *o* invoice

albedrío *nm (arbitrio)* discretion

albergar *vt* to harbour

alborotador, -ra **1** *adj (escandaloso)* disorderly; **le acusaron de borracho y alborotador** = he was charged with being drunk and disorderly **2** *n* troublemaker; *(manifestante)* rioter; *(gamberro)* hooligan; **los alborotadores efectuaron destrozos en bancos y oficinas de correos** = rioters attacked the banks and post offices

alboroto *nm (disturbio)* disturbance *o* mayhem; **le acusaron de armar alboroto en la biblioteca pública** = he was accused of making a disturbance in the public library

alcahueta *nf* bawd *o* procuress

alcahuete *nm* pimp *o* procurer

alcalde *nm* mayor; **alcalde de una gran ciudad** = Lord Mayor; **relativo al alcalde** = mayoral
◊ **alcaldesa** *nf* mayoress
◊ **alcaldía** *nf* mayorality *o* mayor's office

El alcalde preside el ayuntamiento o gobierno de un municipio. Es elegido por los concejales

alcance *nm (ámbito)* scope; *(competencia de una ley parlamentaria)* purview

alcanzar *vt* to reach; **alcanzar algo** = to gain access to something

alcohol *nm* alcohol; **conducir con imprudencia bajo los efectos del alcohol** = drunken driving; **someter a la prueba del alcohol** = to breathalyse
◊ **alcoholemia** *nf* blood-level of alcohol; **medir el grado de alcoholemia** = to breathalyse; **prueba de alcoholemia** = breath test
◊ **alcohólico, -ca 1** *adj* addicted to alcohol *o* alcoholic **2** *n* alcoholic
◊ **alcoholímetro** *nm* breathalyser

aleatorio, -ria *adj* aleatory; **contrato aleatorio** = aleatory contract

alegación *nf* (a) *(alegato)* allegation *o* plea *o* pleadings *o* affirmation; *(en respuesta a la defensa)* reply; **alegación de culpabilidad** = plea of guilty; **alegación de inocencia** = plea of not guilty; **el juez consideró que las alegaciones del demandado no revelaban objeto de litigio** = the judge found that the plaintiff's pleadings disclosed no cause of action; **las alegaciones se deben presentar ante el tribunal cuando la acción esté fijada para juicio** = pleadings must be submitted to the court when the action is set down for trial; **los daños se especifican en las alegaciones** = the damage is itemized in the pleading

alegar *vi* (a) *(invocar)* to allege *o* to adduce *o* to argue; **alegar ignorancia** = to plead ignorance; **alegar pruebas** = to submit evidence; **'la defensa no tiene nada más que alegar'** = the defence rests its case; **la defensa alegó que el acusado estaba en la casa cuando se cometió el delito** = the defence alleged that the accused was in the house when the crime was committed; **el acusador particular alegó razones en contra de conceder la libertad bajo fianza** = the private prosecutor argued against granting bail; **el abogado alegó que el acusado no tenía argumentos para defenderse** = counsel submitted that the defendant had no case to answer; **se alegó que el derecho a la legítima defensa sólo puede ser posible contra un acto de agresión delictiva** = it was submitted that the right of self-defence can be available only against unlawful attack **(b)** *(declarar)* to claim *o* to aver *o* to affirm

alegato *nm* (a) allegation *o* plea *o* pleading *o* submission; **hacer un alegato** = to plead; **alegato en favor del acusado para atenuar la pena** = plea in mitigation; **el alegato ha terminado** = the case rests; **la defensa presentó sus alegatos** = defence counsel put his case; **el tribunal oyó el alegato de la defensa que no había acusación a la que responder** = the court heard the submission of defence counsel that there was no case to answer *o* in the submission of defence counsel there was no case to answer; **los alegatos en contra del acusado son muy convincentes** *o* **existen argumentos de peso en contra del acusado** = there is a strong case against the accused

alentar *vt (estimular)* to encourage

alertar *vt* to warn *o* to alert

alevosía *nf* aggravating circumstance *o* breach of trust; **con alevosía** = maliciously

La alevosía consiste en un agravante en la comisión de un delito contra las personas, mediante el cual el delincuente busca la ocasión adecuada que impide la defensa del atacado (CP art° 22.1)

alfabético, -ca *adj* alphabetical; **guía alfabética** = classified directory; **orden alfabético** = alphabetical order; **se leyeron los nombres de los acusados por orden alfabético** = the names of the accused were read out in alphabetical order

alfabeto *nm* alphabet

alguacil, -la *n* bailiff

alguno, -na *adj y pron* some *o* several NOTA: **algún** delante de nm

alienación *nm* mental derangement

aliento *nm (respiración)* breath

alijo *nm* cache *o* smuggled goods; **alijo de armas** = consignment of smuggled arms; **alijo de drogas** = cache of drugs; **éste es, con mucho, el mayor alijo de drogas que hemos aprehendido** = this is easily the largest consignment of drugs we have seized

alimentación *nf* feed; **alimentación de hojas sueltas** = sheet feed; **alimentación de papel continuo** = continuous feed

alimentar *vt (introducir información en un ordenador)* to feed

alimenticia *adj* **pensión alimenticia** = alimony; **pensión alimenticia pagadera tras la separación o el divorcio** palimony; **pensión alimenticia durante el litigio** = alimony pending suit *o* pendente lite

alistamiento *nm* recruitment *o* conscription

alistar *vt* to enlist *o* to conscript

aliviar *vt* to relieve *o* to mitigate

alivio *nm* relief

allá *adv* there; **más allá de** = beyond

allanamiento *nm* **allanamiento de morada** = forcible entry *o* breaking and entering *o* housebreaking; **robar con allanamiento de morada** = to burgle; **robo con allanamiento de morada** = burglary; **robo con armas y allanamiento de morada** = aggravated burglary; **se le acusó de allanamiento de morada** = he was charged with breaking and entering

El allanamiento de morada consiste en la entrada o permanencia en morada ajena contra la voluntad expresa o tácita del morador.

allí *adv* there; **de allí** = therefrom; **allí dentro** = therein

almacén *nm* warehouse *o* depository; **en almacén** = in stock; **precio en** *o* **de almacén** = price ex warehouse

almacenaje *nm* warehousing; **almacenaje en depósito aduanero** = warehousing in bond; **los costes de almacenaje están subiendo rápidamente** = warehousing costs are rising rapidly

almacenamiento *nm* storage; **capacidad de almacenamiento** = storage capacity

almacenar *vt* to warehouse; *(tener existencias)* to stock

Almirantazgo *nm* **Almirantazgo británico** = Admiralty

alojamiento *nm (vivienda)* dwelling

alojarse *vr (hospedarse)* to stay

alquilado, -da *adj* hired *o* rented; **avión alquilado** = chartered plane; **coche alquilado** = hire car *o* hired car; **propiedad alquilada** = tenement; **conducían un coche alquilado cuando la policía les detuvo** = they were driving a rented car when they were stopped by the police; **todos los coches de nuestra empresa son alquilados** = all our company cars are leased; **tiene alquilada una oficina en el centro de la ciudad** = he rents an office in the centre of town

alquilar *vt* **(a)** *(tomar en arriendo)* to lease *o* to hire *o* to rent; **alquilar material** = to lease equipment; **alquilar un autobús** = to charter a bus; **alquilar un coche** *o* **una grúa** = to hire a car *o* a crane; **alquilar una oficina** *o* **un coche** = to rent an office *o* a car; **alquilar una oficina a una compañía de seguros** = to lease an office from an insurance company; **alquilaron la oficina por un breve periodo de tiempo** = they took the office on a short let **(b)** *(ceder en arriendo)* to lease *o* to hire *o* to rent (out)

alquilar coches *o* **herramientas a otros** = to hire out cars *o* equipment; **alquilar una oficina** = to let an office; **alquilamos parte del edificio a una empresa americana** = we rented part of the building to an American company; **propiedad amueblada** *o* **local amueblado para alquilar** furnished lettings

alquiler *nm* **(a)** *(renta)* rent; *(arrendamiento)* rental; **alquiler anual de una propiedad** = rack rent; **alquiler atrasado** = back rent; **alquiler barato** *o* **alquiler elevado** = low rent *o* high rent; **alquiler exagerado** *o* **exorbitante** = rack rent; **alquiler nominal** = peppercorn rent; **control gubernamental sobre precios de alquiler** = rent controls; **renta por alquiler** *o* **ingresos por alquiler** = income from rents *o* rent income *o* rental

income *o* income from rentals; **subsidio estatal destinado a pagar el alquiler** = rent allowance *o* rent rebate; **pagar tres meses de alquiler por adelantado** = to pay three months' rent in advance **(b)** *(arriendo)* hire *o (flete)* chartering; **alquiler con derecho a compra** = leasehold enfranchisement; **agencia de alquiler de la propiedad** *o* **de viviendas** = letting agency; **coche de alquiler** = hire car *o* hired car; **compañía de alquiler de coches** = car hire firm; **edificio de apartamentos en alquiler** = tenement; **oficinas en alquiler** = offices to let; **(periodo de) alquiler** = let *o* tenancy; **la empresa se ha pasado al campo del alquiler de coches** = the company has branched out into car leasing; **una empresa de alquiler de ordenadores con opción de compra** = a computer-leasing company

alrededor *(prep)* around *o* about; *(cerca de)* **alrededor de** = in the neighbourhood of; **la parte superior de la mesa mide alrededor de 51 cm** = the top of the table is about 20 inches high

alta *nf* **(a)** *(certificado médico)* discharge from hospital **(b)** **darse de alta** =; *(en el trabajo)* to return to work; *(en una asociación)* to join; **dar una propiedad de alta** = to register a property

altamente *adv* highly; **altamente cualificado** = highly qualified; **todos nuestros empleados están altamente cualificados** = all our staff are highly qualified

alteración *nf* **(a)** *(cambio)* alteration *o* change **(b)** *(desorden)* disturbance; **alteración del orden público** = breach of the peace

alterar *vt* **(a)** *(modificar)* to alter **(b)** *(perturbar)* to disturb; **alterar la paz** = to disturb the peace

alternativa *nf* alternative

alto, -ta 1 *adj* high; **alta mar** = high seas; **alta traición** = high treason; **alto cargo** = top executive; **impuestos altos** = high taxation; **los precios están muy altos** = prices are running high; **están diseñando un bloque de oficinas de 30 pisos de alto** = they are planning a 30-storey high office block; **las estanterías miden 30 cm de alto** = the shelves are 30 cm high; **no podemos meter las máquinas en el edificio porque la puerta no es lo bastante alta** = the door is not high enough to let us get the machines into the building **2** *nm* stop *o* halt; *(en el trabajo)* pause; **alto el fuego** = cease-fire

aludir *vi (mencionar)* **aludir a** = to mention

alzado, -da *adj* **(a)** *(elevado)* raised; **a mano alzada** = show of hands; **votación a mano alzada** = show of hands; **la moción se llevó a cabo a mano alzada** *o* **la moción se aprobó a mano alzada** = the motion was carried on a show of hands **(b)** *(precio fijo)* flat rate; **tanto alzado** = lump sum; **acuerdo** *o* **contrato a tanto alzado** = fixed-price agreement; **le pagan un tanto alzado** = he is paid a flat rate

alzamiento *nm* (a) *(militar)* uprising (b) **alzamiento de bienes** = concealment of assets

ama *nf* landlady *o* proprietress

amancebamiento *nm* cohabitation

amañamiento *nm* fiddling; **amañamiento de resultados electorales** = gerrymandering

amañar *vt (falsificar)* to tamper with something *o* to fiddle; **amañar el estado de cuentas de una empresa** = to manipulate the accounts; **amañar una acusación contra alguien** = to frame someone; **le han amañado las pruebas para que la culpa recaiga sobre él** = he has been framed; **intentó amañar su declaración de la renta** = he tried to fiddle his tax returns; **sorprendieron al vendedor amañando su cuenta de gastos** = the salesman was caught fiddling his expense account

amarillo, -lla *adj* **páginas amarillas** = commercial directory *o* trade directory

amarradero *nm (atracadero)* mooring *o* berth

ambiente *nm* background

ambigüedad *nf* ambiguity; **ambigüedad latente (en un contrato)** = latent ambiguity

ambiguo, -gua *adj* ambiguous; **los términos de la cláusula son ambiguos y necesitan ser aclarados** = the wording of the clause is ambiguous and needs clarification

ámbito *nm (alcance)* scope; *(dominio)* domain; **ámbito nacional** = nation-wide; **dentro del ámbito** = within the limit *o* the scope; **la cuestión no entra en el ámbito de los poderes de la autoridad** = the question does not come within the scope of the authority's powers

amenaza *nf* threat *o* menace; **pedir dinero bajo amenazas** = demanding money with menaces

amenazar *vt* to threaten; **amenazó con llevar al inquilino ante los tribunales** = he threatened to take the tenant to court *o* to have the tenant evicted; **alegó que su marido la había amenazado con un cuchillo** = she complained that her husband threatened her with a knife

amigable *adj* friendly; **actuar de amigable componedor** = to play the honest broker

amigo, -ga *n* friend; **'amigo del tribunal'** = amicus curiae

amistoso, -sa *adj* friendly; **acuerdo amistoso** = out-of-court settlement; **se llegó a un acuerdo amistoso entre las partes** = a settlement was reached out of court; **confían en llegar a un acuerdo amistoso** = they are hoping to reach an out-of-court settlement; **se llegó a un acuerdo amistoso** *o* **las dos partes llegaron a un arreglo amistoso** = a settlement was reached out of court *o* the two parties reached an out-of-court settlement

amnistía *nf* amnesty *o* free pardon; **amnistía total e incondicional** = unconditional pardon

La amnistía consiste en el perdón y el olvido de un delito, teniéndose éste por no cometido, mientras que el indulto supone la remisión total o parcial de una pena

amnistiar *vt* to amnesty

amo *nm* proprietor *o* landlord

amonestación *nf* (a) *(reprimenda)* caution; **amonestación escrita** *o* **verbal** = written *o* verbal warning; **firmó su confesión bajo amonestación** = he signed his confession under caution (b) *(proclamas matrimoniales)* **amonestaciones** = banns; **publicar las amonestaciones de Ana Torres y Victor Santos** = to publish the banns of marriage between Ana Torres and Victor Santos

amonestar *vt (llamar al orden)* to caution; **el policía amonestó a los chicos tras sorprenderlos robando fruta** = the policeman cautioned the boys after he caught them stealing fruit

amoroso, -osa *adj* love; **aventura amorosa** = love affair

amortizable *adj* redeemable; **no amortizable** = irredeemable

amortización *nf* depreciation; **amortización de una deuda** = redemption; **plazo de amortización** = payback period; **amortización anticipada** = redemption before due date; **amortización de vacantes de una plantilla** = natural wastage

amortizar *vt* to redeem; **amortizar un préstamo** = to pay off a loan

amotinado, -da 1 *adj* riotous 2 *n* rioter *o* mutineer *o* rebel

amotinador, -ra *n* mutineer

amotinarse *vr (provocar disturbios)* to riot; *(rebelarse)* to mutiny

amparar *vt* to protect; *(a un criminal)* to harbour ◊ **ampararse** *vr* to seek protection

amparo *nm* protection; *(tutela)* guardianship; **amparo fiscal** = tax shield; **amparo legal** *o* **jurídico** = legal protection; **al amparo de los tribunales** = under court protection; **recurso de amparo** = appeal for legal protection

ampliación *nf (plazo)* extension; **ampliación de póliza mediante endoso** = endorsement; **requerimiento de ampliación de plazo** = time summons

ampliado, -da *adj* extended; **condena ampliada** = extended sentence

ampliar *vt* (a) *(aumentar)* to increase; *(extender las actividades)* to expand; **ampliar el negocio a una nueva rama** *o* **a otras actividades** = to branch out **(b)** *(prolongar)* to extend; **le ampliaron la condena a cinco años de prisión** = he was sentenced to five years imprisonment, extended

amueblado, -da *adj* furnished; **piso amueblado** *o* **casa amueblada** = furnished accommodation

amueblar *vt* to furnish; **amuebló la oficina con sillas y mesas de segunda mano** = he furnished his office with secondhand chairs and desks; **la compañía gastó 200.000 ptas en amueblar la oficina del presidente** = the company spent 200,000 ptas on furnishing the chairman's office

analfabeto, -ta *n (persona que firma con una cruz)* marksman

análisis *nm (investigación)* analysis *o* review; **análisis de sangre** = blood test *o* blood grouping test; **análisis financiero** = financial review; **análisis judicial** = judicial review; **hacer un análisis del sistema empleado para dictar sentencias** = to conduct a review of sentencing policy

analista *nmf* analyst; **analista profesional de opinión pública** = pollster

analizar *vt* to analize *o* to sample; **se analizó el aliento del sospechoso y la prueba dio positiva** = the suspect's breath was sampled and the test proved positive

analogía *nf (interpretación de la ley)* construction

Cuando no exista norma aplicable a un caso determinado, pero la razón para aplicar a este caso la consecuencia jurídica prevista en una norma para otro caso similar sea idéntica, entonces se aplicará la norma prevista en el otro caso (CC artº 4.1)

anarquía *nf* anarchy *o* lawlessness; **cuando el presidente fue asesinado, el país se sumió en un estado de anarquía** = when the president was assassinated, the country fell into anarchy

anárquico, -ca *adj* anarchical; **el estado anárquico de las comarcas del país** = the anarchical state of the country districts

anciliario, -ria *n* ancillary

andar *vi (tergiversar)* **andar con rodeos** = to prevaricate

anexar *vt* to attach *o* to annex

anexo *nm* annexe; *(documento adjunto)* enclosure

animar *vt (incitar)* to encourage; **con dejar las ventanas abiertas sólo se consigue animar a los ladrones** = leaving windows open only encourages burglars; **les animaron a continuar** = they were encouraged to go on

ánimo *nm* animus; **ánimo de lucro** = animus lucrandi; **ánimo de permanecer (en un lugar)** = animus manendi; **ánimo de revocar (un testamento)** = animus revocandi; **ánimo de robar** = animus furandi; **ánimo de suprimir** *o* **cancelar** = animus cancellandi; **con ánimo de** = with intent *o* with the intention of; **sin ánimo de lucro** = non profit making

anónimo, -ma *adj* anonymous; **sociedad anónima (SA)** = Public Limited Company (Plc); **sociedad mercantil anónima** = corporation; **autorización para convertirse en sociedad anónima** = certificate of incorporation; **García Hnos., sociedad anónima** García Hnos. Incorporated

anormal *adj* abnormal

anotación *nf* note; *(asiento)* entry; **anotación al dorso** = endorsement; **anotación preventiva** = caveat

anotar *vt (tomar nota)* to note; *(levantar acta)* to minute; **anotar al dorso** = to endorse; **anotar en el haber** = to credit

antagonista *nmf* opponent

ante *prep* before *o* in the presence of; **ante la sala** = in the presence of the court; **ante todo** =; *(en primer lugar)* primarily

antecedente *nm* cause *o* precedent; *(historial)* antecedent *o* record; **antecedentes penales** = criminal record; **una persona sin antecedentes penales** = a person of previous good character; **el acusado no tenía antecedentes penales** = the accused had no criminal record; **el tribunal fue informado de que no poseía antecedentes penales** the court was told she had no previous criminal record **(b)** *(experiencia)* background *o* track record; **explicó los antecedentes de la demanda** = he explained the background to the claim

antecesor, -ra *n* predecessor

antedatar *vt* to antedate *o* to backdate

antedicho *nm* aforesaid *o* aforementioned

antelación *nf* **con antelación** = in advance; **con poco tiempo de antelación** = at short notice; **las retiradas de fondos se deben notificar con siete días de antelación** = you must give seven days' advance notice of withdrawals from the account

antemano *adv;* **de antemano** = beforehand *o* in advance; **las condiciones de pago se acordarán de antemano** = the terms of the payment will be agreed beforehand

antepasado, -da 1 *adj* **la semana antepasada** *o* **el mes antepasado** *o* **el año antepasado** the week *o* month *o* year before last 2 *n* ancestor; **antepasado común** = common ancestor

anteproyecto *nm* draft Bill; **el anteproyecto de ley está en manos de los abogados de los letrados del Congreso** = the draft Bill is with the Congress lawyers

anterior *adj* previous *o* prior; *(en un cargo)* former; **anterior a la causa** = pre-trial; **condena anterior** = spent conviction; **detalles anteriores** = background; **situación anterior** *o* **statu quo anterior** = status quo ante; **actuando como administradores las partes anteriores** = the parties heretofore acting as trustees; **vea el párrafo anterior de mi carta** = see the preceding paragraph of my letter; **pedir al tribunal que considere las seis condenas anteriores del acusado** = to ask for six previous convictions to be taken into consideration
◊ **anteriormente** *adv* ante *o* previously *o* heretofore; **'lo que ha sucedido anteriormente'** = status quo ante; **no pudo aceptar la invitación porque ya se había comprometido anteriormente** = he could not accept the invitation because he had a previous engagement

antes de *prep* aforementioned *o* heretofore *o* before; **antes de aquel tiempo** = theretofore

anti-balas *adj* bullet-proof; **chaleco anti-balas** = bullet-proof jacket

anticipación *nf* anticipation; **con anticipación** = in advance *o* beforehand; **con poca anticipación** = at short notice

anticipado, -da *adj* anticipatory *o* advance; **pago anticipado** = advance payment; **reserva anticipada** = advance booking; **declaración anticipada de incumplimiento de contrato** *o* **violación anticipada de contrato** = anticipatory breach; **poner una fecha anticipada a un documento** = to antedate a document; **por anticipado** = beforehand *o* in advance

anticipar *vt* to advance

anticipo *nm* advance; **anticipo a cuenta** = advance on account; **anticipo de caja** *o* **en efectivo** = cash advance; **anticipo sobre los honorarios (de un abogado)** = retainer; **conceder un anticipo de remuneración** = to pay an advance against next month's salary

anticonstitucional *adj* unconstitutional

anticuado, -da *adj* *(obsoleto)* obsolete; **reglamento anticuado** = dead letter; **la ley ha quedado anticuada a causa de los nuevos adelantos en la ciencia forense** = the law has been made obsolete by new developments in forensic science

antidroga *adj* **la brigada antidroga** = the Drug Squad; **una campaña antidroga** = an anti-drug campaign

antiestatutario, -ria *adj* unconstitutional *o* against statutory rights; **su acción fue antiestatutaria** = their action was ultra vires; **la reelección del presidente por un segundo periodo es antiestutaria** = the re-election of the chairman for a second term is not constitutional

antigüedad *nf* seniority; **se hizo una lista de los directores por orden de antigüedad en la empresa** = the managers were listed in order of seniority

antiguo, -gua *adj* **(a)** *(previo)* former *o* ex-; **el Sr Rubio, el antiguo presidente de la compañía** = Mr Rubio, the ex-chairman of the company **(b)** *(viejo)* old; **(trabajador) más antiguo** = senior; *(de muchos años)* long-standing

antihuelga *adj* **cláusula antihuelga** = no-strike agreement *o* no-strike clause

antijurídico, -ca *adj* unlawful

antilegal *adj* illegal

antimonopolio *adj* anti-trust; **leyes** *o* **legislación antimonopolio** = anti-trust laws *o* legislation

antinomia *nf* **antinomia legal** = conflict of laws

antirrobo *adj* **alarma antirrobo** = burglar alarm; **al introducir la mano por la ventana accionó la alarma antirrobo** = as he put his hand through the window he set off the burglar alarm

antiterrorista *adj* **la brigada antiterrorista** = the anti-terrorist squad

antro *nm* *(edificio)* joint; *(cueva)* den

anual *adj* annual *o* *(al año)* per annum; **alquiler anual de una propiedad** = rack rent; **rendimiento anual** = annual return; **renta anual** *o* **pensión anual** = annuity; **Junta General Anual** = Annual General Meeting (AGM); **¿cuál es su volumen de ventas anual?** = what is their turnover per annum?; **recibe una renta anual del estado** = he has a government annuity *o* an annuity from the government
◊ **anualmente** *adv* annually *o* on an annual basis; **las cifras se revisan anualmente** = the figures are revised annually

anualidad *nf* annuity *o* life annuity *o* annuity for life; **comprar** *o* **suscribir una anualidad** to buy *o* to take out an annuity

anuario *nm* yearbook; *(repertorio)* directory

anuencia *nf* consent

anulable *adj* annullable; *(rescindible)* voidable

anulación *nf* *(invalidación)* annulling *o* annulment *o* nullification *o* abrogation *o* invalidation; *(revocación)* revocation *o* defeasance; **anulación de legado** = lapse *o* ademption; **anulación del matrimonio** = annulment of marriage; **anulación de la resolución de quiebra** = annulment of adjudication; **anulación de un acuerdo** = cancellation of an agreement; **anulación de un contrato** = annulling of a contract; **anulación de una cita** = cancellation of an appointment; **anulación de un testamento** = revocation of probate

anular *vt* to annul *o* to abrogate *o* to cancel *o* to nullify *o* to quash *o* to invalidate; **anular un acuerdo** = to call off a deal; **anular un cheque** = to cancel a cheque; **anular un contrato** = to break (a contract) *o* to void a contract; **anular un fallo** *o* **una decisión** = to render a decision null; **anular un juicio en la instancia de apelación** = to reverse a judgment on appeal; **anular una cláusula de un acuerdo** = to revoke a clause in an agreement; **a causa de la absorción de la empresa, el contrato ha sido anulado** = because the company has been taken over, the contract has been invalidated; **el fallo del árbitro fue anulado en la apelación** = the arbitrator's award was set aside on appeal; **el tribunal anuló el contrato** = the contract was annulled by the court; **la sentencia fue anulada tras el recurso de la defensa** = the verdict was quashed after the defence counsel's appeal; **la compañía espera poder anular el contrato** = the company is hoping to be able to break the contract; **solicitó una revisión del caso para anular la orden judicial** = he applied for judicial review to quash the order; **su matrimonio ha sido anulado** = their marriage has been annulled; **toda declaración de culpabilidad obtenida por medio del fraude o del perjurio de un testigo será anulada** = a conviction obtained by fraud or perjury by a witness will be quashed

anulativo, -va *adj* **cláusula anulativa** = annulling clause

anunciar *vt* to announce; *(promocionar)* to promote; *(advertir)* to warn; **anunciar un aumento** = to post an increase; **anunciar un veredicto** = to hand down a verdict; **anunciar una condena** = to pass sentence; **el presidente del jurado anunció su veredicto** = the foreman of the jury announced their verdict; **el Secretario de Estado anunció las directrices sobre gastos** = the Secretary of State issued guidelines for expenditure

anuncio *nm* announcement *o* notice *o* *(publicidad)* advertisement; **anuncios por palabras** = small ads; **tablón de anuncios** = noticeboard; **la secretaria de la empresa puso un anuncio sobre el plan de pensiones en el tablón** = the company secretary pinned up a notice about the pension scheme; **la lista de electores se coloca en el tablón de anuncios de las oficinas municipales** = the list of electors is put up on the noticeboard in the local offices

añadir *vt* to add *o* to annexe; **el apéndice se añade al contrato** = the appendix is joined to the contract

año *nm* year; **año base** = base year; **año civil** = calendar year; **año fiscal** = fiscal year *o* tax year; *(ejercicio)* financial year; **dos veces al año; cada dos años** = bi-annually; **de muchos años** = long-standing

apaciguar *vt* to appease *o* to calm down

apalabrar *vt* to make a verbal agreement

apalear *vt* to beat; **apalear fuertemente** = to batter

apaño *nm* *(arreglo)* fixing

aparato *nm* *(estratagema)* device; *(mecanismo)* machinery; **aparato administrativo** = administrative machinery

aparecer *vi* to appear; *(presentarse)* to show up

aparentar *vi* to pretend

aparente *adj* apparent *o* ostensible; **socio aparente** = ostensible partner

apartado *nm* **(a)** *(sección de un texto legal)* section **(b)** **apartado de correos** = box number; **número del apartado de correos** = Post Office box number; **por favor escriba al Apartado de Correos número 209** = please reply to Box No. 209

apartar *vt* *(retener)* to retain; **la empresa ha apartado un porcentaje de los beneficios como provisión frente a deudas incobrables** = out of the profits, the company has retained a percentage as provision against bad debts

◊ **apartarse** *vr* *(desistir de una demanda)* to withdraw from a suit

aparte 1 *adv* apart *o* aside *o* separately **2** *nm* new paragraph

apátrida *nmf* stateless person

apelación *nf* appeal; **apelación contra condena** = appeal against conviction; **de apelación** = appellate; **ganó el caso por apelación** = she won her case on appeal; **tribunal de apelación** = court of appeal

La apelación es un recurso interpuesto por la parte agraviada por resolución judicial ante un órgano judicial superior

apelante *nmf* appellant

apelar *vi* to appeal; **ha apelado al Tribunal Supremo** = he has appealed to the Supreme Court

apellido *nm* surname; **las mujeres españolas no adoptan el apellido del marido al casarse** = a Spanish woman doesn't take the surname of her husband when she marries

apenas *adv* barely; **apenas hay suficiente dinero para pagar a los empleados** = there is barely enough money left to pay the staff; **apenas**

tuvo tiempo de llamar a su abogado = she barely had time to call her lawyer

apéndice *nm* appendix *o* schedule; **apéndice relativo a mercados en los que un contrato es de aplicación** *o* **en los que se aplica un contrato** = schedule of markets to which a contract applies; **el apéndice al que nos hemos referido anteriormente** = the schedule before referred to; **los mercados que cubre el contrato de representación se listan en el Apéndice** = the markets covered by the agency agreement are listed in the Appendix; **véase el apéndice correspondiente** = see the attached schedule *o* as per the attached schedule; **véase el Apéndice B para la relación de delitos graves** = see Appendix B for the clear-up rates of notifiable offences

apercibimiento *nm* **(a)** *(citación judicial)* summons *o* subpoena **(b)** *(advertencia)* warning *o* *(aviso oficial)* notice; **recibió un apercibimiento del juez diciendo que si cometía otro delito podía ser encarcelado** = he received a warning from the magistrate that for the next offence he might be sent to prison

apersonarse *vr (comparecer)* to appear

apertura *nf* opening; **apertura de juicio oral** = order for hearing to commence; **apertura de nuevos mercados** = a market opening; **asiento de apertura** = opening entry; **discurso de apertura** = opening speech; **horas de apertura** = opening hours

aplazado, -da *adj* deferred; **pago aplazado** = deferred payment

aplazamiento *nm* postponement *o* adjournment; *(prórroga)* deferment; *(sobreseimiento)* stay; **aplazamiento de un fallo** = deferment of a decision; **aplazamiento de pago** = deferment of payment; **aplazamiento de sentencia** = deferment of sentence; **aplazamiento de la ejecución de una sentencia** = stay of execution; **el acusado ha pedido un aplazamiento** = the defendant has applied for an adjournment; **el acusado solicitó un aplazamiento del proceso hasta que el demandante se hiciera cargo de las costas** = the defendant made an application to stay the proceedings until the plaintiff gave security for costs; **tuve que cambiar mis compromisos a causa del aplazamiento de la reunión del consejo** = I had to change my appointments because of the postponement of the board meeting

aplazar *vt* to postpone *o* to hold over *o* to put off; *(diferir)* to defer; **aplazar indefinidamente** = sine die; **aplazar la sesión** = to adjourn; **aplazar el examen de una moción** = *US* to table; **aplazar el juicio** = to defer judgment; **aplazar una reunión** = to adjourn a meeting; **aplazar el vencimiento de una hipoteca** = to extend a mortgage; **el fallo ha sido aplazado hasta la próxima reunión** = the

decision has been deferred until the next meeting; **el presidente aplazó la vista hasta las tres** = the chairman adjourned the tribunal until three o'clock; **la discusión del punto 4 quedó aplazada para la próxima reunión** = discussion of item 4 was held over until the next meeting; **preguntaron si podían aplazar el pago hasta que la situación de caja fuera mejor** = they asked if they could postpone payment until the cash situation was better; **preguntó si podíamos aplazar la visita hasta mañana** = he asked if we could put the visit off until tomorrow; **aplazó la reunión hasta mañana** = he postponed the meeting until tomorrow; **la vista se aplazó dos semanas** = the hearing was put off for two weeks

aplicable *adj (ejecutorio)* enforceable; **ser aplicable a** = to apply to; **esta cláusula sólo es aplicable fuera de la UE** = this clause applies only to deals outside the EU

aplicación *nf (realización)* implementation; *(cumplimiento)* enforcement; **aplicación de la ley** = law enforcement; **de aplicación inmediata** = self-enforcing

aplicar *vt* to apply; *(un castigo)* to administer; **aplicar la ley** = to enforce the law

apoderado , -da *n* attorney; *(poderhabiente)* proxy; **actuar como apoderado de alguien** = to act as proxy for someone; **nombrar a alguien apoderado** = to nominate someone as proxy; **cuenta administrada por un apoderado** = nominee account; **documento que certifica que alguien es apoderado** = letter of attorney

apología *nf* defence; **apología de delito** = statement in support of a criminal act; **apología del terrorismo** = statement showing approval of terrorism

aporrear *vt (dar un porrazo)* to cosh; **los ladrones aporrearon al tendero y robaron el dinero de la caja** = the burglars coshed the shopkeeper and stole money from the till

aportar *vt* to contribute; **aportar pruebas** = to adduce evidence

apostar *vt* **(a)** *(estacionar)* to station **(b)** *(jugarse)* to bet *o* to wager; **apostó 10.000 ptas por el resultado de las elecciones** = he bet *o* he wagered 10,000 ptas on the result of the election; **te apuesto a que el acusado escapa con una multa** = I bet you the accused will get off with a fine

apoyar *vt* **(a)** *(sostener)* to support *o* to uphold *o* to back up; **apoyar un proyecto de ley** = to back a bill; **apoyar una moción** = to second a motion; **confía en que el resto de los miembros del comité la apoyarán** = she hopes the other members of the committee will support her **(b)** *(defender)* stand by **(c)** *(estar a favor de)* to favour *o* *US* to favor

apoyo *nm* support; **apoyo a una causa** = advocacy; **apoyo económico** = financial support; **carta de apoyo** = letter of comfort *o* comfort letter; **el presidente tiene el apoyo del comité** = the chairman has the support of the committee; **no tenemos apoyo económico de los bancos** = we have no financial support from the banks

apreciación *nf (estimación)* estimate; **según una apreciación prudente** = at a conservative estimate

apreciar *vt (valorar)* to appreciate *o* to value *o* to estimate

◊ **apreciarse** *vr* to increase in value

aprecio *nm* appreciation; **en aprecio por** = in appreciation of

aprehender *vt (persona)* to catch *o (mercancías)* to seize

aprehensión *nf* capture

apremiar *vt* to press *o* to oblige

apremio *nm* court order; **apremio provisional** = interim order

> Se llama apremio a la diligencia judicial sobre los bienes del demandado, a fin de asegurar el pago de una obligación

aprendiz, -za *n* trainee

aprendizaje *nm* apprenticeship; **contrato de aprendizaje** = indentures *o* articles of indenture; **periodo de aprendizaje** = training period; **realizar un contrato de aprendizaje** = to indenture; **se le hizo un contrato de aprendizaje con un maestro de obras** = he was indentured to a builder

apresurarse *vr* to hurry; **los directores se apresuraron a la reunión** = the directors hurried into the meeting

apretado, -da *adj* tight; **el juzgado tiene un horario muy apretado** = the court has a busy schedule

aprobación *nf* (a) *(autorización)* approval *o* assent; **aprobación formal de un proyecto de ley para que se convierta en Ley del Parlamento** *o* **parlamentaria** = Royal Assent; **certificado de aprobación** = certificate of approval; **someter un presupuesto a aprobación** = to submit a budget for approval; **el solar se vende con la aprobación provisional para la construcción de cuatro casas** = the land is to be sold with outline planning permission for four houses (b) *(muestra de conformidad)* acceptance *o* adoption; **tenemos su carta de aprobación** = we have his letter of acceptance; **propuso la aprobación de la resolución** = he moved the adoption of the resolution

aprobar *vt* (a) *(sancionar)* to approve *o* to approve of *o* to sanction *o* to pass *o* to agree *o* to adopt; **aprobar el orden del día** = to adopt the agenda; **aprobar los términos de un contrato** = to approve the terms of a contract; **aprobar una moción** *o* **una resolución** = to pass *o* to adopt a resolution *o (por votación)* to carry a motion; **la junta aprobó la propuesta** = the proposal was approved by the board; **la comisión aprobó la moción** = the motion was approved by the committee; **el director financiero tiene que aprobar las facturas antes de su envío** = the finance director has to pass an invoice before it is sent out; **Las Cortes han aprobado el proyecto de ley que ahora se ha convertido en ley** = Parliament passed the Bill which has now become law; **el préstamo ha sido aprobado por la junta** = the loan has been passed by the board; **la junta aprobó una propuesta para congelar los salarios** = the meeting passed a proposal that salaries should be frozen; **los auditores han aprobado las cuentas con reservas** = the auditors have qualified the accounts; **se aprobaron las propuestas por unanimidad** = the proposals were adopted unanimously (b) *(ratificar)* to endorse; **el tribunal aprobó la opinión del abogado** = the court endorsed counsel's view (c) *(pasar un examen)* to pass; **aprobó el examen de mecanografía** = he passed his typing test; **ha aprobado todos los exámenes y ya es abogada titulada** = she has passed all her exams and now is a qualified solicitor

apropiación *nf* appropriation; **apropiación indebida** *o* **ilícita** = conversion *o* misappropriation; **apropiación ilícita de fondos** = conversion of funds

> La apropiación indebida es un delito consistente en la apropiación y distracción de dinero, efectos o bienes muebles recibidos en depósito, comisión o administración, o por otro título que produzca la obligación de entregarlos o devolverlos, o en la negación de haberlos recibidos (CP artº 252)

apropiado, -da *adj* appropriate *o* suitable; *(pertinente)* relevant; **¿es una multa un castigo apropiado para los delitos contra la libertad sexual?** = is a fine an appropriate punishment for sex offences?; **el miércoles es el día más apropiado para la celebración de la vista** = Wednesday is the most suitable day for the hearing

apropiarse *vr* to take possession; **apropiarse de** = to appropriate; **apropiarse indebidamente de** = to misappropriate; **apropiarse ilícitamente de fondos** = to convert funds to one's own use; **el ayuntamiento se apropió de la tierra para construir las nuevas oficinas municipales** = the town council appropriated the land to build the new municipal offices

aprovechable *adj* available

aprovechado, -da *nmf* profiteer

aprovisionamiento *nm* provision *o* supply

aproximación *nf* estimate *o* approximation

aproximado, -da *adj* rough; **cálculo aproximado** *o* **estimación aproximada** = rough calculation *o* rough estimate; **estas cifras son sólo aproximadas** these figures are only an estimate ◊ **aproximadamente** *adv (más o menos)* roughly; **estimar** *o* **calcular aproximadamente** = to estimate; **calcular los gastos aproximadamente** = to estimate costs; **el volumen de ventas es aproximadamente el doble que el del año pasado** = the turnover is roughly twice last year's

aproximarse *vr* **aproximarse a** = to approach; **la oferta no se aproxima a la cifra que solicita mi cliente** = the offer does not approach the figure my client seeks

aproximativo, -va *adj* **estimación aproximativa** = rough calculation *o* rough estimate

aptitud *nf* **(a)** *(competencia)* competence *o* competency *o* fitness; **aptitud a la finalidad que poseen** = fitness for purpose; **aptitud legal** = legal capacity; **certificado de aptitud** = test certificate **(b)** *(título)* qualification; **aptitud profesional** = professional qualifications

apto, -ta *adj (capacitado)* fit; *(incapacitado)* unfit to plead

apuesta *nf* bet *o* wager; **tenedor de apuestas** = stakeholder

apuntamiento *nm (resumen de las actuaciones en un juicio)* abstract of court record

apuntar *vt* **(a)** *(incitar a alguien a decir algo)* to prompt; **el juez advirtió al abogado que no apuntara al testigo** = the judge warned counsel not to prompt the witness **(b)** *(registrar)* to enter; *(anotar)* to note *o* to make a note of something; **apuntar un nombre en una lista** = to enter a name on a list; **apuntar una cifra en la columna de gastos** = to put down a figure for expenses; **el policía apuntó el número del coche en su libreta** = the policeman noted the number of the car in his notebook

apunte *nm* entry; **tomar apuntes de una reunión** = to take notes of a meeting

apuro *nm* **(a)** *(necesidad)* difficulty *o* distress; **apuro económico** = hardship; **verse en apuros** = to be in trouble **(b)** *(urgencia)* emergency

aquí *adv* here *o* to hand; **tengo la factura aquí** = I have the invoice to hand

arancel *nm* tariff; **arancel de honorarios** = scale of fees; **arancel judicial** = schedule of court costs; **arancel proteccionista** = protective tariff; **aranceles aduaneros** *o* **de aduanas** = customs tariffs

arancelario, -aria *adj* tariff *o* customs; **barrera arancelaria** = customs barrier *o* tariff barrier; **Departamento de Derechos Arancelarios e Impuestos Indirectos** customs *o* Customs and Excise; **imponer barreras arancelarias a un producto** = to impose tariff barriers on a product; **levantar barreras arancelarias a un producto** = to lift tariff barriers from a product

arbitraje *nm* arbitration; **arbitraje extrajudicial** = out-of-court arbitration; **acuerdo de arbitraje** = arbitration agreement; **cámara** *o* **junta** *o* **comisión de arbitraje** = arbitration board *o* arbitration tribunal; **tribunal de arbitraje industrial** = industrial arbitration tribunal; **acudir al arbitraje** = to go to arbitration; **llevar una disputa a arbitraje** = to take a dispute to arbitration; **someter una disputa a arbitraje** = to submit a dispute to arbitration; **aceptar la decisión de la comisión de arbitraje** = to accept the ruling of the arbitration board

arbitral *adj* **cámara** *o* **junta** *o* **comisión arbitral** = arbitration board *o* arbitration tribunal; **laudo arbitral** = arbitration award; **tribunal arbitral** = adjudication tribunal

arbitrar 1 *vi* **arbitrar en una disputa** = to arbitrate in a dispute **2** *vt* to arbitrate

arbitrio *nm (discreción)* discretion; **al arbitrio de alguien** = at the discretion of someone; **el tribunal ejerció su arbitrio** = the court exercised its discretion; **los magistrados tienen arbitrio para permitir que un acusado cambie su elección de un juicio sumario a un juicio ante jurado** = magistrates have a discretion to allow an accused person to change his election from a summary trial to a jury trial

árbitro *nm* arbitrator *o* adjudicator; *(juez especialista en casos técnicos de gran complejidad)* official refereee; **árbitro en una disputa laboral** = adjudicator in an industrial dispute; **árbitro industrial** *o* **laboral** = industrial arbitrator; **aceptar** *o* **rechazar la decisión del juez árbitro** = to accept *o* to reject the arbitrator's ruling; **confiar un asunto a un juez árbitro** = to refer a question to arbitration; **el asunto de la manutención lo lleva un árbitro nombrado por el tribunal** = the question of maintenance payments is with a court-appointed referee

archivador 1 *adj* **caja archivadora** = box file **2** *nm (carpeta)* file; *(fichero)* filing cabinet; *(caja archivadora)* box file

archivar *vt* **(a)** *(guardar documentos)* to save *o* to file; **archivar algo** = to place something on file; **archivar el nombre de alguien** = to keep someone's name on file; **documentos por archivar** = filing; **al finalizar la semana hay que archivar un montón de documentos** = there is a lot of filing to do at the end of the week; **el director hojeó los**

documentos archivados durante la semana para ver qué cartas se habían enviado = the manager looked through the week's filing to see what letters had been sent; **la correspondencia se archiva en la carpeta de 'reclamaciones'** = the correspondence is filed under 'complaints' **(b)** *(aplazar)* to shelve; **archivar diligencias** = to shelve the record of proceedings; **el juez dictó un auto por el que se archiva la denuncia** = the judge ruled there was no case to answer

archivero, -ra *n* filing clerk

archivo *nm* **(a)** *(fichero)* file *o (de ordenador)* computer file; *(armario)* cabinet; *(caja archivadora)* box file; **copia de archivo** = file copy; **sistema de archivo** = filing system; **¿Cómo podemos proteger nuestros archivos del ordenador?** = how can we protect our computer files?; **busca su descripción en el archivo de personas desaparecidas** = look up her description in the missing persons' file; **la correspondencia del año pasado está en el último cajón del archivo** last year's correspondence is in the bottom drawer of the filing cabinet; **la policía guarda un archivo de vehículos desaparecidos** = the police keep a file of missing vehicles **(b)** *(conjunto de documentos guardados)* records; **archivo público** = public records office; **los nombres de los clientes están en los archivos de la empresa** the names of customers are kept in the company's records

ardid *nm (estratagema)* device

área *nf* **área de control y vigilancia de un policía** = beat

argucia *nf* **argucias jurídicas** = legal subtleties

argüir *vi* to argue; **el fiscal arguyó que los acusados debían ser condenados a sentencias ejemplares** = prosecuting counsel argued that the accused should be given exemplary sentences

argumentar *vt/i* to argue

argumento *nm* argument; **argumento basado en la observación** = a posteriori argument; **argumentos a favor y en contra** = pros and cons; **argumentos jurídicos** = case; **exponer argumentos convincentes** = to show cause; **el abogado presentó los argumentos para la acusación** = counsel presented the argument for the prosecution; **al juez le resultaron difíciles de seguir los argumentos de la defensa** = the judge found the defence arguments difficult to follow; **al Tribunal Superior le inquietaba el hecho de que el juez de primera instancia hubiera pronunciado la sentencia sin tener unos argumentos apropiados** = the Court of Appeal was concerned that the judge at first instance had delivered judgment without proper argument

arma *nf* gun *o* weapon; **arma blanca** = sharp instrument; **arma de fuego** = firearm; **arma homicida** = deadly weapon; **arma ofensiva** *o* **peligrosa** = dangerous *o* offensive weapon; **licencia de armas** = firearms certificate; **tenencia ilícita de armas** = carrying offensive weapons; **gritaron a los atracadores que tiraran las armas** = they shouted to the robbers to drop their guns; **la policía no tiene permitido llevar armas** = the police are not allowed to carry guns

armado, -da *adj* armed; **hombre armado** = gunman; **robo a mano armada** = armed robbery; **la furgoneta de seguridad fue asaltada por tres hombres armados** = the security van was held up by three gunmen

armario *nm (archivo)* cabinet

armero *nm (delincuente que proporciona armas para cometer delitos)* armourer

armisticio *nm* armistice

armonía *nf* harmony; **en completa armonía con** = on all fours with

arrancar *vt (extorsionar)* to extort

arrebatar *vt* to snatch

arrebato *nm* rage

arreglar *vt* to arrange; *(reparar)* to repair *o* to fix; **¿puedes arreglar la fotocopiadora?** = can you fix the copying machine?; **el servicio de mantenimiento vendrá a arreglar el teléfono** = the maintenance staff are coming to fix the telephone
◊ **arreglárselas** *vr (hacer frente)* to cope with; *(conseguir hacer algo)* to manage to; **se las arregló para anotar seis pedidos y atender tres llamadas telefónicas en dos minutos** = she managed to write six orders and take three phone calls all in two minutes

arreglo *nm* **(a)** *(acuerdo)* arrangement *o* adjustment *o* settlement; **arreglo extrajudicial** = out-of-court settlement; **llegar a un arreglo** = to compromise **(b)** *(reparación)* repair; **arreglo improvisado** = makeshift

arremeter *vt* to assail *o* to attack

arrendado, -da *adj* **propiedad arrendada** = leasehold property; **propiedades arrendadas** = chattels real

arrendador, -ra *n (de propiedad)* lessor *o (de maquinaria)* hirer; **nuestro arrendador es una compañía de seguros** = our ground landlord is an insurance company

arrendamiento *nm* **(a)** *(contrato)* lease; *(periodo de alquiler)* let; **arrendamiento a largo plazo** *o* **a corto plazo** = long lease *o* short lease; **arrendamiento a voluntad** *o* **cancelable sin plazo fijo** = tenancy at will; **arrendamiento del propietario absoluto al inquilino** = head lease; **arrendamiento en el que todas las reparaciones**

corren por cuenta del arrendatario = full repairing lease; **al término del arrendamiento** = on expiration of the lease; **el arrendamiento finaliza en diez años** = the lease expires *o* runs out in ten years; **tomar en arrendamiento un edificio de oficinas a largo plazo** = to take an office building on a long lease **(b) arrendamiento financiero** = leasing; **utilizar una multicopista en virtud de un contrato de arrendamiento financiero** = to run a copier under a leasing arrangement **(c)** *(alquiler)* rental; **arrendamiento protegido contra desahucio** = protected tenancy; **periodo de arrendamiento** = tenancy; **renta por arrendamiento** = income from rents *o* rent income *o* rental income *o* income from rentals **(d)** *(propiedad arrendada)* leasehold; **arrendamiento con derecho a compra** = leasehold enfranchisement

arrendar *vt (ceder en arriendo)* to lease; *(alquilar)* to let; **arrendar equipo** = to lease equipment; **arrendar una zona del mar del Norte** = to hold a lease in the North Sea; **vendieron el edificio de oficinas para obtener dinero, y luego lo arrendaron por veinticinco años** = they sold the office building to raise cash, and then leased it back for twenty-five years

arrendatario, -ria *n (inquilino)* tenant *o* lessee *o* leaseholder; **las reparaciones corren por cuenta del arrendatario** = the tenant is liable for repairs

arrepentimiento *nm* repentance *o* contrition

arrepentirse *vr* to repent

arrestar *vt* **(a)** *(detener)* to arrest *o* *(encarcelar)* to imprison; **arrestado en cuartel** = confined to barracks **(b)** *(atacar a alguien en prisión)* **arrestar a alguien** = to claim

arresto *nm* arrest *o* detention; **arresto civil** = citizen's arrest; **arresto domiciliario** = house arrest; **arresto ilegal** = false arrest; **arresto mayor** imprisonment for more than one month and a day and less than six months; **arresto menor** = minimum-term imprisonment (maximum of thirty days); **arresto preventivo** = preventive detention; **arresto sin orden de detención** = summary arrest; **delito con pena de arresto** = arrestable offence; **el jefe de la oposición ha estado bajo arresto domiciliario durante seis meses** = the opposition leader has been under house arrest for six months; **el líder de la oposición lleva seis años bajo arresto domiciliario** = the opposition leader has been under house arrest for six years; **el tribunal condenó a sendas penas de cuatro meses y un día de arresto mayor a cuatro personas por cultivar marihuana** = the court sentenced four people to four months and one day of imprisonment each for growing marihuana

El presente Código Penal ha suprimido las penas de arresto menor y mayor y las ha substituído por la pena de arresto de fin de semana con un máximo de veinticuatro fines de semana. Antiguamente el arresto suponía la privación de libertad por un período no superior a seis meses (CP art° 37)

arriba *adv* above; **véase más arriba** = supra; **más arriba** = thereinbefore

arriendo *nm (arrendamiento)* lease *o (cantidad que se paga)* rent; **arriendo exorbitante** = rack rent; **ceder en arriendo** = to lease; **arriendo con opción a compra** = leasing; **propiedad en arriendo** = leasehold property; **ceder oficinas en arriendo para pequeñas empresas** = to lease offices to small firms; **al finalizar el arriendo** = on expiration of the lease; **alquilar un espacio para oficinas con un arriendo de veinte años** = to rent office space on a twenty-year lease; **el arriendo de nuestros locales actuales es a corto plazo** = we have a short lease on our current premises; **vendieron el edificio de oficinas y luego lo recuperaron otra vez por medio de un contrato de arriendo al vendedor** = they sold the office building and then took it back under a lease-back arrangement

arriesgado, -da *adj* risky; *(peligroso)* unsafe; **negocio arriesgado** = risky business; **trabajo arriesgado** = dangerous job

arriesgar *vt (poner en peligro)* to risk *o* to endanger *o* to jeopardize; **arriesgar la vida en el mar** = endangering life at sea
◊ **arriesgarse** *vr* to risk *o* to run a risk; **se arriesga a perder su permiso de conducir** = his driving licence is in jeopardy; **se arriesgó a que le detuvieran por lanzarle un huevo al Primer Ministro** = he risked being arrested *o* he risked arrest by throwing an egg at the Prime Minister

arrojado, -da *adj* **carga arrojada al mar** = jetsam

arruinar *vt* to bankrupt; **la recesión arruinó a mi padre** = the recession bankrupted my father
◊ **arruinarse** *vr* to go bankrupt; **se arruinó tras dos años en el negocio** = he went bankrupt after two years in business

arte *nm* **arte de gobernar** = politics

artículo *nm* **(a)** *(sección de un texto legal)* clause *o* section *o* article; **ver artículo 8 del contrato** = see article 8 of the contract **(b)** *(mercancía)* article *o* item *o* commodity; **artículos** = goods; **artículo de mayor venta** *o* **artículo que más vende** = leader *o* market leader; **artículos de oficina** = office supplies; **artículo de reclamo** *o* **de lanzamiento** = loss-leader; **artículos de uso doméstico** = household goods; **artículos de venta al contado** = cash items; **artículos diversos** = sundry items *o* sundries; **artículos exentos del pago del IVA** = exempt supplies **(c) (editorial); artículo de fondo** = editorial; **un artículo de un periódico** = a report in a newspaper *o* a newspaper report

artificio *nm* trick

asaltador, -ra *n* mugger

asaltante *nmf* attacker

asaltar *vt* to assault *o* to attack *o* to hold up *o* to mug; **fue asaltada por dos atracadores** = she was assaulted by two muggers; **seis hombres armados asaltaron la furgoneta de seguridad** = six gunmen held up the security van

asalto *nm* assault *o* attack *o* mugging *o* holdup; **asalto a mano armada** = armed robbery; **asalto y agresión** = assault and battery; **el número de asaltos a policías está aumentando** = the number of cases of assault *o* the number of assaults on policemen is increasing; **el número de asaltos ha aumentado bruscamente en los últimos años** = the number of muggings has increased sharply over the last few years

asamblea *nf* **(a)** *(reunión)* meeting; **asamblea general** = general meeting *o* meeting of shareholders *o* shareholders' meeting **(b)** *(junta)* assembly; **la Asamblea de la UE** = the Assembly of the EU

ascendencia *nf* **es de ascendencia británica** = he is British by descent *o* he is of British descent

ascender *vi* **(a)** *(promover)* to promote; **fue ascendido de vendedor a director de ventas** = he was promoted from salesman to sales manager **(b)** *(totalizar)* **ascender a** = to run to *o* to total; **los costes ascendieron a millones de ptas** = the costs ran into thousands of ptas

ascenso *nm* **(a)** *(promoción)* promotion; **ganarse el ascenso** = to earn promotion **(b)** **ascenso al trono** = accession to the throne

asegurable *adj* insurable; **interés asegurable** = insurable interest

asegurado, -da 1 *adj* insured; **no asegurado, -da** = uninsured; **acreedor asegurado** = secured creditor; **la persona asegurada** = the life insured; **la suma asegurada** = the sum insured; **estar asegurado a todo riesgo** = to be fully covered; **el conductor del vehículo no estaba asegurado** = the driver of the car was uninsured; **¿está asegurado contra robo?** = do you have cover against theft?; **¿está asegurado contra posibles daños ocasionados por incendios?** = do you have coverage against fire damage? **2** *n* the assured *o* the person insured

asegurador, -ra *n* **(a)** *(seguro de vida)* assurer *o* assuror; *(seguros en general)* insurer **(b)** *(suscriptor)* underwriter; **asegurador de Lloyd** *o*

asegurador de la compañía de seguros Lloyd = Lloyd's underwriter; **asegurador marítimo** *o* **asegurador contra riesgos marítimos** = marine underwriter

asegurar *vt* **(a)** *(suscribir)* to assure *o* to insure; **sin asegurar** = uninsured; **asegurar el equipaje (contra robos y pérdidas)** = to insure baggage against loss; **asegurar una casa contra incendios** = to insure a house against fire; **asegurar una emisión de acciones** = to underwrite a share issue; **estaba asegurado por valor de 50 millones** = he was insured for 50 million **(b)** *(garantizar)* to guarantee; **asegurar el porvenir de** = to make provision for; **aseguró el porvenir de su hija en su testamento** = he provided for his daughter in his will **(c)** *(reforzar)* to secure; **la policía y el ejército han asegurado la frontera** = the police and army have made the border secure
◊ **asegurarse** *vr* to insure *o* to take out insurance; **asegurarse contra el mal tiempo** = to insure against bad weather; **asegurarse contra la pérdida de ingresos** = to insure against loss of earnings

asentar *vt* **(a)** *(establecer)* to settle **(b)** *(anotar un pedido)* to enter

asentir *vt* *(confirmar)* to admit; *(conceder)* to grant

asertorio, -ria *adj* **juramento asertorio** = sworn statement

asesina *nf* murderess

asesinar *vt* to murder; *(a una figura importante)* to assassinate

asesinato *nm* murder *o* (culpable) homicide *o* *(de una figura importante)* assassination; **asesinato en primer grado** *o* **con premeditación** = first degree murder; **asesinato frustrado** *o* **intento de asesinato** = attempted murder; **asesinato premeditado** = intended murder; **fue acusado de asesinato** *o* **se le declaró culpable de asesinato** = he was charged with murder *o* he was found guilty of murder; **se han cometido tres asesinatos durante la última semana** = three murders have been committed during the last week

Se tipifica como asesinato el homicidio en el que concurren alguna de las circunstancias siguientes: alevosía, recompensa, precio o promesa, ensañamiento o aumento deliberado o inhumano del dolor de la víctima (CP 139)

asesino *nm* murderer *o* killer *o* assassin; **la policía está buscando al asesino de la chica** = the police are searching for the girl's killer

asesor, -ra 1 *adj* advisory; **una empresa asesora** = a consultancy firm; **junta asesora** = advisory board; **técnico asesor** = consulting engineer **2** *n* **(a)** *(consejero)* adviser *o* advisor *o* consultant; **asesor administrativo** *o* **de empresa** = management consultant; **asesor financiero** = financial adviser; **asesor fiscal** = tax consultant; **asesor jurídico** = legal adviser *o* counsellor; **asesor técnico** *o* **asesor de ingeniería** = engineering consultant; **está actuando como asesor** *o* **actúa en calidad de asesor** = he is acting in an advisory capacity; **está consultando con el asesor jurídico de la compañía** = he is consulting the company's legal adviser **(b)** *(tasador)* assessor *o* adjuster

asesoramiento *nm* advice *o* *(asesoría)* consultancy; **asesoramiento jurídico** = legal advice; **asesoramiento técnico** = expert advice; **director, -ra de asesoramiento** = non-executive director; **ofrece un servicio de asesoramiento** = he offers a consultancy service

asesorar *vt* to advise *o* to give legal advice ◊ **asesorarse** *vr;* **asesorarse jurídicamente** = to take legal advice

asesoría *nf* consultancy; **una asesoría** = a consultancy firm; **asesoría jurídica** = legal section

aseveración *nf* assertion *o* allegation; **aseveración falsa** = false statement *o* false allegation

asiento *nm* *(entrada)* entry; **asiento de caja** = cash entry; **asiento del débito** = debit entry

asignación *nf* **(a)** *(distribución)* allocation *o* appropriation; **asignación presupuestaria** = allotment; **asignación proporcional** = apportionment; **asignación de acciones** = share allocation *o* allocation of shares; **asignación de fondos para investigar sobre el crimen** = allocation of funds to research into crime **(b)** *(retribución)* allowance; **asignación por carestía de vida** = cost of living allowance

asignar *vt* **(a)** *(destinar)* to assign *o* to earmark *o* to allocate *o* to allot *o* to appropriate; **asignar proporcionalmente** = to apportion; **asignar fondos a un proyecto** = to earmark funds for a project; **el terreno está asignado para la industria ligera** = the land is zoned for industrial use; **se han asignado tres detectives para el caso** = three detectives have been assigned to the case; **se le asignó la tarea de comprobar los números de los coches robados** = he was assigned the job of checking the numbers of stolen cars **(b)** *(delegar)* **asignar un cargo** = to depute **(c)** *(legar)* to settle on; **asignar una propiedad en fideicomiso a futuros propietarios** = to settle property on someone

asilado, -da *n* refugee

asilo *nm* asylum *o* refuge; **asilo político** = political asylum; **pedir asilo político** = to ask for political asylum

asistencia *nf* **(a)** *(acto de presencia)* attendance **(b)** *(auxilio)* aid; **asistencia jurídica** = legal aid; **asistencia letrada** = legal assistance; **asistencia social** = welfare; **programa de asistencia jurídica gratuita** Legal Aid scheme

asistir 1 *vt (ayudar, socorrer)* to assist *o* to help *o* to aid **2** *vi (comparecer)* to attend; *(presentarse)* to report to; **citaron a los testigos para asistir al juicio** = the witnesses were subpoenaed to attend the trial

asociación *nf* **(a)** *(sociedad)* association; *(organización)* organization; **asociación de consumidores** = consumer council; **asociación de empresas** = trust company; **asociación comercial** = trade association; **asociación de empresarios** = employers' organization *o* association; **Asociación Internacional de Abogados** = International Bar Association; **contrato de asociación** = articles of partnership; **escritura de asociación** *o* **estatutos de asociación** = articles of association *o* articles of incorporation **(b)** *(relación)* association; **asociación ilícita** = unlawful assembly; **libertad de asociación** = freedom of association; **culpable por asociación** = guilt by association

asociado, -da 1 *adj* associated; **director asociado** = associate director; **empresa asociada** = associate company; **un convenio que va asociado a la posesión de la tierra** = a covenant which runs with the land **2** *n* associate; *(socio)* partner; **en su declaración nombró a dos asociados** = in his testimony he named six associates

asociar *vt* to associate *o* *(conectar)* to connect ◊ **asociarse** *vr;* **asociarse con alguien** = to go into partnership with someone; **asociarse con un amigo** = to enter into a partnership with a friend

aspirante *nmf* candidate *o* applicant

asumir *vt (una responsabilidad)* to assume; *(un cargo)* to take; **asumir la presidencia de una reunión** = to take the chair; **asumir todos los riesgos** = to assume all risks; **ha asumido la responsabilidad de la comercialización de productos** = he has assumed responsibility for marketing

asunción *nf* assumption; **asunción de riesgos** = assumption of risks

asunto *nm* **(a)** *(negocio)* business; *(cuestión)* matter *o* issue; **asunto colateral** *o* **incidental** = collateral issue; **asuntos a tratar** = agenda; **Ministerio de Asuntos Exteriores** = Foreign (and Commonwealth) Office; **Ministro de Asuntos Exteriores** = Foreign Secretary; **ser asunto de alguien** = at the discretion of someone; **condenar es asunto del juez** = sentencing is at the discretion of the judge; **el asunto más importante del orden del día** = the most important matter on the agenda; **el asunto principal de la reunión se concluyó a**

las 3 de la tarde = the main business of the meeting was finished by 3 p.m.; **es un asunto que preocupa a los miembros del comité** = it is a matter of concern to the members of the committee **(b)** *(enredo)* affair; **¿estás involucrado en el asunto de los derechos de autor?** = are you involved in the copyright affair? **(c)** *('cosa')* res; *(caso)* case

atacar *vt* to attack *o* to assault; **atacar a la competencia por medio de ventas masivas** = to knock the competition; **atacar por sorpresa** = to ambush; **los diputados de la oposición atacaron al gobierno por no gastar suficiente dinero en la policía** = the Opposition attacked the government for not spending enough money on the police

ataque *nm* attack; **ataque cardíaco** = heart attack; **ataque con robo** = mugging; **ataque fulminante** = stroke; **ataque por sorpresa** = raid; **realizar un ataque por sorpresa** = to raid; **el periódico se distingue por sus ataques al gobierno** = the newspaper is known for its attacks to the government

atar *vt* to bind

atareado *adj (ocupado)* busy

atasco *nm (embotellamiento)* bottleneck *o* traffic jam

atención *nf* **(a)** attention; *(cuidado)* care; **atención sanitaria** = health care; **sus pedidos recibirán nuestra máxima atención** = your orders will have our best attention **(b)** *(en correspondencia)* **a la atención de** = care of; **a la atención del Director Gerente** = for the attention of the Managing Director; **Herr Schmidt, a la atención del Sr Matín** = Herr Schmidt, care of Mr Martín **(c)** *(expresión usada al principio de algunos juicios)* **¡atención!** = oyez

atender *vt* to attend to *o* to cater for; **atender a un cliente** = to serve a customer; **atender a las necesidades de** = to make provision for; **atender a las necesidades económicas de alguien** = to make financial provision for someone; **la comisaría tiene que atender a cualquier tipo de delito** = the police station has to cater for every type of crime

atenerse *vr* **atenerse a** = to abide by; **no se atuvo a los términos del contrato** = she did not abide by the terms of the agreement

atentado *nm* attack *o* attempt; **atentado a la intimidad** = invasion of privacy; **atentado contra el pudor** = indecent assault; **atentado terrorista** = terrorist attack

atentamente *adv (en una carta)* **atentamente** *o* **le saluda atentamente** = yours faithfully *o* Yours truly *o* *US* Truly yours

atentar **1** *vt* to attempt; **atentar un delito** = to try to commit a crime **2** *vi;* **atentar contra alguien** = to make an attempt on a person's life; **atentar contra la ley** = to break the law; **atentar contra de un acuerdo** = to derogate from something which has been agreed

atenuación *nf (mitigación)* mitigation

atenuante **1** *adj* **circunstancias** *o* **factores atenuantes** = extenuating circumstances *o* mitigating factors **2** *nm* extenuation; **atenuante de la indemnización por daños** = mitigation of damages; **como atenuante de** = in extenuation of something; **el abogado alegó la edad del acusado como atenuante de los hechos** = counsel pleaded the accused's age in extenuation of his actions

> Un atenuante es una circunstancia que disminuye la gravedad de un acto punible (CP artº 9)

atenuar *vt (mitigar)* to mitigate; **alegato para atenuar la pena** plea in mitigation; **el abogado defensor hizo un discurso para atenuar la pena** = defence counsel made a speech in mitigation

aterrizar *vi* to land; **hacer aterrizar** = to land; **el avión aterrizó diez minutos tarde** = the plane landed ten minutes late

atesoramiento *nm* hoarding

atesorar *vt* to hoard

atestación *nf* attestation; **atestación por notario público** = notarization

atestado *nm* affidavit *o* sworn statement *o* report; **atestado policial** = police report

atestar *vt* to testify

atestiguar *vt* to witness *o* to bear witness

átono, -na *adj* flat

atracadero *nm* mooring

atracador, -ra *n* robber *o* mugger; **la policía mató a uno de los atracadores en el asalto al banco** = the police shot one of the gangsters in the bank raid

atracar **1** *vi* to dock; **el barco atracó a las 17.00** = the ship docked at 17.00 **2** *vt (asaltar)* to hold up *o* to mug; *(robar)* to rob; **atracaron un banco en Zaragoza y robaron un coche para poder huir** = they robbed a bank in Zaragoza and stole a car to make their getaway; **atracó tres gasolineras en dos días** = he committed three petrol station robberies in two days; **la banda se dedicaba a atracar tiendas del centro de la ciudad** = the gang robbed shopkeepers in the centre of the town; **los turistas fueron atracados en la estación** = the tourists were mugged in the station; **se le acusó de atracar a una anciana en la calle** = he was accused of mugging an old lady in the street; **seis hombres armados atracaron el banco** = six gunmen held up the bank

atraco *nm* robbery *o* holdup; **atraco a mano armada** = heist *o* armed robbery; **la banda perpetró tres atracos a mano armada en el mismo día** = the gang committed three armed holdups on the same day

atrás *adv* back

atrasado, -da *adj* back *o (trabajo)* behind schedule; *(pago)* overdue *o* in arrears; **alquiler atrasado** = back rent; **salario atrasado** = back pay; **impuestos atrasados** = back taxes; **intereses atrasados** = back interest; **ponga a la factura fecha atrasada del 1 de abril** = backdate your invoice to April 1st

atrasar *vt* to delay

◊ **atrasarse** *vr* to be late; **atrasarse en los pagos** = to allow the payments to fall into arrears

atraso *nm* **(a)** *(tiempo)* delay; **el avión lleva dos horas de atraso** = the plane is two hours late **(b)** *(pago)* arrears; **los pagos llevan seis meses de atraso** = the payments are six months in arrears **(c)** **atrasos** = back wages *o* back pay

atravesar *vt* to undergo *o (cruzar)* to cross over

atribuible *adj* attributable

atribuir *vt* to attribute *o* to impute; **atribuir un móvil a alguien** = to impute a motive to someone; **observaciones atribuidas al Jefe de Policía** = remarks attributed to the Chief Constable

atropellar *vt* to outrage; *(en un vehículo)* to run over *o* to knock down

atropello *nm* abuse *o* outrage

ATS = AYUDANTE TECNICO SANITARIO

audiencia *nf* **(a)** *(vista)* audience *o* hearing; **audiencia a puerta cerrada** = private hearing; **audiencia pública** = public hearing *o* open court; **en audiencia pública** = in open court; **derecho de audiencia ante un tribunal** = locus standi; **el contribuyente no tiene derecho de audiencia en este tribunal** = the taxpayer does not have locus standi in this court **(b)** *(tribunal de justicia)* high court *o* Crown Court; **Audiencia Nacional** = National Criminal Court (in Madrid); **Audiencia Provincial** = County Court *o* Crown Court

La Audiencia Nacional tiene jurisdicción en toda España y está integrada por las salas de lo Penal, de lo Contencioso-Administrativo y de lo Social, las cuales resuelven casos que afectan a todo el territorio del Estado (LOPJ artº 62-67)
Las audiencias provinciales tienen jurisdicción sobre la provincia. En el orden penal resuelven recursos contra las resoluciones de los Juzgados de Instrucción y de lo Penal, y también juzgan determinados delitos en

primera instancia. En el orden civil resuelven recursos contra las resoluciones de los Juzgados de Primera Instancia (LOPJ art.80)

auditor, -ra *n* **(a)** *(censor jurado)* auditor; **la Junta General Anual nombra a los auditores de la empresa** = the AGM appoints the company's auditors **(b)** *(tribunal militar)* **Auditor General de Guerra** = Judge Advocate-General

auditoría *nf* audit *o* accounting; **auditoría general** = general audit; **falseamiento de auditoría** = false accounting

aumentar 1 *vi* to increase *o* to rise; **aumentar de precio** = to increase in price; **aumentar de tamaño** = to increase in size; **aumentar en valor** = to appreciate *o* to increase in value; **que aumenta** = mounting; **el índice neto de delitos violentos ha aumentado en un 15%** = the clear-up rate for crimes of violence has risen by 15% **2** *vt* to raise *o* to increase; **aumentar proporcionalmente** *o* **a escala** = to scale up; **el gobierno ha aumentado la pena por tráfico de drogas** = the government has raised the penalties for drug smuggling; **está satisfecha; le han aumentado el sueldo** = she is pleased - she has had her raise; **la aduana ha aumentado en un 10% los aranceles sobre artículos eléctricos** = the customs have imposed a 10% tax increase on electrical items; **la empresa aumentó su dividendo en un 10%** = the company raised its dividend by 10%; **los beneficios se vieron aumentados en un 10% durante el año pasado** = profits showed a 10% increase *o* an increase of 10% on last year

aumento *nm* *(incremento)* increase *o* rise; **aumento de sueldo** = increase in salary *o* salary increase *o* rise; **aumento del coste de vida** = cost-of-living increase; **aumento de la rentabilidad** = gain in profitability; **aumento de los impuestos** = increase in tax *o* tax increase; **aumento de los precios** = increase in price *o* price increase; **aumento en valor** *o* **en precio** = appreciation; **aumento salarial por mérito** = merit increase; **en aumento** = increasing *o* on the increase; **beneficios en aumento** = increasing profits; **un aumento del índice de criminalidad** = a rise in the crime rate; **le pidió al jefe un aumento de sueldo** = he asked the boss for a raise; **el gobierno espera ajustar el aumento de sueldos en un 3%** = the government hopes to hold salary increases to 3%; **los precios de la bolsa experimentaron un aumento general** = prices generally advanced on the stock market; **según el informe, el número de delitos de violencia denunciados está en aumento** = the report points to upwards trends in reported crimes of violence; **el robo cometido en comercios va en aumento** = stealing from shops is on the increase

ausencia *nf* absence; **ausencia del trabajo** = leave (from work); **en ausencia de** = in the absence of; **en ausencia de alguien** = in absentia; **por ausencia** = by default; **el juicio tuvo lugar en ausencia del acusado** = the trial took place in the absence of the defendant; **en ausencia del presidente, su adjunto presidió la reunión** = in the absence of the chairman, his deputy took the chair; **fue elegido por ausencia de otros candidatos** = he was elected by default

ausente 1 *adj* absent; *(fuera del trabajo)* off **2** *nmf* absentee

autenticar *vt* to authenticate

autenticidad *nf* authenticity *o* genuineness

auténtico, -ca *adj (verdadero)* real *o* genuine *o* authentic; **el artículo auténtico** = the genuine article; **su maleta es de cuero auténtico** *o* **tiene una maleta de cuero auténtico** = his case is made of real leather *o* he has a real leather case ◊ **auténticamente** *adv* genuinely *o* authentically; **persona auténticamente interesada en comprar** = genuine purchaser

autentificar *vt* to authenticate

auto *nm* **(a)** *(mandamiento)* warrant; **auto de comparecencia** = summons; **auto de detención** = general warrant *o* warrant for arrest; **auto de ejecución** = writ of execution; **auto de ejecución de embargo** = warrant of execution; **auto de hábeas corpus** = writ of habeas corpus; **auto de ingreso en prisión** = commitment; **auto de prerrogativa** = prerogative order *o* writ; **auto de prisión** = warrant of committal *o* committal warrant; **auto de prisión expedido por un tribunal** = bench warrant; **auto de procesamiento** = indictment; **auto interlocutorio** = mesne process; **auto judicial** = writ; **elevación de los autos** *o* **auto de avocación** = order of certiorari; **solicitó una revisión judicial por elevación de los autos** = he applied for judicial review by way of certiorari **(b)** *(actas del proceso)* **autos** = court record *o* proceedings; **autos incidentales** = interlocutory proceedings

autoinculpación *nf* self-incrimination

automático, -ca *adj* automatic; **hay un aumento salarial automático el 1 de enero** = there is an automatic increase in salaries on January 1st ◊ **automáticamente** *adv* automatically; **las multas no pagadas aumentan en un 15% automáticamente** = unpaid fines are automatically increased by 15%

automatismo *nm* automatism

autónomo, -ma *adj y n (que trabaja por su cuenta)* freelance; **trabajador autónomo** = self-employed; **los (trabajadores) autónomos** = the self-employed

autopsia *nf* autopsy *o* post mortem; **la autopsia fue llevada a cabo por el médico forense de la** policía = the post mortem was carried out *o* was conducted by the police pathologist

autor, -ra *n* **(a)** *(de un crimen o delito)* author *o* perpetrator; **autor material** = principal; **autor de** = responsible for; **autor de un daño** = wrongdoer; **autor de una moción** = mover; **era la autora de una serie de robos en oficinas** = she was responsible for a series of thefts from offices **(b)** *(propiedad intelectual)* **derechos de autor** = copyright *o* copyright law; **Ley de los derechos de autor** = Copyright Act; **obra cuyos derechos de autor son del dominio público** = work which is out of copyright; **obra protegida por los derechos de autor** = work still in copyright; **propietario, -ra de los derechos de autor** = copyright owner; **registrado, -da con derechos de autor** = copyrighted; **es ilegal hacer copias de un libro protegido por los derechos de autor** = it is illegal to take copies of a copyright work

autoría *nf* **autoría intelectual** = entrapment

autoridad *nf* authority *o* power; **autoridad local** = local authority; **autoridad pública** = public authority; **'por autoridad'** = quo warranto; **con la autoridad de** = per pro *o* per procurationem; **las autoridades** = the authorities; **autoridades competentes** = the authorities in charge; **un tribunal puede dar órdenes a una autoridad local** = a court can give directions to a local authority; **el Proyecto de Ley pretende dar protección a los niños que están bajo la custodia de una autoridad local** = the Bill aims at giving protection to children in the care of a local authority; **una decisión de la autoridad local de acuerdo con los poderes y obligaciones impuestos por la ley** = a decision of the local authority pursuant to the powers and duties imposed upon it by the statutory code; **el proyecto de ley propone aumentar la autoridad del tribunal** = the Bill plans to increase the scope of the tribunal's authority

autorización *nf* authorization *o* authority *o* sanction *o* permission; **autorización escrita** = written permission; **autorización verbal** = verbal permission; **autorización legal** = warrant; **autorización para constituirse en sociedad anónima** = certificate of incorporation; **ley de autorización** = enabling legislation *o* statute; **¿quién dio la autorización para que se presentaran las acusaciones?** = on whose authority was the charge brought?; **¿tienes autorización para realizar este gasto?** = do you have authorization for this expenditure?; **actuaba con la autorización del tribunal** = she was acting on the authority of the court; **el pago se realizó sin autorización oficial** = the payment was made without official sanction; **mostró al banco su autorización para inspeccionar el contenido de la caja fuerte** = he showed the bank his authorization to inspect the contents of the safe; **necesitará la autorización de las autoridades locales para poder derribar el bloque de oficinas** = you will need the sanction of the local authorities before you can knock down the office block; **no tiene autorización para actuar en nuestro nombre** = he has no authority to act on our behalf

autorizado, -da *adj* authorized *o* accredited; **agente autorizado** = authorized dealer; **capital autorizado** = authorized capital; **cita legalmente autorizada** = fair dealing; **contable autorizado** = certified accountant; **huelga no autorizada** = unofficial strike

autorizar *vt* **(a)** *(dar permiso)* to authorize *o* to sanction *o* to entitle; *(dar poder)* to empower; **autorizar a alguien a hacer algo** = to give someone permission to do something; **autorizar a alguien a actuar en nombre de uno mismo** = to authorize someone to act on your behalf; **autorizar el pago** = to authorize payment; **no está autorizado para actuar en nuestro nombre** = he has no authorization to act on our behalf; **la dirección autorizó el gasto de 12 millones en el plan de desarrollo** = the board sanctioned the expenditure of 12 million on the development plan; **el agente está autorizado a vender la propiedad** = the agent is empowered to sell the property; **la compañía le autorizó a firmar el contrato** = she was empowered by the company to sign the contract; **un policía está autorizado a detener a una persona sospechosa de haber cometido un delito** = a constable is empowered to arrest a person whom he suspects of having committed an offence **(b)** *(certificar)* **autorizar una firma** *o* **un documento** = to authenticate a signature *o* to certify a document

auxiliar 1 *adj* ancillary; **guardia auxiliar** = special constable **2** *nmf;* **auxiliar administrativo, -va** = office junior **3** *vt* to aid

auxilio *nm* assistance *o* aid *o* relief

aval *nm* **(a)** *(garantía)* guarantee *o* security; *(carta de apoyo)* letter of comfort *o* comfort letter; **aval de una letra** = backer of a bill; **el banco le prestó 200.000 ptas sin necesidad de aval** = the bank lent him 200,000 ptas without security **(b)** *(endoso)* endorsement

avalar *vt* *(garantizar)* to guarantee; *(ser garante de alguien)* **avalar a alguien** = to stand guarantor for someone *o* to back someone *o* to stand security for someone; **avalar a una compañía asociada** *o* **empresa afiliada** = to guarantee an associated company; **avalar una deuda** = to guarantee a debt; **avalar una letra** = to back a bill *o* to endorse a bill; **avalar una letra de cambio** = to guarantee a bill of exchange

avalúo *nm* appraisal

avance *nm* *(progreso)* progress *o* development

avanzar *vi* *(progresar)* to proceed *o* to progress; **la investigación avanzó rápidamente una vez que se introdujeron los detalles en el ordenador de la policía** = the investigation progressed rapidly once the details were put onto the police computer; **las negociaciones avanzan con lentitud** = the negotiations are proceeding slowly

avenencia *nf* settlement *o* agreement; *(en situación de quiebra)* **avenencia jurídica** = composition in bankruptcy

aventura *nf* **aventura amorosa** = affair; **tener una aventura amorosa con alguien** = to have an affair with someone

avería *nf* **(a)** *(siniestro)* average; **avería gruesa** = general average; **avería simple** = particular average; **pérdida por avería simple** = particular average; **tasador de averías** = average adjuster **(b)** *(desperfecto)* breakdown *o* fault; **no podemos comunicar con nuestro coche patrulla a causa de una avería en el sistema radiofónico** = we cannot communicate with our squad car because of the breakdown of the radio link

averiarse *vr* to break down; **¿qué haces cuando tu coche patrulla se avería?** = what do you do when your squad car breaks down?

averiguar *vt* to gather *o* to discover *o* to find out; **¿averiguaste quién estará en la reunión?** = did you gather who will be at the meeting?

avisar *vt* **(a)** *(informar)* to advise *o* to notify **(b)** *(advertir)* to warn

aviso *nm* **(a)** *(notificación)* advice *o* notice *o* notification; **aviso de crédito** = credit note; **aviso de desahucio** = notice to quit; **aviso de expedición** *o* **de envío** = advice note; **aviso de huelga** = strike notice; **aviso de pago** = reminder; **aviso de petición** = notice of motion; **aviso de quiebra** = bankruptcy notice; **hasta nuevo aviso** = until further notice; **entregar** *o* **dar un aviso a alguien** = to give someone notice *o* to serve notice on someone; **darle a un inquilino el aviso de que se marche** *o* **darle la notificación de desahucio** *o* **desalojo** = to give a tenant notice to quit *o* to serve a tenant with notice to quit; **se dio un aviso al club para que cediese el ruido** = a noise abatement notice was served on the club **(b)** *(citación)* order; **aviso de comparecencia** = subpoena **(c)** *(anuncio)* announcement; **aviso público** = public announcement **(d)** *(advertencia)* warning

avocación *nf* **auto de avocación** = order of certiorari; **el tribunal ordenó un auto de avocación y la consiguiente revisión judicial, anulando la sentencia dictada por el tribunal de menores** = the court ordered certiorari following judicial review, quashing the order made by the juvenile court

avorecedor, -ra *n* accommodation maker

ayuda *nf* assistance *o* aid *o* help; **ayuda de sepelio** = death grant; **ayuda económica** = support; **ayuda estatal** = subsidy; **ayuda financiera** = financial assistance; **ayuda material** = relief; **prestar ayuda económica** = to support; **el abogado no obtuvo mucha ayuda del testigo** = counsel did not get much help from the witness; **el gobierno ha proporcionado ayuda económica a la industria informática** = the government has provided support to the computer industry; **el ordenador le resulta de gran ayuda para escribir cartas** = she finds the computer a great help in writing letters; **la compañía se estableció con ayuda estatal** = the company was set up with help from the government; **recibe ayuda financiera de las autoridades locales** = she receives financial assistance from the local authority; **ayudas a la exportación de alimentos procedentes de la UE** = export restitution

ayudante *nmf* assistant *o* deputy; **ayudante técnico sanitario (ATS)** = nurse *o* social health worker

ayudar *vt* to assist *o* to help *o* to aid; **ayudar a cometer un delito** = to aid and abet; **esperamos que los bancos nos ayuden durante el periodo de expansión** = we hope the banks will support us during the expansion period; **se ayudó al acusado a llegar al banquillo de los acusados** = the accused had to be assisted into the dock; **su caso no se vio ayudado por la declaración del testigo pericial** = his case was not helped by the evidence of the expert witness; **su declaración no ayudó la defensa del acusado** = his evidence did not help the case for the defendant

ayuntamiento *nm* **(a)** *(casa consistorial)* Town Hall **(b)** *(concejo municipal)* borough council *o* town council; **(antiguamente) secretario del ayuntamiento** = Town Clerk

azotar *vt* to whip *o* to thrash

Bb

B *nf (acciones ordinarias con derechos de voto especiales muchas veces propiedad del fundador y su familia)* **acciones de clase 'B'** = 'B' shares

baja *nf* **(a)** *(descenso o disminución)* decline *o* drop; **durante el año pasado los salarios reales han experimentado una baja** = the last year has seen a decline in real wages **(b)** *(ausencia del trabajo)* leave; **baja incentivada** *o* **voluntaria con derecho a indemnización** = voluntary redundancy; **baja por enfermedad** = sick leave; **está de baja por enfermedad** *o* **por maternidad** = she is away on sick leave *o* on maternity leave

bajar 1 *vi* **(a)** *(descender)* to drop *o* to decrease; **el precio del petróleo ha bajado** = the price of petrol has gone down; **las ventas han bajado en un 10%** = sales show a drop of 10% **2** *vt (reducir)* to cut *o* to lose; **el dólar bajó dos centavos con respecto a la libra** = the dollar lost two cents against the pound; **las acciones del oro bajaron ayer un 5% en el mercado** = gold shares lost 5% on the market yesterday

bajo *prep* under; **bajo coacción** = under duress; **bajo custodia** = under care; **bajo el encabezamiento** = thereinunder; **bajo juramento** = on oath *o* under oath; **bajo los efectos del alcohol** = under the influence of alcohol; **bajo mano** = under the counter; **bajo palabra** = on parole

bala *nf* bullet; **murió de heridas de bala** = he died of gunshot wounds
◊ **balazo** *nm* bullet wound

balance *nm* balance *o* statement; **balance bancario mensual** *o* **trimestral** *o* **anual** = monthly *o* quarterly *o* yearly statement; **balance de liquidación** = statement of affairs; **balance de resultados** = profit and loss statement; **balance general** = financial statement *o* balance sheet; **el balance general de la empresa correspondiente al año anterior muestra pérdidas considerables** = the company balance sheet for the previous year shows a substantial loss; **el contable ha preparado el balance de situación del primer semestre** = the accountant has prepared the balance sheet for the first half-year; **el departamento de cuentas ha preparado un balance general para los accionistas** = the accounts department have prepared a financial statement for the shareholders

balanza *nf* balance; **balanza de pagos** = balance of payments; **balanza trucada** = false weight

bancario , -ria *adj* banking; **cuenta bancaria** = bank account *o US* banking account; **domiciliación bancaria** = banker's order *o* standing order *o* direct debit; **giro bancario** = bank draft *o* banker's draft; **realizar un giro bancario** = to make a draft on a bank; **pago mi suscripción por domiciliación bancaria** = I pay my subscription by standing order

bancarrota *nf* bankruptcy; **(en) bancarrota** = bankrupt; **fue a la bancarrota tras dos años en el negocio** = he went bankrupt after two years in business

banco *nm* **(a)** *(comercial)* bank; **banco central** = central bank; **banco comercial** = clearing bank *o* credit bank; **banco hipotecario** = mortgage loan bank; **Banco Mundial** = World Bank; **banco por acciones** *o* **banco privado constituido en sociedad anónima** = joint-stock bank; **billete de banco** = paper money *o* paper currency *o* bank note *o* banknote; **pago mi suscripción a través del banco** = I pay my subscription by standing order **(b)** *(información)* **banco de datos** = data bank *o* bank of data *o* database; **la policía guarda un banco de huellas dactilares** = the police maintain a database of fingerprints **(c)** *(asiento)* bench; **banco de testigos** = witness box; *(en las Cortes españolas)* **banco azul** = the government front bench

banda *nf* band; **banda armada** = armed band; **banda de criminales** = gang; **miembro de una banda de criminales** = gangster; **una banda de ladrones de joyas** = a gang of jewel thieves; **una banda de traficantes de droga** = a drugs gang

bandeja *nf* tray; **bandeja para documentos** = filing basket *o* filing tray

bandera *nf (pabellón)* flag; **embarcación de bandera española** = ship flying the Spanish flag; **enarbolar una bandera** = to fly a flag

bandidaje *nm* banditry

bandido *nm* bandit; **tras el golpe bajaron grupos de bandidos de las montañas para atacar las comisarías de policía** = after the coup groups of bandits came down from the mountains to attack police stations

bandolerismo *nm* banditry

bandolero *nm* bandit

banquero, -ra *n* banker

banquillo *nm* **banquillo de los acusados** = dock; **el acusado en el banquillo** = the prisoner in the dock

bar *nm (taberna)* public house

barato *adj* cheap; **dinero** *o* **crédito barato** = cheap money

barco *nm (buque)* ship; **barco hundido** *o* **naufragado** = wreck; **derecho de retención de un barco** = maritime lien; **desertar del barco en el que se está enrolado** = to jump ship; **el petróleo salía a raudales de los restos del barco** = oil poured out of the wreck of the ship

baremo *nm (escala)* scale

barón *nm* baron

barrera *nf* barrier; **barreras arancelarias** = customs barriers *o* tariff barriers; **imponer** *o* **levantar barreras arancelarias a un producto** = to impose *o* to lift tariff barriers on a product; **imponer** *o* **levantar barreras comerciales a ciertas mercancías** = to impose *o* to lift trade barriers on certain goods

barrio *nm* **(a)** *(distrito)* district; **barrio residencial** = suburb **(b)** *(vecindad)* neighbourhood; **vivimos en un barrio muy tranquilo** = we live in a very quiet neighbourhood

basado, -da *adj* **basado en** = based on

basar *vt* to base; **basamos nuestros cálculos en el rendimiento del año pasado** = we based our calculations on last year's turnover; **hemos calculado el rendimiento basándonos en un aumento de los precios de un 6%** = we have calculated the turnover on the basis of a 6% price increase
◊ **basarse** *vr* to rely *o* to go on; **la policía sólo cuenta con dos huellas dactilares en las que basarse** = two fingerprints are all the police have to go on

base 1 *adj* basic; **año base** = base year; **impuesto de tipo base** = base rate tax; **salario** *o* **sueldo base** = basic pay *o* basic salary *o* basic wage **2** *nf* **(a)** *(sede)* base; **tiene una oficina en Madrid que utiliza como base mientras viaja por el sur de Europa** = he has an office in Madrid which he uses as a base while he is travelling in Southern Europe; **un ejecutivo de ventas con base en Londres** = a London-based sales executive **(b)** *(fundamento)* basis; **¿en base a qué se formula la reclamación por daños y perjuicios?** = what are the grounds for the claim for damages? **(c)** *(militantes de un partido)* rank and file; **las bases** = grass-roots; **el partido cuenta con el apoyo de las bases** = the

party has considerable support at grass-roots level **(d)** *(informática)* **base de datos** = database

BASIC *nm* BASIC (BEGINNER'S ALL-PURPOSE SYMBOLIC INSTRUCTION CODE)

básico, -ca *adj (fundamental o esencial)* basic *o* fundamental; **lo básico** = basics; **tiene un conocimiento básico del mercado** = he has a basic knowledge of the market
◊ **básicamente** *adv* basically

bastardo, -da *n* bastard

beca *nf* grant
◊ **becado, -da** *n* grantee

benefactor, -ra 1 *nm* benefactor **2** *nf* benefactress **3** *n* volunteer

beneficiario, -ria *adj y n* **(a)** *(destinatario)* beneficiary *o* payee *o* recipient; **beneficiario, -ria de la póliza** = person named in the policy; **propietario beneficiario** = beneficial owner; **los principales beneficiarios del testamento son los familiares del difunto** = the main beneficiaries of the will are the deceased's family **(b)** *(cesionario)* transferee *o* volunteer

beneficiarse *vr* to benefit; **beneficiarse de algo** = to benefit from *o* by something

beneficiencia *nf* charity

beneficio *nm* **(a)** *(rendimiento)* return; *(ganancia)* profit *o* gain; **beneficio bruto** = gross margin *o* gross profit; **beneficio neto** *o* **líquido** = clear profit *o* net profit; **beneficio de explotación** *o* **beneficio comercial** = trading profit *o* operating profit; **beneficio sin deducir los impuestos** = profit before tax *o* pretax profit; **beneficio después de impuestos** = profit after tax; **beneficios de una sociedad** = corporate profits; **beneficios extraordinarios** = excess profits; **realización de beneficios excesivos** = profiteering; **sin beneficios** = at a loss; **sacamos** *o* **obtuvimos un beneficio neto de seis millones por la venta** = we made six million clear profit on the sale; **traficar con objetos robados para sacar un beneficio** = to deal in stolen goods for gain **(b)** *(disfrute de una herencia)* benefit; **beneficio de deliberación** = right of beneficiary to await the outcome of the inventory of an estate before deciding whether or not to accept the inheritance; **beneficio de inventario** = benefit of inventory *o* right of beneficiary to await the outcome of the inventory of an estate before paying any dues related to the inheritance.; **se dejó la propiedad a beneficio de los nietos del propietario** = the estate was left to the benefit of the owner's grandsons **(c)** *(dividendos)* equity

El beneficio de inventario es un derecho concedido al heredero según el cual éste no queda obligado a pagar las deudas y demás cargas de la herencia, más que hasta donde cubran los bienes de la misma (CC artº 1010)

benéfico, -ca *adj* charitable; **institución benéfica** = charity; **sociedad benéfica** = charitable trust *o* charitable corporation

benemérita *nf* the Spanish Civil Guard

beneplácito *nm* assent

bestia *nmf (criminal)* thug
◊ **bestialidad** *nf* bestiality

best-seller *nm (artículo de mayor venta)* best-seller

bi *prefijo* bi-; **bimensual** = bi-monthly; **bimestral** = bi-monthly

bicameralismo nm *(sistema de dos cámaras)* bicameralism

bien *nm* **(a)** *(propiedad)* asset *o* property; *(posesión)* possession; **bien comunal** = common *o* public property; **bienes de capital** = capital goods; **bienes de consumo** = consumer goods; **bienes de equipo** = capital goods; **bienes dotales** = dowry; **bienes heredados** = inherited property; **bienes inmuebles** *o* **bienes raíces** = real estate *o* (real) property *o* immovable property *o* immovables; **bienes intangibles** = incorporeal chattels; **bienes mostrencos** = abeyance; **bienes muebles** = personal property *o* personalty *o* chattels personal *o* personal assets; **bienes vacantes** = bona vacantia; **bienes y servicios** = goods and services; **enseres y bienes muebles** = goods and chattels; **hipoteca sobre bienes muebles** = chattel mortgage; **impuesto sobre los bienes** = property tax *o* tax on property; **ocultación de bienes** = concealment of assets; **el mercado de los bienes comerciales está en decadencia** *o* **en crisis** = the commercial property market is declining

bienestar *nm (asistencia social)* welfare; **estado de bienestar** = welfare state; **es obligación del tribunal de menores velar por el bienestar de los menores tutelados** = it is the duty of the juvenile court to see to the welfare of children in care

bienhechor, -ra **1** *nm* benefactor **2** *nf* benefactress **3** *n* volunteer

bigamia *nf* bigamy

bígamo, -ma **1** *adj* bigamous; **celebraron una ceremonia de matrimonio bígamo** = they went through a bigamous marriage ceremony **2** *n* bigamist

bilateral *adj* bilateral *o* reciprocal; **el ministro firmó un acuerdo de comercio bilateral** = the minister signed a bilateral trade agreement

billete *nm* bill *o (entrada)* ticket; **billete de banco** = bank note *o* banknote *o* currency note *o* paper money *o* paper currency

◊ **billetero, -ra** *n* wallet; **billetera para tarjetas de crédito** = credit card holder

birlar *vt (mangar)* to knock off *o* to nick *o* to pinch

blanco, -ca **1** *adj* **(a)** *(color)* white; **delincuencia de guante blanco** = white collar crime; **enviar un documento en un sobre blanco** = to send a document under plain cover **(b)** *(libertad de acción)* **carta blanca** = carte blanche; **tiene carta blanca para actuar en nombre de la empresa** *o* **la empresa le ha concedido carta blanca para que actúe en su nombre** = he has carte blanche to act on behalf of the company *o* the company has given him carte blanche to act on its behalf **2** *nm* **(a)** *(hueco)* **en blanco** = blank; **espacio en blanco** = blank; **un cheque en blanco** = a blank cheque **(b)** *(hito)* target; **dar en el blanco** = to hit the mark *o* the target **3** *nf (dinero)* money; **estar sin blanca** = to be broke

blando, -da *adj (flojo)* soft; **moneda blanda** = soft currency

blanquear *vt* to launder; **blanquear dinero negro** = to launder money; **las ganancias del robo fueron blanqueadas a través de un banco en el Caribe** = the proceeds of the robbery were laundered through a bank in the Caribbean

blasfemar *vi* to blaspheme

blasfemia *nf* blasphemy

blindado, -da *adj* **puerta blindada** = burglarproof door

bloc *nm* pad; **bloc de notas** = notepad

bloque *nm* block; **un bloque de oficinas** = a block of offices *o* an office block; **reserva en bloque** = block booking; **la empresa tiene una reserva en bloque de veinte asientos de avión** *o* **de diez habitaciones de hotel** = the company has a block booking for twenty seats on the plane *o* for ten rooms at the hotel

bloqueado, -da *adj* blocked; **cuenta de garantía bloqueada** = escrow account; **divisa bloqueada** = blocked currency; **moneda bloqueada** = blocked currency

bloquear *vt* **(a)** *(detener)* to block; **utilizó su voto de calidad para bloquear la moción** = he used his casting vote to block the motion; **la comisión de planificación bloqueó el proyecto de construir una autopista que atravesara el centro de la ciudad** = the planning committee blocked the plan to build a motorway through the middle of the town **(b)** *(inmovilizar créditos o bienes)* to freeze; **bloquear capital** = to lock up capital; **bloquear una cuenta corriente** = to freeze an account; **el tribunal ordenó bloquear la cuenta bancaria de la compañía** = the court ordered the company's bank account to be frozen **(c)** *(cercar)* to blockade;

la armada enemiga bloqueó la ciudad = the town was blockaded by the enemy navy

bloqueo *nm* blockade; **bloqueo económico** = embargo; **el enemigo levantó el bloqueo del puerto durante dos meses para dejar entrar provisiones de necesidad urgente** = the enemy lifted the blockade of the port for two months to let emergency supplies in; **el gobierno hizo entrar las mercancías por aire para combatir el bloqueo** = the government brought in goods by air to beat the blockade

BOE (= BOLETIN OFICIAL DEL ESTADO)

bofia *nf (la palma)* cop; **la bofia** = the fuzz

boicot *o* **boicoteo** *nm* boycott; **el sindicato organizó un boicot contra los coches de importación** = the union organized a boycott against *o* of imported cars

boicotear *vt* to boycott; **estamos boicoteando todas las importaciones de ese país** = we are boycotting all imports from that country; **la dirección ha boicoteado la reunión** = the management has boycotted the meeting; **los productos de la empresa han sido boicoteados por los principales grandes almacenes** = the company's products have been boycotted by the main department stores

boletín *nm* bulletin; **boletín de Bolsa** = Stock Exchange listing; **boletín oficial de la UE** = Official Journal; **Boletín Oficial del Estado (BOE)** = Official Gazette of the Spanish State

boleto *nm* ticket *o* slip

Bolsa *nf* **(a)** *(mercado de valores)* stock market *o* Stock Exchange; **bolsa de contratación** = commodity market *o* commodity exchange; **bolsa de trabajo** = labour exchange; **cotización oficial en la Bolsa** = quotation on the Stock Exchange *o* Stock Exchange quotation; **cotizaciones de la Bolsa** = Stock Exchange listing; **trabaja en la Bolsa** = he works on the Stock Exchange; **las acciones de la empresa se negocian en la Bolsa** = shares in the company are traded on the Stock Exchange **(b)** *(beca)* grant

bonificación *nf* **(a)** *(descuento)* allowance *o* rebate; *(por ausencia de indemnizaciones en una póliza de seguros)* no-claims bonus; **bonificación tributaria** = tax rebate **(b)** *(prima)* bounty

bono *nm* **(a)** *(obligación)* bond; *(de interés fijo)* debenture; **bono basura** = junk bond; **bono con garantía** = secured bond; **bono de confianza** = gilt-edged bond; **bono hipotecario** = mortgage bond; **bono negociable** = marketable bond; **bono nominativo** = registered bond; **bono no transferible** = non-marketable bond; **bono redimible** = callable bond; **bonos del Estado** *o* **del Tesoro** = government bonds *o* treasury bonds **(b)** *(vale)* voucher; **bono de entrega** = delivery order

borde *nm* **estar al borde de una crisis** = to be on the verge of a crisis; **la empresa estaba al borde de la quiebra** = the company was close to bankruptcy

bordo *nm* **a bordo** = on board; **franco a bordo** = free on board (f.o.b.)

borrachera *nf (embriaguez)* intoxication

borracho, -cha 1 *adj* drunk; **borracho e incapacitado** = drunk and incapable; **borracho y alborotador** = drunk and disorderly **2** *n* drunkard; **borracho empedernido** *o* **borracho habitual** = habitual drunkard

borrador *nm* *(copia preliminar)* rough copy; *(de un proyecto)* draft; **borrador de un contrato** = draft of a contract *o* draft contract; **borrador de una orden judicial** = minutes of order; **hacer un borrador** = to rough out *o* to draft; **el primer borrador del contrato lo corrigió el director gerente** = the first draft of the contract was corrected by the managing director; **el consejo de administración rechazó el borrador del contrato propuesto por el sindicato** = the board threw out the draft contract submitted by the union

borrar *vt (levantar)* to remove; *(tachar o suprimir)* to expunge; **borrar del acta** = to strike from the record; **podemos borrar su nombre de la lista de direcciones** = we can remove his name from the mailing list

bosquejar *vt* to outline *o* to draft

bosquejo *nm (borrador)* outline *o* rough draft

botín *nm* loot; *(pillaje)* plunder; **botín de guerra** = spoils of war *o* prize; **llevar como botín** = to loot

brazo *nm* arm; **brazo armado** = armed wing; **brazo derecho** = right-hand man; **huelga de brazos caídos** = sit-down protest

brevedad *nf* **a la mayor brevedad** = at your earliest convenience

brigada *nf* squad *o* brigade; **brigada móvil** = flying squad; **la brigada anticorrupción** = the Fraud Squad; **la brigada antidisturbios** = the riot squad; **la brigada antidroga** *o* **de estupefacientes contra la droga** = the Drug Squad; **la brigada de homicidios** = the Homicide Squad *o* Murder Squad; **brigada de investigación criminal** = criminal investigation department (CID)

británico, -ca *adj* British; **el gobierno británico** Her Majesty's Government; **¿es ciudadano británico?** = is he a UK citizen?; **¿tiene pasaporte británico?** = does she have a UK passport?

broma *nf* joke; **broma pesada** = hoax

brusco, -ca *adj (fuerte)* sharp; **aumento brusco de delitos violentos** = sharp rise in crimes of violence

◊ **bruscamente** *adv (fuertemente)* sharply; **el número de atracos ha aumentado bruscamente durante los últimos años** = the number of mugging cases has risen sharply over the last few years

bruto, -ta 1 *adj (total)* gross; **beneficio bruto** *o* **margen bruto** = gross margin *o* gross profit; **ingresos brutos** *o* **renta bruta** *o* **sueldo bruto** = gross earnings *o* gross income *o* gross salary *o* gross receipts; **peso bruto** = gross weight; **producto interior bruto (PIB)** = gross domestic product (GDP); **producto nacional bruto (PNB)** = gross national product (GNP) 2 *nm* thug

bueno, -na *adj* **(a)** *(apreciable)* good; **buena causa** *o* **buena razón** = good cause; **buen comportamiento** = good behaviour; **buena compra** = good buy; **buena fe** *o* **de buena fe** = bona fides *o* bona fide *o* (in) good faith; **actuó de buena fe** = he acted bona fide; **una oferta de buena fe** = a bona fide offer; **el demandado no actuaba de buena fe** = the respondent was not acting bona fides; **el abogado nos dio muy buenos consejos** = the solicitor gave us some very sound advice (NOTA: se escribe **buen** delante de nm); **un buen número** = a good many; **un buen número de empleados se ha afiliado al sindicato** = a good many staff members have joined the union; **la condenaron a cuatro años de cárcel pero la liberaron pronto por buen comportamiento** = she was sentenced to four years in prison, but was released early for good behaviour; **los jueces le obligaron legalmente a tener buen comportamiento** = the magistrates bound him over to be of good behaviour

La buena fe es la convicción de actuar de forma lícita. La buena fe se presume siempre

bufete *nm* lawyer's office; *(clientela)* practice; *(despacho de abogados)* chambers; **es socio de un bufete de abogados del país** = he is a partner in a country solicitor's practice; **ha puesto un bufete de abogados** = he has set up in practice as a solicitor

buhonero, -ra *n (vendedor)* street vendor *o* pedlar

bulto *nm* package *o* packet

buque *nm* ship

burdel *nm* brothel

burla *nf* trick *o* hoax

burlar *vt* to trick *o* to hoax; **burlar la acción de la justicia** = to outwit *o* to defeat justice

burocracia *nf* paper work; *(papeleo)* red tape

burócrata *nmf* bureaucrat *o* public official

burocrático, -ca *adj* official; **lenguaje burocrático** = officialese

busca *nf* search *o* hunt; **en busca** = in pursuit; **los atracadores del banco escaparon en un coche con la policía en su busca** = the bank robbers escaped in a car with the police in pursuit

buscar *vt (averiguar)* to search *o* to hunt *o* to look for; **el representante buscó en sus archivos un justificante de la venta** = the agent searched his files for a record of the sale; **la policía está buscando pistas del asesinato** = the police are hunting for clues to the murder **(b)** *(esforzarse para encontrar)* **buscar algo** *o* **a alguien** = to seek; **buscar trabajo** = to seek employment; **la policía busca a un hombre alto que fue visto cerca del lugar del crimen** = the police are seeking a tall man who was seen near the scene of the crime; **la policía está buscando a dos hombres** = two men are being sought by the police; **las autoridades locales están buscando alojamiento para un menor bajo la tutela del tribunal** = the local authority is seeking to place the ward of court in accommodation **(c)** *(recoger)* **ir a buscar** = to shop (for) something

búsqueda *nf (inspección)* search; *(caza)* hunt; **búsqueda del asesino** = murder hunt; **búsqueda y arresto** = search and arrest; **la policía ha organizado una búsqueda del oro robado** *o* **de los presos huidos** *o* **del arma homicida** = the police have organized a hunt for the stolen gold *o* for the escaped prisoners *o* for the murder weapon

Cc

cabal *adj (estado mental)* sound; **no estar en sus cabales** = to be out of one's mind

caballo *nm* **(a)** (animal) horse; **a caballo** = mounted **(b)** *(heroína)* heroin

caballero *nm* gentleman; **acuerdo entre caballeros** = gentlemen's agreement *o US* gentleman's agreement

cabecera *nf* head

cabecilla *nmf (jefe)* boss

caber *vi* to contain *o* to hold *o* to fit; **en una bolsa caben veinte kilos de azúcar** = a bag can hold twenty kilos of sugar

cabeza *nm* head; **cabeza de familia** = householder; **estar a la cabeza de** = to lead

cabildear *vt* to lobby; **cabildero,-ra** *n;* **cabildero, -ra que representa a un grupo de presión** = lobbyist

cabina *nf* cabin *o* booth; **cabina electoral** = election booth *o* voting booth *o* polloing booth; **cábina telefónica** = call box

cabo *nm* end; **llevar a cabo** = to effect *o* to carry out; *(poner en práctica)* to implement

cachear *vt* to frisk *o* to search

cachiporra *nf (argot)* cosh *o* life preserver

cacique *nm (en prisión)* baron

caco *nm (argot)* thief; *(carterista)* pickpocket

cadalso *nm* scaffold *o* gallows

cadáver *nm* corpse *o* cadaver

cadena *nf* **cadena perpetua** = life imprisonment

cadete *nm* cadet; **ha entrado en la escuela de cadetes de la policía** = he has entered the police cadet college; **se incorporó al cuerpo de policía como cadete** = she joined the police force as a cadet

caducar *vi* to lapse *o* to expire; **pasaporte caducado** = lapsed passport; **su pasaporte está caducado** = his passport has expired

caducidad *nf (derogación)* lapse; *(vencimiento)* expiry; **fecha de caducidad** = expiry date

caer *vi* to fall; **caer en desuso** = to fall into abeyance; **caer fuera** = to fall outside; **la fiesta nacional cae en lunes** = the national holiday falls on a Monday

caída *nf* drop; **caída repentina** = sharp fall; **la caída del dólar** = the fall in the value of the dollar; **una caída de los precios** = a drop in prices

caja *nf* **(a)** *(recipiente)* box *o* case; **caja archivadora** = box file; **caja de embalaje** = packing case; **las drogas estaban escondidas en cajas de artículos de oficina** = the drugs were hidden in boxes of office stationery; **los sobres vienen en cajas de doscientos** = envelopes come in boxes of two hundred; **se envió la mercancía en cajas de cartón fino** = the goods were sent in thin cardboard boxes **(b)** *(para guardar fondos)* cash box *o* safe; **caja de seguridad** *o* **caja de custodia** = safe deposit *o* safe deposit box; **caja fuerte** *o* **caja de caudales** = safe *o* strongbox; **caja fuerte a prueba de incendios** = fire-proof safe; **caja fuerte empotrada** = wall safe; **caja nocturna** = night safe; **depósito en caja fuerte** = safe deposit; **dinero en caja** = balance in hand *o* cash in hand; **guardamos el dinero para gastos menores en la caja fuerte** = we keep the petty cash in the safe; **pon los documentos en la caja fuerte** = put the documents in the safe **(c)** *(banco)* **caja de ahorros** = Trustee Savings Bank; **caja de pensiones** = pension fund; **Caja Postal de Ahorros** = National Savings

cajero, -ra *n* teller; **cajero automático** = cash dispenser

cajón *nm* **(a)** *(caja grande)* packing case **(b)** *(en un mueble)* drawer

calabozo *nm* dungeon *o* police station cell

calculador, -ra 1 *adj* calculating; **el juez calificó al acusado de criminal frío y calculador** = the judge called the prisoner a cool calculating villain **2** *nf* calculator

calcular *vt* **(a)** *(contar)* to calculate *o* to work out the figures; **calcular mal** = to miscalculate; **que no se pueden calcular** = unquantifiable; **el empleado de banco calculó el tipo de cambio del dólar** = the bank clerk calculated the rate of exchange for the dollar; **calculó que tenían seis minutos para**

escapar antes de que llegara la patrulla de policía = he calculated that they had six minutes left to escape before the police patrol would arrive; **el vendedor calculó mal el descuento, así que apenas cubrimos los gastos en la operación** = the salesman miscalculated the discount, so we hardly broke even on the deal **(b)** *(estimar)* to estimate *o* to quote; **calcular aproximadamente** = to estimate; **calcular los gastos** = to estimate costs; **calcular por lo bajo** = to underestimate; **calculando por lo bajo** = at a conservative estimate; **calcular un precio en dólares** = to quote a price in dollars; **calculó por lo bajo el tiempo necesario para terminar el trabajo** = he underestimated the amount of time needed to finish the work; **me calculó un precio de 100.000 ptas** = he quoted me a price of 100,000 ptas

cálculo *nm* calculation *o* estimate; **cálculo aproximado** = rough estimate; **cálculo de costas** = cost accounting; **cálculo del presupuesto** = estimates of expenditure; **cálculo estimativo** = quotation; **error de cálculo** *o* **cálculo erróneo** = miscalculation; **según un cálculo moderado** = at a conservative estimate; **según mis cálculos, el índice de crímenes resueltos ha aumentado en un 20% en los últimos seis meses** = according to my calculations, the detection rate has increased by 20% over the last six months; **hice unos cálculos aproximados al dorso de un sobre** = I made some rough calculations on the back of an envelope; **el índice de criminalidad ha aumentado al menos un 20% durante el pasado año, y eso haciendo un cálculo moderado** = the crime rate has risen by at least 20% in the last year, and that is a conservative estimate

calendario *nm* calendar; **calendario de trabajo** = desk planner *o* wall planner

calibrar *vt (medir)* to measure

calidad *nf* **(a)** *(cualidad)* quality; **de primera calidad** = select; **de poca calidad** = inferior; **productos de poca calidad** = inferior products *o* products of inferior quality **(b)** *(capacidad)* capacity *o* position; **calidad de socio** *o* **miembro** = membership; **en calidad de presidente** = in his capacity as chairman; **voto de calidad** = casting vote; **el presidente tiene voto de calidad** = the chairman has a casting vote; **utilizó su voto de calidad para bloquear la moción** = he used his casting vote to block the motion

caliente *adj (especulación)* **dinero caliente** = hot money

calificación *nf* description; *(de un delito)* specification

calificado, -da *adj* qualified

calificar *vt* to call *o* to describe; **calificar los hechos delictivos** = bring specific charges

caligrafía *nf* **experto** *o* **perito en caligrafía** = handwriting expert

callar *vt* to suppress

callejero *nm* street directory

calumnia *nf* false accusation; **calumnia oral** = slander
◊ **calumniador, -ra** *n* slanderer
◊ **calumniar** *vt* to slander; *(por escrito)* to libel

El delito de calumnia consiste en la falsa imputación de un delito de los que dan lugar a procedimiento de oficio. El acusado queda exento de pena si se prueba el hecho imputado (CP artº 453).

calzada *nf* carriageway

cámara *nf* **(a)** *(entidad)* house *o* chamber; **Cámara de Comercio** = Chamber of Commerce; **cámara de compensación** = clearing house **(b)** *(parlamento)* **Cámara de los Comunes** = House of Commons; **Cámara de los Lores** = House of Lords; **Cámara de Representantes** = House of Representatives; **sistema de dos cámaras** = bicameralism **(c)** *(sala)* room; **cámara acorazada** = strongroom; **cámara de gas** = gas chamber

camarilla *nf (grupo de presión)* ring *o* lobby *o* pressure group; **camarilla política** = caucus

cambiable *adj* exchangeable

cambiar 1 *vt* **(a)** *(modificar)* to change *o* to alter; **cambiar completamente** = to reverse **(b)** *(enmendar)* to qualify **(c)** *(sustituir)* to exchange an article for another; *(dinero)* to convert; **cambiamos nuestras libras a francos suizos** = we converted our pounds into Swiss francs **2** *vi* **(a)** *(modificar)* to change; **cambiar de partido** = to cross the floor **(b)** *(trasladar)* to move; *(transbordar)* to transfer; **cuando llegue al aeropuerto de Londres, tiene que cambiar a un vuelo nacional** = when you get to London airport, you have to transfer onto an internal flight
◊ **cambiarse** *vr (trasladarse)* to move

cambiario *adj* exchange; **mercados cambiarios** = the foreign exchange markets

cambio *nm* **(a)** *(modificación)* change *o* alteration; **cambio completo** = reversal; **la demandante solicitó un cambio en su orden de manutención** = the petitioner asked for a variation in her maintenance order **(b)** *(sustitución)* **cambio de dueño** *o* **de dirección** = under new management; **cambio de plantilla** = staff turnover *o* turnover of staff; **cambio de rumbo** = departure **(c)** *(finanzas)* exchange; **cambio a plazo** = forward rate; **cambio de moneda** *o* **de divisas** = foreign exchange; **agente de cambio de divisas** = foreign exchange broker; **control de cambio** = exchange controls; **letra de cambio** = bank draft *o* bill of exchange; **operaciones de cambio** = foreign exchange dealing; **operador, -ra de cambios** = dealer; **tipo de cambio** = rate of exchange *o* exchange rate **(d)** *(comercio)* **libre cambio** = free trade; **zona de libre cambio** = free trade area **(e)** *(moneda)* small change *o* loose change

◊ **cambista** *nmf (operador de cambios)* foreign exchange broker *o* dealer

camello *nm (traficante de droga)* drug peddlar

camino *nm* way *o* path; **camino de herradura** = bridleway; *(pedido)* **en camino** = on order

campaña *nf* campaign; **campaña electoral** = electoral campaign; **hacer campaña** = to campaign; **el Gobierno ha lanzado una campaña en contra de las personas que conducen en estado de embriaguez** = the Government has launched a campaign against drunken drivers; **está haciendo campaña por la modificación de la Ley de Secretos Oficiales** = he is campaigning for a revision of the Official Secrets Act; **están haciendo campaña por la abolición de la pena de muerte** *o* **están haciendo campaña contra la pena de muerte** = they are campaigning for the abolition of the death penalty *o* they are campaigning against the death penalty

campo *nm* **(a)** *(materia)* field; **campo de aplicación** = terms of reference **(b)** *(superficie)* camp; **campo de concentración** = concentration camp; **campo de prisión** = convict settlement

canal *nm* channel; **canal de televisión** = TV station

cancelación *nf (anulación)* cancellation *o* annulling *o* annulment *o* *(de un acuerdo)* revocation; **cancelación de una deuda** = redemption; **documento de cancelación de una hipoteca** = memorandum of satisfaction

cancelar *vt* **(a)** *(anular)* to cancel; **cancelar un acuerdo** = to call off a deal; **cancelar un cheque** = to cancel a cheque; **el acuerdo ha sido cancelado** = the agreement is off; **el tratado sobre derechos de pesca ha sido cancelado** = the treaty on fishing rights has been revoked **(b)** *(amortizar)* to redeem **(c)** *(negarse a cumplir)* to repudiate *o* to revoke *o* to countermand; **cancelar una acción legal por incomparecencia del demandante** *o* **otra razón** = to strike out; **la demanda fue cancelada porque revelaba ausencia de causa para la acción** = the statement of claim was struck out because it disclosed no cause of action

candidato, -ta *n* candidate *o* *(aspirante)* applicant; **candidato a un puesto de trabajo** = applicant for a job *o* job applicant; **presentarse como candidato a** = to contest; **¿a qué candidato vas a votar?** = which candidate are you voting for?; **todos los candidatos a la elección aparecieron en la televisión** = all the candidates in the election appeared on television; **entrevistamos a diez candidatos para el puesto** = we interviewed ten candidates for the post; **hay seis candidatos para el puesto de guardia jurado** = there are six candidates for the post of security guard

candidatura *nf* candidature *o* candidacy; **proponer la candidatura de** = to nominate; **elecciones con una única candidatura** = an uncontested election

canje *nm (cambio)* exchange; **canje parcial** = part exchange

canjeable *adj* exchangeable

canjear *vt* to exchange

cánon *nm* tax *o* royalty; **los cánones del petróleo suponen una gran parte de los ingresos del país** oil royalties make up a large proportion of the country's revenue

canónico *adj* **derecho canónico** = canon law

cantar *vt (denunciar)* to grass *o* to shop

cantidad *nf* **(a)** *(cifra)* quantity *o* amount *o* figure; **cantidad apostada** = wager; **gran cantidad** = quantity; **una gran cantidad** = a lot of *o* a great deal of; **compró una gran cantidad de piezas de repuesto** = he bought a large quantity of spare parts; **una pequeña cantidad de drogas ilegales** = a small quantity of illegal drugs; **la empresa hace un descuento cuando se compra en grandes cantidades** = the company offers a discount for quantity purchase **(b)** *(suma)* sum; **cantidad global** = lump sum; **la cantidad asegurada** = the sum insured; **recibió la cantidad de 50 millones de indemnización** = she received the sum of 50 million in compensation

caos *nm* chaos; **tras el golpe de estado, reinó el caos en el país** = after the coup the country was in chaos; **reinó el caos en el centro de la ciudad hasta que llegaron la policía y los coches de bomberos** = chaos reigned in the centre of the town until the police and fire engines arrived

◊ **caótico, -ca** *adj* chaotic; **la situación era caótica hasta que la policía llegó y controló el tráfico** = the situation was chaotic until the police arrived to control the traffic

capacidad *nf* **(a)** *(aptitud jurídica)* capacity *o* competence *o* competency; **capacidad legal** *o* **procesal** = legal capacity; **capacidad para testar** = disposing capacity; **persona con mayoría de edad y plena capacidad** = person of full age and capacity; **su acción se excedía de su capacidad legal** = their action was ultra vires; **el tribunal no tenía capacidad para pronunciar sentencia ya que una de las partes no había terminado de presentar sus pruebas** = the court was unable to adjudicate because one side had not finished presenting its evidence **(b)** *(aptitud comercial)* power; **capacidad de préstamo** *o* **de**

endeudamiento = borrowing power; **capacidad negociadora** = bargaining power **(c)** *(cabida)* capacity; **capacidad de almacenamiento** = storage capacity

capacitación *nf* training; **responsable de la capacitación** = training officer

capacitado, -da *adj* fit *o* competent; **declararse capacitado para ser juzgado** = fit to plead; **el abogado declaró que su cliente no estaba capacitado para declararse culpable** *o* **inocente** = the solicitor stated that his client was not fit to plead; **no está capacitado para firmar el contrato** = he is incompetent to sign the contract

capacitar *vt (formar)* to train

capaz *adj (competente)* capable *o* competent; **capaz de** = capable of; **es capaz de escribir a máquina con una rápidez increíble** = she is capable of very fast typing speeds; **es capaz de realizar fraudes muy complicados** = he is capable of very complicated frauds; **'capaz de intención criminal'** = doli capax

capcioso, -sa *adj* captious; **pregunta capciosa** = leading question

capitación *nf* community charge; **impuesto de capitación** = poll tax

capital 1 *adj* capital; **delito capital** = capital crime *o* offence; **delito no capital** = non-capital crime *o* offence; **pena capital** = capital punishment **2** *nf (ciudad)* capital city **3** *nm* capital; **capital autorizado** = authorized capital; **capital circulante** = working capital; **capital de una deuda** *o* **de un préstamo** *o* **principal de un capital** = principal; **capital disponible** = spare capital; **capital en acciones ordinarias** *o* **capital accionista** *o* **capital propio** = shareholders' equity *o* equity capital; **capital fijo** = fixed capital; **capital que se debe a la empresa** = monies owing to the company; **capital social** *o* **en acciones** *o* **accionario** = share capital; **bienes de capital** = capital goods; **compañía de capital** = corporation; **gastos de capital** = capital expenditure; **pagar capital e intereses** = to repay principal and interest; **pérdidas de capital** = capital loss; **valor de mercado del capital emitido** = market capitalization

capitalización *nf* capitalization

capitulación *nf* surrender; **capitulaciones matrimoniales** = marriage settlement

capítulo *nm* chapter; **capítulo de daños** = head of damage; **capítulo de una ley** = chapter

capturar *vt* to capture; **volver a capturar** = to recapture; **el castillo fue capturado por el enemigo** = the castle was captured by the enemy; **se fugaron seis presos, pero pronto volvieron a ser capturados** = six prisoners escaped, but they were all quickly recaptured

cara *nf* face *o (argot)* mug

carácter *nm* **(a)** *(de una persona)* character **(b)** *(propensión)* **con carácter transitorio** = on a temporary basis; **con carácter vitalicio** = for life **(c)** *(de imprenta)* type *o* typeface

cárcel *nf* **(a)** *(prisión)* jail *o* gaol *o* prison *o* custodial establishment *o* institution; **pasó diez años en la cárcel** = he spent ten years in jail; **la cárcel fue construida hace 150 años** = the prison was built 150 years ago; **el gobierno ha ordenado la construcción de seis nuevas cárceles** = the government has ordered the construction of six new prisons **(b)** *(encarcelamiento)* imprisonment; **un periodo de cárcel** = a term of imprisonment; **el castigo por el primer delito consiste en una multa o seis semanas de cárcel** = the penalty for the first offence is a fine of or six weeks' imprisonment

carcelario *adj* prison; **permiso carcelario** = parole; **dar un permiso carcelario** = to parole; **le concedieron un permiso carcelario de una semana para visitar a su madre en el hospital** = he was given a week's parole to visit his mother in hospital

carcelero, -ra *n* gaoler *o* jailer *o* warder; *(argot)* screw

carecer *vi* to lack; **carece de sentido** = it doesn't make sense; **la policía carece de pistas sobre el asesinato** = the police lack any clues to the murder

carencia *nf* lack

careo *nm* confrontation *o (de sospechosos)* identity parade *o (de testigos)* face to face interview; **someter a careo** = to bring face to face

carestía *nf* shortage *o* scarcity; **carestía de vida** = cost of living; **plus de carestía de vida** = cost-of-living allowance; **incluir un plus de carestía de vida en los salarios** = to allow for the cost of living in salaries

carga *nf* **(a)** *(responsabilidad)* onus *o* burden; *(obligación de probar lo alegado)* **carga de la prueba** = burden of proof *o* onus of proof *o* onus probandi; **la carga de la prueba recae sobre el demandante** = the onus of proof is on the plaintiff **(b)** *(gravamen)* encumbrance *o* charge; **carga fija** = fixed charge **(c)** *(envío)* shipment; *(mercancía)* freight

cargar *vt* to charge; **cargar en cuenta** = to debit an account; **cargaron 10.000 ptas en su cuenta** = his account was debited with the sum of 10,000 ptas ◊ **cargarse** *vr (matar)* to bump off

cargo *nm* **(a)** *(puesto)* title *o* office *o* position *o* post; **cargo principal** prior charge; **alto cargo** = high office; **tiene el cargo de 'Director Ejecutivo'** = he has the title 'Chief Executive'; **tiene** *o* **desempeña el cargo de tesorero** = he holds *o* performs the office of treasurer; **se retiró de su cargo en el departamento de contabilidad** = she retired from her position in the accounts department **(b)** *(acusación)* charge *o* count; **pliego de cargos** = charge sheet; **el secretario del juzgado leyó los cargos** = the clerk of the court read out the charges; **se le declaró culpable de los cuatro cargos** = he was found guilty on all four counts **(c)** *(débito)* charge; **cargo territorial** = charge on land *o* charge over property; **cargo territorial que existe sobre una propiedad por hipoteca legal** = legal charge; **a cargo de** = chargeable; **gastos a cargo del cliente** = charges forward; **letra al propio cargo** = note of hand *o* promissory note; **nota de cargo** = debit note; **porte a cargo del cliente** = carriage forward *o* freight forward; **la concesión de un requerimiento corre a cargo del tribunal** = the granting of an injunction is at the discretion of the court; **las reparaciones del edificio corren a cargo del inquilino** = the tenant is responsible for all repairs to the building **(d)** *(deber)* **hacerse cargo de** = to take over; **el comprador se hace cargo de las obligaciones de la empresa** = the buyer takes over the company's liabilities **(e)** *(custodia)* **persona a cargo** = dependant

caritativo, -va *adj* eleemosynary

carnal *adj* carnal *o* of the whole blood

carnet *nm (permiso de conducir)* driving licence; **los aspirantes al cuerpo de policía deben poseer un carnet de conducir válido** *o* **vigente** = applicants for the police force should hold a valid driving licence; **tiene carnet para conducir un camión** = he is licensed to drive a lorry

carnicería *nf (matanza)* carnage *o* slaughter

caro, -ra *adj* dear *o* expensive; **dinero** *o* **crédito caro** = dear money

carpeta *nf* **(a)** *(encuadernador)* folder *o* binder; **carpeta de anillas** = ring binder **(b)** *(fichero)* file; **coloca estas cartas en la carpeta de los casos sin resolver** = put these letters in the unsolved cases file; **mire en la carpeta que dice 'casos por resolver'** = look in the file marked 'pending'

carrera *nf (profesión, estudio)* degree *o* studies; **terminará la carrera de abogado el año que viene** = he will qualify as a solicitor next year

carretera *nf* carriageway *o* highway

carta *nf* **(a)** *(correo)* letter; **carta adjunta** *o* **explicatoria** *o* **de cobertura** covering letter *o* covering note; **carta amenazadora** = threatening letter; **carta certificada** = registered letter; **carta comercial** = business letter; **carta credencial** = letter of credence; **carta de acuse de recibo** = letter of acknowledgement; **carta de contestación** *o* **de reiteración a otra** *o* **de seguimiento** = follow-up letter; **carta de crédito** = letter of credit; **carta de crédito general** = circular letter of credit; **carta de crédito irrevocable** = irrevocable letter of credit; **carta de intención** = letter of intent; **carta de reclamación** = letter of complaint; **carta de recomendación** = letter of reference; **carta de requerimiento** = letter of demand; **carta de requerimiento de pago** = notice of dishonour; **carta de solicitud** *o* **de suscripción (de acciones)** = letter of application; **carta modelo** = standard (form) letter; **carta personal** = private letter; **carta previa a una actuación judicial** = letter before action; **carta por avión** = airmail letter; **carta privilegiada** *o* **que goza de privilegio** = privileged communication; **las cartas** = the post; **acusar recibo de algo por carta** = to acknowledge receipt by letter; **la carta no llegó en el primer reparto de esta mañana** = the letter did not arrive by first post this morning; **mi secretaria abre las cartas en cuanto llegan** = my secretary opens the post as soon as it arrives **(b)** *(documento)* card; *(constitucional)* charter; **carta de privilegio** *o* **carta real** = royal charter; **Carta Magna** = Magna Carta; **carta verde** = green card **(c)** **carta blanca** = carte blanche; **tiene carta blanca para actuar en nombre de la empresa** *o* **la empresa le ha concedido carta blanca para que actúe en su nombre** = he has carte blanche to act on behalf of the company *o* the company has given him carte blanche to act on its behalf

cartel *nm* **(a)** *(grupo de empresas)* ring *o* cartel **(b)** *(anuncio)* bill *o* notice

cartelera *nf (valla publicitaria)* advertisement hoarding

cartera *nf* **(a)** *(para documentos)* briefcase; **puso todos los archivos en su cartera** = he put all the files into his briefcase **(b)** *(de valores)* portfolio; **capital en cartera** = issued capital; **sociedad de cartera** = holding company; **valores en cartera** = holding; **ha vendido toda su cartera del Extremo Oriente** = he has sold all his holdings in the Far East; **su cartera contiene valores en las principales empresas petroleras** = his portfolio contains shares in the major oil companies **(c)** *(en política)* **ministro sin cartera** = Minister without Portfolio **(d)** *(billetero)* wallet

carterista *nmf (ratero)* pickpocket *o* dip; **en una banda de rateros, el que actúa como carterista** = picker

cartilla *nf* savings book

casa *nf* **(a)** *(residencia)* house *o* home *o* residence; **casa con sus dependencias y tierras** = messuage; **ladrón de casas** = housebreaker; **robo en una casa** = housebreaking; **tiene una casa de campo donde pasa los fines de semana** = he has a country residence where he spends his weekends **(b)** *(empresa, entidad)* company *o* house; **casa comercial** = firm; **casa consistorial** = town hall;

casa de aceptación = accepting house; **casa de empeños** = pawnshop; **casa de la moneda** = mint; **casa de lenocinio** *o* **de prostitución** = brothel; **en la propia casa** = inside; **delito llevado a cabo por un empleado de la casa** = inside job; **llevar una casa de lenocinio** = keeping a disorderly house **(c)** *(familia)* household

casar *vt* **(a)** *(contrato matrimonial)* to marry **(b)** *(revocar)* to annul *o* to abrogate; **casar una sentencia** = to overturn a judgment
◊ **casarse** *vr* to get married

casación *nf* abrogation; **recurso de casación** = appeal to the Supreme Court *o* motion to vacate

El recurso de casación es el que se interpone ante el Tribunal Supremo contra fallo definitivo o laudo en el que se supone infracción de Ley o doctrina legal o quebrantamiento de alguna garantía esencial de procedimiento (LEC artº 1689- LECrim artº 847)

casera *nf (ama)* landlady

casero *nm (amo)* landlord

casi *adv* almost *o* nearly; *(cercano)* close to; *(semi-)* quasi-

caso *nm* **(a)** *(asunto)* case; **caso imprevisto** = emergency; **caso práctico** = moot case; **caso resuelto** = decided case; **juez encargado de un caso** = trial judge; **casos determinantes** *o* **casos que sientan jurisprudencia** = leading cases; **'en el caso de'** = in re; **la policía considera el caso como asesinato** *o* **lo considera un caso de asesinato** = the police are treating the case as murder *o* are treating it as a murder case; **tenemos a tres detectives trabajando en el caso** = we have three detectives working on the case; **tuvimos seis casos de saqueo durante la noche** = we had six cases of looting during the night **(b)** *(ejemplo)* case *o* instance *o* event; **en caso de** *o* **en caso de que** = in the event of *o* in the event that; **en caso de desacuerdo** *o* **en caso de que las partes no lleguen a un acuerdo, se someterá el caso a arbitraje** = in the event of a disagreement *o* in the event that the parties fail to agree, the case will be submitted to arbitration; **en caso necesario** = where necessary; **en su caso** = where appropriate; **en este caso pasaremos por alto el retraso** = in this instance we will overlook the delay; **no hacer caso de** = to override

castigable *adj* penal *o* punishable

castigar *vt* to discipline *o* to punish; *(penalizar)* to penalize; **delitos castigados con penas de prisión** = crimes punishable by imprisonment; **se castigó al empleado por pasar el informe a la prensa** = the clerk was disciplined for leaking the report to the newspapers; **te castigarán por golpear al policía** = you will be punished for hitting the policeman; **la traición se castiga con la muerte** = the punishment for treason is death

castigo *nm* punishment *o* penalty; **castigo corporal** = corporal punishment; **castigo justo** = fair retribution; **que merece castigo** *o* **merecedor de castigo** = punishable; **el castigo por llevar un arma ofensiva es una multa y tres meses de arresto** = the penalty for carrying an offensive weapon is a fine and three months in prison; **el castigo por traición es la muerte** = the punishment for treason is death

casual *adj* accidental

casualidad *nf* chance

casus belli *nm (justificación de declaración de guerra)* casus belli

catalogar *vt (clasificar)* to index; *(notificar oficialmente)* to schedule

catálogo *nm* list; **precio de catálogo** = list price

catastral *adj* **registro catastral** = Land Registry; **valor catastral** = assessed value

catastro *nm* Land Registry *o* land register *o* land registration

categoría *nf* **(a)** *(clase)* category *o* class; **de primera categoría** = first-class *o* A1; **alojarse en hoteles de primera categoría** = to stay in first-class hotels; **el hurto tiene categoría de delito menor** = the theft comes into the category of petty crime **(b)** *(rango)* rank *o* bracket; *(status)* status; **categoría financiera** = financial rating; **pérdida de categoría** = loss of status; **conceder categoría diplomática a alguien** = to grant someone diplomatic status

caución *nf (precaución)* caution; **caución de arraigo** *o* **caución respecto de costas procesales** = security for costs; **caución judicial** = recognizance; **escritura de caución** = bail bond
◊ **caucionar** to caution

caudal *nm* wealth; **caja de caudales** = strongbox

causa *nf* **(a)** *(motivo)* cause *o* reason *o* ground; **causa desconocida** = unknown reason; **causa determinante** = moot case; **buena causa** = good cause; **causas propiciatorias** = contributory causes; **las causas del divorcio** = the grounds for divorce; **según el informe, las malas relaciones entre los miembros de la comunidad fue una de las causas propiciatorias de los disturbios** = the report listed bad community relations as one of the contributory causes to the riot **(b)** *(proceso)* court case; **la causa se verá la semana próxima** = the case is being heard next week **(c)** *(debido a)* **a causa de** = owing to; **el avión llegó tarde a causa de la niebla** the plane was late owing to fog

causar vt (provocar) to cause o to give rise to; (ocasionar) to occasion; **causar estragos** = to take a heavy toll; **causar problemas** = to cause trouble

cautela nf caution; **con cautela** = cautiously

cautelar adj cautionary; **requerimiento cautelar** = interlocutory o temporary injunction

cautiverio nm (cautividad) captivity

cautividad nf (cautiverio) captivity; **los guerrilleros fueron mantenidos en cautividad durante tres meses** = the guerillas were held in captivity for three months

cautivo, -va adj captive

caza nf (búsqueda) hunting o hunt; (presa) game; **caza furtiva** = poaching; **licencia de caza** = game licence
◊ **cazador** nm hunter; **lo enganchó un cazador de talentos** = he was headhunted
◊ **cazar** vt to hunt; **cazar talentos** = to headhunt
◊ **cazatalentos** nmf headhunter

CC = CODIGO CIVIL

CE = COMUNIDAD EUROPEA, CONSTITUCION ESPAÑOLA; **los ministros de la CE se reunieron hoy en Bruselas** = EC ministers met today in Brussels; **los EE UU están incrementando el comercio con la CE** = the USA is increasing its trade with the EC

cebo nm bait

cebra nf zebra; **paso de cebra** = zebra crossing

cedente nmf assignor o transferor

ceder 1 vt (a) (transmitir) to assign o to hand over o to transfer o to vest o to part with something; **ceder un crédito a alguien** = to assign a debt to someone; **ceder un derecho a alguien** = to assign a right to someone; **cedió el puesto a su adjunto** = he handed over to his deputy; **cedió sus acciones a un fideicomiso familiar** he transferred his shares to a family trust **2** vi to give in

cédula nf (a) (título) bond; **cédula hipotecaria** = mortgage debenture o mortgage bond (b) (certificado) certificate (c) (patente de privilegio o de invención)** letters patent

celda nf cell; **celda de los condenados a muerte** = condemned cell; **compañero, -ra de celda** = cellmate; **comparte una celda con otros dos prisioneros** = he shares a cell with two other prisoners; **pasó la noche en una celda pequeña** = she was put in a small cell for the night

celebrar vt to celebrate o to hold; **celebrar un juicio** o **una vista** = to hold a trial o a hearing; **celebrar una reunión** o **una entrevista** = to hold a meeting o a discussion o an interview; **el recaudador judicial celebrará una subasta de los bienes de la compañía** = the receiver will hold an auction of the company's assets

◊ **celebrarse**; (tener lugar) to take place o to be held; **la reunión se celebrará en nuestras oficinas** = the meeting will take place in our offices; **las vistas se celebraron a puerta cerrada** = the hearings were held in camera

célebre adj famous

celo nm zeal; **exceso de celo** = zealous; **hacer huelga de celo** = to work to rule

censo nm (lista) roll; **censo de abogados** = Roll of Solicitors; **censo electoral** = register of electors

censor, -ra n (a) (de censura) censor; **la película fue cortada** o **prohibida por el censor** = the film was cut o was banned by the censor; **la película fue aprobada por el censor** = the film was passed by the censor (b) (auditor) **censor de cuentas** = auditor; **Censor Jurado de Cuentas** = Chartered Accountant

censura nf (a) (reprobación) censorship; **el gobierno ha impuesto una estricta censura de prensa** = the government has imposed strict press censorship o censorship of the press; **los reporteros de televisión se quejaron de la censura gubernamental** = TV reporters complained of government censorship (b) (política) censure; **voto de censura** = vote of censure o censure vote; **la oposición presentó una moción de censura contra el gobierno** = the Opposition put forward a motion to censure the government; **la reunión aprobó un voto de censura al ministro** = the meeting passed a vote of censure on the minister
◊ **censurable** adj blameworthy

censurar vt (a) (reprobar) to censor; **el reportaje televisivo ha sido censurado y sólo se pueden emitir algunas partes** = the TV report has been censored and only parts of it can be shown; **la noticia de los disturbios fue censurada** = the news of the riots was censored; **la película no fue censurada** o **fue pasada por alto por el censor** = the film was passed by the censor; **todos los informes de prensa son censurados por el gobierno** = all press reports are censored by the government (b) (objetar) to censure

central adj central o middle; **oficina central** = central office o general office; **sede central** = head office o main office o headquarters; **sociedad central** = parent company

centralización nf centralization

centralizar vt to centralize; **todas las fichas policiales se han centralizado en la jefatura de policía** = the gathering of all criminal records has been centralized in the police headquarters

centrista adj centre; **partido centrista** = centre party

centro nm centre o institution; **centro de acogimiento para menores** = young offender institution *o* detention centre; **centro de investigación** = research centre; **centro de rehabilitación** = rehabilitation centre; **centro de salud mental** *o* **centro psiquiátrico** = mental institution; **centro financiero y comercial** = business centre; **centro industrial** = industrial centre; **centro penitenciario** = penitentiary; **el centro de la industria del calzado** = the centre for the shoe industry; **se le envió a un centro de detención para delincuentes juveniles** = he was sent to the detention centre for corrective training

ceñirse *vr* **ceñirse al reglamento** = to work to rule

cerca *adv* near *o* nearby; **cerca de** = close to *o* in the neighbourhood of; **estamos muy cerca de resolver el crimen** = we are close to solving the crime; **la fábrica está cerca de la prisión** = the factory is in the neighbourhood of the prison

cercanías *nfpl* **tren de cercanías** = commuter train

cercano, -na *adj* close to *o* neighbouring

cero *nm* zero; *(nada)* nil; **inflación cero** = zero inflation; **el código para llamadas internacionales es cero cero (00)** = the code for international calls is zero zero (00)

cerrado, -da *adj* closed; **mercado cerrado** = closed market; **sobre cerrado** = sealed envelope; **licitaciones en pliego cerrado** = sealed tenders; **a puerta cerrada** = in camera; **sesión a puerta cerrada** = closed session; **la vista del caso se realizó a puerta cerrada** = the case was heard in camera; **se envió la información en sobre cerrado** = the information was sent in a sealed envelope; **la corporación municipal se reunió a puerta cerrada para discutir problemas de personal en el Area de Transportes** = the town council met in closed session to discuss staff problems in the Transport Department; **se desalojó la tribuna pública cuando la reunión pasó a ser a puerta cerrada** = the public gallery was cleared when the meeting went into closed session

cerradura *nf* lock; **cerradura de apertura controlada** = time lock; **forzar una cerradura** *o* **abrir una cerradura con ganzúa** = to pick a lock; **la cerradura de la caja para gastos menores está rota** = the lock is broken on the petty cash box; **he olvidado la combinación de la cerradura de la caja fuerte** = I have forgotten the combination of the lock of the safe

cerrar *vt* **(a)** *(clausurar)* to close; **cerrar con llave** = to lock; **cerrar herméticamente** = to seal; **cerrar una tienda** *o* **una oficina (al finalizar la jornada laboral)** = to lock up a shop *o* an office; **la oficina cierra a las 5.30** = the office closes at 5.30; **la oficina cierra los lunes** = the office is closed on Mondays; **los sábados cerramos temprano** = we

close early on Saturdays; **todos los bancos cierran el día de la fiesta nacional** all the banks are closed on the National Day; **el director olvidó cerrar con llave la puerta de la sala de ordenadores** = the manager forgot to lock the door of the computer room; **la caja para gastos menores no estaba cerrada con llave** = the petty cash box was not locked **(b)** *(liquidar)* to close down; **cerrar una cuenta** = to close an account; **la empresa ha cerrado** = the company has stopped trading; **la empresa va a cerrar su oficina de Londres** = the company is closing down its London office; **las acciones cerraron a 15$** = the shares closed at $15 **(c)** *(concluir)* to conclude; **cerrar un trato** = to clinch a deal; **(es un duro negociador); cerrar un trato con él** = he drives a hard bargain; **ofreció un 5% extra para cerrar el trato** = he offered an extra 5% to clinch the deal; **necesitan la aprobación de la junta antes de poder cerrar el trato** = they need approval from the board before they can clinch the deal

cerrojo *nm* lock

certeza *nf* certainty

certificación *nf* *(certificado)* certificate; **(de una firma)** attestation; **certificación registral** = certificate of registration

certificado, -da 1 *adj* certified *o* registered; **carta certificada** *o* **paquete certificado** = registered letter *o* registered parcel; **copia certificada** = certified copy; **correo certificado** = recorded delivery; **enviar documentos por correo certificado** = to send documents by registered mail *o* registered post; **enviar una carta certificada** = to register; **envié la carta certificada porque contenía dinero** = I registered the letter, because it contained some money **2** *nm* certificate; **certificado de acciones** = share certificate; **certificado de aprobación** = certificate of approval; **certificado de buena conducta** = certificate of good conduct; **certificado de buena salud** = clean bill of health; **certificado de defunción** = death certificate; **certificado de depósito** = certificate of deposit; **certificado de despacho de aduana** = customs clearance certificate; **certificado de ejercicio de la abogacía** = practising certificate; **certificado de inscripción** = certificate of registration *o* registration certificate; **certificado de origen** = certificate of origin; **certificado de propiedad territorial** = land certificate; **certificado provisional de posesión de acciones en una empresa** = scrip; **certificado de registro de buques** = certificate of registry; **certificado de tierras** = land certificate; **certificado sanitario** = bill of health

certificar *vt* to certify *o* to acknowledge *o* *(una firma)* to attest; **el documento está certificado como copia fiel** = the document is certified as a true copy; **certifico que ésta es una copia auténtica** = I certify that this is a true copy; **cláusula que certifica la firma de las partes** = attestation clause

cesación *nf* cessation

cesante *adj* redundant; **lucro cesante** = lost profits

cesantía *nf* severance pay

cesar *vt* to cease *o* to dismiss; *(romper)* to break off; *(interrumpirse)* to break down; **la empresa ha cesado** = the company has stopped trading

cese *nm* cessation; *(de un cargo)* dismissal; **cese de contrato por mutuo acuerdo** = discharge by agreement; **cese de un puesto de trabajo (por dimisión, retiro, o despido)** = *US* termination; **indemnización por cese en el cargo** = compensation for loss of office; **cese por cumplimiento** = discharge by performance

cesión *nf (traspaso)* assignment *o* cession; *(transmisión)* demise; *(donación)* grant; **cesión de acciones** = transfer of shares; **cesión de arrendamiento** = assignment of a lease; **cesión de un derecho** = release; **cesión de una letra de cambio** = delivery; **cesión de una patente** *o* **de los derechos de autor** *o* **de la propiedad intelectual** = assignment of a patent *o* of a copyright; **cesión total del activo en garantía de una deuda** = floating charge; **escritura de cesión** = deed of assignment; **escritura de cesión de bienes** = assignment; **escritura de cesión de acciones** = deed of transfer ◊ **cesión-arrendamiento** *nf* lease-back; **realizar una operación de cesión-arrendamiento** = to lease back

cesionario, -ria *n* assignee *o* transferee; **cesionario de bienes del fallido** = assignee in bankruptcy; **sus herederos y cesionarios** = his heirs and assigns

cesionista *nmf* grantee *o* assignor

CGPJ = CONSEJO GENERAL DEL PODER JUDICIAL

El CGPJ es el máximo órgano de gobierno del Poder Judicial. Su presidente también lo es del Tribunal Supremo.

chaleco *nm* **chaleco anti-balas** = bullet-proof jacket

chanchullo *nm* fiddle *o* sharp practice

chantaje *nm (extorsión)* blackmail *o* racket; *(crimen organizado)* racketeering *o* protection racket; **obtuvieron 25 millones del director gerente por chantaje** = they got 25 million from the managing director by blackmail; **se le acusó de chantaje** = he was charged with blackmail; **la mandaron a la cárcel por chantaje** = she was sent to prison for blackmail; **recibe ingresos superiores a las 10.000 libras de chantajes** his income from

protection rackets runs into five figures *o* he has a five-figure income from protection rackets

chantajear *vt* to blackmail; **fue chantajeado por su antiguo socio** = he was blackmailed by his former partner

chantajista *nmf* blackmailer *o* racketeer

chárter *nm* charter; **avión chárter** = charter plane; **vuelo chárter** = charter flight

cheque *nm* cheque; **abierto** *o* **sin cruzar** = open *o* uncrossed cheque; **cheque al portador** = bearer cheque; **cheque conformado** = certified cheque *o* *US* certified check; **cheque cruzado** = crossed cheque; **cheques de viaje** = traveller's cheques; **cheque en blanco** = blank cheque; **cheque sin fondos** = dud cheque; **detener el pago de un cheque** = to stop a cheque; **el banco devolvió el cheque al librador** = the bank referred the cheque to drawer; **endosar un cheque** = to endorse a cheque; **extender un cheque a alguien** = to make out a cheque to someone; **firmar un cheque** = to sign a cheque; **girar** *o* **extender un cheque** = to draw a cheque; **ingresar** *o* **depositar un cheque** = to pay a cheque into your account; **pagar con cheque** = to pay by cheque

chequeo *nm* check; *(rueda de identificación)* **chequeo de sospechosos** = identification *o* identity parade

chirona *nf (informal)* nick *o* porridge *o* lock-up; **estar en chirona** = to do porridge

chivarse *vr; to grass*; **chivarse de alguien** = to grass on someone

chivatazo *nm* tip-off; **dar el chivatazo** = to grass on someone

chivato *nm* grass

chivo *nm* **chivo expiatorio** = scapegoat

chocar 1 *vt* to shock **2** *vi* to crash *o* to conflict

choque *nf* collision

chorizo *nm (argot)* crook *o* thief

chulo *nm (proxeneta)* pimp

cíclico, -ca *adj* cyclical; **factores cíclicos** = cyclical factors

ciclo *nm* cycle; **ciclo de trabajo** = run; **ciclo económico** = economic cycle

ciencia *nf* science; **estudiar ciencias empresariales** = to study business *o* management

científico, -ca 1 *adj* scientific; **conocimientos científicos** = know-how **2** *n* scientist

cierre *nm* **(a)** *(comercial)* closing; **cierre de ejercicio** = year-end closing; **cierre dominical** = Sunday closing; **hora de cierre** = closing time **(b)** *(conclusión, cese de operaciones)* close *o* closure;

cierre de la fase de alegaciones = close of pleadings; **cierre de un debate** = closure; **cierre patronal** = lockout; **declarar el cierre patronal** = to lock out workers; **al cierre de la sesión bursátil las acciones habían bajado un 20%** = at the close of the day's trading the shares had fallen 20% **(c)** *(fecha límite)* deadline

cierto, -ta *adj (seguro)* certain; **veredicto cierto** = true bill; **un cierto número** *o* **una cierta cantidad** = a certain number *o* a certain quantity

cifra *nf* **(a)** *(cantidad)* figure; **cifras de producción** = figures; **cifras de ventas** = sales figures; **de dos cifras** = in double figures; **dar una cifra** = to quote; **dio las cifras del informe anual** = she quoted figures from the annual report; **las cifras de producción del año pasado** = the figures for last year *o* last year's figures; **la inflación es de dos cifras** = inflation is in double figures; **hemos tenido una inflación de dos cifras durante algunos años** = we have had double-figure inflation for some years **(b)** *(código)* code
◊ **cifrado** nm *(codificación)* coding
◊ **cifrar** vt *(poner en clave)* to code

cinta *nf* tape; **cinta magnética** = magnetic tape *o* mag tape

circulación *nf* **(a)** *(difusión)* circulation; **circulación de capital** = circulation of capital; **libre circulación de bienes** = free circulation of goods; **libre circulación de capital** = free movement of capital; **poner en circulación** =; *(emitir)* to issue; *(circular)* to circulate; **poner dinero en circulación** = to put money into circulation; **la cantidad de dinero en circulación aumentó más de lo previsto** = the amount of money in circulation increased more than had been expected **(b)** *(tráfico)* traffic; **agente de circulación** = traffic warden; **Código de Circulación** = the Highway Code; *(dirección del tráfico)* **control de la circulación** = point duty; **delitos contra el código de la circulación** = traffic offences

circulante 1 *adj* circulating; **activo circulante** = current assets; **costes circulantes** = floating charge **2** nm *(oferta monetaria)* money supply

circular 1 *nf* circular *o* circular letter; **enviar una circular** = to circularize; **enviaron una circular ofreciendo un 10% de descuento** = they sent out a circular offering a 10% discount; **mandaron circulares con una nueva lista de precios a todos sus clientes** = they circularized all their customers with a new list of prices; **el comité ha acordado enviar circulares a los miembros** = the committee has agreed to circularize the members **2** vi *(moverse)* to run; *(poner en circulación)* to circulate

circunscripción *nf* *(distrito electoral)* constituency

En España, las circunscripciones electorales corresponden a la división administrativa provincial, salvo algunas excepciones en las provincias insulares y a las ciudades de Ceuta y Melilla.

circunstancia *nf* circumstance; **circunstancia agravante** = aggravation; **circunstancias atenuantes** *o* **mitigantes** = extenuating *o* mitigating circumstances; **circunstancias causantes** = causation; **circunstancias eximentes de responsabilidad criminal** = exculpatory circumstances; **según las circunstancias, el acusado puede recibir una multa o ser enviado a prisión** = depending on the circumstances, the accused may receive a fine or be sent to prison; **el inspector de policía describió las circunstancias que llevaron al motín** = the police inspector described the circumstances leading to the riot; **el abogado alegó la edad del acusado como circunstancia atenuante de los hechos** = counsel pleaded the accused's age in extenuation of his actions

circunstancial *adj* *(indirecto)* circumstantial; **prueba circunstancial** = circumstantial evidence

cita *nf* **(a)** *(reunión, entrevista)* appointment; **citas** = engagements; **anotó la cita en su agenda** = she noted the appointment in her engagements diary; **darse cita para las dos** = to make *o* to fix an appointment for two o'clock; **llegó tarde a la cita** = he was late for his appointment; **tuvo que anular la cita** = she had to cancel her appointment **(b)** *(como referencia)* citation *o* quote **(c)** *(operaciones comerciales correctas)* **cita legalmente autorizada** = fair dealing

citación *nf* process *o* citation; **citación de un testigo** = subpoena ad testificandum; **citación de un testigo para comparecer con determinadas pruebas** = subpoena duces tecum; *(apercibimiento)* **citación judicial** = subpoena; *(auto de comparecencia)* summons; *(documento de emplazamiento)* writ of summons; **citación judicial por falta de pago** = default summons; **citación para sentencia** = final judgment; **notificador de la citación** *o* **persona que entrega la citación** = process-server; **rompió la citación judicial y se marchó de vacaciones al extranjero** = he tore up the summons and went on holiday abroad

citado, -da *adj* quoted; **citado a continuación** = undermentioned; **obra citada (op. cit.)** = op. cit.

citar vt **(a)** *(notificar)* to call; *(emplazar)* to summon; *(mandar comparecer)* to subpoena; **citar a alguien como testigo** = to call someone as a witness; **el director financiero fue citado por la acusación** = the finance director was subpoenaed by the prosecution **(b)** *(encarcelar)* **citar ante los tribunales** = to commit; **citar a alguien ante los tribunales** = to commit someone for trial; **fue**

citado ante la Audiencia Nacional = he was committed for trial in the National Criminal Court **(c)** *(para una reunión)* to arrange a meeting *o* to make an appointment **(d)** *(textualmente)* to cite *o* to quote; **el abogado citó textualmente de la declaración realizada por el testigo en la comisaría de policía** = counsel quoted from the statement made by the witness at the police station; **el juez citó varios casos precedentes en su discurso final** = the judge cited several previous cases in his summing up

◊ **citarse** *vr* to arrange to meet; **citarse (con alguien) para las dos** = to make *o* to fix an appointment (with someone) for two o'clock

ciudad *nf* town *o* city; **las principales ciudades de Europa están conectades por vuelos que salen cada hora** = the largest cities in Europe are linked by hourly flights

ciudadanía *nf* citizenship; **(concesión de la) ciudadanía** = naturalization; **debe rellenar la carta de ciudadanía** = you must fill in the naturalization papers; **ha solicitado la ciudadanía** = she has applied for naturalization

ciudadano, -na *n (habitante)* citizen; *(súbdito)* national; **el gobierno ordenó la deportación de todos los ciudadanos extranjeros** = the government ordered the deportation of all foreign nationals; **es ciudadano francés de nacimiento** = he is a French citizen by birth

civil *adj* civil; **año civil** = calendar year; **demanda civil** *o* **acción civil** *o* **proceso civil** = civil action; **derecho civil** = civil law; **derechos civiles** = civil rights; **guerra civil** = civil war; **libertades civiles** = civil liberties; **mes civil** = calendar month; **secretario general** *o* **funcionario jefe del registro civil** = Registrar-General; **inscribir un matrimonio en el registro civil** *o* **declarar una defunción en el registro civil** = to register a marriage *o* a death

clandestino, -na *adj* clandestine

clarificación *nf (aclaración)* clarification

clarificar *vt (aclarar)* to clarify

claro, -ra 1 *adj (evidente)* clear *o* apparent; *(flagrante)* flagrant; *(inequívoco)* unequivocal; **dejó bien claro que quería la dimisión del director** = he made it clear that he wanted the manager to resign; **para dejar las cosas en claro** = for the record *o* to keep the record straight **2** *adv* **(a)** *(naturalmente)* of course **(b)** *(claramente)* clearly

clase *nf* **(a)** *(categoría)* class; **de primera clase** = first-class *o* A1; **viajar en primera clase** = to travel first-class; **los viajes en primera clase ofrecen el mejor servicio** = first-class travel provides the best service; **sólo vendemos artículos de primera clase** = we sell only goods in A1 condition; **un billete de primera clase** = a first-class ticket **(b)** *(tipo)* type *o*

kind *o* nature; **de ninguna clase** = whatsoever; **varias clases de asesinato** = several types of murder; **la impresora produce dos clases de impresión** = the printer produces two kinds of printout; **la policía no encontró documentos sospechosos de ninguna clase** = the police found no suspicious documents whatsoever; **no hay solidez de ninguna clase en el informe** = there is no substance whatsoever in the report

clasificación *nf* classification; *(sistema de archivo)* filing system; **clasificación crediticia** = credit rating

clasificado, -da *adj* classified; **directorio comercial clasificado por secciones** = classified directory

clasificar *vt* **(a)** *(ordenar)* to classify *o* to order; *(catalogar)* to index; **clasificar documentos** = to file documents; **ese archivo contiene facturas clasificadas según la fecha** = that filing cabinet contains invoices ordered by date **(b)** *(por clases)* to class; **la revista fue clasificada como publicación obscena** = the magazine was classed as an obscene publication **(c)** *(desglosar)* to break down

cláusula *nf* clause *o* article; **cláusula adicional** = rider; **cláusula de autoexclusión** = opting-out clause; **cláusula de confiscación** *o* **cláusula decomisoria** = forfeit clause; **cláusula de excepción** = escape clause *o* let-out clause *o* saving clause; **cláusula de exclusión** = exclusion clause; **cláusula de exención** = exemption clause; **cláusula de penalización** = penalty clause; **cláusula de reajuste de precios** *o* **salarios** = escalator clause; **cláusula de renuncia** = waiver; **cláusula de rescisión** = cancellation clause; **cláusula de responsabilidad limitada** = liability clause; **cláusula derogatoria** = derogatory clause; **cláusula facultativa** = optional clause; **cláusula penal** = penalty clause; **cláusula que significa que** = clause to the effect that; **cláusula resolutoria** *o* **de nulidad** = termination clause *o* defeasance; **cláusula restrictiva** *o* **de restricción de un contrato** = restrictive covenant; **cláusula suplementaria** *o* **adicional** = rider; **añadir una cláusula adicional a un contrato** = to add a rider to a contract; **de acuerdo con la cláusula seis, el pago no vence hasta el año próximo** = according to clause six, payment will not be due until next year; **hay diez cláusulas en el contrato** = there are ten clauses in the contract

clausura *nf* closure; **moción de clausura** = closure motion

clausurar *vt (terminar)* to wind up

clave *nf* **(a)** *(explicación)* key; **ha desaparecido un testigo clave** = a key witness has disappeared; **palabras clave de una escritura** = operative words **(b)** *(código)* code; *(cifrar)* **poner en clave** = to code; **el espía envió su mensaje en clave** = the spy sent his message in code; **recibimos instrucciones en clave de nuestro agente en Nueva York** = we received coded instructions from our agent in New York

clemencia *nf* clemency *o* mercy; **como acto de clemencia, el presidente concedió la amnistía a todos los presos políticos** = as an act of clemency, the president granted an amnesty to all political prisoners

clemente *adj (poco severo)* lenient

cleptomanía *nf* kleptomania

cleptómano, -na *nmf* kleptomaniac

clerical *adj* clerical

cliché *nm* **cliché para multicopista** = duplicating paper

cliente *nmf* client; **cliente fallido** = bad debtor; **cliente preferencial** = account; **el abogado pagó la multa en nombre de su cliente** = the solicitor paid the fine on behalf of his client
◊ **clientes** *nmpl; (clientela)* practice *o* clientele

clientela 1 *nf* **(a)** *(de una empresa)* clientele *o* custom **(b)** *(fondo de comercio)* goodwill; **pagó 10 millones por la clientela y 4 millones por las existencias** = he paid 10 million for the goodwill of the shop and 4 million for the stock; **perder la clientela** = to lose someone's custom **(b)** *(bufete)* practice

co- *prefijo* co-; **coacreedor, -ra** = co-creditor; **coacusado, -da** = co-defendant; **coarriendo** = joint tenancy; **coaseguro** = co-insurance; **cobeneficiario, -ria** = joint beneficiary; **codemandado, -da** = co-respondent; **codirección** = joint management; **codirector, -ra** = joint managing director; **coheredero, -ra** joint heir

coacción *nf (coerción)* coercion *o* duress; **bajo coacción** = under duress; **la coacción no supone atenuante en una acusación de asesinato** = duress provides no defence to a charge of murder
◊ **coaccionado, -da** *adj (bajo coacción)* under duress; **alegaron que habían cometido el crimen coaccionados por otro de los acusados** = they alleged they had committed the crime under duress from another defendant
◊ **coaccionar** *vt* to coerce; **le coaccionaron para que firmara la confesión** = he signed the confession under duress

Se entiende por coacción la fuerza o violencia contra una persona para obligarla a decir o ejecutar algo (CP art°172).

coalición *nf* coalition; *(cartel de empresas que se ponen de acuerdo para fijar precios)* ring

coartada *nf* alibi

cobertura *nf* **(a)** coverage; **cobertura informativa** *o* **de prensa** *o* **de medios de comunicación** = press coverage *o* media coverage **(b)** *(póliza de seguros)* insurance cover; **cobertura total** = full cover; **nota de cobertura** = cover note; **solicitar cobertura adicional** = to ask for additional cover; **operar sin cobertura suficiente** = to operate without adequate cover **(c)** *(que cubre)* covering; **carta de cobertura** = covering letter *o* covering note

cobijar *vt* to shelter; *(esconder a un delincuente)* to harbour

cobijo *nm* shelter; **dar cobijo (a un delincuente)** = harbouring

cobrador, -ra *n (recaudador)* collector; **(agente) cobrador de morosos** = debt collector

cobrar *vt* **(a)** *(pago)* to charge *o* to be paid *o* to receive; **cobrar a destajo** = to be paid at piece-work rates; **cobrar más de lo debido** *o* **cobrar de más** = to overcharge; **cobrar por horas** = to be paid by the hour; **cobrar por la entrega** = to charge for delivery; **cobrar un sueldo** = to draw a salary; **por cobrar** = receivable; **cuentas a cobrar** *o* **por cobrar** = accounts receivable; **deudas por cobrar** = receivables; **no cobrar por el reparto** *o* **envió** = to make no charge for delivery; **¿cuánto cobra?** = how much does he charge?; **cobra 3.000 ptas por hora** = he charges 3,000 ptas an hour; **hace seis meses que los obreros no cobran** *o* **los obreros no cobran desde hace seis meses** = the workers have not received any salary for six months; **el hotel nos cobró de más por las comidas** = the hotel overcharged us for meals; **pedimos un reembolso porque se nos había cobrado más de lo debido** = we asked for a refund because we had been overcharged **(b)** *(recaudar)* to collect; **cobrar una deuda** = to collect a debt

cobro *nm* **(a)** *(recaudación)* collection; **cobro de morosos** = debt collection *o* collecting; **agencia de cobro de morosos** = debt collection agency *o* collecting agency; **letra al cobro** = bills for collection **(b)** *(pago)* charge; **cobro excesivo** = overcharge; **día de cobro** = pay day **(c)** *(llamada de teléfono)* **a cobro revertido** = collect call; **llamar a cobro revertido** = to make a collect call; **llamó a su oficina a cobro revertido** = he called his office collect

coche *nm* car; **coche-bomba** = car bomb; **coche celular** = police van; **coche patrulla** = patrol car

codicilo *nm* codicil

codificación *nf* codification; *(cifrado)* coding; **la codificación de facturas** = the coding of invoices

codificar *vt* to codify

código *nm* **(a)** *(clave)* code; **códigos en lenguaje de máquina**_o códigos usados por un ordenador *o* **códigos legibles por un ordenador** = machine-readable codes; **código postal** = post code *o US* zip code **(b)** *(norma)* code; **código civil** = civil code; **código de circulación** = the Highway Code; **código de conducta** *o* **de ética profesional** = code of practice; **código de leyes** = statute book; **código de Napoleón** = Code Napoleon; **código mercantil** = merchant law *o* commercial code; **código penal** = the penal code; **códigos comentados** *o* **comentarios a un código** *o* **código con jurisprudencia** = commentary; **nadie pueder ser procesado por no cumplir el código** = failure to observe the code does not render anyone liable to proceedings

coeficiente *nm* rate *o* ratio; *(elemento)* factor

coerción *nf (coacción)* coercion

coger *vt* to catch *o* to pick up; *(pillar)* to nick

cohabitación *nf* cohabitation; *(unión consensual)* common-law marriage

cohabitante *nmf* cohabiter *o* cohabitee

cohabitar *vi (vivir juntos)* to cohabit

cohecho *nm* bribe *o* bribery; *(corrupción a un miembro del jurado)* embracery

---

El cohecho es un delito consistente en la aceptación por un funcionario público de dádivas o promesas u otros beneficios a cambio de la ejecución u omisión de un acto relativo al ejercicio de su cargo (CP artº 420)

---

coincidir *vi* to coincide; **coincidir con** = to agree with *o* to correspond with something

cola *nf* queue; **hacer cola** *o* **ponerse en la cola** = to queue *o* to form a queue *o* to join a queue; **cuando había escasez de alimentos, la gente tenía que hacer cola para conseguir pan** = when food was in short supply, people had to queue for bread; **hicimos cola durante horas para entrar en la sala** = we queued for hours to get into the courtroom; **se formaron colas a la puerta de la Audiencia para ver al acusado** = queues formed at the doors of the Crown Court to see the accused

colaboración *nf* collaboration; **su colaboración en el desarrollo del sistema informático fue muy provechosa** = their collaboration on the development of the computer system was very profitable

colaborador, -ra *n (en un crimen)* accessory

colaborar *vi* to collaborate; **colaboraron en la construcción del nuevo avión** = they collaborated on the new aircraft; **colaborar con una firma francesa en la construcción de un puente** = to collaborate with a French firm on building a bridge

colación *nf (de bienes)* hotchpot

colateral 1 *adj* collateral; **asunto colateral** = collateral issue **2** *nm (prendario)* collateral

colectivo, -va *adj* collective *o* joint; **conflicto colectivo** = industrial dispute; **convenio colectivo (libre)** = (free) collective bargaining; **firmaron un convenio salarial colectivo** = they signed a collective wage agreement; **propiedad colectiva** = collective ownership; **responsabilidad colectiva** = collective responsibility

colega *nmf* colleague; *(homólogo)* counterpart; **el abogado pidió más tiempo para consultar con sus colegas** = counsel asked for more time to consult his colleagues

colegiado, -da *adj* collegiate *o (abogado)* member of the Bar; **contable colegiado** = chartered accountant *o* certified accountant

colegio *nm* college; **colegio de abogados** = Law Society *o GB* the Bar Council *o US* the American Bar Association; **colegio electoral** = electoral college *o* polling station

colgar *vt* to hang; **colgó el paraguas en el respaldo de su silla** = he hung his umbrella over the back of his chair; **cuelga el abrigo en el perchero detrás de la puerta** = hang your coat on the hook behind the door

colindar *vt* to adjoin; **colindar con** = to abut (on)

colisión *nf* collision; **seis personas resultaron heridas en la colisión** = six people were injured in the collision

colocación *nf* **(a)** *(empleo)* situation *o* place; *(oficina de empleo)* **agencia de colocación** = employment office *o* bureau *o* agency **(b)** *(posicionamiento)* placement; **la colocación de una emisión de acciones** = the placing of a line of shares

colocar *vt* **(a)** *(poner)* to place; **colocar un paquete de acciones** = to place a block of shares; **colocar a los empleados** = to place staff; **colocar pruebas falsas con la intención de implicar a alguien en un crimen** = to plant evidence **(b)** *(situar)* to rank **(c)** *(depositar)* to lodge
◊ **colocarse** *vr (ponerse)* to go; **la fecha se coloca en la parte superior de la carta** = the date goes at the top of the letter

columna *nf* column; **columna del debe** = debit column; **columna de debe** *o* **de haber** = debit column *o* credit column

colusión *nf (connivencia)* collusion

colusorio, -ria *adj* collusive; **acción colusoria** = collusive action

comandante *nmf* commander

comandita *nf* sleeping partnership; **sociedad en comandita** = limited partnership

comanditario, -ria *adj* socio comanditario = sleeping partner

comentado, -da *adj* códigos comentados = commentary; sentencia comentada = commentary

comentar *vt (hacer comentarios)* to comment; el periódico comenta el juicio brevemente = the newspaper has some short comments about the trial; los periódicos comentaron el resultado del juicio = the newspapers commented on the result of the trial

comentario *nm (observación)* comment *o* observation; comentario acertado *o* oportuno = fair comment; comentario justo (hecho honestamente y no difamatorio) = fair comment; comentarios a un código = commentary; hacer comentarios = to comment

comenzar *vi* to begin *o* to commence; *(originar)* to originate; comenzar de nuevo = to resume; el proceso comenzó con la toma de juramentos a los testigos = the proceedings commenced with the swearing-in of witnesses; el abogado de la acusación comenzó con una descripción del entorno familiar del acusado = counsel for the prosecution opened with a description of the accused's family background; el informe de los auditores comenzó con una descripción de los principios generales adoptados = the auditors' report began with a description of the general principles adopted; el inspector de policía comenzó el interrogatorio del sospechoso = the police inspector commenced the questioning of the suspect

comercial *adj* (a) *(mercantil)* commercial; acuerdo *o* convenio *o* tratado comercial = trade agreement; asociación comercial = trade association; banco comercial = credit bank; carta comercial = business letter; curso comercial = commercial course; descripción comercial = trade description; directorio comercial *o* guía comercial *o* repertorio comercial = commercial directory *o* trade directory; feria comercial = trade fair; nombre comercial = trademark *o* trade mark *o* trade name; prácticas comerciales justas = fair trading; pedir referencias comerciales a una empresa = to ask a company to supply trade references; transacción *o* trámite *o* operación comercial = business transaction; zona comercial = industrial estate *o* trading estate (b) *(vendible)* marketable

comercialización *nf* commercialization

comercializar *vt* to commercialize

comercialmente *adv* commercially; no viable comercialmente = not commercially viable

comerciante *nmf (agente)* dealer; *(negociante)* trader; comerciante autorizado = licensed trader;

comerciante especializado en productos básicos *o* materias primas = commodity trader; comerciante de artículos de consumo = commodity trader; comerciante de vinos = wine merchant; comerciante individual = sole trader

comerciar *vt (negociar)* to trade; *(vender)* to handle; comerciar con alguien = to have dealings with someone; comerciar con otro país = to trade with another country; no comerciamos en coches extranjeros = we do not handle foreign cars

comercio *nm* (a) *(transacción comercial)* commerce *o* trade *o* trading *o* dealing; comercio de exportación *o* de importación = export trade *o* import trade; comercio fraudulento = fraudulent trading; comercio interior = home trade; comercio justo = fair trading; Cámara de Comercio = Chamber of Commerce; escuela de comercio = commercial college; libre comercio = free trade (b) *(empresa)* business

cometer *vt (perpetrar)* to commit *o* to perpetrate; cometer un crimen *o* un delito = to commit a crime; cometer un error = to make a mistake; sorprendido en el momento de cometer un delito = in flagrante delicto; la banda cometió seis robos antes de ser capturada = the gang committed six robberies before they were caught

cometido 1 *adj* delito cometido = substantive offence **2** *nm (misión)* commission *o* assignment

comienzo *nm (inicio)* commencement; comienzo de ciertos casos en un juzgado municipal = originating application

comisaría *nf* (police) station; comisaría de policía = police station; pasó la noche en la comisaría = he spent the night in the cells; pasó la noche en las celdas de la comisaría = he spent the night in the station cells; prestar declaración en comisaría *o* ser llevado a comisaría para declarar = to help police with their inquiries; seis manifestantes fueron detenidos y llevados a la comisaría = six demonstrators were arrested and taken to the police station

comisario *nm (miembro de una comisión)* deputy *o* delegate; comisario de policía = commissioner of police *o* police commissioner; comisario de la UE = EU commissioner

comisión *nm* (a) *(junta)* commission *o* board *o* committee; *(tribunal de expertos)* panel of experts; comisión asesora *o* consultiva = advisory board; comisión conjunta = joint committee; Comisión de la Comunidad Europea = Commission of the European Community; comisión de trabajo = working party; comisión ejecutiva = executive committee; comisión permanente = standing committee; ser miembro de una comisión = to be a member of a committee *o* to sit on a committee; el gobierno ha formado una comisión para estudiar los problemas de los residuos industriales = the government has set up a working party to study the problems of industrial waste; **el gobierno ha nombrado una comisión de investigación para examinar los problemas de masificación en las cárceles** = the government has appointed a commission of inquiry to look into the problems of prison overcrowding; **es el presidente de la comisión gubernamental sobre la violencia en el fútbol** = he is the chairman of the government commission on football violence **(b)** *(honorarios)* fee; **recibe una comisión del 15% de las ventas** = he has an agent's commission of 15% of sales **(c)** *(soborno)* **comisión ilegal** = kickback **(d)** *(misión)* assignment

◊ **comisionado, -da** *n (comisario de la UE)* commissioner

comisionista *nmf* **(a)** *(persona que recibe una comisión)* commission agent **(b)** *(miembro de una comisión)* commissioner

comité *nm* committee *o* commission; **comité de dirección** = steering group; **presidir un comité** = to chair a committee; **es el presidente del comité de planificación** = he is the chairman of the planning committee; **es la secretaria del comité financiero** = she is the secretary of the finance committee; **fue elegido para el comité de personal del club** *o* **le nombraron miembro del comité del club del personal** = he was elected to the committee of the staff club; **los nuevos planes tienen que ser aprobados por los miembros del comité** = the new plans have to be approved by the committee members

Commonwealth *nf (Comunidad de Naciones)* the Commonwealth

como *adv* as *o* like; *(derecho)* qua; **una decisión del Presidente del Tribunal Supremo como máxima autoridad del poder judicial** = a decision of the President of the Supreme Court qua head of the judiciary

cómodo, -da *adj (conveniente)* convenient; **el préstamo se devuelve en cómodos plazos** = the loan is repayable in easy payments; **un giro bancario es una forma cómoda de enviar dinero al extranjero** = a bank draft is a convenient way of sending money abroad

compañero, -ra *n* companion; *(de trabajo)* colleague; **compañero de celda** = cellmate

compañía *nf (sociedad)* company; **compañía de capital** = corporation; **compañía de seguros** = insurance company; **compañía financiera (que financia la compra a plazos)** = hire-purchase company

comparable *adj* comparable; **los dos delitos no son comparables** = the two crimes are not comparable

comparación *nf* comparison; *(cotejo)* collation; **las ventas han bajado en comparación con las del año pasado** = sales are down in comparison with those of last year; **comparación de declaraciones** = reconciliation

comparado, -da *adj* **comparado con** = compared with; **derecho comparado** = comparative law

comparar *vt (cotejar)* to compare; **comparar con** = to compare with; **¿cuál es la empresa que más se puede comparar con ésta en importancia?** = which is the nearest company comparable to this one in size?; **el director financiero comparó las cifras del primer y segundo trimestre** = the finance director compared the figures for the first and second quarters; **no se pueden comparar las exportaciones con las ventas nacionales** = there is no comparison between export and home sales; **el detective comparó las huellas dactilares de la botella con las del cuchillo** = the detective compared the fingerprints on the bottle and those on the knife; **comparado con el de algunas de las principales ciudades, nuestro porcentaje de delitos es bastante bajo** = compared with that of some major cities, our crime rate is quite low

comparativo, -va *adj* comparative

comparecencia *nf* appearance; **registro de comparecencia por la defensa** = entry of appearance

comparecer *vi* to appear; **no comparecer** = fail to appear

compartir *vt* to share; **compartir el tiempo que se utiliza el ordenador** = to share computer time; **compartir información** *o* **datos** = to share information *o* to share data; **compartir un teléfono** = to share a telephone; **compartir una oficina** = to share an office

compasión *nf (clemencia)* mercy

compendiar *vt* to abstract

compendio *nm* abstract; *(principios de derecho)* = digest

compensación *nf* **(a)** *(indemnización)* compensation *o* amends *o* relief; **compensación extra** = overrider *o* overriding commission; **compensación por aumento del coste de vida** = cost-of-living allowance; **fondo de compensación a clientes por los daños sufridos por las acciones de los abogados** = compensation fund; **compensación por pérdida de ganancias** = compensation for loss of earnings **(b)** *(finanzas)* clearing; **cámara de compensación** = clearing house; **cuenta de compensación de cambios** = Exchange Equalization Account

compensado, -da *adj* balanced; **cuenta compensada** = contra account

compensar *vt* **(a)** *(indemnizar)* to compensate; **compensar a un director por pérdida de comisión** = to compensate a manager for loss of commission **(b)** *(finanzas)* to balance *o* to equalize; **el cheque tardó diez días en ser compensado** *o* **el banco tardó diez días en compensar el cheque** = the cheque took ten days to clear *o* the bank took ten days to clear the cheque

competencia *nf* **(a)** *(concurso)* competition; **competencia desleal** = unfair competition; **libre competencia** = free competition; **hacer la competencia** = to compete; **el contrato de empleo prohíbe a los miembros del personal irse a trabajar para la competencia** = the contract of employment forbids members of staff from leaving to go to work for competitors **(b)** *(capacidad jurídica)* jurisdiction; **áreas de competencia** = terms of reference; **competencia de una ley parlamentaria** = purview; **devolución** *o* **traspaso de competencias (a una Comunidad Autónoma)** = devolution; **traspasar competencias** = to devolve; **dentro de la competencia del tribunal** = within the jurisdiction of the court; **fuera de la competencia del tribunal** = outside the jurisdiction of the court; **el caso es de la competencia del tribunal** = the case falls within the competence of the court; **el prisionero se negó a reconocer la competencia del tribunal** = the prisoner refused to recognize the jurisdiction of the court; **el tribunal no tiene competencia para llevar el caso** = the court is not competent to deal with this case; **las competencias del tribunal no cubren delitos de tráfico** = the tribunal's terms of reference do not cover traffic offences; **se han traspasado competencias a las Comunidades Autónomas** = power is devolved to regional assemblies **(c)** *(aptitud)* competence *o* competency; *(pericia)* expertise; **contratamos al Sr. Smith por su competencia financiera** = we hired Mr Smith because of his financial expertise **(d)** *(ámbito)* scope

competente *adj* *(capacitado)* competent; *(capaz)* capable; **es una abogada muy competente para casos de divorcio** = she is a very capable divorce barrister; **es una secretaria competente** *o* **una directora competente** = she is a competent secretary *o* a competent manager

competición nm *(prueba o lucha)* contest

competidor, -ra *n* competitor; **nuestros principales competidores son dos firmas alemanas** = two German firms are our main competitors

competir *vi* *(hacer la competencia)* to compete; **competir con alguien** *o* **con una empresa** = to compete with someone *o* with a company; **las bandas competían por el control del mercado de drogas** = the gangs were competing for control of the drugs market

compilar *vt* *(acumular)* to consolidate; **compilar las leyes** = to codify

complacencia *nf* **letra de complacencia** = accommodation bill

complejo, -ja **1** *adj* complex; **un sistema complejo de control de las importaciones** = a complex system of import controls; **la normativa sobre la inmigración es muy compleja** = the regulations governing immigration are very complex **2** *nm* complex; **un gran complejo industrial** = a large industrial complex

completar *vt* *(terminar)* to complete; **completar un sobre** = to address; **la fábrica completó el pedido en dos semanas** = the factory completed the order in two weeks

completo, -ta *adj* *(entero)* complete *o* full; *(en su totalidad)* outright; **por completo** = completely; **pago completo de una deuda** = full payment *o* payment in full; **el pedido está completo y listo para enviar** = the order is complete and ready for sending; **el pedido sólo debe entregarse si está completo** = the order should be delivered only if it is complete
◊ **completamente** *adv* *(totalmente)* completely *o* fully; *(íntegramente)* in full

complicado, -da *adj* complicated; **el juez advirtió al jurado de que el caso era complicado y podría durar varias semanas** = the judge warned the jury that the case was a complicated one and might last several weeks; **la normativa del IVA es muy complicada** = the VAT rules are very complicated

cómplice *nmf* accomplice *o* accessory *o* party to a crime; **cómplice del demandado** = co-respondent; **cómplice encubridor** = accessory after the fact; **cómplice instigador** = accessory before the fact; **ser cómplice con incitación al crimen** = to aid and abet

complicidad *nf* complicity; **complicidad e incitación al crimen** *o* **a cometer un crimen** = aiding and abetting

componedor *nm* adjuster; **actuar de amigable componedor** = to play the honest broker

componenda *nf* *(acuerdo)* compromise *o* settlement

componer *vt* *(reparar)* to repair
◊ **componerse** *vr*; **componerse de** = to consist of; **el tribunal se compone normalmente de cinco magistrados** = the Court consists normally of five justices

comportamiento *nm* *(conducta)* conduct; **comportamiento ofensivo** *o* **insultante** = insulting behaviour; **buen comportamiento** = good behaviour; **mal comportamiento** = misbehaviour

comportarse *vr (persona)* to behave; *(máquina)* to perform; **comportarse de un modo engañoso** = to hold out; **se comportaba como si fuera el director de la compañía** = he held himself out as a director of the company

compra *nf (adquisición)* purchase *o* acquisition; **compra a plazos** = hire purchase (HP); **compra con derecho a devolución** = sale or return; **buena** *o* **mala compra** = good buy *o* bad buy; **la compra de una empresa** = the acquisition of a company; **impuesto sobre compras** = purchase tax; **jefe de compras** = head buyer; **orden de compra** = purchase order; **precio de compra** = purchase price; **ese reloj fue una buena compra** = that watch was a good buy; **este coche fue una mala compra** = this car was a bad buy
◊ **compra-venta** *nf* **contrato de compraventa** = bill of sale; **se dedica a la compra-venta de coches de segunda mano** = he is in the secondhand car trade

comprador, -ra *n* buyer *o* purchaser; **agente comprador de deudas** = debt factor

comprar *vt* to buy *o* to purchase; **comprar a crédito** = to buy on credit; **comprar al contado** = to purchase something for cash; **comprar al por mayor y vender al por menor** = to buy wholesale and sell retail; **comprar divisas a plazo** = to buy forward; **comprar un frigorífico a plazos** = to buy a refrigerator on hire purchase; **ir a comprar algo** = to shop (for) something; **volver a comprar** = to buy back; **compró 10.000 acciones** = he bought 10,000 shares; **la compañía ha sido comprada por su principal proveedor** = the company has been bought by its leading supplier; **vendió la tienda el año pasado y ahora está tratando de volver a comprarla** = he sold the shop last year and is now trying to buy it back

comprender *vt/i (entender)* to apprehend *o* to understand *o* to realize; **el presidente comprendió que iba a ser derrotado en la elección** = the chairman realized that he was going to be outvoted

comprensión *nf* realization

comprensivo, -va *adj (razonable)* reasonable

comprobable *adj* verifiable; **deudas comprobables** = provable debts

comprobación *nf (inspección)* check *o* checking; *(verificación)* verification; **balance de comprobación** = trial balance; **muestra de comprobación** = check sample

comprobante *nm (recibo, resguardo)* receipt; **comprobante de deuda** = proof

comprobar *vt (verificar)* to check *o* to prove; *(controlar)* to monitor; **comprobar declaraciones** = to reconcile; **comprobar que una factura es correcta** = to check that an invoice is correct; **comprobar una deuda** = to prove a debt; **comprobó si la impresión de ordenador coincidía con las facturas** = he checked the computer printout against the invoices; **están comprobando el nuevo sistema de resolver el problema de la delincuencia juvenil** = they are monitoring the new system of dealing with young offenders; **la policía está intentando comprobar sus movimientos en la noche del asesinato** = the police are trying to establish his movements on the night of the murder

comprometer *vt* **(a)** *(implicar)* to compromise *o* to bind; **comprometer a alguien a hacer algo por medio de un contrato** = to engage someone to do something; **que compromete** = binding; **es un documento que compromete legalmente** = this document is legally binding *o* it is a legally binding document **(b)** *(arriesgar)* to risk; **comprometió la buena reputación de la empresa** = he put the good name of the firm at risk
◊ **comprometerse** *vr* to get involved *o* to commit oneself; *(prometer)* to undertake

compromiso *nm* **(a)** *(obligación)* obligation *o* bond *o* commitment; **compromiso formal** = formal commitment; **compromiso que hay que cumplir** = undertaking; **compromiso de comparecencia ante la ley para responder de las acusaciones imputadas, personalmente o por delegación, so pena del pago de una multa** = recognizance; **compromisos financieros** = financial commitments; **pérdida del derecho al compromiso de comparecencia ante los tribunales** *o* **pérdida del derecho a la libertad por falta de comparecencia ante los tribunales** = estreated recognizance **(b)** *(cita previa)* appointment *o* engagement; **romper un compromiso** = to break an engagement to do something; **no tengo más compromisos para el resto del día** = I have no engagements for the rest of the day

compulsa *nf* attested *o* true copy
◊ **compulsado, -da** *adj* certified as a true copy

compulsar *vt* to attest

común *adj* **(a)** *(público)* common; *(general)* general; **acreedor, -ra común** = unsecured creditor; **de común acuerdo** = by mutual consent; **delito común** = ordinary offence; **en común** = in common *o* jointly; **propiedad en común** = common ownership; **poseer una propiedad en común** = to own a property jointly; **son responsables de los daños en común** = they are jointly liable for damages; **relativo al derecho común anglosajón** = common-law **(b)** *(la Comunidad Europea CE)* **el Mercado Común Europeo** = the European Common Market

◊ **comunal** *adj* communal; **terreno comunal** = common *o* common land; **bienes comunales** = common property

comunicación   *nf*   communication; **comunicación escrita** = written communication; **establecer comunicación con alguien** = to enter into communication with someone; **hemos establecido comunicación con el departamento del gobierno pertinente** = we have entered into communication with the relevant government department; **tras las inundaciones se cortaron todas las comunicaciones con el exterior** = after the flood all communications with the outside world were broken

comunicado   *nm*   communication   *o* announcement; **comunicado de prensa** = press release; **hemos recibido un comunicado del inspector fiscal de la zona** = we have had a communication from the local tax inspector; **la empresa emitió un comunicado de prensa sobre el lanzamiento del nuevo coche** = the company sent out *o* issued a press release about the launch of the new car

comunicar *vt* (a) *(informar)* to communicate *o* announce *o* to inform; **comunicar algo a alguien** = to notify someone of something; **el Ministerio de Comercio nos ha comunicado que van a entrar en vigor nuevos aranceles** = we have been informed by the Department of Trade that new tariffs are coming into force; **tenemos el placer de** *o* **nos es grato comunicarle que su oferta ha sido aceptada** = we are pleased to inform you that your offer has been accepted; **lamento comunicarle que su oferta no ha sido aceptada** = I regret to inform you that your tender was not acceptable (b) *(por teléfono)* **línea comunicando** = engaged line; **está comunicando** = the line is busy; **no puede hablar con el director - su teléfono comunica** *o* **está comunicando** = you cannot speak to the manager - his line is engaged

◊ **comunicarse** *vr* to communicate; **los miembros del jurado no deben comunicarse con los testigos** = the members of the jury must not communicate with the witnesses

comunidad *nf* community; *(copropiedad)* **comunidad de bienes** = community property *o* tenancy in common; **Comunidad de Naciones** = the Commonwealth; **la Comunidad Europea (CE)** = the European Community (EC); **los ministros de la Comunidad** = the Community ministers; **comunidades autónomas** = self-governing regions *o* autonomous communities

comunitario, -ria *adj* community; **legislación comunitaria** = Community legislation; **servicio comunitario** = community service

con *prep* with; **con costas** = with costs

conceder *vt* (a) *(otorgar)* to award *o* to grant; **conceder a alguien un aumento salarial** = to award someone a salary increase; **conceder crédito a un cliente** = to extend credit to a customer; **conceder la palabra** = to recognize the speaker; **conceder libertad condicional** = to release on parole; **conceder permiso a alguien para construir una casa** *o* **para abandonar el país** = to grant someone permission to build a house *o* to leave the country; **conceder tiempo** *o* **una prórroga**= to allow time; **conceder un préstamo** = to open a loan; **conceder una licencia** *o* **un permiso** = to license; **el gobierno concedió una amnistía a todos los presos políticos** = the government granted an amnesty to all political prisoners; **el gobierno concedió un préstamo sin intereses a la empresa para poner en funcionamiento la nueva fábrica** = the government granted the company an interest-free loan to start up the new factory; **le concedieron la libertad condicional** *o* **libertad bajo palabra** = he was granted parole; **los derechos sobre la propiedad fueron concedidos a los administradores** = the property was vested in the trustees; **se le conceden treinta días para pagar la multa** = you are allowed thirty days to pay the fine (b) *(reconocer)* to concede

concejal, -la *n* councillor

concejo *nm* *(ayuntamiento)* **concejo municipal** = borough council *o* town council

concentración *nf* *(acumulación)* consolidation

concerner *vt* **¿a qué ministerio concierne?** = which is the relevant government department?; *(teniendo en cuenta)* **por lo que concierne a** = having regard to *o* as regards *o* regarding; **por lo que concierne al segundo de los acusados, el jurado no pudo llegar a un veredicto mayoritario** = as regards *o* regarding the second of the accused, the jury was unable to reach a majority verdict

concerniente *adj* **concerniente a** = in re

concernir *vt* *(implicar)* to involve; **su reclamación concierne a dinero gastado en viajes al extranjero** = his claim involves money spent on trips abroad

concertación *nf* *(reconciliación de las partes)* reconciliation

concertar *vt* *(iniciar)* to enter into; **concertar un acuerdo** *o* **un contrato** = to enter into an agreement *o* a contract; **concertamos la reunión en sus oficinas** = we arranged to have the meeting in their offices

concesión *nf* (a) *(agencia exclusiva)* concession; *(licencia)* franchising; **lleva una concesión de joyería en unos grandes almacenes** = she runs a jewellery concession in a department store; **ha adquirido una concesión de venta de perritos calientes** = he has bought a hot dog franchise **(b)** *(cesión)* grant; **concesión de nombramiento de administrador judicial** = grant of letters of administration; **hizo una concesión de tierras a su hijo** = he made a grant of land to his son **(c)** *(desgravación)* concession; **concesión fiscal** = tax concession **(d)** *(reconocimiento)* concession

◊ **concesionario, -ria** *n (persona autorizada)* licensee *o* concessionnaire; *(franquiciado)* franchisee

conciliación *nf* conciliation; *(acuerdo con concesiones recíprocas)* compromise

conciliar *vt* to conciliate *o* to mediate

concluir *vt* **(a)** *(llegar a una conclusión)* to conclude; *(deducir)* to deduce; **la policía concluyó que el ladrón había entrado en el edificio por la puerta principal** = the police concluded that the thief had got into the building through the main entrance **(b)** *(cerrar)* to conclude; *(terminar)* to terminate *o* to wind up; **concluyó la reunión dando las gracias al comité** = he wound up the meeting with a vote of thanks to the committee; **concluyó su periodo de empleo** = his employment was terminated

conclusión *nf* **(a)** *(cierre)* conclusion *o* close; **en conclusión** = in conclusion; **conclusiones finales** = closing speeches; **las conclusiones finales del abogado defensor** = the conclusion of the defence counsel's address **(b)** *(resultado final)* findings *o* conclusion; **las conclusiones de una comisión investigadora** = the findings of a commission of enquiry; **llegar a una conclusión** = to conclude; **sacar la conclusión de que** = to gather; **la policía ha llegado a la conclusión de que el mecanismo de explosión de la bomba fue accionado a distancia** = the police have come to the conclusion *o* have reached the conclusion that the bomb was set off by radio control

concluyente *adj (definitivo)* conclusive
◊ **concluyentemente** *adv; (definitivamente)* conclusively

concordar *vi* to agree with; **concordar con** = to agree with; **la declaración del testigo no concuerda con la del acusado** = the witness' statement does not agree with that of the accused

concreto, -ta *adj (especial)* particular; *(tangible)* tangible

concurrente *adj* concurrent; **negligencia concurrente** = contributory negligence; **fue sentenciado a dos periodos de dos años de prisión, siendo las condenas concurrentes** = he was sentenced to two periods of two years in prison, the sentences to run concurrently
◊ **concurrentemente** *adv* concurrently

concurso *nm* **(a)** competition; **concurso público** = invitation to tender for a contract

concusión *nf* extortion
◊ **concusionario, -ria** *n* extortionist

condado *nm* county; *GB* **juzgado del condado** = County Court; **diputación** *o GB* **consejo del condado** = county council

condena *nf* **(a)** *(acción de condenar)* condemnation **(b)** *(sentencia)* conviction *o* sentence; **condena ampliada** = extended sentence; **condena anterior** = spent conviction; **condena simultánea** = concurrent sentence; **lleva diez condenas por robo con allanamiento de morada** = he has had ten convictions for burglary; **los dos hombres acusados de violación se enfrentan a condenas de hasta doce años de prisión** = the two men accused of rape face sentences of up to twelve years in prison; **se le impusieron dos condenas simultáneas de seis meses de arresto** = he was given two concurrent jail sentences of six months

condenado, -na *n* convicted prisoner *o* con; **celda de los condenados a muerte** = condemned cell

condenar *vt (sentenciar)* to *o* to condemn; **condenar a alguien** = to pass sentence on someone *o* to convict someone of a crime; **condenar a prisión** = to imprison; **volver a condenar** = to re-convict; **el juez le condenó a seis meses de prisión** *o* **le condenaron a seis meses de arresto** = the judge sentenced him to six months in prison *o* he was sentenced to six months' imprisonment; **le condenaron a tres años de prisión** = he received a three-year jail sentence; **los acusados fueron condenados a muerte** = the prisoners were condemned to death

condición *nm* **(a)** *(estado)* condition; **buque en perfectas condiciones** = ship which is A1 at Lloyd's **(b)** *(estipulación)* proviso *o* condition; **condición resolutoria** = condition subsequent; **condición suspensiva** = condition precedent; **a condición de que** = on the understanding that *o* provided that *o* providing *o* on condition that; **aceptamos los términos del contrato, a condición de que sea ratificado por el Consejo de Administración en pleno** = we accept the terms of the contract, on the understanding that it has to be ratified by the full board; **firmamos el contrato con la condición de que los términos puedan ser discutidos de nuevo dentro de seis meses** = we are signing the contract with the proviso that the terms can be discussed again in six months' time; **se les concedió el arrendamiento a condición de que pagaran los gastos legales** = they were granted the lease on condition that they paid the legal costs; **fue puesto en libertad a condición de pagar una multa si no comparecía ante los tribunales** = he was remanded on his own recognizance **(c)**

(requisitos) **condiciones** = term *o* terms; **condiciones de empleo** *o* **de trabajo** *o* **de servicio** = conditions of employment *o* conditions of service; **condiciones de ingreso** = conditions of membership; **condiciones de pago** = terms of payment *o* payment terms; **condiciones de venta** = conditions of sale *o* terms of sale; **se negó a aceptar algunas de las condiciones del contrato** = he refused to agree to some of the terms of the contract; **cerrar un trato en condiciones favorables para uno** *o* **imponer duras condiciones** = to drive *o* to strike a hard bargain; **sin condiciones** = unconditional; **la oferta se aceptó sin condiciones** = the offer was accepted unconditionally

condicionado, -da *adj (con reservas)* qualified; **aceptación condicionada de una letra de cambio** = qualified acceptance of a bill of exchange; **inmunidad condicionada a la ausencia de malicia** = qualified privilege

condicional *adj* **(a)** *(a prueba)* conditional; **honorario condicional** = contingent fee; **dar una aceptación condicional** = to give a conditional acceptance; **hizo una oferta condicional** = he made a conditional offer; **la oferta se hizo terminante** *o* **perdió su carácter condicional el pasado jueves** the offer went unconditional last Thursday **(b)** *(custodia por aplazamiento de caso)* **libertad condicional** = conditional discharge *o* remand; **libertad condicional a prueba** = probation; **conceder la libertad condicional** = to parole; **en** *o* **bajo libertad condicional a prueba** = on probation; *(remisión de condena)* **sentencia condicional** = suspended sentence
◊ **condicionalmente** *adv (con reservas)* conditionally; **aceptar una oferta condicionalmente** = to accept an offer conditionally

condominio *nm* condominium; *(comunidad de bienes)* tenancy in common; *(propiedad mancomunada)* joint ownership *o* common ownership

condonación *nf (perdón)* condonation; **condonación de la pena** = licence *o* license

condonar *vt (perdonar)* to condone

conducción *nf* driving; **conducción en estado de embriaguez** = drunk driving; **conducción imprudente y temeraria** = driving without due care and attention *o* careless driving

conducente *adj* conducive; **la amenaza de acción de huelga no es conducente a una solución fácil de la disputa** = the threat of strike action is not conducive to an easy solution to the dispute

conducir *vi* **(a)** to drive; **conducir con imprudencia** = reckless driving; **conducir en estado de embriaguez** *o* **bajo los efectos del** alcohol = drunken driving; **conducir peligrosamente** *o* **sin el cuidado y la atención debidos** = careless driving *o* driving without due care and attention; **inhabilitación para conducir** *o* **retirada del permiso de conducir** = disqualification; **conduce un coche de la empresa** = she drives a company car; **después del accidente le impusieron una multa de 50.000 ptas y le retiraron el carnet de conducir durante tres meses** = after the accident he was fined 50,000 ptas and disqualified from driving for three months; **iba conduciendo al trabajo cuando oyó la noticia en la radio** = he was driving to work when he heard the news on the car radio **(b)** *(dirigir)* to head; **conduce una delegación del gobierno a China** = he is heading a government delegation to China **(c)** **conducir a** = to lead (up) to; **recibimos una serie de propuestas conducentes a la oferta de adquisición** = we received a series of approaches leading up to the takeover bid

conducta *nf (comportamiento)* conduct *o* behaviour; **conducta conducente a una alteración del orden público** = conduct conducive to a breach of the peace; **conducta criminal** = felony; **conducta indebida** = misconduct; **conducta intachable** = irreprochable conduct; **código de conducta** = code of practice; **mala conducta** = misbehaviour *o* misconduct; **normas de conducta** = code of conduct; **fue detenido por conducta escandalosa** = he was arrested for disorderly conduct in the street; **se divorció de su esposo a causa de su mala conducta** = she divorced her husband because of his conduct; **la condenaron a cuatro años de prisión pero la pusieron en libertad pronto por buena conducta** = she was sentenced to four years in prison, but was released early for good behaviour

conectar *vt (relacionar)* to connect

confabulación *nf (colusión)* collusion; *(connivencia)* connivance

confeccionar *vt (publicar)* to get out; **la Comisión confeccionó el informe a tiempo para la reunión** = the Commission got out the report in time for the meeting

confederación *nf* union

conferencia *nf* **(a)** *(discurso)* speech **(b)** *(congreso)* conference **(c)** *(llamada telefónica)* **conferencia internacional** = overseas call *o* international call; **conferencia (interurbana)** = trunk call *o* long-distance call; **conferencia personal** = person-to-person call

conferir *vi (otorgar)* to confer; **los poderes discrecionales conferidos al tribunal por ley** = the discretionary powers conferred on the tribunal by statute

confesar *vi* to confess *o* to admit; **confesó estar en la casa cuando ocurrió el asesinato** = he admitted to being in the house when the murder took place; **tras seis horas de interrogatorio por la policía, el acusado confesó** = after six hours' questioning by the police the accused man confessed

confesión *nf* confession *o* admission; **confesión espontánea** *o* **voluntaria** = voluntary confession; **confesión de culpabilidad** = admission of guilt; **el acusado puso por escrito su propia confesión** = the accused wrote down his own confession statement; **el sargento de policía le pidió que firmara su confesión** = the police sergeant asked him to sign his confession; **la confesión no fue admitida en juicio, porque el acusado declaró que había sido forzada** = the confession was not admitted in court, because the accused claimed it had been extorted

confianza *nf* confidence *o* trust *o* faith; **confianza implícita** = implied trust; **confianza personal** *o* **confianza que nace del comportamiento de una persona** = constructive trust; **de confianza** = reputable; **de poca confianza** = unreliable; **abuso de confianza** = breach of confidence *o* betrayal of trust; **digno, -na de confianza** = trustworthy; **puesto** *o* **cargo de confianza** = position of trust; **reunión de confianza** = privileged meeting; **tener confianza en algo** *o* **en alguien** = to have faith in something *o* someone; **voto de confianza** = confidence vote *o* vote of confidence; **propuso un voto de confianza en el gobierno** = he proposed a vote of confidence in the government; **es un testigo de confianza** = he is a reliable witness *o* the witness is completely reliable; **¿quién es su persona de confianza en el Ministerio?** = who is your contact in the Ministry?; **la junta tiene plena confianza en el director gerente** = the board has total confidence in the managing director; **los empleados que se ocupan del dinero son de total confianza** = the staff who deal with cash are completely trustworthy; **los equipos de ventas no tienen mucha confianza en su director** = the sales teams do not have much confidence in their manager

confiar *vt* to entrust; **confiar algo a alguien** = to trust someone with something *o* to entrust someone with something *o* to entrust something to someone; **confiar en** = to count on *o* to rely on; **confió el testamento a su abogado** = he deposited his will with his solicitor; **puede confiar en el Sr Tenas, es un abogado excelente** = you can count on Mr Tenas, he is an excellent solicitor
◊ **confiarse** *vr* **¿puede confiársele todo ese dinero?** = can he be trusted with all that cash?

confidencia *nf (confianza)* confidence
◊ **confidencial** *adj* confidential; **ponga en la carta la mención de 'Confidencial'** = please mark

the letter 'Private and Confidential'; **envió un informe confidencial al presidente** = he sent a confidential report to the chairman
◊ **confidencialidad** *nf (secreto)* confidentiality; **violó la confidencialidad de las discusiones** = he broke the confidentiality of the discussions
◊ **confidencialmente** *adv (oficiosamente)* off the record

confidente *nm (delator* o *chivato)* informer *o* grass; **confidente de la policía que informa sobre las actividades de otros delincuentes** = supergrass

confinamiento *nm (reclusión)* confinement

confinar *vt (encerrar)* to confine

confirmación *nf (ratificación)* confirmation *o* acknowledgement; *(de una firma)* attestation; *(verificación)* verification; **confirmación de una reserva** = confirmation of a booking; **recibió confirmación del banco de que se habían depositado las escrituras** = he received confirmation from the bank that the deeds had been deposited

confirmado, -da *adj* confirmed; **no confirmado** = unconfirmed

confirmar *vt (ratificar)* to confirm *o* to acknowledge *o* to affirm *o* to ratify; *(una firma)* to attest; *(refrendar)* to countersign; **confirmar una condena** = to uphold a sentence; **sin confirmar** = unconfirmed; **el Tribunal Supremo confirmó la sentencia** = the Supreme Court upheld the sentence; **el Tribunal Supremo ha confirmado la sentencia dictada por el juez** = the Supreme Court has confirmed the judge's decision; **su secretaria llamó por teléfono para confirmar la habitación de hotel** *o* **el billete** *o* **el acuerdo** *o* **la reserva** = his secretary phoned to confirm the hotel room *o* the ticket *o* the agreement *o* the booking; **hay noticias sin confirmar de que nuestro representante ha sido detenido** = there are unconfirmed reports that our agent has been arrested

confirmatorio, -ria *adj* **pruebas confirmatorias** = corroboration

confiscación *nf (incautación)* confiscation *o* forfeit; *(embargo)* impounding; **cláusula de confiscación** = forfeit clause; **confiscación de una propiedad** = forfeiture *o* sequestration

confiscado, -da *adj* **fianza confiscada** = estreated recognizance

confiscar *vt* to confiscate *o* to impound *o* to seize *o* to sequester *o* to sequestrate; **la mercancía fue confiscada** = the goods were declared forfeit; **el tribunal ordenó que se confiscaran las drogas** = the court ordered the drugs to be confiscated; **los oficiales de aduana confiscaron todo el cargamento** = the customs impounded the whole cargo; **su maleta fue confiscada en el aeropuerto** = his case was seized at the airport

conflicto *nm* conflict *o* strife *o* dispute; **conflicto colectivo** = industrial dispute; **conflicto de intereses** = conflict of interest; **conflicto de leyes** = conflict of laws; **conflicto salarial** = pay dispute; **conflictos civiles** *o* **conflicto entre grupos** = civil strife; **conflictos laborales** *o* **colectivos** = industrial disputes *o* labour disputes; **procedimiento de resolución de conflictos** = complaints procedure *o* grievance procedure; **servir de intermediario en un conflicto** = to adjudicate *o* to mediate in a dispute

conforme *adj* agreed; **conforme a** = in accordance with *o* accordingly *o* in conformity with; *(según)* under *o* pursuant to; **conforme a la norma** = up to standard; **conforme con** = compliant; **no conforme con** = not compliant with; **recibo** *o* **factura conforme** = receipt in due form; **actúa conforme a la regla 23 del estatuto del sindicato** = he is acting under rule 23 of the union constitution; **conforme a lo que nos ordenó, hemos ingresado el dinero en su cuenta corriente** = in accordance with your instructions we have deposited the money in your current account; **ha actuado conforme a las normas** = he has acted in conformity with the regulations

conformidad *nf* conformance *o* compliance; **de conformidad con** = under *o* pursuant to; **no conformidad** = non-conformance; **sentencia de conformidad** = plea bargaining; **asuntos de conformidad con el artículo 124 del tratado de la UE** = matters pursuant to Article 124 of the EU treaty; **en conformidad con las directrices de la Comisión** = in conformance with the directives of the Commission; **fue criticado por falta de conformidad a la normativa** = he was criticized for non-conformance with the regulations

congelado, -da *adj* frozen; **activo congelado** = frozen assets

congelar *vt (bloquear una cuenta)* to freeze (an account)

congresista 1 *nf (diputada)* Congresswoman **2** *nm (diputado) nm* Congressman

congreso *nm* **(a)** *(conferencia)* conference *o* convention; **actas de un congreso** = conference proceedings; **la federación de policía celebra su congreso anual esta semana** = the Police Federation is holding its annual conference this week **(b)** *(asamblea)* Congress; **Congreso de los Diputados** = lower house; *(en GB)* House of Commons; **del Congreso** = Congressional; **una subcomisión del Congreso** = a Congressional subcommittee

El Congreso de los Diputados está formado por un número entre 300 y 400 diputados, elegidos por un sistema de representación proporcional a la población de cada provincia española.

conjunto, -ta *adj (global)* comprehensive; *(colectivo)* joint; **cuenta conjunta** = joint account; **dirección conjunta** = joint management; **propiedad conjunta** = multiple ownership; **signatario conjunto** *o* **firmante conjunto** = joint signatory; **responsabilidad conjunta y solidaria** = joint and several liability; **responsable conjunta y solidariamente** = jointly and severally liable; **negociaciones conjuntas (entre patronal y trabajadores)** = joint discussions; **responsables conjuntos de un agravio** = joint tortfeasors
◊ **conjuntamente** *adv (en común)* jointly; **dirigir una empresa conjuntamente** = to manage a company jointly

conjura *o* **conjuración** *nf* conspiracy

conmorientes *nmpl* commorientes

conmutación *nf* commutation; **privilegio de conmutación** = prerogative of mercy

conmutar *vt* to commute *o* to reprieve; **conmutar una sentencia** = to commute a sentence; **la sentencia de muerte fue conmutada por la de cadena perpetua** = the death sentence was commuted to life imprisonment

connivencia *nf (consentimiento)* connivance; *(colusión)* collusion; **era sospechoso de estar de connivencia desleal con el dueño de la propiedad** = he was suspected of (acting in) collusion with the owner of the property

conocer *vt* to know; **conocer de una causa** = to hear; **¿conoce al Sr Martin, nuestro nuevo director de ventas?** = do you know Mr Martin, our new sales director?

conocido, -da 1 *adj* known; **marca conocida** = brand name; **conocido como** = known as; **Juan Soriano, también conocido como 'el Carnicero'** = Juan Soriano, otherwise known as 'the Butcher' **2** *n; (contacto)* contact

conocimiento *nm* **(a)** *(saber)* knowledge *o* expertise; **conocimientos científicos** = know-how; **conocimiento de causa** *o* **por deducción** *o* **implícito** = constructive knowledge; **sin conocimiento previo** = without prior knowledge; **contratamos al Sr. Ramos por sus conocimientos del mercado africano** = we hired Mr Ramos because of his expertise in the African market; **necesita adquirir conocimientos de informática** = he needs to acquire computer know-how; **se necesitan ciertos conocimientos jurídicos para hacer este trabajo** = you need some legal know-how to do this job **(b)** *(documento)* notice; **conocimiento de embarque** = bill of lading; **conocimiento judicial** = judicial notice; **conocimiento de embarque** = advice note; **según conocimiento de embarque** = as per advice; **conocimiento real** = actual notice; **conocimiento sobre un hecho que la ley da por sentado que una**

persona posee *o* puede poseer = constructive notice

consanguíneo, -nea *adj* blood related; relación consanguínea = blood relationship

consanguinidad *nf* relaciones de consanguinidad que impiden el matrimonio = prohibited degrees; vínculo de consanguinidad = next of kin

consecución *nf* attainment

consecuencia *nf* **(a)** *(resultado)* consequence; a consecuencia de = as a result of *o* following; en consecuencia = accordingly; hemos recibido su carta y hemos modificado el contrato en consecuencia = we have received your letter and have altered the contract accordingly **(b)** *(conclusión)* conclusion; llevar *o* tener como consecuencia = to carry

consecuente *adj (de acuerdo)* consistent; la sentencia es consecuente con la política gubernamental sobre el trato a delincuentes juveniles = the sentence is consistent with government policy on the treatment of young offenders

consecutivo, -va *adj (sucesivo)* consecutive
◊ **consecutivamente** *adv* consecutively

conseguir *vt* **(a)** *(obtener)* to obtain *o* to gain *o* to procure; *(un empréstito)* to raise; que se puede conseguir = obtainable; conseguir el control de un negocio = to gain control of a business; conseguir una propiedad por medio del fraude *o* de la estafa = to obtain a property by fraud *o* by deception; los precios bajan cuando las materias primas son fáciles de conseguir prices fall when raw materials are easily obtainable; nos resulta muy difícil conseguir estos artículos we find these items very difficult to obtain; consiguió el control comprando las acciones pertenecientes a la familia = he obtained control by buying the family shareholding; la empresa consiguió la contrata del proyecto = the company was the successful tenderer for the project; ¿de dónde conseguirá el dinero para empezar su negocio? = where will he raise the money from to start up his business?; el gobierno consigue dinero por medio de los impuestos = the government raises money by taxation; la empresa está tratando de conseguir el capital necesario para invertir en su programa de expansión = the company is trying to raise the capital to fund its expansion programme **(b)** *(asegurar)* to secure; consiguieron la liberación de los rehenes = they secured the release of the hostages **(c)** *(lograr)* conseguir hacer algo = to manage to; ¿conseguiste ver al abogado? = did you manage to see the solicitor?; el abogado consiguió que la vista se aplazara = counsel managed to have the hearing adjourned; con dejar las ventanas abiertas sólo se consigue que entren ladrones = leaving windows open only encourages burglars; el juez consiguió que el testigo admitiera que no había visto el accidente = the magistrate extracted an admission from the witness that he had not seen the accident; el abogado no consiguió convencer al jurado de la inocencia de su cliente = counsel failed to persuade the jury that his client was innocent **(d)** *(capturar)* to capture; la oposición consiguió seis nuevos escaños en las elecciones generales = the Opposition captured six seats in the general election

consejero, -ra *n* adviser *o* advisor; *(director gerente)* consejero delegado = managing director; dos consejeros fueron depuestos de su cargo en la junta general anual = two directors were removed from the board at the AGM; está consultando con el consejero legal de la compañía = he is consulting the company's legal adviser

consejo *nm* **(a)** *(junta directiva)* board *o* council; consejo de administración = board of directors; *GB* consejo del condado = county council; consejo de familia = family council; consejo de Estado = Council of the Realm *o* Privy Council; Consejo de Europa = Council of Europe; consejo de guerra = court-martial; consejo de ministros = cabinet; Consejo de Ministros de Asuntos Exteriores de los países de la UE = Council of Ministers; Consejo de Seguridad = Security Council; consejo de síndicos = board of trustees; consejo editorial *o* de redacción = editorial board; consejo ejecutivo = executive council; consejo escolar = board of governors; Consejo General de la Abogacía Española = General Council of Spanish Advocates; Consejo General del Poder Judicial = General Council of the Judiciary; Consejo Municipal = Town Council *o* borough council; juzgar en consejo de guerra = to court-martial; reunión del consejo de administración = board meeting; el banco tiene dos representantes en el consejo = the bank has two representatives on the board; es el representante del banco en el consejo de administración = he sits on the board as a representative of the bank; el consejo de guerra tuvo lugar en el cuartel general del ejército = the court-martial was held in the army headquarters **(b)** *(asesoramiento)* advice; consejo legal = counsel's advice; enviamos los documentos a la policía siguiendo consejo legal = we sent the documents to the police on the advice of the solicitor *o* we took the solicitor's advice and sent the documents to the police

El Consejo de Estado es el supremo órgano consultivo del Gobierno del Estado

consenso *nm* consensus; política de consenso = consensus politics; en ausencia de consenso, no se podrá alcanzar ninguna decisión = in the absence of a consensus, no decisions could be reached; **hubo consenso entre todos los partidos en cuanto a los pasos que se debían dar** = there was a consensus between all parties as to the next steps to be taken

consensual *adj* consensual; *(relativo al derecho común anglosajón)* common-law; **(contrato) consensual** = simple contract *o* consensus ad idem; *(convivencia)* **unión consensual** = common-law marriage

consentido, -da *adj* **actos consentidos** = consensual acts

consentimiento *nm* **(a)** *(conformidad)* approval *o* assent *o* consent; **consentimiento entre adultos** *o* **entre mayores de edad** = consenting adults; **consentimiento expreso** = express consent; **consentimiento implícito** = constructive consent; **consentimiento tácito** = sufferance; **sin el consentimiento** = against the will; **actos sexuales con consentimiento** = consensual acts; **orden judicial de consentimiento con un tercero** = consent order; **tomó el coche prestado sin el consentimiento del propietario** = he borrowed the car without the owner's consent **(b)** *(confabulación)* connivance; **con el consentimiento de los aduaneros, logró hacer entrar las mercancías en el país** = with the connivance of the customs officers, he managed to bring the goods into the country

consentir *vi* to consent *o* to agree; **el banco nunca consentirá prestar 20 millones a la empresa** = the bank will never agree to lend the company 20 million; **el juez consintió en la petición del abogado para la acusación** = the judge consented to the request of the prosecution counsel

conserje *nmf (portero)* caretaker

conservación *nf* *(mantenimiento)* maintenance; **estado de conservación** = state of repair; **orden de conservación** = preservation order; **la casa estaba en mal estado de conservación cuando la compramos** = the house was in a bad state of repair when he bought it

conservar *vt (mantener)* to maintain; **derecho a conservar un puesto de trabajo** *o* **una vivienda alquilada** = security of tenure

considerable *adj (importante)* considerable *o* substantial; **vendemos cantidades considerables de nuestros productos a África** = we sell considerable quantities of our products to Africa

considerablemente *adv* considerably; *(en gran parte)* largely; **las cifras de delitos son considerablemente más altas que las del año pasado** = crime figures are considerably higher than they were last year

consideración *nf* consideration *o* account; **la consideración debida** *o* **la debida consideración** = good consideration; **tomar algo en consideración** = to take something into consideration; **habiendo tomado en consideración la edad del acusado, el tribunal ha decidido concederle una remisión condicional de la pena** = having taken the age of the accused into consideration, the court has decided to give him a suspended sentence; **confesar un acusado otros delitos aparte del que se le acusa y pedir que también sean tomados en consideración** = to ask for other offences to be taken into consideration

considerando *nm* whereas clause

considerar *vi* to consider; *(creer)* to deem *o* to hold; *(juzgar)* to judge; **el juez pidió al jurado que considerara el veredicto** = the judge asked the jury to consider their verdict; **estamos considerando trasladar la oficina principal a Escocia** = we are giving consideration to moving the head office to Scotland; **las penas sobre difamación en el nuevo Código Penal se consideran demasiado indulgentes** = the punishment for libel in the new Criminal Code is considered too lenient; **de no efectuarse ningún pago, el partido ser considerado deudor moroso** = if no payment is made, the party shall be deemed to have defaulted; **el tribunal consideró que la defensa no tenía suficientes argumentos jurídicos** = the court held that there was no case to answer; **se le considera uno de los mejores abogados en materia de divorcios** = he is considered to be one of the leading divorce lawyers; **el juez consideró necesario ordenar que se desalojara la sala** = the judge deemed it necessary to order the court to be cleared; **el juez no considerar ninguna propuesta de la acusación para retrasar el comienzo de la vista** = the judge will not entertain any proposal from the prosecution to delay the start of the hearing **(b)** **considerando que** = whereas; **considerando que la propiedad se mantiene en fideicomiso** *o* **en depósito para el demandante** = whereas the property is held in trust for the appellant

consignación *nf* appropriation; *(envío)* consignment; *(partida)* consignation; *(registro)* recording; **declaración de consignación** = consignment note; **mercancías en consignación** = goods on consignment; **la consignación de una orden judicial** = the recording of an order

consignado, -da *adj* **mercancías consignadas** = goods on consignment

consignador, -ra *n (remitente)* consignor; **los bienes son propiedad del consignador hasta su venta por parte del consignatario** = the goods remain the property of the consignor until the consignee sells them

consignar *vt* **(a)** *(tomar nota de)* to record; **el tribunal consignó una declaración de inocencia** = the court recorded a plea of not guilty **(b)** *(enviar)* to consign; **consignar mercancías a alguien** = to consign goods to someone **(c)** to appropriate

consignatario, -ria *n (destinatario)* consignee

consiguiente *adj (por lo tanto)* **por consiguiente** = therefor

consistorial *adj (ayuntamiento)* **casa consistorial** = Town Hall

consistorio *nm* Town Council

consolidar *vt (establecer)* to establish
◊ **consolidarse** *vr (afirmarse)* to firm; **las acciones se consolidaron a 500 ptas** = the shares firmed at 500 ptas

consorcio *nm* **(a)** consortium; *(sociedad personal)* partnership; *(coparticipación)* co-ownership **(b)** *(copartícipe)* co-partner

consorte *nmf* **(a)** *(cónyuge)* spouse **(b)** *(cómplice)* accomplice *o* partner in crime

conspiración *nf* conspiracy

conspirar *vi* to conspire

constar *vt* **(a)** *(componerse de)* **constar de** = to consist of **(b)** *(tomar nota de)* **hacer constar** = to record; *(oficialmente)* **que consta** = on record; **para que conste** = for the record *o* to keep the record straight; **una delegación que consta de todos los jefes de los departamentos interesados** = a delegation consisting of all the heads of department concerned

constatación *nf* confirmation

constatar *vt* to confirm

constitución *nf* **(a)** *(reglamento)* constitution; **la Constitución Española** = the Spanish Constitution; **escritura de constitución** = articles of association *o* articles of incorporation *o* memorandum of association; **el nuevo presidente pidió a la asamblea que redactara una nueva constitución** = the new president asked the assembly to draft a new constitution; **la libertad del individuo está garantizada por la constitución del país** = the freedom of the individual is guaranteed by the country's constitution **(b)** *(formación)* formation *o* forming; **constitución de una sociedad** = incorporation
◊ **constitucional** *adj (estatutario)* constitutional; **derecho constitucional** = constitutional law; **derechos constitucionales** = constitutional rights; **Tribunal Constitucional** = Constitutional Court; **la censura de prensa no es constitucional** = censorship of the press is not constitutional

La Constitución es la ley fundamental de organización del Estado y es la fuente suprema del ordenamiento jurídico. La Constitución Española entró en vigor en 1978.

constituir *vt* to constitute *o* to form; **sociedad legalmente constituida** = registered company; **una sociedad constituida legalmente** = an incorporated company; **asociación no constituida como sociedad anónima** = unincorporated association; **una empresa constituida en EE UU** = a company incorporated in the USA; **la conducta que tiende a interferir en el curso de la justicia constituye desacato a los tribunales** = conduct tending to interfere with the course of justice constitutes contempt of court; **los documentos constituyen pruebas fundamentales** = the documents constitute primary evidence; **esta Ley constituye un cambio importante en la política gubernamental** = this Act constitutes a major change in government policy
◊ **constituirse** *vr* **(a)** *(formar una sociedad)* to organise *o* to establish; **constituirse en sociedad** = to incorporate **(b) constituirse parte civil** = to bring a civil action

construcción *nf* construction; **permiso de construcción** = planning permission; **aprobación provisional de un proyecto de construcción** = outline planning permission; **denegarle a alguien la licencia de construcción** = to be refused planning permission; **en construcción** = under construction; **el aeropuerto está en construcción** = the airport is under construction; **la empresa ha presentado una oferta para la construcción del nuevo aeropuerto** = the company has tendered for the contract to construct the new airport; **estamos esperando el permiso de construcción para empezar a construir** = we are waiting for planning permission before we can start building

constructivo, -va *adj (positivo)* constructive; **hizo unas sugerencias constructivas para mejorar las relaciones entre la patronal y los trabajadores** = she made some constructive suggestions for improving management-worker relations

constructor, -ra 1 *adj* construction; **empresa constructora** = construction company **2** *nm* builder *o* constructor; **constructor especulativo** = speculative builder

construir *vt* to construct *o* to build

consuetudinario, -ria *adj* **derecho consuetudinario** = common law *o* common-law *o* unwritten law

consulta *nf* **(a)** *(asesoramiento)* consultation *o* consultancy **(b)** *(referencia)* reference

consultar *vt* to consult *o* to confer; **consultar a un abogado** = to take legal advice; **consultó a su**

abogado sobre la carta = he consulted his solicitor about the letter

consultivo, -va *adj* advisory; **comisión consultiva** = advisory board; **junta consultiva** = an advisory board

consultoría *nf* consultancy firm

consumación *nf* completion; **consumación de traspaso de una propiedad** = completion of a conveyance; **consumación del matrimonio** = consummation

consumado, -da *adj* **matrimonio no consumado** = non-consummation of marriage

consumar *vt* to complete; **consumar una transmisión de propiedad** = to complete a conveyance; **matrimonio sin consumar** = non-consummation of marriage

consumidor, -ra *n* consumer; **asociación de consumidores** = consumer council; **crédito al consumidor** = consumer credit; **legislación del consumidor** = consumer legislation; **protección al consumidor** = consumer protection; **la fábrica es una gran consumidora de agua** = the factory is a heavy consumer of water; **los consumidores de gas protestan por el aumento de precios** = gas consumers are protesting at the increase in prices

consumo *nm* consumption; **consumo de drogas** = drug use; **consumo interior** = domestic consumption; **bienes de consumo** = consumer goods; **el consumo de carbón en la fábrica es muy elevado** = the factory has a heavy consumption of coal; **un coche con un bajo consumo de gasolina** = a car with low petrol consumption

contabilidad *nf* accounting; **contabilidad ficticia** *o* **falseada** *o* **falseamiento de contabilidad** = false accounting

contable *nmf* accountant; **contable colegiado** *o* **autorizado** = certified accountant *o* chartered accountant; **contable jefe** = controller

contacto *nf* (a) *(relación)* contact; *(contactar)* **ponerse en contacto con** = to contact; **¿puede ponerse en contacto con los abogados que representan a los vendedores?** = can you contact the solicitors representing the vendors?; **he perdido contacto con ellos** = I have lost contact with them; **me puse en contacto con un buen abogado** = he put me in contact with a good lawyer; **trató de ponerse en contacto con su oficina por teléfono** = he tried to contact his office by phone (b) *(enchufe)* contact; **¿quién es su contacto en el Ministerio?** = who is your contact in the Ministry?; **tiene muchos contactos en la ciudad** = he has many contacts in the city

contaminación *nf* pollution

contante *adj* **contante y sonante** = hard cash

contar *vt* (a) *(sumar)* to count *o* to calculate; **contar con unos gastos de 5.000 ptas por persona** = allow 5,000 ptas per head for expenses (b) *(esperar)* **contar con** = to count on; **la defensa parece que cuenta con ganarse la compasión del jurado** = the defence seems to be counting on winning the sympathy of the jury

contencioso, -sa **1** *adj* contentious **2** *nm* defended action

contener *vt* to contain *o* to hold; **algunas de las instrucciones contenidas en el testamento son imposibles de llevar a cabo** = some of the instructions contained in the will are quite impossible to carry out; **cada caja contiene 250 hojas de papel** = each box holds 250 sheets of paper; **el contrato contiene algunas cláusulas que pueden dar lugar a interpretaciones equívocas** *o* **erróneas** = the contract contains some clauses which are open to misinterpretation; **la lata** *o* **el bote contiene veinte paquetes** = the tin holds twenty packets

◊ **contenerse** *vr* *(abstenerse)* to hold back

contenido *nm* content *o* contents; **el contenido de la carta** = the contents of the letter; **el contenido de la botella se derramó en el suelo** = the contents of the bottle poured out onto the floor; **los aduaneros inspeccionaron el contenido de la caja** = the customs officials inspected the contents of the box

contestación *nf* (a) *(respuesta)* reply *o* answer; **contestación a la demanda** = answer; **carta de contestación** = follow-up letter; **en contestación a su carta del 24** = in reply to your letter of the 24th; **se ruega contestación** = RSVP (b) *(contrarréplica)* rejoinder

contestar *vi* to answer *o* to reply; **contestar a la demanda** = tender a plea; **contestar a una carta** = to reply to a letter *o* to answer a letter; **contestar el teléfono** = to answer the phone; **contestar con evasivas** = to be evasive *o* to prevaricate; **intenté llamar por teléfono a su oficina pero no me contestaron** = I tried to phone his office but there was no answer; **la empresa ha contestado a la oferta de adquisición ofreciendo a los accionistas dividendos mayores** = the company has replied to the takeover bid by offering the shareholders higher dividends; **no contestaron a mi carta** *o* **a mi llamada de teléfono** = there was no reply to my letter *o* to my phone call; **le escribo contestando a su carta del 6 de octubre** = I am writing in answer to your letter of October 6th

contexto *nm* context; **la actuación de la policía tiene que considerarse en el contexto de los disturbios en contra del gobierno** = the action of the police has to be seen in the context of the riots against the government; **las palabras sólo pueden ser entendidas en el contexto de la frase en la que**

aparecen = the words can only be understood in the context of the phrase in which they occur

contienda *nf* dispute *o* litigation

contiguo, -gua *adj* adjacent; **estar contiguo a** = to adjoin; **los promotores adquirieron el antiguo edificio de correos y las dos propiedades contiguas** = the developers acquired the old post office and two adjoining properties

contingencia *nf (imprevisto)* contingency; **reserva para contingencias** = contingency fund *o* contingency reserve; **plan de contingencia** = contingency plan; **política de contingencia** = contingent policy

contingente 1 *adj* **gastos contingentes** = contingent expenses **2** *nm* import *o* export quota

continuación *nf* continuation; *(más abajo)* **a continuación** = hereunder *o* hereinafter; **las condiciones enumeradas a continuación** = the conditions hereinafter listed; **véanse los documentos enumerados a continuación** = see the documents listed hereunder
◊ **continuadamente** *adv; (sin interrupción)* continuously

continuar *vi* to continue *o* to go on; *(seguir)* to proceed; **los empleados continuaron trabajando a pesar del incendio** = the staff went on working in spite of the fire; **continuaron trabajando, aun cuando el jefe les dijo que pararan** = they kept working, even when the boss told them to stop

continuo, -nua *adj* continual *o* continuous; **alimentación continua** = continuous feed; **papel continuo** = continuous stationery; **tener trabajo continuo** *o* **trabajar durante un periodo continuo sin interrupción** = to be in continuous employment
◊ **continuamente** *adv* continually

contra 1 *adv* **en contra** = v. *o* versus *o* against; **testimonio en contra** = adverse witness; **sin votos en contra** = unopposed **(b)** *prep* against; **contra OPA** = reverse takeover; **en contra de** = counter to; **en contra de la ley** = against the law; **estar en contra de** = to disapprove of something; *(desaprobar)* **ir en contra de** =; **atentar contra** *o* **ir en contra de un acuerdo** = to derogate from something which has been agreed; *(contravenir)* to contravene *o* to oppose; *(quebrantar)* to flout; **acción contra una propiedad, no contra una persona** = action in rem; **la decisión del tribunal va en contra del consejo del secretario del juzgado** = the decision of the court runs counter to the advice of the clerk to the justices; **la secretaria prestó declaración en contra de su anterior jefe** = the secretary gave evidence against her former employer; **estamos todos en contra de la adquisición** = we are all opposed to the takeover; **la compañía actuó en contra de la ley al enviar sustancias peligrosas por correo** = the company

went against the law by sending dangerous goods through the post; **encender hogueras en la calle va en contra de la ley** = lighting fires in the street is against the law; **el juez se manifestó públicamente en contra de los jurados** = the judge openly disapproved of juries

contra - *prefijo* anti- *o* counter-
◊ **contraasiento** *nm* contra entry; **introducir un contraasiento** = to contra an entry; **palabras que indican que se ha realizado un contraasiento** = per contra *o* as per contra

contrabandista *nmf* smuggler; **contrabandista de alcohol** = bootlegger

contrabando *nm* contraband *o* smuggling; **contrabando de alcohol** = bootlegging; **(alcohol) de contrabando** = bootleg (liquor); **mercancías de contrabando** = contraband (goods); **hizo su fortuna con el contrabando de armas** = he made his money in arms smuggling; **pasar de** *o* **hacer contrabando** = to smuggle; **tuvieron que pasar las piezas de recambio de contrabando** = they had to smuggle the spare parts into the country

contractual *adj (por contrato)* contractual; **cumplir las obligaciones contractuales** = to fulfill your contractual obligations; **relación contractual** = privity of contract; **responsabilidad contractual** = contractual liability
◊ **contractualmente** *adv* contractually

contradecir *vt* to contradict; *(negar algo)* to deny; **el testigo se contradijo varias veces** = the witness contradicted himself several times; **la declaración contradice lo publicado en los periódicos** = the statement contradicts the report in the newspapers

contradenuncia *nf (reconvención)* counterclaim

contradicción *nf* contradiction; **existe una contradicción entre la declaración del ministro en el Congreso y las noticias publicadas en los periódicos** = there is a contradiction between the Minister's statement in the Congress and the reports published in the newspapers; **la declaración del testigo fue una pura contradicción** =; **el testimonio de la mujer contradice el del esposo** = the evidence of the wife conflicts with that of her husband

contradictorio, -ria *adj* contradictory; **declaraciones contradictorias** = conflicting evidence; **un montón de pruebas contradictorias** = a mass of contradictory evidence; **el jurado tiene que decidir a quién creer entre un montón de declaraciones contradictorias** = the jury has to decide who to believe among a mass of conflicting evidence

contraer *vt* to incur; **contraer deudas** = to get into debt *o* to incur debts

contraespionaje *nm* counter-intelligence; **los agentes de contraespionaje intervinieron las oficinas con micrófonos ocultos** = the offices were bugged by counter-intelligence agents

contraoferta *nf* counteroffer

contrapartida *nf* **Martínez reclamó 250.000 ptas por daños y perjuicios y Salvador, como contrapartida, reclamó 50.000 por despido** = Martínez claimed 250,000 ptas in damages and Salvador counterclaimed 250,000 ptas for loss of office

contraprestación *nf* consideration; **contraprestación ejecutada** *o* **efectuada** = executed consideration; **contraprestación realizable** *o* **por realizar** *o* **por realizarse** = executory consideration

contrario, -ria 1 *adj* adverse *o* opposite; **posición contraria** = vice versa; **veredicto contrario (a lo que se considera la decisión correcta** *o* **a la opinión del juez)** perverse verdict; **si no se dan instrucciones contrarias** = failing instructions to the contrary **2** *nm* contrary; *(opuesto)* contra; **al contrario** *o* **por el contrario** = on the contrary; **de lo contrario** = otherwise; **el abogado no estaba enfadado con la testigo - al contrario, la elogió** = counsel was not annoyed with the witness - on the contrary, he praised her; **salvo que se acuerde lo contrario** *o* **salvo pacto en contrario** = unless otherwise agreed; **excepto cuando se afirme lo contrario** = except as otherwise stated **(b)** *(adversario)* opponent *o* adversary; **la acusación intentó desacreditar a sus contrarios en el caso** = the prosecution tried to discredit their opponents in the case

contrarréplica *nf (contestación)* rejoinder

contraseña *nf* password; **poner contraseña a** = to check

contraste nm **marca de contraste** = hallmark; **sello de contraste** = assay mark; **poner el contraste a una pieza de oro o plata** = to hallmark; **una cuchara con la marca de contraste** = a hallmarked spoon

contrata *nf* contract; **trabajo a contrata** = contract work; **hacer una contrata** *o* **licitación** to invite tenders for a contract; **sacar una obra a contrata** = to put a project out to tender *o* to ask for *o* to invite tenders for a project

contratación *nf* **(a)** *(negocio)* **hacer una oferta de contratación** = to tender for a contract; **lonja de contratación** *o* **bolsa de contratación** = commodity market *o* commodity exchange **(b)** *(reclutamiento)* recruitment; **sistema de contratación exclusiva de trabajadores sindicados** = closed shop

contratado, -da *adj (empleado)* employed

contratante *nmf* **parte contratante** = contracting party

contratar *vt* **(a)** *(comprometerse por contrato)* to contract; **contratar a otra empresa para que haga un trabajo** = to put work out to contract **(b)** *(emplear)* to hire *o* to engage; **contratar a un abogado** = to instruct a solicitor; **contratar a un abogado para que actúe en el nombre de uno** = to retain a lawyer to act for you; **contratar personal** = to hire staff; **contratar nuevo personal** = to recruit; **contrataron los servicios de una pequeña empresa para que pintara las oficinas** = they hired a small company to paint the offices; **hemos contratado a los mejores abogados para que nos representen** = we have hired the best lawyers to represent us; **hemos contratado al mejor abogado mercantil para que nos represente** = we have engaged the best commercial lawyer to represent us

contratista *nmf* contractor *o* building contractor; **contratista del Estado** = government contractor

contrato *nm* **(a)** *(acuerdo)* contract *o* agreement; **contrato de accionistas** = shareholders' agreement; **contrato de arrendamiento** = lease; **contrato de Bolsa** = contract note; **contrato consensual** = consensus ad idem; **contrato de asociación** = articles of partnership; **contrato de flete** = charterparty; **contrato de servicio** *o* **contrato de servicios** = service contract *o* contract of service *o* contract for services; **contrato de suministro de piezas de repuesto** = contract for the supply of spare parts; **contrato de trabajo** = contract of employment *o* employment contract; **contrato de venta** = bill of sale; **contrato en exclusiva** = exclusive agreement; **un contrato de representación** = an agency agreement; **contrato entre dos** *o* **más partes** = indenture; **contrato exclusivo** *o* **de representación exclusiva** = exclusive agreement; **contrato preliminar** = collateral contract; **derecho de contratos** = contract law *o* law of contract; **condiciones de contrato** = conditions of contract *o* contract conditions; **incumplimiento** *o* **violación de contrato** = breach of contract; **intercambio de contratos** = exchange of contracts **(b)** **adjudicar un contrato a una empresa** = to award a contract to a company *o* to place a contract with a company; **anular un contrato** = to void a contract; **firmar un contrato** = to sign a contract *o* to sign an agreement; **hacer un borrador de un contrato** = to draft a contract; **presentar una oferta para un contrato** = to tender for a contract; **redactar un contrato** = to draw up *o* to draft an agreement; **violar un contrato** = to break an agreement; **la empresa ha incumplido el contrato** = the company is in breach of contract; **el contrato es vinculante para las dos partes** = the contract is binding on both parties; **concertar un contrato para suministrar piezas de repuesto** = to enter into a contract to supply spare parts; **firmar un contrato de suministro de**

repuestos por valor de 10 millones = to sign a contract for 10 million worth of spare parts **(c) bajo contrato** *o* **según contrato** *o* **con contrato** = under contract; **por contrato** = contractual; **por contrato privado** = by private contract; **trabajo por contrato** = contract work; **comprometerse por contrato** = to contract; **comprometerse a suministrar piezas de repuesto por contrato** = to contract to supply spare parts *o* to contract for the supply of spare parts; **según contrato, la empresa debe entregar las mercancías para noviembre** = the firm is under contract to deliver the goods by November; **no está obligado por contrato a comprar** = he is under no contractual obligation to buy; **la empresa está obligada por contrato a pagar sus gastos** = the company is contractually bound to pay his expenses

◊ **contrato-tipo** *nm* standard agreement *o* standard contract; **contrato-tipo formal** = standard form contract

contravención *nf (infracción)* contravention

contravenir *vt (ir en contra de)* to contravene; **que contraviene** in contravention of; **el restaurante contraviene las normas de seguridad** = the restaurant is in contravention of the safety regulations; **el taller ha contravenido el reglamento laboral** = the workshop has contravened the employment regulations; **la dirección del cine cerró las salidas de incendios con llave contraviniendo las normas de seguridad** = the management of the cinema locked the fire exits in contravention of the fire regulations

contribución *nf* contribution; **contribución territorial rústica** = land tax; **contribución para formación profesional** = training levy; **contribuciones especiales** = special levies; **imponer contribuciones a** = to tax

contribuir *vt* to contribute; **contribuir a** = to contribute to; **que contribuye** = contributory; **contribuyó con el 10% de los beneficios** = to contribute 10% of the profits; **contribuyó al fondo de pensiones durante diez años** = he contributed to the pension fund for ten years; **la respuesta del público a la petición de información contribuyó a la captura de la banda** = the public response to the request for information contributed to the capture of the gang

contributivo, -va *adj (que contribuye)* contributory

contribuyente 1 *adj* contributory; **causas contribuyentes** = contributory causes; **factor contribuyente** = contributory factor **2** *nmf* **(a)** *(impuestos)* taxpayer; **contribuyente municipal** *o* **individual** = domestic ratepayer; **contribuyente comercial** = business ratepayer; **contribuyente de a pie** *o* **contribuyente base** *o* **contribuyente que paga el tipo de impuesto base** = basic taxpayer *o*

taxpayer at the basic rate **(b)** *(que aporta capital)* **contribuyente de capital** = contributor of capital

control *nm* **(a)** *(dominio)* control; **bajo control** = under control; **fuera de control** = out of control; **conseguir el control de un negocio** *o* **hacerse con el control de un negocio** = to gain control of a business; **perder el control de un negocio** = to lose control of a business; **la familia perdió el control de su negocio** = the family lost control of its business; **la empresa está bajo el control de tres accionistas** = the company is under the control of three shareholders **(b)** *(inspección)* control *o* check *o* checking; **control de alquileres** = rent control; **control de calidad de un producto** = inspection of a product for defects; **control de divisas** *o* **control de cambio** = exchange control(s); **control de equipaje** = baggage check; **control de la circulación** *o* **punto de control del tráfico** = point duty; **control de precios** = price control; **control presupuestario** = budgetary control; **de control** = supervisory; **mecanismo de control** = surveillance device; **sistemas de control** = control systems; **prueba de control** = control test; **el gobierno tuvo que imponer controles de divisas para detener la compra masiva de dólares** = the government had to impose exchange controls to stop the rush to buy dollars

◊ **controlado, -da** *adj (dirigido)* controlled

controlar *vt* to control; *(comprobar)* to monitor; **controlar un negocio** = to control a business; **el gobierno está luchando por controlar la inflación** *o* **para controlar el aumento del coste de vida** = the government is fighting to control inflation *o* to control the rise in the cost of living; **que controla** = controlling

◊ **controlarse** *vr (dominarse)* to restrain oneself

contumacia *nf* contempt *o* contumacy; **contumacia directa** *o* **indirecta** = direct contempt *o* constructive contempt

contumaz *adj* guilty of contempt

contundente *adj* **(a)** *(prueba)* conclusive; **las huellas dactilares en la pistola fueron pruebas contundentes de que el acusado era culpable** = the fingerprints on the gun were conclusive evidence that the accused was guilty **(b)** *(arma)* offensive; **posesión de objetos contundentes** = carrying offensive weapons

convalidación *nf* validation

convalidar *vt* to validate

convencer *vt* **(a)** *(persuadir)* to convince *o* to persuade; **convencer a alguien de que haga algo** = to prevail upon someone to do something; **convenció al propietario de la tienda de que el edificio necesitaba pintarse** = he convinced the owner of the shop that the building needed painting; **los dos timadores convencieron a la mujer de**

que eran policías vestidos de paisano = the two conmen convinced the woman that they were plainclothes policemen; **el abogado convenció al juez para que concediera un aplazamiento** = counsel prevailed upon the judge to grant an adjournment; **el abogado intentó convencer al jurado de que el acusado no era culpable** = counsel tried to convince the jury that the accused was not guilty; **está convencido de que el demandante ha entablado el pleito maliciosamente** = it is his conviction that the plaintiff has brought the case maliciously **(b)** *(incitar)* to entice; **convencer a los trabajadores de un sindicato de que se asocien a otro** = poaching; **trataron de convencer a los directores para que se unieran a la nueva compañía** = they tried to entice the managers to join the new company **(c)** *(satisfacer)* to satisfy; **el fiscal, al oponerse a la libertad bajo fianza, tuvo que convencer al tribunal de que era probable que el acusado tratara de abandonar el país** = when opposing bail the prosecutor had to satisfy the court that the prisoner was likely to try to leave the country

convencido, -da *adj (seguro)* confident; **estoy convencido de que el volumen de negocios aumentará rápidamente** = I am confident the turnover will increase rapidly

convención *nf* **(a)** *(congreso)* convention *o* assembly; **Convención de Ginebra** = Geneva Convention(s); **la Convención de Ginebra sobre Derechos Humanos** = the Geneva Convention on Human Rights; **el ejército atacante fue acusado de violar la Convención de Ginebra** = the attacking army was accused of violating the Geneva Convention **(b)** *(costumbre)* convention; **convenciones sociales** = social conventions

convenido, -da *adj* agreed; **una cantidad convenida** = an agreed amount

conveniencia *nf* **(a)** *(oportunidad)* suitability **(b)** *(acuerdo)* agreement; **pabellón de conveniencia** = flag of convenience; **embarcación que navega con pabellón de conveniencia** = ship sailing under a flag of convenience

conveniente *adj* *(práctico)* convenient; *(apropiado)* suitable *o* appropriate; **¿les parece las 9.30 de la mañana una hora conveniente para la reunión?** = is 9.30 a.m. a convenient time for the meeting?

convenio *nf* **(a)** *(acuerdo)* arrangement *o* agreement; *(pacto)* covenant; **convenio colectivo (libre)** = (free) collective bargaining; **convenio salarial colectivo** = collective wage agreement; **convenio mútuo** *o* **recíproco** = mutual agreement *o* understanding; **escritura de convenio** = deed of covenant; **un convenio internacional de comercio** = an international agreement on trade; **firmar un**

convenio = to sign an agreement; **firmaron un convenio salarial colectivo** = they signed a collective wage agreement; **firmó un convenio para no subarrendar el local** = he signed a covenant against underletting the premises **(b)** **(acomodamiento entre acreedor y deudor)** composition **(c)** *(negocio)* deal

convenir *vt* to agree; **convenir el pago de una cantidad de dinero al año** = to covenant; **convenir el pago de 10.000 ptas al año a obras de beneficiencia** = to covenant to pay 10,000 ptas per annum to a charity

convertible *adj* convertible; **activos convertibles** = realizable assets; **moneda convertible** = hard currency; **moneda no convertible** = soft currency; **obligaciones convertibles** = convertible loan stock

convertir *vt (transformar)* to convert; **convertir en efectivo** = to realize; **convertir bienes** *o* **activos en efectivo** = to realize property *o* assets

convicción *nf* conviction

convicto, -ta *nf (reo)* convict *o* con; **convicto y confeso** = self-confessed convict

convidar *vt (entretener)* to entertain

convivencia *nf (cohabitación)* common-law marriage; **esposa por convivencia** = common-law wife

convocante *nmf* convener *o* convenor

convocar *vt* to call *o* to convene; **convocar las Cortes** = to summon Parliament; **convocar una junta de accionistas** = to convene a meeting of shareholders

convocatoria *nf* call *o* citation; **convocatoria de acreedores** = creditors' meeting

conyugal *adj* conjugal *o* matrimonial; **derechos conyugales** = conjugal rights; **domicilio conyugal** = matrimonial home

cónyuge *nmf (esposo)* spouse

coopción *nf* co-option; **nombrar por coopción** = to co-opt someone onto a committee

cooperación *nf* co-operation; **el trabajo se finalizó antes de lo previsto con la cooperación de todo el personal** = the work was completed ahead of schedule with the co-operation of the whole staff

cooperar *vi* to co-operate; **las dos firmas han cooperado en la planificación del sistema informático** = the two firms have co-operated on planning the computer system; **los empleados no han cooperado con el plan de reorganización de la dirección** = the staff have not been co-operative over the management's reorganization plan; **los gobiernos están cooperando en la lucha contra la**

piratería = the governments are co-operating in the fight against piracy

cooperativa *nf* co-operative; **cooperativa laboral** = industrial co-operative; **fundar una cooperativa de trabajadores** = to set up a workers' co-operative

cooperativo, -va *adj* co-operative; **sociedad cooperativa** = co-operative society

coordinación *nf* coordination; **centro de coordinación** = incident room

coparticipación *nf (consorcio)* co-ownership *o* co-partnership

copartícipe *nmf (consorcio)* co-partner

copia *nf* copy *o* duplicate; **copia auténtica** *o* **legalizada** *o* **certificada** = certified copy; **copia carbón** = carbon copy; **copia fiel** = true copy; **copia impresa** = printout; **copia legible** = hard copy; **copia de archivo** = file copy; **copia de un contrato de arrendamiento** = counterpart; **copia en limpio** = fair copy *o* final copy; **me envió una copia del contrato** = he sent me the duplicate of the contract

copiadora *nf* copying machine *o* copier *o* duplicating machine

copiar *vt* to copy; **copiar una carta** = to duplicate a letter; **copió el informe de la empresa por la noche y se lo llevó a casa** = he copied the company report at night and took it home

copropiedad *nf (comunidad de bienes)* tenancy in common; *(propiedad mancomunada)* joint ownership *o* co-ownership *o* co-property *o* part-ownership

copropietario, -ria *nmf* co-owner *o* co-proprietor *o* joint owner *o* part-owner; **las dos hermanas son copropietarias de los bienes** = the two sisters are co-owners of the property

cordón *nm* **un cordón policial** = a police cordon

cordura *nf (juicio)* sanity

Corona *nf (el Estado)* **la Corona** = the Crown; *GB* **patrimonio de la Corona** = Crown Lands *o* Crown property

corporación *nf* corporation; **corporación privada** = private corporation; **corporación pública** *o* **municipal** = public corporation *o* Town Council

corporal *adj* corporal; **castigo corporal** = corporal punishment; **daños corporales** = personal injury

corrección *nf* correction *o* amendment; **corrección disciplinaria** = disciplinary measure

correccional *nm* approved school *o* detention centre

correctivo, -va *adj* corrective

correcto, -ta *(exacto)* correct; **operaciones comerciales correctas** = fair dealing; **el balance publicado no ofrece una visión correcta del estado financiero de la empresa** = the published accounts do not give a correct picture of the company's financial position; **las actas de la reunión no eran correctas y tuvieron que modificarse** = the minutes of the meeting were incorrect and had to be changed; **comprobamos cada envío para asegurarnos de que es correcto** = we check each shipment to make sure it is perfect

corrector, -ra *n* proofreader; **corrector de estilo** = editor

corredor, -ra *n* broker; **corredor de bolsa** = stockbroker; **corredor libre** = outside dealer

correduría *nf (corretaje)* brokerage; **correduría de bolsa** = stockbroking

corregir *vt (modificar)* to revise; *(rectificar)* to correct *o* to rectify *o* to amend; **la secretaria tendrá que corregir todos estos errores antes de que usted envíe el contrato** = the secretary will have to correct all these errors before you send the contract

correo *nm* **(a)** *(servicio postal)* post *o* mail; **correo certificado** *o* **servicio de correos con acuse de recibo** = registered mail *o* recorded delivery; **correo electrónico** = e-mail; **correo ordinario** = ordinary mail; **correo postal** = snail mail; **enviar una respuesta** *o* **responder a vuelta de correo** = to send a reply by return of post; **sala de reparto de correo** = post room; **¿ha llegado ya el correo?** = has the post arrived yet?; **el recibo estaba en el correo de esta mañana** = the receipt was in this morning's post; **el cheque se perdió en el correo** = the cheque was lost in the post **(b)** **por correo** = by post *o* by mail; **enviar por correo** *o* **echar al correo** = to post; **enviar una factura por correo** = to send an invoice by post; **entrega de notificación por correo** = postal service; **echó la carta al correo** = he put the letter in the post **(c)** **Administración de Correos** *o* **Correos** = the Post Office; **estafeta de correos** = sub-post office; **funcionarios de correos** *o* **de la administración de correos** = Post Office officials *o* officials of the Post Office; **lista de correos** = poste restante; **número del apartado de correos** = Post Office box number; **oficina de correos** = post office; **envíe cualquier mensaje a 'Lista de Correos, Atenas'** = send any messages to 'Poste Restante, Athens'

correr *vi* to run; **correr un riesgo** = to run a risk; **correr con** = to meet; **la empresa correrá con sus gastos** = the company will meet your expenses; **la empresa corrió con las costas procesales de ambas partes** = the company bore the legal costs of both parties

correspondencia *nf* correspondence; **correspondencia comercial** = business correspondence; **mantener correspondencia con**

alguien = to correspond with someone *o* to be in correspondence with someone

corresponder *vi* **(a)** *(coincidir)* to agree *o* to correspond (with); **corresponder a algo** *o* **con algo** = to agree with something *o* to belong with; **esos documentos corresponden a los informes de ventas** = those documents belong with the sales reports **(b)** *(responder)* to reciprocate; **nos ofrecieron un concesionario en exclusiva de sus coches y nosotros correspondimos ofreciéndoles un concesionario de nuestros autocares** = they offered us an exclusive agency for their cars and we reciprocated with an offer of the agency for our buses

corresponsal *nmf* correspondent; **el corresponsal jurídico de 'El País'** = 'El País' legal correspondent; **un corresponsal financiero** = a financial correspondent; **es el corresponsal en París de 'La Vanguardia'** = he is the Paris correspondent of 'La Vanguardia'

corretaje *nm (correduría de bolsa)* brokerage *o* stockbroking; **una firma de corretaje de bolsa** = a stockbroking firm

corriente 1 *adj* **(a)** *(ordinario)* common *o* normal *o* ordinary *o* average; **ser decomisado en la aduana es muy corriente hoy día** = being caught by the customs is very common these days; **es un trabajador corriente** = he is an average worker **(b)** *(actual)* current; **cuenta corriente** = current account *o* cheque account; **gastos corrientes** = overhead expenses *o* general expenses *o* running expenses **2** *adj y nm (año, mes en curso)* current year *o* month; **de los corrientes** = instant; **nuestra carta del seis del corriente** = our letter of the 6th instant; **su carta del seis del corriente** *o* **de los corrientes** = your letter of the 6th inst

corro *nm (parqué)* ring

corroboración *nf* corroboration

corroborar *vt* to corroborate; **el testigo corroboró la coartada del acusado, diciendo que lo había visto en Pamplona a la hora del asesinato** = the witness corroborated the accused's alibi, saying that at the time of the murder he had seen him in Pamplona

corroborativo, -va *adj* corroborative; **la carta proporciona pruebas corroborativas, mostrando que el acusado sabía que la víctima vivía sola** = the letter provides corroborative evidence, showing that the accused did know that the victim lived alone

corromper *vt* to corrupt; *(depravar)* to deprave; **corromper a alguien** = to corrupt someone's morals; **programas de televisión que pueden corromper las mentes infantiles** = TV programmes which may deprave the minds of children who watch them

corrompido, -da *adj (corrupto)* corrupt

corrupción *nf* corruption; **corrupción a un miembro del jurado** = embracery; **corrupción de funcionarios** = graft; **dinero procedente de la corrupción** = hot money; **el soborno y la corrupción son difíciles de controlar** = bribery and corruption are difficult to control; **el gobierno está deseando erradicar la corrupción del cuerpo de policía** = the government is keen to stamp out corruption in the police force

corrupto, -ta *adj* corrupt; **policía corrupto** = bent copper
◊ **corruptamente** *adv* corruptly

cortes *nfpl* **las Cortes** *o* **Cortes Generales** = (Spanish) Parliament

> El poder legislativo está representado por las Cortes Generales, integradas por una Cámara Baja o Congreso de los Diputados y una Cámara Alta o Senado.

cortesía *nf* **(a)** *(en el trato social)* courtesy *o* politeness **(b)** *(gracia)* grace; **conceder a un acreedor un periodo de cortesía** = = to give a creditor a period of grace

corto, -ta *adj* short; **a corto plazo** *o* **para un corto periodo de tiempo** on a short-term basis; **obligaciones a corto plazo** = current liabilities

cosa *nf (artículo)* item *o* thing *o* chose; **(asunto)** res; **'cosa juzgada'** = res judicata; **'contra una cosa'** = in rem; *(realidades)* **cosas probadas** = matters of fact; **'una cosa por otra'** = quid pro quo

costar *vt* to cost; **¿cuánto cuesta la máquina?** = how much does the machine cost?; **el alquiler de la habitación cuesta 30.000 ptas al mes** = rent of the room will cost 30,000 ptas a month

costas *nfpl* costs; **costas fijas** = fixed costs; **costas judiciales** = legal expenses; **pagar las costas** = to pay costs; **orden judicial de pago de las costas** = costs order; **el juez asignó las costas al demandado** = the judge awarded costs to the defendant; **el tribunal concedió al demandante 800.000 ptas por daños y perjuicios, además de las costas** = the court awarded the plaintiff 800,000 ptas in damages, with costs; **las costas del caso correrán a cargo de la acusación** = costs of the case will be borne by the prosecution

coste *nm* **(a)** *(importe)* cost *o (honorarios)* charge; **coste de producción** *o* **coste básico** = prime cost; **coste fijo** *o* **costes fijos** = fixed charge *o* fixed costs; **costes totales** = full costs; **coste, seguro y flete** = cost, insurance, freight (c.i.f.); **calcular el coste de un producto** = to cost a product **(b)** *(carestía)* **coste de vida** = cost of living; **aumento de salario por coste de vida** = cost-of-living increase; **índice del coste de vida** = cost-of-living index; **subsidio por aumento del coste de vida** = cost-of-living allowance

costear *vt (hacer frente a)* to meet *o* to defray (costs)

costumbre *nf* custom *o* usage *o* convention *o* practice; **costumbre local** *o* **del lugar** = local custom; **es costumbre entre abogados americanos llamarse 'Esquire'** = it is the convention for American lawyers to designate themselves 'Esquire'; **es costumbre que todo el mundo se levante cuando los magistrados entran en la Sala** = it is the custom that everyone stands up when the magistrates enter the courtroom; **tenía la costumbre de llegar al trabajo a las 7.30 y empezar a hacer el recuento de caja** = his practice was to arrive at work at 7.30 and start counting the cash

La costumbre tiene el carácter de norma jurídica, pero solamente regirá en defecto de ley aplicable (CC artº 1.3)

cotejar *vt* to compare

cotejo *nm* collation

cotidiano, -na *adj* day-to-day

cotizable *adj* **valores cotizables** = listed securities

cotización *nf* (a) *(valoración)* quotation *o* price; **cotización al cierre** = closing price; **cotización de apertura** = opening price; **cotización oficial en la Bolsa** = quotation on the Stock Exchange *o* Stock Exchange quotation; **relación de la cotización de una acción y sus beneficios** = price/earnings ratio; **la empresa ha solicitado entrar en la cotización oficial de la Bolsa** = the company is going for a quotation on the Stock Exchange; **la baja cotización de las acciones en el mercado de valores** = the poor performance of the shares on the stock market; **la cotización de las acciones de la empresa descendió** = the company *o* the shares performed badly (b) *(contribución)* contribution; **periodo de cotización necesario para tener derecho a una ayuda o subsidio** = qualifying period

cotizado, -da *adj* **sociedad cotizada en bolsa** = listed company

cotizar *vt* (a) *(valorar)* to quote; **empresa que cotiza en bolsa** = quoted company; **sus precios siempre se cotizan en dólares** = their prices are always quoted in dollars (b) *(contribuir)* **hay que cotizar durante seis meses para poder recibir las prestaciones establecidas en la póliza** = there is a six month qualifying period before you can make use of the assistance covered by the policy
◊ **cotizarse** *vr* to sell for *o* to be quoted at *o* to perform; **las acciones de la empresa se cotizaron**

por debajo de lo normal = the company *o* the shares performed badly

CP = CODIGO PENAL

creación *nf* creation *o* formation *o* forming; **la creación de una nueva empresa** = the formation of a new company; **plan de creación de empleo** = job creation scheme

creado, -da *adj* **intereses creados** = vested interest

crear *vt* to create *o* to form; **crear una sociedad** *o* **una empresa** *o* **una compañía** = to set up a company; **con la adquisición de pequeñas empresas poco rentables pronto creó un gran grupo comercial** = by acquiring small unprofitable companies he soon created a large trading group; **el plan del gobierno tiene como fin crear nuevos puestos de trabajo para la gente joven** = the government scheme aims at creating new jobs for young people; **los hermanos han creado una nueva empresa** = the brothers have formed a new company
◊ **crearse** *vr (establecerse en un negocio)* **crearse una reputación** = to establish oneself in business

crecer *vi* to grow *o* to increase

creciente *adj (en aumento)* increasing *o* mounting; **beneficios crecientes** = increasing profits; **existe una presión creciente en la policía para resolver el crimen** *o* **para combatir la delincuencia en el centro de la ciudad** = there is mounting pressure on the police to solve the murder *o* to combat inner city crime; **la empresa tiene una participación creciente en el mercado** = the company has an increasing share of the market

credibilidad *nf* credibility

crediticio, -cia *adj* credit; **clasificación crediticia** = credit rating

crédito *nm* credit; **crédito al consumidor** = consumer credit; **crédito a largo plazo** = extended credit; **crédito en condiciones muy favorables** = soft loan; **crédito exigible en cualquier momento** = money at call *o* money on call *o* call money; **crédito puente** = bridging loan; **a crédito** = on credit; **carta de crédito** = letter of credit; **carta de crédito irrevocable** = irrevocable letter of credit; **cuenta de crédito** = credit account; **facilidades de crédito** = credit facilities; **límite de crédito** = credit limit *o* lending limit; **periodo de crédito en la Bolsa** = account; **retirada del crédito bancario** = closing of an account; **tarjeta de crédito** = credit card; **petición de informes sobre crédito** = status inquiry; **comprar a crédito** = to buy on credit; **conceder seis meses de crédito a alguien** = to give someone six months' credit; **recibir un crédito bancario** = to receive an advance from the bank; **retirar el crédito comercial a un cliente** = to close an account; **vender en buenas condiciones de crédito** = to sell on good credit terms

creer *vi* to believe *o* to consider *o* to deem; **se cree que el presidente está de negocios en Sudamérica** = the chairman is believed to be in South America on business; **no creemos que los valores bancarios sean una inversión segura** = we do not consider bank shares to be a safe investment

criado, -da *n (sirviente)* servant

criar *vt* to raise; **criar a un hijo adoptivo** = to foster

criba *nf (seleccionar)* selection *o* screening; **pasar los candidatos por la criba** = to screen candidates

crimen *nm (delito)* crime; *(asesinato)* murder; **crimen organizado** = racketeering; **oleada de crímenes** = crime wave

> Se entiende por crimen cualquier delito grave y más específicamente un delito de sangre

criminal 1 *adj* criminal; **acción criminal** = criminal action; **acto criminal** = actus reus; *(difamación)* **calumnia criminal** = criminal libel; **llevó a cabo una acción criminal** = he carried out a felonious act **2** *nmf; (delincuente)* criminal *o* crook; *(ladrón)* villain; **asesinato** *o* **ajuste de cuentas entre criminales** = a gangland murder; **el trabajo de un policía consiste en detener criminales** = the job of the policeman is to catch villains; **la policía ha contactado con conocidos criminales para obtener pistas sobre el asesinato en el hampa** = the police have contacted known criminals to get leads on the gangland murder

criminalidad *nf (delincuencia)* crime; **índice de criminalidad** = crime rate; **ola de criminalidad** = crime wave; **la criminalidad va en aumento** = crime is on the increase

criminalista *nmf* criminal lawyer

criminología *nf* criminology

criterio *nm* criterion; **si aplicamos el criterio de la proporción de casos resueltos sobre el total de casos denunciados, el cuerpo de policía está actuando con más eficacia** = using the criterion of the ratio of cases solved to cases reported, the police force is becoming more efficient

crítica *nf* criticism; **el juez hizo algunas críticas sobre el modo en que la policía había llevado el caso** = the judge made some criticisms of the way in which the police handled the case

criticar *vt* to criticize; **el juez criticó a la policía por la forma en que había llevado el caso de violación** = the judge criticized the police for their handling of the rape case

crónico, -ca *adj* chronic

cronológico, -ca *adj* chronological; **orden cronológico** = chronological order

cruel *adj* cruel

crueldad *nf* cruelty; **fue acusado de crueldad mental** = he was accused of mental cruelty

cruz *nf* mark

cruzado, -da *adj* **cheque cruzado** = crossed cheque; **cheque no cruzado** = uncrossed cheque *o* open cheque

cruzar *vt* to cross; **cruzar un cheque** = to cross a cheque; **cheque sin cruzar** = uncrossed cheque

cuaderno *nm (libreta)* notebook

cuadrar *vt* to balance; **cuadrar una cuenta** = to reconcile; **cuadrar las cuentas** = to reconcile the accounts; **cuadrar una cuenta con otra** = to reconcile one account with another

cuadrilla *nf* gang; **cuadrilla de ladrones** = gang of robbers

cuadro *nm (tabla)* table

cuadruplicado, -da *adj* quadruplicate; **por cuadruplicado** = in quadruplicate; **las facturas están impresas por cuadruplicado** = the invoices are printed in quadruplicate

cuadruplicar *vt* **los beneficios cuadruplican el dividendo pagado** = the dividend is covered four times

cual *pron* **el cual** *o* **la cual** = where-; **de lo cual** = hereof; **en el cual** *o* **en la cual** = wherein; **en fe de lo cual firmo** = in witness whereof I sign my hand; **en confirmación de lo cual adjuntamos un extracto de cuentas bancario** = in confirmation hereof we attach a bank statement

cualificación *nf (título)* qualification; **cualificación profesional** = professional qualifications

cualificado, -da *adj (calificado)* qualified; **altamente cualificado** *o* **muy cualificado** = highly qualified; **es contable cualificado** = he is a trained accountant; **contratan a veintiséis asesores jurídicos sumamente cualificados** = they employ twenty-six highly qualified legal assistants; **todos nuestros empleados están altamente cualificados** = all our staff are highly qualified

cualquier, -ra *adj y pron* whatsoever

cuantía *nf* quantity

cuantificable *adj* quantifiable; **el efecto del cambio en el número de presos no es cuantificable** = the effect of the change on the prison population is not quantifiable

cuantificación *nf (parte)* quantum; **los demandados admitieron su responsabilidad pero el caso se llevó a juicio al no poder llegar a un**

acuerdo sobre la cuantificación de los daños = liability was admitted by the defendants, but the case went to trial because they could not agree the quantum of damages

cuantificar *vt* to quantify; **sin cuantificar** = unquantifiable; **cuantificar el efecto de algo** = to quantify the effect of something; **es imposible cuantificar el efecto de la nueva legislación sobre el índice de criminalidad** = it is impossible to quantify the effect of the new legislation on the crime rate

cuanto *adv* **en cuanto le sea posible** = at your earliest convenience; **¿Puede llamar por teléfono en cuanto consiga la información?** = can you phone immediately you get the information?; **en cuanto a su carta del 25 de mayo** = with reference to your letter of May 25th

cuarentena *nf* quarantine; **poner en cuarentena** = to quarantine; **los animales fueron puestos en cuarentena a su llegada al puerto** = the animals were put in quarantine on arrival at the port; **se han levantado las restricciones de cuarentena con animales importados de aquel país** = quarantine restrictions have been lifted on imported animals from that country; **se hizo un registro en el barco y todos los animales a bordo fueron puestos en cuarentena** = the ship was searched and all the animals on it were quarantined

cuartel *nm* **cuartel general** = headquarters

cuarto, -ta *adj* fourth; **cuarta parte** = quarter; **cuarto trimestre** = fourth quarter *o* last quarter

cuasi *prefijo* quasi-
◊ **cuasi contrato** *nm* *(contrato tácito)* implied contract

cubierto, -ta 1 *adj* **(a)** *(protegido)* covered; **¿está cubierto contra robo?** = do you have cover against theft?; **el dividendo está cubierto cuatro veces** = the dividend is covered four times **(b)** *(secreto)* covert **2** *nf* **(a)** *(de un libro)* cover **(b)** *(de un buque)* deck **3** *nm* place setting *o* piece of cutlery

cubrir *vt* to cover *o* *(hacer frente a)* to meet; **cubrir gastos** = to cover costs; **cubrir los gastos de alguien** = to meet someone's expenses; **cubrir una vacante** = to fill a vacancy; **sólo cubrimos los gastos** = we cleared only our expenses; **el acuerdo cubre todas las agencias** = the agreement covers all agencies; **el seguro cubrió los daños** = the damage was covered by the insurance; **la compañía no cubre sus deudas** = the company is in default; **las ventas no son suficientes para cubrir los gastos de mantenimiento de la tienda** = we do not make enough sales to cover the expense of running the shop; **el seguro cubre incendios, robo y pérdida de trabajo** = the insurance covers fire, theft and loss of work; **esperamos alcanzar pronto el momento en que las ventas cubran todos los**

gastos = we hope to reach the point soon when sales will cover all costs

cuchillo *nm* knife

cuenta *nf* **(a)** *(en un restaurante)* bill; **pagar la cuenta** = to foot the bill; **¿está incluido el servicio en la cuenta?** does the bill include service? =; **¿me puede traer la cuenta por favor?** = can I have the bill please?; **la cuenta asciende a 5.000 ptas con servicio incluido** = the bill comes to 5,000 ptas including service; **el camarero ha añadido un 10% a la cuenta por el servicio** = the waiter has added 10% to the bill for service **(b)** *(en una compañía)* account; **cuenta compensada** = contra account; **cuenta de crédito** = credit account; **cuenta de gastos de representación** = expense account; **cuenta de pérdidas y ganancias** = profit and loss account; **acción por cuenta y razón** *o* **acción sobre rendición de cuentas** = action for an account; **estado de cuentas** = the accounts of a business *o* a company's accounts; **saldo a cuenta nueva** = balance brought forward *o* carried forward; **cerrar** *o* **liquidar una cuenta** = to close an account; **liquidación de una cuenta** = closing of an account; **le ruego me envíe una cuenta detallada** = please send me a detailed *o* an itemized account; **cuentas a cobrar** *o* **cuentas por cobrar** = accounts receivable; **cuentas a pagar** = accounts payable **(c)** *(banco)* account; **cuenta bancaria** = bank account *o* US banking account; **cuenta conjunta** *o* **en participación** = joint account; **cuenta corriente** = cheque account *o* current account; **cuenta de depósito** *o* **cuenta a plazo** = deposit account; **cuenta sin movimiento** *o* **inactiva** = dead account *o* dormant account **(d)** **a cuenta** = on account *o* interim *o* down payment; **dividendo a cuenta** = interim dividend; **pago a cuenta** = interim payment; **entrada a cuenta** = down payment; **el abogado pidió 50.000 ptas a cuenta** = the solicitor asked for a payment of 50,000 ptas on account; **los gastos de electricidad corren a cuenta del inquilino** = electricity charges are payable by the tenant **(e)** *(autónomo)* **que trabaja por su cuenta** = freelance; **trabajador por cuenta propia** = self-employed; **los trabajadores por cuenta propia** = the self-employed; **trabajó en un banco durante diez años pero ahora lo hace por cuenta propia** = he worked in a bank for ten years but now is self-employed **(f)** *(ser responsable ante alguien)* **rendir cuentas a alguien** = to report to someone; **pedir cuentas a alguien** = to bring someone to book **(g)** **tener en cuenta** = to count *o* to note; **tener algo en cuenta** = to take something into consideration; **tener muy en cuenta** = to take note of something; **no tener en cuenta** = to override; **sin tener en cuenta** = regardless of *o* exclusive of; **teniendo en cuenta** = having regard to *o* as regards *o* regarding; **teniendo en cuenta la opinión del Parlamento Europeo** = having regard to the opinion of the European Parliament; **tener en**

cuenta la edad del acusado a la hora de dictar sentencia = to take account of the age of the accused *o* to take the accused's age into account when passing sentence; tener en cuenta un aumento de los gastos en concepto de intereses bancarios = to plan for an increase in bank interest charges; un comportamiento tal constituye desacato a los tribunales sin tener en cuenta la intención = such conduct constitutes contempt of court regardless of intent; el tribunal considera graves los delitos de ese tipo, sin tener en cuenta la edad del acusado = the court takes a serious view of such crimes, regardless of the age of the accused; los miembros del jurado tendrán en cuenta que el acusado no dice que estaba en casa la noche del crimen = members of the jury will note that the defendant does not say he was at home on the night of the crime; el acusado admitió otros seis delitos, y pidió que se tuvieran en cuenta = the accused admitted six other offences, and asked for them to be taken into consideration (h) dar cuenta de = to account for; dar cuenta de una pérdida*o* discrepancia = to account for a loss *o* a discrepancy (i) darse cuenta = to realize; cuando entró en la comisaría no se dio cuenta de que le iban a detener = when he went into the police station he did not realize he was going to be arrested; el abogado se dio cuenta de que el acusado estaba causando una mala impresión en el jurado = counsel realized the defendant was making a bad impression on the jury; los pequeños comerciantes se dieron cuenta de que el supermercado les quitaría una parte de su clientela = the small shopkeepers realized that the supermarket would take away some of their trade

cuerdo, -da *adj* sane

cuerpo *nm* (a) *(físico)* body (b) *(organismo)* cuerpo de policía = police force; el cuerpo de abogados = the legal profession; cuerpo de funcionarios del Estado = civil service; cuerpo de inspectores = inspectorate; cuerpo diplomático = diplomatic corps; cuerpo estatal = public body; cuerpo legislativo = legislative body (c) *(recopilación de leyes)* corpus; cuerpo del delito = corpus delicti

cuestión *nf* question; *(asunto)* matter *o* issue *o* business *o* point; cuestión adicional = collateral issue; cuestión de derecho = point of law *o* question of law; cuestiones de derecho (referentes a un caso) = matters of law; cuestión de hecho = matter of fact *o* point of fact *o* question of fact; cuestiones de hecho (referentes a un caso) = matters of fact; cuestión de orden *o* de procedimiento = point of order; cuestión de procedimiento = procedural problem *o* question; cuestión jurídica = legal matter; cuestión prejudicial = preliminary ruling; cuestión previa = preliminary point *o* prior issue; cuestiones pendientes = matters arising; el abogado planteó

una cuestión de derecho = counsel raised a point of law; el caso ilustra una interesante cuestión de principio legal = the case illustrates an interesting point of legal principle; es una cuestión de hecho si las partes firmaron el contrato, pero es una cuestión de derecho si el contrato es legal o no = it is a matter of fact whether the parties entered into the contract, but it is a matter of law whether or not the contract is legal; planteó una interesante cuestión de orden = he raised an interesting point of order

cuestionar 1 *vt* to question **2** *vi* to dispute

cuestionario *nm* questionnaire; enviar un cuestionario para averiguar las opiniones de los usuarios del sistema = to send out a questionnaire to test the opinions of users of the system; responder *o* rellenar un cuestionario sobre problemas de violencia en el centro de las ciudades = to answer *o* to fill in a questionnaire about problems of inner city violence

cueva *nf* den

cuidado *nm (atención)* care; cuidado y atención razonables = due care and attention; conducir sin cuidado *o* sin el cuidado y la atención debidos = careless driving *o* driving without due care and attention; tener cuidado con = beware of

cuidar *vt* to look after

culpa *nf* (a) *(culpabilidad)* guilt; culpa lata = gross negligence; culpa leve = ordinary negligence; culpa penal = criminal negligence; culpa redimida = spent conviction (b) *(falta)* fault *o* blame; echar la culpa = to blame; *(de buena fe)* libre de culpa = clean hands; el demandante debe estar libre de culpa = the plaintiff must have clean hands; ¿Tuvo la culpa la policía de que la manifestación acabara en disturbios públicos? = was it the fault of the police if the protest march developed into a riot?; echaron la culpa al personal de la sección por las bajas cifras de ventas = the sales staff got the blame for the poor sales figures; el juez de primera instancia echó la culpa de las muertes a la ausencia de un detector de incendios = the lack of fire equipment was blamed by the coroner for the deaths

La culpa o imprudencia es la acción u omisión que incurre en infracción de ley, cometida libremente y sin malicia, por alguna causa que se pudo y se debió evitar

culpabilidad *nf* culpability *o* guilt; confesión *o* reconocimiento de culpabilidad = admission of guilt; admitió su culpabilidad = he admitted his guilt; presunción de culpabilidad de una persona por su relación con otra que es culpable = guilt by association

culpable 1 *adj* culpable *o* guilty; culpable de = responsible for; culpable por asociación = guilt by association; **negligencia culpable** = culpable negligence; **declarar a alguien culpable** = to find someone guilty *o* to return a verdict of guilty *o* to return a guilty verdict; **declarar a alguien culpable de un delito** = to convict someone of a crime; **declararse culpable** = to plead guilty; **declararse culpable de una acusación ante el tribunal** = to answer charges; **el juez le declaró culpable del accidente** = he was found by the judge to be liable for the accident; **fue declarado culpable de homicidio y enviado a prisión** = he was convicted of manslaughter and sent to prison; **la compañía era culpable de evadir las disposiciones del IVA** = the company was guilty of evading the VAT regulations; **le declararon culpable de difamación** = he was found guilty of libel **2** *nmf* culprit

culpar *vt* to blame; **el magistrado culpó a los servicios sociales de no informar del caso rápidamente** = the magistrate blamed the social services for not reporting the case quickly

cumplidor, -ra *adj (digno de confianza)* trustworthy

cumplimentar *vt* to comply with; *(formulario)* to fill in

cumplimiento *nm (ejecución)* enforcement *o* performance; *(observancia)* observance; *(satisfacción)* satisfaction; **cumplimiento de la ley** = law enforcement; **cumplimiento de los términos de un contrato** = enforcement *o* execution of the terms of a contract; **cumplimiento de sentencia** = serving of sentence; **cumplimiento de un contrato** = discharge by performance; **cumplimiento parcial de contrato** = part performance; **imposibilidad de cumplimiento de contrato** = impossibility of performance; **el cumplimiento por parte del gobierno de los acuerdos internacionales** = the government's observance of international agreements; **declaración de cumplimiento de la Ley de sociedades** = declaration of compliance; **fecha de cumplimiento** = completion date; **funcionarios encargados del cumplimiento de la ley** = law enforcement officers; **se les pidió que depositaran 1 millón como fianza de cumplimiento del contrato** = they were asked to put up a 1 million performance bond

cumplir *vt* **(a)** *(realizar una obligación)* to comply with *o* to observe *o* to obey *o* to fulfill *o* to satisfy; **cumplir las instrucciones de una carta** = to act on a letter; **cumplir un contrato** = to fulfill a contract; **cumplir una promesa** = to fulfill *o* to keep a promise; **cumplir con** = to comply with; **cumplir con un deber** = to perform a duty; **no cumplir con algo** = to neglect to do something; **la empresa ha cumplido con la orden del tribunal** = the company has complied with the court order; **la empresa ha cumplido todos los términos del contrato** = the company has fulfilled all the terms

of the agreement; **se le pidió que diera su promesa de que cumpliría la orden judicial** = he was asked to give an undertaking that he would obey the court order; **todos los miembros de la asociación deben cumplir el reglamento de régimen interno** = all members of the association should observe the code of practice; **¿cumple todas las condiciones para que se le conceda la libertad condicional?** = has he satisfied all the conditions for parole?; **el cuerpo de bomberos puede cerrar un restaurante si no cumple con las normas de seguridad** = the fire department can close a restaurant if it contravenes the safety regulations; **la empresa no ha cumplido con todas las condiciones establecidas en el acuerdo** = the company has not satisfied all the conditions laid down in the agreement **(b)** hacer cumplir = to enforce; **hacer cumplir los términos de un contrato** = to enforce the terms of a contract; **(derecho) que no se puede hacer cumplir** = unenforceable; **negarse a cumplir un acuerdo** *o* **un contrato** = to repudiate an agreement *o* a contract **(c)** *(completar)* to complete *o* to accomplish; **cumplir un plazo establecido** = to meet a deadline; **cumplir un requisito** = to meet a requirement; **cumplir una condena** *o* **una sentencia** = to serve a sentence; **la empresa cumple 125 años el año que viene** = the company is 125 years old next year; **le queda todavía la mitad de la sentencia por cumplir** = she still has half her sentence to serve; **no pudieron cumplir el plazo fijado** = they failed to meet the deadline; **cumplió seis meses en una prisión provincial** = he served six months in a local jail; **no pudo cumplir las condiciones de la orden judicial** = he failed to meet the conditions of the court order

cuño *nm* stamp

cuota *nf* **(a)** *(cupo)* quota *o* allocation; **cuota de importación** = import quota; **cuota de mercado** = market share **(b)** *(tasa)* fee; **cuota patronal** = employer's contribution; **cuota tributaria** = tax liability; **cuotas de asociaciones** = membership dues; **cuotas de la Seguridad Social** = National Insurance contributions; **cuotas de pensión** = pension contributions

cupo *nm (cuota)* quota; **sistema de cupos** = quota system; **el gobierno ha impuesto un cupo de importación de coches** = the government has imposed a quota on the import of cars; **se ha aumentado el cupo de coches importados** = the quota on imported cars has been lifted

cupón *nm* coupon *o* dividend

cura *nf* cure *o* remedy

curar *vt* to cure *o* to remedy

curador *nm* guardian for the suit; **curador nombrado para un proceso** = guardian ad litem

currículum nm **currículum vitae** = curriculum vitae *o* *US* résumé; **los candidatos deberán enviar una carta de solicitud con un currículum vitae al departamento de administración** = candidates should send a letter of application with a curriculum vitae to the administrative office

cursar *vt* to file *o* to put in; **cursar una petición** *o* **una demanda** = to file a petition *o* to put in a claim

curso *nm* **(a)** *(estudios)* course; **curso comercial** = commercial course; **está haciendo un curso de dirección** = he is taking a management course; **ha finalizado su curso de secretariado** = she has finished her secretarial course; **la empresa le ha pagado un curso de formación de directores de ventas** = the company has paid for her to attend a course for trainee sales managers **(b)** *(proceso)* process; **el curso formal de la ley** = the due process of the law; **en curso** = in process *o* in progress **(c)** **moneda de curso legal** = legal tender; **dinero de curso forzoso** = fiat money

custodia *nf* **(a)** *(patria potestad)* custody; **custodia judicial** = legal custody; **menor bajo la custodia del Departamento de Bienestar Social** = child in care; **el tribunal concedió a la madre la custodia de ambos hijos** = the court granted the mother custody of both children; **se concedió a la madre la custodia de los hijos** = custody of the children was awarded to the mother; **los niños fueron puestos bajo la custodia del departamento de asuntos sociales** = the children were put in the care of the social services department **(b)** *(protección)* safe keeping **(c)** *(vigilancia)* guard; **custodia preventiva** = protective custody; **custodia por aplazamiento de caso** = remand; **mantener bajo custodia** = to remand; **mantenido bajo custodia** = remanded in custody; **los jóvenes permanecieron bajo custodia durante** *o* **toda la noche** = the young men were kept in police custody overnight; **preso en prisión preventiva a la espera de juicio** = prisoner on remand *o* remand prisoner; **se le mantuvo bajo custodia por dos semanas** = he was remanded in custody for two weeks

custodiar *vt* to guard

CV *nm* = CURRICULUM VITAE; **se ruega presenten la solicitud por escrito, adjuntando un CV actualizado** = please apply in writing, enclosing a current CV

Dd

dactilar *adj* finger; **huellas dactilares** = fingerprints *o* dabs

dádiva *nf* donation *o* gift

damnificar *vt* to injure *o* to harm
◊ **damnificado, -da** *adj y n* injured party; **los damnificados** = the victims

dañado, -da *adj* damaged; **artículos dañados por el incendio** = fire-damaged goods; **existencias dañadas por el agua** = stock which has been damaged by water

dañar *vt* to damage *o* to hurt *o* to harm *o* to injure; **la tormenta dañó la carga** = the storm damaged the cargo; **alegó que el artículo periodístico dañaba la reputación de la compañía** = he alleged that the newspaper article was damaging to the company's reputation; **la noticia de que el presidente ha sido arrestado por fraude ha dañado la reputación de la compañía** = the news that the chairman has been arrested for fraud has harmed the company's reputation

dañino, -na *adj (nocivo)* noxious

daño *nm* **(a)** *(perjuicio)* damage *o* harm *o* wrong *o* prejudice; *(herida)* injury; **daño criminal** *o* **penal** = criminal damage; **daño doloso** = malicious damage; **daño emergente** = general damages; **daño grave a la persona** = grievous bodily harm (GBH); **daño legal** = tort *o* tortious act; **daño material producido por los animales de una persona en la propiedad de otra** = damage feasant; **daño premeditado** = sabotage; **daño privado** *o* **particular** = private nuisance; **daño público** = public nuisance *o* common nuisance; **daño real** *o* **físico a la persona** = actual bodily harm (ABH); **persona que comete una agresión o daño** = tortfeasor; **que causa daño criminal** *o* **penal** = causing criminal damage; **referente a un daño** = tortious **(b) daños calculables** = special damages; **daños causados en accidente laboral** = industrial injuries; **daños causados por tormentas** = storm damage; **daños con agravante** = aggravated damages; **daños efectivos** = actual damages; **daños generales** *o* **directos** = general damages; **daños no importantes** *o* **nominales** = nominal damages; **daños personales** = personal injury; **daños por incendio** = fire damage; **daños punitivos** *o*

ejemplares = exemplary damages; **daños resarcibles** = reparable damages; **causar daños** = to cause damage; **intención de causar daños físicos graves a alguien** = implied malice; **sufrir daños** = to suffer damage; **responsabilidad por daños ocasionados por incumplimiento del deber** = tortious liability; **reclamó 250.000 ptas en concepto de daños por incendio** = he claimed 250,000 ptas for fire damage **(c) daños y perjuicios** = damages; **acción por daños y perjuicios** = action for damages; **acción legal por daños** = action in tort; **indemnización por daños y perjuicios** = compensatory damages; **atenuante** *o* **minoración de la indemnización por daños** = mitigation of damages; **medida** *o* **evaluación de los daños** = measure of damages; **proceso judicial por daños** = proceedings in tort; **estar obligado a indemnizar por daños** = to be liable for *o* in damages; **exigir** *o* **pagar 100.000 ptas por daños y perjuicios** = to claim *o* to pay 100,000 ptas in damages; **presentar una demanda por daños y perjuicios contra alguien** *o* **llevar a los tribunales por daños y perjuicios** = to bring an action for damages against someone

Se entiende por daños el mal ocasionado a persona o cosa, a causa de una lesión que recae directamente sobre ellas. Se entiende por perjuicios la ganancia que ha dejado de obtenerse a consecuencia de los daños. Quienes en el cumplimiento de sus obligacions incurrieren en dolo, negligencia o morosidad deben indemnizar por daños y perjuicios

dar 1 *vt* **(a)** *(ofrecer)* to give *o* to gift *o* to extend; **dar cobijo** = to shelter; **dar derecho** = to entitle; **dar dinero en custodia a alguien** = to lodge money with someone; **dar el visto bueno** = to ratify *o* to give the go ahead; **dar en arriendo** = to lease; **dar en prenda** = to pledge; **dar entrada** = to admit; **dar fe** = to attest; **dar fianza** = to bail; **dar instrucciones** = to instruct; **dar instrucciones a un abogado** = to brief a barrister; **dar poder** = to empower; **¿puede darme alguna información sobre el nuevo sistema informático?** = can you give me some information about the new computer system?; **le dio los documentos al contable** = she gave the documents to the accountant; **no le dé**

ningún detalle a la policía = do not give any details to the police; la compañía dio una fiesta después de ganar el recurso = the company gave a party after they won their appeal (b) *(precio)* to quote; ¿Puede darnos el precio para el suministro de 20.000 sobres? = can you quote for supplying 20,000 envelopes? (c) *(impresión)* to cause *o* to produce; dar a entender = to imply (d) *(proveer)* to furnish; le pidieron que diera pruebas de su identidad al tribunal = he was asked to furnish the court with proof of his identity (e) *(beneficio)* to yield (f) dar a luz = to give birth; dar carpetazo = to shelve; dar parte = to report; dar por hecho = to take for granted; dar por muerto = to consider dead; dar preferencia = to give priority; dar testimonio = to testify; dar una paliza = to beat up 2 *vi;* dar a = to overlook; dar con algo *o* con alguien = to find *o* to meet; su despacho da al jardín = his chambers overlook the garden

◊ darse *vr* darse cuenta = to realize; darse por vencido = to give in *o* to give up; darse a la fuga = to escape; darse de alta *o* de baja =; *(en el trabajo)* to return to work *o* to go sick; *(en una asociación)* to join *o* to resign

dársena *nf* dock; derechos de dársena = dock dues *o* port dues *o* harbour dues

data *nf* date

datar *vt* to date

dato *nm* (a) *(información)* fact *o* piece of information *o* evidence; datos personales = particulars; hoja de datos = fact sheet; el presidente del tribunal quiso examinar con detalle los datos de la reclamación del impuesto sobre la renta = the chairman of the tribunal asked to see all the facts on the income tax claim (b) *(informática)* data; datos de salida = output; base *o* banco de datos = data bank *o* bank of data *o* database; proceso de datos = data processing; protección de datos = data protection; recuperación de datos = information retrieval

de *prep* del que *o* de la que *o* de lo que = whereof; en fe de lo cual firmo = in witness whereof I sign my hand

debajo *prep (menos de)* debajo de *o* por debajo de = under; el número de delitos denunciados que se resuelven está por debajo del 50% = under 50% of reported crimes are solved; el tipo de interés está por debajo del 10% = the interest rate is under 10%

debate *nm* (a) *(discusión)* discussion *o* debate *o* argument; tras un breve debate, el proyecto de ley fue aprobado = the Bill was passed after a short debate; varios diputados criticaron al gobierno durante el debate sobre la ley presupuestaria = several MPs criticized the government in *o* during

the debate on the Finance Bill; el debate se alargó hasta las 3 de la madrugada = the discussion continued until 3 a.m. (b) *(deliberaciones)* deliberations; extracto de los debates = charge

debatir *vt* to debate *o* to argue; los diputados continúan debatiendo el proyecto de ley de Protección de Datos = the MPs are still debating the Data Protection Bill

debe *nm (débito)* debit *o* debit balance *o* debit side *o* debtor side; debe y haber = debit and credit; columna del debe = debit column

deber 1 *vt* to owe; deber dinero = to be in debt; dinero que se debe a los directores = money owing to the directors; debe a la empresa la mercancía que compró = he owes the company for the stock he purchased 2 *vi* to have to 3 nm *(obligación)* duty; deber legal de prevención *o* deber de todo ciudadano de actuar de una manera responsable = duty of care

debido, -da *adj* (a) *(que se debe)* due *o* owing; *(deuda)* debido y no pagado = outstanding debt; debida notificación = due notice; porte debido = carriage forward *o* freight forward; a su debido tiempo = duly *o* in due course; como es debido = in due form; el debido procedimiento legal = the due process of the law; escrito en buena y debida forma = written in due form; conducir sin el cuidado y la atención debidas = driving without due care and attention; contrato redactado en la forma debida = contract drawn up in due form; recibo expedido en la forma debida *o* como es debido = receipt in due form (b) *(a causa de)* debido a = due to *o* owing to; los suministros se han retrasado debido a una huelga en el almacén = supplies have been delayed due to a strike at the warehouse; me temo que debido a un exceso de trabajo, no podemos hacerle entrega de su pedido a tiempo = I am sorry that owing to pressure of work, we cannot supply your order on time

◊ debidamente *adv* duly; representante debidamente autorizado = duly authorized representative; después de considerar la cuestión debidamente = after due consideration of the problem

débil *adj* weak; *(no convertible)* moneda débil = soft currency

debilidad *nf (defecto)* failing

debilitamiento *nm* weakening

débito *nm (debe)* debit; asiento del débito = debit entry

decantarse *vr* to show preference; el acusado se decantó por un juicio con jurado = the accused made his election for jury trial

decapitar *vt* to behead; **se consideró al acusado culpable de traición y fue decapitado** = the accused was found guilty of treason and beheaded

decencia *nf* decency; **la película escandalizó a la decencia pública** = the film shocked public decency

decente *adj* decent; **este libro debería prohibirse - escandalizará a cualquier ciudadano decente** = this book should be banned -it will shock any decent citizen

deceso *nm* death

decidido, -da *adj (decisiones precedentes)* 'a lo decidido' = stare decisis

decidir *vt* to decide *o* to determine; *(judicialmente)* to adjudicate; *(pronunciarse)* to rule; **hemos decidido llevar a nuestros vecinos ante los tribunales** = we have decided to take our neighbours to court; **la comisión de investigación decidió que la empresa estaba incurriendo en incumplimiento de contrato** = the commission of inquiry ruled that the company was in breach of contract
◊ **decidirse** *vr (llegar a una decisión)* to come to a decision *o* to reach a decision /W/ *vt/i* to say *o* to tell; *(mencionar)* to mention *o* to utter; **es decir** = i.e.; **'es decir'** = videlicet; **'diga ser cierto que'** = I put it to you that; **como ya se ha dicho** = as aforesaid; **¿puede decirles que se ha cambiado la fecha de la próxima reunión?** = can you mention to them that the date of the next meeting has been changed?

decisión *nf* **(a)** *(conclusiones)* decision *o* findings; **llegar a una decisión** = to come to a decision *o* to reach a decision; **toma de decisiones** = decision making; **persona que toma las decisiones** = decision maker **(b)** *(fallo arbitral)* award *o* adjudication; **decisión judicial** = rule *o* ruling

decisivo, -va *adj (concluyente)* conclusive *o* final; **factor decisivo** = deciding factor

decisorio, -ria *adj* decisive; **procesos decisorios** = the decision-making processes

declaración *nf* **(a)** *(afirmación)* declaration *o* announcement; **declaración ante el juez** *o* **declaración ante testigos** *o* **declaración estatutaria (ante el Registro Mercantil)** = statutory declaration; **declaración conjunta** = joint tax return; **declaración de aduana** = customs declaration; **declaración de asociación** = declaration of association; **declaración de consignación** = consignment note; **declaración de la renta** = declaration of income; **declaración de quiebra** = declaration of bankruptcy *o* adjudication of bankruptcy; **declaración judicial de quiebra** = adjudication order *o* adjudication of bankruptcy; **declaración del IVA** = VAT declaration; **declaración oficial** = official return; **de**

declaración obligatoria = notifiable; **hacer una declaración de renta** *o* **hacer una declaración a Hacienda** = to make an income tax return *o* to make a return to the tax office; **declaración hecha durante la negociación de un contrato** = representation; **presentar una declaración de quiebra** = to file a petition in bankruptcy; **presentar una declaración a la Delegación de Hacienda** = to file a return to the tax office; **rellenar una declaración del IVA** = to fill in a VAT return; **el presidente hizo unas declaraciones acerca de la oferta de adquisición** = the chairman made an announcement about the takeover bid; **necesitamos la factura para la declaración de la renta** = we need the invoice for tax purposes *o* for the purpose of declaration to the tax authorities; **rellenó el formulario de declaración de siniestros y lo envió a la compañía de seguros** = he filled in the claim form and sent it to the insurance company **(b)** *(testimonio)* testimony *o* assertion *o* statement; **declaración escrita** = deposition; **declaraciones contradictorias** = conflicting evidence; **declaración de culpa** = admission *o* confession; **declaración de derechos del individuo** = Bill of Rights; **declaración de inocencia** = plea of not guilty; **declaración difamante** *o* **difamatoria** = defamatory statement; **declaración escrita de un testigo (de su testimonio en juicio)** = proof of evidence; **declaración falsa** = false representation; **declaración inaugural** = opening statement; **declaración jurada** = affidavit; **derecho a no prestar declaración** = right of silence; **formulario de declaración de siniestro** = claim form; **hacer una declaración a la prensa** *o* **a la policía** = to make a statement; **hacer una declaración falsa** = to make a false statement; **presentar una declaración** = to file; **el abogado hizo una serie de declaraciones que el testigo discutió** = counsel made a series of assertions which were disputed by the witness; **pronunció su declaración en voz baja** = she gave her testimony in a low voice; **el jurado tiene que decidir a quién creer entre un montón de declaraciones contradictorias** = the jury has to decide who to believe among a mass of conflicting evidence

declarado, -da *adj* declared; **declarado, -da en rebeldía** = declared to have absconded *o* in contempt of court; **valor declarado** = declared value

declarante *nmf* deponent

declarar 1 *vt* **(a)** *(revelar)* to declare *o* to state; **declarar a alguien en quiebra** = to declare someone bankrupt; **declarar abierta la sesión** = to declare a court in session; **declarar mercancías en la aduana** = to declare goods to the customs; **declarar un dividendo del 10%** = to declare a dividend of 10%; **no declarar un dividendo** = to pass a dividend; **declarar un interés** = to declare an interest; **se le declaró en quiebra** = he was adjudicated bankrupt; **declarar unos ingresos de 10 millones de ptas a Hacienda** *o* **al fisco** = to return income of 10 million to the tax authorities; **el documento indica que todo ingreso tiene que ser declarado al fisco** = the document states that all revenue has to be declared to the tax office **(b)** *(reconocer)* **la zona fue declarada Parque Nacional** = the area was designated a National Park **(c)** *(emitir un fallo jurídico)* to find; **declarar inocente** = to acquit; **el tribunal declaró al acusado culpable de todos los cargos** = the court found the accused guilty on all charges; **el tribunal declaró culpables a las dos partes** = the tribunal found that both parties were at fault **2** *vi* **(a)** *(afirmar)* to claim *o* to declare *o* to state; *(presentar un informe)* to report; **que hay que declarar a las autoridades** = notifiable; **declara no haber recibido las mercancías** = he claims he never received the goods; **declaró que los daños sufridos eran muy graves** = he asserted that the damage suffered was extremely serious **(b)** *(en un juicio)* to testify; **declarar bajo juramento** = to depose

◊ **declararse** *vr;* **declararse en quiebra** = to file a petition in bankruptcy; **declararse capacitado** *o* **incapacitado para ser juzgado** *o* **para declararse culpable o inocente** = fit *o* unfit to plead; **declararse culpable** = to plead guilty; **declararse culpable** *o* **inocente de una acusación ante el tribunal** = to answer charges; **declararse inocente de los cargos** = to enter a plea of not guilty

declarativo, -va *adj* declaratory; **sentencia declarativa** = declaratory judgment

decomisar *vt (perder el derecho a algo)* to forfeit

decomiso *nm (pérdida de un derecho)* forfeit *o* forfeiture

◊ **decomisorio, -ria** adj **cláusula decomisoria** = forfeit clause

decretar *vt* to decree *o* to enact; *(en un juicio)* to deliver a judgment; **decretar una pena** = to pronounce sentence; **el Presidente decretó que el día 1 de junio sería fiesta nacional** = the President decreed that June 1st should be a National Holiday

decreto *nm* decree *o* act; **decreto legislativo** = Order in Council; **decreto de proscripción** = bill of attainder; **decreto-ley** = decree law; **gobernar por decreto** = to govern by decree

> Un decreto es una disposición o resolución dictada por la Administración en asuntos que le competen.
> Un decreto-ley es una disposición dictada por el Poder Ejecutivo por delegación expresa y especial del Poder Legislativo

dedicar *vt* **dedicar tiempo** = to spend time
◊ **dedicarse** *vr;* **dedicarse a** = to be engaged in; **se dedica a la informática** = he is engaged in work on computers; **la compañía se dedica al comercio**

con Africa = the company is engaged in trade with Africa

deducción *nf* **(a)** *(cantidad)* allowance *o* deduction; **deducción fiscal impositiva** = tax deductions; **deducción impositiva** = tax relief; **deducciones de salario** *o* **en origen** = deductions from salary *o* salary deductions *o* deductions at source; **deducción de impuestos sobre los intereses de una hipoteca** = mortgage relief **(b)** *(razonamiento)* deduction; **conocimiento por deducción** = constructive knowledge; **por deducción, el inspector concluyó que el muerto no ha sido asesinado** = by deduction, the detective came to the conclusion that the dead person has not been murdered

deducible *adj* deductible; **gastos deducibles** = allowable expenses *o* tax deductions

deducir *vt* **(a)** *(descontar)* to deduct; **deducir del sueldo** = to dock (someone's pay); **deducir un 5% de los salarios** = to deduct 5% from salaries; **deducir una cantidad para gastos** = to deduct a sum for expenses; **el sueldo neto es el sueldo bruto después de deducir los impuestos y la contribución a la seguridad social** = net salary is salary after deduction of tax and social security contributions; **impuestos deducidos en origen** = tax deducted at source **(b)** *(concluir)* to deduce *o* to infer; **el abogado dedujo que el testigo no había estado presente en el momento del accidente** = counsel inferred that the witness had not been present at the time of the accident; **por la carta dedujo que el acusado conocía a la víctima del asesinato** = he inferred from the letter that the accused knew the murder victim; **por su atuendo, podemos deducir que la víctima era rica** = from his clothes, we can deduce that the victim was a rich man

defecto *nm (imperfección)* defect *o* fault *o* imperfection; *(debilidad)* failing; **defecto de forma** = formal defect; **en su defecto** = failing that; **por defecto** = by default; **comprobar los defectos de un cargamento** = to check a shipment for imperfect products; **creemos que existe un defecto de base en la elaboración del producto** = we think there is a basic fault in the construction of the product; **el personal del servicio técnico está intentando corregir un defecto en el ordenador** = the technical staff are trying to correct a fault in the computer; **el presidente tiene un defecto - se duerme en las reuniones del consejo de administración** = the chairman has one failing - he goes to sleep at boardmeetings; **la causa del accidente fue un defecto en los frenos** = the accident was caused by faulty brakes

defectuoso, -sa *adj* **(a)** *(imperfecto)* faulty *o* imperfect; **pieza defectuosa** *o* **producto defectuoso** = reject; **venta de artículos defectuosos** = sale of imperfect items; **venta de**

piezas defectuosas = sale of rejects *o* of reject items; **vender existencias defectuosas** = to sell off reject stock; **comprobar los productos defectuosos de un cargamento** = to check a shipment for imperfections **(b)** *(que no funciona)* defective *o* faulty; **el testigo dijo que el accidente se debió al estado defectuoso de la maquinaria** = the witness said the accident was the fault of defective machinery; **la causa del accidente fue una reparación defectuosa de los frenos** = the accident was caused by faulty repairs to the brakes; **la máquina se rompió debido a un sistema de enfriamiento defectuoso** = the machine broke down because of a defective cooling system **(c)** *(sin validez)* defective; **conocimiento de embarque defectuoso** = foul bill of lading

defender *vt* to defend; *(refutar)* to contest; *(abogar)* to plead; **defender una acción** = to defend an action; **defender una causa ante un tribunal** = to defend a lawsuit; **contrató a los mejores abogados para que le defendieran contra las autoridades fiscales** = he hired the best lawyers to defend him against the tax authorities; **la compañía se está defendiendo frente a la oferta de adquisición** = the company is defending itself against the takeover bid

defensa *nf* **(a)** *(protección)* defence *o* US defense; **legítima defensa** *o* **defensa propia** = self-defence; **alegó que había actuado en legítima defensa al golpear al asaltante** = he pleaded that he had acted in self-defence when he had hit the mugger; **su defensa del derecho de los inmigrantes ilegales a permanecer en el país** = his advocacy of the right of illegal immigrants to remain in the country **(b)** *(alegación)* pleading *o* defence; **(caso) sin defensa** = undefended; **caso de divorcio sin defensa** = an undefended divorce case; **presentar una defensa** = to file a defence; **alegó en su defensa que no sabía que los bienes eran robados** = his defence was that he did not know the property was stolen; **el banco mercantil está organizando la defensa de la compañía frente a la oferta de adquisición** = the merchant bank is organizing the company's defence against the takeover bid **(c)** *(abogado defensor)* defence counsel; **entregar documentos en el juzgado por parte de la defensa** *o* **registrar comparecencia por parte de la defensa** = to enter an appearance

defensor *nm* **(a)** *(abogado)* counsel; **abogado defensor** = defence counsel; **defensor de oficio** = counsel appointed by the Legal Aid Board **(b)** *(que investiga las quejas del público contra los ministerios)* **Defensor del Pueblo** = ombudsman *o* Parliamentary Commissioner

> El Defensor del Pueblo es el alto comisionado de las Cortes Generales para la defensa de los derechos fundamentales proclamados en el título primero de la Constitución Española, y está legitimado para interponer recursos de inconstitucionalidad y amparo ante el Tribunal Constitucional (CE artº 54)

deficiencia *nf* deficiency

deficiente *nmf* **deficiente mental** = mentally handicapped

déficit *nm* deficit *o* loss; **anunciar un déficit** = to report a loss

definir *vt* *(precisar)* to define; **las personas inmigrantes tal y como se definen en el apéndice 3** = immigrant persons as defined in appendix 3

definitivo, -va *adj* *(concluyente)* conclusive; *(permanente)* permanent; *(último)* final; **sentencia definitiva** = final judgment
◊ **definitivamente** *adv* **(a)** *(concluyentemente)* conclusively; **la declaración del testigo presencial probó definitivamente que el acusado estaba en la ciudad en el momento en que se cometió el robo** = the evidence of the eye witness proved conclusively that the accused was in the town at the time the robbery was committed **(b)** *(permanentemente)* permanently

deformar *vt* *(falsear)* **deformar los hechos** = to misrepresent

defraudación *nf* **defraudación fiscal** = tax evasion

defraudar *vt* to cheat *o* to defraud; **defraudó miles de euros a Hacienda** = he cheated the Income Tax out of thousands of euros; **defraudó miles de libras a Hacienda** = he defrauded the Inland Revenue of thousands of pounds

defunción *nf* *(muerte)* decease *o* demise; **certificado de defunción** = death certificate; **subsidio de defunción** = death benefit

degradar *vt* to downgrade; **degradar a un oficial** = to reduce someone to the ranks

dejación *nf* *(abandono)* **dejación del deber con resultado de daños** = dereliction of duty

dejar *vt* **(a)** *(abandonar, ceder)* to leave; **dejar constancia** = to put on record; **dejar de cumplir** = to breach; **dejar un empleo** = to quit; **mi abuela me dejó 5 millones en su testamento** = I was left 5 million by my grandmother in her will; **deja marido y tres hijos** = she is survived by her husband and three children; **dejó su trabajo y se compró una granja** = he left his job and bought a farm; **dejó el puesto tras una discusión con el director gerente** = he quit after an argument with the managing director; **varios de los directores dejan sus puestos para establecer su propia empresa** = several of the managers are quitting to set up their own company **(b)** *(permitir)* to let; **dejar de hacer algo** = to omit *o* to neglect to do something; **dejar pasar** = to overlook; **dejar tiempo** = to allow; **deje un margen de veintiocho días para la entrega** = allow twenty-eight days for delivery

delantero, -ra *adj* **parte delantera** = face *o* front

delatar *vt* *(denunciar)* to accuse; *(coloquial)* to shop *o* to squeal; **delatar a alguien** = to inform on someone; **delatar a un cómplice para conseguir una condena más leve** = to turn Queen's evidence *o US* to turn state's evidence

delator, -ra *n* *(confidente de la policía)* informer *o* supergrass

delegación *nf* (a) delegation; **la dirección se reunió con una delegación sindical** = the management met a union delegation; **una delegación china de comercio** = a Chinese trade delegation (b) *(procuración)* proxy

delegado, -da 1 *adj* delegated; **consejero delegado** = managing director; **legislación delegada** = delegated legislation 2 *n* delegate *o* deputy *o* appointee *o* agent; **'el delegado no puede delegar en otro'** = delegatus non potest delegare

delegar *vt* to delegate; **delegar la autoridad** = to delegate authority; **delegar el voto** = to vote by proxy

deliberación *nf* (a) *(de un jurado)* retirement (b) *(discusiones)* **deliberaciones** = deliberations; **se transmitió a los periódicos el resultado de las deliberaciones de la Comisión** = the result of the committee's deliberations was passed to the newspapers

deliberado, -da *adj* *(premeditado)* deliberate; *(intencionado)* intentional; **acto deliberado** = wilful act; **un acto de deliberada crueldad** = an act of intentional cruelty; **negligencia deliberada** = wilful neglect; **la policía insinúa que la carta fue un intento deliberado para provocar disturbios** = the police suggest that the letter was a deliberate attempt to encourage disorder
◊ **deliberadamente** *adv* *(con intención)* deliberately; *(a sabiendas)* knowingly; **se le acusó de haber infringido deliberadamente la ley de Secretos Oficiales publicando el documento en su periódico** = it was charged that he knowingly broke the Official Secrets Act by publishing the document in his newspaper

deliberar *vi* to deliberate; **la comisión estuvo deliberando durante varias horas antes de llegar a una resolución** = the committee deliberated for several hours before reaching a decision

delictivo, -va *adj* criminal *o* felonious; *(que merece castigo)* punishable; **negligencia delictiva** = culpable negligence; **historial delictivo** = criminal record; **la apropiación indebida de fondos es un acto delictivo** = misappropriation of funds is a criminal act; **tiene un historial delictivo que se remonta a sus días de colegio** = he has a criminal record going back to the time when he was still at school

delincuencia *nf* delinquency *o* crime *o* lawlessness; **el gobierno está tratando de luchar contra la delincuencia en las grandes ciudades** = the government is trying to fight lawlessness in large cities

delincuente *nmf* delinquent *o* criminal; *(infractor)* offender; **delincuente fugitivo** = fugitive offender *o US* fugitive from justice; **delincuente condenado y sentenciado** = convicted criminal; **delincuente empedernido** *o* **incorregible** *o* **de difícil reinserción** = hardened criminal; **delincuente habitual** *o* **reincidente** = habitual criminal *o* habitual offender; **delincuente juvenil** = juvenile delinquent *o* young offender; **delincuente juvenil que es juzgado en un tribunal de menores** = juvenile offender; **delincuente sin antecedentes penales** = first offender

delinquir *vi* to commit an offence

delito *nm* *(infracción)* crime *o* criminal offence *o US* offense *o* wrongdoing *o* misdeed; **delito capital** = capital crime *o* offence; **delito común** = ordinary offence; **delitos contra el código de circulación** = road traffic offences; **delito contra el Estado** = offence against the state; **delito contra el orden público** = public order offence *o* offence against public order; **delitos contra la libertad sexual** = sexual offences; **delitos contra la administración de justicia** offences against justice; **delito** *o* **delitos contra las personas** = offence *o* crimes against the person; **delito** *o* **delitos contra la propiedad** = offence *o* crimes against property; **delito de lesiones** = actual bodily harm (ABH); **delito de reunión para llevar a cabo un tumulto** = rout; **delito frustrado** = attempted crime; **delito grave** = felony *o* notifiable offence; **delito menor** = misdemeanour; **delito político** = political offence; **delito reincidente** = second offence; **delitos dolosos** = deliberate crimes; **delitos incompletos** = inchoate offences; **cometer un delito** = to offend; **cometer un delito grave** = to commit a felony; **primer delito** = first offence; **es un delito tener relaciones sexuales con una chica menor de dieciséis años** = it is an offence to have sexual intercourse with a girl under sixteen years of age; **se le acusó de tres delitos graves** = he was charged with three serious offences; **como era el primer delito, le pusieron una multa y no tuvo que ir a prisión** = as it was a first offence, he was fined and not sent to prison; **el ministro fue arrestado y acusado de cometer delitos contra la Ley de Secretos Oficiales** = the minister was arrested and charged with offences against the Official Secrets Act; **los delitos violentos han experimentado un**

aumento = there has been an increase in violent crime; **los delitos violentos han experimentado un aumento del 50%** = there has been a 50% increase in crimes of violence

> Son delitos las acciones u omisiones dolosas o culposas penadas por la ley

demanda *nf* **(a)** *(pleito)* action *o (peticición)* petition *o* claim; **demanda civil** = civil action; **demanda de desahucio** = action for eviction; **demanda de divorcio** = divorce petition; **demanda de menor cuantía** = small claim; **demanda de reivindicación** = action of replevin; **demanda judicial por falta de pago** = default action; **demanda por daños y perjuicios** = action for damages; **demanda por difamación** = action for libel *o* libel suit; **presentar una demanda** = to file; **el matrimonio se había venido abajo y la esposa presentó una demanda de divorcio** = the marriage had broken down and the wife petitioned for divorce; **ha presentado una demanda de 5 millones contra la compañía** he is suing the company for 5 million compensation; **presentó demandas por difamación en relación con declaraciones publicadas en un periódico** = he issued writs for libel in connection with allegations made in a newspaper; **presentó una demanda por las reparaciones del coche** = she put in a claim for repairs to the car **(b)** *(comercial)* demand; **gran demanda** = run; **oferta y demanda** = supply and demand; **ley de la oferta y la demanda** = law of supply and demand; **los precios han bajado debido a una menor demanda de la mercancía** = prices have fallen due to a reduced demand for the goods **(c)** *(protesta)* demand *o* plaint *o* complaint

> La demanda es el escrito por el cual el demandante ejercita la acción. En él se expondrán los hechos y fundamentos de Derecho, se fijará con claridad y precisión lo que se pide y la persona contra quién se interponga la demanda (LEC 524)

demandado, -da 1 *adj* **parte demandada** = defendant; **abogado de la parte demandada** = defence counsel **2** *n (parte demandada)* defendant; **demandado, -da en un caso de divorcio** = respondent; **demandado en una causa de adulterio** = co-respondent; **cómplice del demandado** = co-respondent

demandante 1 *adj (acusación)* **parte demandante** = prosecution **2** *nmf* **(a)** *(querellante)* plaintiff *o* complainant **(b)** *(fiscal)* prosecutor

demandar *vt* to claim *o (entablar un pleito)* to sue; **demandar a alguien** = to bring a lawsuit *o* proceedings against someone; **demandar a alguien en juicio** = to issue a writ against someone; **demandar a alguien por daños y perjuicios** = to sue someone for damages

demencia *nf* insanity

demente *adj* insane non compos mentis; **personas dementes** = persons of unsound mind

democracia *nf* democracy

democrático, -ca *adj* **votación democrática** = popular vote

demora *nf* delay *o* demurrer; **gastos de demora** = demurrage

demorar *vt (atrasar)* to delay; **se demoró el juicio mientras los magistrados pedían peritaje** = judgment was delayed while the magistrates asked for advice; **la compañía demora los pagos** = the company is in default

demostrable *adj* provable

demostrar *vt (probar)* to demonstrate *o* to prove *o* to establish; **la policía demostró cómo fue colocada la bomba** = the police demonstrated how the bomb was planted; **las entradas demostraron que estaba mintiendo** = the tickets proved that he was lying; **está demostrado que el coche no pudo haber sido utilizado porque no tenía gasolina** = it is an established fact that the car could not have been used because it was out of petrol

denegación *nf (negativa)* denial *o* refusal; *(negación)* traverse; **denegación de derechos humanos** = denial of human rights; **denegación de justicia** = denial of justice

denegar *vt* to deny *o* to refuse *o* to disallow; **denegar la libertad bajo fianza** = to withhold bail; **denegar una petición** = to refuse a request; **el préstamo fue denegado por el banco** = the loan was refused by the bank; **pidió 2.000 libras por daños de incendio pero la petición fue denegada** = he claimed £2000 for fire damage, but the claim was disallowed; **pidió un aumento pero se lo denegaron** = he asked for a rise but it was refused; **se le denegó el derecho a ver a su abogado** = he was denied the right to see his lawyer; **su petición fue denegada** = his request met with a refusal

denigrar *vt* to slander

denominación *nf* denomination; **valor nominal** = denomination

dentro de *prep* inside *o* within; **'dentro de lo permitido'** = intra vires; **el caso entra dentro de la jurisdicción del tribunal** = the case falls within the jurisdiction of the court; **la acción del ministro fue calificada como dentro de la autoridad conferida** = the minister's action was ruled to be intra vires; **no había nada dentro del contenedor** = there was nothing inside the container; **tenemos un contacto dentro del departamento de producción de nuestro principal competidor que nos da información muy útil** = we have a contact inside our main competitor's production department who gives us very useful information

denuncia *nf (acusación)* accusation *o* information; *(revelación)* exposure; **hacer una denuncia** = to lay (an) information; **la denuncia en el informe sobre la existencia de corrupción policial** = the report's exposure of corruption in the police force; **se ordenó a los jueces que volvieran a oir la denuncia** = the justices were ordered to rehear the information

denunciar *vt* to accuse; *(delatar)* to squeal *o* to shop; **denunciar a alguien** = to inform on someone; **denunciar un convenio** = to denounce an agreement; **sin denunciar** = unreported; **fue denunciado a la policía por el cabecilla de la otra banda** = he was shopped to the police by the leader of the other gang; **hay miles de casos de robo sin denunciar** = there are thousands of unreported cases of theft; **si no deja de armar ruido le denunciaré** = if you don't stop making that noise I'll have the law on you

denunciante *nmf* informer

departamento *nm* department *o* section; **departamento de contabilidad** = accounts department; **Departamento de Estado** = Department of State; **Departamento de Derechos Arancelarios e Impuestos Indirectos** = customs *o* Customs and Excise; **departamento de visados** = visa section; **departamento jurídico** = legal department *o* legal section; **jefe del departamento** = head of department *o* department head *o* department manager

dependencia *nf* dependency; *(calabozo)* **dependencias policiales** = police station lock-up

depender *vi (estar subordinado)* to depend; **depender de** = to depend on; **depender de alguien** = at the discretion of someone; **dependemos de las ayudas del Estado para pagar los salarios** = we depend on government grants to pay the salary bill; **el contrato depende de la aprobación del gobierno** = the contract is subject to government approval; **el éxito de la campaña anti-droga dependerá de la actitud del público** = the success of the anti-drug campaign will depend on the attitude of the public; **la compañía depende del buen servicio de sus proveedores** = the company depends on efficient service from its suppliers; **la oferta depende de la aceptación de la junta** = the offer is conditional on the board's acceptance

dependiente **1** *adj* dependent; **dependiente de** = appurtenant; *(sujeto a)* subject to; *(subordinado a)* subordinate to; **tierra** *o* **edificaciones dependientes de una propiedad** = appurtenances **2** *n; (persona a cargo)* **familiar dependiente** = dependant; **tiene que mantener a su familia y dependientes con un sueldo muy reducido** = he has to provide for his family and dependants out of a very small salary

deponente *nmf* deponent

deponer *vi* to give evidence *o* to make a statement

deportación *nf (expulsión)* deportation; **orden de deportación** = deportation order; **el ministro firmó la orden de deportación** = the minister signed the deportation order

deportar *vt (expulsar)* to deport; **los inmigrantes ilegales fueron deportados** = the illegal immigrants were deported; **se condenó a los reos a ser deportados** = the convicts were sentenced to deportation

deposición *nf (declaración ante el juez)* deposition

depositante *nmf* depositor *o* bailor

depositar *vt* to lodge *o* to deposit *o* to bank; **depositar dinero en una cuenta** = to place money in an account; **depositar un cheque** = to pay a cheque into your account; **depositar 100.000 ptas en una cuenta corriente** = to deposit 100,000 ptas in a current account; **depositar una garantía en el Registro de la Propiedad para asegurar una propiedad** = to lodge caution; **depositar valores en un banco como garantía para un préstamo** = to lodge securities as collateral; **hemos depositado las escrituras de la casa en el banco** = we have deposited the deeds of the house with the bank

depositario, -ria *n (receptor)* depositary *o* depository *o* receiver *o* pledgee; *(síndico)* liquidator *o* provisional liquidator; **depositario financiero** = licensed deposit-taker

depósito *nm* **(a)** *(dinero)* deposit *o* down payment; **depósito a plazo fijo** = fixed deposit; **depósito en caja fuerte** = safe deposit; **certificado de depósito** = certificate of deposit; **cuenta de depósito** = deposit account; **sólo obtuvo 25 votos y perdió su depósito** = he polled only 25 votes and lost his deposit **(b)** *(fianza)* bailment **(c)** *(mercancías)* deposit; **en depósito** = bonded *o* in escrow; **documento en depósito** = document held in escrow; **mercancías** *o* **géneros en depósito** = bonded goods *o* goods (held) in bond; **retirar mercancías del depósito de aduanas** = to take goods out of bond **(d)** *(almacén)* warehouse *o* storeroom *o* depot; **depósito afianzado** *o* **depósito aduanero** *o* **de aduana** = bonded warehouse **(e)** **depósito de cadáveres** = mortuary; **depósito de objetos incautados** = pound; **depósito policial** = police station lock-up

depravar *vt* to deprave

depreciación *nf* depreciation *o* devaluation; **la depreciación del dólar** = the fall in the value of the dollar

depurar *vt* to purge

derecho *nm* **(a)** *(ciencia, ley)* law; **derecho administrativo** = administrative law; **derecho**

canónico = canon law; **derecho civil** = civil law; **derecho comparado** = comparative law; **derecho constitucional** *o* **político** = constitutional law; **derecho consuetudinario** = common law; **derecho de contratos** = contract law *o* the law of contract; **derecho de empresa** = company law; **derecho de familia** = family law; **derecho de sociedades** = company law; **derecho del trabajo** *o* **derecho laboral** = labour law *o* labour laws *o* labour legislation; **derecho foral** = (local *o* regional) civil law; **derecho hipotecario** = mortgage law; **derecho internacional** = international law; **Derecho Internacional Privado** = Conflict of Laws; **derecho marítimo** = maritime law *o* the law of the sea *o* Admiralty law; **derecho mercantil** = commercial law *o* mercantile law *o* law merchant; **derecho penal** = criminal law; **derecho privado** = private law; **derecho procesal** = law of preocedure; **derecho público** = public law; **abogado especializado en derecho político** = constitutional lawyer; **facultad de derecho** = law school **(b)** *(ley de propiedad intelectual)* **derecho** *o* **derechos de autor** = copyright *o* copyright law; **protegido por los derechos de autor** copyright; **Ley de los derechos de autor** = Copyright Act; **obra cuyos derechos de autor son del dominio público** = work which is out of copyright; **obra protegida por los derechos de autor** = work still in copyright; **propietario, -ra de los derechos de autor** = copyright owner; **registrado, -da con derechos de autor** = copyrighted; **es ilegal hacer copias de un libro protegido por los derechos de autor** = it is illegal to take copies of a copyright work **(c)** *(privilegio)* right *o* entitlement *o* title *o* claim; **derecho a acudir a la vía judicial** *o* **a interponer una demanda** = right of action; **derecho a asistencia letrada** = right to legal representation; **derecho a conservar un puesto de trabajo** *o* **una vivienda alquilada** = security of tenure; **derecho a la huelga** = right to strike; **derecho a la intimidad** = right to privacy; **derecho a la propiedad** = title to property; **derecho a percibir una pensión** = pension entitlement; **derecho a permanecer en silencio** = right against self-incrimination; **derecho a prestaciones sociales** = right of benefit; **derecho a ser oído por el tribunal** = right of audience; **derecho a un periodo de vacaciones** = holiday entitlement; **derecho constitucional** *o* **derechos constitucionales** = constitutional right *o* constitutional rights; **derecho de acción** = chose in action; **derecho de asilo** = right of sanctuary; **derecho de establecimiento** *o* **de fijación de residencia** = right of establishment; **derecho de explotación de la tierra (comunal)** = profit à prendre; **derecho de explotación de una mina** = mining concession; **derecho de hacer leña** *o* **derecho a cortar árboles en un predio arrendado** = estovers; **derecho de ocupación de un alquiler sin interferencias** = quiet enjoyment; **derecho de paso** = right of way *o* easement; **derecho de propiedad** = proprietorship; **derecho de redimir una hipoteca** *o* **de rescate** = equity of redemption; **derecho de renovación de un contrato** = right of renewal of a contract; **derecho de residencia** = right of abode; **derecho de retención** *o* **derecho prendario** = lien (gravamen); **derecho de retención de un barco** = maritime lien; **derecho de retención del trabajador** = repairer's lien; **derecho de retención del transportista** = carrier's lien; **derecho de venta** = put option; **derecho de venta de acciones no pagadas en su totalidad** = lien on shares; **derecho de visita** = access; **derecho de voto** *o* **a votar** = franchise; **derecho expectante** *o* **interino** = contingent remainder; **derecho preferente de compra** = pre-emption; **derecho universal de voto** = universal franchise; **derechos civiles** = civil rights; **derechos conyugales** = conjugal rights; **derechos de propiedad sobre bienes materiales** *o* **tangibles** = corporeal hereditaments; **derechos de propiedad sobre bienes intangibles como patentes** *o* **derechos de autor** = incorporeal hereditaments; **derechos de venta en un país extranjero** = foreign rights; **derechos humanos** = human rights; **derechos individuales** = civil liberties; **derechos preferentes** = prior charge **(d)** **abuso de derecho** = abuse of process; **con derecho a** = eligible; **dar derecho a** = to entitle; **de derecho** = de jure; **declaración de derechos del individuo** = Bill of Rights; **ejercer el derecho a** *o* **de opción** = to exercise an option; **emisión de derechos (a comprar acciones a un precio inferior)** *o* **emisión de acciones con derecho preferente por parte de los accionistas** = rights issue; **ficción de derecho** = legal fiction; **ley de prescripción** *o* **exención de derechos** = statute of limitations; **Tribunal Europeo de Derechos Humanos** = European Court of Human Rights; **es el dueño de derecho de la propiedad** = he is the de jure owner of the property; **tener derecho a** = to qualify for; **tener derecho total a algo** = to have a clear title to something; **tiene derecho a los bienes** = she has a right to the property; **tiene derecho a cuatro semanas de vacaciones** = he is entitled to four weeks' holiday; **tiene derecho a presentarse a reelección** = she is eligible for re-election; **tiene derecho al subsidio de desempleo** = she qualifies for unemployment pay; **tiene justo derecho a la propiedad** = he has a good title to the property; **ejerció su derecho a opción para adquirir derechos exclusivos de comercialización del producto** = he exercised his option to acquire sole marketing rights for the product; **el taller tenía derecho de retención sobre su coche hasta que pagara la factura de reparación** = the garage had a lien on her car until she paid the repair bill; **los empleados tienen derecho a saber lo que está haciendo la empresa** = the staff have a right to know what the company is doing; **no tiene derecho** a la asistencia jurídica gratuita = he does not qualify for Legal Aid; **no tiene derecho a la propiedad** = she has no title to the property; **no tiene derecho alguno sobre la propiedad** *o* **el coche** = he has no legal claim to the property *o* to the car; **no tiene derechos sobre la patente** = he has no right to the patent; **quiero poder ejercer el derecho a opción** = I want to leave my options open **(e)** *(tributos)* dues; **derecho ad valorem** = ad valorem duty; **derecho de autor** *o* **de inventor** *o* **de propietario de tierras** = royalty; **derecho de timbre** = stamp duty; **derecho de usufructo** = beneficial interest; **derechos de aduana** *o* **de importación** = customs duty *o* import duty; **artículos sujetos a derechos de aduana** = dutiable goods *o* dutiable items; **derechos de dársena** = dock dues *o* port dues *o* harbour dues; **derechos de inscripción** *o* **de matrícula** = registration fee; **derechos de sucesión** = death duty *o* death tax; **Departamento de Derechos Arancelarios e Impuestos Indirectos** = customs *o* Customs and Excise **(f)** *(justicia)* jus

◊ **derechohabiente** *nmf (beneficiario)* rightful claimant *o (persona a cargo)* dependant

> El derecho foral es el derecho civil propio de algunas comunidades autónomas, en contraposición al derecho civil común

derivar *vi* to derive; **derivar de** = to arise; **el problema deriva de la dificultad para comprender las disposiciones del IVA** = the problem arises from the difficulty in understanding the VAT regulations

derogación *nf* abolition; *(caducidad)* lapse; **derogación de una ley** = derogation

derogar *vt* to abolish

derogatorio, -ria 1 *adj* derogatory **2** *nf* annulment

derramamiento nm **derramamiento de sangre** = bloodshed

derrelicto *adj* **buque derrelicto** = derelict

derrota *nf* defeat; **el Ministro ofreció su dimisión después de la derrota de la moción en el Congreso** = the minister offered to resign after the defeat of the motion in the Congress

derrotar *vt (vencer)* to beat *o* to defeat; **el gobierno resultó derrotado en una votación sobre el orden público** = the government was defeated in a vote on law and order

desacato *nm* contempt; **desacato a la autoridad** *o* **a la justicia** *o* **a los tribunales** = contempt of court; **persona que comete desacato a los tribunales** = contemnor; **haber mostrado desacato a un tribunal** = to be in contempt; **purgar uno su desacato** = to purge one's contempt; **retractarse de una acción de desacato a los**

tribunales *o* expiar una acción de desacato a los tribunales = to purge one's contempt *o* to purge a contempt of court

desacreditar *vt* to discredit *o* to bring something into disrepute; *(dañar la reputación)* to harm someone's reputation; **la acusación intentó desacreditar a los testigos de la defensa** = the prosecution counsel tried to discredit the defence witnesses

desacuerdo *nm* disagreement; *(malentendido)* misunderstanding; *(disensión)* dissent; *(oposición)* opposition; **en desacuerdo con** = not compliant with; **hubo desacuerdo entre los diputados sobre el modo en que la policía debía enfrentarse a los ataques terroristas** = there was disagreement among the MPs about how the police should deal with terrorist attacks; **los votantes mostraron su desacuerdo con el gobierno votando contra la propuesta en el referéndum** = the voters showed their opposition to the government by voting against the proposal in the referendum

desafiar *vt* to challenge *o* to defy

desafío *nm (recusación)* challenge *o* defiance

desafortunado, -da *adj* unfortunate

desagravio *nm (compensación)* relief

desahuciar *vt* to dispossess *o* to evict *o* to eject; **todos los inquilinos fueron desahuciados por los nuevos propietarios** = all the tenants were evicted by the new landlords

desahucio *nm* dispossession *o* eviction *o* ejection; **acción** *o* **demanda** *o* **proceso de desahucio** = action of ejectment; **notificación** *o* **aviso de desahucio** = notice to quit; **entregar a un inquilino notificación de desahucio** = to serve a tenant with notice to quit

desalojar *vt* to evict; **desalojar la sala** = to clear the court; **desalojar los locales** = to vacate the premises

desamparado, -da *adj* destitute

desamparar *vt* to abandon

desamparo *nm* abandonment; **desamparo de los hijos** = abandonment of children

desaprobación *nf* disapproval

desaparecer *vi* to disappear

desaprobar *vt* to disapprove of something; **el Tribunal de Apelación desaprobó la decisión del Juzgado del Condado** = the Appeal Court disapproved the County Court decision

desarrollar *vt* to develop; **desarrollar un producto nuevo** = to develop a new product; **desarrollar una zona industrial** = to develop an industrial estate

desarrollo *nm* development; **área de desarrollo** = development area *o* development zone

desarticular *vt* to dismantle; **desarticular una banda de criminales** = to dismantle a criminal organisation

desatención *nf (negligencia)* neglect

desatender *vt (abandonar)* to neglect; **desatendió a sus tres hijos** = he neglected his three children

desavenencia *nf (malentendido)* disagreement *o* misunderstanding

desbloquear *vt* **desbloquear las negociaciones** = to break a deadlock

descansar *vi* to rest *o* to take a break; **el tribunal levantó la sesión para descansar durante diez minutos** = the court adjourned for a ten-minute break

descanso *nm* break *o* rest *o* recess

descarga *nf* **gastos de descarga** = landing charges; **permiso de descarga** = landing order

descargar *vt* to land; **coste descargado** = landed costs

descartar *vt (rechazar)* to dismiss *o* to rule out; **los jueces descartaron la declaración del testigo inmediatamente** = the justices dismissed the witness' evidence out of hand

descendencia *nf (hijos)* offspring *o* descent *o* issue; **descendencia en línea directa** = lineal descent; **murió sin descendencia** = she died without issue; **no tienen descendencia** = they have no issue

descender *vi* **(a)** *(bajar)* to drop; **la libra ha descendido tres puntos frente al dólar** = the pound dropped three points against the dollar; **el índice de criminalidad está descendiendo poco a poco** = the crime rate is gradually coming down **(b)** *(sucesión)* to descend; **desciende de la familia real** = he is descended from the royal family

descendiente 2 *nmf* descendant; **su mujer es una descendiente del rey Carlos I** = his wife is a descendant of King Charles I; **tuvo tres descendientes: dos hijos y una hija** = he had issue two sons and one daughter

descenso *nm (baja)* decline; **el descenso del valor de la peseta** = the decline in the value of the peseta

descifrar *vt* to decode

descodificador *nm* decoder

desconectado, -da = *adj* off *o* off-line

desconectar *vt* to disconnect

desconfianza *nf lack of confidence;* **voto de desconfianza** = vote of no confidence; **el presidente dimitió después de que se aprobara la moción de desconfianza en la Junta General Anual** = the chairman resigned after the motion of no confidence was passed at the AGM

desconfiar *vi* **desconfíe de las imitaciones** = beware of imitations

desconocer *vt* not to know

desconocido, -da *adj* **paradero desconocido** = no fixed abode

descontable *adj* bankable

descontado, -da *adj* **por descontado** = of course

descontar *vt* **(a)** *(reducir)* to deduct *o* to discount; **descontar del sueldo** = to dock (someone's pay); **le descontaron 2.000 ptas de su sueldo por llegar tarde** = he had 2,000 ptas docked from his pay for being late; **tendremos que descontarle algo del sueldo si vuelve a llegar tarde al trabajo** = we will have to dock his pay if he is late for work again; **descontamos un 5% por pronto pago** = we give 5% off for quick settlement; **descontar 5.000 ptas del precio** = to take 5,000 ptas off the price *o* to deduct 5,000 ptas from the price **(b)** *(tener en cuenta)* to allow for

descuento *nm* discount; **con descuento** = off

describir *vt* to describe; **describió a su atacante a la policía** = she described her attacker to the police; **describió al juez como un viejo ridículo** = he described the judge as a silly old man

descripción *nf* description; **descripción comercial** = trade description; **descripción detallada** = specification; **descripción engañosa del contenido** = false description of contents; **la policía puso en circulación una descripción del niño desaparecido** *o* **del hombre buscado** = the police circulated a description of the missing boy *o* of the wanted man

descuartizar *vt (desmembrar)* to dismember

descubrimiento *nm* discovery; *(detección)* detection; *(revelación)* exposure; **descubrimiento de las pruebas** = discovery

descubrir *vt* to discover; *(detectar)* to detect; *(desenmascarar)* to expose; **los auditores descubrieron algunos errores en las cuentas** = the auditors discovered some errors in the accounts; **la defensa del acusado se hizo más sólida al descubrirse que el demandante era un quebrado no rehabilitado** = the defendant's case was made stronger by the disclosure that the plaintiff was an undischarged bankrupt

descuento *nm* discount; **descuento para comerciantes del sector** = trade terms; **con**

descuento _o_ **(de) descuento del precio** = off; **hacer un descuento por gastos legales** _o_ **un descuento por diferencia de cambio** = to make an allowance for legal expenses _o_ an allowance for exchange loss; **compra las existencias a precio de descuento y las vende al público a precio de mercado** = he buys stock at a discount and sells at full price to the public; **hacemos un 30% de descuento en pedidos grandes** = we give a 30% discount for large orders; **ofrecemos un descuento del 10% sobre nuestros precios normales** = we give 10% off our normal prices; **estas alfombras se venden con un descuento de 5.000 ptas sobre el precio marcado** = these carpets are sold at 5,000 ptas off the marked price

descuidado, -da _adj (imprudente)_ careless; _(abandonado)_ neglected; _(negligente)_ negligent ◊ **descuidadamente** _adv_ carelessly _o_ negligently

descuidar _vt (abandonar)_ to neglect

descuido _nm (negligencia)_ neglect _o_ negligence; **con descuido** = negligently

desdén _nm (desprecio)_ contempt

desdeñable _adj (insignificante)_ negligible

desechable _adj (de usar y tirar)_ disposable; **envase desechable** = non-returnable packing

desecho nm _(producto defectuoso)_ reject

desembarcar _vt (descargar)_ to land

desembargo _nm (recuperación de bienes muebles bajo fianza)_ replevin

desembarque _nm_ landing; **tarjeta de desembarque** = landing card

desembocar _vi_ **desembocar en** = to lead (up) to; **las negociaciones desembocaron en una gran discusión entre la patronal y el sindicato** = the discussions led to a big argument between the management and the union

desembolsar _vt_ to disburse

desembolso _nm_ disbursement; _(gasto)_ expenditure; **desembolso final** = final discharge; **hacer un desembolso inicial** = to pay money down _o_ to put (money) down

desempeñar _vt_ **(a)** _(cumplir)_ to perform; **desempeñar un trabajo** = to serve; **desempeñar una función** = to carry out **(b)** _(redimir)_ **desempeñar algo** = to take something out of pawn; **garantía sin desempeñar** = unredeemed pledge

desempleado, -da _adj (parado)_ unemployed

desempleo _nm_ _(paro)_ unemployment; **desempleo estacional** = seasonal unemployment; **subsidio de desempleo** = unemployment benefit; **las cifras del desempleo están subiendo** = the unemployment figures _o_ the figures for unemployment are rising

desenmascarar _vt (descubrir)_ to expose; **fue desenmascarado como el jefe de la banda de falsificadores** = he was exposed as the boss of the gang of forgers

desenvolverse _vr (hacer progresos)_ to get on; **¿cómo se desenvuelve el nuevo secretario?** = how is the new secretary getting on?

deserción _nf_ desertion

desertar _vi_ to desert; _(huir)_ to defect; **desertó y se fue a vivir a Sudamérica** = he deserted and went to live in South America

desertor _nm_ deserter

desestimación _nf_ derogation; **desestimación por escritura** = estoppel by deed _o_ estoppel of _o_ by record; **desestimación por razón de conducta** = estoppel by conduct _o_ in pais; **desestimación de una demanda por entrar en contradicción con algo anterior** = estoppel

desestimar _vt_ to put aside _o_ to set aside; _(una causa)_ to dismiss; **el Tribunal Supremo desestimó la sentencia anterior** = the Supreme Court set aside the earlier judgment; **el tribunal desestimó el recurso** _o_ **petición** _o_ **demanda** = the court dismissed the appeal _o_ the application _o_ the action

desfalcador, -ra _n_ embezzler

desfalcar _vt_ to embezzle

desfalco _nm_ embezzlement _o_ defalcation; **le mandaron a la cárcel durante seis meses por desfalco** = he was sent to prison for six months for embezzlement

desfavorable _adj_ adverse; **testigo desfavorable** = adverse witness _o_ hostile witness; **el juez la calificó de testigo desfavorable** = she was ruled a hostile witness by the judge

desfiguración _nf_ misrepresentation

desgaste _nm_ waste; **desgaste natural** _o_ **normal** = fair wear and tear; **la póliza de seguros cubre la mayoría de los daños, pero no el desgaste natural de la máquina** = the insurance policy covers most damage but not fair wear and tear to the machine

desglosar _vt (clasificar)_ to break down; **¿puede desglosar esta factura en piezas de repuesto y mano de obra?** = can you break down this invoice into spare parts and labour?; **desglosamos las cifras en delitos contra las personas y delitos contra la propiedad** = we broke the figures down into crimes against the person and crimes against property

desglose _nm_ breakdown; **hágame un desglose de las últimas cifras netas** = give me a breakdown of the latest clear-up figures

desgracia *nf* misfortune *o* accident

desgravable *adj (deducible de impuestos)* tax-deductible; **gastos desgravables** = allowable expenses; **estos gastos no son desgravables** = these expenses are not tax-deductible

desgravación *nf (concesión)* concession; **desgravación fiscal** = tax rebate *o* allowance; **desgravación impositiva** = tax concession; **desgravaciones fiscales** = allowances against tax *o* tax allowances

desgravar *vt* to reduce tax; **que desgrava** = tax-deductible

deshacer *vr* to undo
◊ **deshacerse** *vr* **deshacerse de** = to dispose of *o* to throw out; *(entregar)* to part with something; **deshacerse de las existencias sobrantes** = to dispose of excess stock; **la Junta General Ordinaria se deshizo del antiguo Consejo de Administración** = the AGM threw out the old board of directors

desheredar *vt* to disinherit; **fue desheredado por su padre** = he was disinherited by his father

deshonesto, -ta *adj* **(a)** *(poco honrado)* dishonest; **negocio deshonesto** = racketeering; **negocio deshonesto (pero no ilegal)** = sharp practice **(b)** *(indecente)* indecent *o* improper; **abusos deshonestos** = indecent assault; **hacer proposiciones deshonestas** = importuning

deshonrar *vt* to dishonour

designación *nf (nombramiento)* nomination

designado, -da *adj* **1** *(nombrado)* designate; **el Presidente designado** = the chairman designate **2** *n* appointee

designar *vt (nombrar)* to appoint *o* to designate; *(proponer la candidatura de)* to nominate; **el gobierno ha designado un equipo especial para encabezar la investigación** = the government has appointed a special team to head the inquiry; **el tribunal designó un depositario judicial** = the court appointed a receiver

desigual *adj* unequal *o* irregular

desistimiento *nm (renuncia)* waiver; **desistimiento de la demanda** = abandonment of a claim

desistir *vt (renunciar)* to waive; **desistir de una demanda** = to abandon a claim

desleal *adj (infiel)* disloyal *o* unfaithful; *(traidor)* treasonable; **competencia desleal** = unfair competition

deslealtad *nf* disloyalty

desliz *nm* slip *o* indiscretion

desmandarse *vr* to get out of control

desmedido, -da *adj* undue; **influencia desmedida** = undue influence

desmembrar *vt* to dismember

desmentir *vt* to deny

desnaturalización *nf (con el fin de que alguien firme un contrato)* misrepresentation

desnaturalizar *vt (desvirtuar)* to pervert

desobedecer *vt* to disobey; **el marido desobedeció el apremio de pagar la manutención a sus hijos** = the husband disobeyed the court order to pay maintenance to his children

desobediencia *nf* disobedience

desocupado, -da *adj (disponible)* vacant; **propiedad** *o* **casa desocupada** = vacant possession

desocupar *vt* to vacate; **desocupar una vivienda** = to quit

desorbitado, -da *adj (exorbitante)* extortionate; **negocio dedicado al préstamo monetario a interés desorbitado** = extortionate credit bargain

desorden *nm* disorder *o* lawlessness
◊ **desordenado, -da** *adj* disorderly; **los magistrados criticaron el comportamiento desordenado de los hinchas del fútbol** = the magistrates criticized the lawless behaviour of the football crowd

desorientador, -ra *adj* misleading; **el texto del testamento es desorientador y debe ser aclarado** = the wording of the will is misleading and needs to be clarified

desorientar *vt (engañar)* to mislead; **el juez desorientó al jurado en su discurso final** = the judge misled the jury in his summing up

despachar *vt* to handle; **despachar en una tienda** = to serve in a shop; **despachar mercancías por la aduana** = to clear goods through the customs

despacho *nm* **(a)** *(oficina)* office; **despacho de billetes** = booking office; **entre en mi despacho** = come into my office; **el despacho del socio principal está en el tercer piso** = the senior partner's office is on the third floor; **tiene un despacho agradable que da al parque** = she has a pleasant office which looks out over the park **(b)** *(bufete)* **despacho de abogados** *o* **de un juez** = chambers **(c)** *(clientela)* practice **(d)** *(envío)* clearance *o* dispatch; **despacho de aduanas** = customs clearance; **despacho de mercancías por la aduana** = clearing of goods through the customs; **certificado de despacho de aduanas** = clearance certificate

despedido, -da *adj* dismissed *o* discharged; **empleados despedidos** = redundant staff; **ser despedido** = to get the sack

despedir *vt* **(a)** *(echar de un trabajo)* to dismiss *o* to pay off; **despedir a alguien** = to sack someone *o* to fire someone *o* to make someone redundant; **despedir a un empleado** = to dismiss an employee *o* to discharge an employee; **cuando la empresa fue absorbida, cerraron la fábrica y despidieron a todos los trabajadores** = when the company was taken over the factory was closed and all the workers were paid off; **el nuevo director gerente despidió a la mitad del personal de ventas** = the new managing director fired half the sales force; **le despidieron por llegar tarde** = he was dismissed for being late; **le despidieron por llegar tarde al trabajo** = he was sacked after being late for work **(b)** *(jurado)* to discharge; **el juez despidió al jurado** = the judge discharged the jury

despejar *vt* to clear *o* to clear up; **despejar la sala** = to clear the court

desperdiciar *vt (malgastar)* to waste

desperfecto *nm* breakage; **los clientes deberán hacerse cargo de cualquier desperfecto** = customers are expected to pay for breakages

despido *nm* dismissal *o* sacking *o* redundancy; *(destitución)* removal; **despido analógico** = constructive dismissal; **despido arbitrario** *o* **improcedente** = wrongful dismissal; **despido injusto** = unfair dismissal; **despido por vencimiento** *o* **por incumplimiento de contrato** = discharge; **indemnización** *o* **compensación por despido** = redundancy payment *o* severance pay *o* compensation for loss of office; **procedimiento de despido** = dismissal procedure; **el sindicato manifestó su protesta por los despidos** = the union protested against the sackings; **la adquisición resultó en 250 despidos** = the takeover caused 250 redundancies; **el despido del director gerente va a ser muy difícil** = the removal of the managing director is going to be very difficult

desplazamiento *nm* travelling; **estudio de desplazamientos y tiempos** = time and motion study; **gastos de desplazamiento** = travelling expenses

despojar *vt (desposeer)* to dispossess; **despojar de** = to oust

despojo *nm (desposeimiento)* spoils *o* ouster

desposeer *vt (desahuciar)* to dispossess

desposeimiento *nm* ouster; **desposeimiento ilegal** = disseisin; **el juez dictó una orden de desposeimiento** = the judge made an ouster order; **tuvo que solicitar una orden de desposeimiento** = he had to apply for an ouster order

déspota *nmf* tyrant

despreciable *adj (insignificante)* negligible; **nada despreciable** = not negligible

desprecio *nm (desdén)* contempt

desprestigiar *vt (desacreditar)* to bring something into disrepute; **le acusaron de desprestigiar el club con su mal comportamiento** = he was accused of bringing the club into disrepute by his bad behaviour

después *prep (más tarde)* after *o* thereafter; *(post)* post-; **después de la muerte** = post-obit

desquitarse *vr* to retaliate

desquite *nm (represalias)* retaliation

destacado, -da *adj* outstanding

destacar *vt* to detail *o* to highlight; **seis inspectores fueron destacados para registrar las instalaciones** = six officers were detailed to search the premises

destajo *nm* **pago** *o* **cobro a destajo** = payment by results

desterrar *vt* to banish; *(expatriar)* to expatriate; **le desterraron durante 10 años** = he was banished for ten years

destierro *nm* banishment

destinar *vt (designar)* to destine *o* to earmark; **la subvención** *o* **la beca está destinada al desarrollo de sistemas informáticos** = the grant is earmarked for computer systems development

destinatario, -ria *n (receptor)* recipient *o* receiver; *(consignatario)* consignee

destitución *nf (despido)* removal

destituir *vt* to remove; **dos directores del consejo de administración fueron destituidos en la Junta General Ordinaria** = two directors were removed from the board at the AGM

destronar *vt* to depose

destrozar *vt (destruir)* to destroy *o* to vandalize; **no funciona ninguna de las cabinas telefónicas porque las han destrozado todas** = none of the call boxes work because they have all been vandalized

destrucción *nf* destruction; **la destrucción de las pruebas al incendiarse en la comisaría hicieron difícil la acusación** = the destruction of the evidence in the fire at the police station made it difficult to prosecute

destruir *vt (destrozar)* to vandalize

desuso *nm* **reglamento en desuso** = dead letter; **esta ley ha caído en desuso** = this law has become a dead letter

desventaja *nf (inconveniente)* disadvantage; **estar en desventaja** *o* **en situación desventajosa** = to be at a disadvantage; **el hecho de no haber**

estudiado derecho le sitúa en desventaja = not having studied law puts him at a disadvantage

desventajoso, -sa *adj* disadvantageous; **estar en situación desventajosa** = to be at a disadvantage

desviación *nf* departure (from); **cualquier desviación de los términos y condiciones del contrato debe notificarse por escrito** = any departure from the terms and conditions of the contract must be advised in writing; **esto constituye una desviación de la práctica establecida** = this forms a departure from established practice

desviarse *vr* to deviate from a course of action

desvirtuar *vt (desnaturalizar)* to pervert

detall *nm* **venta al detall** = retail

detallado, -da *adj* detailed; **cuenta** *o* **factura detallada** = detailed account *o* itemized account; **descripción detallada** = specification; **hoja que da información detallada sobre los artículos en venta** = sheet which gives particulars of the items for sale; **le ruego me envíe una cuenta detallada** = please send me a detailed *o* an itemized account ◊ **detalladamente** *adv; (con todo detalle)* in detail; **anotar algo detalladamente** = to keep the record straight; **enumerar detalladamente** = to detail; **el contrato enumera todos los mercados detalladamente** = the contract lists all the markets in detail

detallar *vt* to detail *o* to itemize; **detallar las cifras de ventas nos llevará unos dos días** = itemizing the sales figures will take about two days; **el documento detalla los acuerdos sobre los pagos de manutención** = the document details the arrangements for maintenance payments; **los términos de la licencia se detallan en el contrato** = the terms of the licence are detailed in the contract

detalle *nm* detail *o* particular; **con todo detalle** = in detail; **detalles anteriores** = background; **el inspector pidió detalles sobre el coche desaparecido** = the inspector asked for particulars of the missing car; **conozco la actual situación contractual, pero ¿podría usted rellenar los detalles anteriores?** = I know the contractual situation as it stands now, but can you fill in the background details?; **el tribunal pidió los detalles anteriores al caso** = the court asked for details of the background to the case

detección *nf (descubrimiento)* detection

detectar *vt (descubrir)* to detect; **la máquina puede detectar explosivos** = the machine can detect explosives

detective *nmf* detective; **detective privado** = private detective; **agencia de detectives** = detective agency

detector *nm* **detector de mentiras** = lie detector

detención *nf* **(a)** *(arresto)* detention *o* arrest *o* apprehension; *(en prisión)* custody; **detención ilegal** = false imprisonment; **detención sin una orden** = summary arrest; **acto de detención** = detainer; **orden de detención** = detention order; **se ha ordenado su detención** = a warrant is out for his arrest; **se le envió a un centro de detención para delincuentes juveniles** = he was sent to the detention centre for corrective training **(b)** *(usurpación)* deforcement **(c)** *(freno)* check

detener *vt* **(a)** *(arrestar)* to detain *o* to apprehend *o* to arrest; *(retener)* to hold; **detuvieron a dos de los huelguistas** = two of the strikers were arrested; **el policía paró el coche y detuvo al conductor** = the constable stopped the car and arrested the driver; **detuvieron a veinte personas en la redada policial** = twenty people were held in the police raid; **los sospechosos fueron detenidos** *o* **detuvieron a los sospechosos** = the suspects were placed in detention; **los sospechosos fueron detenidos por la policía para ser interrogados** *o* **la policía detuvo a los sospechosos para interrogarles** = the suspects were detained by the police for questioning; **se detuvo al sospechoso en la escena del crimen** = the suspect was apprehended at the scene of the crime; **fue detenido por la policía en el aeropuerto** = he was picked up by the police at the airport **(b)** *(parar)* to check; **detener la entrada de contrabando en el país** = to check the entry of contraband into the country; **detener la venta de armas de fuego** = to put a check on the sale of firearms **(c)** *(retirar los cargos)* **detener un proceso** = to drop (charges); **el demandante decidió detener el proceso contra su vecino** = the plaintiff decided to drop the case against his neighbour

detenido, -da **1** *adj* under arrest; **seis miembros de la banda están detenidos en la comisaría** = six of the gang are in the police station under arrest **2** *nmf* detainee

detentar *vt (usurpar la posesión de bienes a un tercero)* to deforce

deteriorar *vt (estropear)* to spoil; **la mitad del cargamento quedó deteriorada a causa del agua** = half the shipment was spoiled by water

determinación *nf* **determinación de los daños** = assessment of damages; **determinación de los hechos** = fact-finding

determinado, -da *adj* certain; **una cantidad determinada** = a certain quantity; **daños no determinados** = unliquidated damages

determinante *adj* **causa determinante** = moot case; *(casos que sientan jurisprudencia)* **casos determinantes** = leading cases

determinar *vt (fijar)* to determine; **las condiciones del contrato están todavía por**

determinar = the conditions of the contract are still to be determined

detrimento *nm (perjuicio)* detriment; **actuar en detrimento de una demanda** = to act to the prejudice of a claim; **sin causar detrimento a su reclamación** = without detriment to his claim

deuda *nf* debt *o* obligation *o* liability; **deuda incobrable** *o* **morosa** = bad debt; **deuda pública** = public debt; **deuda territorial** = charge on land *o* charge over property; **deuda territorial en la que el deudor hipotecario firma una escritura que da al acreedor hipotecario un interés en la propiedad** = charge by way of legal mortgage; **agente comprador de deudas** = debt factor; **gestión de deudas con descuento** = factoring; **liquidación de una deuda** = accord and satisfaction; **situación de deuda** = state of indebtedness; **contraer deudas** = to get into debt; **estar en deuda** = to be in debt; **estar libre de deudas** = to be out of debt; **pagar intereses sobre una deuda** = to service a debt; **pagar todas las deudas propias** = to discharge one's liabilities in full; **en pago total de una deuda** *o* **totalmente libre de deudas** = in full discharge of a debt; **reembolsar** *o* **devolver una deuda** = to pay back a debt; **saldar las deudas** = to meet one's obligations; **la compañía dejó de operar con deudas superiores a diez millones** = the company stopped trading with debts of over 10 million; **no pudo pagar sus deudas** *o* **no pudo hacer frente a sus deudas** = he was not able to meet his liabilities; **salió del país sin pagar sus deudas** = he left the country without paying his bills

deudor, -ra 1 *adj* indebted; **saldo deudor** = debit balance; **nación deudora** = debtor nation **2** *nmf* debtor; **deudor por sentencia judicial firme** *o* **deudor por sentencia firme** *o* **deudor judicial** = judgment debtor; **deudor privilegiado** = chargee

devengar *vt (rendir)* to yield; **devengar intereses** *o* **dividendos** = to earn interest *o* dividends; **¿qué clase de dividendos devengan estas acciones?** = what level of dividend do these shares earn?; **cuenta que devenga intereses al 10%** = account which earns interest at 10%; **las obligaciones devengan un interés del 8%** = the bonds yield 8%

devolución *nf* **(a)** *(reembolso)* repayment *o* refund *o* payback; *(pérdida de una desgravación impositiva que había sido concedida)* clawback; **pedir la devolución de un préstamo** = to call in **(b)** *(reversión)* reversion **(c)** *(reexpedición)* return; **sin devolución** = non-returnable; **el contrato se anula y pierde su valor al producirse la devolución de estos documentos** = the contract becomes null and void when these documents are surrendered

devolver *vt* **(a)** *(reembolsar)* to repay *o* to pay back *o* to refund; **devolver una deuda** = to pay back a debt; **devolver un préstamo** = to pay back a loan; **a devolver** = repayable; **devolverá el dinero en plazos mensuales** = he will pay back the money in monthly instalments; **le presté 10.000 ptas y prometió devolvérmelas en un mes** = I lent him 10,000 ptas and he promised to pay me back in a month; **nunca me ha devuelto el dinero que le presté** = he has never paid me back the money he borrowed; **si los artículos no son de su total satisfacción, le devolveremos el dinero** = all money will be refunded if the goods are not satisfactory; **tenemos que devolver el préstamo pagando la cantidad de 50.000 ptas al mes** = the loan is to be repaid at the rate of 50,000 ptas a month **(b)** *(reenviar)* to return; **devolver existencias defectuosas al mayorista** = to return damaged stock to the wholesaler; **devolver una carta al remitente** = to return a letter to sender; **el banco devolvió el cheque al librador** = the bank referred the cheque to drawer; **la tienda devolvió el cheque al estar la fecha equivocada** = the store sent back the cheque because the date was wrong; **todos estos artículos pueden ser devueltos en caso de no venderse** = these goods are all on sale or return **(c)** *(restituir)* 'devolver todo al estado anterior' = restitutio in integrum; **los oficiales de aduanas nos devolvieron los artículos tras el pago de una multa** = the customs released the goods against payment of a fine

día *nm* day; **día de pago** = pay-day; **día festivo** = bank holiday; **día hábil** *o* **laborable** = working day; **día inhábil** *o* **no laboral** = legal holiday; **días naturales** = calendar days; **al día** = up to date; **poner algo al día** = to bring something up to date; **tener** *o* **mantener algo al día** = to keep something up to date; **orden del día** = agenda; **(indefinidamente); 'sin día'** = sine die; **tres días laborables** *o* **hábiles** = three clear days; **el primer día del mes es festivo** = the first day of the month is a public holiday; **junio tiene treinta días** = there are thirty days in June; **el juicio duró diez días** = the trial lasted ten days; **avisar con diez días laborables de antelación** = to give ten clear days' notice; **cuente con cuatro días laborables para que el cheque sea abonado en cuenta** = allow four clear days for the cheque to be paid into the account

diagrama *nf (organigrama)* flow chart

diario, -ria 1 *adj (cotidiano)* day-to-day; **el secretario organiza el funcionamiento diario de los tribunales** = the clerk organizes the day-to-day running of the courts **2** *nm* **(a)** *(agenda)* diary *o* daybook; **diario de sesiones** = Hansard; **diario oficial** = official register **(b)** *(periódico)* paper ◊ **diariamente** *adv* daily; *(por día* *o* *al día)* per diem

dictáfono *nm* dictating machine

dictamen *nm* **(a)** *(opinión)* opinion; **dictamen consultivo** = advisory opinion; **dictamen jurídico** = legal opinion; **dictamen pericial** = expert opinion; **dictamen de un abogado sobre un caso** = counsel's opinion; **el abogado preparó un dictamen escrito** = counsel prepared a written opinion **(b)** *(mandato)* dictate *o* dictum; **dictámenes accesorios** *o* **accidentales** = obiter dicta

dictaminar *vt* **(a)** *(opinar)* to give an opinion **(b)** *(sentenciar)* to rule *o* to pass (sentence); **el forense dictaminó muerte accidental** = the coroner recorded a verdict of death by misadventure

dictar *vt* **(a)** *(pronunciar)* to dictate; **dictar sentencia** = to pass sentence on someone; **dictar una sentencia** = to deliver a verdict; **el jurado pronunció un veredicto de culpabilidad y el juez dictará sentencia la semana próxima** = the jury returned a verdict of guilty, and the judge will pass sentence next week **(b)** *(establecer)* to lay down; **las directrices establecen normas para hacer frente a los delitos de tráfico** = the guidelines lay down rules for dealing with traffic offences

dietas *nfpl* allowance; **dietas para gastos de viajes** = travel allowance *o* travelling allowance

difamación *nf* libel; **difamación criminal** = criminal libel; **difamación de la reputación** = defamation of character; **difamación escrita** = libel; **difamación oral** = slander; **demanda por difamación** = action for slander *o* slander action; **pleito por difamación** = action for libel *o* libel action

difamador, -ra *n (libelista)* libeller

difamante *adj* defamatory *o* libellous; **declaración difamante** = defamatory statement

difamar *vt* to defame *o* to slander someone; **difamar por escrito a alguien** = to libel

difamatorio, -ria *adj* libellous *o* slanderous; **declaración difamatoria** = defamatory statement; **dijo que la noticia era difamatoria** = he said that the report was libellous; **hizo declaraciones difamatorias sobre el Ministro por televisión** = he made slanderous statements about the Minister on television

diferencia *nf* difference; *(discrepancia)* discrepancy; **con gran diferencia** = easily; **no veo diferencia entre las dos declaraciones** = I see no distinction between the two claims; **la firma es, con gran diferencia, la mayor del mercado** = the firm is easily the biggest in the market

diferente *adj* different; **a no ser que se den instrucciones diferentes** = failing instructions to the contrary

diferido, -da *adj (aplazado)* deferred; **acreedor diferido** = deferred creditor

diferir 1 *vi (ser distinto)* to differ **2** *vt (aplazar)* to defer

difícil *adj* hard; **negocio difícil** = hard bargain; **un caso difícil** = a hard case; **ponerle las cosas difíciles a alguien** = to make things hot for someone; **los oficiales de aduanas están poniendo las cosas difíciles a los traficantes de droga** = customs officials are making things hot for the drug smugglers

dificultad *nf (problema)* trouble

difunto, -ta *n* deceased; **el difunto dejó todas sus propiedades a su viuda** = the deceased left all his property to his widow

difusión *nf (propagación)* dissemination; *(circulación)* circulation; **la empresa trata de mejorar la difusión de información entre departamentos** = the company is trying to improve the circulation of information between departments

digesto *nm (resumen)* digest

dignidad *nf* dignity

dilatorio, -ria *adj* dilatory; **moción dilatoria** = dilatory motion

diligencia *nf* **(a)** *(trámite)* diligence; **diligencias de instrucción** = preparatory enquiries; **diligencias previas** *o* **preliminares** = preliminary hearing **(b)** *(precaución)* care

dimensión *nf* measurement

dimisión *nf (renuncia)* resignation; **dimisión forzada o forzosa** *o* **dimisión bajo presión de la dirección** = constructive dismissal; **presentar la dimisión** = to hand in *o* to give in *o* to send in one's resignation; **presentó su dimisión** = she has handed in *o* given her notice; **escribió su carta de dimisión al presidente** = he wrote his letter of resignation to the chairman; **ha presentado su dimisión con efectos desde el 1 de julio** = he has resigned with effect from July 1st

dimitir *vi (dejar un empleo)* to resign *o* to quit; **dimitió como directora financiera** = she resigned as finance director; **dimitió de su cargo de tesorero** = he resigned from his post as treasurer; **dimitió por razones de salud** = he resigned for medical reasons

dinero *nm* money *o* currency; **dinero caliente** *o* **especulativo** *o* **ilegal** *o* **dinero que pasa de un país a otro** *o* **procedente de la corrupción** = hot money; **dinero efectivo** *o* **dinero líquido** = ready money; **dinero en metálico** *o* **efectivo** = hard cash *o* ready money; **dinero falso** = counterfeit money; **dinero pagadero a petición** = money at call *o* money on call *o* call money; **tipos de interés del dinero** = money rates; **robaron dinero de la oficina de personal** = a sum of money was stolen from the personnel office

diplomado, -da *adj* qualified

diplomático, -ca 1 *adj* diplomatic; **conceder categoría diplomática a alguien** = to grant someone diplomatic status; **inmunidad diplomática** = diplomatic immunity; **invocó la inmunidad diplomática para evitar ser detenido** = he claimed diplomatic immunity to avoid being arrested 2 *n* diplomat *o* diplomatist

diputación *nf* (a) *(delegación)* delegation (b) **diputación provincial** = county council

diputado, -da 1 *n* (a) *(representante)* delegate (b) *(miembro del Parlamento)* Member of Parliament (MP); **diputado, -da del Parlamento Europeo** = Member of the European Parliament (MEP) 2 *nf (congresista)* Congresswoman 3 *nm (congresista)* Congressman

dirección *nf* (a) *(gestión)* administration *o* management; **dirección conjunta** = joint management; **dirección del tráfico** = point duty; **dirección por objetivos** = management by objectives; **alta dirección** = top management; **curso de dirección** = management course; **decisiones tomadas por la dirección** = decisions taken at managerial level; **mala dirección** = mismanagement; **estudiar dirección de empresas** = to study management; **se hizo cargo de la dirección de un importante banco** = he took over the direction of a large bank (b) *(cargo de director)* directorship (c) *(domicilio)* address; **dirección oficial de un litigante** *o* **interesado en un proceso** = address for service; **poner la dirección** = to address; **un paquete con la dirección incorrecta** = an incorrectly addressed package (d) *(rumbo)* direction

directivo, -va 1 *adj (gerencial)* managerial; **equipo directivo** = management team; **junta directiva** = board of directors; **líneas directivas** = guidelines; **ser nombrado para un puesto directivo** = to be appointed to a managerial position 2 *nf* (a) *(orden)* directive (b) *(dirección)* directorate

directo, -ta *adj* direct; **de un modo directo** = directly; **envío** *o* **embarque directo** = drop shipment; **explotador directo (de una propiedad)** = owner-occupier; **impuestos directos** *o* **imposición directa** = direct taxation; **interrogatorio directo** = direct examination; **prueba directa** = direct evidence; **venta directa** = direct selling

◊ **directamente** *adv (de un modo directo)* directly *o* direct; **enviar un pedido directamente al cliente** = to drop ship; **el Director de la Guardia Civil es directamente responsable ante el Ministerio del Interior** = the Head of the Civil Guard is directly responsible to the Home Secretary; **la multa se paga directamente al tribunal** = the fine is paid direct to the court; **pagamos el impuesto sobre la renta directamente**

al gobierno = we pay income tax direct to the government

director, -ra 1 *n* (a) *(de una empresa)* director *o* manager; **Director de la Acusación Pública** = Director of Public Prosecutions (DPP); **director de banco** *o* **de sucursal bancaria** = bank manager; **director de personal** = personnel officer; **director de sucursal** = branch manager; **director de una empresa** = company director; **director general** = general manager; **Director General del servicio oficial de protección al consumidor** = Director-General of Fair Trading; **director ejecutivo** = executive director; **director financiero** = controller; **director gerente** = managing director; **director no ejecutivo** *o* **de asesoramiento** = non-executive director; **director no empleado por la compañía** = outside director; **director regional** = area manager; **directores adjuntos** *o* **directores de departamentos** = junior management; **los directores de una empresa** = the company officers *o* the officers of a company; **cargo de director** = directorship; **presidente y director gerente** = chairman and managing director; **es director de un instituto de gestión estatal** *o* **oficial** = he is the director of a government institute; **le ofrecieron un cargo de director** = he was offered a directorship (b) *(de una institución)* = warden; **director de una prisión** = a prison governor; **los presos solicitaron la libertad condicional al director de la prisión** = the prisoners applied to the governor for parole (c) *(autor de un crimen)* principal 2 *nf (gerente)* manageress; **la nombraron directora de la sociedad benéfica** *o* **de los asuntos de beneficiencia** = she was appointed director of the charity

directorio *nm* directory; *(guía alfabética)* **directorio comercial** = commercial directory *o* trade directory; **directorio comercial (clasificado) por secciones** = classified directory

directriz *nf* guideline; *(directiva)* directive; **el gobierno ha dado directrices sobre aumentos de salarios y precios** = the government has issued guidelines on increases in wages and prices; **el Juez dijo que no estaba exponiendo directrices para formular sentencias** = the Lord Justice said he was not laying down guidelines for sentencing; **el Secretario de Estado puede dar directrices sobre gastos** = the Secretary of State can issue guidelines for expenditure; **el Colegio de Abogados ha dado directrices a sus miembros sobre cómo resolver los casos de violación** = the Law Society has issued guidelines to its members on dealing with rape cases directrices; **el juez dijo que no establecía directrices para formular sentencia** = the judge said he was not laying down guidelines for sentencing

dirigente 1 *adj* leading 2 *nmf* officer; *(jefe)* leader; **dirigente empresarial** = corporate leader;

un dirigente de la patronal = an employers' leader; el dirigente del sindicato de trabajadores de la construcción = the leader of the construction workers' union *o* the construction workers' leader; la elección de los dirigentes de una asociación = the election of officers of an association

dirigido, -da *adj (controlado)* controlled; dirigido por el gobierno = government-controlled; economía dirigida = controlled economy

dirigir *vt* **(a)** *(controlar, encabezar)* to manage *o* to direct *o* to run *o* to lead *o* to head; *(encauzar)* to channel; dirigir un negocio = to control a business; dirigir un departamento = to manage a department *o* to head a department; dirigir mal = to mismanage; el negocio está dirigido por una empresa con base en Luxemburgo = the business is controlled by a company based in Luxembourg; la empresa está dirigida *o* bajo el mando del accionista mayoritario = the company is controlled by the majority shareholder; la acusación está dirigida por el fiscal Herrero = the prosecution is led by J.M. Herrero, QC **(b)** *(mantener)* to conduct; el presidente dirigió los debates muy eficientemente = the chairman conducted the proceedings very efficiently
◊ **dirigirse** *vr;* dirigirse a = to address; *(para hacer una propuesta o una petición)* to approach; dirigirse al banquillo = to take the stand; el acusado pidió permiso para dirigirse al tribunal = the defendant asked permission to address the court; se dirigió al banco para pedir un préstamo = he approached the bank with a request for a loan; el editor americano se dirigió a la empresa para proponer una fusión = the company was approached by an American publisher with the suggestion of a merger

disciplina *nf* discipline; oficial encargado de la disciplina = proctor

disciplinar *vt* to discipline

disciplinario, -ria *adj* disciplinary; procedimiento disciplinario = disciplinary procedure; emprender una acción disciplinaria contra alguien = to take disciplinary action against someone

disco *nm* disk; disco duro = hard disk; disco flexible = floppy disk; unidad de disco = disk drive

disconforme *adj* dissenting

disconformidad *nf (desaprobación)* non-conformance; *(desacuerdo)* disagreement

discordancia *nf* discord

discordia *nf* discord; discordias entre grupos = civil strife

discreción *nf* discretion; la afiliación es a discreción del comité = membership is at the discretion of the committee; lo dejo a su discreción = I leave it to your discretion
◊ **discrecional** *adj* discretionary; fideicomiso discrecional = discretionary trust; el tribunal tiene amplio poder discrecional = the tribunal has wide discretionary power; los poderes discrecionales del ministro = the minister's discretionary powers; el juez rechazó la petición sobre la base de que tenía facultad discrecional para examinar pruebas improcedentes = the judge refused the application, on the ground that he had a judicial discretion to examine inadmissible evidence

discrepancia *nf* discrepancy; hay discrepancia entre el número de delitos publicado por el Ministerio del Interior y el de los sindicatos policiales = there is a discrepancy between the crime figures released by the Home Office and those of the police unions

discrepar *vi (no estar de acuerdo)* to disagree *o* to differ *o* to have a division of opinion

discriminación *nf* discrimination; discriminación sexual = sexual discrimination *o* sex discrimination *o* discrimination on grounds of sex

disculpa *nf* apology *o* excuse; escribir una carta de disculpa = to write a letter of apology; se ordenó al autor del libelo que publicara una disculpa detallada = the writer of the libel was ordered to print a full apology

disculpar *vt* to excuse
◊ **disculparse** *vr* to apologize; disculparse por el retraso en responder = to apologize for the delay in answering

discurso *nm* speech; *(en respuesta a las quejas realizadas por la defensa)* reply; discurso inaugural = opening speech; discurso final de un juez al término de un juicio = instructions to the jury; pronunciar un discurso en el parlamento = to make a speech in Parliament

discusión *nf* discussion *o* argument; *(deliberaciones)* discusiones = deliberations; discusión académica = moot case; entraron en una discusión con el juez acerca de la importancia de los documentos para el caso = they got into an argument with the judge over the relevance of the documents to the case; después de cierta discusión los magistrados acordaron un aplazamiento = after some discussion the magistrates agreed to an adjournment

discutible *adj* debatable

discutir *vt/i (hablar de)* to discuss *o* to argue; *(poner en duda)* to dispute; precio a discutir = or near offer (o.n.o.); el abogado discutió durante horas el significado preciso de la cláusula = counsel spent hours arguing about the precise meaning of the clause; los abogados discutieron la posibilidad de una absolución = the lawyers discussed the possibility of an acquittal; **se pasaron dos horas discutiendo los detalles del contrato** = they spent two hours discussing the details of the contract; **discutieron sobre el precio** = they argued over *o* about the price; **los cargos sindicales discutieron la mejor forma de hacer frente al ultimátum de la dirección** = the union officials argued among themselves over the best way to deal with the ultimatum from the management

disensión *nf (desacuerdo)* dissent

disentimiento nm *(disensión)* dissent

disentir *vi* to dissent; *(no estar de acuerdo)* to differ; **siento disentir** = I beg to differ; **uno de los magistrados disintió** = one of the judges dissented

disfraz *nm* disguise

disfrazar *vt* to disguise; **el espía cruzó la frontera disfrazado** = the spy crossed the border in disguise; **entró en el país disfrazado de policía** = he entered the country disguised as a policeman
◊ **disfrazarse** *vr (disimular)* to disguise; **disfrazarse de alguien** = to disguise yourself as someone

disfrutar *vt/i* to enjoy *o* to make use of; **disfruta de un coche de la empresa** = he has the use of a company car

disfrute *nm (usufructo)* use; *(derecho de ocupación de un alquiler sin interferencias)* **disfrute en privado** = quiet enjoyment; **disfrute privado de la tierra** = quiet enjoyment of land

disidencia *nf* dissent; **la oposición mostró su disidencia votando en contra del proyecto de ley** = the opposition showed its dissent by voting against the Bill

disidente *adj* dissenting *o* dissident; **juicio** *o* **sentencia disidente** = dissenting judgment

disimular *vi* to disguise

diskette *nm* diskette *o* floppy disk

disminución *nf* **(a)** *(baja)* decline *o* drop; **disminución de ventas** = drop in sales; **una disminución del poder adquisitivo** = a decline in buying power **(b)** *(reducción)* decrease; *(de legado)* abetament

disminuido, -da 1 *adj (persona)* = handicapped *o* disabled 2 *n;* **disminuido físico** *o* **disminuida física** = disabled person

disminuir 1 *vi* to decline *o* to drop; **las ventas han disminuido un 10%** = sales have dropped by 10% *o* have dropped 10% 2 *vt (reducir)* to decrease *o* to lessen *o* to diminish; **el gobierno está tomando medidas para disminuir la superpoblación** *o* **el congestionamiento en las cárceles** = the government is taking steps to lessen the

overcrowding in prisons; **el gobierno propone disminuir la cotización del IVA** = the government proposes to decrease the rate of VAT

disolución *nf* liquidation *o* winding up; **disolución de las Cortes** *o* **del Parlamento** = dissolution of Parliament; **disolución de un matrimonio** *o* **una sociedad** = dissolution; **disolución forzosa** = compulsory liquidation; **disolución voluntaria** = voluntary liquidation

disolver *vt* to dissolve; *(acabarse)* to break up; **disolver las Cortes** *o* **el Parlamento** = to dissolve Parliament; **disolver un matrimonio** *o* **una sociedad** *o* **una compañía** = to dissolve a marriage *o* a partnership *o* a company; **disolver una compañía** = to liquidate a company; **la compañía fue disuelta** = the company went into liquidation; **la policía disolvió el mitin de protesta** = the police broke up the protest meeting

disparar *vt* to fire *o* to shoot; **disparó dos tiros a la multitud** = he fired two shots at the crowd

disparo *nm (tiro)* shot *o* gunshot

dispensa *nf (exención)* dispensation; *(exoneración)* exoneration

dispensado, -da *adj (exento)* exempt

dispensar *vt (eximir)* to exempt; *(exonerar)* **dispensar de** = to excuse *o* to exonerate; *(renunciar)* to waive; *(perdonar)* to let off; **el juez dispensó** *o* **despidió al jurado** = the judge discharged the jury; **le dispensaron de actuar como jurado a causa de su sordera** = he was excused jury service because he was deaf

disponer 1 *vi* **disponer de** = to have (available) *o* to have at one's disposal; **poder disponer de algo** = to have access to something; **siempre disponemos de este producto** = we always keep this item in stock 2 *vt* to arrange; **la oficina está dispuesta en un espacio abierto con pequeñas salas aparte para las reuniones** = the office is arranged as an open-plan area with small separate rooms for meetings

disponible *adj* **(a)** *(realizable)* available; **activo disponible** = liquid assets; **renta disponible** = disposable income; **dinero disponible** = balance in hand *o* cash in hand **(b)** *(desocupado)* vacant

disposición *nf* **(a)** *(arreglo)* arrangement *o* disposition; *(transacción previa a la quiebra)* scheme of arrangement; **disposición sucesoria** = settlement of an estate; **disposiciones testamentarias** = devise; **hacer disposiciones testamentarias** = to make testamentary dispositions **(b)** *(reglamentación)* provision *o* regulation; **disposiciones legislativas** = statutory instruments; **las disposiciones de un proyecto de ley** = the provisions of a Bill; **hemos hecho las disposiciones reglamentarias para este fin** = we have made provision to this effect; **las nuevas disposiciones gubernamentales sobre normas de producción de artículos eléctricos** = the new government regulations on standards for electrical goods **(c) poner a disposición de** = to place in custody

dispositivo *nm* device *o* gadget; **dispositivo de seguridad** = safety device

dispuesto, -ta *adj* ready *o* willing

disputa *nf* argument *o* dispute; **despidió a su abogado tras una disputa sobre las costas** = he sacked his solicitor after an argument over costs

disputado, -da *adj* contested; **un caso de divorcio no disputado** = an uncontested divorce case

disputar *vt* to contest *o* to dispute; **oferta de adquisición disputada** = contested takeover; **el escaño es disputado por cinco candidatos** = the seat is being contested by five candidates

disquete *nm* diskette

disquetera *nf (unidad de disco)* disk drive

distancia *nf* distance; **(mantenido) a distancia** = at arm's length; **se pidió a los directores que mantuvieran las distancias con el depositario** = the directors were required to deal with the receiver at arm's length

distinción *nf* distinction; **sin distinciones** = pari passu; **el juez no hizo distinción entre las dos partes** = the judge made no distinction between the parties

distinguir *vt* to distinguish; **distinguir un caso de su precedente** = to distinguish a case ◊ **distinguirse** *vr* to be distinguished *o* to differ; **una empresa que se distingue por la calidad de sus productos** = company with a reputation for quality

distinto, -ta *adj* different; **ser distinto** = to differ

distorsión *nf (falseamiento)* **distorsión de la verdad** *o* **de los hechos** = perverting the course of justice

distraer *vt (robar)* **distraer fondos** = to misappropriate *o* to embezzle

distribución *nf (reparto)* distribution; **distribución de acciones** = share allocation *o* allocation of shares; **distribución de beneficios** = profit sharing

distribuidor, -ra *n* distributor *o (concesionario)* dealer; **distribuidor autorizado** = authorized dealer

distribuir *vt (repartir)* to distribute *o* to apportion *o* to allocate; **distribuir un dividendo** = to pay a dividend; **beneficios no distribuidos** = retained income

distrito *nm* district; *(jurisdicción)* circuit; *(zona)* zone; **distrito electoral** = constituency *US* precinct; **distrito policial** = *US* police precinct; **juez de distrito** = *GB* circuit judge

disturbio *nm* disturbance *o* riot; **delito de reunión para llevar a cabo un disturbio** = rout; **disturbios** = civil disorder *o* public disorder *o* public disorders; **provocar disturbios** = to riot; **los disturbios callejeros forzaron al gobierno a dimitir** = street disturbances forced the government to resign

disuadir *vt* to deter; **se espera que las largas condenas disuadirán a otros del contrabando de droga** = it is hoped that long jail sentences will deter others from smuggling drugs

disuasión *nf* deterrence; **fuerza de disuasión** = deterrent

disuasivo, -va *adj* deterrent

disuasorio, -ria *adj* deterrent; **sentencia disuasoria** = deterrent sentence

disyuntiva *nf* alternative *o* dilemma

diverso, -sa *adj (miscelánea)* miscellaneous; **artículos diversos** = sundry items *o* sundries

dividendo *nm* dividend; **dividendo final** = final dividend; **dividendo provisional** *o* **a cuenta** = interim dividend

dividir *vt* **(a)** *(repartir)* to divide *o* to share; **dividir una herencia** = to break up an estate; **dividir el tiempo que se utiliza el ordenador** = to share computer time; **dividir los beneficios entre los directivos** = to share the profits among the senior executives **(b)** *(separar)* to separate; **el personal se divide entre los que trabajan a tiempo parcial y los que lo hacen con dedicación exclusiva** = the personnel are separated into part-timers and full-time staff; **la empresa se dividió y se vendió cada parte por separado** = the company was broken up and separate divisions sold off

divisa *nf (moneda extranjera)* foreign currency; **divisa bloqueada** = blocked currency; **divisa fuerte** = hard currency; **divisas de reserva** = reserve currency; **cambio de divisas** = foreign exchange; **agente de cambio de divisas** = foreign exchange broker; **control de divisas** = exchange controls; **mercado de divisas** = foreign exchange market; **reservas de divisas** = foreign exchange reserves; **transferencia de divisas** = foreign exchange transfer; **el gobierno tuvo que imponer controles de divisas para detener la gran demanda de compra de dólares** = the government had to impose exchange controls to stop the rush to buy dollars

división *nf* **(a)** *(discordia)* division; **haber división de opiniones** = to have a division of opinion **(b)** *(sección)* branch
◊ **divisional** *adj (divisionario)* divisional
◊ **divisionario, -ria** *adj (divisional)* divisional

divorciarse *vr* to divorce; **se divorció de su mujer y se casó con su secretaria** = he divorced his wife and married his secretary

divorcio *nm* divorce; **divorcio con el consentimiento de las partes** *o* **de mutuo acuerdo** = uncontested divorce *o* divorce by consent; **petición** *o* **demanda de divorcio** = divorce petition; **sentencia de divorcio definitiva** = decree absolute; **sentencia provisional de divorcio** = decree nisi; **le concedieron el divorcio a causa del comportamiento irracional de su marido** = she was granted a divorce on the grounds of unreasonable behaviour by her husband

divulgación *nf* disclosure; **la divulgación de la oferta de adquisición elevó el precio de las acciones** = the disclosure of the takeover bid raised the price of the shares

divulgar *vt (revelar)* to divulge; *(publicar)* to release; *(poner en circulación)* to circulate; **divulgaron una nueva lista de precios entre todos sus clientes** = they circulated a new list of prices to all their customers

doblar 1 *vt* **(a)** *(duplicar)* to double **(b)** *(plegar)* to fold **2** *vi* to turn
◊ **doblarse** *vr (duplicarse)* to double

doble *adj* double *o* dual; **doble imposición** = double taxation; **tratado de doble imposición** = double taxation agreement *o* treaty; **persona con doble nacionalidad** = person of dual nationality *o* person who has dual nationality

doctrina *nf* doctrine

documentación *nf* documentation; *(documentos)* papers; **falsificación y utilización de documentación falsa** = forgery and uttering; **poner en circulación documentación falsa** = to utter; **le ruego me envíe toda la documentación referente a la venta** = please send me the complete documentation concerning the sale

documental *adj* documentary; **prueba documental** = documentary evidence *o* documentary proof

documento *nm* document; *(dictamen)* dictate; **documentos** = papers; **documento adjunto** = annexe; **documento incompleto** *o* **no registrado** = inchoate instrument; *(escritura)* **documento jurídico** = deed; **documento legal** = instrument; **documentos por archivar** = filing; **en este documento** = herein; **lista de documentos relevantes para una acción procesal** = list of documents; **el abogado me envió los documentos**

pertinentes al caso = the solicitor sent me the relevant papers on the case; **las condiciones establecidas en este documento** = the conditions stated herein

dolo *nm (engaño)* fraude; *(intención criminal)* mens rea *o* actual malice; **con dolo** = under false pretences
◊ **doloso** *adj* fraudulent; **daño doloso** = malicious damage; **con intención dolosa** = with malice aforethought

> En Derecho Penal constituye dolo la voluntad maliciosa para la comisión de un delito. En Derecho civil es la voluntad maliciosa y desleal en el cumplimiento de obligaciones

doméstico, -ca *adj* domestic; **efectos domésticos** = household effects; **proceso judicial doméstico** = domestic proceedings

domiciliación *nf (orden de pago regular)* banker's order *o* standing order; **domiciliación bancaria** = direct debit; **pago mi suscripción por domiciliación bancaria** = I pay my subscription by standing order

domiciliado, -da *adj* domiciled; **está domiciliado en Dinamarca** = he is domiciled in Denmark; **letras de cambio domiciliadas en Francia** = bills domiciled in France

domiciliario, -ria *adj* **arresto domiciliario** = house arrest; **el líder de la oposición lleva seis años bajo arresto domiciliario** = the opposition leader has been under house arrest for six years

domicilio *nm (residencia)* residence *o* abode; **domicilio natural** *o* **de origen** = domicile of origin; **domicilio permanente** = domicile; **domicilio real** *o* **verdadero** = domicile of choice; **domicilio social** = registered office *o* headquarters; **domicilio social de una empresa** = a company's registered office; **a domicilio** = house-to-house; **violación de domicilio** = forcible entry

dominante *adj* dominant *o* prevailing; **propiedad** *o* **heredad dominante** = dominant tenement

dominar *vt* to govern *o* to control *o* to override

dominical *adj* Sunday; **cierre dominical** = Sunday closing

dominio *nm* **(a)** *(ámbito)* domain; **dominio público** = public domain; **obra de dominio público** = work which is in the public domain **(b)** *(mandato)* rule; **el país ha soportado diez años de dominio castrense** = the country has had ten years of military rule **(c)** *(propiedad)* **dominio absoluto** *o* **simple** = fee simple; **dominio compartido** = co-ownership; **dominio imperfecto** = qualified ownership; **dominio limitado a herederos directos** = fee tail; **dominio vitalicio** = life estate

donación *nf* bequest; *(cesión)* grant; **donación entre vivos** *o* **inter vivos** = gift inter vivos; **'donación por muerte'** = donatio mortis causa

donante *nmf* donor; *(otorgante)* grantor

donar *vt* to give *o* to donate *o* to gift

donatario, -ria *n* donee

donativo *nm* donation *o* gift

donde *prep* **en donde** = wherein
◊ **dondequiera que** *adv* wheresoever; **el seguro que cubre las joyas dondequiera que se tengan guardadas** = the insurance covering jewels wheresoever they may be kept

dorso *nm* back; **sírvase firmar el cheque al dorso** = please endorse the cheque on the back; **las condiciones de venta figuran al dorso de la factura** = the conditions of sale are printed on the back of the invoice

dos *adj* **sistema de dos partidos** = two-party system

dotación *nf* allowance *o* endowment; **dotación de divisas** = foreign currency allowance

dotal *adj* **póliza dotal** = endowment assurance *o* endowment policy; **hipoteca avalada por una póliza de seguro dotal** = endowment mortgage

dotar *vt* to endow

dote *nf* dowry

droga *nf* drug; **drogas peligrosas** = dangerous drugs; **tráfico de drogas** = drug trafficking; *(la brigada antidroga)* **la brigada de Estupefacientes contra la droga** = the Drug Squad

drogadicción *nf (toxicomanía)* drug addiction

duda *nf* doubt; **fuera de toda duda** *o* **fuera de duda razonable** = beyond reasonable doubt *o* US beyond a reasonable doubt; **poner en duda** = to dispute *o* to query *o* to question; **puso en duda la versión de los hechos que dio el policía** = she disputed the policeman's version of events; **está fuera de duda que** = it is beyond question that; **en un caso criminal, la acusación tiene que demostrar sin que quepa duda alguna que el acusado cometió el crimen** = the prosecution in a criminal case has to establish beyond reasonable doubt that the accused committed the crime; **el abogado puso en duda la fiabilidad de la declaración del testigo** = counsel questioned the reliability of the witness' evidence; **el abogado puso en duda las declaraciones de los testigos de la policía** = counsel queried the statements of the police witnesses; **el acusado puso en duda el resultado de la prueba de alcoholemia** = the accused questioned the result of the breathalyser test; **el acusado puso en duda la declaración** = the defendant disputed the claim

dudar *vi (no estar seguro)* to hesitate; **dudó un momento antes de responder a la pregunta** = she hesitated for some time before answering the question

dudoso, -sa *adj* **(a)** *(equívoco)* equivocal *o* doubtful; **el tribunal decidió que el alegato del acusado era dudoso** = the court took the view that the defendant's plea was equivocal **(b)** *(turbio)* dubious *o* shady

dueño, -ña 1 *n* owner *o* proprietor; **dueño de una casa** = householder *o* owner; **dueño final** = ultimate owner; **único dueño** = sole owner; **cambiar de dueño** = to change hands; **ocupante y dueño de una propiedad** = owner-occupier; **la tienda cambió de dueño por 50 millones de ptas** = the shop changed hands for 50 million ptas **2** *nf (propietaria)* proprietress **2** *nm (propietario)* proprietor

dúplica *nf (contrarréplica)* rejoinder

duplicación *nf* duplication *o* duplicating

duplicado, -da 1 *adj* duplicate; **recibo duplicado** = duplicate receipt *o* duplicate of a receipt **2** *nm (copia)* duplicate; **por duplicado** = in duplicate; **recibo por duplicado** = receipt in duplicate; **escribir una carta por duplicado** = to duplicate a letter; **imprimir una factura por duplicado** = to print an invoice in duplicate

duplicar *vt* to duplicate; **duplicar con otra partida** = to duplicate with another entry; **duplicar el trabajo** = to duplicate work
◊ **duplicarse** *vr* to double

duración *nf (plazo de tiempo)* term *o* period; *(vigencia)* life; **duración de las funciones** = period of appointment; **duración de un préstamo** = the life of a loan

durante *prep (en el transcurso de)* in the course of; **durante el trabajo** = in the course of employment

durar *vi* to last; **la vista empezó en diciembre y duró hasta la segunda semana de enero** = the hearing started in December and lasted until the second week of January

duro, -ra *adj* **(a)** *(inflexible)* hard; **disco duro** = hard disk; **negocio duro** = hard bargain; **imponer duras condiciones** = to drive *o* to strike a hard bargain; **es difícil cerrar un trato con él** *o* **es un duro negociador** = he drives a hard bargain **(b)** *(severo)* harsh *o* stiff *o* heavy; **recibió una dura condena de prisión** = he received a stiff prison sentence; **tuvo que realizar un examen muy duro para sacar el título** = he had to take a stiff test before he qualified

Ee

ebrio, -ria 1 *adj (borracho)* drunk **2** *noun* drunkard; **ebrio habitual** = habitual drunkard

echar *vt (tirar)* to throw *o (deshacerse de)* to throw out; **echar a perder** = to waste; **echar al correo** = to post; **echar la carga al mar** = to jettison; **echar la culpa** = to blame
◊ **echarse** *vr* **echarse atrás** = to back down

echazón *nf (carga arrojada al mar)* jetsam; **pecios y echazón** = flotsam and jetsam

eclesiástico, -ca *adj* ecclesiastical; **Tribunal Eclesiástico** = ecclesiastical court

economía *nf* **(a)** *(sistema económico)* economy; **economía sumergida** = black economy; **economía de libre mercado** = free market economy **(b)** *(ahorro)* *nm* economy *o* saving; **economías de escala** = economies of scale

económico, -ca *adj* **(a)** *(relativo a la economía)* economic; **bloqueo económico** = embargo; **delitos económicos** = white collar crime; **dificultades económicas** *o* **apuros económicos** = hardship; **ejercicio económico** = fiscal year; **sanciones económicas** = economic sanctions; **sistema económico** = economy; **obtener ventajas económicas por estafa** = obtaining a pecuniary advantage by deception; **tener respaldo económico** = to cover a position; **en casos de dificultad económica, los servicios sociales pueden ofrecer alojamiento temporal** = in hardship cases *o* in cases of hardship, the welfare department may offer temporary accommodation; **la orden judicial puede causar dificultades económicas a la familia del acusado** = the court order may cause hardship to the family of the defendant **(b)** *(rentable)* commercial

economizar *vt (ahorrar)* to save

ecu *nm* ecu

edad *nf* age; **edad legal** = legal age; **edad núbil** = age of consent; **edad de responsabilidad penal** = age of criminal responsibility; **mayor de edad** = adult; **menor de edad** = under age

edición *nf* publication *o* edition

edicto *nm* edict; **edictos matrimoniales** = banns of marriage

edificio *nm (propiedad)* property; *(local)* building *o* premises; **edificio declarado de interés artístico o histórico** = listed building; **edificio público** = public building; **en el edificio** = on the premises; **hay un doctor en el edificio a todas horas** = there is a doctor on the premises at all times; **tenemos varios edificios en venta en el centro de la ciudad** = we have several properties for sale in the centre of the town

editar *vt (publicar)* to publish

editor, -ra *n* publisher

editorial 1 *adj* editorial; **consejo editorial** *o* **equipo editorial** = editorial board **2** *nf* publishing house *o* publisher **3** *nm (en periódico, revista)* editorial

educación *nf* **(a)** *(experiencia)* background; *(preparación profesional)* training; **centro de educación especial para delincuentes juveniles** = day training centre **(b)** *(cortesía)* politeness

efectivo, -va 1 *adj* effective *o* actual; **cláusula efectiva desde el 1 de enero** = clause effective as from January 1st; **la policía está intentando encontrar un medio efectivo de resolver el problema de la delincuencia juvenil** = the police are trying to find an effective means of dealing with young offenders; **nuda propiedad efectiva** = vested remainder **2**; *(dinero líquido)* ready money *o* hard cash; **dinero en efectivo** = balance in hand *o* cash in hand

efecto *nm* **(a)** *(consecuencia)* effect; **efecto secundario** *o* **efecto producido por una acción** = knock-on effect; **efecto suspensivo** = stay of execution; **tener efecto sobre** = to bear on *o* to have a bearing on; **sufrimos los efectos de un tipo de cambio elevado** = we are suffering from the influence of a high exchange rate; **le acusaron de conducir bajo los efectos del alcohol** = he was charged with driving under the influence of alcohol **(b)** *(bienes)* effects; **efectos domésticos** = household effects; **efectos personales** = personal effects **(c)** *(valores)* draft *o* bill; **efecto a la vista** = sight draft; **efecto de favor** = accommodation bill; **efecto financiero** = financial bill; **efectos bancarios** = bank paper; **efectos cotizables** = listed securities

efectuado, -da *adj* contraprestación efectuada = executed consideration

efectuar *vt (realizar)* to effect; *(to carry out)* efectuar un pago = to effect a payment

eficaz *adj (efectivo)* effective; *(eficiente)* efficient ◊ **eficazmente** *adv* efficiently; **el presidente dirigió los debates muy eficazmente =; the chairman conducted the proceedings very efficiently**

eficiente *adj (de buen rendimiento)* efficient; **una secretaria eficiente** = an efficient secretary; **la policía hizo frente a la multitud de manifestantes de una manera eficiente** = the police coped efficiently with the crowds of protesters ◊ **eficientemente** *adv* efficiently

ej. *(por ejemplo)* e.g.; **el contrato es válido en algunos países (ej. Francia y Bélgica) pero no en otros** = the contract is valid in some countries (e.g. France and Belgium) but not in others

ejecución *nf* **(a)** *(pena de muerte)* execution; **ejecución en la horca** = hanging; **pelotón de ejecución** = firing squad **(b)** *(cumplimiento)* implementation *o* enforcement *o* execution; **ejecución de la ley** = law enforcement; **ejecución de un contrato según sus términos** = specific performance; **ejecución de un pacto** = deed of covenant; **ejecución forzosa de una hipoteca** = foreclosure *o* repossession; **ejecución de una orden** *o* **de una norma** = execution; **orden de ejecución de pago** = warrant of execution; **orden judicial de ejecución de contrato según sus términos** = specific performance

ejecutable *adj* enforceable

ejecutado, -da *adj* executed; **contraprestación ejecutada** = executed consideration

ejecutar *vt* **(a)** *(condenar a muerte)* to execute; **ejecutar a alguien** = to execute someone; **fue ejecutado por el pelotón de fusilamiento** = he was executed by firing squad **(b)** *(cumplir)* to enforce *o* to perform *o* to implement; **ejecutar los términos de un contrato** = to enforce the terms of a contract; **ejecutar un acuerdo** = to carry out; **ejecutar una orden de detención** = to serve a warrant; **ejecutar una sentencia** = to carry out a sentence; **(derecho) que no se puede hacer ejecutar** = unenforceable

ejecutivo, -va **1** *adj* executive; **comisión ejecutiva** = executive committee; **director ejecutivo** = executive director; **director, -ra no ejecutivo, -va** *o* **director, -ra sin poderes ejecutivos** = non-executive director; **el poder ejecutivo** = the Executive; **poderes ejecutivos** = executive powers **2** *n* executive; **ejecutivo en formación** = management trainee; **jefe ejecutivo** = chief executive; **ejecutivo auxiliar** = junior executive *o* junior manager

ejecutor *nm* **(a)** *(albacea)* ejecutor testamentario = executor **(b)** *(verdugo)* ejecutor de la justicia = hangman

ejecutora *nf (albacea)* ejecutora testamentaria = executrix

ejecutorio, -ria 1 *adj* executory *o* enforceable **2** *nf (auto de ejecución)* writ of execution *o* enforceable judgement

> La ejecutoria es un documento público y solemne en el que se consigna una sentencia firme

ejemplar 1 *adj* exemplary; **condena** *o* **sentencia ejemplar** = exemplary sentence; **daños ejemplares** = exemplary damages; **sentencia ejemplar** = deterrent sentence; **imponer a alguien un castigo ejemplar** = to make an example of someone; **su conducta en el caso fue ejemplar** = her conduct in the case was exemplary; *(indemnización que el acusado debe pagar por daños causados al demandante)* **2** *nm* **(a)** *(publicación)* copy; **¿dónde está mi ejemplar de la guía telefónica?** = where is my copy of the telephone directory?; **lo leí en el ejemplar de 'Fortune' de la oficina** = I read it in the office copy of 'Fortune' **(b)** *(ejemplo)* example

ejemplo *nm* example *o* instance; **dar ejemplo a alguien** = to set an example to someone; **por ejemplo (ej.)** = for example (e.g.); **estas sentencias son un buen ejemplo de la severidad de los tribunales militares** = these sentences are a good example of the harshness of the military tribunals; **las nuevas leyes sobre la piratería informática ofrecen un ejemplo de cómo la ley cambia para mantenerse al día con los nuevos inventos** = new laws on computer copying provide an example of how the law changes to keep in step with new inventions; **se condenó a los alborotadores a prisión a modo de ejemplo para los demás** = the rioters were sentenced to periods of imprisonment as an example to others; **la policía debería dar ejemplo a la comunidad** = the police ought to set an example to the community; **el gobierno tomó medidas para controlar la droga y, por ejemplo, aumentó el número de policías de la brigada antidroga** *o* **de estupefacientes** = the government took steps to control drugs, and, for example, increased the numbers of policemen in the Drug Squad

ejercer 1 *vi* to practise; **ha ejercido durante veinte años** = he has been in practice for twenty years **2** *vt* to exercise; **ejercer un derecho** = to exercise a right; **ejercer un recurso** = to lodge an appeal; **ejercer el derecho a** *o* **de opción** = to exercise an option; **ejerció su derecho a opción para adquirir derechos exclusivos de comercialización del producto** = he exercised his option to acquire sole marketing rights for the product; **ejercer el poder de decisión** = to exercise one's discretion; **los magistrados ejercieron su poder de decisión y dieron al acusado una condena condicional** = the magistrates exercised their discretion and let the accused off with a suspended sentence; **no hubo muchos accionistas que ejercitaran su opción a compra de la nueva emisión de acciones** = not many shareholders exercised their option to buy the new issue of shares

ejercicio *nm* (a) *(ejecución)* exercise *o* practice; **ejercicio del derecho a opción** = exercise of an option; **certificado de ejercicio de la abogacía** = practising certificate; **en el ejercicio de sus funciones como director** = in discharge of his duties as director; **en el ejercicio de sus funciones como juez** = in the exercise of her *o* his powers as a judge; **es un abogado en ejercicio** = he is a practising solicitor (b) *(año civil)* **ejercicio financiero** *o* **ejercicio económico** = financial year *o* fiscal year *o* tax year; **cierre de ejercicio** = year end; **ajuste por cierre de ejercicio** = year-end adjustment; **el departamento de contabilidad ha comenzado a trabajar en la contabilidad de cierre** *o* **en las cuentas de cierre del ejercicio** = the accounts department has started work on the year-end accounts

ejercitar *vt* to exercise

ejido *nm* *(terreno comunal)* common *o* common land

elaboración *nf* *(preparación)* making; *(redacción)* drafting; **elaboración de las leyes** = law-making

elaborar *vt* (a) *(producir)* to produce (b) *(informática)* to process

elección *nf* (a) *(votación)* election; **elecciones** = poll; **elecciones generales** = general election; **elección parcial** = by-election; **elección por correo** = postal ballot; **elecciones primarias** = primaries (b) *(selección)* selection *o* pick; **realizar una elección** = to exercise an option

electo, -ta *adj* -elect; **es la presidenta electa** = she is the president-elect

elector, -ra *n* elector

electorado *nm* electorate

electoral *adj* electoral; **agente electoral** = canvasser; **circunscripción** *o* **distrito electoral** = constituency *o* US precinct; **colegio electoral** = electoral college; **ley electoral** = electoral law *o* GB the Representation of the People Act; **registro electoral** = register of electors; **urna electoral** = ballot box

elegibilidad *nf* eligibility; **el presidente cuestionó su elegibilidad para presentarse a reelección** = the chairman questioned her eligibility to stand for re-election

elegible *adj* *(con derecho a)* eligible

elegir (a) *(votar)* to elect *o* *(diputado)* to return; **elegir a alguien** = to vote someone in; **elegir a los directivos de una asociación** = to elect the officers of an association; **el candidato conservador resultó elegido** = the Tory candidate was voted in; **fue elegida (por votación) miembro del comité** = she was voted on to the committee; **fue elegido por una amplia mayoría** = he was returned with an increased majority; **fue elegida presidenta** = she was elected president (b) *(seleccionar)* to select *o* to pick; **el Consejo General del Poder Judicial ha propuesto a un conocido juez para que sea el nuevo presidente del Tribunal Supremo** = the General council of the Judiciary has proposed a leading judge to be the new chairman of the Supreme Court; **elija a su gusto** = take your pick (c) *(escoger)* to elect *o* to choose; **eligió ser juzgado por un jurado** = he elected to stand trial by jury

elemento *nm* (a) *(parte de algo)* element *o* factor; **elementos de juicio** = background information (b) *(individuo)* person *o* individual

elevación *nf* **elevación de los autos** = order of certiorari; **solicitó una revisión judicial por elevación de los autos** = he applied for judicial review by way of certiorari

elevar *vt* (a) *(presentar)* to forward *o* to refer to *o* to file; **elevar a un tribunal superior** = to refer to a higher court; **elevar un recurso** *o* **una reclamación** = to file a motion *o* a claim (b) *(levantar)* to hand up; **el documento fue elevado al juez** = the exhibit was handed up to the judge (c) *(incrementar)* to raise

eliminación *nf* abatement

eliminar *vt* to abate *o* to eliminate *o* to remove

ello *pron* **a ello** = thereto; **por ello** = thereby; **todo ello** = all of which

eludir *vt* to avoid *o* to evade; **eludir una prohibición** = to beat a ban; **eludiendo toda responsabilidad** = derogation of responsibility

elusión *nf* avoidance; **elusión fiscal** = tax avoidance

embajada *nf* embassy

embajador, ra *n* ambassador

embalaje *nm* packing; **caja de embalaje** = a packing case

embarazada *adj* pregnant

embarazo *nm* pregnancy; **interrupción del embarazo** = child destruction; **interrumpir un embarazo** = to terminate a pregnancy

embarcar *vi* to embark; **los pasajeros embarcaron en Bilbao** = the passengers embarked at Bilbao
◊ **embarcarse** *vr* **(a)** *(subir a bordo)* to board; **los oficiales de aduanas embarcaron en el puerto** = customs officials boarded the ship in the harbour **(b)** *(emprender)* **embarcarse en** = to embark on

embarco *nm* embarkation

embargado, -da *n* garnishee

embargante *nmf* garnisher

embargador, -ra *n* sequestrator

embargar *vt* **(a)** *(confiscar)* to confiscate *o* to impound *o* to seize *o* to arrest; *(secuestrar)* to sequester *o* to sequestrate *o* to attach *o* to distrain; **venta de bienes embargados** = distress sale **(b)** *(prohibir)* to embargo

embargo *nm* **(a)** *(incautación)* impounding *o* seizure *o* arrest; *(secuestro)* sequestration *o* attachment; **embargo preventivo general** = general lien; **embargo preventivo llevado a cabo por una persona sobre la propiedad de otra** = particular lien; **embargo provisorio** = temporary injunction; **embargo suplementario** = second distress; **se le ha retenido la propiedad bajo orden de embargo** = his property has been kept under sequestration **(b)** *(bloqueo económico)* embargo; **imponer un embargo comercial a un país** = to lay *o* put an embargo on trade with a country; **levantar un embargo** = to lift an embargo **(c)** **sin embargo** = notwithstanding

embarque *nm* embarkation; **embarque directo** = drop shipment; **conocimiento de embarque** = bill of lading; **instrucciones de embarque** = shipping instructions; **nota de embarque** = advice note; **puerto de embarque** = port of embarkation; **tarjeta de embarque** = embarkation card *o* boarding card *o* boarding pass

embaucar *vt* to swindle *o* to fiddle; **embaucar a alguien para conseguir dinero** *o* **bienes** = to trick someone; **la banda embaucó al director del banco para sacarle las llaves de la cámara acorazada** = the gang tricked the bank manager into giving them the keys of the vault

embaucador, -ra *n* swindler

embolsar *vt* to pocket

emboscada *nf* ambush

embotellamiento *nm* bottleneck

embriagado, -da *adj* intoxicated

embriaguez *nf* intoxication

embustero, -ra *n* liar *o* cheat; *(impostor)* deceiver

emergencia *nf* emergency; **poderes de emergencia** = emergency powers; **salida de emergencia** = fire escape; **tomar medidas de emergencia excepcionales** = to take emergency measures

emigración *nf* emigration

emigrante *nmf* emigrant

emigrar *vi* to emigrate

emisión *nf* **(a)** *(valores)* issue; *(expedición)* issuance; *(emisor)* issuing; **emisión de acciones nuevas** = issue of new shares *o* share issue; **emisión de derechos** = rights issue; **emisión de obligaciones** = issue of debentures *o* debenture issue; **emisión gratuita** = bonus issue *o* scrip issue; **emisión gratuita de acciones distribuidas entre los accionistas** = scrip issue; **precio de salida de emisión** = issued price **(b)** *(comunicaciones)* broadcast *o* broadcasting

emisor, -ra 1 *adj* issuing; **banco emisor** *o* **casa emisora** = issuing bank *o* issuing house **2** nf **emisora de radio** = radio station

emitido, -da *adj* **capital emitido** = issued capital

emitir *vt* *(poner en circulación)* to issue; **emitir acciones de una empresa nueva** = to issue shares in a new company; **una serie de cheques emitidos por ordenador** = a cheque run **(b)** *(votación)* **emitir un voto** = to cast a vote; **el número de votos emitidos en la elección fue de 125.458** = the number of votes cast in the election was 125,458 **(c)** **emitir un fallo** *o* **un juicio sobre algo** = to pronounce judgment *o* to give one's judgment on something **(d)** *(transmitir)* **emitir un programa** = to broadcast

emolumentos *nmpl* *(honorarios)* fee *o* honorarium

empadronar *vt* *(censo electoral)* to register

empedernido, -da *adj* **borracho empedernido** = habitual drunkard

empeñar *vt* to pawn; **empeñar algo** = to put something in pawn; **empeñar un reloj** = to pawn a watch; **recibo del objeto empeñado** = pawn ticket
◊ **empeñarse** *vr* **(a)** *(endeudarse)* to get into debt; **tuvo que empeñarse hasta la camisa para pagar la multa** = he had to borrow heavily to pay the fine **(b)** *(insistir en algo)* to insist *o* to persist

empeño *nm* *(pignoración)* pledge; **casa de empeños** = pawnshop; **papeleta de empeño** = pawn ticket

empeorar 1 *vt* to make worse **2** *vi* to worsen *o* to get worse
◊ **empeorarse** *vr* to get worse

empezar 1 *vt/i* **(a)** *(comenzar)* to begin *o* to commence *o* to start; **el caso empezó con la lectura del sumario** = the case began with the reading of the indictment **(b)** *(iniciar un caso)* to lead

emplazamiento *nm* **(a)** *(citación judicial)* citation *o* mesne process *o* writ of summons; **emplazamiento judicial** = summons *o* citation; **documento de emplazamiento** = writ of summons

emplazar *vt (citar)* to summon *o* to subpoena; **emplazar a alguien ante el juez** = to issue a writ against someone; **le emplazaron para que compareciera ante la comisión** = he was summoned to appear before the committee

empleado, -da **1** *adj* employed **2** *n; (trabajador)* employee *o* member of staff *o* worker; **empleado de oficina** = clerk; **empleado de fábrica** = inside worker; **empleados y patronos** = employees and employers; **la compañía ha decidido contratar nuevos empleados** = the company has decided to take on new employees; **las relaciones entre la dirección y los empleados han mejorado** = relations between management and employees have improved; **los empleados de la firma tienen derecho a entrar en un plan de participación en los beneficios** = employees of the firm are eligible to join a profit-sharing scheme

emplear *vt* **(a)** *(dar empleo)* to employ *o (contratar)* to hire; **emplear a veinte personas** = to employ twenty staff; **le emplearon para finalizar el contrato** = they hired him to finalise the agreement **(b)** *(usar)* to use; **emplean personal temporal para la mayor parte de su trabajo** = they use temporary staff for most of their work **(c)** *(gastar)* to spend; **emplear tiempo** =; **el tribunal empleó semanas en tomar declaraciones** = the tribunal spent weeks on hearing evidence to spend (time)

empleo *nm* **(a)** *(trabajo)* employment; **empleo fijo** *o* **permanente** = permanent employment; **empleo precario** *o* **estacional** = short term employment *o* seasonal employment; **condiciones de empleo** = conditions of employment; **ley de empleo** = the law of master and servant; **oficina de empleo** = employment office *o* bureau *o* agency **(b)** *(puesto)* job *o* post *o* position *o* appointment *o* place *o* situation; **rechazó tres empleos antes de aceptar el que le ofrecimos** = she turned down three jobs before accepting the one we offered

emprender *vt* **(a)** *(embarcarse en)* to embark on; *(lanzar)* to launch; **la compañía ha emprendido un programa de expansión** = the company has embarked on a development programme; **la policía ha emprendido una campaña contra los conductores en estado de embriaguez** = the police have launched a campaign against drunken drivers **(b)** *(encargarse de)* to undertake; **emprender acciones judiciales** = to take legal action; **emprender una investigación del fraude** = to undertake an investigation of the fraud

empresa *nf* **(a)** *(comercio)* business; *(sociedad)* company *o* corporation; *(firma)* firm; *(negocio)* concern *o* enterprise *o* undertaking; **empresa asociada** *o* **afiliada** = associate company; **empresa comercial** = commercial undertaking; **empresa conjunta** = joint venture; **empresa constructora** = construction company; **empresa cotizada en bolsa** = quoted company; **empresa de tractores** *o* **de aviones** *o* **de chocolate** = a tractor *o* aircraft *o* chocolate company; **empresa familiar** = family company; **empresa naviera** = shipping company; **asesor, -ra de empresa** = management consultant; **derecho de empresa** = company law; **director, -ra de una empresa** = company director; **en la propia empresa** = inside; **libre empresa** = free enterprise; **pagaré de empresa** = debenture bond; **dirige una empresa de ventas por correo** = she runs a mail order enterprise; **una empresa editorial importante** = an important publishing firm; **vendida como empresa en marcha** = sold as a going concern

empresarial *adj* managerial; **planificación empresarial** = corporate planning; **zona empresarial** = enterprise zone; **estudiar ciencias empresariales** = to study management

empresario, -ria *nm (patrón)* employer; **asociación de empresarios** = employers' organization *o* association

empréstito *nm* loan capital; *(préstamo)* borrowing; *(obligaciones convertibles)* convertible loan stock; **empréstito forzoso** = forced loan

en *prep* **en donde** *o* **en que** *o* **en el cual** *o* **en la cual** = wherein; **en el que** *o* **en la que** = whereon; **en sí mismo** = per se; **en funcionamiento** = in operation; **en su defecto** = failing that; **un documento en el que se enumeran las normas** = a document wherein the regulations are listed; **terreno en el que o finca en la que se construye una vivienda** = land whereon a dwelling is constructed

enajenación *nf* **(a)** *(en el matrimonio)* alienation; **enajenación del afecto** = alienation of affection **(b)** *(locura)* **enajenación mental** = insanity **(c)** *(expropiación)* **enajenación de bienes** = disposal of property; **enajenación forzosa** = expropriation

> La enajenación és un acto jurídico en virtud del cual una persona transmite a otra el dominio de una cosa o un derecho que le pertenece

enajenar *vt* to alienate

enarbolar *vt* **enarbolar una bandera** = to fly a flag

encabezamiento *nm (epígrafe)* heading; **encabezamiento de un documento legal** = caption

encabezar *vt (estar a la cabeza de)* to head *o* to lead; **la empresa encabeza el mercado de ordenadores a precio económico** = the company leads the market in cheap computers; **la lista de**

casos por ver está encabezada por dos casos de asesinato = the list of cases to be heard is headed by two murder cases; **las dos compañías petrolíferas más grandes encabezan la lista de resultados de la bolsa** = the two largest oil companies head the list of stock market results

encarcelación *nf (encarcelamiento)* incarceration

encarcelamiento *nm (cárcel)* imprisonment *o* incarceration; **encarcelamiento ilegal** = false imprisonment; **encarcelamiento sin juicio previo** = internment

encarcelar *vt* to incarcerate *o* to imprison *o* to jail *o* to gaol *o* to lock up; *(citar ante los tribunales)* to commit; **fue encarcelada tres años** = she was jailed for three years; **fue encarcelado durante seis años** = he was sent to prison for six years; **estuvo encarcelado por la policía secreta durante seis meses** = he was imprisoned by the secret police for six months

encargado, -da 1 *adj* commissioned 2 *n* person in charge; **encargado de salarios** = wages clerk; **encargado del Registro Mercantil** = Registrar of Companies; **encargado del registro civil** = district registrar; **encargado del registro de marcas** = registrar of trademarks 3 *nf* manageress *o* forewoman 4 *nm* manager *o* foreman

encargar *vt (trabajo)* to commission *o* to put out; **encargar trabajo a una agencia** *o* **a trabajadores independientes** = to put work out to a bureau *o* to freelance workers
◊ **encargarse** *vr* **(a)** *(ocuparse de)* **engargarse de** = to handle *o* to undertake **(b)** *(a cargo de)* 'que el comprador se encargue' = caveat emptor

encargo *nm* commission *o* mandate

encartado, -da *n* accused

encauzar *vt (dirigir)* to channel

encerrar *vt (encarcelar)* to lock up

enchufe *nm (conocido)* contact

encierro *nm (cárcel)* confinement

encima *prep* **por encima de** = in excess

encinta *adj* pregnant

encomendar *vt (confiar)* to entrust; **encomendar algo a alguien** = to trust someone with something

encontrar *vt (hallar)* to find; *(localizar)* to trace; **encontrar apoyo para un proyecto** = to find backing for a project
◊ **encontrarse** *vr* to meet; **encontrarse con** = to meet *o* to run into; **las dos partes se encontraron en el despacho del abogado** = the two sides met in the lawyer's office

encubierto, -ta *adj* hidden; **mandante encubierto** = undisclosed principal

encubridor, -ra *n (de un delito)* accessory; **encubridor, -ra de objetos robados** = receiver *o* fence; **cómplice encubridor** = accessory after the fact

encubrimiento *nm (ocultación)* concealment; *(de un delito)* misprision *o* complicity *o* cover-up; **encubrimiento de activos** = concealment of assets; **encubrimiento de objetos robados** = receiving stolen property; **encubrimiento de nacimiento** = concealment of birth; **encubrimiento de traición** = misprision of treason

encubrir *vt (ocultar)* to conceal; **encubrir a un criminal** = to harbour a criminal; **encubrir objetos robados** = to receive stolen goods

encuesta *nf (sondeo de opinión)* opinion poll

endémico *adj (crónico)* chronic

endeudado, -da *adj* indebted; **país endeudado** = debtor nation; **estar endeudado con una empresa inmobiliaria** = to be indebted to a property company

endeudamiento *nm* borrowing; **capacidad de endeudamiento** = borrowing power

endeudarse *vr (contraer deudas)* to get into debt

endosante *nmf* endorser; **endosante de una letra** = backer of a bill

endosar *vt* to endorse; **endosar un cheque** = to endorse a cheque; **endosó el cheque para que se lo pudieran pagar a su abogado** = he endorsed the cheque over to his solicitor

endosatario, -ria *nmf* endorsee

endoso *nm (anotaciones en un documento legal)* endorsement; *(en auto judicial)* indorsement; **endoso completo** = special indorsement

enemigo, -ga *adj* enemy; *(hostil)* hostile

enemistad *nf* enmity *o* hostility; **enemistad manifiesta** = ill-will; **enemistad entre familias** = feud

enérgico, -ca *adj* **peticiones enérgicas a favor de la abolición de la pena de muerte** = a strong demand for the abolition of capital punishment

enfermedad *nf* illness *o* sickness; **permiso por enfermedad** *o* **baja por enfermedad** = sick leave; **la empresa sigue pagando el sueldo de los empleados que están de baja por enfermedad** = the company continues to pay the wages of staff who are absent due to illness

enfiteusis *nf* ground lease

enfocar *vt* to approach; **modo de enfocar una cuestión** = approach; **tiene un modo profesional**

de enfocar su trabajo = he has a professional approach to his work

enfoque *nm* approach

enfrentamiento *nm* confrontation

enfrentarse *vr (hacer frente a)* to face *o* to confront; **enfrentarse a unos cargos** = to face a charge; **se enfrenta a tres cargos relacionados con armas de fuego** = he faces three charges relating to firearms

engañar *vt (estafar)* to deceive *o* to con; *(desorientar)* to mislead; **engañar a alguien** = to trick someone *o* to take someone in; **las instrucciones del documento engañan** = the instructions in the document are quite misleading; **nos dejamos engañar por su promesa de unos beneficios rápidos** = we were taken in by his promise of quick profits

engaño *nm (estafa)* trick *o* con; *(fraude)* deceit *o* deception; **engaño para que alguien firme un contrato** = fraudulent misrepresentation; **con engaño** = false pretences; **obtener dinero por medio de engaños** = to obtain money by fraud
◊ **engañoso, -sa** *adj* deceptive *o* deceitful; **de un modo engañoso** = dishonestly; **planteamiento** *o* **informe engañoso** = false representation

enjuiciamiento *nm (procesamiento)* prosecution; **delito que puede estar sujeto a** *o* **ser objeto de enjuiciamiento** = triable offence; **ley de enjuiciamiento criminal** = code of criminal procedure

enjuiciar *vt (entablar una acción judicial)* to prosecute; **delito que se puede enjuiciar** = triable offence

enlace *nm* link *o* connection; *(de una banda de carteristas)* runner; **enlace sindical** = shop steward

enmendar *vt (rectificar)* to amend *o* to make amends; *(una ley)* to mark up; **enmendar un contrato** = to make amendments to a contract; **enmendar un proyecto de ley en comisión** = to mark up a bill
◊ **enmendarse** *vr* to go straight

enmienda *nf* amendment

enredar *vt* **(a)** *(comprometer a alguien)* to implicate *o* to involve **(b)** *(complicar un asunto)* to confuse

ensañamiento *nm* extreme cruelty

ensaye *nm* assay; **marca de ensaye** = assay mark

ensayo *nm (prueba)* trial; **muestra de ensayo** = trial sample

enseñar *vt (mostrar)* to show

enseres *nmpl (efectos domésticos)* household effects; **enseres y bienes muebles** = goods and chattels

entablar *vt* **(a)** *(iniciar)* to start *o* to open; **entablar conversaciones** = to open negotiations; **entablar relaciones con alguien** = to enter into relations with someone **(b)** *(recurso legal)* to institute; **entablar demanda de divorcio** = to file for divorce; **entablar juicio** = to sue; **entablar un pleito** = to prefer; **entablar un pleito a alguien** *o* **entablar un proceso contra alguien** = to bring a lawsuit *o* proceedings against someone *o* to take legal action *o* to start legal proceedings against someone *o* to institute proceedings against someone; **entablar una acción judicial** = to prosecute; **entablar una demanda contra alguien** = to lodge a complaint against someone

ente *nm* entity *o* institution; **ente jurídico** = legal entity; **ente público** = public entity

entender *vt* **(a)** *(comprender)* to understand *o* to apprehend; **entender mal** = to misunderstand; **entiendo que usted dice que su cliente tiene una referencia** = I apprehend that you say your client has a reference **(b)** **dar a entender** = to imply; **tener entendido** = to believe *o* to gather; **¿Quiere usted dar a entender que la policía actuó incorrectamente?** = do you wish to imply that the police acted improperly?; **el abogado dio a entender que el testigo no había visto en realidad cómo ocurrió el accidente** = counsel implied that the witness had not in fact seen the accident take place; **tenemos entendido que se ha ofrecido para comprar el 25% de las acciones** = we believe he has offered to buy 25% of the shares; **tengo entendido que ha dejado la oficina** = I gather he has left the office

entendido, -da *n* expert

enterado *nm* acknowledgment of receipt

enterarse *vr (descubrir)* to discover *o* to find out

entero, -ra *adj (completo)* whole *o* clear
◊ **enteramente** *adv; (totalmente)* fully

entidad *nf* **(organización)** entity *o* company; **entidad aseguradora** = insurance company; **entidad financiera** = finance company; **su compañía privada es una entidad separada** = his private company is a separate entity **(b)** **de poca entidad** = of little importance; **demanda** *o* **acción de poca entidad** = frivolous complaint *o* frivolous action

entrada *nf* **(a)** *(ingreso)* entry; *(acceso)* entrance; **entrada ilegal** = trespass; **entrada ilegal en la propiedad de alguien** = trespass to land; **permitir la entrada a** *o* **dar entrada a** = to admit; **segunda entrada** = re-entry; **no existe derecho de entrada por esta puerta** = there is no right of entry through this door; **se debería permitir la entrada a los juzgados a todos los ciudadanos** = access to the courts should be open to all citizens **(b)** *(admisión)* admission; *(espectáculo)* ticket; **precio de entrada**

= admission charge *o* entry charge *o* entrance fee *o* admittance fee; **entrada gratis los domingos** = free admission on Sundays; **entrada gratis al presentar esta tarjeta** = admission is free on presentation of this card; **el precio de la entrada es de quinientas pesetas** = there is a five hundred pesetas admission charge; **la entrada para pensionistas es a mitad de precio** = old age pensioners are admitted at half price **(c)** *(pago)* **entrada a cuenta** = down payment; *(desembolso inicial)* **dar una entrada** = to pay money down; **dar una entrada para la compra de una casa** = to put down money on a house **(d)** *(asiento)* entry; *(ingresos)* **el funcionario copió las entradas en el informe** = the officer copied the entries into the report **(e)** *(input)* input **(f) entrada en vigor** = date of commencement

entrar *vi* **(a)** *(introducirse)* to go in *o* to enter; **entrar a robar** = to break into; **entrar ilegalmente en la propiedad de alguien** = to trespass; **todos se levantaron cuando los jueces entraron en la sala** = they all stood up when the judges entered the courtroom; **el ladrón entró por la ventana** = the burglar gained access through the window; **entraron a robar en su casa mientras estaban de vacaciones** = their house was broken into while they were on holiday; **los saqueadores entraron en el supermercado para robar** looters broke into the supermarket; **la compañía ha gastado millones intentando entrar en el mercado del bricolaje** = the company has spent millions trying to enter the do-it-yourself market; **se prohibe a los niños entrar a!** **banco** = children are not admitted to the bank **(b)** *(ingresar)* to join; **entrar en un despacho de abogados** = to join a firm of solicitors; **le pidieron que entrara en la junta directiva** = he was asked to join the board **(c) entrar dentro** = to fall within; **entrar en funciones** = to come into office; **entrar en posesión** = to take possession; **entrar en vigor** = to come into force; **el artículo periodístico entra dentro de la categoría de difamación** = the newspaper report falls within the category of defamation **(d)** *(informática)* to access

entre *prep* between *o* inter; **'entre otras cosas'** = inter alia; **entre rejas** = behind bars; **estudios comparativos entre compañías** = inter-company comparisons; **operaciones entre compañías** = inter-company dealings

entrega *nf* **(a)** *(distribución)* delivery; **entrega de mercancías a bordo** = goods delivered on board; **entrega de productos** = delivery of goods; **entrega directa de un pedido (a tienda o almacén) sin intermediarios** = drop shipment; **entrega gratuita de productos** = goods delivered free *o* free delivered goods; **aceptar la entrega de mercancías** = to take delivery of goods; **gastos a cobrar a la entrega** = charges forward; **servicio de entrega de cartas certificadas o con acuse de recibo** = recorded delivery; **recogemos tres**

entregas diarias = we take in three deliveries a day; **faltaban cuatro artículos en la última entrega** = there were four items missing in the last delivery **(b)** *(notificación)* service; **entrega (de una notificación) en persona** = service (of process) *o* personal service; **acusar recibo de una entrega** = to acknowledge service; **acuse de recibo de entrega** *o* **acta de reconocimiento de una entrega de notificación** = acknowledgement of service **(c)** *(abandono)* surrender

entregar *vt* **(a)** *(repartir)* to deliver **(b)** *(ceder)* to part with something *o* to hand something over; **entregar un documento** = to surrender a document; **entregar a alguien un mandamiento** *o* **una orden judicial** = to serve someone with a writ *o* to serve a writ on someone; **entregar documentos en el juzgado por parte de la defensa** = to enter an appearance; **entregó los documentos al abogado** = she handed over the documents to the lawyer; **el tribunal le ordenó que entregara su pasaporte** = the court ordered him to surrender his passport ◊ **entregarse** *vr* *(rendirse)* to surrender; **los secuestradores del avión se entregaron a los guardias de seguridad del aeropuerto** = the hijackers surrendered to the airport security guards

entretanto *adv* *(en el interin)* in the interim

entretener *vt* **(a)** *(demorar)* to delay *o* to keep waiting **(b)** *(distraer)* **entretener clientes** = to entertain ◊ **entretenerse** *vr* **(a)** *(tardar)* to delay **(b)** *(distraerse)* to amuse oneself

entrevista *nf* interview; **sala de entrevistas** = interview room

entrevistar *vt* to interview; **entrevistamos a diez candidatos para el puesto** = we interviewed ten candidates for the post

entrometerse *vr* *(interferir)* to interfere

enumerar *vt* *(hacer una lista)* to list; **el catálogo enumera los productos por categorías** = the catalogue lists products by category

envenenar *vt* to poison; **no le dispararon, le envenenaron** = he was not shot, he was poisoned

envergadura *nf* *(importancia)* importance; **la decisión traerá consecuencias de gran envergadura** = the decission will have far-reaching consequences

enviar *vt* **(a)** *(mandar)* to send; **enviar algo a alguien** = to forward something to someone; **enviar dinero** = to remit; **enviar dinero por medio de un cheque** = to remit by cheque; **enviar por correo** = to post; **enviar una carta** *o* **enviar un paquete** = to post a letter *o* to post a parcel; **enviar una carta certificada** = to register; **se ruega enviar los pagos al tesorero** = please send remittances to the treasurer; **el cheque fue enviado ayer a su banco** = the cheque went to your bank yesterday; **la familia**

vive de los giros que semanalmente les envía el padre desde los **EE UU** = the family lives on a weekly remittance from their father in the USA **(b)** *(expedir)* to ship; *(consignar)* to consign; **enviar mercancías a alguien** = to consign goods to someone; **enviar mercancía a los EE UU** = to ship goods to the USA; **la expedición de coches fue enviada al extranjero la semana pasada** = the consignment of cars was shipped abroad last week; **enviamos toda la mercancía por ferrocarril** = we ship all our goods by rail

enviciar *vt* to corrupt
◊ **enviciarse** *vr* to become corrupt

envío *nm* **(a)** *(expedición)* shipping *o* consignment *o* shipment; **envío directo** = drop shipment; **envío agrupado de mercancías (procedentes de diferentes empresas)** = consolidated shipment; **aviso de envío** = advice note; **instrucciones de envío** = shipping instructions; **nota de envío** = shipping note; **ha llegado un envío de mercancías** = a consignment of goods has arrived **(b)** *(giro)* remittance

epígrafe *nm* *(título)* head; *(breve introducción)* heading; **epígrafes de un acuerdo** = heads of agreement

equidad *nf (sistema legal justo)* equity; **hipoteca de equidad (no formalizada que nace con la entrega del dinero)** = equitable mortgage; **jurisdicción de equidad** = equitable jurisdiction

Cuando en un caso concreto la aplicación de una norma jurídica tiene un resultado que la conciencia social puede considerar injusto, el tribunal correspondiente no resuelve conforme a la norma aplicable sino de acuerdo con lo que considera justo para este caso concreto. Pero los tribunales solamente podrán fallar atendiendo a la equidad, cuando lo permita la ley. La equidad deberá ponderarse en la aplicación de las normas: se preferirá la interpretación cuyo resultado sea conforme a la equidad (CC artº 3.2)

equilibrar *vt (compensar)* to equalize *o* to balance; **equilibrar el presupuesto** = to balance the budget

equilibrio *nm* balance; **equilibrio mental** = balance of mind

equipo *nm* **(a)** *(de personas)* team; **equipo editorial** = editorial board; **equipo de rescate** = search party **(b)** *(de material)* equipment; **bienes de equipo** = capital goods

equitativo, -va *adj (igual)* equal; *(justo)* fair *o* equitable; **gravamen equitativo** = equitable lien
◊ **equitativamente** *adv* equally; **las costas se compartirán equitativamente entre las dos partes** = costs will be shared equally between the two parties

equivalencia *nf (paridad)* equivalence

equivalente *adj* equivalent; *(equivaler a)* **ser equivalente a** = to be equivalent to; **el dividendo total pagado es equivalente a un cuarto del beneficio total** = the total dividend paid is equivalent to one quarter of the total profits

equivocación *nf (error)* error *o* mistake; **por equivocación** = by mistake

equivocado, -da *(erróneo)* wrong; **el conductor dio la dirección equivocada al policía** = the driver gave the wrong address to the policeman; **intenté telefonearte, pero llamé a un número equivocado** = I tried to phone you, but I got the wrong number
◊ **equivocadamente** *adv* wrongly

equivocar *vt (engañar)* to mislead; **intenté telefonearte, pero me equivoqué de número** = I tried to phone you, but I got the wrong number
◊ **equivocarse** *vr (cometer un error)* to make a mistake *o* to slip up; **equivocarse en la cuenta** = to miscount; **se equivocaron al contar los votos, así que la votación tuvo que repetirse** = the votes were miscounted, so the ballot had to be taken again

equívoco, -ca **1** *adj* equivocal **2** *nm* *(malentendido)* misunderstanding

erario *nm* treasury; **erario público** = public treasury

errata *nf* corrigendum

erróneo, -nea *adj (incorrecto)* wrong *o* unsound; *(falso)* false; **identificación errónea** = mistaken identity; **unión errónea** = misjoinder; **fue arrestado por robo con allanamiento de morada y liberado después de establecerse que era un caso de identificación errónea** = he was arrested for burglary, but released after it had been established that it was a case of mistaken identity
◊ **erróneamente** *adv; (incorrectamente)* incorrectly *o* wrongly; **informar erróneamente** = to misdirect; **facturó erróneamente a Smith Ltd la cantidad de dos millones, cuando debería haberle abonado la misma cantidad** = he wrongly invoiced Smith Ltd for two million, when he should have credited them with the same amount

error *nm (equivocación)* error *o* mistake *o* slip *o* slip-up; **error de copia** = clerical error; **error de derecho** = mistake of law; **error de hecho** = error of fact; **error de jurisdicción** = mistake in venue; **error de ordenador** = computer error; **error judicial** = miscarriage of justice; **reglamento del Tribunal Supremo que permite la corrección de errores en alegaciones** = slip rule; **cometer un error** = to make a mistake *o* to slip up; **cometimos un grave error al no firmar el acuerdo con la compañía china** = we slipped up badly in not signing the agreement with the Chinese company; **cometió un error al calcular el total** = he made an error in calculating the total; **cometió un par de errores al calcular el descuento** = he made a couple of slips in calculating the discount; **la secretaria ha debido cometer un error de transcripción** = the secretary must have made a typing error; **por error** = by mistake; **salvo error u omisión (s.e.u.o)** = errors and omissions excepted (e. & o.e.)

esbozar *vt (hacer un borrador)* to rough out; **el director financiero esbozó un plan de inversión** = the finance director roughed out a plan of investment

escala *nf* **(a)** *(baremo)* scale; **escala de precios** = scale of charges *o* scale of prices; **escala de salarios** = scale of salaries *o* salary scale; **escala fija de precios** = fixed scale of charges; **escala móvil** = sliding scale; **escalas impositivas** = tax schedules; **economías de escala** = economies of scale; **gran escala** *o* **pequeña escala** = large scale *o* small scale; **empezar un negocio a pequeña escala** = to start in business on a small scale; **reducir** *o* **aumentar a escala** = to scale down *o* to scale up **(b)** *(parada)* stopover

escalada *nf (subida)* escalation; **escalada de precios** = escalation of prices

escalafón *nm* promotion ladder; **escalafón de abogados** = Roll of Solicitors

escalar *vi* to climb *o* to escalate

escalera *nf* **escalera de incendios** = fire escape

escalo *nm* **robar con escalo** = to burgle; **robo con escalo** = burglary; **se le acusó de robo con escalo** = he was charged with burglary

escándalo *nm* **(a)** *(asunto indecente)* scandal; *(abuso)* outrage **(b)** *(alboroto)* row

escandaloso, -sa *adj* disorderly; **le acusaron de conducta escandalosa** = he was charged with disorderly conduct

escaño *nm (parlamento)* seat; **cinco candidatos se disputan el escaño** *o* **hay cinco candidatos en pugna para el escaño** = the seat is being contested by five candidates =

escapar *vi (librarse)* to escape *o* to get off; **los muchachos escaparon con una reprimenda del juez** = the boys got off with a reprimand from the magistrate
◊ **escaparse** *vr (de prisión)* to escape

escapatoria *nf* **(a)** *(solución)* loophole; **encontrar una escapatoria legal** = to find a loophole in the law **(b)** *(fuga)* escape

escasear *vi* to be in short supply; **las piezas de repuesto escasean a causa de la huelga** = spare parts are in short supply because of the strike

escasez *nf (carencia)* lack

escaso, -sa *adj* scarce *o* in short supply

escenario *nm* scene; **el escenario del crimen** = the scene of the crime

escoger *vt* to pick *o* to select *o* to choose; **escoja el que quiera** = take your pick; **la junta escogió al director financiero para suceder al director gerente que se retiraba** = the board picked the finance director to succeed the retiring managing director; **se han escogido tres miembros de la comisión para que hablen en la Junta General Anual** = three members of the committee have been selected to speak at the AGM; **ha sido escogido como candidato de uno de los distritos electorales del norte** = he has been selected as a candidate for a Northern constituency; **la Asociación ha escogido París para su próxima reunión** = the Association has picked Paris for its next meeting

escogido, -da *adj* chosen *o* selected; **lo más escogido** = the pick of the group

escoltar *vt (proteger)* to guard

esconder *vt* to hide *o* to conceal; **el acusado tenía una pistola escondida bajo el abrigo** = the accused had a gun concealed under his coat

escondido, -da *adj* hidden; *(en secreto)* **a escondidas** = on the quiet

escondite *nm* hiding place

escribano *nm (oficial del juzgado)* court clerk

escrito -ta 1 *adj* written; **acuerdo escrito** = written agreement; **acuerdo no escrito** = unwritten agreement; **permiso escrito** *o* **autorización escrita** = written permission; **nos han dado promesa escrita de que no violarán nuestra patente** = they have given us a written undertaking that they will not infringe our patent **2** *nm* **(a)** *(documento)* document *o* text; **escrito legal** = instrument; **presentaron un escrito con un millón de firmas al Congreso, pidiendo que la ley fuera revocada** = they presented a petition with a million signatures to Parliament, asking for the law to be repealed **(b)** **por escrito** = in writing *o* express; **exponer por escrito** = to set out *o* to set forth; **poner por escrito** = to set down

escritor, -ra *n* writer; **escritor jurídico** = legal writer

escritorio *nm* desk; **objetos de escritorio** = stationery

escritura *nf* **(a)** *(título)* deed; **escritura de acuerdo** = deed of arrangement; **escritura de acuerdo entre deudor y acreedor** = deed of arrangement; **escritura de asociación** = articles of association; **escritura de cesión** = deed of assignment; **escritura de cesión de bienes** = assignment; **escritura de constitución** = articles of association *o* articles of incorporation *o* memorandum of association; **escritura de convenio** = deed of covenant; **escritura de fianza** *o* **de caución** = bail bond; **escritura de garantía** = deed of covenant; **escritura de propiedad** = title deeds *o* root of title; **escritura de sociedad** *o* **escritura de constitución de sociedad** = articles of partnership *o* deed of partnership; **escritura de transferencia de acciones** = deed of transfer; **escritura de traspaso** = deed of conveyance; **escritura de venta** = bill of sale; **escritura legal** = deed poll; **escritura legal de declaración unilateral** = deed poll; **escrituras de propiedad** = muniments; **las escrituras, los contratos y los testamentos son todos ellos documentos legales** = deeds, contracts and wills are all legal documents; **hemos depositado la escritura de propiedad de la casa en el banco** = we have deposited the deeds of the house in the bank **(b)** *(letra)* handwriting

escrutador, -ra *n* returning officer; *GB* **escrutador, -ra de la Cámara de los Comunes** = teller

escrutinio nm *(elecciones)* poll

escucha *nf* **escucha telefónica** = telephone tapping

escuchar *vt (intervenir un teléfono)* to tap

escuela *nf* college; **escuela de comercio** = commercial college; **escuela de enseñanza por correspondencia** *o* **a distancia** = correspondence college; **escuela de secretariado** = secretarial college; **escuela empresarial** *o* **de comercio** = business college *o* commercial college

esencial *adj* **(a)** *(imprescindible)* essential; *(para un niño o persona incapacitada)* necessaries **(b)** *(básico)* fundamental *o* basic *o* prime; *(pertinente)* material; **la intención criminal es uno de los elementos esenciales de un delito** = mens rea is one of the essential elements of a crime; **volver a lo esencial** = to get back to basics
◊ **esencialmente** *adv* basically

esfera *nf (ámbito)* domain

eso *pron* there-; **a eso** = thereto; **con eso** = therewith; **con respecto a eso** = in respect thereof; **de eso** = thereof; **por eso** = thereby

espacio *nm* space; **espacio para publicidad en un periódico** = advertisement panel

especial *adj* special; *(particular)* particular; **agente especial** = special agent; **brigada especial** = squad; **comisión especial** = select committee; **depósitos especiales** = special deposits; **resolución especial** = special resolution; **sesiones especiales** = special sessions; **el coche se ofrece a un precio especial** = the car is being offered at a special price; **nos ofreció condiciones especiales** = he offered us special terms

◊ **especialmente** *adv (particularmente)* in particular; **la mercancía frágil, especialmente la cristalería, precisa un embalaje especial** = goods which are easily damaged, in particular glasses, need special packing

especialidad *nf* speciality *o* specialism; *(medicamento de marca registrada)* **especialidad farmacéutica** = proprietary drug

especialista *nmf* specialist; **deberías consultar a un especialista en casos de divorcio** *o* **en divorcios** = you should go to a specialist in divorce cases *o* to a divorce specialist for advice

especializar *vi* to specialize; **esta firma de abogados está especializada en casos de divorcio** = this firm of solicitors specializes in divorce cases; **abogado especializado en casos de contratos internacionales** = QC who specializes in international contract cases
◊ **especializarse** *vr* to specialize; **especializarse en algo** = to specialize in something

especie *nf* kind; **en especie** = in kind; **pago en especie** = payment in kind

especificación *nf (descripción detallada)* specification

específicamente *adv (explícitamente)* specifically; **redactó el testamento específicamente en beneficio de sus nietos** = he drafted the will specifically to benefit his grandchildren

especificar *vt (precisar)* to specify; *(detallar)* to itemize; **el contrato especifica que la mercancía debe ser entregada en Valladolid** = the contract specifies that the goods have to be delivered to Valladolid; **especificar con detalle los motivos de una reclamación** = to specify full details of the grounds for complaint

específico, -ca *adj* specific

espécimen *nm (muestra)* specimen; **dar espécimen de firmas de una orden bancaria** = to give specimen signatures on a bank mandate

especulativo, -va *adj* speculative; **dinero especulativo** = hot money

espera *nf* wait; **a la espera** = waiting; **en espera** = in abeyance; **esta ley está en espera** = this law is in abeyance

esperanza *nf (expectativa)* expectancy *o* expectation; **esperanza de vida** = expectation of life *o* life expectancy

esperar *vt* **(a)** *(aguardar)* to await *o* to expect; **el abogado espera nuestras órdenes** = the solicitor is awaiting our instructions; **esperamos que llegue a las 10.45** = we are expecting him to arrive at 10.45; **esperan un cheque de su agente la semana que viene** = they are expecting a cheque from their agent next week; **estamos esperando la decisión del departamento de planificación** = we are awaiting the decision of the planning department; **están esperando un fallo del tribunal** = they are awaiting a decision of the court; **la casa se vendió a un precio superior al que se esperaba** = the house was sold for more than the expected price **(b)** *(contar con)* to count on *o* to hope; **espero estar de vuelta el sábado** = I hope to be back on Saturday

◊ **esperarse** *vr* to wait

espía *nmf* spy; **trabajar de espía** = to spy; **le acusaron de trabajar de espía para el enemigo** = she was accused of spying for the enemy; **trabajó muchos años de espía para el enemigo** = he spent many years as a spy for the enemy

espionaje *nm* espionage; **espionaje industrial** = industrial espionage; **le arrestaron acusado de espionaje** = he was arrested as a spy

espontáneo, -nea *adj* voluntary

esposado, -da *adj* handcuffed; **el acusado compareció ante el tribunal esposado a dos policías** = the accused appeared in court handcuffed to two policemen

esposas *nfpl* handcuffs

esposo, -sa **1** *n* *(cónyuge)* spouse **2** *nm* *(marido)* husband **3** *nf* wife; **esposa; esposa abandonada** = deserted wife; **esposa por convivencia** = common-law wife

espurio, -ria *n* *(falso)* counterfeit

esquema *nm* scheme

esquirol *nmf* blackleg

estabilidad *nf* *(firmeza)* firmness; **la estabilidad de la libra** = the firmness of the pound; **estabilidad en el trabajo** = security of employment

estable *adj* firm; *(permanente)* permanent

establecer *vt* to establish *o* to arrange; *(formular)* to lay down; *(concertar)* to enter into; *(fijar)* to set; **establecer contacto** = to contact; **establecer impuestos** = to impose tax; **la compañía ha establecido una sucursal en Australia** = the company has established a branch in Australia; **las condiciones se establecen en el documento** = the conditions are laid down in the document

◊ **establecerse** *vr* to get established; **establecerse en un negocio** = to establish oneself in business; **se ha establecido como agente de patentes** = he has set up in practice as a patent agent

establecido, -da *adj* established; **cumplir un plazo establecido** = to meet a deadline; **orden establecida por ley** = statutory instrument

establecimiento *nm* establishment; *(centro)* institution; *(edificio)* premises; **establecimiento comercial** = office premises *o* shop premises;

derecho de establecimiento = right of establishment; **gastos de establecimiento** = establishment charges; **dirige un importante establecimiento tipográfico** = he runs an important printing establishment

estación *nf* station; **el tren sale de la estación central a las 14.15** = the train leaves the Central Station at 14.15

estacionamiento *nm* car park; **infracciones por estacionamiento indebido** = parking offences

estacionar *vt* to station; **seis oficiales de policía fueron estacionados a la puerta de la sala del Tribunal** = six police officers were stationed at the door of the courtroom

estado *nm* **(a)** *(gobierno)* government *o* state *o* *(la Corona)* the Crown; **administración del Estado** = government; **contratista del Estado** = government contractor; **cuerpo de funcionarios del Estado** = civil service; **fiscal del Estado** = Crown prosecutor; **golpe de estado** = coup (d'état); **intervención del estado** = government intervention *o* intervention by the government; **patrimonio del Estado** = Crown Lands *o* Crown property; **secretario de Estado** = Secretary of State *o* Minister of State; **títulos del Estado** = gilt-edged securities *o* government securities; **para ser funcionario del Estado hay que pasar una oposición** = you have to pass an examination to get a job in the civil service *o* to get a civil service job; **el fiscal alegó que se debía aplicar la máxima pena a este caso** = the prosecutor submitted that the maximum sentence should be applied in this case; **el fiscal del Estado alegó que los acusados eran culpables de espionaje** = the Crown case *o* the case for the Crown was that the defendants were guilty of espionage; **el Sr Sala representa al Estado** = Mr Sala is appearing for the Crown **(b)** *(condición)* situation *o* condition *o* state; **estado civil** = marital status; **estado de ánimo** = state of mind; **estado de emergencia** = state of emergency; **artículo vendido en buen estado** = item sold in good condition; **¿cuál era el estado del coche cuando fue vendido?** = what was the condition of the car when it was sold?; **el estado general de la economía** = the general situation of the economy **(c)** *(balance de situación)* **estado de cuenta** *o* **de cuentas** = statement of account *o* bank statement; *(de una empresa)* the accounts of a business *o* a company's accounts; **estado financiero** = financial statement **(d)** *(encinta)* **en estado** = pregnant

estafa *nf* **(a)** *(fraude)* fraud *o* false pretences; **le condenaron por una serie de estafas a compañías aseguradoras** = he was convicted of a series of frauds against insurance companies; **obtener propiedades por estafa** = obtaining property by deception; **se hizo con la propiedad por medio de la estafa** = he got possession of the property by fraud **(b)** *(timo)* swindle *o* racket *o* con *o* confidence trick *o US* confidence game; **fue víctima de una estafa** = he was the victim of a con trick; **intentar que le pagáramos diez horas extraordinarias fue una clara estafa** = trying to get us to pay him for ten hours' overtime was just a con

> Se entiende por estafa la defraudación obtenida por engaño

estafador, -ra *n (timador)* cheat *o* swindler *o* confidence trickster *o US* confidence man; *(extorsionador)* racketeer; *(fullero)* card sharper

estafar *vt (defraudar)* to defraud; *(engañar)* to con *o* to cheat *o* to swindle; **engañar a alguien** = to take someone in; **estafaron al banco para que les prestara 250.000 ptas sin garantía** = they conned the bank into lending them 250,000 ptas with no security; **fue encarcelado por estafar dinero** = he was sent to prison for obtaining money by false pretences; **ganó 5millones estafando a pequeños comerciantes** = he made 5 million by swindling small shopkeepers; **la banda estafó al banco un millón y medio de dólares** = the gang swindled the bank out of £1.5m; **se le acusó de estafar a los clientes que venían a pedirle consejo** = she was accused of cheating clients who came to ask her for advice; **estafó 800.000 ptas a la financiera** = he conned the finance company out of 800,000 ptas

estafeta *nf* estafeta de correos = sub-post office

estamento nm *(clase)* class; *(organismo)* body; **se ha nombrado una comisión para revisar los salarios del estamento judicial** = a committee has been appointed to review judicial salaries

estampilla *nf (tampón)* stamp

estancia *nf (permanencia)* stay; **los turistas estuvieron en la ciudad únicamente durante una breve estancia** = the tourists were in town only for a short stay

estándar *adj (corriente)* standard; **carta estándar** = standard letter

estatal *adj (de propiedad pública)* state-owned; *(gubernamental)* government; **sujeto, -ta a control estatal** = state-controlled; **empresa estatal** = state enterprise; **intervención estatal** = government intervention *o* intervention by the government; **televisión estatal** *o* **sujeta a control estatal** = state-controlled television; **las normas estatales establecen que los artículos caros deben pagar derechos de aduana** = government regulations state that import duty has to be paid on expensive items; **los directores de industrias estatales son nombrados por el gobierno** *o* **los puestos de directores de industrias estatales son de libre designación** = the bosses of state industries are appointed by the government

estatutario, -ria *adj* constitutional; *(reglamentario)* statutory

estatuto *nm* **(a)** *(ley)* statute; **estatuto de autonomía** = statute of autonomy; **estatuto municipal** = bylaw *o* byelaw *o* by-law *o* bye-law **(b)** *(reglamento)* constitution; *(escritura de sociedad)* **estatutos** = articles of incorporation *o* articles of partnership; **estatutos de asociación** = articles of association *o* articles of incorporation; **es director nombrado conforme a los estatutos de la sociedad** = he is a director appointed under the articles of the company; **los estatutos de asociación de la empresa no permiten este procedimiento** = this procedure is not allowed under the articles of association of the company; **los estatutos no permiten que se pague a los directivos de la asociación** = payments to officers of the association are not allowed by the constitution; **según los estatutos de la sociedad, el presidente es elegido por un periodo de dos años** = under the society's constitution, the chairman is elected for a two-year period

> El estatuto de autonomía es la norma institucional básica que rige cada comunidad autónoma, conteniendo la denominación, organización y sede de las instituciones autonómicas así como las competencias asumidas

este *adj* this; **como testigo de este hecho** = as witness hereto; **sobre este punto** *o* **en este documento** = herein; **las partes de este acuerdo** = the parties hereto

estimación *nf* **(a)** *(valoración)* valuation *o* estimate; **estimación baja** = underestimate; **estimación de daños y perjuicios** = liquidated damages; **estimación de la base impositiva** = tax assessment; **estimación presupuestaria** = estimates of expenditure **(b)** *(opinión)* estimation *o* appreciation

estimar *vi* **(a)** *(calcular)* to estimate **(b)** *(valorar)* to rate; **estimar mucho a alguien** = to rate someone highly **(c)** *(aceptar)* to allow; **el Tribunal Supremo estimó el recurso del fiscal** = the Supreme Court allowed the appeal by the prosecution

estimativo, -va *adj* approximate; **cálculo estimativo** = quotation

estimular *vt (animar)* to encourage *o* to promote

estímulo *nm (incentivo)* inducement

estipulación *nf* stipulation; *(condición)* proviso; *(disposición)* provision

estipular *vt* to stipulate; **estipular algo** = to provide for something; **el contrato estipula que el vendedor pagará los costes legales del comprador** = the contract stipulates that the seller pays the buyer's legal costs; **ha sido estipulado en el contrato con este fin** = we have made provision to this effect; **pagos estipulados en el apéndice 6 adjunto** = payments as provided in schedule 6 attached; **la empresa no hizo efectivo el pago en la fecha estipulada** *o* **en la fecha estipulada en el contrato** = the company failed to pay on the stipulated date *o* on the date stipulated in the contract; **pagar el precio estipulado** = to pay the stipulated charges; **estipular que el contrato tenga una validez de cinco años** = to stipulate that the contract should run for five years

esto *pron* this; **a esto** *o* **de esto** = hereto

estorbar 1 *vi* to obstruct= **2** *vi* to be *o* to stand in the way

estorbo *nm* obstruction; **sin estorbo ni obstáculo** = without let or hindrance

estrado *nm* stand; **estrado de testigos** = witness box *o* witness stand

estragos *nmpl* havoc

estraperlista *nmf* profiteer

estraperlo *nm* black market

estratagema *nf* device; **una estratagema para evadir impuestos** = a device to avoid paying tax *o* a tax-saving device

estricto, -ta *(riguroso)* strict; **hacer una interpretación estricta de las normas** = to follow a strict interpretation of the rules
◊ **estrictamente** *adv* strictly; **la policía pide a todos los conductores que sigan estrictamente el nuevo código de circulación** = the police ask all drivers to follow strictly the new highway code

estropear *vt (dañar)* to harm; *(echar a perder)* to spoil; *(manipular)* to tamper with something
◊ **estropearse** *vr (averiarse)* to break down; **se ha estropeado el equipo transmisor-receptor de radio** = the two-way radio has broken down

estudiar *vt* **(a)** *(examinar)* to examine *o* to consider *o* to study; *(investigar)* to investigate; *(profundizar)* to follow up; **el gobierno estudió las propuestas del comité durante dos meses** = the government studied the committee's proposals for two months; **estamos estudiando la posibilidad de abrir una oficina en Nueva York** = we are studying the possibility of setting up an office in New York **(b)** *(educar)* to train *o (cursar estudios)* to study

estudio *nm* **(a)** *(investigación)* study *o* investigation; **el gobierno ha pedido a la comisión que prepare un estudio sobre los sistemas carcelarios de otros países** = the government has asked the commission to prepare a study of prison systems in other countries; **ha leído el estudio del gobierno sobre delincuencia urbana** = he has read the government study on inner city crime; **llevar a cabo un estudio de viabilidad de un proyecto** = to carry out a feasibility study on a project **(b)** *(lugar de trabajo)* studio; **estudios de televisión** = TV station

estupefacientes *nmp* drugs; **la brigada de estupefacientes** = the Drug Squad; **tráfico de estupefacientes** = drug trafficking

estupro *nm* child abuse *o* sexual abuse of children

etc. *abrev* etcétera etc.; **hay que pagar derechos de aduana por los artículos de lujo como coches, relojes, etc.** = the import duty is to be paid on expensive items including cars, watches, etc.

etcétera *adv* etcetera *o* and so on

ética *nf (moralidad)* morals; **ética profesional** = code of practice

etiqueta *nf (normas profesionales)* etiquette

euro 1 *nm (unidad monetaria)* euro **2** *prefijo* Euro
◊ **eurocheque** *nm* Eurocheque
◊ **eurodiputado, -da** *n* member of the European Parliament

europeo, -pea *adj* European; **el Parlamento Europeo** = the European Parliament; **el Sistema Monetario Europeo (SME)** = the European Monetary System (EMS); **la Comunidad Europea (CE)** = the European Community (EC); **Tribunal de Justicia Europeo** = European Court of Justice; **Tribunal Europeo de Derechos Humanos** = European Court of Human Rights; **Unión Europea (UE)** = the European Union (EU)

eutanasia *nf* euthanasia *o* mercy killing

evacuar *vt* **(a)** *(desalojar)* to vacate **(b)** *(realizar)* **evacuar un informe** to issue statement; **evacuar pruebas** = to adduce evidence

evadir *vt (eludir)* to evade; *(de prisión)* to escape; **evadir impuestos** = to evade tax
◊ **evadirse** *vr* to abscond

evaluación *nf (valoración)* evaluation *o* valuation; **evaluación de los daños** = measure of damages; **evaluación de rendimiento** = performance measurement *o* measurement of performance

evaluar *vt (valorar)* to evaluate *o* to appraise; **evaluar los costes** = to evaluate costs

evasión *nf* escape *o* evasion; *(fuga)* jailbreak; **evasión de capitales** = flight of capital; **evasión fiscal** = tax evasion

evasivo, -va *adj* evasive; **contestar con evasivas** = to give evasive answers

eventual *adj (provisional)* temporary *o* casual; **trabajo eventual** = temporary employment; **mano de obra eventual** = casual labour; **personal eventual** = temporary staff; **trabajador, -ra eventual** = casual labourer *o* casual worker; **trabajadores eventuales** = casual labour; **trabajo eventual** = casual work; **tiene trabajo eventual**

como archivero = he has a temporary job as a filing clerk *o* he has a job as a temporary filing clerk

eventualidad *nf (contingencia)* contingency

evidencia *nf (prueba)* evidence

evidenciar *vt (probar)* to evidence; **que evidencia la culpabilidad de alguien** = incriminating

evidente *adj* apparent; *(claro)* clear; *(flagrante)* flagrant; **encontraron en su coche pruebas evidentes de su culpabilidad** = incriminating evidence was found in his car; **no había pruebas evidentes de que estuviera en la casa a la hora del crimen** = there was no clear evidence *o* clear proof that he was in the house at the time of the murder; **la declaración del acusado es una mentira evidente** = the prisoner's statement is a patent lie
◊ **evidentemente** *adv (manifiestamente)* patently

evitación *nf* avoidance; **evitación de un acuerdo** *o* **de un contrato** = avoidance of an agreement *o* of a contract

evitar *vt* **(a)** to avoid; *(soslayar)* to get round; **¿puede aconsejarme sobre cómo podemos evitar el sistema de cuotas?** = can you advise me how we can get round the quota system?; **la empresa está tratando de evitar la quiebra** = the company is trying to avoid bankruptcy; **mi propósito es evitar pagar demasiados impuestos** = my aim is to avoid paying too much tax; **queremos evitar la competencia directa con Puig S.A.** = we want to avoid direct competition with Puig S.A. **(b)** *(prevenir)* to prevent; **hemos cambiado las cerraduras de las puertas para evitar que el anterior director gerente entre en el edificio** = we have changed the locks on the doors to prevent the former managing director from getting into the building

ex- *prefijo* ex; **ex delito** = ex delito; **ex penado** = ex convict; **reclamó la manutención a su ex-marido** = she claimed maintenance from her ex-husband

exacción *nf (de impuestos)* levy

exacto, -ta *adj* exact *o* precise *o* correct; *(riguroso)* strict; *(verdadero)* true; **compulsa** *o* **copia exacta** = true copy

exagerado, -da *adj (exorbitante)* **alquiler exagerado** = rack rent

examen *nm* **(a)** *(inspección)* examination *o* inspection; **examen general** = review; **examen judicial** = judicial review; **someter a un examen riguroso** = to vet; **se ordenó que el examen de documentos tuviera lugar siete días después de su presentación** = inspection was ordered to take place seven days after discovery **(b)** *(prueba)*

examination *o* test; **examen de viabilidad** = feasibility test; **aprobó los exámenes de derecho** = he passed his law examinations; **suspendió el examen y por eso tuvo que dejar el trabajo** = he failed his examination and so had to leave his job; **sacó la mejor nota en el examen de final de curso** = she came first in the final examination for the course

examinador, -ra *n* examiner

examinar *vt* to examine; *(comprobar)* to check; *(estudiar)* to consider; *(investigar)* to explore; *(inspeccionar)* to inspect; **examinar a fondo** = to go into; **examinar rigurosamente** = to vet; **examinar los términos de un contrato** = to consider the terms of a contract; **examinar y firmar por la mercancía** = to check and sign for goods; **volver a examinar un caso** = to retry a case; **el banco quiere examinar a fondo los detalles de los préstamos entre compañías** = the bank wants to go into the details of the inter-company loans; **la policía está examinando los papeles de la caja fuerte del director gerente** = the police are examining the papers from the managing director's safe; **el ministro ha solicitado que el proyecto del nuevo supermercado sea examinado por el ministerio** = the minister has called in the plans for the new supermarket

excarcelar *vt* to set free *o* to release from prison; **el Fiscal General solicitó al Tribunal Constitucional que encarcelara al ex-senador** = the Attorney General asked the Constitutional Court to release the former senator from prison

excedencia *nf* leave of absence

excedente *nm* **(a)** *(de capital)* excess *o* surplus; **tiene que pagar un excedente de 10.000 ptas y los daños ascendieron a más de 200.000** = he has to pay a 10,000 ptas excess, and the damage amounted to over 200,000 **(b)** *(de personal)* redundant; **excedente de plantilla** = redundancy

exceder *vt (sobrepasar)* to exceed
◊ **excederse** *vr* to exceed; **excederse en sus funciones** = to exceed one's powers; **el juez se excedió en sus funciones al criticar al tribunal de apelación** = the judge exceeded his powers in criticizing the court of appeal

excelente *adj* excellent *o* first-class; **es un contable excelente** = he is a first-class accountant

excepción *nf* **(a)** *(proviso)* exception; **excepción dilatoria** = dilatory plea; **excepción perentoria** = demurrer; **cláusula de excepción** = escape clause *o* let-out clause; **con excepción de** = except; **se incluye el IVA en todos los artículos y servicios, con excepción de libros, periódicos y ropa infantil** = VAT is levied on all goods and services except books, newspapers and children's clothes; **añadió una cláusula de excepción al efecto de**

que los pagos se revisarían si el tipo de cambio bajaba más de un 5% = he added a let-out clause to the effect that the payments would be revised if the exchange rate fell by more than 5% **(b)** *(renuncia)* waiver; **si quiere trabajar sin permiso, tendrá que solicitar una excepción** = if you want to work without a permit, you will have to apply for a waiver **(c)** *(emergencia)* **estado de excepción** = state of emergency; **el gobierno declaró el estado de excepción** = the government declared a state of emergency

excepcional *adj (extraordinario)* exceptional; **registros** *o* **partidas excepcionales** = exceptional items

excepto *adv (con excepción de)* except *o* with the exception of *o* excluding *o* excepted; **la norma se aplica en todos los casos excepto en donde se indique lo contrario** = the rule applies in all cases, except where otherwise stated; **las ventas están aumentando en todos los mercados excepto en el Extremo Oriente** = sales are rising in all markets except the Far East; **todos los acusados fueron absueltos excepto uno que fue condenado a tres meses de arresto** = all the accused were acquitted with one exception who was sent to prison for three months

exceptuando *adv (salvo)* **exceptuando a** = excluding *o* except; **las reglas se aplican a los miembros del público, exceptuando a aquéllos que están en los servicios de emergencia** = the regulations apply to members of the public, excluding those serving in the emergency services

excesivo, -va *adj* excessive; *(innecesario)* redundant; **realización de ganancias** *o* **beneficios excesivos** = profiteering; **el conductor tenía una cantidad excesiva de alcohol en la sangre** = the driver had an excessive amount of alcohol in his blood; **encontramos la relación de gastos excesiva y pedimos un descuento** = we found the bill for costs excessive and applied to have it reduced

exceso *nm* excess; **exceso de alcohol en la sangre** = excess alcohol in the blood; **exceso de contratación** = overbooking; **exceso de jurisdicción** = excess of jurisdiction; **exceso de velocidad** = speeding; **en exceso** = in excess

excluido, -da *adj* excepted

excluir *vt (no admitir)* to exclude *o* to preclude; **sin excluir** = not excluding; **excluir a alguien de la lista de abogados** = to strike someone off the rolls; **este acuerdo no excluye un acuerdo entre las partes en el futuro** = this agreement does not preclude a further agreement between the parties in the future

exclusión *nf* exclusion; **cláusula de exclusión** = exclusion clause; **con exclusión de** = to the exclusion of *o* excluding

exclusiva *nf (exclusividad)* exclusivity; **contrato en exclusiva** = exclusive agreement; **licencia en exclusiva** = exclusive licence

exclusividad *nf* exclusivity; **firmaron un acuerdo de exclusividad con una empresa americana** = they signed a closed market agreement with an American company

exclusivo, -va *adj* closed; *(único)* sole; **comerciante exclusivo** = sole trader; **concesión** *o* **agencia exclusiva** = concession; **derechos exclusivos de venta de un producto** = exclusive right to market a product

excluyendo *adv (sin tener en cuenta)* exclusive of

exculpación *nf* acquittal

exculpar *vt* to acquit

excusa *nf* excuse *o* apology; **¿qué excusa dio por llegar tarde a la audiencia?** = what was his excuse for arriving late in court?; **el juez se negó a aceptar** *o* **rechazó la excusa del acusado** = the judge refused to accept the defendant's excuse; **presentar excusas** = to apologize; **adjunto un cheque por 10 libras y le presento mis excusas por el retraso en contestar a su carta** = I enclose a cheque for £10 with apologies for the delay in answering your letter; **presentó sus excusas ante el tribunal por la ausencia del principal testigo** = he apologized to the court for the absence of the chief witness

exención *nf* exemption; **cláusula de exención** = exemption clause; **exención arancelaria** = exemption from customs; **exención fiscal** *o* **tributaria** = exemption from tax *o* tax exemption *o* allowance; **exención del servicio militar** = discharge; **como organización no lucrativa, puedes reclamar exención fiscal** = as a non profit-making organization you can claim tax exemption

exento, -ta *adj* exempt *o* free; **exento, -ta de impuestos** = exempt from tax *o* tax-exempt *o* free of tax *o* tax-free; **exento de derechos de aduana** = free of duty *o* duty-free; **'exentos de poder** *o* **jurisdicción'** = functus officio; **artículos exentos del pago del IVA** *o* **suministros exentos del IVA** = exempt supplies; **el secretario del juzgado afirmó que los jueces estaban exentos de jurisdicción** = the justices' clerk asserted that the justices were functi officio; **las organizaciones no lucrativas están exentas de impuestos** = non profit-making organizations are exempt(ed) from tax; **los alimentos están exentos del impuesto sobre las ventas** = food is exempt(ed) from sales tax

exhibición *nf* exhibition; **exhibición de documentos entre las partes antes del comienzo de la vista (de un proceso civil)** = discovery

exhibicionismo *nm* indecent exposure

exhibir *vt* to exhibit *o* to display; **todos los vehículos deben exhibir un permiso de aparcamiento vigente** = all cars must display a valid parking permit

exhortar *vt* to exhort

exhorto *nm* rogatory letter

exhumación *nf* disinterment

exhumar *vt* to exhume

exigencia *nf* demand *o* requirement; **exigencia bajo amenazas** = demanding with menaces

exigible *adj* due *o* enforceable; **activo exigible** = accounts receivable

exigir *vt* (a) *(reclamar)* to claim; **exigió a su compañía de seguros el pago de las reparaciones del coche** = she claimed for repairs to the car against her insurance; **exigió 100.000 ptas por daños y perjuicios a la empresa de limpieza** = she claimed 100,000 ptas damages against the cleaning firm (b) *(requerir)* to require *o* to demand; **exigir el pago de una deuda** = to call in *o* to enforce a debt; **exigir garantía** = to demand security; **exigir una aclaración total de los gastos** = to require a full explanation of expenditure; **el proyecto de ley exige que los asistentes sociales busquen permiso del tribunal de menores antes de entrar en acción** = the Bill requires social workers to seek the permission of the juvenile court before taking action; **la ley exige declarar todos los ingresos a las autoridades fiscales** = the law requires you to submit all income to the tax authorities (c) *(imponer)* to levy

exilar *vt* to exile

exiliado, -da *n* exile

exiliar *vt* to exile; **le exiliaron de por vida** = he was exiled for life

exilio *nm* exile; **los diez miembros del partido de la oposición fueron enviados al exilio** = the ten members of the opposition party were sent into exile

eximente *nm* defence; **eximente de necesidad** = defence of necessity; **eximente especial** = special defence; **circunstancia eximente por tener las facultades disminuidas** = diminished responsibility

eximir *vt* to exempt; *(renunciar)* to waive; **eximir de** = to excuse; **eximir de un pago** = to waive a payment; **el gobierno eximió de impuestos a los fideicomisos** = the government exempted trusts from tax

existencia *nf* existence

existencias *nfpl* stock; **existencias al cierre de un periodo contable** = closing stock; **existencias al comienzo de un periodo contable** = opening stock; **control de existencias** = stock control; *(en almacén)* **en existencia** = in stock; **tener existencias** = to stock; **valoración** *o* **tasación de existencias** = stock valuation; **comprar una tienda con las existencias según valoración** = to buy a shop with stock at valuation

existir *vi* to exist; **empezar a existir** = to come into existence; **mientras exista el acuerdo** = during the life of the agreement; **el derecho de paso ha existido desde comienzos del siglo XIX** = the right of way has existed since the early nineteenth century

éxito *nm* success; **sin éxito** = unsuccessful

exoneración *nf* (a) *(de una obligación)* exoneration; **exoneración parcial concedida a una nueva empresa** = tax holiday (b) *(absolución)* release *o* discharge

exonerar de *vt* to exonerate; **el juez exoneró al conductor de toda responsabilidad por el accidente** = the judge exonerated the driver from all responsibility for the accident

exorbitante *adj* extortionate; **alquiler exorbitante** = rack rent; **respondió a nuestra carta con peticiones exorbitantes de dinero** = his answer to our letter consisted of a number of unreasonable demands for money

expansión *nf* *(desarrollo)* development; **expansión industrial** = industrial development

expatriación *nf* expatriation

expatriado, -da *n* expatriate; **hay una gran comunidad de expatriados en Génova** = there is a large expatriate community *o* a large community of expatriates in Genoa

expatriar *vt* to expatriate

expectación *nf* expectation *o* expectancy

expectativa *nf* expectancy *o* expectation; **expectativa de vida** = expectation of life *o* life expectancy

expedición *nf* (a) delivery; *(envío)* shipping; **aviso de expedición** = advice note; **orden de expedición** = delivery order; **las escrituras surten efecto únicamente desde el momento de la expedición** = deeds take effect only from the time of delivery (b) *(consignación)* consignment; **estamos esperando una expedición de coches de Japón** = we are expecting a consignment of cars from Japan (c) *(emisión)* issuance; **tras la expedición del mandato, los alguaciles embargaron la propiedad** = upon issuance of the order, the bailiffs seized the property

expedidor, -ra *n (transportista)* shipper

expediente *nm* **(a)** *(recurso)* proceedings; **expediente administrativo** = administrative enquiry; **expediente de apremio** = collection proceedings; **expediente disciplinario** = disciplinary action; **abrir un expediente** = to start proceedings *o* to take disciplinary action **(b)** *(informe)* brief **(c)** *(hoja de servicios)* **expediente profesional** = record *o* file

expedir *vt* **(a)** *(enviar)* to ship; **expedir algo a alguien** = to forward something to someone **(b)** *(poner en circulación)* to issue; **expedir una carta de crédito** = to issue a letter of credit

experiencia *nf* **(a)** *(conocimiento, práctica)* experience *o* background; **adquirió la mayor parte de su experiencia jurídica en el Extremo Oriente** = he gained most of his legal experience in the Far East; **es un abogado con mucha experiencia** = he is a lawyer of considerable experience; **tiene diez años de experiencia** = he is ten years' call; **tiene mucha experiencia en casos de divorcio** = she has a lot of experience of dealing with divorce cases **(b)** *(vivencia)* experience; **el accidente fue una experiencia horrible para ella** = the accident was a terrible experience for her **(c)** *(historial)* track record; **la empresa no tiene experiencia en el mercado de la informática** = the company has no track record in the computer market

experimentado, -da *adj* experienced

experimentar *vt* to experience

experto, -ta 1 *adj* experienced; **es el negociador más experto que conozco** = he is the most experienced negotiator I know **2** *n* expert *o* professional; **hemos nombrado directora de ventas a una gran experta** = we have appointed a very experienced woman as sales director; **experto en derecho** *o* **experto jurídico** = legal expert; **experto tributario** = tax expert; **la compañía pidió consejo a un experto en finanzas** = the company asked a financial expert for advice *o* asked for expert financial advice; **un experto en huellas dactilares** = an expert in the field of fingerprints *o* a fingerprints expert

expiar *vt* to purge; **expiar una acción de desacato a los tribunales** = to purge one's contempt *o* to purge a contempt of court

expiración *nf (caducidad)* expiration *o* expiry; *(terminación)* termination; **expiración de una póliza de seguros** = expiration of an insurance policy

expirar *vi (caducar)* to expire; **al expirar el arriendo** = on expiration of the lease; **el arrendamiento expira en cinco años** = the lease expires in five years' time; **pagar antes de que expire el plazo establecido** = to repay before the

expiration of the stated period; **permitir que una oferta expire** = to let an offer lapse

explicación *nf (aclaración)* explanation; *(razón)* reason; **la defensa no dio explicación de sus objeciones al jurado** = the defence gave no reason for their objections to the juror; **no supo dar explicación de cómo las drogas habían llegado a su maleta** = he could give no explanation of how the drugs came to be in his suitcase

explicar *vi* to explain; **¿puede explicar al jurado cómo es que estaba usted en la casa el jueves 13 de julio?** = can you explain to the jury how you came to be in the house on Thursday 13th July?; **explicó a los oficiales de aduanas que los dos ordenadores eran regalos de amigos** = he explained to the customs officials that the two computers were presents from friends

explicativo, -va *adj (aclaratorio)* explanatory

explicatorio, -ria *adj* explanatory; **carta explicatoria** = covering letter *o* covering note

explícito, -ta *adj* explicit; *(expreso)* express; **término explícito (de un contrato)** = express term; **su intención explícita era dejar la casa a su mujer** = his explicit intention was to leave his house to his wife
◊ **explícitamente** *adv* explicitly; *(específicamente)* specifically; *(expresamente)* expressly; **el contrato excluye explícitamente a los Estados Unidos** = the contract specifically excludes the USA; **el contrato prohíbe explícitamente la venta de productos en Europa** = the contract explicitly prohibits sale of the goods in Europe

explorar *vt (investigar)* to explore

exploratorio, -ria *adj* exploratory; **moción exploratoria** = early day motion

explosivo *nm* explosive; **el coche estaba lleno de explosivos** = the car was full of explosives; **un artefacto explosivo** = an explosive device

explotación *nf* exploitation; *(con abuso)* abuse; **gastos de explotación** = business expenses; **resultado de la explotación** *o* **beneficio de explotación** = trading profit

explotar *vt* to exploit

expoliar *vt* to loot *o* to pillage

expolio *nm* pillage

exponer *vt* **(a)** *(mostrar)* to expose *o* to exhibit *o* to display **(b)** *(comunicar por escrito)* to set out *o* to set forth; **el argumento está expuesto en el documento del Tribunal Europeo** = the argument is set forth in the document from the European Court; **la demanda está expuesta en el documento adjunto** = the claim is set out in the enclosed document; **las cifras están expuestas en las tablas**

de la parte posterior del libro = the figures are set out in the tables at the back of the book **(c)** *(arriesgar)* to risk; **un acto así le expone a una multa** *o* **tal acto le expone a pagar una multa** = such an act renders him liable to a fine

◊ **exponerse** *vr (arriesgarse)* to run a risk

exportación *nf* export; **licencia de exportación** = export licence

exportar *vt* to export; **la mayoría de los productos de la compañía se exportan a los EE UU** = most of the company's products are exported to the USA

exposición *nf* **(a)** *(feria)* show **(b)** *(en un juicio)* exposición de la demanda = statement of claims; exposición de motivos = stated purpose; exposición oral = delivery

expresamente *adv (explícitamente)* expressly

expresar *vt* to express; *(redactar)* to word; **este gráfico muestra el crimen en Bilbao expresado como porcentaje del crimen total del País Vasco** = this chart shows crime in Bilbao expressed as a percentage of total crime in the Basque Country

expresión *nf* expression; **expresión jurídica** = legal expression; **libertad de expresión** = freedom of speech

expreso, -sa *adj (explícito)* express; **término expreso** = express term; **el contrato tiene una prohibición expresa que prohibe la venta en Africa** = the contract has an express condition forbidding sale in Africa

expropiación *nf* expropriation *o* condemnation; **expropiación forzosa** = compulsory purchase; **orden de expropiación** = compulsory purchase order; **juicio de expropiación forzosa** = condemnation proceeding
◊ **expropiado, -da** *n* condemnee
◊ **expropiador, -ra** *n* condemnor *o* expropriator
◊ **expropiar** *vt* to expropriate

expuesto, -ta *adj* on display; **expuesto a** = liable to

expulsar *vt (deportar)* to deport; *(desalojar)* to evict; *(desahuciar)* to eject; **expulsar del Colegio de Abogados** = to disbar

expulsión *nf (deportación)* deportation; *(desahucio)* ejection; **orden de expulsión** = deportation order

extender *vt* **(a)** *(ampliar, prolongar)* to extend *o* to expand **(b)** *(escribir)* **extender un cheque** = to draw a cheque; **extender un cheque a alguien** = to make out a cheque to someone; **extender un cheque bancario** = to draw a cheque on a bank

extensión *nf* **(a)** *(amplitud)* extent; **están evaluando la extensión de los daños tras el incendio** = they are assessing the extent of the

damage after the fire **(b)** *(prolongación)* extension; **extensión telefónica** = telephone extension; **¿me puede poner con la extensión 21? - la extensión 21 está comunicando** = can you get me extension 21? - extension 21 is engaged; **el departamento jurídico está en la extensión 53** = the legal department is on extension 53

extensivo, -iva *adj* extensive

extenso, -sa *adj* extensive; **el juzgado tiene que hacerse cargo de una extensa lista de casos** = the court has to deal with a full list of cases; **posee un extenso conocimiento en materia de drogas** = he has an extensive knowledge of drugs

exterior *adj* exterior *o* external; **comercio exterior** = foreign trade; **inversiones exteriores** = foreign investments; **Ministerio de Asuntos Exteriores** = Foreign (and Commonwealth) Office; **Ministro de Asuntos Exteriores** = Foreign Secretary

extinción *nf* **(a)** *(anulación)* extinction *o* extinguishment; **extinción de un contrato** = discharge; **la extinción de un derecho jurídico** = the extinction of a legal right **(b)** *(terminación)* termination

extinguir *vt* to extinguish; *(incendio)* to put out; **extinguir una hipoteca** = to clear a mortgage

extirpar *vt (suprimir)* to excise

extorsión *nf* extortion; **negocio sucio dedicado a la extorsión** = extortion racket

extorsionador, -ra *nmf; (chantajista)* racketeer

extorsionar *vt (sacar por la fuerza)* to extort; **extorsionó 200.000 ptas a los comerciantes locales** = he extorted 200,000 ptas from local shopkeepers

extra 1 *adj* extra; **horas extras** = overtime **2** *nm (adicional)* extra **3** *prefijo* extra-

extracontractual *adj* outside the contract

extracto *nm* extract *o* abstract; **extracto de cuenta** = bank statement; **extracto de los debates** = charge; **extracto de título** = abstract of title; **el abogado envió un extracto de las escrituras** = the solicitor sent an extract of the deeds

extradición *nf* extradition; **tratado de extradición** = extradition treaty; **los EE UU pidieron la extradición del dirigente de la banda de narcotraficantes** = the USA requested the extradition of the leader of the drug gang

extraditar *vt* to extradite; **le detuvieron en Francia y le extraditaron para ser juzgado en Alemania** = he was arrested in France and extradited to stand trial in Germany

extrajudicialmente *adv* out of court; **las dos partes llegaron a un arreglo extrajudicialmente** = a settlement was reached out of court *o* the two parties reached an out-of-court settlement

extranjero, -ra **1** *adj* foreign; **inversiones extranjeras** = foreign investments; **moneda extranjera** = foreign currency *o* foreign exchange; **productos extranjeros** = foreign goods; **estamos incrementando el comercio con países extranjeros** = we are increasing our trade with foreign countries; **los coches extranjeros han inundado nuestro mercado** = foreign cars have flooded our market **2** *nm* abroad; **en el extranjero** = overseas **3** *n* foreigner *o* alien

extraoficial *adj (no oficial)* unofficial

◊ **extraoficialmente** *adv; (oficiosamente)* unofficially *o* off the record; **oficialmente no sabe nada acerca del problema, pero extraoficialmente nos ha dado buenos consejos** = officially he knows nothing about the problem, but unofficially he has given us a lot of advice about it; **hizo algunos comentarios extraoficialmente sobre el aumento de la criminalidad** = he made some remarks off the record about the rising crime figures; **la delegación de Hacienda le dijo extraoficialmente a la compañía que sería procesada** = the tax office told the company, unofficially, that it would be prosecuted

extraordinario, ria *adj* extraordinary; **beneficios extraordinarios** = excess profits; **gastos** *o* **partidas extraordinarias** = extraordinary items; **negarse a hacer horas extraordinarias** = to work to rule; **Junta General Extraordinaria** = Extraordinary General Meeting (EGM); **partidas extraordinarias** = extraordinary items *o* non-recurring items; **los auditores observaron varias partidas extraordinarias en las cuentas** = the auditors noted several extraordinary items in the accounts

extrarradio *nm* **vive en el extrarradio de la ciudad** = he lives in the commuter belt

extraterritorialidad *nf* extraterritoriality

extrínseco, -ca *adj* extrinsic; **prueba extrínseca** = extrinsic evidence

Ff

fábrica *nf* factory *o (taller)* shop; **precio de fábrica** = price ex works *o* ex factory

facción *nf* **(a)** *(banda)* faction

faccioso, -sa *n (alborotador)* troublemaker *o* seditious person

fácil *adj* easy; **fácil de manejar** *o* **de fácil manejo** *o* **fácil para el usuario** = user-friendly; **escoger el camino más fácil** = to take the soft option
◊ **fácilmente** *adv; (sin problemas)* easily; **la moción fue aprobada por el Congreso fácilmente** = the motion was passed by the Congress easily

facilidad *nf* facility; **facilidades de crédito** = credit facilities; **facilidades de pago** = easy terms

facilitar *vt* **(a)** *(proporcionar)* to furnish *o* to provide; **facilitar información** = to provide information **(b)** *(hacer más fácil)* to facilitate

facineroso, -sa *adj y n* criminal

facsímil *nm* facsimile (copy)

factible *adj* feasible

fáctico *adj* real; **fundamentos fácticos** = particulars of claim; **poderes fácticos** = de facto powers

factor *nm (elemento)* factor; **factores cíclicos** = cyclical factors; **factor contribuyente** = contributory factor; **factor decisivo** = deciding factor; **factores de producción** = factors of production; **el aumento del paro es un factor importante en el aumento del índice de criminalidad** = the rise in unemployment is an important factor in the increased crime rate

factura *nf* bill *o* invoice *o* note of costs; **factura conforme** = receipt in due form; **factura proforma** = pro forma invoice; **presentar** *o* **enviar una factura** = to bill; **le ruego me envíe la factura** = please send me your invoice; **¿lleva la factura el IVA incluido?** = does the bill include VAT?; **el constructor mandó la factura** = the builder sent in his bill; **el contratista le envió una factura por las reparaciones en la casa de su vecino** = the builders billed him for the repairs to his neighbour's house; **el vendedor extendió la factura** = the salesman wrote out the bill; **la factura se ha extendido a nombre de Smith Ltd** = the bill is made out to Smith Ltd

facturación *nf (volumen de ventas)* turnover

facturar *vt* to bill *o* to invoice

facultad *nf* **(a)** *(capacidad)* faculty *o* capacity; *(autoridad)* power; **facultad legislativa** = legislative power *o* capacity; **facultad procesal** = legal capacity to sue; **facultad que permite nombrar a un beneficiario para disponer de una propiedad** = power of appointment; **facultad que permite a la demanda elegir sus recursos** = power of election; **las facultades de una autoridad local en relación a la custodia de menores** = the powers of a local authority in relation to children in care **(b)** *(universidad)* faculty; **facultad de derecho** = Faculty of Law *o* law school

facultar *vt (autorizar)* to empower

facultativo, -va *adj* **(a)** *(optativo)* optional **(b)** *(profesional)* professional

falacia *nf* deceit *o* fraud

falaz *adj* fallacious *o* deceitful

fallar *vi* **(a)** *(fracasar)* to fail **(b)** *(pronunciarse)* to rule; **fallar a favor** *o* **en contra** = to find for *o* to rule against; **el juez falló a favor del acusado** = the judge found for the defendant

fallecido, -da *adj (muerto)* dead *o* deceased

fallecimiento *nm* death; *(defunción)* decease *o* demise; **indemnización por fallecimiento** = death benefit; **indemnización** *o* **subsidio por fallecimiento de un trabajador durante su trabajo en una empresa** = death in service; **legado anulado por fallecimiento del legatario** = lapsed legacy

fallo *nm* **(a)** *(decisión)* decision *o* rule *o* ruling; **fallo que establece un importante precedente** = landmark decision; **el fallo del Tribunal Supremo es irrevocable** = the decision of the Supreme Court is final; **según el fallo del tribunal, el contrato era ilegal** = according to the ruling of the court, the contract was illegal **(b)** *(sentencia)* judgment *o* judgement *o* findings *o (de un tribunal de lo social)* award; **fallo arbitral** = arbitration award; **fallo condenatorio** = conviction; **fallo del jurado** =

verdict; **fallo por falta de comparecencia** = judgment by default *o* default judgment; **declarar** *o* **emitir un fallo jurídico** = to find **(c)** *(incumplimiento)* failure **(d)** *(defecto)* defect

falseado, -da *adj (erróneo)* false; **contabilidad falseada** = false accounting

falseamiento *nm* misrepresentation; **falseamiento con ánimo de fraude** = fraudulent misrepresentation; **falseamiento de contabilidad** *o* **de auditoría** = false accounting

falsear *vt (falsificar)* to forge *o* to fiddle; *(deformar los hechos)* to misrepresent; **falsear el estado de cuentas de una empresa** = to manipulate the accounts; **falsear las pruebas con la intención de implicar a alguien en un crimen** = to plant evidence

falsedad *nf (mentira)* falsehood; *(en documento)* forgery *o* misrepresentation

falsificación *nf* **(a)** *(acto de falsear)* falsification *o* counterfeiting *o* forgery; **falsificación de cuentas** = falsification of accounts; **falsificación de pruebas** = fabrication of evidence; **falsificación y utilización de documentación falsa** = forgery and uttering; **le enviaron a la cárcel acusado de falsificación** = he was sent to prison for forgery **(b)** *(objeto falso)* fake

falsificado, -da *adj* counterfeit

falsificar *vt (falsear)* to falsify *o* to fiddle; *(moneda)* to counterfeit; *(firma)* to forge *o* to fake; **falsificar cuentas** = to falsify accounts; **falsificar pruebas** = to tamper with the evidence; **la policía fue acusada de falsificar las pruebas** = the police were accused of tampering with the evidence; **se probó que la firma era falsificada** = the signature was proved to be a forgery

falso, -sa *adj* **(a)** *(falsificado)* counterfeit; **documento** *o* **billete falso** *o* **moneda falsa** = forgery; **hacer una entrada falsa en el registro** = to make a false entry in the record; **el billete de 10.000 ptas era falso** = the 10,000 ptas note was a dud; **quiso pagar la cuenta con un billete falso** = she wanted to pay the bill with a forged note; **se le acusó de poner billetes falsos en circulación en tiendas** = he was charged with passing counterfeit notes in shops; **trató de entrar en el país con documentación falsa** = he tried to enter the country with forged documents; **el envío llegó con documentación falsa** = the shipment came with fake documentation **(b)** *(erróneo)* false *o* untrue; **falso testimonio** = perjury; **declaración falsa** = false representation; **prestar falso testimonio** *o* **jurar en falso** = to perjure yourself; **realizó una declaración falsa en el juzgado** = he made an untrue statement in court **(c)** *(peso trucado)* **peso falso** = false weight

falta *nf* **(a)** *(carencia)* absence *o* lack; **falta de fondos** = lack of funds; **falta de información** = lack of data *o* lack of information; **falta de respeto** = disrespect; **falta de pago** = default; **a falta de** = in the absence of; **por falta de** = by default; **por falta de pago** = in default of payment; **negarse a pagar** *o* **aceptar por falta de fondos** = to dishonour; **citación judicial** *o* **demanda judicial por falta de pago** = default summons *o* default action; **juicio por falta de comparecencia** = judgment by default *o* default judgment; **no se pueden formular acusaciones por falta de pruebas** = charges cannot be brought for lack of evidence; **el proyecto fue suspendido por falta de fondos** = the project was cancelled because of lack of funds; **la decisión ha sido aplazada por falta de información actualizada** = the decision has been put back for lack of up-to-date information; **la investigación ha sido suspendida por falta de información** = the investigation has been held up by lack of information **(b)** *(delito menor)* fault *o* misdemeanour; **falta de ética** = misconduct; **falta grave** = gross misconduct; **falta leve** = petty offence **(c)** *(infracción)* breach; **se acusó al soldado de haber cometido una falta grave de disciplina** = the soldier was charged with a serious breach of discipline **(d)** *(error)* mistake

faltar *vi* **(a)** to fail *o* *(incumplir un pago)* to default; *(incumplir un juramento)* to break; **faltar a la palabra** = to go back on one's word; **faltar al juramento** = to break one's word; **faltó a su promesa de no ver a la chica** = he went back on his promise not to see the girl **(b)** *(ofender)* to offend; **faltar al respeto** = to be disrespectful; **le acusaron de faltar al respeto al juez** = he was accused of showing disrespect to the judge **(c)** *(carecer de)* **faltarle a uno** = to lack

fama *nf (reputación)* reputation; **tiene fama de ser una persona con la que es difícil negociar** = he has a reputation for being difficult to negotiate with

familia *nf* **(a)** family; *(casa)* household; *(parientes)* kin; **familia y amigos íntimos** = extended family; **derecho de familia** = family law; **reliquia** *o* **joya de familia** = heirloom; **los ladrones robaron algunas joyas de familia** = the burglars stole some family heirlooms; **el acusado procede de buena familia** = the accused is from a good background **(b)** *(Mafia)* **la familia** = the family ◊ **familiar 1** *adj (de la familia)* family *o* familiar; **empresa familiar** family company; **proceso familiar** = domestic proceedings; **reliquia** *o* **joya familiar** = heirloom **2** *nmf; (pariente)* relative; **familiar dependiente** = dependent; **se autoriza la desgravación de impuestos por tener familiares a cargo** = tax relief is allowed for dependent relatives

fatal *adj* **(a)** *(mortal)* fatal **(b)** *(crónico)* chronic

favor *nm* **(a)** *(ayuda, servicio)* favour *o* US favor; 'como favor' = ex gratia; **como favor** *o* **como un favor especial** = as a favour; **le pidió a la secretaria un préstamo como favor especial** = he asked the secretary for a loan as a favour **(b)** *(apoyo)* **a favor de** = in favour of; **estar a favor de** = to favour *o* US to favor; **la mayoría de los trabajadores está a favor de una jornada laboral más corta** = most of the workers are in favour of shorter working hours; **los jueces están a favor de las sentencias disuasorias para los gamberros** = judges favour deterrent sentences for hooligans; **seis miembros del gabinete están a favor de la propuesta y tres en contra** = six members of the cabinet are in favour of the proposal, and three are against it **(c)** *(a cargo propio)* accommodation; **pagaré de favor** = accommodation bill; **saldo a favor** = credit balance; **saldo a nuestro favor** = balance due to us

favorable *adj* favourable *o* in favour; **cerrar un trato en condiciones favorables para uno** = to drive *o* to strike a hard bargain; **comprar algo en condiciones favorables** = to buy on favourable terms

favorecer *vt* to favour; **(juez o miembro del jurado) que favorece a una de las partes en un juicio** = biased

favorecido, -da *adj* favoured; **nación más favorecida** = most-favoured nation; **cláusula de nación más favorecida** = most-favoured-nation clause

favorito, -ta *adj* **(a)** *(preferido)* favourite **(b)** *(bolsa)* **acción favorita** = leader; **las acciones favoritas subieron en la Bolsa** = leading shares rose on the Stock Exchange

fe *nf* **(a)** *(confianza)* faith; **buena fe** = good faith; **de buena fe** *o* **de mala fe** = in good faith *o* in bad faith; 'de total buena fe' = uberrimae fidei; **un contrato de seguros es de total buena fe** = an insurance contract is uberrimae fidei; **actuó de buena fe** *o* **de mala fe** he acted in good faith *o* in bad faith; **comprar algo de buena fe** = to buy something in good faith; **compró el coche de buena fe, sin saber que había sido robado** = he bought the car in good faith, not knowing that it had been stolen; **tener fe en algo** *o* **en alguien** = to have faith in something *o* someone **(b)** *(certificado)* **fe de óbito** = death certificate; **fe de vida** = official proof that a person is living; **fe pública** = notary's attestation **(c)** *(testimoniar)* **dar fe de** = to witness; **en fe de lo cual** = in witness whereof

fecha *nf* date; **fecha límite** = deadline; **fecha de caducidad** *o* **vencimiento** = expiry date; **fecha de entrada en vigor (de una ley parlamentaria)** = date of commencement; **fecha de finalización** *o* **de cumplimiento** = completion date; **fecha de presentación** = date of filing; **fecha de recepción** *o*

de registro = date of receipt *o* of record; **fecha de vencimiento** = due date; **fecha de vencimiento de pago** = final date for payment; **con fecha** = dated; **con fecha futura** = postdated; **con la misma fecha de cierre** = coterminous; **en fecha próxima** = at an early date; **hasta la fecha** = to date; **intereses hasta la fecha** = interest to date; **el cheque tenía fecha del 24 de marzo** = the cheque was dated March 24th; **la carta del asesino tenía fecha del 15 de junio** = the murderer's letter was dated June 15th; **nos mandó un cheque con una fecha futura** = he sent us a postdated cheque; **su cheque llevaba fecha del próximo mes de junio** = his cheque was postdated to June

fechador *nm* date stamp

fechar *vt* to date; **olvidó fechar el cheque** = he forgot to date the cheque; **se fechó la factura con efecto retroactivo al 1 de enero** = the invoice was antedated to January 1st

fedatario *nm* commissioner for oaths

federación *nf* federation

federal *adj* federal; **Oficina Federal de Investigación (FBI)** = Federal Bureau of Investigation (FBI); **tribunal federal** *o* **leyes federales** = federal court *o* federal laws

federalismo *nm* federalism

fehaciente *adj* *(testimonio)* reliable *o* authentic

feria *nf* **(a)** *(exposición)* fair *o* show; **feria comercial** = trade fair **(b)** *(descanso)* **feria judicial** = judicial vacation

festivo, -va *adj* **día festivo** = bank holiday; **el Lunes de Pascua es día festivo** = Easter Monday is a bank holiday

fiabilidad *nf* reliability; **el tribunal tiene que decidir sobre la fiabilidad de los testigos** = the court has to decide on the reliability of the witnesses

fiable *adj* reliable

fiador, -ra *n* *(garante)* guarantor *o* warrantor *o* bondsman *o* cautioner *o* surety; **fiador judicial** = person who stands bail; **fiador en bancarrota** = bankruptcy surety; **salir fiador de alguien** = to stand surety for someone *o* to bail someone out

fianza *nf* **(a)** *(garantía)* security *o* guarantee *o* surety *o* bond; **fianza de administración** = administration bond; **fianza de aduana** = customs bond; **fianza de pago** = payment bond; **sin fianza** = unsecured; **dejar títulos de acciones como fianza** *o* **garantía** = to leave share certificates as a guarantee; **el banco le prestó 2 millones sin fianza** = the bank lent him 2 million without security **(b)** *(carcelaria)* bail *o* bond; **fianza confiscada** = estreated recognizance; **fianza de comparecencia** = bail bond; **fianza policial** = police bail; **bajo**

fianza o con fianza = on bail; depositario, -ria de fianza = bailee; escritura de fianza = bail bond; depositar una fianza de 500.000 ptas por alguien = to stand bail of 500,000 ptas for someone; obtener la libertad de alguien bajo fianza = to bail someone out; perder la fianza (por no comparecer ante los tribunales) = to estreat; poner en libertad bajo fianza = to remand; quebrantar la libertad bajo fianza o huir estando bajo fianza = to jump bail; la policía se opuso a la libertad bajo fianza pretextando que el acusado podría intentar salir del país = the police opposed bail on the grounds that the accused might try to leave the country; pagó 3 millones por su fianza = she paid 3 million to bail him out; se le concedió la libertad bajo fianza de 100.000 ptas = he was granted bail on his own recognizance of 100,000 ptas; se le liberó bajo fianza de 2 millones = he was remanded on bail of 2 million

fiar vt (a) (garantizar) to bail o to bond (b) (confiar) to rely; de fiar = reliable o trustworthy; que no es de fiar = unreliable; la acusación trató de demostrar que la declaración del conductor no era de fiar = the prosecution tried to show that the driver's evidence was unreliable; la defensa llamó a dos testigos y ninguno era de fiar = the defence called two witnesses and both were unreliable
◊ fiarse vr (tener confianza) to rely on o to trust; fiarse de = to have faith in something o someone; nos fiamos de sus afirmaciones = we took his statement on trust

fiat nm (autorización) fiat

ficción nf fiction; ficción de derecho o legal = fiction of law o legal fiction

ficha nf file o filing card o card file; ficha de ordenador = computer file; ficha policial = police file o record
◊ fichado, -da adj delincuente fichado por la policía = suspect with a police record

fichero nm (a) (ficha) card index; llevamos un fichero de clientes = we keep a card index of clients (b) (archivo informático) computer file (c) (archivador) filing cabinet

ficticio, -cia adj fictitious; activo ficticio = fictitious assets; beneficio ficticio = paper profit; contabilidad ficticia = false accounting; pérdida ficticia = paper loss

fidedigno, -na adj (fiable) reliable; la policía tiene información fidedigna sobre los movimientos de la banda = the police have reliable information about the gang's movements

fideicomisario, -ria nmf (administrador) trustee; fideicomisario judicial = judicial trustee; actuaba de fideicomisario = he was acting in a fiduciary capacity

fideicomiso nm trust o (asociación de empresas) trust company; fideicomiso discrecional = discretionary trust; fideicomiso familiar = family trust; fideicomiso por disposición legal = constructive trust; contrato de fideicomiso o acto de constitución de un fideicomiso = trust deed o instrument; en fideicomiso = in trust; fondo de fideicomiso = trust fund; propiedad objeto de fideicomiso = settled land; dejó sus bienes en fideicomiso para sus nietos = he left his property in trust for his grandchildren
◊ fideicomitente nmf (a) (que encarga el fideicomiso) beneficiary (b) (que recibe el fideicomiso) settlor

fidelidad nf allegiance; juramento de fidelidad = oath of allegiance; juró fidelidad al nuevo presidente = he swore an oath of allegiance to the new president

fiduciario, -ria adj beneficiary o fiduciary; fondo fiduciario = trust fund; moneda fiduciaria = fiat money; tierra vinculada a la Ley de la Propiedad Fiduciaria = settled land; un director de empresa tiene una obligación fiduciaria para con la compañía = a company director owes a fiduciary duty to the company

fiel adj (a) (de confianza) faithful o trustworthy o loyal; fiel cumplimiento = faithful performance; copia fiel = true copy; certifico que ésta es una copia fiel = I certify that this is a true copy

fiesta nf holiday; fiesta nacional = public holiday; fiesta oficial = legal holiday; fiesta oficial o legal = statutory holiday

figurar vi to appear o to figure; el caso figura para ser visto la semana próxima = the case is listed to be heard next week; su nombre figura en la lista = his name appears in the list

fijación nf fixing o pricing o (valoración) assessment; fijación del interés de una hipoteca = fixing of a mortgage rate; fijación de los precios o tarifas = price fixing o fixing of charges; fijación ilegal de precios entre empresas = common pricing; fijación del valor de una propiedad = assessment of property; derecho de fijación de residencia = right of establishment

fijar vt (a) (establecer) to fix o to set o to determine; (programar) to arrange o to schedule; fijar la fecha de un juicio = to set down; fijar precios o cantidades = to determine prices o quantities; fijar un acuerdo = to arrange a deal o to set up a deal o to do a deal; fijar un presupuesto = to fix a budget; fijar una fecha = to set a date; fijar una fianza = to set bail; fijar una reunión a las 3 de la tarde = to fix a meeting for 3 p.m.; el precio del oro se fijó en 300 dólares = the price of gold was fixed at $300; la fecha de la vista todavía está por fijar = the date of the hearing has still to be fixed; la pena por delitos relacionados con drogas ha sido fijada por el Código Penal = the punishment for drug offences has been fixed by the Penal Code; **la vista se fijó para abril** = the hearing was arranged for April; **las alegaciones deben presentarse ante el tribunal cuando esté fijada la fecha del juicio** = pleadings must be submitted to the court when the action is set down for trial **(b)** *(poner)* to put **(c)** *(valorar)* to assess; **fijar el valor de una propiedad para asegurarla** = to assess a property for the purposes of insurance

◊ **fijarse** *vr* to notice; *(tener en cuenta)* **fijarse en** = to note

fijo, -ja *adj* **(a)** *(establecido)* fixed; **activo fijo** = capital assets *o* fixed assets; **capital fijo** = fixed capital; **carga fija** *o* **precio fijo** *o* **coste fijo** = fixed charge; **costes fijos** = fixed costs; **escala fija de precios** = fixed scale of charges; **gastos fijos** = fixed expenses; **plazo fijo** = fixed term; **depósito a plazo fijo** = fixed deposit; **puesto fijo como funcionario** = established post; **renta fija** = fixed income; **inversiones de renta fija** = fixed-interest investments; **sin residencia fija** = no fixed abode **(b)** *(uniforme)* flat; **porcentaje fijo** *o* **cuota fija** = flat rate; **pagamos una cantidad fija por la electricidad cada trimestre** = we pay a flat rate for electricity each quarter **(c)** *(permanente)* permanent; **empleo fijo** = secure job; **hacer fijo a alguien en un trabajo** = to confirm someone in a job; **tiene trabajo fijo** = she is in permanent employment; **ha encontrado un trabajo fijo** = he has found a permanent job

filiación *nf* affiliation; **sentencia de filiación** = affiliation order; **procedimientos de filiación** = affiliation proceedings

filial *nf* *(sucursal)* branch *o* branch office; *(empresa subsidiaria)* subsidiary company; **la compañía de seguros ha cerrado sus filiales en Sudamérica** = the insurance company has closed its branches in South America; **una filial propiedad de la empresa** = a wholly-owned subsidiary

filtración *nf* leak; **el gobierno está investigando la última filtración de documentos relacionada con el juicio por espionaje** = the government is investigating the latest leak of documents relating to the spy trial

filtrar *vi* to leak
◊ **filtrarse** *vr* to leak; **la información sobre los planes del gobierno se ha filtrado a los periódicos** = information about the government plans has been leaked to the papers

fin *nm* **(a)** *(cierre)* closure *o* end; **fin de año** = year end; **fin de plazo** = closing date; **al fin** = in the end; **por fin** = finally *o* at last **(b)** *(objetivo)* objective *o* aim
◊ **final 1** *adj* *(último)* final *o* closing; **conclusiones finales** = closing speeches; **consumidor final** = ultimate consumer; **demanda**

final = final demand; **dividendo final** = final dividend; **dueño final** = ultimate owner; **pago** *o* **desembolso final** = final discharge; **reembolso final** = final discharge; **sentencia final** = final judgment **2** *nm* *(cierre)* end *o* close; **al final** = in the end

◊ **finalmente** *adv* finally; **el contrato se firmó finalmente ayer** = the contract was finally signed yesterday; **tras diez horas de debate, el Congreso finalmente levantó la sesión a las dos en punto de la madrugada** = after ten hours of discussions, the Congress finally rose at two o'clock in the morning

finalización *nf* *(conclusión)* completion; **finalización de un arrendamiento colectivo** *o* **coarriendo** = severance; **finalización de un contrato** = discharge by performance; **finalización de un contrato de trabajo** = severance; **finalización de contrato por mutuo acuerdo** = discharge by agreement; **fecha de finalización** = completion date

finalizar 1 *vi* *(expirar)* to expire; **la oferta finaliza al morir el oferente** = the offer terminates on the death of the offeror; **que puede finalizar** = terminable **2** *vt* *(terminar)* to terminate; **finalizar un acuerdo** = to terminate an agreement

financiar *vt* to finance; **el nuevo edificio debe ser financiado por el Ayuntamiento** = the new building must be financed by the local Council; **un programa de construcción de prisiones financiado por el gobierno** = a government-financed programme of prison construction

financiero, -ra *adj* financial; **ayuda financiera** = financial assistance; **compañía financiera (que financia la compra a plazos)** = hire-purchase company; **depositario financiero** *o* **entidad financiera** = licensed deposit-taker; **director financiero** = controller; **estado financiero** = financial statement; **intermediario financiero** = broker; **institución financiera** = financial institution; **sociedad financiera** = finance corporation; **es el secretario de la comisión de finanzas del Ayuntamiento** = he is the secretary of the local Council finance committee; **atender a las necesidades financieras de alguien** = to make financial provision for someone; **recibe ayuda financiera de las autoridades locales** = she receives financial assistance from the local authority; **tiene un interés financiero por la compañía** = he has a financial interest in the company
◊ **financieramente** *adv* financially; **financieramente, la empresa es muy fuerte** *o* **sólida** = the company is financially very strong; **está metido financieramente en la empresa inmobiliaria** = he is financially involved in the property company

finanzas *nfpl (recursos)* finance *o* finances; **Ley de Finanzas** = Finance Act

fingido, -da *adj (falso)* sham

fingir *vi (simular)* to pretend; **fingió que tenía gripe y pidió el día libre** = she pretended she had 'flu and asked to have the day off; **consiguió entrar fingiendo ser un ingeniero de la telefónica** = he got in by pretending to be a telephone engineer

finiquito *nm* settlement; **finiquito por consenso** = discharge by agreement

firma *nf* (a) *(rúbrica)* signature; **aceptar una firma** *o* **reconocer una firma** = to honour a signature; **se ha pasado a limpio el contrato listo para la firma** = the contract has been engrossed ready for signature; **todos los cheques de la empresa necesitan dos firmas** = all the company's cheques need two signatures; **un montón de cartas a la espera de la firma del director gerente** = a pile of letters waiting for the managing director's signature; **un testamento necesita la firma del testador y dos testigos** = a will needs the signature of the testator and two witnesses (b) *(empresa)* firm; **es socio de un bufete de abogados** = he is a partner in a law firm; **una firma de auditores** *o* **asesores contables** = a firm of accountants

firmante *nmf (signatario)* signatory; **firmante por acomodamiento** = accommodation maker; **si desea cambiar los términos del acuerdo tiene que conseguir el permiso de todos los firmantes** = you have to get the permission of all the signatories to the agreement if you want to change the terms

firmar *vt* to sign; **firmar un contrato** *o* **un acuerdo** *o* **un convenio** = to sign a contract *o* an agreement *o* a deal; **firmar un contrato como testigo** = to witness an agreement; **firmar un acuerdo con alguien** = to conclude an agreement with someone; **firmar una carta** *o* **un documento** *o* **un cheque** = to sign a letter *o* a document *o* a cheque; **firmar un recibo** *o* **una carta en nombre de alguien** = to p.p. a receipt *o* a letter; **persona que firma con una cruz** = marksman; **en fe de lo cual, firmo la presente** = in witness whereof, I set my hand; **la empresa no ha firmado el acuerdo** = the company is not a party to the agreement; **el cheque carece de validez si no está firmado por el director financiero** = the cheque is not valid if has not been signed by the finance director; **la carta está firmada por el director gerente** = the letter is signed by the managing director; **la secretaria firmó la carta en nombre del director, mientras éste estaba comiendo** = the secretary p.p.'d the letter while the manager was at lunch

firme *adj* (a) *(fuerte)* strong; **el país necesita un cuerpo de policía firme** = the country needs a strong police force (b) *(estable)* firm; **la libra se mostró más firme en los mercados de divisa extranjera** = the pound was firmer on the foreign exchange markets; **las acciones se mantuvieron firmes** = shares remained firm (c) *(sólido)* **en firme** = firm; **enviar un pedido en firme** = to send a formal order; **están cotizando un precio en firme por caja** = they are quoting a firm price per case; **hacer una oferta en firme** = to make a firm offer for something; **hacer una oferta en firme por dos aviones** = to place a firm offer for two aircraft; **no firme** = unsafe

firmeza *nf* firmness

fiscal 1 *adj* (a) *(del fisco)* fiscal; **año** *o* **ejercicio fiscal** = tax year *o* fiscal year; **asesor fiscal** = tax adviser *o* tax consultant; **código fiscal** = tax code; **concesión fiscal** = tax concession; **deducción fiscal impositiva** = tax deductions; **desgravaciones fiscales** = allowances against tax *o* tax allowances; **elusión fiscal** = tax avoidance; **evasión (ilegal) fiscal** *o* **fraude fiscal** = tax evasion; **exención fiscal** = tax exemption *o* exemption from tax; **desgravación fiscal** = tax allowance *o* allowance against tax; **franquicia fiscal** = tax holiday; **inspector fiscal** = tax inspector *o* inspector of taxes; **laguna fiscal** = tax loophole; **medidas fiscales** = fiscal measures; **planificación fiscal** = tax planning; **la política fiscal del gobierno** = the government's fiscal policies; **paraíso fiscal** = tax haven; **como organización no lucrativa, puedes reclamar exención fiscal** = as a non profit-making organization you can claim tax exemption (b) *(tribunal de justicia)* **ministerio fiscal** = prosecution **2** *nmf; (acusador público)* public prosecutor *o (abogado de la acusación)* prosecution counsel *o* counsel for the prosecution; **fiscal de distrito** = district attorney; **fiscal del Estado** = Crown prosecutor; **Fiscal General del Estado** = *GB* Attorney-General

Al Fiscal General del Estado le corresponde la jefatura del Ministerio Fiscal. Es nombrado por el Rey a propuesta del Gobierno, entre juristas con experiencia en el ejercicio de su profesión (artº 124 CE)

fiscalía *nf* public prosecutor's office; **fiscalía general del estado** = Crown Prosecution Service (CPS)

Fisco *nm (Hacienda)* the Inland Revenue *o US* the Internal Revenue Service

fisgar *o* **fisgonear** *vi* to pry *o* to spy on

físico, -ca *adj* physical; **disminuido físico** *o* **disminuida física** = disabled person; **incapacidad física** = disability; **persona física** = natural person; **el testador gozaba de buena salud física, pero era mentalmente incapaz de comprender los términos del testamento** = the testator was physically fit, but mentally incapable of understanding the terms of the will; **se informó al tribunal de actos de violencia física contra la**

policía = the court was told of acts of physical violence committed against the police

◊ **físicamente** *adv* physically; **persona disminuida físicamente** = disabled person

flaco, -ca *adj (débil)* weak; **punto flaco** = failing

flagrante 1 *adj (evidente)* flagrant; **un caso flagrante de desacato a los tribunales** = a flagrant case of contempt of court; **una violación flagrante de los derechos humanos** = a flagrant violation of human rights **2** *adv;* **en flagrante** = red-handed; **le sorprendieron en flagrante** = he was caught red-handed

fletado, -da *adj* chartered; **vuelo fletado** = charter flight; **barco fletado por el Sr Soler** = boat on charter to Mr Soler

fletador, -ra *n* charterer

fletamento *nm* charter *o* chartering; **fletamento de un barco sin tripulación** = demise charter

fletamiento *nm* charter

fletar *vt* to charter; **fletar un avión** *o* **un barco** = to charter a plane *o* a boat

flete *nm* **(a)** *(fletamento)* chartering; **contrato de flete** = charterparty **(b)** *(transporte)* freight; **cuotas** *o* **tarifas de flete** = freight charges *o* freight rates

flojo, -ja *adj (blando)* soft

floppy nm *(disco flexible)* floppy disk

flotante *adj* floating; **costes flotantes** = floating charge; **restos flotantes de un naufragio** = flotsam; **póliza flotante** = open policy

FMI = FONDO MONETARIO INTERNACIONAL

folio *nm* sheet *o* folio; **papel tamaño folio** = foolscap; **sobre para folios** = a foolscap envelope; **la carta estaba escrita en seis folios** = the letter was on six sheets of foolscap

folleto *nm* leaflet *o* pamphlet; **folleto informativo** *o* **explicativo de las condiciones de una emisión** = prospectus

fomentar *vt (estimular)* to encourage *o* to promote; **algunas personas creen que las condenas indulgentes fomentan el crimen** = some people believe that lenient sentences encourage crime

fondo *nm* **(a)** *(reserva)* fund; **fondo de comercio** = goodwill; **fondo de compensación territorial** = interterritorial compensation fund; **fondo de pensiones** = pension fund; **fondo de reserva** = reserve fund; **Fondo Europeo de Desarrollo (FED)** = European Development Fund (EDF); **fondo para gastos menores** = petty cash; **Fondo Monetario Internacional (FMI)** = International Monetary Fund (IMF); **fondo social** = partnership property; **Fondo Social Europeo (FSE)** =

European Social Fund (ESF); **a fondo perdido** = (loan) without security **(b)** *(esencia de algo)* **a fondo** = in depth *o* in detail; *(cuestión de derecho)* **fondo del caso** = merits of the case; **examinar a fondo** = to go into; **el banco quiere examinar a fondo los detalles de los préstamos entre compañías** = the bank wants to go into the details of the inter-company loans; **la brigada contra el fraude está investigando a fondo los datos sobre las transacciones de propiedad** = the fraud squad is going into the facts behind the property deals

◊ **fondos** *nmpl* finance *o* funds *o (dinero)* monies; **fondos públicos** = public funds; **apropiación ilícita** *o* **indebida de fondos** = conversion of funds; **apropiarse de fondos ajenos en beneficio propio** = to convert funds to one's own use; **recaudar fondos a nuestro favor** = to collect monies due; **estar sin fondos** = to bounce; **pagó el coche con un cheque sin fondos** = he paid for the car with a cheque that bounced; **¿Dónde conseguirán las autoridades fondos para pagar el aumento de salarios** *o* **los salarios más altos?** = where will the authority find the finance to pay the higher salaries?

forajido, -da *n* fugitive *o* outlaw

forastero, -ra *adj y n (extranjero)* foreigner

forcejear *vi* to struggle

forcejeo *nm* struggle

forense *adj* forensic; **medicina forense** = forensic medicine; **médico forense** = pathologist; **ciencia forense** = forensic science

forma *nf* form; **de forma implícita** = constructively *o* implicitly; **de forma legal** = legally; **en forma de** = by way of; **recibo expedido en la forma debida** = receipt in due form; **dar la forma final** = to settle; **el abogado tiene instrucciones de dar la forma final a la defensa** = counsel is instructed to settle the defence

formación *nf* **(a)** *(creación)* formation *o* forming **(b)** *(preparación profesional)* training; **ejecutivo,-va en formación** = management trainee; **formación de mandos** = management training; **jefe de formación** = training officer; **periodo de formación** = qualifying period *o* period of qualification; **el director tiene una formación americana** = the director is American-trained

formal *adj* formal; **contrato formal** = specialty contract; **hacer una solicitud formal** = to make a formal application

◊ **formalmente** *adv* formally

formalidad *nf* **(a)** *(requisito)* formality *o* technicality; **formalidades procesales debidas** = due process of law **(b)** *(seriedad)* **con formalidad** = responsibly

formalizar *vt* to formalize; **formalizar un acuerdo** = to enter into an agreement

formar *vt* **(a)** *(crear, constituir)* to form; **formar parte de** = to be part of; **formar parte de un tribunal** = to sit on a tribunal; **formar una sociedad** = to incorporate **(b)** *(capacitar)* to train ◊ **formarse** *vr* **(a)** *(prepararse profesionalmente)* to train *o* to be trained **(b)** *(hacerse)* to form; **formarse un opinión** = to form an opinion

fórmula *nf* formula; **fórmulas judiciales utilizadas en un documento legal** = form of words

formular *vt* to formulate; *(establecer)* to lay down; **formular acusaciones contra alguien** = to press charges against someone; **formular una pregunta** = to pose a question; **formular una protesta** = to raise an objection; **formular reparos** = to raise objections; **se enfadó mucho cuando el hijo de su vecino incendió su coche, pero decidió no formular acusaciones** = he was very angry when his neighbour's son set fire to his car, but decided not to press charges

formulario *nm* form; **formulario de declaración aduanera** = customs declaration form; **formulario de declaración de siniestro** = claim form; **formulario de inscripción** *o* **de solicitud** = application form; **formulario de reclamación** = claim form; **rellenó el formulario de declaración de siniestros y lo envió a la compañía de seguros** = he filled in the claim form and sent it to the insurance company

foro *nm* forum; **el juzgado de instrucción no es el foro adecuado para esta petición** = the magistrates' court is not the appropriate forum for this application

fortuito, -ta *adj* accidental

forzado, -da *adj* *(actuar bajo protesta)* forced; **hacer algo forzado** = to do something under protest; **trabajos forzados** = hard labour *o* penal servitude

forzar *vt* **(a)** *(aplicar fuerza)* to force; **forzar una casa** *o* **un edificio** = to break in; **forzar una cerradura** = to pick a lock **(b)** *(obligar)* to force *o* to compel *o* to oblige **(c)** *(violar)* to rape

forzoso, -sa *adj* **(a)** compulsory; **adquisición forzosa** = compulsory purchase; **orden de adquisición forzosa** = compulsory purchase order; **alimentación forzosa (en un caso de huelga de hambre)** = forcible feeding; **liquidación forzosa** = compulsory liquidation *o* compulsory winding up; **orden de liquidación forzosa** = compulsory winding up order; **moneda de curso forzoso** = fiat money; **trabajos forzosos** = hard labour *o* penal servitude; **venta forzosa** = forced sale **(b)** *(obligado)* compellable; **un testigo forzoso** = a compellable witness ◊ **forzosamente** *adv;* *(por necesidad)* of necessity; **un juez debe ser forzosamente imparcial** = a judge must of necessity be impartial

fotografía *nf* *(para los archivos policiales)* mug shot

fracasar *vi* **(a)** *(fallar)* to fail **(b)** *(naufragar)* to wreck

fracaso *nm* *(interrupción)* failure

fracturas *nfpl* *(roturas)* breakages

franco, -ca *adj* free *o* franco; **franco a bordo** = free on board (f.o.b.); **zona franca** = free port *o* free trade zone *o* free trade area

franqueadora *nf* *(correos)* **máquina franqueadora** = franking machine

franquear *vt* *(poner sellos)* to stamp *o* to frank; **carta** *o* **tarjeta a franquear en destino** = reply paid card *o* letter; **máquina de franquear** = franking machine

franqueo *nm* *(tarifa postal)* postage; **franqueo de cartas** *o* **de paquetes** = letter rate *o* parcel rate; **con franqueo pagado** = post free; **el folleto se puede obtener con franqueo pagado del colegio de abogados** = the leaflet is obtainable post free from the Law Society; **sobre con dirección y franqueo** = stamped addressed envelope (s.a.e.)

franquicia *nf* **(a)** *(licencia)* franchise; *(franquiciador)* **persona que concede franquicias** = franchiser; **ha adquirido una franquicia de imprenta** = he has bought a printing franchise; **lleva su cadena de bocaterías en régimen de franquicia** = he runs his sandwich chain as a franchising operation; **su bocatería tuvo tanto éxito que decidió explotarlo en régimen de franquicia** = his sandwich bar was so successful that he decided to franchise it **(b)** *(exención)* freedom from duty; **franquicia fiscal** *o* **tributaria** = tax holiday

franquiciado, -da *n* *(concesionario)* franchisee

franquiciador, -ra *n* *(persona que concede franquicias)* franchiser

franquiciar *vt* *(conceder una licencia de explotación)* to franchise

fraude *nm* fraud; *(engaño)* deceit *o* deception *o* false pretences; *(estafa)* confidence trick *o* US confidence game; **fraude de ley** = fraud in equity *o* in law; **fraude electoral** = ballot-rigging; **fraude fiscal** = tax evasion; **fraude informático** = computer fraud; **brigada contra el fraude** = Fraud Squad; **caso de fraude** = scam; **obtener dinero por medio de fraude** = to obtain money by fraud; **obtener propiedades por fraude** = obtaining property by deception; **le encarcelaron por obtener dinero por fraude** = he was sent to prison for obtaining money by false pretences; **representación falsa con ánimo de fraude** = fraudulent misrepresentation; **se le acusó de fraude**

de divisas = he was accused of frauds relating to foreign currency

El fraude de ley consiste en la realización de un acto permitido al amparo de una norma dictada con finalidad distinta, con objeto de conseguir un resultado prohibido por otra norma. En tal caso el acto realizado será nulo (CC art° 6.4)

fraudulento, -ta *adj* fraudulent; *(deshonesto)* dishonest; **comercio fraudulento** = fraudulent trading; **de un modo fraudulento** = dishonestly; **medios fraudulentos** = false pretences; **quiebra fraudulenta** = criminal bankruptcy; **transmisión fraudulenta de una sociedad** = fraudulent conveyance
◊ **fraudulentamente** *adv* fraudulently; **mercancías importadas fraudulentamente** = goods imported fraudulently; **se le acusó de adquirir las joyas fraudulentamente** = he was accused of dishonestly acquiring the jewels; **le encarcelaron por obtener dinero fraudulentamente** = he was sent to prison for obtaining money by false pretences

frecuencia *nf (incidencia)* incidence; '**con la frecuencia necesaria'** = toties quoties; **la frecuencia de casos de violación ha aumentado durante los últimos años** = the incidence of cases of rape has increased over the last years

frecuentar *vt (trato)* **frecuentar la compañía de** = to associate with; **frecuentaba la compañía de criminales** = she associated with criminals

frenar *vt (restringir)* to restrain

freno *nm (fuerza de disuasión)* deterrent; **una condena larga de prisión actuará como freno para otros posibles criminales** = a long prison sentence will act as a deterrent to other possible criminals

frente 1 *nm* front *o* face; **hacer frente** = to cope; **hacer frente a** = to meet; **hacer frente a una acusación** = to face a charge; **¿cómo puede la policía hacer frente a toda la violencia del centro de la ciudad sin tener personal suficiente?** = how can the police cope with inner city violence when they do not have enough staff?; **no pudo hacer frente a los pagos de la hipoteca** = he was unable to meet his mortgage repayments **2** *prep; (en contra de)* counter to

frontera *nf* border; *(límite)* boundary (line)

fructífero, -ra *adj* profitable; **discusiones fructíferas** = productive discussions

frustración *nf* frustration

frustrado, -da *adj* attempted; **homicidio frustrado** = attempted murder

frustrar *vt* to frustrate *o* to thwart

fruto *nm* fruit; **frutos de la tierra** = emblements

fuego *nm* fire; **arma de fuego** = firearm; **la policía abrió fuego contra la multitud** = the police opened fire on the crowd

fuente *nf (origen)* source; **fuente fidedigna** *o* **fuente solvente** = reliable source; **fuente de información** = source of information *o* informant; **fuente de ingresos** = source of income; **se tienen que declarar todas las fuentes de ingresos al fisco** = you must declare income from all sources to the Inland Revenue

fuera *adv y prep* outside; **fuera de** = ex *o* outside; **fuera de actas** = off the record; **fuera de horas de oficina** = outside office hours; **fuera de la empresa** = outside; **fuera de la ley** = outlaw; **fuera de peligro** = out of danger; **fuera del trabajo** = off; **trabajador, -ra que trabaja fuera de la empresa** = outside worker; **enviar trabajo para que se realice fuera de la empresa** = to send work to be done outside

fuero *nm* **(a)** *(ley)* law **(b)** *(inmunidad)* privilege *o* absolute privilege

fuerte *adj* **(a)** *(firme)* strong *o* hard; **caja fuerte** = safe *o* strongbox; **moneda fuerte** = hard currency; **divisas fuertes** = hard currency *o* reserve currency **(b)** *(brusco)* sharp
◊ **fuertemente** *adv* **(a)** *(duramente)* heavily **(b)** *(bruscamente)* sharply **(c)** *(severamente)* severely

fuerza *nf* **(a)** *(poder)* force *o* power; **fuerza de disuasión** = deterrent; **fuerza de la ley** = power of the law; **fuerza de negociación** = bargaining power; **fuerza legal** = force of law *o* validity; **fuerza mayor** = act of God *o* force majeure *o* vis major; **a la fuerza** *o* **por fuerza** = forcible; **por fuerza mayor** = a fortiori; **sacar por la fuerza** = to extort; **toda la fuerza de la ley** = the full power of the law; **aplicaremos toda la fuerza de la ley para recuperar la posesión de nuestra propiedad** = we will apply the full power of the law to regain possession of our property; **las nuevas normas tienen fuerza legal** = the new regulations have the force of law **(b)** *(policía)* **fuerza pública** = police force

La fuerza mayor es una circunstancia imprevisible que impide el cumplimiento de una obligación

fuga *nf* **(a)** *(evasión)* escape; *(de prisión)* jailbreak; **fuga múltiple** = mass jailbreak **(b)** *(pérdida)* leak; **fuga de cerebros** = brain drain; **fuga de información secreta** = security leak

fugarse *vr* to abscond; *(de prisión)* to escape *o* to break out of prison; **tres presos se fugaron saltando el muro** = three prisoners escaped by climbing over the wall

fugitivo, -va 1 *adj* fugitive; **delincuente fugitivo** = fugitive offender *o US* fugitive from justice 2 *n* fugitive *o* outlaw

fullero, -ra *n* card sharper

función *nf* **(a)** *(cargo)* function *o* duty; **función pública** = official duty *o* civil service; **en funciones** = acting; **hacer las funciones de otro** = to act as deputy for someone *o* to act as someone's deputy; **Primer Ministro** *o* **presidente en funciones** = caretaker Prime Minister *o* caretaker chairman **(b) en función de** = according to; **pensión calculada en función del salario** = earnings-related pension

Se entiende por función pública la función ejercida por personas físicas capaces de voluntad, las cuales por medio de su actividad realizan los fines del Estado

funcionamiento *nm* **(a)** *(operación)* operating; *(de una máquina)* run; **costes de funcionamiento** = operational costs; **periodo de funcionamiento de un ordenador** = a computer run; **presupuesto de funcionamiento** = operating budget **(b)** *(rendimiento)* performance **(c) en funcionamiento** = in operation; **el sistema entrará en funcionamiento en junio** = the system will be in operation by June

funcionar *vt* to operate *o* to perform; **empezar a funcionar** = to become operative; **hacer funcionar** = to run; **hacer funcionar una máquina** = to operate a machine; **máquina que funciona perfectamente** = machine in full working order; **negocio que funciona bien** = going concern; 'no funciona' = out of order; **si eso no funciona** = failing that; **el sistema empezó a funcionar el 1 de junio** = the system became operational on June 1st; **el teléfono no funciona** = the telephone is out of order; **las nuevas condiciones del servicio funcionarán a partir del 1 de enero** = the new terms of service will operate from January 1st

funcionariado *nm* civil service

funcionario, -ria *n (oficial)* official *o* officer; **funcionario del Estado** = civil servant; **funcionario de prisiones** = warder; **funcionario judicial** = court officer; **funcionario subalterno** *o* **de poca categoría** = minor official; **alto funcionario** = high official; **cuerpo de funcionarios del Estado** = civil service; **los funcionarios del aeropuerto inspeccionaron el envío** = airport officials inspected the shipment; **los funcionarios del gobierno suspendieron la licencia de importación** = government officials stopped the import licence; **para ser funcionario del Estado hay que pasar una oposición** = you have to pass an examination to get a job in the civil service *o* to get a civil service job

funda *nf* holder; **funda de la tarjeta de crédito** = credit card holder; **funda protectora de tarjetas** *o* **mensajes** = card holder *o* message holder

fundación *nf* foundation; **fundación de una empresa** = promotion of a company

fundador, -ra *n* founder; **fundador de una mercantil** = company promoter; **acciones de fundador** = founder's shares

fundamental *adj* fundamental *o* material *o* primary *o* prime; **alteración fundamental hecha en un documento legal** = material alteration; **incumplimiento de un término fundamental de un contrato** = fundamental breach; **ley fundamental** = Bill of Rights; **testigo fundamental** = material witness

fundamento *nm* substance; *(razones)* grounds; **fundamentos de derecho** = legal grounds; **fundamentos fácticos** = particulars of claim; **caso criminal con poco fundamento** = weak case; **sin fundamento** = unjustified *o* groundless; **las historias sobre su dimisión no tienen ningún fundamento** = there is no substance to the stories about his resignation

fundar *vt* to establish; **fundar una sociedad** *o* **una empresa** *o* **una compañía** = to set up a company; **el negocio se fundó en Valencia en 1823** = the business was established in Valencia in 1823

fungible *adj* fungible; **bienes fungibles** *o* **material fungible** = fungible goods *o* fungibles

furgón *nm* van; **furgón policial** = police van

furtivo, -va *adj* **caza** *o* **pesca furtiva** = poaching

fusil *nm* gun
◊ **fusilar** *vt (ejecutar)* to shoot *o* to execute
◊ **fusilamiento** *nm* execution

fusión *nf* **(a)** *(de empresas)* merger; **como resultado de la fusión, la empresa es la más grande del sector** = as a result of the merger, the company is the largest in the field **(b)** *(de procedimientos, demandas)* = joinder

fusionar *vt* to merge
◊ **fusionarse** *vr* to merge; **la firma se fusionó con su principal competidor** = the firm merged with its main competitor; **las dos empresas se han fusionado** = the two companies have merged

fútil *adj* **demanda** *o* **acción fútil** = frivolous complaint *o* frivolous action

futuro, -ra 1 *adj* future; **en fecha futura** = forward; **entrega futura** = future delivery; **especulación** *o* **compras para entrega futura** = forward buying *o* buying forward; **tipos de cambio futuros** = forward (exchange) rate; **ventas futuras** = forward sales 2 *nm* future; **para el futuro** = forward; **en el futuro todos los informes deberán**

enviarse a Australia por avión = in future all reports must be sent to Australia by air

◊ **futuros** *nmpl* futures; **de futuros** = forward *o* futures; **bienes comercializados en el mercado de futuros** = commodity futures; **mercado de futuros** = forward market; **la plata subió ayer un 5% en el mercado de futuros** = silver rose 5% on the commodity futures market yesterday; **comprar divisas a futuros** = to buy forward; **vender divisas a futuros** = to sell forward; **transacciones de futuros** = forward dealings

Gg

gabinete *nm (consejo de ministros)* cabinet

gajes *nmpl* **gajes del oficio** = occupational hazards

galería *nf* corridor; *(de una cárcel)* prison wing

gamberrismo *nm* thuggery

gamberro *nm (alborotador)* thug *o* hooligan; **un grupo de gamberros adolescentes atacó a la pareja cuando salía de la tienda** = a group of teenage thugs attacked the couple as they left the shop

ganancia *nf* **(a)** *(beneficio)* gain *o* profit *o* return; *(ingresos)* **ganancias** = earnings *o* proceeds; **ganancias del capital** = capital gains; **impuesto sobre las ganancias del capital** = capital gains tax; **realización de ganancias excesiva** profiteering; **cuenta de pérdidas y ganancias** = profit and loss account **(b)** *(comisión)* turn *o* commission; **ganancia del intermediario** *o* **del corredor de Bolsa** = jobber's turn

ganar *vt* **(a)** *(percibir)* to earn; **la verdad es que nuestro agente de París no se gana su comisión** = our agent in Paris certainly does not earn his commission; **ganar 30.000 ptas a la semana** = to earn 30,000 ptas a week **(b)** *(conseguir)* to gain; *(en una disputa)* to win; **ganar un pleito** = to win a case

ganga *nf* bargain *o* a good buy

gángster *nm* gangster *o* hoodlum

ganzúa 1 *nf* picklock; *(forzar una cerradura)* **abrir una cerradura con ganzúa** = to pick a lock

garante *nmf (fiador)* guarantor *o* surety *o* bailor; **ser garante de alguien** = to stand guarantor for someone; **salir garante de alguien** = to stand surety for someone

garantía *nf* **(a)** *(seguridad)* collateral *o* cover; **garantía subsidiaria** = collateral security; **garantía prendaria** = collateral; **¿tienes garantía suficiente para este préstamo?** = do you have sufficient cover for this loan? **(b)** *(fianza)* security *o* pledge *o* surety; *(caución)* caution; **garantía hipotecaria** = mortgage security; **garantía no rescatada** *o* **garantía sin rescatar** *o* **sin desempeñar** = unredeemed pledge; **acciones con garantía** = qualifying shares; **acreedor con garantía** = secured creditor; **acreedor, -ra sin garantía** = unsecured creditor; **préstamo con garantía** = secured loan; **préstamo sin garantía** = unsecured loan; **títulos** *o* **valores de máxima garantía** = gilt-edged securities *o* gilts *o* government securities; **utilizar una casa como garantía de un préstamo** = to use a house as security for a loan; **el banco le adelantó 10 millones con la garantía de su casa** = the bank advanced him 10 million against the security of his house; **el funcionario encargado de examinar el caso ordenó que el demandante depositara 200.000 ptas como garantía del pago de las costas del demandado** = the master ordered that the plaintiff should deposit 200,000 ptas as security for the defendant's costs **(c)** *(aval)* guarantee *o* warranty; **garantía de indemnización** = letter of indemnity; **certificado de garantía** = certificate of guarantee *o* guarantee certificate; **persona que recibe una garantía** = warrantee; **violación de garantía** = breach of warranty; **el coche se vende con doce meses de garantía** = the car is sold with a twelve-month warranty; **el coche tiene garantía de estar en perfectas condiciones** = the car is warranted in perfect condition; **el coche todavía está en periodo de garantía** = the car is still under guarantee; **la garantía cubre las piezas de repuesto pero no la mano de obra** = the warranty covers spare parts but not labour costs; **la garantía tiene una duración de dos años** *o* **tiene una garantía de dos años** = the guarantee lasts for two years; **el ordenador se vende con dos años de garantía** = the computer is sold with a two-year guarantee; **dejar títulos de acciones como garantía** = to leave share certificates as a guarantee

garantizado, -da *adj* guaranteed; **deuda no garantizada** = unsecured debt; **deudas garantizadas** = secured debts *o* secured loans; **obligaciones garantizadas por los activos de la compañía** = debenture capital *o* debenture stock; **emisión de obligaciones garantizada por los activos de la compañía** = debenture issue *o* issue of debentures

garantizar *vt* **(a)** *(avalar)* to guarantee *o* to warrant; *(responder de)* to vouch for; **el producto está garantizado por doce meses** = the product is guaranteed for twelve months; **todas las piezas de**

repuesto están garantizadas = all the spare parts are warranted **(b)** *(asegurar)* to secure *o* to underwrite; **garantizar el pago** = to underwrite; **garantizar un préstamo** = to secure a loan; **garantizar una deuda** = to give something as security for a debt; **garantizar una emisión de acciones** = to underwrite a share issue; **garantizar una póliza de seguros** = to underwrite an insurance policy; **el gobierno ha garantizado el pago de los costes de ampliación del edificio** = the government has underwritten the development costs of the building; **la emisión fue garantizada por tres sociedades** = the issue was underwritten by three underwriting companies

garrote *nm* **garrote vil** = garrote (execution using a strangulation method)

gas *nm* gas; **cámara de gas** = gas chamber

gastar *vi* **gastar dinero** = to spend; **se gastaron todos sus ahorros en la compra de la tienda** = they spent all their savings on buying the shop; **la empresa se gasta millones en investigación** = the company spends millions on research

gasto *nm (coste)* cost; *(desembolso)* expenditure *o* expense; **gastos de capital** = capital expenditure; **gastos de demora** = demurrage; **gastos de descarga** = landing charges; **gastos de desplazamiento** = travelling expenses; **gastos de establecimiento** = establishment charges; **gastos de explotación** = business expenses; **gastos de manipulación** *o* **de transporte interno** = handling charges; **gastos de plantilla** *o* **gastos de personal** *o* **gastos de establecimiento** = establishment charges; **gastos de representación** = entertainment expenses; **gastos de transporte** = carriage charges; **gastos deducibles** = allowable expenses *o* tax deductions; **gastos imprevistos** = incidental expenses; **gastos fijos** = fixed expenses; **gastos generales** *o* **gastos corrientes** = overhead expenses *o* general expenses *o* running expenses; **con mucho gasto** = at great expense; **con todos los gastos pagados** = all expenses paid; **correr con los gastos** = to foot the bill; **cubrir gastos** = to cover costs; **cuenta de gastos de representación** = expense account; **esperamos alcanzar pronto el momento en que las ventas cubran todos los gastos** = we hope to reach the point soon when sales will cover all costs; **las ventas no son suficientes para cubrir los gastos de mantenimiento de la tienda** = we do not make enough sales to cover the expense of running the shop; **no podemos permitirnos el gasto de dos teléfonos** = we cannot afford the cost of two telephones

gemelo, -la 1 *adj y n* twin

general *adj* **(a)** *(global)* general *o* comprehensive; **Acuerdo General sobre Aranceles Aduaneros y Comercio** = the General Agreement on Tariffs and Trade (GATT); **auditoría**

general *o* **intervención general** = general audit; **carta de crédito general** = circular letter of credit; **cuartel general de la policía** = police headquarters; **director general** = general manager; **elecciones generales** = general election; **embargo preventivo general** = general lien; **gastos generales** = overhead expenses *o* general expenses *o* running expenses; **huelga general** = general strike; **junta general** = general meeting; **junta general anual** = Annual General Meeting (AGM); **Junta General Extraordinaria** = Extraordinary General Meeting (EGM); **negativa general** = blanket refusal; **total general** = grand total; **explicar en términos generales** *o* **dar una idea general de** = to outline **(b)** *(corriente)* standard; **tenemos un precio general de 5.000 ptas por cada sesión de treinta minutos** = we have a standard charge of 5,000 ptas for a thirty minute session **(c)** *(generalmente)* **en general** = ordinarily; **por lo general** = generally; **por regla general** = on an average; **resultar por regla general** = to average; **los crímenes políticos son, por lo general, tratados con más dureza en los tribunales militares** political crimes are generally dealt with more harshly in the military courts; **la oficina cierra en general entre Navidad y Año Nuevo** = the office is generally closed between Christmas and the New Year

◊ **generalmente** *adv (por lo general)* generally; *(en general)* ordinarily

género *nm* **(a)** *(clase)* nature; **¿qué clase de género contiene el paquete?** = what is the nature of the contents of the parcel? **(b)** *(artículos)* goods

genocidio *nm* genocide

genuino, -na *adj (verdadero)* genuine *o* real; **esta mesa antigua es genuina** = this old table is genuine

gerencia *nf* management; **gerencia lineal** = line management
◊ **gerencial** *adj (administrativo)* managerial

gerente *nmf; (encargado)* manager; *(encargada)* manageress; **director gerente** = managing director; **presidente y director gerente** = chairman and managing director

gestión *nf* **(a)** *(administración)* administration *o* management; **gestión financiera** = financial management; **buena gestión** *o* **gestión eficiente** = good management *o* efficient management; **contable de gestión** = management accountant; **cuentas de gestión** = management accounts; **curso de gestión empresarial** = management course **(b)** *(diligencia)* transaction; **hacer gestiones** = to take steps

gestionar *vt* **(a)** *(dirigir un negocio)* to manage **(b)** *(negociar)* to negotiate **(c)** *(tramitar)* **gestionar una causa** = to conduct a case

gestor, -ra *n* promoter

Ginebra *nf* Geneva; **Convención de Ginebra** = Geneva Convention(s); **el ejército atacante fue acusado de violar la Convención de Ginebra** = the attacking army was accused of violating the Geneva Convention

girar *vt (dar vueltas)* to turn; **girar un cheque** = to draw

giro *nm* **(a)** *(pago)* order; *(remesa)* remittance; **giro bancario** = bank draft *o* banker's draft; **giro internacional** = foreign money order *o* international money order *o* overseas money order; **giro postal** = money order; **nos envió un giro a través del Banco Comercial** = he sent us an order on the Chartered Bank; **realizar un giro bancario** = to make a draft on a bank **(b)** *(cambio)* development; **la declaración del testigo representó un nuevo giro en el caso** = the testimony of the witness represented a new development in the case

global *adj (general)* comprehensive; **acuerdo global** = package deal *o* blanket agreement; **suma global** = lump sum

glosa *nf (acalaración)* gloss

gobernador, -ra *n* governor; *(antiguamente)* **gobernador civil** = civil governor *o* UK Chief Constable

gobernar *vt (dirigir)* to govern *o* to rule; **gobernar por decreto** = to govern by decree; **el país está gobernado por un grupo de dirigentes militares** *o* **por un grupo de oficiales del ejército** = the country is governed by a group of military leaders *o* is ruled by a group of army officers

gobierno *nm (administración del Estado)* government *o* ministry *o* administration; *(estado)* state; **gobierno autonómico** = autonomous government; **gobierno municipal** = local authority; **fue Ministra de Educación con el gobierno anterior** = she was Minister of Education in the last administration; **funcionarios del gobierno no le permitieron salir del país** = government officials prevented him leaving the country; **la política del gobierno está resumida en el libro** = government policy is outlined in the book; **se promulgó la ley bajo el gobierno anterior** = the Act became law under the previous administration

golpe *nm* blow *o* knock *o* stroke; **golpe de estado** = coup (d'état); **de golpe** = suddenly; **lo habían matado a golpes con un martillo** = the dead man had been battered to death with a hammer

golpear *(pegar)* to beat *o* to knock *o* to strike; **golpear fuertemente** = to batter; **dos policías fueron golpeados con botellas** = two policemen were struck by bottles; **la policía golpeaba fuertemente la puerta del piso** = police were battering on the door of the flat; **los prisioneros fueron golpeados con palos** = the prisoners were beaten with sticks; **se golpeó la cabeza contra el archivo** = she knocked her head on the filing cabinet; **le golpearon en la cabeza con una porra** = he was struck on the head by a cosh

gordo, -da *adj* fat; **hacer la vista gorda ante algo** *o* **con respecto a algo** = to connive at something

gorila *nm (coloquial)* bodyguard *o* henchman

gozar *vt (disfrutar)* to enjoy

gracia *nf* **(a)** *(perdón)* mercy *o* clemency; **medida de gracia** = free pardon **(b)** *(prórroga)* grace; **conceder a un acreedor un periodo de gracia** = to give a creditor a period of grace

el derecho de gracia es una prerrogativa del Jefe del Estado por la cual se deja sin efecto una resolución judicial. La amnistía consiste en el perdón y el olvido de un delito, teniéndose éste por no cometido, mientras que el indulto supone la remisión total o parcial de una pena. La Constitución española contiene la prohibición expresa de autorizar indultos generales

grado *nm (categoría)* rank *o* degree; **grado de parentesco** = degree of kinship; **le ascendieron al grado de Comisario jefe** = he was promoted to the rank of Chief Superintendent

gráfico *nm* chart

grafología *nf* graphology; **experto** *o* **perito en grafología** = handwriting expert

gran *adj (contracción de 'grande' delante de un nombre singular)* grand; **hurto de gran cuantía** = grand larceny; **gran jurado** = grand jury; **gran volumen de ventas** = high volume (of sales)

grande *adj* **(a)** *(importante)* great *o* high *o (grave)* gross; **grandes ingresos por ventas** = high sales; **tuvo que contraer grandes deudas para pagar la multa** = he had to borrow heavily to pay the fine **(b)** *(tamaño)* large *o* big; **¿por qué tiene ella un despacho más grande que el mío?** = why has she got an office which is larger than mine?

gratificación *nf* **(a)** *(recompensa)* reward **(b)** *(propina)* gratuity

gratificar *vt (recompensar)* to reward

gratis *adv (gratuito)* free of charge; *(sin pagar)* gratis; **el servicio es gratis** = there is no charge for service *o* no charge is made for service; **entramos en la exposición gratis** = we got into the exhibition gratis

gratuito, -ta *adj* **(a)** *(gratis)* free *o* free of charge; **muestra gratuita** = free sample; **emisión gratuita de acciones distribuidas entre los accionistas** = scrip issue; **prueba gratuita y sin**

compromiso de compra = free trial; a título gratuito = voluntary; organización a título gratuito = voluntary organization; el servicio es gratuito = there is no charge for service *o* no charge is made for service; el transporte de la mercancía es gratuito = goods are delivered free; le dieron una entrada gratuita para la exposición = he was given a free ticket to the exhibition; solicite envío gratuito de lista de precios = price list sent free on request (b) *(sin fundamento)* gratuitous; promesa gratuita = gratuitous promise

gravamen *nm (carga)* encumbrance; *(derecho de retención)* lien; gravamen equitativo = equitable lien; gravamen sobre las importaciones = import levy

gravar *vt (imponer)* to impose *o* to levy; gravar impuestos = to impose taxes; gravar el tabaco = to put a duty on cigarettes; gravar las bicicletas con un impuesto = to impose a tax on bicycles; el gobierno ha decidido gravar los coches importados con un impuesto = the government has decided to levy a tax on imported cars

grave *adj* heavy *o* serious *o* severe *o* gross; impusieron condenas de prisión graves a los saqueadores = the looters were given heavy jail sentences; reclama que ha habido un grave error judicial = she claims there has been a serious miscarriage of justice; se enfrenta a seis acusaciones graves *o* tiene que hacer frente a seis acusaciones graves = he faces six serious charges ◊ gravemente *adv* severely *o* seriously; le hirieron gravemente en la batalla contra el ejército rebelde = he was severely wounded in the battle with the rebel army

gravedad *nf (seriedad)* seriousness; *(severidad)* severity; de gravedad = severely; el jefe superior de policía solicitó un informe sobre la gravedad de la situación en el centro de la ciudad = the Police Commissioner asked for a report on the seriousness of the situation in the centre of town; la duración de la pena de prisión depende de la gravedad del delito = the length of the prison sentence depends on the seriousness of the crime

gremio *nm (industria)* trade

grueso, -sa 1 *adj* thick *o* bulky 2 *nf* gross; avería gruesa = general average; fianza de contrato a la gruesa = bottomry bond

grupo *nm* group; *(categoría)* bracket; grupo de presión = lobby; grupo de redactores = editorial board; grupo de trabajo = working party; grupo de expertos = panel of experts; grupo impositivo = income bracket *o* tax bracket; el presidente del grupo = the group chairman *o* the chairman of the group; facturación *o* producción del grupo = group turnover *o* turnover for the group; pleito *o* acción legal en beneficio de un grupo de personas = class suit; resultados del grupo de empresas = group results; el catedrático Smith es el presidente del grupo de trabajo sobre drogodependencia = Professor Smith is the chairman of the working party on drug abuse; un grupo de empleados ha enviado una nota al presidente quejándose del ruido que hay en la oficina = a group of staff members has sent a memorandum to the chairman complaining about noise in the office

guante *nm (soborno)* hush money

guarda *nmf* guard *o* keeper; *(conserje)* caretaker; guarda de noche *o* guarda nocturno = night watchman; guarda jurado = security guard ◊ guardaespaldas *nm* bodyguard *o* henchman *o* minder; al ministro le seguían sus tres guardaespaldas = the minister was followed by his three bodyguards ◊ guardamuebles *nm* furniture depository

guardar *vt (a) (mantener)* to keep *o* to hold; *(proteger)* to ward (b) *(archivar)* to save

guardia 1 *nf (custodia)* custody; guardia de noche = night duty; abogado de guardia = duty solicitor; juzgado de guardia = police court; sargento de guardia = duty sergeant; servicio de guardia nocturna = night duty; estar de guardia = to be on duty *o* to be on call; el policía Martínez hace las guardias de noche de esta semana = PC Martínez is on night duty this week 2 *nmf* guard; *(policía)* policeman *o* police constable *o* woman police constable *o US* patrolman; guardia auxiliar = special constable; guardia civil = the Spanish Civil Guard; guardia de tráfico = traffic warden; guardia jurado = security guard; guardia urbana = municipal police; guardia urbano = municipal police officer; el prisionero fue tiroteado por los guardias al intentar escapar = the prisoner was shot by the guards as he tried to escape; había tres guardias de servicio en la puerta del banco = there were three guards on duty at the door of the bank *o* three bank guards were on duty (b) *(ujier)* guardia de sala = usher

guardián, -ana *n* custodian *o* warden

gubernamental *adj (del estado)* government *o* governmental; una prohibición gubernamental sobre la importación de armamento = a government ban on the import of arms

gubernativo, -va *adj (gubernamental)* governmental

guerra *nf* war; guerra civil = civil war; consejo de guerra = court-martial; declarar la guerra a un país = to declare war on a country; juzgar en consejo de guerra = to court-martial; prisionero, -ra de guerra = prisoner of war; los dos países están en guerra = the two countries are at war; el consejo de guerra tuvo lugar en el cuartel

general del ejército = the court-martial was held in the army headquarters

guerrillero, -ra *n* guerilla; **el llamamiento fue hecho por una emisora de radio perteneciente a guerrilleros** = the appeal was made by a guerilla radio station; **el tren fue asaltado por guerrilleros** = the train was attacked by guerillas

guía *nf* **guía alfabética** = classified directory; **guía comercial** = commercial directory *o* trade directory; **guía telefónica** *o* **de teléfonos** = phone book *o* telephone book *o* telephone directory; **guía urbana** = street directory

guiar *vt* **(a)** *(regir)* to govern **(b)** *(inducir a)* to lead

guillotina *nf* guillotine

guillotinar *vt* to guillotine

gustar *vi* to like *o* to appreciate; **una persona que gusta a mucha gente** = a very popular person; **éste es el modelo que más gusta** = this is our most popular model

Hh

habeas *nm* **habeas corpus** = habeas corpus; **orden de habeas corpus** = writ of habeas corpus

Habeas corpus es una frase latina que designa el derecho de un ciudadano detenido a comparecer ante el juez para que decida dentro de un plazo límite sobre su libertad o detención

haber 1 *nm* credit balance *o* credit side; **abonar 100.000 ptas en el haber del Sr García** = to pay in 100,000 ptas to the credit of Mr García; **anotar 100.000 ptas en el haber de alguien** = to enter 100,000 ptas to someone's credit; **debe y haber** = debit and credit **2** *vt* to have *o* to possess **3** *v aux;* **han prestado juramento** = they have been duly sworn **4** *v impersonal;* **hay** = there is *o* there are; **no ha lugar a procedimiento** = stay of proceedings

hábil *adj* **(a)** *(inteligente)* clever **(b)** *(experto)* skilful **(c)** *(días laborables)* **tres días hábiles** = three clear days; **cuente con tres días hábiles para que el cheque sea depositado en su banco** = allow three clear days for the cheque to be paid into your account

habilidad *nf* **(a)** *(aptitud)* capacity *o* skill; **tiene una habilidad especial para los negocios** = he has a particular capacity for business; **tiene una gran habilidad para los negocios** = she has great business skills **(b)** *(competencia)* expertise

habilitación *nf* *(autorización)* authorisation *o* qualification

habilitar *vt* *(autorizar)* to authorize *o* to enable *o* to entitle

habitante *nmf* inhabitant; *(de un país)* citizen; *(de una residencia)* resident *o* occupant

habitual *adj* habitual; *(corriente)* ordinary *o* usual; **criminal habitual** = hardened criminal; **delincuente habitual** = habitual criminal *o* habitual offender; **residencia** *o* **domicilio habitual** = habitual residence; **con residencia habitual** = ordinarily resident
◊ **habitualmente** *adv (generalmente)* ordinarily

habla *nf (palabra)* speech

hablar *vt/i* to speak *o* to talk; *(discutir)* **hablar de** = to discuss

hacer *vt* **(a)** *(producir)* to do *o* to make *o* to render; **hacer acto de presencia** = to be present; **hacer algo** = to take action; **hacer balance** = to balance; **hacer concesiones** = to make allowances; **hacer caso** = to take notice; **hacer caso omiso** *o* **no hacer caso a** = to ignore; **hacer frente a** = to confront; **hacer justicia** = to do justice; **hacer juramento** = to take an oath; **hacer juramento en falso** = to commit perjury; **hacer un pedido** = to place an order; **hacer una oferta por algo** = to put in a bid for something; **hacer una oferta para realizar una obra** = to put in a tender *o* to submit a tender; **hacer un presupuesto** = to estimate; **hacer una advertencia** = to warn; **hacer una redada** = to raid; **el ordenador estuvo haciendo facturas toda la noche** = the computer was running invoices all night; **de no cumplirse las condiciones de la fianza el acusado se hace susceptible de arresto** = failure to observe the conditions of bail renders the accused liable to arrest; **el estado de salud del testigo hace imposible su aparición ante los tribunales** = the state of health of the witness renders his appearance in court impossible; **la impresora hará gráficos en color** = the printer will output colour charts **(b)** *(plantear)* to raise; **hacer objeciones** = to raise an objection; **los representantes del sindicato hicieron una serie de objeciones sobre la redacción del acuerdo** = the union representatives raised a series of objections to the wording of the agreement **(c)** *(celebrar)* to hold; **hacer una reunión** = to hold a meeting **(d)** *(publicar)* to get out *o* to issue; **hizo una serie de demandas por difamación relacionadas con declaraciones realizadas a un periódico** = he issued writs for libel in connection with allegations made in a newspaper **(e)** **hacer falta** = to take; **hicieron falta seis policías para arrestarle** = it took six policemen to arrest him **(f)** **hacer constar** = to note *o* to record; **hacer cumplir** = to enforce; **hacer saber** = to inform
◊ **hacerse** *vr;* **hacerse cargo de** = to take over; **hacerse pasar por** = to impersonate; **hacerse socio** = to join *o* to become a member; **hacerse un seguro contra robo** = to take out insurance against theft; **el comprador se hace cargo de las obligaciones de la empresa** = the buyer takes over the company's liabilities

Hacienda *nf* **(a)** *(Fisco)* the Inland Revenue *o* US the Internal Revenue Service; **la Hacienda Pública** *o* **el Ministerio de Hacienda** = the Treasury; **delegado de Hacienda** = revenue officer; **inspector de Hacienda** = tax inspector *o* inspector of taxes; **Ministro de Hacienda** = Chancellor of the Exchequer; **Secretario de Hacienda** Secretary to the Treasury *o* Treasury Secretary; **hacer una declaración a Hacienda** = to make a declaration to the Inland Revenue **(b)** *(finca)* property; *(heredad)* US homestead

hallar *vt* to find; **hallar culpable** = to find guilty; **visto y hallado conforme** = acknowledged and agreed

hambre *nf* hunger; **huelga de hambre** = hunger strike; **se declaró en huelga de hambre hasta que las autoridades de prisiones le permitieron recibir el correo** = he went on hunger strike until the prison authorities allowed him to receive mail

hampa *nf* underworld *o* gangland; **la policía tiene confidentes en el hampa de la ciudad** = the police has informers in the city's underworld; **todos las indicios apuntan a que se trata de una matanza del hampa** *o* **de un ajuste de cuentas** = the indications are that it is an underworld killing; **tiene múltiples contactos en el mundo del hampa** = she has extensive contacts in the underworld

hasta *prep* until *o* pending; **hasta nuevo aviso** = until further notice; **hasta recibir asesoramiento de nuestros abogados** = pending advice from our lawyers; **pensión de manutención provisional hasta la celebración del juicio** = maintenance pending suit

hecho *nm* *(realidad)* fact; **hecho consumado** = fait accompli; **hecho establecido** = a matter of record; **de hecho** = de facto; *(en realidad)* in fact *o* in point of fact; **por este mismo hecho** *o* **el hecho mismo nos muestra** = ipso facto; **el hecho de haber escrito la carta fue ya de por sí una admisión de culpabilidad** = the writing of the letter was ipso facto an admission of guilt; **le encontraron en el vehículo en el momento del accidente y por este mismo hecho le creyeron culpable del mismo** = he was found in the vehicle at the time of the accident and ipso facto was deemed to be in charge of it; *(situación en la que los hechos son tan obvios que es el acusado el que tiene que demostrar que no fue negligente y no el demandante probar su reclamación)* 'el hecho habla por sí solo' = res ipsa loquitur **(b)** *(realidades)* **hechos** = matters of fact; **hechos probados** = case stated; **apeló por exposición de hechos probados** = he appealed by way of case stated; **el Tribunal Superior desestimó el recurso por medio de exposición de hechos probados** = the Higher Court dismissed the appeal by way of case stated **(c)** *(evidencia)* **hechos** = evidence

heredad *nf* *(hacienda)* homestead

heredar *vt* to inherit *o* to succeed; **heredar una propiedad** = to succeed to a property; **heredó 10 millones de su abuelo** = he inherited 10 million from his grandfather; **heredó la tienda a la muerte de su padre** = when her father died she inherited the shop

heredera *nf* heiress *o* inheritor *o* devisee

heredero *nm* heir *o* inheritor *o* devisee; **heredero absoluto** = heir unconditional; **heredero del remanente** = residuary legatee; **heredero forzoso** = heir apparent; **heredero legítimo** = rightful heir; **heredero universal** = residuary legatee; **presunto heredero** = heir presumptive; **único heredero** = universal heir *o* sole heir; **herederos y cesionarios** = heirs and assigns; **sus herederos y cesionarios** = his heirs and assigns; **sus herederos dividieron la propiedad entre ellos** = his heirs split the estate between them

hereditario, -ria *adj* hereditary; **cargo hereditario** = hereditary office; GB **par hereditario** = hereditary peer

herencia *nf* estate *o* inheritance; **herencia conjunta** = co-inheritance; **bienes que pueden ser objeto de herencia** = hereditament; **impuesto sobre herencias y donaciones** = estate tax; **su herencia se valoró en 100 millones** *o* **dejó una herencia valorada en 100 millones** = his estate was valued at 100 million *o* he left estate valued at 100 million

herida *nf* **(a)** *(lesión)* wound; **tiene una herida de arma blanca en la pierna** = she has a knife wound in her leg; **le causaron heridas de muerte** = she was fatally wounded **(b)** *(perjuicio)* injury

herido, -da *adj y n* wounded *o* injured; **resultar gravemente herido** = to be seriously injured; **dos trabajadores resultaron heridos en el incendio** = two workers were injured in the fire; **resultó herido en la pelea** = he was wounded in the fight; **no hubo heridos en el accidente** = nobody was injured in the accident

herir *vt* **(a)** *(lesionar)* to injure *o* to wound *o* to hurt; **herir de muerte** = to cause fatal injuries **(b)** *(perjudicar)* to injure

hermanamiento *nm* *(entre ciudades de distintos países)* twinning; **el comité del ayuntamiento que organiza el hermanamiento de dos ciudades** = the district council's town-twinning committee

hermanar *vt* to twin; **hermanar una ciudad con otra similar de un país distinto** = to twin a town with another town

heroína *nf* heroin

herramienta *nf* implement *o* instrument; **le golpearon la cabeza con una herramienta pesada** = he was hit on the head with a heavy implement

hijo, -ja 1 *nf* daughter 2 *nm* son; **José Pérez, hijo** = José Pérez, Junior 3 *n* child *o* offspring; **hijo adoptivo** = adopted child; **hijo legítimo** = legitimate child; **sus hijos heredaron sus bienes** *o* **propiedades** = his offspring inherited the estate; **tuvieron dos hijos** = they had two offspring

hincha *nmf* fan *o* supporter; *(gamberro)* hooligan; **la policía colocó barricadas para impedir que los hinchas más violentos del fútbol causaran destrozos** = the police put up barriers to prevent the football hooligans from damaging property

hipoteca *nf* mortgage; *(gravamen)* encumbrance; **hipoteca avalada por una póliza de seguro dotal** = endowment mortgage; **hipoteca de equidad (no formalizada que nace con la entrega del dinero)** = equitable mortgage; **hipoteca naval** = bottomry; **hipoteca secundaria en la que la escritura de propiedad no se ha entregado al prestamista** = puisne mortgage; **hipoteca sobre bienes muebles** = chattel mortgage; **ejecución de una hipoteca** = foreclosure; **pagos de una hipoteca** = mortgage (re)payments; **primera hipoteca** = first mortgage; **segunda hipoteca** = second mortgage; **título garantizado por hipoteca** = mortgage debenture; **ejecutar la hipoteca de una propiedad** = to foreclose on a mortgaged property; **obtener una hipoteca sobre una casa** = to take out a mortgage on a house; **redimir una hipoteca** = to pay off a mortgage; **comprar una casa con una hipoteca de 20 millones de ptas** = to buy a house with a 20 million ptas mortgage
◊ **hipotecado, -da** *adj* mortgaged; **la casa está hipotecada al banco** = the house is mortgaged to the bank; **vender una propiedad hipotecada por orden judicial** = to foreclose on a mortgaged property

hipotecar *vt* to mortgage; **hipotecó su casa para establecerse por cuenta propia** = he mortgaged his house to set up in business

hipotecario, -ria *adj* **acreedor hipotecario** *o* **acreedora hipotecaria** = mortgagee; **bono hipotecario** *o* **cédula hipotecaria** = mortgage bond *o* mortgage debenture; **deudor hipotecario** *o* **deudora hipotecaria** = mortgagor; **juicio hipotecario** = foreclosure; **entablar juicio hipotecario** = to foreclose; **obligación no hipotecaria** = debenture bond

historial *nm (experiencia)* track record; **historial delictivo** = criminal record; **historial profesional** = curriculum vitae; **el historial de la empresa en cuanto a relaciones laborales** = the company's record in industrial relations; **¿nos podría decir algo sobre el historial familiar de la chica?** = can you tell us something of the girl's family

background?; **tiene un buen historial como detective** = he has a good track record as a detective; **tiene un historial delictivo que se remonta a los últimos veinte años** = he has a criminal record stretching back twenty years

hogar *nm (vivienda)* home; **hogar adoptivo** *o* **de adopción** = foster home; **hogar tutelar de menores** = community home; **sin hogar** = homeless

hoja *nf* **(a)** *(papel)* sheet *o* leaf; *(formulario)* form; **hoja de reclamación** = claim form; **hoja de solicitud** = application form; **hoja suelta** = leaflet; **un bloc de hojas de pedidos** = a pad of order forms **(b) hoja de servicios** = record; **la hoja de servicios del empleado** = the clerk's record of service *o* service record

hombre *nm* man; **hombre de confianza** = right-hand man; **hombre de paja** = front man

homicida 1 *adj* homicidal; **arma homicida** = murder weapon *o* deadly weapon 2 *nm* murderer 3 *nf* murderess

homicidio *nm* murder *o* homicide *o* culpable homicide; **homicidio culposo** *o* **imprudente** *o* **por imprudencia** *o* **no premeditado** *o* **sin premeditación** *o* **involuntario** = (involuntary) manslaughter *o* *US* second degree murder; **homicidio intencionado con circunstancias atenuantes** = voluntary manslaughter; **homicidio frustrado** = attempted murder; **homicidio justificable** *o* **homicidio justificado** = justifiable homicide; **homicidio premeditado** = murder *o* *US* first degree murder; **La Brigada de Homicidios** = the Homicide Squad; **el índice de homicidios ha bajado en el último año** = the murder rate has fallen over the last year; **el índice de homicidios se ha duplicado en los diez últimos años** = the homicide rate has doubled in the last ten years; **fue acusado de homicidio involuntario** = he was accused of manslaughter; **le declararon culpable de homicidio** = he was found guilty of homicide; **se le declaró culpable del homicidio involuntario de su marido** = she was convicted of the manslaughter of her husband

El homicidio es un delito consistente en quitar la vida a otra persona (CP artº 138). El homicidio culposo o imprudente también está penado por la ley (CP artº 142)

homologar *vt* to bring into line; **homologar un testamento** = to prove a will

homólogo, -ga *nmf (colega)* counterpart; **John es mi homólogo en Smith's** = John is my counterpart in Smith's

honesto, -ta *adj* honest *o* straight
◊ **honestamente** *adv* **actuar honestamente con alguien** = to play straight *o* to act straight with someone

honorable *adj (ilustre)* honourable

honorario, -ria *adj* honorary; **miembro honorario** = honorary member; **presidente honorario** = honorary president; **secretario honorario** = honorary secretary

honorarios *nmpl (emolumentos)* fee *o* honorarium *o (coste)* charge; **honorarios condicionales** = contingent fee; **honorarios suplementarios** = refresher; **honorarios de un abogado** = solicitors' charges *o* barrister's fees; **anticipo sobre los honorarios** = retainer; **el abogado cobró 200.000 ptas por la preparación del expediente más honorarios suplementarios de 50.000 ptas por día** = counsel's brief fee was 200,000 ptas with refreshers of 50,000; **cobramos unos pequeños honorarios por nuestros servicios** = we charge a small fee for our services

honradez *nf* honesty

honrado, -da *adj* honest *o* straight; **se ha advertido al público que tenga cuidado con los comerciantes poco honrados** = the public has been warned to look out for dishonest shopkeepers
◊ **honradamente** *adv* honestly

hora *nf* **(a)** *(horario)* time; **hora de cierre** = closing time; **hora normal** = Standard Time; **la hora de llegada viene indicada en la pantalla** = the time of arrival *o* the arrival time is indicated on the screen **(b)** *(parte del día)* hour; **horas de trabajo** *o* **horas laborables** = business hours; **horas extraordinarias** *o* **horas extra** = overtime; **paga por horas extra** = overtime pay; **hacer horas extraordinarias** = to work overtime; **hacer seis horas extraordinarias** = to work six hours' overtime; **la tarifa por horas extraordinarias es una vez y media la tarifa del salario normal** = the overtime rate is one and a half times normal pay; **prohibición de hacer horas extraordinarias** = overtime ban

horario *nm* **(a)** *(hora)* time *o* hour; **horario comercial** = opening hours; **horario de oficina** = business hours *o* office hours; **horario de verano** = Summer Time *o* Daylight Saving Time; **el horario de salida lleva un retraso de hasta quince minutos debido a la cantidad de tráfico** = departure times are delayed by up to fifteen minutes because of the volume of traffic **(b)** *(programa)* nm timetable *o* schedule; **preparar** *o* **realizar un horario** = to timetable; **según el horario, debería haber un tren a Valencia a las 10.22** = according to the timetable, there should be a train to Valencia at 10.22; **la empresa de autobuses ha publicado su nuevo horario para los próximos doce meses** = the bus company has brought out its new timetable for the next twelve months; **su secretaria intentó hacerme un hueco en su horario** = his secretary tried to fit me into his schedule

horca *nf (cadalso)* gallows; **ejecución en la horca** = hanging

horizontal *adj* horizontal; **propiedad horizontal** = condominium

hospedarse *vr (alojarse)* to stay; **el presidente se hospeda en el Hotel Continental** = the chairman is staying at the Hotel Continental

hospital *nm* hospital; **hospital psiquiátrico** = asylum

hostigamiento *nm* harassment

hostigar *vt* to harass

hostil *adj (enemigo)* hostile; **testigo hostil** = adverse witness *o* hostile witness; **oferta pública de adquisición hostil** = hostile takeover bid

huelga *nf* strike; **huelga de brazos caídos** = sit-down protest; **huelga de celo** = work to rule; **huelga de hambre** = hunger strike; **huelga de protesta** = protest strike; **huelga general** = general strike; **huelga ilegal** *o* **no aprobada por el sindicato** = unofficial strike; **huelga oficial** *o* **aprobada por los sindicatos** = official strike; **huelga simbólica** = token strike; **fondo de huelga** = strike fund; **llamada a la huelga** *o* **convocatoria de huelga** = strike call; **subsidio de huelga** = strike pay; **voto de huelga** = strike ballot *o* strike vote **(b)** **declararse en huelga** *o* **ir a la huelga** = to strike *o* to come out on strike *o* to go on strike *o* to take strike action; **declararse en huelga de solidaridad con los trabajadores de correos** = to strike in sympathy with the postal workers; **declararse en huelga en protesta por malas condiciones laborales** = to strike in protest against bad working conditions; **declararse en huelga para conseguir aumentos salariales** *o* **una reducción de la jornada laboral** = to strike for higher wages *o* for shorter working hours; **llamar a los trabajadores a la huelga** *o* **convocar una huelga de trabajadores** = to call the workers out on strike; **los oficinistas están en huelga en petición de un aumento de salario** = the office workers are on strike for higher pay; **se declaró en huelga de hambre hasta que las autoridades de prisiones le permitieron recibir el correo** = he went on hunger strike until the prison authorities allowed him to receive mail

huella *nf* trace; **huella dactilar** *o* **huellas dactilares** = fingerprints; **tomar las huellas dactilares** = to fingerprint; **huella de pisada** = footprint; **tomar las huellas dactilares a alguien** = to take someone's fingerprints; **el tribunal oyó el testimonio presentado por un experto en huellas dactilares** = the court heard evidence from a fingerprint expert; **encontraron sus huellas dactilares en el arma homicida** = they found his fingerprints on the murder weapon; **la policía tomó las huellas dactilares al sospechoso después de**

haberle expuesto los cargos = the police fingerprinted the suspect after charging him

huérfano, -na *n* orphan

huir *vi (escapar)* to escape *o* to run away; *(desertar)* to defect; **huir de la justicia** = to abscond; **huir de los acreedores** = to avoid creditors; **huir estando bajo fianza** = to jump bail; **se le acusó de huir de la justicia** = he was charged with absconding from lawful custody

humano, -na *adj* human; **error humano** = human error; **derechos humanos** = human rights; **Tribunal Europeo de Derechos Humanos** = European Court of Human Rights

hundimiento *nm* **los inversores perdieron miles de libras en el hundimiento de la sociedad**

inversora = investors lost thousands of pounds in the wreck of the investment company

hundirse *vr (naufragar)* to wreck

hurtar *vt (robar)* to steal *o* to pilfer; *(informal)* to lift

hurto *nm* theft *o* larceny *o* pilferage *o* pilfering; **hurto de menor cuantía** = petty larceny; **hurto de gran cuantía** = grand larceny; **hurto en las tiendas** = shoplifting; **hurto menor** = petty theft; **fue condenado por hurto** = he was convicted of larceny

El hurto es un delito consistente en la sustracción de cosas muebles ajenas con ánimo de lucro y sin la voluntad de su dueño, sin que exista intimidación en las personas, ni fuerza en las cosas (CP art° 234)

Ii

ibídem *adv* ibid *o* ibidem

ídem *pron* idem

idéntico, -ca *adj* identical *o* the same; **idéntico a** = on all fours with; **este caso es idéntico al anterior** = this case is on all fours with the previous one

identidad *nf* identity; **identidad de las partes** = identity of parties; **cambió de identidad** = he changed his identity; **carnet** *o* **carné de identidad** = identity card *o* ID card; **documento** *o* **tarjeta nacional de identidad** = national identity card; **documentos de identidad** = proof of identification; **placa de identidad** =; identity disk; **le pidieron que diera pruebas de su identidad** = he was asked for proof of identity

identificación *nf* identification; **identificación errónea** = mistaken identity; **caso de identificación errónea** = case of mistaken identity; **identificación positiva** = positive identification; **prueba de identificación** = proof of identification; **rueda de identificación** = identification *o* identity parade; **fue arrestado por robo con allanamiento de morada y liberado después de establecerse que era un caso de identificación errónea** = he was arrested for burglary, but released after it had been established that it was a case of mistaken identity

identificar *vt* to identify; **sin identificar** = unascertained *o* unidentified; **víctima** *o* **cadáver sin identificar** = unidentified victim *o* body; **pudo identificar a su atacante** = she was able to identify her attacker; **el comprador no puede obtener el título de propiedad de bienes hasta que no hayan sido identificados** = title to unascertained goods cannot pass to the buyer until the goods have been ascertained; **se identificó al fallecido por sus huellas dactilares** = the dead man was identified by his fingerprints; **se pidió a los pasajeros que identificaran sus maletas** = passengers were asked to identify their suitcases
◊ **identificarse** *vr* to identify oneself; **el policía le pidió que se identificara** = the policeman asked him for proof of identification

idioma *nm* language

idóneo, -nea *adj* suitable *o (muy apto)* highly qualified; **tuvimos que poner de nuevo el anuncio del trabajo porque no se presentó ningún candidato idóneo** = we had to advertise the job again because there were no suitable candidates

ignominia *nf (injusticia)* injustice *o* unfairness; **cometerieron una ignominia al acusarle sin pruebas** = it was unfair of them to accuse him without proof

ignorancia *nf* ignorance; **'la ignorancia de la ley no exime su cumplimiento'** = ignorantia legis non *o* neminem *o* haud excusat *o* ignorance of the law is no excuse

ignorar *vt* to ignore *o* not to know *o* to be unaware of

igual 1 *adj* equal *o* similar; **por igual** = equally; **ser igual a** = to equal; **los trabajadores del sexo masculino y femenino reciben igual salario** = male and female workers have equal pay **2** *nmf* equal *o* peer
◊ **igualmente** *adv* equally *o* likewise; **el mandante está de acuerdo en reembolsar el dinero al mandatario e igualmente el mandatario está de acuerdo en reembolsarlo al mandante** = the principal agrees to reimburse the agent, and likewise the agent agrees to reimburse his principal

iguala *nf* retainer

igualar *vt* to equal *o* to equalize; **igualar dividendos** = to equalize dividends; **la producción de este mes ha igualado a la del mejor mes que hemos tenido** = production this month has equalled our best month ever

igualdad *nf* parity *o* equality; **igualdad de tratamiento** *o* **en igualdad de condiciones** = pari passu *o* on an equal basis; **Comisión de Igualdad de Oportunidades** = Equal Opportunities Commission; **programa de igualdad de oportunidades** = equal opportunities programme; **el personal femenino quiere igualdad de condiciones con los hombres** = the female staff want parity with the men

ilegal *adj* **(a)** *(ilícito)* illegal *o* unlawful *o* lawless; **acto ilegal** *o* **conducta ilegal** = malfeasance; **acto**

legal realizado con un fin ilegal = misfeasance; acto sexual ilegal = unlawful sexual intercourse; asociación ilegal = unlawful assembly; **contrato ilegal** = illegal contract; **declarar ilegal** = to outlaw; **huelga ilegal** = unofficial strike; **retención ilegal** *o* **detención ilegal** = false imprisonment; **violación ilegal de una propiedad** = unlawful trespass on property; **es ilegal despedir a un trabajador sin ninguna razón** = dismissing a worker without reason is against the law; **los inmigrantes ilegales son deportados** = illegal immigrants are deported **(b)** *(deshonesto)* bent *o* wrong *o* wrongful; **dinero ilegal** = hot money; **trato ilegal** = bent job; **la copia de datos informáticos es ilegal** = copying computer data is wrong

◊ **ilegalmente** *adv* illegally *o* unlawfully *o* wrongfully *o (bajo mano)* under the counter; **la acusaron de retener el dinero de sus clientes ilegalmente** = she was accused of wrongfully holding her clients' money; **le acusaron de introducir ilegalmente armas de fuego en el país** = he was accused of illegally bringing firearms into the country

ilegalidad *nf* illegality

ilegitimidad *nf* illegitimacy

ilegítimo, -ma *adj* illegitimate *o* unlawful; **posesión ilegítima** = adverse possession

ileso, -sa *adj* unharmed *o* unhurt; **salir ileso** = to come out unharmed

ilícito, -ta *adj* illegal *o* illicit *o* unlawful *o* lawless; **acto ilícito civil** = tort; **apropiación ilícita** = conversion; **apropiación ilícita de fondos** = conversion of funds; **comercio ilícito de alcohol** = trade in illicit alcohol; **negocio ilícito** = racketeering; **tenencia ilícita de armas** = the illegal carrying of arms; **venta ilícita de alcohol** = illicit sale of alcohol; **le acusaron de tenencia ilícita de armas de fuego** = he was charged with unlawfully carrying firearms

ilimitado, -da *adj* unlimited; **responsabilidad ilimitada** = unlimited liability; **el banco le ofreció crédito ilimitado** = the bank offered him unlimited credit; **empresa cuyos accionistas tienen responsabilidad ilimitada** = unlimited company

ilocalizable *adj* of unknown whereabouts

ilustre *adj* honourable

imitación *nf* imitation; **desconfíe de las imitaciones** = beware of imitations

imitar *vt* to imitate; **esta nueva banda está imitando todos los trucos de la famosa banda china de los años treinta** = this new gang is imitating all the tricks of the famous Chinese gang of the 1930s

impagado, -da *adj* unpaid; **deuda impagada** = unpaid debt *o* bad debt

impagar *vt* to dishonour; **impagar un cheque por falta de fondos** = to dishonour a cheque *o* to bounce a cheque

impago *nm* non-payment *o* dishonour; **impago de una deuda** = non-payment of a debt; **el impago del cheque paralizó sus negocios** = the dishonour of the cheque brought her business to a stop

imparcial *adj* impartial *o* just; **un juicio debe ser imparcial** = a judgment must be impartial; **ofrecer a alguien un juicio justo e imparcial** = to give someone a fair and impartial hearing

◊ **imparcialidad** *nf* impartiality; **la prensa dudó de la imparcialidad del juez** = the newspapers doubted the impartiality of the judge

◊ **imparcialmente** *adv* impartially; **el juez tiene que decidir imparcialmente entre las dos partes** = the adjudicator has to decide impartially between the two parties

impedido, -da *adj* handicapped

impedimento *nm* **(a)** *(obstáculo)* impediment *o* obstacle *o* bar; **impedimento legal** = estoppel; **impedimento por escritura** = estoppel by deed; **impedimento por falta de declaración** = estoppel by silence; **impedimento por razón de conducta** = estoppel by conduct *o* in pais; **impedimento por el que no se pueden cumplir los términos de un contrato** = frustration **(b)** *(circunstancia que impide el matrimonio)* **impedimento dirimente** = diriment impediment; **impedimento impediente** = prohibitive impediment; **impedimento de matrimonio por consanguinidad** = prohibited degrees **(c)** *(invalidez)* **impedimento físico** = handicap *o* disability **(d)** *(prevención)* prevention

impedir *vt* **(a)** *(obstaculizar)* to preclude *o* to bar *o* to restrain; **impedir que se cumplan los términos de un contrato** = to frustrate; **orden judicial que impide la acción al acusado mientras el tribunal esté decidiendo** = restraining order; **el tribunal garantizó al demandante un requerimiento que impidiera al acusado la infracción en materia de derechos de autor** = the court granted the plaintiff an injunction restraining the defendant from breaching copyright **(b)** *(prohibir)* **relaciones de consanguinidad que impiden el matrimonio** = prohibited degrees **(c)** *(prevenir)* to prevent; **debemos intentar impedir la oferta de absorción** = we must try to prevent the takeover bid; **la policía impidió que nadie saliera del edificio** = the police prevented anyone from leaving the building

imperativo, -va **1** *adj* mandatory; **requerimiento imperativo** = mandatory injunction **2** *nm* **imperativo legal** = legal requirement

imperfección *nf* fault *o* imperfection

imperfecto, -ta *adj* imperfect *o* faulty; **título imperfecto** = qualified title

imperio *nm* rule *o* authority; **el imperio de la ley** = the rule of law

impersonal *adj* impersonal; **un estilo de dirección impersonal** = an impersonal style of management

impertinente *adj* irrelevant

implantar *vt* to establish *o* to introduce; **implantaron un horario nuevo** = they introduced a new timetable

implicar *vt* **(a)** *(comprometer)* to involve *o* to compromise; **el ministro se vio implicado en un caso de soborno** = the minister was compromised in the bribery case; **las muertes en las que policías están implicados son siempre motivo de investigación** = deaths involving policemen *o* deaths where policemen are involved are always the subject of an inquest **(b)** *(suponer)* to entail

implícito, -ta *adj* implied *o* implicit; **condiciones implícitas** = implied terms and conditions; **conocimiento implícito** = constructive knowledge; **fideicomiso implícito** = implied trust

imponer *vt* **(a)** *(obligar o forzar a alguien a cumplir algo)* to enforce *o* to impose; **imponer un embargo comercial a un país** = to lay an embargo on trade with a country; **imponer una pena** = to pass a sentence; **que no se puede imponer** = unenforceable; **los sindicatos han pedido al gobierno que imponga barreras comerciales a los coches extranjeros** = the unions have asked the government to impose trade barriers on foreign cars; **trataron de imponer una prohibición sobre el uso del tabaco** = they tried to impose a ban on smoking **(b)** *(gravar)* to impose *o* to levy; **imponer una multa** = to impose a fine; **imponer un impuesto** = to impose a tax; **el gobierno impuso un impuesto especial sobre el petróleo** = the government imposed a special duty on oil; **el tribunal impuso una multa de 10.000 ptas** = the court imposed a fine of 10,000 ptas; **imponer un arancel a las importaciones de piezas informáticas** = to levy a duty on the import of computer parts
◊ **imponerse** *vr* to prevail

imponible *adj* taxable; **base imponible** = taxable base; **no imponible** = non-taxable; **renta imponible** = taxable income; **renta no imponible** = personal allowances; **valor imponible de la propiedad** = rateable value

importación *nf* import; **gravamen sobre las importaciones** = import levy; **permiso *o* licencia de importación** = import licence; **la importación de armas de fuego está prohibida** = the import of firearms is forbidden; **todas las importaciones deben declararse en la aduana** = all imports must be declared to the customs

importancia *nf* importance; **de menor importancia** = subsidiary; **de poca importancia** = minor; **sin importancia** = petty *o* immaterial; **una pérdida de poca importancia** = a loss of minor importance; **con la reorganización de la compañía redujeron la importancia de su cargo** = his job was downgraded in the company reorganization; **el banco da mucha importancia al acuerdo *o* a la transacción** = the bank attaches great importance to the deal; **se enfrenta a una acusación grave y a varias de menor importancia derivadas de la acusación principal** = he faces one serious charge and several subsidiary charges arising out of the main charge

importante *adj* **(a)** *(prioritario)* important *o* major; **accionista importante** = major shareholder; *(principal)* **más importante** = superior *o* leading *o* head; **menos importante** = sub-; **poco importante** = unimportant; **daños poco importantes** = nominal damages; **tiene una reunión muy importante a las 10.30** = she has an important meeting at 10.30; **le ascendieron a un puesto más importante** = he was promoted to a more important position **(b)** *(considerable)* substantial *o* considerable; **perdieron una importante cantidad de dinero en la bolsa de contratación** = they lost a considerable amount of money on the commodity market; **adquirir un importante número de acciones de una empresa** = to acquire a substantial interest in a company; **le concedieron una importante cantidad por daños y perjuicios** = she was awarded substantial damages **(c)** *(grande)* grand *o* large *o* heavy; **proyecto importante** = grand plan; **es nuestro cliente más importante** = he is our largest customer; **se dejó un montón de papeles importantes en el taxi** = he left a pile of important papers in the taxi; **le condenaron a pagar una multa importante** = he was sentenced to pay a heavy fine

importar 1 *vt* to import **2** *vi* to matter; **¿importa si las ventas de un mes son bajas?** = does it matter if one month's sales are down?

importunar *vt* to importune *o* *(abordar)* to solicit; **importunar sexualmente a alguien bajo amenazas** = to molest; **persona que importuna sexualmente a otra persona** = molester; **orden judicial que prohíbe importunar sexualmente al cónyuge bajo amenazas** = non-molestation order

imposibilidad *nf* impossibility; **imposibilidad de cumplimiento** = impossibility of performance; **imposibilidad material** = physical impossibility

imposibilitar *vt* to preclude; **el Tribunal Superior está imposibilitado por ley para revisar dicho fallo** = the High Court is precluded by statute from reviewing such a decision

imposible *adj* impossible; **a la policía le resulta imposible trabajar más de lo que lo hacen ya** = it is impossible for the police force to work harder than they are working already; **la reglamentación oficial nos hace imposible la venta de nuestras piezas de ordenadores** = government regulations make it impossible for us to sell our computer parts; **se está haciendo imposible conseguir personal cualificado** = getting skilled staff is becoming impossible

imposición *nf* **(a)** *(impuestos)* imposition *o* taxation; **imposición de costas** = taxation of costs; **imposición directa** = direct taxation; **doble imposición** = double taxation; **tratado de doble imposición** = double tax treaty *o* double taxation agreement **(b)** *(depósito)* deposit

impositivo, -va *adj* **código impositivo** tax code; **deducción fiscal impositiva** = tax deductions; **desgravación impositiva** = tax concession *o* tax exemption; **desgravación impositiva por gastos** = tax deductions; **grupo impositivo** = income bracket *o* tax bracket; **reducción impositiva** = tax relief; **retención impositiva en origen** = tax deducted at source; **sistema impositivo** = tax system

impositor, -ra *n (depositante)* depositor

impostor, -ra *n* impostor *o* deceiver

impostura *nf* jactitation *o* *(engaño)* fraudulent misrepresentation

impremeditado, -da *adj* unpremeditated

imprescindible *adj* essential; **es imprescindible que todos los datos del caso se presenten lo más claramente posible** = it is essential that all the facts of the case should be presented as clearly as possible

impresión *nf* **(a)** *(opinión creada sobre algo)* impression; **el discurso del abogado causó una fuerte impresión en el jurado** = counsel's speech made a strong impression on the jury; **el juez tuvo la impresión de que el testigo trabajaba en un banco** = the judge got the impression that the witness worked in a bank; *(pensar que)* **tener la impresión de que** = to take the view that **(b)** *(copia impresa)* printing; **impresión de salida** = printout **(c)** *(marca)* **impresión digital** = fingerprint

impreso, -sa **1** *adj* printed; **hoja impresa** = (printed) form; **copia impresa** *o* **texto impreso (de un texto en ordenador o microfilm)** = hard copy; **material impreso** = printed matter **2** *nm* *(formulario)* form; **impreso de inscripción** *o* **de matrícula** = admissions form *o* registration form; **impreso de solicitud** = application form; **rellenar un impreso de solicitud para un trabajo** = to fill in an application (form) for a job *o* a job application (form); **tiene que rellenar el impreso por duplicado** = you have to fill in the form in duplicate

impresor *nm* printer; **impresor de títulos** *o* **de documentos de valor** = security printer

impresora *nf (informática)* printer

imprevisión *nf* negligence

imprevisto, -ta **1** *adj (incidental)* incidental *o* contingent; **gastos imprevistos** = contingent expenses *o* incidental expenses **2** *nm (eventualidad)* contingency; **dinero para imprevistos** = emergency reserves; **fondo** *o* **reserva para imprevistos** = contingency fund *o* contingency reserve; **reservar dinero para imprevistos** = to provide

improbabilidad *nf* remoteness

ímprobo, -ba *adj (malvado)* dishonest *o* corrupt

improcedente *adj* unfair *o* wrongful; **despido improcedente** = unfair dismissal *o* wrongful dismissal; **(prueba) improcedente** = inadmissible

improperio *nm* insult; **improperios** = abuse; **lanzar improperios** = to abuse

impropio, -pia *adj* improper; **conducta impropia (contraria a la ética profesional)** = unprofessional conduct; **(comportamiento** *o* **vestido) impropio** = unbecoming
◊ **impropiamente** *adv* improperly

imprudencia *nf* negligence; *(culpa penal)* criminal negligence; **imprudencia temeraria** = recklessness *o* gross negligence; **conducir con imprudencia** = reckless driving; **conducir con imprudencia en estado de embriaguez** *o* **bajo los efectos del alcohol** = drunken driving

imprudente *adj* reckless *o* careless; **conducción imprudente** = reckless driving; **peatón imprudente** = jaywalker
◊ **imprudentemente** *adv* recklessly; **cruzar la calle imprudentemente** = jaywalking; **la empresa gastó imprudentemente millones en una nueva fábrica** = the company recklessly spent millions on a new factory

impúber *adj* underage *o* minor

impúdico, -ca *adj* obscene *o* lecherous

impuesto **1** *nm* **(a)** tax *o* duty; **impuesto a cuenta** = PAYE *o* pay-as-you-earn; **impuesto ad valorem, por porcentaje fijo del valor** *o* **impuesto sobre el precio** = ad valorem tax; **impuesto atrasado** = back tax; **impuesto básico** = basic rate tax; **impuesto de carretera** *o* **de vehículos rodados** = road tax; **impuesto de circulación** = vehicle tax; **impuesto de patrimonio** *o* **impuesto de plusvalía** *o* **impuesto sobre las ganancias del capital** = capital gains tax *o* Schedule A; **impuesto de sucesión** = death tax *o* *US* death duty; **impuesto de timbre** = stamp duty; **impuesto desgravable** *o* **deducible de impuestos** = tax-deductible; **impuesto municipal abonado por comerciantes o**

empresas = uniform business rate (UBR); **impuesto sobre beneficios extraordinarios** = excess profits tax; **impuesto sobre el capital** = capital levy; **impuesto (específico) sobre el consumo** *o* **sobre la venta** = excise duty *o* tax; **impuesto sobre el valor** = ad valorem duty *o* ad valorem tax; **impuesto sobre el valor añadido (IVA)** = Value Added Tax (VAT); **impuesto sobre la renta** = income tax; **impuesto sobre la renta de las personas físicas (IRPF)** = personal income tax; **impuesto sobre las transmisiones** *o* **las transferencias de capital** = capital transfer tax (CTT); **impuesto sobre las ventas** = sales tax; **impuesto sobre las ventas de bienes** *o* **de servicios** = output tax; **impuesto sobre sucesiones** *o* **impuesto sobre herencias y donaciones** = inheritance tax *o* estate tax *o* estate duty; **impuestos locales** *o* **municipales sobre la propiedad** = the rates **(b) exento, -ta de impuestos** = exempt from tax *o* tax-exempt *o* non-taxable; **libre de impuestos** = tax-free *o* duty-free *o* non-taxable; **recaudador, -ra de impuestos** = exciseman; **sujeto a impuesto** = taxable; **artículos sujetos a impuesto** = taxable items; **administración de aduanas e impuestos sobre el consumo** = Customs and Excise *o* Excise Department; **elusión de impuestos** = tax avoidance; **beneficio después de impuestos** *o* **utilidad después de impuesto** = profit after tax; **beneficio sin deducir los impuestos** *o* **utilidad antes de impuesto** = profit before tax *o* pretax profit; **crédito por impuestos pagados** = tax credit; **deducción del salario en concepto de impuesto** = tax deductions; **momento en el que se empieza a aplicar un impuesto** = tax point; **productos con impuestos aduaneros pagados** = duty-paid goods; **productos sujetos a impuesto** = goods which are liable to duty; **sociedad sujeta al pago de impuestos** = corporate taxpayers; **tienda libre de impuestos (en aeropuertos y barcos)** = duty-free shop; **estos artículos están sujetos a un impuesto elevado** these items are heavily taxed; **la renta está sujeta a un impuesto del 29%** = income is taxed at 29%; **compró un reloj, libre de impuestos, en el aeropuerto** = he bought a duty-free watch at the airport *o* he bought the watch duty-free **(c) establecer un impuesto** = to levy a tax *o* to impose a tax; **establecer un impuesto legal** = to set a legal rate; **gravar con un impuesto** = to tax; **gravar las empresas con un impuesto del 50%** = to tax businesses at 50%; **suprimir un impuesto** = to lift a tax; **suprimir los impuestos sobre el alcohol** = to take the duty off alcohol; **el gobierno ha establecido un impuesto del 15% sobre la gasolina** = the government has imposed a 15% tax on petrol **(d)** *(imposición)* imposition **2** *nmpl* taxation; **impuestos directos** = direct taxation

impugnable *adj* open to appeal

impugnación *nf* rebuttal *o* objection

impugnar *vt* to rebut; **impugnar una herencia** = to dispute an inheritance; **impugnar una sentencia** = to appeal against a sentence

impulso *nm* impulse; **impulso irresistible** = irresistible impulse

impune *adj* unpunished
◊ **impunemente** *adv* with impunity; **nadie puede burlarse de la ley impunemente** = no one can flout the law with impunity

imputable *adj* chargeable

imputación *nf* imputation *o* charge *o* accusation

imputado, -da *adj* charged *o* accused

imputar *vt* to impute *o* to charge *o* to accuse

inactivo, -va *adj* *(latente)* dormant *o* dead; *(átono)* flat; **cuenta inactiva** = dead account; **la bolsa estuvo inactiva hoy** = the market was flat today

inadecuado, -da *adj* improper

inadmisible *adj* inadmissible

inalienable *adj* inalienable

inapelable *adj* unappealable *o* not open to appeal

inaplazable *adj* which cannot be postponed

inauguración *nf* opening; **la inauguración de una nueva sucursal** *o* **de un nuevo mercado** *o* **de una nueva oficina** = the opening of a new branch *o* of a new market *o* of a new office

inaugural *adj* opening

incalculable *adj* unquantifiable; **daños incalculables** = unquantifiable damages *o* losses

incapacidad *nf* incapacity; **incapacidad absoluta permanente** = permanent total disability; **incapacidad absoluta temporal** = temporary total disability; **incapacidad física** = physical disability; **incapacidad jurídica** = legal disability; **incapacidad laboral transitoria** = temporary disability; **incapacidad parcial** = partial disability; **incapacidad permanente y absoluta** = total disability; **el juzgado tuvo que actuar** *o* **tomar cartas en el asunto a causa de la incapacidad de los administradores** = the court had to act because of the incapacity of the trustees

incapacitado, -da *adj* **(a)** *(físicamente imposibilitado)* disabled; **incapacitado mental** = mentally disabled **(b)** *(no apto para ser juzgado)* incapable *o* incompetent *o* legally incompetent; **incapacitado para ser juzgado** = unfit to plead; **persona incapacitada jurídicamente** = person under a disability; **borracho e incapacitado** = drunk and incapable; **un menor está considerado legalmente incapacitado para cometer un delito** = a child is considered legally incapable of committing a crime

incapacitar *vt (inhabilitar)* to disqualify

incapaz *adj* (a) *(incapacitado)* incapable *o* unable; **incapaz de intención criminal** = doli incapax; **fue incapaz de cumplir los términos del contrato** = he was incapable of fulfilling the terms of the contract (b) *(incompetente)* incompetent

incautación *nf* attachment *o* seizure *o* confiscation; **incautación de ingresos** = attachment of earnings; **orden de incautación de ingresos** = attachment of earnings order; **el tribunal ordenó la incautación de los fondos de la compañía** = the court ordered the company's funds to be seized; **el tribunal ordenó la incautación del envío** *o* **de los fondos de la compañía** = the court ordered the seizure of the shipment *o* of the company's funds

incautar *vt* to arrest *o* to attach
◊ **incautarse** *vr* to impound; **incautarse de** = to seize *o* to confiscate; **los oficiales de aduanas se incautaron del cargamento de libros** = the customs seized the shipment of books

incendiar *vt* to burn down *o* to set on fire; **incendiar una casa** = an arson attack on a house *o* to set a house on fire
◊ **incendiarse** *vr* to catch fire; **los papeles de la papelera se incendiaron** = the papers in the waste paper basket caught fire

incendiario, -ria *n* fire-raiser *o* arsonist *o* pyromaniac

incendio *nm* fire; **incendio doloso** *o* **incendio provocado** *o* **premeditado** *o* **intencionado** = fire-raising *o* arson; **a prueba de incendios** = fireproof; **artículos dañados en un incendio** = fire-damaged goods; **daños por incendio** = fire damage; **delito de incendio intencionado** *o* **provocado** = arson; **peligro** *o* **riesgo de incendio** = fire hazard *o* fire risk; **regulaciones en materia de incendios** = fire regulations; **seguro contra incendios** = fire insurance; **se le acusó de incendio intencionado** = he was charged with arson; **reclamó 250.000 ptas en concepto de daños por incendio** = he claimed 250,000 ptas for fire damage; **durante el motín hubo diez casos de robo y dos incendios intencionados** = during the riot there were ten cases of looting and two of arson; **el envío resultó dañado en el incendio que se declaró a bordo del carguero** = the shipment was damaged in the fire on board the cargo boat; **es imposible conseguir que la oficina esté completamente a prueba de incendios** = it is impossible to make the office completely fireproof; **ese almacén lleno de papel es un peligro en caso de incendio** = that warehouse full of paper is a fire hazard; **la mitad de las existencias quedaron destruidas en el incendio del almacén** = half the stock was destroyed in the warehouse fire; **la policía que investiga el incendio sospecha que**

fue intencionado = the police who are investigating the fire suspect arson

incentivado, -da *adj* **baja incentivada** = voluntary redundancy

incentivo *nm (estímulo)* inducement; **le ofrecieron un coche de la empresa como incentivo para que se quedara** = they offered him a company car as an inducement to stay

incesto *nm* incest

incidencia *nf* (a) *(frecuencia)* incidence; **una alta incidencia de accidentes relacionados con conductores en estado de embriaguez** = a high incidence of accidents relating to drunken drivers (b) *(suceso)* incident; **sala de incidencias de una comisaría** = incident room (c) *(impacto)* impact; **las advertencias han tenido poca incidencia** = the warnings have had little impact

incidental *adj* incidental; **asunto incidental** = collateral issue; **autos incidentales** = interlocutory proceedings

incidente *nm* incident; **incidente fatal** = a fatal incident; **se dio parte de tres incidentes cuando los vehículos policiales fueron atacados por una multitud** = three incidents were reported when police vehicles were attacked by a crowd

incitación *nf* incitement; **incitación al odio racial** = incitement to racial hatred; **complicidad e incitación a cometer un crimen** = aiding and abetting

incitador, -ra *n* inciter *o (al crimen)* abettor

incitar *vt* (a) *animar* to incite *o* to encourage; **incitar a alguien a decir algo** = to prompt; **incitar a cometer un crimen** = to abet (b) *(provocar)* to provoke; **los huelguistas incitaron a la policía a tomar represalias** = the strikers provoked the police to retaliate

inclinación *nf* bias *o* tendency; **tener inclinaciones criminales** = to have criminal tendencies; **tiene tendencia a robar** = he has a tendency to steal

inclinar *vt* to bias *o* to incline; **la falta de dinero le inclinó a robar** = the lack of money induced him to steal

incluido, -da *adj (inclusive)* inclusive; **no incluido** = exclusive of; **todo incluido** = all-in; **impuestos incluidos** *o* **IVA no incluido** = inclusive of tax *o* not inclusive of VAT; **el transporte va incluido en el precio** = the price includes free delivery; **los gastos de envío no están incluidos** = delivery is not allowed for

incluir *vt* (a) *(tener en cuenta)* to include *o* to count; **incluir en** = to cut someone in on; **precio que incluye todos los gastos** = inclusive sum *o* inclusive charge; **incluyendo este artículo pero sin**

excluir a otros = including, but not limited to; **el IVA está incluido en el precio** = the charge includes VAT; **el total asciende a 500.000 ptas incluido el transporte** = the total comes to 500,000 ptas including freight; **el total es de 140.000 ptas sin incluir seguro y flete** = the total is 140,000 ptas not including insurance and freight; **¿incluyó en la defensa que el dinero de la caja robado por el acusado formaba parte del robo total?** = did the defence count the accused's theft of money from the till as part of the total theft?; **se incluyó la moción en el orden del día** = the motion was noted on the agenda **(b)** *(incorporar)* to incorporate; **incluir a alguien en una acción** = to join someone to an action; **la lista de mercados está incluida en el contrato principal** = the list of markets is incorporated into the main contract; **la renta procedente de la adquisición de 1984 está incluida en las cuentas** = income from the 1984 acquisition is incorporated into the accounts

inclusive *adj* inclusive *o (sin excluir)* not excluding; **los funcionarios del gobierno, inclusive los jueces, están protegidos** *o* **amparados por el proyecto de ley** = government servants, not excluding judges, are covered by the Bill; **la cuenta cubre los servicios hasta el mes de junio inclusive** = the account covers services up to and including the month of June; **la reunión durará desde el 12 al 16 ambos inclusives** = the meeting runs from the 12th to the 16th inclusive

inclusivo, -va *adj* inclusive

incoar *vt (iniciar)* to institute; **incoar un proceso contra alguien** = to institute proceedings against someone

incobrable *adj (irrecuperable)* irrecoverable; **deuda incobrable** = irrecoverable debt *o (obligación perpetua)* irredeemable bond; **ser incobrable (por falta de fondos)** = to bounce

incógnito *nm* incognito; *(de paisano)* **de incógnito** = plainclothes; **en el tren viajaba un detective de incógnito** = a plainclothes detective travelled on the train

incombustible *adj (ininflamable)* fireproof

incomparecencia *nf* absence *o* failure to appear (in court)

incompatible *adj* incompatible; **la legislación del Reino Unido es incompatible con las directrices de la UE** = the UK legislation conflicts with the directives of the EU; **ser juez es incompatible con ser diputado** = being a judge disqualifies you from being a Member of Parliament

incompetencia *nf* incompetency *o* maladministration

incompetente *adj* incompetent; **el director de ventas es totalmente incompetente** = the sales

manager is quite incompetent; **la empresa tiene un director de ventas incompetente** = the company has an incompetent sales director

incompleto, -ta *adj* defective *o* inchoate; **documento incompleto** = inchoate instrument; **delitos incompletos** = inchoate offences

incomunicación *nf* isolation *o (en prisión)* solitary confinement

incomunicado, -da *adj* in solitary confinement; **le mantuvieron incomunicado durante seis meses** = he was kept in solitary confinement for six months

incondicional *adj* unconditional; **aceptación incondicional de la oferta por parte del Consejo de Administración** = unconditional acceptance of the offer by the board
◊ **incondicionalmente** *adv* unconditionally; **la oferta se aceptó incondicionalmente** = the offer was accepted unconditionally

inconfeso, -sa *adj* suspect who does not confess *o* who denies the charges

inconsciente *adj* **(a)** *(sin reflexionar)* reckless **(b)** *(sin conocimiento)* unconscious

inconstitucional *adj (anticonstitucional)* unconstitutional; **el presidente decidió que la reunión era inconstitucional** = the chairman ruled that the meeting was unconstitutional; **el Tribunal Constitucional decidió que la acción del fiscal general era inconstitucional** = the Constitutional Court ruled that the action of the Attorney-General was unconstitutional

incontestable *adj* undeniable *o* undisputable

incontestado, -da *adj (indisputable)* unchallenged *o* uncontested; **elecciones incontestadas** = an uncontested election; **un caso de divorcio incontestado** = an uncontested divorce case

incontrolable *adj* uncontrollable; **inflación incontrolable** = uncontrollable inflation; **tenía impulsos incontrolables que le inducían al robo** = he had an uncontrollable impulse to steal

incontrovertible *adj* indisputable

inconveniente *nm* **(a)** *(desventaja)* disadvantage; **para un abogado especializado en impuestos es un inconveniente no haber estudiado contabilidad** = it is a disadvantage for a tax lawyer not to have studied to be an accountant **(b)** *(molestia)* inconvenience; **la manifestación de protesta causó algunos inconvenientes a los comerciantes de la zona** = the protest march caused some inconvenience to the local shopkeepers

inconvertible *adj* irredeemable

incorporar vt (incluir) to incorporate; (en un documento) to annex
◊ **incorporarse** vr **incorporarse a un despacho de abogados** = to join a firm of solicitors; **se incorporó el 1 de enero** = he joined on January 1st; **Casado S.A. ha solicitado incorporarse a la asociación comercial** = Casado Ltd has applied to join the trade association

incorpóreo, -rea adj incorporeal

incorrecto, -ta adj **(a)** (equivocado) incorrect o incorrectly o wrong; **un paquete con la dirección incorrecta** = an incorrectly addressed package; **el total de la última columna es incorrecto** = the total in the last column is wrong **(b)** (impropio) improper
◊ **incorrectamente** adv **(a)** (erróneamente) incorrectly; **la acusación estaba redactada incorrectamente** = the indictment was incorrectly worded **(b)** (indebidamente) improperly; **el informe del policía estaba redactado incorrectamente** = the police constable's report was improperly made out

incorrupto, -ta adj uncorrupt

incrementar vt (aumentar) to increase

incremento nm increase; **incremento del coste de vida** = increase in the cost of living; **incremento del patrimonio** = capital gains

incriminar vt to incriminate; **incriminar a alguien** = to frame; **le han incriminado** = he has been framed; **le incriminaron por el mensaje grabado que envió a la víctima** = he was incriminated by the recorded message he sent to the victim

incruento, -ta adj bloodless

inculpable adj not guilty o innocent

inculpado, -da n accused

inculpar vt to accuse o to incriminate

incumbencia nf **es de su incumbencia** = it is incumbent upon him; **es incumbencia de los jueces advertir de sus dudas sobre un caso** = it is incumbent upon justices to give some warning of their doubts about a case

incumbir vi to be incumbent upon; **le incumbe a él** = it is incumbent upon him

incumplido, -da adj (estar en situación de) **haber incumplido** = in breach of

incumplimiento nm (negligencia) neglect o (fallo) failure; **incumplimiento de pago** = default of payment; **incumplimientio de contrato** = breach of contract; (antiguamente) **incumplimiento de pago** = default; **incumplimiento de palabra** o **de promesa matrimonial** = breach of promise; **incumplimiento del procedimiento correcto** = failure to observe the correct procedure; **delito por incumplimiento** = nonfeisance; **por incumplimiento de pago** = in default of payment; **su incumplimiento de la orden judicial** = his failure to comply with the court order; **su incumplimiento de respetar el plazo fijado** = their failure to meet the deadline; **su incumplimiento en el pago de una factura** = her failure to pay a bill

incumplir vt to fail to observe o to fail to fulfill; **incumplir la ley** = to break the law; **incumplir un contrato** o **un pago** = to dishonour o to default on payments; **el demandado ha incumplido sus obligaciones legales** = the defendant is in breach of his statutory duty; **la empresa ha incumplido el contrato** = the company is in breach of contract

incuria nf malpractice

incurrir vi to incur o to commit; **incurrir en delito** = to commit a crime o a felony; **incurrir en gastos** = to incur costs; **incurrir en perjurio** o **en soborno** = to commit perjury o to commit bribery; **incurrir en el riesgo de una multa** = to incur the risk of a penalty; **la empresa ha incurrido en gastos elevados para llevar a cabo el programa de desarrollo** = the company has incurred heavy costs to implement the development programme

indagación nf enquiry o inquiry

indagar vt to enquire o to investigate

indagatorio, -ria 1 adj investigatory **2** nf **(a)** (declaración sin juramento) preliminary investigation **(b)** **indagatoria del forense** = coroner's inquest

indebido, -da adj improper o illegal; **apropiación indebida** = conversion o misappropriation; **unión indebida** = misjoinder; **uso indebido** = misuse; **uso indebido de fondos o de activos** o **de bienes** = misuse of funds o of assets
◊ **indebidamente** adv improperly; **apropiarse indebidamente de** = to misappropriate; **le acusaron de actuar indebidamente al ir a ver al padre del acusado** = he was accused of acting improperly in going to see the prisoner's father

indecencia nf indecency o obscenity

indecente adj indecent o obscene

indecoroso, -sa adj indecent; (comportamiento o vestido) **indecoroso** = unbecoming

indefenso, -sa adj without a defence o defenceless

indefinido, -da adj indefinite; **por un periodo indefinido de tiempo** = for an indefinite period of time
◊ **indefinidamente** adv (sin día) sine die

indemnidad nf indemnity

indemnización *nf* (a) *(acción)* indemnification (b) *(pago)* indemnity *o* compensation *o* benefit *o* relief; **indemnización doble (por muerte accidental)** = double indemnity; **indemnización por daños** = insurance claim *o* damages; **indemnización por daños y perjuicios** = compensation for damage *o* compensatory damages *o* restitution; **indemnización por despido** *o* **por cese en el cargo** = severance pay *o* compensation for loss of office; **indemnización por enfermedad** *o* **por baja laboral** = sick pay *o* statutory sick pay; **indemnización por fallecimiento** = death benefit; **indemnización que el acusado debe pagar por daños causados al demandante** = exemplary damages; **indemnización suplementaria** = aggravated damages; **atenuante** *o* **minoración de la indemnización por daños** = mitigation of damages; **garantía de indemnización** = letter of indemnity; **orden de indemnización** = compensation order; **reclamar** *o* **pedir una indemnización** = to put in a claim; **la Audiencia puede conceder indemnización ilimitada** = unlimited compensation may be awarded in the Crown Court; **la agencia de seguros envía cheques de indemnización todas las semanas** = the insurance office sends out benefit cheques each week; **la indemnización que el demandante solicitaba consistía en una intimación y daños** = the relief the plaintiff sought was an injunction and damages; **pidió una indemnización de 250.000 ptas por daños y perjuicios al conductor del otro coche** = she put in a claim for 250,000 damages against the driver of the other car; **tuvo que pagar una indemnización de 100.000 ptas** = he had to pay an indemnity of 100, 000 ptas

indemnizar *vt* to indemnify; **indemnizar a alguien por una pérdida** = to indemnify someone for a loss; **indemnizar un siniestro** = to settle. a claim; **la compañía aseguradora se negó a indemnizar los daños causados por el temporal** = the insurance company refused to settle his claim for storm damage

independiente *adj* independent *o* *(que trabaja por su cuenta)* freelance; **comerciante independiente** *o* **comercio independiente** = independent trader *o* independent shop; **contratista independiente** = independent contractor; **empresa independiente** = independent company; **los trabajadores independientes** = the self-employed; **trabaja para el periódico local como reportera independiente** = she is a freelance reporter for the local newspaper
◊ **independientemente** *adv* independently; **los dos detectives llegaron a la misma conclusión independientemente del otro** = the two detectives reached the same conclusion independently of each other; **trabaja independientemente como agente publicitario** = he works freelance as an advertising agent

indicación *nf* (a) *(señal)* indication *o* *(pista)* lead (b) *(sugerencia)* suggestion *o* advice; **enviamos los documentos a la policía por indicación del abogado** = we sent the documents to the police on the advice of the solicitor *o* we took the solicitor's advice and sent the documents to the police

indicador *nm* indicator

indicar *vt* (a) *(señalar)* to indicate *o* to show *o* **indicar un aumento** *o* **un descenso** = to show a gain *o* a fall; *(marcar)* to mark; *indicar en un producto 'sólo para la exportación'* = to mark a product 'for export only' (b) *(especificar)* to specify

índice *nm* (a) *(repertorio)* index; **índice de materias** = table of contents (b) *(ritmo)* rate *o* index *o* indicator; **índice de criminalidad** = crime rate; **índice del coste de vida** = cost-of-living index; **índice de errores** = error rate; **índice de inflación** = rate of inflation *o* inflation rate; **índice de mortalidad** *o* **de natalidad** = death toll *o* birth rate; **índices económicos oficiales** = government economic indicators; **el índice de natalidad ha descendido al doce por ciento** = the birth rate has fallen to twelve per hundred

indicio *nm* evidence *o* clue; **indicio claro** = conclusive evidence; **indicio dudoso** = inconclusive evidence; **indicio leve** = light presumption; **indicios racionales de criminalidad** = reasonable *o* sufficient evidence; **indicios razonables** = prima facie evidence; **indicios vehementes** = strong evidence; **pruebas por indicio** = presumptive evidence

indigente *adj* destitute; **como persona indigente** = in forma pauperis

indirecto, -ta *adj* indirect *o* vicarious *o* circumstantial; **daños indirectos** = special damages; **ejecución de un contrato de un modo indirecto** = vicarious performance; **prueba indirecta** *o* **circunstancial** = circumstantial evidence; **responsabilidad indirecta** = vicarious liability
◊ **indirectamente** *adv* vicariously

indispensable *adj* **lo indispensable (para un niño o persona incapacitada)** = necessaries; **requisito indispensable** = necessity; **'sin lo que nada': requisito indispensable** = sine qua non

indisputable *adj* unchallenged *o* uncontested

individual *adj* individual; **libertad individual** = liberty of the subject; **derechos individuales** = civil liberties; **se tiene a los presos en celdas individuales** = the prisoners are kept in individual cells
◊ **individualmente** *adv* **son responsables individualmente** = they are jointly and severally liable

individuo, -dua 1 *adj* individual 2 *nm* individual; **declaración de derechos del individuo** = Bill of Rights; **libertad del individuo** = liberty of the subject; **se le acercaron dos individuos que vestían abrigos blancos** = he was approached by two individuals in white coats

índole *nf* nature

inducción *nf* inducement; **inducción dolosa a la comisión de un delito (para poder detener al delincuente)** = entrapment; **inducción al quebrantamiento de un contrato** = inducement to break contract

> La inducción consiste en instigar, persuadir o mover a otra persona a realizar una acción constitutiva de delito. Para que la inducción sea punible ha de probarse la relación de causalidad entre ésta y la comisión del delito

inducir *vt* to induce; **inducir a** = to lead; **el abogado no debe inducir al testigo** = counsel must not lead the witness

indulgencia *nf* leniency

indulgente *adj* lenient
◊ **indulgentemente** *adv* leniently; **los acusados fueron tratados indulgentemente por el tribunal militar** = the accused were treated leniently by the military tribunal

indultar *vt* to pardon *o* to reprieve; **le condenaron a muerte pero fue indultado por el presidente** = he was sentenced to death but was reprieved by the president; **los presos políticos fueron indultados por el presidente** = the political prisoners were pardoned *o* were amnestied by the president

indulto *nm* pardon; **indulto general** = general amnesty; **indulto en caso de sentencia y condena nulas** = free pardon

> La amnistía consiste en el perdón y el olvido de un delito, teniéndose éste por no cometido, mientras que el indulto supone la remisión total o parcial de una pena. La Constitución española contiene la prohibición expresa de autorizar indultos generales

industria *nf* industry *o* (ramo) trade
◊ **industrial** *adj* industrial; **propiedad industrial** = industrial property; **polígono industrial** = industrial estate *o* trading estate

inédito, -ta *adj* unpublished *o* new

inepto, -ta *adj* (incompetente) inept

inequívoco, -ca *adj* unequivocal

inevitable *adj* unavoidable *o* inevitable; **accidente inevitable** = inevitable accident; **los vuelos están sujetos a retrasos inevitables** = planes are subject to unavoidable delays

◊ **inevitablemente** *adv* unavoidably; **la vista se retrasó inevitablemente** = the hearing was unavoidably delayed

inexcusable *adj* unforgivable

infame *adj* infamous

infanticida *nmf* infanticide *o* child-killer

infanticidio *nm* infanticide

inferencia *nf* deduction

inferior *adj* (a) (calidad, rango) inferior *o* substandard; **tribunal inferior** = inferior court (b) (menor) junior *o* puisne

inferir *vt* to infer

infidencia *nf* (a) (acto legal realizado con un fin ilegal) misfeasance (b) (abuso de confianza) breach of confidence

inflación *nf* inflation; **índice de inflación** = rate of inflation *o* inflation rate

infligir *vt* **infligir daño** = to inflict harm; **infligir un castigo** = to inflict punishment

influencia *nf* influence; **influencia desmedida** *o* **indebida** = undue influence

influenciar *vt* to influence; **el fallo del tribunal se vio influenciado por la juventud del acusado** = the court was influenced in its decision by the youth of the accused; **la decisión del tribunal no se vio influenciada por el discurso del Primer Ministro** = the decision of the court was not influenced by the speech of the Prime Minister

influir *vt* to influence *o* to affect; **tratar de influir sobre los testigos** = to interfere with witnesses; **el precio del petróleo ha influido en el precio de los productos industriales** = the price of oil has influenced the price of industrial goods; **le acusaron de tratar de influir sobre los magistrados** = he was accused of trying to influence the magistrates

influyente *adj* **persona influyente** = influential person

información *nf* (a) (informe) information; **información confidencial** = confidential information *o* (en la bolsa) a tip; **información falsa** = false information; **información privada** *o* **privilegiada** = inside information *o* insider dealing *o* insider trading; **información secreta** *o* **reservada** = classified information; **agencia de información** = news agency; **empleado, -da del servicio de información** = information officer; **fuente de información** = informant; **oficina de información** = information bureau *o* information office; **revelación de información confidencial** = disclosure of confidential information; **sesión de información** = briefing; **ofrecer** *o* **dar información** = to volunteer information; **ofrecer** *o* dar información completa sobre algo = to give full particulars of something; **pedir información** = to inquire; **responder a una petición de información** = to answer a request for information; **revelar una información** = to disclose a piece of information; **sacar u obtener información de alguien** = to extract information from someone; **solicitó información sobre el número de crímenes resueltos** = she inquired about the rate of crimes solved; **todos los detectives del caso asistieron a una sesión de información que dio el comandante** = all the detectives on the case attended a briefing given by the commander; **para mayor información, por favor escriba a la sección 27** = for further information, please write to Department 27; **¿Tiene usted información sobre las cuentas de depósito?** = have you any information on *o* about deposit accounts?; **adjunto remito este folleto para su información** = I enclose this leaflet for your information **(b)** *(datos)* data

informal *adj* casual *o* informal; **el jefe de la Brigada Criminal se reunió de una manera informal con oficiales de la Interpol** = the head of the CID had an informal meeting with officers from Interpol
◊ **informalmente** *adv* informally; **apareció ante el tribunal *o* en el juicio vistiendo informalmente** = he appeared in court wearing casual clothes

informante *nmf* informant; **¿su informante es de confianza?** = is your informant reliable?

informar *vt* **(a)** *(comunicar)* to inform *o* to brief *o* to advise *o* to report; **informar erróneamente** = to misdirect; **el Comisario jefe informó a la prensa de los progresos de la investigación** = the superintendent briefed the press on the progress of the investigation; **informó que el acusado no era en realidad un súbdito británico** = he informed that the defendant was not in fact a British subject; **se nos informa que el envío llegará la semana próxima** = we are advised that the shipment will arrive next week **(b)** *(abarcar)* to cover; **los periódicos han informado exhaustivamente sobre el juicio por asesinato** = the newspapers have covered the murder trial **(c)** *(dar instrucciones)* to brief; **informar a un abogado de un caso** = to brief a barrister
◊ **informarse** *vr (pedir información)* to inquire

informática *nf* information technology

informático, -ca *adj* **archivo informático** = computer file; **fraude informático** = computer fraud; **lenguaje informático** = computer language; **oficina de servicios informáticos** = computer bureau

informativo, -va *adj* informative; **prospecto *o* folleto informativo** = prospectus; **restricciones informativas (sobre un caso en la prensa)** = reporting restrictions; **se levantaron las restricciones informativas** = reporting restrictions were lifted

informatizar *vt* to computerize; **los archivos policiales han sido totalmente informatizados** = the police criminal records have been completely computerized

informe *nm* **(a)** *(declaración)* report *o* memorandum *o* statement; **informe confidencial** = confidential report; **informe de un abogado sobre un caso** = counsel's advice *o* counsel's opinion; **informe de gastos de compra-venta de una propiedad** = completion statement; **informe del tesorero** = the treasurer's report; **informe engañoso** = false representation; **informe pericial** = expert's report; **informe sobre la marcha de los trabajos** = progress report; **hacer un informe** = to make a report; **presentar un informe *o* enviar un informe** = to report *o* to present a report *o* to send in a report; **el gobierno ha publicado un informe sobre los problemas de la violencia en el centro de las ciudades** = the government has issued a report on the problems of inner city violence; **el oficial encargado de la custodia presentó un informe sobre el progreso de los dos delincuentes juveniles** = the probation officer reported on the progress of the two young criminals; **el presidente ha recibido un informe de la compañía aseguradora** = the chairman has received a report from the insurance company; **el tribunal oyó un informe del oficial encargado de la libertad condicional** = the court heard a report from the probation officer **(b)** *(memoria)* report; **informe anual del consejo de administración** = directors' report; **el informe anual de la empresa *o* el informe del presidente *o* el informe del director** = the company's annual report *o* the chairman's report *o* the directors' report **(c)** *(referencias)* reference; **informe a favor** = letter of comfort *o* comfort letter; **agencia de informes comerciales** = credit agency *o* credit bureau; **persona que da informes de otra** = referee *o* reference; **dar un buen informe sobre alguien** = to give someone a character reference; **pedimos al banco un informe sobre su estado financiero** = we asked the bank to report on his financial status **(d)** *(actas de un tribunal)* record

infracción *nf* **(a)** *(violación)* infringement *o* breach *o* violation *o* contravention; **infracción de los derechos de autor** = infringement of copyright *o* copyright infringement; **ha aumentado el número de infracciones de tráfico** = the number of traffic violations has increased **(b)** *(delito)* wrongdoing *o* offence *o* US offense; **infracción menor** = misdemeanour; **infracciones por estacionamiento indebido** = parking offences; **primera infracción** = first offence; **fue acusado de varias infracciones, entre ellas la de conducir sin permiso vigente y la de provocar disturbios** = he was charged with several misdemeanours, including driving without a valid licence and creating a disturbance

infractor, -ra *n* *(delincuente)* offender *o* *(intruso)* trespasser

infravaloración *nf* underestimate; **la cifra de 500.000 ptas por las costas legales fue una infravaloración considerable** *o* **fue calculada muy por lo bajo** = the figure of 500,000 ptas in legal costs was a considerable underestimate

infravalorar *vt* to underestimate

infringir *vt* to infringe; **infringir la ley** = to break the law *o* to offend; **el ayuntamiento ha infringido las normas de planificación urbanística** = the council has violated the planning regulations; **si pegas a un policía infringirás la ley** = if you hit a policeman you will be breaking the law

infringir *vt* to break *o* to violate; **infringir los derechos de autor** = to infringe a copyright

infructuoso, -sa *adj* unsuccessful; **la policía llevó a cabo una búsqueda infructuosa del sospechoso** = the police carried out an unsuccessful search for the suspect

ingerencia *nf* interference

ingresar 1 *vi* to join; **ingresar en el Colegio de Abogados** = call to the Bar **2** *vt* **(a)** to bank *o* to credit *o* to deposit; **ingresar un cheque** = to pay a cheque into your account; **ingresar 100.000 ptas en una cuenta** = to credit an account with 100,000 ptas *o* to credit 100,000 ptas to an account **(b)** **ingresar cadáver** = to be dead on arrival

ingreso *nm* **(a)** *(entrada)* admission; **ingreso en prisión** = committal; **auto de ingreso en prisión** = commitment; **orden de ingreso en prisión** = committal order; **orden judicial de ingreso en prisión** = committal warrant; **Turquía ha solicitado el ingreso en la UE** = Turkey has applied for membership of the EU **(b)** *(dinero)* deposit *o* receipts; **ingresos (de una tienda)** = take; **detallar los ingresos y los gastos** = to itemize receipts and expenditure; **los ingresos han bajado en comparación con el mismo periodo del año pasado** = receipts are down against the same period of last year
◊ **ingresos** *nmpl* *(salario)* income *o* earnings *o* *(renta)* revenue *o* *(ganancias)* proceeds; **indemnización por pérdida de ingresos** = compensation for loss of earnings

inhabilitación *nf* disqualification *o* disability; **inhabilitación para el cargo** = disqualification from office; **inhabilitación para conducir** = disqualification from driving; **inhabilitación perpetua** = civil death; **inhabilitación total** = total disability; **le condenaron por conducir un vehículo en periodo de inhabilitación** = he was

convicted for driving a motor vehicle while disqualified

> La inhabilitación es una pena consistente en la prohibición de obtener cargos públicos o de ejercitar derechos civiles o políticos. La inhabilitación en caso de quiebra priva al quebrado de la administración de sus bienes

inhabilitar *vt* **(a)** *(descalificar)* to disqualify **(b)** *(privar de los derechos civiles o del derecho de votación)* to disenfranchise *o* to disfranchise

inherente *adj* inherent; **inherente a** = incident to something; **comprar algo con todos los derechos inherentes** = to purchase something outright *o* to make an outright purchase

inhibitoria *nf* abstention *o* restraining order

iniciado *nm* insider; **operaciones de iniciado** = insider dealing

inicial 1 *adj* *(primero, de apertura)* initial *o* opening; **asiento inicial** = opening entry; **capital inicial** = initial capital; **oferta** *o* **puja inicial** = opening bid; **parte inicial** premises; **saldo inicial** = opening balance; **los comentarios iniciales del juez** = the judge's opening remarks; **comenzó el negocio con un gasto inicial** *o* **con una inversión inicial de 5 millones** = he started the business with an initial expenditure *o* initial investment of 5 million **2** *nf* *(rúbrica)* initial; **poner** *o* **marcar** *o* **firmar con las iniciales** = to initial; **¿Qué significan las iniciales QC?** = what do the initials QC stand for?; **el presidente marcó con sus iniciales todas las modificaciones efectuadas en el contrato que estaba firmando** = the chairman wrote his initials by each alteration in the contract he was signing

iniciar *vt* to open *o* to initiate *o* to start *o* to enter into *o* to institute; **iniciar acciones judiciales** = to serve proceedings; **iniciar negociaciones** = to open negotiations; **iniciar un caso** = to lead; **iniciar una causa contra alguien** = to proceed against someone; **iniciar una conversación** = to open a discussion; **iniciar un proceso** *o* **un procedimiento legal contra alguien** = to take legal action *o* to start legal proceedings against someone; **el Sr Ramos inició la acusación =; iniciar negociaciones con un gobierno extranjero** = to enter into negotiations with a foreign government Mr Ramos led for the prosecution; **el presidente inició la reunión a las 10.30** = the chairman opened the meeting at 10.30; **el Ministro del Interior iniciará el debate extraordinario en nombre del Gobierno** = the Home Secretary will lead for the Government in the emergency debate; **inició las discusiones con una descripción del producto** = he opened the discussions with a description of the product

iniciativa *nf* iniciative; **iniciativa popular** = proposal for a bill backed by a petition; **iniciativa propia** = own initiative; **iniciativa privada** = private sector

> La iniciativa popular es la potestad de formular una proposición de ley ante el Congreso o el Senado, mediante la presentación de 500.000 firmas acreditadas. Dicha iniciativa no procede en materias propias de ley orgánica, tributarias, de carácter internacional ni en lo relativo a la prerrogativa de gracia

inicio *nm* commencement

inimputable *adj* immune from prosecution

ininflamable *adj* fireproof *o* fire-resistant

injerencia *nf* interference; **la autoridad local se quejó de continua injerencia por parte del gobierno central** = the local authority complained of continual interference from the central government

injuria *nf* abuse *o* insult

injuriar *vt* to abuse *o* to insult; **injuriar a** to abuse

injurioso, -sa *adj* injurious; **mentira injuriosa** = injurious falsehood

injustamente *adv* unjustly; **reclamó que fue injustamente despedido** = he claimed he was wrongfully dismissed; **se le acusó injustamente de malgastar el tiempo de la policía** = she was unjustly accused of wasting police time

injusticia *nf* injustice *o* tort; **injusticia notoria** = manifest injustice

injustificado, -da *adj* unjustified *o* unwarranted; **detención** *o* **retención injustificada** = false imprisonment

injusto, -ta *adj* unjust; **despido injusto** = unfair dismissal *o* wrongful dismissal; **término injusto de un contrato** = unfair contract term

inmediato, -ta *adj* immediate *o* instant *o* prompt; **el juez ordenó su liberación inmediata** = the judge ordered her immediate release ◊ **inmediatamente** *adv* immediately *o* directly *o* forthwith *o* promptly *o* urgently *o* (*sin miramientos*) out of hand; **el demandado presentó inmediatamente una demanda en respuesta a la del demandante** = the defendant promptly counterclaimed against the plaintiff; **el ministro negó inmediatamente las alegaciones contra él** = the minister issued a prompt denial of the allegations against him; **en cuanto se enteró de la noticia llamó inmediatamente a su oficina** = as soon as he heard the news he immediately phoned his office; **escribió una carta de reclamación inmediatamente** = he wrote an immediate letter of complaint; **la citación judicial fue entregada inmediatamente después que el juez firmara la orden judicial** = the summons was served directly after the magistrate had signed the warrant; **los magistrados desestimaron la prueba inmediatamente** = the justices dismissed his evidence out of hand

inmemorial *adj* immemorial; **tiempo inmemorial** *o* **existencia inmemorial** = immemorial existence *o* time immemorial; **desde tiempo inmemorial** = from time immemorial; **esta práctica ha existido desde tiempo inmemorial** = this practice has existed from before the time of legal memory

inmigración *nf* immigration; **leyes de inmigración** = Immigration Laws

inmigrante *nmf* immigrant; **inmigrante en situación ilegal** = illegal immigrant

inmigrar *vi* to immigrate

inminente *adj* imminent *o* impending; **está intentando evitar la inminente absorción de la empresa** = he is trying to prevent the imminent takeover of the company; **la prensa difundió rumores sobre el inminente caso de divorcio** = the newspapers carried stories about the impending divorce case

inmobiliario, -ria 1 *adj* property; **agencia inmobiliaria** estate agency; **agente inmobiliario** = estate agent *o* house agent; **propiedad inmobiliaria** = real estate *o* real property *o* immovable property *o* immovables; **sociedad inmobiliaria** = property company; **sociedad de préstamo inmobiliario** = building society **2** *nf* real estate company *o* property company

inmóvil *adj* immovable; **permanecer inmóvil** = to remain motionless

inmovilización *nf* locking up; **la inmovilización de dinero en acciones** = the locking up of money in stock

inmovilizar *vt* to lock up; **inmovilizar capital** = to lock up capital

inmueble 1 *adj* (*inmóvil*) immovable **2** *nm* building *o* property; **inmuebles residenciales** = house property; **bienes inmuebles** = real estate *o* real property *o* realty *o* immovable property *o* immovables

inmunidad *nf* immunity *o* privilege; **inmunidad condicionada a la ausencia de malicia** = qualified privilege; **inmunidad diplomática** = diplomatic immunity; **inmunidad judicial** = judicial immunity; **inmunidad parlamentaria** = parliamentary privilege; **inmunidad por ostentar cargo público** = absolute privilege; **que goza de inmunidad** = privileged; **carta que goza de inmunidad** = privileged communication; **Comisión de la Cámara de los Comunes que examina casos de de violación de inmunidad** =

Committee of Privileges; **violación de la inmunidad parlamentaria** = breach of parliamentary privilege; **cuando se ofreció a dar información a la policía, le garantizaron la inmunidad judicial** = when he offered to give information to the police, he was granted immunity from prosecution; **invocó la inmunidad diplomática para evitar ser detenido** = he claimed diplomatic immunity to avoid being arrested

innecesario, -ria *adj* unnecessary *o* redundant; **un cláusula innecesaria en un contrato** = a redundant clause in a contract

innegable *adj* undeniable; **acción innegable** = estoppel

inocencia *nf* innocence

inocencia *nf* innocence; **demostrar la inocencia de alguien** = to clear someone of charges; **trató de demostrar su inocencia** = he tried to establish his innocence

inocente *adj y nmf* innocent *o* not guilty; **declararse inocente** = to plead not guilty; **declararse inocente de una acusación ante el tribunal** = to answer charges; **el acusado fue declarado inocente por falta de pruebas** = the accused was found to be innocent *o* was acquitted for lack of evidence; **según la ley, el acusado es considerado inocente hasta que no se demuestre lo contrario** = in law, the accused is presumed to be innocent until he is proved to be guilty; **el acusado se declaró inocente de la acusación de asesinato, pero culpable del cargo menor de homicidio involuntario** = the accused pleaded not guilty to the charge of murder, but pleaded guilty to the lesser charge of manslaughter; **fue declarado inocente de todas las acusaciones** *o* **de todos los cargos que había contra él** = he was cleared of all charges *o* he was cleared on all counts; **una declaración en apariencia inocente puede ser difamatoria si contiene una insinuación** = an apparently innocent statement may be defamatory if it contains an innuendo

inquietud *nf* concern

inquilino, -na *nmf* tenant *o* lessee *o* householder *o* occupier; **inquilino a término** = tenant for years; **inquilino a voluntad (cuyo arrendamiento está sujeto a la voluntad del propietario)** = tenant at will; **inquilino de una propiedad que se ha vendido** = sitting tenant; **inquilino vitalicio** *o* **que ocupa una propiedad de por vida** = tenant for life; **las reparaciones corren por cuenta del inquilino** *o* **el inquilino es responsable de las reparaciones** = the tenant is liable for repairs

inscribir *vt* to enter *o* to register; **inscribir un nombre en una lista** = to enter a name on a list
◊ **inscribirse** *vr* to register *o* to enrol

inscripción *nf* registration *o* entering; **certificado de inscripción** = certificate of registration *o* registration certificate; **derechos de inscripción** = registration fee; **formulario de inscripción** = application form; **número de inscripción** = registration number; **inscripción de una marca en el registro** = registration of a trademark

inscrito, -ta *adj* recorded; **no inscrito** = unrecorded; **asociación no inscrita en registro** = unincorporated association

insignificante *adj* negligible *o* petty

insinuación *nf* innuendo

insistir *vi* to insist; **insistir en** = to hold out for *o* to insist on; **insistió en que se le diera un 50% de descuento** = he held out for a 50% discount; **el sindicato insiste en un aumento de los salarios del 10%** = the union is holding out for a 10% wage increase; **insistió en que se debía hacer algo para ayudar a la familia del demandante** = he insisted on something being done *o* he insisted that something should be done to help the family of the plaintiff

insolvencia *nf* insolvency *o* bankruptcy; **la empresa se encontraba en un estado de insolvencia** = the company was in a state of insolvency

insolvente *adj* insolvent *o* bankrupt; **empresa insolvente** = wreck; **la empresa fue declarada insolvente** = the company was declared insolvent

inspección *nf* **(a)** *(control)* inspection *o* check *o* checking; **inspección judicial de la escena del crimen** = viewing the scene; **dar una orden de inspección** = to issue an inspection order; **efectuar una inspección** *o* **llevar a cabo la inspección de una nueva cárcel** = to make an inspection *o* to carry out an inspection of a new prison; **realizar una visita de inspección** = to carry out a tour of inspection; **muestra de inspección** = check sample; **sello de la inspección** = inspection stamp; **una inspección rutinaria del equipo contra incendios** = a routine check of the fire equipment; **los auditores realizaron una inspección del libro de caja** = the auditors carried out checks on the petty cash book; **los inspectores encontraron algunos defectos durante la inspección del edificio** = the inspectors found some defects during their checking of the building **(b)** *(registro)* search

inspeccionar *vt* to inspect; **inspeccionar una cárcel** = to inspect a machine *o* a prison; **todas las solicitudes son rigurosamente inspeccionadas por el Ministerio del Interior** = all applications are vetted by the Home Office

inspector, -ra *n* inspector; **inspector de fábricas** = inspector of factories *o* factory inspector; **inspector de guardia** = duty officer; **inspector de**

Hacienda = inspector of taxes *o* tax inspector; **inspector de pesos y medidas** = inspector of weights and measures; **inspector de policía** = police inspector; **inspector jefe** = Chief Inspector; **cuerpo de inspectores** = inspectorate; **el cuerpo de inspectores de fábricas** = the factory inspectorate

instalación *nf* installation; **instalaciones destinadas a viviendas** = domestic premises; **instalaciones fijas y accesorios** = fixtures and fittings; **instalaciones y bienes de equipo** = plant

instancia *nf* (a) *(petición)* petition *o* request; **en última instancia** = as a last resort; **prestamista en última instancia** = lender of the last resort (b) *(grado jurídico)* instance; **juzgado de primera instancia** = court of first instance; **tribunal de primera instancia** *o* **tribunal de última instancia** = court of first instance *o* court of last resort; **tribunal federal de primera instancia** = district court (c) *(solicitud)* application form; **mande una instancia por duplicado** = please send the application in duplicate

instantáneo, -nea *adj* instant; **crédito instantáneo** = instant credit

instante *nm* instant *o* moment; **al instante** = instantly

instigador, -ra *n* abettor; **cómplice instigador** = accessory before the fact

instigar *vt* to instigate *o* to abet *o* to incite

institución *nf* institution; **institución financiera** = financial institution; **institución penitenciaria** = penal institution

institucional *adj* institutional; **venta institucional** = institutional selling; **inversores institucionales** = institutional investors

instituto *nm* institute; **instituto de investigación** = research institute

instrucción 1 *nf* instruction *o* directive; **instrucción de una causa** = pre-trial proceedings; **juez de instrucción** = examining justice *o* magistrate; **juzgado de instrucción** = magistrates' court **2** *nfpl* instructions *o* directions; **instrucciones de envío** *o* **de transporte** = forwarding instructions *o* shipping instructions; **dar instrucciones** = to instruct *o* to issue instructions; **esperar instrucciones** = to await instructions; **salvo instrucciones contrarias** = failing instructions to the contrary; **según las instrucciones** = in accordance with *o* according to instructions; **dio instrucciones a su corredor de bolsa para que vendiera las acciones inmediatamente** = he gave instructions to his stockbroker to sell the shares immediately

instructor, -ra *n* instructor

instruir *vt* to instruct; **instruir diligencias** = to open an enquiry; **instruir un sumario** = to investigate *o* to draw up evidence; **instruir mal (al jurado)** = to misdirect; **'ser instruido'** = certiorari

instrumental *adj* instrumental; **prueba instrumental** = primary evidence

instrumento *nm* instrument *o* implement *o* tool; **instrumento legal** = instrument; **instrumento negociable** = negotiable instrument; **los empleados del servicio técnico poseen instrumentos para medir la potencia eléctrica** = the technical staff have instruments to measure the output of electricity

insuficiencia *nf* *(deficiencia)* inadequacy; **insuficiencia de la prueba** = lack of proof

insultante *adj* insulting; **comportamiento insultante** = insulting behaviour

insultar *vt* to insult *o* to abuse; **el prisionero insultó al juez** = the prisoner shouted abuse at the judge; **insultó a la policía antes de ser conducido a la celda** = he abused the police before being taken to the cells

insulto *nm* insult *o* assault *o* abuse

insumiso *nm* *(servicio militar)* insubmissive

intangible *adj* incorporeal

intangible *adj* intangible; **activo intangible** = intangible assets; **bienes intangibles (patentes** *o* **derechos de autor)** = incorporeal chattels

íntegro, -gra *adj* full *o* complete; **devolución íntegra** = full refund *o* refund paid in full; **juicio íntegro organizado según el procedimiento correcto** = full trial; **título íntegro de una ley parlamentaria** = full title; **el demandante aceptó 50.000 ptas como pago íntegro y final de su reclamación de 60.000 para evitar ir a juicio** = the plaintiff accepted 50,000 in full and final settlement of his claim for 60,000 to avoid going to court
◊ **íntegramente** *adv* in full; **le reembolsaron íntegramente cuando se quejó del servicio** = he got a full refund when he complained about the service

intelectual *adj* intellectual; **propiedad intelectual** = copyright *o* intellectual property; **leyes sobre la propiedad intelectual** = copyright law; **violación de la propiedad intelectual** = infringement of copyright *o* copyright infringement

inteligente *adj* clever; **los accionistas inteligentes han obtenido mucho dinero en la transacción** = clever shareholders have made a lot of money on the deal

intención *nf* intention *o* intent *o* animus *o* purpose *o* effect; **intención de permanecer (en un lugar)** = animus manendi; **intención de revocar (un**

testamento) = animus revocandi; **intención de robar** = animus furandi; **intención de suprimir** *o* **cancelar** = animus cancellandi; **intención delictuosa** = malice *o* implied malice; **intención dolosa** *o* **criminal** = mens rea; **carta de intención** = letter of intent; **con intención** = deliberately; **con intención delictuosa** = with malice aforethought; **segunda intención** = ulterior motive; **tener la intención** *o* **tener intención de** = to intend *o* to propose to; **la empresa tiene la intención de ir a juicio por daños** = the company intends to sue for damages; **la intención de crear una relación legal es uno de los elementos esenciales de un contrato** = intention to create a legal relationship is one of the essential elements of a contract; **le acusaron de perjurio con la intención de incriminar a su patrono** = he was accused of perjury with the intention of incriminating his employer; **tenemos la intención de ofrecer trabajo a 250 jóvenes parados** = we intend to offer jobs to 250 unemployed young people; **tengo intención de pagar el préstamo a 5.000 ptas al mes** = I propose to repay the loan at 5,000 ptas a month; **tiene la intención de disfrazarse de policía** = he plans to disguise himself as a policeman

◊ **intencionado, -da** *adj* intentional; **acto intencionado** = wilful act

◊ **intencionadamente** *adv* intentionally *o* on purpose *o* wilfully; **le acusaron de prender fuego a la tienda intencionadamente** = he was accused of deliberately setting fire to the shop; **prendió fuego al edificio intencionadamente** = he wilfully set fire to the building; **cambió la fecha en el contrato intencionadamente** = he intentionally altered the date on the contract

intentar *vt* to attempt; **el abogado intentó que se retiraran los cargos** = the solicitor attempted to have the charge dropped; **la empresa intentó penetrar en el mercado americano** = the company made an attempt to break into the American market

intento *nm* attempt; **intento de asesinato** *o* **de homicidio** = attempted murder; **intento de robo** = attempted robbery; **todos sus intentos de encontrar un trabajo han sido fallidos** = all his attempts to get a job have failed

inter- *prefijo* inter-

interbancario *adj* inter-bank; **préstamo interbancario** = inter-bank loan

intercambiable *adj* exchangeable

intercambiar *vt* to exchange (an article for another); **intercambiar contratos** = to exchange contracts

intercambio *nm* exchange; **intercambio de contratos** = exchange of contracts

interdicto *nm* interdict *o* injunction; **interdicto prohibitivo** = prohibitory injunction

interés *nm* (a) *(valor)* interest; **interés compuesto** = compound interest; **interés personal** = vested interest; **de interés público** = of public interest; **conflicto de intereses** = conflict of interest; **tiene un interés personal en hacer que el negocio siga funcionando** = she has a vested interest in keeping the business working; **la policía mostró un gran interés por el coche abandonado** = the police showed a lot of interest in the abandoned car; **el director gerente no tiene ningún interés por el club de los empleados** = the managing director takes no interest in the staff club (b) *(renta)* interest; **interés acumulado** *o* **devengado (pero no pagado o cobrado)** = accrued interest; **interés atrasado** = back interest; **interés compuesto** = compound interest; **interés de usufructo** = beneficial interest; **interés elevado** *o* **bajo interés** = high *o* low interest; **interés fijo** = fixed interest; **interés simple** = simple interest; **acumulación de interés** = accrual of interest; **cargos en concepto de interés** = interest charges; **crédito** *o* **préstamo sin intereses** = interest-free credit *o* loan; **tipo** *o* **tasa de interés** = interest rate *o* rate of interest; **recibir un interés del 5%** = to receive interest at 5%; **cuenta que recibe un 10% de interés** = account which earns interest at 10% *o* which earns 10% interest; **el banco paga un 10% de interés sobre las imposiciones a plazo fijo** = the bank pays 10% interest on deposits; **el préstamo paga un 5% de interés** = the loan pays 5% interest; **imposición que da un interés del 5%** = deposit which yields *o* gives *o* produces *o* bears 5% interest; **imposiciones con interés** *o* **que producen intereses** = interest-bearing deposits; **la empresa concede a sus empleados préstamos sin intereses** = the company gives its staff interest-free loans (c) *(participación)* interest; **tener un interés mayoritario en una empresa** = to have a controlling interest in a company; **tiene un interés mayoritario en la compañía** = he has a controlling interest in the company

interesado, -da *adj* interested; **interesado, -da en** = interested in; **parte interesada** *o* **persona interesada** = interested party *o* person concerned

interesante *adj* interesting; **nos hicieron una oferta muy interesante por la fábrica** = they made us a very interesting offer for the factory

interesar *vt* to interest; **el director gerente está únicamente interesado en aumentar la rentabilidad** = the managing director is interested only in increasing profitability; **trató de que varias empresas se interesaran por su nuevo invento** = he tried to interest several companies in his new invention

◊ **interesarse** *vr* to take an interest; **interesarse por** = to inquire about

interferir *vt* to interfere *o* to pervert; **tratar de interferir el curso de la justicia** = to attempt to pervert the course of justice

ínterin *nm* interim; **en el ínterin** = in the interim

interino, -na 1 *adj* temporary *o* acting; **director interino** = acting manager; **es interina en un bufete de abogados** = she has a temporary job *o* post with a firm of solicitors **2** *n* locum (tenens); **se necesitan interinos en Madrid** = locums wanted in Madrid

interior 1 *adj* **(a)** *(nacional)* domestic *o* inland; **consumo interior** = domestic consumption; **correo interior** = inland postage; **costes del flete interior** = inland freight charges; **mercado interior** = domestic market; **producto interior bruto (PIB)** = gross domestic product (GDP) **(b)** *(dentro de una empresa)* inside **2** *nm* **(a)** *(en un país)* interior; **en el interior y en el extranjero** = at home and abroad; **Ministerio del Interior** = Home Office *o* Ministry of the Interior *o* Interior Ministry; **Ministro, -tra del Interior** = Home Secretary **(b)** *(en una compañía)* **en el interior de la empresa** = internally

interlocutorio, -ria 1 *adj* interlocutory; **acciones** *o* **reuniones interlocutorias** = interlocutory proceedings; **asunto interlocutorio** = interlocutory matter; **auto interlocutorio** = mesne process; **juicio interlocutorio** = interlocutory judgment; **requerimiento interlocutorio** = interlocutory *o* temporary injunction *o* provisional injunction; **vista interlocutoria** = interlocutory proceedings **2** *nm* temporary injunction

intermediario, -ria *adj y nm* intermediary *o* mediator *o (agente)* middleman; **intermediario financiero** = broker; **servir de intermediario en** = to mediate; **servir de intermediario entre el director y sus empleados** = to mediate between the manager and his staff; **se negó a actuar de intermediario entre los dos directores** = he refused to act as an intermediary between the two directors; **vendemos directamente de la fábrica al cliente y así suprimimos al intermediario** = we sell direct from the factory to the customer and cut out the middleman

intermedio, -dia *adj* intermediate *o* mesne; **mandos intermedios** = middle management

interno, -na 1 *adj* internal; **intervención externa** = external audit *o* independent audit; **intervención interna** = internal audit **2** *n; (preso)* inmate *o* prisoner

internacional *adj* international; **Asociación Internacional de Abogados** = International Bar Association; **derecho internacional** = international law; **en aguas internacionales** = outside territorial waters; **llamada internacional** = international call; **Organización Internacional del Trabajo** = International Labour Organization; **Tribunal Internacional de Justicia** = International Court of Justice

internado, -da *n* internee

internamiento *nm* confinement *o* committal; **orden de internamiento psiquiátrico de un delincuente** = hospital order

internar *vt* to intern *o* to commit

interno, -na *n (en una cárcel)* inmate

interpelar *vt* to plea *o* to ask for an explanation

Interpol *nf* Interpol; **avisaron a la Interpol de que los criminales podían estar disfrazados de mujeres** = they warned Interpol that the criminals might be disguised as women

interponer *vt* to file *o* to interpose; **interponer un recurso de apelación** = to file *o* to lodge an appeal; **interponer una querella** = to sue *o* to bring a charge

interpretación *nf (de una ley o de un precedente)* interpretation *o* construction *o (formalidad)* technicality; **interpretación deductiva** = construction; **dar** *o* **hacer una interpretación de algo** = to put an interpretation on something; **cláusula de interpretación** = interpretation clause; **cláusula que se presta a una interpretación errónea** = clause which is open to misinterpretation; **derecho de interpretación de una pieza musical protegida por propiedad intelectual** = performing right; **mala interpretación** *o* **interpretación errónea** = misconstruction *o* misinterpretation; **su decisión da una interpretación bastante diferente de la responsabilidad de los administradores** = his ruling puts quite a different interpretation on the responsibility of trustees

interpretar *vt (una ley o un precedente)* = to interpret *o* to construe; **interpretar las palabras** = to put a construction on words; **interpretar mal** = to misinterpret; **el tribunal interpretó las palabras como que había un contrato entre las partes** = the court construed the words to mean that there was a contract between the parties; **los alborotadores interpretaron mal las instrucciones de la policía** = the rioters misinterpreted the instructions of the police; **una opinión escrita no es admisible como prueba para interpretar una escritura de liquidación** = written opinion is not admissible as evidence for the purposes of construing a deed of settlement

interpretativo, -va *adj* interpretative; **sentencia interpretativa de una escritura o un documento** = declaratory judgment

intérprete *nmf* interpreter; **mi secreteria actuará de intérprete** = my secretary will act as interpreter; **mi ayudante sabe griego, así que**

actuará de intérprete para nosotros = my assistant knows Greek, so he will interpret for us; **el testigo no sabía hablar inglés y el tribunal tuvo que contratar a un intérprete** = the witness could not speak English and the court had to appoint an interpreter

interrogador, -ra *n* interrogator

interrogar *vt* to interrogate *o* to question; **interrogar testigos (para tratar de desarmar sus argumentos)** = to cross-examine; **volver a interrogar** = to re-examine; **interrogó al presidente sobre la política de inversiones de la empresa** = she questioned the chairman about the company's investment policy; **la policía interrogó a los contables durante cuatro horas** = the police questioned the accounts staff for four hours; **llevaron al hombre a la comisaría de policía para ser interrogado** = the man was taken to the police station for questioning; **los acusados fueron interrogados por espacio de tres horas** = the prisoners were interrogated for three hours

interrogatorio *nm* interrogation *o* questioning *o* examination *o* interrogatory; **interrogatorio directo** = direct examination; **interrogatorio directo de los testigos** = examination in chief *o* *US* direct examination; **interrogatorio hecho a testigos (para tratar de desarmar sus argumentos)** = cross-examination; **interrogatorio policial** = police questioning; **nuevo interrogatorio** = re-examination; **sometida a interrogatorio, dio los nombres de sus cómplices** = under interrogation, she gave the names of her accomplices; **confesó el crimen durante el interrogatorio** = he confessed to the crime during his interrogation; **durante el interrogatorio de la policía, confesó el crimen** = during questioning by the police, she confessed to the crime; **el testigo se desconcertó durante el interrogatorio del fiscal** = the witness became confused during questioning by counsel for the prosecution

interrumpir *vt* to break off *o* to suspend; **interrumpimos la discusión a medianoche** = we broke off the discussion at midnight
◊ **interrumpirse** *vr* to break down; **las negociaciones se interrumpieron después de seis horas** = negotiations broke down after six hours

interrupción *nf* **(a)** *(detener)* interruption; **interrupción del proceso** = stay of proceedings; **sin interrupción** = continuously; **la junta discutió el problema de los presupuestos durante cinco horas sin interrupción** = the meeting discussed the problem of budgets continuously for five hours **(b)** *(fracaso)* failure *o* breakdown; **la interrupción de las negociaciones** = the failure of the negotiations **(c)** *(aborto)* **interrupción del embarazo** = child destruction

interurbano, -na *adj* inter-city; **llamada interurbana** = long-distance call; **los servicios ferroviarios interurbanos son buenos** = the inter-city rail services are good

intervalo *nm* **intervalo de tiempo** = a lapse of time

intervención *nf* intervention; **intervención de cuentas** = audit; **intervención del estado** *o* **intervención estatal** = government intervention *o* intervention by the government; **intervención general** = general audit; **intervención interna** = internal audit; **intervención judicial** = receivership; **precio de intervención** = intervention price; **la intervención de la asociación en el conflicto laboral** = the association's intervention in the labour dispute; **la intervención del banco central en la crisis bancaria** = the central bank's intervention in the banking crisis; **la intervención estatal en el mercado de divisas** = the government's intervention in the foreign exchange markets

intervenir 1 *vi (mediar)* to intervene *o* to take part; **intervenir a favor** *o* **en contra de alguien** = to intercede for *o* against somebody; **intervenir en un conflicto** = to intervene in a dispute **2** *vt (las cuentas)* to audit

interventor, -ra *n* auditor *o* controller; **Interventor y Auditor General** = Controller and Auditor General; **interventor externo** = external auditor; **interventor interno** = internal auditor; **interventor judicial** = Official Receiver; **el Tribunal de Protección nombró un interventor para que administrara los asuntos del cliente** = the Court of Protection appointed a receiver to administer the client's affairs

intestado, -da *adj* intestate; **bienes intestados** = residuary estate; **morir intestado** = to die intestate; **hecho de morir intestado** = intestacy
◊ **ab intestato** *adv* intestate; **morir ab intestato** = intestate succession

intimación *nf* **intimación de pago** = request for payment

intimar *vt* to order *o* to require; **le intimó a que devolviera el dinero** = she ordered him to return the money

intimidación *nf* intimidation; **intimidación violenta** = battery

intimidad *nf* privacy; **privación** *o* **violación del derecho a la intimidad** = invasion of privacy

intimidar *vt* to intimidate; **se dijo que el acusado había intimidado a los testigos** = the accused was said to have intimidated the witnesses

intransferible *adj* non-negotiable

intransigente *adj* intransigent; **adoptar una postura intransigente en las negociaciones**

sindicales = to take a hard line in trade union negotiations

intriga *nf* plot

intrigar *vi* to plot

intrínseco, ca *adj* intrinsic; **prueba intrínseca** = intrinsic evidence

introducción *nf* introduction; **breve introducción** = *nf* heading

introducir *vt* **(a)** *(meter)* to introduce; **introducir datos** *o* **información en un ordenador** = to input *o* to feed; **introducir medidas de seguridad** = to adopt safety measures; **introducir mercancías de contrabando** = to smuggle in **(b)** *(presentar)* to introduce
◊ **introducirse** *vr* to enter; **la compañía ha gastado millones intentando introducirse en el mercado del bricolaje** = the company has spent millions trying to enter the do-it-yourself market

intromisión *nf* interference; **intromisión en la vida privada** = invasion of privacy

intrusión *nf* encroachment *o* trespass

intruso, -sa *n* intruder *o* trespasser

inútil *adj* useless

inutilidad *nf* incapacity; **inutilidad física** = physical incapacity

invalidación *nf* invalidation *o* avoidance

invalidado, -da *adj* void; **voto invalidado** = spoilt ballot paper

invalidar *vt* to invalidate *o* to annul *o* to override; **invalidar un contrato** = to void a contract; **el tribunal superior invalidó la decisión del tribunal inferior** = the higher court overrode the decision of the lower court

invalidez *nf* invalidity; **invalidez absoluta** = total disability; **pensión de invalidez** = disability pension

inválido, -da 1 *adj (nulo)* invalid *o* void *o* null and void **2** *n (minusválido)* invalid

invención *nf* invention; **cédula** *o* **patente de invención** = letters patent

inventar *vt* to invent; **¿Quién inventó la taquigrafía?** = who invented shorthand?; **el jefe de contabilidad ha inventado un nuevo sistema de clasificación de clientes** = the chief accountant has invented a new system of customer filing; **inventó un nuevo tipo de teclado de ordenador** = she invented a new type of computer keyboard

inventariar *vt* to inventory

inventario *nm* inventory; **le ruego me envíe un inventario** = please send me a detailed *o* an itemized account

invento *nm* invention; **intentó vender su último invento a una empresa automovilística norteamericana** = he tried to sell his latest invention to a US car company; **presentó una solicitud de patente para su invento** = she filed a patent application for her invention

inventor, -ra *n* inventor; **es el inventor del coche fabricado enteramente de plástico** = he is the inventor of the all-plastic car

inverosímil *adj* unlikely

inversión *nf* investment *o* capital expenditure; **fondos mutuos de inversión** *o* **sociedades de inversión** = mutual fund; **inversiones exteriores** *o* **extranjeras** = foreign investments; **inversiones de renta fija** = fixed-interest investments; **sociedad general de inversiones** = discretionary trust; **perdió todo su dinero en inversiones arriesgadas en la Bolsa** = he lost all his money in risky investments on the Stock Exchange
◊ **inversionista** *nmf* investor

inverso, -sa *adj* inverse *o* reverse; **adquisición inversa** = reverse takeover

inversor,-ra *n* investor

invertir *vt* to invest; **invertir en un negocio** = to put money into a business; **invirtió todo su dinero en una tienda** = he invested all his money in a shop; **le aconsejaron que invirtiera en bienes raíces** *o* **en propiedad inmobiliaria** = she was advised to invest in real estate

investigación *nf* investigation; **investigación oficial** = inquiry; **investigación preliminar** = preliminary investigation; **investigación que da como resultado la poca fiabilidad de una persona** = positive vetting; **delegación** *o* **misión de investigación** = fact-finding delegation *o* mission; **pedir información** *o* **hacer investigaciones** = to inquire; **realizar una investigación sobre posibles irregularidades en operaciones con valores** = to conduct an investigation into irregularities in share dealings; **la comisión está haciendo investigaciones sobre la corrupción dentro del cuerpo de policía** = the commission is inquiring into corruption in the police force; **se ha realizado una investigación gubernamental sobre la pérdida de documentos secretos** there has been a government inquiry into the loss of the secret documents

investigador, -ra *n* investigator; **un investigador oficial** *o* **estatal** *o* **del gobierno** = a government investigator

investigar *vt* **(a)** *(indagar)* to investigate *o* to inquire into **(b)** *(examinar)* to examine *o* to explore *o* *(examinar rigurosamente)* to vet; **estamos investigando la posibilidad de abrir una oficina en Londres** = we are exploring the possibility of opening an office in London **(c)** *(estudiar)* to research

inviolabilidad *nf* immunity

invitación *nf* invitation; **extender una invitación a alguien para que forme parte del consejo** = to issue an invitation to someone to join the board

invitado, -da *n* invitee

invitar *vt* to invite; **invitar a alguien a formar parte del consejo** = to invite someone to join the board; **invitar a alguien a una reunión** = to invite someone to a meeting; **invitar a los accionistas a que suscriban una nueva emisión** = to invite shareholders to subscribe to a new issue

involucrar *vt* to involve ; **involuntario, -ria** *adj* involuntary; **comportamiento involuntario** = involuntary conduct; **homicidio involuntario** = involuntary manslaughter
◊ **involuntariamente** *adv* involuntarily; **la defensa del acusado consistía en que actuó involuntariamente** = the accused's defence was that he acted involuntarily

ir *vi* to go; **ir a juicio** = go to law; **ir bien** = to get on; **ir con** = to belong with; **ir contra** = to go against; **el avión va a Francfort, luego a Roma** = the plane goes to Frankfurt, then to Rome; **fuimos a juicio para tratar de recuperar nuestros bienes** = we went to law to try to regain our property; **va a nuestra oficina de Lagos** = he is going to our Lagos office; **a mi hijo le va muy bien - le acaban de ascender** = my son is getting on well - he has just been promoted
◊ **irse** *vr* to go away *o* to leave

irracional *adj* unreasonable
◊ **irracionalmente** *adv* unreasonably; **la aprobación no será negada irracionalmente** = approval shall not unreasonably be withheld

irreconciliable *adj* irreconcilable; **ruptura matrimonial irreconciliable** *o* **diferencias irreconciliables entre marido y mujer** = = irretrievable breakdown of a marriage

irrecuperable *adj* irrecoverable *o* irretrievable

irrecurrible *adj* unappealable

irrecusable *adj* unchallengeable

irredimible *adj* irredeemable ; **irrefutable** *adj* irrefutable *o* conclusive

irregular *adj* irregular *o* abnormal; **documentación irregular** = irregular documentation; **este procedimiento es muy irregular** = this procedure is highly irregular

irregularidad *nf* irregularity; **la irregularidad del reparto del correo** = the irregularity of the postal deliveries; **investigar irregularidades en operaciones de valores** = to investigate irregularities in the share dealings

irrelevante *adj* irrelevant

irremediable *adj* irremediable *o* without remedy

irreparable *adj* irretrievable; **de un modo irreparable** = irretrievably; **se resolvió que el matrimonio se había deshecho de un modo irreparable** = it was agreed that the marriage had broken down irretrievably

irresistible *adj* irresistible; **impulso irresistible** = irresistible impulse; **su impulso irresistible de prender fuego a las zapaterías** = his irresistible impulse to set fire to shoe shops

irresponsabilidad *nf* irresponsibility

irresponsable *adj* irresponsible

irrevocable *adj* irrevocable; **aceptación irrevocable** = irrevocable acceptance; **carta de crédito irrevocable** = irrevocable letter of credit; **derecho irrevocable** = indefeasible right

irritar *vt* **(a)** *(molestar)* to irritate **(b)** *(anular)* to void

irrogar *vt* to cause damage *o* to punish

irrumpir *vi* **irrumpir en** = to burst into

Islam *nm* Islam
◊ **islámico, -ca** *adj y n* Islamic; **Derecho Islámico** = Islamic Law

IVA *nm* = *impuesto sobre el valor añadido* Value Added Tax (VAT) *o* input tax; **artículos exentos del pago del IVA** = exempt supplies; **momento en el que se suministran los artículos y se paga el IVA** = tax point; **suministros exentos del IVA** = exempt supplies

izquierdo, -da 1 *adj* left 2 *nf* the left; **el ala izquierda de un partido** = the left wing of a party; **la izquierda ha exigido una reforma política** = the left have demanded political reform; **han detenido a muchos miembros de la izquierda** = many members of the left have been arrested; **pertenecen al ala izquierda del partido conservador** = they are on the left of the Conservative Party

Jj

jactancia *nf* jactitation

jaula *nf (calabozo)* nick

jefatura *nf* headquarters; **jefatura de policía** = police headquarters

jefe, -fa *n* **(a)** *(persona que dirige)* head *o* chief *o* *(director, gerente)* manager; **jefe de comedor** *o* **de camareros** = head waiter; **jefe de compras** = head buyer; **jefe de contabilidad** = accounts manager; **jefe de departamento** *o* **jefe de sección** = head of department *o* department head *o* department manager; **jefe de estado** = head of state; **jefe de formación** = training officer; **jefe de información** = information officer; **jefe de oficina** = chief clerk *o* head clerk; **jefe de personal** = personnel officer; **conserje jefe** = head porter; **jefe ejecutivo** = chief executive; **(en) jefe** = chief; **vendedor en jefe** = head salesman; **es el contable jefe de un grupo industrial** = he is the chief accountant of an industrial group **(b)** *(en autoridad)* governor *o (de una familia de mafiosos o banda criminal)* boss **(c)** *(policía)* **jefe de policía** = Chief Constable; **ayudante del jefe de policía** *o* **jefe de policía adjunto** = Assistant Chief Constable *o* Deputy Chief Constable; **inspector jefe** = Chief Inspector *o* Chief Superintendent **(d)** *(autor de un crimen)* principal **(e)** *(líder)* leader; **el ministro era el jefe del grupo de abogados en una visita a los juzgados españoles** = the minister was the leader of the party of lawyers on a tour of Spanish courts; **es la jefa de la delegación comercial para Nigeria** = she is the leader of the trade delegation to Nigeria

jerga *nf* jargon; **jerga jurídica** = legal jargon

jeta *nf (cara)* mug

jornada *nf* day; **jornada laboral** = working day

jornal *nm* daily wage
◊ **jornalero, -ra** *n* day worker

joven 1 *adj* juvenile; **más joven** = junior; **persona joven** = young person **2** *nmf; (mayor de catorce años y menor de diecisiete)* youth *o* young person

joya *nf* jewel; **joya familiar** *o* **de familia** = heirloom
◊ **joyería** *nf* jewellery *o (tienda)* jewellers
◊ **joyero, -ra** *n* jeweller

jubilación *nf* **(a)** *(retiro)* retirement; **acogerse a la jubilación anticipada** = to take early retirement; **edad de jubilación** *o* **de retiro** = pensionable age *o* retiring age *o* retirement age; **dar la jubilación** = to retire someone **(b)** *(pensión de retiro)* retirement pension *o* old age pension; **con derecho a jubilación** = pensionable; **fondo de jubilaciones** = pension fund

jubilado, -da *n (pensionista)* old age pensioner

jubilar *vt* **jubilar a alguien** = to retire someone *o* to pension someone off; **decidieron jubilar a todos los empleados mayores de 50 años** = they decided to retire all staff over 50 years of age
◊ **jubilarse** *vr* to retire; **se jubiló con una pensión de 2 millones de ptas** = she retired with a pension of 2 million ptas

judicatura *nf* judicature *o* judiciary

judicial *adj* judicial *o* legal; **acción judicial** = court action *o* court case; **acreedor judicial** = judgment creditor; **agente judicial** = bailiff; **citación judicial** *o* **emplazamiento** *o* **requerimiento judicial** = summons; **conocimiento judicial** = judicial notice; **costas judiciales** = legal costs *o* legal charges *o* legal expenses; **deudor judicial** = judgment debtor; **error judicial** = miscarriage of justice; **fórmulas judiciales utilizadas en un documento legal** = form of words; **inmunidad judicial** = judicial immunity; **interventor** *o* **administrador judicial** = the Official Receiver; **orden judicial** = court order; *(la magistratura)* **el poder judicial** = the judiciary; **precedente judicial** = judicial precedent; **procedimientos judiciales** = judicial processes; **revisión** *o* **análisis** *o* **examen judicial** = judicial review; **el tribunal ordenó a los agentes judiciales que embargaran sus bienes porque no había pagado la multa** = the court ordered the bailiffs to seize his property because he had not paid his fine; **el tribunal dictó una orden judicial de manutención** = the court made an order for maintenance *o* made a maintenance order; **se negó a obedecer la orden judicial y fue enviado a prisión por desacato** = he refused to obey the court order and was sent to prison for contempt

juego *nm* game *o* gaming *o* gambling; **juego de azar** = game of chance; **licencia de juego** = gaming licence; **impuesto sobre el juego** = betting duty *o* tax

juez, -za *n* **(a)** judge *o (magistrado)* magistrate *o* justice; **juez de distrito** *o* **juez comarcal** *o* **juez titular** = circuit judge *o* district judge; **juez de guardia** = duty magistrate; **juez de instrucción** = examining justice *o* magistrate; **juez de paz** = justice of the peace *o* lay magistrate; **juez de primera instancia** = examining magistrate; **juez de vigilancia penitenciaria** = prison judge; **juez letrado** = stipendiary magistrate; **juez que ve un caso en privado** = judge in chambers; **el juez le condenó a prisión por malversación de fondos** *o* **desfalco** = the judge sent him to prison for embezzlement; **ser juez** = to sit on the bench **(b)** *(árbitro)* adjudicator; **actuar de juez en una disputa** = to adjudicate in a dispute

> Un juez está a cargo de un órgano judicial unipersonal, mientras que un magistrado forma parte de un órgano judicial colegiado

juicio *nm* **(a)** *(proceso)* trial *o (pleito)* lawsuit *o* hearing; **juicio con jurado** = trial by jury; **juicio de amparo** = restraining order; **juicio de deshaucio** = eviction proceedings; **juicio de faltas** = summary trial; **juicio de mayor cuantía** *o* **de cuantía indeterminada** = suit for a case exceeding a limiting amount; **juicio de menor cuantía** = suit for a case not exceeding a limiting amount; **juicio de quiebra** = bankruptcy proceedings; **juicio declarado nulo** = mistrial; **juicio hipotecario** = foreclosure; **juicio imparcial** = fair trial; **juicio oral** = oral proceedings; **juicio testamentario** = probate proceedings; **entablar juicio hipotecario** = to foreclose; **juicio que hace jurisprudencia** *o* **que sienta precedente para posibles casos posteriores** = test case; **durante el juicio** = pendente lite; **nuevo juicio** = retrial; **pendiente de juicio** *o* **en espera de juicio** = pending action; **presente en el juicio** = in court; **demandar a alguien en juicio** = to issue a writ against someone; **ir a juicio** = go to law; **recusar** *o* **poner en tela de juicio** = to impeach; **fuimos a juicio para tratar de recuperar nuestros bienes** = we went to law to try to regain our property; **el acusado estuvo presente en el juicio durante tres horas** = the defendant was in court for three hours; **el juez ordenó la celebración de un nuevo juicio cuando se supo que uno de los miembros del jurado era el hermano del acusado** = the judge ordered a new trial when one of the jurors was found to be the accused's brother; **juicio de faltas** = complaints procedure *o* grievance procedure **(b)** *(sentencia)* judgment *o* judgement *o* adjudication *o (veredicto)* verdict; **juicio interlocutorio** = interlocutory judgment; **juicio en rebeldía** *o* **por falta de comparecencia** = judgment by default *o* default judgment **(c)** *(opinión)* estimation; **a mi juicio es el mejor abogado mercantil de la ciudad** = in my estimation, he is

the best commercial lawyer in town; **lo dejo a su a su juicio** = I leave it to your discretion **(d)** *(cordura)* sanity

> En un juicio de menor cuantía se deciden demandas cuyos intereses económicos excedan de 800.000 ptas. y no sobrepasen los 160.000.000 ptas y las demandas relativas a filiación, maternidad o paternidad y estado civil de las personas, y las demandas cuya cuantía es inestimable o de difícil determinación. El juicio de mayor cuantía resuelve las demandas cuyos intereses económicos excedan de 160.000.000 ptas o las relativas a derechos honoríficos de las personas.
> El juicio oral es la fase del proceso penal, llamada también fase de plenario, en la que las partes exponen la calificación provisional del hecho, se practican las pruebas y se pronuncia sentencia

junta *nf* **(a)** *(consejo)* board; **junta asesora** = advisory board; **junta de síndicos** = board of trustees; **junta directiva** = board of directors **(b)** *(reunión)* meeting; **dirigir una junta** = to conduct a meeting; **junta de accionistas** = general meeting *o* meeting of shareholders *o* shareholders' meeting; **junta de acreedores** = creditors' meeting; **junta de dirección** = management meeting; **junta general** = general meeting; **Junta General Anual** *o* **junta general ordinaria** = Annual General Meeting (AGM); **Junta General Extraordinaria** = Extraordinary General Meeting (EGM)

juntar 1 *vi (reunir)* to assemble *o* to gather **2** *vt (unir)* to join; **abrieron una puerta en la pared para juntar las oficinas** = the offices were joined together by making a door in the wall
◊ **juntarse** *vr* to assemble *o* to associate with

junto, -ta 1 *adj* united *o* joined *o* together; **poner juntos** = to bracket together

jurado, -da 1 *adj* **(a)** *(en profesión)* chartered; **censor jurado de cuentas** = chartered accountant; **vigilante jurado** = security guard **(b)** *(en juicio)* sworn; **no jurado, -da** = unsworn; **declaración jurada** = affidavit; **una declaración no jurada** = an unsworn statement **2** *nm* jury; **gran jurado** *o* **jurado de acusación** = grand jury; **miembro del jurado** = juror *o* juryman; **'Miembros del Jurado'** = 'Members of the Jury'; **selección de los miembros del jurado** = jury vetting; **panel** *o* **tribuna** *o* **estrado del jurado** = jury box; **el presidente del jurado** = the foreman of the jury; **sala del jurado** = jury room; **Tribunal del Jurado** = the jury; **juicio con jurado** = trial by jury *o* jury trial; **condena por juez sin jurado** = summary conviction; **le han llamado para actuar como jurado** = he has been called for jury service *o* US he has been called for jury duty

> Son competencia del Tribunal del Jurado los delitos contra las personas, los cometidos por

los funcionarios públicos en el ejercicio de sus cargos, los delitos contra el honor y los delitos contra el medio ambiente (Ley Orgánica 5/1995). Los tribunales del jurado constan de nueve miembros y un magistrado.

La Jurisprudencia es la doctrina emanada de las resoluciones del Tribunal Supremo, requiriéndose por lo menos dos de idéntica interpretación. La jurisprudencia constituye una de las fuentes del derecho

juramento *nm* oath; **juramento de fidelidad** = oath of allegiance; **juramento de un cargo** = swearing-in; **juramento de un testigo** = swearing of a witness; **juramento falso** = perjury; **juramento solemne** = solemn oath; **encargado de tomar juramento** = commissioner for oaths; **tomar juramento a alguien** = to administer an oath to someone *o* to swear someone in; **sin juramento** = unsworn; **una declaración sin juramento** = an unsworn statement; **estaba bajo juramento** *o* **había prestado juramento** = he was on oath *o* under oath; **le tomaron juramento como Consejero de Estado** = he was sworn in as a State Councillor

jurar *vt* to swear; **juró decir la verdad** = he swore to tell the truth; **'juro decir la verdad, toda la verdad y nada más que la verdad'** = 'I swear to tell the truth, the whole truth and nothing but the truth'

jurídico, -ca *adj* legal *o* juridical; **asesor jurídico** = counsellor *o* legal adviser; **asesoría jurídica** *o* **departamento jurídico** = legal department *o* legal section; *(perteneciente al Instituto de Ejecutivos Jurídicos)* **experto jurídico** = legal expert; **incapacidad jurídica** = disability; **persona jurídica** = legal personality *o* artificial person; **personalidad jurídica** = corporate personality; **este contrato tiene fuerza jurídica** = the contract is legally binding

◊ **jurídicamente** *adv* **asesorarse jurídicamente** = to take legal advice; **persona incapacitada jurídicamente** = person under a (legal) disability

jurisconsulto, -ta *n* legal consultant *o* legal adviser

jurisdicción *nf* **(a)** *(competencia)* jurisdiction; **jurisdicción administrativa** = jurisdiction for cases involving administrative law; **jurisdicción contenciosa administrativa** = jurisdiction for suits involving the Administration; **jurisdicción civil** = civil jurisdiction; **jurisdicción criminal** = criminal jurisdiction; **jurisdicción justa** *o* **de equidad** = equitable jurisdiction **(b)** *(distrito)* circuit; **error de jurisdicción** = mistake in venue

jurisdiccional *adj* jurisdictional; **aguas jurisdiccionales** = territorial waters; **terreno jurisdiccional** = exclusion zone

jurisprudencia *nf* jurisprudence; *(precedentes)* case law; **código con jurisprudencia** = commentary; **juicio que hace jurisprudencia** = test case

jurista *nmf* jurist *o* legal expert

justicia *nf* justice *o* *(sistema legal justo)* equity; **justicia natural** = natural justice; **administración de justicia** = dispensation of justice; **administrar justicia** = to administer justice *o* to dispense justice; **citar ante la justicia a alguien** = to take someone to law; **llevar a un criminal ante la justicia** = to bring a criminal to justice; **el ministro de Justicia** = the Minister of Justice *o* the Justice Minister; **Ministerio de Justicia** = Department of Justice *o* Justice Department; **tribunal de justicia** = adjudication tribunal; **Tribunal de Justicia Europeo** = European Court of Justice; **Tribunal Internacional de Justicia** = International Court of Justice; **'que se haga justicia'** = fiat justicia

justiciable *adj* actionable

justificable *adj* justifiable; **homicidio justificable** = justifiable homicide

justificación *nf* justification; **como justificación** = in justification; **el acusado declaró, como justificación, que el ladrón le había atacado con un hacha** = in justification, the accused claimed that the burglar had attacked him with an axe; **tacha con** *o* **sin justificación** *(objeción a un miembro del jurado con causa* *o* *sin causa)* = challenge for cause *o* without cause

justificado, -da *adj* justifiable; **homicidio justificado** = justifiable homicide

justificante *nm* *(comprobante)* receipt

justificar *vt* to justify; **justificar un trato monetario** = to account for; **el fin no justifica los medios** = the end does not justify the means

justo, -ta *adj* *(equitativo)* fair *o* equitable *o* *(imparcial)* just; **justo derecho** = perfect right; **jurisdicción justa** = equitable jurisdiction; **mostrar causa justa** = to show just cause; **prácticas comerciales justas** = fair trading *o* fair dealing; **precio justo** = fair price; **sistema legal justo** = equity; **trato justo** = fair deal

juvenil *adj* juvenile; **delincuente juvenil** = juvenile delinquent *o* young offender *o* *US* youthful offender; **delincuente juvenil que es juzgado en un tribunal de menores** = juvenile offender

juzgado *nm* court of law *o* law court; *(tribunal)* tribunal *o* sessions; **juzgado de guardia** = police court *o* duty magistrates' court; **juzgado de instrucción** = magistrates' court; **juzgado de lo civil** *o* **de lo criminal** = civil court *o* criminal court; **juzgado de lo social** = industrial tribunal; **juzgado de primera instancia** = court of first instance;

juzgado de paz = magistrates' court; **juzgado de segunda instancia** = court of appeal; **juzgado local** *o* **del condado** = local court *o* County Court; **reglamento interno de los juzgados locales** *o* **del condado** = County Court Rules; **secretario de juzgado** = justices' clerk *o* clerk to the justices; **los juzgados están en el centro de la ciudad** = the law courts are in the centre of the town; **trabaja en los juzgados como portero de estrados** = she works in the law courts as an usher

Los Juzgados de Primera Instancia e Instrucción tienen su sede en la capital del partido judicial y pueden tener un único titular o -en el caso de las grandes ciudades- son dos órganos distintos. Los Juzgados de primera Instancia se ocupan de casos de orden civil en primera instancia, mientras que los de Instrucción conocen de la instrucción de las causas por delitos cuyo enjuiciamiento corresponde a las Audiencias Provinciales y a los Juzgados de lo Penal, de los juicios de faltas y de los procedimientos de "habeas corpus"

Los Juzgados de lo Penal tienen jurisdicción sobre la provincia y juzgan determinados delitos (LOPJ artº 89).
Los Juzgados de lo Social, anteriormente conocidos como Magistraturas de Trabajo tienen jurisdicción sobre la provincia y conocen en primera o única instancia de las materias que afectan a intereses de los trabajadores y empresarios (LOPJ artº 92)

juzgar *vt* **(a)** *(someter a juicio)* to try; *(prejuzgar)* **juzgar de antemano** = to prejudge; **juzgar en consejo de guerra** = to court-martial; **el tribunal carece de competencia para juzgar el caso** = the court is not competent to try the case; **fue juzgado por asesinato y condenado a cadena perpetua** = he was tried for murder and sentenced to life imprisonment; **se le juzga por desfalco** = he is on trial *o* is standing trial for embezzlement **(b)** *(formar juicio)* to judge *o* to adjudicate; **juzgar una demanda** = to adjudicate a claim; **juzgar erróneamente** = misjudge; **juzgó que era hora de poner fin a las discusiones** = he judged it was time to call an end to the discussions; **juzgar la actuación del gobierno** = to measure the government's performance

LI

labor *nf (trabajo)* work *o* labour *o (tarea)* task
◊ **laborable** *adj* working; **tres días laborables** = three clear days
◊ **laboral** *adj* industrial *o* occupational *o* laboral; **accidente laboral** = occupational *o* industrial accident; **conflictos laborales** = labour disputes; **derecho laboral** *o* **legislación laboral** = labour law *o* labour laws *o* labour legislation; **jornada laboral** = (working) day; **leyes laborales** = labour laws; **relaciones laborales** = labour relations; **riesgos laborales** = occupational hazards

lacerar *vt (herir)* to cause physical harm; *(desacreditar)* to harm someone's reputation

lacrado, -da *adj* sealed; **ofertas lacradas** = sealed tenders; **la empresa ha pedido ofertas lacradas para el almacén** = the company has asked for sealed bids for the warehouse

lacrar *vt* to seal (with wax)

lado *nm* side; **al lado de** = next to; **a un lado** = aside; **dejar de lado** = to set aside; **el demandante se sentó al lado de su abogado** = the plaintiff sat next to his solicitor; **el fuego se extendió a la propiedad de al lado** = the fire spread to the adjoining property

ladrón, -na *n* burglar *o* thief *o* villain *o (atracador)* robber *o (timador)* crook; **ladrón de cajas fuertes** = cracksman; **ladrón de casas** = housebreaker; **ladrón de ganado** = rustler *o* cattle rustler; **ladrón que roba en las tiendas** = shoplifter; **entraron ladrones en la oficina y robaron el dinero** = thieves broke into the office and stole the money
◊ **ladronzuelo, -la** *n* pilferer

laguna *nf* gap *o* loophole; **encontrar una una laguna legal** = to find a loophole in the law; **encontrar una laguna fiscal** = to find a tax loophole

lamentar *vt* to regret; *(en carta)* **lamentamos informarles de la muerte del presidente** = we regret to inform you of the death of the chairman

lanzamiento *nm* **(a)** *(desposesión)* dispossession *o* eviction **(b)** *(en el mercado)* launch; **lanzamiento de un producto** = promotion of a product; **artículo de lanzamiento** = loss-leader; **gastos de lanzamiento** = promotional budget

lanzar *vt* **(a)** *(desalojar)* to dispossess *o* to evict **(b)** *(comercial)* to launch; **lanzar al mercado** = to market

lapso *nm* lapse; **un lapso de tiempo** = a lapse of time

lapsus *nm* slip; **lapsus linguae** = slip of the tongue

largo, -ga 1 *adj* long; **a largo plazo** *o* **para un largo periodo de tiempo** = on a long-term basis; **crédito a largo plazo** = extended credit; **crédito de larga duración** = long credit; **deudas a largo plazo** = long-term debts; **letras** *o* **valores con vencimiento a largo plazo** = long-dated bills *o* paper; **objetivos a largo plazo** = long-term objectives; **planificar a largo plazo** = to take the long view; **préstamo a largo plazo** = long-term loan; **previsión a largo plazo** = long-term forecast; **títulos del estado a largo plazo** = longs **2** *nf* **a la larga** = in the long term

latente *nm* latent; **ambigüedad latente en un contrato** = latent ambiguity

látigo *nm* whip

latín *nm* Latin

latrocinio *nm* larceny

laudo *nm* award; **laudo arbitral** = arbitration award; **laudo de indemnización** = compensatory award; **el laudo del juez fue desestimado tras el recurso** = the arbitrator's award was set aside on appeal

> El Laudo es un fallo que dicta un árbitro en los asuntos que le son sometidos voluntariamente por las partes

leal *adj* fair; **prácticas comerciales leales** = fair trading *o* fair dealing; **según mi leal saber y entender** = to the best of my knowledge and belief
◊ **lealtad** *nf* loyalty *o* allegiance

LEC = LEY DE ENJUICIAMIENTO CIVIL

LECri = LEY DE ENJUICIAMIENTO CRIMINAL

lectura *nf* reading; **lectura de la acusación** = arraignment

leer *vt* to read; **leer entre líneas** = to read between the lines; **leer textualmente** = to quote; **leer la acusación** = to arraign; **leer los derechos al detenido** = to caution a suspect

legado *nm* legacy *o* bequest *o (de bienes raíces)* devise; **legado diferido** = executory bequest; **legado en fideicomiso** = trust legacy; **legado preferente con cargo a fondo particular** = demonstrative legacy; **hizo varios legados a sus empleados** = he made several bequests to his staff; **recibió un pequeño legado en el testamento de su tío** = she received a small legacy in her uncle's will

legajo *nm* roll (of papers); **legajo de sentencia** = judgment roll

legal *adj* **(a)** *(lícito)* legal *o (legítimo)* lawful *o* statutory; *(judicial)* judicial; **escritura legal** = deed poll; **ficción legal** = legal fiction; **impedimento legal** = estoppel; **moneda de curso legal** = legal currency *o* legal tender; **reivindicación legal** *o* **reclamación legal** = legal claim; **separación legal** = legal separation *o* judicial separation; **con capacidad legal** = sui juris; **la acción de la empresa fue totalmente legal** = the company's action was completely legal **(b)** *(forense)* forensic; **ciencia legal** = forensic science; **medicina legal** = forensic medicine
◊ **legalmente** *adv* legally *o* lawfully; **este contrato es legalmente vinculante** *o* **compromete legalmente** = the contract is legally binding

legalidad *nf* legality; **garantía de legalidad de un testamento** *o* **concesión de legalidad de un testamento** = grant of probate; **puede que la empresa no haya actuado dentro de la legalidad al despedirle** = there is doubt about the legality of the company's action in dismissing him; **se comunicó al albacea la legalidad del testamento** = the executor was granted probate *o* obtained a grant of probate

legalización *nf* legalization; **legalización de un documento** *o* **legalización de un testamento** = probate; **la campaña para la legalización del aborto** = the campaign for the legalization of abortion; **registro de legalización de testamentos** = Probate Registry

legalizado, -da *adj* **copia legalizada** *o* **certificada** = certified copy

legalizar *vt* to legalize *o (certificar un documento ante notario)* to authenticate; **legalizar un matrimonio** = to legalize a marriage; **legalizar una firma** = to attest a signature

legar *vt (dejar)* to leave *o* to bequeath *o* to devise *o (asignar)* to settle on; **legó la casa a su mujer** = he left his house to his wife; **legó las acciones a su hija** = he bequeathed his shares to his daughter;

legó sus bienes a sus hijos = he settled his property on his children

legatario, -ria *n* legatee *o* devisee *o (de bienes raíces)* heir to an estate; **legatario remanente** = residuary legatee

legislación *nf* legislation; **legislación del consumidor** = consumer legislation; **legislación delegada** = delegated legislation; **legislación comunitaria** = Community legislation; **legislación laboral** = labour legislation

legislar *vt* to legislate; **el Congreso ha legislado en contra de la venta de drogas** = Congress has legislated against the sale of drugs

legislativo, -va *adj* legislative; **cuerpo legislativo** = legislature; **procesos legislativos** = legislative processes; **el Parlamento es el órgano legislativo en Gran Bretaña** = Parliament is the law-making body in Great Britain; **las Cortes tienen una función legislativa** = Parliament has a legislative function

legislatura *nf* **(a)** *(periodo de tiempo)* term **(b)** *(cuerpo legislativo)* legislature

legista *nmf* jurist *o* legist

legítima *nf (parte de una herencia)* share of an estate (approximately two thirds); **legítima estricta** = one third of the value of the estate divided among the lawful inheritents; **legítima larga** = normally two thirds of the estate

> Son legitimarios, y por ello tienen derecho a recibir una parte del patrimonio del difunto o legítima, los hijos y descendientes y en su defecto los padres y ascendientes y el cónyuge viudo (CC artº 807)

legitimación *nf* legitimation *o* legitimization *o* legalization

legitimar *vt* to legitimate *o* to legalize; **juicio para legitimar a alguien** = legitimacy

legitimidad *nf* legitimacy; **el tribunal dudó de la legitimidad de su demanda** = the court doubted the legitimacy of his claim

legítimo, -ma *adj* **(a)** *(legal)* legitimate *o* lawful *o* rightful; **legítima defensa** = self-defence; **comercio legítimo** = lawful trade; **hijo legítimo, hija legítima** = legitimate child; **práctica legítima** = lawful practice; **propietario, legítimo, propietaria legítima** = rightful owner; **tiene derecho legítimo a la propiedad** = he has a legitimate claim to the property; **no tiene derecho legítimo alguno sobre la propiedad** = he has no legal claim to the property; **legó la propiedad a su hijo legítimo** = he left his property to his legitimate offspring **(b)** *(auténtico)* genuine; **un monedero de cuero legítimo** = a genuine leather purse
◊ **legítimamente** *(adv) (legalmente)* lawfully

La legítima defensa es una circunstancia eximente o atenuante de la responsabilidad criminal, consistente en un acto de defensa necesario para impedir o repeler una agresión injusta contra las personas, los derechos o los bienes, propios o ajenos

lego *nm* lay *o* layman

lengua *nf* language; **lengua materna** = mother tongue *o* native language

lenguaje *nm* language; **lenguaje informático** *o* **de programación** = computer language *o* programming language; **lenguaje ofensivo** *o* **difamatorio** = offensive language *o* abusive language; **fue acusado de utilizar un lenguaje ofensivo con un policía** = he was accused of using offensive language to a policeman

lenidad *nf* leniency

lenocinio *nm* *(prostitución)* procuring; **casa de lenocinio** = brothel; **llevar una casa de lenocinio** = keeping a disorderly house

lesión *nf* injury; **lesión cerebral** = brain damage; **lesión grave** = grievous bodily harm (GBH); **delito de lesiones** = actual bodily harm (ABH); **sin lesiones apreciables** = no visible injuries; **subsidio** *o* **indemnización por lesiones** = injury benefit

lesionar *vt* to hurt *o* to injure *o* *(herir)* to wound; **el artículo publicado en el periódico ha lesionado en gran medida la reputación de la firma** = the newspaper report has done a lot of harm to the firm's reputation

letra *nf* **(a)** *(forma de pago)* bill *o* draft; **letra al cobro** = bills for collection; **letra de cambio** = bill of exchange *o* bank draft; **letra de cambio a la vista** = sight draft; **letra de complacencia** = accommodation bill; **letra a cargo propio** *o* **letra al propio cargo** = promissory note *o* note of hand; **aceptar una letra** = to accept a bill for payment; **devolver una letra** = to dishonour a bill; **protestar una letra** = to note a bill **(b)** *(escritura)* writing *o* handwriting; **en fe de lo cual firmo de mi puño y letra** = in witness whereof, I set my hand; **falsificó la letra de su padre** = he faked *o* forged his father's handwriting **(c)** *(de imprenta)* letra; **ajustarse a la letra del reglamento** = to stick to the rules; **al pie de la letra** = literally; **escriba su nombre y dirección en letras de molde** *o* **letras mayúsculas** = write your name and address in block letters *o* in capital letters

letrero *nm* sign *o* notice

levantamiento *nm* **(a)** *(suspensión)* lifting; **documento de levantamiento de una hipoteca** *o* **de liquidación de un pago** = memorandum of satisfaction; **levantamiento del secreto del sumario** = lifting of subjudice rule **(b)** **levantamiento del cadáver** = removal of the body

in the presence of the judge **(c)** *(alzamiento)* uprising

levantar *vt* **(a)** *(suprimir)* to lift *o* to remove; **el gobierno ha levantado el embargo sobre las importaciones de material informático** = the government has removed the ban on imports of computer equipment; **el ministro ha levantado el embargo a la exportación de armas de fuego** = the minister has lifted the embargo on the export of firearms **(b)** *(aplazar)* to adjourn

levantar **levantar la sesión** = to adjourn *o* to close the meeting; **se levanta la sesión** = the meeting stands adjourned **(c)** **levantar acta** = to take the minutes; **levantar acta de acusación** = to prefer an indictment; **levantar acta notarial (por falta de pago)** = to note (a bill) ◊ **levantarse** *vr* **(a)** *(ponerse de pie)* to get up *o* to stand up **(b)** *(aplazarse)* to adjourn; **la reunión se levantó a mediodía** = the meeting adjourned at midday

ley *nf* *(derecho)* lex *o* law *o* *(parlamento)* act; **Ley de Enjuiciamiento Civil** = Code of Civil Law Procedure; **Ley de Enjuiciamiento Criminal** = Code of Criminal Procedure; **ley de extranjería** = immigration laws; **ley de prescripción** = statute of limitations; **ley de propiedad intelectual** = copyright law; **Ley de Sociedades** = Companies Act; **ley del foro** *o* **del tribunal** = lex fori; **ley del lugar del acto** = lex loci actus; **ley del lugar del contrato** = lex loci contractus; **ley del lugar del delito** = lex loci delicti; **ley del patrono y del obrero** *o* **ley de empleo** = the law of master and servant; **Ley de los derechos de autor** = Copyright Act; **ley electoral** = the Representation of the People Act; **ley fundamental** = Bill of Rights; **ley orgánica** = constitutional law; **ley orgánica del poder judicial** = constitutional law relating to the judiciary; **ley parlamentaria** = act of Parliament *o* statute *o* enactment; **ley recopiladora** = Consolidating Act; **ley vigente** = law in force; **ley por la que se debe regir un contrato** = proper law of the contract; **leyes de Oleron: (primeras leyes marítimas (de 1216), utilizadas como base para posteriores leyes internacionales)** = Laws of Oleron; **leyes federales** federal laws; **leyes laborales** = labour laws; **leyes sobre la propiedad intelectual** = copyright law; **medida de ley** = measure; **proposición de ley** = Member's bill; **proyecto de ley** = bill; **una ley ha de ser aprobada por el Parlamento** = a law has to be passed by Parliament; **la cámara está discutiendo el proyecto de ley de prevención del ruido** = the house is discussing the Noise Prevention Bill; **el gobierno ha propuesto una nueva ley para regular la venta de mercancías los domingos** = the government has proposed a new law to regulate the sale of goods on Sundays **(b)** **la ley** = the law; **bajo la ley sub judice; contra la ley** *o* **fuera de la ley** = against the law *o* outside the law; **dentro de la**

ley *o* **según la ley** = in law *o* inside the law *o* within the law; **el brazo fuerte de la ley** = the strong *o* long arm of the law; **infractor de la ley** = lawbreaker; **mantener la ley** = to keep the law; **por la ley** = statutorily; **recurrir a la ley** = to go to law; **vacaciones establecidas por ley** = statutory holiday; **violación de la ley** *o* **transgresión de la ley** = law-breaking; **violar la ley** *o* **infringir la ley** *o* **quebrantar la ley** = to break the law; **violando una ley** = in violation of a law; **los directores son responsables ante la ley** = the directors are legally responsible; **tarde o temprano tendrá que vérselas con la ley** = the law will catch up with him in the end; **un inquilino protegido por la ley** = a statutorily protected tenant; **¿cuáles son las obligaciones de un tutor según la ley?** = what are the duties in law of a guardian?; **despedir a un trabajador sin razón va contra la ley** = dismissing a worker without reason is against the law; **está quebrantando la ley vendiendo mercancías el domingo** = he is breaking the law by selling goods on Sunday; **infringirás la ley si intentas sacar ese ordenador del país sin una licencia de exportación** = you will be breaking the law if you try to take that computer out of the country without an export licence; **la empresa está actuando en contra de la ley** = the company is operating outside the law; **las autoridades tienen una obligación establecida por ley de ofrecer educación gratuita a todos los niños** = the authority has a statutory obligation to provide free education to all children **(c)** *(economía)* **ley de la oferta y la demanda** = law of supply and demand

Las leyes orgánicas son las relativas al desarrollo de los derechos fundamentales y de las libertades públicas, las que aprueban los estatutos de autonomía y el régimen electoral y las previstas en la Constitución. Requieren mayoría absoluta del Congreso, en una votación sobre el conjunto del proyecto (CE 81)

libelista *nmf* libeller

libelo *nm* libel; **libelo difamatorio** = libel; **acción** *o* **demanda** *o* **pleito por libelo** = action for libel *o* libel action; **declaró que la noticia era un libelo** = he claimed that the newspaper report was a libel

liberación *nf* release; **liberación de un prisionero** *o* **liberación parcial de un contrato** = discharge; **liberación de la mujer** = women's liberation

liberalizar *vt* to decontrol *o* *(mercado)* to deregulate; **liberalizar el precio de la gasolina** = to decontrol the price of petrol

liberar *vt* **(a)** *(poner en libertad)* to free *o* to release *o* *(absolver)* to discharge *o* *(mantener bajo custodia)* to remand; **liberar a alguien** = to set someone free; **el nuevo presidente liberó a todos**

los presos políticos = the new president freed all political prisoners; **la multitud asaltó la comisaría de policía y liberó a los tres prisioneros** = the crowd attacked the police station and set the three prisoners free **(b)** *(librar)* to exempt; **liberar a alguien de una deuda** *o* **de un contrato** = to release someone from a debt *o* from a contract; **liberar de impuestos** = to exempt from tax; **liberar a alguien de un deber** = to free someone of a duty

libertad *nf* freedom *o* liberty *o* *(liberación)* release; **libertad bajo fianza** = on bail; **libertad bajo palabra** = parole; **libertad condicional (a prueba)** *o* **libertad vigilada** = probation *o* conditional discharge *o* release on licence *o* *(custodia por aplazamiento de caso)* remand; **libertad de asociación** = freedom of association; **libertad de elección** = freedom of choice; **libertad de expresión** = freedom of speech; **libertad de prensa** = freedom of the press *o* liberty of the press; **libertad de reunión** = freedom of assembly *o* of meeting; **libertad del ciudadano** *o* **libertad individual** = liberty of the subject; **libertad del individuo** *o* **de la persona (de actuar según la ley)** = liberty of the individual; **libertad incondicional** = absolute discharge; **libertad provisional** = release on-trial; **libertad provisional bajo fianza** = bail; **libertad provisional sin fianza** = release without bail; **libertades civiles** = civil liberties; **conceder la libertad condicional** *o* **la libertad vigilada** = to parole; **en libertad** = free *o* at large *o* at liberty; **en libertad condicional a prueba** *o* **bajo libertad vigilada** = on probation; **orden judicial de libertad vigilada** *o* **de libertad condicional** = probation order; **persona que está en libertad vigilada** = probationer; **poner en libertad** = to free *o* to release *o* to liberate *o* to set someone free; **poner en libertad bajo fianza** = to remand; **después de seis meses de buena conducta en la cárcel, puede concedérsele la libertad condicional** = after six month's good conduct in prison she is eligible for parole; **el apelante será puesto en libertad condicional después de ocho meses** = the appellant will be released on licence after eight months; **el juez dejó a los chicos en libertad con una amonestación** = the magistrate let the boys off with a warning; **el presidente dio la libertad al acusado** = the president gave the accused man his freedom; **el presidente puso en libertad al líder de la oposición** = the president released the opposition leader from prison; **están todavía en libertad mientras esperan a que se formulen las acusaciones** = they are still at liberty while waiting for charges to be brought; **le concedieron la libertad condicional e inmediatamente entró a robar en una casa** = he was let out on parole and immediately burgled a house; **le concedieron la libertad vigilada durante un año** = she was sentenced to probation for one year; **le pusieron en libertad bajo fianza por dos semanas** = he was remanded in custody *o* remanded on bail for two weeks; **si tienes suerte te concederán la libertad condicional antes de Navidad** = if you're lucky you will be paroled before Christmas; **tres prisioneros escaparon - dos fueron capturados, pero uno está todavía en libertad** = three prisoners escaped - two were recaptured, but one is still at large; **tres presos fueron puestos en libertad** = three prisoners were liberated

libertar *vt* to liberate

librado, -da 1 *adj* **pagó la factura con un cheque librado contra un banco egipcio** = he paid the invoice with a cheque drawn on an Egyptian bank 2 *n (tomador)* drawee

librador, -ra *n* drawer; **el banco devolvió el cheque al librador** = the bank returned the cheque to drawer

librar *vt (de una responsabilidad)* to free *o* to release *o* to exempt
◊ **librarse** *vr (escaparse)* to get off

libre *adj* **(a)** *(liberado)* free *o* **(en libertad)** at large *o* at liberty; **libre albedrío** = free will; **libre absolución** = absolute discharge; **libre de cargas** = acquitted; **estar libre de culpa** = to have clean hands; **estar libre de sospechas** = to be in the clear; **el demandante debe estar libre de culpa** = the plaintiff must have clean hands **(b)** *(sin restricciones)* **libre circulación de capital** = free movement of capital; **libre circulación de mercancías** = free circulation of goods; **libre comercio** *o* **libre cambio** = free trade; **libre competencia** = free competition; **libre empresa** = free enterprise; **convenio colectivo libre** = free collective bargaining; **mercado libre** = free market *o* open market; **moneda de libre circulación** = free currency; **zona de libre cambio** = free trade area **(c)** *(independiente)* **por libre** = freelance; **trabajar por libre** = to work freelance; **trabaja por libre como agente publicitario** = he works freelance as an advertising agent; **tenemos tres personas trabajando por libre** = we have three people working on a freelance basis **(d)** *(disponible)* free *o* vacant *o* for hire; **propiedad libre de inquilinos** = vacant possession; **¿Hay alguna mesa libre en el restaurante?** = are there any tables free in the restaurant?; **la casa está en venta y libre de inquilinos** = the house is for sale with vacant possession; **la propiedad debe venderse libre de inquilinos** = the property is to be sold with vacant possession **(e)** *(franco)* franco; **libre de impuestos** = free of tax *o* tax-free *o* free of duty *o* duty-free; **tienda libre de impuestos** = duty-free shop; **compró un reloj, libre de impuestos, en el aeropuerto** = he bought a duty-free watch at the airport *o* he bought the watch duty-free **(f)** **tiempo libre** = free time *o* spare time; **tomarse tiempo libre durante el trabajo** = to take time off work; **tomarse tres días libres** = to take three days off;

mañana es el día libre de la secretaria = it is the secretary's day off tomorrow
◊ **libremente** *adv; (sin restricciones)* freely; **el dinero debería circular libremente dentro de la Unión Europea** = money should circulate freely within the European Union

librecambista *nmf* free trader

librería *nf* bookshop

librero, -ra 1 *n* bookseller *o* stationer 2 *nm* bookcase

libreta *nf* notebook; **libreta de ahorros** = savings book

libro *nm* book; **libro de actas** = minute book; **libro de consultas** = reference book; **libro de familia** = family register (equivalent to copy of marriage and birth certificates); **libros del registro civil** = records held at the public registry office; **libro registro** = register; **libro verde (informe del gobierno británico sobre un proyecto de ley presentado al Parlamento)** = Green Paper; **libros de cuentas de una compañía** = a company's books; **libros del derecho civil romano** = corpus legis; **según nuestros libros la factura número 1234 no ha sido pagada** = we find from our records that our invoice number 1234 has not been paid; **valor del activo de una compañía según sus libros de cuentas** = book value

licencia *nf* **(a)** *(permiso)* licensing *o* licence *o* US license *o* **licencia de armas** = firearms certificate; **licencia de exportación** = export permit *o o* export licence; **licencia de importación** = import permit *o* import licence; **licencia de juego** = gaming licence; **licencia de obras** = building permit; **licencia en exclusiva** = exclusive licence; **licencia matrimonial** = marriage licence; **licencia para vender alcohol** = licence to sell liquor *o* liquor licence; **licencia paterna** = parents' consent; **acuerdo** *o* **contrato de concesión de licencia** = licensing agreement; **conceder una licencia a una empresa para fabricar piezas de repuesto** = to license a company to produce spare parts; **productos fabricados con licencia** = goods manufactured under licence; **tiene licencia para dirigir una oficina de empleo** *o* **una agencia de colocación** = she is licensed to run an employment agency **(b)** *(concesión de franquicia)* franchising *o* franchise; **conceder una licencia de explotación** = to franchise **(c)** **licencia por maternidad** = maternity leave; **licencia temporal** = leave of absence
◊ **licenciatario, -ria** *n (concesionario)* franchisee

licitación *nf* tender *o* tendering; **licitaciones en pliego cerrado** = sealed tenders; **hacer una licitación** = to invite tenders for a contract; **presentar una oferta de licitación** = to tender for a contract; **sacar una obra a licitación** = to put a project out to tender *o* to ask for *o* to invite tenders for a project

licitador, -ra *n* tenderer *o* bidder *o* postor

licitante *nmf* tenderer *o* bidder *o* postor

licitar *vt* to bid for something; **licitar para un contrato** = to tender for a contract; **licitar para la construcción de un hospital** = to tender for the construction of a hospital

lícito, -ta *adj* lawful *o* legal *o* licit *o* (*permitido*) allowable; **práctica lícita** = lawful practice

líder *nm* leader; **líder de la oposición** = Leader of the Opposition; **empresa líder de un sector del mercado** = a market leader; **es la empresa líder del sector** = they are the leading company in the field

limitación *nf* limitation; **limitación al libre comercio** = restraint of trade; **limitación de la responsabilidad** = limitation of liability

limitado, -da *adj* limited; **no limitado** *o* **no limitado de antemano** = unlimited *o* open-ended *o* US open-end; **responsabilidad limitada** = limited liability; **sociedad de responsabilidad limitada (SRL)** = limited liability company *o* close company; **sociedad limitada (SL)** = private limited company *o* (Singapore) proprietary company (Pty); **sociedad personal de responsabilidad limitada** = limited partnership; **título limitado de una propiedad** = qualified title; **un acuerdo no limitado de antemano** = an open-ended agreement

limitar *vt* (a) (*restringir*) to limit *o* to restrict *o* (*ajustarse a*) to hold to; **limitar las importaciones** = to set limits to imports *o* to impose limits on imports *o* to restrict imports; **los bancos han limitado su crédito** = the banks have limited their credit; **el acuerdo limita la capacidad de ventas de la empresa** = the agreement restricts the company's ability to sell its products; **el gobierno espera limitar el aumento de salarios a un 5%** = the government hopes to hold wage increases to 5%; **el tribunal limitó los daños y perjuicios a 25.000 ptas** = the court limited damages to 25,000 ptas (b) (*lindar*) to border on

limitativo, -va *adj* limiting

límite *nm* (a) (*acotación*) limit; **límite de crédito** = credit limit *o* lending limit; **límite de peso** = weight limit; **límite de velocidad** = speed limit; **límite legal** = legal limit; **poner límite a** = to set a limit to; **sin límites fijos** = open-ended *o* US open-end; **plazo de tiempo límite** = time limitation; **imponer límites a las importaciones** = to set limits to imports *o* to impose limits on imports; **ha excedido su límite de crédito** = he has exceeded his credit limit (b) (*frontera*) boundary (line); **la disputa en los juzgados sobre los límites de tierra se hizo interminable** = the boundary dispute dragged through the courts for years

limítrofe *adj* bordering; **ser limítrofe con** = to adjoin

limpio, -pia 1 *adj* clean *o* (*honrado*) honest; **juego limpio** = fair play; **tener las manos limpias** = to have clean hands 2 *nm* (a) (*neto*) **en limpio** = net (b) **copia en limpio** = fair copy *o* final copy

linaje *nm* descent

linchamiento *nm* lynch; **ley de lynch** = lynch law

linchar *vt* to lynch

lindar *vi* **lindar con** = to abut (on) *o* to border on

línea *nf* line; **línea de acción** *o* **de conducta** = course of action; **línea externa** = outside line; **línea de descendencia** *o* **en línea directa** = lineal descent; **línea marítima** = shipping line; **línea ocupada** = engaged line; **línea programática** = policy; **líneas directivas** = guidelines; **líneas generales** = outline; **¿cuál es la mejor línea de conducta que debe tomar el demandado?** = what is the best course of action the defendant should take?; **trazaron las líneas generales de un proyecto** = they drew up the outline of a plan *o* an outline plan

lío *nm* (a) (*enredo*) muddle; **meterse en un lío** = to get into trouble; **el testigo se hizo un lío** = the witness got into a muddle; **los papeles están hechos un lío** = the papers are all mixed up (b) (*relación amorosa*) affair; **tener un lío con alguien** = to have an affair with someone

liquidación *nf* (a) (*disolución*) liquidation *o* winding up *o* (*cumplimiento*) satisfaction; **liquidación de activos** *o* **valor en liquidación** = realization of assets; **liquidación de una cuenta** = closing of an account; **liquidación de una deuda** = liquidation *o* clearing of a debt *o* accord and satisfaction; **liquidación forzosa** = compulsory liquidation *o* compulsory winding up; **liquidación voluntaria** = voluntary winding up; **documento de liquidación de un pago** = memorandum of satisfaction; **orden de liquidación forzosa** = compulsory winding up order; **solicitud de liquidación judicial de una empresa** = winding up petition; **la compañía entró en (periodo de) liquidación** = the company went into liquidation *o* went into receivership (b) (*bolsa*) settlement; **de liquidación** = closing; **día** *o* **fecha de liquidación** = settlement day *o* settlement date (c) (*rebajas*) sale; **liquidación de existencias** = clearance sale

liquidar *vt* (a) (*saldar*) to settle *o* to pay *o* to pay off *o* to close *o* to adjust; **liquidar una cuenta** = to settle *o* to close an account; **liquidar una deuda** = to pay off a debt; **liquidar una reclamación** = to settle a claim (b) (*vender*) to liquidate *o* to get out *o* (*negocio*) to sell out; **liquidar activo** = to liquidate assets; **liquidar existencias** = to clear stock; **liquidar una compañía** *o* **una empresa** *o* **una**

sociedad = to liquidate a company *o* to wind up a company *o* to put a company into liquidation; **el tribunal ordenó liquidar la empresa** = the court ordered the company to be wound up

liquidez *nf* liquidity

líquido *adj y nm* liquid; **líquido imponible** = taxable income; **activo líquido** = liquid assets; **saldo líquido** = balance in hand

lista *nf* **(a)** *(repertorio)* list *o* schedule; *(censo)* roll *o (programa)* calendar; *(tabla)* table; **lista abierta** *o* **lista cerrada** = open *o* closed list; **lista de casos para ver** = list of cases to be heard; **lista de causas** *o* **de pleitos** *o* = cause list *o* docket *o* court calendar; **lista de causas alzadas** = calendar of appeals; **lista de deudores** = list of debtors; **lista de direcciones** *o* **de destinarios** = address list *o* mailing list; **lista de pasajeros de un barco** *o* **avión** = passenger manifest; **lista de precios** = tariff *o* scale of charges *o* schedule of charges *o* price list; **lista de productos** = list of products *o* product list; **lista de socios** list of members; **lista del contenido de un paquete** = docket; **lista electoral** = electoral roll; **lista negra** *o* **lista de particulares, empresas y países con los que se hallan prohibidas las relaciones comerciales** = black list; **añadir un artículo a una lista** = to add an item to a list; **hacer una lista** = to list; **poner en la lista negra** = to blacklist; **tachar el nombre de alguien de una lista** = to cross someone's name off a list; **el gobierno puso su empresa en la lista negra** = his firm was blacklisted by the government **(b)** **lista de correos** = poste restante; **envíe cualquier mensaje a 'Lista de Correos, Atenas'** = send any messages to 'Poste Restante, Athens'
◊ **listado** *nm* listing

listo, -ta *adj* **(a)** *(inteligente)* clever; **pasarse de listo** = to be too clever; **es muy listo para encontrar gangas** he is very clever at spotting a bargain **(b)** *(preparado)* ready; **estar siempre listo** = to be always ready

literal *adj* literal; **una transcripción literal del juicio** = a verbatim transcript of the trial
◊ **literalmente** *adv* literally *o* verbatim

literario, -ria *adj* literary; **propiedad literaria** = copyright; **registrado, -da como propiedad literaria** = copyrighted; **registrar como propiedad literaria** = to copyright

litigante *nmf* litigant; **litigante en persona** = litigant in person; **litigante oneroso** *o* **vejatorio** = vexatious litigant

litigar *vt* to litigate

litigio *nm* litigation *o* dispute *o* lawsuit *o* suit *o (litis)* lis; **litigio internacional** = international dispute; **litigio pendiente** = lis pendens; **litigio vejatorio** = vexatious action; **en litigio** = in dispute
◊ **litigios** *nmpl* courtroom battles

◊ **litigioso, -sa** *adj* litigious

litis *nm* lis; **litis pendencia** = lis pendens

litisconsorcio *nm* joint litigation

llamada *nf* **(a)** *(llamamiento)* call; **llamada al orden** = caution *o* call to order; **llamada de atención** = reprimand; **los muchachos fueron puestos en libertad con una llamada al orden** = the boys were let off with a caution **(b)** *(teléfono)* **llamada a cobro revertido** = transferred charge call; **llamada a larga distancia** = long-distance call; **llamada internacional** = overseas call *o* international call; **llamada local** *o* **urbana** = local call; **llamada telefónica** = telephone call **(c)** *(nombrado)* called; **una propiedad llamada 'Los Pinos'** = a property called 'Los Pinos'

llamamiento *nm* call; **llamamiento de pago de acciones** = call

llamar *vt* **(a)** *(hacer una llamada)* to call *o (a la puerta)* to knock; **llamar a** = to call in; **llamar a cobro revertido** = to make a collect call; **llamar a alguien a declarar** = to call upon someone to give evidence; **llamar a filas** = to call up (for military service); **llamar a la huelga** = to call out to strike; **llamar al orden** = call to order; **persona que llama** *o* **el que llama (por teléfono)** = caller; **llamó a la puerta y entró** = he knocked on the door and went in; **te llamaré mañana a tu despacho** = I shall call you at your office tomorrow **(b)** *(hacer volver)* to recall; **el testigo fue llamado a declarar de nuevo** = the witness was recalled to the witness box **(c)** *(nombrar)* to name

llave *nf* key; **hemos perdido las llaves de la sala de ordenadores** = we have lost the keys to the computer room; **operación llaves en mano** = turnkey operation; **se ha llevado las llaves de la oficina, así que nadie puede entrar** = he has taken the office keys home with him, so no one can get in

llegar *vi* **(a)** *(a un sitio)* to arrive *o* to get to; **por fin llegó a la sala del tribunal a las 10.30** = she finally got to the courtroom at 10.30; **el cargamento llegó a Canadá seis semanas tarde** = the shipment got to Canada six weeks late **(b)** **llegar a** = to reach; **llegar a un acuerdo** = to reach an agreement *o* a settlement; **llegar a un acuerdo extrajudicial** = to settle out of court; **llegar a un acuerdo sobre los precios o salarios** = to reach an agreement *o* to come to an agreement on prices or salaries; **llegar a un arreglo** = to compromise; **llegar a una conclusión** = to conclude; **llegar a una decisión** = to reach a decision; **las dos partes llegaron a un acuerdo al margen de los tribunales** *o* **llegaron a un acuerdo amistoso** = the two parties settled out of court; **el jurado no pudo llegar a una decisión unánime** = the jury was unable to reach a unanimous decision

lleno, -na *adj* full; **los presos tienen que compartir las celdas por estar las prisiones**

demasiado llenas *o* porque las prisiones están demasiado llenas = prisoners have to share cells because the prisons are too full

llevar *vt* **(a)** *(de un sitio a otro)* to carry *o* to take *o* *(traer)* to bring; **llevar a** = to lead (up) to; **llevar a alguien a juicio** to take someone to court; **llevar a la prostitución** = to procure; **llevar a los tribunales** = to commit; **el abogado llevó a su secretaria para que tomara nota de la reunión** = the solicitor brought his secretary to take notes of the meeting; **el tren llevaba un cargamento de coches** = the train was carrying a consignment of cars **(b)** *(dirigir)* to manage *o* to run *o* *(tramitar)* to conduct; **llevar la contabilidad** *o* **los libros de una empresa** = to keep the books of a company *o* to keep a company's books; **llevar negociaciones** = to conduct discussions *o* negotiations; **llevar un negocio** = to run a business; **llevar una casa de lenocinio** *o* **de prostitución** = keeping a disorderly house; **llevar una causa** = to conduct a case; **llevar una sucursal** = to manage a branch office; **lleva un negocio de pedidos por correo desde su casa** = he runs a mail-order business from home; **lleva una empresa multimillonaria** = she is running a multimillion-pound company **(c)** *(realizar)* **llevar a cabo** = to carry out; **la policía llevó a cabo la redada a gran velocidad** = the police carried out the raid with great speed; **la investigación se llevará a cabo en Londres durante el mes de junio** = the inquiry will be held in London in June; **llevan un club deportivo para los empleados** = they run a staff sports club; **los agentes judiciales tuvieron que llevar a cabo la orden del tribunal de embargar los bienes de la mujer** = the bailiffs had to carry out the order of the court and seize the woman's property **(d)** *(tener como consecuencia)* to carry; **el delito lleva una pena máxima de dos años de prisión** = the offence carries a maximum sentence of two years' imprisonment **(e)** *(transcurrir)* **llevar tiempo** = to take time; **le llevará toda la mañana pasar mis cartas a máquina** = it will take her all morning to type my letters **(f)** *(someter)* to put; **llevar una propuesta al consejo de dirección** = to put a proposal to the board

◊ **llevarse** *vr* **(a)** *(robar, secuestrar)* to carry off *o* to steal; **los saqueadores se llevaron todos los televisores que había en el almacén** = the looters carried off all the stock of television sets; **uno de nuestros directores se fue para formar su propia empresa y se llevó la lista de direcciones de nuestros clientes** = one of our managers left to form his own company and stole the list of our clients' addresses **(b)** **llevarse bien con alguien** = to get on (well) with someone; **no se lleva bien con su nuevo jefe** she does not get on with her new boss

local 1 *adj* local; **autoridad local** = local authority; **derecho local** = municipal law; **juzgado local** = local court *o* *GB* County Court; **oficinas**

locales = municipal offices; **proyecto de ley de interés local** = Private Bill; **reglamento interno de los juzgados locales** = County Court Rules; **un tribunal puede dar instrucciones a una autoridad local en lo que se refiere al ejercicio de sus poderes en materia de tutela infantil** = a court can give instructions to a local authority as to the exercise of its powers in relation to children in care **2** *nm* *(edificio)* premises *o* *(lugar)* site; **local comercial** = business premises *o* commercial premises; **local sin vivienda incorporada** = lock-up premises; **en el local** = on the premises; **hay un doctor en el local** = there is a doctor on the premises at all times

◊ **localización** *nf* **(a)** *(situación)* *nf* situation **(b)** *(muestreo)* **localización de contribuyentes** = canvassing

localizar *vt* to trace; **hemos localizado los documentos que faltaban** = we have traced the missing documents

loco, -ca 1 *adj* insane *o* mad *o* crazy **2** *nf* madwoman *o* lunatic **3** *nm* madman *o* lunatic

locura *nf* insanity *o* madness

locutorio *nm* *(de una cárcel)* booth *o* visiting room

lograr *vt* to obtain; **lograr algo** = to procure

lonja *nf* commodity market; **lonja de contratación** = commodity exchange

LOPJ = LEY ORGANICA DEL PODER JUDICIAL

lote *nm* lot; **al final de la subasta la mitad de los lotes no se habían vendido** = at the end of the auction half the lots had not been sold; **hizo una oferta por el lote 23** = he put in a bid for lot 23; **vender acciones en pequeños lotes** = to sell shares in small lots

lotería *nf* lottery

lucha *nf* **(a)** *(conflicto)* fight *o* struglle *o* battle *o* strife **(b)** *(competición)* contest

luchar *vi* to fight *o* *(hacer campaña)* to campaign

lucrativo, -va *adj* lucrative *o* profitable; **empleo lucrativo** = gainful employment; **organización no lucrativa** = non-profit corporation; **existe un lucrativo mercado negro de piezas de repuesto de coche** = there is a lucrative black market in car spare parts; **firmó un contrato lucrativo con una compañía de televisión** = he signed a lucrative contract with a TV company

◊ **lucrativamente** *adv* profitably

lucro *nm* **lucro cesante** = loss of profit *o* lost profits; **organización sin fines de lucro** = non-profit corporation; **lucro cesante** = claim for damages for loss of profit

> El lucro cesante es la ganancia dejada de obtener por el acreedor, en materia de indemnización por daños y perjuicios

luego *adv* then *o* later; **desde luego** = of course; **¿quieres ir a Australia en viaje de negocios? - ¡desde luego!** = are you willing to go on a sales trip to Australia? - of course!

lugar *nm* (**sitio**) place *o* site; **lugar de ejecución** = place of performance; **lugar de encuentro** *o* **de reunión** = meeting place; **lugar de trabajo** = place of work; **lugar del crimen** = scene of the crime; **lugar donde un caso se puede llevar a juicio** = *US* venue; **lugar público** = public place; **lugar seguro** = safe keeping; **en el lugar citado** = loc. cit.; **proceso judicial iniciado en otro lugar** *o* **litigio pendiente en otro lugar** = lis alibi pendens; **la** solicitud de planificación incluye una fotografía del lugar = the planning application includes a photograph of the site; **el juez y el jurado visitaron el lugar del crimen** = the judge and jury visited the site of the crime; **he perdido el lugar en el que estaba y no puedo recordar hasta dónde había archivado** = I have lost my place and cannot remember where I have reached in my filing **(b)** *(situación)* locus; **en lugar de** = in lieu of; **en lugar del padre** = in loco parentis; **dar a alguien dos meses de sueldo en lugar del aviso de despido** = to give someone two months' salary in lieu of notice; **el tribunal actúa en lugar del padre** = the court is acting in loco parentis **(c)** *(en un juicio)* **no ha lugar** = case dismissed *o* objection overruled **(d)** *(suceder)* **tener lugar** = to occur *o* to take place

luz *nf* light; **luz verde** = green light; **servidumbre de luces (y vistas)** = ancient lights

Mm

madre *nf* mother; **madre política** = mother-in-law; **madre portadora** = surrogate mother
◊ **madrastra** *nf* step-mother
◊ **madrina** *nf* godmother

madrugada *nf* early morning; **se fue a París en un vuelo de madrugada** = he took an early flight to Paris

mafia *nf* mafia; **la mafia** = the mafia *o* the mob; **miembro de la mafia** = mobster

magistrado, -da *n* magistrate *o* senior judge *o* justice *o* (argot) beak; **magistrado en funciones** = acting judge; **magistrado municipal** = recorder; **el magistrado Sr Ortega** = Mr Justice Ortega; **es magistrado** = he is on the bench; **ser magistrado** = to sit on the bench

> Un juez está a cargo de un órgano judicial unipersonal, mientras que un magistrado forma parte de un órgano judicial colegiado

magistratura *nf* judiciary *o* justiciary; **Magistratura de Trabajo** = industrial tribunal

magnético, -ca *adj* magnetic; **cinta magnética** = magnetic tape *o* mag tape

magnicidio *nm* assassination of a political figure

majestad *nf* Majesty

mal 1 *adj (apócope de malo delante nms)* bad; **mal asunto** = nasty business; **mal comportamiento** = misbehaviour; **mal momento** = wrong time *o* bad timing; **mal uso** = misuse **2** *adv* **administrar mal** *o* **dirigir mal** = to mismanage; **calcular mal** = to miscalculate; **instruir mal (al jurado)** = to misdirect; **interpretar mal** = to misinterpret **3** *nm* evil

maldad *nf* malice *o* villainy

maleante *nmf* villain *o* (vagabundo) vagrant; **gente maleante** = underworld; **le acusaron de ser un maleante** = he was charged with vagrancy

malentendido *nm* misunderstanding; **hubo un malentendido con mis billetes** *o* **con mis entradas** = there was a misunderstanding over my tickets

malgastar *vt* to waste

malhechor, -ra *n* malefactor

malicia *nf* malice; **malicia expresa** = express malice; **malicia premeditada** = malice aforethought; **acusación de malicia** *o* **existencia de malicia** = imputation of malice
◊ **malicioso, -sa** *adj* malicious; **denuncia maliciosa** = malicious prosecution; **mentira maliciosa** = malicious falsehood
◊ **maliciosamente** *adv* maliciously; **declaró que había sido denunciado maliciosamente** = he claimed that he had been prosecuted maliciously

malintencionado, -da *adj* malicious; **conducta malintencionada** *o* **negligencia malintencionada** = wilful misconduct

malo, -la *adj* bad *o* wrong; **mala administración** = maladministration; **mala conducta** = misconduct; **mala dirección** = mismanagement; **malas instrucciones (al jurado)** = misdirection; **mala intención** = maliciousness; **malo per se: actos (como el asesinato) que constituyen delitos por sí mismos** = mala in se; **malo por razón de ley: actos (como pisar el césped de un parque) prohibidos aunque no constituyen delitos por sí mismos** = mala prohibita; **malos tratos** = cruelty; **de mala fama** *o* **de mala reputación** = of ill fame *o* of ill repute; **demanda de mala fe** = malicious prosecution; **con** *o* **sin mala intención** = de dolo *o* bona fide

maltratado, -da *adj* ill-treated; **hijo maltratado** *o* **mujer maltratada** = battered child *o* battered wife

maltratar *vt* to abuse

maltrato *nm* abuse *o* ill-treatment; **le acusaron de maltrato de menores** = he was accused of child abuse

malversación *nf* misappropriation; **malversación de fondos** = embezzlement *o* conversion of funds

> La malversación de fondos consiste en invertir ilícitamente bienes muebles públicos en usos distintos de aquellos para los que están destinados

malversador, -ra *n* embezzler

malversar *vt* to embezzle *o* to misappropriate; **le mandaron a la cárcel durante seis meses por malversar el dinero de sus clientes** = he was sent to prison for six months for embezzling his clients' money

mancha *nf* blemish; *(conducta)* **sin mancha** = unblemished

mancomunado, -da *adj* joint; **mancomunada y solidariamente** = joint and several; **propiedad mancomunada** = joint ownership; **signatario mancomunado** = joint signatory

mancomunar *vt (asumir responsabilidad conjunta)* to assume joint responsibility

mancomunidad *nf* joint responsibility *o* Commonwealth

mandamás *nmf* boss *o (coloquial)* baron

mandamiento *nm* warrant; **mandamiento de ejecución** *o* **de pago** = warrant of execution; **mandamiento de prerrogativa** = prerogative order *o* writ; **mandamiento judicial** = writ (of summons) *o* mandamus; **la empresa presentó un mandamiento judicial para impedir que el sindicato fuera a la huelga** = the company issued a writ to prevent the trade union from going on strike

mandante *nm* principal; **mandante encubierto** = undisclosed principal; **el mandatario ha venido a Londres a ver a sus mandantes** = the agent has come to London to see his principals

mandar *vt* **(a)** *(ordenar)* to command *o* to order *o* to instruct *o* to direct; **el presidente mandó al jefe de policía que arrestara a los diputados** = the President commanded the Chief of Police to arrest the Members of Parliament **(b)** *(gobernar)* to rule **(c)** **(citar en juicio)** to subpoena

Mandarín *nm* Mandarin; **mandarines de la prensa** = press barons

mandatario, -ria *n* **(a)** *(representante)* agent *o (apoderado)* proxy **(b)** *(de un país)* **el primer mandatario** = head of state

mandato *nm* **(a)** *(orden)* order *o* mandate *o* command **(b)** *(mando)* rule *o (periodo en un mando)* term *o* tenure; **durante su mandato como presidente** = during his term of office as chairman *o* during his tenure of the office of chairman **(c)** **(campo de aplicación)** terms of reference; **el mandato del tribunal no incluye delitos de tráfico** = the tribunal's terms of reference do not cover traffic offences; **conforme a su mandato, el comité no puede investigar quejas del público** = under the terms of reference of the committee, it cannot investigate complaints from the public **(d)** *(documento legal)* writ *o* dictate; **mandato judicial** = injunction; **mandato judicial de quiebra** = receiving order; **mandato judicial para el pago de**

los impuestos locales = precept; **notificar un mandato judicial a alguien** = to serve someone with a writ

mando *nm* control; **estar al mando de** = to be in charge of; **estar bajo el mando de** = to be controlled by; **mandos intermedios** = middle management; **formación de mandos** = management training; **la empresa está bajo el mando del accionista mayoritario** = the company is controlled by the majority shareholder

manejable *adj* manageable

manejar *vt* to manipulate *o (hacer funcionar una máquina)* to operate a machine; **fácil de manejar** = user-friendly; **estos programas son realmente fáciles de manejar** = these programs are really user-friendly

manejo *nm* handling; **manejo de objetos robados** = handling stolen goods; **de fácil manejo** = user-friendly

manera *nf* manner *o* way; **de la misma manera** = equally; **de ninguna manera** = no way

mangar *vt (robar)* to lift *o (birlar)* to pinch *o* to knock off

maníaco, -ca *n* maniac; **maníaco sexual** = sex maniac

manicomio *nm* mental institution *o* asylum

manifestación *nf* **(a)** *(protesta)* demonstration *o* protest march; **hacer una manifestación** = to demonstrate; **la policía disolvió la manifestación estudiantil** = police broke up the student demonstration **(b)** *(declaración)* statement

manifestante *nmf* demonstrator *o* protester *o (alborotador)* rioter

manifestar *vt* to demonstrate *o* to declare
◊ **manifestarse** *vr (hacer una manifestación)* to demonstrate; **multitud de estudiantes se manifestaban en contra del gobierno** = crowds of students were demonstrating against the government

manifiesto, -ta *adj* apparent *o* manifest *o* patent *o* overt; **defecto manifiesto** = apparent defect; **una injusticia manifiesta** = a manifest injustice; **acto con intención delictiva manifiesta** = overt act
◊ **manifiestamente** *adv* patently; **hizo una declaración al tribunal que era manifiestamente incierta** he made a patently false statement to the court

maniobra *nf* manoeuvre; **maniobra de Bolsa** = stock market manipulation

manipulación *nf* manipulation; **manipulación de la justicia** = perverting the course of justice; **manipulación de objetos robados** = handling stolen goods; **manipulación de precios** *o* **de votos** = price-rigging *o* ballot-rigging; **gastos de**

manipulación *o* **gastos de transporte interno** = handling charges

manipulador *nm* manipulator; **manipulador de Bolsa** = stock market manipulator

manipular *vt* **(a)** *(manejar)* to manipulate; **manipular el mercado de la Bolsa** = to manipulate the market **(b)** *(amañar)* to tamper with something; **se le acusa de manipular las ruedas del coche de la víctima** = the charges state that he tampered with the wheels of the victim's car

mano *nf* **(a)** hand; **a mano alzada** = show of hands; **dar la mano** *o* **estrechar la mano** = to shake hands; **darse la mano para sellar un trato** *o* **cerrar un trato con un apretón de manos** = to shake hands on a deal; **tener las manos limpias** = to have clean hands; **la moción se llevó a cabo a mano alzada** = the motion was carried on a show of hands; **la empresa está en manos del receptor** = the company is in the hands of the receiver **(b) a mano** = by hand *o* *(aquí)* to hand; **entregar una carta a** *o* **en mano** = to send a letter by hand *o* to hand *o* in person; **este importante paquete debe ser entregado al presidente en mano** = this important package is to be delivered to the chairman in person; **el caso de fraude ha sido puesto en manos de la legislación de protección al consumidor** = the fraud case has been covered by the consumer protection legislation; **¿cómo llegó a sus manos?** = how did it come into his possession *o* how did he get possession of it? **(c)** **escrito, -ta a mano** = handwritten; **letra a mano** = longhand; **envíe carta de solicitud escrita a mano** = send a letter of application in your own handwriting; **las solicitudes deberán escritas a mano y enviarse al jefe de contratación** = applications should be written in longhand and sent to the recruitment officer; **es más profesional enviar una carta de solicitud a máquina que a mano** = it is more professional to send in a typed rather than a handwritten letter of application **(d)** **robo a mano armada** = armed robbery; **bajo mano** = under the counter; **trabajo entre manos** = work in hand; **con las manos en la masa** = red-handed; **le cogieron con las manos en la masa** = he was caught red-handed
◊ **mano de obra** *nf* labour *o* labor *o* labour force; **mano de obra barata** = cheap labour; **mano de obra especializada** = skilled labour; **mano de obra local** = local labour; **cobrar los materiales y la mano de obra** = to charge for materials and labour; **abriremos una nueva fábrica en Extremo Oriente para aprovechar la mano de obra local barata** = we are opening a new factory in the Far East because of the cheap local labour force; **industria que utiliza mucha mano de obra** *o* **industria con un alto coeficiente de mano de obra** = labour-intensive industry

manta *nf* blanket

mantener (a) *(conservar, preservar)* to keep *o* to maintain *o* to uphold; **mantener buenas relaciones** = to maintain good relations; **mantener contacto con** = to maintain contact with; **mantener discusiones** *o* **negociaciones** = to conduct discussions *o* negotiations; **mantener la ley** *o* **la paz** = to keep the law *o* the peace; **mantener un dividendo** = to maintain a dividend; **mantener un tipo de interés al 5%** = to maintain an interest rate at 5%; **mantener una sentencia** = to uphold a sentence; **el precio del petróleo ha mantenido la libra alta** = the price of oil has kept the pound at a high level; **debemos mantener nuestra lista de direcciones al día** = we must keep our mailing list up to date; **el gobierno está alentando a las empresas a mantener los precios bajos** = the government is encouraging firms to keep prices low; **la escasa demanda ha mantenido los precios bajos** = lack of demand has kept prices down; **se trajo a la policía montada para mantener la ley y el orden** = mounted police were brought in to maintain law and order; **la empresa ha mantenido el mismo volumen de negocios a pesar de la recesión** = the company has maintained the same volume of business in spite of the recession **(b)** *(manutención)* to maintain; **mantener a alguien** = to provide for someone; **se ordenó al ex-marido a que mantuviera a su mujer y tres hijos** = the ex-husband was ordered to maintain his wife and three children **(c)** *(idea, opinión)* to hold *o* to maintain
◊ **mantenerse** *vr* to hold to *o* to hold up; **las ventas se mantuvieron durante la época turística** = sales held up during the tourist season; **los precios de las acciones se han mantenido bien** = share prices have held up well

mantenimiento *nm* maintenance; **mantenimiento del orden** = policing; **contrato de mantenimiento** = maintenance contract; **el buen mantenimiento del orden en el centro de las ciudades** = the efficient policing of city centres; **el mantenimiento de la ley y el orden está en manos del cuerpo de policía local** = the maintenance of law and order is in the hands of the local police force; **el Ayuntamiento está debatiendo el sistema de mantenimiento del orden propuesto por el jefe de policía local** = the council is debating the local Chief Constable's policing policy

manual *adj* manual; **trabajo manual** = manual labour

manuscrito, -ta *adj* handwritten; **envíe carta de solicitud manuscrita** = send a letter of application in your own handwriting; **las solicitudes deberán ser manuscritas y enviadas al jefe de contratación** = applications should be written in longhand and sent to the recruitment officer

manutención *nf* maintenance; **orden de manutención** = maintenance order; **manutención pendiente de litigio** = maintenance pending suit; **los abogados que representaban a la esposa solicitaron una orden de manutención** = solicitors acting for the wife made an application for a maintenance order

manzana *nf* block

maña *nf* skill; **mañas** = sharp practice

mañana *nf* (a) *(parte del día)* morning; **por la mañana** = a.m. *o* ante meridiem; **antes de las 6 de la mañana, las llamadas telefónicas se cobran a tarifa reducida** = telephone calls before 6 a.m. are charged at the cheap rate; **el vuelo sale a las 9.20 de la mañana** = the flight leaves at 9.20 a.m. (b) *(el día después de hoy)* tomorrow

máquina *nf* machine; **código de máquina** = machine code *o* machine language; **códigos en lenguaje de máquina** = machine-readable codes; **escribir a máquina** = to type; **sabe escribir a máquina a mucha velocidad** = he can type quite fast
◊ **maquinaria** *nf* machinery *o (instalaciones y bienes de equipo)* plant; **el inspector consideró que la maquinaria de la fábrica era peligrosa** = the inspector found that the machinery in the factory was dangerous
◊ **maquinista** *nmf* machinist *o* operative

maquinar *vt* to plot *o* to conspire
◊ **maquinación** *nf* conspiration

marca *nf* (a) *(nombre comercial)* brand *o* make; **marca comercial** *o* **marca conocida** = brand name; **marca registrada** = trademark *o* trade mark; **artículos de marca** = branded goods; **de marca registrada** = proprietary; **medicamento de marca registrada** = proprietary drug; **poner una marca** = to brand; **oficina** *o* **registro de patentes y marcas** = patents office (b) *(señal)* mark; **marca de contraste** = hallmark; **marca de ensaye** = assay mark; **hacer una marca** = to check

marcar *vt* (a) *(dar nombre)* to brand (b) *(señalar)* to mark; **artículo marcado con (un precio de) 1.500 ptas** = article marked at 1,500 ptas (c) *(teléfono)* to dial

marcha *nf* (a) *(progreso)* progress; **el comisario informó a la prensa sobre la marcha de la investigación** = the superintendent briefed the press on the progress of the investigation (b) **en marcha** = in progress *o* in working order; **empresa en marcha** = going concern; **vender un negocio en marcha** *o* **vendida como empresa en marcha** = to sell a business as a going concern *o* sold as a going concern (c) *(manifestación)* **marcha de protesta** = protest march
◊ **marcharse** *vr (irse)* to leave *o* to depart

marcial *adj* martial; **ley marcial** = martial law; **el gobierno suprimió la ley marcial** = the government lifted martial law; **el presidente declaró la ley marcial en dos provincias** = the president imposed *o* declared martial law in two provinces

margen *nm* (a) *(comercial)* margin; **margen bruto** = gross margin; **margen de beneficio** = profit margin; **margen de cobertura** = backwardation; **margen de seguridad** = safety margin; **margen neto** = net margin (b) *(borde)* edge *o* border; **mantenerse al margen** = to keep out

marginado, -da *n* **marginado social** = social outcast

marido *nm* husband; **marido y mujer** = husband and wife

mariguana o **marihuana** o **marijuana** *nf* grass

marino, -na 1 *adj* marine; **compañía aseguradora de riesgos marinos** = marine underwriter 2 *nf* marine *o* navy; **la marina mercante** = the merchant marine; **Ministerio de Marina** = Admiralty 3 *nm* marine *o* naval officer

marital *adj* marital *o* matrimonial

marítimo, -ma *adj* marine *o* maritime; **asegurador marítimo** = marine underwriter; **comercio marítimo** = maritime trade; **derecho marítimo** = Admiralty law *o* maritime law *o* the law of the sea; **abogado especializado en derecho marítimo** = maritime lawyer; **línea marítima** = shipping company *o* shipping line; **seguro marítimo** = marine insurance; **tribunal marítimo** = Admiralty Court

más *adj y adv* more; **más de** = more than; **más o menos** = roughly; **cobrar más de lo debido** *o* **cobrar de más** = overcharge; **el coste del desarrollo del proyecto será de 25 millones más o menos** = the development cost of the project will be roughly 25 million; **el hotel nos cobró de más por las comidas** = the hotel overcharged us for meals; **pedimos un reembolso porque se nos había cobrado más de lo debido** = we asked for a refund because we had been overcharged; **devolver lo que se se ha cobrado de más** = to pay back an overcharge

matanza *nf* slaughter *o* mass killing

matar *vt* to kill *o* to hit; **intención de matar a alguien** = express malice; **fue acusado de matar a su novia con un cuchillo** = he was accused of killing his girl friend with a knife

materia *nf* (a) *(asunto)* matter (b) *(material)* = material; **materias primas** = raw materials

material 1 *adj* material; **daños materiales** = damage to property *o* property damage; **la tormenta causó importantes daños materiales** =

the storm caused considerable damage to personal property **2** *nm* **(a)** *(materia)* material *o (suministro)* supply; **material de exposición** = display material; **material de oficina** = office supplies; **materiales de construcción** = building materials; **tienda que vende material de oficina** = shop selling office stationery **(b)** *(sustancia)* matter *o* substance; **material peligroso** = dangerous substance

maternidad *nf* maternity; **permiso** *o* **licencia por maternidad** = maternity leave

matón *nm (gángster)* heavy *o* hoodlum

matricidio *nm* matricide

matrícula *nf* registration; **derechos de matrícula** = registration fee; **impreso de matrícula** = admissions form; **número de matrícula** = registration number

matrimonial *adj* matrimonial *o* marital; **capitulaciones matrimoniales** = marriage settlement; **domicilio matrimonial** = matrimonial home; **pleitos** *o* **juicios matrimoniales** = matrimonial causes; **privilegios matrimoniales (de no testimoniar en contra del cónyuge en ciertos procesos)** = marital privileges

matrimonio *nm* matrimony *o* marriage; **matrimonio civil** = civil marriage; **matrimonio de conveniencia** *o* **de interés** = sham marriage *o* marriage of convenience; **matrimonio de hecho** = common-law marriage; **matrimonio por poderes** = marriage by proxy; **matrimonio rato** *o* **no consumado** = unconsummated marriage; **por matrimonio** = by marriage; **pasó a ser ciudadana española por matrimonio** = she became a Spanish citizen by marriage

matriz *nf (sede de una empresa)* **casa matriz** = head office; **sociedad matriz** = parent company

máximo, -ma 1 *adj* maximum *o (récord)* record *o (completo)* full; **edad máxima** = age limit; **índice de criminalidad máximo** *o* **pérdidas máximas** *o* **beneficios máximos** = record crime figures *o* record losses *o* record profits; **tarifa máxima del impuesto** = maximum rate of tax; **tarifa máxima del impuesto sobre la renta** = maximum income tax rate; **fue sentenciado a la máxima pena de cárcel** = he was sentenced to the maximum sentence of imprisonment **2** *nm* maximum; **aumentar la producción al máximo** = to increase production to the maximum level; **hasta un máximo de 10.000 ptas** = up to a maximum of 10,000 ptas **3** *nf (norma)* maxim

mayor *adj* **(a)** *(más grande)* largest; **nuestra empresa es una de las mayores proveedoras de ordenadores del gobierno** = our company is one of the largest suppliers of computers to the government **(b) al por mayor** = wholesale; **venta al por mayor** = wholesale; **compra al por mayor y vende al por menor** = he buys wholesale and sells

retail **(c)** *(más edad)* senior; **mayor de edad** = adult *o* of age

◊ **mayoría** *nf* **(a)** *(cantidad)* majority *o* most; **mayoría de acciones** = majority shareholding; **mayoría de los accionistas** = majority of the shareholders; **mayoría de votos** = majority of votes; **mayoría escasa** = bare majority; **sin mayoría** = hung; **veredicto por mayoría (al menos diez miembros del jurado)** = majority verdict; **la junta aceptó la propuesta por una mayoría de tres sobre dos** = the board accepted the proposal by a majority of three to two **(b)** *(persona)* **mayoría de edad** = legal age *o* age of consent

mayorista *nmf (comerciante al por mayor)* wholesaler *o* wholesale dealer *o* buyer

mayoritario, -ria *adj* majority; **accionista mayoritario** = majority shareholder; **decisión mayoritaria** = majority decision; **interés mayoritario** = majority interest; **participación mayoritaria** = majority shareholding; **socio mayoritario** = senior partner; **voto mayoritario** = majority vote; **tener un interés mayoritario en una empresa** = to have a controlling interest in a company

mayúsculas *nfpl* capital letters *o* block capitals *o* block letters; **escriba su nombre y dirección en mayúsculas** = write your name and address in block letters; **escriba su nombre con mayúsculas en la parte superior del formulario** = write your name in block capitals at the top of the form

mazmorra *nf (calabozo)* dungeon

mecanismo *nm* *(aparato)* machinery; **mecanismo de control** = surveillance device

mechera *nf (que roba en las tiendas)* shoplifter

media *nf* average; **la media de los tres últimos meses** = the average for the last three months *o* the last three months' average

mediación *nf* mediation; **la disputa se resolvió a través de la mediación de los cargos sindicales** = the dispute was ended through the mediation of union officials; **los empresarios rehusaron una oferta de mediación del gobierno** = the employers refused an offer of government mediation

mediador, -ra mediator *o* intervener *o (agente)* intermediary; **mediador, -ra; mediador del gobierno en una disputa laboral** = official mediator; **mediador en conflictos laborales** = troubleshooter; **ser mediador en** = to mediate

medianero, -ra *n* **(a)** *(pared)* party wall **(b)** *(persona)* mediator

mediar *vi* to mediate *o* to intervene; **mediar en una disputa** *o* **conflicto** = to intervene in a dispute; **el gobierno se ofreció a mediar en el conflicto** = the government offered to mediate in the dispute

medicamento *nm (medicina)* medicine *o* drug

medicina *nf* medicine; **medicina forense** *o* **legal** = forensic medicine

medición *nf* measurement; **medición de la rentabilidad** = measurement of profitability

médico, -ca 1 *adj* medical; **certificado médico** = medical certificate; **inspección médica (de un lugar de trabajo)** = medical inspection; **reconocimiento médico** *o* **revision médica** = medical; **seguro médico** = medical insurance **2** *n* doctor; **médico forense** = forensic surgeon

medida *nf* (a) *(disposición)* measure; **medida cautelar** = precaution; **medida de ahorro** = economy measure; **medida de control** *o* **de seguridad** = safety measure; **medida de gracia** = pardon; **medida de prevención** = contingency plan; **medida de protección** = protective measure; **medida de seguridad** = safety precaution *o* safety measure; **medida preventiva** = preventive *o* precautionary measure; **como medida preventiva** *o* **de precaución** = as a precautionary measure; **medidas fiscales** = fiscal measures; **tomar medidas** = to take action; **tomar medidas de emergencia** = to take emergency measures; **tomar medidas preventivas** = to take measures to prevent something happening (b) *(medición)* measure *o* measurement; **medida de áridos** = dry measure; **medida de superficie** = square measure; **medida de volumen** = cubic measure; **inspector de pesas y medidas** = inspector of weights and measures; **anotar las medidas de un paquete** = to write down the measurements of a package; **tomar las medidas** = to measure

medio, -dia 1 *adj* (a) *(promedio)* average *o* middle; **por término medio** = on an average; **ser por término medio** = to average; **coste medio de gastos por empleado** = average cost of expenses per employee; **el aumento medio de precios** = the average increase in prices; **las cifras medias de los últimos tres meses** = the average figures for the last three months; **los aumentos de precios son por término medio de un 10% por año** = price increases have averaged 10% per annum (b) *(mitad)* half; **media pensión** = half board **2** *adv* **por medio del cual** *o* **por medio de la cual** = whereby; **por este medio** *o* **por la presente** = hereby; **una escritura por medio de la que se traspasa la posesión de la propiedad** = a deed whereby ownership of the property is transferred **3** *nmpl* (a) *(método)* means; **medios de transporte** = means of transport; **medios fraudulentos** = false pretences; **medios legales** = legal means; **le encarcelaron por obtener dinero con medios fraudulentos** = he was sent to prison for obtaining money under false pretences (b) *(recursos)* means; **medios económicos** *o* **medios de vida** = financial resources *o* economic means

mediodía *nm* **antes de las doce del mediodía** = a.m. *o* ante meridiem; **después de las 12 del mediodía** = p.m. *o* post meridiem

medir *vt/i* to measure; **medir el tamaño de un paquete** = to measure the size of a package; **un paquete que mide 10cm por 25cm** = a package which measures 10cm by 25cm *o* a package measuring 10cm by 25cm

mejor *adj* better *o* best; **mejor postor** = highest bidder; **el mejor del grupo** = the pick of the group; **la mejor prueba: documento original utilizado como prueba** = best evidence

mejora *nf* (a) *(recuperación)* recovery *o* *(propiedad)* improvement (b) *(en testamento)* **mejora hereditaria** = part of inheritance that lawful heirs may receive over and above their legitimate entitlement; **tercio de mejora** = third for betterment (above the legitimate entitlement of inheritance)
◊ **mejoramiento** *nm* improvement

mejorar *vt* (a) *(recuperar)* to recover *o* to improve *o* *(negocios)* to pick up; **el comercio está mejorando** = business *o* trade is picking up (b) *(en testamento)* to add to the legal share of an inheritance

membrete *nm* letterhead *o* letter heading *o* heading on notepaper; **papel con membrete** = headed paper

memorándum *nm* memorandum

memoria *nf* *(informe)* report; **memoria anual del consejo de administración** = directors' report

memorial *nm* *(escrito)* written statement (such as a proposal or a petition); **memorial de agravios** = list of grievances

mencionado, -da *adj* mentioned; **mencionado más abajo** = undermentioned; **ya mencionado** = aforementioned; **la compañía antes mencionada** = the aforementioned company

mención *nf* mention; **hacer mención** = to mention

mencionar *vt* to mention *o* to name *o* to refer; **el programa mencionado con anterioridad** = the schedule before referred to; **el jefe de policía fue mencionado en el caso de divorcio** = the Chief Constable was named in the divorce case; **el juez mencionó la necesidad de que el jurado examinara todos los documentos** = the judge mentioned the need for the jury to examine all the documents

menor *adj* (a) *(pequeño)* minor *o* *(más pequeño)* lesser *o* *(inferior)* puisne; **acusación menor** *o* **cargo menor** = holding charge; **delito menor** *o* **delitos menores** = summary offence *o* petty crime; **fondo** *o* **caja para gastos menores** = petty cash; **gastos menores** = minor expenditure; **hurto menor** =

petty theft; **se declaró culpable del cargo menor de homicidio involuntario** = he pleaded guilty to the lesser charge of manslaughter **(b) al por menor** = retail; **precio al por menor** = retail price; **venta al por menor** = retail **(c)** *(persona)* child *o* infant *o* junior *menor de edad* = minor *o* under age; **menor bajo custodia o tutela** *o* **niño internado en un centro de protección de menores** = child in care; **menor bajo la protección de un Tribunal** = ward of court; **menor tutelado** = ward; **tribunal de menores** = juvenile court; **el tribunal superior anuló la orden de retirada de la patria potestad dictada por el tribunal de menores** = the appeal court quashed the care order made by the juvenile court; **una persona no está obligada a pagar las deudas contraídas cuando era menor de edad** = a person is not liable for debts contracted during his minority

menos *adj y adv;* **menos de** = under; **gastar lo menos posible** = to keep expenses to a minimum; **a menos que** = unless

menoscabo *nm* **en menoscabo de**= to the detriment of

menospreciar *vt (despreciar)* to minimize; **no menosprecie los posibles riesgos** = do not minimize the risks involved

menosprecio nm *(falta de respeto)* derogation *o* contempt

mensual *adj* monthly; **pagó la deuda en plazos mensuales** = she paid off the debt in monthly instalments
◊ **mensualmente** *adv* monthly; **se le ordenó que pagara mensualmente un suma de dinero a su mujer** = he was ordered to pay a sum of money to his wife monthly

mensualidad *nf* monthly payment

mental *adj* mental; **equilibrio mental** = balance of mind; **estado mental alterado** = disturbed balance of mind; **trastorno mental** = mental disorder; **los criminales con trastornos mentales son internados en instituciones especializadas** = mentally ill criminals are committed to special establishments; **el veredicto del forense fue suicidio en situación de trastorno mental** = the verdict of the coroner's court was suicide while the balance of mind was disturbed
◊ **mentalmente** *adv* mentally; **persona mentalmente inestable** = of unsound mind

mente *nf* mind; **de mente sana** = of sound mind

mentira *nf* lie *o* falsehood; **mentira maliciosa** *o* **injuriosa** = injurious falsehood *o* malicious falsehood; **mentira piadosa** = white lie

mentir *vi* to lie *o* to deceive

mercadear *vt/i* to bargain

mercado *nm* **(a)** *(comercio)* market; **mercado abierto** *o* **mercado libre** = open market *o* free market; **mercado cerrado** *o* **controlado** *o* **cautivo** = closed market; **mercado en expansión** *o* **en crecimiento** = growth market; **mercado favorable al comprador** = buyer's market; **mercado favorable al vendedor** = seller's market; **mercado interior** *o* **nacional** = home *o* domestic market; **mercado limitado** *o* **con escaso movimiento** = limited market; **economía de libre mercado** = free market economy; **lanzar al mercado** = to market; **precio de mercado** = market price **(b)** *(en la clandestinidad)* **mercado negro** = black market; **comerciante del mercado negro** = black marketeer; **pagar precios de mercado negro** = to pay black market prices; **ventas en el mercado negro** = under-the-counter sales; **vivían bien de las mercancías del mercado negro** = they lived well on black-market goods; **compraron monedas de oro en el mercado negro** = they bought gold coins on the black market; **hay un lucrativo mercado negro de piezas de recambio de coches** = there is a lucrative black market in spare parts for cars **(c)** *(bolsa)* **mercado de capitales** = capital market; **mercado de divisas** *o* **mercado cambiario** = foreign exchange market; **mercados de futuros** = forward markets; **mercado de valores** = stock market; **mercado de valores sin cotización oficial** = over-the-counter market; **comprar acciones en el mercado libre** = to buy shares in the open market; **valor de mercado del capital emitido** = market capitalization **(d)** *(lonja)* market; **mercado público** = market overt *o* open market; **cuota por un puesto en el mercado** = market dues; **día de mercado** *o* **día en que hay mercado** = market day **(e)** *(unión europea)* **mercado único** = single market; **el Mercado Común** = the Common Market; **el Mercado Común Europeo** = the European Common Market

mercancía *nf* **(a)** *(género)* merchandise *o* goods *o* *(materias primas y alimentos)* commodity; **mercancías consignadas** *o* **en consignación** = goods on consignment; **tren de mercancías** = goods train; **retención de mercancías en la aduana** = goods (held) in bond **(b)** *(carga)* freight

mercantil *adj* commercial; **derecho mercantil** = commercial law *o* mercantile law *o* law merchant; **tribunal mercantil** = Commercial Court

merced *nf* **estar a la merced de** = to be at the mercy of; **vuestra merced** = your honour

merecer *vt* to deserve; **lo que se merece (regla según la cual una de las partes tiene derecho al cobro por trabajo realizado, cuando existe incumplimiento de contrato)** = quantum meruit

mérito *nm* merit; **mérito procesal** *o* **méritos de la causa** = merits of the case; **aumento salarial por méritos** = merit increase; **prima** *o* **bonificación**

por **méritos** = merit award *o* merit bonus; **valoración de méritos** = merit rating

merodear *vi* to loiter *o* to prowl; **merodear con fines delictivos** *o* **con intenciones criminales** = loitering with intent

mes *nm* month; **mes civil** = calendar month; **cada dos meses** = bi-monthly; **acordamos pagar el alquiler cada tres meses** = we agreed to pay the rent quarterly *o* on a quarterly basis

mesa *nf* table; **mesa electoral** = polling station; **mesa redonda** = round table conference

metálico *nm (dinero)* cash; **dinero en metálico** = hard cash; **pagó 10.000 ptas en metálico por la silla** = he paid out 10,000 ptas in hard cash for the chair

metropolitano, -na *adj* metropolitan; **la policía metropolitana de Londres** = the Metropolitan Police *o* the Met

microficha *nf* microfiche; **guardamos nuestros informes en microficha** = we hold our records on microfiche

microfilm *nm* microfilm; **guardamos nuestros informes en microfilm** = we hold our records on microfilm

microfilmar *vt* to microfilm; **mande esta correspondencia a que sea microfilmada** = send this correspondence to be microfilmed *o* for microfilming

micrófono *nm* microphone; **micrófono oculto** = bug *o* bugging device; **ocultar un micrófono en** = to bug; **el personal de limpieza colocó un micrófono oculto bajo la mesa del abogado** = the cleaners planted a bug under the lawyer's desk; **los agentes colocaron un micrófono oculto en el despacho del Presidente** = the agents bugged the President's office; **la policía encontró un micrófono oculto bajo la mesa del abogado** = police found a bugging device under the lawyer's desk

miedo *nm* fear; *(alegato)* **miedo insuperable** = unconquerable fear

> El miedo insuperable es una circunstancia eximente de la responsabilidad penal

miembro *nm* member *o (socios)* membership; **miembro honorario** = honorary member; **miembro ordinario** = ordinary member; **miembros de la profesión** = profession; **nuevo miembro** = recruit; **los miembros de las Naciones Unidas** = the members of the United Nations; **los países miembros** *o* **los estados miembros de la UE** = the member countries *o* the member states of the EU; **los nuevos miembros tienen que realizar un curso especial de entrenamiento** *o* **formación** = new recruits have to take a special training course

mientras *adv* **mientras el juicio continúa** = pending suit

militar *adj* military; **tribunal militar** = court-martial; **fue declarado culpable por el tribunal militar y sentenciado a prisión** = he was found guilty by the court-martial and sentenced to imprisonment

minimizar *vt* to minimize; **siempre minimiza la dificultad del proyecto** = he always minimizes the difficulty of the project

mínimo, -ma *adj* minimum *o* minimal *o (indispensable)* basic; **mínimo de actividad económica** = trough; **condena mínima** = minimum sentence; **dividendo mínimo** = minimum dividend; **pago mínimo** = minimum payment; **precio mínimo** = knockdown price; **precio mínimo aceptable** = reserve (price); **requisitos mínimos necesarios** *o* **periodo mínimo de tiempo cotizable para poder ser beneficiario de una prestación o ayuda** = period of qualification; **salario mínimo** = minimum wage; **arrendar una propiedad por un alquiler mínimo** = to lease a property for *o* at a peppercorn rent; **gastar lo mínimo** = to keep expenses to a minimum; **reducir al mínimo** = to minimize; **reducir el riesgo de pérdidas al mínimo** = to reduce the risk of a loss to a minimum; **el cuadro fue retirado al no alcanzar el precio mínimo** = the painting was withdrawn when it did not reach its reserve; **la cantidad de defectos del nuevo surtido de mercancías era mínima** = there was a minimal quantity of imperfections in the new stock; **la oficina central ejerce un control mínimo sobre las sucursales** = the head office exercises minimal control over the branch offices; **para trabajar en la caja, se necesitan unos conocimientos mínimos de matemáticas** = to work at the cash desk, you need a basic qualification in maths

ministerial *adj* ministerial; **tribunal ministerial** = ministerial tribunal

ministerio *nm* ministry *o* office; **Ministerio de Asuntos Exteriores** = Foreign Office; **Ministerio de Educación y Ciencia** = Department of Education and Science; **Ministerio de Industria y Comercio** = Department of Trade and Industry; **Ministerio del Interior** = Home Office *o* Ministry of the Interior *o* Interior Ministry; **Ministerio de Marina** = Admiralty; **ministerio estadounidense de Asuntos Exteriores** = State Department; **ministerio fiscal** = prosecution; **está al cargo del ministerio de Información** = he is in charge of the Ministry of Information *o* of the Information Ministry; **trabaja en el ministerio de Hacienda** = he works in the Ministry of Finance *o* the Finance Ministry; **un funcionario del ministerio** = a ministry official *o* an official from the ministry

El ministerio fiscal ejerce sus funciones por medio de órganos propios y no forma parte del Poder Judicial. Su función consiste en promover la acción de la justicia en defensa de la legalidad y del interés público (CE art° 124)

ministro, tra *n* minister; **ministro, -tra con cartera** Secretary of State; **ministro, -tra del gobierno** = a government minister *o* secretary; **Ministro, -tra de Asuntos Exteriores** = Foreign Secretary *o* Minister of Foreign Affairs *o* Foreign Minister *o* US Secretary of State; **Ministro, -tra de Educación** = Education Secretary; **Ministro, -tra de Hacienda** = Chancellor of the Exchequer *o* Secretary of the Treasury; **Ministro, tra de Información** = Minister of Information *o* the Information Minister; **Ministro, -tra del Interior** = Home Secretary; **Ministro, -tra de Justicia** = Minister of Justice *o* the Justice Minister *o* US Attorney-General; **ministro, -tra sin cartera** = minister without portofolio; **consejo de ministros** = cabinet

minoración *nf (atenuante) nm* mitigation; **minoración de la indemnización por daños** *o* **minoración de la indemnización de perjuicios** = mitigation of damages

minoría *nf* minority; **minoría de edad** = minority; **en la minoría** = in the minority; **los pequeños partidos son una minoría en el concejo municipal** = the small parties are in the minority on the local council; **una minoría de miembros de la junta se opuso al presidente** = a minority of board members opposed the chairman

minorista *nmf* retailer

minoritario, -ria *adj* minority; **accionista minoritario** = minority shareholder; **interés minoritario** *o* **participación minoritaria en las acciones** = minority shareholding *o* minority interest

minusvalía *nf* capital loss

minuta *nf* (a) *(nota escrita)* memo *o* draft (b) *(honorarios)* fee; *(de un abogado)* solicitors' charges (c) *(anticipo sobre los honorarios)* retainer

minuto *nm* minute; **el fiscal interrogó a los testigos durante cincuenta minutos** = counsel for the prosecution cross-examined the witness for fifty minutes

miramiento *nm* consideration; **sin miramientos** = without consideration *o* out of hand

mirar *vt* to look at *o* to watch *o (ver)* to view

misceláneo, -nea **1** *adj* miscellaneous **2** *nf* *(artículos diversos)* sundry items *o* sundries

misión *nf* mission *o* assignment *o (cometido)* commission; **hemos puesto a tres policías en esa**
misión especial = we have put six constables on that particular assignment

mismo, -ma *adj* same; **asi mismo** *o* **del mismo modo** *o* **lo mismo** = likewise; **de lo mismo** = hereof; **uno mismo** = personally; **él mismo abrió el sobre** = he personally opened the envelope

mitad *nf* half *o* moiety; **los domingos cobra la mitad más** = he is paid time and a half on Sundays

mitigación *nf* mitigation; **mitigación de daños** = mitigation of damages

mitigador, -ra *n* abator

mitigar *vt* to mitigate

mixto, -ta *adj* mixed *o* joint; **comisión mixta de investigación** = joint commission of inquiry *o* joint committee; **póliza mixta** = endowment assurance *o* endowment policy

mobiliario, -ria *adj* *(bienes muebles)* **propiedad mobiliaria** = personalty *o* personal estate *o* personal property

moción *nf* motion; **moción de censura** = vote of no confidence; **moción de clausura** = closure motion; **moción de clausura de un debate (para acabar con un filibustero), que requiere dieciséis senadores para presentarla y dos tercios para aprobarla; moción exploratoria** = US early day motion cloture; **autor, -ra de una moción** = mover; **apoyar una moción** = to speak for a motion; **criticar** *o* **hablar en contra de una moción** = to speak against a motion; **presentar una moción** = to table a motion; **proponer una moción** = to propose *o* to move a motion; **la junta votó la moción** = the meeting voted on the motion; **la moción fue aprobada** *o* **rechazada por 220 votos contra 196** = the motion was carried *o* was defeated by 220 votes to 196; **el presidente dimitió después de que se aprobara la moción de desconfianza en la Junta General Anual** = the chairman resigned after the motion of no confidence was passed at the AGM

moda *nf* fashion; **de moda** = popular; **la costa del Sur es la zona de moda para las vacaciones** = the South Coast is the most popular area for holidays

modelo *nm* (a) *(muestra)* specimen *o* example (b) *(patrón)* standard *o* pattern

moderación *nf* **moderación salarial** = pay restraint *o* wage restraint

moderado, -da *adj* moderate *o* reasonable; **el restaurante ofrece buena comida a precios moderados** = the restaurant offers good food at reasonable prices

módico, -ca *adj* reasonable; **el restaurante ofrece buena comida a precios módicos** = the restaurant offers good food at reasonable prices

modificable *adj* modifiable; **acuerdo modificable** = open-ended agreement

modificación *nf* modification *o* revision; **el presidente del Tribunal Supremo ha propuesto una modificación de los procedimientos de divorcio** = the President of the Supreme Court has proposed a revision of the divorce procedures

modificación *nf* adjustment *o* alteration; **realizar *o* llevar a cabo modificaciones del plan** = to make *o* to carry out modifications to the plan; **se ha publicado la modificación de los procedimientos de instrucción** = the revised examination procedures have been published

modificado, -da *adj* modified; **éste es el nuevo acuerdo modificado** = this is the new modified agreement

modificar *vt* to alter *o* to modify *o* to revise *o* to adjust *o* to make alterations; **modificar los términos de un contrato** = to alter the terms of a contract; **pedimos que se modificara el contrato** = we asked for modifications to the contract; **el coche tendrá que ser modificado para pasar las pruebas oficiales** = the car will have to be modified to pass the government tests; **el juez modificó su anterior decisión de no tener en cuenta una alegación del abogado defensor** = the judge revised his earlier decision not to consider a submission from defence counsel; **el presidente modificó el sistema de elaboración de informes** = the chairman modified the reporting system; **ha modificado su testamento seis veces en los últimos diez años** = he has altered his will six times in the last ten years; **modificamos en parte los términos de un contrato** we made some alterations to the terms of a contract

modo *nm* way; **modo de actuar de un criminal por el que se le puede identificar** = modus operandi

mojado, -da *adj* damp *o* wet; **papel mojado** = dead letter

mojón *nm* landmark

molestar **1** *vt (causar molestias)* to inconvenience *o* to annoy; **juicio entablado para molestar al demandado** = vexatious action *o* litigation **2** *vi (estorbar)* to intrude *o* to get in the way
◊ **molestarse** *vr* to get annoyed

molestia *nf* inconvenience; **molestia pública** = public nuisance; **causar molestias** = to inconvenience

molesto, -ta *adj* vexatious; **sentirse molesto** = to feel uncomfortable *o* embarrassed; **estar molesto con alguien** = to be annoyed with someone

momento *nm* moment *o* occasion; **momento procesal** = stage of a trial; **hasta el momento** = hereto; **por el momento** = pro tem *o* pro tempore

moneda *nf* **(a)** *(dinero)* coin *o* money; **moneda falsa** = counterfeit money; **moneda fiduciaria *o* de curso forzoso** = fiat money; **necesito monedas para el teléfono** = I need some coins for the telephone; **me devolvió dos monedas de 10 ptas** he gave me two 10 ptas coins in my change **(b)** *(divisa)* currency; **moneda bloqueada** = blocked currency; **moneda convertible *o* moneda fuerte** = hard currency; **moneda de curso legal** = legal tender *o* legal currency; **moneda de libre circulación *o* exenta de restricciones** = free currency; **moneda débil *o* no convertible** = soft currency; **moneda extranjera** = foreign currency *o* foreign exchange

monetario, -ria *adj* monetary; **Fondo Monetario Internacional (FMI)** = International Monetary Fund (IMF); **mercados monetarios** = money markets; **oferta monetaria** = money supply; **Sistema Monetario Europeo (SME)** = European Monetary System (EMS); **unidad monetaria** = monetary unit

monitor *nm* monitor *o* instructor

monogamia *nf* monogamy

monopolio *nm* monopoly; **monopolio de demanda** = monopsony; **monopolio público *o* estatal** = public monopoly *o* state monopoly; **tener el monopolio de las ventas de alcohol *o* el monopolio del alcohol** = to have the monopoly of alcohol sales *o* to have the alcohol monopoly; **la empresa tiene el monopolio absoluto de las importaciones de vino francés** = the company has the absolute monopoly of imports of French wine

monopolización *nf* monopolization

monopolizar *vt* to monopolize

monopsonio *nm* monopsony

montado, -da *adj* mounted; **policía montada** = mounted police; **se mandó llamar a la policía montada para controlar a la multitud** = mounted police were brought in to control the crowd

montar *vt* **(a)** *(establecer)* to set up; **montar una casa** = to set up house; **montar un negocio de coches robados** = to set up a stolen car business **(b)** *(construir)* to assemble; **montó el motor con piezas robadas** = he assembled the engine with stolen parts

monte *nm (casa de empeños)* **monte de piedad** = pawnshop; **papeleta del monte de piedad** = pawn ticket

mora *nf* delay; **en mora** = in arrears

morada *nf* abode; **allanamiento de morada** = forcible *o* unlawful entry; **robo con allanamiento de morada** = burglary; **robo con armas y allanamiento de morada** = aggravated burglary

moral *adj* moral *o* *(moralidad)* morals; **el alto nivel moral que debería ser fijado por los jueces**

= the high moral standard which should be set by judges

moratoria *nf* moratorium *o* deferment; **los bancos pidieron una moratoria en los pagos** = the banks called for a moratorium on payments

La moratoria consiste en el plazo que se concede para solventar una deuda vencida

morir *vi* to die *o* to decease; **morir antes que** = to predecease; **morir en el acto** = to die instantly; **murió antes que su padre** = he predeceased his father; **heredó la fortuna de una tía que murió** = she inherited the estate of a deceased aunt; **su herencia es donada a su hija, pero en el caso de que ésta muera antes, se dejará en depósito para los hijos de la misma** = his estate is left to his daughter, but should she predecease him, it will be held in trust for her children

moroso, -sa *adj y n* in arrears *o* in default *o* *(persona)* defaulter *o* slow payer; **cobro de morosos** = debt collection *o* debt collecting; **agencia de cobro de morosos** = debt collection agency *o* collecting agency; **agente cobrador de morosos** = debt collector; **la compañía es morosa** = the company is in default

mortal *adj* fatal; **durante la primera semana del año hubo seis accidentes mortales** = there were six fatal accidents in the first week of the year; **tomó una dosis mortal de drogas** = he took a fatal dose of drugs

mortalidad *nf* mortality; **tabla de mortalidad** = mortality tables; **tasa de mortalidad** = mortality rate

mortandad *nf* slaughter *o* carnage

mostrador *nm* counter

mostrar *vt* to show *o* to produce *o* *(indicar)* to indicate; **mostrar un beneficio** *o* **una pérdida** = to show a profit *o* a loss; **la policía mostró una serie de armas incautadas durante los disturbios** = the police produced a number of weapons seized during the riot; **las últimas cifras muestran un descenso del índice de criminalidad** = the latest figures indicate a fall in the crime rate
◊ **mostrarse** *vr* **(a)** *(adoptar cierta actitud)* to represent *o* to appear; **se le mostró como hombre de gran honor** = he was represented as a man of great honour **(b) mostrarse parte** = to enter a caveat

mostrenco *adj* in abeyance

motín *nm* **(a)** *(disturbio)* riot **(b)** *(rebelión)* mutiny

motivado,-da *adj* motivated

motivo *nm* **(a)** *(causa)* cause *o* motive *o* ground; **motivo de apelación** = ground of appeal; **motivos de divorcio** = grounds for divorce; **motivo**

fundado *o* **con motivo** = reasonable grounds *o* with a motive; **motivo suficiente** = good cause; **sin motivo** = without motive *o* unfounded; **¿tiene motivos fundados para quejarse?** = does he have good grounds for complaint? **(b)** *(razón)* reason *o* subject; **por motivo de salud** = for health reasons; **el motivo de la acción era la responsabilidad del acusado frente a los daños del demandante** = the subject of the action was the liability of the defendant for the plaintiff's injuries; **el juez le preguntó el motivo de su nuevo retraso** = the judge asked him for the reason why he was late again

mover *vt* to move *o* *(provocar)* to provoke; **mover pleito a una persona** = to take someone to court *o* to take proceedings against someone

movible *adj* movable *o* moveable

móvil *nm* **(a)** *(motivo)* motive **(b)** *(movible)* movable *o* moveable

movimiento *nm* movement *o* motion; **movimientos cíclicos del comercio** = cyclical movements of trade; **movimientos de capital** = movements of capital; **movimientos en los mercados monetarios** = movements in the money markets; **cuenta sin movimiento** = dormant account

mucho, -cha 1 *adj y pron* a lot *o* a great deal *o* a good deal *o* a good many; **pedir mucho** = to drive *o* to strike a hard bargain; **el abogado perdió mucho tiempo interrogando al padre del fallecido** = counsel wasted a great deal *o* a good deal of time cross-examining the dead man's father; **ganó mucho dinero en la Bolsa** = he made a great deal *o* a good deal of money on the Stock Exchange; **hay mucha gente desempleada** *o* **en el paro** *o* **sin trabajo** = a lot of people *o* lots of people are out of work; **la compañía tuvo que pagar mucho dinero por el edificio** = the company had to pay a good deal of money for the building; **habrá que trabajar mucho para que la compañía sea verdaderamente rentable** there is a great deal of work to be done before the company can be made really profitable 2 *adv;* **con mucho** = easily; **él es, con mucho, el criminal internacional más importante que se ha detenido este año** = he is easily the most important international criminal to have been arrested this year; **éste es, con mucho, el mayor alijo de drogas que hemos aprehendido** = this is easily the largest consignment of drugs we have seized

mudanza *nf* removal; **compañía de mudanzas** = removal company

mueble 1 *adj* movable; **bienes muebles** = movables *o* movable property *o* chattels (personal) *o* *(propiedad mobiliaria que se puede transmitir por herencia)* personal estate *o* personal property *o* personal assets *o* personalty; **bienes muebles e**

inmuebles real property; **enseres y bienes muebles** = goods and chattels; **hipoteca sobre bienes muebles** = chattel mortgage **2** *nm* furniture; **muebles y enseres** = furniture and fixtures

muelle *nm* dock

muerte *nf* death *o* demise; **muerte accidental** = accidental death *o* death by misadventure; **muerte a mano armada** *o* **muerte violenta** = violent death; **muerte natural** = natural death; **muerte repentina** = sudden death; **donación por muerte** = donatio mortis causa; **pena de muerte** = death penalty *o* capital punishment; **presunción de muerte** = presumption of death; **estar en peligro de muerte** = to be in danger; **el tribunal pronunció un veredicto de muerte accidental** = the court returned a verdict of death by misadventure; **a su muerte, la fortuna pasó a su hija** = on his demise the estate passed to his daughter; **a su muerte, todas sus propiedades pasarán a su viuda** = on his decease all his property will go to his widow; **heredamos la casa a la muerte de mi abuelo** = we inherited the house from my dead grandfather

muerto, -ta 1 *adj* dead; **punto muerto** = deadlock; **estar en punto muerto** = to deadlock; **seis personas resultaron muertas como consecuencia del accidente** = six people were dead as a result of the accident **2** *n* dead *o* deceased *o* victim; **hubo seis muertos en el accidente** = six people were killed in the accident; **cargar con el muerto** = to take the blame; **dar por muerto** = to give up for dead; **echarle a alguien el muerto** = to make someone carry the can

muestra *nf* **(a)** *(prueba)* sample *o* *(simbólica)* token; **muestra aleatoria** = random sample; **muestra de inspección** *o* **comprobación** = check sample; **muestra gratuita** = free sample; **muestras disponibles a petición del interesado** 'samples available on request'; **analizar una muestra** *o* **tomar una muestra para examen** = to sample; **libro de muestras** = pattern book **(b)** *(espécimen)* specimen; **muestra de sangre** = blood specimen; **muestra de orina** = urine specimen **(c)** *(indicación)* indication; **no dio muestras de estar mintiendo** = he gave no indication that he was lying; **muestras disponibles a petición del interesado** 'samples available on request'

muestreo *nm* sample *o* *(sondeo de opinión)* canvassing

mujer *nf* woman *o* *(esposa)* wife; **mujer casada** = married woman; **mujer soltera** = unmarried woman

multa *nf* fine *o* penalty; **tuvimos que pagar una multa por aparcamiento indebido** = we had to

pay a parking fine; **el tribunal le condenó a pagar 250.000 ptas de multa** = the court sentenced him to pay a 250,000 ptas fine; **la condena por conducir con imprudencia temeraria consiste en una multa de 200.000 ptas o dos meses de arresto** = the sentence for dangerous driving is a 200,000 ptas fine or two months in prison

multar *vt* to fine; **multar a alguien por estafar dinero** = to fine someone for obtaining money by false pretences

multicopista *nf* duplicator *o* duplicating machine; **cliché para multicopista** = duplicating paper

múltiple *adj* multiple; **visado de entradas múltiples** = multiple entry visa; **tiene múltiples contactos en el mundo del hampa** = she has extensive contacts in the underworld

multipropiedad *nf* time share

municipal *adj* municipal *o* local; **concejo municipal** *o* **consejo municipal** = borough council *o* town council; **estatuto** *o* **reglamento** *o* **ordenanza municipal** = bylaw *o* byelaw *o* by-law *o* bye-law; **gobierno municipal** = local authority; **impuestos municipales** = municipal taxes; **magistrado municipal** = recorder; **oficinas municipales** = municipal offices; **una decisión del gobierno municipal conforme a los poderes y deberes impuestos sobre él por decreto** = a decision of the local authority pursuant to the powers and duties imposed on it by the Act
◊ **municipalidad** *nf* municipality

municipio *nm* borough *o* municipality

murmurar *vt* to gossip

musulmán, -ana *adj y n* Muslim

mutilado, -da 1 *adj* crippled *o* disabled **2** crippled *o* disabled person

mutilación *nf* mutilation; **mutilación criminal de una de las extremidades del cuerpo** = mayhem

mutilar *vt* to mutilate *o* to cripple *o* to disable

mutuo, -tua 1 *adj* mutual *o* joint *o* reciprocal; **mutua decisión** = joint decission; **fondos mutuos** = mutual fund; **divorcio de mutuo acuerdo** = undefended divorce case; **separación de mutuo acuerdo** = separation by mutual consent; **sociedad de ayuda mutua (en caso de enfermedad o de dificultades financieras)** = friendly society; **testamentos mutuos** mutual wills **2** *nf* **mutua de seguros** = mutual (insurance) company
◊ **mutualidad** *nf* mutuality *o* friendly society *o* *(fondos de inversión)* mutual fund
◊ **mutualista** *nmf*; **mutualistas de inversión** = mutual fund

Nn

nacer *vi* to be born *o* to come into existence; **la costumbre nació durante el siglo XVIII** = the custom came into existence during the eighteenth century

nacimiento *nm* birth; **encubrimiento de nacimiento** = concealment of birth; **fecha y lugar de nacimiento** = date and place of birth; **partida de nacimiento** = birth certificate; **es británico de nacimiento** = he is British by birth

nación *nf* nation; **nación deudora** = debtor nation; **Naciones Unidas (NN.UU)**= United Nacions (UN)
◊ **nacional (a)** *(de la nación)* national; **fiesta nacional** = public holiday; **Himno Nacional** = National Anthem; **producto nacional bruto (PNB)** = gross national product (GNP) **(b)** *(interior)* domestic *o* home *o* inland; **mercado nacional** = domestic market; **producción nacional** = domestic production; **productos nacionales** = home-produced products
◊ **nacionalidad** *nf* nationality *o* citizenship; **es de nacionalidad española** = he is of Spanish nationality; **tiene doble nacionalidad** = he has dual nationality
◊ **nacionalismo** *nm* nationalism
◊ **nacionalista** *nmf* nationalist
◊ **nacionalización** *nf* nationalization
◊ **nacionalizado, -da** *adj* nationalized *o* *(naturalizado)* naturalized; **industria nacionalizada** = nationalized industry; **es un ciudadano americano nacionalizado** = he is a naturalized American citizen
◊ **nacionalizar** *vt* to nationalize

nada 1 *adj y pron* anything *o* nothing; **de nada** = don't mention it; **no sirve para nada** = it's useless; **no ha dicho nada** = he hasn't said anything *o* he has said nothing **2** *adv* at all *o* as soon as; **no es nada fácil** = it isn't at all easy; **nada más llegar al país, fue arrestada por la policía del aeropuerto** = as soon as she arrived in the country, she was immediately arrested by the airport police **3** *nf* **salieron de la nada** = they came out of nowhere

nadie *adj y pron* anybody *o* nobody; **no había nadie** = there was nobody *o* there wasn't anybody; **sin nadie más** = in isolation

Napoleón *nm* **código de Napoleón** - Code Napoleon

narcótico *nm* drug
◊ **narcotraficante** *nmf* drug dealer *o* peddlar

narcotráfico *nm* drug trafficking

nato *adj* **(a)** *(de hecho)* born; **un criminal nato** = a born criminal **(b)** *(por derecho)* ex officio; **el juez es miembro nato de la comisión** = the judge is ex officio a member of the committee

natural 1 *adj* natural; **derecho natural** = natural justice *o* natural right; **desgaste natural** = fair wear and tear; **fibra natural** = natural fibre; **hijo, -ja natural** = natural child; **justicia natural** = natural justice; **padres naturales** = natural parents; **recursos naturales** = natural resources; **la póliza de seguros cubre la mayoría de los daños a excepción del desgaste natural de la máquina** = the insurance policy covers most damage, but not fair wear and tear to the machine **2** *nmf* native *o* inhabitant
◊ **naturaleza** *nf* nature *o* *(ciudadanía)* naturalization; **debe rellenar la carta de naturaleza** = you must fill in the naturalization papers
◊ **naturalización** *nf* *(concesión de la ciudadanía)* naturalization
◊ **naturalizado, -da** *adj* *(nacionalizado)* naturalized
◊ **naturalmente** *adv* **(a)** *(de manera natural)* naturally **(b)** *(por supuesto)* of course

> La naturalización es un acto del poder público por el cual se concede a una persona extranjera la cualidad de ciudadano o nacional en el estado que el poder representa

naufragado, -da *adj* wrecked; **están tratando de salvar el barco naufragado** = they are trying to salvage the wrecked ship

naufragar *vt* to wreck

naufragio *nm* wreck *o* shipwreck; **restos de un naufragio** *o* **de una colisión** = wreck; **salvaron la carga del naufragio** = they saved the cargo from the wreck

naval *adj* naval; **hipoteca naval** = bottomry

Navidad *nf* Christmas; **Día de Navidad** = Christmas Day

naviero, -ra 1 *adj* shipping; **compañía naviera** = shipping company **2** *nm* ship owner

necesario, -ria *adj* necessary; **acciones necesarias para ser director de una empresa** *o* **para obtener determinados derechos** = qualifying shares; **requisitos mínimos necesarios para poder ser beneficiario de una prestación o ayuda** = period of qualification; **debe reunir la documentación necesaria antes de solicitar una ayuda** = you must have all the necessary documentation before you apply for a subsidy; **fueron necesarios seis policías para atrapar al ladrón** = it took six policemen to hold the burglar
◊ **necesariamente** *adv* necessarily; **la imposición de una multa no es necesariamente el único camino abierto al tribunal** = the imposition of a fine is not necessarily the only course open to the court

necesidad *nf* necessity *o* need *o* *(requisito)* requirement; **necesidad de endeudamiento del sector público** = public sector borrowing requirement; **atender a las necesidades de** = to make provision for; **atender a las necesidades económicas de alguien** = to make financial provision for someone; **de primera necesidad** = basic; **los bienes de primera necesidad** = the necessities of life; **productos de primera necesidad** = basic commodities; **por necesidad** = of necessity

necesitar *vt* to need *o* *(requerir)* to require

necropsia o **necroscopia** *nf* autopsy *o* post-mortem

negación *nf* **(a)** *(negativa)* denial; **la concesión de cualquier préstamo no será negada irracionalmente** = approval of any loan will not be unreasonably withheld **(b)** *(denegación de hechos)* traverse

negatoria *nf* negative easement

negar *vt* **(a)** *(rechazar)* to deny *o* to refuse; **negar los hechos** = to deny the facts; **negar una acusación** = to deny *o* to refute an accusation; **negó haber estado en la casa a la hora del asesinato** = he denied being in the house at the time of the murder
◊ **negarse** *vr* **(a)** *(rechazar)* to decline *o* to refuse; **negarse a admitir** = to disclaim; **negarse a cumplir** = to repudiate; **negarse a cumplir un acuerdo o un contrato** = to repudiate an agreement *o* a contract; **negarse a dar información** = to withhold; **negarse a hacer horas extraordinarias** = to work to rule; **negarse a pagar** = to dishonour; **el acusado se negó a prestar juramento** = the accused refused to take the oath; **el testigo se negó a prestar juramento** = the witness declined to take the oath; **el banco se negó a prestar más dinero a**

la empresa = the bank refused to lend the company any more money; **el banco se negó a pagar su cheque** = the bank dishonoured his cheque; **el cliente se negó a aceptar los artículos** = the customer refused the goods *o* refused to accept the goods; **el tribunal se negó a permitir que el testigo hiciera uso de la palabra** = the court refused to allow the witness to speak; **le acusaron de negarse a dar información a la policía** *o* **de negarse a colaborar con la policía** = he was charged with withholding information from the police; **se negó a admitir cualquier conocimiento sobre la bomba** = he disclaimed all knowledge of the bomb

negativo, -va 1 *adj* negative; **prescripción negativa** = laches; **la respuesta fue negativa** = the answer was in the negative; **la prueba del alcoholímetro dio negativa** = the breathalyser test was negative **2** *nf* denial *o* refusal; **negativa global** *o* **negativa general** = blanket refusal; **negativa a aceptar una responsabilidad** *o* **un derecho** = disclaimer; **a pesar de sus negativas le declararon culpable** = in spite of his denials he was found guilty

negligencia *nf* neglect *o* negligence *o* dereliction of duty *o* *(incuria)* malpractice *o* *(mala conducta)* misconduct; **negligencia concurrente** = contributory negligence; **negligencia deliberada** = wilful neglect; **negligencia delictiva** *o* **culpable** *o* **inexcusable**= culpable negligence; **negligencia malintencionada** = wilful misconduct; **negligencia profesional** = professional misconduct; **responsabilidad por negligencia profesional** = tortious liability; **le declararon culpable de gran negligencia** = he was found guilty of gross dereliction of duty
◊ **negligente** *adj* negligent; **el demandado incurrió en conducta negligente al llevar a cabo sus obligaciones como fideicomisario** = the defendant was negligent in carrying out his duties as a trustee
◊ **negligentemente** *adv* negligently; **el tutor actuó negligentemente hacia su pupilo** = the guardian acted negligently towards his ward

negociabilidad *nf* negotiability

negociable *adj* negotiable *o* bankable; **cheque negociable** = negotiable cheque; **documento negociable** = negotiable instrument; **instrumento negociable** = negotiable instrument; **no negociable** = not negotiable; **documento no negociable** = non-negotiable instrument

negociación *nf* negotiation *o* bargaining; **negociación entre la defensa y la acusación con respecto a los cargos** = plea bargaining; **contrato en negociación** = contract under negotiation; **entablar negociaciones** = to enter into negotiations *o* to start negotiations; **interrumpir las negociaciones** = to break off negotiations;

mantener *o* **llevar a cabo negociaciones** = to conduct negotiations; **poder de negociación** = bargaining power; **reanudar las negociaciones** = to resume negotiations

negociado nm *(agencia)* office *o* department; **negociado de asuntos generales** = service department

negociador, -ra 1 *adj* negotiating; **comité negociador** *o* **comisión negociadora** = negotiating committee; **poder negociador** = bargaining power; **posición negociadora** = bargaining position **2** *n* negotiator; **es un negociador experimentado** = he is an experienced negotiator

negociante *nmf* trader

negociar 1 *vt* to negotiate; **negociar un acuerdo** = to arrange a deal *o* to set up a deal *o* to do a deal; **negociar los términos y las condiciones de un contrato** *o* **negociar un contrato** = to negotiate terms and conditions *o* to negotiate a contract **2** *vi* **(a)** *(tratar)* to negotiate *o* to deal *o* to bargain; **negociar con alguien** = to negotiate with someone; **negociar en la Bolsa** = to trade on the Stock Exchange; **una cuestión para ser negociada** = a matter for negotiation; **la patronal se negó a negociar con el sindicato** = the management refused to negotiate with the union **(b)** *(comerciar)* to trade

negocio nm **(a)** *(actividad comercial)* business *o* *(empresa)* enterprise *o* concern; **negocio ilícito** *o* **deshonesto** = racketeering; **negocio sucio que utiliza la estafa** *o* **la extorsión** = racket; **llevar a cabo un negocio** *o* **hacer negocios** = to transact business; **meterse en negocios** *o* **abrir** *o* **emprender un negocio** = to go into business; **(por asuntos) de negocios** = on business; **empezó el negocio vendiendo coches** = he went into business selling cars; **emprendió un negocio a medias con su hijo** = she went into business in partnership with her son; **es dueño de un pequeño negocio de reparación de coches** = he owns a small car repair business; **lleva un negocio desde su casa** = she runs a business from her home; **su negocio marcha bien** = his business is a going concern; **sus negocios eran tan difíciles de entender que los abogados tuvieron que pedir consejo a contables** = his affairs were so difficult to understand that the lawyers had to ask accountants for advice **(b)** *(transacción)* deal *o* bargain; **negocio duro** *o* **difícil** = hard bargain; **negocio sucio** *o* **negocio turbio** = shady deal; **un buen negocio** = a bargain; **hacer negocios con alguien** = to have dealings with someone **(c)** *(asunto)* affair

negro,-gra *adj* black; **dinero negro** = undeclared earnings; **lista negra** = black list; **poner en la lista negra** = to blacklist; **mercado negro** = black market; **comerciante del mercado negro** = black marketeer; **pagar precios de mercado negro**

= to pay black market prices; **ventas en el mercado negro** = under-the-counter sales; **hay un lucrativo mercado negro de piezas de recambio para coches** = there is a lucrative black market in spare parts for cars; **se pueden comprar monedas de oro en el mercado negro** = you can buy gold coins on the black market; **un mercado negro en prendas de vestir importadas** = a black market in imported articles of clothing; **vivían bien de las mercancías del mercado negro** = they lived well on black-market goods

neto, -ta *adj* net; **beneficio neto** = clear profit *o* net profit; **renta neta** *o* **salario neto** = real income *o* real wages *o* net income; **sacamos** *o* **obtuvimos un beneficio neto de 600.000 ptas por la venta** = we made 600.000 ptas clear profit on the sale

nexo nm link; **nexo causal** = causation

ningún = NINGUNO

ninguno, -na *adj y pron* nobody *o* no-one *o* none; **no se rechazar ninguna oferta** = no reasonable offer refused NOTA: ningún delante de nm singular

niño, -ña *n* child; **niño expósito** = foundling; **secuestro de un niño** = child stealing

nivel nm level; **nivel de vida** = standard of living *o* living standards; **al mismo nivel** = pari passu; **las nuevas acciones se situarán al mismo nivel que las ya existentes** = the new shares will rank pari passu with the existing ones

nivelar *vt* to balance; **nivelar el presupuesto** = to balance the budget

NN.UU = NACIONES UNIDAS

no *adv* non-; **no caucionable** = non-bailable; **no premeditado** = unintended; **política de no intervención** = non-intervention policy

nocivo, -va *adj* noxious *o* harmful; **sustancia nociva** = noxious substance

nocturno,-na *adj* late-night; **servicio nocturno** *o* **servicio de guardia nocturna** = night duty; **hay un avión nocturno entre Londres y Madrid** = there is an evening plane running between London and Madrid; **sus negociaciones nocturnas finalizaron con un acuerdo firmado a las 3 de la madrugada** = their late-night negotiations ended in an agreement which was signed at 3 a.m.

nombrado, -da *adj* designate

nombramiento *nm* appointment *o* *(designación)* nomination; **nombramiento de administrador judicial** = letters of administration; **notificación del nombramiento para un puesto** *o* **carta de nombramiento** = letter of appointment; **en su nombramiento como magistrado** = on his appointment as magistrate

nombrar *vt* to appoint *o (designar)* to nominate *o* to designate *o* to name; **nombrar a alguien apoderado o representante** = to nominate someone as proxy; **nombrar a alguien para un puesto** = to nominate someone to a post; **nombrar a Juan Serra director** = to appoint Juan Serra to the post of manager

nombre *nm* name; **nombre, apellidos y dirección** = full name and address *o* name and address in full; **nombre comercial** = trade name *o* corporate name; **nombre supuesto** *o* **por otro nombre** = alias; **con el nombre de** = under the name of; **en nombre de** = on behalf of *o* ex parte; **actúa en mi nombre** = she is acting on my behalf; **abogados que actúan en nombre de la empresa argentina** = solicitors acting on behalf of the Argentinian company; **el estafador utilizaba varios nombres falsos** = the confidence trickster used several aliases; **escribo en nombre de los accionistas minoritarios** = I am writing on behalf of the minority shareholders

nómina *nf* payroll

nominal *adj* nominal; **alquiler nominal** = peppercorn rent; **capital nominal** = nominal capital; **valor nominal** = face value *o* nominal value; **pagan un alquiler nominal** = they are paying a nominal rent

nominativo, -va *adj* **póliza de seguros nominativa** = insurance policy which covers a named person; **cheque nominativo** = personal cheque *o* cheque not transferable

nonato, -ta *adj* unborn

norma *nf* (a) *(regla)* rule *o* regulation *o (ley)* law; **norma programática** = policy; **normas de la empresa** = company rules (and regulations); **normas de seguridad en el lugar de trabajo** = safety regulations which apply to places of work; **tenemos por norma que la asesoría jurídica examine todos los contratos** = our policy is to submit all contracts to the legal department (b) *(patrón)* standard; **normas de producción** = production standards; **conforme a la norma** = up to standard (c) *(código)* **normas** = code; **normas de conducta** = code of conduct; **normas procesales** = rules of court; **normas profesionales** = etiquette (d) *(modelo)* pattern
◊ **normal** *adj* (a) *(estándar)* standard; **tasa de impuesto normal** = standard rate; **el precio normal por consulta es de 5.000 ptas** = the standard charge for consultation is 5,000 ptas (b) *(corriente)* usual *o* common; **el horario normal de trabajo es de 9 a 1 y de 3 a 7** = the usual hours of work are from 9 to 1 and from 3 to 7; **lo normal es que el contrato sea firmado por un director de la empresa** = the usual practice is to have the contract signed by a director of the company; **nuestras condiciones normales consisten en un crédito de**

treinta días = our usual terms *o* usual conditions are thirty days' credit (c) *(natural)* natural

nota *nf* (a) *(escrito informal)* note *o* memo *o* memorandum; **nota al margen** = marginal note; **bloc de notas** = notepad; **el presidente del jurado le pasó una nota al juez** = the foreman of the jury passed a note to the judge (b) **tomar nota de** = to note *o* to record; **tomar nota de algo** = to make a note of something *o* to take note of something; **tomar notas de una reunión** = to minute *o* to take notes of a meeting; **se ha tomado nota de su reclamación** = your complaint has been noted; **hemos tomado nota de su reclamación y será investigada** = your complaint has been recorded and will be investigated; **se pidió al jurado que tomara nota de las pruebas dadas por el patólogo** = the jury was asked to take note of the evidence given by the pathologist (c) *(recibo)* slip; **nota de abono** *o* **de crédito** = credit note; **nota de adeudo** *o* **de cargo** = debit note *o* note of costs; **nota de cobertura** = cover note; **nota de compraventa de acciones** = contract note; **nota de embarque** = advice note; **nota sobre los derechos de autor** = copyright notice; **según nota de expedición** = as per advice (d) *(en un restaurante)* ¿me puede dar la nota por favor? = can I have the bill please?

notar *vt* to observe

notaría *nf* notary's office

notarial *adj* notarial; **acta notarial** = affidavit *o* notarial act *o* jurat; **poder notarial** = power of attorney

notario, -ria *n* notary public; **notario público** = commissioner for oaths

noticia *nf* (a) *(comunicación)* item *o* piece of news; **noticias** = news; **tener noticias de** = to hear from; **esperamos tener noticias de los abogados dentro de breves días** = we hope to hear from the lawyers within a few days; **hace algún tiempo que no tenemos noticias de ellos** = we have not heard from them for some time (b) *(en un periódico)* a report in a newspaper *o* a newspaper report

notificación *nf* notice *o* notification; **notificación de adjudicación (de acciones)** = letter of allotment *o* allotment letter; **notificación de desahucio** = notice to quit; **notificación del nombramiento para un puesto** = letter of appointment; **notificación de pago** = reminder; **periodo de notificación (de despido** *o* **de dimisión)** = period of notice; **pagó la pensión alimenticia tras varias notificaciones** = he paid the maintenance after several reminders; **el alquiler quedó rescindido por una notificación de desalojo** = the tenancy was determined by a notice to quit

notificador *nm (agente judicial)* process-server

notificar *vt* to notify; **notificar oficialmente** = to schedule; **notificar a alguien un mandamiento** *o* **una orden judicial** = to serve someone with a writ *o* to serve a writ on someone; **notificar una apelación (iniciar los trámites oficiales para la presentación de una apelación)** to give notice of appeal; **se les notificó el inminente proceso judicial** = they were notified of the impending court action

notorio *adj* self-evident *o* well-known

novación *nf* novation

novedad *nf* novelty *o* (new) departure; **la venta de discos será una novedad para la librería local** = selling records will be a departure for the local bookshop; **sin novedad** = nothing new

nudo, -da *adj* **nudo pacto** = nudum pactum; **nuda propiedad** = legal ownership; **nuda propiedad efectiva** = vested remainder; **nudo propietario** = remainder *o* legal owner

> La nuda propiedad es la propiedad de la que se ha separado o deducido el usufructo

nuevo, -va *adj* new; **nueva emisión** = new issue; **nuevo juicio** = new trial *o* rehearing; **nuevo miembro** *o* **nuevo socio** = new member *o* recruit; **nueva orientación comercial** = new departure; **de nuevo** = re-; **comenzar de nuevo** = de novo

nulidad *nf* nullity *o* invalidity; **nulidad de actuaciones** = annulment of proceedings; **nulidad matrimonial** = void marriage; **la nulidad del contrato** = the invalidity of the contract; **cláusula de nulidad** = defeasance

nulo, -la *adj* null *o* void *o* invalid; **nulo y sin efecto** *o* **nulo y sin valor** = null and void; **inflación nula** = zero inflation; **matrimonio nulo** = void marriage; **permiso nulo** = permit that is invalid; **voto nulo** = spoilt ballot paper; **declarar un rendimiento nulo** = to make a nil return; **reclamación que ha sido declarada nula** = claim which has been declared invalid; **el contrato fue declarado nulo y sin valor** = the contract was declared null and void

numérico, -ca *adj* numeric *o* numerical; **orden numérico** = numerical order; **los documentos están archivados por orden numérico** = the documents are filed in numerical order

número *nm* number *o* (*cifra*) figure; **en números redondos** = in round figures; **el número de presos encarcelados es de 45.000 en números redondos** = the number of prisoners in jail is 45,000 in round figures

Oo

obedecer *vt/i* to obey *o* to comply with; **no obedecer** = to disobey; **se negó a obedecer el requerimiento** = she refused to comply with the injunction; **la multitud se negó a obedecer las órdenes de la policía** = the crowd refused to obey the police instructions; **se dejó a los presos incomunicados como castigo por no haber obedecido las órdenes del director de la prisión** = the prisoners were put in solitary confinement as punishment for their disobedience of the governor's orders

obediencia *nf* obedience; **obediencia debida** = allegiance; **el ejército juró obediencia al presidente** = the army swore obedience to the president; **todo ciudadano debería mostrar obediencia a las leyes del estado** = every citizen should show obedience to the laws of the state

óbito *nm* demise

objeción *nf* (a) *(recusación)* objection *o* exception *o* challenge; **objeción al jurado exponiendo las razones** = challenge for cause; **objeción al jurado sin dar razones** *o* **sin exponer las razones** = peremptory challenge *o* challenge without cause; **objeción de conciencia** = conscientious objection; **hacer objeciones a algo** = to raise an objection to something (b) *(protesta)* demur; **hacer objeciones** = to demur; **el abogado no hizo ninguna objeción a la propuesta** = counsel made no demur to the proposal; **el abogado expuso que no había motivos para continuar el juicio, pero el juez hizo objeciones** = counsel stated that there was no case to answer, but the judge demurred

objetar *vt* (a) *(recusar)* to object *o* to challenge *o* to take exception to something; **objetar a un jurado** = to object to a juror (b) *(protestar)* to demur; **tener algo que objetar** = to demur

objetivo, -va 1 *adj* objective; **debe ser objetivo al evaluar la actuación del personal** = you must be objective in assessing the performance of the staff; **el juez pidió al jurado que fuera objetivo al considerar las pruebas que se le presentaban** = the judge asked the jury to be objective in considering the evidence put before them; **llevar a cabo una revisión objetiva de la legislación actual** = to carry out an objective review of current legislation 2 *nm* objective *o* purpose; **objetivo a largo plazo** *o* **a corto plazo** = long-term objective *o* short-term objective; **dirección por objetivos** = management by objectives

objeto *nm* (a) *(cosa)* object *o* thing; **objeto abandonado** = unattendend property; **objeto en posesión** = chose in possession; **estar en posesión de objetos contundentes** = carrying offensive weapons; **la dirección no se hace responsable de los objetos de valor que el cliente deje en las habitaciones del hotel** = the management is not responsible for property left in the hotel rooms (b) *(propósito)* purpose *o* object *o* aim; **objeto de litigio** = cause of action; **ser objeto de un asalto** = to be the target of an attack

objetor *nm* **objetor de conciencia** = conscientious objector

obligación *nf* (a) *(deber)* obligation *o* duty *o* engagement; **obligación legal** = legal obligation; **obligaciones** = commitments; **obligación de probar lo alegado** = burden of proof *o* onus of proof *o* onus probandi; **cumplir con las obligaciones contractuales** = to fulfil one's contractual obligations; **cumplir con las obligaciones de uno** = to honour one's commitments; **tener la obligación de hacer algo** *o* **verse en la obligación de hacer algo** = to be under an obligation to do something; **todo ciudadano tiene la obligación de actuar como jurado en caso de ser convocado** = it is the duty of every citizen to serve on a jury if called; **el gobierno tiene la obligación de proteger a los ciudadanos de los criminales** = the government has a duty to protect the citizens from criminals; **no tiene obligación contractual de comprar** = he is under no contractual obligation to buy (b) *(pagaré)* bond; **obligación de interés fijo** = debenture; **obligación no hipotecaria** = debenture bond; **obligaciones** = loan stock *o* *(deudas)* liabilities; **obligaciones a corto plazo** = current liabilities; **obligaciones convertibles** = convertible loan stock; **obligaciones de interés fijo** = loan stock; **obligaciones de renta fija** = debenture stock; **obligaciones garantizadas por los activos de la compañía** = debenture capital *o* debenture stock;

emisión de obligaciones garantizada por los activos de la compañía = debenture issue *o* issue of debentures; **tenedor de obligaciones** = debenture holder *o* bondholder; **títulos u obligaciones** = equities

◊ **obligacionista** *nmf (tenedor de obligaciones)* debenture holder *o* bondholder; **registro de obligacionistas** = debenture register *o* register of debentures

obligado, -da *adj* compellable *o* duty bound; **obligado a** = liable to; **de obligado complimiento** = legally binding; **estar obligado a hacer algo** = *US* to be obligated to do something; **un testigo obligado** = a compellable witness; **los testigos bajo juramento están obligados a decir la verdad** = witnesses under oath are duty bound to tell the truth

obligar *vt (forzar)* to oblige *o* to compel *o* to force *o (por contrato)* to bind; **obligar a alguien a hacer algo** = to oblige someone to do something; **obligar a alguien a hacer algo por medio de un contrato** = to engage someone to do something; **obligar legalmente a (comparecer ante el tribunal)** = to bind over; **se le obligó a mantener la paz** = he was bound over to keep the peace; **se vio** *o* **se sintió obligado a anular el contrato** = he felt obliged to cancel the contract; **se le obligó (a mantener la paz** *o* **a llevar una buena conducta) durante seis meses** = he was bound over (to keep the peace *o* to be of good behaviour) for six months; **el contrato obliga a la compañía a realizar un mínimo de compras anuales** *o* **a comprar una cantidad mínima de productos anualmente** = the contract engages the company to purchase minimum annual quantities of goods; **la competencia ha obligado a la empresa a bajar los precios** = competition has forced the company to lower its prices; **la empresa está obligada a respetar sus estatutos** = the company is bound by its articles of association; **la Ley obliga a todos los conductores a tener un seguro adecuado** = the Act compels all drivers to have adequate insurance; **no se considera obligado al acuerdo firmado por su predecesor** = he does not consider himself bound by the agreement which was signed by his predecessor

obligatoriedad *nf* compellability

obligatorio, -ria *adj* obligatory *o* compulsory *o* mandatory *o (vinculante)* binding; **reunión** *o* **junta obligatoria** = mandatory meeting; **todas las personas deben pasar un examen médico obligatorio** = each person has to pass an obligatory medical examination

obra *nf* work; **obras públicas** = public works; **mano de obra** = labour force; **abriremos una nueva fábrica en Extremo Oriente para aprovechar la mano de obra local barata** = we are opening a new factory in the Far East because of the cheap local labour force

obrar *vt* to act; **obrar con conocimiento de causa** = to be responsible for one's actions; **obrar con precaución** = to act with caution; **obrar conforme a** *o* **de acuerdo con** = to act on; **obrar de acuerdo con una carta** = to act on a letter; **los abogados están obrando conforme a nuestras órdenes** = the lawyers are acting on our instructions; **obra en mi poder** = in receipt of

obrero, -ra *n* labourer *o* worker; **patrón y obrero** = master and servant; **ley del patrono y del obrero** = the law of master and servant; **obreros** = labour force; **la dirección ha ofrecido un aumento a los obreros** = the management has made an increased offer to the labour force

obscenidad *nf* obscenity

obsceno, -na *adj* obscene; **la revista fue clasificada como publicación obscena** = the magazine was classed as an obscene publication

obsequio *nm* present *o* giveaway

observación *nf* observation *o* comment; **hacer observaciones** = to comment; **el juez hizo algunas observaciones sobre la conducta del acusado durante el juicio** = the judge made some observations about the conduct of the accused during the trial; **el juez hizo una observación sobre las pruebas presentadas por la defensa** = the judge made a comment on the evidence presented by the defence; **el juez hizo observaciones sobre la falta de pruebas** = the judge commented on the lack of evidence

observador, -ra *n* observer; **a la reunión asistieron dos observadores oficiales** = two official observers attended the meeting

observancia *nf* observance

observar *vt* to observe *o* to note; **observar la ley** = to be law-abiding; **se les ha pedido a los funcionarios que observen cómo se desarrollan las elecciones** = officials have been instructed to observe the conduct of the election

obsoleto, -ta *adj* obsolete

obstaculizar *vt* to obstruct; **obstaculizar la labor de la policía** = obstructing the police; **es un delito obstaculizar la labor de la policía** = obstruction of the police is an offence

obstáculo *nm* obstruction *o* obstacle *o* bar *o* hurdle; **sin estorbo ni obstáculo** = without let or hindrance; **las leyes gubernamentales son un obstáculo para el comercio exterior** = government legislation is a bar to foreign trade; **el acusado tendrá que superar dos obstáculos si quiere que su apelación prospere** = the defendant will have to overcome two hurdles if his appeal is to be successful

obstante *adv* **no obstante** = notwithstanding

obstinado, -da *adj* obstinate *o* wilful

obstrucción *nf* obstruction; **el coche causó una obstrucción del tráfico** = the car caused an obstruction to the traffic

obstruir *vt* to obstruct; **los coches aparcados obstruyen el tráfico** = the parked cars are obstructing the traffic

obtener *vt* **(a)** *(lograr)* to obtain *o* to get *o* *(fondos)* to raise; **obtener por estafa** = obtaining by deception; **obtener suministros del extranjero** = to obtain supplies from abroad; **obtener un requerimiento contra una compañía** = to obtain an injunction against a company; **obtener ventajas económicas por estafa** = obtaining a pecuniary advantage by deception; **obtener votos en unas elecciones** to poll; **su partido obtuvo sólo 123 votos en las elecciones generales** = their party polled only 123 votes in the general election; **que se puede obtener** = obtainable **(b)** *(recuperar)* to recover; **obtener daños y perjuicios del conductor del coche** = to recover damages from the driver of the car **(c)** *(sacar)* to derive

obtenible *adj* obtainable

ocasión *nf* occasion *o* chance
◊ **ocasional** *adj* occasional *o* casual; **trabajo ocasional** = casual work
◊ **ocasionalmente** *adv* occasionally

ocasionar *vt* to occasion *o* to give rise to; **se declaró culpable de agresión ocasionando lesiones a la persona** = he pleaded guilty to assault occasioning actual bodily harm; **el fallo ha ocasionado quejas por parte de la familia del acusado** = the decision has given rise to complaints from the family of the defendant

ocular *adj* eye; **testigo ocular** = eye witness; **contó su versión del atraco al banco, como testigo ocular** = he gave an eye witness account of the bank hold-up

ocultación *nf* concealment *o* suppression; **ocultación de bienes** = concealment of assets; **ocultación de delito** = misprision; **ocultación de nacimiento** = concealment of birth; **ocultación de traición** = misprision of treason; **la ocultación de la verdad sobre un caso** = the suppression of the truth about the case

ocultar *vt* to conceal *o* to suppress *o* to withhold; **ocultar la verdad** = suppressio veri; **ocultar objetos robados** = to conceal stolen goods; **ocultar un micrófono** = to bug; **el gobierno trató de ocultar la noticia sobre el motín de la prisión** = the government tried to suppress the news about the prison riot; **se le acusó de ocultar información** = he was accused of concealing information

oculto, -ta *adj* hidden *o* latent; **ayuda oculta en un juicio** = champerty; **defecto oculto en el programa** = hidden defect in the program;

micrófono oculto = bug *o* bugging device; **colocar un micrófono oculto** = to bug; **reservas ocultas** = hidden reserves; **la policía encontró un micrófono oculto bajo la mesa del abogado** = police found a bugging device under the lawyer's desk; **los agentes colocaron un micrófono oculto en el despacho del Presidente** = the agents bugged the President's office

ocupa *o* **okupa** *nmf* squatter

ocupación *nf* **(a)** *(trabajo)* employment *o* occupation; **ocupación de un cargo** = tenure; **su principal ocupación es la construcción de casas** = his main occupation is house building **(b)** *(tenencia)* occupancy; **ocupación de un edificio** = occupation of a building; **ocupación ilegal de un edificio** = squatting; **de ocupación inmediata** = vacant possession *o* with immediate occupancy

ocupado, -da *adj* busy; **línea ocupada** = engaged line; **la policía estaba muy ocupada tratando de controlar a la muchedumbre** = the police were kept busy dealing with the crowds

ocupante *nmf* occupant *o* occupier; **ocupante y dueño de una propiedad** = owner-occupier; **ocupante legal de una vivienda** = legal occupier; **ocupante ilegal de una vivienda** = squatter

ocupar *vt* to occupy *o* to hold; **ocupar un puesto** = to occupy a post; **ocupar ilegalmente una vivienda** = to squat; **que ocupa ilegalmente una vivienda** = squatter; **sin ocupar** = free; **el edificio está siendo ocupado ilegalmente** = squatters are occupying the building; **tiene ocupados 200.000 metros cuadrados en Asturias** = he holds fifty acres in Asturias; **la empresa ocupa tres pisos de un edificio de oficinas** = the company occupies three floors of an office block; **los rebeldes ocuparon la oficina de Correos** = the rebels occupied the Post Office; **todas las habitaciones del hotel están ocupadas** = all the rooms in the hotel are occupied
◊ **ocuparse** *vr* ocuparse de = to handle *o* to attend to; **la brigada contra el fraude se ocupa de casos de negligencia empresarial** = the fraud squad handles cases of business malpractice; **los tribunales se encontraron con dificultades para ocuparse de todos los casos** = the courts had difficulty in handling all the cases; **el director gerente se ocupará de su reclamación personalmente** = the managing director will attend to your complaint personally; **el tribunal no se ocupa del valor de los artículos robados** = the court is not concerned with the value of the items stolen

ocurrir *vi* to happen *o* to occur; **que ocurre de vez en cuando** = occasional

odio *nm* hatred; **odio racial** = racial hatred; **su odio por la injusticia y la desigualdad** = his hatred of injustice *o* of inequality

ofensivo, -va *adj* injurious; **arma ofensiva** = offensive weapon; **comportamiento ofensivo** = insulting behaviour

oferente *nmf* offeror

oferta *nf* **(a)** *(propuesta)* offer; **oferta de compra** = offer to buy; **oferta de pago en efectivo** = cash offer; **oferta de venta** = offer to sell; **oferta especial** = special offer; **oferta para suscribir nuevas acciones** = invitation to subscribe to a new issue; **oferta pública de acciones** = offer for sale; **precio de oferta de acciones** = offer price; **ofertas de empleo (jurídico)** = legal appointments vacant; **ofertas de trabajo** = situations vacant *o* appointments vacant; **aceptar una oferta de 800.000 ptas por el coche** = to accept an offer of 800.000 ptas for the car; **admitimos toda clase de ofertas** = we are open to offers; **hacer una oferta por una empresa** = to make an offer for a company; **hicimos una oferta por la casa por escrito** = we made a written offer for the house; **recibió seis ofertas de trabajo** = he received six offers of jobs *o* six job offers; **se ha hecho una oferta por la casa** = the house is under offer; **solicitud de ofertas de compra** = invitation to treat; **su oferta fue mucho más baja que las demás** = his quotation was much lower than all the others **(b)** *(licitación)* bid *o* tender; **oferta pública de adquisición de una empresa (OPA)** = takeover bid *o* offer; **hacer una oferta pública de acciones** *o* **sacar acciones a oferta escrita** = to sell shares by tender; **ofertas cerradas** *o* **ofertas lacradas** = sealed tenders; **hacer una oferta de compra** *o* **presentar una oferta** = to make *o* to enter a bid for something *o* to put in a bid for something; **hacer una oferta de contratación** *o* **presentar una oferta de licitación** = to tender for a contract; **hacer una oferta para la construcción de un hospital** = to tender for the construction of a hospital; **hacer una oferta pública de acciones** *o* **sacar acciones a oferta escrita** = to sell shares by tender; **presentar una oferta de adquisición** = to make a takeover bid for a company; **presentó la oferta más baja** *o* **más barata por el trabajo** = he made the lowest bid for the job; **retirar una oferta de adquisición de una empresa** = to withdraw a takeover bid; **receptor de la oferta** = offeree; **solicitaron ofertas para el suministro de piezas de repuesto** = they asked for bids for the supply of spare parts **(c)** *(suministro)* supply; **oferta monetaria** = money supply; **oferta y demanda** = supply and demand; **la ley de la oferta y la demanda** = the law of supply and demand; **precio de oferta** = supply price

◊ **ofertar** *vt* to offer *o* to tender; **ofertar acciones** = to sell shares by tender

oficial 1 *adj* official; **Boletín Oficial del Estado (BOE)** Official Journal; **fiesta oficial** = legal holiday; **no oficial** = unofficial; **mercado no oficial de valores** *o* **mercado de valores sin cotización**

oficial = over-the-counter market; **precios** *o* **tarifas oficiales** = scheduled prices *o* scheduled charges; **hemos solicitado permiso oficial de construcción para el recinto de la nueva zona comercial** = we have formally applied for planning permission for the new shopping precinct; **la huelga se hizo oficial** = the strike was made official; **en asuntos oficiales** = on official business; **cursar** *o* **hacer una petición oficial** = to file a petition; **una investigación oficial sobre el crimen organizado** = a government investigation into organized crime; **venta de valores sin cotización oficial** = over-the-counter sales; **ésta debe de ser una orden oficial - está escrita en papel de la empresa** = this must be an official order - it is written on the company's notepaper; **recibió una carta oficial explicatoria** = she received an official letter of explanation; **se dejó documentos oficiales en el coche** = he left official documents in his car **2** *nm* officer *o* official; **oficial a cargo de los que están bajo libertad vigilada** = probation officer; **oficial de aduanas** = customs officer *o* customs official; **oficial de justicia** = marshal; **oficial mayor** = chief clerk *o* head clerk; **agente oficial** = officer; **es oficial de las fuerzas armadas** = he has a commission in the armed forces

◊ **oficialmente** *adv* officially *o* on record; **oficialmente hablando** *o* **hablando oficialmente** = speaking in an official capacity; **oficialmente no sabe nada acerca del problema, pero extraoficialmente nos ha dado buenos consejos** = officially he knows nothing about the problem, but unofficially he has given us a lot of advice about it; **el presidente ha dicho oficialmente que los beneficios van a aumentar** = the chairman is on record as saying that profits are set to rise

oficina *nf* **(a)** *(centro de trabajo)* office *o* centre *o* *(agency)* agency *o* bureau; **oficina central** = central office *o* general office *o* head office; **oficina de correos** = post office; **oficina de empleo** = employment office *o* bureau *o* agency *o* Job Centre; **oficina de información** = information bureau *o* information office *o* inquiry office; **oficina de servicios informáticos** = computer bureau; **Oficina del Registro Civil** = Registry Office; **Oficina Federal de Investigación (FBI)** = Federal Bureau of Investigation (FBI); **oficina principal** = head office *o* main office *o* general office **(b) de oficina** = clerical; **empleado de oficina** = clerk; **horario de oficina** = office hours; **jefe de oficina** = chief clerk *o* head clerk; **personal de oficina** = clerical staff *o* office staff; **trabajo de oficina** = clerical work; **bloque de oficinas** = office block *o* a block of offices; **espacio para oficinas** *o* **espacio ocupado por oficinas** = office space *o* office accommodation **(c)** *(sucursal)* branch; **el director de nuestra oficina en Santander** = the manager of our branch in Santander *o* of our Santander branch

◊ **oficinista** *nmf* clerk *o* clerical worker; **oficinistas** = clerical staff

oficio *nm* **(a)** *(profesión)* profession *o* occupation; **gajes del oficio** = occupational hazards; **de oficio** = ex officio; **el tesorero es un miembro de oficio de la comisión financiera** = the treasurer is ex officio a member *o* an ex officio member of the finance committee **(b)** *(comunicado escrito)* **oficio judicial** = official letter
◊ **oficioso, -sa** *adj* unofficial
◊ **oficiosamente** *adv* off the record *o* unofficially

ofrecer *vt* **(a)** *(comprar,vender)* to offer; **100.000 ptas es lo máximo que puedo ofrecer** = 100,000 ptas is the best offer I can make; **ofreció 2.000 ptas por acción** he made an offer of 2,000 ptas a share; **ofrecer a alguien 50 millones por su casa** = to offer someone 50 million for his house **(b)** *(en subasta)* to tender *o* to bid for something; **ofreció 100.000 ptas por las joyas** = he bid 100,000 ptas for the jewels **(c)** *(facilitar)* **ofrecer excusas** = to apologize; **ofrecer servicios** = to solicit orders; **ofrecer a alguien un trabajo** = to offer someone a job; **ofrecer compensación por daños causados** = to offer to pay compensation for damages; **ofrecer crédito por un periodo continuado** = to roll over credit
◊ **ofrecerse** *vr* to offer; **seis hombres se ofrecieron para entrar en la casa incendiada** = six men volunteered to go into the burning house

ofrecimiento *nm* offer; **ofrecimiento de compensación** *o* **de reparación de daños** = offer of amends

oír *vt* to hear; **oír un caso** = to hear; *(en un juicio)* **¡oíd!** = oyez; **el tribunal ha oído al testigo de descargo** = the court has heard the evidence for the defence; **el tráfico hace tanto ruido que no puedo oír si el teléfono suena** = the traffic makes so much noise that I cannot hear my phone ringing; **se puede oír la impresora de la oficina contigua** *o* **de al lado** = you can hear the printer in the next office

OIT = ORGANIZACION INTERNACIONAL DEL TRABAJO International Labour Organization (ILO)

ola *nf* wave; **ola de criminalidad** = crime wave
◊ **oleada** *nf* big wave; **oleada de crímenes** = crime wave

Oleron *nm* *(primeras leyes marítima)* **leyes de Oleron** = Laws of Oleron

ológrafo *nm* holograph; **dejó un testamento ológrafo** = he left a holograph will

olvidar *vt* to forget *o* *(omitir)* to omit; **olvidar hacer algo** = to neglect to do something
◊ **olvidarse** *vr* to omit; **olvidarse de hacer algo** = to forget to do something; **se me olvidó dejar el mensaje** = I forgot to give the message

olvido *nm* oversight *o* omission

omisión *nf* omission; **omisión de pago** = default; **omisión dolosa** = negligent act; **omisión de deberes** *o* **delito por omisión** = nonfeisance; **salvo error u omisión (s.e.u.o.)** = errors and omissions excepted; **el secretario leyó las acusaciones sin omisiones** = the clerk read out the charges in full

omitir *vt* to omit *o* to leave out; **omitió poner la fecha en la carta** = she left out the date on the letter; **el contrato omite cualquier detalle sobre acuerdos de marketing** = the contract leaves out all details of marketing arrangements; **la secretaria omitió la fecha al pasar a máquina el contrato** = the secretary omitted the date when typing the contract

oneroso, -sa *adj* onerous; **litigante oneroso** = vexatious litigant; **transmisión onerosa** *o* **título oneroso** = valuable consideration; **las condiciones de pago son especialmente onerosas** = the repayment terms are particularly onerous

ONU = ORGANIZACION DE LAS NACIONES UNIDAS United Nations Organization (UN)

op. cit. *frase latina que significa 'obra citada'* op. cit.

OPA = OFERTA PUBLICA DE ADQUISICION takeover bid *o* offer

opción *nf* **(a)** *(alternativa)* option; **opción de compra** *o* **de venta** = option to purchase *o* to sell; **primera opción** = first option *o* first refusal; **dar a alguien primera opción** = to give someone first refusal; **ejercer el derecho a opción** *o* **realizar una opción** *o* **consolidar el mercado de opción** = to take up an option *o* to exercise an option; **quiero poder ejercer el derecho a opción** = I want to leave my options open; **conceder a alguien una opción de seis meses para ser el agente** *o* **para fabricar un producto** = to grant someone a six-month option on a product; **ejerció su derecho a opción para adquirir derechos exclusivos de comercialización del producto** = he exercised his option *o* he took up his option to acquire sole marketing rights to the product; **no hubo muchos accionistas que ejercitaran su opción a compra de la nueva emisión de acciones** = not many shareholders exercised their option to buy the new issue of shares **(b)** *(en bolsa)* option; **opción de compra de acciones** = call option; **opción de venta de acciones** *o* **prima de opción de venta de acciones en una fecha determinada** = put option; **opción de compra** *o* **venta de acciones a cierto precio para el futuro** = share option; **derecho de opción de compra** *o* **de venta de acciones a precio fijo** = option contract; **operación de opción** = option dealing *o* option trading; **prima de opción para compra de acciones (ofrecida a los empleados de una compañía)** = stock option

operación *nf* operation *o* *(explotación)* operating; **operación al contado** = cash transaction; **operación comercial** = business transaction; **operación de Bolsa** *o* **bursátil** = Stock Exchange operation *o* a transaction on the Stock Exchange; **operación en divisas** = exchange transaction; **operación fraudulenta** = fraudulent transaction; **operaciones en bolsa** = dealing; **operaciones comerciales correctas** = fair dealing; **operaciones de iniciado** = insider dealing; **análisis** *o* **investigación de operaciones** = operations review; **dirige las operaciones en el Norte de España** = he heads up the operations in Northern Spain; **el periódico publica una lista diaria de operaciones bursátiles** = the paper publishes a daily list of Stock Exchange transactions; **las operaciones de la compañía en Africa occidental** = the company's operations in West Africa

◊ **operacional** *adj* operational

operador, -ra *n* **(a)** *(maquinista)* operator *o* *(telefonista)* switchboard operator **(b)** *(cambista)* broker *o* dealer; **operador de cambios** = foreign exchange broker

operante *adj* operative

operar *vi* to operate *o* to transact; **el reglamento opera en los servicios postales del territorio nacional** = the rules operate on inland postal services; **la compañía opera bajo un nombre nuevo** = he trades under a new name

operario, -ria *n* worker *o* operative

operativo, -va *adj* operative *o* operational; **investigación** *o* **planificación operativa** = operational research *o* planning; **sistema operativo** = operating system

opinar *vi* to be of the opinion; **el juez opinaba que si las pruebas eran dudosas la demanda se debía desestimar** = the judge was of the opinion that if the evidence was doubtful the claim should be dismissed

opinión *nf* opinion *o* view *o* *(dictamen expresado por un juez)* obiter dicta; **opinión pública** = public opinion; **dar una opinión** = to give an opinion; **pedir una opinión** = to ask for an opinion; **sondeo de opinión** = opinion poll *o* opinion research; **persona que hace sondeos de opinión** = canvasser; **pedir a un asesor su opinión sobre un caso** = to ask an adviser for his opinion on a case; **tener una opinión sobre algo** = to take a view on something; **ser de la opinión** = to be of the opinion; **el tribunal es de la opinión que el acusado no publicó la difamación maliciosamente** = the court takes the view that the defendant did not publish the defamation maliciously; **los abogados dieron su opinión** = the lawyers gave their opinion

oponente *nmf* opponent

oponer *vt* to oppose; **oponer resistencia** = to resist *o* to obstruct

◊ **oponerse** *vr* **(a)** *(objetar)* to oppose *o* to object (to); **oponerse a una cláusula de un contrato** = to object to a clause in a contract; **la policía se opuso a la libertad bajo fianza** = the police opposed bail *o* opposed the granting of bail; **el abogado del demandante se opuso a la petición de aplazamiento por parte del demandado** = counsel for the plaintiff opposed the defendant's application for an adjournment; **una minoría de los miembros del consejo se opuso a la moción** = a minority of board members opposed the motion **(b)** *(estar en pugna)* to conflict

oportunidad *nf* opportunity *o* chance; **el fiscal aprovechó la oportunidad y pidió al testigo que repitiera la conversación que había mantenido con el acusado** = the prosecuting counsel seized his chance and asked the witness to repeat the conversation which he had had with the accused

oportuno, -na *adj* **comentario oportuno** = fair comment
◊ **oportunamente** *adv* duly

oposición *nf* **(a)** *(actitud contraria)* opposition; **líder de la oposición** = Leader of the Opposition; **partido de la oposición** = opposition; **sin oposición** = uncontested; **elecciones sin oposición** = an uncontested election; **hubo una oposición considerable al proyecto para reorganizar los tribunales de divorcio** = there was considerable opposition to the plan for reorganizing the divorce courts; **la oposición intentó proponer un voto de censura contra el Primer Ministro** = the opposition tried to propose a vote of censure on the Prime Minister **(b)** *(concurso público)* public *o* open competition *o* examination

opositor, -ra *n* opponent

optar *vi* to decide

optativo, -va *adj* optional; **la póliza de seguros es optativa** = the insurance cover is optional

óptimo, -ma *adj* optimal *o* optimum; **el mercado ofrece condiciones óptimas para las ventas** = the market offers optimum conditions for sales

opuesto, -ta *adj* **(a)** *(lado)* opposite *o* reverse; *(opinión)* opposed *o* contra *o* contrary *o* adverse

oral *adj* oral *o* parol *o* *(de viva voz)* viva voce; **testimonio oral** = oral evidence *o* parol evidence
◊ **oralmente** *adv* orally

orden 1 *nf* **(a)** *(documento legal)* order *o* warrant *o* *(mandamiento judicial)* writ (of summons); **orden de arresto por incomparecencia** = bench warrant; **orden de comparecencia (como testigo)** = subpoena; **orden de conservación** = preservation order; **orden de desahucio** = eviction order; **orden de detención** *o* **de arresto** = detention order *o* arrest warrant; **orden de ejecución** = warrant of execution; **orden de ejecución de la pena de**

muerte = death warrant; **orden de ejecución de pago** = warrant of execution; **orden de embargo** = garnishee order; **orden de expulsión** *o* **de deportación** = deportation order; **orden de habeas corpus** = writ of habeas corpus; **orden de indemnización** = compensation order; **orden de ingreso en prisión** = warrant of committal *o* committal warrant; **orden de ingreso en prisión por desacato** = committal order; **orden de intervención judicial** = receiving order; **orden de manutención** = maintenance order; **orden de prisión** = custodial sentence; **orden de registro** = search warrant; **orden de rehabilitación de la quiebra** = order of discharge; **orden judicial** = court order; **orden judicial de libertad vigilada** *o* **condicional** = probation order; **orden provisional** = interim order; **orden reglamentaria** *o* **establecida por ley** = statutory instrument; **extender una orden de detención de alguien** = to issue a warrant for the arrest of someone *o* to issue an arrest warrant for someone; **el ministro firmó la orden de deportación** = the minister signed the deportation order; **el preso fue trasladado por orden judicial** = the prisoner was removed by order of the court; **el tribunal dictó una orden judicial de manutención** = the court made an order for maintenance *o* made a maintenance order; **se negó a obedecer la orden judicial y fue enviado a prisión por desacato** = he refused to obey the court order and was sent to prison for contempt **(b)** *(documento comercial)* order; **orden de compra** = purchase order; **orden de compra de un importador** = indent; **orden de expedición** = delivery order; **orden de pago** = bank mandate; **orden de pago regular** = banker's order *o* standing order; **presentó una orden de compra para importar una nueva partida de piezas de repuesto** = he put in an indent for a new stock of spare parts **(c)** *(mandato)* command *o* directive *o* order; **órdenes** = directions; **órdenes ministeriales** = orders; **estar a las órdenes de alguien** = to report to someone; **está a las órdenes del director gerente** = he reports direct to the managing director; **la fábrica fue vendida por orden del administrador judicial** = the factory was sold by order of the receiver; **el tribunal no está capacitado para dar órdenes a la autoridad local** = the court is not able to give directions to the local authority **2** *nm* **(a)** *(clasificación)* order *o* arrangement; **orden alfabético** = alphabetical order; **orden cronológico** = chronological order; **orden de importancia** = ranking; **orden numérico** = numerical order **(b)** *(armonía, normalidad)* **¡orden! ¡orden!** = order! order!; **orden público** = public order *o* law and order; **cuestión de orden** = point of order; **llamada al orden** = caution; **llamar al orden** = to caution; **llamar al orden en una reunión** = to bring a meeting to order; **mantener el orden** = to police; **perturbación** *o* **alteración del orden público** = breach of the peace; **planteó una**

cuestión de orden = he raised a point of order; **se alteró el orden público después del asesinato del presidente** = there was a breakdown of law and order following the assassination of the president; **delito contra el orden público** = offence against public order *o* public order offence; **los muchachos fueron puestos en libertad con una llamada al orden** = the boys were let off with a caution; **hubo una seria alteración del orden público** = there was a serious breakdown of law and order **(c)** *(en una reunión)* **orden del día** = agenda; **el orden del día de la reunión del comité** = the committee meeting agenda *o* the agenda of the committee meeting; **después de dos horas, estábamos todavía discutiendo el primer asunto del orden del día** = after two hours we were still discussing the first item on the agenda; **la secretaria puso las finanzas como asunto prioritario del orden del día** = the secretary put finance at the top of the agenda

ordenación *nf (planificación urbana)* zoning

ordenador *nm* computer; **error de ordenador** = computer error; **programa de ordenador** = computer program; **códigos usados por un ordenador** = machine-readable codes

ordenanza *nf* ordinance; **ordenanza municipal** = bylaw *o* byelaw *o* by-law *o* bye-law; **según las ordenanzas municipales, se debe reducir el ruido en el centro de la ciudad** = according to the local bylaws, noise must be limited in the town centre

ordenar *vt* **(a)** *(mandar)* to order *o* to direct *o* to command *o* *(dar instrucciones)* to instruct; **ordenar a alguien que haga algo** = to instruct someone to do something; **el juez ordenó que se despejase la tribuna del público** = the judge commanded that the public gallery should be cleared; **ordenó a la policía que registrara el local** = he ordered the police to search the premises; **ordenó al inspector de préstamos que tomara cartas en el asunto** = he instructed the credit controller to take action; **el gobierno ordenó al ejército que ocupara la estación de radio** = the government ordered the army to occupy the radio station; **el juez ordenó al jurado que absolviera a todos los acusados** = the judge directed the jury to acquit all the defendants; **el Tribunal Superior ordenó al juez de primera instancia la revisión del caso** = the Crown Court directed the justice to rehear the case **(b)** *(clasificar)* to arrange *o* to order; **ordenar los documentos por fechas** = to arrange the documents in order of their dates; **la lista de direcciones está ordenada por países** = the address list is ordered by country; **los archivos están ordenados por orden alfabético** = the files are arranged in alphabetical order

ordinario, -ria *adj* ordinary; **acciones ordinarias** = ordinary shares *o* equities; **accionista ordinario** = ordinary shareholder; **miembro**

ordinario = ordinary member; **resolución ordinaria** = ordinary resolution; **vía ordinaria** = ordinary proceedings

organigrama *nm* flow chart *o* organization chart

organismo *nm* agency; **organismo asesor** = advisory body; **organismo paraestatal** = quango; **organismo público** = government agency

organización *nf* **(organismo)** organization; **Organización de las Naciones Unidas (ONU)** = United Nations (UN); **Organización Internacional del Trabajo (OIT)** = International Labour Organization (ILO); **dirige una organización para la rehabilitación de delincuentes** = he runs an organization for the rehabilitation of criminals **(b)** *(planificación)* organization *o* organizing; **la organización de un mitin de protesta** = the organization of a protest meeting **(c)** *(aparato)* machinery; **la organización del gobierno local** = the local government machinery *o* the machinery of local government

organizado, -da *adj* organized; **crimen organizado** = organized crime *o* racketeering

organizador, -ra *n* organizer *o* convener *o* convenor

organizar *vt* to organize *o* to arrange; **organizó un coche para que le recogiera en el aeropuerto** = she arranged for a car to meet him at the airport

órgano *nm* body *o* agency; **órgano decisorio** = decision-making body; **órgano directivo** = steering committee; **órgano jurisdiccional colegiado** = bench of judges

orientación *nf* direction; **nueva orientación comercial** = departure

origen *nm* **(a)** *(procedencia)* origin; **certificado de origen** = certificate of origin; **país de origen** = country of origin **(b)** *(fuente)* source; **ingresos sujetos a retención en el origen** = income which is taxed at source

original 1 *adj* original; **copia original** = master copy *o* top copy; **copia original de un archivo informático** = master copy of a file; **enviaron una copia de la factura original** = they sent a copy of the original invoice **2** *nm* original *o* master; **el original** = the genuine article; **envíe el original y archive dos copias** = send the original and file two copies

originar *vi* comenzar *o* empezar *o* originar to originate

originariamente *adv* originally

orina *nf* urine; **análisis de orina** = urine test

ostentar *vt* *(cargo, título)* to hold *o* to possess; **ostentar un cargo público** = to hold office

otorgamiento *nm* granting *o* conferring; **otorgamiento de un documento legal** = execution of an instrument

otorgante *nmf* grantor

otorgar *vt* to grant *o* to confer *o* to extend; **otorgar un testamento** = to make a will; **otorgar una escritura** = to execute a deed; **otorgar una licencia** *o* **una patente** = to grant a licence *o* a patent

otro, -tra *adj y pron* **(a)** *(alternativo)* alternative *o* other *o* another; **de otra manera** *o* **de otro modo** = otherwise; **conseguir a alguien otro trabajo** = to find someone alternative employment **(b)** *(adicional)* further; **'y otros'** *o* **'y otras cosas'** = et al. *o* et alia **(c)** *(indirectamente)* **por otro** = vicariously

Pp

pabellón *nm* flag; **pabellón de conveniencia** = flag of convenience; **embarcación que navega con pabellón de conveniencia** = ship sailing under a flag of convenience *o* ship flying a flag of convenience

pactar *vt* to agree; **pactar el pago de una cantidad de dinero al año** = to covenant
◊ **pacto** *nm* covenant *o* compact; **pacto de no agresión** = non-aggression pact; **pacto de retro** *o* **retroventa** = repurchase agreement; **pacto entre caballeros** = gentlemen's agreement; **ejecución de un pacto** = deed of covenant; **pacto social** = social contract

padrastro *nm* step-father

padre *nm* father; **Luis Solá padre** = Luis Solá, Senior; **padres** = parents
◊ **padrastro** *nm* step-father
◊ **padrino** *nm* godfather

padrón *nm* **padrón municipal** = census

paga *nf* pay; **paga extraordinaria** = bonus; **los domingos cobra paga y media** = she is paid time and a half on Sundays
◊ **pagadero, -ra** *adj* payable *o* due; **pagadero a la entrega** = payable on delivery; **pagadero a la vista** = payable on demand; **pagadero a sesenta días** = payable at sixty days; **pagadero por adelantado** = payable in advance; **acciones pagaderas en el momento de la suscripción** = shares payable on application; **cheque pagadero al portador** = cheque made payable to bearer

pagado, -da paid; **con porte pagado** *o* **con franqueo pagado** = post free

pagador, -ra *n* payer

pagar *vt* **(a)** *(gastos)* to pay *o* to bear *o* to defray; **pagar a la vista** = to pay on demand; **pagar al contado** *o* **en efectivo** = to pay cash; **pagar a plazos** = to pay in instalments; **pagar con cheque** = to pay by cheque; **pagar intereses sobre una deuda** = to service a debt; **pagar por adelantado** = to pay in advance; **pagar un interés** = to pay interest; **pagar un cheque** *o* **una letra de cambio** = to honour a cheque *o* a bill; **pagar una deuda** = to honour a debt *o* to pay up; **pagar una entrada** = to pay money down; **pagar una reclamación** = to settle a claim; **pagó finalmente con seis meses de retraso** = he finally paid up six months late; **las empresas constructoras pagan un interés del 10%** = building societies pay interest of 10%; **páguese al Sr Ramos o según indique éste** = pay to Mr Ramos or order; **páguese directamente a la cuenta del Sr Ramos** = pay to the order of Mr Ramos; **¿cuánto dinero más hay que pagarle a la empresa?** = how much is still owing to the company? **(b) a pagar** due *o* payable; **cuentas a pagar** *o* **efectos a pagar** = accounts payable *o* bills payable; **no pagar** = to default; **no pagar los plazos** *o* **las deudas** = to default on payments; **por pagar** = outstanding *o* unpaid; **sin pagar** = gratis *o* outstanding *o* unpaid; **deudas sin pagar** = outstanding debts; **negarse a pagar** = to dishonour; **el banco se negó a pagar su cheque** = the bank dishonoured his cheque; **la empresa no pagó la deuda hasta que nuestro abogado no les envió una carta** = the company paid up only when we sent them a letter from our solicitor **(c)** *(por trabajo realizado)* to pay; **pagamos buenos salarios a los trabajadores especializados** = we pay good wages for skilled workers; **¿cuánto te pagan por hora?** = how much do they pay you per hour?; **pagamos 2.000 ptas por hora** = we pay 2,000 ptas per hour; **no se ha pagado a los trabajadores durante tres semanas** = the workers have not been paid for three weeks **(d)** *(amortizar)* to redeem **(e)** *(reembolsar)* to repay

pagaré *nm* IOU *o* note of hand *o* promissory note; **un pagaré** = a promise to pay; **pagaré de empresa** = debenture bond; **pagaré de favor** = accommodation bill; **pagaré de interés fijo** = debenture; **hacer efectivos un montón de pagarés** = to pay a pile of IOUs

página *nf* page; **páginas amarillas** = commercial directory *o* trade directory

pago *nm* **(a)** *(retribución)* payment *o* settlement; **pago a cuenta** = payment on account; **pago al contado** = cash terms *o* payment in cash *o* cash payment; *(en cheques)* **'pago al contado'** = 'pay cash'; **pago al recibo de la factura** = payment on invoice; **pago aplazado** = deferred payment; **pago atrasado** = back payment; **pago contra reembolso** = cash on delivery; **pago de intereses** = payment of interest *o* interest payment; **pago de liquidación** *o* **de saldo** = payoff; **pago en efectivo** = settlement in cash *o* cash settlement; **pago inicial** = down payment; **pago mediante cheque** *o* **talón** = payment by cheque; **pago parcial** = interim payment *o* part payment; **pago simbólico** = token payment; **pago total** *o* **pago íntegro** *o* **pago de liberación** *o* **pago único** = full payment *o* payment in full *o* lump sum; **acciones de pago preferente** = redeemable preference shares; **aceptar algo como pago íntegro** = to accept something in full settlement; **acuerdo de pago** = accord and satisfaction; **demanda de pago** = call; **día de pago** *o* **de cobro** = pay day; **recibió un pago total de 500.000 ptas** = he received a lump sum payment of 500,000 ptas; **nuestro descuento normal es de un 20% pero ofrecemos un 5% más por pronto pago** = our basic discount is 20% but we offer an extra 5% for rapid settlement **(b)** *(reembolso)* discharge *o* repayment; **en pago total de una deuda** = in full discharge of a debt; **exigir el pago de una deuda** = to call in; **incumplimiento** *o* **omisión** *o* **falta de pago** = default; **incumplir** *o* **retrasar los pagos** = to default on payments; **mandamiento de pago** *o* **orden de ejecución de pago** = warrant of execution; **por falta de pago** *o* **por incumplimiento de pago** = in default of payment; **último pago** = final discharge; **no pudo hacer frente a los pagos de la hipoteca** = he was unable to meet *o* to keep up with his mortgage repayments

país *nm* country *o* nation; **país de origen** = country of origin; **país desarrollado** = developed country; **país endeudado** = debtor nation; **país en vías de desarrollo** = developing country; **productos del país** = home-produced products; **algunos países africanos exportan petróleo** = some African countries export oil; **el contrato cubre las ventas en los países de la Unión Europea** = the contract covers sales in the countries of the European Union

paisano, -na *n* **(a)** *(de un país)* compatriot *o* fellow countryman (*o* countrywoman) **(b)** *(sin uniforme)* **de paisano** = in plain clothes

palabra *nf* word *o* promise *o* *(habla)* speech; **(de) palabra** = parol; **palabra por palabra** = verbatim; **amonestación de palabra** = verbal warning; **bajo palabra (de honor)** = on parole; **ceder la palabra** = to invite someone to speak; **dar la palabra** = to give one's word; **de palabra** = orally; **incumplimiento de palabra** = breach of promise; **una transcripción del juicio palabra por palabra** = a verbatim transcript of the trial
◊ **palabrota** *nf* swearword

paliar *vt* to mitigate; **paliar los daños** *o* **las pérdidas** = to mitigate damages *o* losses

paliza *nf* beating; **recibir una paliza** = to take a beating

palma *nf (bofia)* fuzz

pandilla *nf* gang

panel *nm* panel; **panel de exposición** = display panel

pantalla *nf* screen *o* monitor

papel *nm* **(a)** *(hoja)* paper; **papel carbón** = carbon paper; **papel con membrete** = headed paper; **papel continuo** = continuous stationery; **papel de escribir y sobres** = stationery; **papel de impresora** = copier paper; **papel grueso de los documentos judiciales** = engrossment paper *o* judicature paper; **papel mojado** = dead letter; **papel para máquina de escribir** = typing paper; **papel para multicopista** = duplicating paper; **papel rayado** = lined paper; **papel sellado** *o* **timbrado** = stamped paper; **alimentador del papel** = paper feed; **beneficio sobre el papel** = paper profit; **sobre el papel** = on paper; **pérdida sobre el papel** = paper loss **(b)** *(billete)* **papel moneda** = paper money *o* paper currency **(c)** *(actuación)* **hacer un buen** *o* **mal papel** = to make a good *o* bad impression
◊ **papeles** *nmpl;* *(documentos)* papers; **ha perdido los papeles de la aduana** = he has lost the customs papers; **la oficina requiere los papeles del IVA** = the office is asking for the VAT papers

papeleo *nm* paperwork *o* *(burocracia)* red tape; **la solicitud se ha retrasado por el papeleo** = the application has been held up by red tape

papelera *nf* waste paper basket

papelería *nf* stationery
◊ **papelero** *nm* stationer

papeleta *nf* **(a)** *(para votar)* voting paper *o* ballot paper **(b)** *(recibo)* ticket; **papeleta de empeño** = pawn ticket **(c)** *(asunto difícil de resolver)* **¡Vaya papeleta!** = this is a difficult task!

paquete *nm* **(a)** *(artículos)* lot *o* block *o* pack *o* packet; **compró un paquete de 6.000 acciones** = he bought a block of 6,000 shares **(b)** *(del gobierno)* package; **paquete de medidas** = set of measures

par 1 *nf (valor nominal)* par; **acciones vendidas sobre la par** = shares sold at a premium; **el dólar está sobre la par** = the dollar is at a premium **2** *nm (persona)* peer; *GB* **par hereditario** = hereditary peer; **par vitalicio (miembro vitalicio de la Cámara de los Lores)** = life peer
◊ **paresa** *nf* peeress

para *prep* **para esto** *o* **para el caso** = ad hoc; **un comité para el caso** = an ad hoc committee; '**para la vida de otra persona**' = per autre vie

paradero *nm* whereabouts; **paradero desconocido** = no fixed abode

parado, -da 1 *adj (sin trabajo)* **estar parado** = to be unemployed *o* to be out of work **2** *n*

unemployed person; **los parados** = the unemployed
3 *nf* stop *o* check

paraíso *nm* **paraíso fiscal** *o* **paraíso tributario** =
tax haven

paralizar *vt* to deadlock *o* to paralyze; **la huelga
paralizó el transporte ferroviario** = the strike
closed down the railway system; **las negociaciones
están paralizadas desde hace diez días** = talks
have been deadlocked for ten days

parar *vt* **(a)** *(detener)* to stop *o* to check; **sin parar**
= non-stop *o* without a break; **el juicio duro cinco
horas sin parar** = the case went on for five hours
without a break **(b)** *(reducir)* to cut

parcela *nf* parcel; **se vende una parcela cerca de
la playa** = for sale: a parcel of land near the sea

parcial *adj* **(a)** *(en parte)* partial; **acreedores con
garantía parcial** = partly-secured creditors; **canje
parcial** = part exchange; **cumplimiento parcial de
contrato** = part performance; **elección parcial** =
by-election; **pago parcial** = part payment; **pérdida
parcial** = partial loss; **le concedieron una
indemnización parcial por los daños sufridos en
su casa** = he was awarded partial compensation for
the damage to his house **(b)** *(predispuesto)* partial *o*
prejudiced; **el demandado se quejó de que el juez
era parcial** = the defendant complained that the
judge was partial
◊ **parcialmente** *adv* partly; **acreedores
parcialmente asegurados** = partly-secured
creditors; **capital parcialmente desembolsado** =
partly-paid capital

parcialidad *nf* prejudice

parecer **1** *nm* *(opinión)* view; **al parecer** =
apparently; **ser del parecer** = to be of the opinion;
lo dejo a su parecer = I leave it to your discretion **2**
vi to appear *o* to seem; **'parece'** (palabra utilizada
para discutir una sentencia judicial en la que hay
cierta incertidumbre sobre la intención del
tribunal *o* la validez de la misma) = semble; **hacer
lo que a uno le parezca** *o* **obrar como mejor le
parezca a uno** = to exercise one's discretion; **el
testigo parecía tener dificultad para recordar lo
que había pasado** = the witness appeared to have
difficulty in remembering what had happened

pareja *nf* *(par)* couple; *(en una relación)* partner;
pareja de hecho = common-law marriage *o*
domestic partnership

parentesco *nm* kinship *o* relationship;
parentesco íntimo = close relationship; **grado de
parentesco** = degree of kinship

paridad *nf* parity *o* equivalence; **la libra bajó
hasta alcanzar la paridad con el dólar** = the
pound fell to parity with the dollar

pariente *nmf* relative; **pariente más cercano**
next of kin; **parientes** = relatives *o* relations *o* kin;

parientes consanguíneos = blood relations; **su
único pariente es una tía que vive en Mallorca** =
his only next of kin is an aunt living in Mallorca; **la
policía ha informado a los parientes más
cercanos de las personas muertas en el accidente**
= the police have informed the next of kin of the
people killed in the accident

parlamentario, -ria 1 *adj* parliamentary;
inmunidad parlamentaria = parliamentary
privilege; **Ley Parlamentaria** = Act of Parliament
2 *n* parliamentarian *o* member of parliament

parlamento *nm* parliament; **parlamento
autonómico** = parliament of an autonomous region;
el Parlamento Europeo = the European
Parliament; **conducta que desprestigia al
Parlamento** = contempt of Parliament; **miembro
del Parlamento** = Member of Parliament

paro *nm* unemployment; **en paro** = unemployed;
paro breve = token strike; **paro estacional** =
seasonal unemployment; **paro general** = general
strike; **paro técnico** = work to rule; **subsidio de
paro** = unemployment benefit

párrafo *nm* paragraph; **párrafo de una
disposición legal** = paragraph; **el primer párrafo
de su carta** = the first paragraph of your letter *o*
paragraph one of your letter; **le rogamos se remita
al párrafo del contrato sobre 'instrucciones de
envío'** = please refer to the paragraph in the
contract on 'shipping instructions'

parricidio *nm* patricide

parroquia *nf* parish

parte 1 *nf* **(a)** *(sección)* part *o* cut *o* *(proporción)*
proportion; **parte delantera** = face; **parte inicial** =
premises; **parte superior** = head; **en parte** = in
part; **en gran parte** = largely; **parte del personal
hace horas extraordinarias** = part of the staff is on
overtime; **contribuir a parte de las costas** = to
contribute in part to the costs; **introduce nuevos
clientes y recibe una parte de la comisión del
vendedor** = he introduces new customers and gets a
cut of the salesman's commission; **pagar una parte
de las costas** = to pay the costs in part; **posee la
mayor parte de las acciones de la empresa** = he
has a controlling interest in the company; **se
estropeó una parte del envío** = part of the
shipment was damaged; **se reembolsará una parte
de los gastos** = part of the expenses will be
refunded; **sólo una pequeña parte de nuestras
ventas procede de tiendas al por menor** = only a
small proportion of our sales comes from retail
shops; **una parte de los beneficios brutos se
reserva para imprevistos** = a proportion of the
pretax profit is set aside for contingencies **(b)**
(persona) party; **parte demandada** = defendant;
parte culpable = guilty party; **parte perjudicada** =
aggrieved party; **actuar de parte de alguien** = to
represent; **de una de las partes** *o* **de parte de** = ex

parte; **identidad de las partes** = identity of parties; **'entre las partes'** (vista de un caso en el que las dos partes están representadas) = inter partes; **mostrarse parte en el procedimiento** = to enter a caveat; **según el tribunal el caso debería verse entre las partes lo antes posible** = the court's opinion was that the case should be heard inter partes as soon as possible; **solicitud de una de las partes** = an ex parte application; **una de las partes litigantes ha fallecido** = one of the parties to the suit has died **(c)** *(cuantificación)* quantum **(d)** *(elemento)* element; **las partes de un acuerdo** = the elements of a settlement **2** *nm* report; **parte de un accidente** = accident report; **parte de la policía** = police report; **parte médico** = medical report; **dar parte de** = to report; **dio parte de los daños a la compañía aseguradora** = he reported the damage to the insurance company

partición *nf* partition

participación *nf (interés)* interest *o* share; **participación de capital en una sociedad** = equity; **participación en el mercado** = share in the market; **participación en los beneficios** = share in profits; **participación mayoritaria** *o* **participación minoritaria** = majority interest *o* minority interest; **cuenta en participación** = joint account; **negocio en participación** = joint adventure; **adquirir una participación substancial en una empresa** = to acquire a substantial interest in the company; **declarar una participación en una compañía** = to declare *o* disclose an interest; **tiene una participación mayoritaria en una cadena de supermercados** = he has a majority interest in a supermarket chain

participar *vi* to participate *o* to take part
◊ **partícipe** *nmf* partner; **partícipe en un crimen** *o* **en un delito** = partner in a crime; **hacer partícipe a alguien** = to cut someone in

particular *adj* **(a)** *(personal)* private; **acusación particular** = private prosecution; **daño** *o* **perjuicio a un particular** = private nuisance; **propiedad particular** = private property; **relación particular de las partes contratantes** = privity of contract; **viviendas particulares** = house property **(b)** *(especial)* particular
◊ **particularmente** *adv* in particular

partida *nf* **(a)** *(registro)* certificate; **partida de defunción** = death certificate; **partida de nacimiento** = birth certificate **(b)** *(asiento)* entry *o* item; **partida de gasto** = item of expenditure; **partidas extraordinarias** = extraordinary items; **los auditores observaron varias partidas extraordinarias en las cuentas** = the auditors noted several extraordinary items in the accounts **(c)** *(remesa)* consignment

partido *nm* **(a)** *(política)* party; **partido político** = political party; **partido centrista** = centre party;

cambiar de partido = to cross the floor **(b)** **partido judicial** = legal *o* administrative area; **tomar partido** = to take sides; **sacar partido** = to benefit

partir 1 *vt* **(a)** *(dividir)* to divide *o* to share **(b)** *(cortar)* to split; **partir la diferencia** = to split the diffrence; **le partieron el cráneo** = his skull was split open **2** *vi* to depart; **partir de** = to go on; **a partir de** = starting from; **a partir del 1 de enero los precios aumentarán un 10%** = prices are increased 10% with effect from January 1st

pasado, -da 1 *adj* past *o* previous *o* last; **la semana pasada** *o* **el mes pasado** *o* **el año pasado** = last week *o* last month *o* last year; **la contabilidad del año pasado tiene que estar lista para la Junta General Ordinaria** = last year's accounts have to be ready by the AGM **2** *nm* the past *o* the background

pasante *nmf* junior clerk *o* trainee *o* law clerk; **pasante de abogado** = articled clerk *o* legal executive; **trabajar como pasante (servir bajo contrato a un abogado para aprender derecho)** = to serve articles

pasantía *nf* clerkship *o* pupillage

pasaporte *nm* passport; **titular de un pasaporte** = passport holder; **su pasaporte ha expirado** = his passport is out of date; **tiene pasaporte británico** = she is a British passport holder; **tuvimos que mostrar los pasaportes en el puesto de aduana** = we had to show our passports at the customs post; **el oficial selló mi pasaporte** = the passport officer stamped my passport

pasar 1 *vt* **(a)** *(transmitir)* to pass *o* to hand *o* *(propiedad)* to hand down; **pasar información** = to pass on *o* to leak information; **la casa ha ido pasando de padres a hijos desde el siglo XIX** = the house has been handed down from father to son since the nineteenth century **(b)** *(de un lugar a otro)* **pasar algo por la aduana** = to effect customs clearance; **pasar contrabando** = to smuggle **(c)** *(dedicar tiempo)* to spend (time); **el presidente se pasó la tarde de ayer con los auditores** = the chairman spent yesterday afternoon with the auditors; **pasaron cinco meses en el extranjero** = they spent five months abroad **(d)** *(suplantar)* **hacer pasar una cosa por otra** = to pass something off as something else **(e)** *(cambiar de actividad, ramificarse)* **la banda pasó al robo de coches** = the gang branched out into car theft **(f)** **pasar por alto** *o* **dejar pasar** = to overlook; **en este caso pasaremos por alto el retraso** = in this instance we will overlook the delay; **el tribunal pasó por alto el hecho de que el coche del demandado no estaba asegurado** = the court overlooked the fact that the defendant's car was not insured **(g)** *(cuentas)* **pasar factura** = to invoice; **pasar un asiento a una cuenta** = to post an entry **(h)** *(informática)* **pasar a máquina** = to type *o* to keyboard; **pasar datos al**

ordenador = to input information *o* to key in data
(i) *(aprobar)* **pasar una prueba** *o* **un examen** = to
pass an exam *o* examination **2** *vi* **(a)** *(atravesar)* to
go though; **el autobús pasa por el centro** = the bus
goes through the centre; **pasar por la aduana** = to
go through customs; **pasar el control de aduanas** =
to clear customs; **no se puede pasar** = you can't go
through **(b)** *(suceder)* to happen; **¿qué ha pasado?**
= what happened?; **¿qué pasa?** = what is going on?
(c) *(exceder)* **pasar de la raya** = to overstep the
mark **(d)** *(impersonar)* **hacerse pasar por otra
persona** = to impersonate; **consiguió entrar en la
casa haciéndose pasar por un inspector de las
autoridades locales** = he gained entrance to the
house by impersonating a local authority inspector;
**le acusaron de haberse hecho pasar por un
oficial de policía** = he was charged with
impersonation of a police officer **(e) pasar a
disposición judicial** = to be brought before a
magistrate's court; **pasar a la clandestinidad** = to
go into hiding
◊ **pasarse** *vr* **(a)** *(excederse)* to go too far *o* to
overdo it **(b)** *(cambiar)* to switch over; **pasarse al
campo contrario** = to switch to the opposite side

pase *nm* pass *o* permit; **necesita un pase para
entrar en las oficinas del ministerio** = you need a
pass to enter the ministry offices; **todos los
miembros del personal deben mostrar su pase** =
all members of staff must show a pass

pasivo, -va 1 *adj* **resistencia pasiva** = civil
disobedience **2** nm *(deudas)* liabilities; **pasivo a
largo plazo** = long-term liabilities; **pasivo
circulante** = current liabilities; **el balance general
muestra el activo y el pasivo de la empresa** = the
balance sheet shows the company's assets and
liabilities; **el grupo planeó una campaña de
resistencia pasiva en protesta contra las
restricciones a los** *o* **de inmigrantes** = the group
planned a campaign of civil disobedience as a
protest against restrictions on immigrants

paso *nm* **(a)** *(camino)* way; **paso de peatones** =
zebra-crossing; **servidumbre de paso** *o* **derecho de
paso** = access *o* right of way *o* easement **(b)**
(movimiento) **paso a paso** = step by step; **dar el
primer paso** = to make the first move; **dar un paso
en falso** = to make a false move *o* to take a false step

patentado, -da *adj* patented *o* proprietary

patentar *vt* **patentar un invento** = to patent an
invention *o* to take out a patent for an invention

patente 1 *adj* *(evidente)* patent **2** *nf* patent **(a)**
(licencia) **patente de navegación** = certificate of
registry; **patente de sanidad** = bill of health **(b)** *(de
inventos y marcas)* patent; **patente de invención** =
letters patent; **patente solicitada** *o* **patente en
trámite** *o* **pendiente de patente** = patent applied
for *o* patent pending; **agente de patentes y marcas**
= patent agent; **derechos de patente** = patent

rights; **descripción de una patente** = patent
specification; **encargado, -da de examinar
patentes** = patent examiner; **número de patente** =
patent number; **oficina** *o* **registro de patentes y
marcas** = patents office; **poseedor, -ra de una
patente** = patentee; **pérdida legal de una patente
(por falta de pago)** = to forfeit a patent; **sacar la
patente de un invento** = to take out a patent for an
invention; **sacar una patente para un nuevo tipo
de bombilla** = to take out a patent for a new type of
light bulb; **solicitar la patente de un nuevo
invento** = to apply for a patent for a new invention;
solicitar una patente = to file a patent application;
titular de una patente = patent holder; **violación
de patente** = infringement of patent *o* patent
infringement; **violar una patente** = to infringe a
patent; **se le ha concedido la patente de su invento**
= he has received a grant of patent for his invention

paternidad *nf* paternity; **litigio de paternidad** =
paternity action *o* suit; **permiso** *o* **licencia por
paternidad** = paternity leave

patíbulo *nm* *(cadalso)* scaffold *o* gallows

patología *nf* pathology
◊ **patólogo, -ga** *n* pathologist

patria *nf* **(a)** *(país de origen)* native country; **sin
patria** = stateless person **(b)** *(custodia)* **patria
potestad** = custody *o* care and control; **juicio para
otorgar la patria potestad** = care proceedings;
**orden que retira la patria potestad y otorga la
custodia de un menor a una autoridad local** =
care order

La patria potestad consiste en el conjunto
deberes y derechos que tienen los
progenitores para con sus hijos menores de
edad no emancipados

patrimonio *nm* patrimony *o* heritage;
patrimonio cultural = cultural heritage;
Patrimonio del Estado = Crown Lands;
Patrimonio Nacional = Crown property *o* national
heritage; **impuesto sobre el patrimonio** = property
tax *o* tax on property

Los bienes muebles e inmuebles propiedad
del Estado y adscritas al uso de la Corona
forman el Patrimonio Nacional, antiguamente
Patrimonio Real. Los demás bienes del
Estado constituyen el Patrimonio del Estado

patrón *nm* **(a)** *(empresario)* employer **(b)**
(modelo) standard; **patrón oro** = gold standard

patronal 1 *adj* *(del empresario)* **cuota patronal**
= employer's contribution; **organización patronal**
= employer's association **2** *nf* the management; **los
sindicatos y la patronal** = the unions and the
management

patronato *nm* (a) *(corporación)* employer's organization *o* management (b) *(fundación)* trust *o* board of trustees

patrono, -na *n* employer; **patrono y empleado** = master and servant

patrulla *nf* patrol; **patrulla de policía** = police patrol; **coche patrulla** = patrol car *o* squad car; **de patrulla** = on patrol

patrullar *vt* to patrol; **patrullando** = on patrol; **patrullando a pie** = on foot patrol; **grupos de policía antidisturbios patrullaban por el centro de la ciudad** = groups of riot police were patrolling the centre of the town; **tenemos seis coches patrullando en el centro de la ciudad** = we have six squad cars on patrol in the centre of the town

pauta *nf* (a) *(directrices)* guidelines (b) *(norma)* pattern; **la pauta general del crimen en el centro de las ciudades es diferente de la del campo** = the pattern of crime in the inner cities is different from the pattern in the country

paz *nf* peace; **juez de paz** justice of the peace *o* lay magistrate; **juzgado de paz** = magistrates' court; **mantener la paz** = to keep the peace; **se le obligó a mantener la paz** = he was bound over to keep the peace; **ambos lados afirman que la otra parte rompió el acuerdo de paz** = both sides claimed the other side broke the peace agreement; **ayer se firmó el tratado de paz** = the peace treaty was signed yesterday; **tras seis años de guerra civil, el país está ahora en paz** = after six years of civil war, the country is now at peace

P.D. = POSDATA post scriptum (P.S.)

peaje *nm* toll

peaton *nm* pedestrian; **zona reservada para peatones** = pedestrian precinct
◊ **peatonal** *adj* pedestrian; **zona peatonal** = pedestrian precinct

pecios *nmpl* **pecios y echazón** = flotsam and jetsam

peculio *nm* one's own money *o* savings

pecuniario, -ria *adj* pecuniary; **no sacó ninguna ventaja pecuniaria** = he gained no pecuniary advantage

pedido, -da 1 *adj (encargado)* on order 2 *nm* order *o (orden de compra de un importador)* = indent; **pedidos pendientes** = back orders *o* outstanding orders; **pedidos por teléfono** = telephone orders; **pedidos por servir** = dues; **hacer un pedido** = to order *o* to indent for something; **libro de pedidos** = order book; **el departamento ha cursado un pedido para comprar un nuevo ordenador** = the department has indented for a new computer; **hacer un pedido de veinte archivos** = to give someone an order *o* to place an order with

someone for twenty filing cabinets; **servir** *o* **entregar un pedido** = to fill *o* to fulfil an order

pedir *vt* (a) *(solicitar)* to ask *o* ask for *o* to solicit *o* to request; **pedir ayuda al Estado** = to request assistance from the government; **pedir la palabra** = to request the floor *o* to ask to be allowed to speak; **pedir información** = to inquire; **pedir perdón** = to ask forgiveness *o* to apologize; **pedir prestado** = to borrow; **pedir un préstamo** = to ask for a loan /; **pedir la devolución de un préstamo** = to call in a loan; **pedir un trabajo** = to apply for a job; **el juez pidió al testigo que escribiera el nombre en un papel** = the judge asked the witness to write the name on a piece of paper; **el testigo pidió permiso para prestar declaración sentado** = the witness requested permission to give evidence sitting down; **los agentes de policía pidieron a los manifestantes que se fueran a casa** = the police officers asked the marchers to go home; **los funcionarios de la aduana le pidieron que abriera su maleta** = the customs officials asked him to open his case; **pidió a su secretario que fuera a buscar un archivo del despacho del director gerente** = she asked her secretary to fetch a file from the managing director's office (b) *(exigir)* to require *o* to claim *o* to seek; **pedir una indemnización por daños** *o* **pérdida** = to put in a claim for damage *o* loss; **piden una indemnización por la pérdida de ingresos** = they are seeking damages for loss of revenue; **acreedor que pide una orden de intervención judicial según la legislación sobre quiebras** = a creditor seeking a receiving order under the Bankruptcy Act; **el proyecto de ley exige que un asistente social pida permiso al tribunal de menores** = the Bill requires a social worker to seek permission of the Juvenile Court; **el solicitante pidió una revisión judicial para anular la orden** = the applicant sought judicial review to quash the order (c) *(cobrar)* to charge; **¿cuánto pide?** = how much does he charge?; **piden 24.000 libras por el coche** = they are asking £24,000 for the car (d) *(hacer un pedido)* to order (e) *(acudir a)* **pedir a** = to call on; **el ministro pidió a los dirigentes de la comunidad que ayudaran en la prevención de los delitos callejeros** = the minister called on community leaders to help prevent street crime (f) *(rogar)* to pray *o* to beg

pegar *vt* to strike *o* to beat *o* to knock; **los guardianes pegaron al prisionero para hacerle confesar** = the warders beat the prisoner to make him confess

peinar *vt* to comb; **peinar la zona** = to comb the area

peligro *nm* (a) *(riesgo)* danger *o* hazard *o* peril *o* risk; **peligro de incendio** = fire hazard *o* fire risk; **peligros del mar** = perils of the sea *o* maritime perils; **peligros no previstos** = unforeseen hazards;

en peligro de = in danger of; **estar en peligro** = to be in jeopardy *o* in danger; **poner en peligro** = to risk *o* to endanger *o* to jeopardize; **poner en peligro a los pasajeros de un tren** = endangering railway passengers; **daño criminal en el que se pone en peligro la vida** = criminal damage endangering life; **está poniendo en peligro su trabajo al quejarse a la policía** = he is risking his job by complaining to the police; **no hay peligro que la vista del caso sea a corto plazo** = there is no danger of the case being heard early; **su arresto por conducir en estado de embriaguez puede poner en peligro su trabajo como médico especialista en puericultura** = her arrest for drunken driving may jeopardize her work as a doctor specializing in child care **(b) sin peligro** = safely

◊ **peligroso, -sa** *adj* dangerous *o* unsafe; *(arriesgado)* risky; **arma peligrosa** = dangerous weapon *o* offensive weapon; **drogas peligrosas** = dangerous drugs; **trabajo peligroso** = dangerous job

◊ **peligrosamente** *adv* dangerously; **conducir peligrosamente** = careless driving *o* driving without due care and attention

peligrosidad *nf* danger; **plus de peligrosidad** = danger money; **los trabajadores han hecho un paro laboral en petición de un plus de peligrosidad** = the workers have stopped work and asked for danger money

pelotón *nm* squad; **pelotón de ejecución** *o* **de fusilamiento** = firing squad

pena *nf (castigo)* punishment *o* penalty; **pena ampliada** = extended sentence; **pena capital** *o* **pena de muerte** = capital punishment *o* death penalty; **condena a** *o* **sentencia de muerte** = death sentence; **pena máxima** = maximum sentence; **el presidente ha introducido la pena de muerte por determinados delitos contra el estado** = the president has introduced the death penalty for certain crimes against the state

penal 1 *adj* penal *o* criminal; **antecedentes penales** = criminal record; **cláusula penal** = penalty clause; **código penal** = penal code; **culpa penal** = criminal negligence; **daño penal** = criminal damage; **derecho penal** = criminal law; **edad de responsabilidad penal** = age of criminal responsibility; **institución penal** = penal institution; **las leyes penales** = penal laws; **sistema penal** = the penal system; **tribunal penal** *o* **juzgado de lo penal** = criminal court; **el acusado no tenía antecedentes penales** = the accused had no criminal record **2** *nm (penitenciaría)* prison *o* penal *o* convict settlement *o* penal colony *o* (US) penitentiary

◊ **penalidad** *nf* penalty

◊ **penalista** *nmf* criminal lawyer *o* expert in criminal law

penalización *nf* penalty; **cláusula de penalización** = penalty clause; **el contrato contiene una cláusula de penalización que multa a la empresa en un 1% por cada semana que se retrasa la fecha de cumplimiento** = the contract contains a penalty clause which fines the company 1% for every week the completion date is late

penalizar *vt* to penalize; **se les penalizó por un servicio deficiente** = they were penalized for bad service; **penalizar a un proveedor por entregas tardías** = to penalize a supplier for late deliveries

penar *vt (castigar)* to penalize

pendiente *adj (sin resolver)* pending *o* outstanding *o* unsolved; **pendiente de resolución** = sub judice *o* pending decision; **cuestiones pendientes** = matters arising; **cuestiones pendientes de la reunión anterior** = matters outstanding from the previous meeting; **delitos pendientes** = outstanding offences; **deudas pendientes** = outstanding debts; **esta ley está pendiente** = this law is in abeyance; **manutención pendiente de litigio** = maintenance pending suit; **pedidos pendientes** = outstanding orders; **reclamación pendiente de pago** = unliquidated claim

penetrar *vi* to enter; **penetrar por la fuerza (para robar)** = to break in; **la compañía ha gastado millones intentando penetrar el mercado del bricolaje** = the company has spent millions trying to enter the do-it-yourself market; **los ladrones penetraron a través de una ventana trasera de la casa** = burglars broke in through a window at the back of the house

penitenciaría *nf* prison *o* (US) penitentiary; **la penitenciaría del estado de Pensilvania** = the Pennsylvania State Penitentiary

penitenciario, -ria 1 *adj* **centro penitenciario** = prison; **institución penitenciaria** = penal institution; **director de un centro penitenciario** = prison governor **2** *nm* prison

penología *nf* penology

pensar *vt* to think; **pensar que** = to take the view that; **sin pensar** = without thinking; **sin pensarlo dos veces** = out of hand

pensión *nf (a) (anualidad)* pension; **pensión anual** = annuity; **pensión de jubilación** *o* **pensión de retiro** *o* **pensión de vejez** = retirement pension *o* old age pension; **pensión de manutención provisional hasta la celebración del juicio** = maintenance pending suit; **pensión de viudedad** = widow's pension; **pensión vitalicia** = life annuity *o* annuity for life; **cuotas de pensión** *o* **contribuciones al fondo de pensiones** = pension contributions; **derecho a percibir una pensión** = pension entitlement; **fondo de pensiones** = pension fund; **plan de pensiones** = pension plan *o* pension scheme; **plan de pensiones de la empresa** *o* **pensión laboral** occupational pension; **plan de pensiones con contribución del empleado** *o* **plan de pensiones contributivo** = contributory pension scheme; **plan de pensiones gratuito** = non-contributory pension scheme; **plan de pensiones personal** = personal pension plan; **plan de pensiones proporcional** = graduated pension scheme **(b)** *(manutención)* maintenance; **pensión alimenticia (entre cónyuges)** = alimony; **pensión alimenticia durante el litigio** = alimony pending suit *o* pendente lite; **pensión alimenticia pagadera al compañero, -ra o excónyugue tras la separación o el divorcio** palimony; **volvió a solicitar la pensión alimenticia** = she reapplied for a maintenance order **(b)** *(subsidio)* benefit; **pensión de invalidez** = disability benefit; **pensión de jubilación** = old age pension; **la pensión por enfermedad se paga mensualmente** = the sickness benefit is paid monthly

◊ **pensionista** *nmf* **(a)** *(jubilado)* pensioner *o* old age pensioner *o* OAP **(b)** *(que recibe anualidad)* annuitant

peón *nm* labourer

peor *adj* worse

pequeño, -ña *adj* **(a)** *(menor)* small *o* minor; **accionistas pequeños** = minor shareholders; **a pequeña escala** = small-scale; **más pequeño** = lesser **(b)** *(insignificante)* petty

per cápita *adv* per capita; **gastos per cápita** = per capita expenditure; **ingresos medios per cápita** = average income per capita *o* per capita income

percibir *vt* **(a)** *(recibir)* to earn; **sin percibir sueldo** = voluntarily **(b)** *(notar)* to perceive

perder *vt* **(a)** *(dejar de tener)* to lose; **perder el derecho a algo** = to forfeit; **perder el tiempo** = to waste time; **perder la dirección** *o* **la participación mayoritaria** *o* **el control de una empresa** = to lose control of a company; **perder la fianza (por no comparecer ante los tribunales)** = to estreat; **perder un pedido** = to lose an order; **perder una entrada** *o* **un depósito** = to forfeit a deposit; **salir perdiendo** = to lose out; **perdió 25 millones de ptas en la empresa de ordenadores de su padre** = he lost 25 million ptas in his father's computer company; **perdió el juicio por indemnización** = she lost her case for compensation; **perdió su empleo cuando la fábrica cerró** = she lost her job when the factory closed; **perdió el recurso presentado al Tribunal Supremo** = he lost his appeal to the Supreme Court; **durante la huelga, la empresa perdió seis pedidos frente a competidores americanos** = during the strike, the company lost six orders to American competitors; **la libra ha perdido valor** = the pound has lost value; **perdió todo lo que tenía cuando su empresa fue disuelta** = he lost all he possessed

when his company was put into liquidation; **la empresa ha salido perdiendo al precipitarse a fabricar ordenadores a bajo precio** = the company has lost out in the rush to make cheap computers; **le acusaron de hacer perder el tiempo al tribunal** *o* **a la policía** = he was accused of wasting the court's time *o* of wasting police time **(b)** **hacer perder a alguien** = to vote out; **el gobierno perdió las elecciones al cabo de un año** = the government was voted out of office within a year **(b)** **echar a perder** = to spoil; **los resultados de la empresa se echaron a perder por el último trimestre** = the company's results were spoiled by the last quarter

pérdida *nf* **(a)** *(acción de perder)* loss; **pérdida de la nacionalidad** = loss of nationality; **pérdida de peso** = loss in weight; **pérdida del puesto de trabajo** = loss of employment *o* redundancy; **pérdida del derecho a unas acciones por no haberlas reclamado** = forfeiture of shares; **pérdida de un derecho** = forfeiture; **pérdida de un familiar** = bereavement; **pérdida de una desgravación impositiva que había sido concedida** = clawback; **pérdida de valor de un terreno por deterioro o desgaste** = waste; **pérdida legal de algún derecho como castigo** = forfeit; **pérdida durante el transporte** = loss in transport; **pérdida parcial** = partial loss; **pérdida por siniestro** = accidental loss; **pérdida total** = dead loss; **indemnización por pérdida de empleo** = compensation for loss of office **(b)** *(reducción de beneficios)* loss; **pérdida de beneficios** = loss of profits; **pérdida de capital** = capital loss; **pérdida del ejercicio** = trading loss; **compensación por pérdida de ganancias** = compensation for loss of earnings; **cuenta de pérdidas y ganancias** = profit and loss account; **frenar las pérdidas** = to cut one's losses; **hacer constar una pérdida en el balance de resultados** = to report a loss; **la empresa sufrió pérdidas** = the company suffered a loss **(c)** **con pérdidas** = at a loss *o* out of pocket; **la empresa opera con pérdidas** = the company is trading at a loss; **vendió la tienda con pérdida** = he sold the shop at a loss **(d)** *(cosas que se pierden)* **pérdidas** wastage

perdón *nm* **(a)** *(condonación)* forgiveness *o* condonation *o* pardon *o* *(indulto)* free pardon **(b)** *(disculpa)* **pedir perdón** = to apologize; **pidió perdón por llegar tarde** = she apologized for being late

perdonar *vt/i* **(a)** *(condonar)* to condone *o* to pardon *o* to remit; **perdonar la vida a alguien** = to spare someone's life; **perdonar una deuda** = to remit a debt **(b)** *(disculpar)* to excuse *o* to forgive **(d)** *(dispensar de)* to let off

perentorio, -ria *adj* peremptory; **excepción perentoria** = demurrer

perfeccionar *vt* to perfect; **perfeccionó el proceso para fabricar acero de alta calidad** = he perfected the process for making high quality steel

perfecto, -ta *adj* perfect; **perfecto derecho** = perfect right; **comprobamos cada envío para asegurarnos de que está en perfecto estado** = we check each shipment to make sure it is perfect; **hizo una prueba de mecanografía perfecta** = she did a perfect typing test
◊ **perfectamente** *adv* perfectly; **le oyó perfectamente** = she heard it perfectly

perfilar *vt* to outline; **el presidente perfiló los planes de la empresa para el próximo año** = the chairman outlined the company's plans for the coming year

pergeñar *vt* to draft

pericia *nf* expertise
◊ **pericial** *adj* **informe pericial** = expert's report; **testigo pericial** = expert witness *o* professional witness

periferia *nf (extrarradio de la ciudad)* periphery; **vive en la periferia** = he lives in the commuter belt

periódico, -ca 1 *adj* periodic *o* periodical; **arrendamiento periódico** *o* **alquiler periódico** = periodic tenancy; **pagos periódicos** = periodical payments; **revista periódica** *o* **publicación periódica** = periodical 2 *nm (diario)* paper; **periódico gratuito** = free paper *o* giveaway paper

periodo *nm (plazo de tiempo)* period *o* term
◊ **periodo contable** = accounting period; **periodo de arrendamiento** = term of a lease; **periodo de conservación de un producto** = shelf life of a product
◊ **periodo de cotización necesario para tener derecho a una ayuda o subsidio** = qualifying period; **periodo de gracia** = period of grace; **periodo de prueba** = qualifying period; **periodo de prueba (en un empleo)** = probation; **periodo fijo de tiempo (de un arrendamiento)** = term of years; **periodo mínimo de tiempo cotizable para poder ser beneficiario de una prestación o ayuda** = period of qualification; **para un corto periodo de tiempo** = on a short-term basis; **para un largo periodo de tiempo** = on a long-term basis; **por un periodo de meses** *o* **de tiempo** = for a period of months *o* of time; **se le ha nombrado para un breve periodo de tiempo** = he has been appointed on a short-term basis

perito, -ta 1 *adj* expert *o* skilled 2 *n* (a) *(experto)* expert; **perito testigo** = expert witness (b) *(tasador)* adjuster; **perito de averías** = average adjuster *o* loss adjuster

perjudicado, -da *adj* damaged *o* injured; **parte perjudicada** = injured party

perjudicar *vt* to prejudice *o* to affect *o* to damage to hurt *o* to harm *o* to injure; **perjudicar la demanda de alguien** = to prejudice someone's claim; **alegó que el artículo periodístico perjudicaba la reputación de la compañía** = he alleged that the newspaper article was damaging to the company's reputation; **el mal tiempo perjudicó la venta de ropa de verano** = sales of summer clothes were hurt by the bad weather; **la compañía no se ha visto perjudicada por la recesión** *o* **la recesión no ha perjudicado a la compañía** = the company has not been hurt by the recession

perjudicial *adj* (a) *(dañino)* detrimental *o* injurious; **acción perjudicial para el mantenimiento del orden público** = action detrimental to the maintenance of public order (b) *(ofensivo)* noxious; **olor perjudicial** = noxious smell

perjuicio *nm* (a) *(detrimento)* prejudice *o* detriment; **actuar en perjuicio de una demanda** = to act to the prejudice of a claim; **la falsificación es la copia de un documento verdadero, de manera que es aceptado como auténtico en perjuicio de alguien** = forgery is the copying of a real document, so that it is accepted as genuine to someone's prejudice; **sin perjuicio** = without prejudice; **sin causar perjuicio a su reclamación** = without detriment to his claim; **su acción causó perjuicio al demandante** = his action was to the detriment of the plaintiff (b) *(daño)* damage *o* harm *o* wrong *o* injury; **perjuicio de derechos** = miscarriage of justice; **perjuicio material** = real injury; **daños y perjuicios** = damages; **acción por daños y perjuicios** = action for damages; **causar perjuicios** = to cause damage; **entablar una demanda** *o* **llevar a los tribunales por daños y perjuicios** = to bring an action for damages against someone; **exigir** *o* **pagar 100.000 ptas por daños y perjuicios** = to claim *o* to pay 100,000 ptas in damages; **indemnización por daños y perjuicios** = compensatory damages; **presentar una demanda por daños y perjuicios contra alguien** = to bring an action for damages against someone (c) **perjuicio privado o particular** = private nuisance; **perjuicio público** = public nuisance *o* common nuisance

perjurar *vt (dar falso testimonio)* to perjure oneself
◊ **perjurio** *nm (falso testimonio)* perjury; **compareció ante el tribunal por una acusación de perjurio** = she appeared in court on a charge of perjury *o* on a perjury charge; **se le condenó a prisión por perjurio** = he was sent to prison for perjury

permanecer *vi* **hospedarse** *o* **permanecer** *o* **quedarse** *o* **alojarse** to remain *o* to stay

permanencia *nf* stay *o* permanency
◊ **permanente** *adj* standing *o* permanent *o* chronic; **comisión (parlamentaria) permanente** = standing committee

◊ **permanentemente** *adv* permanently

permiso *nm* **(a)** *(autorización)* permission *o* sanction *o* leave; **permiso carcelario** = parole; **permiso escrito** = written permission; **conceder un permiso** = to license; **dar permiso a alguien para hacer algo** = to give someone permission to do something; **dar un permiso carcelario** = to parole; **dio permiso a su vecino para utilizar su campo** = he granted his neighbour a licence to use his field; **el abogado solicitó permiso del tribunal para mostrar una película que se tomó del accidente** = counsel asked leave of the court to show a film taken of the accident **(b)** *(licencia)* permit *o* licence *o* (US) license; **permiso de conducir** = driving licence; **permiso de construcción** = building permit; **permiso de descarga** = landing order; **permiso de entrada** = entry permit; **permiso de residencia en EE.UU** = green card; **permiso de trabajo** = work permit; **permiso provisional de un proyecto de planeamiento urbanístico** *o* **permiso provisional para edificar** = outline planning permission **(c)** *(baja)* leave *o* leave of absence; **permiso por enfermedad** = sick leave; **permiso por maternidad** = maternity leave; **con su permiso** = 'by your leave'; **estar de permiso** = to go on leave *o* to be on leave

permitir *vt* **(a)** *(autorizar)* to permit *o* to enable *o* to allow *o* to let; **este documento permite la exportación de veinticinco sistemas informáticos** = this document permits the export of twenty-five computer systems; **el billete permite la entrada de tres personas a la exposición** = the ticket permits three people to go into the exhibition; **no está permitido** = it is not allowed; **no se permite el paso de visitantes a las celdas de los prisioneros** = visitors are not allowed into the prisoners' cells; **el juez permitió que el detenido hablase con su mujer** = the magistrate let the prisoner speak to his wife **(b)** *(aprobar)* to sanction

permuta *nf* exchange

perpetrador, -ra *n* perpetrator

perpetrar *vt* to perpetrate *o* to commit; **perpetrar un delito** = to commit a crime

perpetuo, -tua *adj* **(a)** *(condena)* life; **cadena perpetua** = life imprisonment *o* life sentence; **condenado a cadena perpetua** = lifer **(b)** **obligación perpetua** = irredeemable bond

per se *frase latina* **procesable per se** = actionable per se

persecución *nf* **en persecución** = in pursuit

persona *nf* **(a)** person *o* persona; **persona a cargo** = dependant; **persona autorizada** = licensee; **persona con derecho a protección** = protected person; **persona física** = individual; **persona jurídica** = legal person *o* legal personality *o* artificial person; **persona no grata** = persona non

grata; **a la persona** = bodily; **daño físico a la persona** = actual bodily harm (ABH); **daño grave a la persona** = grievous bodily harm (GBH); 'contra una persona' = in personam; **acción contra una persona** = personal action *o* action in personam; **en persona** = in person *o* in chief *o* personally; **hacerse pasar por otra persona** = to impersonate; **la persona asegurada** = the life assured *o* the life insured; **las personas que figuran en el contrato** = the persons named in the contract; **litigante en persona, que inicia un proceso judicial y defiende personalmente su causa ante el tribunal** = litigant in person; **este importante paquete debe ser entregado al presidente en persona** = this important package is to be delivered to the chairman in person **(b)** /G (cabeza) head; **calcula 5.000 ptas para gastos por persona** = allow 5,000 ptas per head for expenses; **los representantes cuestan por término medio 5 millones de ptas al año por persona** = representatives cost on average 5 million ptas per head per annum **(c)** *(parte interesada)* party; **por persona interpuesta** = through the agency of a third party

personal 1 *adj* *(propio de una persona)* personal *o* private; **acción personal** = personal action *o* action in personam; **bienes muebles personales** = personal assets; **efectos personales** = private effects; **daños personales** = personal injury; **deducciones personales** = personal allowances; **ordenador personal** = personal computer; **renta personal** *o* **ingresos personales** = personal income **(b)** *(privado)* private *o* personal; **cliente personal** = private client *o* private customer; **secretario, -ria personal** = personal assistant; **quiero ver al director para un asunto personal** = I want to see the director on a personal matter **2** *nm* **(a)** *(plantilla)* establishment; **formar parte del personal** = to be on the establishment; **gastos de personal** = establishment charges **(b)** *(empleados)* *nmpl* personnel *o* staff; **personal administrativo** *o* **de oficina** = office staff *o* clerical staff; **director de personal** *o* **jefe de personal** = personnel officer; **la dirección ha ofrecido un aumento al personal** = the management has made an increased offer to the labour force; **todo el personal tiene que firmar la Ley relativa a los Secretos Oficiales** = all the personnel have to sign the Official Secrets Act

◊ **personalmente** *adv* personally *o* in person; **me escribió personalmente** = she wrote to me personally; **vino a verme personalmente** = he came to see me in person

personalidad *nf* personality; **personalidad jurídica** = legal personality *o* legal status; **personalidad jurídica de una sociedad anónima** = corporate personality; **personalidad procesal** = legal capacity; **suplantar la personalidad** to impersonate *o* personate; **suplantación** *o*

usurpación de la personalidad = impersonation *o* personation

personarse *vr (comparecer)* to appear; **personarse en el procedimiento** = to enter a caveat

personificación *nf* impersonation

persuadir *vt* (a) *(convencer)* to persuade *o* to convince; **persuadir a alguien para hacer algo** = to prevail upon someone to do something; **tras diez horas de debate, persuadieron al demandante para que aceptara un acuerdo amistoso** = after ten hours of discussion, they persuaded the plaintiff to accept an out-of-court settlement; **no pudimos persuadir a la empresa francesa para que firmara el contrato** = we could not persuade the French company to sign the contract (a) *(inducir)* to induce; **le persuadieron de que robara los planos ofreciéndole una gran suma de dinero** = he was induced to steal the plans by an offer of a large amount of money

pertenecer *vi* to belong to *o* to belong with; **pertenecer a la judicatura** = to be on the bench; **pertenecer a la plantilla** = to be on the staff; **la empresa pertenece a una tradicional familia americana de banqueros** = the company belongs to an old American banking family; **la patente pertenece al hijo del inventor** = the patent belongs to the inventor's son
◊ **perteneciente** *adj* **perteneciente a** = appurtenant; **tierra** *o* **edificaciones pertenecientes a una propiedad** = appurtenances
◊ **pertenencias** *nfpl* appurtenances

pertinencia *nf* relevance

pertinente *adj (apropiado)* relevant *o* material; **¿puede darme los documentos pertinentes?** can you give me the relevant papers?; **la pregunta no es pertinente** = the question is not relevant to the case; **prueba pertinente** = material evidence

perturbación *nf* **perturbación del orden público** = breach of the peace

perturbado, -da *adj* unsound; **perturbado mental** = of unsound mind *o* mentally unbalanced

perturbador, -ra *n* agitator

perturbar *vt* to disturb the peace

pervertido, -da *n* pervert

pervertir *vt* to deprave *o* to pervert

pesado, -da *adj* onerous

pesar *nm* **a pesar de** = notwithstanding; **el juicio prosiguió a pesar de las objeciones del acusado** = the case proceeded notwithstanding the objections of the defendant *o* the defendant's objections notwithstanding

pesca *nf* **pesca furtiva** = poaching

pescar *vt (argot)* (a) *(pillar)* to cop *o* to nick (b) *(agarrar)* to pinch

peso *nm* weight; **peso trucado** *o* **peso falso** false weight; **demanda** *o* **acción de poco peso** = frivolous complaint *o* frivolous action; **límite de peso** *o* **peso máximo** = weight limit

petición *nf* (a) *(solicitud)* petition *o* application *o* appeal; **petición de divorcio** = divorce petition; **petición de orden judicial** = motion; **petición de nuevo juicio** = motion for a new trial; **aviso de petición al tribunal** = notice of motion; **petición de quiebra** = bankruptcy petition; **petición de un trabajo** = application for a job *o* job application; **cursar** *o* **hacer una petición oficial** = to file; **dirigir una petición** = to petition; **presentar una petición de quiebra** = to file a petition in bankruptcy (b) *(demanda)* request; **petición de dinero** = claim; **petición de pago de acciones** = call; **a petición** = on request; **dinero pagadero a petición** = money at call *o* money on call *o* call money; **muestras disponibles a petición del interesado** = we will send samples on request *o* 'samples available on request'
◊ **peticionario, -ria** *n (solicitante)* petitioner

pez *nm (argot)* **pez gordo** = baron

PIB = PRODUCTO INTERIOR BRUTO gross domestic product (GDP)

picapleitos *nm* litigious person

pie *nm* **al pie de la letra** = literally *o* verbatim; **justicia aplicada al pie de la letra** = rough justice; **ponerse en** *o* **de pie** = to stand up *o* to rise

pieza *nf* piece; **pieza de recambio** *o* **de repuesto** spare part

pignoración *nf* pledge

pignorador *nm* pledger

pignorar *vt* to pledge; **pignorar acciones** = to pledge share certificates

pignoraticio *nm* **acreedor pignoraticio** = secured creditor

pillaje *nm* plunder *o* loot; **cometer pillaje** = to plunder *o* to loot

pillar *vt* (a) *(saquear)* to plunder *o* to loot (b) *(argot)* to nick *o* to cop; **me has pillado** = it's a fair cop

PIN = PRODUCTO INTERIOR NETO net domestic product (NDP)

pinchar *vt (argot)* **pinchar un teléfono** = to bug a phone

piquete *nm* **piquete de huelga** = picket; **piquete de vigilancia** = picket line; **formación de piquetes laborales a la entrada de una fábrica** = picketing; **formación de piquetes laborales en una huelga legal** *o* **piquetes pacíficos** = lawful *o* peaceful picketing; **formación de piquetes múltiples** *o* **en masa** = mass picketing; **formación de piquetes secundarios** = secondary picketing; **organizar piquetes a la entrada de una fábrica** = to picket a factory

pirata 1 *adj* pirate; **copia pirata** = pirate copy; **edición pirata** = piracy; **emisora de radio pirata** = pirate radio station; **una edición pirata de un libro** *o* **diseño pirata** = a pirated book *o* a pirated design **2** *nmf* pirate; **pirata del aire** = hijacker
◊ **pirateador, -ra** *n* pirate
◊ **piratear** *vt (hacer una edición pirata)* to pirate; **los dibujos para la nueva colección de vestidos fueron pirateados en Extremo Oriente** = the drawings for the new dress collection were pirated in the Far East
◊ **piratería** *nf* piracy; **piratería de discos** *o* **de cintas de música** = bootlegging; **leyes para prohibir la piratería editorial** = laws to ban book piracy

piso *nm* flat; **piso de la empresa** = company flat; **está comprando un piso cerca de su oficina** = she is buying a flat close to her office; **tiene un piso en el centro de la ciudad** = he has a flat in the centre of town

pista *nf* clue *o* lead; **pista falsa** = false trail *o* red herring; **la policía está siguiendo diversas pistas en la investigación del asesinato** = the police are following up several leads in the murder investigation; **la policía ha registrado la habitación en busca de pistas** = the police have searched the room for clues; **la policía tiene diversas pistas en cuanto a la identidad del asesino** = the police have several clues to the identity of the murdered

pistola *nf* gun *o* handgun; **a punta de pistola** = at gunpoint; **cuando la policía registró el coche encontró seis pistolas** = the police found six handguns when they searched the car; **le obligaron a abrir la caja fuerte a punta de pistola** = he was forced at gunpoint to open the safe

pistolero *nm* gunman

plagiar *vt* to plagiarize
◊ **plagio** *nm* plagiarism

plan *nm* plan *o* arrangement; **plan de emergencia** = contingency plan; **plan de pensiones de la empresa** = occupational pension scheme; **un plan quinquenal** = a Five-Year Plan; **los planes económicos del gobierno** = the government's economic plans

planeamiento *nm* **planeamiento urbanístico** planning; **organismo local que regula el planeamiento urbanístico** = planning authority; **solicitud o tramitación de un proyecto de planeamiento urbanístico** = planning inquiry

planear *vt* to plan; **el atraco al banco fue minuciosamente planeado con antelación** = the bank robbery was carefully planned in advance

planificación *nf* planning; **planificación económica** = economic planning; **planificación empresarial** = corporate planning; **planificación familiar** = family planning; **planificación urbana** = planning *o* zoning; **departamento de planificación urbana** = planning department

planificar *vt* to plan
◊ **planificado, -da** *adj* planned; **economía planificada** = planned economy

planificador, -ra *n* planner; **los planificadores económicos** = the government's economic planners

planificar *vt* to plan; **planificar a largo plazo** = to take the long view; **planificar las inversiones** = to plan investments

plano *nm* plan; **plano de la ciudad** = street plan *o* town plan; **plano de la planta** = floor plan

planteamiento *nm* **planteamiento engañoso** = false representation; **planteamiento encaminado a convencer a alguien de la firma de un contrato** = representation

plantear *vt* to raise *o* to bring up; **plantear una cuestión** *o* **un asunto en una reunión** = to raise a question *o* a point at a meeting; **en relación a las cuestiones planteadas por el Sr. Sala** = in answer to the point of order raised by Mr Sala

plantilla *nf* personnel *o* establishment; **estar en plantilla** = to be on the establishment; **excedente de plantilla** = redundancy; **gastos de plantilla** = establishment charges; **personal de plantilla** = staff; **puesto de plantilla** = established post; **oficina con una plantilla de quince empleados** = office with an establishment of fifteen; **el personal de plantilla trabaja treinta y cinco horas a la semana** = the permanent staff work a thirty-five hour week

plazo *nm* **(a)** *(periodo de tiempo)* period *o* term *o* time; **plazo de espera** *o* **plazo de entrega** = lead time; **plazo de un préstamo** = life of a loan; **plazo fijo (de un contrato)** = fixed term; **plazos y condiciones** = terms and conditions; **ampliación** *o* **prórroga de plazo** = extension of time; **el plazo de amortización del préstamo es de quince años** = the term of the loan is fifteen years; **el plazo de entrega de este artículo es de más de seis semanas** = the lead time on this item is more than six weeks; **obtener un préstamo por un plazo de quince años** = to have a loan for a term of fifteen years; **por un plazo de seis años** = for a six-year period; **tiene que dar un plazo de siete días para sacar dinero** = you must give seven days' notice of withdrawal **(b)** *(fecha futura)* **a plazo** = forward; **a corto plazo** = short-term *o* on a short-term basis; **a largo plazo** = long-term *o* on a long-term basis; **a**

plazo medio = medium-term; **contrato a plazo fijo** = forward contract; **crédito a largo plazo** = extended credit; **cuenta a plazo** = deposit account; **depósito a plazo** = term deposit; **depósito a plazo fijo** = fixed deposit; **depósito a plazo fijo de una sociedad de préstamo inmobiliario** = term shares; **divisas a plazo** = forward (exchange) rate; **entrega a plazo** _o_ **entregas a plazo** = future delivery _o_ futures; **mercado a plazo fijo** = forward market; **obligaciones a corto plazo** = current liabilities; **préstamo a plazo fijo** = term loan; **depositar dinero a plazo fijo** = to deposit money for a fixed period **(c)** _(término)_ time limit; **plazo de prescripción** = time limit for legal action; **plazo de vencimiento** = expiry date; **cumplir el plazo estipulado** = to keep within the time limits _o_ within the time schedule **(d)** _(fecha tope)_ deadline; **acabar algo en el plazo previsto** _o_ **cumplir un plazo establecido** = to meet a deadline; **no acabar algo en el plazo previsto** _o_ **no cumplir un plazo establecido** = to miss a deadline **(e)** _(forma de pago)_ instalment _o_ periodical payment; **compra** _o_ **venta a plazos** = hire purchase (HP) _o_ installment plan; **comprar un frigorífico a plazos** = to buy a refrigerator on hire purchase; **firmar un contrato de venta a plazos** = to sign a hire-purchase agreement; **pagó a sus acreedores en doce plazos** = he paid off his creditors in twelve instalments; **se paga una entrada de 25.000 ptas y el resto en doce plazos mensuales de 20.000 ptas** = you pay 25,000 ptas down and twelve monthly instalments of 20,000 ptas; **los plazos se pagan a últimos de cada trimestre** = the instalments are payable at the end of each quarter

pleitear _vi_ to litigate

pleito _nm_ **(a)** _(juicio)_ suit _o_ lawsuit _o_ cause _o_ court case _o_ litigation; **pleitos matrimoniales** = matrimonial causes; **entablar un pleito** = to bring a lawsuit _o_ to take legal action _o_ to start legal proceedings; **lista de pleitos** = cause list; **se ha metido en un pleito con la Diputación** = he has got into litigation with the county council

plenario, -ria _adj_ plenary _o_ full session

plenipotenciario _nm_ plenipotentiary

pleno _nm_ plenary _o_ full session _o_ plenum; **pleno municipal** = town council plenum

plica _nf_ escrow

pliego _nm_ **pliego de cargos** = charge sheet; **pliego de condiciones** = specifications; **pliego de defensa** = plea of defence; **pliego de descargo** = written reply to charges

pluriempleado, -da _n_ moonlighter

pluriempleo _nm_ moonlighting; **practicar** _o_ **ejercer el pluriempleo** = to moonlight; **gana miles al año por medio del pluriempleo** = he makes thousands a year from moonlighting

plus _nm_ bonus; **plus de peligrosidad** = danger money; **los trabajadores han hecho un paro en petición de un plus de peligrosidad** = the workers have stopped work and asked for danger money

plusvalía _nf_ capital gains; **impuesto sobre la plusvalía** = capital gains tax

PNB = PRODUCTO NACIONAL BRUTO gross national product (GNP)

PNN = PRODUCTO NACIONAL NETO Net National Product (NNP)

población _nf_ population; **población delincuente** _o_ **criminal** _o_ **población con antecedentes penales** = the criminal population; **población reclusa** = prison population

poder 1 _nf_ **(a)** _(fuerza)_ power; **poder adquisitivo** = earning power; **poder ejecutivo** = executive power; **el poder ejecutivo** = the Executive; **el poder judicial** = the judiciary; **poder negociador** _o_ **de negociación** = bargaining power =; **poder notarial** = power of attorney _o_ letter of attorney; **poderes y deberes conferidos al tribunal por ley** = powers and duties conferred on the tribunal by the statutory code; **dar poder** = to empower; **dar poderes a alguien** = to nominate someone as proxy; **ejercer el poder de decisión** = to exercise one's discretion; **'más allá de los poderes'** = ultra vires; **se excedía de sus poderes legales** = their action was ultra vires; **su abogado recibió poder (notarial)** = his solicitor was granted power of attorney; **concedieron al presidente amplios poderes según la constitución** = the president was granted wide powers under the constitution **(b) por poder** _o_ **poderes** = per pro _o_ proxy; **firmar por poderes** = to sign by proxy; **voto por poderes** = proxy vote; **el secretario firmó por poderes del director** = the secretary signed per pro the manager **(c)** _(tenencia)_ nf **en poder** = in possession; **los documentos están en su poder** = the documents are in his possession; **obra en mi poder** = in receipt of; **obra en nuestro poder una carta de reclamación** = we are in receipt of a letter of complaint **2** _vi_ to be able to; **poder con** = to cope; **no poder hacer algo** = to be unable to do something; **todos los interesados pueden solicitar el trabajo** = the job is open to all applicants; **los jueces no pueden con todos los casos de divorcio** = the judges have difficulty in coping with all the divorce cases

poderdante _nm_ principal

poderhabiente _nm_ proxy

poli _nmf_ _(informal)_ cop _o_ copper _o_ bobby

policía 1 _nf_ **(a)** _(guardia)_ **mujer policía** = policewoman _o_ woman police constable; **la mujer policía Martínez estaba en el lugar del accidente** = Woman Police Constable Martínez was at the scene of the accident **(b)** _(fuerza pública)_ police _o_ police force; **policía judicial** = criminal investigation department (CID); **policía de tráfico** = traffic police; **policía militar** = military police; **policía nacional** = state police; **policía secreta** = secret police; **agente de policía** = police officer *o* police constable; **comisaría de policía** = police station; **comisario de policía** = Police Commissioner; **cuerpo de policía** = police force; **inspector de policía** = police inspector; **jefatura de policía** = police headquarters; **jefe de policía** = Chief Constable; **jefe de policía adjunto** = Deputy Chief Constable =; **ayudante del jefe de policía** = Assistant Chief Constable; **sargento de policía** = police sergeant; **comité de quejas a la policía** = Police Complaints Board; **el gobierno confía en la policía para mantener el orden público durante las elecciones** = the government is relying on the police to keep law and order during the elections; **la policía de Madrid está buscando nuevos agentes** = the Madrid police force is looking for more recruits; **la policía ha acordonado el centro de la ciudad** = the police have cordoned off the town centre; **los atracadores del banco fueron detenidos por la policía en la estación de ferrocarril** = the bank robbers were picked up by the police at the railway station; **miembros de varios cuerpos de policía local han colaborado en la búsqueda del asesino** = members of several local police forces have collaborated in searching for the murderer **2** *nf* policeman *o* police constable *o* (US) patrolman *o* lawman *o* (informal) bobby; **policía vestido de paisano** = plain clothes policeman; **policía de servicio** = duty officer; **el policía Martínez se encontraba en el lugar del accidente** = (US) Patrolman Martínez was at the scene of the accident; **el sargento y tres policías registraron el local** = the sergeant and six constables searched the premises; **los policías Salinas y Ramírez están de patrulla** = Police Constables Salinas y Ramírez are on patrol

◊ **policíaco, -ca** *adj* police; **novela policíaca** = detective story

◊ **policial** *adj* police; **cordón policial** = police cordon; **distrito policial** = (US) police precinct

polígamo, -ma *adj* polygamous; **una sociedad polígama** = a polygamous society

poligamia *nf* polygamy

polígono *nm* estate; **polígono industrial** = industrial estate *o* trading estate

política *nf* **(a)** *(arte de gobernar)* politics; **política de agresión** = power politics; **política local** = local politics; **política nacional** *o* **internacional** = national *o* international politics **(b)** *(norma)* policy; **política exterior** = foreign policy; **política presupuestaria** = budgetary policy; **la política de precios del gobierno** = the government's prices policy; **la política del gobierno sobre salarios** = government policy on wages *o* government wages policy; **la política económica del gobierno** = the country's economic policy; **la política fiscal del gobierno** = the government's fiscal policies; **el gobierno hizo una declaración pública sobre su política** = the government made a policy statement *o* made a statement of policy

político, -ca 1 *n* politician **2** *adj* political; **asilo político** = political asylum; **crimen político** = political crime; **derecho político** = constitutional law; **partido político** = political party; **preso político** = political prisoner; **abogado especializado en derecho político** = constitutional lawyer; **fondos que un sindicato destina a fines políticos** = political funds

póliza *nf* policy; **póliza de seguros** = insurance policy *o* insurance cover; **póliza de seguros a todo riesgo** = comprehensive *o* all-risks policy *o* blanket insurance policy; **póliza de seguro de vida** = life insurance policy; **póliza de seguros dotal** = endowment policy; **póliza flotante** *o* **no valorada** = open policy; **póliza marítima con vencimiento fijo** = time policy; **póliza mixta** *o* **póliza dotal** = endowment assurance *o* endowment policy; **póliza para imprevistos** = contingent policy; **póliza provisional** = cover note; **hipoteca avalada por una póliza de seguro dotal** = endowment mortgage; **tenedor de una póliza de seguros** = policy holder

ponderar *vt* **ponderar pruebas** = to weigh evidence

ponencia *nf* delivery of leading opinion of a bench of judges for consideration

◊ **ponente** *nmf* judge responsible for delivering the leading opinion for consideration

poner *vt* **(a)** *(colocar)* to put *o* to lay *o* to place *o* to set; **poner aparte** = to put aside; **poner bajo fianza** = to put on bail; **poner el precio** = to mark the price; **poner en el orden del día un asunto a tratar** = to put an item on the agenda; **poner entre rejas** = to put behind bars; **poner un anuncio** = to post up a notice; **poner un anuncio en un periódico** = to put an ad in a paper; **poner por escrito** = to put in writing *o* to set down; **le pusieron entre rejas durante diez años** = he was put away for ten years; **puesto que no sabía escribir, puso una 'X' en lugar de su firma** = because he could not write he marked an 'X' in place of his signature **(b)** *(disponer)* **poner a disposición** = to make available; **poner al día** = to update; **poner a prueba** = to try out *o* to test; **poner en circulación** = to circulate; **poner en conocimiento** = to inform; **poner en duda** = to cast doubt *o* to challenge; **poner en entredicho** = to question; **poner en evidencia** = to make clear *o* to demonstrate *o* (ridiculizar) to make a fool of; **poner en libertad** = to discharge; **poner en peligro** = to endanger; **pner en tela de juicio** = to challenge; **poner fin** = to end; **poner reparos a algo** = to raise an objection to something; **poner trabas** = to obstruct; **poner un negocio** = to open a business; **poner una multa** = to impose a fine; **ha puesto una tienda en la calle Mayor** = she has opened a shop in the High Street; **le pusieron una multa de 25.000 ptas** *o* **una multa de aparcamiento** = he got a 25,000 ptas fine *o* he got a parking ticket; **estaba en su derecho al poner en duda la declaración realizada por el oficial de policía** = he was within his rights when he challenged the statement made by the police officer

◊ **ponerse** *vr* **ponerse en contacto** = to contact

popular *adj* popular; **acción popular** = class action *o* class suit; **base popular (de un partido o de una sociedad)** = grass-roots; **precios populares** = popular prices; **votación popular** = popular vote; **el presidente es elegido por votación popular** = the president is elected by popular vote

por *prep* per; **por cabeza** *o* **por persona** = per head *o* per capita; **por ciento** = per cent; **por día** = per day *o* per diem; **por hora** *o* **por semana** *o* **por año** = per hour *o* per week *o* per year; **por el que** *o* **por la que** *o* **por medio del cual** *o* **por medio de la cual** = whereby; **por lo que** *o* **por lo cual** = per quod; **por el tribunal (en pleno)** = per curiam; **por estirpes** *o* **por ramas (en testamentos)** = per stirpes; **'por falta de cuidado'** = per incuriam; **por poder** = per procurationem; **por sí mismo** *o* **per se** = per se; **los dividendos por acción** = the earnings per share; **mercancías vendidas al por menor** = goods sold over the counter; **el ochenta por ciento (80%) de los delitos se resuelven** = eighty per cent (80%) of crimes are solved; **el personal de confianza cuesta una media de 3 millones de ptas por persona y año** = reliable staff cost on average 3 million ptas per head per annum; **la proporción de artículos defectuosos es de aproximadamente veinticinco por mil** = the rate of imperfect items is about twenty-five per thousand

porcentaje *nm* percentage; **porcentaje de aumento** = percentage increase; **porcentaje de venta anual** = turnover; **porcentaje por el servicio (en un restaurante)** = service charge; **¿cuál es el porcentaje de delitos cometidos por la noche?** = what is the percentage of crimes committed at night?

porcentual *adj* percentage; **aumento** *o* **incremento porcentual** = percentage increase; **un punto porcentual** = a percentage point; **el número de delitos con violencia ha caído en dos puntos porcentuales en los tres últimos años** = the number of crimes of violence has fallen by two percentage points over the last three years

pormenor *nm* detail; **pormenores** = particulars; **petición de los pormenores de la demanda** = request for further and better particulars

pornografía *nf* pornography

◊ **pornográfico, -ca** *adj* pornographic *o* obscene; **leyes referentes a publicaciones** *o* **películas pornográficas** = obscenity laws; **la policía se incautó de una serie de películas pornográficas** = the police seized a number of obscene films

porqué *nm* the reason why; **el juez le preguntó el porqué de su nuevo retraso** = the judge asked him for the reason why he was late again

porra *nf* **(a)** *(de policía)* truncheon **(b)** *(de ladrón)* cosh **(c)** *(cachiporra)* life preserver

porrazo *nm* blow; **dar un porrazo** = to cosh

portador, -ra *n* bearer *o* holder *o* payee; **cheque al portador** = bearer cheque; **el cheque se paga al portador** = the cheque is payable to bearer; **título al portador** = bearer bond

portafolio *nm* portfolio

portavoz *nmf* spokesperson; **portavoz del gobierno (y responsable de las relaciones con el Parlamento) ante una de las dos Cámaras** = *GB* Leader of the House; **portavoz del jurado** = foreman *o* forewoman *o* foreperson of the jury

porte *nm* **(a)** *(transporte)* freight *o* carriage **(b)** *(correos)* postage; **con porte pagado** = post free

portero, -ra *n* caretaker; **portero de estrados** = usher

porvenir *nm* future; **asegurar el porvenir de** = to make provision for; **aseguró el porvenir de su hija en su testamento** = he provided for his daughter in his will

posdata *nf* **¿Leyó la posdata al final de la carta?** = did you read the P.S. at the end of the letter?

posdata *nf* post scriptum (P.S.)

poseedor, -ra *n* holder; **poseedor de acciones** = stockholder; **poseedor de buena fe** = bona fide possessor; **poseedor de mala fe** = mala fide possessor; **poseedor de obligaciones** = bondholder

poseer *vt* **(a)** *(tener)* to own *o* to possess *o* to hold; **la brigada contra el fraude no posee el personal necesario para llevar a cabo la investigación** = the fraud squad lacks the necessary staff to undertake the investigation; **posee el 10% de las acciones de la compañía** = he holds 10% of the company's shares; **la empresa posee propiedades en el centro de la ciudad** = the company possesses property in the centre of the town; **perdieron todo lo que poseían en el incendio** = they lost all their possessions in the fire

posesión *nf* **(a)** *(bienes)* asset *o* possession; **posesión de hecho** = naked possession; **posesión ilegítima** = unlawful possession *o* adverse possession; **posesión legal** *o* **de jure** = legal possession *o* possession in law; **posesión real** *o* efectiva = actual possession; **posesiones** = possessions; **objeto en posesión** = chose in possession **(b)** *(propiedad)* ownership; **posesión de tierra** = seisin; **en posesión legal de una propiedad en dominio absoluto** = seised of a property **(c)** *(ocupación)* tenure

posesorio, -ria *adj* possessory

posfechar *vt* to postdate

posibilidad *nf* likelihood *o* chance; **posibilidad de que un juicio no sea imparcial a causa de la conexión entre un miembro del tribunal y una de las partes** = likelihood of bias; **¿existe alguna posibilidad de que la vista tenga lugar antes del verano?** = is there any chance of the hearing taking place before the summer?; **quiero tener la posibilidad de elección** = I want to leave my options open

posible *adj* **en cuanto le sea posible** = at your earliest convenience

posibilitar *vt* to enable

posición *nf* **(a)** *(postura)* position; **posición negociadora** = bargaining position **(b)** *(en un tribunal)* **posiciones** = pleadings **(d)** *(categoría)* status

positivo, -va *adj* **(a)** *(afirmativo)* positive *o* *(opinión)* constructive; **la prueba de alcoholemia dio positiva** = the breath test was positive **(b)** *(real)* substantive; **derecho positivo** = substantive law

posponer *vt* to postpone *o* to hold over *o* to stand over; **la apelación se pospuso hasta que se obtuvieran nuevas declaraciones juradas** = the appeal was adjourned for affidavits to be obtained; **el caso se ha pospuesto hasta el mes próximo** = the case has been stood over to next month

post *prefijo* post-; **servicio de post-venta** after-sales service

postal *adj* postal; **código postal** = post code *o* (US) zip code; **paquete postal** = postal packet; **servicio de cartas postales** *o* **paquetes postales** = letter post *o* parcel post; **servicio postal** = postal service; **tarifa postal** = postage

posterior *adj* **poner fecha posterior a la del día** = to postdate; **poner a una factura fecha posterior a la actual** = to date an invoice forward

postor *nm* bidder *o* tenderer; **el lote se vendió al mejor postor** = the lot was sold to the highest bidder

póstumo, -ma *adj* posthumous

postura *nf* position; **postura negociadora** = bargaining position

potestad *nf* **patria potestad** = custody *o* care and control; **juicio para otorgar la patria potestad** = care proceedings; **orden que retira la**

patria potestad y otorga la custodia de un menor a una autoridad local = care order

práctica *nf* practice; **prácticas comerciales leales** *o* **justas** = fair trading *o* fair dealing; **prácticas empresariales** *o* **industriales** *o* **comerciales** = business practices *o* industrial practices *o* trade practices; **prácticas establecidas** = standard practice; **prácticas restrictivas** = restrictive practices; **en la práctica** = in practice; **poner en práctica** = to implement; **poner en práctica un acuerdo** *o* **una decisión** = to implement an agreement *o* a decision; **puesta en práctica** = implementation; **la puesta en práctica de las nuevas normas** = the implementation of new rules; **fue apartado de la práctica de la abogacía** = he was struck off the roll; **el proyecto para acabar con la delicuencia juvenil parece muy interesante, pero ¿qué costará en la práctica?** = the scheme for dealing with young offenders seems very interesting, but what will it cost in practice?

practicar *vt* to practice; **practicar una autopsia** = to perform an autopsy

práctico, -ca *adj* convenient; **caso práctico** = moot case

preámbulo *nm* preamble

preaviso *nm* notice; **periodo de preaviso** = period of notice

precaución *nf* precaution; **la empresa no tomó las debidas precauciones contra incendios** = the company did not take proper fire precautions; **tomar precauciones** = to take precautions; **tomar precauciones para evitar robos en la oficina** = to take precautions to prevent thefts in the office

precautorio, -ria *adj* precautionary; **tomar medidas precautorias** = to take precautionary measures

precaverse *vr* to take precautions *o* to provide

precedente 1 *adj* preceding *o* former; **caso precedente** = decided case; **decisiones precedentes** = stare decisis; **la cláusula precedente da detalles de los acuerdos de representación** = the preceding clause gives details of the agency arrangements **2** *nm* precedent *o* decided case; **precedente convincente** *o* **precedente a tener en cuenta (no vinculante pero importante para dictar sentencia)** = persuasive authority *o* persuasive precedent; **precedente judicial** *o* **precedente que sólo puede ser revocado por un tribunal superior** = judicial precedent; **precedente vinculante** = binding precedent; **caso que sienta un precedente** *o* **que puede ser utilizado como precedente legal** = reported case; **caso sin precedentes** = case of first impression; **casos que representan precedentes jurídicos** = *GB* Law Reports; **fallo que establece un importante precedente** = landmark decision;

juicio que sienta precedente para posibles casos posteriores = test case; **que no constituyen precedentes jurídicos** = unreported; **seguir un precedente** *o* **basarse en un precedente** = to follow a precedent; **sentar un precedente** = to set a precedent; **sin precedentes** = unprecedented; **en una maniobra sin precedentes, el tribunal pidió al acusado que cantara una canción** = in an unprecedented move, the tribunal asked the witness to sing a song; **el abogado remitió al juez a una serie de casos relevantes que no constituían precedentes jurídicos** = counsel referred the judge to a number of relevant unreported cases; **la decisión del juez sienta un precedente para futuros casos de desacato a los tribunales** = the judge's decision sets a precedent for future cases of contempt of court; **el fallo del tribunal sienta precedente** = the tribunal's ruling has established a precedent

◊ **precedentes** *nmpl* case law

preceder *vt/i* to precede

preceptivo, -va *adj* mandatory; **mandamiento preceptivo** = mandatory injunction

precepto *nm* precept *o* prescription

precintar *vt* to seal; **la aduana precintó el envío** = the customs sealed the shipment; **los discos del ordenador fueron enviados en un paquete precintado** = the computer disks were sent in a sealed container

precinto *nm* seal; **precinto aduanero** *o* **de aduana** = customs seal; **entrada de mercancías bajo precinto aduanero** = entry of goods under bond; **han forzado los precintos de la urna** = the seals on the ballot box had been tampered with; **mercancías bajo precinto aduanero** = goods (held) in bond

precio *nm* price *o* cost *o* charge *o* rate; **precio al por menor** = retail price; **precio convenido** *o* **acordado** = agreed price; **precio de entrega inmediata** = spot price; **precio de fábrica** = price ex works *o* ex factory; **precio en almacén** = price ex warehouse *o* price ex works; **precio fijo** *o* **definitivo** = firm price *o* fixed charge; **precio justo** = fair price; **precio íntegro** *o* **sin descuento** = full rate; **precio neto** = net price; **precio ofrecido** = asking price; **precio razonable** = reasonable price; **precio solicitado** = asking price; **precio todo incluido** *o* **precio total** = all-in price *o* all-in rate; **precios oficiales** *o* **precios según tarifa** = scheduled prices *o* scheduled charges; **control de precios** = price control; **estabilización de precios** *o* **fijación de precios (entre competidores)** = common pricing *o* price fixing; **lista de precios** = scale of charges; **política de precios** = pricing policy; **relación precio-ganancias** *o* **relación de la cotización de una acción y sus beneficios** = price/earnings ratio; **poner precio a** = to price;

alquilar algo a bajo precio = to make a small charge for rental; **dar un precio para el suministro de material de oficina** = to quote a price for supplying stationery; **los precios de los ordenadores bajan cada año** = computer costs are falling each year; **precios mínimos** *o* **precios de saldo** *o* **precios por los suelos** = knockdown prices

precipitación *nf (prisa)* haste *o* hurry

precipitado, -da *adj* hasty *o* hurried
◊ **precipitadamente** *adv* hastily; **el presidente no quiere que le obliguen a tomar una decisión precipitadamente** = the chairman does not want to be hurried into making a decision

precisar *vt* to define *o* to specify; **el médico forense fue incapaz de precisar la hora del asesinato** = the pathologist was unable to give a precise time for the murder; **el juez pidió al acusado que precisase lo que quería decir con 'incapaz'** = the judge asked counsel to define what he meant by 'incapable'

preciso, -sa *adj* precise; **el testamento da instrucciones precisas sobre el acuerdo de traspaso de la propiedad** = the will gives precise instructions about the settlement of the estate; **es preciso rellenar el formulario debidamente** = it is necessary to fill in the form correctly

predecesor, -ra *n* predecessor; **sustituyó a su predecesor el pasado mes de mayo** = he took over from his predecessor last May; **adquirió la lista de clientes de su predecesor** = she acquired her predecessor's list of clients

predio *nm* estate *o* property; **predio dominante** = dominant tenement; **predio sirviente** = servient tenement

predisposición *nf* bias; **sin predisposición** = unprejudiced

predisponer *vt* to predispose

predispuesto, -ta *adj* prejudiced; **el juez parecía predispuesto contra los extranjeros** = the judge seemed to be prejudiced against foreigners

predominante *adj* predominant; **interés predominante** = overriding interest

predominar *vi* to prevail *o* to predominate; **su mujer estableció un interés sobre la propiedad que predominaba sobre la hipoteca del banco en la misma** = his wife established an overriding interest in the property against the bank's charge on it

preferencia *nf* preference
◊ **preferencial** *adj* preferential; **arancel preferencial** *o* **tarifa preferencial** = preferential duty *o* preferential tariff; **condiciones preferenciales** *o* **trato preferencial** = preferential terms *o* preferential treatment; **pago preferencial** = preferential payment; **pago preferencial de una**

empresa insolvente a un acreedor = fraudulent preference

preferente *adj* preferential; **acciones preferentes** = preference shares *o* (US) preferred stock; **acciones preferentes acumulativas** = cumulative preference shares *o* cumulative preferred stock; **accionistas preferentes** = preference shareholders; **acreedor preferente** = preferential creditor *o* preferred creditor; **derecho preferente de compra** = pre-emption; **derechos preferentes** = prior charge; **tipo de interés preferente** = prime rate

preferir *vt* to prefer; **prefiere tratar él mismo directamente con sus clientes** = he prefers to deal directly with his clients himself; **la mayoría de la gente prefiere evitar llevar a sus vecinos a juicio** = most people prefer to avoid taking their neighbours to court

prefijo *nm* area code

pregunta *nf* question *o* query *o* *(interrogatorio)* questioning; **pregunta capciosa** *o* **tendenciosa (hecha de tal manera que sugiere la respuesta deseada)** = leading question; **el abogado hizo preguntas al testigo sobre sus cuentas bancarias** = counsel asked the witness questions about his bank accounts; **el contable jefe tuvo que responder a un montón de preguntas de los auditores** = the chief accountant had to answer a mass of queries from the auditors; **el director gerente se negó a responder preguntas sobre despidos** = the managing director refused to answer questions about redundancies; **el fiscal hizo tres preguntas al inspector de policía** = counsel for the prosecution put three questions to the police inspector; **el equipo de investigación de mercado preparó una serie de preguntas destinadas a analizar las reacciones del público hacia problemas de orden público** = the market research team prepared a series of questions to test the public's attitude to problems of law and order

preguntar *vt* **(a)** *(una explicación, información)* to ask *o* to inquire; **preguntar por** = to ask for; **el fiscal preguntó al acusado por qué el bidón de petróleo estaba en su coche** = prosecuting counsel asked the accused why the can of petrol was in his car; **hay un señor en el teléfono que pregunta por el Sr. Torres** = there is a man on the phone asking for Mr Torres; **preguntó si pasaba algo** = he inquired if anything was wrong **(b)** *(poner en duda)* to query *o* to question

prejuicio *nm* prejudice; **prejuicio racial** = racial prejudice; **con** *o* **sin prejuicio** = prejudiced *o* unprejudiced

prejuzgar *vt* to prejudge; **no prejuzgue la cuestión - escuche lo que el abogado defensor tiene que decir** = do not prejudge the issue - hear what defence counsel has to say

preliminar *adj* preliminary *o* *(sin terminar)* rough; **borrador** *o* **copia preliminar** = rough copy; **contrato preliminar** = collateral contract; **discusión preliminar** *o* **reunión preliminar** = preliminary discussion *o* preliminary meeting; **investigación preliminar de un caso** = preliminary enquiry *o* investigation; **investigación preliminar relativa a una compraventa de propiedad llevada a cabo por el abogado del futuro comprador** = preliminary inquiries; **vista preliminar** *o* **diligencias preliminares** = preliminary hearing; **vista preliminar de un caso** = committal proceedings

premeditación *nf* premeditation; **con premeditación** = with malice aforethought; **sin premeditación** = involuntary *o* without malice; **asesinato con premeditación** = wilful murder *o* premeditated murder; **homicídio sin premeditación** = involuntary manslaughter

premeditado, -da *adj* premeditated *o* deliberate; **asesinato premeditado** = intended murder *o* premeditated murder; **el crimen fue premeditado** = the crime was premeditated
◊ **premeditadamente** *adv* with premeditation

premeditar *vt* to premeditate

premio *nm* reward

premisas *nfpl* *(parte inicial)* premises

prenda *nf* pledge *o* earnest *o* pawn; **prenda no rescatada** = unredeemed pledge; **dejar algo en prenda** = to put something in pawn; **rescatar una prenda** = to redeem a pledge
◊ **prendar** *vt* to pledge *o* to pawn

prendario, -ria *adj* **garantía prendaria** = collateral

prender *vt* **(a)** *(apresar)* to arrest *o* to apprehend **(b)** *(encender)* to light *o* to switch on; **prender fuego** = to set fire
◊ **prenderse** *vr* *(incendiarse)* to catch fire

prendimiento *nm* apprehension

prensa *nf* press; **prensa local** = local press; **prensa nacional** = national press; **agencia de prensa** = news agency; **cobertura de prensa** = press coverage; **comunicado de prensa** = press release *o* news release; **rueda de prensa** = press conference; **libertad de prensa** = freedom of the press

preocupación *nf* concern; **la dirección no mostró ninguna preocupación por la seguridad de los trabajadores** = the management showed no concern at all for the workers' safety

preparación *nf* **(a)** *(elaboración)* preparation *o* drafting; **la preparación de un recurso interpuesto al Tribunal Supremo** = the organization of an appeal to the Supreme Court **(b)** *(formación)* training

preparado, -da *adj* ready *o* prepared

preparar *vt (elaborar)* to prepare *o (redactar)* to draw up *o (tramitar)* to process **(b)** *(formar)* to train
◊ **prepararse** *vr* to get ready

preparativos *nmpl* preparations *o* arrangements; **la secretaria de la empresa está haciendo todos los preparativos para la Junta General Anual** the company secretary is making all the arrangements for the AGM

prerrogativa *nf* prerogative *o* privilege; **prerrogativa real** = royal prerogative; **auto de prerrogativa** *o* **mandamiento de prerrogativa** = prerogative order *o* writ

presa *nf* prize; **presa de guerra** = loot

prescindir *vt* to dispense; **prescindir de algo** = to dispense with something; **el acusado decidió prescindir de los servicios de un abogado** = the accused decided to dispense with the services of a lawyer; **el presidente del tribunal prescindió de la formalidad de levantar actas** = the chairman of the tribunal dispensed with the formality of taking minutes

prescribir *vt* to prescribe

prescripción *nf* **(a)** *(restricción)* prescription *o* limitation; **prescripción adquisitiva** = adverse possession; **prescripción del delito** = lapsing of time to bring prosecution; **normas sobre prescripción para ejercer acciones legales** = limitation of actions *o* statute of limitations; **plazo de prescripción** = time during which prosecution may be brought **(b)** *(extinción)* lapse *o* extinguishment; **plazo de prescripción** = **(c)** *(negligencia en actuar)* **prescripción negativa** = laches

prescrito, -ta *adj* statute-barred

presencia *nf* presence; **el testamento fue firmado en presencia de dos testigos** = the will was signed in the presence of two witnesses
◊ **presencial** *adj* **testigo presencial** = eye witness

presentación *nf* presentation *o* production *o (de personas)* introduction; **presentación de un documento** = presentment; **presentación de un documento en un juzgado** = filing; **presentación de nuevas pruebas para un caso** = introduction of new evidence into a case; **presentación de un proyecto de ley ante el Congreso** = introduction of a Bill; **presentación de una letra de cambio** = presentation of a bill of exchange; **cheque pagadero a su presentación** = cheque payable on presentation; **hemos pedido a dos empresas de relaciones públicas que hagan presentaciones de las campañas de publicidad propuestas** = we have asked two PR firms to make presentations of proposed advertising campaigns; **la empresa de márketing hizo una presentación de los servicios**

que ofrecía = the marketing company made a presentation of the services they could offer

presentar *vt* **(a)** to present *o* to promote *o* to produce; **presentar al tribunal** = to arraign; **presentar la dimisión** = to tender one's resignation; **presentar motivos justificantes de que un decreto condicional no debe hacerse definitivo** = to show cause; **presentar oficialmente** = to file *o* to submit; **presentar pruebas** = to adduce evidence; **presentar pruebas ante un tribunal** = to lead; **presentar un alegato** = to serve a pleading; **presentar un documento en un juzgado** = to file; **presentar un proyecto de ley ante la Cámara** = to lay a proposal before the House; **presentar una declaración a la delegación de Hacienda** = to file a return to the tax office; **presentar una letra a aceptación** *o* **al pago** = to present a bill for acceptance *o* for payment; **presentar una moción** = to table a motion; **presentar una propuesta al comité** = to submit a proposal to the committee; **al presentar** = on production of; **entrada gratuita al presentar esta tarjeta** = free admission on presentation of this card; **la mercancía se puede intercambiar solamente al presentar el recibo de venta** = goods can be exchanged only on production of the sales slip; **persona que presenta una proposición de ley** = promoter; **la citación le exigía presentar cierto documento ante el tribunal** = the summons required him to produce a certain document before the court; **se presentó el informe del comité financiero** = the report of the finance committee was tabled; **presentó una reclamación a los aseguradores** = he submitted a claim to the insurers **(b)** *(entablar un pleito)* to prefer; **presentar cargos** = to prefer charges; **presentar una demanda contra alguien** = to lodge a complaint against someone; **presentar una denuncia** = to lay (an) information **(c)** *(introducir)* to introduce *o* to put in; **presentar un presupuesto** = to put in an estimate for something; **está presentando una proposición de ley ante el Congreso para prevenir la venta de drogas** = he is introducing a Bill in Parliament to prevent the sale of drugs; **la acusación ha presentado nuevas pruebas** = the prosecution has introduced some new evidence; **presentar una reclamación por daños** *o* **pérdidas** = to put in a claim for damage *o* loss **(d)** *(inscribir)* to enter; **el acusado presentó defensa en un juicio por difamación** = the defendant entered defence of justification **(e)** *(elevar)* to hand up
◊ **presentarse** *vr (asistir)* to report; **presentarse a una entrevista** = to report for an interview; **la aduana devolverá la maleta al presentarse los documentos pertinentes** = the case will be released by the customs on production of the relevant documents; **la defensa debe presentarse en el juzgado y notificarse a la otra parte en un plazo de siete días** = the defence must be filed and served in seven days; **libertad bajo fianza**

significa que tiene que presentarse en la comisaría de policía una vez a la semana = a condition of bail is that he has to report to the police station once a week; **le rogamos se presente en nuestra oficina de Londres para los cursos de formación** = please report to our London office for training; **no se presentó en la oficina de control de personas en libertad condicional** = he failed to appear at the probation office

presente 1 *adj* present; **presente en el juicio** = in court; **dos policías estaban presentes cuando los agentes judiciales embargaron los bienes** = two police officers were present when the bailiffs seized the property; **el acusado estuvo presente en el juicio durante tres horas** = the defendant was in court for three hours; **solamente seis directores estuvieron presentes en la reunión del consejo** = only six directors were present at the board meeting **2** *adj y n;* **con la presente** = herewith; **del presente mes** = instant; **en la presente** = herein; **la presente** *o* **el presente documento** = these presents; **por la presente** = hereby; **comuníquese por la presente** *o* **sépase por el presente documento** = know all men by these presents; **por la presente revocamos el acuerdo del 1 de enero de 1992** = we hereby revoke the agreement of January 1st 1992

preservación *nf* preservation; **orden de preservación** = preservation order

preservar *vt* to retain

presidencia *nf* chair *o* chairmanship; **ocupar la presidencia** = to be in the chair; **el comité se reunió bajo la presidencia del Sr Martínez** = the committee met under the chairmanship of Mr Martínez

presidenta *nf* president *o* (de una reunión) chairwoman *o* chairperson; **fue elegida presidenta** = she was voted into the chair; **Señora Presidenta** = Madam Chairman

presidente *nmf* (a) (de un país, organización) president *o* (de una reunión) chairman *o* chairperson; **presidente de comisión** = convener *o* convenor; **presidente de la Cámara** = speaker; **presidente de los magistrados** *o* **del tribunal** = chairman of the magistrates *o* of the bench; **presidente en funciones** = acting president; **presidente y director gerente** = chairman and managing director; **dirigirse al presidente** = to address the chair; **Señor Presidente** = Mr Chairman; **el Presidente de los Estados Unidos** = the President of the United States; **Luis Solá ha sido nombrado presidente de la compañía** = Luis Solá has been appointed president of the company; **el presidente del consejo de administración** *o* **de la empresa** = the chairman of the board *o* the company chairman; **el Sr Ribas fue presidente** *o* **actuó como presidente** = Mr Ribas was chairman *o* acted as chairman; **fue elegido presidente del club**

deportivo = he was elected president of the sports club **(b)** (portavoz) speaker *o* (de un jurado) foreman of the jury

presidente

presidiario, -ria *n* convict; **ex-presidiario reincidente** = old lag

presidio *nm* jail *o* prison; **presidio correccional** = reformatory; (antiguamente) **presidio mayor** = imprisonment (for a term of six years and one day to twelve years); **presidio menor** = imprisonment (for a term of six months and one day to six years)

presidir *vt* to chair *o* to preside *o* to be in the chair; **presidir una reunión** = to preside over a meeting; **en ausencia del presidente presidió su adjunto** = in the absence of the chairman his deputy took the chair; **la reunión estuvo presidida por la Sra Tenas** = the meeting was chaired by Mrs Tenas; **el Sr Torres presidió** = Mr Torres took the chair; **la reunión se celebró en la sala de juntas y fue presidida por el Sr Sala** = the meeting was held in the committee room, Mr Sala presiding

presión *nf* pressure; **grupo de presión** = lobby; **grupo de presión ecologista** = environmentalist lobby; **cabildero,-ra que representa a un grupo de presión** = lobbyist; **ejercer presión** = to lobby; **ejercer presión sobre** = to nobble; **un grupo de empresarios de la localidad ha ido a Madrid para ejercer presión sobre los diputados acerca de los problemas del desempleo en la región** = a group of local businessmen has gone to Madrid to lobby their MPs on the problems of unemployment in the area

presionar *vt* to press *o* to put pressure *o* to lobby

preso, -sa *n* prisoner; **preso preventivo** *o* **en custodia a la espera de juicio** = prisoner on remand *o* remand prisoner; **preso reincidente** = jailbird; **presos peligrosos** = category 'A' prisoners

prestación *nf* (a) (préstamo) loan (b) (en un contrato) consideration (c) (ayuda) benefit; **prestación social** = social service (d) **prestación de juramento** = swearing *o* taking an oath

prestado, -da *adj* **pedir prestado** = to borrow; **pidieron prestados 25 millones con la garantía de la fábrica** = they borrowed 25 million against the security of the factory; **el contable mandó la factura por los servicios prestados** = the accountant sent in his bill for professional services

prestamista *nmf* lender *o* moneylender *o* pawnbroker; **prestamista en última instancia** *o* **de último recurso** = lender of the last resort

préstamo *nm* loan *o* borrowing *o* advance *o* accommodation; **préstamo a corto plazo** *o* **préstamo a largo plazo** = short-term loan *o* long-term loan; **préstamo bancario** *o* **préstamos bancarios** = bank loan *o* bank borrowings;

préstamo hipotecario = mortgage loan; **préstamo sin garantía** = unsecured loan; **préstamo sin interés** = soft loan; **conceder un préstamo de 100.000 ptas a alguien** = to make an advance of 100,000 ptas to someone; **concesión de un préstamo** = lending; **pedir la devolución de un préstamo** = to call in; **recibir un préstamo bancario** = to receive an advance from the bank; **sociedad de préstamo inmobiliario** = building society; **tomar a préstamo** = to borrow; **financiaron la nueva fábrica con préstamos bancarios** = the new factory was financed by bank borrowing; **la empresa tuvo que tomar grandes cantidades de dinero a préstamo para pagar sus deudas** = the company had to borrow heavily to repay its debts; **los préstamos de la empresa se han duplicado** = the company's borrowings have doubled

prestar *vt* **(a)** *(dinero)* to lend *o* to loan *o* to advance; **prestar dinero con garantía** = to lend money against security; **el banco le prestó 10 millones con la garantía de su casa** = the bank advanced him 10 million against the security of his house; **el banco le prestó 500.000 ptas para iniciar su negocio** = the bank lent him 500,000 ptas to start his business; **prestó dinero a la empresa** = he lent the company money *o* he lent money to the company **(b)** *(ayuda, servicio)* the lend; **prestar algo a alguien** = to lend something to someone *o* to lend someone something; **prestar atención a** = to attend to; **prestar sevicio como jurado** = to serve on a jury; **le prestó el coche de la empresa a su hija** = she lent the company car to her daughter **(c)** **prestar declaración** *o* **juramento** to declare *o* to swear; **el testigo ha prestado juramento** = the witness has been duly sworn

prestatario, -ria *n* borrower *o* debtor; **los prestatarios del banco pagan un interés del 12%** = borrowers from the bank pay 12% interest

presumir *vt* to presume; **el tribunal presume que los pagos de la manutención se están efectuando puntualmente** = the court presumes the maintenance payments are being paid on time

presunción *nf* presumption; **presunción de muerte** *o* **de fallecimiento** = presumption of death; **presunción de inocencia** = presumption of innocence; **presunción legal** = presumption of law

presunto , -ta *adj* presumptive *o* presumed; **presunto culpable** = presumed guilty; **presunto heredero** = heir presumptive; **presunto inocente** = presumed innocent
◊ **presuntamente** *adv* presumed; **dos marineros han desaparecido, presuntamente ahogados** = two sailors are missing, presumed drowned

presuntivo, -va *adj* presumptive; **pruebas presuntivas** = presumptive evidence

presuponer *vt* to imply *o* to presuppose

presupuestación *nf* budgeting

presupuestario, -ria *adj* budgetary; **control presupuestario** = budgetary control; **estimación presupuestaria** = estimates of expenditure; **política presupuestaria** = budgetary policy; **requisitos presupuestarios** = budgetary requirements; **comisión presupuestaria del Congreso** = Committee of Ways and Means

presupuesto *nm* **(a)** *(cálculo anticipado)* budget *o* estimate *o* quotation; **presupuesto sobre emisión de acciones** = prospectus; **el Presupuesto** = the Budget; **proyecto de ley de Presupuestos del Estado** = Supply Bill; **cálculo del presupuesto** = estimates of expenditure; **preparación del presupuesto** = budgeting; **equilibrar el presupuesto** = to balance the budget; **hacer un presupuesto de un trabajo** = to estimate for a job; **preparar** *o* **confeccionar un presupuesto** = to draw up a budget; **presentar un presupuesto** = to put in an estimate; **aceptamos el presupuesto más bajo** = we accepted the lowest quotation; **antes de conceder la subvención debemos tener un presupuesto de los costes totales en juego** = before we can give the grant we must have an estimate of the total costs involved; **el ministro presentó un presupuesto encaminado a ralentizar la economía** = the minister put forward a budget aimed at slowing down the economy; **el presidente proyecta un presupuesto equilibrado** = the president is planning for a balanced budget; **hemos acordado los presupuestos para el año que viene** = we have agreed the budgets for next year; **pedir presupuestos para la construcción de una nueva sala de vistas** = to ask for quotations for building a new courtroom; **pedir a un constructor presupuesto para la construcción del almacén** = to ask a builder for an estimate for building the warehouse; **presentaron su presupuesto para el trabajo** = they sent in their quotation for the job **(b)** *(supuesto)* assumption; **presupuestos procesales** = prerequisites of procedure

pretender *vt* to claim

pretensión *nf* pretence; **pretensión con fundamento jurídico** *o* **con derecho legal** = legal claim; **pretensión sin fundamento** = unfounded claim; **falsa pretensión al estado de matrimonio** = jactitation of marriage

preterintencionalidad *nf* plea or defence that the damage caused was greater than that intended

La preterintencionalidad es una circunstancia atenuante de la responsabilidad criminal consistente en causar un mal o un daño mayor del que se tenía intención de causar

pretexto *nm* pretence

prevalecer *vi* to prevail

prevaricación *nf* breach of trust

La prevaricación es el quebrantamiento malicioso de las obligaciones propias de su cargo por parte de un juez u otro funcionario

prevención *nf* prevention; **prevención de incendios** = fire safety; **encargado de la prevención de incendios** = fire safety officer; **prevención del terrorismo** = prevention of terrorism; **detención para la prevención de actos criminales** = preventive detention

prevenir *vt* **(a)** *(advertir)* to warn; **prevenir a un detenido de sus derechos** = to caution a suspect **(b)** *(evitar)* to prevent

preventivo, -va *adj* preventive; **arresto preventivo** = preventive detention; **medidas preventivas contra la corrupción** = prevention of corruption; **preso preventivo** = prisoner on remand *o* remand prisoner; **prisión preventiva** = remand centre; **como medida preventiva** = as a precautionary measure; **tomar medidas preventivas contra el robo** = to take preventive measures against theft

prever *vt* **(a)** *(tener en cuenta)* to make provision for; **prever algo** = to provide for something; **prever un aumento de los gastos en concepto de intereses bancarios** = to plan for an increase in bank interest charges; **estos gastos no han sido previstos** = these expenses have not been provided for; **el contrato prevé un incremento anual de los gastos** = the contract provides for an annual increase in charges; **no está previsto un aparcamiento de coches en los planos del bloque de oficinas** = there is no provision for *o* no provision has been made for car parking in the plans for the office block; **se han previsto 10 millones en el presupuesto** = 10 million has been provided for in the budget **(b)** *(anticipar)* to foresee; **el cierre de la compañía no fue previsto por los empleados** = the closure of the company was not foreseen by the staff; **no previó que su carta podía entenderse como una amenaza** = he did not foresee that his letter could be taken as a threat **(c)** *(programar)* to schedule; **está previsto que el edificio se termine en mayo** = the building is scheduled for completion in May

previo, -via *adj* pre- *o* previous *o* prior; **previa cita** = by appointment; **previo aviso** = prior notice; **sin previo aviso** = without notice; **acuerdo previo** = prior agreement; **diligencias previas** = preliminary hearing; **discusión previa al contrato** = pre-contract discussion; **sin conocimiento previo** = without prior knowledge; **habrá una reunión del consejo previa a la junta general ordinaria** = there will be a pre-AGM board meeting; **una venta previa al recuento de existencias** = a sale prior to stocktaking

◊ **previamente** *adv* previously

previsibilidad *nf* foreseeability; **prueba de previsibilidad** = foreseeability test

previsión *nf* foresight; **plan de previsión social** = pension plan *o* pension scheme

previsto, -ta *adj* expected; **tener prevista la llegada** = to be due; **acabar algo en el plazo previsto** = to meet a deadline; **no acabar algo en el plazo previsto** = to miss a deadline; **ir al ritmo previsto** = to be on schedule; **llegar antes de lo previsto** = to be ahead of schedule; **el proyecto de ley se desarrolla al ritmo previsto** = the Bill is on schedule; **el avión tiene prevista su llegada a las 10.30** = the plane is due to arrive at 10.30 *o* is due at 10.30; **el proyecto de ley se debatió por segunda vez antes de lo previsto** = the Second Reading was completed ahead of schedule

prima *nf* premium *o* bounty *o* free gift; **prima adicional** = additional premium; **prima cambiaria** = exchange premium; **prima de opción de venta de acciones en una fecha determinada** = put option; **prima de seguros** = insurance premium; **acciones vendidas con prima de emisión** = shares sold at a premium; **la prima anual es de 150.000 ptas** = the annual premium is 150,000 ptas; **renta anual: 2 millones - prima: 100.000 ptas** = annual rent: 2 million - premium: 100,000 ptas; **usted paga una prima anual de 120.000 ptas o doce primas mensuales de 10.000 ptas** = you pay either an annual premium of 120,000 ptas or twelve monthly premiums of 10,000 ptas

primario, -ria *adj* primary; **pruebas primarias** = primary evidence

primer *adj* *(apócope de primero)* first; **primer arrendamiento** = headlease; **primer delito** = first offence; **primer semestre** = first half *o* first half-year; **primer trimestre** = first quarter; **primer trimestre del año** = first quarter; **el Primer Ministro** *o* **la Primera Ministra** = the Prime Minister *o* the Premier; **en primer lugar** = primarily; **ir en primer lugar** = to lead; **él es el primer responsable de sus deudas** = he is primarily liable for his debts

primero, -ra 1 *adj* first *o* initial *o* original; **primera clase** = first-class; **primera licencia** = head licence; **a primera vista** = prima facie; **a primera vista, existe motivo de demanda** = there is a prima facie case to answer; **de primera calidad** = select; **de primera clase** *o* **categoría** first-class *o* A1; **administrativo de primera** = junior clerk; **alojarse en hoteles de primera categoría** = to stay in first-class hotels; **efectos de primera clase** *o* **primeras de cambio** = prime bills; **viajar en primera clase** = to travel first-class; **un billete de primera clase** = a first-class ticket; **los viajes en primera clase ofrecen el mejor servicio** = first-class travel provides the best service; **juzgado** *o* **tribunal de primera instancia** = court of first instance; **tribunal federal de primera instancia** = *US* district court; **sólo vendemos artículos de primera clase** = we sell only goods in A1 condition **2** *n* the first; **nuestra empresa fue una de las primeras en introducirse en el mercado europeo** = our company was one of the first to sell into the European market

primo, -ma *adj y n (informal)* mug *o* fool

primogénito, -ta *n* first-born; **derechos del primogénito** = primogeniture

primogenitura *nf* primogeniture

primordial *adj* prime

principado *nm* principality

principal 1 *adj* **(a)** *(más importante, dirigente)* principal *o* chief *o* leading *o* head; **abogado principal** = leader *o* leading counsel; **cargo principal** = prior charge; **director principal** = senior manager *o* senior executive; **oficina principal** = head office *o* main office; **socio principal** = senior partner; **vendedor principal** = head salesman; **ser el abogado principal** = to lead; **valor principal de los cotizados en la bolsa** = leader; **los accionistas principales pidieron una reunión** = the principal shareholders asked for a meeting; **los principales accionistas de la compañía impusieron un cambio en la dirección** = leading shareholders in the company forced a change in management policy; **los productos principales del país son el papel y la madera** = the country's principal products are paper and wood **(b)** *(fundamental)* primary *o* prime **2** *nm (préstamo)* principal *o* capital; **principal de un capital** = principal ◊ **principalmente** *adv (en primer lugar)* primarily

principio *nm* **(a)** *(regla)* principle *o* policy; **principio fundamental** = basic principle; **principios jurídicos** = legal principles; **principio de admisión de pruebas** = rule of evidence; **principio de derecho** = rule of law **(b)** *(precepto)* principle; **acuerdo de principio** = agreement in principle; **en principio** = in principle; **va en contra de sus principios** = it is against his principles **(c)** *(comienzo)* **al principio** = originally; **desde el principio** = ab initio *o* a priori; **escriba el nombre de la compañía al principio de la lista** = write the name of the company at the head of the list

> Los Principios Generales del Derecho informan el ordenamiento jurídico, ya que en caso de duda la interpretación de una norma debe atenerse a estos principios. Por ootra parte tienen el carácter de norma jurídica, ya que los principios regirán en caso de no existir ley ni costumbre aplicable al caso (CC artº 1.4)

prioridad *nf* priority *o* preference; **cláusula de prioridad** = pre-emption clause; **dar prioridad a**

(un acreedor) = to prefer; **dar prioridad absoluta a algo** = to give something top priority; **tener prioridad** = to have priority; **tener prioridad sobre algo** = to have priority over *o* to take priority over something; **el gobierno ha dado prioridad absoluta al mantenimiento del orden público** = the government has given the maintenance of law and order top priority; **los tenedores de obligaciones tienen prioridad sobre los accionistas ordinarios** = debenture holders have priority over ordinary shareholders

prioritario, -ria *adj* priority *o* major; **asunto prioritario** = top priority

prisa *nf* hurry; **de prisa** = in a hurry; **darse prisa** = to hurry; **no tenemos prisa por conocer los resultados, no los necesitamos hasta la semana que viene** = there is no hurry for the figures, we do not need them until next week

prisión *nf* **(a)** *(cárcel)* prison *o* custodial establishment or institution *o (coloquial)* jail *o* gaol; **prisión abierta** = open prison; **prisión de alta seguridad** = top security prison; **prisión de régimen abierto** = attendance centre; **prisión mayor** imprisonment (for a term of six years and one day to twelve years); **prisión menor** imprisonment (for a term of six months and one day to six years); **campo de prisión** = convict settlement; **en prisión** = inside; **enviar a prisión** = to put away; **funcionario de prisiones** = prison officer; **reformatorio; se escapó de la prisión escalando el muro** = he escaped from prison by climbing over the wall; **han pasado los últimos seis meses en prisión** = they have spent the last six months in prison; **sentencia de ingreso en prisión** = custodial sentence **(b)** *(detención)* custody; **prisión ilegal** = wrongful imprisonment; **prisión preventiva** = in remand ◊ **prisionero/ -ra** *n* prisoner *o* inmate *o* con; **prisionero de guerra** = prisoner of war

> La pena de prisión tendrá una duración mínima de seis meses y máxima de veinte años, salvo excepciones previstas en el Código (CP artº 37). Anteriormente se dividían las penas de privación de libertad por un tiempo superior a seis meses en: prisión o presidio menor (de 6 meses y un día a 6 años), prisión o presidio mayor (de 6 años y un día a 12 años), reclusión menor (de 12 años y un día a 20 años) y reclusión mayor (de 20 años y un día a 30 años)

privación *nf* ban; **privación de libertad** = imprisonment; **privación del derecho a la intimidad** = invasion of privacy; **privación del permiso de conducir** = to suspend *o* to take away a driving licence

privado, -da *adj* **(a)** *(personal)* personal *o* private; **asunto privado** = private business; **banco privado constituido en sociedad anónima** =

joint-stock bank; **carta privada y confidencial** = letter marked 'private and confidential'; **derecho privado** = private law; **detective privado** = private detective *o US* private eye; **disfrute en privado** = quiet enjoyment; **empresa privada** = private enterprise; **sector privado** = private sector; **sociedad privada** = private (limited) company; **el comité celebró una reunión especial para discutir unos asuntos privados** = the committee held a special meeting to discuss some private business **(b) en privado** = privately *o* in private *o (extraoficialmente)* off the record *o (juicio)* in chambers; **propiedad privada** = private property; **el juez vio el caso** *o* **oyó la petición en privado** = the judge heard the case *o* the application in chambers; **el trato fue negociado en privado** = the deal was negotiated privately; **pidió ver al director gerente en privado** = he asked to see the managing director in private **(c)** *(falto de algo)* **privado de juicio** *o* **de razón** = of unsound mind
◊ **privadamente**
◊ **adv** *(en privado)* privately

privar *vt* to deprive *o* to ban
◊ **privar a alguien de algo** = to deprive someone of something; **privar de los derechos civiles o del derecho de votación** = disenfranchise *o* disfranchise; **privar de un título** *o* **derecho** = to disentitle; **privar temporalmente de sus funciones** = to suspend; **el nuevo proyecto de ley priva a los extranjeros del derecho de apelación** = the new Bill deprives aliens of the right to appeal; **la compañía ha tratado de privar a los accionistas ordinarios del derecho de votación** = the company has tried to disenfranchise the ordinary shareholders; **se privó a los prisioneros del contacto con sus familias** = the prisoners were deprived of contact with their families

privatizar *vt* to deregulate *o* to privatise

privilegiado, -da *adj* privileged; **deuda privilegiada** = preferential debt; **deudor privilegiado** = chargee; **información privilegiada** = insider dealing *o* insider trading

privilegio *nm* privilege *o* prerogative; **privilegio contra la autoincriminación** = right not to say anything that might be incriminating; **privilegio de conmutación** = prerogative of mercy; **carta que goza de privilegio** = privileged communication; **conceder un privilegio** = to allow

pro 1 *nm* pro; **examinemos los pros y los contras antes de tomar una decisión** = let's analise the pros and cons before taking our final decision **2** *prep;* **en pro de** = pro **3** *prefijo* pro-; **pro-europeo** = pro-European
◊ **pro forma** *o* **proforma** *nf* pro forma; **carta pro forma** *o* **informe proforma** = pro forma letter *o* report; **necesitamos una factura pro forma** = we need a pro forma invoice

probabilidad *nf* likelihood *o* chance

probable *adj* probable; **un ataque al corazón fue la causa probable de la muerte** *o* **es probable que muriera a causa de un ataque al corazón** = a heart attack was the probable cause of death
◊ **probablemente** *adv* probably; **el juez se va a retirar probablemente el próximo año** = the judge is probably going to retire next year; **su muerte fue causada probablemente por un ataque al corazón** = his death was probably caused by a heart attack

probado, -da *adj* proven; **hechos probados** = case stated

probar *vt* **(a)** *(demostrar)* to prove *o* to establish *o* to demonstrate *o* to evidence; **probar algo alegado en juicio** = to discharge a burden of proof; **obligación de probar (lo alegado)** = burden of proof *o* onus of proof *o* onus probandi; **sin probar** = not proven; **el abogado pudo probar que al acusado le habría sido imposible subir por la ventana** = counsel was able to demonstrate how it was impossible for the accused to climb through the window; **el demandante es quien debe probar que lo que alega es cierto** = the onus of proof is on the plaintiff; **es la acusación quien debe probar que lo que alega es cierto** = the burden of proof is on the prosecution; **la ausencia de buena voluntad tal y como se ha probado por el comportamiento del acusado en el estrado** = the lack of good will, as evidenced by the defendant's behaviour in the witness stand; **si hay acusación, el acusador tendrá que probar la veracidad de las alegaciones en juicio** = if there is a prosecution the onus will normally be on the prosecutor to prove the case **(b)** *(tantear)* to test; **probar un sistema informático** = to test a computer system

probatorio, -ria *adj* probationary

problema *nm* **(a)** *(dificultad)* trouble *o* problem; **sin problemas** = easily; **hubo algunos problemas en la sala de audiencias tras el anuncio del veredicto** = there was some trouble in the courtroom after the verdict was announced; **la empresa tiene problemas de flujo de caja** *o* **problemas laborales** = the company suffers from cash flow problems *o* staff problems; **la policía teme que haya problemas durante el partido de fútbol** = the police are expecting trouble at the football match **(b)** *(asunto)* problem *o* question *o* matter; **problemas de procedimiento** = procedural problems; **resolver un problema** = to solve a problem; **el principal problema es el tiempo** = the main question is that of time; **el tribunal discutió el problema de las indemnizaciones por despido** = the tribunal discussed the question of redundancy payments; **la vista se interrumpió mientras el abogado discutía sobre problemas de procedimiento** = the hearing was held up while counsel argued over procedural problems; **planteó**

el problema del coste del proceso judicial = he raised the question of the cost of the lawsuit

◊ **problemático, -ca** *adj* problem *o* problematic; **área problemática** *o* **asunto problemático** = problem area; **los delitos relacionados con las drogas son un asunto problemático en las grandes ciudades** = drug-related crime is a problem area in large cities

procedencia *nf* origin; **país de procedencia** = country of origin; **piezas de recambio de procedencia europea** = spare parts of European origin

proceder *vi* to derive; **proceder a la vista de un caso** = to hear; **proceder contra alguien** = to proceed against someone; **esta ley procede del antiguo derecho romano de propiedad** = this law derives from *o* is derived from the former Roman law of property

procedimiento *nm* procedure *o* practice *o* modus operandi; **procedimiento civil** = civil procedure; **procedimiento criminal** = criminal procedure; **procedimiento de despido** = dismissal procedure; **procedimiento de quiebra** = bankruptcy proceedings; **procedimiento de resolución de conflictos** = complaints procedure *o* grievance procedure; **procedimiento de revisión** = review proceedings; **procedimiento de toma de decisiones** = decision-making processes; **procedimiento de urgencia** = emergency procedure; **procedimiento disciplinario** = disciplinary procedure; **procedimiento especial** = special procedure; **procedimiento legal** = process *o* legal proceedings; **procedimiento ordinario** = ordinary procedure; **procedimiento penal** = trial *o* criminal proceedings; **procedimiento verbal** = oral proceedings; **procedimientos de despido** = dismissal procedures; **procedimientos laborales** = industrial processes; **procedimientos judiciales** = judicial processes; **cuestión de procedimiento** = point of order *o* procedural question; **de procedimiento** = procedural; **iniciar un procedimiento legal contra alguien** = to institute *o* to start proceedings against someone; **seguir el procedimiento adecuado** = to follow the proper procedure; **la vista se interrumpió mientras el abogado discutía sobre problemas de procedimiento** = the hearing was held up while counsel argued over procedural problems; **este procedimiento es muy irregular** = this procedure is very irregular; **se aplazó la reunión por una cuestión de procedimiento** = the meeting was adjourned on a point of order; **según las reglas de procedimiento, el Sr Sala pidió al presidente que estableciera una norma sobre si el comité podía aprobar sus propias cuentas** = on a point of order, Mr Sala asked the chairman to give a ruling on whether the committee could approve its own accounts; **según las reglas de procedimiento, Sr Presidente, ¿puede este comité aprobar sus**

propias cuentas? on a point of order, Mr Chairman, can this committee approve its own accounts? proceso judicial

procesable *adj* actionable; **procesable por sí mismo** *o* **per se** = actionable per se; **agravios procesables de por sí** = torts which are actionable per se

procesado, -da *n* accused *o* on trial

procesal *adj* procedural; **derecho procesal** = procedural law

procesamiento *nm* **(a)** *(enjuiciamiento)* prosecution *o* arraignment; **procesamiento por malversación de fondos** = prosecution for embezzlement **(b)** *(tratamiento)* processing; **procesamiento de datos** *o* **de información** = data processing *o* information processing; **procesamiento de textos** = word processing *o* text processing

procesar *vt* *(enjuiciar)* to prosecute *o* to try *o* to arraign; **fue procesado por malversación de fondos** = he was prosecuted for embezzlement **(b)** *(elaborar)* to process; **procesar las cifras** = to process figures; **las cifras de ventas se están procesando en nuestro departamento de contabilidad** = the sales figures are being processed by our accounts department; **los datos están siendo procesados en nuestro ordenador** = data is being processed in our computer

proceso *nm* **(a)** *(acción judicial)* trial *o* court action *o* court case *o* arraignment; **proceso cautelar** = preventive action; **proceso civil** = civil action; **proceso criminal** = criminal prosecution; **proceso disciplinario** = disciplinary proceedings; **proceso judicial** = legal proceedings *o* lawsuit; **proceso sumario** = summary process; **proceso testamentario** = probate proceedings; **iniciar un proceso** = to take legal action *o* to start legal proceedings; **entablar un proceso** = to institute *o* to start proceedings against someone; **entablar un proceso contra alguien** = to take proceedings against someone; **el proceso fue suspendido** = the court proceedings were adjourned; **el proceso duró seis días** = the trial lasted six days **(b)** para el proceso = ad litem; **tutor para el proceso** = guardian ad litem **(c)** *(transcurso)* **proceso de fabricación** = industrial processes; **el debido proceso legal** = the due process of the law; **proceso de fabricación** = industrial processes; **procesos decisorios** = the decision-making processes **(d)** *(elaboración)* processing; **proceso de datos** = data processing; **proceso de datos** = data processing *o* information processing

proclama *nf* **(a)** *(amonestación)* banns **(b)** *(declaración)* public notice

procuración *nf* proxy

procurador *nm* legal representative; **procurador general** = Solicitor-General; **el demandante compareció en juicio con su procurador y dos abogados** = the plaintiff appeared in court with his solicitor and two counsel

procurar *vt* to seek

producción *nf* production *o* output *o* yield; **producción en serie** *o* **producción a gran escala** = mass production; **producción nacional** = domestic production; **factores de producción** = factors of production; **ritmo de producción** = rate of production *o* production rate; **el 25% de nuestra producción se exporta** = 25% of our output is exported; **esperamos acelerar la producción con la instalación de nueva maquinaria** = we are hoping to speed up production by putting in new machinery; **la producción ha aumentado en un 10%** = output has increased by 10%; **la producción probablemente se interrumpirá por la huelga** = production will probably be held up by industrial action

producir *vt* **(a)** *(elaborar)* to produce **(b)** *(rendir)* to yield *o* realize; **la venta produjo 100.000 ptas** = the sale realized 100,000 ptas **(c)** *(por ordenador)* to output
◊ **producirse** *vr* to arise *o* to occur; **la situación se ha producido porque ninguna de las partes puede pagar las costas del caso** = the situation has arisen because neither party is capable of paying the costs of the case; **el testigo narró cómo se produjo la discusión** = the witness described how the argument occurred; **no se han producido infracciones desde que se dictó la orden judicial** = no infringements have occurred since the court order was made

productividad *nf* productivity *o* efficiency

productivo, -va *adj* productive *o* *(rentable)* commercial *o* *(lucrativo)* profitable; **capital productivo** = productive capital
◊ **productivamente** *adv* profitably *o* productively

producto *nm* product *o* article *o* *(materias primas y alimentos)* commodity; **producto acabado** = finished product; **producto básico** = basic product; **producto final** = end product *o* final product; **producto interior bruto (PIB)** = gross domestic product (GDP); **producto nacional bruto (PNB)** = gross national product (GNP); **producto secundario** = byproduct; **el producto de una venta** = the proceeds of a sale; **productos de primera necesidad** = staple commodity; **productos nacionales** = home-produced products; **productos primarios** *o* **básicos** = primary *o* basic commodities; **productos sobrantes** = goods left on hand; **responsabilidad legal por un producto** = product liability
◊ **productor, -ra 1** *adj* productive **2** *n* producer

profanar *vt* to profane *o* to desecrate
◊ **profanación** *nf* desecration

profano, -na 1 *adj* profane **2** *n* lay; **profano en derecho** = layman

profesión *nf* **(a)** *(ocupación)* profession *o* occupation; **la profesión médica** = the medical profession; **miembros de la profesión** = profession; **¿cuál es su profesión?** = what is her occupation? **(b) de profesión** = professional *o* by profession; **el director gerente es abogado de profesión** = the managing director is a lawyer by profession
◊ **profesional 1** *adj* professional *o* occupational *o* industrial; **enfermedad profesional** = occupational disease; **ética profesional** = code of practice; **conducta contraria a la ética profesional** = unprofessional conduct; **historial profesional** = curriculum vitae; **negligencia profesional** = professional misconduct; **normas profesionales** = etiquette; **títulos profesionales** = professional qualifications; **tuvimos que pedirle a nuestro abogado asesoramiento profesional sobre el contrato** = we had to ask our lawyer for professional advice on the contract **2** *nmf* professional; **un profesional** *o* **una profesional** = a professional man *o* a professional woman; **profesional de la abogacía** = law practitioner; **profesionales** = people in professional occupations

proforma = PRO FORMA

prófugo *nm* fugitive *o* deserter; **un prófugo de la justicia** = a fugitive from justice

profundizar *vt* to follow up *o* to go into

programa *nm* **(a)** *(plan)* programme *o* schedule *o* timetable; **programa de un congreso** = conference timetable; **el director gerente tiene un programa de entrevistas muy apretado** = the managing director has a busy schedule of appointments; **el Sr. Sala tiene un programa muy apretado, dudo que pueda recibirle a usted hoy** = Mr Sala has a very full timetable, so I doubt if he will be able to see you today **(b)** *(informática)* program; **programa de ordenador** *o* **programa informático** = computer program
◊ **programación** *nf* **(a)** *(planificación)* planning **(b)** *(informática)* programming; **lenguaje de programación** = programming language
◊ **programador, -ra** *n* *(informática)* computer programmer

programar *vt* **(a)** *(planificar)* to schedule **(b)** *(informática)* to program; **el ordenador está programado para buscar cierto tipo de huella dactilar en los archivos policiales** = the computer is programmed to search the police records for a certain type of fingerprint

progresar *vi* to progress

progreso *nm* progress; **hacer progresos** = to get on; **la brigada contra el fraude está haciendo progresos en el caso de la falsificación de la póliza de seguros** = the fraud squad is making progress in the false insurance case

prohibición *nf* ban *o* prohibition *o* interdict *o* *(bloqueo económico)* embargo; **levantar la prohibición de fumar** = to lift the ban on smoking; **prohibición de utilizar información confidencial al cambiar de trabajo** = restraint of trade; **prohibición oficial sobre la venta de armas** = a government ban on the sale of weapons; **prohibición sobre la copia de material informático de programas de ordenador** = a ban on the copying of computer software

prohibido, -da *adj* banned *o* prohibited; **estar prohibido** = to be under an embargo; **bienes que tienen prohibida la importación** = prohibited goods; **el ayuntamiento ha prohibido (todos los planes encaminados a) hacer manifestaciones de protesta en el centro de la ciudad** = the council has vetoed all plans to hold protest marches in the centre of town

prohibir *vt* **(a)** *(vetar)* to prohibit *o* to ban *o* to bar *o* to forbid *o* to veto; **prohibir a un abogado que ejerza la profesión** = disbar; **prohibir fumar** = to impose a ban on smoking; **prohibir el comercio de ciertas mercancías** *o* **con ciertos proveedores** = to black; **el gobierno prohibió el comercio con tres empresas** = three firms were blacked by the government; **el sindicato ha prohibido el comercio con una empresa marítima** = the union has blacked a shipping firm; **el comisario de policía prohibió el uso de armas de fuego** = the police commissioner barred the use of firearms; **el contrato prohíbe la venta de los productos a los EE UU** = the contract forbids sale of the goods to the USA; **el gobierno ha prohibido la venta de alcohol** = the government has banned the sale of alcohol; **el juez prohibió cualquier alusión al acusado en los medios de comunicación** = the judge forbade any reference to the defendant in the media; **los empleados tienen prohibido el uso de la entrada principal** = the staff are forbidden to use the front entrance; **se ha prohibido la venta de discos piratas** = the sale of pirated records has been banned; **se le prohibió asistir a la reunión** = he was barred from attending the meeting; **se prohíbe la mendicidad en la estación** = begging is not allowed in the station; **se prohíbe a los niños entrar al banco** = children are not admitted to the bank; **se prohíbe aparcar frente al garaje** = parking is prohibited in front of the garage **(b)** *(declarar ilegal)* to outlaw *o* to prohibit; **la legislación prohíbe la venta de alcohol a menores de edad** = the law prohibits the sale of alcohol to minors; **el gobierno ha propuesto un proyecto de ley para prohibir el consumo de bebidas en público** = the government has proposed a bill to outlaw drinking in public; **está prohibido por ley conducir por el lado contrario de la carretera** = the law does not allow you to drive on the wrong side of the road **(c)** *(embargar)* to embargo; **prohibir el comercio** = to put an embargo on trade; **prohibir el comercio con un país** = to lay *o* put an embargo on trade with a country; **el gobierno no ha prohibido el comercio con el país agresor** = the government has not embargoed trade with the aggressor country

◊ **prohibitivo, -va** *adj* prohibitive; **interdicto prohibitivo** = prohibitory injunction

◊ **prohibitorio, -ria** *adj* prohibitory; **requerimiento prohibitorio** = prohibitory injunction

prohijamiento *nm* adoption

prohijar *vt* to adopt

proindiviso *adv* undivided; **beneficiario proindiviso** = joint beneficiary

prolongación *nf* extension; **prolongación de un contrato** = extension of a contract

prolongar *vt* to extend; **prolongar el arrendamiento a alguien** = to hold over

promedio *nm* average; **promedio de ventas** = sales average *o* average of sales; **alcanzar un promedio** = to average

promesa *nf* promise *o* undertaking; **promesa gratuita** = gratuitous promise; **promesa hecha en respuesta a otra promesa** = counter-promise; **promesa solemne** = affirmation; **cumplir una promesa** = to keep a promise; **faltar a una promesa** = to go back on a promise; **tenedor de una promesa** = promisee; **el juez aceptó la promesa del acusado de no acosar al demandante** = the judge accepted the defendant's undertaking not to harass the plaintiff

prometedor, -ra *adj* promisor

prometer *vt* to promise *o* to undertake *o* *(dar la palabra)* to give one's word; **los miembros del jurado han prometido no leer los periódicos** = the members of the jury have undertaken not to read the newspapers; **prometió presentarse en la comisaría una vez al mes** = he undertook to report to the police station once a month; **prometió que el asunto permanecería confidencial** = he gave his word that the matter would remain confidential; **el director de personal prometió examinar las quejas de los empleados de la oficina** = the personnel manager promised to look into the grievances of the office staff; **prometieron pagar el último plazo la semana próxima** = they promised to pay the last instalment next week

promisorio, -ria *adj* promissory; **impedimento promisorio** = promissory estoppel

promoción *nf* **(a)** promotion; **promoción de un producto** = promotion of a product; **de promoción** *o* **en promoción** = promotional; **presupuesto de promoción** = promotional budget

promocionar *vt* to promote; **promocionar un nuevo producto** = to promote a new product

promotor, -ra *n* promoter; **promotor de una mercantil** = company promoter; **promotor de viviendas** *o* **promotor inmobiliario** = property developer

promover *vt* to promote

promulgación *nf* enactment

promulgar *vt* to enact

prontitud *nf* **con prontitud** promptly

pronto 1 *adj* prompt; **a falta de pronto pago** = failing prompt payment **2** *adv* **(a)** *(rápidamente)* promptly **(b)** *(temprano)* early; **muy pronto** = at an early date; **esperamos una pronta reanudación de las negociaciones** = we hope for an early resumption of negotiations

pronunciar *vt* **(a)** *(decir algo)* to utter; **pronunciar un discurso** = deliver a speech; **el acusado no pronunció palabra alguna cuando se leyó la sentencia** = the prisoner did not utter a word when the sentence was read out **(b)** *(emitir juicio)* to bring in; **pronunciar sentencia** = to pronounce judgment; **pronunciar un veredicto** = to return a verdict; **el jurado pronunció un veredicto de inocencia** = the jury returned a verdict of not guilty; **la investigación pronunció un fallo sobre el caso** = the inquiry gave a ruling on the case
◊ **pronunciarse** *(decidir)* *vr* to rule; **sin pronunciarse** = withholding a final decision; **estamos esperando que el juez se pronuncie sobre la admisibilidad de las pruebas de la defensa** = we are waiting for the judge to rule on the admissibility of the defence evidence

propagación *nf* dissemination

propaganda *nf* publicity; **folleto de propaganda** = prospectus; **el restaurante tiene chicas contratadas para repartir propaganda en la calle** = the restaurant has girls handing out prospectuses in the street

propiciatorio, -ria *adj* propitiatory; **causas propiciatorias** = contributory causes; **según el informe, las malas relaciones entre los miembros de la comunidad fue una de las causas propiciatorias de los disturbios** = the report listed bad community relations as one of the contributory causes to the riot

propiedad *nf* **(a)** *(bienes)* property *o* estate *o* *(posesión de bienes)* ownership; **propiedad absoluta de un inmueble** = fee simple; **propiedad colectiva** = collective ownership; **propiedad conjunta** = multiple ownership; **propiedad de**

dominio absoluto = freehold property; **propiedad en común** = common ownership *o* ownership in common; **propiedad horizontal** = condominium; **propiedad inmobiliaria** = (real) property *o* real estate *o* immovable property *o* immovables *o* real property *o* realty; **propiedad industrial** = industrial property; **propiedad mobiliaria** = personal property *o* personalty; **propiedad privada** *o* **propiedad particular** = private property *o* private ownership; **propiedad pública** = public ownership *o* state ownership; **propiedades arrendadas** = chattels real **(b)** **derecho de propiedad** = proprietary right *o* proprietorship; **derecho de la propiedad** = law of property; **derechos de propiedad sobre bienes materiales o tangibles** = corporeal hereditaments; **escritura** *o* **títulos de propiedad** = title deeds; **impuesto sobre la propiedad** = property tax *o* tax on property; **nuda propiedad efectiva** = vested remainder; **registro de la propiedad** = land register; **título de una propiedad** = possessory title *o* deducing title; **tener la propiedad absoluta de un inmueble** = to hold an estate in fee simple; **propiedad objeto de fideicomiso** = settled land; **la propiedad de la empresa ha pasado a los bancos** = the ownership of the company has passed to the banks; **la empresa ha pasado a ser propiedad del estado** = the company has been put into state ownership **(c)** *(derechos de autor)* **propiedad intelectual** = copyright *o* intellectual property; **derechos de propiedad sobre bienes intangibles como patentes o derechos de autor** = incorporeal hereditaments; **ley de propiedad intelectual** *o* **leyes sobre la propiedad intelectual** = copyright law; **registrado como propiedad literaria** = copyrighted; **registrar como propiedad literaria** = to copyright; **violación de la propiedad intelectual** *o* **de los derechos de autor** = infringement of copyright *o* copyright infringement

propietaria *nf* owner *o* proprietress *o* *(vivienda)* landlady; **la propietaria de una empresa asesora en publicidad** = the proprietress of an advertising consultancy

propietario, -ria 1 *adj* proprietary **2** *nm* owner *o* proprietor *o* *(vivienda)* landlord; **propietario absoluto** *o* **nudo propietario** = ground landlord *o* freeholder; **propietario beneficiario** = beneficial owner; **propietario de los derechos de autor** = copyright owner; **propietario legítimo** = rightful owner; **propietario rural** = landowner; **propietario único** = sole owner; **registro de propietarios** = proprietorship register; **el propietario de un hotel** = the proprietor of a hotel *o* a hotel proprietor; **mercancías enviadas por cuenta y riesgo del propietario** = goods sent at owner's risk

propina *nf* gratuity *o* *(en un restaurante)* service charge; **los empleados tienen órdenes de no**

aceptar propinas = the staff are instructed not to accept gratuities

propio, -pia *adj* (a) *(apropiado)* proper; **propio de** = incident to something; **'de su propia clase': sui generis** = sui generis (b) *(de uno)* own; **trabajan en beneficio propio** = they work for themselves *o* for their own benefit

proponer *vt* to propose *o* to move *o* to suggest *o* *(ofrecerse)* to offer; **proponer a un candidato** *o* **proponer una candidatura** = to nominate a candidate; **proponer a alguien para presidente** = to propose someone as president; **proponer una enmienda** = to move an amendment; **proponer una moción** = to propose a motion; **el proyecto de ley propone que cualquier parte en el proceso pueda apelar** = the Bill proposes that any party to the proceedings may appeal; **propongo que se suspenda la reunión durante diez minutos** = I move that the meeting should adjourn for ten minutes; **propusimos al Sr Campos para el puesto de tesorero** = we suggested Mr Campos for the post of treasurer; **propuso comprar la casa** = he offered to buy the house; **propuso que se acordase el estado de cuentas** = he moved that the accounts be agreed
◊ **proponerse** *vr* to propose to *o* to set out; **la acusación se ha propuesto desacreditar al testigo de la defensa** = counsel for the prosecution has set out to discredit the defence witness

proporción *nf* proportion; **en proporción con** = in proportion to
◊ **proporcional** *adj* proportional; **asignación proporcional** = apportionment; **representación proporcional** = proportional representation; **sistema de representación proporcional** = proportional representation
◊ **proporcionalmente** *adv* proportionately *o* *(prorrata)* pro rata; **aumentar** *o* **reducir proporcionalmente o a escala** = to scale up *o* to scale down; **repartir** *o* **asignar proporcionalmente** = to apportion; **los costes se asignan proporcionalmente según los ingresos planificados** = costs are apportioned according to planned revenue

proporcionar *vt* to provide *o* to supply

proporcionar algo a alguien = to provide someone with something; **el demandado proporcionó al tribunal un informe detallado de sus movimientos** = the defendant provided the court with a detailed account of his movements; **el departamento de personal puede proporcionar detalles sobre la dirección y el número de teléfono de los empleados** = details of staff addresses and phone numbers can be supplied by the personnel department; **la acusación proporcionó al tribunal un mapa detallado de la zona en la que ocurrió el crimen** the prosecution supplied the court with a detailed map of the area where the crime took place

proposición *nf* proposal; **proposición de ley** = Private Member's Bill; **proposición no de ley** = motion

propósito *nm* (a) *(objeto)* object *o* effect; **cláusula sobre el propósito de una empresa** = objects clause (b) *(intención)* purpose *o* intent *o* intention; **a propósito** = on purpose *o* knowingly *o* intentionally; **escondió el cuchillo a propósito** = she hid the knife on purpose; **tener el propósito de hacer algo** = to intend

propuesta *nf* (a) *(proposición)* offer *o* proposal *o* approach; **propuesta de seguro** = proposal form; **presentar** *o* **hacer una propuesta** = to make a proposal *o* to put forward a proposal; **la empresa ha recibido una propuesta de un consorcio australiano** = the company has had an approach from an Australian consortium; **tenemos una propuesta de cooperación procedente de una naviera de Italia** = we had a constructive proposal from a shipping company in Italy; **el comité rechazó la propuesta** = the committee turned down the proposal (b) *(sugerencia)* suggestion (c) *(transacción previa a la quiebra)* **propuesta de concordato** = scheme of arrangement

prorrata *nf* **a prorrata** = pro rata; **pagar a alguien a prorrata** = to pay someone pro rata; **un pago a prorrata** = a pro rata payment
◊ **prorratear** *vt* to share *o* to apportion
◊ **prorrateo** *nm* apportionment

prórroga *nf* (a) *(extensión)* extension; **conseguir una prórroga del plazo de pago** = to get an extension of credit; **el tribunal concedió una prórroga de catorce días al acusado para ejercer su defensa** = the court extended the defendant's time for serving his defence by fourteen days; **la acusada solicitó una prórroga para ejercer su defensa** = the defendant applied for an extension of time in which to serve her defence (b) *(aplazamiento)* deferment *o* stay of execution; **prórroga del pronunciamiento de una sentencia** = arrest of judgment; **prórroga especial** = period of grace; **conceder a un acreedor dos semanas de prórroga (especial)** = to give a creditor two weeks' grace; **el tribunal concedió a la empresa dos semanas de prórroga** = the court granted the company a two-week stay of execution (c) *(renovación)* renewal; **prórroga de un arrendamiento** = renewal of a lease

prorrogar *vt* (a) *(prolongar)* to extend; **prorrogar un contrato por dos años** = to extend a contract for two years (b) *(renovar)* to renew

proscribir *vt* to proscribe *o* to ban

proscripción *nf* attainder; **decreto de proscripción** = bill of attainder

proscrito, -ta 1 *adj* proscribed; **un partido político proscrito** = a proscribed political party 2 *n* outlaw

proseguir *vt/i* to pursue *o* to continue; **proseguir algo** = to proceed with something; **la vista prosiguió después de que los grupos de protesta fueran expulsados de la sala** = the hearing proceeded after the protesters were removed from the courtroom

prospecto *nm* prospectus

prostíbulo *nm* brothel; **delito de ser propietario de *o* dirigir un prostíbulo** = keeping a disorderly house

prostitución *nf* prostitution; **ingresos obtenidos ejerciendo la prostitución** = immoral earnings; **llevar a la prostitución** = to procure; **llevar una casa de prostitución** = keeping a disorderly house; **vivir de la prostitución** = living off immoral earnings

prostituta *nf* prostitute

protección *nf* (a) *(amparo)* protection *o* safeguard; **protección al consumidor** = consumer protection; **protección de datos** data protection; **protección judicial** = legal custody; **protección policial** = police protection; **organización criminal que demanda dinero a cambio de 'protección'** = protection racket; **la legislación propuesta ofrecerá protección contra comerciantes ilegales** = the proposed legislation will provide a safeguard against illegal traders; **le dieron protección policial al ministro** = the minister was given police protection (b) *(tutela de menores)* *nf* guardianship; **menor bajo la protección de un Tribunal** = ward of court ◊ **proteccionista** *adj* protective; **arancel proteccionista** = protective tariff

protector, -ra 1 *adj* protective; **funda protectora** = protective cover 2 *n* protector

proteger *vt* to protect *o* to guard *o* to safeguard *o* to ward; **proteger una industria por medio de la imposición de barreras arancelarias** = to protect an industry by imposing tariff barriers; **el tribunal intervino para proteger los intereses de los accionistas** = the court acted to safeguard the interests of the shareholders; **dos perros guardianes protegen el edificio** = the building is guarded by two guard dogs; **la legislación estatal protege a los trabajadores contra el despido injusto** = the workers are protected from unfair dismissal by government legislation; **la funda protege la máquina del polvo** = the cover protects the machine from dust; **una funda de plástico protege el ordenador** = the computer is protected by a plastic cover ◊ **protegido, -da** *adj* protected; **arrendamiento protegido contra desahucio** = protected tenancy; **protegido por los derechos de autor** = copyright;

es ilegal hacer copias de un libro protegido por los derechos de autor = it is illegal to take copies of a copyright work

protesta *nf* (a) *(queja)* protest; **actuar bajo protesta** = to do something under protest; **en protesta por** = in protest at; **formular *o* elevar una protesta a** = to make representations; **hacer una protesta contra los precios altos** = to make a protest against high prices; **manifestación *o* marcha de protesta** = protest march; **los empleados ocuparon las oficinas en protesta por los bajos salarios ofrecidos** = the staff occupied the offices in protest at the low pay offer (b) *(objeción)* demur

protestar 1 *vt* to protest; **protestar una letra *o* una letra de cambio** = to protest a bill *o* to note a bill 2 *vi* to protest *o* to take exception to something *o* to demur; **protestar contra algo** = to protest against something; **el abogado defensor protestó por los comentarios del testigo** = counsel for the defence took exception to the witness' remarks; **ha protestado por los artículos del juicio publicados en los periódicos** = he has taken exception to the reports of the trial in the newspapers; **los minoristas protestan contra la prohibición de importar mercancías** = the retailers are protesting against the ban on imported goods

protesto *nm* protest; **protesto por falta de pago** = protest for non-payment; **documento *o* certificado de protesto** = certificate of protest

protocolario, -ria *adj* formal *o* by protocol; *(en un documento legal)* **términos protocolarios** = form of words

protocolo *nm* protocol *o* etiquette; **sin protocolos** = informally *o* without formalities; **el protocolo exige que el presidente presida la mesa** = protocol requires that the president sits at the head of the table

provecho *nm* benefit ◊ **provechoso, -sa** *adj* lucrative

proveedor, -ra *n* supplier

proveer *vt* to supply *o* to furnish; **proveer a alguien de algo** = to provide someone with something

providencia *nf* court order *o* ruling; **providencia de ejecución** writ of execution; **dictar una providencia** = to issue a ruling

provisión *nf* provision *o* reserve *o* supplies; **provisión de fondos** = allocation of funds; **se han reducido las provisiones de carbón** = supplies of coal have been reduced

provisional *adj* (a) *(temporal)* provisional *o* interim *o* temporary; **dividendo provisional** = interim dividend; **empleo provisional** = temporary employment; **fallo provisional del Tribunal**

Europeo = preliminary ruling; **informe provisional** = interim report; **orden** *o* **apremio provisional** = interim order; **póliza provisional** = cover note; **presupuesto provisional** = provisional budget; **requerimiento provisional** = temporary injunction *o* provisional injunction; **la policía cerró la calle al tráfico como medida provisional** = the police took temporary measures to close the street to traffic; **le concedieron un requerimiento provisional** = he was granted a temporary injunction; **escribieron para dar su aceptación provisional del contrato** = they wrote to give their provisional acceptance of the contract **(b)** *(a prueba)* tentative; **llegaron a un acuerdo provisional sobre la propuesta** = they reached a tentative agreement over the proposal; **sugerimos el miércoles 10 de mayo como fecha provisional para la próxima reunión** = we suggested Wednesday May 10th as a tentative date for the next meeting

◊ **provisionalmente** *adv* **(a)** *(temporalmente)* provisionally *o* temporarily; **el contrato ha sido aceptado provisionalmente** = the contract has been accepted provisionally; **fue nombrado director provisionalmente** = he was provisionally appointed director **(b)** *(a modo de prueba)* tentatively; **sugerimos provisionalmente el miércoles como fecha de nuestra próxima reunión** = we tentatively suggested Wednesday as the date for our next meeting **(c)** *(por el momento)* pro tem *o* pro tempore

provocación *nf* provocation; **actuó por provocación** = he acted under provocation

provocador, -ra *adj* provocative *o* provoking; **agente provocador** = agent provocateur

provocar *vt* to provoke *o* to cause *o* to occasion; **el comienzo del juicio provocó protestas por parte de la familia del acusado** = the opening of the trial was the occasion of protests by the family of the accused; **la recesión provocó cientos de quiebras** = the recession caused hundreds of bankruptcies; **los asesinatos provocaron una campaña para aumentar la protección policial de los políticos** = the murders provoked a campaign to increase police protection for politicians; **actuó porque se le provocó** = he acted under provocation

proxeneta *nm* procurer *o* pimp

proxenitismo *nm* procuring *o* procurement; **dedicarse al proxenetismo** = to procure

próximo, -ma *adj (siguiente)* next; **en fecha próxima** = at an early date

proyectar *vt* to schedule

proyecto *nm* **(a)** *(plan)* plan *o* project *o* *(planificación)* planning; **proyecto de acuerdo** = scheme of arrangement **(b)** *(borrador)* draft; **hacer un proyecto** = to draft; **redactó el proyecto del**

acuerdo en el reverso de un sobre = he drew up the draft agreement on the back of an envelope **(c)** *(parlamento)* **proyecto de ley** = bill *o* measure; **presentar un proyecto de ley ante la Cámara** = to lay a proposal before the House; **la cámara está discutiendo el proyecto de ley de prevención del ruido** = the house is discussing the Noise Prevention Bill; **un proyecto de ley del gobierno para reducir la criminalidad en el centro de las ciudades** = a government measure to reduce crime in the inner cities

prudencia *nf* caution *o* care *o* sound judgement; **prudencia razonable** = due and considerable care; **conducir sin la prudencia debida** = to drive recklesssly *o* without care

prudente *adj* sound *o* cautious

prueba *nf* **(a)** *(testimonio)* evidence *o* proof; **prueba admisible** = admissible evidence; **prueba contundente** = conclusive evidence; **prueba de cargo** = evidence for the prosecution; **prueba de descargo** = evidence for the defence; **prueba de entrega de notificación** = proof of service; **prueba de la identidad** = proof of identity; **prueba de oídas** = hearsay evidence; **prueba directa** = direct evidence; **prueba documentada** *o* **prueba documental** = documentary proof *o* documentary evidence; **prueba escrita** = written evidence; **prueba extrínseca** = extrinsic evidence; **prueba falsa** *o* **falsificada** = false evidence; **prueba indirecta** *o* **circunstancial** = circumstantial evidence; **prueba instrumental** = primary evidence; **prueba intrínseca** = intrinsic evidence; **prueba irrefutable** = irrefutable evidence; **prueba pericial** = evidence; **prueba presunta** = probable cause; **prueba testifical** = testimony *o* evidence of a witness; **pruebas aportadas por la policía** = police evidence; **pruebas confirmatorias** = corroboration; **pruebas primarias** = primary evidence; **carga de la prueba** = burden of proof *o* onus of proof *o* onus probandi; **falta de pruebas** = weakness; **por falta de pruebas** *o* **veredicto de absuelto por falta de pruebas** = not proven; **poner pruebas falsas con la intención de implicar a alguien** = to plant evidence; **presentar pruebas ante un tribunal** = to lead; **principio de admisión de pruebas** = rule of evidence; **el testigo fue incapaz de proporcionar pruebas que corroborasen lo que le había dicho a la policía** = the witness was unable to provide corroboration of what he had told the police; **las pruebas parecen indicar que el incendio fue provocado** = all the evidence points to arson; **se suspendió la vista por falta de pruebas de la acusación** *o* **contra el acusado** = the hearing was abandoned because of the weakness of the prosecution case **(b)** *(examen)* trial *o* test *o* test run; **prueba de alcoholemia** = breath test; **prueba de control** = control test; **prueba de viabilidad** = feasibility test; **prueba gratuita** *o* **prueba sin compromiso de compra** =

free trial; **someter a la prueba del alcohol** = breathalyse **(c)** *(ensayo)* **a prueba** = on trial *o* on probation *o* *(venta)* on approval; **bajo libertad condicional a prueba** = on probation; **contratar a alguien a prueba** = to take someone on probation; **empleado a prueba** = probationer; **está a prueba durante un periodo de tres meses** = he is on three months' probation; **el producto está siendo sometido a prueba en nuestros laboratorios** = the product is on trial in our laboratories **(d)** *(protegido)* **a prueba de** = -proof; **a prueba de balas** = bulletproof; **a prueba de incendios** = fireproof; **a prueba de robos** = burglarproof; **a prueba de incendios** = fireproof; **es imposible conseguir que la oficina esté completamente a prueba de incendios** = it is impossible to make the office completely fireproof; **guardamos los papeles en una caja a prueba de incendios** = we packed the papers in a fireproof safe **(e)** *(probatorio)* **de prueba** = probationary; **a modo de prueba** = tentatively; **muestra de prueba** = trial sample; **periodo de prueba** = probation *o* trial period *o* qualifying period; **un periodo de prueba de tres meses** = a probationary period of three months; **después del periodo de prueba la empresa decidió ofrecerle un contrato a jornada completa** = after the probationary period the company decided to offer him a full-time contract; **enviar un aparato por un periodo de prueba de dos semanas** = to send a piece of equipment for two weeks' free trial **(f)** *(competición)* contest **(g)** *(símbolo)* token

psiquiatra *nmf* psychiatrist

psiquiatría *nf* psychiatry

psiquiátrico, -ca *adj* psychiatric; **centro psiquiátrico** = mental institution; **hospital psiquiátrico** = psychiatric hospital; **informe psiquiátrico** = psychiatric report; **tratamiento psiquiátrico** = psychiatric treatment; **le enviaron al hospital para que recibiera tratamiento psiquiátrico** = he was sent to hospital for psychiatric treatment; **se enseñó al tribunal un informe psiquiátrico** = the court was shown a psychiatric report

publicación *nf* publication; **publicación obscena** = obscene publication; **publicación periódica no diaria** = review; **la publicación de los documentos del Consejo de Ministros tiene lugar transcurridos treinta años** = publication of Cabinet papers takes place after thirty years; **la revista fue clasificada como publicación obscena y retirada de la circulación por los oficiales de aduanas** = the magazine was classed as an obscene publication and seized by the customs

publicar *vt* **(a)** *(poner en circulación)* to publish *o* to release *o* to issue; **el gobierno no ha publicado las cifras en las que se basan sus propuestas** = the government has not published the figures on which

its proposals are based; **la sociedad publica una lista de sus miembros anualmente** = the society publishes its list of members annually; **la empresa publicó información sobre la nueva mina de Australia** = the company released information about the new mine in Australia; **el gobierno publicó un informe sobre el tráfico de Barcelona** = the government issued a report on Barcelona's traffic **(b)** *editar* to publish; **la empresa publica seis revistas para el mercado financiero** = the company publishes six magazines for the business market

publicidad *nf* publicity *o* advertising; **publicidad agresiva** *o* **publicidad que critica los productos competidores** = knocking copy; **espacio para publicidad en un periódico** = advertisement panel

publicitario, -ria *adj* **valla publicitaria** = advertisement hoarding

público, -ca 1 *adj* public *o* common; **acusador público** = public prosecutor; **administración pública** = public administration *o* civil service; **administrador público** = Public Trustee; **bien público** = public policy; **daño público** = common nuisance *o* public nuisance; **derecho público** = public law; **dominio público** = public domain; **fondos públicos** = public funds; **fuerza pública** = police force; **gasto público** = public expenditure; **hacienda pública** = public finance; **imagen pública** = public image; **juicio público** = open court; **lugar público** = public place; **orden público** = law and order *o* public order; **perjuicio público** = public nuisance; **propiedad pública** = public ownership *o* state ownership; **relaciones públicas** = public relations (PR); **sector público** = public sector; **transporte público** = public transport; **vía pública** = highway; **de propiedad pública** = state-owned; **delito contra el orden público** = offence against the public order *o* public order offence; **departamento de relaciones públicas** = public relations department; **funcionario encargado de las relaciones públicas** = public relations officer; **empresa de transportes públicos** = common carrier; **en audiencia pública** = in open court; **obra de dominio público** = work in the public domain; **perturbación del orden público** *o* **alteración del orden público** = breach of the peace; **la empresa va a hacer públicas algunas de sus acciones** = the company is going public; **trabaja en la administración pública** = he has a job in the civil service; **necesidad de endeudamiento del sector público** = public sector borrowing requirement; **un informe sobre aumento de salarios en el sector público** = a report on wage rises in the public sector *o* on public sector wage settlements; **la policía está intentando mejorar su imagen pública** = the police are trying to improve their public image **2** *nm* the public; **el**

público en general = the general public; **en público** = in public

pucherazo *nm* ballot-rigging

pudor *nm* **atentado contra el pudor** = indecent assault

pueblo *nm (nación)* people; **defensor del pueblo** = ombudsman *o* Parliamentary Commissioner

puente *nm* bridge; **crédito** *o* **préstamo puente** = bridging loan

puerta *nf* **(a)** door; **puerta de incendios** *o* **de emergencia** = fire door; **de puerta en puerta** = house-to-house; **la policía llevó a cabo una búsqueda de los presos evadidos de puerta en puerta** = the police carried out a house-to-house search for the escaped prisoners **(b) a puerta cerrada** = in camera; **sesión a puerta cerrada** = closed session; **la vista del caso se realizó a puerta cerrada** = the case was heard in camera; **se desalojó la tribuna pública cuando la reunión pasó a ser a puerta cerrada** the public gallery was cleared when the meeting went into closed session; **el pleno municipal se reunió a puerta cerrada para discutir problemas de personal en el departamento de Transportes** = the town council met in closed session to discuss staff problems in the Transport Department

puerto *nm* port *o* harbour; **el puerto** = the docks; **puerto de embarque** = port of embarkation; **puerto de registro de un buque** = port of registry *o* registry port; **puerto franco** = free port

puesta *nf* **puesta a disposición del juzgado** = committal; **puesta a disposición de un tribunal superior** = committal for trial; **puesta en libertad** release

puesto *nm* **(a)** *(cargo)* position *o* post *o* place; **puesto de confianza** = position of trust; **puesto de plantilla** *o* **puesto fijo como funcionario** established post; **puesto de trabajo** = job *o* post *o* place of work; **puesto fijo** = permanency; **puesto vacante** = vacancy; **solicitar un puesto de director** = to apply for a position as manager; **solicitar un puesto de pasante** = to apply for a post as legal executive; **anunciamos tres puestos de trabajo en 'La Vanguardia'** = we advertised three posts in 'La Vanguardia'; **le ofrecieron un puesto en una agencia de seguros** = he was offered a place with an insurance company; **tenemos tres puestos vacantes** *o* **tenemos varios puestos vacantes** = we have three posts vacant *o* we have several positions vacant; **todos los puestos vacantes han sido cubiertos** = all the vacant positions have been filled; **todos nuestros puestos han sido cubiertos** = all our posts have been filled **(b)** *(posición)* position

pugna *nf* conflict; **estar en pugna oponerse** = to conflict

puja *nf* bid

pujar *vt* to bid for something

punible *adj* penal

punitivo, -va *adj* punitive; **daños punitivos** = exemplary damages

punto *nm* **(a)** *(en discusión)* point *o* item; **punto de vista** = viewpoint; **puntos a tratar** = items on the agenda; **puntos de consulta** = terms of reference; **punto flaco** = failing; **punto muerto** = deadlock; **estar en punto muerto** = to deadlock; **hasta cierto punto** = up to a point *o* to a certain extent; **sobre este punto** = herein; **discutiremos ahora el punto cuatro del orden del día** = we will now take item four on the agenda; **tenía razón hasta cierto punto** = he was correct to a certain extent; **véase la referencia sobre este punto más arriba** = see the reference herein above; **se llevaron a cabo las recomendaciones del informe hasta cierto punto** = the recommendations of the report were carried out to a certain extent **(b)** *(lugar)* place; **punto de reunión** = venue; **señaló en rojo el punto del texto en donde se había quedado** she marked her place in the text with a red pen **(c)** *(en actividad económica)* **punto más bajo** = trough

puntual *adj* **el avión fue puntual** = the plane was on time

◊ **puntualmente** *adv* on time

pupilaje *nm* pupillage *o* wardship

pupilo, -la *n* ward; **el Sr. Rosanas actuando en representación de su pupila, la Srta. Bonet** Mr Rosanas acting on behalf of his ward, Miss Bonet

purgar *vt* to purge

putativo, -va *adj* putative; **padre putativo** = putative father

Qq

quebrado, -da 1 *adj* bankrupt **2** *n* bankrupt; **quebrado no rehabilitado** = undischarged bankrupt; **quebrado rehabilitado** = discharged bankrupt; **rehabilitación del quebrado** = discharge in bankruptcy

quebrantamiento *nm* breaking; **quebrantamiento de condena** = breach of sentence; **quebrantamiento de forma** = breaking legal formalities

> El quebrantamiento de forma es motivo de recurso de casación y supone la infracciòn de las leyes procesales en cuanto a la forma de las resoluciones judiciales, así como de los trámites a seguir en el curso de los autos

quebrantar *vt* **(a)** *(violar)* to break *o* to violate; **quebrantar la ley** = to break the law; **quebrantar un testamento** = to revoke a will; **la acción del gobierno quebranta el tratado internacional sobre transporte comercial** = the action of the government violates the international treaty on commercial shipping **(b)** *(ir en contra)* to flout; **la tienda está deliberadamente quebrantando la ley al vender alcohol a menores** = by selling alcohol to minors, the shop is deliberately flouting the law **(c)** **quebrantando una norma** *o* **un acuerdo** = in violation of a rule *o* an agreement; **el gobierno ha actuado quebrantando el acuerdo** = the government has acted in violation of its agreement

quebrar *vi* to fail *o* to go bankrupt; **la compañía quebró** = the company failed; **quebró tras dos años en el negocio** = he went bankrupt after two years in business

quedar *vi* *(sobrar)* to remain; **la mitad de las existencias quedó sin vender** = half the stock remained on the shelves
◊ **quedarse** *vr* **(a)** *(permanecer)* to remain *o* to stay; **se quedó en la oficina pasadas las 6.30 para terminar su trabajo** = she remained behind at the office after 6.30 to finish her work **(b)** *(retener)* to retain

queja *nf* complaint *o* protest *o* *(agravio)* grievance; **queja infundada** = unjustified complaint; **presentar una queja contra alguien** = to make *o* lodge a complaint against someone; **tramitación de quejas** = complaints procedure; **procedimiento de tramitación de quejas** = grievance procedure
◊ **quejarse** *vr* to complain; **si quiere quejarse, escriba al director** = if you want to complain, write to the manager; **hace tanto frío en la oficina que el personal ha empezado a quejarse** = the office is so cold the staff have started complaining; **se quejan de que nuestros precios son demasiado altos** = they are complaining that our prices are too high; **se quejó del servicio** = she complained about the service

quemar *vt* to burn; **el contable jefe quemó los documentos antes de que llegara la policía** = the chief accountant burned the documents before the police arrived

querella *nf* dispute *o* action for damages; **querella por difamación** = action for defamation
◊ **querellante** *nmf;* *(demandante)* plaintiff *o* complainant *o* prosecutor

> La querella es la acusación con la que se inicia un proceso penal a instancia de parte

quiebra *nf* bankruptcy *o* failure; **(en) quiebra** = bankrupt; **quiebra comercial** = commercial failure; **quiebra fraudulenta** = criminal bankruptcy; **quiebra fortuita** = fortuitous bankruptcy; **quiebra voluntaria** = voluntary bankruptcy; **aviso de quiebra** = bankruptcy notice; **declaración de quiebra** = adjudication of bankruptcy *o* declaration of bankruptcy; **juicio de quiebra** = bankruptcy proceedings; **petición de quiebra** = bankruptcy petition; **rehabilitación de quiebra** = discharge in *o* of bankruptcy; **tribunal de quiebras** = Bankruptcy Court; **disposición** *o* **transacción previa a la quiebra** = scheme of arrangement; **fue declarado en quiebra** = he was adjudicated *o* declared bankrupt; **hacer una petición de quiebra** *o* **solicitar una declaración de quiebra** = to file a petition in bankruptcy; **la empresa está en quiebra** = the company is in the hands of the receiver; **la recesión ha provocado miles de quiebras** = the recession has caused thousands of bankruptcies; **la recesión llevó a mi padre a la quiebra** = the recession bankrupted my father; **perdió todo el dinero en la quiebra bancaria** = he lost all his money in the bank failure; **un promotor**

inmobiliario en quiebra = a bankrupt property developer

quitar *vt* to remove

quórum *nm* quorum; **con quórum** = quorate; **haber quórum** = to have a quorum; **¿hay quórum?** = do we have a quorum?; **sin quórum** = inquorate; **la decisión no tuvo validez porque la reunión de los accionistas no tenía quórum** = the resolution was invalid because the shareholders' meeting was not quorate; **la reunión se pospuso al no haber quórum** = the meetingwas adjourned since there was no quorum; **la reunión se suspendió por falta de quórum** = the meeting was declared inquorate and had to be abandoned

Rr

racial *adj* racial; **discriminación racial** = racial discrimination; **incitación al odio racial** = incitement to racial hatred; **odio racial** = racial hatred; **prejuicio racial** = racial prejudice; **relaciones raciales** = race relations

racista *adj y nmf* racist

racismo *nm* racism

radicar *vi* base
◊ **radicarse** *vr* to become established

raíz *nf* **a raíz de** = as a result of *o* as a consequence of; **bienes raíces** = real estate *o* real property *o* realty

ramera *nf* whore *o* prostitute

ramo *nm* sector *o* trade; **es muy conocida dentro del ramo de la confección** = she is very well known in the clothing trade

rango *nm* rank; **grupo de personas del mismo rango** = peer group

rápido, -da *adj* (a) *(inmediato)* quick *o* prompt; **divorcio rápido** = quickie (divorce); **el contable echó una rápida ojeada al montón de facturas** = the accountant quickly looked through the pile of invoices; **espera que el juicio sea rápido** = he is hoping for a quick trial; **la empresa tuvo una recuperación rápida** = the company made a quick recovery (b) *(urgente)* express (c) *(repentino)* sharp
◊ **rápidamente** *adv* quickly *o* promptly; **el caso de divorcio pasó por los tribunales rápidamente** = the divorce case went through the courts quickly

raptar *vt* to kidnap *o* to abduct; **los ladrones raptaron a la heredera y pidieron un rescate por ella** = the robbers abducted the heiress and held her to ransom
◊ **rapto** *nm* abduction *o* kidnapping
◊ **raptor, -ra** *n* abductor *o* kidnapper

rastrear *vt* to trace; **rastrear la zona** = to comb the area

rastro *nm* trace *o* trail; **desaparecieron sin dejar rastro** = they disappeared leaving no trace; **le siguieron el rastro** = they followed his trail

ratear *vt* to pilfer
◊ **ratería** *nf* pilferage *o* pilfering *o* petty theft

◊ **ratero, -ra** *n* pilferer *o* petty thief *o* pickpocket; **ratero de tiendas** = shoplifter; **en una banda de rateros, el que actúa como carterista** = picker

ratificación *nf* ratification *o* confirmation; **ratificación de la sentencia** = upholding of sentence

ratificar *vt* to ratify *o* to endorse *o* to confirm; **ratificar una sentencia** = to uphold a sentence; **aunque los directores habían actuado sin la debida autoridad, la empresa ratificó sus acciones** = although the directors had acted without due authority, the company ratified their actions; **el acuerdo tiene que ser ratificado por el consejo de dirección** = the agreement has to be ratified by the board; **el Tribunal Supremo ratificó la sentencia** = the Supreme Court upheld the sentence

rato *nm* *(matrimonio)* marriage which has not been consummated

raza *nf* race

razón *nf* (a) *(explicación)* reason; **'razón para decidir'** = ratio decidendi; **buena razón** = good cause; **dar razón de** = to account for; **le preguntaron al testigo las razones por las que volvió al lugar del incendio** = the witness was asked for his reasons for returning to the fire (b) *(motivo)* grounds; **razones fundadas** = supporting reasons; **no hay razones por las que nos puedan demandar** = there are no grounds on which we can be sued (c) *(nombre comercial)* **razón social** = corporate name *o* business name
◊ **razonable** *adj* reasonable *o* sound *o* proper; **precio razonable** = fair price; **poco razonable** = unreasonable; **los jueces se mostraron muy razonables cuando ella explicó que necesitaba el permiso de conducir para su trabajo** = the magistrates were very reasonable when she explained that the driving licence was necessary for her work
◊ **razonado, -da** *adj* reasoned; **después de tres meses, el juez emitió un juicio razonado** = after three months, the judge delivered a reasoned judgment
◊ **razonamiento** *nm* reasoning; **es difícil de entender el razonamiento que llevó a la decisión del juez** = it is difficult to understand the reasoning behind the judge's decision

◊ **razonar** *vt/i* to reason *o* to argue

re- *prefijo* re-
◊ **reabrir** *vt* to reopen
◊ **reactivación** *nf* recovery
◊ **reajustar** *vt* to adjust
◊ **reajuste** *nm* adjustment; **reajuste de averías** = average adjustment; **cláusula de reajuste de precios** *o* **de salarios** = escalator clause; **reajuste ministerial** = cabinet reshuffle

real *adj* **(a)** *(verdadero, efectivo)* real *o* actual; **conocimiento real** = actual notice; **daño real** = actual damage; **pérdida real** = actual loss; **renta real** *o* **salario real** = real income *o* real wages; **valor real** = actual value; **en términos reales** = in real terms; **él es el dueño real de la propiedad** = he is the de facto owner of the property; **las ventas han subido un 3% pero con una inflación del 5% supone un descenso en términos reales** = sales have gone up by 3% but with inflation running at 5% that is a fall in real terms **(b)** *(positivo, sólido)* substantive *o* hard **(c)** *(perteneciente a la realeza)* royal
◊ **Real Orden** = Order in Council; **indulto real** = Royal pardon **(d)** *(de ordenador)* **tiempo real** = real time; **sistema a tiempo real** = real-time system
◊ **realmente** *adv* in real terms

realidad *nf* fact; **en realidad** = in real terms *o* in fact *o* in point of fact *o* *(en la práctica)* in practice; **realidades** = matters of fact

realizable *adj* **activos realizables** = realizable assets

realización *nf* realization *o* implementation; **la realización de un proyecto** = the realization of a project; **el plan avanzó hacia su realización al firmarse los contratos** = the plan moved a stage nearer realization when the contracts were signed

realizado, -da *adj* **delito realizado** = substantive offence

realizar *vt* to realize *o* to effect *o* to carry out; **realizar un acuerdo entre dos partes** = to effect a settlement between two parties; **realizar un control de calidad** = to inspect products for defects; **realizar un proyecto** *o* **un plan** = to realize a project *o* a plan; **realizar un pago** = to effect a payment; **realizar una determinada acción** = to take an action; **realizar una opción** = to exercise an option; **no se realizará el pago hasta que se haya firmado el contrato** = payment will be held back until the contract has been signed
◊ **realquilar** *vt* to sublet *o* to sublease *o* to underlet

reanudación *nf* resumption; **esperamos una pronta reanudación de las negociaciones** = we expect an early resumption of negotiations

reanudar *vt* to resume; **las discusiones se reanudaron tras un descanso de dos horas** = the discussions resumed after a two hour break

reaseguro *nm* reinsurance

rebaja *nf* reduction *o* cut; **rebaja de precios** = price reductions; **conceder una rebaja** = to allow for; **rebaja proporcional de legados** = abatement
◊ **rebajas** *nfpl* sale; **las rebajas** = the sales; **rebajas a mitad de precio** = half-price sale; **la tienda ha organizado unas rebajas para liquidar las existencias antiguas** = the shop is having a sale to clear old stock
◊ **rebajado, -da** *adj* reduced

rebajar *vt* to reduce *o* to allow for *o* to abate *o* to knock off

rebajar; **el precio rebajado es el 50% del precio normal** = the sale price is 50% of the normal price; **rebajó 2000 ptas el precio por pago en efectivo** = he knocked 2000 ptas off the price for cash; **hemos rebajado los precios de todos nuestros modelos** = we are cutting prices on all our models

rebasar *vt* to exceed *o* to overrun; **ha rebasado su límite de crédito** = he has exceeded his credit limit

rebatido, -da *adj* contested; **oferta de adquisición rebatida** = contested takeover

rebatir *vt* to contest *o* to rebut; **deseo rebatir la declaración hecha por el testigo** = I wish to contest the statement made by the witness; **intentó rebatir las afirmaciones realizadas por el testigo de la acusación** = he attempted to rebut the assertions made by the prosecution witness

rebelarse *vr* to rebel *o* to mutiny

rebelde *nmf* **(a)** *(amotinador)* rebel *o* mutineer; **los rebeldes opuestos al gobierno han tomado seis ciudades** = anti-government rebels have taken six towns; **los contribuyentes rebeldes han ocupado el ayuntamiento** = rebel ratepayers have occupied the town hall **(b)** *(persona que comete desacato a los tribunales)* contemnor

rebeldía *nf* absence; **juicio en rebeldía** = judgment by default *o* default judgment; **sentencia en rebeldía** = judgment by default *o* default judgment; **fue juzgada y condenada a muerte en rebeldía** = she was tried and sentenced to death in absentia *o* in her absence

rebelión *nf* rebellion *o* mutiny; **el ejército ha aplastado la rebelión en el sur** = the army has crushed the rebellion in the southern province

recaer *vi* **recaer en** = to vest

recambio *nm* spare; **pieza de recambio** = spare part

recargo *nm* overcharge

recaudación *nf* collection; **recaudación de impuestos** = levy

recaudador, -ra *n* collector; **recaudador de impuestos** = exciseman *o* collector of taxes *o* tax collector

recaudar *vt* to collect *o* to levy

recaudo *nm* **buen recaudo** = safe keeping

recepción *nf (recibo)* receipt *o* receiving; **oficina de recepción** = receiving office; **servicio de recepción** = receiving department; **las facturas deberán abonarse dentro de los treinta días siguientes a su recepción** = invoices are payable within thirty days of receipt
◊ **recepcionista** *nmf (mercancías)* receiving clerk

receptación *nf (crimen)* receiving; **receptación de objetos robados** = receiving stolen property; **le acusaron de receptación de cheques robados** = he was accused of being in receipt of stolen cheques

La receptación es un delito que consiste en el aprovechamiento que hace para sí un tercero no participante como autor ni cómplice en la comisión de un delito contra los bienes, de los efectos de este delito, aunque tales efectos le fueron entregados con la mera finalidad de su custodia

receptáculo *nm* holder

receptador, -ra *n* receiver (of stolen goods)

receptar *vt* to deal in stolen goods

receptor *m* **(a)** *(destinatario)* recipient; **el receptor de una ayuda procedente de la empresa** = the recipient of an allowance from the company **(b)** *(de una empresa)* receiver; **receptor por delegación o nombramiento** *o* **receptor oficial de una empresa** = Official Receiver; **el tribunal nombró un receptor para la empresa** = the court appointed a receiver for the company; **la empresa está en manos del receptor** = the company is in the hands of the receiver **(c)** *(de objetos robados)* fence

recesión *nf* recession; **la recesión ha dejado a mucha gente sin trabajo** = the recession has put many people out of work; **perdió todo su dinero durante la recesión** = he lost all his money in the recession

rechazar *vt* **(a)** *(descartar)* to reject *o* to throw out *o* to turn down *o* to dismiss; **rechazar un recurso** = to reject an appeal *o* to uphold a sentence; **rechazar una moción** = to vote down; **el Tribunal Supremo rechazó el recurso** = the Supreme Court upheld the sentence; **se rechazó la propuesta** = the proposal was voted down; **el recurso fue rechazado por el Tribunal Supremo** = the appeal was rejected by the Supreme Court; **el banco rechazó su petición de préstamo** = the bank turned down their request for a loan; **el comité de planificación rechazó la propuesta** = the proposal was thrown out by the planning committee; **la**

solicitud de licencia fue rechazada = the application for a licence was turned down **(b)** *(denegar)* to disallow *o* to reject *o* to refuse; **el juez rechazó la prueba de la defensa** = the judge disallowed the defence evidence; **el juez rechazó una petición del acusado** = the magistrate rejected a request from the defendant; **el cliente rechazó los artículos** = the customer refused the goods; **la empresa rechazó la oferta de adquisición** = = the company rejected the takeover bid; **el sindicato rechazó las propuestas de la patronal** = the union rejected the management's proposals; **se rechazó su solicitud de un requerimiento judicial** = his application for an injunction was refused **(c)** *(anular)* to defeat; **el proyecto de ley fue rechazado por el Senado por 52 votos a favor y 64 en contra** = the bill was defeated in the Senate by 52 to 64
◊ **rechazo** *nm* **(a)** *(repudio)* rejection *o* repudiation; **el rechazo del recurso por parte del tribunal** = the rejection of the appeal by the tribunal; **el rechazo de la petición del acusado** = the rejection of the defendant's request **(b)** *(denegación)* **rechazo global** = blanket refusal; **rechazo de una letra de cambio** = non-acceptance

recibir *vt* **(a)** *(obtener)* to receive *o* to get *o* to take; **recibí** = 'received with thanks'; **recibir instrucciones de un cliente** = to take instructions; **cuando la defensa ofreció 1.000 dólares, el abogado del demandante dijo que tendría que recibir instrucciones de su cliente** = when the defence offered £1,000, the plaintiff's solicitor said he would take his client's instructions; **he recibido** *o* **habiendo recibido** = in receipt of; **recibimos su carta del 21 de octubre a su debido tiempo** = we duly received his letter of 21st October; **al recibir la notificación, la empresa interpuso un recurso** = on receipt of the notification, the company lodged an appeal; **la mercancía se recibió en buen estado** = the goods were received in good condition; **recibimos el pago hace diez días** = we received the payment ten days ago; **recibimos una carta del abogado esta mañana** = we got a letter from the solicitor this morning **(b)** *(entretener clientes)* to entertain **(c)** *(en un juicio)* **recibir a prueba** = to admit as evidence

recibo *nm* **(a)** *(acto de recibir)* receipt; **acuse de recibo** = to acknowledge service; **acusar recibo de** *o* **dar un recibo por** = to acknowledge receipt; **acusar recibo de una carta** = to acknowledge receipt of a letter; **acusamos recibo de su carta del 15 del corriente** = we acknowledge receipt of your letter of the 15th; **acuso recibo de su carta de 21 de octubre** = we duly received his letter of 21st October; **en caso de que quiera cambiar los artículos comprados se ruega presentar el recibo** = please produce your receipt if you want to exchange items **(b)** *(resguardo)* receipt *o* slip; **recibo conforme** = receipt in due form; **recibo de**

aduana = customs receipt; **recibo de compra (de artículos)** = receipt for items purchased; **recibo de venta** = bill of sale; **recibo del alquiler** = rent receipt; **recibo duplicado** = duplicate receipt *o* duplicate of a receipt; **talonario de recibos** = receipt book *o* book of receipts; **la mercancía se suministrará dentro de los treinta días siguientes al recibo del pedido** = goods will be supplied within thirty days of receipt of order

reciente *adj* **más reciente** = latest; **aquí están las cifras de accidentes más recientes** = here are the latest accident figures

recinto *nm* precinct

reciprocidad *nf* reciprocity *o* mutuality; **convenio internacional de reciprocidad arancelaria** = fair trade

recíproco, -ca *adj* reciprocal; **comercio recíproco** = reciprocal trade; **propiedad de acciones recíproca** = cross holdings; **tenencia recíproca de acciones** = reciprocal holdings; **testamentos recíprocos** = mutual wills *o* reciprocal wills

reclamación *nf* **(a)** *(de pago)* claim *o* demand; **reclamación interpuesta inmediatamente a otra anterior** *o* **reclamación recíproca por daños y perjuicios** = counterclaim; **reclamación por fraude** = bill for fraud; **hoja** *o* **formulario de reclamación** = claim form; **liquidar una reclamación** = to settle a claim; **la tramitación de una reclamación al seguro** = the processing of a claim for insurance; **presentar una reclamación como respuesta a otra interpuesta por otra persona** = to counterclaim **(b)** *(queja)* complaint; **presentar una reclamación** = to make *o* lodge a complaint against someone; **procedimiento de reclamación** = complaints procedure; **cuando haga una reclamación, cite siempre el número de referencia** = when making a complaint, always quote the reference number; **envió su carta de reclamación al director gerente** = she sent her letter of complaint to the managing director

reclamar (a) *(exigir)* to demand *o* to ask for **(b)** *(propiedad)* to claim *o* to reclaim; **reclamar daños y perjuicios** = to claim damages; **reclamar la devolución de un dinero** = claim back; **nadie reclamó el paraguas que se encontró en mi despacho** = no one claimed the umbrella found in my office; **reclama la propiedad de la casa** = he is claiming possession of the house

reclamo *nm* **artículo de reclamo** = loss-leader

reclusión *nf* confinement; **reclusión perpetua** = life imprisonment; *(antiguamente)* **reclusión mayor** = imprisonment (for a term of twenty years and a day to thirty years) with loss of civil rights during the sentence period; **reclusión menor** = imprisonment (for a term of twelve years and a day

to twenty years) with loss of civil rights during the sentence period

recluso, -sa *n* prisoner *o* jailbird *o* inmate

recluta *nmf* recruit
◊ **reclutamiento** *nm* recruitment; **el índice de reclutamiento está subiendo** = the recruitment rate is rising

reclutar *vt* to recruit *o* to conscript; **veinticinco mujeres fueron reclutadas en el cuerpo de policía local** = twenty-five women were recruited into the local police force

recobrar *vt* to get back; **recobrar desgravaciones impositivas** = to claw back; **recobrar un objeto comprado a plazos por falta de pago de los mismos** = to repossess; **acción para recobrar la posesión de bienes muebles** = action in detinue

recoger *vt* **(a)** *(ir a buscar)* to collect; **recoger fondos** = to raise money; **¿puedes recoger mis cartas en recepción?** = can you collect my letters from the reception desk?; **la recogida de cartas se hace dos veces al día** = letters are collected twice a day; **tenemos que recoger la mercancía del almacén** = we have to collect the stock from the warehouse **(b)** *(recopilar)* to gather; **recogió todos sus papeles antes de que empezara la reunión** = he gathered his papers together before the meeting started

recogida *nf* collection; **gastos** *o* **costes de recogida** = collection charges *o* collection rates; **hay seis recogidas de cartas al día** = there are six collections a day from the letter box

recomendación *nf* recommendation; **carta de recomendación** = letter of reference; **fue condenado a cadena perpetua, con la recomendación de que debería cumplir, al menos, veinte años** = he was sentenced to life imprisonment, with a recommendation that he should serve at least twenty years; **fue puesto en libertad por recomendación del comité encargado de la libertad condicional** = he was released on the recommendation of the Parole Board *o* on the Parole Board's recommendation; **lo nombramos por recomendación de su anterior jefe** = we appointed him on the recommendation of his former employer

recomendar *vt* to recommend; **¿me puede recomendar un buen hotel en Amsterdam?** = can you recommend a good hotel in Amsterdam?; **el abogado nos recomendó enviar los documentos a la policía** = the solicitor advised us to send the documents to the police; **la reunión del consejo recomendó un dividendo de 10 peniques por acción** = the board meeting recommended a dividend of 10p a share; **el comité** *o* **la junta recomendó al preso para la libertad condicional**

= the Parole Board recommended him for parole; **yo nunca recomendaría a la Srta.Smith para el trabajo** = I certainly would not recommend Miss Smith for the job

recompensa *nf* (a) *(premio)* reward; **la policía ha ofrecido una recompensa a cambio de información sobre el hombre visto en el banco** = the police have offered a reward for information about the man seen at the bank; **ofreció una recompensa de 5000 ptas a quien encontrara su reloj** = she offered a 5000 ptas reward to anyone who found her watch **(b)** *(prima)* bounty

recompensar *vt* to reward

reconciliación *nf* reconciliation; **reconciliación contable** = reconciliation; **reconciliación de las partes** = reconciliation; **estado de reconciliación** = reconciliation statement

reconciliar *vt* reconcile

reconocer *vt (distinguir)* **¿Reconoce la letra de la carta?** = do you recognize the handwriting on the letter?; **reconocí su voz antes de que dijera quién era** = I recognized his voice before he said who he was; **reconoció al hombre que la atacó** = she recognized the man who attacked her **(b)** *(admitir)* to recognize *o* to concede *o* to acknowledge *o* to admit to recognize; **reconocer a un hijo** = to acknowledge an illegitimate child; **reconocer un gobierno** = to recognize a government; **reconocer un sindicato** = to recognize a union *o* to grant a trade union recognition; **reconocer una firma** = to honour a signature; **aunque todos los empleados pertenecían al sindicato, la dirección se negó a reconocerlo** = although all the staff had joined the union, the management refused to recognize it; **reconoció su error** *o* **su responsabilidad** = he admitted his mistake *o* his liability **(c)** *(examinar)* **reconocer el terreno** = to case the joint

◊ **reconocido, -da** *adj* recognized; **representante reconocido** = recognized agent

◊ **reconocimiento** *nm* **(a)** *(agradecimiento)* recognition *o* appreciation *o* acknowledgement; **en reconocimiento de** = in appreciation of **(b)** *(aceptación)* admission *o* concession; **reconocimiento de culpabilidad** = admission of guilt **(c)** *(identificación)* **reconocimiento en rueda** = identity parade

reconstrucción *nf* reconstruction; **reconstrucción de los hechos** = reconstruction of a crime

reconvención *nf* counterclaim

reconvenir *vt* **(a)** *(presentar una reclamación)* counterclaim **(b)** *(reprender)* to reprimand

recopilación *nf* summary *o* consolidation; **recopilación de leyes** = corpus *o* law digest

recopilador, ra **1** *adj* **ley recopiladora** = Consolidating Act **2** *n* compiler

recopilar **ha estado recopilando información de varias fuentes sobre los controles a la importación** she has been gathering information on import controls from various sources

recopilar *vt* to gather *o* to compile; **recopilar datos** = to gather information; **recopilar pruebas documentales** = to compile documentary evidence

récord *nm* record *o* high; **el número de accidentes de tráfico ocurridos este año ha igualado al récord de 1997** = road accidents this year equalled the record of 1997; **el número de asaltos ha establecido un nuevo récord** = the figure for muggings has set a new record *o* has broken all previous records; **el volumen de ventas ha alcanzado un récord nunca visto** = sales volume has reached an all-time high

recordar *vt* **(a)** *(acordarse de)* to remember *o* to recall; **¿recuerda si vio al acusado en la casa?** = do you remember seeing the defendant in the house?; **el testigo no podía recordar si había visto al acusado** = the witness could not recall having seen the accused; **lo último que recordaba era el sonido de la sirena de la policía** = the last thing he remembered was the sound of the police siren; **no puede recordar dónde dejó las joyas** = she cannot remember where she left the jewels; **recuerdo que cerré con llave la caja de seguridad** = I remember locking the door of the safe; **recordó la matrícula del coche** = he remembered the registration number of the car **(b)** *(algo a alguien)* to remind; **¿me puedes recordar que cierre con llave la caja de seguridad?** = can you remind me to lock the safe?; **debo recordar al tribunal los detalles de la relación del acusado con el demandante** = I must remind the court of the details of the defendant's relationship with the plaintiff

◊ **recordatorio** *nm* reminder

recortar *vt* to reduce

◊ **recorte** *nm* cut; **recorte presupuestario** = budget cut; **recortes salariales** = salary cuts *o* cuts in salaries

rectificación *nf* amendment *o* rectification; **proponer una rectificación al borrador del acuerdo** = to propose an amendment to the draft agreement

rectificar *vt* to rectify *o* to amend *o* to correct; **rectificar un contrato** = to make amendments to a contract; **el tribunal rectificó su error** = the court rectified its mistake; **le ruego rectifique su copia del contrato en consecuencia** = please amend your copy of the contract accordingly

rectitud *nf* honesty; **el tribunal alabó a la testigo por su rectitud al informar a la policía del crimen** = the court praised the witness for her honesty in informing the police of the crime

recto, -ta *adj* straight *o* honest

rector, -ra 1 *adj* governing **2** *n* **rector de Universidad** rector *o* Vice Chancellor

recuperable *adj* recoverable

recuperación *nf* **(a)** *(reactivación)* recovery; **la economía mostró síntomas de recuperación** = the economy showed signs of a recovery; **la recuperación de la economía tras la recesión** = the recovery of the economy after a recession **(b)** *(rescate)* recovery *o* *(propiedad)* repossession; **recuperación de bienes muebles bajo fianza** = replevin; **recuperación de datos** = information retrieval; **recuperación de una propiedad** = re-entry; **derecho de recuperación de una propiedad** = right of re-entry; **nuestro propósito es la recuperación total del dinero invertido** = we are aiming for the complete recovery of the money invested

recuperar *vt* to recover *o* to get back; **recuperar un objeto comprado a plazos por falta de pago de los mismos** = to repossess; **acción para recuperar una propiedad** = possessive action; **iniciar una acción judicial para recuperar bienes** = to start a court action to recover property; **nunca se recuperó el desembolso inicial** = the initial investment was never recovered; **nunca recuperó su dinero** = he never recovered his money; **recuperará la propiedad al terminar el arrendamiento actual** = he has the reversion of the estate; **recuperé el dinero después de quejarme al director** = I got my money back after I had complained to the manager; **recuperó su inversión inicial en dos meses** = he got his initial investment back in two months; **recuperar los artículos retenidos en la aduana** = to release goods from customs

recuperarse *vr* to recover *o* to pick up; **los negocios se recuperan** = business *o* trade is picking up; **el mercado no se ha recuperado de la subida de los precios del petróleo** = the market has not recovered from the rise in oil prices; **la bolsa bajó por la mañana, pero se recuperó en el transcurso de la tarde** = the stock market fell in the morning, but recovered during the afternoon

recurrente *nmf* appelant

recurrir 1 *vi* **(a)** *(en un pleito)* to appeal; **decidir recurrir a los tribunales** = to decide to have recourse to the courts; **la empresa recurrió contra la decisión de los funcionarios de planificación** = the company appealed against the decision of the planning officers **(b) recurrir a** = to call in *o* to resort to; **los trabajadores no deben recurrir a la violencia en los conflictos laborales** = workers must not resort to violence in industrial disputes; **tuvo que recurrir a la amenaza de emprender una acción judicial para conseguir la devolución del dinero que le debían** = he had to resort to

threats of court action to get repayment of the money owing **2** *vt* **recurrir una sentencia** = to appeal against a sentence

recurso *nm* **(a)** *(en un pleito)* appeal; **recurso contra condena** = appeal against conviction; **recurso de amparo** = appeal for legal protection; **recurso de apelación** = appeal against sentence; **recurso de casación** = appeal to the Supreme Court; **recurso de queja** = appeal of complaint against refusal to accept appeal; **recurso de reposición** = appeal for reversal of interlocutory order; **recurso por quebrantamiento de forma** = appeal on grounds of breaking legal formalities; **perdió el recurso por daños y perjuicios contra la compañía** = he lost his appeal for damages against the company; **se presentará el próximo mes el recurso contra la resolución de planificación** *o* **el recurso de la sentencia del tribunal** = the appeal from the court order *o* the appeal against the planning decision will be heard next month **(b)** *(petición)* petition **(c)** *(medio para hacer algo)* resort; **prestamista de último recurso** = lender of the last resort **(d)** *(medios económicos)* **recursos** = means *o* finance; **declaración de recursos económicos** = statement of means

> El recurso es la acción que la ley concede a quien se considera perjudicado por una resolución judicial o administrativa, para formular reclamación contra ella ante el organismo correspondiente
> El recurso de amparo es un mecanismo procesal para recabar del Tribunal Constitucional la tutela de las libertades y drechos reconocidos en los artículos 14 al 30 de la Constitución Española frente a violaciones originadas por disposiciones emanadas de los poderes públicos

recusación *nf* objection *o* challenge; **recusación de un juez** = objection to a judge; **recusación del jurado** = objection to a jury; **recusación por falta de competencia** = challenge propter defectum; **recusación sin causa** = peremptory challenge ◊ **recusado, -da** *adj* unchallenged; **pruebas no recusadas** unchallenged evidence

recusar *vt* to challenge *o* to impeach; **recusar una sentencia aprobada por el juez de primera instancia por recurso ante el Tribunal Supremo** = to challenge a sentence passed by magistrates by appeal to the Crown Court

red *nf* network; **red de prostitución** = prostitution ring

redacción *nf* **(a)** *(documento)* drafting *o* wording; **redacción definitiva** = final wording *o* engrossment; **el periodo de redacción de un proyecto de ley parlamentaria** = the drafting stage of a parliamentary Bill; **la redacción del contrato duró seis semanas** = the drafting of the contract took six weeks **(b)** *(equipo de redactores)* editorial office; **consejo de redacción** = editorial board; **jefe de redacción** = editor

redactar *vt* to word *o* to draw up; **redactar un contrato** *o* **un acuerdo** *o* **un documento** *o* **un escrito** = to draft a contract *o* an agreement *o* a document *o* a bill; **redactar los estatutos de una compañía** = to draw up a company's articles of association; **el contrato estaba mal redactado** = the contract was incorrectly worded; **todavía estamos redactando el contrato** = the contract is still being drafted *o* is still in the drafting stage a contract
◊ **redactor, -ra** *n* **(a) redactor de documentos** = drafter; **redactor de proyectos de ley** = parliamentary draftsman **(b)** *(en un periódico, revista)* **equipo de redactores** = editorial board; **redactor jefe** = chief editor

redada *nf* raid; **redada policial** = police raid; **redada por sorpresa** = to raid; **la policía ha realizado redadas en varias casas de la ciudad** = the police have raided several houses in the town; **se encontraron drogas durante la redada policial en el club** = drugs were found when the police raided the club

redención *nf* redemption *o* ransom; **redención de una hipoteca** = settlement of a mortgage

redimir *vt* to redeem *o* to pay off; **redimir una hipoteca** = to pay off a mortgage; **privar del derecho de redimir una hipoteca** = foreclose

rédito *nm* return

redondo, -da *adj* round; **en números redondos** = in round figures; **el número de presos encarcelados es de 45.000 en números redondos** = the number of prisoners in jail is 45,000 in round figures

reducción *nf (rebaja)* reduction *o* cut; **reducción de gastos** = reduction of expenditure; **reducción de impuestos** = tax reductions; **reducción de la demanda** = reduction in demand; **reducción de personal** = staff reductions; **reducción de precios** = price cuts *o* cut in prices; **reducción de una condena** = remission; **reducción natural de la mano de obra por jubilación o baja voluntaria** = natural wastage; **una reducción en el capital nominal de una sociedad limitada requiere la autorización del tribunal** = a reduction in the nominal capital of a limited company requires the leave of the court

reducido, -da *adj* reduced

reducir *vt* **(a)** *(recortar)* to cut *o* to reduce *o* *(disminuir)* to decrease *o* to lessen; **reducir el empleo** *o* **los puestos de trabajo** = to cut jobs; **reducir el gasto en prisiones** *o* **en investigaciones criminales** = to reduce expenditure on prisons *o* on crime detection; **reducir la producción** = to cut

(back) production; **reducir los gastos al mínimo** = to keep spending to a minimum; **reducir proporcionalmente** *o* **a escala** = to scale down; **una medida para reducir gastos** = an economy measure; **recurrió y le redujeron la condena** = he received a reduced sentence on appeal; **hemos despedido a algunos empleados para reducir gastos** = we have made some staff redundant to reduce costs; **el tamaño de nuestras oficinas hace que el número de empleados quede reducido a veinte** = we are restricted to twenty staff by the size of our offices; **el Tribunal Supremo redujo la multa impuesta por el juzgado de primera instancia** *o* **redujo la condena a siete años de prisión** = the Appeal Court reduced the fine imposed by the magistrates *o* reduced the sentence to seven years' imprisonment; **la política del gobierno es reducir la inflación al 5%** = the government's policy is to reduce inflation to 5% **(b)** *(restringir)* to restrain; **el detenido opuso resistencia y tuvo que ser reducido por dos policías** = the prisoner fought and had to be restrained by two policemen

reembolsable *adj* repayable; **gastos reembolsables** = out-of-pocket expenses; **no reembolsable** = non-refundable; **el préstamo es reembolsable en cinco años** = the loan is repayable over five years

reembolsar *vt* to refund *o* to reimburse *o* to repay *o* to pay back; **devolver una deuda** = to pay back a debt; **reembolsar los gastos de franqueo** = to refund the cost of postage; **los gastos de desplazamiento de los testigos serán reembolsados** = witnesses' travelling expenses will be reimbursed to pay off
◊ **reembolsarse** *vr* to claw back; **de los diez millones de pesetas asignados para el desarrollo del sistema, el gobierno se reembolsó 1 millón en impuestos** = of the 10 million pesetas allocated to the development of the system, the government clawed back 1 million in taxes

reembolso *nm* rebate *o* repayment *o* refund *o* payback; **reembolso de una desgravación impositiva que había sido concedida** = clawback; **reembolso de una deuda** = redemption; **reembolso final** = final discharge; **cláusula de reembolso de un préstamo** = payback clause ; **pago contra reembolso** = cash on delivery; **plazo de reembolso** = payback period; **reembolso íntegro** *o* **total** = full refund *o* refund in full

reemplazar *vt* to replace *o* to supersede; **el gobierno ha publicado un proyecto de ley que reemplaza la legislación actual** = the government has published a Bill to supersede the current legislation
◊ **reemplazo** *nm* replacement

reestructuración *nf* restructuring; **la reestructuración de una empresa** = the reconstruction of a company

reexpedición *nf* return

referencia *nf* **(a)** *(recomendación)* reference; **dar referencias de alguien** = to write someone a reference *o* to give someone a reference; **dar el nombre de alguien como referencia** = to give someone's name as referee; **dio el nombre de su jefe como referencia** = she gave the name of her boss as a referee; **al hacer la solicitud se ruega incluir el nombre de tres personas como referencia** = when applying please give the names of three referees; **pedir a los candidatos que proporcionen sus referencias** = to ask applicants to supply references; **pedir a una empresa referencias comerciales** *o* **referencias bancarias** = to ask a company for trade references *o* for bank references; **persona que da referencias** = referee *o* reference; **puedes dar mi nombre como referencia si lo deseas** = please use me as a reference if you wish **(b) con referencia a** = in relation to; **con referencia a su carta del 25 de mayo** = with reference to your letter of May 25th; **hacer referencia a un número** = to quote; **referencia: informe de García de ayer** = re: García's memorandum of yesterday; **el informe no hace referencia a la imparcialidad del juez** = the report does not concern itself with the impartiality of the judge; **gracias por su carta (referencia 1234)** = thank you for your letter (reference 1234); **nuestra referencia es: PC/MS 1234** = our reference: PC/MS 1234; **sírvanse indicar esta referencia en su correspondencia** = please quote this reference in all correspondence **(c) prueba testimonial por referencia** = hearsay evidence

referéndum *nm* referendum; **el gobierno decidió hacer un referéndum sobre la abolición de la pena de muerte** = the government decided to hold a referendum on the abolition of capital punishment

referente *adj* **referente a** = in relation to; **la ley referente al orden público** = the law pertaining to public order; **referente a la orden judicial del 4 de junio** = referring to the court order dated June 4th

referirse **el precedente legal se refiere únicamente a los casos en los que los padres del niño estén divorciados** = the legal precedent applies to cases where the parents of the child are divorced

referir *vt* to refort *o* to refer
◊ **referirse** *vr* **(a)** *(remitirse)* to refer *o* to advert; **no se ha referido este caso en Santos** = this case was not adverted to in Santos; **se refirió a un artículo que había visto en 'La Vanguardia'** he referred to an article which he had seen in 'La Vanguardia' **(b) referirse a** = to apply *o* to concern *o* to pertain to *o* to bear on *o* to have a bearing on

reforma *nf* reform; **reforma de la ley** = law reform; **reforma judicial** = law reform; **han firmado un recurso para la reforma del sistema de detención preventiva** = they have signed an appeal for the reform of the remand system; **la reforma de la legislación se hizo con la intención de simplificar los procedimientos judiciales** = the reform in the legislation was intended to make the court procedure more straightforward

reformar *vt* to reform; **el grupo está presionando para que se reforme el régimen penitenciario** = the group is pressing for the prison system to be reformed; **el recluso ha cometido tantos delitos violentos que no podrán reformarle nunca** = the prisoner has committed so many crimes of violence that he will never be reformed

reformatorio *nm* reformatory *o* remand centre; **reformatorio de menores** = young offender institution

refrendar *vt* to countersign; **el pago tiene que ser refrendado por el deudor hipotecario** = the payment has to be countersigned by the mortgagor; **los comunicados oficiales del rey serán refrendados por el presidente del Gobierno** = the King's official communications shall be countersigned by the Prime Minister

refrendo *nm* authentication

refriega *nf* affray

refugiado, -da *n* refugee

refugiarse *vr* to take refuge *o* to shelter; **se refugiaron en un país vecino** = they seeked asylum in a neighbouring country

refugio *nm* refuge *o* shelter; **refugio tributario** = tax shelter

refundición *nf* revision *o* codification

refutación *nf* rebuttal

refutar *vt* to rebut *o* to contest

regalar *vt* to give *o* to give away *o* to present; **en la oficina le regalaron un reloj cuando se jubiló** = the office gave him a clock when he retired; **le regalaron un reloj al cumplir los veinticinco años de servicio a la empresa** = he was presented with a watch on completing twenty-five years' service with the company; **regalamos una calculadora de bolsillo por cada 5.000 pesetas de compra** = we are giving away a pocket calculator with each 5,000 pesetas of purchases

regalía *nf* royalty; **recibe regalías por su invención** = he is receiving royalties from his invention

regalo *nm* gift *o* present *o* free gift *o* giveaway; **la oficina le hizo un regalo cuando se casó** = the office gave her a present when she got married;

estas calculadoras son un buen regalo = these calculators make good presents

regateador, -ra *n* bargain hunter

regatear *vt/i* to bargain over; **se pasaron dos horas regateando** = they spent two hours bargaining about *o* over the discount; **tendrás que regatear con el comerciante si quieres que te haga descuento** = you will have to bargain with the dealer if you want a discount

regateo *nm* bargaining

régimen *nm* **régimen abierto** = open-plan; **régimen jurídico** = legal system

región *nf* region *o* area *o* district

regir 1 *vt (dominar)* to rule *o* to govern *o* to obtain; **que rige** = ruling; **ley por la que se debe regir un contrato** = proper law of the contract; **los precios que rigen en el momento actual** = prices which are ruling at the moment; **este derecho no rige en procesos judiciales** = this right does not obtain in judicial proceedings; **una norma que rige en el derecho internacional** = a rule obtaining in international law **2** *vi (vigente)* to be in force

registrado, -da *adj* registered; **registrado oficialmente** = registered; **registrado, -da como propiedad literaria** *o* **con derechos de autor** = copyrighted; **marca registrada** = trademark *o* trade mark *o* registered trademark *o* trade name; **de marca registrada** = proprietary; **medicamento de marca registrada** = proprietary drug; **propiedad registrada** = registered land; **sociedad registrada** = listed company; **valores registrados** = listed securities; **no registrado, -da** = unregistered; **documento no registrado** = inchoate instrument; **persona** *o* **empresa autorizada a usar una marca registrada** = registered user

registrador, -ra *n* registrar

registrar *vt* **(a)** *(inscribir en un registro)* to register *o* to enter *o* to record; **registrar en el haber** = to credit; **registrar un buque** = to flag a ship; **registrar una marca comercial** = to register a trademark; **registrar una propiedad** = to register a property; **registrar una venta** = to register a sale; **registrar como propiedad literaria** = to copyright; **sin registrar** = unregistered; **registrar la sentencia** = to enter judgement *o* to take judgment; **registrar la sentencia por alguien** *o* **en nombre de alguien** = to enter judgment for someone; **registrar comparecencia por parte de la defensa** = to enter an appearance; **el demandante registró la sentencia** = the plaintiff entered judgment; **el empleado registró la objeción en las actas** = the clerk entered the objection in the records; **se registró la sentencia en nombre del demandante** = judgment was entered for the plaintiff; **la empresa ha registrado un año más de aumento de ventas** = the company has

recorded another year of increased sales **(b)** *(examinar)* to examine *o* to search *o* to inspect *o* to frisk; **la policía registró la zona de alrededor de la casa en busca de pistas** = the police searched the area round the house for clues; **los oficiales de aduanas quisieron registrar el interior del coche** = the customs officials asked to examine the inside of the car; **todos los conductores y sus vehículos son registrados en el puesto de aduanas** = all drivers and their cars are searched at the customs post **(c)** *(catalogar)* to schedule *o* to set down

◊ **registrarse** *vr* to register; **se registraron en el hotel con el nombre de Mamano** = they registered at the hotel under the name of Mamano

registro *nm* **(a)** *(inscripción)* registry *o* register; **registro catastral** *o* **de la propiedad** = land registry *o* land registration; **registro central de penados y rebeldes** = central register of convicted offenders; **registro civil** = district registry *o* registry office; **registro de cargas** *o* **registro de gravámenes** = register of charges; **registro de empresas** = companies' register *o* register of companies; **registro de la propiedad intelectual** = copyright office; **registro de la sentencia** = entry of judgment; **Registro General de Actos de Ultima Voluntad** = Probate Registry; **registro de Lloyds** = Lloyd's register; **registro de obligaciones** *o* **de obligacionistas** = debenture register *o* register of debentures; **registro de patentes** = patents office; **registro de sumarios de causas** = docket; **registro de un buque** = registry; **registro de buques en naciones extranjeras** = flag of convenience; **registro electoral** = register of electors; **Registro Mercantil** = register of companies *o* companies' register; **secretario del Registro Mercantil** = Registrar of Companies; **secretario general** *o* **funcionario jefe del registro civil** = Registrar-General; **registro público** = public records office; **apuntar algo en un registro** = to enter something in a register; **certificado de registro de un buque** = certificate of registry; **declarar una defunción en el registro civil** = to register a death; **inscribir en un registro** = to register; **inscribir a una empresa en el registro** = to register a company; **inscribir un matrimonio en el registro civil** = to register a marriage; **inscripción de una marca en el registro** = registration of a trademark; **mantener un registro al día** = to keep a register up to date; **sociedad inscrita en el registro mercantil** = registered company **(b)** *(acto de registrar)* recording *o* entering *o* registration; **registro de la sentencia** = entry of judgment; **registro de tierras** = land registration; **registro de una transferencia de acciones** = registration of a share transaction; **derecho de registro** = registration fee; **número de registro** = registration number **(c)** *(inspección)* search *o* examination *o* inspection; **registro aduanero** = customs examination; **registro**

domiciliario = search of a house *o* search of premises; **orden de registro** = search warrant

regla *nf* **(a)** *(reglamento)* rule *o* law; **en regla** = in order *o* valid; **¿está toda la documentación en regla?** = is all the documentation in order?; **llevaba un pasaporte en regla** = he was carrying a valid passport **(b) por regla general** = as a rule *o* on an average; **resultar por regla general** = to average
◊ **reglamentación** *nf* regulations; **reglamentación en materia de importación y exportación** = regulations concerning imports and exports; **reglamentación en materia de incendios** = fire regulations

reglamentar *vt* to regulate
◊ **reglamentario, -ria** *adj* statutory; **instrumento reglamentario** *o* **orden reglamentaria** = statutory instrument; **libros reglamentarios** = statutory books; **obligación reglamentaria** = statutory duty; **orden reglamentaria** = statutory instrument; **vacaciones reglamentarias** = statutory holiday; **declaración reglamentaria ante el encargado del Registro Mercantil** = statutory declaration; **seguir el conducto reglamentario** = to go through official channels ; **existe** *o* **hay un periodo reglamentario de prueba de trece semanas** = there is a statutory period of probation of thirteen weeks
◊ **reglamentariamente** *adv* statutorily

reglamento *nm* regulations; **reglamento anticuado** *o* **en desuso** = dead letter; **reglamento del Tribunal Supremo** = Rules of the Supreme Court; **reglamento de una empresa** = company rules *o* code of practice; **reglamento general** = standing orders; **reglamento interno** = code of conduct; **reglamento municipal** = bylaw *o* byelaw *o* by-law *o* bye-law; **reglamento municipal efectivo sólo en esa jurisdicción** = ordinance; **ceñirse al reglamento** = to work to rule; **el reglamento prohíbe jugar al balón en los jardines públicos** = the bylaws forbid playing ball in the public gardens; **el Secretario de Estado ha hecho público el reglamento sobre piquetes** = the code of practice on picketing has been issued by the Secretary of State

regreso *nm* return; **viaje de regreso** = return journey

regulación *nf* regulation; **la regulación de las prácticas comerciales** = the regulation of trading practices

regular 1 *adj* regular *o* standard *o* average; **la actuación de la empresa ha sido sólo regular** = the company's performance has been only average **2** *vt* **(a)** *(ajustar)* to regulate; **precio regulado por el gobierno** = government-regulated price; **los precios se regulan por la oferta y la demanda** = prices are regulated by supply and demand **(b)** *(regir)* to govern; **la cuantía de los daños viene**

regulada según la gravedad de las heridas sufridas = the amount of damages is governed by the seriousness of the injuries suffered

rehabilitación *nf* rehabilitation; **rehabilitación de quiebra** = discharge in *o* of bankruptcy; **rehabilitación del quebrado** = discharge in bankruptcy; **centro de rehabilitación** = detention centre; **rehabilitación de delincuentes** = rehabilitation of offenders

rehabilitado, -da *adj* rehabilitated; **quebrado rehabilitado** = discharged bankrupt; **quebrado no rehabilitado** = undischarged bankrupt

rehabilitar *vt* to rehabilitate; **rehabilitar al quebrado** = to discharge a bankrupt

rehén *nmf* hostage; **los bandidos se llevaron al director del banco y lo tuvieron de rehén** = the bandits took away the bank manager and kept him hostage; **los guerrilleros le tomaron como rehén** = he was taken hostage by the guerillas; **los terroristas liberaron a tres rehenes** = the terrorists released three hostages

rehusar *vt* to refuse

Reina *nf* Queen *o* Regina; **la reina madre** = the queen mother; **por orden de la reina** = by Royal Command
◊ **reinado** *nm* reign; **bajo el reinado de** = in the reign of; **una ordenanza que se remonta al reinado de Carlos III** = a byelaw dating back to the reign of Charles the third
◊ **reinar** *vi* to reign; **el caos reinaba en el centro de la ciudad hasta que llegó la policía** = chaos reigned in the centre of town until the police arrived

reincidencia *nf* relapse

reincidente *nmf* recidivist; **criminal reincidente** = persistent offender *o* habitual criminal *o* hardened criminal; **condena a un reincidente** = re-conviction; **el índice de condenas a reincidentes está aumentando** = the re-conviction rate is rising; **ex-presidiario reincidente** = old lag

reincidir *vi* to relapse *o* to repeat an offence

reingreso *nm* re-entry

reinserción *nf* **reinserción social** = rehabilitation
◊ **reinsertar** *vt* rehabilitate

reintegrar *vt* to refund; **se reintegrarán los gastos de desplazamiento a los testigos que presten declaración ante el tribunal** = travelling expenses will be refunded to witnesses giving evidence to the tribunal
◊ **reintegro** *nm* refund *o* withdrawal

reiteración *nf* repetition; **carta de reiteración** = follow-up letter

reivindicación *nf* claim; **reivindicación salarial** = wage claim; **su gobierno ha formulado una reivindicación sobre parte de nuestro territorio** = their government has laid claim to part of our territory

reivindicar *vt* to claim; **el sindicato reivindicó un aumento salarial del 6%** = the union put in a 6% wage claim

reja *nf* bar; **entre rejas** = behind bars

relación *nf* (a) *(vínculo entre personas)* relation *o* relationship; **relación consanguínea** = blood relationship; **relaciones laborales** = industrial relations *o* labour relations; **relaciones públicas** = public relations (PR); **relaciones sexuales** = sexual intercourse; **departamento de relaciones públicas** = public relations department; **responsable de relaciones públicas** *o* **funcionario encargado de las relaciones públicas** = public relations officer; **entablar relaciones comerciales con alguien** = to enter into relations with someone; **tuvo una relación adúltera con la Srta. X** = he had an adulterous relationship with Miss X; **¿qué relación existe entre el acusado y el testigo?** = what is the relationship between the accused and witness?; **relación contractual** *o* **relación particular de las partes contratantes** = privity of contract; **interrumpir las relaciones comerciales con alguien** = to break off relations with someone; **mantener relaciones sexuales con una menor de doce años es constitutivo de delito** = sexual intercourse with a girl under twelve is an offence (b) *(conexión)* connection *o* relevance; **relación precio-ganancias** *o* **relación entre la cotización de una acción y sus beneficios** = price/earnings ratio; **no hay relación alguna entre los dos delitos** = there is no connection between the two crimes; **¿existe alguna relación entre la pérdida de los documentos y la muerte del abogado?** = is there a connection between the loss of the documents and the death of the lawyer?; **el abogado discutió con el juez si los documentos tenían alguna relación con el caso** = counsel argued with the judge over the relevance of the documents to the case (c) *(lista)* index *o* list; **relación de accionistas** = register of members *o* of shareholders *o* share register; **relación de directivos de una empresa** = register of directors (d) *(relativo a)* **con relación a** = in relation to; **tener alguna relación con** = to relate to; **se le ha pedido que declare como testigo en relación con la estafa** = he has been asked to give evidence concerning the fraud (e) *(contacto)* contact

◊ **relacionado, -da** *adj* related *o* relevant; **relacionado con** = relating to; **estar relacionado con** = to concern; **daños que no están suficientemente relacionados con un caso** *o* **principio legal según el cual los daños que no están suficientemente relacionados con un caso no obligan al acusado** = remoteness of damage; **el**

tribunal decidió que los daños no estaban lo suficientemente relacionados con el caso como para que el demandante pudiera tener derecho a reparación = the court decided that the damage was too remote to be recoverable by the plaintiff; **delitos relacionados con drogas** = offences related to drugs *o* drug-related offences; **documentos relacionados con el caso** = documents relating to the case; **la pregunta no está relacionada con el caso** = the question is not relevant to the case; **personas bien relacionadas** = connected persons

◊ **relacionar** *vt* to connect; **la empresa está relacionada con el gobierno porque el hermano del presidente es ministro** = the company is connected to the government because the chairman's brother is a minister

◊ **relacionarse** *vr* **relacionarse con** = to relate to *o* to pertain to

relacionarse; referirse a *o* relacionarse con

relativo , -va *adj* relative; **relativo a** = in relation to *o* relating to *o* against *o* re; **documentos relativos al caso** = documents in relation to the case; **los poderes judiciales relativos a la custodia de los hijos** = the court's powers in relation to children in care; **relativo a: el orden del día de la Junta General Ordinaria** = re: the agenda for the AGM; **la legislación relativa a la conducción en estado de embriaguez** = the law which relates to drunken driving

relato *nm* account; **relato de los hechos** = particulars of claim

relevante *adj* relevant; **daños no relevantes** = nominal damages

relevar *vt* to remove; **relevar a alguien de un cargo** = to relieve someone from his /her post

◊ **relevo** *nm* take-over *o* relief; **el periodo de relevo siempre es difícil** = the take-over period is always difficult; **se retrasó el relevo** *o* **el relevo llegó con retraso** = the relief was delayed *o* arrived late

reliquia *nf* **reliquia familiar** *o* **de familia** = heirloom

remanente *adj* remaining; **legatario, -ria remanente** = residuary devisee *o* residuary legatee

remarcar *vt* to flag; **el funcionario del comité remarcó todas las referencias a las obras de reparación** = the committee clerk flagged all the references to building repairs

remediar *vt* to remedy

remedio *nm* remedy; **sin remedio** = irretrievably; **el demandante está buscando remedio a través de los tribunales** = the plaintiff is seeking remedy through the courts

remesa *nf* consignment *o* remittance; **remesa documental** = documentary remittance

remisión *nf* remission; **remisión de condena** = suspended sentence; **remisión de la pena** = licence *o* license; **remisión del procedimiento a la Audiencia** *o* **puesta a disposición de un tribunal superior** = committal for trial; **remisión de una sentencia** = prerogative of mercy; **le condenaron a cinco años, pero con la remisión sólo cumplirá tres** = he was sentenced to five years, but should serve only three with remission

remite *nm* return address
◊ **remitente** *nmf* sender *o* consignor *o* shipper *o* return address

remitir *vt* **(a)** *(devolver)* 'remitir al librador' = 'refer to drawer'; **remítase al destinatario** *o* **a las nuevas señas** = please forward *o* to be forwarded **(b)** *(referir)* to refer; **remitir un caso a un tribunal inferior** = to remand; **remitir un problema a un comité** = to refer a question to a committee; **el banco remitió el cheque al librador** = the bank referred the cheque to drawer; **hemos remitido su queja al tribunal** = we have referred your complaint to the tribunal **(b)** *(perdonar)* to remit; **le remitieron seis meses de pena por buena conducta** = she got six months' remission for good behaviour
◊ **remitirse** *vr* to refer to; **nos remitimos a su carta del 26 de mayo** = we refer to your letter of May 26th

remoción *nf* dismissal

remoto, -ta *adj* remote

remuneración *nf* remuneration; **no recibe remuneración por su trabajo como secretario honorario del club de fútbol** = he receives no remuneration for his work as honorary secretary of the football club

remunerado, -da *adj* paid; **empleo remunerado** = gainful employment; **no ejerce un empleo remunerado** *o* **no tiene un trabajo remunerado** = he is not gainfully employed

rencor *nm* resentment

rendimiento *nm* **(a)** *(actuación)* performance; **rendimiento del personal en relación a los objetivos marcados** = performance of personnel against objectives; **de buen rendimiento** = efficient; **como medida del rendimiento de la empresa** = as a measure of the company's performance; **entrevista anual entre empleado y director para revisar el rendimiento del primero** = performance review **(b)** *(beneficio)* yield *o* return; **rendimiento anual** = annual return; **rendimiento de la inversión** *o* **del capital** = return on investment *o* on capital; **rendimiento nulo** = nil return; **rendimiento sobre el capital** return against capital employed; **tasa de rendimiento** = rate of return **(c)** *(producción)* capacity *o* output; **estamos trabajando a pleno rendimiento** = we are working at full capacity

rendir 1 *vt* **(a)** *(producir)* to produce; **rendir cuentas** = to render an account; **rendir interés** = to yield **(b)** *(actuar)* to perform **2** *vi* to produce *o* to yield; **tuvieron que cerrar porque el negocio no rendía** = they had to close down because the business didn't pay
◊ **rendirse** *vr* to surrender *o* to submit

renovación *nf* renewal; **aviso de renovación de un seguro** = renewal notice; **¿cuándo es la fecha de renovación de la letra?** = when is the renewal date of the bill?; **prima sucesiva** *o* **de renovación** = renewal premium; **renovación de un contrato de arrendamiento** *o* **de una subscripción** *o* **de una letra** = renewal of a lease *o* of a subscription *o* of a bill

renovar *vt* to renew; **renovar una letra de cambio** *o* **un contrato de arrendamiento** = to renew a bill of exchange *o* to renew a lease; **renovar una póliza de seguros** = to renew an insurance policy; **renovar una subscripción** *o* **un abono** = to renew a subscription; **habrá que renovar el contrato de arrendamiento el mes que viene** = the lease is up for renewal next month

renta *nf* income *o* rent *o* revenue; **renta anual** = annuity; **renta de la tierra** *o* **del terreno** = ground rent; **renta disponible** = disposable income; **renta fija** = fixed income; **renta nacional** = national income; **renta no imponible** = personal allowances; **renta nominal** = nominal rent; **renta vitalicia** = life interest *o* life annuity *o* annuity for life; **declaración de la renta** = tax return *o* tax declaration; **impuesto sobre la renta** = income tax; **inversiones de renta fija** = fixed-interest investments
◊ **rentabilidad** *nf* yield *o* profitability; **rentabilidad económica** = earning power; **valoración de la rentabilidad** = measurement of profitability
◊ **rentable** *adj* commercial *o* profitable; **una proposición no rentable** = not a commercial proposition
◊ **rentista** *nmf* annuitant

renuncia *nf* **(a)** *(dimisión de un cargo)* renunciation *o* resignation; **carta de renuncia** = letter of renunciation **(b)** *(en un contrato)* disclaimer *o* waiver; **cláusula contractual de renuncia de responsabilidad** = disclaimer; **cláusula de renuncia** = waiver clause **(c)** *(abandono)* abandonment *o* waiver *o* abjuration; **renuncia de citación** = waiver of notice; **renuncia de un derecho** = release; **renuncia al derecho de juicio con jurado** = waiver of jury **(d)** *(rescate)* surrender

renunciar *vt* **(a)** *(desistir)* to renounce; **renunciar a** = to abandon *o* to waive *o* to abjure; **renunciar a un derecho** = to surrender a right; **renunció a su derecho a la herencia** = he waived his claim to the estate; **el gobierno ha renunciado**

al uso de la fuerza en el trato con terroristas internacionales = the government has renounced the use of force in dealing with international terrorists **(b)** *(negarse a admitir)* to disclaim

reo *nmf* culprit *o* prisoner; **reo de muerte** = prisoner under death sentence

reorganización *nf* reorganization; **la reorganización de una empresa** = the reorganization of a company *o* a company reorganization

reorganizar *vt* to reorganize

reparación *nf* repair *o* relief; **reparación de los daños** = recovery *o* compensation; **reparación presentada ante los tribunales** = relief; **arrendamiento en el que las reparaciones corren por cuenta del arrendatario** = full repairing lease; **el propietario efectuó reparaciones en el tejado** = the landlord carried out repairs to the roof; **la cuenta por la reparación del coche ascendía a 150.000 ptas** = the bill for repairs to the car came to 150,000 ptas
◊ **reparador** *nm* repairer; **derecho de retención de un reparador sobre el artículo reparado hasta no haber cobrado por ello** = repairer's lien

reparar *vt* to repair *o* to fix; **reparar una injusticia** = to repair an injustice

reparo *nm* **(a)** *(arreglo)* repair **(b)** *(objeción)* **poner reparos a algo** = to raise an objection to something; **los delegados del sindicato pusieron reparos al texto del acuerdo** = the union delegates raised an objection to the wording of the agreement

repartir *vt* **(a)** *(dividir y distribuir)* to share *o* to divide *o* to distribute *o* to allot; **repartir acciones** = to allot shares; **repartir acciones a alguien** = to assign shares to someone; **repartir proporcionalmente** = to apportion; **el mercado está repartido entre tres empresas** = three companies share the market; **el dinero de la herencia se debe repartir entre los familiares del difunto** = the money in the estate is to be distributed among the members of the deceased's family **(b)** *(entregar)* to deliver
◊ **repartirse** *vr* to share out; **las dos compañías acordaron repartirse el mercado entre ellas** = the two companies agreed to divide the market between them

reparto *nm* **(a)** *(distribución)* distribution; **reparto de bienes** = distribution of assets; **reparto de bienes muebles** = partition of chattels; **reparto de tierra** = partition **(b)** *(entrega)* delivery; **reparto de productos** = delivery of goods

repatriación *nf* repatriation

repatriar *vt* to repatriate

repentino, -na *adj* sharp; **baja repentina de precios** = sharp drop in prices

◊ **repentinamente** *adv* sharply

repercusión *nf* knock-on effect

repercutir *vi* **repercutir en** = to to have an effect on; **la huelga de los oficiales de aduana ha repercutido en la producción de coches al retrasar las exportaciones** = the strike by customs officers has had a knock-on effect on car production by slowing down exports of cars

repertorio *nm* index

repetición *nf* repetition; **la repetición de una difamación es un delito** = repetition of a libel is an offence

repetir *vt* to repeat; **repitió su declaración más despacio para que el oficial de policía pudiera tomar nota** = he repeated his evidence slowly so that the police officer could write it down; **cuando se le preguntó qué pensaba hacer, el presidente de los magistrados repitió 'Nada'** = when asked what he planned to do, the chairman of the magistrates repeated 'Nothing'
◊ **repetirse** *vr* to recur; **espero que nunca vuelva a repetirse** = I hope it will never recur

réplica *nf* answer *o* reply; **derecho de réplica** = right of reply; **exigió el derecho de réplica a las alegaciones realizadas por el periódico** = he demanded the right of reply to the newspaper allegations

replicar *vt/i* to reply *o* to answer

reportaje *nm* **la empresa dispuso de amplios reportajes en los medios de comunicación para el lanzamiento de su nuevo modelo** = the company had good media coverage for the launch of its new model

repregunta *nf* cross-examination

repreguntar *vt* to cross-examine

reprender *vt* to reprimand *o* to reprehend; **fue reprendido por el juez** = he was reprimanded by the magistrate
◊ **reprensible** *adj* reprehensible

reprensión *nf* reprimand; **el oficial de policía recibió una reprensión oficial tras la investigación del accidente** = the police officer received an official reprimand after the inquiry into the accident

represalia *nf* retaliation; **tomar represalias** = to retaliate; **el tribunal concedió un requerimiento a los trabajadores y la dirección tomó represalias cerrando las puertas de la oficina** = the court granted an injunction to the workers, and the management retaliated by locking the office doors; **los atracadores dispararon a los empleados del banco y la policía respondió del mismo modo como represalia** = the robbers fired at the bank staff, and the police fired back in retaliation

representación *nf* representation *o (agencia)* agency; **sistema de representación proporcional** = proportional representation; **representación a cargo de un abogado** = representation; **gastos de representación** = entertainment expenses; **cuenta de gastos de representación** = expense account; **firmaron un contrato de representación** = they signed an agency agreement *o* an agency contract; **representación falsa con ánimo de fraude** *o* **de engaño** *o* **de impostura** = fraudulent misrepresentation

representante *nmf* representative *o* delegate *o* agent; **representante exclusivo** = sole agent; **representante testamentario** = personal representative *o* albacea; **representante en la cámara baja del Congreso** = *US* representative; **nombrar a alguien representante** = to nominate someone as proxy; **Cámara de Representantes** = *US* the House *o* House of Representatives; **sistema de elección de representantes en el parlamento** = representation; **el solicitante carecía de representante legal** = the applicant had no legal representation; **el tribunal oyó al representante de la compañía de seguros** = the court heard the representative of the insurance company; **la dirección se negó a reunirse con los representantes de los sindicatos** = the management refused to meet the trade union delegates

representar *vt* to represent; **representar a** = to appear; **representar a alguien** = to act for someone *o* to act on someone's behalf; **el acusado está representado por su abogado** = the defendant is represented by his solicitor; **el Sr. Rosanas representa al demandado** = Mr Rosanas is appearing on behalf of the defendant; **los abogados que representaban a la esposa solicitaron una orden de manutención** = solicitors acting for the wife made an application for a maintenance order

reprimenda *nf* caution

reprochar *vt* to blame *o* to reproach

reproducción *nf* reproduction; **derechos de reproducción** = mechanical reproduction rights; **la ley prohíbe la reproducción de material sujeto a derechos de autor sin el permiso de éste** *o* **del mismo** the reproduction of copyright material without the permission of the copyright holder is banned by law

reproducir *vt* to reproduce; **los documentos relacionados con las vistas están reproducidos en el reverso del informe** = the documents relating to the hearings are reproduced in the back of the report
◊ **reproducirse** *vr* **(a)** *(propagar)* to reproduce *o* to breed **(b)** *(volver a producirse)* to recur

repudiar *vt* to repudiate; **repudiar una herencia** = to reject a will
◊ **repudio** *nm* repudiation

repuesto *nm* spare part; **pieza de repuesto** = spare part

reputación *nf* reputation *o* standing *o* character; **empresa de muy buena reputación** = company of good standing; **es un hombre de buena reputación** = he is a man of good character; **llevar testigos a un juicio para que testifiquen sobre la reputación de alguien** = to introduce character evidence; **mala reputación** = disrepute
◊ **reputado, -da** *adj* reputable

requerimiento *nm* demand *o* summons *o* injunction; **requerimiento de ampliación de plazo** = time summons; **requerimiento de pago** = demand; **requerimiento de pago de acciones** = call; **requerimiento final** *o* **último requerimiento** = final demand; **requerimiento imperativo** = mandatory injunction; **requerimiento interlocutorio** *o* **cautelar** = interlocutory *o* temporary injunction; **requerimiento judicial** = injunction *o* summons; **requerimiento judicial de pago** *o* **en su defecto de ingreso en prisión** = judgment summons; **requerimiento prohibitorio** *o* **interdicto prohibitivo** = prohibitory injunction; **requerimiento provisional** = interim injunction; **carta de requerimiento** = letter of demand; **la empresa solicitó un requerimiento que impidiera a la competencia comercializar un producto parecido** = the company applied for an injunction to stop their competitor from marketing a similar product; **recibió un requerimiento impidiendo que la empresa vendiera su coche** = he got an injunction preventing the company from selling his car; **la empresa volvió a solicitar un requerimiento en contra de los sindicatos** = the company reapplied for an injunction against the union

requerir *vt* **(a)** *(necesitar)* to require; **el documento requiere un estudio en profundidad** *o* **un examen cuidadoso** = the document requires careful study; **para escribir el programa se requiere un especialista en informática** = to write the program requires a computer specialist **(b)** *(exigir)* to demand; **les acusaron de requerir el pago con amenazas** = they were accused of demanding payment with threats

requisar *vt* to requisition; **el ejército requisó todos los camiones para llevar provisiones** = the army requisitioned all the trucks to carry supplies

requisito *nm* requirement; **requisitos mínimos necesarios** = minimum requirement; **requisitos mínimos para poder ser beneficiario de una prestación o ayuda** period of qualification; **requisitos para hacerse socio** = membership qualifications; **requisitos presupuestarios** = budgetary requirements; **que satisface los requisitos** = up to standard; **'sin lo que nada':** **requisito indispensable** = sine qua non; **el acuerdo por parte de la dirección es un requisito**

indispensable de todos los contratos de trabajo = agreement by the management is a sine qua non of all employment contracts

requisitoria *nf* warrant for the arrest of a wanted person; **requisitoria del título de propiedad =** requisition on title; **requisitoria judicial =** bench warrant

resarcimiento *nm* compensation
◊ **resarcir** *vt* to compensate *o* to repay
◊ **resarcirse** *vr* to claw back *o* to recover; **con el impuesto sobre la renta, el Estado se resarce del 25% de lo que paga en pensiones =** income tax claws back 25% of pensions paid out by the government

rescatable *adj* redeemable

rescatado, -da *adj* redeemed; **prenda** *o* **garantía no rescatada =** unredeemed pledge

rescatar *vt* to redeem *o* to rescue *o* to buy back; **rescatar una póliza de seguros =** to surrender a policy
◊ **rescate** *nm* **(a)** *(salvamento)* rescue *o* ransom *o* salvage; **nota de rescate =** ransom note; **operación de rescate =** rescue operation; **pagar un rescate =** to ransom; **pedir** *o* **exigir rescate por alguien =** to hold someone to ransom; **la hija del banquero fue retenida por los secuestradores que pedían un rescate de cien millones de ptas =** the daughter of the banker was held by kidnappers who asked for a ransom of one hundred million ptas; **su familia pagó el rescate por su liberación =** she was ransomed by her family **(b)** *(redención)* surrender; **rescate anticipado =** redemption before due date; **rescate de un empréstito =** redemption; **derecho del propietario al rescate de un bien hipotecado mediante el pago de la deuda (incluso una vez iniciada la ejecución) =** equity of redemption; **fecha de rescate =** redemption date; **valor de rescate =** redemption value *o* surrender value

reiscindible *adj* annullable *o* voidable

reiscindir *vt* to annul *o* to cancel *o* to rescind; **rescindir un contrato** *o* **un acuerdo =** to void a contract *o* to rescind an agreement

rescisión *nf* **(a)** *(cancelación)* annulling *o* annulment *o* rescinding *o* rescission; **cláusula de rescisión =** cancellation clause **(b)** *(expiración)* termination; **la rescisión de una oferta =** the termination of an offer

reserva *nf* **(a)** *(hotel, avión)* reservation *o* booking; **llamó a la sección de reservas** *o* **a recepción y pidió una habitación para cuatro noches =** he phoned reservations and asked to book a room for four nights **(b)** *(provisión)* reserve *o* provision; **reservas bancarias =** bank reserves; **reservas de divisas =** currency reserves *o* foreign exchange reserves; **reservas en metálico** *o* **reservas de capital =** cash reserves; **reservas**

ocultas = hidden reserves; **reserva para deudas incobrables =** reserve for bad debts; **reserva para imprevistos =** contingency reserve *o* emergency reserve; **divisas de reserva =** reserve currency; **en reserva** *o* **de reserva =** in reserve *o* in hand; **fondo reserva =** fund; **fondos de reserva =** reserve fund; **las reservas de divisas de un país =** a country's foreign currency reserves **(c)** *(suministro)* supply *o* stock; **tenemos grandes reservas de petróleo** *o* **carbón =** we have large stocks of oil *o* coal; **las reservas del país de mantequilla** *o* **azúcar =** the country's stocks of butter *o* sugar **(d) cláusula de reserva de dominio =** reservation of title clause; **con reservas =** conditionally *o* qualified; **aceptar una oferta con reservas =** to accept an offer conditionally; **cuentas aprobadas con reservas =** qualified accounts; **sin reservas =** without reservations; **aceptó todas nuestras condiciones sin reservas =** he accepted all our conditions in full; **el plan recibió la aprobación del consejo con reservas =** the plan received qualified approval from the board; **los auditores han aprobado las cuentas con reservas =** the auditors have qualified the accounts; **manifestó sus reservas con respecto a la legalidad de la acción =** he expressed reservations about the legality of the action; **el plan fue aceptado por el comité con ciertas reservas =** the plan was accepted by the committee with some reservations **(e)** *(deducción)* allowance

reservado, -da *adj* **(a)** *(hotel, avión)* booked *o* reserved **(b)** *(secreto)* closed; **reservado para uso oficial =** for official use only; **reservados todos los derechos =** all rights reserved; **información reservada =** classified information

reservar *vt* to reserve *o* to book; **reservar una habitación** *o* **una mesa** *o* **un billete =** to reserve a room *o* a table *o* a seat; **reservar una habitación de hotel** *o* **una mesa en un restaurante** *o* **un billete de avión =** to book a room in a hotel *o* a table at a restaurant *o* a ticket on a plane; **reservar una habitación de hotel** *o* **un billete de avión para alguien =** to book someone into a hotel *o* onto a flight; **reservé una mesa para las 7.45 =** I booked a table for 7.45; **¿puede su secretaria reservarme un billete de tren para Sevilla? =** can your secretary reserve a seat for me on the train to Sevilla?; **quiero reservar una mesa para cuatro personas =** I want to reserve a table for four people; **reservó un billete hasta El Cairo =** he booked a ticket through to Cairo **(b)** *(asignar)* to earmark; **la empresa ha reservado 2 millones de libras para deudas incobrables =** the company has made a £2m provision for bad debts; **reservamos el derecho a sus servicios por un pago de 100.000 ptas al año =** we pay him a retainer of 100,000 ptas per annum; **se reservan 250.000 ptas para deudas incobrables =** 250,000 ptas are provided against bad debts; **reservar dinero para imprevistos =** to provide

◊ **reservarse** *vr* to reserve; **reservarse el derecho de hacer algo** = to reserve the right to do something; **reservarse el juicio** = to reserve judgment; **reservarse la defensa en espera del juicio definitivo** = to reserve one's defence; **nos reservamos el derecho de apelar contra el fallo del tribunal** = we reserve the right to appeal against the tribunal's decision; **se reservó el derecho de interrogar a los testigos** = he reserved the right to cross-examine witnesses

resguardo *nm* receipt *o* slip; **resguardo provisional** = binder

residencia *nf* residence; **residencia habitual** = habitual residence; **derecho de residencia** = right of abode; **permiso de residencia** = residence permit; **sin residencia fija** = no fixed abode; **ha solicitado un permiso de residencia** = he has applied for a residence permit; **la empresa tiene su residencia en Valencia** = the company is resident in Valencia; **le concedieron un permiso de residencia de un año** = she was granted a residence permit for one year; **persona con residencia habitual en España** = person ordinarily resident in Spain

◊ **residencial** adj **inmuebles residenciales** = house property

◊ **residente** *nmf* resident; **no residente** = non-resident; **le concedieron un visado de no residente** = she was granted a non-resident visa; **tiene una cuenta de no residente en un banco español** = he has a non-resident account with a Spanish bank

residual *adj* residual *o* residuary; **bienes residuales** = residue; **legatario, -ria residual** = residuary devisee *o* residuary legatee; **patrimonio hereditario residual** = residuary estate; **después de pagar varios legados, los bienes residuales de su fortuna se dividieron entre sus hijos** = after paying various bequests the residue of his estate was split between his children

residuo *nm* residue

resistencia *nf* resistance; **resistencia a la autoridad** = resisting arrest; **resistencia pasiva** = civil disobedience; **el grupo planeó una campaña de resistencia pasiva en protesta contra las restricciones a los inmigrantes** = the group planned a campaign of civil disobedience as a protest against restrictions on immigrants; **había mucha resistencia al nuevo plan por parte de los funcionarios de prisiones** = there was a lot of resistance from the prison officers to the new plan; **la propuesta del ministro del interior provocó una gran resistencia por parte del servicio encargado de la libertad condicional** = the Home Secretary's proposal met with strong resistance from the probation service

◊ **resistente** adj *(a prueba de)* -proof

resistir *vt* to resist; **pensión que resiste la inflación** = inflation-proof pension; **el acusado resistió todas las presiones para obligarle a confesar** = the accused resisted all attempts to make him confess

◊ **resistirse** *vr* to resist; **la empresa se resiste a la oferta de adquisición** = the company is resisting the takeover bid

resolución *nf* resolution *o* order; **resolución extraordinaria** *o* **especial** = extraordinary *o* special resolution; **resolución judicial de quiebra** = adjudication order *o* adjudication of bankruptcy; **resolución ordinaria** = ordinary resolution; **presentar una resolución en una reunión** = to put a resolution to a meeting

◊ **resolutorio, -ria** *adj* subsequent; **cláusula resolutoria** = termination clause *o* defeasance; **condición resolutoria** = condition subsequent

resolver *vt* **(a)** *(solucionar)* to solve *o* to clear up; **resolver un crimen** = to solve a crime; **sin resolver** = outstanding *o* unsolved *o* pending; **la mitad de los crímenes cometidos quedan sin resolver** = half the crimes committed are never cleared up **(b)** *(decidir)* to determine

respaldar *vt* to back someone *o* to support

◊ **respaldo** *nm* backing; **tener respaldo económico** = to cover a position

respectivamente *adv* respectively *o* severally

respecto *nm* respect

respecto a = re; **respecto a su petición del 29 de mayo** = re your inquiry of May 29th; **con respecto a** = in connection with *o* with respect to *o* in respect of; **con respecto a su carta del 25 de mayo** = with reference to your letter of May 25th; **el acusado reclamó por su parte los daños debidos a rotura y extravío con respecto a una máquina que el acusado le había vendido** = the defendant counterclaimed for loss and damage in respect of a machine sold to him by the plaintiff; **la policía quiere interrogar al hombre con respecto a los robos perpetrados el pasado noviembre** = the police want to interview the man in connection with burglaries committed last November; **su derecho a indemnización con respecto a desembolsos anteriores** = his right to an indemnity in respect of earlier disbursements

respetar *vt* to respect; **hacer respetar** = to uphold; **hacer respetar la ley** = to uphold the law; **que no se puede hacer respetar** = unenforceable; **respetar una cláusula de un acuerdo** = to respect a clause in an agreement; **la empresa no ha respetado los términos del contrato** = the company has not respected the terms of the contract

◊ **respeto** *nm* respect; **falta de respeto** = disrespect; **le acusaron de faltar al respeto al juez** = he was accused of showing disrespect to the judge

respiración *nf* breath

responder *vt* to answer *o* to reply; **responder a** = to answer to; **responder de** = to vouch for; **no puedo responder de la exactitud de la transcripción de las actas** = I cannot vouch for the correctness of the transcript of proceedings

responsabilidad *nf* responsibility *o* liability *o* onus *o* accountability; **responsabilidad civil** = civil liability; **responsabilidad civil subsidiaria** = vicarious liability; **responsabilidad colectiva** = collective responsibility; **responsabilidad conjunta y solidaria** = joint and several liability; **responsabilidad contractual** = contractual liability; **responsabilidad del inquilino de que los visitantes no sufran daños** = occupier's liability; **responsabilidad legal por un producto** = product liability; **responsabilidad limitada** = limited liability; **cláusula de responsabilidad limitada de los socios** = liability clause; **edad de responsabilidad penal** = age of criminal responsibility; **sociedad de responsabilidad limitada** = close company *o* limited liability company; **un trabajo** *o* **puesto de responsabilidad** = a responsible job; **aceptar** *o* **admitir la responsabilidad de algo** = to accept *o* to admit liability for something; **rechazar** *o* **no admitir la responsabilidad de algo** = to refuse liability for something; **el inquilino tiene la responsabilidad de mantener el interior del edificio en buen estado** = keeping the interior of the building in good order is the responsibility of the tenant; **las responsabilidades de su cargo como director gerente le resultan demasiado pesadas** = he finds the responsibilities of being managing director too heavy ; **sus aseguradores han admitido la responsabilidad pero la cantidad de los daños aún no ha sido acordada** = his insurers have admitted liability but the amount of damages has not yet been agreed

> Toda persona responsable criminalmente de un delito o falta también lo es civilmente

responsable 1 *adj* responsible *o* answerable *o* liable *o* accountable; **responsable ante alguien** = responsible to someone; **responsable de** = responsible for *o* liable (for); **responsable de la capacitación** = training officer; **ser responsable ante alguien** = to report to someone; **se negó a ser responsable de las decisiones de la comisión** = she refused to be held answerable for the committee's decision; **si desaparece dinero, el cajero es considerado responsable** = if money is lost, the person at the cash desk is held accountable; **el cliente es responsable de los desperfectos** = the customer is liable for breakages; **el consignatario se hace responsable de los artículos recibidos** = the consignee is held responsible for the goods he has received on consignment; **el líder será responsable de las acciones del grupo** = the group leader will be held accountable for the actions of the group; **el presidente era personalmente responsable de las deudas de la empresa** = the chairman was personally liable for the company's debts; **es responsable ante el jefe de policía del comportamiento de los agentes de su cuerpo** = he is answerable to the Police Commissioner for the conduct of the officers in his force; **la dirección se hace responsable total de la pérdida de artículos en depósito** = the management accepts full responsibility for loss of goods in storage; **la empresa no se hace responsable de la pérdida de objetos pertenecientes a los clientes** = there is no responsibility on the company's part for loss of customers' property; **en Inglaterra, los jueces son responsables ante el presidente de la Cámara de los Lores mientras que en España lo son ante el Consejo Superior del poder Judicial** = In England, magistrates are responsible to the Lord Chancellor while in Spain they are responsible to the General Council of the Judiciary **2** *nmf* person in charge; **responsable del sistema contra incendios** = fire safety officer; **responsable sindical** = convener *o* convenor; **'que el superior sea responsable'** = respondeat superior

respuesta *nf* answer *o* reply; **cupón de respuesta internacional** = international postal reply coupon; **la respuesta de la empresa a la oferta de adquisición** = the company's reply to the takeover bid; **le escribo en respuesta a su carta del 6 de octubre** = I am writing in answer to your letter of October 6th; **mi carta no obtuvo respuesta** = my letter got no answer *o* there was no answer to my letter

restablecer *vt* to restore; **restablecer el diálogo** = to break a deadlock; **restablecer el orden** = to restore order

restitución *nf* restitution; **orden de restitución** = restitution order; **el tribunal ordenó la restitución de los bienes a la empresa** = the court ordered the restitution of assets to the company

restituir *vt* to reinstate

restitutio *nm* restitutio in integrum (**cumplimiento de una obligación cuya prestación consiste en la reparación del agravio como si la infracción no hubiera tenido lugar**) = restitutio in integrum

resto *nm* remainder *o* balance *o* residue; **restos de edición** = remainders; **el resto de las existencias se liquidará a mitad de precio** = the remainder of the stock will be sold off at half price; **puede pagar 100 libras de depósito y el resto en un plazo de sesenta días** = you can pay £100 deposit and the balance within sixty days

restricción *nf* restraint *o* restriction *o* limitation; **restricción de libertad** = restraint of liberty; **restricción mental** = mental reservation; **restricciones a la importación** = import restrictions *o* restrictions on imports; **restricciones informativas** *o* **sobre la publicación de información** = reporting restrictions; **restricciones laborales** *o* **profesionales** = restraint of trade; **cláusula de restricción de un contrato** = restrictive covenant; **convenio de restricción (del comercio)** = restrictive covenant; **sin restricciones** = freely; **imponer restricciones a la venta de armas de fuego** = to put a check on the sale of firearms; **el contrato impone restricciones sobre el número de coches que se pueden importar** = the contract imposes limitations on the number of cars which can be imported; **imponer restricciones a la importación** *o* **imponer restricciones de crédito** = to impose restrictions on imports *o* on credit; **levantar las restricciones crediticias** *o* **suavizar las restricciones de crédito** = to lift credit restrictions; **se levantaron las restricciones informativas** = reporting restrictions were lifted

restrictivo, -va *adj* restrictive *o* limiting; **cláusula restrictiva** = restrictive covenant; **prácticas restrictivas** = restrictive practices; **una cláusula restrictiva de un contrato** = a limiting clause in a contract; **la corta temporada de vacaciones es un factor restrictivo en la industria hotelera** = the short holiday season is a limiting factor on the hotel trade

restringir *vt* to restrict *o* to restrain; **restringir el flujo comercial** = to restrict the flow of trade

resuelto, -ta *adj* **caso resuelto** = decided case; **índice de crímenes resueltos** = detection rate; **tasa de delitos resueltos** = clear-up rate

resultado *nm* **(a)** *(conclusión)* outcome *o* balance; **el resultado del juicio era dudoso** = the outcome of the trial was in doubt; **estamos esperando el resultado de la investigación** = we are waiting for the outcome of the enquiry **(b)** *(beneficio, producto)* profit; **resultado de la explotación** = trading profit; *(cifras de produción)* **resultados** = figures **(c)** **si no da resultado** = failing that; **prueba con la secretaria de la empresa, y si no da resultado, con el presidente** = try the company secretary, and failing that the chairman

resultar *vi* to result *o* to prove to be *o* to work out; **la demanda resultó ser falsa** the claim was proved to be false

resumen *nm* **(a)** *(sumario)* summary *o* digest *o* *(discurso final del juez al término de un juicio)* summing up; **el inspector de policía dio un resumen de los acontecimientos que desembocaron en el asalto a la casa** = the police inspector gave a summary of events leading to the raid on the house; **el presidente dio un resumen de sus conversaciones con la delegación alemana** = the chairman gave a summary of his discussions

with the German delegation **(b)** *(esquema)* abstract *o* outline

resumir *vt* to summarize *o* to abstract ◊ **resumirse**; **el caso se resumió en los periódicos locales** the case was summarized in the local papers

retención *nf* **(a)** *(impuestos)* tax deduction *o* withholding; **sistema fiscal de retención directa** *o* **en origen** = pay as you earn (PAYE) *o* (US) pay-as-you-go **(b)** *(sueldo)* deduction; **retención del salario** *o* **salarial** *o* **de la paga** = attachment of earnings **(c)** *(detención)* detention; **retención ilegal** *o* **injustificada** = false imprisonment; **retención ilegal de bienes muebles** = detinue; **retención ilegal de enseres ajenos** = detention

retener *vt* **(a)** *(detener)* to hold *o* to hold up; **el cargamento ha sido retenido en la aduana** = the shipment has been held up at the customs; **fue retenida durante seis días sin que pudiera ver a su abogado** = she was held for six days without being able to see her lawyer; **retienen a los presos en comisaría** = the prisoners are being held in the police station **(b)** *(preservar)* to retain

retirada *nf* withdrawal

retirada; **retirada de fondos de una cuenta a plazo fijo sin recargo, siempre que se avise con siete días de antelación** = withdrawal without penalty at seven days' notice; **retirada del crédito bancario** = closing of an account; **retirada masiva de fondos de un banco** = a run on the bank

retirado, -da *n* old age pensioner; **la tienda pertenece a un policía retirado** = the shop is owned by a retired policeman

retirar *vt* **(a)** *(sacar)* to withdraw; **retirar el crédito comercial a un cliente** = to close an account; **retirar los cargos** = to drop (charges); **retirar un cargo** *o* **una acusación** = withdraw; **retirar una oferta** = to withdraw an offer; **retirar una oferta de absorción** = to withdraw a takeover bid; **le retiraron la acusación** *o* **retiraron los cargos contra él** = the charges against him were withdrawn *o* dropped; **la acusación ha retirado los cargos contra él** = the prosecution has withdrawn the charges against him; **la acusación retiró todos los cargos contra el acusado** = the prosecution dropped all charges against the accused; **el presidente le pidió que retirara las observaciones que había hecho sobre el director financiero** = the chairman asked him to withdraw the remarks he had made about the finance director; **uno de los capitalistas de la sociedad ha retirado su apoyo** = one of the company's backers has withdrawn **(b)** *(jubilar)* to retire ◊ **retirarse** *vr* to retire *o* *(de un cargo)* to stand down; **el jurado se retiró durante cuatro horas** = the jury retired for four hours; **el tesorero se retira después de seis años** = the treasurer retires after six years; **la mujer de uno de los candidatos está enferma y él se ha retirado** = the wife of one of the candidates is ill and he has stood down; **los jueces se retiraron a considerar su veredicto** = the magistrates retired to consider their verdict; **el presidente de la empresa se retiró a la edad de 65 años** = the chairman of the company retired at the age of 65

retiro *nm* **(a)** *(jubilación)* retirement; **edad de retiro** = pensionable age; **pensión de retiro** = retirement pension *o* old age pension **(b)** *(retirada)* withdrawal

reto *nm* challenge

retoque *nm* correction; **dio algunos retoques al borrador del contrato** = he made some corrections to the draft contract

retornable *adj* returnable; **envase no retornable** = non-returnable packing

retractar *vt* to withdraw
◊ **retractarse** *vr* to go back on; **retractarse de una acción de desacato a los tribunales** = to purge one's contempt *o* to purge a contempt of court; **dos meses más tarde se retractaron del acuerdo** = two months later they went back on the agreement; **los diputados de la oposición obligaron al ministro a retractarse de su declaración** = the opposition MPs forced the minister to withdraw his statement
◊ **retracto** *nm* **retracto legal** = right of pre-emption

retrasado, -da *adj* **(a)** *(con retraso)* behind time *o* late; **ir retrasado** = to be behind schedule; **pago retrasado** = overdue payment **(b)** *(persona, país)* backward; **retrasado mental** = mentally retarded

retrasar *vt* to delay *o* to hold up; **retrasar los pagos** = to default on payments; **se retrasará el pago hasta la firma del contrato** = payment will be held up until the contract has been signed; **la huelga retrasará el reparto algunas semanas** = the strike will hold up delivery for some weeks
◊ **retrasarse** *vr* **el avión se retrasó dos horas** = the plane was two hours late; **la vista se retrasó al no haber ninguna sala libre** = the hearing was delayed because there was no courtroom free

retraso *nm* delay *o* hold-up *o* late; **retraso en reclamar un derecho** = laches; **hay un recargo por retraso en la entrega** = there is a penalty for late delivery; **la huelga causó retrasos en el envío de la mercancía** = the strike caused hold-ups in the shipment of goods; **rogamos disculpen el retraso en la llegada del avión procedente de Amsterdam** = we apologize for the late arrival of the plane from Amsterdam; **siento comunicarle que llevamos tres meses de retraso** = I am sorry to say that we are three months behind schedule; **la vista empezó con treinta minutos de retraso** =

there was a delay of thirty minutes before the hearing started *o* the hearing started after a thirty minute delay

retrato *nm* portrait *o* photograph; **retrato robot** = identikit; **la policía puso en circulación un retrato robot del atracador** = the police issued an identikit picture of the mugger

retribución *nf* payment *o* compensation *o* consideration; **por una pequeña retribución** = for a small consideration

retribuido, -da *adj* paid; **no retribuido** = unpaid

retroactivo, -va *adj* retroactive; **con efecto retroactivo** = ex post facto *o* with retrospective effect; **legislación con efecto retroactivo** = retrospective legislation; **el aumento de sueldo es retroactivo al 1 de enero** = the pay increase is backdated to January 1st; **las disposiciones se aplican con efecto retroactivo** = the ruling is applied retrospectively; **las disposiciones sobre impuestos tienen efecto retroactivo** = the tax ruling has retrospective effect; **recibieron un aumento de sueldo con efecto retroactivo desde el pasado enero** = they received a pay rise retroactive to last January
◊ **retroactivamente** *adv* retroactively

retrospectivo, -va *adj* retrospective; **legislación retrospectiva** = retrospective legislation
◊ **retrospectivamente** *adv* retrospectively

reunión *nf* **(a)** *(junta)* meeting *o* assembly *o* conference; **reunión del consejo de dirección** *o* **de la junta de directores** = board meeting; **reunión del personal** = staff meeting; **reunión ilegal** = unlawful assembly; **reunión plenaria** = plenary session; **celebrar una reunión** = to hold a meeting; **dirigir una reunión** = to conduct a meeting; **delito de reunión para llevar a cabo un acto ilegal** *o* **disturbio** *o* **tumulto** = rout; **libertad de reunión** = freedom of assembly *o* freedom of meeting; **presentar una propuesta a voto en una reunión** = to put a resolution to a meeting; **la reunión se celebrará en la sala de juntas** = the meeting will be held in the committee room **(b)** *(acumulación de acciones)* joinder

reunir *vt* to assemble *o* to gather; **la policía está todavía reuniendo todas las pruebas** = the police are still assembling all the evidence; **el tribunal estuvo reunido desde las once hasta las cinco** = the court sat from eleven to five o'clock
◊ **reunirse (a)** *(encontrarse)* to meet *o* to assemble; **reunirse con un comité negociador** = to meet a negotiating committee; **reunirse con un representante en su hotel** = to meet an agent at his hotel; **la multitud se reunió delante de la comisaría de policía** = the crowd assembled in

front of the police station **(b)** *(celebrar sesión)*
reunirse un tribunal = to sit

revalorización *nf* appreciation

revalorizar *vt* to revalue
◊ **revalorizarse** *vr* to appreciate; **el valor de la
propiedad se ha revalorizado en un 20% en los
dos últimos años** = property values have
appreciated by 20% over the last two years

revelación *nf* exposure *o* disclosure; **revelación
de datos** *o* **de pruebas** = disclosure of information *o*
of evidence

revelar *vt* **(a)** *(divulgar)* to disclose *o* to reveal *o* to
expose *o* to divulge; **sin revelar** = undisclosed;
mandante sin revelar = undisclosed principal; **el
banco no tiene derecho a revelar detalles de mi
cuenta a la oficina de recaudación de impuestos**
= the bank has no right to disclose details of my
account to the tax office; **el gobierno se ha negado
a revelar las cifras referentes al número de
mujeres en paro** = the government has refused to
release figures for the number of unemployed
women; **el jardín reveló varias pistas del
asesinato** = the garden revealed several clues to the
murder; **el jefe de policía no reveló el informe al
resto de la plantilla** = the Chief Constable kept the
report secret from the rest of the force; **la
investigación policial reveló que había
corrupción dentro del gobierno** = the police
investigation exposed corruption in the
government; **reveló que había estado con el
acusado la noche del asesinato** = she divulged that
she had been with the accused on the evening of the
murder; **se negó a revelar información alguna
sobre su cuenta bancaria** = he refused to divulge
any information about his bank account; **un estudio
de la cuenta bancaria reveló que en agosto
habían sido retiradas grandes sumas de dinero** =
examination of the bank account revealed that large
sums had been drawn out in August **(b)** *(delatar)* to
betray; **reveló el secreto al enemigo** = he betrayed
the secret to the enemy

reversión *nf* reversion; **bienes de reversión** =
reversionary

reverso *nm* back

revertible *adj* reversionary annuity; **derechos de
autor revertibles a los herederos de un escritor a
su muerte** = reversionary right

revertido, -da **(llamada de teléfono) a cobro
revertido** collect

revertido, -da *adj* **llamada a cobro revertido**
= reverse charge call *o* transferred charge call;
llamar a cobro revertido = to reverse the charges *o*
to make a collect call; **llamó a su oficina a cobro
revertido** = he called his office collect

revertir *vi* to revert; **los bienes revierten a su
propietario inicial en tres años** = the property
reverts to its original owner in three years

revés *nm* reversal *o* check; **la empresa sufrió un
revés en Extremo Oriente** = the company suffered
a reversal in the Far East

revisar *vt* **(a)** *(cuentas)* to audit *o* to check *o* to
inspect; **revisar las cuentas** = to audit the accounts;
revisar las cuentas de una empresa = to inspect
the accounts of a company; **los libros aún no han
sido revisados** = the books have not yet been
audited **(b)** *(to examine)* to review *o* to examine *o* to
inspect; **revisar un caso** = to rehear *o* to retry; **el
Tribunal Superior ha revisado el fallo** = the High
Court has reviewed the decision; **revisar una
máquina** *o* **una cárcel** = to inspect a machine *o* a
prison **(c)** *(corregir)* to revise

revisión *nf* **(a)** *(examen)* review *o* examination;
revisión de un caso = rehearing *o* retrial; **revisión
judicial** = judicial review; **revisión salarial** = wage
review *o* salary review; **llevar a cabo una revisión**
= to make an inspection *o* to carry out an inspection;
el tribunal ordenó la revisión del caso = the court
ordered the case to be retried; **el Tribunal
Supremo ordenó la revisión del caso** = the
Supreme Court ordered a retrial **(b)** *(cuentas)* audit;
revisión contable por un técnico independiente =
external audit *o* independent audit; **efectuar una
revisión de cuentas anual** = to carry out an annual
audit

revisor, -ra *n* inspector; **revisor de cuentas** =
auditor

revista *nf* review; **revista comercial** = trade
paper

revocable *adj* revocable *o* annullable

revocación *nf* repeal *o* reversal *o* abrogation *o*
annulling *o* annulment; **revocación de algún
contrato** = defeasance; **revocación de un legado** =
ademption; **la revocación del fallo del Tribunal
Superior por el Tribunal Supremo** = the reversal
of the High Court ruling by the Supreme Court

revocar *vt* to revoke *o* to countermand *o* to repeal
o to abrogate *o* to reverse *o* to annul; **revocar un
legado** = to adeem; **revocar una orden** = to
countermand an order; **con poder de revocar** =
annulling; **el proyecto de ley está encaminado a
revocar la legislación existente** = the Bill seeks to
repeal the existing legislation; **el Tribunal
Supremo revocó el fallo del Tribunal Superior** =
the Supreme Court reversed the decision of the
High Court

revolución *nf* revolution; **el gobierno fue
derrocado por una revolución encabezada por el
jefe del ejército** = the government was overthrown
by a revolution led by the head of the army

revolver *vt* to disturb *o* to cause unrest

Rey *nm* Rex; **el Rey** = the king; **por orden del rey** = by Royal Command

reyerta *nf* affray

rezagarse *vr* to fall behind

ribereño, -ña *adj* riparian; **derechos ribereños** = riparian rights

riesgo *nm* risk *o* danger *o* hazard *o* peril; **riesgo de incendio** = fire hazard; **por cuenta y riesgo del propietario** = at owner's risk; **póliza de seguros a todo riesgo** = blanket insurance policy; **seguro a todo riesgo** = full cover *o* comprehensive insurance; **correr un riesgo** = to run a risk; **corre el riesgo de caer en desacato a los tribunales** = he is in danger to being in contempt of court; **los trabajadores corren un riesgo al usar maquinaria antigua** = there is danger to the workers in using old machinery; **él es un gran riesgo** = he is a bad risk; **es probable que muera pronto, por eso es un gran riesgo para una compañía de seguros** = he is likely to die soon, so is a bad risk for an insurance company; **al permitirle conservar su pasaporte, el tribunal corre el riesgo de que el acusado intente huir a los EEUU** = in allowing him to retain his passport, the court runs the risk that the accused may try to escape to the USA

rigidez *nf* rigidity *o* stiffness; **'rigidez cadavérica'** (estado de rigidez al que se llega después de la muerte y que, en algunos casos, puede permitir a un patólogo calcular la hora de la muerte) = rigor mortis

rígido, -da *adj* stiff

riguroso, -sa *adj* strict; **responsabilidad rigurosa** *o* **responsabilidad total** = strict liability; **por riguroso orden de antigüedad** = in strict order of seniority
◊ **rigurosamente** *adv* strictly

ritmo *nm* rate

robado, -da *adj* bent *o* hot; **manipulación** *o* **receptación de objetos robados** = handling *o* receiving stolen goods; **joyas robadas** = hot jewels; **mercancía robada** *o* **objetos robados** = stolen goods; **un coche robado** = a hot car; **receptor, -ra de objetos robados** = fence; **traficar con objetos robados** = to fence

robar *vt* to rob *o* to steal *o* to lift *o* to borrow *o* (saquear) to plunder; **robar algo del bolsillo de alguien** = to pick someone's pocket; **robar con escalo** *o* **con allanamiento de morada** = to burgle; **robar ganado** = to rustle; **entrar a robar** = to break into *o* to burgle; **entraron a robar en el colegio mientras el vigilante estaba de vacaciones** = the school was burgled when the caretaker was on holiday; **dos ladrones asaltaron** la oficina y robaron el dinero suelto que había en aquel momento = two burglars broke into the office and stole the petty cash

robo *nm* theft *o* robbery *o* stealing *o* larceny; **robo en las tiendas** = shoplifting; **robo a mano armada** = armed robbery *o* robbery with violence; **robo con armas y allanamiento de morada** = aggravated burglary; **robo con escalo** *o* **con allanamiento de morada** = burglary; **robo de ganado** = rustling; **robo de menor cuantía** *o* **robo de cuantía mayor** = petty larceny *o* grand larceny; **robo de una casa** = break-in; **en una semana ha habido tres robos en nuestra calle** = there have been three break-ins in our street in one week; **ha habido una ola de robos contra quioscos de prensa** = there has been a wave of thefts from newsagents; **ha habido varios robos en nuestra calle** = there has been a series of burglaries in our street; **hacerse un seguro contra robo** = to take out insurance against theft; **hemos puesto guardias de seguridad para proteger la tienda contra robos** = we have brought in security guards to protect the store against theft; **la empresa está tratando de reducir las pérdidas causadas por robos** = the company is trying to reduce losses caused by theft; **se le acusó de robo con escalo** = he was charged with burglary; **uno de nuestros mayores problemas es el robo en el departamento de vinos** = one of our biggest problems is stealing in the wine department

> El robo es un delito consistente en la sustracción de cosas muebles ajenas, con ánimo de lucro, empleando fuerza en las cosas para acceder al lugar donde éstas se encuentran o violencia o intimidación en las personas (CP 237)

rogar *vt* to pray

rollo *nm* roll; **la calculadora de mesa lleva un rollo de papel** = the desk calculator uses a roll of paper

romano, -na *adj y n* **derecho romano** = Roman law

romper *vt* to break *o* to break off; **romper el trato** = to break up *o* to break off relations; **romper un acuerdo** = to break an agreement; **romper un compromiso** = to break an engagement to do something; **(garantía) que no se puede romper** = copper-bottomed (guarantee); **la compañía ha roto el contrato** *o* **el acuerdo** = the company has broken the contract *o* the agreement; **la dirección rompió las negociaciones con el sindicato** = management broke off negotiations with the union

ronda *nf* watch *o* beat; **ronda policial** = police patrol; **el policía en su ronda** = the constable on the beat

rotación *nf* rotation; **rotación de personal** = staff turnover *o* turnover of staff

rótulo *nm* sign

rotura *nf* breaking *o* breakage; **roturas** = breakages; **en el caso de rotura o extravío** = in the event of breakage or loss

rubricar *vt* to initial; **rubricar una enmienda de un contrato** = to initial an amendment to a contract; **por favor rubrique el acuerdo en el lugar marcado con una X** = please initial the agreement at the place marked with an X

rueda *nf* **rueda de prensa** = press conference; **rueda de identificación** *o* **rueda de presos** = identification *o* identity parade

ruego *nm* request; **ruegos y preguntas** = any other business (AOB)

rufián *nm* hoodlum

ruina *nf* ruin; **declarar en ruina** = to condemn; **consiguió salvar de la ruina de la empresa algo de lo que había invertido** = he managed to save some of his investment from thewreck of the company; **empresa en ruinas** = wreck

rumbo *nm* direction; **la nueva prueba cambió el rumbo de la vista** = the newevidence changed the direction of the hearing

rumor *nm* rumour *o* hearsay; **¿puede confirmar el rumor sobre la posible acusación?** = can you confirm the report that charges are likely to be brought?; **se suprimieron del informe las pruebas basadas en rumores inadmisibles** = inadmissible hearsay evidence was expunged from the report

ruptura *nf* breakdown *o* severance; **ruptura de contrato** = breach of contract; **ruptura matrimonial irreconciliable** = irretrievable breakdownof a marriage; **pidió el divorcio alegando ruptura de matrimonio** = she petitioned for divorce on account of the breakdown of their marriage; **una ruptura en las negociaciones salariales** = a breakdown in wage negotiations

rutina *nf* routine
◊ **rutinario, -ria** *adj* day-to-day; **llamada rutinaria** = routine call

Ss

S.A. = SOCIEDAD ANONIMA

saber 1 *nm* knowledge; **saber y entender** = knowledge and belief; **según mi leal saber y entender** *o* **por lo que yo sé** *o* **que yo sepa** = to the best of my knowledge; **el testigo dijo que, según su leal saber y entender, el acusado no había salido en ningún momento de la habitación** = the witness said that to the best of his knowledge the accused had never left the room **2** *vt/i* to know; **saber de alguien** = to hear from someone; **por lo que yo sé** *o* **que yo sepa** = to the best of my knowledge; **¿sabe cuánto se tarda en llegar al aeropuerto?** = does he know how long it takes to get to the airport?; **la secretaria no sabe dónde está el socio principal** = the senior partner's secretary does not know where he is; **no sabía que el contrato existía** = he had no knowledge of the contract; **no sé cómo funciona un ordenador** = I do not know how a computer works
◊ **sabiendas** *adv* **a sabiendas** = knowingly

sabotaje *nm* sabotage; **se cometieron diversas acciones de sabotaje contra emisoras de radio** = several acts of sabotage were committed against radio stations

sacar *vt* **(b)** *(extraer)* to draw *o* to withdraw *o* to take out *o* to get out; **sacar dinero de una cuenta** = to draw money out of an account; **sacar dinero del banco** *o* **de la cuenta propia** = to withdraw money from the bank *o* from your account; **sacar información de alguien** = to extract information from someone; **sacar la patente de un invento** = to take out a patent for an invention; **sacar una conclusión** = to draw a conclusion; **se pueden sacar hasta 10.000 ptas de cualquier banco sólo con presentar la tarjeta de crédito** = you can withdraw up to 10,000 ptas from any bank on presentation of a banker's card; **el presidente sacó a relucir el tema de la corrupción en el cuerpo de policía** = the chairman brought up the question of corruption in the police force **(b)** *(ganar)* to produce *o* to derive; **sacar provecho de algo** = to benefit from *o* by something; **sacó beneficios económicos de la transacción** = he derived financial benefit from the transaction; **sacar un 10% neto** *o* **$5.000 netas en la transacción** = to clear 10% *o* $5,000 on the deal

saco *nm* sack; **los ladrones se llevaron un saco lleno de relojes de la tienda** = the burglars carried a sack of clocks from the shop

sala *nf* room; **sala de interrogatorios** = detention room; **sala de juntas** = boardroom; **sala de lo civil** = civil court; **sala de lo contencioso-administrativo** = court that hears appeals against administrative decisions; **sala de lo penal** = criminal court; **sala de un tribunal** = courtroom; **sala de vacaciones** = court that deals with urgent matters during the recess period

salario *nm* pay *o* earnings; **salario atrasado** = back pay; **salario neto** = take-home pay; **cheque de salario** = pay cheque
◊ **salarial** *adj* wage; **negociaciones salariales** = pay negotiations *o* pay talks

saldar *vt* **(a)** *(pagar)* to pay off *o* to pay up; **saldar una cuenta** = to settle an account; **saldar una deuda** = to pay *o* settle *o* liquidate a debt **(b)** *(hacer balance final)* to balance

saldar las cuentas = to close the accounts; **he terminado de saldar las cuentas de marzo** = I have finished balancing the accounts for March **(c)** *(liquidar)* **saldar las deudas propias** = to discharge one's liabilities *o* to meet one's obligations; **saldar libros** = to remainder books

saldo *nm* **(a)** *(resultado)* balance; **saldo a favor** *o* **saldo acreedor** = credit balance; **saldo a nuestro favor** = balance due to us; **saldo de una cuenta** = bank balance; **saldo deudor** = debit balance; **saldo líquido** = balance in hand *o* cash in hand **(b)** *(liquidación)* **saldo de una deuda** = clearing *o* liquidation of a debt **(c)** *(rebajas)* sales; **de saldo** = giveaway; **precios de saldo** = knockdown prices; **vender a precio de saldo** = to sell at giveaway prices; **me vendió el coche a un precio de saldo** = he sold me the car at a knockdown price

salida *nf* **(a)** *(avión, tren)* departure; **la salida del avión se retrasó dos horas** = the plane's departure was delayed by two hours **(b)** *(informática)* **datos de salida** = output; **dar salida** = to output; **impresión de salida** = printout; **ésa es la información de salida del ordenador** = that is the information outputted from the computer **(c)** *(lugar* *y acto de salir)* exit; **salida de incendios** *o* **de emergencia** = fire escape

salir *vi* to go *o* to depart *o* to leave; *(circular)* to run; **el avión sale a las 11.15** = the plane departs at 11.15; **este tren sale los días laborables** = this train runs on weekdays; **el próximo avión sale a las 10.20** = the next plane leaves at 10.20; **salió de su despacho temprano para ir a la reunión** = he left his office early to go to the meeting
◊ **salirse** *vr* to fall outside; **salirse de la norma** = to depart from normal practice; **el caso se sale de la jurisdicción de la audiencia** = the case falls outside the jurisdiction of the court

salón *nm* **salón del automóvil** = motor show; **salón de la informática** = computer show

saltarse *vr* to leave out

salud *nf* health

saluda *nm* compliments slip

saludar *vt* *(en carta)* **le saluda atentamente** = Yours sincerely *o* Yours faithfully *o* Yours truly *o* US sincerely yours *o* Truly yours

salvamento *nm* *(rescate)* salvage; **acuerdo de salvamento de un barco en peligro de naufragio** = salvage agreement; **buque de salvamento** = salvage vessel; **premio de salvamento** = salvage (money); **ponemos a la venta un almacén lleno de objetos procedentes de un salvamento** = we are selling off a warehouse full of salvaged goods

salvar *vt* **(a)** *(recuperar)* to salvage; **el administrador judicial consiguió salvar algo de la ruina de la empresa** = the receiver managed to salvage something from the failure of the company; **la empresa está tratando de salvar su reputación tras el envío a prisión del director gerente por fraude** = the company is trying to salvage its reputation after the managing director was sent to prison for fraud **(b)** *(informática)* to save; **no te olvides de salvar los archivos cuando hayas terminado de corregirlos** = do not forget to save your files when you have finished correcting them
◊ **salvado, -da** *adj* salvaged; **mercancías salvadas de un naufragio** *o* **de un incendio** = salvage; **liquidación de objetos salvados de una inundación** = a sale of flood salvage items

salvedad *nf (excepción)* proviso

salvo *adv* except *o* excepted; **salvo error u omisión (s.e.u.o.)** = errors and omissions excepted (e. & o.e); **salvo instrucciones al contrario** = failing instructions to the contrary; **salvo pronto pago** = failing prompt payment; **salvo que se disponga lo contrario** = except as otherwise provided

salvoconducto *nm* safe-conduct

sanción *nf* **(a)** *(castigo)* sanction; **sanciones económicas** = (economic) sanctions; **imponer sanciones a un país** = to impose sanctions on a country; **levantar las sanciones impuestas** = to lift sanctions **(b)** *(permiso)* sanction *o* enactment

sancionar *vt* **(a)** *(penalizar)* penalize **(b)** *(autorizar)* endorse *o* ratify

sangrado *nm* indent

sangrar *vt* to indent; **sangra tres espacios en la primera línea** = indent the first line three spaces

sangre *f* blood; **análisis de sangre** = blood test *o* blood grouping test; **muestra de sangre** = blood sample; **a sangre fría** = in cold blood

sanidad *nf* health *o* public health; **inspector de sanidad** = health inspector; **jefe de sanidad municipal** = medical officer of health (MOH); **patente de sanidad** = bill of health

sano, -na *adj* healthy; **sano y salvo** = safe and sound; **en su sano juicio** = sane *o* of sound mind *o* compos mentis; **¿estaba en su sano juicio al hacer el testamento?** = was he sane when he made the will?

saquear *vt* *(pillaje)* to loot *o* to plunder; **las tiendas fueron saqueadas por una pandilla de gamberros** = the stores were looted by a mob of hooligans
◊ **saqueador, -ra** *n* looter
◊ **saqueo** *nm* looting; **la policía acordonó la zona para evitar el saqueo** = the police cordoned off the area to prevent looting

sargento *nmf* sergeant; **sargento de policía** = police sergeant; **sargento de servicio** *o* **de guardia** = duty sergeant

satisfacción *nf* satisfaction *o* amends; **dar cumplida satisfacción** = to make amends; **satisfacción en el trabajo** = job satisfaction

satisfacer *vt* to satisfy *o* to fulfil; *(cumplir)* to meet (requirements); **satisfacer a un cliente** = to satisfy a client; **satisfacer la demanda de un nuevo producto** = to meet the demand for a new product; **satisfacer los requisitos de un cliente** = to meet a customer's requirements; **satisfacer una demanda** = to settle a claim; **que satisface los requisitos** = up to standard; **un cliente satisfecho** = a satisfied customer; **no podemos producir lo suficiente para satisfacer la demanda del producto** = we cannot produce enough to satisfy the demand for the product

sea = SER

s.e.u.o. = SALVO ERROR U OMISION

sección *nf* **(a)** *(apartado)* article *o* section; **sección de daños** = head of damage; **sección de un texto legal** = clause; **sección de una disposición legal** = paragraph; **la fusión no es legal según el**

capítulo VIII, sección 2 de la Ley de Sociedades Anónimas = the merger is not legal under Chapter 8, section 2 of the Companies Act **(b)** *(división)* branch *o* division; **el Derecho de Contratos y la Ley de Agravios son secciones del derecho civil** = the Law of Contract and the Law of Tort are branches of civil law **(c)** *(departamento)* department; **sección de muebles** = furniture department; **sección de reclamaciones** = complaints department

secretaría *nf* secretariat; **la secretaría de las Naciones Unidas** = the United Nations secretariat ◊ **secretariado** *nm* secretariat *o* secretarial; **escuela de secretariado** = secretarial college; **está haciendo un curso de secretariado** = she is taking a secretarial course

secretario, -ria *n* secretary; **Secretario, -ria de Estado** = Minister of State *o* Secretary of State; **secretario de juzgado** = clerk to the justices *o* associate of the Crown Office; **secretario de la compañía** = company secretary; **secretario de una empresa** *o* **compañía** = company secretary; **secretaria de una firma de abogados** *o* **del departamento jurídico de una empresa** = legal secretary; **secretario del Registro Mercantil** = Registrar of Companies; **secretario honorario** = honorary secretary; **secretaria y ayudante personal** = secretary and personal assistant; **de secretario** *o* **de secretaria** = secretarial; **está buscando un trabajo de secretario** = he is looking for secretarial work; **entre las funciones de un secretario de juzgado se incluye la de aconsejar sobre el derecho, la práctica y el procedimiento** = the functions of a justices' clerk include giving advice about law, practice and procedure; **necesitamos más secretarios para que se ocupen de los envíos por correo** = we need extra secretarial help to deal with the mailings; **el secretario advirtió al juez de primera instancia que el caso debía ser juzgado por la Audiencia** = the clerk advised the magistrates that the case had to be passed to the Crown Court for trial; **mi secretaria se ocupa de las visitas** = my secretary deals with visitors; **su secretaria telefoneó para decir que llegaría tarde** = his secretary phoned to say he would be late

secreto, -ta 1 *adj* covert *o* secret; **acción secreta** = covert action; **agente secreto** = special agent *o* undercover agent; **información secreta** = classified information; **reunión secreta** = privileged meeting; **firmaron un acuerdo secreto con su principal competidor** = they signed a secret deal with their main competitor **2** *nm* secret *o* confidentiality *o* security; **secreto de estado** = official secret; **Ley de Secretos Oficiales** = Official Secrets Act; **secreto del sumario** = sub judice rule; **secreto profesional** = trade secret; **guardar un secreto** to keep a secret **(b) en secreto** = in secret *o* on the quiet *o* in confidence *o* secretly; **el jefe de la banda se reunió** con el inspector detective en secreto = the gang leader met the detective inspector in secret; **el tratado fue firmado en secreto por el Primer Ministro y el Presidente** = the treaty was signed secretly by the Prime Minister and the President; **fotografió el plano de la cámara acorazada del banco en secreto** = he photographed the plan of the bank vault in secret; **se ofreció a copiar los planos en secreto y venderlos a otra firma** = he offered to copy the plans secretly and sell them to another firm; **te mostraré el informe en secreto** = I will show you the report in confidence; **transfirió su cuenta bancaria a Suiza en secreto** = he transferred his bank account to Switzerland on the quiet

sector *nm* sector; **sector privado** = private sector; **sector público** = public sector; **necesidad de endeudamiento del sector público** = public sector borrowing requirement (PSBR) ◊ **sectorial** *nf* **agrupación sectorial** = trade association

secuestrador, -ra *n (de personas)* abductor *o* kidnapper; *(avión)* hijacker

secuestrar *vt* **(a)** *(raptar)* to kidnap *o* to abduct *o* *(avión, tren)* to hijack; **secuestraron al director del banco a punta de pistola** = the bank manager was abducted at gunpoint; **el avión fue secuestrado por seis terroristas armados** = the plane was hijacked by six armed terrorists; **los bandidos secuestraron el camión y mataron al conductor** = the bandits hijacked the lorry and killed the driver **(b)** *(confiscar)* to seize *o* to sequester *o* to sequestrate **(c)** *(llevarse)* to carry off

secuestro *nm* **(a)** *(rapto)* kidnapping *o* abduction *o* *(avión)* hijack *o* hijacking; **secuestro de un niño** *o* **secuestro de menores** = child stealing; **el secuestro fue organizado por un grupo de opositores al gobierno** = the hijack was organized by a group of opponents to the government; **el secuestro se produjo nada más despegar el avión** = the hijacking took place just after the plane took off; **en lo que va de año se han producido seis secuestros** = there have been six hijackings so far this year **(b)** *(embargo)* sequestration; **secuestro de bienes** = sequestration of goods

secundario, -ria *adj* **(a)** *(subsidiario)* secondary *o* subsidiary *o* minor **(b)** *(incidental)* incidental

seda *nf* silk

sede *nf* base; **sede central** =; head office *o* main office *o* social headquarters; **establecer sede en** = base; **la empresa tiene su sede en Londres y sucursales en todos los países europeos** = the company has its base in London and branches in all European countries; **nuestra sucursal extranjera tiene su sede en Las Bahamas** = our foreign branch is based in the Bahamas

sedición *nf* sedition

◊ **sedicioso, -sa** *adj* seditious; **reunión sediciosa** = riotous assembly; **comunicación escrita de carácter sedicioso** = seditious libel

seguir 1 *vi* to follow *o* to proceed *o* to go on *o* to keep; **seguir con algo** = to proceed with something; **seguir los trámites** = follow the procedure; **el presidente siguió hablando durante dos horas** = the chairman went on speaking for two hours; **la inflación sigue siendo alta a pesar de los esfuerzos del gobierno por reducirla** = inflation has stayed high in spite of the government's efforts to bring it down; **en la discusión que siguió el acusado golpeó al demandante con una botella** = in the ensuing argument, the defendant hit the plaintiff with a bottle **2** *vt* **(a)** *(continuar)* to follow; **seguir una iniciativa** = to follow up an initiative **(b)** *(buscar)* to trace; **la policía siguió a los dos hombres hasta un hotel de Londres** = the police traced the two men to a hotel in London; **la policía está siguiendo varias pistas** = the police are following up several leads **(c)** *(suceder)* to succeed ◊ **seguido, -da 1** *adj* continuous *o* without interruption **2** *nf* **en seguida** = forthwith *o* out of hand

según *prep* according to *o* under *o* pursuant to *o* as per; **según factura** = as per invoice; **según muestra** = as per sample; **según pedido anterior** = as per previous order; **oferta según disponibilidad** = offer subject to availability; **los pagos se hicieron según la sentencia de pago de manutención** = the payments were made according to the maintenance order; **según el testigo, el acusado transportó el cuerpo en el asiento trasero de su coche** = according to the witness, the accused carried the body on the back seat of his car; **según el artículo 2 de la ley de 1979, no reúne las condiciones necesarias** = she does not qualify under section 2 of the 1979 Act; **según los poderes conferidos a las autoridades locales** = pursuant to the powers conferred on the local authority; **según los términos del acuerdo, la mercancía debe ser entregada en octubre** = under the terms of the agreement, the goods should be delivered in October

segundo, -da *adj* second; **segunda hipoteca** = second mortgage; **segunda instancia** = appeal; **segunda intención** = ulterior motive; **segundo trimestre** = second quarter; **en segundo lugar** = secondarily; **la persona que realiza un aval es responsable en segundo lugar si la persona responsable en primer lugar deja de cumplir el pago** = the person making a guarantee is secondarily liable if the person who is primarily liable defaults

seguridad *nf* **(a)** *(garantía)* security *o* safety; **seguridad de permanencia en el empleo** = security of employment; **seguridad jurídica** = legal certainty; **seguridad social** = National Insurance *o* social security; **cotizaciones a la seguridad social** = National Insurance contributions (NIC); **caja de seguridad** = safe deposit *o* safe deposit box; **cárcel de máxima seguridad** = escape-proof prison; **casi con toda seguridad** = to the best of my knowledge; **cerradura de seguridad** = time lock; *(Naciones Unidas)* **Consejo de Seguridad** = Security Council; **guardia de seguridad** = security guard; **Ordenanza General de Seguridad e Higiene en el Trabajo** = Health and Safety at Work Act; **margen de seguridad** = safety margin; **medidas de seguridad en aeropuertos** = airport security; **medidas de seguridad en oficinas** = office security; **normas de seguridad** = safety regulations; **para mayor seguridad** = for safety; **prisión de máxima seguridad** = top security prison; **tomar medidas de seguridad** = to take safety measures; **la seguridad en esta oficina es nula** = security in this office is nil; **vive de la paga que recibe de la seguridad social** = he lives on social security payments; **coloca los documentos en el armario para mayor seguridad** = put the documents in the cupboard for safety; **guardamos los documentos en el banco para mayor seguridad** = we put the documents into the bank for safe keeping **(b)** *(confianza)* confidence *o* certainty

seguro, -ra 1 *adj* **(a)** *(protegido)* safe *o* secure; **empleo seguro** *o* **fijo** = secure job; **inversión segura** *o* **inversiones seguras** = secure investment *o* safe investments; **lugar seguro** = safe keeping; **guarda los documentos en lugar seguro** = keep the documents in a safe place; **los documentos deben guardarse en lugar seguro** = the documents should be kept in a secure place **(b)** *(cierto)* certain *o* confident; **no estar seguro** = to hesitate; **el comisario jefe está seguro de que el jefe de la banda está todavía en libertad** = the superintendent is certain that the head of the gang is still at large; **el jurado no está seguro del veredicto** = the jury is hesitating about its verdict; **¿está seguro de que el equipo de ventas es capaz de vender este producto?** = are you confident the sales team is capable of handling this product? **(c)** *(de confianza)* reliable *o* sound; **poco seguro** = unreliable; **las pruebas presentadas por la policía no son muy seguras** = the evidence brought forward by the police is not very sound **2** *nm* insurance *o* assurance *o* policy; **seguro a todo riesgo** *o* **contra todo riesgo** = all-in-policy *o* comprehensive insurance *o* full cover; **seguro contra incendios** = fire insurance; **seguro contra terceros** = third-party insurance; **seguro corriente de vida** = whole-life insurance; **seguro de accidentes** *o* **contra accidentes** = accident policy *o* accident insurance; **seguro de automóviles** = car insurance *o* motor insurance; **seguro de vida** = life insurance; **seguro médico** = medical insurance; **seguro que cubre los gastos de un juicio** = legal expenses insurance; **seguro temporal** *o* **seguro de vida por un periodo determinado** = term insurance; **póliza de seguros** = insurance cover; **hacer un seguro de vida a alguien** = to insure someone's life; **hacerse un seguro contra incendios** = to take out an insurance against fire; **sin seguro** = uninsured; **solicitar un seguro adicional** = to ask for additional cover; **póliza de seguros** = insurance policy

selección *nf* selection *o* pick; **la selección de candidatos** = the screening of candidates; **comisión de selección** = selection board *o* selection committee; **procedimiento de selección** = selection procedure

seleccionar *vt* to pick; **seleccionar candidatos** = to screen candidates; **seleccionar un jurado** = to empanel a jury

selecto, -ta *adj* select; **lo más selecto** = the pick of the group; **nuestros clientes son muy selectos** = our customers are very select; **un grupo selecto de clientes** = a select group of clients

sellar *vt* to seal *o* to stamp; **los funcionarios de aduana sellaron los documentos** = the documents were stamped by the customs officials
◊ **sellado, -da** adj **contrato sellado** = contract under seal; **documento firmado y sellado** = sealed instrument

sello o precinto *m* seal

sello *nm* stamp *o* *(de lacre)* seal; **sello de la compañía** = common seal *o* company's seal; **sello de la inspección** = inspection stamp; **sello de contraste** = assay mark *o* hallmark; **sello de goma** = rubber stamp; **un sello de 100 ptas** a 100 ptas stamp; **un sello de correos** = a (postage) stamp; **poner sellos** = to stamp; **poner el sello de la compañía a un documento** = to attach the company's seal to a document; **ponerle a una factura el sello de 'pagado'** *o* **'recibí'** = to stamp an invoice 'Paid'; **la factura tiene el sello del recibí** = the invoice has the stamp 'Received with thanks' on it; **el oficial de aduanas le miró los sellos del pasaporte** = the customs officer looked at the stamps in his passport

semestre *nm* half-year; **primer semestre** = first half *o* first half-year
◊ **semestral** *adj* half-yearly *o* bi-annual *o* bi-annually
◊ **semestralmente** *adv* half-yearly *o* bi-annually

semi- *prefijo* quasi-
◊ **semijudicial** *adj* **una investigación semijudicial** = a quasi-judicial investigation
◊ **semioficial** *adj* **un organismo semioficial** = a quasi-official body

senado *nm* senate; **el Senado de los EE UU** = the Senate of the USA; **la comisión de relaciones**

exteriores del Senado = the Senate Foreign Relations Committee; **las Cortes Españolas se componen de dos Cámaras: el Congreso y el Senado** = the Spanish Parliament consists of two Houses: the Congress and the Senate

El Senado es la Cámara de representación territorial. Está compuesto por 208 senadores elegidos en cada provincia por un sistema mayoritario con representación de minorías y por un número de senadores designado por cada asamblea de las Comunidades Autónomas en proporción a su población

senador, -ra *n* senator

sencillo, -lla *adj* simple; **el caso parece sencillo** = the case appears to be a simple one

sensatez *nf* soundness

sensato, -ta *adj* reasonable

sentada *nf* sit-down protest

sentencia *nf* (a) sentence *o* award *o* judgment *o* judgement *o* adjudication; **sentencia absolutoria** = acquittal; **sentencia acordada** *o* **de conformidad** *o* **de negociación** = plea bargaining; **sentencia coincidente** = concurrent sentence; **sentencia comentada** = commentary; **sentencia condenatoria** = verdict of guilty; **sentencia de ingreso en prisión** = custodial sentence; **sentencia de muerte** = death sentence; **sentencia declarativa** *o* **interpretativa de una escritura** *o* **de un documento** = declaratory judgment; **sentencia definitiva** *o* **final** *o* **firme** = final judgment; **sentencia disuasoria** *o* **ejemplar** = deterrent sentence; **sentencia en rebeldía** = judgment by default *o* default judgment; **sentencias sucesivas** = consecutive sentences; **una sentencia de la magistratura de trabajo** = an award by an industrial tribunal (b) **acreedor por sentencia firme** = judgment creditor; **aplazamiento de una sentencia** = stay of execution; **deudor por sentencia firme** = judgment debtor; **persona que dicta sentencia** = sentencer; **pronunciar** *o* **dictar sentencia** = to pronounce judgment *o* to pass sentence on someone; **registrar la sentencia** = to enter judgement *o* to take judgment; **registrar la sentencia de aceptación o no aceptación de una demanda** = to enter judgment for *o* against the plaintiff; **registrar la sentencia por alguien** *o* **en nombre de alguien** = to enter judgment for someone; **registro de la sentencia** = entry of judgment; **testimonio de sentencia** = certificate of judgment; **el jurado emitió un veredicto de homicidio involuntario y el juez dictará sentencia la semana que viene** = the jury returned a verdict of manslaughter and the judge will pass sentence next week ; **sentenciar 1** *vi* to sentence *o* to adjudicate *o* to decide; **a los magistrados les pueden pagar los gastos cuando sentencien** = magistrates may be paid expenses when adjudicating; **el juez sentenció a favor del demandante** = the judge decided in favour of the plaintiff; **el tribunal sentenció en contra de la concesión de daños y perjuicios** = the tribunal decided against awarding any damages **2** vt **sentenciar a alguien** = to pass sentence on someone; **el acusado fue declarado culpable de asesinato y será sentenciado la semana que viene** = the accused was convicted of murder and will be sentenced next week

sentido *nm (intención)* effect

señal *nf* **(a)** *(depósito)* deposit *o* token *o* earnest (money); **dejar una señal** = to pay money down *o* to leave a deposit; **perder una señal** = to forfeit a deposit; **dejó una señal de 50 libras y el resto lo pagó en plazos mensuales** = he paid £50 down and the rest in monthly instalments; **entregó 1.000 libras al abogado como señal de su intención de compra** = he deposited £1,000 with the solicitor as earnest of his intention to purchase **(b)** *(indicación)* indication *o* sign *o* mark; **los conductores ignoraron las señales de peligro** = drivers paid no attention to the warning signs; **señal de socorro** = distress signal

señalar *vt* to mark *o* to flag; **señalar el día de la vista** = set a day for the trial

Señor *nm* Mr *o* Mister *o* Sir; **Señor Don (Sr.D.)** = Mr *o* esquire; **carta dirigida al Señor Don P.Tenas** = letter addressed to Mr P.Tenas *o* P.Tenas Esq.; **Muy Sr mío** = Dear sir

Señora *nf* Mrs *o* Madam *o* Lady; **Señora Presidenta** = Madam Chairman; **Muy Sra. mía** = Dear madam

separación *nf* separation; **separación legal** = legal separation *o* judicial separation; **separación conyugal** *o* **matrimonial** = separation; **separación de bienes** = separation of estates
◊ **separado, -da** *adj* **por separado** separate *o* separately *o* severally *o* seriatim; **enviar** *o* **mandar algo por separado** = to send something under separate cover; **son responsables en grupo y por separado** = they are jointly and severally liable; **se cobró a los dos hermanos por separado** = the two brothers were charged separately
◊ **separadamente** *adv* separately *o* severally

separar *vt* to separate

sepelio *nm* burial; **ayuda de sepelio** = death grant

ser *vi* to be; **siendo** = in esse; **o sea** = i.e.; **las restricciones sobre importación se aplican a artículos caros, o sea artículos que cuestan más de 2.500 dólares** = the import restrictions apply to expensive items, i.e. items costing more than $2,500

sereno *nm* night watchman

seriedad *nf* seriousness; **con seriedad** = responsibly; **el juez felicitó al jurado por haber actuado con seriedad** = the judge congratulated the jury on acting responsibly

serio, -ria *adj* serious

servicio *nm* **(a)** *(labor)* service *o* accommodation; **servicio comunitario** = community service; **servicio de entrega de cartas certificadas** *o* **con acuse de recibo** = recorded delivery; **servicio nocturno** *o* **servicio de guardia nocturna** = night duty; **contrato de servicio** = contract of service *o* service contract; **estar de servicio** *o* **de guardia** = to be on duty; **orden de servicio a la comunidad** = community service order; **prestación de servicio como jurado** = jury service; **sargento de servicio** *o* **de guardia** = duty sergeant; **sentencia que condena a realizar servicios sociales** = community service order **(b)** *(en un restaurante)* service charge **(c)** **cuota de servicios (en una comunidad de vecinos)** = service charge; **cubrir el servicio** = to run

servidumbre *nf* access *o* right of way *o* easement

servidumbre; **servidumbre de aguas** = water rights; **servidumbre de luces y vistas** = ancient lights; **servidumbre de paso** = right of way; **servidumbre legal** = easement of necessity; **servidumbre tácita** = easement by implication

La servidumbre es un gravamen que se impone sobre una finca en favor de otra perteneciente a dueño distinto

servir *vt* **servir un pedido** = to deal with an order *o* to fill *o* to fulfil an order; **servir mesas en un restaurante** = to serve in a restaurant; **servir de algo** = to be useful; **no sirve para nada** = it is useless

sesgo *nm* bias

sesión *nf* session *o* sitting; **sesión a puerta cerrada** = closed session; **sesión de apertura** *o* **sesión de clausura** = opening session *o* closing session; **sesión de información** = briefing; **sesión parlamentaria** = session; **sesión plenaria** = plenary session; **sesiones (jurídicas)** = sittings; **abrir una sesión** = to open a meeting; **levantar una sesión** = to close a meeting; **el gobierno piensa introducir el proyecto de ley en la próxima sesión parlamentaria** = the government is planning to introduce the Bill at the next session of Parliament; **la sesión de la mañana** *o* **de la tarde tendrá lugar en la sala de conferencias** = the morning session *o* the afternoon session will be held in the conference room

seudónimo *nm* pseudonym

severidad *nf* severity *o* harshness; **la policía ha pedido que se trate a la banda con severidad** =

the police has asked for the gang to be treated severely; **la prensa comentó la severidad de la condena** o **la severidad de las penas** = the newspapers commented on the harshness of the sentence o on the severity of the sentences; **con severidad** = severely; **la ley trata a los culpables de violación con gran severidad** = the law treats convicted rapists with great severity

severo, -ra adj severe o harsh; **justicia severa** = rough justice; **poco severo** = lenient; **de forma poco severa** = leniently; **el juez dictó severas condenas contra los violadores** = the judge passed severe sentences on the rapists; **el juez fue poco severo ante el delito** = the judge took a lenient view of the offence; **dada la edad del acusado, el tribunal dictó una sentencia poco severa** = because of the accused's age, the court passed a lenient sentence; **el juez impuso severas condenas a los alborotadores** = the magistrate gave harsh sentences to the rioters
◊ **severamente** adv severely o harshly

severamente o de un modo violento

sexual adj sexual; **delitos contra la libertad sexual** = sexual offences; **relaciones sexuales** = sexual intercourse; **tener contactos sexuales con un menor de 12 años** = to commit an act of gross indecency; **es un delito tener relaciones sexuales con una chica menor de doce años** = it is an offence to have sexual intercourse with a girl under twelve years of age

sheriff nm (jefe de la policía del condado) (US) sheriff

sida nm AIDS

siempre adv; **siempre que** = provided that o providing o on the understanding that; **el juez sentenciará al reo la próxima semana siempre que el informe del psiquiatra se reciba a tiempo** = the judge will sentence the convicted man next week provided (that) o providing the psychiatrist's report is received in time

sigilosamente adv on the quiet

signatario, -ria m signatory
◊ **significado** nm meaning; **el significado de la carta** = the content of the letter

significar vt to mean; **cláusula que significa que** = clause to the effect that

signo nm mark

siguiente adj y pron next o ensuing; **'y lo siguiente'** = et seq. o et sequenter; **el primer caso de esta mañana fue de asesinato, el siguiente de intento de asesinato** = the first case this morning was one of murder, the next of attempted murder; **la siguiente decisión del tribunal se consideró inconstitucional** = the court's next decision was judged to be unconstitutional; **llegó a Londres el**

miércoles y el día siguiente intentó asesinar al Primer Ministro = on Wednesday he arrived in London and the next day tried to assassinate the Prime Minister

silencio nm silence; **derecho a guardar silencio** = right of silence; **el acusado se mantuvo en silencio durante todo el juicio** = the accused maintained silence throughout the trial

silla nf chair; **silla eléctrica** = electric chair o the chair

simbólico, -ca adj nominal; **alquiler simbólico** = peppercorn rent; **huelga simbólica** = token strike; **pagar un alquiler simbólico** = to pay a peppercorn rent; **pago simbólico** = token payment; **precio simbólico** = token charge; **renta simbólica** = token rent; **cobramos un precio simbólico por nuestros servicios** = we make a nominal charge for our services; **pagan un alquiler simbólico** o **una renta simbólica** = they are paying a nominal rent; **se cobra un precio simbólico por la calefacción** = a token charge is made for heating

símbolo nm token

similar adj de un modo similar = similiter

simple adj simple; **avería simple** = particular average; **pérdida por avería simple** = particular average; **contrato simple** = simple contract; **dominio simple** = fee simple; **interés simple** = simple interest; **fue una simple malinterpretación de las normas gubernamentales** = it was a simple misunderstanding of the government regulations

simular vt to fake o to pretend; **simularon forzar la entrada para que la policía creyera que habían robado los documentos** = they faked a break-in to make the police believe the documents had been stolen

simultáneo, -nea adj **condena simultánea** = concurrent sentence; **se le impusieron dos condenas simultáneas de seis meses de cárcel** = he was given two concurrent jail sentences of six months

sin prep without o ex; **sin beneficios** = at a loss; **'sin día'** = sine die; **sin perjuicio** = without prejudice; **'sin recurso'** = sans recours; **acción cotizada sin dividendos** = share quoted ex dividend; **sin fijación de precio mínimo** = without reserve

sin menoscabo o **sin perjuicio** = without prejudice

sincero, -ra adj honest
◊ **sinceramente** adv honestly

sindicado, -da adj unionized; **trabajadores sindicados** = organized labour

sindical adj **acuerdo sindical** = union agreement; **cuota de inscripción sindical** = union dues *o* union subscription; **reconocimiento sindical** = union recognition

◊ **sindicalista** *nmf* unionist

sindicato *nm* union *o* trade union *o* trades union; **sindicato de trabajadores** = (US) labor union; **Confederación de Sindicatos en G.B.** = Trades Union Congress; **están afiliados a un sindicato** = they are members of a trade union *o* they are trade union members; **ha solicitado la afiliación a un sindicato** = he has applied for trade union membership *o* he has applied to join a trade union; **reconocimiento de un sindicato** = union recognition

síndico *nm* liquidator *o* trusteeship; **síndico de una quiebra** = Official Receiver *o* trustee in bankruptcy; **síndico nombrado por un tribunal** = provisional liquidator

sine *frase* **la vista se pospuso sine die** = the hearing was adjourned sine die

siniestro *nm* accident; **siniestro pendiente** = loss incurred; **siniestro total** = dead loss; **indemnizar un siniestro** = to settle a claim; **declararon el coche siniestro total** = the car was written off as a dead loss

sirviente *adj y nm* servant; **predio sirviente** = servient tenement

sisa *nf* pilferage *o* pilfering

sisar *vt* to pilfer

sistema *nm* system; **sistema de archivo** = filing system; **sistema de control para verificar que un ordenador funciona debidamente** = control system; **sistema económico** = economy; **sistema fiscal de retención directa** = pay as you earn (PAYE) *o* (US) pay-as-you-go; **sistema informático** = computer system; **Sistema Monetario Europeo (SME)** = European Monetary System (EMS); **análisis de sistemas** = systems analysis; **analista de sistemas** = systems analyst; **utilizar un sistema de cupos** = to operate a quota system; **el sistema jurídico británico ha servido de modelo para muchos otros sistemas jurídicos** = the British legal system has been taken as the standard for many other legal systems
◊ **sistemático, -ca** *adj* systematic; **pidió un informe sistemático del servicio de libertad condicional** = he ordered a systematic report on the probation service

sitio *nm* site *o* place

situación *nf* **(a)** *(localización)* situation *o* locus; **situación anterior** = status quo ante; **la fábrica tiene una situación muy agradable al lado del mar** = the factory is in a very pleasant situation by the sea **(b)** *(reputación)* situation *o* standing; **la situación financiera de una empresa** = financial situation of a company *o* the financial standing of a

company **(c)** *(postura)* position; **situación difícil** = difficult position

situado, -da *adj* situated; **su propiedad está situada cerca de Andorra** = his property is situated near Andorra

situar *vt* to rank; **las nuevas acciones se situarán al mismo ritmo que las ya existentes** = the new shares will rank pari passu with the existing ones

SL = SOCIEDAD LIMITADA

SME = SISTEMA MONETARIO EUROPEO

soberano, -na *n* sovereign; **estado soberano** = sovereign state
◊ **soberanía** *nf* sovereignty; **tener soberanía sobre un territorio** = to have sovereignty over a territory

sobornar *vt* to bribe *o* to nobble *o* to corrupt *o* to tamper; **intentó sobornar a uno de los miembros del jurado** = he tried to nobble one of the jurors; **sobornó al oficial para que se retiraran los cargos** = he corruptly offered the officer money to get the charges dropped

soborno *nm* bribe *o* bribery *o* kickback *o* hush money; **soborno con el fin de que otro cometa perjurio** = subornation of perjury; **soborno a un miembro del jurado** = embracery

soborno de funcionarios = graft; **dinero para sobornos** = slush fund; **el sargento de policía fue despedido por aceptar sobornos** = the police sergeant was dismissed for taking bribes; **es imposible acabar con el soborno en el almacén de seguridad** = bribery in the security warehouse is impossible to stamp out

sobrante *adj* remainder; **productos sobrantes** = goods left on hand

sobrar *vi* to remain; **pondremos a la venta las existencias antiguas a mitad de precio y lo que sobre lo tiraremos** = we will sell off the old stock at half price and anything remaining will be thrown away

sobre 1 *nm* envelope; **enviar un documento en un sobre blanco** = to send a document under plain cover **2** *prep* over *o* above; **sobre todo** = largely **3** *prefijo* super- *o* over-
◊ **sobreentender** *vt* to infer
◊ **sobreentendido, -da** *adj* implicit; **contrato sobreentendido** = implied contract
◊ **sobrepasar** *vt* to exceed; **le arrestaron por sobrepasar el límite de velocidad** = he was arrested for exceeding the speed limit
◊ **sobresaliente** *adj* first-class
◊ **sobreseimiento** *nm* **(a)** *(aplazamiento)* stay (of proceedings) **(b)** *(desestimación)* to be nonsuit *o* nonsuited

sobrestimar *vt* to overestimate; **sobrestimó la cantidad de tiempo necesaria para preparar su**

caso = he overestimated the amount of time needed to prepare his case

◊ **sobrevalorar** *vt* to overestimate

◊ **sobrevivir** *vi* to survive; **sobrevivió a su mujer** = he survived his wife; **le sobreviven el marido y tres hijos** = she is survived by her husband and three children

> El sobreseimiento consiste en el cese en la instrucción sumarial dejando sin curso ulterior el procedimiento

social *adj* social *o* corporate; **asistente** *o* **asistenta social** = social worker; **bienestar** *o* **asistencia social** = welfare; **capital social** = share capital; **cotizaciones a la seguridad social** = National Insurance contributions (NIC); **domicilio social** = registered office; **domicilio social de una empresa** = headquarters *o* a company's registered office; **razón social** = corporate name *o* business name; **seguridad social** = National Insurance *o* social security; **servicios sociales** = social services

sociedad *nf* **(a)** *(empresa)* company *o* partnership *o* corporation; **sociedad anónima (SA)** public limited company (Plc) *o* joint-stock company; **sociedad anónima privada** private (limited) company; **sociedad benéfica** = charitable trust *o* charitable corporation; **sociedad central** = parent company; **sociedad cooperativa** = co-operative society; **sociedad cotizada en bolsa** = listed company; **sociedad de cartera** = holding company; **sociedad de inversión** = investment trust; **sociedad de inversión mobiliaria (SIM)** = security investment company; **sociedad de préstamo inmobiliario** = building society; **sociedad (de responsabilidad) limitada (S.R.L)** = limited (liability) company *o* close company; **sociedad en comandita** limited partnership; **sociedad financiera** = finance company; **sociedad inversora por obligaciones** = unit trust; **sociedad limitada (SL)** = private limited company (Ltd); **sociedad matriz** *o* **central** = parent company; **sociedad mercantil anónima** = corporation; **sociedad personal de responsabilidad limitada** = limited partnership; **sociedad por acciones** joint-stock company; **sociedad registrada** listed company; **sociedad sin límite de tiempo establecido** = partnership at will **(b) beneficios de una sociedad** = corporate profits; **constituido en sociedad** = corporate; **constituirse en sociedad** *o* **formar una sociedad** = to incorporate; **derecho de sociedades** = company law; **disolver una sociedad** = to dissolve a partnership; **escritura de sociedad** *o* **escritura de constitución de sociedad** = articles of partnership; **la Ley de Sociedades Anónimas** = the Companies Act; **liquidar una sociedad** = to put a company into liquidation

socio, -cia *n* **(a)** *(de una empresa o asociación)* associate *o* partner; **socio activo** = active partner *o* working partner; **socio comanditario** *o* **en**

comandita = sleeping partner *o* dormant partner *o* limited partner; **socio minoritario** *o* **socio subalterno** *o* **de menor antigüedad** = junior partner; **socio mayoritario** *o* **socio principal** = senior partner; **tomar a alguien como socio** = to offer someone a partnership *o* to take someone into partnership with you; **pasó a ser socio de un despacho** *o* **bufete de abogados** **(b)** *(de un club)* member; **socio fundador** = founding member; **hacerse socio de una asociación** *o* **de un grupo** = to join an association *o* a group; **los socios** = the members *o* membership; **pagar la cuota de socio** = to pay your membership *o* your membership fees; **se pidió a los socios que votaran a un nuevo presidente** = the membership was asked to vote for the new president; **el club tiene quinientos socios** = the club has a membership of five hundred

socorro *nm* relief

sodomía *nf* buggery

sojuzgar *vt* to subject to

solemne *adj* solemn; **acuerdo solemne y obligatorio** = solemn and binding agreement

solicitación *nf* requesting; **solicitación de votos** = canvassing

solicitado, -da *adj* requested; **patente solicitada** = patent pending; **no solicitado, -da** = unsolicited; **mercancía no solicitada** = unsolicited goods; **testimonio no solicitado** = unsolicited testimonial; **un regalo no solicitado** = an unsolicited gift; **acciones pagaderas al ser solicitadas** = shares payable on application

solicitante *nmf* applicant *o* petitioner; **solicitante de un trabajo** = applicant for a job *o* job applicant

solicitar *vt* **(a)** *(pedir)* to ask for *o* to request *o* to solicit *o* to apply; **solicitó el archivo de los deudores de 1997** = he asked for the file on 1997 debtors; **solicitó una entrevista con el ministro** = she sought an interview with the minister; **el abogado solicitó más tiempo para consultar con sus colegas** = counsel asked for more time to consult with his colleagues; **solicite envío de muestras** = 'samples available on request' **(b)** **solicitar acciones** = to apply for shares; **solicitar ayuda del gobierno** = to request assistance from the government; **solicitar pedidos** = to solicit orders; **solicitar personalmente** = to apply in person; **solicitar por escrito** = to apply in writing; **solicitar que se conceda la libertad bajo fianza** = to ask for bail to be granted; **solicitar un trabajo** = to apply for a job; **solicitar una entrevista** = to seek an interview; **solicitar un seguro o una cobertura adicional** = to ask for additional cover; **solicitar votos** to canvass; **persona que solicita votos** = canvasser; **volver a solicitar** = to reapply ;

al ver que el puesto seguía vacante, volvió a solicitarlo = when he saw that the job had still not been filled, he reapplied for it; **la empresa volvió a solicitar un requerimiento en contra de los sindicatos** = the company reapplied for an injunction against the union **(c)** *(al tribunal)* to move; **dirigirse al tribunal para solicitar algo** = to apply to the Court; **mi cliente desea solicitar defensa de oficio** = my client wishes to apply for Legal Aid; **solicitó un requerimiento** *o* **un interdicto al tribunal** = he applied to the Court for an injunction; **solicitó revisión judicial** *o* **indemnización** *o* **un aplazamiento** = he applied for judicial review *o* for compensation *o* for an adjournment; **los abogados que representaban a la esposa solicitaron una orden de manutención** = solicitors acting for the wife made an application for a maintenance order **(d)** *(presentar una solicitud)* to petition; **solicitó una pensión especial al gobierno** = he petitioned the government for a special pension

solicitud *nf* application *o* request *o* petition; **solicitud de acciones** = application for shares; **solicitud de liquidación** = winding up petition; **solicitud de un trabajo** = application for a job *o* job application; **solicitud de algo al tribunal** = application; **solicitud de inclusión de un crédito en la masa de la quiebra** = proof of debt; **solicitud requisitoria del título de propiedad** *o* **solicitud del título de propiedad** = requisition on title; **solicitud unilateral** *o* **solicitud de una de las partes** = an ex parte application; **solicitudes de trabajo** = situations wanted; **aviso de solicitud al tribunal** = notice of motion; **carta de solicitud** *o* **de suscripción (de acciones)** = letter of application; **hacer la solicitud de una patente** = to file an application for a patent; **hoja** *o* **impreso de solicitud** = application form; **presentar una solicitud** = to petition; **segunda solicitud** = reapplication; **presentaron una solicitud para una ayuda estatal** = they put in a request for a government subsidy; **su solicitud de aplazamiento fue rechazada por el juez de primera instancia** = his request for an adjournment was turned down by the coroner

solidario, -ria *adj* **responsabilidad conjunta y solidaria** = joint and several liability

◊ **solidariamente** *adv* **mancomunada y solidariamente** = joint and severally; **responsable conjunta y solidariamente** = jointly and severally liable; **son responsables solidariamente** = they are jointly and severally liable

sólido *adj* **(a)** *(duro)* hard **(b)** *(firme)* firm *o* sound; **la situación financiera de la empresa es muy sólida** = the company's financial situation is very sound; **caso criminal con pruebas poco sólidas** = weak case

soltar *vt* to release *o* to let go of; **le engañaron para que soltara las llaves de la caja fuerte** = he was tricked into parting with the keys to the safe

soltero, -ra 1 *adj* single *o* unmarried; **una madre soltera** = a single mother *o* an unmarried mother **2** *nf* single woman *o* spinster; **apellido de soltera** = maiden name **3** *nm* bachelor

solución *nf* solution; **solución jurídica** = remedy; **después de discutir la cuestión, se llegó a una solución que beneficiaba a todos** = after some discussion a compromise solution was reached

solucionar *vt* to solve; **solucionar un problema** = to solve a problem; **el préstamo solucionará algunos de nuestros problemas a corto plazo** = the loan will solve some of our short-term problems

solvencia *nf* solvency

◊ **solvente** *adj* solvent; **la empresa apenas era solvente cuando la compró** = when he bought the company it was barely solvent

someter *vt* to submit; **someter a** = to subject to; **someter a juicio** = to try; **someter a votación** = to put to a vote; **sometió a su marido a malos tratos** = she subjected her husband to bad treatment; **le sometieron a tortura** = he was subjected to torture; **someter una propuesta a voto** = to put a proposal to the vote

◊ **someterse** *vr* to submit; **someterse a** = to abide by; **someterse a juicio** = to stand trial; **prometió someterse a la decisión del tribunal** = he promised to abide by the decision of the court; **se negó a someterse a la jurisdicción del tribunal** = he refused to submit to the jurisdiction of the court

sondear *vt* to poll; **sondear a una muestra de la población** = to poll a sample of the population; **sondear la opinión pública** = to canvass; **sondear la opinión de los socios del club sobre un asunto** = to poll the members of the club on an issue

◊ **sondeo** *nm* canvassing; **sondeo de opinión** = opinion poll *o* opinion research; **persona que hace sondeos de opinión** = canvasser; **hicieron un sondeo de opinión entre un grupo de votantes** = they polled a sample group of voters

sopesar *vt* to weigh *o* to measure; **sopesar la actuación del gobierno** = to measure the government's performance

soplón, -ona *n* nark *o* supergrass

soporte *nm* holder

sorteo *n m* ballot; **la subscripción de acciones se cubrió con exceso, por lo que hubo que proceder a un sorteo** = the share issue was oversubscribed, so there was a ballot for the shares

soslayar *vt* to get round; **intentamos soslayar el embargo enviando el cargamento desde Canadá** = we tried to get round the embargo by shipping from Canada

sospecha *nf* suspicion; **sospecha fundada** = absolute presumption; **le arrestaron bajo sospecha de encubrimiento** *o* **de complicidad** = he was arrested on suspicion of being an accessory after the fact; **lo arrestaron bajo sospecha de espionaje** = he was arrested as a suspected spy

sospechar 1 *vt* to suspect; **la policía sospecha que los robos fueron cometidos por uno de los empleados de la tienda** = the police suspect that the thefts were committed by a member of the shop's staff **vi**; **sospechar de** = to be suspicious of ◊ **sospechoso, -sa 1** *adj* suspect *o* suspicious *o* shady; **la policía está investigando el paquete sospechoso encontrado en el coche** = the police are dealing with the suspicious package found in the car; **encontraron substancias sospechosas en el bolsillo del hombre** = suspicious substances were found in the man's pocket **2** *n* suspect; **chequeo de sospechosos** = identification *o* identity parade; **la policía tiene a seis sospechosos bajo custodia** = the police have taken six suspects into custody; **la policía está interrogando al sospechoso sobre sus movimientos a la hora en que se cometió el crimen** = the police are questioning the suspect about his movements at the time the crime was committed

sostener *vt* to hold *o* to uphold *o* to maintain *o* to assert; **el juez de apelación sostuvo que el acusado no incurría en incumplimiento de deber** = the appeal judge held that the defendant was not in breach of his statutory duty ◊ **sostenerse** *vr* to hold up

Sres *abrev* = *SEÑORES* Messrs; **los Sres Mamano y Solá** = Messrs Mamano & Solá

statu quo *nm* status quo; **statu quo anterior** = status quo ante; **el contrato no altera el statu quo** = the contract does not alter the status quo

sub- *prefijo* sub-
◊ **subagencia** *nf* sub-agency
◊ **subagente** *nmf* sub-agent
◊ **subalterno, -na** *adj y n* junior *o* office junior
◊ **subarrendador, -ra** *n* sublessor
◊ **subarrendamiento** *nm* underlease
◊ **subarrendar** *vt* to underlet *o* to sublet *o* to sublease; **hemos subarrendado parte de nuestra oficina a una asesoría financiera** = we have sublet part of our office to a financial consultancy; **subarrendaron una pequeña oficina en el centro de la ciudad** = they subleased a small office in the centre of town
◊ **subarrendatario, -ria** *n* sublessee *o* subtenant *o* undertenant
◊ **subarriendo** *nm* underlease *o* sublease *o* subtenancy

subasta *nf* auction; **poner en pública subasta** = to put something up for auction
◊ **subastador, -ra** *n* auctioneer

subastar *vt* to auction *o* to put something up for auction; **cerraron la fábrica y subastaron la maquinaria** = the factory was closed and the machinery was auctioned off

subcomisión *nf* sub-committee; **es el presidente de la subcomisión de finanzas** = he is chairman of the Finance Sub-Committee

subcomité *nm* sub-committee

subcontratar *vt* to subcontract; **subcontratar trabajo** = to put work out to contract; **la instalación eléctrica ha sido subcontratada a Smith Ltd** = the electrical work has been subcontracted to Smith Ltd
◊ **subcontratista** *nmf* subcontractor; **solicitaremos ofertas a subcontratistas para la instalación eléctrica** = we will put the electrical work out to subcontract
◊ **subcontrato** *nm* subcontract; **ceder en subcontrato** = to subcontract; **les han concedido el subcontrato para toda la instalación eléctrica del nuevo edificio** = they have been awarded the subcontract for all the electrical work in the new building

súbdito, -ta *n* subject *o* national; **súbdito de nacimiento** = natural-born subject; **súbditos extranjeros** = foreign nationals; **es un súbdito español** = he is a Spanish subject; **los súbditos españoles no necesitan visado para visitar los países de la UE** Spanish subjects do not need visas to visit EU countries

subestimar *vt* to underestimate *o* to minimize; **subestimaron los efectos de las sanciones en las ventas** = they underestimated the effects of the sanctions on their sales

subgobernador *nm* **subgobernador civil** = undersheriff

subida *nf* **(a)** *(aumento)* rise *o* increase; **subida de los impuestos** = increase in tax *o* tax increase; **subida de precios** *o* **subida de los precios** = escalation of prices *o* increase in price *o* price increase; **subida de sueldo** = increase in pay *o* pay increase; **una subida del tipo de interés** = a rise in interest rates **(b) subida al trono** = accession to the throne

subir *vt* **(a)** *(escalar)* to escalate *o* to advance **(b)** *(aumentar)* to increase *o* to rise; **le subieron el sueldo a 20.000 libras** = his salary was increased to £20,000; **los precios suben más deprisa que la inflación** = prices are rising faster than inflation **(c)** **subir a** = to board

sub judice *adj* *(bajo secreto sumarial)* sub judice; **'bajo la ley': sub judice** = sub judice; **la prensa no puede informar sobre el caso porque todavía está sub judice** = the papers cannot report the case because it is still sub judice

sublevación *nf* rebellion

sublevarse *vr* to rebel *o* to mutiny

subordinado, -da 1 *adj* subordinate *o* ancillary; **subordinado a** = subordinate to **2** *n* subordinate; **a sus subordinados les resultaba difícil trabajar con él** = his subordinates find him difficult to work with

subrogación *nf* subrogation

subsanar *vt* to put right

subsidiario, -ria *adj* subsidiary *o* ancillary; **bancos subsidiarios** = secondary banks; **empresa subsidiaria** = subsidiary company; **garantía subsidiaria** = collateral security; **piquete subsidiario** = secondary action *o* secondary picketing; **responsabilidad subsidiaria** = vicarious liability

subsidio *nm* benefit *o* subsidy *o* *(beca)* grant; **subsidio de defunción** = death benefit; **subsidio de desempleo** *o* **de paro** = unemployment pay; **recibe un subsidio de paro de 20.000 ptas. a la semana** = she receives 20,000 ptas. a week as unemployment benefit; **subsidio por aumento del coste de vida** = cost-of-living allowance

subsiguiente *adj* subsequent

substancial *adj* substantial *o* essential; **prueba substancial** = material evidence

subvención *nf* **(a)** *(subsidio)* subsidy *o* *(beca)* grant; **subvención a fondo perdido** = non-recoverable grant; **precio de subvención** = support price; **el gobierno ha aumentado la subvención a la industria automovilística** = the government has increased its subsidy to the car industry; **el instituto tiene una subvención estatal para cubrir el coste del programa de desarrollo** = the institute has a government grant to cover the cost of the development programme; **la industria depende de las subvenciones estatales** = the industry exists on government subsidies; **el Gobierno ha asignado subvenciones para sufragar los gastos del proyecto** = the Government has allocated grants towards the costs of the scheme **(b)** *(prima)* bounty

subvencionado, -da *adj* subsidized; **alojamiento subvencionado** *o* **vivienda subvencionada** = subsidized accommodation; **proyecto subvencionado** = grant-aided scheme

subvencionar *vt* to subsidize *o* to support; **el gobierno se ha negado a subvencionar la industria automovilística** = the government has refused to subsidize the car industry; **el gobierno subvenciona la industria informática a razón de 2 millones de dólares al año** = the government is supporting the computer industry to the tune of $2m per annum

subversivo, -va *adj* subversive; **la policía mantiene bajo control elementos subversivos** = the police are keeping subversive elements under surveillance

suceder *vt/i* **(a)** *(tener lugar)* to take place **(b)** *(seguir)* to succeed

sucesión *nf* succession; **sucesión ab intestato** = intestate succession; **sucesión testada** = testamentary succession; **derechos de sucesión** *o* **impuesto sobre sucesiones** = death duty *o* death tax; **impuesto de sucesión** *o* **impuesto sobre transmisiones** *o* **impuesto sobre herencias y donaciones** = estate tax; **ley de sucesión** = law of succession

sucesivo, -va *adj* consecutive; **sentencias sucesivas** = consecutive sentences; **prima sucesiva** = renewal premium; **procura ser más cuidadoso en lo sucesivo** = try to be more careful in future; **fue sentenciado a dos periodos de dos años de cárcel, siendo las sentencias sucesivas** = he was sentenced to two periods of two years in jail, the sentences to run consecutively
◊ **sucesivamente** *adv* seriatim

suceso *nm* event; **la policía está intentando reconstruir los sucesos de la noche anterior** = the police are trying to piece together the events of the previous evening; **los artículos periodísticos informaron de los sucesos ocurridos tras el partido de fútbol** = the newspaper reports covered the events following the football match

sucesor, -ra *n* successor; **el sucesor del Sr. Cervera como presidente será el Sr. Sala** = Mr Cervera's successor as chairman will be Mr Sala

sucio, -cia *adj* dirty; **negocio sucio** = shady deal; **negocio sucio que utiliza la estafa** *o* **la extorsión** = racket; **lleva un negocio sucio de reventa de entradas** = he runs a cheap ticket racket

sucursal *nf* branch *o* branch office *o* division; **sucursal de correos** = sub-post office; **director de sucursal** = branch manager; **encargado, -da de una sucursal** = sub-agent; **es el director de nuestra sucursal local del banco Lloyds** = he is the manager of our local branch of Lloyds bank; **hemos decidido abrir una sucursal en Chicago** = we have decided to open a branch office in Chicago; **la empresa tiene su sede en Londres y sucursales en todos los países europeos** = the company has its base in London and branches in all European countries; **nuestra sucursal extranjera tiene su sede en Las Bahamas** = our foreign branch is based in the Bahamas; **el banco** *o* **el almacén tiene sucursales en la mayoría de las ciudades del sur del país** = the bank *o* the store has branches in most towns in the south of the country; **Smith's es ahora una sucursal del grupo de compañías Brown** = Smith's is now a division of the Brown group of companies

suegra *nf* mother-in-law

suegro *nm* father-in-law

sueldo *nm* pay *o* earnings; **sueldo base** = basic pay; **sueldo neto** = take-home pay; **asesino a sueldo** = hired killer *o* hit man; **cheque de sueldo** = pay cheque *o* paycheck

suelo *nm* ground

suelto, -ta *adj* at large

suerte *nf* luck; **buena** *o* **mala suerte** = good *o* bad luck; **tuvieron mucha suerte** = they were very lucky

suficiente *adj* sufficient *o* adequate; **motivo suficiente** = good cause; **actuar sin cobertura suficiente** = to operate without adequate cover; **no dar suficientes instrucciones a un jurado** = non-direction; **el tribunal pidió al acusado que justificara una causa suficiente para no ir a la cárcel** = the court asked the accused to show good cause why he should not be sent to prison; **garantizó suficientes fondos para su mujer** = he made adequate provision for his wife; **la empresa tiene fondos suficientes para pagar su programa de expansión** = the company has sufficient funds to pay for its expansion programme; **le dan lo suficiente para vivir** = they provide for him

sufragar *vt* to defray; **la compañía accedió a sufragar las costas del juicio** = the company agreed to defray the costs of the prosecution

sufragio *nm* suffrage; **sufragio universal** = universal suffrage

sufrir *vt/i* to experience *o* to suffer; **sin sufrir daño alguno** = safely; **la mercancía fue descargada del barco que se hundía sin sufrir daño alguno** = the cargo was unloaded safely from the sinking ship

sugerencia *nf* suggestion; **buzón de sugerencias** = suggestion box

sugerir *vt* to suggest; **el presidente sugirió que la siguiente reunión se celebrara en octubre** = the chairman suggested (that) the next meeting should be held in October

sui generis *adj (de su propia clase)* sui generis

suicida 1 *adj* suicidal; **los funcionarios de prisiones deberían vigilar estrechamente a ese interno; puede tener intenciones suicidas** = the warders should keep close watch on that prisoner - we think he may be suicidal **2** *nmf* suicide

suicidarse *vr* to commit suicide; **después de disparar a su mujer, se suicidó en la habitación** = after shooting his wife, he committed suicide in the bedroom

suicidio *nm* suicide; **pacto de suicidio** = suicide pact; **la policía considera la muerte como suicidio, no como asesinato** = the police are treating the death as suicide, not murder

sujetar *vt* to attach

sujeto, -ta 1 *adj* **sujeto a** = subject to *o* liable to; **acuerdo sujeto a contrato** *o* **venta sujeta a contrato** = agreement *o* sale subject to contract; **estos artículos están sujetos a tasas de importación** = these articles are subject to import tax; **ventas que están sujetas a impuesto del timbre** = sales which are liable to stamp duty **2** *n* individual

suma *nf* sum; **suma global** = lump sum; **sumas** = monies; **la empresa ofreció una suma total de 10 millones si se acordaba no llevar el caso a los tribunales** = the company offered a lump sum of 10 million as an out-of-court settlement; **perdió grandes sumas de dinero en la bolsa** = he lost large sums on the Stock Exchange

sumamente *adv* highly; **contrataron a un equipo de asesores jurídicos sumamente cualificados** they employed a team of highly qualified legal assistants

sumar 1 *vt* to count; **sumó las ventas de los seis meses hasta diciembre** = he counted up the sales for the six months to December **2** *vt/i* to add up *o* to total; **costes que suman más de £25.000** costs totalling more than £25,000

sumario, -ria 1 *adj* summary; **despido sumario** = summary dismissal; **juicio sumario** = summary judgment; **jurisdicción sumaria** = summary jurisdiction **2** *nm* summary *o* abstract; **sumario del fallo de un tribunal** = abstract of judgment; **hacer un sumario de las escrituras de una propiedad** = to make an abstract of the deeds of a property

sumergido, -da *adj* hidden; **economía sumergida** = black economy

suministrador, -ra *n* supplier

suministrar *vt* to supply *o* to furnish; **suministrar piezas de repuesto a una fábrica** = to supply a factory with spare parts

suministro *nm* supply; **el suministro de piezas de repuesto fue adjudicado a Bonet S.A.** = the supply of spare parts was contracted out to Bonet S.A.; **la fábrica se está quedando sin suministro de carbón** = the factory is running short of supplies of coal; **suministros exentos del IVA** = exempt supplies

señal *nf (pago de una pequeña parte de la deuda)* token payment

superar *vt* to beat *o* to exceed *o* to overcome; **han superado a sus competidores relegándoles al segundo puesto en el mercado informático** = they have beaten their competitors into second place in the computer market

superfluo, -flua *adj* redundant; **esta ley es superflua** = this law is now redundant; **la nueva legislación ha convertido la cláusula 6 en**

superflua = the new legislation has made clause 6 redundant

superior 1 *adj* **(a)** *(en cantidad)* higher; **superior a** = in excess; **cantidades superiores a los veinticinco kilos** = quantities in excess of twenty-five kilos **(b)** *(en calidad)* superior; **nuestro producto es superior a todos los productos de la competencia** = our product is superior to all competing products; **sus ventas son más elevadas porque ofrecen un servicio superior** = their sales are higher because of their superior service **(c)** *(en posición)* **cámara superior de un parlamento bicameral** = upper house; **parte superior** = head; **Tribunal Superior (de una Comunidad Autónoma)** = High Court (of Justice); **su caso se verá en un tribunal superior** = the case will be heard in a superior court; **trató de chantajear a un oficial superior** = he tried to blackmail a superior officer **2** *nm* superior *o* senior; **cada encargado es responsable ante su superior de informar con exactitud de las ventas** = each manager is responsible to his superior for accurate reporting of sales
◊ **superioridad** *nf* seniority

supervisar *vt* to supervise *o* to police *o* to superintend; **el traslado a las nuevas oficinas fue supervisado por el director administrativo** = the move to the new offices was supervised by the administrative manager; **supervisa a seis chicas en el departamento jurídico** = she supervises six girls in the legal department; **supervisa las ventas de la empresa en el extranjero** = he superintends the company's overseas sales

supervisión *nf* supervision; **de supervisión** = supervisory; **personal de supervisión** = supervisory staff; **el personal de nueva contratación trabaja bajo supervisión durante los tres primeros meses** = new staff work under supervision for the first three months; **realiza un trabajo de supervisión** he works in a supervisory capacity; **el recuento del dinero se hizo bajo la supervisión del director financiero** = the cash was counted under the supervision of the finance director; **tiene mucha experiencia y se le puede dejar trabajar sin necesidad de supervisión** = she is very experienced and can be left to work without any supervision

supervisor, -ra *n* supervisor *o* superintendent *o* comptroller; **trabaja en calidad de supervisor** = he works in a supervisory capacity

superviviente *nmf* survivor; **derecho del superviviente de un coarriendo a la propiedad, antes que los herederos del arrendatario fallecido** = survivorship

suplantación *nf* **suplantación de la personalidad** = impersonation

suplantar *vt* to take the place of *o* to forge; **suplantar la personalidad** = to impersonate

suplementario, -ria adj **indemnización suplementaria** = aggravated damages

suplemento *nm* excess fare *o* additional charge

suplente *nmf* **(a)** *(delegado)* deputy *o* vice- **(b)** *(interino)* locum (tenens); **se necesitan suplentes en el Sur** locums wanted in the South **(c)** *(sustituto)* substitute

súplica *nf* prayer; **palabras de súplica** = precatory words
◊ **suplicante 1** *adj* precatory **2** *nmf* petitioner
◊ **suplicatoria** *nf* rogatory letter
◊ **suplicatorio** *nm* petition

> El suplicatorio es el despacho que un juez o tribunal de carácter penal dirige a otro superior en petición de auxilio judicial

suponer *vt* to imply *o* to entail *o* to assume *o* to presume; **la coacción no supone atenuante en una acusación de asesinato** = duress provides no defence to a charge of murder; **se supone que la empresa es todavía solvente** = the company is presumed to be still solvent; **suponemos que el envío ha sido robado** = we presume the shipment has been stolen; **todo el mundo supuso que era culpable** = everyone assumed he was guilty; **detallar las cifras de ventas supondrá unos diez días de trabajo** = itemizing the sales figures will entail about ten days' work

suposición *nf* presumption

supremo *adj* supreme; **Tribunal Supremo** Supreme Court (of Judicature)

supresión *nf* abolition *o* abatement; **supresión del ruido** = noise abatement

suprimir *vt* **(a)** *(eliminar)* to delete *o* to excise *o* to expunge *o* to omit; **los abogados han suprimido la cláusula segunda del contrato** = the lawyers have deleted clause two from the contract; **el tribunal ordenó al periódico que suprimiera toda referencia al caso de divorcio** = the court ordered the newspaper to delete all references to the divorce case; **el presidente ordenó que se suprimieran los comentarios del informe oficial** = the chairman ordered the remarks to be excised from the official record; **se suprimieron del informe las pruebas basadas en rumores inadmisibles** = inadmissible hearsay evidence was expunged from the report **(b)** *(anular)* to abate *o* to abolish; **el Ministro de Economía y Hacienda se negó a pedir al Parlamento que suprimiese el impuesto sobre el alcohol** = the Chancellor of the Exchequer refused to ask Parliament to abolish the tax on alcohol **(c)** *(levantar)* to lift; **el gobierno ha suprimido la prohibición a las importaciones de equipo**

técnico = the government has lifted the ban on imports of technical equipment

supuesto *nm* **nombre supuesto** = alias; **por supuesto** = of course; **por supuesto que la empresa está interesada en los beneficios** = of course the company is interested in profits

surgir *vi* to arise

surtido *nm* stock

surtir *vt* to produce; **surtir efecto** = to have the desired effect

suscribir *vt* to subscribe; **suscribir acciones** = to subscribe for shares; **quien esto suscribe** = the undersigned
◊ **suscribirse** *vr* to subscribe to something; **suscribirse a acciones** = to apply for shares; **suscribirse a una revista** to subscribe to a magazine

suscripción *nf* subscription; **suscripción de acciones** = application for shares; **acciones a pagar por suscripción** = shares payable on application; **carta de suscripción (de acciones)** = letter of application

suscriptor, -ra *n* subscriber *o* underwriter; **había miles de suscriptores de acciones en la nueva compañía** = there were thousands of applicants for shares in the new company

suscrito, -ta *n* undersigned

susodicho, -cha *adj y n* aforesaid

suspender *vt* (a) *(cancelar)* to suspend *o* to cancel *o* to call off; **suspender una cita** to cancel an appointment; **suspender una reunión** = to adjourn *o* to cancel a meeting; **la reunión se suspendió a mediodía** = the meeting adjourned at midday; **la vista se suspendió por término indefinido** the hearing was adjourned sine die; **hemos suspendido los pagos en espera de noticias de nuestro agente** = we have suspended payments while we are waiting for news from our agent; **la dirección decidió suspender las negociaciones** = the management decided to suspend negotiations; **le suspendieron de empleo y sueldo mientras tenían lugar las investigaciones policiales** = he was suspended on full pay while the police investigations were proceeding; **se ha suspendido el trabajo sobre la preparación del caso** = work

on the preparation of the case has been suspended; **se ha suspendido la búsqueda de los niños desaparecidos** = the search for the missing children has been called off (b) *(indultar)* to reprieve; **suspender la ejecución de una sentencia** = to reprieve
◊ **suspendido, -da** *adj* off; **la huelga ha sido suspendida** = they called the strike off

suspensión *nf* suspension *o* adjournment; **suspensión de entregas** = suspension of deliveries; **suspensión de la ejecución de una sentencia** = stay of execution; **suspensión de la vista** = adjournment of the hearing; **suspensión del pronunciamiento de una sentencia** = arrest of judgment; **suspensión de pagos** = suspension of payments; **suspensión de sesiones** = recess; **suspensión temporal de una pena** *o* **orden judicial** = reprieve; **la suspensión duró dos horas** = the adjournment lasted two hours; **el tribunal garantizó a la empresa dos semanas de prórroga para la ejecución de la sentencia** = the court granted the company a two-week stay of execution

suspensivo, -va *adj* **condición suspensiva** = condition precedent

suspenso *adj* **esta ley está en suspenso** = this law is in abeyance

sustancial *adj* substantial; **adquirir una participación sustancial en una compañía** to acquire a substantial interest in a company

sustentar *vt* to maintain

sustituir *vt* to substitute *o* to stand in for *o* to supersede *o* to take over; **sustituir a alguien** = to deputize for someone; **la Srta. Tenas sustituyó al Sr. Cervera el 1 de mayo** Miss Tenas took over from Mr Cervera on May 1st; **el Sr. Smith sustituye al presidente que se encuentra de vacaciones** = Mr Smith is standing in for the chairman who is away on holiday

sustituto, -ta *n* substitute; **actuar como sustituto, -ta de alguien** = to act as deputy for someone *o* to act as someone's deputy

sustracción *nf* abstraction *o* theft; **sustracción de menores** = kidnapping *o* child abduction

sustraer *vt* to abstract; **sustraer dinero** = to steal

Tt

taberna *nf* public house

tabla *nf* **(a)** *(cuadro)* table; **tabla de mortalidad** = actuarial tables **(b)** *(gráfico)* chart
◊ **tablón** nm **tablón de anuncios** = noticeboard

tachar *vt (borrar)* to strike off *o* to cross off *o* to cross out *o* to expunge; **puede tacharle de nuestra lista de direcciones** = you can cross him off our mailing list; **tachó 250 libras y puso 500 libras** = she crossed out £250 and put in £500; **tachó mi nombre de su lista** = he crossed my name off his list **(b)** *(desafiar)* to challenge; **tachar a un jurado** = to challenge a jury

tácito, ta *adj (implícito)* tacit *o* implied; **contrato tácito** = implied contract; **fideicomiso tácito** = implied trust; **consentimiento tácito** = sufferance *o* tacit agreement; **el comité dio su tácito consentimiento a la propuesta** = the committee gave its tacit agreement to the proposal
◊ **tácitamente** *adv* **alquiler tácitamente prorrogado** = tenancy at sufferance

tajantemente *adv* **queda tajantemente prohibido** = it is absolutely forbidden

tal *adj y pron* such; **con tal que** = on the understanding that *o* provided that *o* providing

taller *nm* shop *o* workshop; **taller de reparaciones** = repair shop; **taller mecánico** = machine shop

talón *nm* cheque; **talón conformado** = certified cheque; **hemos recibido un talón sin fondos** = we have received a bad cheque

tamiz *nm* **pasar los candidatos por el tamiz** = to screen candidates

tampón *nm* stamp *o* rubber stamp

tanatorio *nm* mortuary

tangible *adj* tangible; **activo tangible** *o* **bienes tangibles** tangible assets *o* property

tantear *vt* to test
◊ **tanteo** nm **de tanteo** tentatively

tanto *nm* **(a)** **tanto alzado** = lump sum *o* flat rate; **acuerdo** *o* **contrato a tanto alzado** fixed-price agreement; **le pagan un tanto alzado de 500 ptas por mil** = he is paid a flat rate of 500 ptas per thousand; **tanto por ciento** = percentage **(b)** **por lo tanto** = therefor

tapa *nf* cover
◊ **tapadera** *nf* front; **el restaurante es la tapadera de una organización que trafica en drogas** = the restaurant is a front for a drugs organization

taquigrafía *nf* shorthand; **los periodistas sabían escribir en taquigrafía** = the reporters could take notes in shorthand
◊ **taquigráficamente** *adv* **se tomó nota taquigráficamente de las actas del tribunal** = the court proceedings were taken down in shorthand
◊ **taquígrafo, -fa** *n* shorthand writer *o* stenographer

taquilla *nf* box office *o* ticket office *o* booking office

tara *nf* defect

tardar *vi* to delay; **tardar tiempo** = to take time; **el jurado tardó seis horas en llegar a un veredicto** = it took the jury six hours to reach a verdict *o* the jury took six hours to reach a verdict

tarde 1 *adv* late; **más tarde** = thereafter; **de lo que se ha concluido más tarde** = a posteriori; **el cargamento fue desembarcado tarde** = the shipment was landed late; **la vista comenzó tarde** = the hearing started late **2** *nf (parte del día)* afternoon *o* evening *o* p.m.; **las llamadas a Nueva York después de las seis de la tarde son más baratas** if you phone New York after 6 p.m. the calls are at a cheaper rate; **el tren sale a las 6.50 de la tarde** the train leaves at 6.50 p.m.

tardío *adj* late

tarea *nf* assignment *o* undertaking *o* occupation

tarifa *nf* tariff *o* rate; **tarifa de carga** *o* **de flete** = freight rate; **tarifa de seguros** = insurance rate; **tarifa especial para empleados** = concessionary fare; **tarifa fija** = fixed rate; **tarifa reducida** *o* reduced rate *o* concessionary fare; **tarifa telefónica de noche** *o* **nocturna** = night rate; **tarifa uniforme** = flat rate; **tarifas oficiales** *o* **precios según tarifa** = scheduled charges *o* prices; **Acuerdo General sobre Tarifas y Comercio** = General Agreement on Tariffs and Trade (GATT); **la tarifa es de 1.000**

ptas por hora = the rate is 1,000 per hour; utilizamos la tarifa normal de correos para toda la correspondencia = we use second-class mail for all our correspondence

tarjeta *nf* card; **tarjeta de crédito** = credit; **tarjeta de desembarque** = landing; **tarjeta de embarque** = boarding card *o* boarding pass *o* embarkation card; **tarjeta verde** = green card

tasa *nf* fee *o* rate; **tasa de cambio** = exchange rate *o* rate of exchange; **tasa de rendimiento** = rate of return

tasación *nf* assessment *o* valuation; **tasación de averías** = average adjustment; **tasación de costas procesales** = taxation of costs; **tasación de existencias** = stock valuation; **tasación de los precios** = pricing; **tasación de acciones basada en su valor actual en bolsa** = stock market valuation

tasador, -ra *n* estimator *o* valuer *o* appraiser *o* *(funcionario del Tribunal Supremo que valora las costas procesales)* Taxing Master; **tasador de daños** = average adjuster *o* loss adjuster; **costas procesales fijadas por el tasador** = taxed costs

tasar *vt* to value *o* to price *o* to appraise *o* to assess *o* to tax *o* to adjust; **nos están tasando las joyas para el seguro** = we are having the jewellery valued for insurance; **el tribunal ordenó que se tasaran las costas si no se llegaba a un acuerdo** = the court ordered the costs to be taxed if not agreed

tecla *nf* key; **tecla de control** = control key; **tecla de mayúsculas** = shift key; **hay sesenta y cuatro teclas en el teclado** = there are sixty-four keys on the keyboard
◊ **teclado** *nm* keyboard

tecnicismo *nm* technicality

técnico, -ca **1** *adj* technical; **estar en paro técnico** = to work to rule; **conocimientos técnicos especializados** = know-how; **se concedieron daños no relevantes al juzgarse que el daño era más técnico que real** = nominal damages were awarded as the harm was judged to be technical rather than actual **2** *nm* technician

técnico asesor consulting engineer **3** *nf* technique; **técnica especial** = special technique

telefónico, -ca *adj* telephone; **extensión telefónica** = (telephone) extension; **guía telefónica** = telephone directory

tema *nf* matter *o* issue; **tema adicional** = collateral issue; **tema de disputa secundario que se trata antes de un juicio** = interlocutory matter; **el tema en discusión** = point at issue; **el tema en discusión es la posesión de los bienes** = the point at issue is the ownership of the property; **veremos primero el tema de la baja de precios del mes pasado** = we shall consider first the matter of last month's fall in prices

temerario, -ria *adj* reckless; **conducción temeraria** = reckless driving; **imprudencia temeraria** = gross negligence *o* recklessness; **le acusaron de conducción temeraria** he was accused of driving recklessly

temeridad *nf* recklessness

temor *nm* *(miedo)* fear *o* *(recelo)* suspicion

temporal *adj* temporary *o* interim; **interdicto temporal** = temporary injunction; **trabajo temporal** = temporary employment; **requerimiento** *o* **intimación temporal** = interim injunction; **seguro temporal** = term insurance
◊ **temporalmente** *adv* temporarily

temporero, ra *n* casual labourer *o* casual worker

temporizador *nm* time lock

temprano, -na *adj y adv* early

tendencia *nf* trend *o* tendency; **hay una tendencia en contra de los métodos de supervisión tradicionales** = there is a trend away from old-style policing methods; **observamos una tendencia general a vender al mercado estudiantil** = we notice a general tendency to sell to the student market; **tendencias económicas** = economic trends; **una tendencia al alza** *o* **a la baja en las inversiones** = an upward *o* a downward trend in investment

tenedor, -ra *n* holder *o* bearer *o* *(portador)* payee; **tenedor de acciones** = shareholder *o* stockholder; **tenedor de buena fe** = holder in due course; **tenedor de obligaciones** = bondholder *o* debenture holder; **tenedor de una letra de cambio** *o* **de un pagaré** = holder; **tenedor legal** = lawful owner; **tenedores de bonos del estado** = holders of government bonds *o* bondholders

tenencia *nf* **(a)** *(ocupación)* occupation *o* occupancy *o* tenure; **tenencia de tierras** = land tenure **(b)** *(posesión)* possession; **tenencia de drogas** = possession of drugs; **tenencia ilícita de armas** = unlawful possession of weapons *o* carrying offensive weapons **(c)** *(de acciones)* shareholding; **una tenencia de acciones mayoritaria** *o* **una tenencia de acciones minoritaria** = a majority shareholding *o* a minority shareholding

tener *vt* **(a)** *(poseer)* to have *o* to hold *o* to own *o* to possess; **tener y poseer** = to have and to hold; **tener derecho a** = to have a right to; **tener noticias de alguien** = to hear from someone; **tener una cuenta bancaria** = to bank; **tener una discusión** *o* **una charla** = to hold a discussion; **tiene la tierra en arrendamiento de la compañía inmobiliaria** = she holds the land under a lease from the property company; **la compañía tiene valores de sociedades manufactureras alemanas** = the company has holdings in German manufacturing companies; **tiene pasaporte británico** = she is a British passport holder *o* she is the holder of a

British passport; **perdió todo lo que tenía cuando su empresa fue disuelta** = he lost all he possessed when his company was put into liquidation; **no tener** = not to have *o* to lack; **no tenía conocimiento de la existencia del contrato** = he had no knowledge of the contract **(b)** *(mantener)* to keep; **tener el nombre de alguien archivado** *o* **en archivo** = to keep someone's name on file **(c) tener conocimiento de** = to know; **tener cuidado** = to beware; **tener efecto** = to take effect; **tener en cuenta** = to take into account; **tener que ver con** = to bear on *o* to have a bearing on

tentación *nf* enticement

tentativa *nf* attempt; **la junta rechazó la tentativa de absorción de la empresa** = the takeover attempt was turned down by the board; **homicidio en grado de tentativa** = homicide attempt

> A los autores de tentativa de delito se les impondra la pena inferior en uno o dos grados a la señalada por la Ley para el delito consumado, en la extensión que se estime adecuada, atendiendo al peligro inherente al intento y al grado de ejecución alcanzado (CP art° 62)

teoría nf **en teoría** = on paper; **en teoría el sistema es perfecto, pero tenemos que verlo en funcionamiento antes de firmar el contrato** = on paper the system is ideal, but we have to see it working before we will sign the contract

tercer *adj (contracción de tercero)* third; **tercer trimestre** = third quarter

tercería *nf* third party proceedings; **tercería de dominio** = third party claim to ownership

tercero, -ra 1 *adj* third; **vender todo por la tercera parte de su valor** = to sell everything at one third off **2** *nm* third party; **el caso está en manos de un tercero** = the case is in the hands of a third party; **notificación de inclusión de un tercero** = third party notice; **proceso en el que se incluye un tercero** = third party proceedings; **seguro contra terceros** = third-party insurance; **un tercero debería dar fe del documento** = the document should be witnessed by a third person

tercio *nm* third

tergiversación *nf* misrepresentation; **tergiversación fraudulenta** = fraudulent misrepresentation; **tergiversación de los hechos** = false information

tergiversar *vt* to misrepresent *o* to prevaricate; **tergiversar los hechos** = to give false information

terminable *adj* terminable

terminación *nf* **(a)** *(término)* termination; **la terminación de un arrendamiento** = the

termination of a lease; **apelar contra la terminación de una orden judicial de adopción** = to appeal against the termination of a foster order **(b)** *(expiración)* expiration

terminante *adj* unconditional; **la oferta se hizo terminante el pasado jueves** = the offer went unconditional last Thursday

◊ **terminantemente** *adv* expressly; **el franquiciado tiene terminantemente prohibida la venta de cualquier otro producto que no le sea directamente suministrado por el franquiciador** = the franchisee is expressly forbidden to sell goods other than those supplied by the franchisor; **según el contrato queda terminantemente prohibido vender a los EE UU** = the contract expressly forbids sales to the United States

terminar 1 *vt* to complete *o* to terminate *o* to wind up; **terminar un mandato** = to retire; **¿cuánto tiempo le llevará terminar el trabajo?** = how long will it take you to complete the job? **2** *vi* **(a)** *(acabar)* to end *o* to finish; **terminar de trabajar** = to knock off; **el abogado terminará en unos minutos** = the solicitor will be free in a few minutes **(b)** *(caducar)* to expire; **terminar de pagar una deuda** = to pay off a debt **(c) para terminar** = in conclusion; **para terminar, el juez dio las gracias al jurado por su largo y paciente servicio** in conclusion, the judge thanked the jury for their long and patient service ; **sin terminar** = rough

término *nm* **(a)** *(plazo)* term *o* deadline *o* time limit; **término contractual secundario (a la finalidad principal del contrato)** = warranty **(b)** *(expresión)* wording *o* form of words; **explicar en términos generales** = to outline; **¿entendiste los términos del contrato?** = did you understand the wording of the contract? **(c)** *(condiciones)* term *o* terms; **términos generales (de un acuerdo)** = basis; **términos y condiciones implícitos de un contrato** = implied terms and conditions; **según los términos del contrato, la empresa es responsable de todos los daños contra la propiedad** = by *o* under the terms of the contract, the company is responsible for all damage to the property **(d)** *(frontera)* boundary (line); **término municipal** = municipal area **(e) acordar un término medio** = to compromise; **él pedía más de lo que yo le ofrecía y acordamos un término medio** he was asking more than I was prepared to pay and we compromised **(f) por término medio** = on average; **ser por término medio** = to average; **los días perdidos por enfermedad han resultado ser veintidós por término medio durante los últimos cuatro años** = days lost through sickness have averaged twenty-two over the last four years

terna *nf* short list of three candidates

terrateniente *nm* landowner

terreno *nm* lot *o* land; **terreno comunal** = common *o* common land; **terreno jurisdiccional** = exclusion zone

terrible *adj (terrible)* chronic

territorial *adj* territorial; **aguas territoriales** = territorial waters; **cargo territorial** *o* **deudas territoriales** = charge on land *o* charge over property *o* land charges; **deuda territorial en la que el deudor hipotecario firma una escritura que da al acreedor hipotecario un interés en la propiedad** = charge by way of legal mortgage; **impuestos territoriales** = land taxes; **reivindicaciones territoriales** = territorial claims

territorio *nm* territory; **su gobierno ha formulado una reivindicación sobre parte de nuestro territorio** = their government has laid claim to part of our territory

terrorismo *nm* terrorism

terrorista *nmf* terrorist; **acto terrorista** = act of terrorism; **atentado terrorista** = terrorist attack; **la bomba fue puesta por un grupo terrorista** *o* **por un grupo de terroristas** = the bomb was planted by a terrorist group *o* by a group of terrorists

tesorero, -ra *n* treasurer; **tesorero honorario** = honorary treasurer

tesoro *nm* treasure; **tesoro descubierto** treasure trove; **entraron ladrones en el palacio y robaron el tesoro del rey** thieves broke into the palace and stole the king's treasure; **el Tesoro** = the Treasury; **bono del tesoro** *o* **pagaré del tesoro** = Treasury Bill; **bonos del tesoro (a largo plazo) de los EE UU** = treasury bonds

testado *adj* testate; **¿murió habiendo testado?** = did he die testate?

testador *nm* testator

testadora *nf* testatrix

testaferro *nm* front man

testamentaría *nf* execution of a will *o* testamentary execution

testamentario, -ria *adj* testamentary; **disposiciones testamentarias** = testamentary dispositions *o* devise; **hacer disposiciones testamentarias** = to make testimentary dispositions; **ejecutor testamentario** = executor; **ejecutora testamentaria** = executrix; **representante testamentario** = personal representative

testamento *nm* will *o* last will and testament; **testamento abierto** = nuncupative will; **testamento cerrado** = sealed will; **testamento ológrafo** = holograph will; **legalización de un testamento** = probate; **garantía de legalidad de un testamento** *o* **concesión de legalidad de un**

testamento = grant of probate; **hacer testamento** = to make testimentary dispositions *o* to make a will; **según el testamento, todos los bienes pasan a sus hijos** = according to her will, all her property is left to her children

testar *vi* to make a will; **capacidad de testar** = testamentary capacity; **morir sin haber testado** = to die intestate

testifical *adj* **prueba testifical** = primary evidence

testificar *vti* to testify *o* to give evidence

testigo, -ga *n* witness; **testigo de cargo** *o* **de la acusación** = prosecution witness *o* witness for the prosecution; **testigo de conducta** = character witness; **testigo de descargo** *o* **de la defensa** = defence witness *o* witness for the defence; **testigo desfavorable** *o* **hostil** = adverse witness *o* hostile witness; **testigo favorable** = friendly witness; **testigo instrumental** = attesting witness; **testigo ocular** *o* **presencial** = eye witness; **testigo pericial** = expert *o* professional *o* skilled witness; **testigo testamentario** = witness to a will; **banco de testigos** = witness box; **actuar como testigo de la veracidad de un documento** *o* **firma** = to act as a witness to a document *o* a signature; **firmar como testigo de un acuerdo** *o* **firmar un contrato como testigo** = to witness an agreement; **ser testigo de una firma** = to witness a signature; **'ahora que la escritura ha sido presenciada por testigos'** = 'now this deed witnesseth'; **contó su versión del atraco al banco, como testigo ocular** = he gave an eye witness account of the bank hold-up; **el contrato tiene que firmarse en presencia de** *o* **ante dos testigos** = the contract has to be signed in the presence of two witnesses; **el juez la calificó de testigo desfavorable** = she was ruled a hostile witness by the judge

testimonial *adj* **cláusula testimonial** = testimonium clause

testimonio *nm* **(a)** *(declaración)* testimony; **testimonio de sentencia** = certificate of judgment; **testimonio oral** = oral evidence **(b)** *(testigo)* witness; **testimonio en contra** = adverse witness

texto *nm* text *o* wording; **texto impreso** = hard copy; **texto íntegro** = transcript; **escribió anotaciones al margen del texto del acuerdo** = he wrote notes at the side of the text of the agreement; **libro de texto** = textbook; **procesamiento de textos** = text processing; **tratamiento de textos** = word processing

◊ **textualmente** *adv* textually; **citar** *o* **leer textualmente** = to quote; **el abogado citó textualmente de la declaración realizada por el testigo en la comisaría de policía** = counsel quoted from the statement made by the witness at the police station

tiempo *nm* **(a)** *(duración de una acción)* time; **tiempo completo** = full-time; **tiempo libre** = spare time; **tiempo parcial** = part-time; **tiempo real** = real time; **tiempo de utilización de un ordenador (pagado a horas)** = computer time; **límite de tiempo** *o* **plazo de tiempo término** = time limit; **fletamento por tiempo determinado** = time charter; **conceder tiempo** *o* **dejar tiempo** = to allow time; **el tribunal aplazó la sesión para dejar tiempo a la acusación para encontrar al testigo desaparecido** = the court adjourned to allow the prosecution time to find the missing witness **(b) a tiempo** = on time; **al mismo tiempo** = at the same time *o* coterminous; **de hace tiempo** = long-standing; **(desde) tiempo inmemorial** = time immemorial; **por mucho tiempo** = for a long time; **tendrás que apresurarte si quieres llegar a tiempo a la vista** = you will have to hurry if you want to get to the hearing on time *o* if you want to be on time for the hearing; **los arrendamientos finalizan al mismo tiempo** = the leases are coterminous

tienda *nf* shop; **tienda al por menor** = retail shop; **una tienda de artículos de electricidad** = an electrical goods shop; **una tienda de informática** = a computer shop; **tienda sin vivienda incorporada** = lock-up shop; **ladrón que roba en las tiendas** *o* **ratero, -ra de tiendas** = shoplifter; **robo** *o* **hurto en las tiendas** = shoplifting; **abrió una tienda de moda femenina** = she opened a women's wear shop; **todas las tiendas del centro cierran los domingos** = all the shops in the centre of town close on Sundays

tierra *nf* land *o* ground; **certificado de tierras** = land certificate; **registro de tierras** = land registration

timador, -ra *n* **(a)** *(estafador)* cheat *o* swindler *o* confidence trickster *o* (US) confidence man **(b)** *(ladrón)* crook **(c)** *(chantajista)* racketeer

timar *vt* to con *o* to cheat *o* to swindle; **timaron a la anciana 25.000 libras** = they tricked the old lady out of £25,000

timbre *nm* stamp; **derecho** *o* **impuesto de timbre** = stamp duty

timo *nm* con *o* swindle *o* fiddle *o* confidence trick *o* (US) confidence game; **no es más que un timo** = it's all a fiddle

tipo *nm* **(a)** *(clase)* type *o* kind *o* nature; **la ley distingue varios tipos de delito contra la persona** = the law distinguishes several kinds of crime against the person; **se desconoce el tipo de negocios a los que se dedica** = the nature of his business is not known; **un nuevo tipo de droga** = a new type of drug; **de ninguna clase** *o* **de ningún tipo** = whatsoever **(b)** *(tasa)* rate; **tipo de cambio** = rate of exchange *o* exchange rate; **tipo de interés** = interest rate *o* rate of interest; **tipos de cambio**

futuros = forward (exchange) rate **(c)** *(estándar)* **carta tipo** = standard letter

tirada *nf* circulation

tirado, -da 1 *adj* *(precio)* giveaway **2** *nf* *(prensa)* circulation; **aumentar la tirada de un periódico** = to improve the circulation of a newspaper

tirador *nm* marksman

tirar *vt* **(a)** *(deshacerse de)* to throw out; **tiramos todos los teléfonos antiguos e instalamos un sistema informático** = we threw out the old telephones and put in a computerized system

tiro *nm* gunshot; **matar a tiros** = to gun down; **le mataron a tiros en la calle delante de su oficina** = he was gunned down in the street outside his office

titulación *nf* **tener la titulación adecuada para el trabajo** = to have the right qualifications for the job

titulado, -da *adj* qualified

titular *nmf* *(de un cheque)* holder *o* *(de un cargo oficial)* incumbent; **titular de un juzgado** = judge in charge of a court of first instance; **titular de una póliza de seguros** = holder of an insurance policy *o* policy holder; **titular de una tarjeta de crédito** = credit card holder

título *nm* **(a)** *(derecho)* title; **título absoluto** = full legal ownership; **título de privilegio** = letters patent; **título de propiedad** = deducing title *o* title deeds; **título de propiedad (con plenos derechos)** = good title; **título nobiliario** = title; **tener un título de propiedad de algo saneado y sin cargas** = to have a clear title to something; **título imperfecto** *o* **limitado de una propiedad** *o* **título no absoluto** = qualified title; **título garantizado por hipoteca** = mortgage debenture **(b)** *(cualificación)* qualification; **título académico** *o* **profesional** = academic degree *o* professional qualification; **sacar** *o* **obtener el título de** = to qualify as; **ha sacado el título de contable** = she has qualified as an accountant; **obtendrá el título de abogado el año que viene** = he will qualify as a solicitor next year; **tiene el título de abogado** = she is a qualified solicitor **(c)** *(valores)* bond *o* paper *o* securities; **título al portador** = bearer bond; **título de acción** = share certificate; **títulos de crédito de primerísima clase** = gilt-edged securities; **títulos del Estado** = government stocks *o* government securities; **título negociable** negotiable paper; **títulos u obligaciones** = equities; **comerciante en títulos** = securities trader **(d)** *(encabezamiento)* head *o* heading; **título abreviado** = short title; **título completo de una ley parlamentaria** = full title *o* long title; **título de una ley parlamentaria** = title; **título válido** = good title; **los artículos están clasificados por títulos** = items are listed under several headings; **observen la cifra bajo el título 'Costes 95-96'** = look at the figure under the heading 'Costs 95-96' **(e) a título de** = in the capacity of

todo, -da 1 *adj* all *o (entero)* whole; **todo incluído** = all-in; **seguro a todo riesgo** = fully comprehensive insurance; **toda la evidencia apunta a que fue una banda de tres personas quien atracó el banco** = all the evidence suggests that it was a gang of three people who held up the bank; **todos los testigos dicen que vieron al acusado con el bidón de petróleo** all the witnesses say they saw the accused with the can of petrol **2** *adv* all *o* largely; **nuestras ventas se dirigen sobre todo al mercado nacional** = our sales are largely in the home market

toga *nf* gown *o* robe; **tomar la toga** = to take silk

tolerancia *nf* tolerance *o* condonation *o* sufferance

tolerar *vt* to allow *o* to tolerate *o* to condone; **se le ha tolerado que viva en la casa** = he has been allowed to live in the house on sufferance; **el tribunal no puede tolerar su trato hacia sus hijos** = the court cannot condone your treatment of your children

toma *nf* **toma de decisiones** = decision making; **toma de declaración** = taking of statement *o* evidence; **toma de razón** = recording; **toma de posesión** = inauguration *o* taking over

tomar *vt* to take; **tomar juramento a** = to administer an oath; **tomar medidas** = to take action; **tomar nota** =; **to minute; tomar partido** = to take sides; **tomar posesión** = to take over; **tomar posesión de un cargo** = to take office; **tomar precauciones** = to take safety precautions; **tomar represalias** = to retaliate *o* to take revenge; **el nuevo presidente toma posesión el 1 de julio** = the new chairman takes over on July 1st; **debe tomar medidas de inmediato si quiere frenar los robos** = you must take immediate action if you want to stop thefts

tomo *nm* volume; **mira el tomo de disposiciones correspondiente al año 1996** = look in the 1996 volume of the regulations

tongo *nm (fraude electoral)* ballot-rigging *o* gerrymandering

tope *nm* limit; **a tope** = at full capacity; **estamos trabajando a tope** = we are working at full capacity

tortura *nf* torture; **sacaron la confesión mediante torturas** *o* **usaron torturas para sacar la confesión** the confession was extracted under torture

torturar *vt* to torture

total 1 *adj* total *o* outright; **cantidad total** = total amount; **cobertura total** = full cover; **coste total** =

total cost; **producción total** = total output; **reembolso total** = full refund *o* refund paid in full; **renta total** = total income; **responsabilidad total** = strict liability; **siniestro total** = total loss; **suma total** = grand total; **activos totales** = total assets; **costes totales** = full costs; **gastos totales** = total expenditure; **ingresos totales** = total revenue; **tener derecho total a algo** = to have a clear title to something **2** *nm* total *o* sum; **total general** *o* **total global** = grand total; **el total de los gastos asciende a más de £1.000** the total of the charges comes to more than £1,000; **le condenaron a un total de doce años de prisión** = he was sentenced to a total of twelve years' imprisonment

◊ **totalmente** *adv* totally *o* fully *o* completely; **totalmente libre de deudas** = in full discharge of a debt; **acciones no liberadas totalmente** = partly-paid up shares; **capital totalmente desembolsado** *o* **cubierto** = fully paid-up capital; **el agua arruinó totalmente el cargamento** = the cargo was completely ruined by water; **el almacén quedó totalmente destruido por el incendio** = the warehouse was completely destroyed by fire; **la fábrica quedó totalmente destruida en el incendio** = the factory was totally destroyed in the fire; **la mercancía quedó totalmente estropeada por el agua** = the cargo was totally ruined by water

totalidad *nf* total; **en su totalidad** = outright

totalizar *vti* to total

toxicomanía *nf* drug addiction *o* drug abuse
◊ **toxicómano, -na** *n* drug addict *o* addicted to drugs

trabajador, -ra *n* labourer *o* worker; **trabajador autónomo** *o* **por cuenta propia** self-employed; **trabajador eventual** = casual labourer; **trabajador manual** = manual labourer; **trabajadores eventuales** = casual labour; **trabajadores sindicados** *o* **organizados** = organized labour

trabajar *vi* to work; **estar trabajando en** = to be engaged in; **seguir trabajando** = get on with

trabajo *nm* employment *o* work *o* labour *o* labor; **trabajo arriesgado** *o* **peligroso** = dangerous job; **trabajo de oficina** = clerical work; **trabajo manual** = manual labour; **trabajo ocasional** *o* **eventual** = casual work; **accidente de trabajo** = occupational accident; **condiciones de trabajo** = conditions of employment; **contrato de trabajo** = contract of employment *o* employment contract; **estabilidad en el trabajo** = security of employment; **ofertas de trabajo** = situations vacant; **Magistratura del Trabajo** = industrial tribunal; **personas que tienen un trabajo** = the employed; **solicitudes de trabajo** = situations wanted; **no interrumpir el trabajo** = get on with; **los empleados no interrumpieron su trabajo y**

terminaron el pedido a tiempo = the staff got on with the work and finished the order on time

◊ **trabajos** *nmpl* occupations; **trabajos forzados** *o* **forzosos** = penal servitude *o* hard labour

traer *vt* to bring; **trajo sus documentos consigo** = he brought his documents with him

traficar *vt* to traffic; **traficar con objetos robados** = to fence; **traficar en algo** = to traffic in something

tráfico *nm* **(a)** *(circulación)* traffic; **delitos de tráfico** = traffic offences; **dirección del tráfico** *o* **punto de control del tráfico** = point duty; **policía de tráfico** = traffic police **(b)** *(negocio ilegal)* **tráfico de drogas** *o* **de estupefacientes** = drug trafficking; **le acusaron de tráfico de estupefacientes** *o* **tráfico de drogas** = he was charged with trafficking in drugs *o* with drug trafficking; **tráfico de objetos robados** handling stolen goods **(c)** *(soborno)* **tráfico de influencias** = graft

traición *nf* treason; **alta traición** = high treason; **delito grave de traición** = treason felony; **acusación de traición** = impeachment; **acusar a una persona de traición ante el parlamento** = to impeach; **ejecutaron a tres hombres por traición** = three men were executed for treason; **el juicio por traición duró tres semanas** = the treason trial lasted three weeks; **se le acusó de traición** = he was accused of treason; **le acusaron de hacer comentarios que podían incurrir en delito de traición** = he was accused of making treasonable remarks; **ocultación** *o* **encubrimiento de traición** = misprision of treason

traicionar *vt* to betray; **traicionar al país propio** *o* **a un amigo** = to betray one's country *o* a friend

traidor, -ra *adj* treasonable

trama *nf* plot *o* conspiracy

tramitación *nf* processing *o* procedure; **tramitación de quejas** = complaints procedure; **tramitación legal** = legal procedure; **la tramitación de una indemnización por daños** *o* **de una reclamación al seguro** = the processing of a claim for insurance

tramitar *vt* to process; **tramitar el pago de un cheque** = to clear a cheque; **tramitar una reclamación al seguro** = to process an insurance claim; **la sala de incidencias está tramitando la información recibida del público** = the incident room is processing information received from the public

◊ **trámite** *nm* transaction *o* procedure *o* formality; **trámite comercial** = business transaction; **trámites aduaneros** = customs formalities; **trámites de despido** = dismissal procedures; **trámites judiciales** = court proceedings; **patente en trámite** = patent pending; **el presidente prescindió del**

trámite de leer las actas = the chairman dispensed with the formality of reading the minutes; **los trámites para conceder los contratos del gobierno** = the machinery for awarding government contracts

trampa *nf* fiddle; **hace trampa** = he's on the fiddle

tranquilidad *nf* peace

◊ **tranquilo, -la** *adj* quiet *o* calm; **el acusado parecía muy tranquilo cuando el secretario le leyó los cargos** = the prisoner seemed very quiet when the clerk read out the charges

◊ **tranquilamente** *adv* easily *o* quietly; **pasaron la aduana tranquilamente** = they went through customs easily

transacción *nf* deal *o* business transaction; **transacción con concesiones recíprocas** = compromise; **transacción amigable** = amicable settlement; **transacción previa a la quiebra** = scheme of arrangement; **transacciones de futuros** = forward dealings; **transacciones en bolsa** = dealing; **formulario de transacciones bursátiles** = stock transfer form

transbordar *vt* to transfer

◊ **transbordo** *nm* transfer; **hacer transbordo** to transfer ; **cuando llegue al aeropuerto de Londres, tiene que hacer transbordo** when you get to London airport, you have to transfer

transcribir *vt* to settle

◊ **transcripción** *nf* transcript; **una transcripción literal del juicio** = a verbatim transcript of the trial; **el juez pidió una transcripción completa de la declaración** = the judge asked for a full transcript of the evidence; **las transcripciones de las sentencias se pueden consultar en el ARANZADI** = transcripts of sentences are available at the ARANZADI (a privately published digest of sentences)

transcurrir *vi* to elapse; **transcurrió el plazo** the deadline expired; **debemos dejar transcurrir el tiempo suficiente antes de presentar una queja** = we must allow sufficient time to elapse before making a complaint; **transcurrieron seis semanas hasta que la orden judicial entró en vigor** = six weeks elapsed before the court order was put into effect

transcurso *nm* **en el transcurso de** = in the course of; **en el transcurso de la vista, el demandado hizo varias alegaciones nuevas** = in the course of the hearing, several new allegations were made by the defendant

transeúnte *nmf* **(a)** *(ciudadano)* non-resident **(b)** *(que pasa por la calle)* passer-by

transferencia *nf* transfer; **transferencia bancaria** = bank transfer *o* credit transfer; **transferencia de dinero de una cuenta a otra** *o* **de**

una sección del presupuesto a otra = virement; **transferencia de divisas** = foreign exchange transfer; **transferencia de fondos** = transfer of funds; **transferencia de propiedad** *o* **de acciones** = transfer of property *o* transfer of shares; **transferencia de una letra de cambio** = delivery; **impuesto sobre las transferencias de capital** = capital transfer tax

◊ **transferible** *adj* transferable; **votación única transferible** = single transferable vote; **el billete de abono no es transferible** = the season ticket is not transferable

transferir *vt* to transfer *o* to assign *o* to attorn; **transfirió su dinero a una cuenta de depósito** = she transferred her money to a deposit account

transformar *vt* to convert

tránsfuga *nmf (nación)* defector; *(ejército)* desertor; *(partido)* turncoat

transgredir *vt* to trespass; **transgredir la ley** = to break the law

transgresión *nf* trespass; **transgresión de bienes** = trespass to goods; **transgresión de la propiedad** = trespass; **transgresión de los derechos de la persona** = trespass to the person; **acción de transgresión** = action in tort

transigir *vt* to compromise

tránsito *nm* **mercancía en tránsito** = goods in transit

transitorio, -ria *adj* temporary

transmisión *nf* demise *o* assignment; **transmisión de propiedad** *o* **de acciones** transfer of property *o* transfer of shares; **transmisión del título de propiedad** conveyance; **transmisión fraudulenta de propiedad** = fraudulent conveyance; **impuesto sobre transmisiones** = estate tax; **orden de transmisión de propiedad** = vesting order

transmitir *vt* to hand down *o* to hand over

transportar *vt* to carry *o* to convey; **transportar mercancías** = to carry goods

transporte *nm* **(a)** *(de personas)* transport; **transporte público** = public transport; **medio de transporte** = means of transport **(b)** *(envío)* shipping; **transporte aéreo** = carriage by air; **agente** *o* **agencia de transporte** = shipping agent; **empresa de transportes** = carrier *o* removal company; **empresa de transportes privada** = private carrier; **empresa de transportes públicos** = common carrier **(c)** *(porte)* carriage *o* freight; **gastos de transporte** = carriage charges; **gastos de transporte interno** = handling charges

◊ **transportista** *nmf* shipper *o* carrier; **derecho de retención del transportista** = carrier's lien

trapichear *vi (argot)* to be on the fiddle

◊ **trapicheo** *nm (argot)* shady deal

trasladar *vt* to transfer *o* to move; **el contable fue trasladado a nuestra sucursal de Escocia** = the accountant was transferred to our Scottish branch; **hemos decidido trasladar nuestra fábrica a un solar cerca del aeropuerto** = we have decided to move our factory to a site near the airport

◊ **trasladarse** *vr* to move; **la empresa se traslada de Toledo a Madrid** = the company is moving from Toledo to Madrid

◊ **traslado** *nm* transfer *o (mudanza)* removal; **traslado de mercancías** = stock movements; **traslado de una causa** = transfer of a case

traspasar *vt* to transfer; **traspasar competencias** = to devolve; **traspasar un negocio** = to transfer a business; **traspasar una propiedad a un comprador** = to convey a property to a purchaser; **se han traspasado competencias a las comunidades autónomas** = power is devolved to autonomous regions

traspaso *nm* **(a)** *(venta)* transfer *o* cession *o* disposal; **traspaso de bienes** = assignment *o* alienation; **traspaso de dominio** = conveyance; **traspaso de un negocio** = disposition; **traspaso de propiedad** = disposal of property; **redacción de una escritura de traspaso** *o* **ley y procedimiento de un traspaso de propiedad** = conveyancing; **redacción de una escritura de traspaso sin la ayuda de un abogado** = do-it-yourself conveyancing; **notario que hace escrituras de traspaso** = conveyancer **(b)** *(pago de entrada)* key money *o* premium; **piso para alquilar con traspaso de 10.000 libras** = flat to let with a premium of £10,000 **(c)** *(devolución)* **traspaso de competencias** = devolution

trastorno *nm* disorder; **trastorno mental** = mental disorder *o* disturbed balance of mind

tratado *nm* treaty; **tratado comercial** = commercial treaty; **tratado cultural** = cultural treaty; **Tratado de Adhesión a la UE** = Treaty of Accession to the EU; **tratado de doble imposición** = double taxation agreement; **tratado de extradición** = extradition treaty; **Tratado de Roma (UE)** = Treaty of Rome (EU)

tratamiento *nm* **(a)** *(informática)* processing; **tratamiento de información** *o* **de cifras** = processing of information *o* of figures; **tratamiento de textos** = word processing *o* text processing **(b)** *(trato)* usage

tratar 1 *vi* to discuss; **tratar con** = to deal with *o* to associate with; **tratar de** = to attempt; **se le acusó de tratar de ponerse en contacto con un miembro del jurado** = he was accused of attempting to contact a member of the jury **2** *vt* to handle; **las Salas de lo Penal no tratan causas civiles** = Crown Courts do not deal with civil cases

trato *nm* **(a)** *(negocio)* deal *o* bargain; **hacer un trato** = to arrange *o* to set up *o* to do a deal; **trato hecho** = it's a deal; **trato justo** = fair deal **(b)** *(tratamiento)* treatment; **trato preferente** = special treatment; **trato vejatorio** = abuse; **malos tratos** = rough treatment *o* cruelty; **tiene un trato agradable** = she has a pleasant manner

tregua *nf* truce; **tregua laboral** = cooling off period *o* *(US)* cooling time

trena *nf (cárcel)* nick

treta *nf (trampa)* trick

tren *nm* train; **tren de cercanías** = commuter train

tribunal *nm* tribunal *o* court *o* sessions *o* bench; **tribunal administrativo** = administrative tribunal; **tribunal arbitral** *o* **tribunal de justicia** = adjudication tribunal; **tribunal civil** = Civil Court; **Tribunal Constitucional** = Constitutional Court; **tribunal de apelación** = Court of Appeal *o* Appeal Court; **Tribunal de Cuentas** = National Audit Office; **tribunal de expertos** = panel of experts; **tribunal de instrucción** = petty sessions; **tribunal de justicia** = law court; **Tribunal de Justicia Europeo** = European Court of Justice; *GB* **tribunal de magistrados** = magistrates' court *o* bench of magistrates; **tribunal (tutelar) de menores** = juvenile court; **tribunal de patentes** = patents court; **tribunal de primera instancia** = court of first instance *o* petty sessions; **tribunal de segunda instancia** = court of appeal; **tribunal de última instancia** = court of last resort; **tribunal desautorizado** = kangaroo court; **Tribunal Europeo de Derechos Humanos** = European Court of Human Rights; **tribunal federal** = federal court; *US* **tribunal federal de primera instancia** = district court; **Tribunal Internacional de Justicia** = International Court of Justice; **tribunal laboral** = industrial tribunal; **tribunal marítimo** = Admiralty Court; **tribunal mercantil** = Commercial Court; **tribunal militar** = court-martial *o* military tribunal; **tribunal penal** = Criminal Court; **Tribunal Superior de Justicia (de las Comunidades Autónomas)** = High Court of Justice (of an Autonomous Community); **Tribunal Supremo** = Supreme Court (of Judicature); **sala de un tribunal** = courtroom; **forma parte del tribunal** = he is on the bench; **llevar a alguien ante los tribunales** = to take someone to law *o* to take someone to court; **llevar a un criminal ante los tribunales** = to bring a criminal to justice; **el tribunal se retirará durante treinta minutos** = the court will retire for thirty minutes; **fue declarado culpable por el tribunal militar y sentenciado a prisión** = he was found guilty by the court-martial and sentenced to imprisonment

El Tribunal Constitucional como intérprete supremo de la Constitución, tiene jurisdicción sobre todo el territorio español y conoce de los procedimientos de declaración de inconstitucionalidad y enjuicia la conformidad o disconformidad con la Constitución de las disposiciones legales. También tiene competencia para conocer de los recursos de amparo y de los conflictos de competencias entre el Estado y las Comunidades Autónomas o entre los diferentes órganos constitucionales (CE artºs 161-163).
El Tribunal Superior de Justicia de cada comunidad autónoma es el tribunal de última instancia dentro del territorio de la comunidad. Está compuesto por una sala de lo Civil y Penal, otra de lo Contencioso- Administrativo y otra de lo Social (LOPJ artº 70).
El Tribunal Supremo es el órgano jurisdiccional superior, a excepción de las competencias del Tribunal Constitucional en relación a las garantías constitucionales. Está compuesto por cinco salas: de lo Penal, de lo Civil, de lo Contencioso-Administrativo, de lo Social y de lo Militar. El Tribunal Supremo se ocupa de los recursos de casación (LOPJ artºs 53-60)

tributario, -ria *adj* tax; **exención tributaria** = tax exemption; **franquicia tributaria** = tax holiday; **paraíso tributario** = tax haven; **privilegio tributario** = tax concession; **sistema tributatrio** = tax system

tributos *nmpl* dues

trimestre *nm* term *o* quarter; **primer trimestre** *o* **segundo trimestre** *o* **tercer trimestre** *o* **cuarto trimestre** *o* **último trimestre** = first quarter *o* second quarter *o* third quarter *o* fourth quarter *o* last quarter; **primer trimestre del año** first quarter; **día final del trimestre para el pago de la renta** = quarter day; **el alquiler correspondiente al primer trimestre se paga por adelantado** = the first quarter's rent is payable in advance; **el trimestre de otoño comienza en septiembre** = the autumn term starts in September; **los gastos de electricidad se pagan por trimestres** = there is a quarterly charge for electricity
◊ **trimestral** *adj* quarterly; **audiencia trimestral** = Quarter Sessions
◊ **trimestralmente** *adv* quarterly; **acordamos pagar el alquiler trimestralmente** = we agreed to pay the rent quarterly *o* on a quarterly basis; **el banco nos manda un extracto de cuenta trimestralmente** = the bank sends us a quarterly statement

tríplica *nf* plaintiff's answer

triplicado *adj* **por triplicado** = in triplicate; **facturación por triplicado** = invoicing in triplicate; **hacer una factura por triplicado** = to print an invoice in triplicate

triplicarse *vr* to treble; **los préstamos de la empresa se han triplicado** = the company's borrowings have trebled

tripulación *nf* crew; **fletamento de un barco sin tripulación** = demise charter

◊ **tripulante** *nmf* crew member

trivial *adj* '**la ley no trata asuntos triviales**' = de minimis non curat lex

trizas *nfpl* **hacer algo** *o* **a alguien trizas** = to tear something *o* someone to shreds; **el argumento de la defensa quedó hecho trizas por el comportamiento del acusado ante el tribunal** = the defence case was wrecked by the defendant's behaviour in court

trono *nm* throne

trucado, -da *adj (falseado)* **peso trucado** = false weight

truco *nm* trick *o* gimmick

trueque *nm* exchange

tumulto *nm* riot; **delito de reunión para llevar a cabo un tumulto** rout

turbio, -bia *adj* shady

turno *nm* **(a)** *(rotación)* rotation; **ocupar la presidencia por turno** to fill the post of chairman by rotation; **dos directores se retiran por haber concluido su turno** two directors retire by rotation **(b)** *(programa de asistencia legal)* **abogado de turno** = legal aid lawyer; **turno de oficio** = Legal Aid (scheme)

tutela *nf* guardianship *o* wardship *o* protection; **el tribunal puso a la niña bajo su tutela** = the court warded the girl; **el Tribunal puso a la niña bajo su tutela, para protegerla de su tío que quería sacarla del país** = the Court declared the girl ward of court, to protect her from her uncle who wanted to take her out of the country; **menor bajo la tutela del Departamento de Bienestar Social** = child in care; **el juez tiene poder para ejercer la jurisdicción de tutela** = the judge has discretion to exercise the wardship jurisdiction; **tutela de los derechos** = protection of rights

tutelar *vt* to ward *o* to protect

tutor, -ra *n* guardian; **tutor para el proceso** = guardian ad litem

tutoría *nf* wardship

Uu

UE *nf* = *UNION EUROPEA* EU; **los ministros de la UE se reunieron hoy en Bruselas** = EU ministers met today in Brussels

ujier *nm* usher

último, -ma *adj* **(a)** *(final)* final *o* last *o* ultimate *o* closing; **último pago** = final discharge; **prestamista en última instancia** *o* **de último recurso** = lender of the last resort; **tribunal de última instancia** = court of last resort; **última notificación de pago** = final demand; **última voluntad y testamento** = last will and testament; **última voluntad verbal ante testigos** = nuncupative will; **dar los últimos toques a un documento** = to put the final details on a document; **efectuar el último pago** = to make the final payment; **pagar el último plazo** = to pay the final instalment; **de una cola de veinte personas, me sirvieron el último** = out of a queue of twenty people, I was served last; **el último caso fue de intento de asesinato, éste es de robo** = the last case was one of attempted murder, this one is for theft; **ésta es la última reunión de la junta antes de mudarnos a las nuevas oficinas** = this is our last board meeting before we move to our new offices **(b) en último lugar** *o* **por último** = last; **último trimestre** = fourth quarter *o* last quarter **(c)** *(más reciente)* late *o* latest; **a última hora de la noche** = late-night; **siempre lleva el último modelo de coche** = he always drives the latest model of car; **tuvieron una reunión a última hora de la noche en el aeropuerto** = they had a late-night meeting at the airport; **última fecha para la firma del contrato** = latest date for signature of the contract **(d) por último** = finally

ultimátum *nm* ultimatum; **los cargos sindicales discutieron entre ellos sobre la mejor manera de hacer frente al ultimátum de la dirección** = the union officials argued among themselves over the best way to deal with the ultimatum from the management

ultrajar *vt* to outrage *o* to abuse

ultraje *nm* outrage *o* insult

unánime *adj* unanimous; **veredicto unánime** = unanimous verdict; **el jurado pronunció un veredicto unánime de inocencia** = the jury reached a unanimous verdict of not guilty; **llegaron a un acuerdo unánime** = they reached unanimous agreement; **hubo un voto unánime contra la propuesta** = there was a unanimous vote against the proposal

◊ **unánimemente** *adv* unanimously *o* nemine contradicente *o* nem con; **las propuestas fueron adoptadas unánimemente** = the proposals were adopted unanimously

◊ **unanimidad** *nf* **por unanimidad** = unanimously *o* nemine contradicente *o* nem con; **la moción fue aprobada por unanimidad** = the motion was adopted nem con; **el tribunal de apelación pronunció su sentencia a favor del acusado por unanimidad** = the appeal court decided unanimously in favour of the defendant

único, ca *adj* sole; **propietario** *o* **dueño único** = sole owner *o* sole proprietor

unido, -da *adj* **(a)** *(conjunto)* joint; **Reino Unido** = United Kingdom (UK); **vinieron a estudiar al Reino Unido** = they came to the UK to study; **los Estados Unidos de América (EE UU)** = United States of America (USA); **recopilación de las leyes vigentes en los Estados Unidos de América** = the United States Code; **Organización de las Naciones Unidas (ONU)** = United Nations *o* United Nations Organization (UNO *o* UN)

uniforme 1 *adj* flat *o* uniform **2** *nm* uniform; **un grupo de policías sin uniforme entró en la casa** = a group of plainclothes police went into the house

unilateral *adj* unilateral *o* ex parte; **solicitud unilateral** = an ex parte application; **tomaron la decisión unilateral de anular el contrato** = they took the unilateral decision to cancel the contract

◊ **unilateralmente** *adv* unilaterally; **anularon el contrato unilateralmente** = they cancelled the contract unilaterally

unión *nf* **(a)** *(confederación)* union; **unión aduanera** = customs union; **Unión Europea (UE)** = the European Union (EU); **los Estados miembros de los EE UU** = the States of the Union; **los EE UU están incrementando el comercio con la Unión Europea** = the USA is increasing its trade with the European Union **(b)** *(acumulación de acciones)* joinder **(c)** *(amancebamiento)* **unión**

consensual = common-law marriage; *(matrimonio)* **unión conyugal** = marriage

unir *vt* to attach *o* to merge *o* to join
◊ **unirse** *vr* to join *o* to merge; **unirse con alguien para formar una sociedad** = to join with someone to form a partnership

universal *adj* universal; **heredero universal** = residuary legatee; **sufragio universal** = universal suffrage

urbano, -na *adj* urban; **guía urbana** = street directory; **guardia urbana** = police; **ordenación** *o* **planificación urbana** = town planning *o* zoning
◊ **urbanismo** *nm* town planning
◊ **urbanista** *nm* town planner
◊ **urbanizar** *vt* to develop

urgencia *nf* emergency
◊ **urgente** *adj* (a) *(inmediato)* urgent *o* pressing; **compromisos urgentes** = pressing engagements; **facturas urgentes** = pressing bills (b) *(rápido)* express; **carta urgente** = express letter; **entrega urgente** *o* **envío urgente** = express delivery; **enviar por transporte** *o* **correo urgente** = to express; **enviamos el pedido al almacén del cliente por transporte urgente** = we expressed the order to the customer's warehouse
◊ **urgentemente** *adv* urgently

urna *nf* **urna electoral** = ballot box; **ir a las urnas** = to go to the polls

usar *vt* (a) *(emplear)* to use; **de usar y tirar** = disposable (b) *(ejercer)* to exercise

uso *nm* use *o* usage; **uso de nombre supuesto** = impersonation; **artículos de uso personal** = items for personal use; **instrucciones de uso** = directions for use; **mal uso** *o* **uso indebido** = misuse; **uso indebido de fondos** *o* **de activos** *o* **de bienes** = misuse of funds *o* of assets; **tierra planificada para uso industrial** = land zoned for industrial use; **los**

usos comerciales *o* **de un comercio** = the customs of the trade; **usos y costumbres** = custom and usage

usual *adj* usual *o* common

usuario, -ria *n* user; **usuario final** = end user; **fácil para el usuario** = user-friendly; **guía del usuario** = user's guide *o* handbook; **usuario con permiso oficial de una marca registrada** = registered user

usufructo *nm* use *o* usufruct *o* beneficial use; **usufructo vitalicio** = life interest; **derecho de usufructo** = beneficial interest; **interés de usufructo** = beneficial interest
◊ **usufructuario, -ria** *adj y n; (de una propiedad)* beneficial occupier *o* beneficial owner

usura *nf* usury *o* profiteering

usurpación *nf* (a) *(intrusión)* usurpation *o* encroachment; **usurpación de bienes** = trespass to goods; **usurpación de funciones** = impersonation of a public officer; **usurpación de personalidad** = personation (b) *(detención)* deforcement

usurpar *vt* to usurp *o* encroach; **usurpar la posesión de bienes a un tercero** = to deforce

utilidad *nf* (a) *(servicio)* usefulness; **utilidad pública** = public utility (b) *(beneficio)* **utilidad después de impuesto** = profit after tax; **utilidad antes de impuesto** = profit before tax *o* pretax profit

utilizar *vt* to use; **utilizar algo** = to make use of something; **utilizaba los tribunales para desahuciar a sus inquilinos** = he used the courts to evict his tenants; **puede utilizarlo como prueba** = you can use it in evidence; **el derecho de auto-defensa sólo se puede utilizar contra un ataque ilícito** = the right of self-defence is only available against unlawful attack

utilización *nf* usage *o* use; **falsificación y utilización de documentación falsa** = forgery and uttering

Vv

vacación *nf* vacation

◊ **vacaciones** *nfpl* holiday *o* vacation; **vacaciones judiciales** = legal vacation; **vacaciones parlamentarias** = recess; **vacaciones universitarias** = vacation; **las vacaciones de verano** = the summer holidays; **el trabajo ofrece cinco semanas de vacaciones** = the job carries five weeks' holiday; **damos al personal cuatro días de vacaciones por Navidad** = we give the staff four days off at Christmas; **tomarse unas vacaciones** *o* **irse de vacaciones** = to take a holiday *o* to go on holiday; **¿Cuándo se toma las vacaciones el director?** = when is the manager taking his holidays?; **estará de vacaciones durante dos semanas** = he is away on holiday for two weeks; **mi secretaria empieza sus vacaciones mañana** = my secretary is off on holiday tomorrow

vacante 1 *adj* vacant *o* unoccupied **2** *nf* vacancy; **amortización de vacantes de una plantilla** = natural wastage; **bienes vacantes** = bona vacantia; **puestos** *o* **plazas vacantes** = job openings

vacío, -cía 1 *adj* empty **2** *nm* vacuum; **vacío legal** = legal vacuum

vacuo *adj* vacant

vagabundeo *nm* vagrancy

vagabundo, -da *n* vagrant *o* vagrancy; **le acusaron de ser un vagabundo** = he was charged with vagrancy

vagancia *nf* vagrancy

vago *nm* unreliable person *o* vagrant

vale *nm* voucher *o* *(pagaré)* IOU

valedero, ra *adj* valid; **billete valedero para tres meses** = ticket which is valid for three months

validación *nf* validation

validar *vt* to validate; **validar un testamento** = to probate; **los documentos de importación tienen que ser validados por los oficiales de aduana** = the import documents have to be validated by the customs officials

validez *nf* validity; **validez legal** = legal validity; **periodo de validez** = period of validity; **el alquiler tiene una validez de seis meses** *o* **de veinte años** = the lease has only six months to run *o* the lease runs for twenty years; **comprobar la validez de** *o* **dar validez a** = to validate; **la validez del documento fue comprobada por el banco** = the document was validated by the bank

válido, -da *adj* **(a)** *(valedero)* valid; **válido hasta nueva orden** *o* **hasta nuevo aviso** = good until cancelled; **el contrato no es válido si no ha sido firmado por un testigo** = the contract is not valid if it has not been witnessed; **ése no es un argumento válido** *o* **ésa no es una excusa válida** = that is not a valid argument *o* excuse **(b)** ser válido to run

valioso, -sa *adj* valuable; **nos reveló una información valiosa** = he disclosed a valuable piece of information

valla *nf* fence; **valla publicitaria** = advertisement hoarding

valor *nm* **(a)** *(precio)* value *o* worth; **valor actual** = present value *o* present worth; **valor al vencimiento** = maturity value; **valor asignado** = rating; **valor contable** = book value; **valor de activo** = asset value; **valor de mercado** = market value; **valor de reposición** = replacement value *o* replacement cost; **valor de rescate** = surrender value; **valor declarado** = declared value; **valor fiscal** = rateable value; **valor nominal** = face value *o* nominal value; **valor verdadero** = true value; **aumentar en valor** = to appreciate; **fijación del valor de una propiedad** = assessment of property; **fijar el valor de una propiedad para asegurarla** = to assess a property for the purposes of insurance; **calculó muy por debajo** *o* **infravaloró el valor del arrendamiento** = he put a very low figure on the value of the lease; **importó mercancías por valor de £250** = he imported goods to the value of £250 **(b)** **sobre el valor** = ad valorem; **impuesto sobre el valor** = ad valorem duty *o* ad valorem tax; **valor añadido** = value addeed; **impuesto sobre el valor añadido (IVA)** = Value Added Tax (VAT) **(c)** **sin valor** = worthless; **sin valor ni efecto** = null and void **(d)** **objetos de valor** = valuable property *o* valuables; **billetes de pequeño valor** = small denomination banknotes

◊ **valores** *nmpl* *(bolsa)* securities; **valores de máxima garantía** = gilt-edged securities; **valores** cotizables *o* registrados = listed securities; **valores mobiliarios** = stocks and shares; **valores públicos** = government stocks; **valores realizables** = quick assets; **valores transmisibles** = negotiable securities; **bolsa de valores** = Stock Exchange; **comerciante en valores** = securities trader; **mercado de valores** = stock market *o* securities market; **monedas de todos los valores** = coins of all denominations; **valores aceptados por un banco en garantía de un préstamo** = bankable paper

valoración *nf* valuation *o* evaluation *o* appreciation *o* assessment; **valoración de daños** = assessment of damages; **valoración de existencias** = stock valuation; **valoración de la rentabilidad** = measurement of profitability; **valoración de los precios** = pricing; **valoración de puestos de trabajo** = job evaluation; **valoración de resultados** = performance rating; **valoración fiscal** = assessment of rateable value; **solicitar la valoración de una propiedad antes de hacer una oferta** = to ask for a valuation of a property before making an offer for it

valorar *vt* **(a)** *(calcular)* to value *o* to assess *o* to price; **valoró las existencias en £25.000** = he valued the stock at £25,000; **valorar daños en 1.000 libras** = to assess damages at £1,000 **(b)** *(evaluar)* to appraise *o* to appreciate; **un juez siempre valora un caso bien documentado** = a judge always appreciates a well-documented case
◊ **valorado, -da** adj **artículos valorados en £250** = goods valued at £250; **coche valorado en 5.000 libras** = car priced at £5,000

vandalismo *nm* vandalism

vándalo *nm* vandal; **unos vándalos han arrancado los teléfonos de las cabinas** = vandals have pulled the telephones out of the call boxes

variación *nf* variation *o* movement

variado, -da *adj* miscellaneous; **una caja de piezas variadas** = a box of miscellaneous pieces of equipment

variar *vt* to vary

varios, -riaa *adj* **(a)** *(diversos)* miscellaneous *o* sundry; **artículos varios** = miscellaneous items; **gastos varios** = miscellaneous expenditure **(b)** *(algunos)* several; **este año se retiran varios jueces** = several judges are retiring this year

vástago *nm* offspring

vecindad *nf* neighbourhood

vecindario *nm* neighbourhood

vecino, -na 1 *adj* next *o* neighbouring; **el juicio fue trasladado a la sala vecina** = the trial was adjourned to the next courtroom; **vive en la calle vecina** = he lives in the neighbouring street; **la fábrica está en la ciudad vecina** = the factory is in the neighbouring town 2 *n* neighbour; **demandó al vecino de al lado por daños y perjuicios** = she sued her next door neighbour for damages; **se le acusó de incendiar el coche de su vecino** = he was accused of setting fire to his neighbour's car

veda *nf* prohibition
◊ **vedar** *vt* to prohibit
◊ **vedado, -da** *adj* prohibited *o* off limits

vejatorio *adj* **(a)** *(molesto)* vexatious; **pleito vejatorio** = vexatious action *o* litigation; **litigante vejatorio** = vexatious litigant **(b)** *(ofensivo)* offensive; **trato vejatorio** = abuse

vejez *nf* old age; **pensión de vejez** = old age pension

vencer 1 *vt* **(a)** *(superar)* to overcome *o* to beat; **el acusado tendrá que vencer dos obstáculos si quiere que su recurso prospere** = the defendant will have to overcome two hurdles if his appeal is to succeed **(b)** *(derrotar)* to defeat; **vencer en una votación** = to outvote 2 *vi* *(plazo)* to mature *o* to fall due *o* to become due; **el pago de los intereses venció hace tres semanas** = interest payments are three weeks overdue; **la letra venció** = the bill fell due; **letra que vencerá en tres meses** = bill which will mature in three months **(b)** *(caducar)* to expire
◊ **vencido, -da** *adj* due *o* overdue; **vencido y pagadero** = due and payable
◊ **vencidos** *nmpl* arrears
◊ **vencimiento** *nm* maturity *o* expiry *o* expiration; **fecha de vencimiento (de pago)** = expiry date *o* final date for payment; **vencimiento de una póliza de seguros** = expiry of an insurance policy; **letra con vencimiento el 1 de mayo** = bill due on May 1st; **póliza marítima con vencimiento fijo** = time policy

vendedor, -ra *n* seller *o* sales clerk *o* vendor; **vendedor, -ra ambulante** street vendor; **mercado favorable al vendedor** = seller's market; **el abogado que actúa en nombre del vendedor** = the solicitor acting on behalf of the vendor; **había pocos vendedores en el mercado, por eso los precios se mantuvieron altos** = there were few sellers in the market, so prices remained high

vender *vt* **(a)** *(comerciar)* to sell *o* to offer *o* to handle; **vender a término** *o* **a futuros** *o* **para entrega futura** = to sell forward; **vender algo a crédito** = to sell something on credit; **vender coches** *o* **vender frigoríficos** = to sell cars *o* to sell refrigerators; **vender el negocio propio** = to dispose of one's business; **vender un bono** = to redeem a bond; **su casa es difícil de vender** = her house is difficult to sell; **sus productos son fáciles de vender** = their products are easy to sell; **han decidido vender su casa** = they have decided to sell their house; **intentaron vender su casa por 100.000 libras** = they tried to sell their house for £100,000; **no venderán mercancía producida por otras firmas** = they will not handle goods produced by other firms **(b)** *(liquidar)* to get out; **no le gustó el informe anual, por eso vendió sus acciones antes de que la compañía se declarara insolvente** = he didn't like the annual report, so he got out before the company became insolvent **(c)** *(deshacerse de)* to dispose of; **vender las existencias sobrantes** = to dispose of excess stock **(d)** *(vendible)* **producto que se vende bien** = steady seller; **este libro se vende bien** = this book is a good seller; **este producto se vende en todos los países europeos** = this product is being marketed in all European countries

vendible *adj* marketable; **título vendible (sin gravámenes)** = marketable title

veneno *nm* poison; **mató a la anciana poniéndole veneno en el té** = she killed the old lady by putting poison in her tea

venganza *nf* revenge

vengarse *vr* to retaliate *o* to take revenge

venia *nf* **con la venia de la corte** = with the court's permission

venta *nf* sale *o* selling *o* **venta a plazos** = hire purchase; **venta apresurada de la libra** = a run on the pound; **venta de ocasión** = bargain offer; **venta de valores** = disposal of securities; **venta directa** = direct selling; **venta de un lote de acciones en la Bolsa** = bargain; **venta forzosa** = forced sale; **venta por correo** = direct mail *o* mail-order selling; **venta y posterior arrendamiento de una propiedad al comprador** = sale and lease-back **(b)** *(traspaso)* disposal; **arrendamiento en venta** = lease for disposal; **negocio en venta** = business for disposal **(c)** **artículo de mayor venta** = best-seller; **cifra de ventas** = sales figures; **condiciones de venta** = conditions of sale *o* terms of sale; **contrato de venta a plazos** = hire purchase agreement; **factura de venta** = bill of sale; **de venta libre** = over the counter; **departamento de ventas** = sales department; **derecho de venta** *o* **prima de opción de venta de acciones en una fecha determinada** = put option; **en venta** = for sale; **escritura** *o* **contrato de venta** = bill of sale; **impuesto sobre la venta** = sales tax; **ley de venta de mercancías** = Sale of Goods Act; **precio de venta** = selling price; **poner en venta** *o* **a la venta** = to market; **poner algo en venta** = to offer something for sale *o* to put something up for sale; **pusieron la fábrica en venta** = they put the factory up for sale; **reunión de profesionales de ventas** = sales conference *o* sales meeting; **estos artículos no están a la venta al gran público** = these items are not for sale to the general public; **pusimos la casa en venta** = we offered the house for sale; **su tienda está en venta** = his shop is for sale

◊ **ventas** *nfpl* sales; **agente de ventas** = factor; **ventas a plazos** *o* **ventas futuras** *o* **ventas para**

entrega futura = forward sales; **ventas nacionales** = domestic sales *o* home sales

ventaja *nf* advantage; **ventajas adicionales** = fringe benefits; **obtener ventajas económicas por estafa** = obtaining a pecuniary advantage by deception
◊ **ventajoso, -sa** *adj* advantageous; **trato poco ventajoso** = hard bargain; **enterarse de algo que es ventajoso para uno** = to learn something to your advantage

ventanilla *nf* counter

ver *vt* to see *o* to view; **visto y hallado conforme** = acknowledged and agreed; **sin ser visto** = unseen; **ver una causa** = hear a case; **éste es el último caso que los magistrados verán antes de la comida** this is the last case which the magistrates will hear before lunch; **'que ve'** = q.v. *o* quod vide; **véase;** *(documento)* **véase al dorso** = please turn over

veraz *adj (declaración)* truthful

verbal *adj* verbal *o* oral *o* parol; **acuerdo verbal** = verbal agreement *o* parol agreement; **contrato verbal** = verbal contract; **amonestación verbal** = verbal warning; **declaración verbal** = oral evidence; **llegaron a un acuerdo verbal sobre las condiciones y seguidamente comenzaron a redactar el contrato** = they agreed to the terms verbally, and then started to draft the contract
◊ **verbalmente** *adv* verbally

verdad *nf* truth; **el abogado defensor dijo que el demandante no estaba diciendo la verdad** = counsel for the defence said that the plaintiff was not telling the truth; **el tribunal está tratando de averiguar la verdad sobre los pagos** = the court is trying to find out the truth about the payments; **los testigos tienen que jurar decir la verdad** = witnesses have to swear to tell the truth
◊ **verdadero, -ra** *adj* **(a)** *(auténtico)* genuine *o* real *o* actual; **es una verdadera ganga** = is a real bargain **(b)** *(exacto)* true; **dueño verdadero** = ultimate owner

verde *adj* green; **carta verde** *o* **tarjeta verde** = green card; **libro verde (informe del gobierno británico sobre un proyecto de ley presentado al Parlamento)** = Green Paper

verdugo *nm* executioner *o* torturer *o* hangman

veredicto *nm* verdict; **veredicto absolutorio** = not guilty verdict; **veredicto de muerte por causa desconocida** = open verdict; **veredicto por mayoría (al menos diez miembros del jurado)** majority verdict; **anunciar un veredicto** = to hand down a verdict; **llegar a un veredicto** = to come to a verdict *o* to reach a verdict; **pronunciar un veredicto** = to bring in *o* to return a verdict; **el jurado pronunció un veredicto de inocencia** = the jury brought in *o* returned a verdict of not guilty; **el jurado tardó dos horas en llegar a un veredicto** =

the jury took two hours to reach their verdict; **el tribunal dio un veredicto que no especificaba las circunstancias de la muerte del policía** = the court recorded an open verdict on the dead policeman

vergajo *nm* life preserver

verificación *nf* verification

verificar *vt* **(a)** *(comprobar)* to verify *o* to check; **se permitió la entrada del cargamento en el país después de que la aduana verificara los documentos** = the shipment was allowed into the country after verification of the documents by the customs; **se pudo verificar el envío del paquete mediante el recibo de la oficina de Correos** = dispatch of the packet was proved by the Post Office receipt **(b)** *(demostrar)* to prove

verosímil *adj* probable

versión *nf* version; **puso en duda la versión de los hechos que dio el policía** = she disputed the policeman's version of events

vetar *vt* to veto; **la resolución fue vetada por el presidente** = the resolution was vetoed by the president
◊ **veto** *nm* veto; **el Presidente tiene derecho de veto sobre los proyectos de ley aprobados por el Congreso** = the President has the power of veto over Bills passed by Congress; **el Reino Unido hizo uso de su veto en el Consejo de Seguridad** = the UK used its veto in the Security Council

vez *nf* time; **cada vez más** = increasingly; **de vez en cuando** = occasionally; **en vez de** = in lieu of; **admitió que de vez en cuando visitaba la casa** = he admitted that he occasionally visited the house; **la empresa tiene que depender cada vez más del mercado de consumo interior** = the company has to depend increasingly on the home consumer market

vía *nf* way *o* channel; **vía ordinaria** = ordinary proceedings; **vía penal** = criminal proceedings; **vía pública** = highway *o* public way; **vía sumaria** = summary proceedings; **actuar por la vía oficial** = to go through the official channels; **crear nuevas vías de comunicación** = to open up new channels of communication
◊ **viabilidad** *nf* viability *o* feasibility
◊ **viable** *adj* viable; **alternativa viable** = viable alternative; **no viable comercialmente** = not commercially viable

viajar *vi* to travel; **viajar diariamente al trabajo** = to commute; **viaja diariamente del campo a su oficina, que se encuentra en el centro de la ciudad** = he commutes from the country to his office in the centre of town

viaje *nm* trip; **viaje de negocios** = business trip
◊ **viajero, -ra** *n* traveller; **viajero diario** *o* **viajera diaria** = commuter

Vicecanciller *nm* *(magistrado presidente de la Chancery Division del Tribunal Superior)* Vice Chancellor

vicepresidencia *nf* **fue designada para que ocupara la vicepresidencia del comité** = she was appointed to the vice-chairmanship of the committee
◊ **vicepresidenta** *nf* vice-president *o* vice-chairwoman *o* vice-chairperson
◊ **vicepresidente** *nm* vice-president *o* vice-chairman *o* vice-chairperson; **es el vicepresidente de un grupo industrial** = he is the vice-chairman of an industrial group

viceversa *adv* vice versa; **las responsabilidades del contratante para con la persona contratada y viceversa** = the responsibilities of the employer towards the employee and vice versa

vicio *nm* flaw *o* defect; **vicio de forma** = procedural defect; **vicio manifiesto** = patent defect; **vicio oculto** = hidden deffect; **su título de la propiedad tiene vicios jurídicos** = his title to the property is defective

víctima *nf* victim; **el asaltante dejó a su víctima tirada en la carretera** = the mugger left his victim lying in the road; **las víctimas del accidente fueron trasladadas al hospital** = the accident victims *o* victims of the accident were taken to hospital

vida *nf* life; **aumento de salario por coste de vida** = cost-of-living increase; **cliente de toda la vida** = long-standing customer *o* customer of long standing; **de por vida** *o* **para toda la vida** = for life; **esperanza de vida** = life expectancy; **índice del coste de vida** = cost-of-living index; **plus de carestía de vida** *o* **subsidio por aumento del coste de vida** = cost-of-living allowance; **seguro de vida** = life assurance *o* life insurance; **seguro corriente de vida** = whole-life insurance *o* whole-life policy; **dejó sus bienes a los parientes con vida** = he left his estate to his surviving relatives; **su pensión le da unos cómodos ingresos de por vida** = his pension gives him a comfortable income for life; **el accidente le dejó inválido para toda la vida** = he was permanently disabled by the accident

viejo, -ja *adj* old; **hemos decidido deshacernos del viejo sistema de ordenadores e instalar uno nuevo** = we have decided to get rid of our old computer system and put in a new one

vigencia *nf* *(vida)* life *o* *(periodo)* period *o* *(plazo)* term; **la vigencia de un préstamo** = the life of a loan; **continuar en vigencia** to remain in effect **(b)** *(validez)* validity

vigente *adj* **(a)** *(en vigor)* ruling *o* in operation; **estar vigente** = to be in force *o* to run; **seguir vigente** = to remain in effect; **tipo de interés vigente** = standard rate **(b)** *(en regla)* valid; **llevaba un pasaporte vigente** = he was carrying a valid passport

vigilado, -da *adj* under surveillance; **libertad vigilada** = parole; **mantener vigilado a alguien** = to place under surveillance; **libertad vigilada** = probation; **bajo libertad vigilada** = on probation; **oficial a cargo de los que están bajo libertad vigilada** = probation officer; **orden judicial de libertad vigilada** = probation order; **persona que está en libertad vigilada** = probationer

vigilancia *nf* surveillance *o* policing *o* supervision *o* watch; **vigilancia controlada por medio de aparatos electrónicos** = electronic surveillance; **comosión de vigilancia** = watch committee; **cuerpo de vigilancia (en especial de departamentos gubernamentales *o* firmas comerciales para que no se transgredan las normas)** = watchdog body; **mecanismo de vigilancia** = surveillance device; **los diplomáticos fueron puestos bajo vigilancia policial** = the diplomats were placed under police surveillance; **los acusados fueron llevados a la sala del tribunal bajo vigilancia armada** = the prisoners were brought into the courtroom under armed guard; **se ha incrementado la vigilancia en los aeropuertos internacionales** = surveillance at international airports has been increased

vigilante *nm* warden *o* caretaker *o* proctor *o* watchman; **vigilante de seguridad *o* vigilante jurado** = security guard; **vigilante nocturno** = night watchman

vigilar *vt* to guard *o* to police; **los presos están vigilados día y noche** = the prisoners are guarded night and day; **la reunión fue vigilada por policías sin uniforme** = the meeting was policed by plainclothes men

vigor *nm* (a) *(energía)* force (b) *(vigente)* **en vigor** = in operation; **fecha de entrada en vigor** = effective date; **entrar en vigor** = to operate *o* to come into force *o* to become operative; **el nuevo sistema entró en vigor el 1 de junio** = the new system came into operation on June 1st; **términos de un contrato que entran en vigor el 1 de enero** = terms of a contract which take effect *o* come into effect from January 1st; **estar en vigor** = to be in force; **el reglamento está en vigor desde 1945** = the rules have been in force since 1945; **las nuevas normas entrarán en vigor el 1 de enero** = the new regulations will come into force on January 1st
◊ **vigoroso, -sa** *adj* strong

villanía *nf* villainy

vinculante *adj* binding; **este contrato es legalmente vinculante** = this document is legally binding *o* it is a legally binding document; **juicio *o* opinión no vinculante** = obiter dictum; **precedente vinculante** = binding precedent

vincular *vt* to bind; **el acuerdo vincula a todas las partes** = the agreement is binding on all parties

vínculo *nm* connection *o* entail; **vínculo *o* dominio limitado a herederos directos** = fee tail; **vínculo de consanguinidad** = next of kin

vindicar *vt* to avenge

violación *nf* (a) *(infracción)* violation *o* infringement *o* breach; **violación de contrato** = breach of contract; **violación de garantía** = breach of warranty; **violación de patente** infringement of patent *o* patent infringement; **violación de la libertad condicional** = breaking bail; **el tribunal criticó las violaciones del tratado sobre los derechos humanos** = the court criticized the violations of the treaty on human rights; **violación de la propiedad intelectual *o* de los derechos de autor** = infringement of copyright *o* copyright infringement (b) *(persona)* rape; **fue llevado ante los tribunales y acusado de violación** = he was brought to court and charged with rape; **la incidencia de casos de violación ha aumentado durante los últimos años** = the incidence of cases of rape has increased over the last years; **violación del derecho a la intimidad** = invasion of privacy (c) *(entrada ilegal)* **violación de domicilio** = forcible entry; **violación de la propiedad** = trespass

violar *vt* (a) *(infringir)* to violate *o* to break *o* to infringe; **violar la ley** = to offend; **violando una ley** = in violation of a law; **violar un contrato** = to break an agreement; **la compañía violó la sección 26 de la Ley de Sociedades** = the company broke section 26 of the Companies Act

violar una patente = to infringe a patent (b) *(persona)* to rape

violencia *nf* violence *o* assault *o* battery

violencia contra la persona = violence against the person; **robo con violencia** = robbery with violence

violento, -ta *adj* violent *o* harsh; **de un modo violento** = harshly; **un ataque violento a la policía** = a violent attack on the police; **el prisionero se mostró violento** = the prisoner became violent; **los presos se han quejado de recibir trato violento en las prisiones militares** = the prisoners have complained that they are harshly treated in the military prisons; **se quejaron de tratamiento violento por parte de los carceleros** = they complained of harsh treatment on the part of the warders
◊ **violentamente** *adv* violently

virtud *nf* **'en virtud de su cargo'** = virtute officii

visado *nm* visa *o* entry permit; **visado de entrada** = entry visa; **visado de entrada múltiple *o* de entradas múltiples** = multiple entry visa; **visado de tránsito** = transit visa; **visado turista** = tourist visa; **necesitarás un visado para poder entrar en los EE UU** = you will need a visa before you go to the USA; **rellenó el formulario de solicitud de visado** = he filled in his visa application form

visita *nf* call *o* visit *o* *(person)* caller; **visita de negocios** = business call; **derecho de visita** = access; **horario de visitas** = visiting hours; **los vendedores realizan seis visitas diarias** = the salesmen make six calls a day
◊ **visitador, -ra** *n* visitor; **visitador, -ra de prisiones** = prison visitor
◊ **visitante** *nmf* visitor

visitar *vt* to visit *o* to call in *o* to call on; **el representante de ventas nos visitó dos veces la semana pasada** = the sales representative called in twice last week; **los oficiales encargados de la libertad condicional visitan a sus clientes dos veces al mes** = the probation officers call on their clients twice a month

vista *nf* **(a)** *(en una causa)* hearing; **vista a puerta cerrada** = hearing in camera; **vista interlocutoria** = interlocutory proceedings; **vista preliminar de un caso** = committal proceedings; **vista pública** = public hearing; **vista de corta duración** *o* **vista rápida** = mention; **vista de un caso judicial** = hearing; **proceder a la vista de un caso** = to hear; **la vista duró diez días** = the hearing lasted ten days; **la vista del caso tendrá lugar el mes próximo** = the case will be heard next month; **el juez realizó la vista del caso en privado** = the judge heard the case in chambers; **se han suspendido las vistas durante dos semanas** = the hearings have been suspended for two weeks **(b)** **dar a** *o* **tener vista a** = to overlook; **en vista de** = in view of; **en vista de la edad del acusado, los jueces le concedieron una remisión de condena** = in view of the age of the accused the magistrates gave him a suspended sentence; **hacer la vista gorda ante algo** *o* **con respecto a algo** = to connive at something **(c)** **efecto** *o* **letra de cambio a la vista** = sight draft *o* demand bill; **pagadero a la vista** = payable on demand

visto 1 *adj* **(a)** **visto que** = whereas; **visto que el contrato entre las dos partes estipulaba que cualquiera de las dos partes podía retirarse con previo aviso de seis meses** = whereas the contract between the two parties stipulated that either party may withdraw at six months' notice **(b)** **visto para sentencia** = words pronounced by the judge indicating that the trial is at an end **2** *nm* **dar el visto bueno a** = to pass

vitalicio, -cia 1 *adj* **con carácter vitalicio** = for life; **renta vitalicia** = life interest; **par vitalicio (miembro vitalicio de la Cámara de los Lores)** = life peer; **pensión vitalicia** *o* **renta vitalicia** = life annuity *o* annuity for life; **usufructo vitalicio** = life interest **2** *nm* life annuity *o* annuity for life

vitrina *nf* cabinet

viuda *nf* widow

viudo *nm* widower

vivienda *nf* house *o* dwelling *o* home; **el impuesto sobre la vivienda ha aumentado** = the tax on dwellings has been raised; **instalaciones destinadas a viviendas** = domestic premises; **viviendas particulares** = house property

vivir *vi* **(a)** *(estar vivo)* to live *o* to be alive; **vivir juntos** = to cohabit; **'los que viven'** = vivos

vivir (b) *(ocupar)* **vivir en** = to occupy **(c)** *(experimentar)* to experience
◊ **vivo, -va** *adj* alive; **de viva voz** = viva voce
◊ **vivos** nm **entre vivos** = inter vivos; **donación entre vivos** = gift inter vivos

volumen *nm* **(a)** *(capacidad)* volume; **volumen de ventas** *o* **de negocios** *o* **facturación** = turnover; **tener un volumen de ventas de** = to turn over; **basamos nuestros cálculos en el volumen de ventas del año pasado** = we based our calculations on last year's turnover; **el volumen de ventas de la empresa ha aumentado en un 23,5%** = the company's turnover has increased by 23.5%; **tenemos un volumen de ventas de 2.000 libras a la semana** = we turn over £2,000 a week **(b)** *(tomo)* volume

voluntad *nf* will; **última voluntad** = last will and testament; **última voluntad ante testigos, formalizada posteriormente** = nuncupative will; **arrendamiento a voluntad** = tenancy at will; **si hay voluntad no existe injuria (norma según la cual si alguien accede a aceptar el riesgo de resultar herido no puede interponer una demanda por ello, como por ejemplo puede ocurrir en el boxeo)** = volenti non fit injuria
◊ **voluntariamente** *adv* voluntarily; **ofrecerse voluntariamente** = to volunteer; **se entregó a la policía voluntariamente** = he voluntarily gave himself up to the police

voluntario, -ria 1 *adj* voluntary; **baja voluntaria con derecho a indemnización** = voluntary redundancy; **confesión voluntaria** = voluntary confession; **liquidación** *o* **disolución voluntaria** = voluntary liquidation *o* winding up; **organización voluntaria** = voluntary organization; **traspaso de propiedad voluntario** *o* **donación voluntaria** = voluntary disposition **2** *n* volunteer

volver *vi* to return; **volver a** = to revert; **volver a solicitar** = to reapply; **volvió a solicitar la pensión alimenticia** = she reapplied for a maintenance order; **al ver que el puesto seguía vacante, volvió a solicitarlo** = when he saw that the job had still not been filled, he reapplied for it; **la empresa volvió a solicitar un requerimiento en contra de los sindicatos** = the company reapplied for an injunction against the union; **hacer volver** = to recall

votación *nf* ballot *o* voting *o* vote *o* poll; **votación a mano alzada** = show of hands; **votación**

fraudulenta = ballot-rigging; **votación popular** = popular vote; **votación por correo** = postal ballot; **votación secreta** = secret ballot; **el presidente es elegido por votación popular** = the president is elected by popular vote; **en la votación sobre el proyecto de Ley del Orden Público el gobierno obtuvo una amplia mayoría** = in the division on the Law and Order Bill, the government had a comfortable majority; **someter a votación** = to ballot; **someter una propuesta a votación** = to take a vote on a proposal *o* to put a proposal to the vote; **vencer en una votación** = to outvote; **el presidente perdió en la votación** = the chairman was outvoted

◊ **votante** *nmf* voter

votar *vt/i* to vote *o* to ballot; **derecho a votar** = franchise; **ir a votar** = to go to the polls; **votar a favor de una propuesta** = to vote for a proposal; **votar en contra de una propuesta** = to vote against a proposal; **el 52% de los socios votaron al Sr. Smith como presidente** = 52% of the members voted for Mr Smith as chairman; **el sindicato está votando para el cargo de presidente** = the union is balloting for the post of president; **en la Junta General Anual se votó a favor del cese de dos directores** = two directors were voted off the board at the AGM; **la Cámara votó a las 10.30** = the House divided at 10.30; **la junta votó a favor del cierre de la fábrica** = the meeting voted to close the factory

voto *nm* vote; **voto de calidad** = casting vote; **voto de castigo** = vote of no confidence; **voto de** censura = vote of censure *o* censure vote *o* vote of no confidence; **voto de confianza** = confidence vote; **voto de gracias** *o* **voto de agradecimiento** = vote of thanks; **voto por correo** = postal vote; **voto por delegación** *o* **por representación** = block vote; **derecho a voto** = voting rights; **derecho al voto** = suffrage; **derecho de voto** = franchise; **derecho universal de voto** = universal franchise; **acciones sin derecho a voto** = non-voting shares; **conceder el derecho de voto** = to enfranchise; **concesión del derecho de voto** = enfranchisement; **solicitar votos** = to canvass; **persona que solicita votos** = canvasser; **el presidente tiene el voto de calidad** = the chairman has the casting vote; **utilizó su voto de calidad para bloquear la moción** = he used his casting vote to block the motion; **el presidente dimitió cuando la Junta General Anual emitió el voto de no confianza** *o* **el voto de castigo** = the chairman resigned after the vote of no confidence in him was passed by the AGM; **la reunión aprobó un voto de censura al ministro** = the meeting passed a vote of censure on the minister; **propuso un voto de confianza en el gobierno** = he proposed a vote of confidence in the government

vuelta *nf* **(a)** *(regreso)* return; **tarifa de ida y vuelta** = return fare; **contestó a vuelta de correo** = he replied by return of post; **de vuelta** = back **(b)** *(giro)* turn; **dar vueltas** = to turn

vulnerar *vt* to break *o* to trespass; **vulnerar la ley** = to break the law

Xx Yy Zz

xenofobia *nf* xenophobia

yacente *adj (herencia)* unclaimed

yacer *vi* to lie

yerno *nm* son-in-law

yerro *nm* error *o* mistake

zona *nf* **(a)** *(área)* area *o* zone; **zona comercial** = shopping precinct *o* trading estate; **zona de libre** cambio *o* **zona franca** = free trade area; **zona de peligro** = danger area; **zona de desastre** = disaster area; **zona reservada para peatones** *o* **zona peatonal** = pedestrian precinct; **zona residencial** = residential area; **zona verde** = green belt **(b)** *(territorio)* area *o* territory *o* region *o* zone; **zona empresarial** = enterprise zone; **zona franca** = free port *o* free trade zone enterprise zone; **dividir en zonas** = to zone

ENGLISH-SPANISH DICTIONARY
DICCIONARIO INGLÉS-ESPAÑOL

Aa

A [eɪ] *first letter of the alphabet;* **category 'A' prisoners** = presos *mpl* peligrosos; **Schedule A** = impuesto *m* de plusvalía; **Table A** = escritura modelo de constitución de una sociedad limitada descrita en la Ley de Sociedades de 1985; **'A' shares** = acciones *fpl* de clase A (con derecho a voto limitado)
◊ **A1** [ˈeɪ ˈwɒn] *adjective* **(a)** *(best)* de primera clase *or* de primera categoría *or* excelente; **we sell only goods in A1 condition** = sólo vendemos artículos de primera clase **(b)** **ship which is A1 at Lloyd's** = barco *m* que está en condiciones óptimas (según el Registro Lloyd's)

A.B.A. [ˈeɪ ˈbiː ˈeɪ] = AMERICAN BAR ASSOCIATION

abandon [əˈbændən] *verb* **(a)** *(to give up)* abandonar *or* renunciar a; **to abandon an action** = abandonar un caso; **to abandon a claim** = desistir de una demanda **(b)** *(to leave)* desamparar *or* abandonar; **he abandoned his family and went abroad** = abandonó a su familia y se marchó al extranjero; **the crew abandoned the sinking ship** = la tripulación abandonó el barco que se hundía
◊ **abandonment** [əˈbændənmənt] *noun* abandono *m or* renuncia *f;* **abandonment of a claim** = desistimiento *m* de la demanda; **abandonment of children** = desamparo *m* de los hijos

COMMENT: abandoning a child under two years old is a notifiable offence

abate [əˈbeɪt] *verb* **(a)** *(to remove or to stop a nuisance)* eliminar *or* suprimir **(b)** *(to reduce)* rebajar; *(of a legacy)* ser rebajado
◊ **abatement** [əˈbeɪtmənt] *noun* **(a)** *(removal of a nuisance)* eliminación *f or* supresión *f;* **noise abatement** = supresión *f* del ruido; **a noise abatement notice was served on the club** = se dio un aviso al club para que redujera el ruido **(b)** *(reduction of a legacy)* rebaja *f* proporcional de legados
◊ **abator** [əˈbeɪtə] *noun* mitigador, -ra; **tax abatement** = desgravación *f* fiscal

abduct [əbˈdʌkt] *verb* secuestrar *or* raptar; **the bank manager was abducted at gunpoint** = secuestraron al director del banco a punta de pistola; **the robbers abducted the heiress and**

held her to ransom = los ladrones raptaron a la heredera y pidieron un rescate por ella
◊ **abduction** [əbˈdʌkʃn] *noun* rapto *m or* secuestro *m;* **child abduction** = sustracción *f* de menores
◊ **abductor** [əbˈdʌktə] *noun* secuestrador, -ra *or* raptor, -ra

abet [əˈbet] *verb* incitar *or* instigar; **aiding and abetting** = complicidad *f* e incitación *f* a cometer un crimen (NOTE: **abetting - abetted**)
◊ **abettor** [əˈbetə] *noun* instigador, -ra *or* incitador, ra

abeyance [əˈbeɪəns] *noun* **(a)** *(not enforced)* **in abeyance** = mostrenco *m;* **to fall into abeyance** = caer en desuso; **this law is in abeyance** = esta ley está en suspenso *or* pendiente *or* en espera **(b)** *(property without owner)* bienes *mpl* mostrencos

ABH [ˈeɪ ˈbiː ˈeɪtʃ] = ACTUAL BODILY HARM

abide by [əˈbaɪd ˈbaɪ] *verb* atenerse a *or* someterse a; **to abide by the law** = acatar la ley; **he promised to abide by the decision of the court** = prometió someterse a la decisión del tribunal; **she did not abide by the terms of the agreement** = no se atuvo a los términos del contrato

ab initio [ˈæb ɪˈnɪʃɪəu] *Latin phrase* desde el principio

abjure [əbˈdʒuə] *verb US* abjurar *or* renunciar a
◊ **abjuration** [æbdʒuˈreɪʃn] *noun* abjuración *f or* renuncia *f*

abnormal [æbˈnɔːməl] *adjective* anormal *or* irregular

abode [əˈbəud] *noun* domicilio *m or* morada *f;* **right of abode** = derecho *m* de residencia

abolish [əˈbɒlɪʃ] *verb* abolir *or* suprimir *or* derogar; **the Chancellor of the Exchequer refused to ask Parliament to abolish the tax on alcohol** = el Ministro de Economía y Hacienda se negó a pedir al Parlamento que suprimiese el impuesto sobre el alcohol; **the Senate voted to abolish the death penalty** = el Senado votó para abolir la pena de muerte
◊ **abolition** [æbəˈlɪʃn] *noun* abolición *f or* derogación *f or* supresión *f;* **to campaign for the**

abolition of the death penalty = hacer campaña por la abolición de la pena de muerte

abortion [ə'bɔːʃn] *noun* aborto *m;* **legal abortion** = aborto despenalizado; **illegal abortion is a notifiable offence** = el aborto ilegal es un delito grave

abridged [ə'brɪdʒd] *adjective* abreviado, -da

abrogate ['æbrəgeɪt] *verb* revocar *or* anular *or* casar
◊ **abrogation** [æbrə'geɪʃn] *noun* revocación *f or* anulación *f* casación *f*

abscond [əb'skɒnd] *verb* evadirse *or* fugarse *or* huir de la justicia; **he was charged with absconding from lawful custody** = se le acusó de huir de la justicia

absence ['æbsəns] *noun* ausencia *f or* falta *f or* incomparecencia *f or* rebeldía *f;* **in the absence of** = en ausencia de *or* a falta de; **in the absence of the chairman, his deputy took the chair** = en ausencia del presidente, su adjunto presidió la reunión; **the trial took place in the absence of the defendant** = el juicio tuvo lugar en ausencia del acusado; **she was sentenced to death in her absence** = fue condenada a muerte en rebeldía; **leave of absence** = permiso *m or* licencia *f* temporal; *see also* IN ABSENTIA
◊ **absent** ['æbsənt] *adjective* ausente
◊ **absentee** [æbsən'tiː] *noun* ausente *mf;* **absent without leave** = incomparecencia no justificada
◊ **absenteeism** [æbsən'tiːɪzm] *noun* absentismo *m*

absolute ['æbsəluːt] *adjective* absoluto, -ta; **absolute discharge** = libre absolución *or* libertad incondicional; **absolute monopoly** = monopolio *m* absoluto; **absolute privilege** = privilegio *m* absoluto *or* inmunidad; **absolute title** = título absoluto *or* de plena propiedad; *see also* DECREE, FORECLOSURE

abstain [æb'steɪn] *verb* abstenerse de; **sixty MPs abstained in the vote on capital punishment** = sesenta diputados se abstuvieron de votar sobre la pena capital
◊ **abstention** [æb'stenʃn] *noun* **(a)** *(voting)* abstención *f;* **the motion was carried by 200 votes to 150, with 60 abstentions** = la moción se aprobó por 200 votos contra 150, con 60 abstenciones **(b)** *US* inhibitoria *f*

abstract ['æbstrækt] **1** *noun* extracto *m or* sumario *m;* **abstract of court record** = apuntamiento *m;* **abstract of judgment** = sumario del fallo de un tribunal; **to make an abstract of the deeds of a property** = hacer un sumario de las escrituras de una propiedad; **abstract of title** = extracto de título **2** *verb* **(a)** *(to make a summary)* resumir *or* compendiar **(b)** *(steal)* sustraer
◊ **abstraction** [əb'strækʃn] *noun* sustracción *f*

abuse 1 [ə'bjuːs] *noun* **(a)** *(using something wrongly)* abuso *m;* **abuse of power** = abuso de poder; **abuse of process** = abuso de derecho; **drug abuse** = toxicomanía *f* **(b)** *(insult)* injuria *f or* improperios *mpl or* insultos *mpl;* **the prisoner shouted abuse at the judge** = el prisionero insultó al juez **(c)** *(bad treatment)* abuso *m or* atropello *m or* mal trato *m or* trato vejatorio; **child abuse** *or* **sexual abuse of children** = abusos deshonestos de menores *or* estupro *m* **(d)** *(exploitation)* explotación *f* **2** [ə'bjuːz] *verb* **(a)** *(to misuse)* abusar de; **to abuse one's authority** = abusar de la autoridad de uno **(b)** *(to insult)* injuriar a *or* lanzar improperios contra *or* insultar *or* ultrajar; **he abused the police before being taken to the cells** = insultó a la policía antes de ser conducido a la celda **(c)** *(to mistreat)* abusar de *or* maltratar; **he had abused small children** = había abusado de menores

abut (on) [ə'bʌt] *verb* *(of a piece of land)* lindar con *or* colindar con (NOTE: **abutting - abutted**)

ACAS ['eɪkæs] = ADVISORY CONCILIATION AND ARBITRATION SERVICE

ACC ['eɪ 'siː 'siː] = ASSISTANT CHIEF CONSTABLE

accept [ək'sept] *verb* aceptar; **to accept a bill for payment** = aceptar una letra; **she accepted the offer of a job in Australia** = aceptó la oferta de un trabajo en Australia; **he accepted £200 for the car** = aceptó 200 libras por el coche; **to accept an offer conditionally** = aceptar una oferta condicionalmente *or* con reserva
◊ **acceptable** [ək'septəbl] *adjective* aceptable; **the offer is not acceptable to both parties** = la oferta no es aceptable para ambas partes
◊ **acceptance** [ək'septəns] *noun* **(a)** *(approval)* aceptación *f or* aprobación *f;* **acceptance of an offer** = aceptación de una oferta *or* de una propuesta; **we have his letter of acceptance** = tenemos su carta de aprobación; *see note at* CONTRACT **(b)** *(agreement to pay)* aceptación *f*
◊ **accepting house** [ək'septɪŋ 'haus] *noun* casa de aceptación *or* entidad *f* financiera
◊ **acceptor** [ək'septə] *noun* aceptante *mf*

access ['ækses] **1** *noun* **(a)** *(of land)* acceso *or* servidumbre *f* de paso; **he complained that he was being denied access to the main road** = se quejó de que se le negaba acceso de paso a la carretera principal **(b)** **to have access to something** = tener acceso a algo *or* poder disponer de algo; **to gain access to something** = acceder *or* alcanzar algo; **access to the courts should be open to all citizens** = se debería permitir la entrada a los juzgados a todos los ciudadanos; **the burglar gained access through the window** = el ladrón entró por la ventana **(c)** *(right of a child to see a parent)* derecho *m* de visita **2** *verb* acceder *or* tener acceso a
◊ **accession** [ək'seʃn] *noun* adhesión *f or* accesión *f;* **accession to the throne** = ascenso *m or or*

subida *f* al trono; **Treaty of Accession** = Tratado *m* de Adhesión

◊ **accessory** [ək'sesəri] *noun* **(a)** *(incidental)* accesorio, -ria **(b)** *(accomplice)* cómplice *mf or* encubridor, -ra; **accessory after the fact** = cómplice encubridor; **accessory before the fact** = cómplice instigador

accident ['æksɪdənt] *noun* accidente *m or* desgracia *f*; **industrial accident** = accidente laboral; **accident insurance** = seguro *m* contra accidentes; **fatal accident** = accidente mortal; **road accident** = accidente de circulación

◊ **accidental** [æksɪ'dentl] *adjective* accidental *or* fortuito, -ta; **a case of accidental death** = un caso de muerte accidental

accommodate [ə'kɒmədeɪt] *verb* acomodar

accommodation [əkɒmə'deɪʃn] *noun* **(a)** *(money lent)* crédito *m or* préstamo *m* **(b)** *(something done to help someone)* favor *m or* servicio *m*; **to reach an accommodation with creditors** = llegar a un acuerdo con los acreedores; **accommodation address** = dirección *f* para recibir el correo exclusivamente; **accommodation bill** = pagaré *m or* efecto *m* de favor *or* letra *f* de complacencia; **accommodation maker** = firmante *mf* por acomodamiento *or* avorecedor, -ra

accompany [ə'kʌmpni] *verb* acompañar; **they sent a formal letter of complaint, accompanied by an invoice** = enviaron una carta formal de queja acompañada de una factura (NOTE: **accompanied by** something)

accomplice [ə'kʌmplɪs] *noun* cómplice *mf or* consorte *mf*

accord and satisfaction [ə'kɔːd ən sætɪs'fækʃn] *noun* acuerdo de pago *or* liquidación de una deuda

accordance [ə'kɔːdəns] *noun* **in accordance with** = de acuerdo con *or* conforme a; **in accordance with your instructions we have deposited the money in your current account** = conforme a lo que nos ordenó, hemos ingresado el dinero en su cuenta corriente; **I am submitting the claim for damages in accordance with the advice of our legal advisers** = presento la demanda por daños y perjuicios de acuerdo con las instrucciones de nuestros asesores legales

◊ **according to** [ə'kɔːdɪŋ 'tʊ] *preposition* según *or* en función de; **according to the witness, the accused carried the body on the back seat of his car** = según el testigo, el acusado transportó el cuerpo en el asiento trasero de su coche; **the payments were made according to the maintenance order** = los pagos se hicieron según la sentencia de pago de manutención

◊ **accordingly** [ə'kɔːdɪŋli] *adverb* de acuerdo con *or* conforme a *or* en consecuencia; **we have received your letter and have altered the contract accordingly** = hemos recibido su carta y hemos modificado el contrato en consecuencia

account [ə'kaʊnt] **1** *noun* **(a)** *(notice of payment due)* factura *f or* cuenta *f*; **please send me your account** *or* **a detailed** *or* **an itemized account** = le ruego me envíe la factura *or* un inventario *or* una cuenta detallada; **accounts payable** = cuentas a pagar; **accounts receivable** = cuentas a cobrar; **action for an account** = acción *f* por cuenta y razón *or* acción sobre rendición de cuentas **(b)** *(in a shop)* cuenta **(c)** *(regular client)* cliente *mf* (preferencial) **(d)** *(financial balance sheet)* **the accounts of a business** *or* **a company's accounts** = estado *m* de cuentas *or* balance (de una empresa) *m* **(e)** **bank account** *or* *US* **banking account** = cuenta bancaria; **current account** *or* **cheque account** = cuenta corriente **(f)** *(Stock Exchange)* periodo de crédito en la Bolsa **(g)** *(consideration)* cuenta *or* consideración *f*; **to take account of the age of the accused** *or* **to take the accused's age into account when passing sentence** = tener en cuenta la edad del acusado a la hora de dictar sentencia **2** *verb* **to account for** = dar razón de *or* dar cuenta de *or* justificar un trato monetario; **to account for a loss** *or* **a discrepancy** = dar cuenta de una pérdida *or* discrepancia

◊ **accountable** [ə'kaʊntəbl] *adjective* responsable; **if money is lost, the person at the cash desk is held accountable** = si desaparece dinero, el cajero es considerado responsable; **the group leader will be held accountable for the actions of the group** = el líder será responsable de las acciones del grupo

◊ **accountability** [əkaʊntə'bɪliti] *noun* responsabilidad *f*

◊ **accountant** [ə'kaʊntənt] *noun* contable *mf*; **Chartered Accountant** = Censor *m* Jurado de Cuentas (GB) *or* contable colegiado

◊ **accounting** [ə'kaʊntɪŋ] *noun* contabilidad *f or* auditoría *f*; **cost accounting** = cálculo *m* de costas; **false accounting** = falseamiento *m* de contabilidad *or* de auditoría

accredited [ə'kredɪtɪd] *adjective* autorizado, -da *or* acreditado, -da

accretion [ə'kriːʃn] *noun* acrecentamiento *m*

accrual [ə'kruːəl] *noun* acumulación *f*; **accrual of interest** = acumulación del interés

◊ **accrue** [ə'kruː] *verb (of interest or dividends)* acumular *or* percibir *or* devengar

accumulate [ə'kjuːmjəleɪt] *verb* acumular *or* acumularse

accuse [ə'kjuːz] *verb* acusar *or* delatar *or* denunciar *or* imputar *or* inculpar; **she was accused of stealing £25 from her boss** = se le acusó de robarle 25 libras a su jefe; **he was accused of murder** = fue acusado de asesinato; **of what has she been accused?** *or* **what has she been accused of?** = ¿de qué se le ha acusado? (NOTE: you accuse someone **of** a crime)

◊ **accusation** [ækjuːˈzeɪʃn] *noun* acusación *f or* denuncia *f;* **false accusation** = calumnia *f*
◊ **accusatorial procedure** [ækjuːzəˈtɔːriəl prəˈsiːdʒə] *noun* procedimiento acusatorio; *compare* INQUISITORIAL
◊ **accused** [əˈkjuːzd] **1** *adjective* inculpado, -da *or* imputado, -da *or* acusado, -da **2** *noun* **the accused** = el acusado *or* la acusada *or* los acusados *or* las acusadas; **all the accused pleaded not guilty** = todos los acusados se declararon inocentes; **the police brought the accused into the court** = la policía condujo al acusado al juzgado (NOTE: can be singular or plural: **the six accused all pleaded guilty** = los seis acusados se confesaron culpables)

acknowledge [əkˈnɒlɪdʒ] *verb* **(a)** *(accept)* reconocer *or* confirmar *or;* *(admit)* admitir; **to acknowledge a signature** = admitir una firma; **acknowledged and agreed** = visto y hallado conforme **(b)** *(confirm that something has been received)* acusar recibo de; **to acknowledge service** = acuse *m* de recibo
◊ **acknowledgement** [əkˈnɒlɪdʒmənt] *noun* reconocimiento *m or* confirmación *f;* **acknowledgement of service** = aceptación *f* de la defensa

acquire [əˈkwaɪə] *verb* adquirir
◊ **acquisition** [ækwɪˈzɪʃn] *noun* adquisición *f or* compra *f;* **the acquisition of Smith & Sons by Jones Ltd** = la adquisición *or* compra de Smith & Sons por Jones Ltd

acquit [əˈkwɪt] *verb* absolver *or* exculpar; **he was acquitted of the crime** = se le absolvió del delito; **the court acquitted two of the accused** = el tribunal absolvió a dos de los acusados (NOTE: **acquitting - acquitted.** Note also that you acquit someone **of** a crime)
◊ **acquittal** [əˈkwɪtəl] *noun* absolución *f or* exculpación *f;* **after his acquittal he left the court smiling** = tras haber sido absuelto, salió del juzgado sonriendo
◊ **acquitted** [əˈkwɪtɪd] *adj* libre de cargas

act [ækt] **1** *noun* **(a)** *(statute)* ley *f or* decreto *m;* **Act of Parliament** = Ley parlamentaria; **Companies Act** = Ley de Sociedades; **Finance Act** = Ley anual del Parlamento británico que concede al gobierno poder para aumentar los impuestos según lo expuesto en el presupuesto (NOTE: use **under** when referring to an Act of Parliament: **a creditor seeking a receiving order under the Bankruptcy Act; she does not qualify under section 2 of the 1979 Act**) **(b)** *(action)* acto *m or* acción *f;* **act of God** = fuerza *f* mayor (NOTE: acts of God are usually not covered by an insurance policy); **act or default** = acción u omisión; **contested act** = acto impugnado; **legal act** = acto jurídico; **unlawful act** = acción delictiva **2** *verb* **(a)** *(to work)* actuar; **to act as an agent for an American company** = actuar como representante de una empresa americana; **to act for someone** *or* **to act on someone's behalf** = representar a *or* actuar

en nombre de alguien **(b)** *(to do something)* actuar *or* obrar; **to act in good faith** = actuar de buena fe; **to act with caution** = obrar con precaución; **the lawyers are acting on our instructions** = los abogados están obrando conforme a nuestras órdenes; **to act on a letter** = obrar de acuerdo con *or* cumplir las instrucciones de una carta
◊ **acting** [ˈæktɪŋ] *adjective* en funciones

> COMMENT: before an Act becomes law, it is presented to Parliament in the form of a Bill. See notes at BILL

action [ˈækʃn] *noun* **(a)** *(thing which has been done)* acción *f;* **to take action** = hacer algo *or* tomar medidas **(b)** *(case in a law court)* **court action** = proceso *m or* acción *f* judicial; **legal action** = acción procesal; **to take legal action** = iniciar *or* abrir un proceso *or* acción judicial; **letter before action** = carta *f* previa a una actuación judicial; **action in personam** = acción personal; **action in rem** = acción contra la cosa; **action in tort** = acción de lesión jurídica; **action for damages** = acción *or* demanda por daños y perjuicios; **to bring an action for damages against someone** = entablar una demanda *or* llevar a los tribunales por daños y perjuicios; **action for eviction** = demanda de deshaucio; **action for libel** *or* **libel action** = acción por libelo *or* demanda por difamación; **action of replevin** = demanda de reivindicación; **chose in action** = derecho *m* de acción; **civil action** = demanda civil *or* acción civil *or* proceso civil; *US* **class action** = acción popular; **criminal action** = acción criminal; **personal action** = agravio *or* acción personal; *(in common law)* acción contra una persona resultante de un contrato
◊ **actionable** [ˈækʃnəbl] *adjective* procesable *or* justiciable; **torts which are actionable per se** = agravios procesables de por sí
◊ **active** [ˈæktɪv] *adjective* activo, -va; **active partner** = socio, -cia activo, -va
◊ **actively** [ˈæktɪvli] *adverb* activamente
◊ **activity** [əkˈtɪvɪti] *noun* actividad *f*

actual [ˈæktʃuəl] *adjective* real *or* efectivo, -va *or* verdadero, -ra; **actual bodily harm (ABH)** = delito *m* de lesiones; **actual loss** *or* **damage** = pérdida *f* real *or* daño *m* real; **actual total loss** = pérdida efectiva total; **actual notice** = conocimiento *m* real; **actual value** = valor *m* real

actuary [ˈæktʃuəri] *noun* actuario *m* (de seguros)
◊ **actuarial** [æktʃuˈeəriəl] *adjective* actuarial; **the premiums are worked out according to actuarial calculations** = las primas se calculan por métodos actuariales; **actuarial tables** = cuadros *mpl or* tablas *fpl* actuariales

actus reus [ˈæktəs ˈreɪəs] *Latin phrase* acto *m* criminal *or* acción u omisión culposa; *compare* MENS REA; *See note at* CRIME

addendum [əˈdendəm] *noun* adición *f*

addict [ˈædɪkt] *noun* adicto, -ta; **drug addict** = toxicómano, -na
◊ **addicted** [ˈædɪktɪd] *adjective;* **addicted to alcohol** *or* **drugs** = alcohólico, -ca *or* toxicómano, -na
◊ **addiction** [əˈdɪkʃn] *noun* **drug addiction** = toxicomanía *f*

additional [əˈdɪʃənəl] *adjective* adicional; **to ask for additional cover** = solicitar un seguro *or* solicitar cobertura adicional

address [əˈdres] **1** *noun* **(a)** *(where a person lives)* dirección *f;* **address for service** = dirección oficial de un litigante *or* interesado en un proceso **(b)** *(formal speech)* discurso *m or* alocución *f;* **address of thanks** = discurso oficial de agradecimiento; **in his address to the meeting, the mayor spoke of the problems facing the town** = en su discurso a los presentes, el alcalde habló de los problemas a los que la ciudad debería enfrentarse **(c)** *(Parliament)* UK **humble address** = comunicado oficial del Parlamento a la Reina; **debate on the address** = debate parlamentario tras el discurso inaugural de la Reina en la apertura del Parlamento **(d)** **form of address** = tratamiento *m* **2** *verb* **(a)** *(a letter or a parcel)* completar un sobre *or* dirigir *or* poner la dirección; **an incorrectly addressed package** = un paquete con la dirección incorrecta **(b)** *(to speak to)* dirigirse a; **the defendant asked permission to address the court** = el acusado pidió permiso para dirigirse al tribunal; **the Leader of the Opposition will address the meeting** = el líder de la oposición se dirigirá a los presentes **(c)** *(to speak about a particular issue)* tratar *or* abordar; **he then addressed the question of finance** = después trató la cuestión financiera; **to address oneself to a problem** = afrontar un problema; **the government will have to address itself to problems of international trade** = el gobierno tendrá que afrontar los problemas del comercio internacional

adduce [əˈdjuːs] *verb* alegar *or* aducir *or* presentar; **to adduce evidence** = aportar *or* presentar *or* aducir pruebas

adeem [əˈdiːm] *verb* anular *or* revocar (un legado)
◊ **ademption** [əˈdempʃn] *noun* anulación *f or* revocación *f* de un legado

adequate [ˈædɪkwət] *adjective* suficiente; **to operate without adequate cover** = actuar sin cobertura suficiente; **he made adequate provision for his wife** = garantizó suficientes fondos para su mujer

ad hoc [ˈæd ˈhɒk] *Latin phrase* para esto *or* para el caso; **an ad hoc committee** = un comité *m* para el caso; *see also* STANDING

ad idem [ˈæd ˈaɪdem] *Latin phrase* de acuerdo *or* en acuerdo

adjacent [əˈdʒeɪsnt] *adjective* contiguo, -gua

adjective law [ˈædʒektɪv ˈlɔː] *noun* ley adjetiva *or* derecho procesal

adjoin [əˈdʒɔɪn] *verb (of a property)* colindar *or* ser limítrofe con *or* estar contiguo a; **the developers acquired the old post office and two adjoining properties** = los promotores adquirieron el antiguo edificio de correos y las dos propiedades contiguas; **the fire spread to the adjoining property** = el fuego se extendió a la propiedad de al lado

adjourn [əˈdʒəːn] *verb* aplazar *or* levantar la sesión; **to adjourn a meeting** = aplazar *or* suspender una reunión; **the chairman adjourned the tribunal until three o'clock** = el presidente aplazó la vista hasta las tres; **the meeting adjourned at midday** = la reunión se levantó *or* se suspendió a mediodía; **the appeal was adjourned for affidavits to be obtained** = la apelación se pospuso hasta que se obtuvieran nuevas declaraciones juradas; **the meeting stands adjourned** = se levanta la sesión; **the hearing was adjourned sine die** = la vista se suspendió por término indefinido
◊ **adjournment** [əˈdʒəːnmənt] *noun* **(a)** *(of a session)* suspensión *f or* aplazamiento *m;* **the adjournment lasted two hours** = la suspensión duró dos horas; **the defendant has applied for an adjournment** = el acusado ha pedido un aplazamiento **(b)** UK suspensión de una sesión parlamentaria hasta el día siguiente; **motion for adjournment of the debate** = moción para aplazar la sesión; **motion for the adjournment of the House** = moción para aplazar la sesión parlamentaria hasta el día siguiente; **adjournment debate** *or* **debate on the adjournment** = debate sobre la moción presentada para aplazar una sesión parlamentaria **(c)** US **adjournment sine die** = aplazamiento indefinido de una sesión del Congreso; **adjournment to a day certain** = aplazamiento de una sesión del Congreso hasta fecha indicada

adjudicate [əˈdʒuːdɪkeɪt] *verb* sentenciar *or* juzgar *or* decidir (judicialmente); **to adjudicate a claim** = juzgar una demanda; **to adjudicate in a dispute** = actuar de juez en una disputa; **magistrates may be paid expenses when adjudicating** = a los magistrados les pueden pagar los gastos cuando sentencien; **he was adjudicated bankrupt** = se le declaró en quiebra
◊ **adjudication** [ədʒuːdɪˈkeɪʃn] *noun* decisión *f or* juicio *m or* sentencia *f;* **adjudication order** *or* **adjudication of bankruptcy** = resolución *f or* declaración judicial de quiebra; **adjudication tribunal** = tribunal *m* de justicia *or* tribunal arbitral
◊ **adjudicator** [əˈdʒuːdɪkeɪtə] *noun* juez *m or* árbitro *m;* **an adjudicator in an industrial dispute** = un árbitro en una disputa laboral

adjust [ə'dʒʌst] *verb* **(a)** *(to change to fit new conditions)* ajustar *or* reajustar *or* modificar *or* acomodar **(b)** *(to settle an account)* liquidar *or* tasar
◊ **adjuster** [ə'dʒʌstə] *noun* tasador, -ra *or* perito, -ta *mf;* **average adjuster** *or* **loss adjuster** = tasador de daños *or* perito de averías
◊ **adjustment** [ə'dʒʌsmənt] *noun* ajuste *m or* reajuste *m or* arreglo *m or* modificación *f;* **average adjustment** = tasación *f or* reajuste de averías
◊ **adjustor** [ə'dʒʌstə] *noun* = ADJUSTER

ad litem ['æd 'laɪtəm] *Latin phrase* para el proceso; **guardian ad litem** = tutor *m* para el proceso

administer [æd'mɪnɪstə] *verb* **(a)** *(court)* to **administer justice** = administrar justicia; **to administer an oath** = tomar juramento a **(b)** *(to organize or to manage)* administrar *or* dar; **he administers a large pension fund** = administra grandes fondos de pensiones **(c)** *(to give someone a medecine or a drug)* administrar; **she was accused of administering a poison to the old lady** = se le acusó de administrar un veneno a la anciana **(d)** *(punishment)* aplicar (un castigo)
◊ **administration** [ədmɪnɪ'streɪʃn] *noun* **(a)** *(management)* administración *f or* gestión *f or* dirección *f or* control *m;* **the administration of justice** = la administración de justicia; **letters of administration** = nombramiento *m* de Administrador Judicial (NOTE: not used in the singular); **administration bond** = fianza *f* de administración; **administration order** = sentencia *f* de administración **(b)** *(government)* gobierno *m or* administración *f;* **the Act became law under the previous administration** = se promulgó la ley bajo el gobierno anterior; **she was Minister of Education in the last administration** = fue Ministra de Educación con el gobierno anterior
◊ **administrative** [əd'mɪnɪstrətɪv] *adjective* administrativo, -va; **administrative law** = derecho *m* administrativo; **administrative tribunal** *or* US **administrative hearing** = tribunal *m* administrativo
◊ **administrator** [əd'mɪnɪstreɪtə] *noun* **(a)** *(in a business)* administrador, -ra **(b)** *(appointed by a court)* albacea testamentario
◊ **administratrix** [əd'mɪnɪstrətrɪks] *noun* administradora *f or* albacea *f*

Admiralty ['ædmərəlti] *noun* Ministerio *m* de Marina *or* Almirantazgo *m* británico; **Admiralty Court** = tribunal *m* marítimo; **Admiralty law** = derecho *m* marítimo

admit [əd'mɪt] *verb* **(a)** *(to allow someone to go in)* admitir *or* permitir la entrada a *or* dar entrada a; **children are not admitted to the bank** = se prohibe a los niños entrar al banco; **old age pensioners are admitted at half price** = la entrada para pensionistas es a mitad de precio **(b)** *(to allow someone to practise as a solicitor)* admitir como

abogado; **he was admitted in 1978** = se le admitió como abogado en 1978 **(c)** *(to allow evidence to be used in court)* aceptar *or* admitir *or* reconocer como prueba; **the court agreed to admit the photographs as evidence** = el tribunal admitió las fotografías como prueba **(d)** *(to agree that an allegation is correct)* reconocer *or* admitir *or* confesar; **he admitted his mistake** *or* **his liability** = reconoció su error *or* su responsabilidad; **she admitted having stolen the car** = admitió haber robado el coche; **he admitted to being in the house when the murder took place** = confesó haber estado en la casa cuando ocurrió el asesinato (NOTE: **admitted - admitting**. Note also that you admit **to** something, or admit **having done** something)
◊ **admissibility** [əmɪsə'bɪlɪti] *noun* admisibilidad *f;* **the court will decide on the admissibility of the evidence** = el tribunal decidirá sobre la admisibilidad de la evidencia
◊ **admissible** [əd'mɪsəbl] *adjective* admisible *or* aceptable; **the documents were not considered relevant to the case and were therefore not admissible** = los documentos no se consideraron relevantes al caso y por consiguiente no fueron admisibles
◊ **admission** [əd'mɪʃn] *noun* **(a)** *(allowing someone to go in)* entrada *f or* ingreso *m;* **there is a £1 admission charge** = el precio de la entrada es de una libra; **admission is free on presentation of this card** = entrada gratis al presentar esta tarjeta; **free admission on Sundays** = entrada gratis los domingos **(b)** *(in education)* **admissions form** = impreso *m* de matrícula **(c)** *(confession)* confesión *f or* reconocimiento *m;* **admission of guilt** = confesión *or* reconocimiento de culpabilidad **(d)** *(in civil cases)* declaración *f* admisión *f* de culpa

adopt [ə'dɒpt] *verb* **(a)** *(to become a legal parent)* adoptar *or* prohijar **(b)** *(to approve or to accept)* aprobar; **to adopt a legal measure** = adoptar una medida judicial; **to adopt a resolution** = aprobar una resolución; **to adopt the agenda** = aprobar el orden del día; **the proposals were adopted unanimously** = se aprobaron las propuestas por unanimidad
◊ **adoption** [ə'dɒpʃn] *noun* **(a)** *(of children)* adopción *f;* **adoption order** = sentencia *f* de adopción; **adoption proceedings** = procedimientos *mpl* de adopción **(b)** *(of ideas or suggestions)* aprobación *f;* **he moved the adoption of the resolution** = propuso la aprobación de la resolución
◊ **adoptive** [ə'dɒptɪv] *adjective* adoptivo, -va; **adoptive child** = hijo *m* adoptivo *or* hija *f* adoptiva; **adoptive parent** = padre *m* adoptivo *or* madre *f* adoptiva

COMMENT: if a child's parents divorce, or if one parent dies, the child may be adopted by a step-father or step-mother

adult ['ædʌlt] *noun* adulto, -ta *or* mayor de edad

adulterate [ə'dʌltəreɪt] *verb* adulterar; **to adulterate the truth** = adulterar la verdad

adulteration [ədʌltə'reɪʃn] *noun* adulteración *f*

adultery [ə'dʌltri] *noun* adulterio *m;* **his wife accused him of committing adultery with Miss X** = su mujer le acusó de cometer adulterio con la Srta. X
◊ **adulterous** [ə'dʌltrəs] *adjective* adúltero, -ra; **he had an adulterous relationship with Miss X** = tuvo una relación adúltera con la Srta. X

ad valorem ['æd və'lɔːrem] *Latin phrase* sobre el valor; **ad valorem duty** *or* **ad valorem tax** = impuesto *m* sobre el valor

advance [əd'vɑːns] **1** *adjective* anticipado, -da *or* adelantado, -da; **advance booking** = reserva anticipada; **advance payment** = pago anticipado; **you must give seven days' advance notice of withdrawals from the account** = las retiradas de fondos se deben notificar con siete días de antelación **2** *noun* **(a)** *(loan)* préstamo *m or* anticipo *m or* crédito *m;* **a cash advance** = un anticipo (en efectivo) *or* un adelanto; **to receive an advance from the bank** = recibir un préstamo *or* crédito bancario; **an advance on account** = un anticipo a cuenta; **to make an advance of £100 to someone** = conceder un préstamo de 100 libras a alguien **(b) in advance** = por adelantado *or* por anticipado *or* de antemano; **to pay in advance** = pagar por adelantado *or* con antelación; **freight payable in advance** = flete a pagar por adelantado **2** *verb* **(a)** *(to lend money)* prestar *or* anticipar; **the bank advanced him £10,000 against the security of his house** = el banco le prestó 10.000 libras con la garantía de su casa **(b)** *(to increase)* subir; **prices generally advanced on the stock market** = los precios de la bolsa experimentaron un aumento general **(c)** *(to make something happen earlier)* adelantar *or* anticipar; **the date of the hearing has been advanced to May 10th** = la fecha de la vista se ha adelantado al 10 de mayo
◊ **advancement** [əd'vɑːnsmənt] *noun* anticipo *m or* donación *f* de la herencia en vida; **power of advancement** = poder que tienen los fideicomisarios para hacer un anticipo de la herencia

advantage [əd'vɑːntɪdʒ] *noun* ventaja *f;* **to learn something to your advantage** = enterarse de algo que es ventajoso para uno; **obtaining a pecuniary advantage by deception** = estafar

adversary ['ædvəsəri] **1** *noun* adversario, -ria *or* contrario, -ria **2** *adjective;* **adversary procedure** *see* ACCUSATORIAL PROCEDURE

adverse ['ædvɜːs] *adjective* **(a)** adverso, -sa *or* contrario, -ria *or* opuesto, -ta *or* desfavorable; **adverse possession** = prescripción *f* adquisitiva; **adverse witness** = testigo *m* desfavorable *or* hostil *

testimonio *m* en contra **(b)** *(in a court case)* **adverse party** = parte contraria

advert [əd'vɜːt] *verb* referirse a; **this case was not adverted to in** *Smith v. Jones Machines Ltd* = no se ha referido este caso en *Smith v. Jones Machines Ltd*

advertisement [əd'vɜːtɪzmənt] *noun* anuncio *m*

advice [əd'vaɪs] *noun* **(a)** *(notice)* **advice note** = conocimiento *m or* nota *f* de embarque *or* aviso *m* de expedición *or* envío; **as per advice** = según conocimiento de embarque *or* nota de expedición **(b)** *(opinion)* consejo *m or* asesoramiento *m;* **expert advice** = asesoramiento técnico; **legal advice** = asesoramiento jurídico; **to give legal advice** = asesorar; **to take legal advice** = consultar a un abogado; **counsel's advice** = consejo legal; **we sent the documents to the police on the advice of the solicitor** *or* **we took the solicitor's advice and sent the documents to the police** = enviamos los documentos a la policía por indicación del abogado *or* siguiendo consejo legal

advise [əd'vaɪz] *verb* **(a)** *(to inform)* informar *or* advertir *or* avisar; **we are advised that the shipment will arrive next week** = se nos informa que el envío llegará la semana próxima **(b)** *(to suggest what should be done)* aconsejar; **we are advised to take the shipping company to court** = nos han aconsejado llevar a la compañía naviera a los tribunales; **the solicitor advised us to send the documents to the police** = el abogado nos recomendó enviar los documentos a la policía
◊ **advise against** [əd'vaɪz ə'genst] *verb* aconsejar en contra; **the bank manager advised against closing the account** = el director del banco aconsejó no cerrar *or* saldar la cuenta; **our lawyers have advised against suing the landlord** = nuestros abogados han aconsejado no demandar al propietario
◊ **adviser** *or* **advisor** [əd'vaɪzə] *noun* consejero, -ra *or* asesor, -ra; **he is consulting the company's legal adviser** = está consultando con el asesor jurídico *or* consejero legal de la compañía; **financial adviser** = asesor financiero *or* fiscal
◊ **advisory** [əd'vaɪzəri] *adjective* asesor, -ra *or* consultivo, -va; **advisory body** = organismo asesor; **he is acting in an advisory capacity** = está actuando como asesor *or* actúa en calidad de asesor; **an advisory board** = junta *f* consultiva; *GB* **the Advisory Conciliation and Arbitration Service (ACAS)** = Servicio *m* Asesor de Arbitraje y Conciliación

advocacy ['ædvəkəsi] *noun* **(a)** *(pleading a case before a court)* defensa *f* **(b)** *(support for a cause)* defensa *f or* apoyo *m;* **his advocacy of the right of illegal immigrants to remain in the country** = su defensa del derecho de los inmigrantes ilegales a permanecer en el país

advocate 1 [ˈædvəkət] *noun (in Scotland)* abogado *m* (con derecho a alegar en los tribunales superiores) *US* abogado; **Faculty of Advocates =** Colegio *m* Oficial de Abogados de Escocia; **Judge Advocate-General =** Auditor *m* General de Guerra **2** [ˈædvəkeɪt] *verb* abogar *or* defender
◊ **Advocate General** [ˈædvəkət ˈdʒenrəl] *noun* **(a)** *(in Scotland)* uno de los dos Fiscales del Estado en Escocia **(b)** *(in the European Court of Justice)* abogado general

advowson [ədˈvausən] *noun* derecho *m* a nombrar sacerdote de parroquia a una persona

affair [əˈfeə] *noun* **(a)** *(business or dealings)* asunto *m or* negocio *m;* **are you involved in the copyright affair? =** ¿estás involucrado en el asunto de los derechos de autor?; **his affairs were so difficult to understand that the lawyers had to ask accountants for advice =** sus negocios eran tan difíciles de entender que los abogados tuvieron que pedir consejo a contables **(b)** *(adultereous relationship)* aventura *f* amorosa; **to have an affair with someone =** tener un lío *or* una aventura amorosa con alguien

affect [əˈfekt] *verb* afectar *or* perjudicar *or* influir; **the new government regulations do not affect us =** las nuevas regulaciones *or* reglamentaciones oficiales no nos afectan; **the company's sales in the Far East were seriously affected by the embargo =** las ventas de la compañía en el Extremo Oriente se vieron seriamente afectadas por el embargo
◊ **affection** [əˈfekʃn] *noun* afecto *m; see also* ALIENATION

affidavit [æfiˈdeɪvɪt] *noun* declaración *f* jurada *or* afidávit *m or* acta *f* notarial *or* atestado *m*

affiliation [əfiliˈeɪʃn] *noun* afiliación *f;* **affiliation order =** sentencia *f* de filiación; **affiliation proceedings =** procedimientos *mpl* de filiación

affirm [əˈfɜːm] *verb* **(a)** *(to state that you are telling the truth)* declarar *or* alegar **(b)** *(to confirm that something is correct)* confirmar
◊ **affirmation** [æfəˈmeɪʃn] *noun* **(a)** *(without swearing an oath)* declaración *f or* alegación *f* **(b)** *(statement by an MP, showing allegiance to the Queen)* promesa *f* solemne
◊ **affirmative** [əˈfɜːmətɪv] *adjective* afirmativo, -va; **the answer was in the affirmative =** la respuesta fue afirmativa

affix [əˈfɪks] *verb (attach)* añadir *(signature)* suscribir

affray [əˈfreɪ] *noun* reyerta *f or* refriega *f*

COMMENT: a person is guilty of affray if he uses or threatens to use unlawful violence towards another, and his conduct is such that a reasonable person who happened to be present might fear for his safety

aforementioned [əfɔːˈmenʃənd] *adjective* antes *or* ya mencionado, -da *or* antedicho, -cha; **the aforementioned company =** la compañía antes mencionada

aforesaid [əfɔːˈsed] *adjective* susodicho, -cha *or* antedicho, -cha; **as aforesaid =** como ya se ha dicho

aforethought [əˈfɔːθɔːt] *adjective;* **with malice aforethought =** con intención delictuosa

a fortiori [ˈeɪ fɔːtiˈɔːraɪ] *Latin phrase* por fuerza *f* mayor; **if the witness was present at the scene of the crime, then a fortiori he must have heard the shot =** si el testigo estaba presente en la escena del crimen, entonces debe haber oído el disparo por fuerza mayor

against [əˈgenst] *preposition* **(a)** contra *or* sobre; **against the law =** en contra de la ley; **against the will =** sin el consentimiento; **lighting fires in the street is against the law =** encender hogueras en la calle va en contra de la ley; **the company went against the law by sending dangerous goods through the post =** la compañía actuó en contra de la ley al enviar sustancias peligrosas por correo **(b)** *(relating to)* de *or* relativo a; **to pay an advance against next month's salary =** conceder un anticipo de remuneración; **the bank advanced him £10,000 against the security of his house =** el banco le adelantó 10.000 libras con la garantía de su casa

age [eɪdʒ] *noun* edad *f;* **age of consent** *or* **legal age =** edad núbil *or* edad legal *or* mayoría de edad; **under age =** menor de edad; *see* CONSENT, DISCRIMINATION

agency [ˈeɪdʒənsi] *noun* **(a)** *(in contractual matters)* representación *f* **(b)** *(in an area)* oficina *f;* **they signed an agency agreement** *or* **an agency contract =** firmaron un contrato de representación **(c)** *(branch of government)* agencia *f or* organismo *m;* **government agency =** organismo *m* público; **the Atomic Energy Agency =** la Agencia de Energía Atómica; **a counter-intelligence agency =** una agencia de contraespionaje

agenda [əˈdʒendə] *noun* orden *m* del día *or* asuntos *mpl* a tratar; **the committee meeting agenda** *or* **the agenda of the committee meeting =** el orden del día de la reunión del comité; **after two hours we were still discussing the first item on the agenda =** después de dos horas, estábamos todavía discutiendo el primer asunto del orden del día; **the secretary put finance at the top of the agenda =** la secretaria puso las finanzas como asunto prioritario del orden del día

agent [ˈeɪdʒənt] *noun* **(a)** *(in matters relating to contracts)* representante *mf or* delegado, -da; **land**

agent = administrador, -ra **(b)** *(in charge of an agency)* agente *mf;* **advertising agent** = agente publicitario *or* de publicidad; **commission agent** = comisionista *mf;* **estate agent** = agente inmobiliario; **sole agent** = administrador único *or* representante exclusivo; **travel agent** = agente de viajes **(c)** *(who works for a government)* agente *mf;* **secret agent** = agente secreto

◊ **agent provocateur** [ˈæʒɒn prəvɒkəˈtəː] *French expression* agente provocador

aggravation [ægrəˈveɪʃn] *noun* agravante *m or* circunstancia *f* agravante

◊ **aggravated** [ˈægrəveɪtɪd] *adjective* agravado, -da; **aggravated assault** = agresión *f* grave; **aggravated burglary** = hurto *m* con circunstancias agravantes; **aggravated damages** = daños *mpl* con agravantes *or* indemnización *f* suplementaria

aggression [əˈgreʃn] *noun* agresión *f or* acometimiento *m*

aggressive [əˈgresɪv] *adjective* agresivo, -va; **aggressive behaviour** = conducta agresiva

aggrieved [əˈgriːvd] *adjective* dañado, -da *or* perjudicado, -da *or* agraviado, -da

AGM [ˈeɪ ˈdʒiː ˈem] = ANNUAL GENERAL MEETING

agree [əˈgriː] *verb* **(a)** *(to approve)* acordar *or* convenir *or* aprobar; **the figures were agreed between the two parties** = se acordaron las cifras entre las dos partes; **terms of the contract are still to be agreed** = se tienen que acordar todavía los términos del contrato **(b)** *(to accept)* acceder *or* consentir *or* aceptar; **it has been agreed that the lease will run for twenty-five years** = se ha accedido a que el contrato de arrendamiento tenga una validez de veinticinco años; **after some discussion he agreed to our plan** = después de discutirlo un poco, aceptó nuestro plan; **the bank will never agree to lend the company £250,000** = el banco nunca consentirá prestar 250.000 libras a la empresa **(c)** **to agree to do something** = aceptar hacer algo *or* acceder (NOTE: you agree **to** or **on** a plan or agree **to do** something)

◊ **agree with** [əˈgriː ˈwɪθ] *verb* **(a)** *(to be of the same opinion)* estar de acuerdo con **(b)** *(to be the same as)* concordar con *or* corresponder a *or* coincidir; **the witness' statement does not agree with that of the accused** = la declaración del testigo no concuerda con la del acusado

◊ **agreed** [əˈgriːd] *adjective* acordado, -da *or* convenido, -da; **an agreed amount** = una cantidad convenida; **on agreed terms** *or* **on terms which have been agreed upon** = según los términos acordados

◊ **agreement** [əˈgriːmənt] *noun* acuerdo *m or* contrato *m or* convenio *m;* **knock-for-knock agreement** = acuerdo (entre dos compañías de seguros); **in agreement** = acorde; **written agreement** = acuerdo escrito; **unwritten** *or* **verbal agreement** = acuerdo verbal; **to draw up** *or* **to draft an agreement** = redactar un contrato; **to break an agreement** = quebrantar *or* violar un contrato *or* romper un acuerdo; **to sign an agreement** = firmar un contrato *or* un acuerdo *or* un convenio; **to witness an agreement** = firmar un contrato como testigo; **an agreement has been reached** *or* **concluded** *or* **come to** = se ha llegado a un acuerdo; **to reach an agreement** *or* **to come to an agreement on prices** *or* **salaries** = llegar a un acuerdo sobre los precios *or* salarios; **an international agreement on trade** = un convenio internacional de comercio; **collective wage agreement** = convenio salarial colectivo; **an agency agreement** = un contrato de representación; **a marketing agreement** = un acuerdo comercial *or* de comercialización; **blanket agreement** = acuerdo global *or* general; **exclusive agreement** = contrato exclusivo *or* de representación exclusiva; **shareholders' agreement** = contrato de accionistas; **agreement in principle** = acuerdo con las condiciones básicas de una propuesta; **gentleman's agreement** = acuerdo verbal *or* pacto entre caballeros

COMMENT: a gentleman's agreement is not usually enforceable by law

aid [eɪd] **1** *noun* ayuda *f or* asistencia *f* auxilio *m;* **Legal Aid** = asesoramiento *m* jurídico gratuito *or* asistencia jurídica *or* defensa de oficio; **to pray in aid** = acogerse a; **I pray in aid the Statute of Frauds in support of the defendant's case** = me acojo a la Ley Anti-fraude en favor del caso del procesado **2** *verb* ayudar *or* auxiliar *or* asistir; **to aid and abet** = ayudar a cometer un crimen *or* ser cómplice con incitación al crimen

◊ **aiding and abetting** [ˈeɪdɪŋ ənd əˈbetɪŋ] *noun* complicidad *f* e incitación *f* al crimen

AIDS [eɪdz] *noun* sida *m*

a. k. a. [ˈeɪ ˈkeɪ ˈeɪ] = ALSO KNOWN AS

al. [æl] *see* ET AL.

alarm [əˈlɑːm] *noun* alarma *f;* **as he put his hand through the window he set off an alarm bell** = al meter la mano por la ventana, activó la alarma; **burglar alarm** = alarma antirrobo; **fire alarm** = alarma contra incendios

alcohol [ˈælkəhɒl] *noun* alcohol *m;* **blood level of alcohol** = alcoholemia *f*

aleatory [æliˈeɪtəri] *adjective* aleatorio, -ria; **aleatory contract** = contrato *m* aleatorio

alert [əˈləːt] *verb* alertar

alia [ˈeɪliə] *see* ET ALIA, INTER ALIA

alias [ˈeɪliəs] **1** *noun* alias *m or* nombre *m* supuesto; **the confidence trickster used several aliases** = el estafador utilizaba varios nombres falsos **2** *adverb* alias *or* por otro nombre; **John**

Smith, alias Reginald Jones = John Smith, alias Reginald Jones

alibi ['ælɪbaɪ] *noun* coartada *f*

alien ['eɪliən] *noun (in the UK)* extranjero, -ra; **resident alien** = extranjero con permiso de residencia; **illegal alien** = inmigrante ilegal

alienate ['eɪliəneɪt] *verb* enajenar

alienation [eɪliə'neɪʃn] *noun* enajenación *f or* traspaso *m* (de bienes); **alienation of affection** = enajenación del afecto (en el matrimonio)

alimony ['ælɪməni] *noun* pensión *f* alimenticia (entre cónyuges); **alimony pending suit** *or* **pendente lite** = pensión alimenticia durante el litigio; *see also* PALIMONY (NOTE: in British English is usually referred to as **maintenance**)

alive [ə'laɪv] *adjective* vivo, -va

all [ɔːl] *adjective & pronoun* todo, -da *or* todos, -das; **all the witnesses say they saw the accused with the can of petrol** = todos los testigos dicen que vieron al acusado con el bidón de petróleo; **all the evidence suggests that it was a gang of three people who held up the bank** = toda la evidencia apunta a que fue una banda de tres personas quien atracó el banco; **on all fours with** = en completa armonía con *or* idéntico a; **this case is on all fours with** *Donoghue v. Stevenson* = este caso es idéntico a *Donoghue v. Stevenson*
◊ **All England Law Reports (All E.R.)** ['ɔːl 'ɪŋlənd 'lɔː rɪ'pɔːts] *plural noun* informes de casos *or* pleitos en los tribunales superiores ingleses
◊ **all-in** ['ɔːl'ɪn] *adjective* todo incluido; *US* **all-in-policy** = seguro *m* contra todo riesgo

allege [ə'ledʒ] *verb* alegar *or* afirmar *or* declarar; **the prosecution alleged that the accused was in the house when the crime was committed** = la acusación alegó que el acusado estaba en la casa cuando se cometió el crimen
◊ **allegation** [ælɪ'geɪʃn] *noun* alegación *f or* alegato *m or* aseveración *f;* **false allegation** = aseveración falsa

allegiance [ə'liːdʒəns] *noun* lealtad *f or* fidelidad *f or* obediencia *f;* **oath of allegiance** = juramento *m* de fidelidad; **he swore an oath of allegiance to the new president** = juró fidelidad al nuevo presidente

All E. R. ['ɔːl 'iː 'ɑː] = ALL ENGLAND LAW REPORTS

allocate ['æləkeɪt] *verb* asignar *or* distribuir
◊ **allocation** [ælə'keɪʃn] *noun* **(a)** *(a sum of money)* asignación *f or* cuota *f;* **allocation of funds to research into crime** = asignación de fondos para investigar sobre el crimen **(b)** *share allocation or* **allocation of shares** = asignación *or* distribución de acciones

◊ **allocatur** [æloɪkæ'tuːə] *Latin word* cúmplase *or* certificado que confirma que una parte ha de pagar a otra tras un proceso

allocution [ælokjuːʃn] *noun US* palabras que emite el juez para pedir al acusado que manifieste lo que estime conveniente antes de que se dicte la sentencia

allot [ə'lɒt] *verb* adjudicar *or* asignar *or* repartir; **to allot shares** = repartir *or* distribuir acciones (NOTE: **allotting - allotted**)
◊ **allotment** [ə'lɒtmənt] *noun* **(a)** *(sharing out)* reparto *m or* asignación *f or* repartimiento *m* **(b)** *(distribution of a share issue)* adjudicación *f* de acciones

allow [ə'laʊ] *verb* **(a)** *(to permit)* permitir *or* tolerar; **the law does not allow you to drive on the wrong side of the road** = está prohibido por ley conducir por el lado contrario de la carretera; **begging is not allowed in the station** = se prohíbe la mendicidad en la estación; **visitors are not allowed into the prisoners' cells** = no se permite el paso de visitantes a las celdas de los prisioneros **(b)** *(to give time or a privilege)* conceder tiempo *or* dejar tiempo *or* conceder un privilegio; **the court adjourned to allow the prosecution time to find the missing witness** = el tribunal aplazó la sesión para dejar tiempo a la acusación para encontrar al testigo desaparecido; **you are allowed thirty days to pay the fine** = se le conceden treinta días para pagar la multa **(c)** *(to agree or to accept legally)* admitir *or* aceptar; **to allow a claim** *or* **an appeal** = aceptar una demanda *or* una apelación
◊ **allow for** [ə'laʊ 'fɔː] *verb* descontar *or* rebajar *or* conceder una rebaja; **delivery is not allowed for** = los gastos de envío no están incluidos; **allow twenty-eight days for delivery** = deje un margen de veintiocho días para la entrega
◊ **allowable** [ə'laʊəbl] *adjective* lícito, -ta *or* permitido, -da; **allowable expenses** = gastos *mpl* desgravables *or* deducibles
◊ **allowance** [ə'laʊəns] *noun* **(a)** *(money given for special reason)* bonificación *f or* dietas *fpl or* dotación *f;* **travel allowance** *or* **travelling allowance** = dietas para gastos de viajes; **foreign currency allowance** = dotación de divisas; **cost-of-living allowance** = subsidio *m or* compensación *f* por aumento del coste de vida *or* asignación *f* por carestía de vida **(b)** *(tax)* exención *f or* desgravación *f* fiscal; **personal allowances** = renta *f* no imponible; **allowances against tax** *or* **tax allowances** = desgravaciones fiscales; **wife's earned income allowance** = desgravación *f* por los ingresos recibidos por la esposa **(c)** *(proportion of money removed)* reserva *f or* deducción *f;* **to make an allowance for legal expenses** *or* **an allowance for exchange loss** = hacer un descuento por gastos legales *or* un descuento por diferencia de cambio

alphabet ['ælfəbet] *noun* alfabeto *m*

◊ **alphabetical order** [ælfə'betɪkl 'ɔːdə] *noun* orden *m* alfabético; **the names of the accused were read out in alphabetical order** = se leyeron los nombres de los acusados por orden alfabético

alter ['ɒltə] *verb* cambiar *or* modificar *or* alterar; **to alter the terms of a contract** = modificar los términos de un contrato; **he has altered his will six times in the last ten years** = ha modificado su testamento seis veces en los últimos diez años
◊ **alteram** ['ɔːltərəm] *see* AUDI
◊ **alteration** [ɔːltə'reɪʃn] *noun* cambio *m or* modificación *f or* alteración *f*; **we made some alterations to the terms of a contract** = modificamos en parte los términos de un contrato

alternative [ɔːl'tɜːnətɪv] **1** *adjective* otro, -tra *or* alternativo, -va; **to find someone alternative employment** = conseguir a alguien otro trabajo **2** *noun* alternativa *f or* disyuntiva *f*; **pleading in the alternative** *or* **US alternative pleading** = presentación de dos o más alegatos en un mismo caso
◊ **alternative vote (AV)** [ɔːl'tɜːnətɪv 'vəut] *noun* (*in Australia*) sistema de votación que incluye una segunda vuelta en que los votos pueden ser redistribuidos entre los candidatos

a.m. *or* **ante meridiem** ['eɪ 'em] *Latin phrase* por la mañana *or* antes de las doce del mediodía; **the flight leaves at 9.20 a.m.** = el vuelo sale a las 9.20 de la mañana; **telephone calls before 6 a.m. are charged at the cheap rate** = antes de las 6 de la mañana, las llamadas telefónicas se cobran a tarifa reducida

ambassador [æm'bæsədə] *noun* embajador, -ra; **she is the wife of the Spanish Ambassador** = es la esposa del embajador de España; **our ambassador in Spain** = nuestro embajador en España; **the government has recalled its ambassador** = el gobierno ha retirado a su embajador
◊ **ambassadorial** [æmbæsə'dɔːriel] *adjective* diplomático, -ca *or* de embajador; **the ambassadorial Rolls-Royce** = el Rolls-Royce del embajador
◊ **ambassadress** [æmbæsə'dres] *noun* (**a**) embajadora *f* (**b**) la esposa del embajador

ambiguous [æm'bɪgjuəs] *adjective* ambiguo, -gua *or* equívoco, -ca; **the wording of the clause is ambiguous and needs clarification** = los términos de la cláusula son ambiguos y necesitan ser aclarados
◊ **ambiguity** [æmbɪ'gjuːɪti] *noun* ambigüedad *f*; **latent ambiguity** = ambigüedad latente

ambush ['æmbuʃ] **1** *noun* emboscada *f* **2** *verb* atacar por sorpresa

amend [ə'mend] *verb* enmendar *or* rectificar *or* corregir; **please amend your copy of the contract**

accordingly = le ruego rectifique su copia del contrato en consecuencia
◊ **amendment** [ə'mendmənt] *noun* (**a**) (*in a document*) rectificación *f or* corrección *f*; **to propose an amendment to the draft agreement** = proponer una rectificación al borrador del acuerdo; **to make amendments to a contract** = rectificar *or* enmendar un contrato (**b**) (*to a Bill in Parliament*) enmienda *f*
◊ **amends** [ə'mendz] *plural noun* compensación *f or* satisfacción *f*; **to make amends** = dar cumplida satisfacción *or* enmendar; **offer of amends** = ofrecimiento *m* de compensación *or* de reparación de daños

American Bar Association [ə'merɪkən 'bɑːr əsəusi'eɪʃn] *noun* asociación *f* norteamericana de abogados *or* Colegio *m* Oficial de Abogados de los EE UU

amicus curiae [ə'maɪkəs 'kjuəriaɪ] *Latin phrase* 'amigo del tribunal': abogado que no representa a ninguna de las partes en un caso pero que es llamado a dirigirse al tribunal para ayudarle a clarificar una dificultad legal *or* para explicar algo que es de interés público

amnesty ['æmnəsti] **1** *noun* amnistía *f*; **general amnesty** = indulto general **2** *verb* amnistiar; **they were amnestied by the president** = fueron indultados por el presidente

analyze ['ænəlaɪz] *verb* analizar

analyst ['ænəlɪst] *noun* analista *mf*

anarchy ['ænəki] *noun* anarquía *f*; **when the president was assassinated, the country fell into anarchy** = cuando el presidente fue asesinado, el país se sumió en un estado de anarquía
◊ **anarchic** *or* **anarchical** [ə'nɑːkɪk *or* ə'nɑːkɪkl] *adjective* anárquico, -ca; **the anarchical state of the country districts** = el estado anárquico de las comarcas del país

ancestor ['ænsestə] *noun* antepasado, -da; **common ancestor** = antepasado común; **Mr Smith and the Queen have a common ancestor in King Henry VIII** = el Sr. Smith y la Reina tienen a Enrique VIII como antepasado común

ancient lights ['eɪntʃənt 'laɪts] *plural noun* servidumbre *f* de luces (y vistas)

ancillary [æn'sɪləri] *adjective* subordinado, -da *or* auxiliar *or* subsidiario, -ria *or* anciliario, -ria; **ancillary relief** = estipulación financiera *or* ajuste de derechos de propiedad que un tribunal dispone para un cónyuge o hijo en trámites de divorcio

animus ['ænɪməs] *noun* ánimo *m or* intención *f*; **animus cancellandi** = intención *or* ánimo de suprimir *or* cancelar; **animus furandi** = intención *or* ánimo de robar; **animus lucrandi** = ánimo de lucro; **animus manendi** = intención *or* ánimo de permanecer (en un lugar); **animus revocandi** =

intención *or* ánimo de revocar (un testamento) (NOTE: when used to mean 'with the intention of', use **animo: animo revocandi =** with the intention of revoking a will)

annexe *or US* **annex 1** ['æneks] *noun* anexo *m or* documento *m* adjunto **2** [ə'neks] *verb* adjuntar *or* añadir *or* anexar

announce [ə'naʊns] *verb* anunciar *or* declarar *or* comunicar; **the foreman of the jury announced their verdict** = el presidente del jurado anunció su veredicto
◊ **announcement** [ə'naʊnsmənt] *noun* anuncio *m or* declaración *f or* aviso *m or* comunicado *m;* **public announcement** = aviso público; **the chairman made an announcement about the takeover bid** = el presidente hizo unas declaraciones acerca de la oferta de adquisición

annoy [ə'nɔɪ] *verb* molestar; **to be annoyed with someone** = estar molesto con alguien; **to get annoyed** = molestarse

annual ['ænjʊəl] *adjective* anual; **Annual General Meeting (AGM)** = Junta *f* General Anual; **annual return** = rendimiento *m* anual; **on an annual basis** = anualmente
◊ **annually** ['ænjʊəli] *adverb* anualmente; **the figures are revised annually** = las cifras se revisan anualmente

annuity [ə'njuːəti] *noun* anualidad *f or* renta *f* anual *or* pensión *f* anual; **he has a government annuity** *or* **an annuity from the government** = recibe una renta anual del estado; **to buy** *or* **to take out an annuity** = comprar *or* suscribir una anualidad
◊ **annuitant** [ə'njuːɪtənt] *noun* rentista *mf or* pensionista *mf*

annul [ə'nʌl] *verb* **(a)** *(to cancel or to stop)* revocar *or* cancelar *or* rescindir **(b)** *(to declare that something never existed or had legal effect)* anular *or* invalidar; **the contract was annulled by the court** = el tribunal anuló el contrato; **their marriage has been annulled** = su matrimonio ha sido anulado (NOTE: **annulling - annulled**)
◊ **annullable** [ə'nʌləbl] *adjective* anulable *or* revocable *or* rescindible
◊ **annulling** [ə'nʌlɪŋ] **1** *adjective* anulativo, -va *or* que anula *or* con poder de anular *or* revocar; **annulling clause** = cláusula anulativa *or* abrogatoria **2** *noun* anulación *f or* revocación *f or* cancelación *f or* rescisión *f;* **the annulling of a contract** = la anulación de un contrato
◊ **annulment** [ə'nʌlmənt] *noun* anulación *f or* revocación *f or* cancelación *f or* rescisión *f;* **annulment of adjudication** = anulación de la resolución de quiebra; **annulment of marriage** = anulación del matrimonio

annum ['ænəm] *see* PER ANNUM

anonymous [ə'nɒnɪməs] *adjective* anónimo, -ma

answer ['ɑːnsə] **1** *noun* **(a)** *(reply in a letter)* respuesta *f or* contestación *f;* **I am writing in answer to your letter of October 6th** = le escribo en respuesta a *or* contestando a su carta del 6 de octubre; **my letter got no answer** *or* **there was no answer to my letter** = mi carta no obtuvo respuesta; **I tried to phone his office but there was no answer** = intenté llamar por teléfono a su oficina pero no me contestaron **(b)** *(in court)* contestación a la demanda *or* réplica *f* **2** *verb* **(a)** *(to respond)* responder (a) *or* contestar (a); **to answer a letter** = contestar una carta; **to answer the telephone** = contestar el teléfono **(b)** *(formally in court)* contestar a la demanda; **to answer charges** = declararse inocente o culpable de una acusación; **the judge ruled there was no case to answer** = el juez decidió que no existía nada en contra del acusado *or* defendido
◊ **answerable** ['ɑːnsrəbl] *adjective* responsable; **he is answerable to the Police Commissioner for the conduct of the officers in his force** = es responsable ante el jefe de policía del comportamiento de los agentes de su cuerpo; **she refused to be held answerable for the consequences of the police committee's decision** = se negó a ser responsable de las consecuencias de la decisión del comité de policía (NOTE: you are answerable **to** someone **for** an action)

ante ['ænti] *Latin adverb* 'lo que ha sucedido anteriormente' *or* 'antes'; **status quo ante** = el estado *m or* la situación *f* anterior

antecedents [ænti'siːdənts] *plural noun* antecedentes *mpl*

antedate [ænti'deɪt] *verb* antedatar *or* poner una fecha anticipada a un documento; **the invoice was antedated to January 1st** = se fechó la factura con efecto retroactivo al 1 de enero

anti- ['ænti] *prefix* contra; **an anti-drug campaign** = una campaña antidroga; **the anti-terrorist squad** = la brigada antiterrorista
◊ **anti-trust** ['ænti'trʌst] *adjective* antimonopolio; **anti-trust laws** *or* **legislation** = leyes *or* legislación antimonopolio

anticipation [æntɪsɪ'peɪʃn] *noun* anticipación *f*
◊ **anticipatory** [æntɪsɪ'peɪtəi] *adjective* anticipado, -da; **anticipatory breach** = declaración *f* anticipada de incumplimiento de contrato *or* violación *f* anticipada de contrato

Anton Piller order ['æntɒn 'pɪlə 'ɔːdə] *noun* mandato *m or* auto *m* judicial en un proceso civil por el cual se permite a una parte examinar y llevarse los documentos de un defendido, en especial cuando éste pudiera destruir pruebas

COMMENT: called after the case of *Anton Piller K.G. v. Manufacturing Processes Ltd*

AOB ['eɪ 'əʊ 'biː] = ANY OTHER BUSINESS

apologize [ə'pɒlədʒaɪz] *verb* disculparse *or* pedir perdón *or* presentar excusas; **to apologize for the delay in answering** = disculparse por el retraso en responder; **she apologized for being late** = pidió perdón por llegar tarde; **he apologized to the court for the absence of the chief witness** = presentó sus excusas ante el tribunal por la ausencia del principal testigo

◊ **apology** [ə'pɒlədʒi] *noun* disculpa *f or* excusa *f;* **to write a letter of apology** = escribir una carta de disculpa; **I enclose a cheque for £10 with apologies for the delay in answering your letter** = adjunto un cheque por 10 libras y le ruego acepte mis excusas por el retraso en contestar a su carta; **the writer of the libel was ordered to print a full apology** = se ordenó al autor del libelo que publicara una disculpa detallada

a posteriori ['eɪ pɒsteri'ɔːraɪ] *Latin phrase* a posteriori *or* 'de lo que se ha concluido más tarde'; **a posteriori argument** = argumento *m* basado en la observación

apparent [ə'pærənt] *adjective* aparente *or* claro, -ra *or* evidente *or* manifiesto, -ta; **apparent defect** = defecto *m* manifiesto; **heir apparent** = heredero *m* forzoso *or* presunto heredero

appeal [ə'piːl] **1** *noun* apelación *f or* recurso *m* petición *f;* **appeal against conviction** = recurso *or* apelación contra condena; **appeal against sentence** = recurso de apelación; **appeal for legal protection** = recurso de amparo; **Appeal Court** *or* **Court of Appeal** = Tribunal *m* de Apelación; **Lord of Appeal in Ordinary** = uno de los once lores que actúa como miembro de la Cámara de los Lores cuando ésta funciona como Tribunal de Apelación; **appeal to the Supreme Court** = recurso de casación; **open to appeal** = impugnable; **not open to appeal** = inapelable; **the appeal from the court order** *or* **the appeal against the planning decision will be heard next month** = se presentará el próximo mes el recurso contra la resolución de planificación *or* el recurso de la sentencia del tribunal; **he lost his appeal for damages against the company** = perdió el recurso por daños y perjuicios contra la compañía; **she won her case on appeal** = ganó el caso por apelación **2** *verb* recurrir *or* apelar; **to appeal against a sentence** = impugnar una sentencia; **the company appealed against the decision of the planning officers** = la empresa recurrió contra la decisión de los funcionarios de planificación; **he has appealed to the Supreme Court** = ha apelado al Tribunal Supremo (NOTE: you appeal **to** a court or **against** a decision; an appeal is **heard** and **allowed** or **dismissed**);

COMMENT: in English law, in the majority of cases decisions of lower courts and of the High Court can be appealed to the Court of Appeal. The Court of Appeal is divided into the Civil Division and the Criminal Division. The Civil Division hears appeals from the County Court and the High Court; the Criminal Division hears appeals from the Crown Court. From the Court of Appeal, appeal lies to the House of Lords. When the remedies available under English law are exhausted, it is in certain cases possible to appeal to the European Court of Justice. For many countries (especially Commonwealth countries) appeals may be heard from the highest court of these countries by the Privy Council

appear [ə'pɪə] *verb* **(a)** *(to seem)* parecer *or* mostrarse; **the witness appeared to have difficulty in remembering what had happened** = el testigo parecía tener dificultad para recordar lo que había pasado **(b)** *(show up)* aparecer *or* apersonarse *or* personarse; *(to stand trial)* comparecer; **failure to appear** = no comparecer ante los tribunales **(c)** *(to represent a client in court)* representar a; **Mr A. Clark QC is appearing on behalf of the defendant** = el Sr. Clark QC representa al demandado

◊ **appearance** [ə'pɪərəns] *noun* comparecencia *f;* **to enter an appearance** = entregar documentos en el juzgado por parte de la defensa *or* registrar comparecencia por parte de la defensa; **entry of appearance** = entrega de documentos en el juzgado por parte del defendido *or* registro de comparecencia por la defensa

appease [ə'piːz] *verb* apaciguar

appellant [ə'pelənt] *noun* apelante *mf or* recurrente *mf*

appellate [ə'pelət] *adjective* de apelación; **appellate jurisdiction** = jurisdicción *f* en apelación: competencia de la Cámara de los Lores británica para ver apelaciones; **appellate court;** *see* APPEAL COURT

appendix [ə'pendɪks] *noun* apéndice *m;* **the markets covered by the agency agreement are listed in the Appendix** = los mercados que cubre el contrato de representación se listan en el Apéndice; **see Appendix B for the clear-up rates of notifiable offences** = véase el Apéndice B para la relación de delitos graves (NOTE: plural is **appendices**)

apply [ə'plaɪ] *verb* **(a)** *(to ask for)* solicitar; **to apply for a job** = solicitar *or* pedir un trabajo; **to apply for shares** = suscribirse a *or* solicitar acciones; **to apply in writing** = solicitar por escrito; **to apply in person** = solicitar personalmente; **my client wishes to apply for Legal Aid** = mi cliente desea solicitar defensa de oficio; **he applied for judicial review** *or* **for**

compensation *or* for an adjournment = solicitó revisión judicial *or* indemnización *or* un aplazamiento; **to apply to the Court** = dirigirse al tribunal para solicitar algo; **he applied to the Court for an injunction** = solicitó un requerimiento *or* un interdicto al tribunal **(b)** *(affect)* afectar *or* ser aplicable a *or* referirse a; **this clause applies only to deals outside the EU** = esta cláusula sólo es aplicable fuera de la UE; **the legal precedent applies to cases where the parents of the child are divorced** = el precedente legal se refiere únicamente a los casos en los que los padres del niño estén divorciados

◊ **applicant** ['æplɪkənt] *noun* solicitante *mf or* aspirante *mf or* candidato, -ta; **applicant for a job** *or* **job applicant** = solicitante de un trabajo *or* candidato a un puesto de trabajo; **there were thousands of applicants for shares in the new company** = había miles de suscriptores de acciones en la nueva compañía

◊ **application** [æplɪ'keɪʃn] *noun* **(a)** *(asking for something in writing)* solicitud *f or* petición *f;* **application for shares** = solicitud *or* suscripción de acciones; **shares payable on application** = acciones a pagar por suscripción *or* pagaderas al ser solicitadas; **application for a job** *or* **job application** = solicitud *or* petición de un trabajo; **application form** = impreso *m* de solicitud; **to fill in an application (form) for a job** *or* **a job application (form)** = rellenar un impreso de solicitud para un trabajo; **letter of application** = *(job)* carta de solicitud; *(shares)* carta de suscripción (de acciones) **(b)** *(asking the court to make an order)* solicitud de algo al tribunal; **his application for an injunction was refused** = se rechazó su solicitud de un requerimiento judicial; **solicitors acting for the wife made an application for a maintenance order** = los abogados que representaban a la esposa solicitaron una orden de manutención

appoint [ə'pɔɪnt] *verb* nombrar *or* designar; **to appoint James Smith to the post of manager** = nombrar a James Smith director; **the government has appointed a QC to head the inquiry** = el gobierno ha designado un abogado de prestigio para encabezar la investigación; **the court appointed a receiver** = el tribunal designó un depositario judicial (NOTE: you appoint a person **to** a job or **to do** a job)

◊ **appointee** [əpɔɪn'tiː] *noun* designado, -da *or* delegado, -da

◊ **appointment** [ə'pɔɪntmənt] *noun* **(a)** *(meeting)* cita *f or* compromiso *m;* **by appointment** = previa cita; **to make** *or* **to fix an appointment for two o'clock** = darse cita *or* citarse para las dos; **to make an appointment with someone for two o'clock** = citarse con alguien para las dos; **he was late for his appointment** = llegó tarde a la cita; **she had to cancel her appointment** = tuvo que anular

la cita; **appointments book** = agenda **(b)** *(to a job)* nombramiento *m;* **on his appointment as magistrate** = en su nombramiento como magistrado; **letter of appointment** = carta *f or* notificación *f* del nombramiento para un puesto de trabajo **(c)** *(job)* puesto *m or* empleo *m;* **legal appointments vacant** = ofertas *fpl* de empleo (jurídico) **(d)** **power of appointment** = poder *m* que tiene el apoderado para disponer de una propiedad

apportion [ə'pɔːʃn] *verb* repartir *or* asignar proporcionalmente *or* distribuir; **costs are apportioned according to planned revenue** = los costes se asignan proporcionalmente según los ingresos planificados

◊ **apportionment** [ə'pɔːʃnmənt] *noun* asignación *f* proporcional *or* prorrateo *m*

appraisal [ə'preɪzl] *noun* avalúo *m*

appraise [ə'preɪz] *verb* tasar *or* valorar *or* evaluar

◊ **appraiser** [ə'preɪzə] *noun* tasador *m* persona que hace una evaluación

appreciate [ə'priːʃɪeɪt] *verb* **(a)** *(quality)* apreciar *or* valorar; **a judge always appreciates a well-documented case** = un juez siempre valora un caso bien documentado **(b)** *(value)* revalorizarse *or* aumentar en valor; **property values have appreciated by 20% over the last two years** = el valor de la propiedad se ha revalorizado en un 20% en los dos últimos años

◊ **appreciation** [əpriːʃɪ'eɪʃn] *noun* **(a)** *(increase in value)* revalorización *f or* aumento *m* en valor *or* en precio **(b)** *(valuing something highly)* aprecio *m or* valoración *f or* estimación *f or* reconocimiento *m;* **in appreciation of** = en aprecio por *or* en reconocimiento de

apprehend [æprɪ'hend] *verb formal* **(a)** *(to understand)* comprender *or* entender; **I apprehend that you say your client has a reference** = entiendo que usted dice que su cliente tiene una referencia **(b)** *(to arrest)* prender *or* detener; **the suspect was apprehended at the scene of the crime** = se detuvo al sospechoso en la escena del crimen

◊ **apprehension** [æprɪ'henʃn] *noun formal* prendimiento *m or* detención *f*

approach [ə'prəʊtʃ] **1** *noun* **(a)** *(proposal)* propuesta *f or* proposición *f;* **the company has had an approach from an Australian consortium** = la empresa ha recibido una propuesta de un consorcio australiano **(b)** *(method)* enfoque *m or* aproximación *f or* modo *m* de enfocar una cuestión *or* de abordar un problema; **he has a professional approach to his work** = tiene un modo profesional de enfocar su trabajo **2** *verb* **(a)** *(to make a proposal)* dirigirse a (para hacer una propuesta *or* una petición); **he approached the bank with a request for a loan** = se dirigió al banco para pedir un préstamo; **the company was approached by an Australian publisher with the suggestion of a merger** = el editor australiano se dirigió a la empresa para proponer una fusión **(b)** *(to come or to bring closer)* acercarse a *or* aproximarse a; **the offer does not approach the figure my client seeks** = la oferta no se aproxima a la cifra que solicita mi cliente

appropriate 1 [əˈprəʊprɪət] *adjective* apropiado, -da *or* conveniente; **where appropriate** = en su caso; **is a fine an appropriate punishment for sex offences?** = ¿es una multa un castigo apropiado para los delitos contra la libertad sexual? **2** [əˈprəʊprɪeɪt] *verb* asignar *or* consignar *or* apropiarse de; **the town council appropriated the land to build the new municipal offices** = el ayuntamiento se apropió de la tierra para construir las nuevas oficinas municipales
◊ **appropriation** [əprəʊprɪˈeɪʃn] *noun* asignación *f or* consignación *f or* apropiación *f;* **appropriations committee** = comité *m* que inspecciona los gastos del gobierno

approve [əˈpruːv] *verb* **(a)** *(to agree something officially)* aprobar; **to approve the terms of a contract** = aprobar los términos de un contrato; **the proposal was approved by the board** = la junta aprobó la propuesta; **the motion was approved by the committee** = la comisión aprobó la moción **(b) to approve of** = aprobar
◊ **approval** [əˈpruːvl] *noun* **(a)** *(agreement)* aprobación *f or* consentimiento *m;* **to submit a budget for approval** = someter un presupuesto a aprobación; **certificate of approval** = certificado *m* de aprobación **(b) on approval** = (venta) *f* a prueba
◊ **approved school** [əˈpruːvd ˈskuːl] *noun* correccional *m*

appurtenant [əˈpɜːtɪnənt] *adjective* dependiente de *or* perteneciente a
◊ **appurtenances** [əˈpɜːtɪnənsɪz] *plural noun* pertenencias *fpl or* tierra *f or* edificaciones *fpl* dependientes de o pertenecientes a una propiedad

a priori [ˈeɪ praɪˈɔːraɪ] *Latin phrase* 'desde el principio' *or* a priori; **a priori argument** = razonamiento *m* basado en ideas *or* suposiciones, no en casos reales

arbitrate [ˈɑːbɪtreɪt] *verb* arbitrar; **to arbitrate in a dispute** = arbitrar en una disputa
◊ **arbitration** [ɑːbɪˈtreɪʃn] *noun* arbitraje *m;* **to submit a dispute to arbitration** = someter una disputa a arbitraje; **to refer a question to arbitration** = confiar un asunto a un juez árbitro; **to take a dispute to arbitration** = llevar una disputa a arbitraje; **to go to arbitration** = acudir al arbitraje; **arbitration agreement** = acuerdo *m* de arbitraje; **arbitration award** = laudo *m* arbitral; **arbitration board** *or* **arbitration tribunal** = cámara *f or* junta *f or* comisión *f* de arbitraje *or* arbitral; **industrial arbitration tribunal** = tribunal *m* de arbitraje

industrial; **to accept the ruling of the arbitration board** = aceptar la decisión de la comisión de arbitraje; **out-of-court arbitration** = arbitraje extrajudicial
◊ **arbitrator** [ˈɑːbɪtreɪtə] *noun* árbitro *m or* juez *m* árbitro; **industrial arbitrator** = árbitro industrial *or* laboral; **to accept** *or* **to reject the arbitrator's ruling** = aceptar *or* rechazar la decisión del juez árbitro

area [ˈeərɪə] *noun* zona *f;* **danger area** = zona de peligro; **disaster area** = zona de desastre; **residential area** = zona residencial

argue [ˈɑːgjuː] *verb* **(a)** *(to discuss)* discutir *or* debatir; **they argued over** *or* **about the price** = discutieron sobre el precio; **counsel spent hours arguing about the precise meaning of the clause** = el abogado discutió durante horas el significado preciso de la cláusula; **the union officials argued among themselves over the best way to deal with the ultimatum from the management** = los cargos sindicales discutieron la mejor forma de hacer frente al ultimátum de la dirección **(b)** *(to give reasons)* razonar *or* argüir *or* alegar; **prosecuting counsel argued that the accused should be given exemplary sentences** = el fiscal arguyó que los acusados debían ser condenados a sentencias ejemplares; **the police solicitor argued against granting bail** = el abogado de la policía alegó razones en contra de conceder la libertad bajo fianza (NOTE: you argue with someone about or over something)
◊ **argument** [ˈɑːgjumənt] *noun* **(a)** *(discussing without agreing)* discusión *f or* disputa *f or* debate *m;* **they got into an argument with the judge over the relevance of the documents to the case** = entraron en una discusión con el juez acerca de la importancia de los documentos para el caso; **he sacked his solicitor after an argument over costs** = despidió a su abogado tras una disputa sobre las costas **(b)** *(giving reasons)* argumento *m;* **the judge found the defence arguments difficult to follow** = al juez le resultaron difíciles de seguir los argumentos de la defensa; **counsel presented the argument for the prosecution** = el abogado presentó los argumentos para la acusación; **the Court of Appeal was concerned that the judge at first instance had delivered judgment without proper argument** = al Tribunal de Apelación le inquietaba el hecho de que el juez de primera instancia hubiera pronunciado la sentencia sin tener unos argumentos apropiados (NOTE: can be used without the)

arise [əˈraɪz] *verb* surgir *or* producirse *or* derivar de; **the situation has arisen because neither party is capable of paying the costs of the case** = la situación se ha producido porque ninguna de las partes puede pagar las costas del caso; **the problem arises from the difficulty in understanding the VAT regulations** = el problema deriva de la dificultad para comprender las disposiciones del IVA; **matters arising** = cuestiones pendientes (NOTE: **arising - arose - arisen**)

aristocracy [ærɪs'tɒkrəsi] *noun* aristocracia *f;* **the aristocracy supported the military dictatorship** = la aristocracia apoyó la dictadura militar
◊ **aristocrat** ['ærɪstəkræt] *noun* aristócrata *mf;* **many aristocrats were killed during the revolution** = mataron a muchos aristócratas durante la revolución

arm [ɑːm] *noun* brazo *m*
◊ **arm's length** ['ɑːmz 'leŋθ] *noun* **at arm's length** = (mantenido) a distancia; **to deal with someone at arm's length** = mantener las distancias; **the directors were required to deal with the receiver at arm's length** = se pidió a los directores que mantuvieran las distancias con el depositario
◊ **armed** ['ɑːmd] *adj* armado, -da; **armed robbery** = robo a mano armada; **armed wing** = brazo armado

armistice ['ɑːmɪstɪs] *noun* armisticio *m*

armoured ['ɑːməd] *adj* acorazado, -da

armourer ['ɑːmərə] *noun (slang)* armero *m or* delincuente *mf* que proporciona armas para cometer delitos

arraign [ə'reɪn] *verb* procesar *or* presentar al tribunal *or* leer la acusación
◊ **arraignment** [ə'reɪnmənt] *noun* proceso *m or* procesamiento *m or* acusación *f* formal en un juicio

arrange [ə'reɪnʒ] *verb* **(a)** *(to put in order)* ordenar *or* arreglar *or* disponer; **the office is arranged as an open-plan area with small separate rooms for meetings** = la oficina está dispuesta en un espacio abierto con pequeñas salas aparte para las reuniones; **the files are arranged in alphabetical order** = los archivos están ordenados por orden alfabético; **to arrange the documents in order of their dates** = ordenar los documentos por fechas **(b)** *(to organize)* fijar *or* señalar *or* establecer; **the hearing was arranged for April** = la vista se fijó para abril; **we arranged to have the meeting in their offices** = concertamos la reunión en sus oficinas; **she arranged for a car to meet him at the airport** = organizó un coche para que le recogiera en el aeropuerto (NOTE: you arrange **for** someone to do something or you arrange **for** something to be done)
◊ **arrangement** [ə'reɪnʒmənt] *noun* **(a)** *(way in which something is organized)* arreglo *m or* disposición *f or* orden *m or* plan *m;* **the company secretary is making all the arrangements for the AGM** = la secretaria de la empresa está haciendo todos los preparativos para la Junta General Anual **(b)** *(financial)* acuerdo *m or* convenio *f* ajuste *m or* acomodo *m;* **to come to an arrangement with the**

creditors = llegar a un acuerdo con los acreedores; **deed of arrangement** = escritura *f* de acuerdo; **scheme of arrangement** = proyecto *m* de acuerdo

arrears [ə'rɪəz] *plural noun* atrasos *mpl or* vencidos *mpl;* **to allow the payments to fall into arrears** = atrasarse en los pagos; **in arrears** = atrasado en los pagos *or* en mora; **the payments are six months in arrears** = los pagos llevan seis meses de atraso; **he is six weeks in arrears with his rent** = lleva seis semanas de atraso en el pago de su alquiler

arrest [ə'rest] **1** *noun* **(a)** *(to take and charge someone with a crime)* detención *f or* arresto *m;* **citizen's arrest** = arresto civil; **house arrest** = arresto domiciliario; **false arrest** = arresto *or* detención ilegal; **summary arrest** = detención sin una orden; **a warrant is out for his arrest** = se ha ordenado su detención; **under arrest** = detenido, -da; **six of the gang are in the police station under arrest** = seis miembros de la banda están detenidos en la comisaría; **the opposition leader has been under house arrest for six months** = el jefe de la oposición ha estado bajo arresto domiciliario durante seis meses **(b) arrest of judgment** = prórroga *f or* suspensión *f* del pronunciamiento de una sentencia **2** *verb* **(a)** *(people)* detener *or* prender; *(with confinment)* arrestar; **two of the strikers were arrested** = detuvieron a dos de los huelguistas; **the constable stopped the car and arrested the driver** = el policía paró el coche y detuvo al conductor **(b)** *(to seize a ship or cargo)* incautar *or* embargar
◊ **arrestable offence** [ə'restəbl ə'fens] *noun* delito *m* con pena de arresto
◊ **arrest warrant** [ə'rest 'wɒrənt] *noun* orden *m* de detención *or* de arresto

COMMENT: any citizen may arrest a person who is committing a serious offence, though members of the police force have wider powers, in particular the power to arrest persons on suspicion of a serious crime or in cases where an arrest warrant has been granted. Generally a policeman is not entitled to arrest someone without a warrant if the person does not know or is not told the reason for his arrest

arson ['ɑːsən] *noun* incendio *m* intencionado o provocado; **he was charged with arson** = se le acusó de incendio intencionado; **during the riot there were ten cases of looting and two of arson** = durante el motín hubo diez casos de robo y dos incendios intencionados; **the police who are investigating the fire suspect arson** = la policía que investiga el incendio sospecha que fue intencionado; **an arson attack on a house** = incendiar una casa
◊ **arsonist** ['ɑːsənɪst] *noun* incendiario, -ria

article ['ɑːtɪkl] *noun* **(a)** *(product)* artículo *m or* producto *m;* **a black market in imported articles of clothing** = un mercado negro en prendas de vestir importadas **(b)** *(section of a legal agreement)* artículo *or* sección *f or* cláusula *f;* **see article 8 of the contract** = ver artículo 8 del contrato **(c)** *(in a company)* **articles of association** *or* **US articles of incorporation** = escritura *f* de constitución *or* estatutos *mpl* de asociación; **articles of partnership** = contrato *m* de asociación; **he is a director appointed under the articles of the company** = es director nombrado conforme a los estatutos de la sociedad; **this procedure is not allowed under the articles of association of the company** = los estatutos de asociación de la empresa no permiten este procedimiento **(d)** *(legal profession)* **articles** = periodo *m* durante el cual un pasante trabaja para un despacho de abogados aprendiendo derecho; **articles of indenture** = contrato por el cual un artesano aprendiz trabaja para un maestro durante algunos años para aprender un oficio; **to serve articles** = servir bajo contrato a un abogado para aprender derecho **(e)** *US* **articles of impeachment** = formulación *f* de cargos contra un alto funcionario
◊ **articled** ['ɑːtɪkld] *adjective;* **articled clerk** = pasante *mf* de abogado

artificial person ['ɑːtɪfɪʃl 'pɜːsən] *noun* persona *f* jurídica

aside [ə'saɪd] *adverb* a un lado *or* aparte; **to put aside** *or* **to set aside** = desestimar; **the appeal court set aside the earlier judgment** = el tribunal de apelación desestimó la sentencia anterior

ask [ɑːsk] *verb* **(a)** *(to question)* preguntar *or* pedir (una explicación, etc.); **prosecuting counsel asked the accused why the can of petrol was in his car** = el fiscal preguntó al acusado por qué el bidón de petróleo estaba en su coche **(b)** *(to tell someone to do something)* pedir; **the police officers asked the marchers to go home** = los agentes de policía pidieron a los manifestantes que se fueran a casa; **she asked her secretary to fetch a file from the managing director's office** = pidió a su secretario que fuera a buscar un archivo del despacho del director gerente; **the customs officials asked him to open his case** = los funcionarios de la aduana le pidieron que abriera su maleta; **the judge asked the witness to write the name on a piece of paper** = el juez pidió al testigo que escribiera el nombre en un papel
◊ **ask for** ['ɑːsk 'fɔː] *verb* **(a)** *(to say that you want or need)* solicitar *or* reclamar *or* preguntar por; **to ask for a loan** = pedir un préstamo; **he asked for the file on 1993 debtors** = solicitó el archivo de los deudores de 1993; **counsel asked for more time to consult with his colleagues** = el abogado solicitó más tiempo para consultar con sus colegas; **there is a man on the phone asking for Mr Smith** = hay un señor en el teléfono que pregunta por el Sr.

Smith; **to ask for bail to be granted** = solicitar que se conceda la libertad bajo fianza **(b)** *(price)* pedir; **they are asking £24,000 for the car** = piden 24.000 libras por el coche

assail [ə'seɪl] *verb* arremeter

assassin [ə'sæsɪn] *noun* asesino, -na
◊ **assassinate** [ə'sæsɪneɪt] *verb* asesinar
◊ **assassination** [əsæsɪ'neɪʃn] *noun* asesinato *m;* *(of a political figure)* magnicidio *m*

assault [ə'sɒlt] **1** *noun* violencia *f or* asalto *m or* agresión *f or* insulto *m;* **simple assault** = acometimiento *m;* **assault and battery** = acometimiento y agresión; **sexual assault** = agresión sexual; **he was sent to prison for assault** = se le envió a prisión por asalto; **the number of cases of assault** *or* **the number of assaults on policemen is increasing** = el número de asaltos a policías está aumentando; *see also* BATTERY (NOTE: as a crime or tort, assault has no plural; when it has a plural this means 'cases of assault') **2** *verb* asaltar *or* atacar *or* acometer; **she was assaulted by two muggers** = fue asaltada por dos atracadores

COMMENT: assault should be distinguished from battery, in that assault is the threat of violence, whereas battery is actual violence. However, because the two are so closely connected, the term 'assault' is frequently used as a general term for violence to a person. 'Aggravated assault' is assault causing serious injury or carried out in connection with another serious crime. The term 'common assault' is frequently used for any assault which is not an aggravated assault

assay [ə'seɪ] *noun* ensaye *m;* **assay mark** = sello *m* de contraste *or* marca *f* de ensaye

assemble [ə'sembl] *verb* **(a)** *(to put something together)* reunir *or* juntar *or* montar; **he assembled the engine with stolen parts** = montó el motor con piezas robadas; **the police are still assembling all the evidence** = la policía está reuniendo todas las pruebas **(b)** *(to gather)* reunirse *or* juntarse *or* congregar; **the crowd assembled in front of the police station** = la multitud se congregó delante de la comisaría de policía
◊ **assembly** [ə'sembli] *noun* **(a)** *(group of people)* reunión *f or* asamblea *f;* **freedom of assembly** = libertad *f* de reunión; **unlawful assembly** = reunión ilegal **(b)** *(the Assembly of the EU* = la Asamblea de la UE *or* el Parlamento Europeo; **the General Assembly of the United Nations** = la Asamblea General de las Naciones Unidas
◊ **assemblyman** [ə'sembliman] *noun* miembro de una asamblea (legislativa) (NOTE: many national legislatures are called 'National Assemblies' in English)

assent [ə'sent] *noun* consentimiento *m or* aprobación *f;* **Royal Assent** = aprobación formal de un proyecto de ley para que se convierta en Ley del Parlamento *or* parlamentaria

assert [ə'sə:t] *verb* afirmar *or* declarar *or* sostener *or* asegurar; **he asserted that the damage suffered was extremely serious** = declaró que los daños sufridos eran muy graves
◊ **assertion** [ə'sə:ʃn] *noun* afirmación *f or* declaración *f or* aseveración *f;* **counsel made a series of assertions which were disputed by the witness** = el abogado hizo una serie de declaraciones que el testigo discutió

assess [ə'ses] *verb* valorar *or* tasar *or* fijar; **to assess damages at £1,000** = valorar daños en 1.000 libras; **to assess a property for the purposes of insurance** = fijar el valor de una propiedad para asegurarla
◊ **assessment** [ə'sesmənt] *noun* valoración *f or* tasación *f or* fijación *f;* **assessment of damages** = valoración de daños *or* determinación de los daños; **assessment of property** = fijación del valor de una propiedad; **tax assessment** = estimación *f* de la base impositiva
◊ **assessor** [ə'sesə] *noun* asesor, -ra

asset ['æsɪt] *noun* posesión *f or* activo *m or* bien *m;* **he has an excess of assets over liabilities** = su activo supera el pasivo; **her assets are only £640 as against liabilities of £24,000** = sus activos son de 640 libras únicamente, frente a unos pasivos de 24.000 libras; **concealment of assets** = ocultación *f* de bienes; **capital assets** *or* **fixed assets** = activo fijo; **current assets** = activo circulante; **fictitious assets** = activo ficticio; **frozen assets** = activo congelado; **intangible assets** = activo intangible; **liquid assets** = activo líquido; **personal assets** = bienes muebles; **tangible assets** = activo tangible; **asset value** = valor *m* de activo

assign [ə'saɪn] *verb* **(a)** *(to give legally)* ceder *or* transferir; **to assign a right to someone** = ceder un derecho a alguien; **to assign shares to someone** = repartir acciones a alguien; **to assign a debt to someone** = ceder un crédito a alguien **(b)** *(to give a job)* asignar; **he was assigned the job of checking the numbers of stolen cars** = se le asignó la tarea de comprobar los números de los coches robados; **three detectives have been assigned to the case** = se han asignado tres detectives para el caso
◊ **assignee** [əsaɪ'ni:] *noun* cesionario, -ria; **assignee in bankruptcy** = cesionario de bienes del fallido
◊ **assignment** [ə'saɪnmənt] *noun* **(a)** *(legal transfer of property)* cesión *f or* traspaso *m or* trasmisión *f;* **assignment of a patent** *or* **of a copyright** = cesión de una patente *or* de los derechos de autor *or* de la propiedad intelectual; **assignment of a lease** = cesión de arrendamiento; **deed of assignment** = escritura *f* de cesión **(b)** *(document)* escritura de cesión de bienes **(c)** *(particular job)* cometido *m or* misión *f or* tarea *f;*

we have put six constables on that particular assignment = hemos puesto a tres policías en esa misión especial
◊ **assignor** [ə'saɪnə] *noun* cedente *mf or* cesionista *mf*
◊ **assigns** [ə'saɪnz] *plural noun* cesionarios *mpl;* **his heirs and assigns** = sus herederos y cesionarios

assist [ə'sɪst] *verb* ayudar *or* asistir; **the accused had to be assisted into the dock** = se ayudó al acusado a llegar al banquillo de los acusados; **assisted person** = persona que recibe asistencia jurídica gratuita bajo el sistema de 'Legal Aid'
◊ **assistance** [ə'sɪstəns] *noun* ayuda *f or* auxilio *m;* **financial assistance** = ayuda financiera; **legal assistance** = asistencia letrada; **litigants who receive assistance under the Legal Aid scheme** = litigantes que reciben asistencia jurídica gratuita bajo el sistema de 'Legal Aid'
◊ **assistant** [ə'sɪstənt] *noun* asistente *mf or* auxiliar *mf or* ayudante *mf*

Assizes *or* **Assize Courts** [ə'saɪzɪz *or* ə'saɪz 'kɔ:ts] *plural noun* antiguo nombre para lo que ahora es el *Crown Court*

associate [ə'səʊʃieɪt] **1** *adjective* asociado, -da; **associate company** = empresa *f* asociada; **associate director** = director *m* asociado **2** *noun* asociado, -da *or* socio, -cia; **in his testimony he named six associates** = en su declaración nombró a seis asociados; **associate of the Crown Office** = secretario *m* de juzgado **3** *verb* juntarse *or* tratar con *or* frecuentar la compañía de; **she associated with criminals** = frecuentaba la compañía de criminales
◊ **Associate Justice** *noun US* juez suplente
◊ **associated** [ə'səʊʃieɪtɪd] *adjective* asociado, -da *or* afiliado, -da; **Smith Ltd and its associated company, Jones Brothers** = Smith Ltd y su empresa afiliada, Jones Brothers
◊ **association** [əsəʊʃi'eɪʃn] *noun* **(a)** *(group of people or companies)* asociación *f or* agrupación *f;* **trade association** = asociación comercial; **employers' association** = asociación de empresarios; **freedom of association** = libertad *f* de asociación; **guilt by association** = culpable por asociación **(b)** **articles of association** = escritura *f* de asociación; **memorandum of association** = escritura de constitución **(c)** *(in prison)* recreo *m or* paseo *m*

assume [ə'sju:m] *verb* **(a)** *(to believe something without any proof)* suponer; **everyone assumed he was guilty** = todo el mundo supuso que era culpable **(b)** *(to take on)* asumir; **to assume all risks** = asumir todos los riesgos; **he has assumed responsibility for marketing** = ha asumido la responsabilidad de la comercialización de productos
◊ **assumption** [ə'sʌmpʃn] *noun* asunción *f;* **assumption of risks** = asunción de riesgos

assure [ə'ʃʊə] *verb* asegurar; **the assured** = el asegurado
◊ **assurance** [ə'ʃʊrəns] *noun* seguro *m*
◊ **assurer** *or* **assuror** [ə'ʃʊərə] *noun* asegurador, -ra

COMMENT: **assure** and **assurance** are used in Britain for insurance policies relating to something which will certainly happen (such as death or the end of a given period of time); for other types of policy use **insure** and **insurance**

asylum [ə'saɪləm] *noun* **(a)** *(hospital)* manicomio *m* or hospital *m* psiquiátrico **(b)** *(safe place)* asilo *m;* **to ask for political asylum** = pedir asilo político

at issue ['æt 'ɪʃuː] *see* ISSUE

attach [ə'tætʃ] *verb* **(a)** *(to fasten or to join)* sujetar *or* unir *or* adjuntar; **I am attaching a copy of my previous letter** = le adjunto una copia de mi carta anterior; **attached is a copy of my letter of June 24th** = le envío adjunta una copia de mi carta del 24 de junio **(b)** *(to arrest)* embargar *or* incautar
◊ **attachment** [ə'tætʃmənt] *noun* **(a)** *(action)* embargo *m* or incautación *f;* **attachment of earnings** = incautación de ingresos; **attachment of earnings order** = orden *f* de incautación de ingresos **(b)** *(document)* **warrant of attachment** = mandato *m* que autoriza al alguacil a detener a una persona por desacato al juez

attack [ə'tæk] **1** *noun* **(a)** *(harm)* agresión *f* or asalto *m;* **there has been an increase in attacks on police** *or* **in terrorist attacks on planes** = los actos de agresión contra la policía *or* los asaltos terroristas a los aviones van en aumento **(b)** *(criticism)* ataque *m;* **the newspaper published an attack on the government** = el periódico publicó un ataque al gobierno **2** *verb (to hurt or to harm)* agredir *or* asaltar *or* acometer *or* arremeter; **the security guard was attacked by three men carrying guns** = tres hombres armados agredieron al guardia de seguridad **(b)** *(to criticize)* atacar; **MPs attacked the government for not spending enough money on the police** = los diputados atacaron al gobierno por no gastar suficiente dinero en la policía (NOTE: you attack someone, but make an attack on someone)
◊ **attacker** [ə'tækə] *noun* agresor, -ra *or* asaltante *mf;* **she recognized her attacker and gave his description to the police** = reconoció a su agresor y dio su descripción a la policía

attainder [ə'teɪndə] *noun* proscripción *f;* **bill of attainder** = decreto *m* de proscripción

attempt [ə'tempt] **1** *noun* **(a)** *(try)* intento *m* or tentativa *f;* **the company made an attempt to break into the American market** = la empresa intentó penetrar en el mercado americano; **the takeover attempt was turned down by the board** = la junta rechazó la tentativa de absorción de la empresa; **all his attempts to get a job have failed** = todos sus intentos de encontrar un trabajo han sido fallidos **(b)** *(assault)* atentado *m;* **to make an attempt on a person's life** = atentar contra alguien; **attempt is a crime even if the attempted offence has not been committed** = el atentado es un crimen aunque el delito no se haya cometido **2** *verb* intentar *or* tratar de; **the solicitor attempted to have the charge dropped** = el abogado intentó que se retiraran los cargos; **he was accused of attempting to contact a member of the jury** = se le acusó de tratar de ponerse en contacto con un miembro del jurado; **attempted murder** = intento de asesinato *or* homicidio frustrado

attend [ə'tend] *verb* asistir; **the witnesses were subpoenaed to attend the trial** = citaron a los testigos para asistir al juicio
◊ **attend to** [ə'tend 'tʊ] *verb* atender *or* ocuparse de *or* prestar atención a; **the managing director will attend to your complaint personally** = el director gerente se ocupará de su reclamación personalmente
◊ **attendance** [ə'tendəns] *noun* asistencia *f;* **attendance centre** = prisión de régimen abierto
◊ **attention** [ə'tenʃn] *noun* atención *f;* **for the attention of the Managing Director** = a la atención del Director Gerente; **your orders will have our best attention** = sus pedidos recibirán nuestra máxima atención

attest [ə'test] *verb* certificar *or* confirmar (una firma) *or* compulsar *or* dar fe; **to attest a signature** = legalizar una firma
◊ **attestation** [æte'steɪʃn] *noun* certificación *f or* confirmación *f* (de una firma) *or* atestación *f;* **attestation clause** = cláusula *f* que certifica la firma de las partes

COMMENT: the attestation clause is usually written: 'signed sealed and delivered by ... in the presence of ...'

attorn [ə'tɜːn] *verb* trasferir *or* ceder
◊ **attorney** [ə'tɜːni] *noun* **(a)** *(legally allowed to act on behalf of someone else)* apoderado, -da; **letter of attorney** = documento *m* que certifica que alguien es apoderado; **power of attorney** = poder *m* (notarial); **his solicitor was granted power of attorney** = su abogado recibió poder (notarial) **(b)** *US* abogado, -da
◊ **Attorney-General** [ə'tɜːni'dʒenrl] *noun GB* Fiscal *mf* de la Corona *US* Ministro, -tra de Justicia *or* Fiscal General del Estado

COMMENT: in the US Federal Government, the Attorney-General is in charge of the Department of Justice

attribute [ə'trɪbjuːt] *verb* atribuir; **remarks attributed to the Chief Constable** = observaciones atribuidas al Jefe de Policía
◊ **attributable** [ə'trɪbjʊtəbl] *adjective* atribuible

auction ['ɔːkʃn] **1** *noun* subasta *f;* **mock auction** = simulacro *m* de subasta; **to put something up for auction** = subastar *or* poner en pública subasta **2** *verb* subastar; **the factory was closed and the machinery was auctioned off** = cerraron la fábrica y subastaron la maquinaria
◊ **auctioneer** [ɔːkʃə'niːə] *noun* subastador, -ra

audi alteram partem ['aʊdi 'ælterəm 'paːtəm] *Latin phrase* 'oír la otra parte': regla en derecho natural por la que toda persona tiene derecho a hablar en su propia defensa y a que le expliquen las acusaciones alegadas contra ella

audience ['ɔːdiəns] *noun* audiencia *f or* derecho *m* a hablar a un tribunal; **a barrister has right of audience in any court in England and Wales** = un abogado tiene derecho de audiencia en cualquier tribunal de Inglaterra y Gales (NOTE: solicitors now have right of audience in some courts)

audit ['ɔːdɪt] **1** *noun* revisión *f or* intervención *f* de cuentas *or* auditoría *f;* **to carry out an annual audit** = efectuar una revisión de cuentas anual; **external audit** *or* **independent audit** = revisión contable por un técnico independiente *or* intervención externa; **general audit** = intervención general; **internal audit** = intervención interna **2** *verb* revisar *or* intervenir (las cuentas); **to audit the accounts** = revisar las cuentas; **the books have not yet been audited** = los libros aún no han sido revisados
◊ **auditor** ['ɔːdɪtə] *noun* interventor, -ra *or* revisor, -ra de cuentas *or* auditor, -ra; **the AGM appoints the company's auditors** = la Junta General Anual nombra a los auditores de la empresa; **Comptroller and Auditor General** = Interventor y Auditor General; **external auditor** = auditor externo o independiente *or* interventor externo o independiente; **internal auditor** = interventor *or* auditor interno

authentic [ɔː'θentɪk] *adjective* auténtico, -ca; *(reliable)* fehaciente
◊ **authentically** [ɔː'θentɪkli] *adverb* auténticamente
◊ **authenticity** [ɔːθen'tɪsɪti] *noun* autenticidad *f*

authenticate [ɔː'θentɪkeɪt] *verb* autenticar *or* autentificar *or* legalizar; **to authenticate a signature** = autorizar una firma

authority [ɔː'θɒrəti] *noun* **(a)** *(official power given to someone to do something)* autoridad *f or* autorización *f;* **public authority** = autoridad pública; **he has no authority to act on our behalf** = no tiene autorización para actuar en nuestro nombre; **she was acting on the authority of the court** = actuaba con la autorización del tribunal; **on whose authority was the charge brought?** = ¿quién dio la autorización para que se presentaran las acusaciones? **(b)** *(administration)* **local authority** = autoridad *f* local *or* gobierno *m* municipal; **a court can give directions to a local authority** = un tribunal puede dar órdenes a una

autoridad local; **a decision of the local authority pursuant to the powers and duties imposed upon it by the statutory code** = una decisión de la autoridad local de acuerdo con los poderes y obligaciones impuestos por la ley; **the Bill aims at giving protection to children in the care of a local authority** = el Proyecto de Ley pretende dar protección a los niños que están bajo la custodia de una autoridad local **(c) the authorities** = las autoridades
◊ **authoritarian** [ɔːθɒrɪ'teəriən] *adjective* autoritario, -ria; **authoritarian regime** = régimen autoritario
◊ **authoritarianism** [ɔːθɒrɪ'teəriənɪzm] *noun* autoritarismo *m*

authorize ['ɔːθəraɪz] *verb* **(a)** *(to give permission)* autorizar; **to authorize payment of £10,000** = autorizar el pago de 10.000 libras **(b)** *(to enable)* habilitar **(c)** *(to give authority)* autorizar; **to authorize someone to act on your behalf** = autorizar a alguien a actuar en nombre de uno mismo
◊ **authorization** [ɔːθəraɪ'zeɪʃn] *noun* **(a)** *(official permission)* autorización *f;* **do you have authorization for this expenditure?** = ¿tienes autorización para realizar este gasto?; **he has no authorization to act on our behalf** = no está autorizado para actuar en nuestro nombre **(b)** *(document)* autorización; **he showed the bank his authorization to inspect the contents of the safe** = mostró al banco su autorización para inspeccionar el contenido de la caja fuerte
◊ **authorized** ['ɔːθəraɪzd] *adjective* autorizado, -da; **authorized capital** = capital *m* autorizado; **authorized dealer** = agente *m* autorizado

automatic [ɔːtə'mætɪk] *adjective* automático, -ca; **there is an automatic increase in salaries on January 1st** = hay un aumento salarial automático el 1 de enero
◊ **automatically** [ɔːtə'mætɪkli] *adverb* automáticamente; **unpaid fines are automatically increased by 15%** = las multas no pagadas aumentan en un 15% automáticamente

automatism [ɔː'tɒmətɪzm] *noun* automatismo *m*

autonomy [ɔː'tɒnəmi] *noun* autonomía *f;* **the separatists are demanding full autonomy for their state** = los separatistas exigen el estado de autonomía para su país; **the government has granted the region a limited autonomy** = el gobierno ha concedido una autonomía limitada a la región
◊ **autonomous** [ɔː'tɒnəməs] *adjective* autónomo, -ma; **an autonomous regional government** = un gobierno regional autónomo; **the former Soviet Union was formed of several autonomous republics** = la antigua Unión Soviética estaba formada por varias repúblicas autónomas; **semi-autonomous** = semiautónomo, -ma

autopsy ['ɔːtɒpsi] *noun* autopsia *f or* necropsia *f or* necroscopia *f;* **to perform an autopsy** = practicar una autopsia

autrefois acquit ['əʊtrəfwæ ə'kiː] *French phrase meaning* 'ya absuelto': declaración de que un acusado ya ha sido absuelto del delito del que se le acusa
◊ **autrefois convict** ['əʊtrəfwæ kɒn'vɪkt] *French phrase meaning* 'ya condenado': declaración de que un acusado ya ha sido condenado por el delito del que se le acusa

AV ['eɪ 'viː] = ALTERNATIVE VOTE

available [ə'veɪləbl] *adjective* disponible *or* aprovechable; **the right of self-defence is only available against unlawful attack** = el derecho de auto-defensa sólo se puede utilizar contra un ataque ilícito

avenge [ə'venʒ] *verb* vindicar

aver [ə'vɜː] *verb* declarar *or* alegar (NOTE: **averring - averred)**
◊ **averment** [ə'vɜːmənt] *noun* declaración *f or* alegación *f*

average ['ævrɪdʒ] **1** *adjective* **(a)** *(middle figure)* medio, -dia; **average cost of expenses per employee** = coste medio de gastos por empleado; **the average figures for the last three months** = las cifras medias de los últimos tres meses; **the average increase in prices** = el aumento medio de precios **(b)** *(not very good)* regular *or* corriente; **the company's performance has been only average** = la actuación de la empresa ha sido sólo regular; **he is an average worker** = es un trabajador corriente **2** *noun* **(a)** *(number)* media *f or* promedio *m;* **the average for the last three months** *or* **the last three months' average** = la media de los tres últimos meses; **sales average** *or* **average of sales** = promedio de ventas; **on an average** = por regla general *or* por término medio; **on an average, £15 worth of goods are stolen every day** = por término medio, cada día se roban productos por valor de 15 libras **(b)** *(maritime law)* avería *f;* **average adjuster** = tasador, -ra de averías; **general average** = avería gruesa; **particular average** = pérdida *f* por avería simple **3** *verb* ser por término medio *or* resultar por regla general *or* alcanzar un promedio; **price increases have averaged 10% per annum** = los aumentos de precios son por término medio de un 10% por año; **days lost through sickness have averaged twenty-two over the last four years** = los días perdidos por enfermedad han resultado ser veintidós por término medio durante los últimos cuatro años
◊ **averager** ['ævrɪdʒə] *noun* persona que compra la misma acción en distintos momentos para conseguir un precio medio

avoid [ə'vɔɪd] *verb* **(a)** *(to try not to do something)* evitar *or* eludir; **the company is trying to avoid bankruptcy** = la empresa está tratando de evitar la quiebra; **my aim is to avoid paying too much tax** = mi propósito es evitar pagar demasiados impuestos; **we want to avoid direct competition with Smith Ltd** = queremos evitar la competencia directa con Smith Ltd; **to avoid creditors** = huir de los acreedores **(b)** *(to make something void)* anular *or* invalidar (NOTE: you avoid something or someone or avoid **doing** something)
◊ **avoidance** [ə'vɔɪdəns] *noun* **(a)** *(trying not to do something)* evitación *f or* elusión *f;* **avoidance of an agreement** *or* **of a contract** = evitación de un acuerdo *or* de un contrato; **tax avoidance** = elusión fiscal; *see also* EVASION **(b)** *(confession to a charge, suggesting that it should be cancelled)* invalidación *f or* anulación *f*

await [ə'weɪt] *verb* esperar *or* aguardar; **we are awaiting the decision of the planning department** = estamos esperando la decisión del departamento de planificación; **they are awaiting a decision of the court** = están esperando un fallo del tribunal; **the solicitor is awaiting our instructions** = el abogado espera nuestras órdenes

award [ə'wɔːd] **1** *noun* laudo *m or* fallo *m or* decisión *f or* sentencia *f;* **compensatory award** = laudo de indemnización; **an award by an industrial tribunal** = una sentencia de la magistratura de trabajo; **the arbitrator's award was set aside on appeal** = el laudo del juez *or* árbitro fue desestimado tras el recurso; **arbitration award** = fallo arbitral **2** *verb* conceder *or* adjudicar; **to award someone a salary increase** = conceder a alguien un aumento salarial; **to award damages** = adjudicar los daños; **the judge awarded costs to the defendant** = el juez adjudicó las costas al acusado; **to award a contract to a company** = adjudicar un contrato a una empresa

AWOL ['eɪwɒl] = ABSENT WITHOUT LEAVE

aye [aɪ] = YES; *(in the House of Commons)* **the ayes lobby** = grupo parlamentario que vota a favor de una moción; **the Ayes have it** = la moción ha sido aprobada por una mayoría a favor; *see also* DIVISION

Bb

B [bi:] *second letter of the alphabet;* **category 'B' prisoners** = presos menos peligrosos, pero que deben ser vigilados cuidadosamente; **Schedule B** = división *f* de las leyes tributarias referente a los impuestos sobre las rentas de los bosques; **Table B** = escritura *f* de constitución modelo de una sociedad limitada descrita en la Ley de Sociedades de 1985; **'B' shares** = acciones *fpl* de clase 'B' *or* ordinarias con derechos de voto especiales (muchas veces propiedad del fundador y su familia)

bachelor [ˈbætʃələ] *noun* soltero *m*

back [bæk] **1** *adjective* atrasado, -da; **back interest** = intereses atrasados; **back rent** = alquiler *m* atrasado; **back taxes** = impuestos *mpl* atrasados; **back wages** *or* **back pay** = atrasos *mpl* **2** *adverb* de nuevo *or* atrás *or* de vuelta; **he will pay back the money in monthly instalments** = devolverá el dinero en plazos mensuales; **the store sent back the cheque because the date was wrong** = la tienda devolvió el cheque al estar la fecha equivocada; **he went back on his promise not to see the girl** = faltó a su promesa de no ver a la chica **3** *noun* dorso *m or* reverso *m;* **the conditions of sale are printed on the back of the invoice** = las condiciones de venta figuran al dorso de la factura; **please endorse the cheque on the back** = sírvase firmar el cheque al dorso **4** *verb* **(a) to back someone** = apoyar *or* respaldar *or* avalar a alguien **(b) to back a bill** = *(financially)* avalar una letra *(in Parliament)* apoyar un proyecto de ley

◊ **backdate** [bækˈdeɪt] *verb* antedatar; **to backdate your invoice to April 1st** = poner a la factura fecha atrasada del 1 de abril; **the pay increase is backdated to January 1st** = el aumento de sueldo es retroactivo al 1 de enero

◊ **back down** [ˈbæk ˈdaʊn] *verb* echarse atrás

◊ **backer** [ˈbækə] *noun* **backer of a bill** = endosante *mf or* aval *m* de una letra

◊ **background** [ˈbækgraʊnd] *noun* **(a)** *(work or family history)* experiencia *f or* ambiente *m or* educación *f;* **the accused is from a good background** = el acusado procede de buena familia; **can you tell us something of the girl's family background?** = ¿nos podría decir algo sobre el historial familiar de la chica? **(b)** *(past details)* antecedentes *mpl or* detalles *mpl* anteriores *or* bases *fpl or* pasado *m;* **he explained the background to the claim** = explicó los antecedentes de la demanda; **the court asked for details of the background to the case** = el tribunal pidió los detalles anteriores al caso; **I know the contractual situation as it stands now, but can you fill in the background details?** = conozco la actual situación contractual, pero ¿podría usted rellenar los detalles anteriores?

◊ **backsheet** [ˈbækʃi:t] *noun* última hoja de un auto que, al ser plegada, pasa a ser la primera y contiene el resumen del mismo

backwardation [bækwəˈdeɪʃn] *noun* margen *m* de cobertura

bad [bæd] *adjective* malo, -la; **bad debt** = deuda *f* incobrable *or* morosa; **bad timing** = mal momento; **in bad faith** = de mala fe

bail [beɪl] **1** *noun* fianza *f;* **on bail** = bajo fianza; **to set bail** = fijar una fianza; **to stand bail of £3,000 for someone** = depositar una fianza de 3.000 libras por alguien; **to withhold bail** = denegar la libertad bajo fianza; **he was granted bail on his own recognizance of £1,000** = se le concedió la libertad bajo fianza de 1.000 libras; **the police opposed bail on the grounds that the accused might try to leave the country** = la policía se opuso a la libertad bajo fianza pretextando que el acusado podría intentar salir del país; **police bail** = fianza policial; **he was remanded on bail of £3,000** = se le liberó bajo fianza de 3.000 libras; **to jump bail** = quebrantar la libertad bajo fianza *or* huir estando bajo fianza; **bail bond** = escritura *f* de fianza *or* de caución *or* fianza de comparecencia **2** *verb* dar fianza; **to bail someone out** = *(a prisoner)* obtener la libertad de alguien bajo fianza *(to rescue financially)* salir fiador por alguien; **she paid £3,000 to bail him out** = pagó 3.000 libras por su fianza

◊ **bailee** [beɪˈli:] *noun* depositario, -ria de fianza

◊ **bailment** [ˈbeɪlmənt] *noun* depósito *m*

◊ **bailor** [beɪˈlɔ:] *noun* fiador, -ra *or* depositante *mf*

Bailey [ˈbeɪli] *see* OLD BAILEY

bailiff [ˈbeɪlɪf] *noun* **(a)** *GB (employed by the court)* agente *mf* judicial; **the court ordered the bailiffs to seize his property because he had not paid his fine** = el tribunal ordenó a los agentes judiciales que embargaran sus bienes porque no había pagado la multa **(b)** US *(deputy to a sheriff)* alguacil, -la

bait [beɪt] *noun* cebo *m*

balance ['bæləns] **1** *noun* **(a)** *(in an account)* saldo *m or* resultado *m;* **credit balance** = saldo a favor *or* saldo acreedor *or* haber *m;* **debit balance** = saldo deudor *or* debe *m* **(b)** *(rest of an amount owed)* resto *m;* **you can pay £100 deposit and the balance within sixty days** = puede pagar 100 libras de depósito y el resto en un plazo de sesenta días **(c)** **bank balance** = saldo de una cuenta **(d) balance of mind** = equilibrio *m* mental; **disturbed balance of mind** = estado *m* mental alterado *or* trastorno *m* mental; **the verdict of the coroner's court was suicide while the balance of mind was disturbed** = el veredicto del forense fue suicidio en situación de trastorno mental **2** *verb* **(a)** *(account)* saldar *or* hacer balance *or* cuadrar; **I have finished balancing the accounts for March** = he terminado de saldar las cuentas de marzo **(b)** *(budget)* equilibrar *or.*nivelar el presupuesto

◊ **balance sheet** ['bæləns 'ʃiːt] *noun* balance *m* general; **the company balance sheet for 1997 shows a substantial loss** = el balance general de la empresa correspondiente a 1997 muestra pérdidas considerables; **the accountant has prepared the balance sheet for the first half-year** = el contable ha preparado el balance de situación del primer semestre

ballot ['bælət] **1** *noun* **(a)** *(election)* votación *f;* **ballot paper** = papeleta *f* (para votar); **ballot box** = urna *f* electoral; **postal ballot** = elección *f or* votación *f* por correo; **secret ballot** = votación secreta **(b)** *(selection)* votación *or* sorteo *m;* **the share issue was oversubscribed, so there was a ballot for the shares** = la subscripción de acciones se cubrió con exceso, por lo que hubo que proceder a un sorteo **2** *verb* votar *or* someter a votación; **the union is balloting for the post of president** = el sindicato está votando para el cargo de presidente

◊ **ballot-rigging** ['bælət'rɪgɪŋ] *noun* manipulación *f* de votos *or* votación fraudulenta *or* pucherazo *m or* fraude *m* electoral *or* tongo *m*

ban [bæn] **1** *noun* prohibición *f;* **a government ban on the sale of weapons** = prohibición oficial sobre la venta de armas; **a ban on the copying of computer software** = prohibición sobre la copia de material informático de programas de ordenador; **to impose a ban on smoking** = prohibir fumar; **to lift the ban on smoking** = levantar la prohibición de fumar **2** *verb* prohibir *or* proscribir; **the government has banned the sale of alcohol** = el gobierno ha prohibido la venta de alcohol; **the sale of pirated records has been banned** = se ha prohibido la venta de discos piratas (NOTE: **banning - banned)**

bandit ['bændɪt] *noun* bandido *m;* **after the coup groups of bandits came down from the mountains to attack police stations** = tras el golpe bajaron grupos de bandidos de las montañas para atacar las comisarías de policía

◊ **banditry** ['bændɪtri] *noun* bandolerismo *m or* bandidaje *m*

banish ['bænɪʃ] *verb* desterrar; **he was banished for ten years** = le desterraron durante 10 años

◊ **banishment** ['bænɪʃmənt] *noun* destierro *m*

bank [bæŋk] **1** *noun* banco *m;* **central bank** = banco central; **clearing bank** = banco comercial **2** *verb* depositar *or* ingresar *or* tener una cuenta bancaria

◊ **bankable** ['bæŋkəbl] *adjective* descontable *or* negociable

◊ **bank account** ['bæŋk ə'kaunt] *noun* cuenta *f* bancaria

◊ **bank draft** ['bæŋk 'drɑːft] *noun* giro *m* bancario *or* letra *f* de cambio

◊ **banker** ['bæŋkə] *noun* banquero, -ra; **banker's draft** = giro bancario

◊ **bank holiday** ['bæŋk 'hɒlɪdeɪ] *noun* día *m* festivo; **Easter Monday is a bank holiday** = el Lunes de Pascua es día festivo

◊ **banking** ['bæŋkɪŋ] *adjective* bancario, -ria

◊ **bank note** *or* **banknote** ['bæŋknəut] *noun* billete *m* de banco (NOTE: US English is **bill**)

◊ **bank statement** ['bæŋk 'steɪtmənt] *noun* extracto *m* de cuenta *or* estado *m* de cuentas

bankrupt ['bæŋkrʌpt] **1** *adjective & noun* (en) quiebra *f or* (en) bancarrota *f or* quebrado, -da *or* insolvente *mf;* **he was adjudicated** *or* **declared bankrupt** = fue declarado en quiebra; **to go bankrupt** = arruinarse; **a bankrupt property developer** = un promotor inmobiliario en quiebra; **he went bankrupt after two years in business** = fue a la bancarrota *or* quebró *or* se arruinó tras dos años en el negocio; **certificated bankrupt** = quebrado rehabilitado por haberse demostrado su inocencia; **discharged bankrupt** = quebrado rehabilitado; **undischarged bankrupt** = quebrado no rehabilitado **2** *verb* arruinar; **the recession bankrupted my father** = la recesión llevó a mi padre a la quiebra *or* arruinó a mi padre

> COMMENT: a bankrupt cannot serve as a Member of Parliament, a Justice of the Peace, a director of a limited company, and cannot sign a contract or borrow money

◊ **bankruptcy** ['bæŋkrʌpsi] *noun* quiebra *f or* bancarrota *f or* insolvencia *f;* **the recession has caused thousands of bankruptcies** = la recesión ha provocado miles de quiebras; **bankruptcy notice** = aviso *m* de quiebra; **bankruptcy petition** = petición *f* de quiebra; **bankruptcy proceedings** = juicio *m* de quiebra; **adjudication of bankruptcy** *or* **declaration of bankruptcy** = declaración *f* de quiebra; **criminal bankruptcy** = quiebra criminal *or* fraudulenta; **discharge in bankruptcy** = rehabilitación *f* del quebrado; **to file a petition in bankruptcy** = hacer una petición de quiebra *or* solicitar una declaración de quiebra

◊ **Bankruptcy Court** [ˈbæŋkrʌpsi ˈkɔːt] *noun* tribunal *m* de quiebras

banns [bænz] *plural noun* amonestaciones *fpl or* proclama *f*; **to publish the banns of marriage between Anne Smith and John Jones** = publicar las amonestaciones de Anne Smith y John Jones

bar [bɑː] **1** *noun* **(a)** *(obstacle)* obstáculo *m or* impedimento *m*; **government legislation is a bar to foreign trade** = las leyes gubernamentales son un obstáculo para el comercio exterior **(b)** *(barristers)* **the Bar** = la abogacía *f or* el cuerpo de abogados; **to be called to the bar** = comenzar a ejercer como abogado ante los tribunales; *(barristers)* **the Bar Council** = Colegio de abogados de Inglaterra y Gales; **the American Bar Association** = Colegio Profesional de abogados estadounidenses; **member of the Bar** = colegiado, -da **(c)** *(rails in a court)* tribunal *m*; **prisoner at the bar** = acusado, -da **(d)** *(in prison)* **behind bars** = entre rejas **2** *verb (to forbid)* prohibir *or* impedir; **he was barred from attending the meeting** = se le prohibió asistir a la reunión; **the police commissioner barred the use of firearms** = el comisario de policía prohibió el uso de armas de fuego

barely [ˈbeəli] *adverb* apenas; **there is barely enough money left to pay the staff** = apenas hay suficiente dinero para pagar a los empleados; **she barely had time to call her lawyer** = apenas tuvo tiempo de llamar a su abogado

bargain [ˈbɑːgɪn] **1** *noun* **(a)** *(agreement between two people)* trato *m or* negocio *m* **(b)** *(cheaper than usual)* ganga *f*; **bargain hunter** = regateador, -ra *or* persona que busca gangas **(c)** *(shares)* venta *f* de un lote de acciones en la Bolsa; **bargains done** = volumen *m* de contratación diario **2** *verb* regatear *or* negociar *or* mercadear; **you will have to bargain with the dealer if you want a discount** = tendrás que regatear con el comerciante si quieres que te haga descuento; **they spent two hours bargaining about *or* over the discount** = se pasaron dos horas regateando

◊ **bargaining** [ˈbɑːgɪnɪŋ] *noun* negociación *f or* regateo *m*; **(free) collective bargaining** = convenio *m* colectivo; **bargaining power** = poder *m* negociador *or* de negociación; **bargaining position** = posición *f* negociadora; **plea bargaining** = negociación *or* trato con la acusación

baron [ˈbærən] *noun* **(a)** *(slang)* barón *m or* pez *m* gordo *or* cacique *m* **(b)** *(in jail)* prisionero con poder sobre otros prisioneros porque vende tabaco y organiza otros negocios sucios en la cárcel; **press barons** = mandarines de la prensa

barratry [ˈbærətri] *noun* **(a)** *(ship)* baratería *f* **(b)** *US (lawsuits)* embrollo *m* jurídico *or* propensión *f* a pleitar

barrier [ˈbæriə] *noun* barrera *f*; **customs barriers** *or* **tariff barriers** = barreras arancelarias; **to impose trade barriers on certain goods** = imponer barreras comerciales a ciertas mercancías; **to lift trade barriers from imports** = levantar las barreras comerciales a las importaciones

barrister [ˈbærɪstə] *noun GB* abogado, -da (que actúa únicamente en el juicio oral)

COMMENT: in England and Wales, a barrister is a member of one of the Inns of Court; he has passed examinations and spent one year in pupillage before being called to the bar. Barristers have right of audience in all courts in England and Wales. Note also that barristers are instructed only by solicitors and never by members of the public. A barrister or a group of barristers is referred to as 'counsel'

base [beɪs] **1** *noun* **(a)** *(initial position)* base *f*; **base year** = año *m* base **(b)** *(centre of operations)* base *or* sede *f*; **the company has its base in London and branches in all European countries** = la empresa tiene su sede en Londres y sucursales en todos los países europeos; **he has an office in Madrid which he uses as a base while he is travelling in Southern Europe** = tiene una oficina en Madrid que utiliza como base mientras viaja por el sur de Europa **2** *verb* **(a)** *(start to calculate from)* basar; **we based our calculations on last year's turnover** = basamos nuestros cálculos en el rendimiento del año pasado; **based on** = basado en **(b)** *(in a place)* adscribir *or* radicar *or* establecer sede en; **the European manager is based in our London office** = el director de la sección europea está adscrito a nuestra oficina de Londres; **our foreign branch is based in the Bahamas** = nuestra sucursal extranjera tiene su sede en Las Bahamas; **a London-based sales executive** = un ejecutivo de ventas con base en Londres

basic [ˈbeɪsɪk] **1** *adjective* **(a)** *(normal)* base *or* básico, -ca; **basic pay** *or* **basic salary** *or* **basic wage** = salario *m or* sueldo *m* base; **basic rate tax** = impuesto *m* de tipo base **(b)** *(most important)* básico *or* de primera necesidad; **basic commodities** = productos *mpl* de primera necesidad **(c)** *(simple)* básico, -ca *or* esencial *or* mínimo, -ma; **he has a basic knowledge of the market** = tiene un conocimiento básico del mercado; **to work at the cash desk, you need a basic qualification in maths** = para trabajar en la caja, se necesitan unos conocimientos mínimos de matemáticas

◊ **basics** [ˈbeɪsɪks] *plural noun* lo básico *or* lo esencial; **to get back to basics** = volver a lo esencial

◊ **basically** [ˈbeɪsɪkli] *adverb* esencialmente *or* básicamente

◊ **BASIC** ['beɪsɪk] *noun* = *BEGINNER'S ALL-PURPOSE SYMBOLIC INSTRUCTION CODE*; *(programming language)* BASIC *m*

basis ['beɪsɪs] *noun* **(a)** *(in calculation terms)* base *f;* **we have calculated the turnover on the basis of a 6% price increase** = hemos calculado el rendimiento basándonos en un aumento de los precios de un 6% **(b)** *(general terms of agreement)* términos *mpl or* condiciones *fpl* generales (de un acuerdo); **on a short-term** *or* **long-term basis** = a corto plazo *or* a largo plazo *or* para un corto *or* largo periodo de tiempo; **he has been appointed on a short-term basis** = se le ha nombrado para un breve periodo de tiempo; **we have three people working on a freelance basis** = tenemos tres personas trabajando por libre (NOTE: the plural is **bases)**

bastard ['bɑːstəd] *noun* bastardo, -da

batter ['bætə] *verb* apalear *or* golpear fuertemente; **the dead man had been battered to death with a hammer** = lo habían matado a golpes con un martillo; **police were battering on the door of the flat** = la policía golpeaba fuertemente la puerta del piso; **battered child** *or* **battered wife** = hijo maltratado *or* mujer maltratada
◊ **battery** ['bætri] *noun* violencia *f or* agresión *f or* intimidación *f* violenta; **assault and battery** = asalto *m* y agresión *f; compare* ASSAULT

battle ['bætl] *noun* lucha *f;* **courtroom battles** = litigios *mpl*

beak [biːk] *noun (slang)* magistrado, -da *or* juez, -za

bear [beə] *verb* **(a)** *(to pay costs)* pagar *or* correr con; **the company bore the legal costs of both parties** = la empresa corrió con las costas procesales de ambas partes **(b)** *(to refer to)* **to bear on** *or* **to have a bearing on** = tener que ver con *or* referirse a *or* tener efecto sobre; **the decision of the court bears on** *or* **has a bearing on future cases where immigration procedures are disputed** = la decisión del tribunal afectará futuros casos referentes a los trámites de inmigración **(c) to bear witness** = atestiguar (NOTE: **bearing - bore - borne)**
◊ **bearer** ['beərə] *noun* portador, -ra *or* tenedor, -ra; **the cheque is payable to bearer** = el cheque se paga al portador
◊ **bearer bond** ['beərə 'bɒnd] *noun* título *m* al portador
◊ **bearer cheque** ['beərə 'tʃek] *noun* cheque *m* al portador

beat [biːt] **1** *noun (area of regular patrol)* ronda *f or* área de control y vigilancia de un policía; **the constable on the beat** = el policía en su ronda **2** *verb* **(a)** *(to hit)* golpear *or* pegar *or* apalear; **the prisoners were beaten with sticks** = los prisioneros fueron golpeados con palos; **the warders beat the prisoner to make him confess** =

los guardianes pegaron al prisionero para hacerle confesar **(b)** *(to win in a fight)* vencer *or* derrotar *or* superar; **they have beaten their competitors into second place in the computer market** = han superado a sus competidores relegándoles al segundo puesto en el mercado informático **(c)** *(to escape)* **to beat a ban** = eludir una prohibición
◊ **beating** ['biːtɪŋ] *noun* paliza *f;* **to take a beating** = recibir una paliza
◊ **beat up** ['biːt 'ʌp] *verb* dar una paliza (NOTE: **beating - beat - has beaten)**

beforehand [bɪ'fɔːhænd] *adverb* de antemano *or* por anticipado *or* con anticipación; **the terms of the payment will be agreed beforehand** = las condiciones de pago se acordarán de antemano

beg [beg] *verb* rogar

begin [bɪ'gɪn] *verb* empezar *or* comenzar; **the case began with the reading of the indictment** = el caso empezó con la lectura del sumario; **the auditors' report began with a description of the general principles adopted** = el informe de los auditores comenzó con una descripción de los principios generales adoptados (NOTE: **beginning - began - begun)**

behalf [bɪ'hɑːf] *noun* **on behalf of** = en nombre de; **I am writing on behalf of the minority shareholders** = escribo en nombre de los accionistas minoritarios; **she is acting on my behalf** = actúa en mi nombre; **solicitors acting on behalf of the American company** = abogados que actúan en nombre de la empresa americana

behead [bɪ'hed] *verb* decapitar; **the accused was found guilty of treason and beheaded** = se consideró al acusado culpable de traición y fue decapitado

believe [bɪ'liːv] *verb* creer *or* tener entendido; **we believe he has offered to buy 25% of the shares** = tenemos entendido que se ha ofrecido para comprar el 25% de las acciones; **the chairman is believed to be in South America on business** = se cree que el presidente está de negocios en Sudamérica

belli ['beliː] *see* CASUS BELLI

bellman ['belmən] *noun (slang)* criminal *m* especializado en desconectar sistemas de alarma

belong [bɪ'lɒŋ] *verb* **(a) to belong to** = pertenecer; **the company belongs to an old American banking family** = la empresa pertenece a una tradicional familia americana de banqueros; **the patent belongs to the inventor's son** = la patente pertenece al hijo del inventor **(b) to belong with** = corresponder *or* pertenecer *or* ir con; **those documents belong with the sales reports** = esos documentos corresponden a los informes de ventas

bench [benʃ] *noun* **(a)** *(in court)* tribunal *m;* **bench of judges** *or* **magistrates** = órgano jurisdiccional colegiado *or* tribunal de magistrados;

he is on the bench = forma parte del tribunal *or* es magistrado; **bench warrant** = auto *m* de prisión expedido por un tribunal; **Queen's Bench Division** = una de las principales divisiones del Tribunal Superior; *(Inns of Court)* **Masters of the Bench** = miembros de la junta de gobierno de uno de los cuatro Colegios de Abogados de Londres **(b)** *(seat)* banco *m; (in Parliament)* escaño *m; GB* **the back benches** = escaños de atrás donde se sientan los diputados que no tienen cargo en el gobierno; **the front benches** = escaños de la primera fila donde se sientan los ministros con cargo en el gobierno; **the Opposition front bench** = escaños de la primera fila donde se sientan las figuras eminentes de la Oposición; **the government front bench** *or* **the Treasury bench** = banco azul; **an Opposition front bench spokesman asked why the Government had been so slow in investigating the affair** = uno de los portavoces de la Oposición en primera fila preguntó por qué el gobierno había tardado tanto en investigar el asunto

◊ **Bencher** ['benʃə] *noun (Inns of Court)* uno de los miembros más antiguos de un Colegio de Abogados

benefactor ['benɪfæktə] *noun* bienhechor *m or* benefactor *m*
◊ **benefactress** ['benɪfæktrəs] *noun* bienhechora *f or* benefactora *f*

beneficial [benɪ'fɪʃl] *adjective* beneficioso, -sa; **beneficial interest** = interés *m* de usufructo; **beneficial occupier** = usufructuario, -ria (de una vivienda); **beneficial owner** = nudo-propietario *m;* **beneficial use** = usufructo *m*
◊ **beneficiary** [benɪ'fɪʃəri] *noun* **(a)** *(of a will)* beneficiario, -ria; **joint beneficiary** = beneficiario proindiviso; **the main beneficiaries of the will are the deceased's family** = los principales beneficiarios del testamento son los familiares del difunto **(b)** *(property)* fideicomitente *mf or* fiduciario, -ria

COMMENT: in a trust, the trustee is the legal owner of the property, while the beneficiary is the equitable owner who receives the real benefit of the trust

benefit ['benɪfit] **1** *noun* **(a)** *(money or advantage gained from something)* beneficio *m* provecho *m;* **the estate was left to the benefit of the owner's grandsons** = se dejó la propiedad a beneficio de los nietos del propietario **(b)** *(payments)* subsidio *m or* pensión *f or* indemnización *f;* **disability benefit** = pensión de invalidez; **she receives £20 a week as unemployment benefit** = recibe un subsidio de paro de 20 libras a la semana; **the sickness benefit is paid monthly** = la pensión por enfermedad se paga mensualmente; **the insurance office sends out benefit cheques each week** = la agencia de seguros envía cheques de indemnización todas las semanas; **death benefit** = indemnización por

fallecimiento *or* subsidio de defunción **2** *verb* sacar partido; **to benefit from** *or* **by something** = beneficiarse de *or* sacar provecho de algo

bent [bent] *adjective; (slang)* corrupto, -ta *or* robado, -da *or* ilegal; **bent copper** = policía corrupto; **bent job** = trato *m* ilegal

bequeath [bɪ'kwiːð] *verb* legar; **he bequeathed his shares to his daughter** = legó las acciones a su hija
◊ **bequest** [bɪ'kwest] *noun* legado *m or* donación *f;* **executory bequest** = legado diferido; **he made several bequests to his staff** = hizo varios legados a sus empleados

COMMENT: freehold land given in a will is a **devise**

bereavement [bɪ'riːvmənt] *noun* aflicción *f or* pérdida de un familiar

berth [bəːθ] *noun* amarradero *m*

BES ['biː 'iː 'es] = BUSINESS EXPANSION SCHEME

best [best] **1** *adjective* (el *or* la) mejor; **best evidence** = la mejor prueba: documento original utilizado como prueba **2** *noun* lo mejor *or* lo más adecuado; **the lawyers did their best, but the jury was not convinced by the evidence** = los abogados hicieron todo lo posible, pero las pruebas no convencieron al jurado
◊ **best evidence rule** ['best 'evɪdəns 'ruːl] *noun* norma que rige la admisión de la mejor prueba

bestiality [besti'ælɪti] *noun (buggery with an animal)* bestialidad *f*

bet [bet] **1** *noun* apuesta *f* **2** *verb* apostar; **he bet £100 on the result of the election** = apostó 100 libras por el resultado de las elecciones; **I bet you £25 the accused will get off with a fine** = te apuesto 25 libras a que el acusado escapa con una multa; **betting duty** *or* **tax** = impuesto *m* sobre el juego

betray [bɪ'treɪ] *verb* traicionar *or* revelar; **he betrayed the secret to the enemy** = reveló el secreto al enemigo; **to betray one's country** *or* **a friend** = traicionar al país propio *or* a un amigo
◊ **betrayal** [bɪ'treɪəl] *noun* **betrayal of trust** = abuso *m* de confianza

beware [bɪ'weə] *verb* tener cuidado con *or* desconfiar de; **beware of imitations** = desconfíe de las imitaciones

beyond [bɪ'jɒnd] *adverb* más allá de; **it is beyond question that** = está fuera de duda que; **beyond reasonable doubt** = fuera de duda razonable: prueba casi decisiva para condenar a una persona en un caso penal

BFP ['biː 'ef 'piː] *US* = BONA FIDE PURCHASER

bi- [baɪ] *prefix* bi *or* dos veces *fpl;* **bi-monthly** = *(twice a month)* bimensual; *(every two months)* bimestral *or* cada dos meses; **bi-annual** *or* **bi-annually** = *(twice a year)* semestral *or* dos veces al año; *(every two years)* cada dos años

◊ **bicameralism** [baɪˈkæmərəlɪzm] *noun* bicameralismo *m or* sistema *m* de dos cámaras

bias [ˈbaɪəs] *noun* inclinación *f or* predisposición *f or* sesgo *m;* **likelihood of bias** = posibilidad de que un juicio no sea imparcial a causa de la conexión entre un miembro del tribunal y una de las partes

◊ **biased** [ˈbaɪəst] *adjective* (juez o miembro del jurado) que favorece a una de las partes en un juicio

bid [bɪd] **1** *noun* **(a)** *(offer to buy)* oferta *f or* puja *f;* **to make a bid for something** = presentar *or* hacer una oferta de compra; **to put in a bid for something** *or* **to enter a bid for something** = presentar *or* hacer una oferta **(b)** *(offer to do work)* oferta; **he made the lowest bid for the job** = presentó la oferta más baja *or* más barata por el trabajo **(c)** *US (offer to sell)* oferta de venta; **they asked for bids for the supply of spare parts** = solicitaron ofertas para el suministro de piezas de repuesto **(d)** **takeover bid** = oferta pública de adquisición de una empresa; **to make a takeover bid for a company** = presentar una oferta de adquisición de una empresa *or* OPA; **to withdraw a takeover bid** = retirar una oferta de adquisición de una empresa **2** *verb (at an auction)* **to bid for something** = pujar *or* ofrecer *or* licitar; **he bid £1,000 for the jewels** = ofreció 1.000 libras por las joyas (NOTE: **bidding - bid**)

◊ **bidder** [ˈbɪdə] *noun* postor *m or* licitador, -ra; **the lot was sold to the highest bidder** = el lote se vendió al mejor postor

bigamy [ˈbɪgəmi] *noun* bigamia *f; see also* MONOGAMY, POLYGAMY

◊ **bigamist** [ˈbɪgəmɪst] *noun* bígamo, -ma

◊ **bigamous** [ˈbɪgəməs] *adjective* bígamo, -ma; **they went through a bigamous marriage ceremony** = celebraron una ceremonia de matrimonio bígamo

bilateral [baɪˈlætərəl] *adjective* bilateral; **bilateral contract** = contrato bilateral; **the minister signed a bilateral trade agreement** = el ministro firmó un acuerdo de comercio bilateral

bilking [ˈbɪlkɪŋ] *noun* estafa *f or* fraude *m*

bill [bɪl] **1** *noun* **(a)** *(list of charges to be paid)* factura *f;* **the salesman wrote out the bill** = el vendedor extendió la factura; **does the bill include VAT?** = ¿lleva la factura el IVA incluido?; **the bill is made out to Smith Ltd** = la factura se ha extendido a nombre de Smith Ltd; **the builder sent in his bill** = el constructor mandó la factura; **he left the country without paying his bills** = salió del país sin pagar sus deudas; **to foot the bill** = pagar la cuenta *or* correr con los gastos **(b)** *(in a restaurant)* cuenta *f;* **can I have the bill please?** = ¿me puede dar la nota *or* traer la cuenta por favor?; **the bill comes to £20 including service** = la cuenta asciende a 20 libras con servicio incluido; **does the bill include service?** = ¿está incluido el servicio en la cuenta?; **the waiter has added 10% to the bill for service** = el camarero ha añadido un 10% a la cuenta por el servicio **(c)** *(written promise to pay)* letra *f;* **bill of exchange** = letra de cambio; **accommodation bill** = efecto *m* de favor **(d)** **bill of health** = patente *f* de sanidad *or* certificado *m* sanitario; **clean bill of health** = certificado de buena salud; **bill of indictment** = acta *f* de acusación *or* US lista de cargos que se le da a un jurado, solicitando que se condene a un acusado; **bill of lading** = conocimiento *m* de embarque **(e)** *US (banknote)* billete **(f)** **bill of sale** = *(sale)* escritura *f or* contrato *m* de venta; *(loan)* recibo *m* de venta **(g)** *(in Parliament)* proyecto *m* de ley; **the house is discussing the Noise Prevention Bill** = la cámara está discutiendo el proyecto de ley de prevención del ruido; **the Finance Bill had its second reading yesterday** = el proyecto de ley de finanzas pasó ayer su segunda lectura; **Private Member's Bill** = proposición *f* de ley; **Private Bill** = proyecto de ley que se refiere a una persona *or* corporación *or* institución en particular; **Public Bill** = proyecto de ley ordinario, presentado por un ministro y referente a un asunto con interés para el público en general **(h)** *US* **Bill of Rights** = declaración *f* de derechos del individuo *or* ley *f* fundamental **(i)** *(notice)* cartel *m* **2** *verb* presentar *or* enviar una factura *or* facturar; **the builders billed him for the repairs to his neighbour's house** = el contratista le envió una factura por las reparaciones en la casa de su vecino

COMMENT: a Bill passes through the following stages in Parliament: **First Reading, Second Reading, Committee Stage, Report Stage** and **Third Reading.** The Bill goes through these stages first in the House of Commons and then in the House of Lords. When all the stages have been passed the Bill is given the Royal Assent and becomes law as an Act of Parliament. In the USA, a Bill is introduced either in the House or in the Senate, passes through **Committee Stage** with public hearings, then to general debate in the full House. The Bill is debated section by section in **Second Reading** and after being passed by both House and Senate is engrossed and sent to the President as a **joint resolution** for signature (or veto)

bind [baɪnd] *verb* vincular *or* obligar (por contrato) *or* comprometer *or* atar; **the company is bound by its articles of association** = la empresa está obligada a respetar sus estatutos; **he does not consider himself bound by the agreement which was signed by his predecessor** = no se considera obligado al acuerdo firmado por su predecesor;

High Court judges are bound by the decisions of the House of Lords = los jueces de Tribunales Superiores se hallan vinculados a las decisiones de la Cámara de los Lores

◊ **binder** ['baɪndə] *noun* **(a)** *(cover for papers)* carpeta *f;* **ring binder** = carpeta de anillas **(b)** *(temporary cover note) US* resguardo *m* provisional (NOTE: the British English for this is **cover note**)

◊ **binding** ['baɪndɪŋ] *adjective* vinculante *or* que compromete *or* obligatorio, -ria; **legally binding** = de obligado cumplimiento; **this document is legally binding** *or* **it is a legally binding document** = este documento es legalmente vinculante *or* es un documento que compromete legalmente; **the agreement is binding on all parties** = el acuerdo vincula a todas las partes; **binding precedent** = precedente *m* vinculante

◊ **bind over** ['baɪnd 'əʊvə] *verb* **(a)** *GB* obligar legalmente a (comparecer ante el tribunal); **he was bound over (to keep the peace** *or* **to be of good behaviour) for six months** = se le obligó (a mantener la paz *or* a llevar una buena conducta) durante seis meses **(b)** *US* ordenar la custodia de un acusado antes de su comparecencia ante el tribunal

◊ **bind-over order** ['baɪnd'əʊvə 'ɔːdə] *noun* sentencia *f* judicial (que obliga a comparecer ante el tribunal); **the applicant sought judicial review to quash the bind-over order** = el solicitante intentó conseguir una revisión judicial para anular la sentencia

birth [bɜːθ] *noun* nacimiento *m;* **he is British by birth** = es británico de nacimiento; **date and place of birth** = fecha *f* y lugar *m* de nacimiento; **birth certificate** = partida *f* de nacimiento; **concealment of birth** = encubrimiento *m* de nacimiento; **to give birth** = dar a luz

black [blæk] **1** *adjective* negro,-gra **(a) black market** = mercado *m* negro; **there is a lucrative black market in spare parts for cars** = hay un lucrativo mercado negro de piezas de recambio para coches; **you can buy gold coins on the black market** = se pueden comprar monedas de oro en el mercado negro; **they lived well on black-market goods** = vivían bien de las mercancías del mercado negro; **to pay black market prices** = pagar precios de mercado negro; **black marketeer** = comerciante *mf* del mercado negro **(b) black economy** = economía *f* sumergida **2** *verb* prohibir el comercio de ciertas mercancías *or* con ciertos proveedores; **three firms were blacked by the government** = el gobierno prohibió el comercio con tres empresas; **the union has blacked a shipping firm** = el sindicato ha prohibido el comercio con una empresa marítima

◊ **blackleg** ['blækleg] *noun* esquirol *mf*

◊ **black list** ['blæk 'lɪst] *noun* lista *f* negra

◊ **blacklist** ['blæklɪst] *verb* poner en la lista negra; **his firm was blacklisted by the government** = el gobierno puso su empresa en la lista negra

◊ **Black Maria** ['blæk mə'raɪə] *noun (informal)* vehículo *m* celular destinado al transporte de detenidos

Black Rod ['blæk 'rɒd] *noun GB (Gentleman Usher)* funcionario formalmente encargado de mantener el orden en la Cámara de los Lores

COMMENT: like the Sergeant at Arms in the Commons, Black Rod is responsible for keeping order in the House. His best-known duty is to go from the Lords to summon the Commons to attend the opening of Parliament and hear the Queen's Speech

blackmail ['blækmeɪl] **1** *noun* chantaje *m;* **he was charged with blackmail** = se le acusó de chantaje; **they got £25,000 from the managing director by blackmail** = obtuvieron 25.000 libras del director gerente por chantaje; **she was sent to prison for blackmail** = la mandaron a la cárcel por chantaje **2** *verb* chantajear; **he was blackmailed by his former partner** = fue chantajeado por su antiguo socio

◊ **blackmailer** ['blækmeɪlə] *noun* chantajista *mf*

blag [blæg] *noun (slang)* robo *m* por banda armada *or* atraco *m* a mano armada

blame [bleɪm] **1** *noun* culpa *f;* **to take the blame** = cargar con el muerto; **the sales staff got the blame for the poor sales figures** = echaron la culpa al personal de la sección por las bajas cifras de ventas **2** *verb* culpar *or* echar la culpa *or* reprochar; **the magistrate blamed the social services for not reporting the case quickly** = el magistrado culpó a los servicios sociales de no informar del caso rápidamente; **the lack of fire equipment was blamed by the coroner for the deaths** = el juez de primera instancia echó la culpa de las muertes a la ausencia de un detector de incendios

◊ **blameworthy** ['bleɪmwɜːði] *adjective* censurable

blanche [blɑːnʃ] *see* CARTE

blank [blæŋk] **1** *adjective* en blanco; **a blank cheque** = un cheque *m* en blanco **2** *noun* espacio *m* en blanco

blanket ['blæŋkɪt] *noun* manta *f;* **blanket agreement** = acuerdo *m* global; **blanket insurance policy** = póliza *f* de seguros a todo riesgo; **blanket refusal** = negativa *f* general

blasphemy ['blæsfəmi] *noun* blasfemia *f*

◊ **blaspheme** [blæs'fiːm] *verb* blasfemar

bloc [blɒk] *noun (group of countries linked together)* bloque *m;* **the Western bloc** = el bloque occidental; **the pro-Communist bloc** = el bloque pro-comunista

block [blɒk] **1** *noun* **(a)** *(series of items grouped together)* bloque *m or* paquete *m;* **he bought a**

block of 6,000 shares = compró un paquete de 6.000 acciones; **block booking** = reserva *f* en bloque; **the company has a block booking for twenty seats on the plane** *or* **for ten rooms at the hotel** = la empresa tiene una reserva en bloque de veinte asientos de avión *or* de diez habitaciones de hotel; **block vote** = voto *m* por representación **(b)** *(streets)* manzana *f or* bloque; **a block of offices** *or* **an office block** = un bloque de oficinas **(c)** *(in prison)* bloque; **H-block** = bloque en forma de H: edificio en una cárcel construido con una sección central y dos alas, formando una H; **hospital block** = sección de una prisión donde se encuentra el hospital **(d)** *(capital letters)* **block capitals** *or* **block letters** = mayúsculas *fpl;* **write your name and address in block letters** = escriba su nombre y dirección en mayúsculas **2** *verb (to stop something)* bloquear; **he used his casting vote to block the motion** = utilizó su voto de calidad para bloquear la moción; **the planning committee blocked the plan to build a motorway through the middle of the town** = la comisión de planificación bloqueó el proyecto de construir una autopista que atravesara el centro de la ciudad; **blocked currency** = moneda *f* bloqueada

blockade [blɒˈkeɪd] **1** *noun* bloqueo *m;* **the government brought in goods by air to beat the blockade** = el gobierno hizo entrar las mercancías por aire para combatir el bloqueo; **the enemy lifted the blockade of the port for two months to let emergency supplies in** = el enemigo levantó el bloqueo del puerto durante dos meses para dejar entrar provisiones de necesidad urgente **2** *verb* bloquear; **the town was blockaded by the enemy navy** = la armada enemiga bloqueó la ciudad

blood [blʌd] *noun* sangre *f;* **blood related** = consanguíneo, -nea; **blood relationship** = relación *f* consanguínea; **blood sample** = muestra *f* de sangre; **blood test** *or* **blood grouping test** = análisis *m* de sangre

◊ **bloodless** [ˈblʌdləs] *adjective* incruento, -ta

◊ **bloodshed** [ˈblʌdʃed] *noun* derramamiento *m* de sangre

blotter [ˈblɒtə] *noun US* libro *m* en el que se recogen los arrestos en una comisaría

blow [bləʊ] *noun* golpe *m or* porrazo *m*

blue [bluː] *adjective* azul

◊ **blue bag** [ˈbluː ˈbæg] *noun* bolsa *f* azul en la que un abogado joven lleva su toga; *see also* RED BAG

◊ **Blue Book** [ˈbluː ˈbʊk] *noun GB* informe *m* oficial de una Comisión Real

◊ **blue chip investments** *or* **blue chip stock** [ˈbluː ˈtʃɪp ɪnˈvesmənts] *noun* inversiones *fpl or* valores *mpl* de toda confianza

◊ **blue laws** [ˈbluː ˈlɔːz] *plural noun US* leyes *fpl* sobre el descanso dominical

◊ **blue sky laws** [ˈbluː ˈskaɪ ˈlɔːz] *plural noun US* leyes que protegen a los inversores contra operadores de bolsa fraudulentos

board [bɔːd] **1** *noun* **(a)** *(group of directors)* consejo *m or* junta *f;* **board of directors** = consejo *m* de administración *or* junta *f* directiva; **the bank has two representatives on the board** = el banco tiene dos representantes en el consejo; **he sits on the board as a representative of the bank** = es el representante del banco en el consejo de administración; **two directors were removed from the board at the AGM** = en la Junta General Anual, dos consejeros fueron depuestos de su cargo; **board meeting** = reunión *f* del consejo de administración **(b)** *(group of people who run a trust or a society)* junta *f or* consejo *m or* comisión *f;* **board of trustees** = junta *or* consejo de síndicos; **advisory board** = comisión consultiva *or* junta asesora; **editorial board** = consejo editorial *or* de redacción; **parole board** = junta del régimen y administración del centro penitenciario que regula la concesión de la libertad condicional; **board of visitors** = junta de inspección de prisiones **2** *verb* abordar *or* embarcarse en *or* subir a; **customs officials boarded the ship in the harbour** = los oficiales de aduanas embarcaron en el puerto

◊ **boarding card** *or* **boarding pass** [ˈbɔːdɪŋ ˈkɑːd *or* ˈpɑːs] *noun* tarjeta *f* de embarque

◊ **boardroom** [ˈbɔːdruːm] *noun* sala *f* de juntas

bobby [ˈbɒbi] *noun (informal) GB* 'poli' *mf or* policía *mf*

body [ˈbɒdi] *noun* **(a)** *(organization)* cuerpo *m;* **public body** = cuerpo estatal; **legislative body** = cuerpo legislativo; **decision-making body** = órgano *m* decisorio; **Parliament is an elected body** = el Parlamento es un órgano representativo; **the governing body of the university has to approve the plan to give the President a honorary degree** = el organismo rector de la universidad tiene que aprobar el plan para que se le conceda el título honoris causa al presidente **(b)** *(large group)* en masa *or* en bloque; **body of opinion** = corriente de opinión; **there is a considerable body of opinion which believes that capital punishment should be reintroduced** = hay una corriente de opinión importante a favor del restablecimiento de la pena de muerte **(c)** *(corpse)* cadáver *m;* **they found the dead body** = encontraron el cadáver; **over my dead body!** = ¡de ninguna manera!

◊ **bodily** [ˈbɒdɪli] *adverb* a la persona; **actual bodily harm (ABH)** = daño *m* real *or* físico a la persona; **grievous bodily harm (GBH)** = daño grave a la persona

◊ **bodyguard** [ˈbɒdigɑːd] *noun* guardaespaldas *m (slang)* gorila *m;* **the minister was followed by his three bodyguards** = al ministro le seguían sus tres guardaespaldas

◊ **the body politic** [ˈbɒdi ˈpɒlɪtɪk] *noun* el estado

boilerplate ['bɔɪləpleɪt] *noun US* impreso *m* con huecos que se rellenan en cada caso

bona fides *or* **bona fide** ['bəʊnə 'faɪdiːz] *Latin phrase* 'buena fe' *or* 'de buena fe'; **bona fide purchaser** = que compra de buena fe; **he acted bona fide** = actuó de buena fe; **the respondent was not acting bona fides** = el demandado no actuaba de buena fe; **a bona fide offer** = una oferta *f* de buena fe

bona vacantia ['bəʊnə və'kæntiə] *noun* bienes *mpl* vacantes

bond [bɒnd] *noun* **(a)** *(debt of a company or government)* bono *m or* obligación *f;* **callable bond** = bono redimible; **gilt-edged bond** = bono de confianza; **government bonds** *or* **treasury bonds** = bonos del Estado *or* del Tesoro; **junk bond** = bono basura; **marketable bond** = bono negociable; **non-marketable bond** = bono no transferible; **payment bond** = fianza de pago; **secured bond** = bono con garantía **(b)** *(borrowing by a person)* título *m or* obligación *or* cédula *f;* **bearer bond** = título al portador; **debenture bond** = obligación no hipotecaria *or* pagaré *m* de empresa; **mortgage bond** = bono hipotecario *or* cédula hipotecaria **(c)** *(legal document which is binding)* contrato *m or* compromiso *m;* **bail bond** = escritura *f* de fianza *or* de caución; **goods (held) in bond** = mercancías *fpl* bajo precinto aduanero *or* en depósito; **entry of goods under bond** = entrada de mercancías bajo precinto aduanero; **to take goods out of bond** = retirar mercancías del depósito de aduanas
◊ **bonded** ['bɒndɪd] *adjective* en depósito; **bonded goods** = mercancías *or* géneros en depósito; **bonded warehouse** = depósito *m* aduanero
◊ **bondholder** ['bɒndhəʊldə] *noun* obligacionista *mf or* tenedor *m* de obligaciones
◊ **bondsman** ['bɒndzmən] *noun* fiador *m*

book [bʊk] **1** *noun* libro *m;* **a company's books** = libros de cuentas de una compañía; **book value** = valor *m* del activo de una compañía según sus libros de cuentas; **minute book** = libro de actas; **phone book** *or* **telephone book** = guía *f* telefónica *or* de teléfonos; **reference book** = libro de consultas **(b)** **to bring someone to book** = pedir cuentas a alguien *or* acusar de un delito **2** *verb* **(a)** *(to order or to reserve)* reservar; **to book a room in a hotel** *or* **a table at a restaurant** *or* **a ticket on a plane** = reservar una habitación de hotel *or* una mesa en un restaurante *or* un billete de avión; **I booked a table for 7.45** = reservé una mesa para las 7.45; **he booked a ticket through to Cairo** = reservó un billete hasta El Cairo; **to book someone into a hotel** *or* **onto a flight** = reservar una habitación de hotel *or* un billete de avión para alguien **(b)** *(informal)* acusar a uno de un delito; **he was booked for driving on the wrong side of the road** = se le acusó de conducir por el lado contrario de la carretera
◊ **booking** ['bʊkɪŋ] *noun* reserva *f*

booth [buːð] *noun* **(a)** *(small cabin)* cabina *f;* **election booth** *or* **polling booth** *or* **voting booth** = cabina electoral **(b)** *(visiting room)* locutorio *m* (de una cárcel)

bootleg ['buːtleg] *adjective* (alcohol) de contrabando
◊ **bootlegger** ['buːtlegə] *noun* contrabandista *mf* de alcohol
◊ **bootlegging** ['buːtlegɪŋ] *noun* **(a)** *(of alcohol)* contrabando *m* de alcohol **(b)** *(of records and tapes)* piratería *f* de discos *or* cintas de música

border ['bɔːdə] **1** *noun* frontera *f* **2** *verb* **to border on** = lindar *or* limitar con
◊ **bordering** ['bɔːdrɪŋ] *adjective* limítrofe

born [bɔːn] **1** *adjective* nato, -ta; **a born criminal** = un criminal nato **2** *verb* **to be born** = nacer

borough ['bʌrə] *noun* municipio *m;* **borough council** = consejo *m* municipal

borrow ['bɒrəʊ] *verb* **(a)** *(to take for a time)* pedir prestado *or* tomar a préstamo; **he borrowed £1,000 from the bank** = pidió prestadas 1.000 libras al banco; **the company had to borrow heavily to repay its debts** = la empresa tuvo que tomar grandes cantidades de dinero a préstamo para pagar sus deudas; **they borrowed £25,000 against the security of the factory** = pidieron prestadas 25.000 libras con la garantía de la fábrica **(b)** *(slang)* robar
◊ **borrower** ['bɒrəʊə] *noun* prestatario, -ria; **borrowers from the bank pay 12% interest** = los prestatarios del banco pagan un interés del 12%
◊ **borrowing** ['bɒrəʊɪŋ] *noun* **(a)** *(action)* préstamo *m or* empréstito *m;* **the new factory was financed by bank borrowing** = financiaron la nueva fábrica con préstamos bancarios; **borrowing power** = capacidad *f* de endeudamiento **(b)** **borrowings** = préstamos; **the company's borrowings have doubled** = los préstamos de la empresa se han duplicado; **bank borrowings** = préstamos bancarios

borstal ['bɔːstəl] *noun (formerly)* reformatorio *m* de menores (NOTE: now replaced by **Young Offender Institutions**)

boss [bɒs] *noun* jefe, -fa mandamás *mf or* cabecilla *mf* (de una familia de mafiosos *or* banda criminal)

bottleneck ['bɒtlnek] *noun* embotellamiento *m or* atasco *m;* **there are serious bottlenecks in the divorce courts** = hay una gran cantidad de casos por resolver en los tribunales de divorcio

bottomry ['bɒtəmri] *noun* hipoteca *f* naval; **bottomry bond** = fianza *f* de contrato a la gruesa

bounce [baʊns] *verb (of a cheque)* ser incobrable (por falta de fondos) *or* estar sin fondos; **he paid for the car with a cheque that bounced** = pagó el coche con un cheque sin fondos

bound [baʊnd] *see* BIND, DUTY

boundary (line) ['baʊndri] *noun* límite *m* or término *m* or frontera *f;* **the boundary dispute dragged through the courts for years** = la disputa en los juzgados sobre los límites de tierra se hizo interminable
◊ **Boundary Commission** ['baʊndri kə'mɪʃn] *noun* comisión *f* parlamentaria que revisa periódicamente los límites de los distritos electorales

bounty ['baʊnti] *noun* **(a)** *(subsidy)* prima *f* or subvención *f* bonificación *f* **(b)** *(reward)* recompensa *f*

bourgeois ['bʊəʒwɑ:] *adjective* **(a)** burgués, -esa; **petty bourgeois** = pequeño burgués **(b)** *(used as criticism)* burgués, -esa or aburguesado, -da; **the Party is trying to reduce its bourgeois image by promoting young activists to the Central Committee** = el partido intenta reducir su imagen aburguesada con la promoción de jóvenes activistas dentro de la Comisión Central
◊ **bourgeoisie** [bʊəʒwɑ:'zi:] *noun* burguesía *f;* **petty bourgeoisie** = pequeña burguesía

box [bɒks] *noun* **(a)** *(container)* caja *f;* **ballot box** = urna *f;* **the goods were sent in thin cardboard boxes** = se envió la mercancía en cajas de cartón fino; **the drugs were hidden in boxes of office stationery** = las drogas estaban escondidas en cajas de artículos de oficina; **envelopes come in boxes of two hundred** = los sobres vienen en cajas de doscientos; **box file** = archivador *m* **(b)** *(in court)* **witness box** = banco *m* de testigos (NOTE: American English is **witness stand**) **(c)** *(postal)* **box number** = apartado *m* de correos; **please reply to Box No. 209** = por favor escriba al Apartado de Correos número 209; **our address is: P.O. Box 74209, Edinburgh** = nuestra dirección es: Apartado de Correos 74209, Edimburgo

boycott ['bɔɪkɒt] **1** *noun* boicot *m* or boicoteo *m;* **the union organized a boycott against** or **of imported cars** = el sindicato organizó un boicot contra los coches de importación **2** *verb* boicotear; **the company's products have been boycotted by the main department stores** = los productos de la empresa han sido boicoteados por los principales grandes almacenes; **we are boycotting all imports from that country** = estamos boicoteando todas las importaciones de ese país; **the management has boycotted the meeting** = la dirección ha boicoteado la reunión

bracelets ['breɪsləts] *plural noun (slang)* esposas *fpl*

bracket ['brækɪt] **1** *noun* or grupo *m* or categoría *f;* **income bracket** or **tax bracket** = grupo impositivo **2** *verb* **to bracket together** = agrupar or poner juntos

branch [brɑ:nʃ] **1** *noun* **(a)** *(local office)* sucursal *f* or filial *f* or oficina *f;* **the bank** or **the store has branches in most towns in the south of the country** = el banco or el almacén tiene sucursales en la mayoría de las ciudades del sur del país; **the insurance company has closed its branches in South America** = la compañía de seguros ha cerrado sus filiales en Sudamérica; **he is the manager of our local branch of Lloyds bank** = es el director de nuestra sucursal local del banco Lloyds; **we have decided to open a branch office in Chicago** = hemos decidido abrir una sucursal en Chicago; **the manager of our branch in Lagos** or **of our Lagos branch** = el director de nuestra oficina en Lagos; **branch manager** = director de sucursal **(b)** *(separate section)* sección *f* or división *f* or rama *f;* **the Law of Contract and the Law of Tort are branches of civil law** = el Derecho de Contratos y la Ley de Agravios son secciones del derecho civil **2** *verb* **to branch out** = extender las actividades de un negocio or ampliar el negocio a una nueva rama or a otras actividades; **from dealing in stolen bicycles, the gang branched out into car theft** = de tratar con bicicletas robadas, la banda pasó al robo de coches

brand [brænd] **1** *noun* marca *f* **2** *verb* marcar or poner una marca
◊ **branded** ['brændɪd] *adjective;* **branded goods** = artículos *mpl* de marca

breach [bri:tʃ] **1** *noun* **(a)** *(terms of agreement)* incumplimiento *m* or violación *f;* **breach of sentence** = quebrantamiento *m* de condena; **in breach of** = (estar en situación de) haber incumplido; **the defendant is in breach of his statutory duty** = el demandado ha incumplido sus obligaciones legales; **breach of confidence** or **of trust** = abuso *m* de confianza or alevosía *f;* **breach of contract** = incumplimiento or ruptura *f* de contrato; **the company is in breach of contract** = la empresa ha incumplido el contrato; **breach of promise** = antiguamente, incumplimiento de promesa matrimonial; **breach of warranty** = violación de garantía **(b)** *(failure to obey the law)* infracción *f* or violación *f* or falta *f;* **the soldier was charged with a serious breach of discipline** = se acusó al soldado de haber cometido una falta grave de disciplina; **breach of the peace** = perturbación *f* or alteración *f* del orden público **2** *verb* dejar de cumplir

break [breɪk] **1** *noun* descanso *m;* **to take a break** = descansar; **without a break** = sin parar; **the court adjourned for a ten-minute break** = el tribunal levantó la sesión para descansar durante diez minutos **2** *verb* **(a)** *(to do something against the law)* violar or infringir or quebrantar; **to break the law** = quebrantar la ley or atentar contra la ley; **if you hit a policeman you will be breaking the law** = si pegas a un policía infringirás la ley; **he is breaking the law by selling goods on Sunday** =

está quebrantando la ley vendiendo mercancías en domingo; **the company broke section 26 of the Companies Act** = la compañía violó la sección 26 de la Ley de Sociedades **(b)** *(to fail to carry out the duties of a contract)* romper *or* incumplir *or* violar; **the company has broken the contract** *or* **the agreement** = la compañía ha roto el contrato *or* el acuerdo; **to break an engagement to do something** = romper un compromiso **(c)** *(to cancel a contract)* anular (un contrato); **the company is hoping to be able to break the contract** = la compañía espera poder anular el contrato (NOTE: breaking - broke - broken)

◊ **breakages** ['breɪkɪdʒɪz] *plural noun* fracturas *fpl or* roturas *fpl or* desperfectos *mpl;* **customers are expected to pay for breakages** = los clientes deberán hacerse cargo de cualquier desperfecto

◊ **break down** ['breɪk 'daʊn] *verb* **(a)** *(machine)* averiarse *or* estropearse; **the two-way radio has broken down** = se ha estropeado el equipo transmisor-receptor de radio; **what do you do when your squad car breaks down?** = ¿qué haces cuando tu coche patrulla se avería? **(b)** *(talks)* cesar *or* terminar *or* interrumpirse; **negotiations broke down after six hours** = las negociaciones se interrumpieron después de seis horas; **their marriage broke down and they separated** = su matrimonio se vino abajo y se separaron **(c)** *(itemize)* clasificar *or* agrupar *or* desglosar; **we broke the crime figures down into crimes against the person and crimes against property** = desglosamos las cifras en delitos contra las personas y delitos contra la propiedad; **can you break down this invoice into spare parts and labour?** = ¿puede desglosar esta factura en piezas de repuesto y mano de obra?

◊ **breakdown** ['breɪkdaʊn] *noun* **(a)** *(mechanical)* avería *f;* **we cannot communicate with our squad car because of the breakdown of the radio link** = no podemos comunicar con nuestro coche patrulla a causa de una avería en el sistema radiofónico **(b)** *(work or discussions)* ruptura *f or* interrupción *f;* **a breakdown in wage negotiations** = una ruptura en las negociaciones salariales; **she petitioned for divorce on account of the breakdown of their marriage** = pidió el divorcio alegando ruptura de matrimonio; **irretrievable breakdown of a marriage** = ruptura matrimonial irreconciliable **(c)** *(itemize)* desglose *m;* **give me a breakdown of the latest clear-up figures** = hágame un desglose de las últimas cifras netas

◊ **break in** ['breɪk 'ɪn] *verb* forzar (una casa *or* un edificio) *or* penetrar por la fuerza (para robar); **burglars broke in through a window at the back of the house** = los ladrones penetraron a través de una ventana trasera de la casa

◊ **break-in** ['breɪkɪn] *noun (informal)* robo *m* de una casa; **there have been three break-ins in our**

street in one week = en una semana ha habido tres robos en nuestra calle

◊ **breaking** ['breɪkɪŋ] *noun* quebrantamiento *m;* **breaking and entering** = allanamiento *m* de morada; **he was charged with breaking and entering** = se le acusó de allanamiento de morada; *see also* HOUSEBREAKING

◊ **break into** ['breɪk 'ɪntu] *verb* entrar a robar; **their house was broken into while they were on holiday** = entraron a robar en su casa mientras estaban de vacaciones; **looters broke into the supermarket** = los saqueadores entraron en el supermercado para robar

◊ **break off** ['breɪk 'ɒf] *verb* cesar *or* interrumpir *or* romper; **we broke off the discussion at midnight** = interrumpimos la discusión a medianoche; **management broke off negotiations with the union** = la dirección rompió las negociaciones con el sindicato

◊ **break up** ['breɪk 'ʌp] *verb* **(a)** *(to split)* dividir; **to break up an estate** = dividir una herencia; **the company was broken up and separate divisions sold off** = la empresa se dividió y se vendió cada parte por separado **(b)** *(to come to an end)* acabar con *or* acabarse *or* disolver *or* romper; **the meeting broke up at 12.30** = la reunión se acabó a las 12.30; **the police broke up the protest meeting** = la policía disolvió el mitin de protesta

breath [breθ] *noun* respiración *f or* aliento *m;* **breath test** = prueba *f* de alcoholemia

◊ **breathalyse** ['breθəlaɪz] *verb* medir el grado de alcoholemia *or* someter a la prueba del alcohol

◊ **breathalyser** ['breθəlaɪzə] *noun* alcoholímetro *m*

bribe [braɪb] **1** *noun* soborno *m or* cohecho *m;* **to take bribes** = aceptar sobornos; **the police sergeant was dismissed for taking bribes** = el sargento de policía fue despedido por aceptar sobornos **2** *verb* sobornar; **he bribed the police sergeant to get the charges dropped** = sobornó al sargento de policía para que retirara los cargos

◊ **bribery** ['braɪbri] *noun* soborno *or* cohecho; **bribery in the security warehouse is impossible to stamp out** = es imposible acabar con el soborno en el almacén de seguridad

bridewell ['braɪdwel] *noun (slang)* celdas *fpl* de una comisaría

bridging loan ['brɪdʒɪŋ 'ləʊn] *noun* crédito *m or* préstamo *m* puente

bridleway ['braɪdlweɪ] *noun* camino *m* de herradura

brief [briːf] **1** *noun* **(a)** *(details of a client's case)* expediente *m* **(b)** *(slang)* abogado, -da **2** *verb* informar; **the superintendent briefed the press on the progress of the investigation** = el superintendente informó a la prensa de los progresos de la investigación; **to brief a barrister**

= dar instrucciones a un abogado *or* informarle de un caso

◊ **briefcase** ['bri:fkeɪs] *noun* cartera *f;* **he put all the files into his briefcase** = puso todos los archivos en su maletín

◊ **briefing** ['bri:fɪŋ] *noun* sesión *f* de información; **all the detectives on the case attended a briefing given by the commander** = todos los detectives del caso asistieron a una sesión de información que dio el comandante

bring [brɪŋ] *verb* traer *or* llevar *or* conducir; **he brought his documents with him** = trajo sus documentos consigo; **the solicitor brought his secretary to take notes of the meeting** = el abogado llevó a su secretaria para que tomara nota de la reunión; **to bring a charge** = interponer una querella; **to bring a civil action** = constituirse parte civil; **to bring a lawsuit** = entablar un pleito *or* demandar a alguien (NOTE: **bringing - brought**)

◊ **bring forward** ['brɪŋ 'fɔ:wəd] *verb* adelantar; **to bring forward the date of repayment** = adelantar la fecha del reembolso; **the date of the hearing has been brought forward to March** = han adelantado la fecha de la vista a marzo

◊ **bring in** ['brɪŋ 'ɪn] *verb* pronunciar; **the jury brought in a verdict of not guilty** = el jurado pronunció un veredicto de inocente

◊ **bring up** ['brɪŋ 'ʌp] *verb* plantear; **the chairman brought up the question of corruption in the police force** = el presidente sacó a relucir el tema de la corrupción en el cuerpo de policía

broadcast ['brɔ:dkɑ:st] **1** *noun* emisión *f or* transmisión *f* **2** *verb* emitir *or* transmitir (un programa)

◊ **broadcasting** ['brɔ:dkɑ:stɪŋ] *noun* emisión *f*

broke [brəʊk] *adjective;* **to be broke** = estar sin blanca

broker ['brəʊkə] *noun* corredor, -ra *or* intermediario financiero *or* agente *mf;* **insurance broker** = agente de seguros

◊ **brokerage** ['brəʊkrɪdʒ] *noun* corretaje *m or* correduría *f*

brothel ['brɒθl] *noun* prostíbulo *m or* burdel *m or* casa *f* de lenocinio *or* casa de prostitución

budget ['bʌdʒɪt] *noun* **(a)** presupuesto *m;* **to draw up a budget** = preparar *or* confeccionar un presupuesto; **we have agreed the budgets for next year** = hemos acordado los presupuestos para el año que viene **(b) the Budget** = el Presupuesto; **the minister put forward a budget aimed at slowing down the economy** = el ministro presentó un presupuesto encaminado a ralentizar la economía; **to balance the budget** = equilibrar el presupuesto; **the president is planning for a balanced budget** = el presidente proyecta un presupuesto equilibrado

◊ **budgetary** ['bʌdʒɪtrɪ] *adjective* presupuestario, -ria; **budgetary policy** = política *f*

presupuestaria; **budgetary control** = control *m* presupuestario; **budgetary requirements** = requisitos *mpl* presupuestarios

◊ **budgeting** ['bʌdʒɪtɪŋ] *noun* presupuestación *f or* preparación *f* del presupuesto

bug [bʌg] **1** *noun* micrófono *m* oculto; **the cleaners planted a bug under the lawyer's desk** = el personal de limpieza colocó un micrófono oculto bajo la mesa del abogado **2** *verb* ocultar un micrófono; *(a phone)* pinchar un teléfono; **the agents bugged the President's office** = los agentes colocaron un micrófono oculto en el despacho del Presidente; **bugging device** = micrófono oculto; **police found a bugging device under the lawyer's desk** = la policía encontró un micrófono oculto bajo la mesa del abogado

buggery ['bʌgri] *noun* sodomía *f*

builder ['bɪldə] *noun* constructor, -ra; **speculative builder** = constructor especulativo

building ['bɪldɪŋ] *noun* edificio *m;* **listed building** = edificio declarado de interés público

◊ **building contractor** ['bɪldɪŋ kən'træktə] *noun* contratista *mf* (de obras)

◊ **building society** ['bɪldɪŋ sə'saɪəti] *noun GB* sociedad *f* de préstamo inmobiliario

bullet ['bʊlɪt] *noun* bala *f*

◊ **bullet-proof** ['bʊlɪt'pru:f] *adjective* a prueba de balas *or* anti-balas; **bullet-proof jacket** = chaleco *m* anti-balas

◊ **bullet wound** ['bʊlɪt 'wu:nd] *noun* balazo *m*

bulletin ['bʊlətɪn] *noun* boletín *m*

bump off ['bʌmp 'ɒf] *verb* matar *or* cargarse (a alguien)

bumping ['bʌmpɪŋ] *noun US* situación en la que un empleado con más antigüedad en un trabajo ocupa el puesto de otro de más reciente incorporación

bunco ['bʌŋkəʊ] *noun (slang)* estafa *f* (normalmente en naipes)

burden of proof ['bɜ:dən əv 'pru:f] *noun* carga *f* de la prueba *or* obligación *f* de probar; **to discharge a burden of proof** = probar algo alegado en juicio; **the burden of proof is on the prosecution** = la acusación debe probar que lo que alega es cierto

bureau ['bjʊərəʊ] *noun* oficina *f or* agencia *f;* **computer bureau** = oficina de servicios informáticos; **employment bureau** = oficina de empleo; **information bureau** = oficina de información *US* **Federal Bureau of Investigation (FBI)** = Oficina Federal de Investigación (FBI) (NOTE: plural es **bureaux**)

◊ **bureaucrat** ['bjʊərəkræt] *noun* burócrata *mf*

burglar ['bɜ:glə] *noun* ladrón, -na; **burglar alarm** = alarma *f* antirrobo; **as he put his hand**

through the window he set off the burglar alarm = al introducir la mano por la ventana activó la alarma antirrobo

◊ **burglarize** ['bɜːgləaɪz] *verb US (informal)* robar con escalo *or* con allanamiento de morada *or* entrar a robar en

◊ **burglary** ['bɜːgləri] *noun* robo *m* con escalo *or* con allanamiento de morada; **he was charged with burglary** = se le acusó de robo con escalo; **there has been a series of burglaries in our street** = ha habido varios robos en nuestra calle; **aggravated burglary** = robo con armas y allanamiento de morada

◊ **burgle** ['bɜːgl] *verb* robar con escalo *or* con allanamiento de morada *or* entrar a robar en; **the school was burgled when the caretaker was on holiday** = entraron a robar en el colegio mientras el vigilante estaba de vacaciones

burial ['beriəl] *noun* sepelio *m*

burn [bɜːn] *verb* quemar; **the chief accountant burned the documents before the police arrived** = el contable jefe quemó los documentos antes de que llegara la policía (NOTE: **burning - burned** *or* **burnt**)

◊ **burn down** ['bɜːn 'daʊn] *verb* incendiar

burst into ['bɜːst 'ɪntʊ] *verb* irrumpir en

business ['bɪznəs] *noun* **(a)** *(commerce)* negocios *mpl*; **on business** = (por asuntos) de negocios **(b)** *(commercial company)* negocio *m or* comercio *m or* empresa *f or* compañía *f*; **he owns a small car repair business** = es dueño de un pequeño negocio de reparación de coches; **she runs a business from her home** = lleva un negocio desde su casa; **he set up in business as an insurance broker** = montó una agencia de seguros *or* se estableció como agente libre de seguros; **Business Expansion Scheme (BES)** = Programa *m* de Expansión Financiera; **business hours** = horas *fpl* laborables *or* de trabajo; **business name** = razón *f* social **(c)** *(items on the agenda)* asunto *m or* cuestión *f or* tema *m;* **nasty business** = mal asunto; **the main business of the meeting was finished by 3 p.m.** = el asunto principal de la reunión se concluyó a las 3 de la tarde; **any other business (AOB)** = ruegos y preguntas **(d)** *(in the House of Commons)* **the business of the House** *or* **business of the day** = asuntos a tratar; **business committee** = comisión parlamentaria que planifica el orden del día; **order of business** = orden del día

COMMENT: the normal order of business of the House of Commons begins with prayers, followed by messages from the Queen or official messages from foreign governments; then motions for writs to hold by-elections; private business; Question Time, when ministers answer questions about the work of their departments. Following this, various matters can be discussed, including debate on motions and public Bills

busy ['bɪzi] *adjective* ocupado, -da *or* atareado, -da; **the police were kept busy dealing with the crowds** = la policía estaba muy ocupada tratando de controlar a la muchedumbre; **the court has a busy schedule** = el juzgado tiene un horario muy apretado; **the line is busy** = está comunicando

buy [baɪ] **1** *noun* compra *f;* **good buy** *or* **bad buy** = buena *or* mala compra; **that watch was a good buy** = ese reloj fue una buena compra; **this car was a bad buy** = este coche fue una mala compra **2** *verb* comprar; **he bought 10,000 shares** = compró 10.000 acciones; **the company has been bought by its leading supplier** = la compañía ha sido comprada por su principal proveedor; **to buy wholesale and sell retail** = comprar al por mayor y vender al por menor; **to buy forward** = comprar divisas a plazo (NOTE: **buying - bought**)

◊ **buy back** ['baɪ 'bæk] *verb* volver a comprar *or* rescatar; **he sold the shop last year and is now trying to buy it back** = vendió la tienda el año pasado y ahora está tratando de volver a comprarla

◊ **buyer** ['baɪə] *noun* **(a)** *(person)* comprador, -ra **(b)** *(wholesaler)* mayorista *mf;* **head buyer** = jefe de compras

by-election ['baɪɪ'lekʃn] *noun* elección *f* parcial

bylaw *or* **byelaw** *or* **by-law** *or* **bye-law** ['baɪlɔː] *noun* **(a)** *(of a club)* reglamento *m* **(b)** *US* estatutos de asociación (NOTE: in the UK, called **Articles of Association) (c)** *(law made by a local authority)* estatuto *m or* reglamento *m or* ordenanza *f* municipal; **the bylaws forbid playing ball in the public gardens** = el reglamento prohíbe jugar al balón en los jardines públicos; **according to the local bylaws, noise must be limited in the town centre** = según las ordenanzas municipales, se debe reducir el ruido en el centro de la ciudad

COMMENT: bylaws must be made by bodies which have been authorized by Parliament, before they can become legally effective

byproduct ['baɪprɒdʌkt] *noun* producto *m* secundario

Cc

C [si:] *third letter of the alphabet;* **category 'C' prisoners** = reclusos, -sas poco peligrosos pero que no gozan de régimen de prisión abierto; **Schedule C** = división *f* de las leyes tributarias referente al impuesto sobre los beneficios de los títulos del estado *or* los valores públicos; **Table C** = escritura *f* de constitución y estatutos *mpl* modelo descritos en la Ley de Sociedades de 1985 para una sociedad limitada con garantía y capital no accionario

CAB ['si: 'eɪ 'bi:] = CITIZENS' ADVICE BUREAU

cabinet ['kæbɪnət] *noun* **(a)** *(piece of furniture)* armario *m or* vitrina *f or* archivo *m;* **last year's correspondence is in the bottom drawer of the filing cabinet** = la correspondencia del año pasado está en el último cajón del archivo **(b)** *(committee)* gabinete *m or* consejo *m* de ministros; *GB* **Cabinet Office** = sección *f* de funcionarios al servicio directo del Primer Ministro Británico y del Gabinete

cache [kæʃ] *noun* alijo *m;* **cache of drugs** = alijo de drogas

cadaver [kəˈdævə] *noun US* cadáver *m (NOTE: GB English is* **corpse)**

cadet [kəˈdet] *noun* cadete *m;* **he has entered the police cadet college** = ha entrado en la escuela de cadetes de la policía; **she joined the police force as a cadet** = se incorporó al cuerpo de policía como cadete

calculate ['kælkjuleɪt] *verb* **(a)** *(to add up numbers)* calcular; **the bank clerk calculated the rate of exchange for the dollar** = el empleado de banco calculó el tipo de cambio del dólar **(b)** *(to estimate)* calcular *or* suponer; **he calculated that they had six minutes left to escape before the police patrol would arrive** = calculó que tenían seis minutos para escapar antes de que llegara la patrulla de policía
◊ **calculating** ['kælkjuleɪtɪŋ] *adjective* calculador, -ra; **the judge called the prisoner a cool calculating villain** = el juez calificó al acusado de criminal frío y calculador
◊ **calculation** [kælkjuˈleɪʃn] *noun* cálculo *m;* **I made some rough calculations on the back of an envelope** = hice unos cálculos aproximados al

dorso de un sobre; **according to my calculations, the detection rate has increased by 20% over the last six months** = según mis cálculos, el índice de crímenes resueltos ha aumentado en un 20% en los últimos seis meses
◊ **calculator** ['kælkjuleɪtə] *noun* calculadora *f*

calendar ['kæləndə] *noun* **(a)** calendario *m;* **calendar days** = días *mpl naturales;* **calendar month** = mes *m* civil; **calendar year** = año *m* civil **(b) Parliamentary calendar** = calendario parlamentario **(c)** *US* lista *f* de proyectos de ley que la Cámara de Representantes y el Senado deben considerar; **calendar Wednesday** = miércoles en el que se debaten proyectos de ley en la Cámara de Representantes; **calendar of appeals** = lista de causas alzadas **(d)** *US* **Consent Calendar** = calendario de debates sobre proyectos de ley no polémicos

> COMMENT: the Senate has only one calendar, but the House of Representatives has several: the Consent Calendar for uncontroversial bills; the Discharge Calendar for motions to discharge a committee of its responsibility for a bill; the House Calendar for bills which do not involve raising revenue or spending money; and the Union Calendar for bills which raise revenue or appropriate money for expenditure

call [kɔːl] **1** *noun* **(a)** *(on telephone)* llamada *f* telefónica; **local call** = llamada local *or* urbana; **trunk call** *or* **long-distance call** = conferencia *f* (interurbana); **overseas call** *or* **international call** = conferencia *or* llamada internacional; **person-to-person call** = conferencia personal **(b)** *(demand for repayment of a loan)* demanda *f* de pago *or;* *(demand to pay for shares)* requerimiento *m or* llamamiento *m or* petición *m* de pago de acciones; **money at call** *or* **money on call** *or* **call money** = dinero *m* pagadero a petición *or* crédito *m* exigible en cualquier momento; **call option** = opción *f* de compra de acciones **(c)** *(admission to the Bar)* ingreso *m* de un abogado en el ejercicio de la abogacía **(d)** *(years at the Bar)* años de experiencia de un abogado; **he is ten years' call** = tiene diez años de experiencia **(e)** *(visit)* visita *f;* **the salesmen make six calls a day** = los vendedores realizan seis visitas diarias; **business call** = visita de negocios **(f)** **to be on call** = estar de guardia **2** *verb* **(a)** *(to phone)* llamar a *or* llamar por teléfono a; **I shall call you at your office tomorrow** = te llamaré mañana a tu despacho **(b)** *(to admit someone to the bar)* admitir en el ejercicio de la abogacía *or* ingresar en el Colegio de Abogados; **he was called (to the bar) in 1994** = se le admitió en el Colegio de Abogados en 1994 **(c)** *(trial)* **to call someone as a witness** = citar a alguien como testigo

◊ **call box** ['kɔːl 'bɒks] *noun* cabina *f* telefónica

◊ **called** [kɔːld] *adjective* llamado, -da; **a property called 'High Trees'** = una propiedad llamada 'High Trees'

◊ **caller** ['kɔːlə] *noun* **(a)** *(person who phones)* persona *f* que llama (por teléfono) **(b)** *(visitor)* visita *f*

◊ **call in** ['kɔːl 'ɪn] *verb* **(a)** *(to visit)* visitar; **the sales representative called in twice last week** = el representante de ventas nos visitó dos veces la semana pasada **(b)** *(to ask for help)* llamar a *or* recurrir a; **the local police decided to call in the CID to help in the murder hunt** = la policía local decidió llamar a la brigada de investigación criminal para que ayudase en la búsqueda del asesino **(c)** *(to ask for plans to be examined)* solicitar que un plan *or* proyecto sea examinado por el ministerio; **the minister has called in the plans for the new supermarket** = el ministro ha solicitado que el proyecto del nuevo supermercado sea examinado por el ministerio **(d)** *(to ask for a debt to be paid)* exigir el pago de una deuda *or* pedir la devolución de un préstamo

◊ **call off** ['kɔːl 'ɒf] *verb* cancelar *or* suspender; **they called the strike off** = suspendieron la huelga; **the search for the missing children has been called off** = se ha suspendido la búsqueda de los niños desaparecidos

◊ **call on** *or* **upon** ['kɔːl 'ɒn] *verb* **(a)** *(to visit)* visitar a; **the probation officers call on their clients twice a month** = los oficiales de seguridad de la libertad condicional visitan a sus clientes dos veces al mes **(b)** *(to appeal to)* pedir a *or* acudir a; **to call upon someone to give evidence** = llamar a alguien a declarar; **the minister called on community leaders to help prevent street crime** = el ministro pidió a los dirigentes de la comunidad que ayudaran en la prevención de los delitos callejeros

◊ **call out** ['kɔːl 'aut] *verb* **to call out to strike** = llamar a la huelga

◊ **call up** ['kɔːl 'ʌp] *verb* *(for military service)* llamar a filas

calm [kɑːm] *adjective* tranquilo, -la

calm down ['kɑːm 'daun] *verb* apaciguar

camera ['kæmrə] *see* BICAMERALISM, IN CAMERA

camp [kæmp] *noun* campo *m;* **concentration camp** = campo de concentración

campaign [kæm'peɪn] **1** *noun* campaña *f;* **the Government has launched a campaign against drunken drivers** = el Gobierno ha lanzado una campaña en contra de las personas que conducen en estado de embriaguez; **electoral campaign** = campaña *f* electoral **2** *verb* hacer campaña *or* luchar; **they are campaigning for the abolition of the death penalty** *or* **they are campaigning against the death penalty** = están haciendo campaña por la abolición de la pena de muerte *or* están haciendo campaña contra la pena de muerte; **he is campaigning for a revision of the Official Secrets Act** = está haciendo campaña por la modificación de la Ley de Secretos de Estado

cancel ['kænsəl] *verb* cancelar *or* anular *or* suspender *or* rescindir; **to cancel an appointment** *or* **a meeting** = suspender una cita *or* una reunión; **to cancel a cheque** *or* **a contract** = cancelar un cheque *or* anular un contrato (NOTE: GB English is **cancelling** - **cancelled** but US English **canceling** - **canceled**)

◊ **cancellandi** [kænsə'lændiː] *see* ANIMUS

◊ **cancellation** [kænsə'leɪʃn] *noun* cancelación *f* *or* anulación *f;* **cancellation of an appointment** = anulación de una cita; **cancellation of an agreement** = anulación de un acuerdo; **cancellation clause** = cláusula *f* de rescisión

candidate ['kændɪdət] *noun* candidato, -ta *or* aspirante *mf;* **there are six candidates for the post of security guard** = hay seis candidatos para el puesto de guardia jurado; **we interviewed ten candidates for the post** = entrevistamos a diez candidatos para el puesto; **all the candidates in the election appeared on television** = todos los candidatos a la elección aparecieron en la televisión; **which candidate are you voting for?** = ¿a qué candidato vas a votar?

canon law ['kænən 'lɔː] *noun* derecho *m* canónico

canvass ['kænvəs] *verb* solicitar votos *or* sondear la opinión pública

◊ **canvasser** ['kænvəsə] *noun* agente *mf* electoral *or* persona *f* que solicita votos *or* hace sondeos de opinión

◊ **canvassing** ['kænvəsɪŋ] *noun* muestreo *m* *or* localización *f* de contribuyentes *or* sondeo *m* *or* solicitación *f* de votos

capable ['keɪpəbl] *adjective* **(a)** *(able)* **capable of** = capaz de; **she is capable of very fast typing speeds** = es capaz de escribir a máquina con una rápidez increíble; **he is capable of very complicated frauds** = es capaz de realizar fraudes muy complicados **(b)** *(efficient)* capaz *or* competente; **she is a very capable divorce barrister** = es una abogada muy competente para casos de divorcio

capacity [kə'pæsɪti] *noun* **(a)** *(production)* capacidad *f* *or* rendimiento *m;* **at full capacity** = a tope **(b)** *(space)* capacidad; **storage capacity** =

capacidad de almacenamiento **(c)** *(ability)* aptitud *f* *or* capacidad *or* habilidad *f;* **he has a particular capacity for business** = tiene una habilidad especial para los negocios **(d)** *(essential element of a contract)* **legal capacity** = aptitud *or* capacidad legal; **person of full age and capacity** = persona con mayoría de edad y plena capacidad **(e) in the capacity of** = a título de; **in his capacity as chairman** = en calidad de presidente; **speaking in an official capacity** = oficialmente hablando

capax ['kæpæks] *see* DOLI

capias ['kæpiæs] *Latin word* 'con esta orden judicial'; **writ of capias** = orden *f* judicial para el cumplimiento o ejecución de una sentencia; **capias ad respondendum** = orden judicial de arresto con citación para presentarse ante el tribunal

capita ['kæpitə] *see* PER CAPITA

capital ['kæpitəl] **1** *adjective* capital; **capital crime** *or* **offence** = delito *m* capital; **capital punishment** = pena *f* capital **2** *noun* **(a)** *(money or property)* capital *m;* **capital gains** = plusvalías *fpl or* ganancias *fpl* del capital; **capital gains tax (CGT)** = impuesto *m* sobre las plusvalías *or* sobre las ganancias del capital; **capital loss** = minusvalías *fpl or* pérdidas *fpl* de capital; **capital transfer tax (CTT)** = impuesto *m* sobre las transmisiones de capital (NOTE: no plural for this meaning) **(b) to make political capital out of something** = sacar partido de algo para obtener ventajas en la política; **the Opposition made a lot of capital out of the Minister's mistake on TV** = la oposición se benefició de los errores cometidos por el ministro en la televisión; *see also* EXPENDITURE **(c)** *(main town)* capital *f;* **London is the capital of England and Madrid the capital of Spain** = Londres es la capital de Inglaterra y Madrid la capital de España **(d) capital letters** *or* **block capitals** = mayúsculas *fpl;* **write your name in block capitals at the top of the form** = escriba su nombre con mayúsculas en la parte superior del formulario
◊ **capitalism** ['kæpitəlizm] *noun* capitalismo *m*
◊ **capitalist** ['kæpitəlist] **1** *noun (sometimes used as criticism)* capitalista *mf* **2** *adjective;* **capitalist countries** = países capitalistas; **the capitalist system** = el sistema capitalista
◊ **capitalization** [kæpitəlaɪˈzeɪʃn] *noun* capitalización *f;* **market capitalization** = valor *m* de mercado del capital emitido

> COMMENT: in the UK the only capital crime is now treason

capitol ['kæpitəl] *noun* US **(a)** *(building in Washington)* Capitolio *m* sede *f* del Senado y la Cámara de Representantes de los EE UU; **Capitol Hill** = colina de Washington donde se hallan el Capitolio y otros edificios oficiales; **on Capitol Hill** = en el Senado o en la Cámara de

Representantes **(b)** *(in the main city of a State)* **State Capitol** = sede de la legislatura de un estado de los EE UU

caption ['kæpʃn] *noun* encabezamiento *m* de un documento legal

captious ['kæpʃəs] *adjective* capcioso, -sa

captive ['kæptɪv] *adjective* cautivo, -va
◊ **captivity** [kæpˈtɪvɪti] *noun* cautividad *f or* cautiverio *m;* **the guerillas were held in captivity for three months** = los guerrilleros fueron mantenidos en cautividad durante tres meses

capture ['kæptʃə] **1** *noun* aprehensión *f or* captura *f* **2** *verb* capturar *or* conseguir *or* acaparar; **the castle was captured by the enemy** = el castillo fue capturado por el enemigo; **the Opposition captured six seats in the general election** = la oposición consiguió seis nuevos escaños en las elecciones generales

car [kɑː] *noun* coche *m;* **car bomb** = coche bomba; **patrol car** = coche patrulla

card [kɑːd] *noun* tarjeta *f;* **party card** = carnet *m* de un partido; **card vote** = sistema *m* de votación en el que se muestra preferencia con una tarjeta

care [keə] *noun* **(a)** *(looking after someone)* cuidado *m or* atención *f or* asistencia *f;* **care and control** = patria *f* potestad; **under care** = bajo custodia; **the children were put in the care of the social services department** = los niños fueron puestos bajo la custodia del departamento de bienestar social; *compare* CUSTODY; **child in care** = menor *mf* bajo la custodia o tutela del departamento local de asuntos sociales *or* menor internado en un centro de protección de menores; **care order** = orden *f* que retira la patria potestad y otorga la custodia de un menor a una autoridad local; **care proceedings** = juicio *m* para otorgar la patria potestad **(b)** *(making sure that someone is not harmed)* cuidado; **due care and attention** = cuidado y atención razonables; **duty of care** = deber *m* de no actuar con negligencia; **to drive without care** = conducir sin la prudencia debida; **driving without due care and attention** = conducción *f* imprudente y temeraria *or* conducir peligrosamente
◊ **careless** ['keələs] *adjective* descuidado, -da *or* imprudente; **careless driving** = conducción *f* imprudente y temeraria *or* conducir peligrosamente
◊ **carelessly** ['keələsli] *adverb* descuidadamente
◊ **care of** ['keə 'ɒv] *phrase; (in an address)* a la atención de; **Herr Schmidt, care of Mr W Brown** = Herr Schmidt, a la atención del Sr W Brown

caretaker ['keəteɪkə] *noun* portero, -ra *or* conserje *mf or* vigilante *mf or* guarda *mf;* **caretaker Prime Minister** *or* **caretaker chairman** = Primer Ministro *or* presidente provisional *or* en funciones

carnage ['kɑːnɪdʒ] *noun* matanza *f or* carnicería *f or* mortandad *f*

carry ['kærɪ] *verb* **(a)** *(to take from one place to another)* llevar *or* transportar; **to carry goods** = transportar mercancías; **the train was carrying a consignment of cars** = el tren llevaba un cargamento de coches; **carrying offensive weapons** = tenencia *f* ilícita de armas **(b)** *(to approve by vote)* aprobar (por votación); **the motion was carried** = se aprobó la moción **(c)** *(to be punishable by)* llevar *or* tener como consecuencia; **to make someone carry the can** = echarle a alguien el muerto; **the offence carries a maximum sentence of two years' imprisonment** = el delito lleva una pena máxima de dos años de prisión
◊ **carriage** ['kærɪdʒ] *noun* transporte *m or* porte *m;* **carriage charges** = gastos *mpl* de transporte; **carriage by air** = transporte aéreo
◊ **carriageway** ['kærɪdʒweɪ] *noun* calzada *f or* carretera *f*
◊ **carrier** ['kærɪə] *noun* transportista *m or* empresa *f* de transportes; **common carrier** = empresa de transportes públicos; **private carrier** = empresa de transportes privada; **carrier's lien** = derecho *m* de retención del transportista
◊ **carry off** ['kærɪ 'ɒf] *verb* llevarse *or* secuestrar; **the looters carried off all the stock of television sets** = los saqueadores se llevaron todos los televisores que había en el almacén
◊ **carry out** ['kærɪ 'aut] *verb* llevar a cabo *or* realizar *or* ejecutar (un acuerdo) *or* desempeñar (una función); **to carry out a sentence** = ejecutar una sentencia; **the police carried out the raid with great speed** = la policía llevó a cabo la redada a gran velocidad; **the bailiffs had to carry out the order of the court and seize the woman's property** = los agentes judiciales tuvieron que llevar a cabo la orden del tribunal de embargar los bienes de la mujer

carte blanche ['kɑːt 'blɒnʃ] *French phrase* carta *f* blanca; **he has carte blanche to act on behalf of the company** *or* **the company has given him carte blanche to act on its behalf** = tiene carta blanca para actuar en nombre de la empresa *or* la empresa le ha concedido carta blanca para que actúe en su nombre

case [keɪs] **1** *noun* **(a)** *(suitcase)* maleta *f;* **the customs made him open his case** = los oficiales de aduana le hicieron abrir la maleta; **she had a small case which she carried onto the plane** = tenía una pequeña maleta que llevó en el avión **(b)** *(box for packing or for alcohol)* caja *f;* **a packing case** = cajón *m or* caja de embalaje **(c)** *(crime under investigation)* caso *m or* asunto *m;* **we have three detectives working on the case** = tenemos a tres detectives trabajando en el caso; **the police are treating the case as murder** *or* **are treating it as a murder case** = la policía considera el caso como

asesinato *or* lo considera un caso de asesinato; **we had six cases of looting during the night (d)** **court case** = causa *f or* pleito *m or* proceso *m;* **the case is being heard next week** = la causa se verá la semana próxima; **case law** = precedentes *mpl or* jurisprudencia *f* **(e)** *(arguments or facts)* argumentos *mpl or* caso; **case stated** = hechos *mpl* probados; **he appealed by way of case stated** = apeló por exposición de hechos probados; **the Appeal Court dismissed the appeal by way of case stated** = el Tribunal de Apelación desestimó la apelación por medio de exposición de hechos probados; **the case rests** = el alegato ha terminado; **defence counsel put his case** = la defensa presentó sus alegatos; **the defence rests its case** = la defensa no tiene nada más que alegar; **there is a strong case against the accused** = los alegatos en contra del acusado son muy convincentes *or* existen argumentos de peso en contra del acusado; **no case to answer** = alegato de la defensa (tras la intervención de la acusación) para que el caso se desestime **2** *verb (slang)* **to case the joint** = reconocer el terreno

COMMENT: a case is referred to by the names of the parties, the date and the reference source where details of it can be found: *Smith v. Jones [1985] 2 W.L.R. 250* This shows that the case involved Smith as plaintiff and Jones as defendant, it was heard in 1985, and is reported in the second volume of the Weekly Law Reports for that year on page 250

cash [kæʃ] *noun* dinero *m;* **hard cash** = dinero efectivo *or* en metálico

cast [kɑːst] *verb* **to cast a vote** = emitir un voto; **to cast doubt** = poner en duda; **the number of votes cast in the election was 125,458** = el número de votos emitidos en la elección fue de 125.458; **under proportional representation, the number of seats occupied by each party is related to the number of votes cast for that party** = según la representación proporcional, el número de escaños ocupados por cada partido es afín al número de votos conseguido por ese partido; **casting vote** = voto *m* de calidad; **the chairman has a casting vote** = el presidente tiene voto de calidad; **he used his casting vote to block the motion** = utilizó su voto de calidad para bloquear la moción (NOTE: **casting - cast - has cast**)

casual ['kæʒuəl] *adjective* **(a)** *(not permanent)* eventual *or* ocasional; **casual labour** = mano de obra eventual; **casual work** = trabajo ocasional *or* eventual; **casual labourer** *or* **casual worker** = trabajador, -ra eventual *or* temporero, -ra **(b)** *(not formal)* informal; **he appeared in court wearing casual clothes** = apareció ante el tribunal vestido de manera informal

casus belli [ˈkɑːzʊs ˈbeliː] *Latin phrase* casus *m* belli: justificación *f* de declaración de guerra

category [ˈkætəgəri] *noun* categoría *f;* **the theft comes into the category of petty crime** = el hurto tiene categoría de delito menor; **category 'A' prisoners** = presos, -as muy peligrosos, -as; **category 'B' prisoners** = presos, -as peligrosos, -as; **category 'C' prisoners** = reclusos, -as poco peligrosos, -as pero que no gozan de régimen de prisión abierto; **category 'D' prisoners** = reclusos, -as en régimen de prisión abierto

cater for [ˈkeɪtə ˈfɔː] *verb* atender *or* abarcar *or* abastecer; **the police station has to cater for every type of crime** = la comisaría tiene que atender a cualquier tipo de delito

caucus [ˈkɔːkəs] *noun* **(a)** camarilla *f* política **(b)** *US* comité *m* electoral de un partido político *or* reunión *f* de miembros de un partido para nominar un candidato NOTE: plural is **caucuses**

causa [ˈkauzə] *see* DONATIO

causation [kɔːˈzeɪʃn] *noun* circunstancias *fpl* causantes *or* nexo *m* causal

cause [kɔːz] **1** *noun* **(a)** *(the reason for something happening)* causa *f or* motivo *m;* **cause of action** = objeto *m* de litigio; **challenge for cause** *or* **without cause** = tacha con *or* sin justificación (objeción a un miembro del jurado con causa *or* sin causa); **contributory causes** = causas propiciatorias; **probable cause** = prueba presunta; **the report listed bad community relations as one of the contributory causes to the riot** = según el informe, las malas relaciones entre los miembros de la comunidad fue una de las causas propiciatorias de los disturbios; **to show cause** = exponer argumentos convincentes; **the judgment debtor was given fourteen days in which to show cause why the charging order should not be made absolute** = se le dieron catorce días al deudor por sentencia judicial para que expusiera sus razones *or* le dieron 14 días al deudor judicial para exponer sus razones por las que la orden de acusación no se debía hacer absoluta **(b)** *(legal proceedings)* causa *or* pleito *m;* **cause list** = lista *f* de causas *or* de pleitos; **matrimonial causes** = pleitos matrimoniales **2** *verb* causar *or* provocar; **to cause trouble** = causar problemas; **the recession caused hundreds of bankruptcies** = la recesión provocó cientos de quiebras

caution [ˈkɔːʃn] **1** *noun* **(a)** *(warning)* advertencia *f or* reprimenda *f or* llamada *f* al orden *or* amonestación *f;* **the boys were let off with a caution** = los muchachos fueron puestos en libertad con una llamada al orden **(b)** *(warning from the police)* advertencia *f;* **he signed his confession under caution** = firmó su confesión bajo amonestación **(c)** *(document lodged at Land Registry)* caución *f or* garantía *f* **(d)** *(care)* cautela *f*

(NOTE: in meanings (b) and (c) caution can be used without the or a: **to lodge caution**) **2** *verb* **(a)** *(to warn someone that he has done wrong)* advertir *or* amonestar *or* llamar al orden; **the policeman cautioned the boys after he caught them stealing fruit** = el policía amonestó a los chicos tras sorprenderlos robando fruta **(b)** *(to warn someone that he will be charged)* caucionar *or* leer los derechos a alguien acusado de un delito, como el derecho a permanecer en silencio y la advertencia de que todo lo que declare podrá ser utilizado en su contra; **the accused was arrested by the detectives and cautioned** = el acusado fue arrestado por los detectives e informado sobre sus derechos

> COMMENT: the person who is cautioned has the right not to answer any question put to him

◊ **cautioner** [ˈkɔːʃənə] *noun* fiador, -ra
◊ **cautious** [ˈkɔːʃəs] *adjective* prudente
◊ **cautiously** [ˈkɔːʃəsli] *adverb* con cautela

caveat [ˈkæviæt] *noun* advertencia *f* aviso *m or* anotación preventiva; **to enter a caveat** = mostrarse parte *or* personarse en el procedimiento *or* hacer una advertencia
◊ **caveat emptor** [ˈkæviæt ˈemptɔː] *Latin phrase* 'que el comprador se encargue': por cuenta y riesgo del comprador
◊ **caveator** [ˈkæviætə] *noun* persona *f* que advierte al tribunal de no otorgar garantía de legalidad de un documento sin consultarle

CB [ˈsiː ˈbiː] *(in the armed forces)* = CONFINED TO BARRACKS

CC [ˈsiː ˈsiː] = CHIEF CONSTABLE

CD [ˈsiː ˈdiː] = CERTIFICATE OF DEPOSIT

cease and desist order [ˈsiːs ən dɪˈzɪst ˈɔːdə] *noun US* orden *f* de cese de una determinada acción, conducta o práctica comercial

cell [sel] *noun* celda *f;* **condemned cell** = celda de los condenados a muerte; **she was put in a small cell for the night** = pasó la noche en una celda pequeña; **he shares a cell with two other prisoners** = comparte una celda con otros dos prisioneros; **he spent the night in the cells** = pasó la noche en la comisaría (NOTE: often used in the plural, meaning the cells in a police station)
◊ **cellmate** [ˈselmeɪt] *noun* compañero, -ra de celda

censor [ˈsensə] **1** *noun* censor, -ra; **the film was cut** *or* **was banned by the censor** = la película fue cortada *or* prohibida por el censor; **the film was passed by the censor** = la película no fue censurada *or* la película fue aprobada por el censor **2** *verb* censurar; **all press reports are censored by the government** = todos los informes de prensa son censurados por el gobierno; **the news of the riots was censored** = la noticia de los disturbios fue censurada; **the TV report has been censored and**

only parts of it can be shown = el reportaje televisivo ha sido censurado y sólo se pueden emitir algunas partes

◊ **censorship** ['sensəʃɪp] *noun* censura *f*; TV reporters complained of government censorship = los reporteros de televisión se quejaron de la censura gubernamental; the government has imposed strict press censorship *or* censorship of the press = el gobierno ha impuesto una estricta censura de prensa

censure ['senʃə] 1 *noun* censura *f*; vote of censure *or* censure vote = voto *m* de censura; the meeting passed a vote of censure on the minister = la reunión aprobó un voto de censura al ministro 2 *verb* censurar; the Opposition put forward a motion to censure the government = la oposición presentó una moción de censura contra el gobierno

census ['sensəs] *noun* padrón *m* municipal

central ['sentrəl] *adjective* central; central office = oficina *f* central; Central Criminal Court = sede *f* central del Tribunal Penal o Tribunal de lo Penal situado en Londres (= THE OLD BAILEY)
◊ **centralization** [sentrəlaɪˈzeɪʃn] *noun* centralización *f*
◊ **centralize** ['sentrəlaɪz] *verb* centralizar; the gathering of all criminal records has been centralized in the police headquarters = todas las fichas oficiales se han centralizado en la jefatura de policía
◊ **centre** *or* US **center** ['sentə] *noun* (a) *(political position between right and left)* centro *m*; centre party = partido *m* centrista; left of centre = centro izquierda *or* con tendencias socialistas; right of centre = centro derecha *or* con tendencias conservadoras; a left-of-centre political group = un grupo político de centro izquierda; the Cabinet is formed mainly of right-of-centre supporters of the Prime Minister = el gabinete está compuesto de una mayoría de centro derecha partidaria del primer ministro (NOTE: usually used with **the: the centre combined with the right to defeat the motion**) (b) *(of a town)* centro *m*; business centre = centro *m* financiero y comercial; an industrial centre = un centro industrial; the centre for the shoe industry = el centro de la industria del calzado (c) *(office)* centro *or* oficina *f*; Job Centre = oficina de empleo; Law Centre = cuerpo *m* de abogados de oficio; Legal Aid Centre = centro de asistencia jurídica; rehabilitation centre = centro de rehabilitación
◊ **centrist** ['sentrɪst] 1 *adjective* centrista; the group advocates a return to centrist politics = el grupo propugna el retorno a una política centrista 2 *noun* centrista *mf*

ceremony ['serəməni] *noun* ceremonia *f*; the mayor presided at the ceremony to open the new council offices = el alcalde presidió la ceremonia de inauguración de las nuevas oficinas del ayuntamiento; special police were present at ceremonies to mark the National Day = los cuerpos especiales de policía estuvieron presentes en las ceremonias de celebración del Día Nacional
◊ **ceremonial** [serɪˈməuniəl] 1 *adjective* ceremonial; the mayor wore his ceremonial robes for the opening ceremony = el alcalde llevaba las vestiduras ceremoniales en la ceremonia inaugural; the President rode in a ceremonial procession = el presidente cabalgó en una procesión ceremonial 2 *noun* ceremonias oficiales; the book lays out the rules for court ceremonial = el libro recoge las normas que rigen las ceremonias oficiales de la corte; there is a lot of ceremonial attached to the job of Lord Mayor = la labor de alcalde va acompañada de mucho ceremonial

certain ['sɜːtən] *adjective* (a) *(sure)* cierto, -ta *or* seguro, -ra; the superintendent is certain that the head of the gang is still at large = el superintendente está seguro de que el jefe de la banda está todavía en libertad (b) *(one particular)* a certain = determinado, -da; a certain number *or* a certain quantity = un cierto número *or* una cierta cantidad
◊ **certainty** ['sɜːtnti] *noun* seguridad *f* *or* certeza *f*

certificate [səˈtɪfɪkət] *noun* certificado *m* *or* certificación *f*; certificate of deposit (CD) = certificado de depósito; certificate of good conduct = certificado de buena conducta; birth certificate = acta *f* *or* partida *f* de nacimiento; clearance certificate = certificado de despacho de aduana; death certificate = fe de óbito *or* certificado de defunción; fire certificate = certificación municipal de que un edificio está debidamente protegido contra incendios; land certificate = certificado de propiedad territorial; marriage certificate = acta matrimonial *or* de matrimonio; practising certificate = certificado de ejercicio de la abogacía; share certificate = certificado de acciones *or* título *m* de acción; certificate of approval = certificado de aprobación; certificate of deposit = certificado de depósito; certificate of incorporation = autorización *f* para constituirse en sociedad anónima; certificate of judgment = testimonio *m* de sentencia; certificate of origin = certificado de origen; certificate of registration = certificación registral; certificate of registry = certificado de registro de buques *or* patente *f* de navegación
◊ **certificated** [səˈtɪfɪkeɪtɪd] *adjective*; certificated bankrupt = quebrado rehabilitado por haberse demostrado su inocencia (mediante un certificado)

certify ['sɜːtɪfaɪ] *verb* certificar *or* acreditar; to certify a document = autorizar un documento; I certify that this is a true copy = certifico que ésta es una copia auténtica *or* fiel; the document is certified as a true copy = el documento está certificado como copia fiel; certified accountant = contable *mf* colegiado *or* autorizado; certified

cheque *or US* **certified check** = cheque *m* conformado; **certified copy** = copia *f* legalizada *or* certificada

certiorari [səːtiəˈrɑːri] *Latin word* 'ser instruído'; **order of certiorari** = elevación *f* de los autos *or* auto *m* de avocación; **he applied for judicial review by way of certiorari** = solicitó una revisión judicial por elevación de los autos; **the court ordered certiorari following judicial review, quashing the order made by the juvenile court** = el tribunal ordenó un auto de avocación y la consiguiente revisión judicial, anulando la sentencia dictada por el tribunal de menores

cessate grant [ˈseseɪt ˈɡrɑːnt] *noun* garantía *f* especial de legalidad de un testamento a causa de la incapacidad de un albacea *or* garantía de legalidad que renueva otra que ya no es válida

cesser [ˈsesə] *noun* (a) *(ending)* cesación *f* (de responsabilidad) (b) *(mortgage, charter)* extinción *f* anticipada

cession [ˈseʃn] *noun* cesión *f or* traspaso *m*

CGT [ˈsiː ˈdʒiː ˈtiː] = CAPITAL GAINS TAX

chair [tʃeə] **1** *noun* (a) *(piece of furniture)* silla *f;* **electric chair** *or* **the chair** = silla eléctrica (b) *(president)* presidencia *f;* **to be in the chair** = ocupar la presidencia *or* presidir; **she was voted into the chair** = fue elegida presidenta; **Mr Jones took the chair** = el Sr Jones presidió; **to address the chair** = dirigirse al presidente **2** *verb* presidir; **the meeting was chaired by Mrs Smith** = la reunión estuvo presidida por la Sra Smith
◊ **chairman** [ˈtʃeəmən] *noun* (a) *(of a meeting)* presidente, -ta; **chairman of the magistrates** *or* **of the bench** = presidente de los magistrados *or* del tribunal; **Mr Howard was chairman** *or* **acted as chairman** = el Sr Howard fue presidente *or* actuó como presidente; **Mr Chairman** *or* **Madam Chairman** = Señor Presidente *or* Señora Presidenta (b) *(of a company)* presidente, -ta; **the chairman of the board** *or* **the company chairman** = el presidente del consejo de administración *or* de la empresa
◊ **chairmanship** [ˈtʃeəmənʃɪp] *noun* presidencia *f;* **the committee met under the chairmanship of Mr Jones** = el comité se reunió bajo la presidencia del Sr Jones
◊ **chairperson** [ˈtʃeəpəːsən] *noun* presidente, -ta
◊ **chairwoman** [ˈtʃeəwʊmən] *noun* presidenta
(NOTE: the word **chair** is now often used to mean the person, as it avoids making a distinction between men and women)

challenge [ˈtʃælɪnʒ] **1** *noun* recusación *f or* objeción *f or* desafío *m or* reto *m;* **challenge for cause** = objeción al jurado exponiendo las razones; **challenge propter defection** = recusación por falta de competencia; **peremptory challenge** *or* **challenge without cause** = recusación sin causa *or* objeción al jurado sin exponer las razones **2** *verb* recusar *or* objetar *or* desafiar *or* poner en duda *or* poner en tela de juicio; **to challenge a jury** = tachar a un jurado; **to challenge a sentence passed by magistrates by appeal to the Crown Court** = recusar una sentencia aprobada por los magistrados por apelación al Tribunal de la Corona

chamber [ˈtʃeɪmbə] *noun* cámara *f or* sala *f;* **the Upper Chamber** = la Cámara de los Lores *or* el Senado
◊ **Chamber of Commerce** *or* **Chamber of Trade** [ˈtʃeɪmbə əv ˈkɒməːs *or* treɪd] *noun* Cámara *f* de Comercio
◊ **chambers** [ˈtʃeɪmbəz] *plural noun* (a) *(of barristers)* despacho *m* de abogados *or* bufete *m* (NOTE: actually called 'a set of chambers') (b) *(of judge)* despacho de un juez; **the judge heard the case in chambers** = el juez vio el caso en privado

champerty [ˈtʃæmpəti] *noun (formerly)* ayuda *f* oculta en un juicio

chance [tʃɑːns] (a) *(being possible)* posibilidad *f or* probabilidad *f;* **is there any chance of the hearing taking place before the summer?** = ¿existe alguna posibilidad de que la vista tenga lugar antes del verano? (b) *(opportunity to do something)* oportunidad *f or* ocasión *f;* **the prosecuting counsel seized his chance and asked the witness to repeat the conversation which he had had with the accused** = el fiscal aprovechó la oportunidad y pidió al testigo que repitiera la conversación que había mantenido con el acusado

Chancellor [ˈtʃɑːnsələ] *noun* (a) *(in the United Kingdom)* **Chancellor of the Exchequer** = Ministro, -tra de Hacienda (b) *US* juez, -za que preside un tribunal de equidad
◊ **Lord Chancellor** [ˈlɔːd ˈtʃɑːnsələ] *noun* Presidente *m* de la Cámara de los Lores y Ministro de Justicia

> COMMENT: the Lord Chancellor is a member of the Cabinet; he presides over debates in the House of Lords; he is the head of the judicial system and advises on the appointment of judges

Chancery [ˈtʃɑːnsri] *noun* **the Chancery Bar** = cuerpo *m* de abogados especializados en la *Chancery Division;* **Chancery Court** = antiguo tribunal *m* de justicia, que establecía la jurisprudencia y el derecho; **Chancery Division** = sección *f* del Tribunal Superior, que se encarga de testamentos, asociaciones y empresas, tributación, quiebras, etc.

change [tʃeɪnʒ] **1** *noun* cambio *m* **2** *verb* cambiar

channel [ˈtʃænəl] **1** *noun* canal *m;* **to go through the official channels** = actuar por la vía oficial; **to open up new channels of communication** = crear nuevas vías de comunicación **2** *verb* encauzar *or* dirigir

chaos ['keɪɒs] *noun* caos *m;* **after the coup the country was in chaos** = tras el golpe de estado, reinó el caos en el país; **chaos reigned in the centre of the town until the police and fire engines arrived** = reinó el caos en el centro de la ciudad hasta que llegaron la policía y los coches de bomberos
◊ **chaotic** [keɪ'ɒtɪk] *adjective* caótico, -ca; **the situation was chaotic until the police arrived to control the traffic** = la situación era caótica hasta que la policía llegó y controló el tráfico

chaplain ['tʃæplɪn] *noun* capellán *m or* sacerdote *m;* **prison chaplain** = capellán de prisión

chapter ['tʃæptə] *noun* **(a)** *(act of Parliament)* término *m* oficial para una ley parlamentaria **(b)** *US* capítulo *m* de una ley

character ['kærəktə] *noun* carácter *m or* reputación *f;* **he is a man of good character** = es un hombre de buena reputación; **to give someone a character reference** = dar un buen informe sobre alguien; **to introduce character evidence** = llevar testigos a un juicio para que testifiquen sobre la reputación de alguien

charge [tʃɑːdʒ] **1** *noun* **(a)** *(price of a service)* coste *m or* precio *m or* honorarios *mpl;* **additional charge** = suplemento *m;* **to make no charge for delivery** = no cobrar por el reparto *or* envió; **to make a small charge for rental** = alquilar algo a bajo precio; **there is no charge for service** *or* **no charge is made for service** = el servicio es gratis *or* gratuito; **admission charge** *or* **entry charge** = entrada *f or* precio de entrada; **scale of charges** = lista *f* de precios; **free of charge** = gratis *or* gratuito, -ta; **solicitors' charges** = minuta *f or* honorarios de un abogado **(b)** *(on land or property)* deuda *f or* cargo *m* territorial; **community charge** = capitación *f;* **fixed charge** = carga *f* fija *or* precio fijo; **floating charge** = cesión *f* total del activo en garantía de una deuda; **charge by way of legal mortgage** = deuda territorial en la que el deudor hipotecario firma una escritura que da al acreedor hipotecario un interés en la propiedad **(c)** *(in court)* cargo *m or* acusación *f;* **he appeared in court on a charge of embezzling** *or* **on an embezzlement charge** = compareció ante el tribunal acusado de malversación de fondos; **the clerk of the court read out the charges** = el secretario del juzgado leyó los cargos; **charge sheet** = pliego *m* de cargos; **to answer charges** = declararse culpable *or* inocente de una acusación ante el tribunal; **to bring specific charges** = calificar los hechos delictivos; **the charges against him were withdrawn** *or* **dropped** = le retiraron la acusación *or* retiraron los cargos contra él; **to press charges against someone** = formular acusaciones contra alguien; **he was very** angry when his neighbour's son set fire to his car, but decided not to press charges = se enfadó mucho cuando el hijo de su vecino incendió su coche, pero decidió no formular acusaciones; **holding charge** = cargo menor por el que se acusa a alguien para mantenerlo en prisión preventiva **(d)** *(instructions from judge to jury)* extracto *m* de los debates **2** *verb* **(a)** *(to ask for payment)* cobrar; pedir; **to charge £5 for delivery** = cobrar 5 libras por la entrega; **how much does he charge?** = ¿cuánto cobra *or* pide?; **he charges £6 an hour** = cobra 6 libras por hora **(b)** *(in a court)* acusar *or* imputar; **he was charged with embezzling his clients' money** = se le acusó de malversar el dinero de sus clientes; **they were charged with murder** = se les acusó de asesinato (NOTE: you charge someone with a crime)
◊ **chargeable** ['tʃɑːdʒəbl] *adjective* **(a)** *(cost)* a cargo de **(b)** *(in court)* acusable *or* imputable
◊ **charged** ['tʃɑːdʒd] *adjective* acusable *or* imputado, -da
◊ **chargee** [tʃɑː'dʒiː] *noun* deudor privilegiado *or* persona *f* que tiene una deuda territorial sobre una propiedad
◊ **charging order** ['tʃɑːdʒɪŋ 'ɔːdə] *noun* orden *f* judicial de ejecución en favor de un acreedor por sentencia firme concediéndole un embargo sobre la propiedad del deudor

charity ['tʃærəti] *noun* institución *f* benéfica *or* beneficiencia *f;* **the Charity Commissioners** = cuerpo *m* regulador de instituciones benéficas
◊ **charitable trust** *or* *US* **charitable corporation** ['tʃærɪtəbl trfist *or* kɔːpə'reɪʃn] *noun* sociedad *f* benéfica

chart [tʃɑːt] *noun* tabla *f or* gráfico *m* gráfica *f;* **flow chart** = organigrama *m or* diagrama *m;* **organization chart** = organigrama

charter ['tʃɑːtə] **1** *noun* **(a)** *(document)* carta *f* (constitucional); **bank charter** = documento *m* de constitución de un banco **(b)** *(hiring)* fletamento *m or* fletamiento *m;* **charter flight** = vuelo *m* chárter *or* vuelo fletado; **charter plane** = avión *m* chárter; **boat on charter to Mr Smith** = barco fletado por el Sr Smith **2** *verb* *(ship, plane)* fletar; *(bus, train)* alquilar; **to charter a plane** *or* **a boat** = fletar un avión *or* un barco; **to charter a bus** = alquilar un autobús
◊ **chartered** ['tʃɑːtəd] *adjective* **(a)** **chartered accountant** = censor jurado de cuentas *or* perito mercantil *or* contable *mf* colegiado **(b)** *(company)* sociedad fundada antiguamente por cédula real **(c)** **chartered ship** *or* **plane** = barco *or* avión alquilado; **chartered bus** = autobús fletado
◊ **charterer** ['tʃɑːtrə] *noun* fletador, -ra
◊ **chartering** ['tʃɑːtrɪŋ] *noun* flete *m or* fletamento *m or* fletamiento *m or* alquiler *m*
◊ **charterparty** ['tʃɑːtəpɑːti] *noun* contrato *m* de flete

chattel mortgage ['tʃætəl 'mɔːɡɪdʒ] *noun US* hipoteca *f* sobre bienes muebles

◊ **chattels** ['tʃætəlz] *plural noun* bienes *mpl* muebles; **goods and chattels** = enseres *mpl* y bienes *mpl* muebles; **chattels real** = propiedades *fpl* arrendadas; **chattels personal** = bienes muebles; **incorporeal chattels** = bienes intangibles (como patentes *or* derechos de autor)

cheat [tʃiːt] **1** *noun* estafador, -ra *or* timador, -ra *or* embustero, -ra **2** *verb* estafar *or* timar *or* defraudar; **he cheated the Income Tax out of thousands of pounds** = defraudó miles de libras a Hacienda; **she was accused of cheating clients who came to ask her for advice** = se le acusó de estafar a los clientes que venían a pedirle consejo (NOTE: you cheat someone **out of** money)

check [tʃek] **1** *noun* **(a)** *(sudden stop)* detención *f* *or* parada *f or* revés *m;* **to put a check on the sale of firearms** = detener *or* imponer restricciones a la venta de armas de fuego **(b) check sample** = muestra de inspección *or* comprobación **(c)** *(inspection)* inspección *f or* comprobación *f or* chequeo *m;* **the auditors carried out checks on the petty cash book** = los auditores realizaron una inspección del libro de caja; **a routine check of the fire equipment** = una inspección rutinaria del equipo contra incendios; **baggage check** = control *m* de equipaje **(d)** *US* = CHEQUE **2** *verb* **(a)** *(to stop or delay)* parar *or* contener *or* detener; **to check the entry of contraband into the country** = detener la entrada de contrabando en el país **(b)** *(to examine or investigate)* comprobar *or* examinar *or* verificar; **to check that an invoice is correct** = comprobar que una factura es correcta; **to check and sign for goods** = examinar y firmar por la mercancía; **he checked the computer printout against the invoices** = comprobó si la impresión de ordenador coincidía con las facturas **(c)** *(to mark with a sign) US* poner contraseña a *or* hacer una marca

◊ **checking** ['tʃekɪŋ] *noun* control *m or* inspección *f or* comprobación *f;* **the inspectors found some defects during their checking of the building** = los inspectores encontraron algunos defectos durante la inspección del edificio

cheque *or US* **check** [tʃek] *noun* cheque *m or* talón *m;* **cheque account** = cuenta *f* corriente; **cheque (guarantee) card** = tarjeta bancaria; **certified cheque** = talón conformado; **crossed cheque** = cheque cruzado; **open** *or* **uncrossed cheque** = cheque abierto *or* sin cruzar; **blank cheque** = cheque en blanco; **traveller's cheques** = cheques de viaje; **to endorse a cheque** = endosar un cheque; **to make out a cheque to someone** = extender un cheque a alguien; **to pay by cheque** = pagar con cheque; **to pay a cheque into your account** = ingresar *or* depositar un cheque; **to dishonour a cheque** *or;* *(informal)* **to bounce a cheque** = impagar un cheque por falta de fondos; **the bank referred the cheque to drawer** = el

banco devolvió el cheque al librador; **to sign a cheque** = firmar un cheque; **to stop a cheque** = detener el pago de un cheque

chief [tʃiːf] *adjective* **(a)** *(most important)* principal *or* (en) jefe; **he is the chief accountant of an industrial group** = es el contable jefe de un grupo industrial *GB* **Lord Chief Justice** = Presidente *mf* del Tribunal Supremo y miembro *mf* del Tribunal de Apelación *US* **Chief Justice** = Presidente de la Sala; **Chief Constable** = jefe *mf* de policía; **Assistant Chief Constable** *or* **Deputy Chief Constable** = ayudante *mf* del jefe de policía *or* jefe de policía adjunto; **Chief Inspector** *or* **Chief Superintendent** = inspector jefe **(b) in chief** = en persona; **examination in chief** = interrogatorio *m* directo de los testigos

child ['tʃaɪld] *noun* niño, -ña; **child benefit** = prestación que recibe la persona responsable por el cuidado de un menor *US* **child support** = manutención *f* que recibe la persona responsable del cuidado de los hijos en caso de divorcio; **child destruction** = aborto *m or* interrupción *f* del embarazo; **child stealing** = secuestro *m* de un menor; **adopted child** = hijo, -ja adoptivo, -va; **legitimate child** = hijo, -ja legítimo, -ma

COMMENT: In Great Britain a child does not have full legal status until the age of eighteen. A contract is not binding on a child, and a child cannot own land, cannot make a will, cannot vote, cannot drive a car (under the age of seventeen). A child cannot marry before the age of sixteen. A child who is less than ten years old is not considered capable of committing a crime; a child between ten and fourteen years of age may be considered capable to committing a crime if there is evidence of malice or knowledge.

chose [ʃəʊz] *French word meaning* cosa *f or* artículo *m;* **chose in action** = derecho *m* de acción; **chose in possession** = objeto *m* en posesión

choose [tʃuːz] *verb* escoger

Christmas Day ['krɪsməs 'deɪ] *noun* Día *m* de Navidad (uno de los días de pago de arrendamiento)

chronic ['krɒnɪk] *adjective* crónico, -ca *or* permanente *or* endémico, -ca *or* terrible *or* fatal

chronological order [krɒnə'lɒdʒɪkl 'ɔːdə] *noun* orden *m* cronológico

CID ['siː 'aɪ 'diː] = CRIMINAL INVESTIGATION DEPARTMENT

c.i.f. ['siː 'aɪ 'ef] = COST, INSURANCE, FREIGHT

circuit ['səːkɪt] *noun* distrito *m or* jurisdicción *f;* **he is a judge on the Welsh Circuit** = es juez del distrito de Gales; **circuit judge** = juez *m* de distrito

COMMENT: the six circuits are: Northern, North-Eastern, Midland and Oxford, Wales and Chester, South-Eastern, and Western

circular ['sɔːkjʊlə] **1** *adjective* circular; **circular letter of credit** = carta *f* de crédito general **2** *noun* circular *f;* **they sent out a circular offering a 10% discount** = enviaron una circular ofreciendo un 10% de descuento

◊ **circularize** ['sɔːkjʊləraɪz] *verb* enviar una circular; **the committee has agreed to circularize the members** = el comité ha acordado enviar circulares a los miembros; **they circularized all their customers with a new list of prices** = mandaron circulares con una nueva lista de precios a todos sus clientes

◊ **circulate** ['sɔːkjʊleɪt] *verb (information)* poner en circulación *or* circular *or* divulgar; **they circulated a new list of prices to all their customers** = divulgaron una nueva lista de precios entre todos sus clientes

◊ **circulating** ['sɔːkjʊleɪtɪŋ] *adjective* circulante

◊ **circulation** [sɔːkjuˈleɪʃn] *noun* **(a)** *(movement)* circulación *f or* difusión *f;* **the company is trying to improve the circulation of information between departments** = la empresa trata de mejorar la difusión de información entre departamentos; **circulation of capital** = circulación de capital; **free circulation of goods** = libre circulación de bienes; **to put money into circulation** = poner dinero en circulación; **the amount of money in circulation increased more than had been expected** = la cantidad de dinero en circulación (se) aumentó más de lo previsto **(b)** *(of newspapers)* tirada *f;* **a circulation battle** = lucha *f* entre publicaciones para conseguir *or* alcanzar la mayor tirada; **to improve the circulation of a newspaper** = mejorar la tirada de un periódico

circumstances ['sɔːkəmstænsɪz] *plural noun* circunstancias *fpl;* **extenuating** *or* **mitigating circumstances** = circunstancias atenuantes *or* mitigantes; **exculpatory circumstances** = circunstancias eximentes de responsabilidad criminal; **the police inspector described the circumstances leading to the riot** = el inspector de policía describió las circunstancias que llevaron al motín; *see also* EXTENUATING

◊ **circumstantial** [sɔːkəmˈstænʃl] *adjective* indirecto, -ta *or* circunstancial; **circumstantial evidence** = prueba *f* indirecta *or* circunstancial

cite [saɪt] *verb* **(a)** *(to summon)* citar **(b)** *(to quote or to refer to)* citar; **the judge cited several previous cases in his summing up** = el juez citó varios casos precedentes en su discurso final

◊ **citation** [saɪˈteɪʃn] *noun* **(a)** *(official request to appear in court)* citación *f or* emplazamiento *m* *(NOTE: used mainly in the Scottish and US courts)* **(b)** *(quotation)* cita *f*

citizen ['sɪtɪzən] *noun* **(a)** *(resident)* ciudadano, -na *or* habitante *mf;* **Citizens' Advice Bureau** = Oficina de Ayuda al Ciudadano; **citizen's arrest** = arresto *m* de un delincuente sospechoso por un ciudadano **(b)** *(national)* ciudadano, -na; **he is a French citizen by birth** = es ciudadano francés de nacimiento

◊ **citizenship** ['sɪtɪzənʃɪp] *noun* ciudadanía *f*

COMMENT: a person has British citizenship if he is born in the UK and his father or mother is a British citizen, or if his father or mother has settled in the UK, or if he is adopted in the UK by a British citizen; British citizenship can also be granted to spouses of British citizens

city ['sɪti] *noun* **(a)** *(large town)* ciudad *f;* **the largest cities in Europe are linked by hourly flights** = las principales ciudades de Europa están conectadas por vuelos que salen cada hora; **capital city** = capital *f* **(b) the City** = la 'City', centro financiero de Londres

civil ['sɪvl] *adjective* civil; **civil action** = demanda *f* civil *or* acción *f* civil; **civil code** = código civil; **civil court** = sala *f or* juzgado *m* de lo civil; **civil death** = inhabilitación perpetua; **civil disorder** = disturbios *mpl;* **civil law** = derecho *m* civil; **civil liberties** = libertades *fpl* civiles *or* derechos *mpl* individuales; *(in UK)* **Civil List** = presupuesto asignado a la familia real; **civil rights** = derechos *mpl* civiles; **civil strife** = conflicto *m or* discordias *fpl* entre grupos; **civil war** = guerra *f* civil

◊ **civil service** ['sɪvl 'sɔːvɪs] *noun* administración *f* pública *or* cuerpo *m* de funcionarios del Estado; **he has a job in the civil service** = trabaja en la administración pública; **you have to pass an examination to get a job in the civil service** *or* **to get a civil service job** = para ser funcionario del Estado hay que pasar una oposición

◊ **civil servant** ['sɪvl 'sɔːvənt] *noun* funcionario, -ria (del Estado)

CJ ['siː 'dʒeɪ] = CHIEF JUSTICE

claim ['kleɪm] **1** *noun* **(a)** *(assertion of legal rights)* derecho *m; (documents)* demanda *f;* **particulars of claim** = fundamentos *mpl* fácticos *or* relato *m* de los hechos **(b)** *(statement of right to a property)* reivindicación *f or* reclamación *f;* **legal claim to something** = pretensión *f* con fundamento jurídico *or* derecho legal; **to put in a claim** = cursar una demanda; **he has no legal claim to the property** *or* **to the car** = no tiene derecho alguno sobre la propiedad *or* el coche **(c)** *(asking for money)* petición *f or* reivindicación de dinero; **wage claim** = reivindicación *f* salarial; **the union put in a 6% wage claim** = el sindicato reivindicó un aumento salarial del 6%; **she put in a claim for £250,000 damages against the driver of the other car** = pidió una indemnización de 250.000 libras por daños y perjuicios al conductor del otro coche **(d)** *(for damage or loss)* **insurance claim** =

indemnización *f* por daños; **no claims bonus** = bonificación *f;* **to put in a claim** = reclamar *or* pedir una indemnización; **claim form** = formulario *m* de declaración de siniestro; **she put in a claim for repairs to the car** = presentó una demanda por las reparaciones del coche; **he filled in the claim form and sent it to the insurance company** = rellenó el formulario de declaración de siniestros y lo envió a la compañía de seguros; **to settle a claim** = indemnizar un siniestro *or* liquidar una reclamación **(e) small claim** = demanda de menor cuantía (de menos de 500 libras); **small claims court** = juzgado *m* de pequeñas demandas **2** *verb* **(a)** *(to state a grievance in a court)* demandar **(b)** *(to ask for money)* exigir *or* pedir; **he claimed £100,000 damages against the cleaning firm** = exigió 100.000 libras por daños y perjuicios a la empresa de limpieza; **she claimed for repairs to the car against her insurance** = exigió a su compañía de seguros el pago de las reparaciones del coche **(c)** *(to state the right to a property)* reclamar *or* reivindicar; **he is claiming possession of the house** = reclama la propiedad de la casa; **no one claimed the umbrella found in my office** = nadie reclamó el paraguas que se encontró en mi despacho **(d)** *(to state that something is a fact)* declarar *or* afirmar *or* alegar *or* pretender; **he claims he never received the goods** = declara no haber recibido las mercancías; **she claims that the shares are her property** = afirma que las acciones son de su propiedad **(e)** *(to attack)* atacar a alguien en prisión **(f)** *(to arrest)* arrestar a alguien

◊ **claimant** ['kleɪmənt] *noun* demandante *mf;* **rightful claimant** = derechohabiente *mf*

◊ **claim back** ['kleɪm 'bæk] *verb* reclamar la devolución de un dinero

clandestine [klæn'destɪn] *adjective* clandestino, -na

clarify ['klærɪfaɪ] *verb* aclarar *or* clarificar; **the Opposition asked the minister to clarify his statement** = la oposición pidió al ministro que aclarase su afirmación

◊ **clarification** [klærɪfɪ'keɪʃn] *noun* aclaración *f or* clarificación *f;* **the wording of the clause is ambiguous and needs clarification** = el texto de la cláusula es ambiguo y necesita una aclaración

class [klɑːs] **1** *noun* clase *f or* categoría *f;* **first-class** = primera clase; **Class F charge** = adeudo *m* sobre una propiedad registrada a nombre de la esposa que reclama el derecho a vivir en la propiedad no siendo dueña de la misma; **class gift** = legado *m* a favor de un grupo definido de personas *or* acción *f* popular *US* **class action** *or* **class suit** = pleito *m or* acción *f* legal en beneficio de un grupo de personas **2** *verb* clasificar; **the magazine was classed as an obscene publication** = la revista fue clasificada como publicación obscena

classify ['klæsɪfaɪ] *verb* clasificar; **classified directory** = guía alfabética *or* directorio *m* comercial clasificado por secciones; **classified information** = información *f* secreta *or* reservada

◊ **classification** [klæsɪfɪ'keɪʃn] *noun* clasificación *f*

clause [klɔːz] *noun* **(a)** *(section of a contract)* cláusula *f;* **there are ten clauses in the contract** = hay diez cláusulas en el contrato; **according to clause six, payment will not be due until next year** = de acuerdo con la cláusula seis, el pago no vence hasta el año próximo; **derogatory clause** = cláusula derogatoria; **escape** *or* **let out** *or* **saving clause** = cláusula de excepción; **exclusion clause** = cláusula de exclusión; **forfeit clause** = cláusula de confiscación; **liability clause** = cláusula de responsabilidad limitada; **opting-out clause** = cláusula de autoexclusión; **optional clause** = cláusula facultativa; **penalty clause** = cláusula penal *or* de penalización; **termination clause** = cláusula resolutoria **(b)** *(section of a bill or constitution)* artículo *m or* sección *f*

claw back ['klɔː 'bæk] *verb* reembolsarse *or* resarcirse; *(of the Inland Revenue)* recobrar desgravaciones impositivas; **income tax claws back 25% of pensions paid out by the government** = con el impuesto sobre la renta, el Estado se resarce del 25% de lo que paga en pensiones; **of the £1m allocated to the development of the system, the government clawed back £100,000 in taxes** = del millón de libras asignadas para el desarrollo del sistema, el gobierno se reembolsó 100.000 libras en impuestos

◊ **clawback** ['klɔːbæk] *noun* devolución *f or* reembolso *m or* pérdida *f* de una desgravación impositiva que había sido concedida

clean bill ['kliːn 'bɪl] *noun US* proyecto *m* de ley revisado que se presenta de nuevo ante la Cámara de los Representantes en el Congreso

clean hands ['kliːn 'hændz] *plural noun* de buena fe *or* libre de culpa; **the plaintiff must have clean hands** = el demandante debe estar libre de culpa

COMMENT: from the maxim: 'he who comes to equity must come with clean hands'

clear ['klɪə] **1** *adjective* **(a)** *(easily understood)* claro, -ra *or* evidente; **he made it clear that he wanted the manager to resign** = dejó bien claro que quería la dimisión del director; **there was no clear evidence** *or* **clear proof that he was in the house at the time of the murder** = no había pruebas evidentes de que estuviera en la casa a la hora del crimen **(b)** *(clear profit)* = beneficio *m* neto; **we made $6,000 clear profit on the sale** = sacamos *or* obtuvimos un beneficio neto de 6.000 dólares por la venta; **to have a clear title to something** = tener derecho total a algo **(c)** *(free or total period of time)* completo, -ta *or* entero, -ra; **three clear days** = tres días laborables *or* hábiles; **allow three clear days for the cheqᵘᵉ to be paid into your account** = cuente con treᵣ dᵢ ᵢs hábiles para que el cheque sea depositado en su banco **2** *noun* **to be in the clear** = estar libre de sospechas **3** *verb* **(a)** *(to get rid of stock)* liquidar existencias **(b)** *(to pass through customs)* **to clear goods through the customs** = despachar mercancías por la aduana **(c)** *(to make a profit)* **to clear 10%** *or* **$5,000 on the deal** = sacar un 10% neto *or* 5.000 dólares netos en la transacción; **we cleared only our expenses** = sólo cubrimos los gastos **(d) to clear a cheque** = tramitar el pago de un cheque; **the cheque took ten days to clear** *or* **the bank took ten days to clear the cheque** = el cheque tardó diez días en ser compensado *or* el banco tardó diez días en compensar el cheque **(e)** *(to find someone not guilty)* absolver; **to clear someone of charges** = probar *or* demostrar la inocencia de alguien; **he was cleared of all charges** *or* **he was cleared on all counts** = fue declarado inocente de todas las acusaciones *or* de todos los cargos que había contra él **(f)** *(to clear up)* desalojar *or* despejar; **to clear the court** = despejar la sala

◊ **clearance** ['klıırəns] *noun* **customs clearance** = despacho *m* de aduanas; **clearance certificate** = certificado *m* de despacho de aduanas

◊ **clearing** ['klıəːrıŋ] *noun* **(a) clearing of goods through the customs** = despacho de mercancías por la aduana **(b) clearing of a debt** = liquidación *f* *or* saldo *m* de una deuda **(c) clearing bank** = banco *m* comercial (en Gran Bretaña); **clearing house** = cámara *f* de compensación

◊ **clear up** ['klıə 'ʌp] *verb* aclarar *or* resolver; **half the crimes committed are never cleared up** = la mitad de los delitos cometidos quedan sin resolver; **clear-up rate** = tasa *f* de delitos resueltos

COMMENT: clear up can be divided into two categories: **primary clear up**, when a crime is solved by arresting the suspect, and **secondary clear up**, where a person charged with one crime then confesses to another which had not previously been solved

clemency ['klemənsi] *noun* clemencia *f* US **executive clemency** = indulto concedido por el Presidente; **as an act of clemency, the president granted an amnesty to all political prisoners** = como acto de clemencia, el presidente concedió la amnistía a todos los presos políticos

clerical ['klerıkl] *adjective* **(a)** *(work)* de oficina; **clerical error** = error *m* de copia; **clerical staff** = personal *m* de oficina *or* oficinistas *mfpl*; **clerical work** = trabajo *m* de oficina; **clerical worker** = oficinista *mf* **(b)** *(of the church)* clerical

clerk [klɑːk] *noun* oficinista *mf or* empleado, -da de oficina *or* administrativo, -va; **accounts clerk** = agente *mf* de bolsa; **court clerk** = escribano, -na;

law clerk = pasante *mf*; **sales clerk** = vendedor, -ra; **wages clerk** = encargado, -da de salarios; **articled clerk** = pasante; **chief clerk** *or* **head clerk** = jefe, -fa de oficina *or* oficial *mf* mayor; **Clerk of the House (of Commons** *or* **of Lords)** = Secretario, -ria de la Cámara (de los Comunes *or* de los Lores); **clerk to the justices** = secretario, -ria de juzgado; **the functions of a justices' clerk include giving advice about law, practice and procedure** = entre las funciones de un secretario de juzgado se incluye la de aconsejar sobre el derecho, la práctica y el procedimiento; **the clerk advised the magistrates that the case had to be passed to the Crown Court for trial** = el secretario advirtió *or* anunció a los magistrados que el caso debía ser juzgado por el Tribunal de la Corona

◊ **clerkess** ['klɑːkes] *noun* *(in Scotland)* oficinista *f or* administrativa *f*

◊ **clerkship** ['klɑːkʃıp] *noun* US pasantía *f*

clever ['klevə] *adjective* inteligente *or* listo, -ta *or* hábil; **to be too clever** = pasarse de listo; **he is very clever at spotting a bargain** = es muy listo *or* tiene un talento especial para encontrar *or* reconocer gangas *or* un buen negocio; **clever shareholders have made a lot of money on the deal** = los accionistas inteligentes han obtenido mucho dinero en la transacción

client ['klaıənt] *noun* **(a)** *(of a professional person)* cliente *mf* **(b)** *(represented by a lawyer)* cliente; **the solicitor paid the fine on behalf of his client** = el abogado pagó la multa en nombre de su cliente

◊ **clientele** [kliːɒn'tel] *noun* clientela *f* clientes *mfpl* (NOTE: not plural in English)

clinch [klınʃ] *verb* *(a deal)* cerrar un trato; **he offered an extra 5% to clinch the deal** = ofreció un 5% extra para cerrar el trato; **they need approval from the board before they can clinch the deal** = necesitan la aprobación de la junta antes de poder cerrar el trato

close 1 [kləus] *adjective;* **close to** = cercano, -na *or* cerca de *or* casi; **the company was close to bankruptcy** = la empresa estaba al borde de la quiebra; **we are close to solving the crime** = estamos muy cerca de resolver el crimen **2** ['kləuz] *noun (end)* final *m or* cierre *m or* conclusión *f;* **at the close of the day's trading the shares had fallen 20%** = al cierre de la sesión bursátil las acciones habían bajado un 20% **3** ['kləuz] *verb* **(a)** *(to stop business for the day)* cerrar; **the office closes at 5.30** = la oficina cierra a las 5.30; **we close early on Saturdays** = los sábados cerramos temprano **(b)** *(end of an accounting period)* **to close the accounts** = saldar las cuentas **(c)** *(to stop credit)* **to close an account** = retirar el crédito comercial a un cliente; *(of bank)* cerrar *or* liquidar una cuenta **(d) the shares closed at $15** = las acciones cerraron a 15 dólares

◊ **close company** or   *US*   **close(d) corporation** [ˈkləʊs ˈkɒmpni or ˈkləʊzd kɔːpəˈreɪʃn] *noun* sociedad *f* privada con pequeña participación de accionistas

◊ **closed** [kləʊzd] *adjective* **(a)** *(shut)* cerrado, -da; **the office is closed on Mondays** = la oficina cierra los lunes; **all the banks are closed on the National Day** = todos los bancos cierran el día de la fiesta nacional **(b)** *(restricted to a few people)* exclusivo, -va or reservado, -da; **closed shop** or *US* **union shop** = empresa *f* que emplea exclusivamente a trabajadores sindicados; **closed shop agreement** = acuerdo *m* para contratar únicamente a trabajadores sindicados or un acuerdo de sindicación obligatoria; **the union is asking the management to agree to a closed shop** = el sindicato pide a la dirección que contrate sólo a trabajadores sindicados; **closed market** = mercado *m* cerrado; **they signed a closed market agreement with an American company** = firmaron un acuerdo de exclusividad con una empresa americana; **closed session** = sesión *f* a puerta cerrada; **the town council met in closed session to discuss staff problems in the Education Department** = la corporación municipal se reunió a puerta cerrada para discutir problemas de personal en el Área de Educación; **the public gallery was cleared when the meeting went into closed session** = se desalojó la tribuna pública cuando la reunión pasó a ser a puerta cerrada

◊ **close down** [ˈkləʊz ˈdaʊn] *verb* cerrar; **the company is closing down its London office** = la empresa va a cerrar su oficina de Londres; **the strike closed down the railway system** = la huelga paralizó el transporte ferroviario

◊ **closing** [ˈkləʊzɪŋ] **1** *adjective* **(a)** *(final)* final or último, -ma; **closing date** = fin *m* de plazo; **closing speeches** = conclusiones *fpl* finales or clausura *f* de la acusación y la defensa al término de un juicio **(b)** *(at the end of an accounting period)* final or al cierre or (de) liquidación *f* **2** *noun* **(a)** *(of a shop)* cierre *m;* **Sunday closing** = cierre dominical; **closing time** = hora *f* de cierre; **early closing day** = día *f* en que las tiendas cierran por la tarde **(b)** **closing of an account** = retirada *f* del crédito bancario or liquidación *f* de una cuenta

◊ **closure** [ˈkləʊʒə] *noun* **(a)** cierre *m* or fin *m* **(b)** *(in the House of Commons)* cierre de un debate; **closure motion** = moción *f* de clausura

> COMMENT: when an MP wishes to end the debate on a motion, he says 'I move that the question be now put' and the Speaker immediately puts the motion to the vote

cloture [ˈkləʊtʃə] *noun US* moción *f* de clausura de un debate (para acabar con un filibustero), que requiere dieciséis senadores para presentarla y dos tercios para aprobarla

clue [kluː] *noun* pista *f* or indicio *m;* **the police have searched the room for clues** = la policía ha registrado la habitación en busca de pistas; **the police have several clues to the identity of the murdered** = la policía tiene diversas pistas en cuanto a la identidad del asesino

Cmnd = COMMAND PAPERS

c/o [ˈsiː ˈəʊ] = CARE OF

Co [kəʊ] = COMPANY; **J. Smith & Co Ltd** = J. Smith & Sociedad Limitada

co- [kəʊ] *prefix* co-; **co-creditor** = coacreedor, -ra; **co-defendant** = coacusado, -da; **co-director** = codirector, -ra; **co-heir** = coheredero, -ra; **co-inheritance** = herencia conjunta; **co-insurance** = coaseguro *m;* **co-ownership** = dominio compartido

coalition [kəʊəˈlɪʃn] *noun* coalición *f;* **the coalition government fell when one of the parties withdrew support** = el gobierno de coalición fracasó cuando uno de los partidos retiró su apoyo

c.o.d. [ˈsiː ˈəʊ ˈdiː] = CASH ON DELIVERY *US* COLLECT ON DELIVERY

code [kəʊd] **1** *noun* **(a)** *(official set of laws or regulations)* código *m;* **the Highway Code** = código de circulación; **the penal code** = código penal; **failure to observe the code does not render anyone liable to proceedings** = nadie pueder ser procesado por no cumplir el código **(b)** *(set of laws of a country or state)* código; *US* **the Louisiana Code** = el código de Louisiana; **Code Napoleon** = código de Napoleón **(c)** *(set of semi-official rules)* código or normas *fpl;* **code of conduct** = normas de conducta; **code of practice** = reglamento *m* or reglamento de régimen interno; **the Code of Practice on Picketing has been issued by the Secretary of State** = el Secretario de Estado ha hecho público el reglamento sobre piquetes **(d)** *(system of signs, numbers and letters with a hidden meaning)* código or clave *f* or cifra *f;* **the spy sent his message in code** = el espía envió su mensaje en clave; **area code** = prefijo *m;* **machine-readable codes** = códigos legibles por un ordenador; **post code** or *US* **zip code** = código postal **2** *verb* cifrar or poner en clave; **we received coded instructions from our agent in New York** = recibimos instrucciones en clave de nuestro agente en Nueva York

◊ **coding** [ˈkəʊdɪŋ] *noun* codificación *f* or cifrado *m;* **the coding of invoices** = la codificación de facturas

codicil [ˈkəʊdɪsɪl] *noun* codicilo *m*

codify [ˈkəʊdɪfaɪ] *verb* codificar or compilar las leyes

◊ **codification** [kəʊdɪfɪˈkeɪʃn] *noun* **(a)** *(putting all laws together into a formal legal code)* codificación *f* **(b)** *(making a single Act of*

Parliament) codificación *f or* refundición *f* (en una misma ley de diferentes normas sobre una misma cuestión); *see also* CONSOLIDATION

coerce [kəʊˈɔːs] *verb* coaccionar

coercion [kəʊˈɔːʃn] *noun* coacción *f or* coerción *f*

coexist [kəʊɪgˈzɪst] *verb* coexistir *or* convivir
◊ **coexistence** [kəʊɪgˈzɪstəns] *noun* coexistencia *f or* convivencia *f;* **peaceful coexistence** = coexistencia pacífica

cohabit [kəʊˈhæbɪt] *verb (of a man and a woman)* cohabitar *or* vivir juntos
◊ **cohabitation** [kəʊhæbɪˈteɪʃn] *noun* cohabitación *f* amancebamiento *m*
◊ **cohabiter** *or* **cohabitee** [kəʊˈhæbɪtə or kəʊhæbɪˈtiː] *noun* cohabitante *mf*

coin [kɔɪn] *noun* moneda *f;* **he gave me two 10-cent coins in my change** = me devolvió dos monedas de 10 centavos; **I need some 10p coins for the telephone** = necesito monedas de 10 peniques para el teléfono
◊ **coinage** [ˈkɔɪnɪdʒ] *noun* acuñación *f or* sistema *m* de monedas utilizado en un país

collaborate [kəˈlæbəreɪt] *verb* colaborar; **to collaborate with a French firm on building a bridge** = colaborar con una firma francesa en la construcción de un puente; **they collaborated on the new aircraft** = colaboraron en la construcción del nuevo avión
◊ **collaboration** [kəlæbəˈreɪʃn] *noun* colaboración *f;* **their collaboration on the development of the computer system was very profitable** = su colaboración en el desarrollo del sistema informático fue muy provechosa

collateral [kəˈlætərəl] **1** *noun (guarantee)* garantía *f or* colateral *m* **2** *adjective* **(a)** *(security)* colateral *or* prendario, -ria; **collateral security** = garantía subsidiaria; **collateral contract** = contrato *m* preliminar **(b) collateral issue** = asunto *m* colateral *or* incidental

collation [kəˈleɪʃn] *noun* cotejo *m* or comparación *f*

colleague [ˈkɒliːg] *noun* colega *mf or* compañero, -ra de trabajo; **counsel asked for more time to consult his colleagues** = el abogado pidió más tiempo para consultar con sus colegas

collect [kəˈlekt] **1** *verb* **(a)** *(money)* recaudar *or* cobrar; **to collect a debt** = cobrar una deuda **(b)** *(to fetch)* recoger; **we have to collect the stock from the warehouse** = tenemos que recoger la mercancía del almacén; **can you collect my letters from the typing pool?** = ¿puedes recoger mis cartas del servicio de mecanografía?; **letters are collected twice a day** = la recogida de cartas se hace dos veces al día **2** *adverb & adjective US* (llamada de teléfono) a cobro revertido; **to make a collect call** =

llamar a cobro revertido; **he called his office collect** = llamó a su oficina a cobro revertido
◊ **collecting** [kəˈlektɪŋ] *noun* **collecting agency** = agencia *f* de cobro de morosos
◊ **collection** [kəˈlekʃn] *noun* **(a)** *(payment of money)* recaudación *f or* cobro *m;* **debt collection** = cobro de morosos; **debt collection agency** = agencia de cobro de morosos; **bills for collection** = letra *f* al cobro **(b)** *(fetching)* recogida *f;* **the stock is in the warehouse awaiting collection** = la mercancía está en el almacén lista para ser recogida; **collection charges** *or* **collection rates** = gastos *mpl or* costes *mpl* de recogida; **to hand something in for collection** = dejar algo para que sea recogido **(c)** *(money collected)* **collections** = cobros *mpl or* recaudaciones *fpl* **(d)** *(of post)* recogida *f;* **there are six collections a day from the letter box** = hay seis recogidas de cartas al día
◊ **collective** [kəˈlektɪv] *adjective* colectivo, -va; **(free) collective bargaining** = convenio *m* colectivo (libre); **collective ownership** = propiedad *f* colectiva; **collective responsibility** = responsabilidad *f* colectiva; **they signed a collective wage agreement** = firmaron un convenio salarial colectivo
◊ **collector** [kəˈlektə] *noun* cobrador, -ra *or* recaudador, -ra; **collector of taxes** *or* **tax collector** = recaudador de impuestos; **debt collector** = (agente) cobrador de morosos

college [ˈkɒlɪdʒ] *noun* **(a)** *(where people can study)* facultad *f or* escuela *f;* **business college** *or* **commercial college** = escuela empresarial *or* de comercio; **correspondence college** = escuela de enseñanza por correspondencia *or* a distancia; **secretarial college** = escuela de secretariado **(b)** *(elections) US* **electoral college** = comisión *f* electoral de compromisarios

collision [kəˈlɪʒn] *noun* colisión *f or* choque *f;* **six people were injured in the collision** = seis personas resultaron heridas en la colisión

collusion [kəˈluːʒn] *noun* colusión *f or* connivencia *f or* confabulación *f;* **he was suspected of (acting in) collusion with the owner of the property** = era sospechoso de estar de connivencia desleal con el dueño de la propiedad
◊ **collusive action** [kəˈluːsɪv ˈækʃən] *noun* acción *f* colusoria

colony [ˈkɒləni] *noun* colonia *f;* **Australia was originally a group of British colonies** = Australia era originariamente un grupo de colonias británicas; **the Romans established colonies in North Africa** = los romanos establecieron colonias en el Norte de África
◊ **colonial** [kəˈləʊniəl] **1** *adjective* colonial; **granting of independence ended a period of a hundred years of colonial rule** = con la concesión de independencia se puso fin a cien años de dominio colonial; **the colonial government was overthrown by a coup led by the local police**

force = el gobierno colonial fue derrocado por un golpe encabezado por la policía local; **colonial dependency** = colonia *f* *or* territorio *m* bajo dependencia **2** *noun* colono, -na

◊ **colonialism** [kə'ləunıəlızm] *noun* colonialismo *m;* **the meeting denounced colonialism, and demanded independence** = la asamblea denunció el colonialismo y reclamó la independencia

◊ **colonist** ['kɒlənıst] *noun* colono, -na

◊ **colonization** [kɒlənaı'zeıʃn] *noun* colonización *f*

◊ **colonize** ['kɒlənaız] *verb* colonizar *or* establecer una colonia; **the government was accused of trying to colonize the Antarctic Region** = acusaron al gobierno de intentar colonizar la región antártica

column ['kɒləm] *noun* columna *f;* **debit column** *or* **credit column** = columna de debe *or* de haber

comb [kəum] *verb* rastrear *or* peinar; **to comb the area** = rastrear la zona *or* hacer un peinado de la zona

come [kʌm] *verb* **to come into force** = entrar en vigor; **to come into office** = entrar en funciones; **to come to the rescue** = acudir a una llamada

comfort ['kʌmfət] *noun* **letter of comfort** *or* **comfort letter** = aval *m* *or* informe *m* favorable sobre una persona que ha solicitado un préstamo

comity ['kɒmıti] *noun* **comity of nations** = acuerdo *m* entre naciones

command [kə'mɑ:nd] **1** *noun* orden *m* *or* mandato *m;* **by Royal Command** = por mandato real; **Command papers** = informes *mpl* presentados al Parlamento por el gobierno **2** *verb* mandar *or* ordenar; **the judge commanded that the public gallery should be cleared** = el juez ordenó que se despejase la tribuna del público; **the President commanded the Chief of Police to arrest the Members of Parliament** = el presidente mandó al jefe de policía que arrestara a los diputados

commander [kə'mɑ:ndə] *noun* comandante *mf*

commence [kə'mens] *verb* comenzar *or* empezar; **order for hearing to commence** = apertura *f* de juicio oral; **the proceedings commenced with the swearing-in of witnesses** = el proceso comenzó con la toma de juramentos a los testigos; **the police inspector commenced the questioning of the suspect** = el inspector de policía comenzó el interrogatorio del sospechoso

◊ **commencement** [kə'mensmənt] *noun* comienzo *m* *or* inicio *m;* **date of commencement** = entrada *f* en vigor

comment ['kɒment] **1** *noun* comentario *m* *or* observación *f;* **the judge made a comment on the evidence presented by the defence** = el juez hizo

una observación sobre las pruebas presentadas por la defensa; **the newspaper has some short comments about the trial** = el periódico comenta el juicio brevemente; **fair comment** = comentario justo (hecho honestamente y no difamatorio) **2** *verb* comentar *or* hacer comentarios *or* observaciones; **the judge commented on the lack of evidence** = el juez hizo observaciones sobre la falta de pruebas; **the newspapers commented on the result of the trial** = los periódicos comentaron el resultado del juicio

◊ **commentary** ['kɒməntri] *noun* **(a)** *(textbook which comments on law)* códigos *mpl* comentados *or* comentarios *mpl* a un código *or* código con jurisprudencia **(b)** *(brief notes which comment on the main points of a judgment)* sentencia *f* comentada

commerce ['kɒmə:s] *noun* comercio *m;* **Chamber of Commerce** = Cámara *f* de Comercio

◊ **commercial** [kə'mə:ʃl] **1** *adjective* **(a)** *(referring to business)* comercial *or* mercantil; **commercial college** = escuela *f* de comercio; **commercial course** = curso *m* comercial; **Commercial Court** = tribunal *m* mercantil; **commercial directory** = guía *f* comercial *or* páginas *fpl* amarillas; **commercial law** = derecho *m* mercantil **(b)** *(profitable)* rentable *or* productivo, -va *or* económico, -ca; **not a commercial proposition** = una proposición no rentable

◊ **commercialization** [kəmə:ʃlaı'zeıʃn] *noun* comercialización *f*

◊ **commercialize** [kə'mə:ʃlaız] *verb* comercializar

◊ **commercially** [kə'mə:ʃli] *adverb* comercialmente; **not commercially viable** = no viable comercialmente

commission [kə'mıʃn] *noun* **(a)** *(official order giving authority)* cometido *m* *or* misión *f;* **he has a commission in the armed forces** = es oficial de las fuerzas armadas **(b)** *(mandate)* encargo *m* **(c)** *(payment)* comisión *f;* **he has an agent's commission of 15% of sales** = recibe una comisión del 15% de las ventas **(d)** *(group of people)* comisión *or* comité *m;* **the government has appointed a commission of inquiry to look into the problems of prison overcrowding** = el gobierno ha nombrado una comisión de investigación para examinar los problemas de masificación en las cárceles; **he is the chairman of the government commission on football violence** = es el presidente de la comisión gubernamental sobre la violencia en el fútbol; **Commission of the European Community** = Comisión de la Comunidad Europea; **Law Commission** = Comisión de Derecho: comité permanente que revisa el derecho inglés; **Royal Commission** = comisión oficial (nombrada por un ministro)

◊ **commissioner** [kə'mıʃənə] *noun* comisionado, -da *or* comisionista *mf* *or* comisario,

-ria de la UE; **the Commissioners of Inland Revenue** = la comisión de Hacienda; **commissioner for oaths** = notario, -ria público, -ca *or* encargado, -da de tomar juramento; **commissioner of police** *or* **police commissioner** = comisario de policía; **Metropolitan Police Commissioner** = comisario de la Policía Metropolitana

commit [kə'mɪt] *verb* **(a)** *(to prison)* encarcelar *or* internar; *(to a court)* citar ante los tribunales *or* llevar a los tribunales; **he was committed for trial in the Central Criminal Court** = fue citado ante el Tribunal Central de lo Penal; **the magistrates committed her for trial at the Crown Court** = los magistrados la enviaron a juicio ante el Tribunal de la Corona **(b)** *(to carry out)* cometer *or* perpetrar; **to commit an offence** = delinquir; **to commit bribery** = incurrir en soborno; **to commit perjury** = hacer juramento en falso *or* incurrir en perjurio; **to try to commit a crime** = atentar un crimen; **to commit suicide** = suicidarse; **the gang committed six robberies before they were caught** = la banda cometió seis robos antes de ser capturada **(c)** *(to get involved)* **to commit oneself** = comprometerse (NOTE: **committing - committed**)
◊ **commitment** [kə'mɪtmənt] *noun* **(a)** *(order)* auto *m* de ingreso en prisión **(b)** *(responsibilities)* **commitments** = obligaciones *fpl or* compromisos *mpl;* **to honour one's commitments** = cumplir con las obligaciones de uno; **financial commitments** = compromisos financieros
◊ **committal** [kə'mɪtəl] *noun* puesta *f* a disposición del juzgado *or* ingreso *m* en prisión *or* internamiento *m;* **committal order** = orden *m* de ingreso en prisión; **committal proceedings** = vista *f* preliminar de un caso; **committal for trial** = remisión *f* del procedimiento a la Audiencia *or* puesta a disposición de un tribunal superior; **committal for sentence** = poner a disposición de un tribunal superior a una persona declarada culpable por un tribunal de magistrados; **committal warrant** = orden judicial de ingreso en prisión

committee [kə'mɪti] *noun* **(a)** *(official group of people)* comité *m;* **joint committee** = comisión conjunta; **standing committee** = comisión permanente; **steering committee** = órgano directivo; **to be a member of a committee** *or* **to sit on a committee** = ser miembro de una comisión; **he was elected to the committee of the staff club** = fue elegido para el comité de personal del club *or* le nombraron miembro del comité del club del personal; **the new plans have to be approved by the committee members** = los nuevos planes tienen que ser aprobados por los miembros del comité; **to chair a committee** = presidir un comité; **he is the chairman of the planning committee** = es el presidente del comité de planificación; **she is the secretary of the finance committee** = es la secretaria del comité financiero **(b)** *(in the House of*

Commons) Comisión *f;* **Committee Stage** = una de las etapas en la discusión de un proyecto de ley, en la que se examina con detalle una cláusula; **select committee** = Comisión de la Cámara de los Comunes que examina la labor de un ministro; **standing committee** = Comisión permanente que examina proyectos (de ley) que no son enviados a otros comités; **Committee of the Whole House** = la Cámara de los Comunes actuando como comisión que examina las cláusulas de un proyecto de ley; **Committee of Privileges** = Comisión de la Cámara de los Comunes que examina casos de ruptura de privilegio; **Public Accounts Committee** = comisión de gastos públicos; *US* **Committee of Ways and Means** = comisión presupuestaria del Congreso

commodity [kə'mɒdɪti] *noun* mercancía *f or* producto *m or* artículo *m* (principalmente materias primas y alimentos); **primary** *or* **basic commodities** = productos primarios *or* básicos; **staple commodity** = productos de primera necesidad; **commodity market** *or* **commodity exchange** = lonja *f or* bolsa *f* de contratación; **commodity futures** = bienes *mpl* comercializados en el mercado de futuros; **silver rose 5% on the commodity futures market yesterday** = la plata subió ayer un 5% en el mercado de futuros; **commodity trader** = comerciante especializado en productos básicos *or* materias primas

common ['kɒmən] **1** *noun* terreno *m* comunal *or* ejido *m* (NOTE: now usually used in place names such as **Clapham Common**) **2** *adjective* **(a)** *(frequent)* normal *or* usual *or* frecuente; **putting the carbon paper in the wrong way round was a common mistake** = poner el papel carbón al revés era un error muy normal; **being caught by the customs is very common these days** = ser decomisado en la aduana es muy corriente hoy día **(b)** *(referring to more than one person)* público, -ca *or* común; **common assault** = delito *m* de actuación temeraria; **common carrier** = empresa *f* de transportes públicos; **common land** = terreno *m* comunal *or* ejido *m;* **common nuisance** = daño *m* público; **common ownership** = propiedad *f* en común *or* condominio *m;* **common pricing** = fijación *f* ilegal de precios entre empresas; **common property** = bienes comunales; **common seal** = sello *m* de la compañía **(c)** *US* **common stock** = acciones ordinarias **(d)** **in common** = en común; **ownership in common** = COMMON OWNERSHIP; **tenancy in common** = copropiedad *f or* comunidad *f* de bienes *or* condominio *m; compare* JOINT TENANCY
◊ **common law** ['kɒmən 'lɔː] *noun* **(a)** *(non statutory)* derecho *m* consuetudinario **(b)** *(former general system of laws in England)* derecho común anglosajón (NOTE: you say **at common law** when referring to something happening according to the principles of common law)

◊ **common-law** ['kɒmənlɔ:] *adjective* consensual *or* consuetudinario *or* relativo, -va al derecho común anglosajón; **common-law marriage** = convivencia *f or* cohabitación *f or* unión *f* consensual *or* matrimonio *m* de hecho; **common-law wife** = esposa *f* por convivencia

◊ **Common Market** ['kɒmən 'mɑ:kɪt] *noun* **the European Common Market** = el Mercado Común Europeo; **the Common Market finance ministers** = los ministros *mpl* de Finanzas del Mercado Común

◊ **Commons** ['kɒmənz] *plural noun* = HOUSE OF COMMONS; **the Commons voted against the Bill** = los Comunes votaron en contra del Proyecto de Ley; **the majority of the Commons are in favour of law reform** = la mayoría de los Comunes está a favor de la reforma del derecho

◊ **Common Serjeant** ['kɒmən 'sɑ:dʒənt] *noun* abogado, -da que actúa de juez en el centro financiero de Londres

◊ **Commonwealth** ['kɒmənwelθ] *noun* mancomunidad *f;* **the Commonwealth** = la 'Commonwealth' *or* Comunidad *f* de Naciones

commorientes [kəʊmɒri'enti:z] *plural noun* conmorientes *mfpl*

COMMENT: the law assumes that the younger person has died after the older one

commune ['kɒmju:n] *noun* **(a)** *(community)* comuna *f* **(b)** *(administrative area in some countries)* comuna *f*

communicate [kə'mju:nɪkeɪt] *verb* comunicar(se); **the members of the jury must not communicate with the witnesses** = los miembros del jurado no deben comunicarse con los testigos

◊ **communication** [kəmju:nɪ'keɪʃn] *noun* **(a)** *(passing of information)* comunicación *f;* **written communication** = comunicación escrita; **to enter into communication with someone** = establecer comunicación con alguien; **we have entered into communication with the relevant government department** = hemos establecido comunicación con el departamento del gobierno pertinente **(b)** *(message)* comunicado *m;* **we have had a communication from the local tax inspector** = hemos recibido un comunicado del inspector fiscal de la zona; **privileged communication** = carta *f* que goza de privilegio **(c) communications** = comunicaciones *fpl;* **after the flood all communications with the outside world were broken** = tras las inundaciones se cortaron todas las comunicaciones con el exterior

community [kə'mju:nɪti] *noun* **(a)** comunidad *f;* **the local business community** = los empresarios de la localidad; **community charge** = impuesto *m* municipal; **community home** = centro *m* de acogida para menores tutelados; **community policing** = acción *f* conjunta de la policía y los miembros de una comunidad para el mantenimiento de la ley y el orden; **community service** = servicio *m* comunitario; **community service order** = sentencia *f* que condena a realizar servicios sociales **(b) the European Community** = la Comunidad Europea; **Community legislation** = legislación *f* comunitaria; **the Community ministers** = los ministros *or* las ministras de la Comunidad **(c)** *(in the USA, Canada, France and many other countries)* **community property** = comunidad de bienes

commute [kə'mju:t] *verb* **(a)** *(to travel to work)* viajar diariamente al trabajo; **he commutes from the country to his office in the centre of town** = viaja diariamente del campo a su oficina, en el centro de la ciudad **(b)** *(to exchange)* conmutar *or* cambiar un derecho de crédito por una suma de dinero **(c)** *(to reduce a sentence)* conmutar; **the death sentence was commuted to life imprisonment** = la sentencia de muerte fue conmutada por la de cadena perpetua

◊ **commutation** [kɒmju'teɪʃn] *noun* conmutación *f*

◊ **commuter** [kə'mju:tə] *noun* viajero diario *or* viajera diaria; **he lives in the commuter belt** = vive en la periferia *or* extrarradio de la ciudad; **commuter train** = tren *m* de cercanías

compact ['kɒmpækt] *noun (agreement)* pacto *m or* convenio *m*

company ['kʌmpni] *noun* **(a)** *(business)* empresa *f or* compañía *f or* sociedad *f;* **to put a company into liquidation** = liquidar una sociedad; **to set up a company** = fundar *or* crear una sociedad *or* una empresa *or* una compañía; **associate company** = empresa asociada *or* afiliada; **close company** = sociedad de responsabilidad limitada; **family company** = empresa familiar; **holding company** = 'holding' *m or* sociedad de cartera; **joint-stock company** = sociedad por acciones *or* sociedad anónima; **limited (liability) company** = sociedad (de responsabilidad) limitada; **listed company** = sociedad registrada *or* cuyas acciones se cotizan en la bolsa; **parent company** = sociedad matriz *or* central; **private (limited) company** = sociedad anónima *or* privada; **public limited company (plc)** = sociedad anónima (SA); **subsidiary company** = filial *f or* empresa subsidiaria **(b) finance company** = sociedad financiera; **insurance company** = compañía de seguros; **shipping company** = empresa naviera; **a tractor *or* aircraft *or* chocolate company** = empresa de tractores *or* de aviones *or* de chocolate **(c) company director** = director, -ra de una empresa; **company law** = derecho *m* de sociedades; **company member** = accionista *mf* de una sociedad *or* empresa; **company secretary** = secretario, -ria de una empresa *or* compañía **(d) the Companies Act** = la Ley de Sociedades Anónimas; **Registrar of Companies** = encargado, -da del Registro Mercantil; **register of companies** *or* **companies'**

register = Registro Mercantil; **Companies House** = oficina *f* (del Registro Mercantil) que guarda información referente a sociedades anónimas **(e)** *(organization in the City of London)* organización *f* benéfica del centro financiero de Londres derivada de las antiguas asociaciones comerciales; **the Drapers' Company** = la asociación *f* de los pañeros; **the Grocers' Company** = la asociación de los tenderos

compare [kəm'peə] *verb* comparar *or* cotejar; **the finance director compared the figures for the first and second quarters** = el director financiero comparó las cifras del primer y segundo trimestre; **the detective compared the fingerprints on the bottle and those on the knife** = el detective comparó las huellas dactilares de la botella con las del cuchillo
◊ **compare with** [kəm'peə 'wɪð] *verb* comparar con; **compared with that of some major cities, our crime rate is quite low** = comparado con el de algunas de las principales ciudades, nuestro porcentaje de delitos es bastante bajo
◊ **comparable** ['kɒmprəbl] *adjective* comparable; **the two crimes are not comparable** = los dos delitos no son comparables; **which is the nearest company comparable to this one in size?** = ¿cuál es la empresa que más se puede comparar con ésta en importancia?
◊ **comparative** [kəm'pærətɪv] *adjective* comparativo, -va; **comparative law** = derecho *m* comparado
◊ **comparison** [kəm'pærɪsən] *noun* comparación *f*; **sales are down in comparison with those of last year** = las ventas han bajado en comparación con las del año pasado; **there is no comparison between export and home sales** = no se pueden comparar las exportaciones con las ventas nacionales

compel [kʌm'pel] *verb (to force)* obligar; **the Act compels all drivers to have adequate insurance** = la Ley obliga a todos los conductores a tener un seguro adecuado (NOTE: **compelling - compelled**)
◊ **compellable** [kɒm'peləbl] *adjective* forzoso, -sa *or* obligado, -da; **a compellable witness** = un testigo obligado *or* forzoso
◊ **compellability** [kɒmpelə'bɪlɪti] *noun* obligatoriedad *f*

compensate ['kɒmpənseɪt] *verb (to pay for damages)* compensar *or* resarcir; **to compensate a manager for loss of commission** = compensar a un director por pérdida de comisión
◊ **compensation** [kɒmpən'seɪʃn] *noun* **(a)** *(payment)* compensación *f or* indemnización *f or* resarcimiento *m*; **compensation for damage** = indemnización por daños y perjuicios; **to offer to pay compensation for damages** = ofrecer compensación por daños causados; **compensation for loss of office** = indemnización por despido *or* por cese en el cargo; **compensation for loss of**

earnings = compensación por pérdida de ganancias; **compensation fund** = fondo *m* de compensación a clientes por los daños sufridos por las acciones de los abogados; **compensation order** = orden *f* de indemnización; **unlimited compensation may be awarded in the Crown Court** = el Tribunal de la Corona puede conceder indemnización ilimitada **(b)** *US* retribución *f*; **compensation package** = paquete *m* de beneficios ofrecidos con un trabajo
◊ **compensatory** [kɒmpən'seɪtəri] *adjective* compensatorio, -ria; **compensatory damages** = indemnización por daños y perjuicios

compete [kʌm'piːt] *verb* competir *or* hacer la competencia; **to compete with someone** *or* **with a company** = competir con alguien *or* con una empresa; **the gangs were competing for control of the drugs market** = las bandas competían por el control del mercado de drogas
◊ **competition** [kɒmpə'tɪʃn] *noun* **(a)** *(trading)* competencia *f*; **free competition** = libre competencia; **unfair competition** = competencia desleal **(b)** *(contest)* concurso *m*; **open** *or* **public competition** = oposición *f*
◊ **competitor** [kəm'petɪtə] *noun* competidor, -ra; **two German firms are our main competitors** = nuestros principales competidores son dos firmas alemanas; **the contract of employment forbids members of staff from leaving to go to work for competitors** = el contrato de empleo prohíbe a los miembros del personal irse a trabajar para la competencia

competence *or* **competency** ['kɒmpɪtəns] *noun* aptitud *f or* competencia *f or* capacidad *f*; **the case falls within the competence of the court** = el caso es de la competencia del tribunal
◊ **competent** ['kɒmpɪtənt] *adjective* **(a)** *(efficient or able)* adecuado, -da *or* capaz *or* competente; **she is a competent secretary** *or* **a competent manager** = es una secretaria competente *or* una directora competente **(b)** *(legally able)* competente *or* capacitado, -da; **the court is not competent to deal with this case** = el tribunal no tiene competencia para llevar el caso; **most people are competent to give evidence** = la mayoría de la gente está capacitada para prestar declaración

compile [kəm'paɪl] *verb* recopilar; **to compile documentary evidence** = recopilar pruebas documentales

complain [kəm'pleɪn] *verb* quejarse; **the office is so cold the staff have started complaining** = hace tanto frío en la oficina que el personal ha empezado a quejarse; **she complained about the service** = se quejó del servicio; **they are complaining that our prices are too high** = se quejan de que nuestros precios son demasiado altos;

if you want to complain, write to the manager = si quiere quejarse, escriba al director

◊ **complainant** [kəm'pleɪnənt] *noun* demandante *mf or* querellante *mf*

◊ **complaint** [kəm'pleɪnt] *noun* **(a)** *(statement that you feel something is wrong)* queja *f or* reclamación *f*; **when making a complaint, always quote the reference number** = cuando haga una reclamación, cite siempre el número de referencia; **she sent her letter of complaint to the managing director** = envió su carta de reclamación al director gerente; **to make** *or* **lodge a complaint against someone** = presentar una reclamación *or* queja contra alguien; **complaints procedure** = procedimiento *m* de reclamación *or* tramitación *f* de quejas; **Police Complaints Committee** = comité que investiga quejas contra la policía **(b)** *(document signed to start proceedings in a magistrates' court)* demanda *f* **(c)** *(before a tribunal)* acusación *f*

complete [kəm'pliːt] **1** *adjective* completo, -ta; **the order is complete and ready for sending** = el pedido está completo y listo para enviar; **the order should be delivered only if it is complete** = el pedido sólo debe entregarse si está completo **2** *verb* **(a)** *(to finish)* terminar *or* acabar *or* completar; **the factory completed the order in two weeks** = la fábrica completó el pedido en dos semanas; **how long will it take you to complete the job?** = ¿cuánto tiempo le llevará terminar el trabajo? **(b) to complete a conveyance** = consumar una transmisión de propiedad

◊ **completely** [kəm'pliːtli] *adverb* completamente *or* totalmente *or* por completo; **the cargo was completely ruined by water** = el agua arruinó totalmente el cargamento; **the warehouse was completely destroyed by fire** = el almacén quedó totalmente destruido por el incendio

◊ **completion** [kəm'pliːʃn] *noun* finalización *f or* conclusión *f*; **completion date** = fecha *f* de finalización *or* de cumplimiento; **completion of a conveyance** = consumación *f* de traspaso de una propiedad; **completion statement** = informe *m* de gastos de compra-venta de una propiedad

complex ['kɒmpleks] **1** *noun* complejo *m; a* **large industrial complex** = un gran complejo industrial **2** *adjective* complejo, -ja; **a complex system of import controls** = un sistema complejo de control de las importaciones; **the regulations governing immigration are very complex** = la normativa sobre la inmigración es muy compleja

compliance [kəm'plaɪəns] *noun* conformidad *f or* acuerdo *m;* **the documents have been drawn up in compliance with the provisions of the Act** = los documentos han sido redactados de acuerdo con las disposiciones de la Ley; **declaration of compliance** = declaración *f* de cumplimiento de la Ley de sociedades

◊ **compliant** [kəm'plaɪənt] *adjective* de acuerdo con *or* conforme con; **not compliant with** = en

desacuerdo con *or* no conforme con; **the settlement is not compliant with the earlier order of the court** = el acuerdo no es conforme con la anterior sentencia del tribunal

complicated ['kɒmplɪkeɪtɪd] *adjective* complicado, -da; **the VAT rules are very complicated** = la normativa del IVA es muy complicada; **the judge warned the jury that the case was a complicated one and might last several weeks** = el juez advirtió al jurado de que el caso era complicado y podría durar varias semanas

complicity [kəm'plɪsɪti] *noun* complicidad *f*

comply [kəm'plaɪ] *verb* **to comply with** = obedecer *or* cumplir con *or* cumplimentar; **the company has complied with the court order** = la empresa ha cumplido con la orden del tribunal; **she refused to comply with the injunction** = se negó a obedecer el requerimiento

composition [kɒmpə'zɪʃn] *noun* acuerdo *m or* convenio *m or* acomodamiento *m* entre acreedor y deudor (para la liquidación de una deuda pagando sólo una parte); **composition in bankruptcy** = avenencia jurídica

compos mentis ['kɒmpɒs 'mentɪs] *Latin phrase* en su sano juicio

compound 1 ['kɒmpaund] *adjective* compuesto, -ta; **compound interest** = interés *m* compuesto **2** [kəm'paund] *verb* **(a)** *(agree with creditors)* ponerse de acuerdo *or* avenirse *or* transigir *or* liquidar una deuda pagando sólo una parte **(b)** *(to agree something in return for money)* **to compound an offence** = desistir *or* apartarse del procedimiento *or* renunciar al procedimiento a causa de cohecho (NOTE: formerly 'to compound a felony', which is still used in the USA)

comprehensive [kɒmprɪ'hensɪv] *adjective* general *or* global *or* de conjunto; **comprehensive insurance** = seguro *m* a todo riesgo

compromise ['kɒmprəmaɪz] **1** *noun* transacción *f or* conciliación *f or* componenda *f or* acuerdo *m* con concesiones recíprocas; **management offered £5 an hour, the union asked for £9, and a compromise of £7.50 was reached** = la dirección ofreció 5 libras por hora, el sindicato pedía 9 libras, y se llegó a un acuerdo de 7,50 libras; **after some discussion a compromise solution was reached** = después de discutir la cuestión, se llegó a una solución que beneficiara a todos **2** *verb* **(a)** *(to reach an agreement)* transigir *or* acordar un término medio *or* llegar a un arreglo; **he asked £15 for it, I offered £7 and we compromised on £10** = pedía 15 libras por él, yo le ofrecí 7 y acordamos un término medio de 10 libras **(b)** *(to involve someone in something)* comprometer *or* implicar; **the minister was compromised in the bribery case** = el ministro se vio implicado en un caso de soborno

comptroller [kən'trəʊlə] *noun* supervisor, -ra *or* interventor, -ra; **Comptroller and Auditor General** = Interventor y Auditor General

compulsory [kəm'pʌlsəri] *adjective* obligatorio, -ria; **compulsory liquidation** *or* **compulsory winding up** = liquidación *f* forzosa; **compulsory purchase** = adquisición *f* forzosa; **compulsory purchase order** = orden *f* de adquisición forzosa; **compulsory winding up order** = orden de liquidación forzosa (NOTE: in the USA, this is **expropriation**)

computer [kəm'pju:tə] *noun* ordenador *m;* **computer bureau** = oficina *f* de servicios informáticos; **computer error** = error *m* de ordenador; **computer file** = archivo *m* informático *or* fichero *m;* **computer fraud** = fraude *m* informático; **computer language** = lenguaje *m* informático; **computer program** = programa *m* de ordenador; **computer programmer** = programador, -ra
◊ **computerize** [kəm'pju:təraɪz] *verb* informatizar; **the police criminal records have been completely computerized** = los archivos policiales han sido totalmente informatizados

con [kɒn] **1** *noun* **(a)** *(informal)* engaño *m or* estafa *f or* timo *m;* **trying to get us to pay him for ten hours' overtime was just a con** = intentar que le pagáramos diez horas extraordinarias fue una clara estafa **(b)** *(slang)* convicto, -ta *or* prisionero, -ra *or* **(c)** *(conviction)* condena *f* **2** *verb (informal)* engañar *or* estafar *or* timar; **they conned the bank into lending them £25,000 with no security** = estafaron al banco para que les prestara 25.000 libras sin garantía; **he conned the finance company out of £100,000** = estafó 100.000 libras a la financiera (NOTE: **con - conning - conned.** Note also you con someone **into** doing something)

conceal [kən'si:l] *verb* ocultar *or* encubrir *or* esconder; **he was accused of concealing information** = se le acusó de ocultar información; **the accused had a gun concealed under his coat** = el acusado tenía una pistola escondida bajo el abrigo
◊ **concealment** [kən'si:lmənt] *noun* ocultación *f or* encubrimiento *m;* **concealment of assets** = encubrimiento de activos *or* alzamiento *m* de bienes; **concealment of birth** = ocultación de nacimiento

concede [kən'si:d] *verb* conceder *or* reconocer *or* admitir; **counsel conceded that his client owed the money** = el abogado admitió que su cliente debía el dinero; **the witness conceded under questioning that he had never been near the house** = el testigo admitió durante el interrogatorio que nunca había estado cerca de la casa; **to concede defeat** = admitir la derrota

concern [kən'sə:n] **1** *noun* **(a)** *(business)* empresa *f or* negocio *m;* **his business is a going concern** = su negocio marcha bien; **sold as a going concern** = vendida como empresa en marcha **(b)** *(worry)* preocupación *f or* inquietud *f;* **the management showed no concern at all for the workers' safety** = la dirección no mostró ninguna preocupación por la seguridad de los trabajadores **2** *verb* referirse a *or* ocuparse de *or* estar relacionado con; **the court is not concerned with the value of the items stolen** = el tribunal no se ocupa del valor de los artículos robados; **the report does not concern itself with the impartiality of the judge** = el informe no hace referencia a la imparcialidad del juez; **he has been asked to give evidence to the commission of inquiry concerning the breakdown of law and order** = se le ha pedido que declare como testigo para la comisión de investigación en relación con el quebrantamiento de la ley y el orden; **the contract was drawn up with the agreement of all parties concerned** = se redactó el contrato con el acuerdo de todas las partes interesadas

concert party ['kɒnsət 'pɑ:ti] *noun* grupo *m* de dos o más personas que actúan juntas en secreto para absorber una sociedad

concession [kən'seʃn] *noun* **(a)** *(right to operate)* concesión *f;* **mining concession** = derecho *m* de explotación de una mina **(b)** *(exclusive right to distribution)* concesión *or* agencia exclusiva; **she runs a jewellery concession in a department store** = lleva una concesión de joyería en unos grandes almacenes **(c)** *(allowance)* desgravación *f or* concesión; **tax concession** = concesión fiscal **(d)** *(admission)* reconocimiento *m or* concesión
◊ **concessionnaire** [kənseʃə'neə] *noun* concesionario, -ria
◊ **concessionary** [kə'seʃnənri] *adjective;* **concessionary fare** = tarifa *f* reducida *or* tarifa especial para empleados

conciliate [kən'sɪlieɪt] *verb* conciliar

conciliation [kənsɪli'eɪʃn] *noun* conciliación *f;* **the Conciliation Service** = ADVISORY, CONCILIATION AND ARBITRATION SERVICE

conclude [kən'klu:d] *verb* **(a)** *(to complete successfully)* concluir *or* cerrar *or* firmar; **to conclude an agreement with someone** = firmar un acuerdo con alguien **(b)** *(to believe from evidence)* concluir *or* llegar a una conclusión; **the police concluded that the thief had got into the building through the main entrance** = la policía concluyó que el ladrón había entrado en el edificio por la puerta principal
◊ **conclusion** [kən'klu:ʒn] *noun* **(a)** *(deciding from evidence)* conclusión *f or* consecuencia *f;* **the police have come to the conclusion** *or* **have reached the conclusion that the bomb was set off**

by radio control = la policía ha llegado a la conclusión de que el mecanismo de explosión de la bomba fue accionado a distancia **(b)** *US* **conclusion of fact** = conclusión final del juez basada en los hechos; **conclusion of law** = conclusión final del juez basada en los principios de derecho **(c)** *(final completion)* conclusión *or* terminación *f;* **the conclusion of the defence counsel's address** = las conclusiones finales del abogado defensor; **in conclusion** = en conclusión *or* para terminar; **in conclusion, the judge thanked the jury for their long and patient service** = para terminar, el juez dio las gracias al jurado por su largo y paciente servicio

◊ **conclusive** [kən'kluːsɪv] *adjective* concluyente *or* irrefutable *or* definitivo, -va *or* decisivo, -va; **the fingerprints on the gun were conclusive evidence that the accused was guilty** = las huellas dactilares en la pistola fueron pruebas contundentes de que el acusado era culpable

◊ **conclusively** [kən'kluːsɪvli] *adverb* concluyentemente *or* definitivamente; **the evidence of the eye witness proved conclusively that the accused was in the town at the time the robbery was committed** = la declaración del testigo presencial probó definitivamente que el acusado estaba en la ciudad en el momento en que se cometió el robo

concur [kən'kəː] *verb* estar de acuerdo; **Smith LJ dismissed the appeal, Jones and White LJJ concurring** = su señoría el Juez Smith rechazó la apelación, estando sus señorías los magistrados Jones y White de acuerdo

◊ **concurrence** [kən'kʌrəns] *noun* acuerdo *m;* **in concurrence with the other judges, Smith LJ dismissed the appeal** = de acuerdo con los otros magistrados, su señoría el Juez Smith rechazó la apelación

concurrent [kən'kʌrənt] *adjective* concurrente; **concurrent sentence** = condena *f* simultánea; **he was given two concurrent jail sentences of six months** = se le impusieron dos condenas simultáneas de seis meses de arresto

◊ **concurrently** [kən'kʌrəntli] *adverb* concurrentemente; **he was sentenced to two periods of two years in prison, the sentences to run concurrently** = fue sentenciado a dos periodos de dos años de prisión, siendo las condenas concurrentes; *see also* CONSECUTIVE, CONSECUTIVELY

condemn [kən'dem] *verb* **(a)** *(to sentence)* condenar; **the prisoners were condemned to death** = los acusados fueron condenados a muerte; **condemned cell** = celda *f* de los condenados a muerte **(b)** *(property)* declarar en ruina

◊ **condemnation** [kɒndem'neɪʃn] *noun* **(a)** *(sentence)* condena *f* **(b)** *(property)* expropiación *f*

◊ **condemnee** [kɒndem'niː] *noun* expropiado, -da

condition [kən'dɪʃn] *noun* **(a)** *(terms)* condición *f;* **conditions of employment** *or* **conditions of service** = condiciones de empleo *or* de servicio; **conditions of sale** = condiciones de venta; **on condition that** = a condición de que; **they were granted the lease on condition that they paid the legal costs** = se les concedió el arrendamiento a condición de que pagaran los gastos legales; **condition precedent** = condición suspensiva; **condition subsequent** = condición resolutoria **(b)** *(general state)* condición *or* estado *m;* **item sold in good condition** = artículo vendido en buen estado; **what was the condition of the car when it was sold?** = ¿cuál era el estado del coche cuando fue vendido?

◊ **conditional** [kən'dɪʃənl] *adjective* condicional; **to give a conditional acceptance** = dar una aceptación condicional; **the offer is conditional on the board's acceptance** = la oferta depende de la aceptación de la junta; **he made a conditional offer** = hizo una oferta condicional; **conditional discharge** = libertad *f* condicional

◊ **conditionally** [kən'dɪʃənli] *adverb* condicionalmente *or* con reservas; **to accept an offer conditionally** = aceptar una oferta condicionalmente

condominium [kɒndə'mɪniəm] *noun US* **(a)** *(rule of a colony or protected territory)* condominio *m* **(b)** *(system of ownership)* propiedad *f* horizontal

condone [kən'dəʊn] *verb* condonar *or* perdonar *or* tolerar; **the court cannot condone your treatment of your children** = el tribunal no puede tolerar su trato hacia sus hijos

◊ **condonation** [kɒndə'neɪʃn] *noun* condonación *f or* perdón *m or* tolerancia *f*

conducive [kən'djuːsɪv] *adjective* conducente; **the threat of strike action is not conducive to an easy solution to the dispute** = la amenaza de acción de huelga no es conducente a una solución fácil de la disputa

conduct 1 ['kɒndʌkt] *noun* **(a)** *(way of behaving)* conducta *f or* comportamiento *m;* **irreproachable conduct** = conducta intachable; **he was arrested for disorderly conduct in the street** = lo detuvieron por conducta escandalosa; **code of conduct** = normas *fpl* de conducta **(b)** *(bad way of behaving)* mala conducta; **she divorced her husband because of his conduct** = se divorció de su esposo a causa de su mala conducta; **conduct conducive to a breach of the peace** = conducta conducente a una alteración del orden público **2** [kən'dʌkt] *verb* mantener *or* dirigir *or* llevar; **to conduct a case** = gestionar una causa; **to conduct discussions** *or* **negotiations** = mantener discusiones *or* llevar negociaciones; **the chairman conducted the proceedings very efficiently** = el presidente dirigió los debates muy eficazmente

confederation or confederacy

[kənfedə'reɪʃn or kən'fedərəsi] *noun* confederación *f;* **the Confederation of British Industry (CBI)** = la confederación de organizaciones empresariales en el Reino Unido

> COMMENT: a confederation (as in Switzerland) is a less centralized form of government than a federation (such as Germany)

◊ **Confederacy** or **Confederate States** [kən'fedərəsi or kən'fedərət 'steɪts] *(American History)* la Confederación *f*

confer [kən'fɜː] *verb* **(a)** *(to give power)* conferir *or* otorgar; **the discretionary powers conferred on the tribunal by statute** = los poderes discrecionales conferidos al tribunal por ley **(b)** *(to discuss)* consultar; **the Chief Constable conferred with the Superintendent in charge of the case** = el jefe de policía consultó con el superintendente a cargo del caso

conference ['kɒnfərəns] *noun* congreso *m or* conferencia *f or* reunión *f;* **the Police Federation is holding its annual conference this week** = la federación de policía celebra su congreso anual esta semana; **conference proceedings** = actas *fpl* de un congreso; **press conference** = rueda *f or* conferencia de prensa

confess [kən'fes] *verb* confesar; **after six hours' questioning by the police the accused man confessed** = tras seis horas de interrogatorio por la policía, el acusado confesó

◊ **confession** [kən'feʃn] *noun* confesión *f or* declaración *f* de culpa; **voluntary confesion** = confesión espontánea *or* voluntaria; **confession and avoidance** = confesión y anulación *f or* defensa *f* de descargo; **the police sergeant asked him to sign his confession** = el sargento de policía le pidió que firmara su confesión; **the accused typed his own confession statement** = el acusado escribió a máquina su propia confesión; **the confession was not admitted in court, because the accused claimed it had been extorted** = la confesión no fue admitida en juicio, porque el acusado declaró que había sido forzada

confidence ['kɒnfɪdəns] *noun* **(a)** *(feeling sure)* confianza *f or* seguridad *f;* **the sales teams do not have much confidence in their manager** = los equipos de ventas no tienen mucha confianza en su director; **the board has total confidence in the managing director** = la junta tiene plena confianza en el director gerente; **confidence vote** = voto *m* de confianza; **vote of no confidence** = voto de desconfianza *or* moción *f* de censura; **he proposed a vote of confidence in the government** = propuso un voto de confianza en el gobierno; **the chairman resigned after the motion of no confidence was passed at the AGM** = el presidente dimitió después

de que se aprobara la moción de desconfianza en la Junta General Anual **(b)** *(trusting someone)* confidencia *f or* confianza *f;* **breach of confidence** = abuso de confianza *or* infidencia *f;* **in confidence** = en secreto; **I will show you the report in confidence** = te mostraré el informe en secreto

◊ **confidence trick** or *US* **confidence game** ['kɒnfɪdəns 'trɪk or 'geɪm] *noun* estafa *f or* fraude *m or* timo *m*

◊ **confidence trickster** or *US* **confidence man** ['kɒnfɪdəns 'trɪkstə] *noun* estafador, -ra *or* timador, -ra

◊ **confident** ['kɒnfɪdənt] *adjective* seguro, -ra *or* convencido, -da; **I am confident the turnover will increase rapidly** = estoy convencido de que el volumen de negocios aumentará rápidamente; **are you confident the sales team is capable of handling this product?** = ¿está seguro de que el equipo de ventas es capaz de vender este producto?

◊ **confidential** [kɒnfɪ'denʃl] *adjective* confidencial; **he sent a confidential report to the chairman** = envió un informe confidencial al presidente; **please mark the letter 'Private and Confidential'** = ponga en la carta la mención de 'Confidencial'

◊ **confidentiality** [kɒnfɪdenʃi'æliti] *noun* confidencialidad *f or* secreto *m;* **he broke the confidentiality of the discussions** = violó la confidencialidad de las discusiones

confine [kən'faɪn] *verb* confinar *or* encerrar; **confined to barracks** = arrestado en cuartel

◊ **confinement** [kən'faɪnmənt] *noun* confinamiento *m or* encierro *m or* reclusión *f or* internamiento *m;* **solitary confinement** = incomunicación *f;* **he was kept in solitary confinement for a week** = le mantuvieron incomunicado durante una semana

confirm [kən'fɜːm] *verb* confirmar *or* ratificar *or* constatar; **the Court of Appeal has confirmed the judge's decision** = el Tribunal de Apelación ha confirmado la sentencia dictada por el juez; **his secretary phoned to confirm the hotel room or the ticket or the agreement or the booking** = su secretaria llamó por teléfono para confirmar la habitación de hotel *or* el billete *or* el acuerdo *or* la reserva; **to confirm someone in a job** = hacer fijo a alguien en un trabajo

◊ **confirmation** [kɒnfə'meɪʃn] *noun* **(a)** *(being certain)* confirmación *f or* constatación *f;* **confirmation of a booking** = confirmación de una reserva **(b)** *(document)* confirmación *or* ratificación *f;* **he received confirmation from the bank that the deeds had been deposited** = recibió confirmación del banco de que se habían depositado las escrituras

confiscate ['kɒnfɪskeɪt] *verb* confiscar *or* incautarse de; **the court ordered the drugs to be confiscated** = el tribunal ordenó que se confiscaran las drogas

◊ **confiscation** [kɒnfɪsˈkeɪʃn] *noun* confiscación *f or* incautación *f*

conflict 1 [ˈkɒnflɪkt] *noun* conflicto *m or* pugna *f;* **conflict of interest** = conflicto de intereses; **Conflict of Laws** = Derecho *m* Internacional Privado *or* antinomia legal **2** [kənˈflɪkt] *verb* oponerse *or* estar en pugna *or* chocar; **the evidence of the wife conflicts with that of her husband** = el testimonio de la mujer contradice el del esposo; **the UK legislation conflicts with the directives of the EU** = la legislación del Reino Unido es incompatible con las directivas de la UE; **conflicting evidence** = declaraciones *fpl* contradictorias; **the jury has to decide who to believe among a mass of conflicting evidence** = el jurado tiene que decidir a quién creer entre un montón de declaraciones contradictorias

conform [kənˈfɔːm] *verb* ajustarse *or* estar de acuerdo; **the proposed Bill conforms to the recommendations of the Royal Commission** = el proyecto de ley propuesto se ajusta a las recomendaciones de la Comisión Real
◊ **conformance** [kənˈfɔːməns] *noun* conformidad *f;* **in conformance with the directives of the Commission** = en conformidad con las directivas de la Comisión; **he was criticized for non-conformance with the regulations** = se le criticó por no ajustarse a las normas
◊ **conformity** [kənˈfɔːmɪti] *noun* **in conformity with** = conforme a; **he has acted in conformity with the regulations** = ha actuado conforme a las normas

confront [kənˈfrʌnt] *verb* enfrentarse *or* hacer frente
◊ **confrontation** [kɒnfrʌnˈteɪʃn] *noun* enfrentamiento *m*

Congress [ˈkɒŋgres] *noun* Congreso *m;* **the President is counting on a Democrat majority in Congress** = el Presidente confía en una mayoría Demócrata en el Congreso; **he was first elected to Congress in 1970** = le eligieron al Congreso por primera vez en 1970; **at a joint session of Congress, the President called for support for his plan** = en una sesión mixta del Congreso, el Presidente pidió que se apoyara su plan (NOTE: often used without **the** except when referring to a particular legislature: **the US Congress met in emergency session; the Republicans had a majority in both houses of the 1974 Congress)**
◊ **Congressional** [kənˈgreʃənl] *adjective* del Congreso; **a Congressional subcommittee** = una subcomisión del Congreso; **the Congressional Record** = las actas del Congreso
◊ **Congressman** [ˈkɒŋgresmən] *noun* congresista *m or* diputado *m* del Congreso (de los EE.UU) (NOTE: when used with a name, **Congressman Smith,** it refers to a member of the House of Representatives)

◊ **Congresswoman** [ˈkɒŋgreswumən] *noun* congresista *f or* diputada *f*

conjugal [ˈkɒndʒəgəl] *adjective* conyugal; **conjugal rights** = derechos *mpl* conyugales

conman [ˈkɒnmæn] *noun* *(informal)* = CONFIDENCE TRICKSTER

connect [kəˈnekt] *verb* *(to join or to link)* relacionar *or* asociar *or* conectar; **the company is connected to the government because the chairman's father is a minister** = la empresa está relacionada con el gobierno porque el padre del presidente es ministro; **connected persons** = personas *fpl* bien relacionadas; *(slang)* personas con enchufe
◊ **connection** [kəˈnekʃn] *noun* *(link)* vínculo *m or* relación *f or* enlace *m;* **is there a connection between the loss of the documents and the death of the lawyer?** = ¿existe alguna relación entre la pérdida de los documentos y la muerte del abogado?; **in connection with** = con respecto a; **the police want to interview the man in connection with burglaries committed last November** = la policía quiere interrogar al hombre con respecto a los robos perpetrados el pasado noviembre

connive [kəˈnaɪv] *verb* **to connive at something** = hacer la vista gorda ante algo *or* con respecto a algo
◊ **connivance** [kəˈnaɪvəns] *noun* connivencia *f or* consentimiento *m or* confabulación *f or* acuerdo *m* para realizar una acción; **with the connivance of the customs officers, he managed to bring the goods into the country** = con el consentimiento de los aduaneros, logró hacer entrar las mercancías en el país

consecutive [kənˈsekjutɪv] *adjective* consecutivo, -va *or* sucesivo, -va; **consecutive sentences** = sentencias *fpl* sucesivas
◊ **consecutively** [kənˈsekjutɪvli] *adverb* consecutivamente; **he was sentenced to two periods of two years in jail, the sentences to run consecutively** = fue sentenciado a dos periodos de dos años de cárcel, siendo las sentencias sucesivas; *see also* CONCURRENT, CONCURRENTLY

consensus [kəˈsensəs] *noun* consenso *m;* **there was a consensus between all parties as to the next steps to be taken** = hubo consenso entre todos los partidos en cuanto a los pasos que se debían dar; **in the absence of a consensus, no decisions could be reached** = en ausencia de consenso, no se podrá alcanzar ninguna decisión; **consensus politics** = política *f* de consenso
◊ **consensus ad idem** [kɒnˈsensəs ˈæd ˈɪdem] *Latin phrase* contrato *m* consensual
◊ **consensual** [kənˈsensjuəl] *adjective* consensual; **consensual acts** = actos *mpl* consentidos *or* actos sexuales con consentimiento

consent [kən'sent] **1** *noun* consentimiento *m or* anuencia *f;* **by mutual consent** = de común acuerdo; **constructive consent** = consentimiento explícito; **express consent** = consentimiento expreso; **he borrowed the car without the owner's consent** = tomó el coche prestado sin el consentimiento del propietario; **the age of consent** = edad núbil; **consent judgment** = sentencia acordada; **consent order** = orden *f* judicial de consentimiento con un tercero; *US* **Consent Calendar;** *see comment at* CALENDAR **2** *verb* consentir; **the judge consented to the request of the prosecution counsel** = el juez consintió en la petición del abogado para la acusación
◊ **consenting** [kən'sentɪŋ] *adjective;* **consenting adults** = consentimiento entre adultos *or* entre mayores de edad

consider [kən'sɪdə] *verb* **(a)** *(to think seriously)* considerar *or* examinar *or* estudiar; **to consider the terms of a contract** = examinar los términos de un contrato; **the judge asked the jury to consider their verdict** = el juez pidió al jurado que considerara el veredicto **(b)** *(to believe)* considerar *or* creer; **he is considered to be one of the leading divorce lawyers** = se le considera uno de los mejores abogados en materia de divorcios; **the law on libel is considered too lenient** = la ley sobre difamación se considera demasiado indulgente
◊ **consideration** [kənsɪdə'reɪʃn] *noun* **(a)** *(serious thought)* consideración *f;* **without consideration** = sin miramientos; **we are giving consideration to moving the head office to Scotland** = estamos considerando trasladar la oficina principal a Escocia; **to take something into consideration** = tomar algo en consideración *or* tener algo en cuenta; **to ask for other offences to be taken into consideration** = confesar un acusado otros delitos aparte del que se le acusa y pedir que también sean tomados en cosideración; **the accused admitted six other offences, and asked for them to be taken into consideration** = el acusado admitió otros seis delitos, y pidió que se tuvieran en cuenta; **having taken the age of the accused into consideration, the court has decided to give him a suspended sentence** = habiendo tomado en consideración la edad del acusado, el tribunal ha decidido concederle una remisión condicional de la pena **(b)** *(price paid, but not necessarily money)* retribución *f or* prestación *f or* contraprestación *f;* **for a small consideration** = por una pequeña retribución; **executed consideration** = contraprestación ejecutada *or* efectuada *or* realizada; **executory consideration** = contraprestación realizable *or* por realizar

considerable [kən'sɪdərəbl] *adjective* considerable *or* importante; **we sell considerable quantities of our products to Africa** = vendemos cantidades considerables de nuestros productos a África; **they lost a considerable amount of money on the commodity market** = perdieron una

importante cantidad de dinero en la bolsa de contratación
◊ **considerably** [kən'sɪdərəbli] *adverb* considerablemente; **crime figures are considerably higher than they were last year** = las cifras de delitos son considerablemente más altas que las del año pasado

consign [kən'saɪn] *verb* enviar *or* consignar; **to consign goods to someone** = consignar *or* enviar mercancías a alguien
◊ **consignation** [kɒnsaɪ'neɪʃn] *noun* consignación *f or* partida *f or* envío *m*
◊ **consignee** [kɒnsaɪ'niː] *noun* consignatario *m or* destinatario, -ria
◊ **consignment** [kən'saɪnmənt] *noun* **(a)** *(sending of goods)* consignación *f or* envío *m or* expedición *f;* **consignment note** = nota *f* de expedición *or* de envío; **goods on consignment** = mercancías consignadas *or* en consignación **(b)** *(quantity of goods sent)* envío *or* remesa *f* partida *f;* **a consignment of goods has arrived** = ha llegado un envío de mercancías; **we are expecting a consignment of cars from Japan** = estamos esperando una expedición de coches de Japón
◊ **consignor** [kən'saɪnə] *noun* consignador, -ra *or* remitente *mf;* **the goods remain the property of the consignor until the consignee sells them** = los bienes son propiedad del consignador hasta su venta por parte del consignatario

consist of [kən'sɪst əv] *verb* componerse de *or* constar de; **the Magistrates' Court consists normally of three justices** = el tribunal de magistrados se compone normalmente de tres jueces; **a delegation consisting of all the heads of department concerned** = una delegación que consta de todos los jefes de los departamentos interesados

consistent [kən'sɪstənt] *adjective* consecuente *or* de acuerdo; **the sentence is consistent with government policy on the treatment of young offenders** = la sentencia es consecuente con la política gubernamental sobre el trato a delincuentes juveniles

consolidate [kən'sɒlɪdeɪt] *verb* compilar *or* acumular; **the judge ordered the actions to be consolidated** = el juez ordenó que las acciones se acumularan
◊ **Consolidated Fund** [kən'sɒlɪdeɪtɪd 'fʌnd] *noun* fondo consolidado *or GB* fondos públicos; *see also* EXCHEQUER
◊ **Consolidating Act** [kən'sɒlɪdeɪtɪŋ 'ækt] *noun* ley *f* recopiladora; *see also* CODIFICATION
◊ **consolidation** [kənsɒlɪ'deɪʃn] *noun* **(a)** *(bringing together various acts)* recopilación *f* **(b)** *(set of proceedings heard in court)* acumulación *f or* concentración *f*

consortium [kən'sɔːtiəm] *noun* consorcio *m*

conspire [kən'spaɪə] *verb* conspirar

◊ **conspiracy** [kən'spɪrəsi] *noun* conspiración *f*
or trama *f*

> COMMENT: conspiracy to commit a crime is
> itself a crime

constable ['kʌnstəbl] *noun* agente *mf* de policía;
police constable = policía *mf or* guardia *mf;*
woman police constable = mujer policía; **the
sergeant and six constables searched the
premises** = el sargento y seis policías registraron el
local (NOTE: constable can be used to address a
policeman; also used with a name: **Constable Smith**; it is
usually abbreviated to PC or WPC)

constituency [kən'stɪtjuənsi] *noun*
circunscripción *f or* distrito *m* electoral; **he
represents one of the northern constituencies** =
representa a una de las circunscripciones del norte

constitute ['kɒnstɪtjuːt] *verb* constituir; **the
documents constitute primary evidence** = los
documentos constituyen pruebas fundamentales;
**this Act constitutes a major change in
government policy** = esta Ley constituye un
cambio importante en la política gubernamental;
**conduct tending to interfere with the course of
justice constitutes contempt of court** = la
conducta que tiende a interferir en el curso de la
justicia constituye desacato a los tribunales

constitution [kɒnstɪ'tjuːʃn] *noun* constitución *f*
or estatutos *mpl;* **the freedom of the individual is
guaranteed by the country's constitution** = la
libertad del individuo está garantizada por la
constitución del país; **the new president asked the
assembly to draft a new constitution** = el nuevo
presidente pidió a la asamblea que redactara una
nueva constitución; **under the society's
constitution, the chairman is elected for a
two-year period** = según los estatutos de la
sociedad, el presidente es elegido por un periodo de
dos años; **payments to officers of the association
are not allowed by the constitution** = los estatutos
no permiten que se pague a los directivos de la
asociación
◊ **constitutional** [kɒnstɪ'tjuːʃnl] *adjective*
constitucional *or* estatutario, -ria; **censorship of the
press is not constitutional** = la censura de prensa
no es constitucional; **constitutional law** = derecho
político *or* constitucional; **constitutional lawyer** =
abogado, -da especializado, -da en derecho político;
constitutional rights = derechos constitucionales;
**the re-election of the chairman for a second term
is not constitutional** = la reelección del presidente
por un segundo periodo es antiestatutaria

> COMMENT: most countries have written
> constitutions, usually drafted by lawyers,
> which can be amended by an Act of the
> country's legislative body. The United States
> constitution was drawn up by Thomas
> Jefferson after the country became

independent, and has numerous amendments
(the first ten amendments being the Bill of
Rights). Great Britain is unusual in that it has
no written constitution, and relies on precedent
and the body of laws passed over the years to
act as a safeguard of the rights of the citizens
and the legality of government

construct [kən'strʌkt] *verb* construir; **the
company has tendered for the contract to
construct the new airport** = la empresa ha
presentado una oferta para la construcción del
nuevo aeropuerto
◊ **construction** [kən'strʌkʃn] *noun* **(a)**
(building) construcción *f;* **construction company** =
empresa *f* constructora; **under construction** = en
construcción; **the airport is under construction** =
el aeropuerto está en construcción **(b)**
(interpretation) interpretación *f; (de la ley)* analogía
f; **to put a construction on words** = interpretar las
palabras
◊ **constructive** [kən'strʌktɪv] *adjective* **(a)**
(helpful) constructivo, -va *or* positivo, -va; **she
made some constructive suggestions for
improving management-worker relations** = hizo
unas sugerencias constructivas para mejorar las
relaciones entre la patronal y los trabajadores; **we
had a constructive proposal from a shipping
company in Italy** = tenemos una propuesta de
cooperación procedente de una naviera de Italia;
constructive dismissal = dimisión forzada *or*
forzosa; **constructive knowledge** = conocimiento
m por deducción *or* implícito; **constructive notice** =
conocimiento *m* que la ley da por sentado que una
persona posee o puede poseer; **constructive trust** =
fideicomiso *m* por disposición legal **(b)** *(insurance)*
constructive total loss = pérdida total constructiva

construe [kən'struː] *verb* interpretar; **the court
construed the words to mean that there was a
contract between the parties** = el tribunal
interpretó las palabras como que había un contrato
entre las partes; **written opinion is not admissible
as evidence for the purposes of construing a deed
of settlement** = una opinión escrita no es admisible
como prueba para interpretar una escritura de
liquidación

consult [kən'sʌlt] *verb* consultar; **he consulted
his solicitor about the letter** = consultó a su
abogado sobre la carta
◊ **consultancy** [kən'sʌltənsi] *noun*
asesoramiento *m or* consulta *f;* **a consultancy firm**
= una asesoría *or* consultoría *or* una empresa
asesora; **he offers a consultancy service** = ofrece
un servicio de asesoramiento
◊ **consultant** [kən'sʌltənt] *noun* asesor, -ra;
engineering consultant = asesor técnico *or* asesor
de ingeniería; **legal consultant** = jurisconsulto, -ta;
management consultant = asesor administrativo *or*
de empresa; **tax consultant** = asesor fiscal
◊ **consultation** [kɒnsʌl'teɪʃn] *noun* consulta *f*

◊ **consulting** [kən'sʌltɪŋ] *adjective* asesor, -ra; **consulting engineer** = técnico asesor

consumer [kən'sjuːmə] *noun* consumidor, -ra; **gas consumers are protesting at the increase in prices** = los consumidores de gas protestan por el aumento de precios; **the factory is a heavy consumer of water** = la fábrica es una gran consumidora de agua; **consumer council** = asociación *f* de consumidores; **consumer credit** = crédito *m* al consumidor; **consumer goods** = bienes *mpl* de consumo; **consumer legislation** = legislación *f* del consumidor; **consumer protection** = protección *f* al consumidor

consummation [kɒnsə'meɪʃn] *noun* consumación *f* del matrimonio

consumption [kən'sʌmpʃn] *noun* consumo *m*; **a car with low petrol consumption** = un coche con un bajo consumo de gasolina; **the factory has a heavy consumption of coal** = el consumo de carbón en la fábrica es muy elevado *or* la fábrica consume mucho carbón

contact 1 ['kɒntækt] *noun* **(a)** *(person)* contacto *m or* conocido *m or* relación *f or; (slang)* enchufe *m;* **he has many contacts in the city** = tiene muchos contactos en la ciudad; **who is your contact in the Ministry?** = ¿quién es su persona de confianza *or* su contacto en el Ministerio? **(b)** *(getting in touch)* contacto *or* relación; **I have lost contact with them** = he perdido contacto con ellos; **he put me in contact with a good lawyer** = me puso en contacto con un buen abogado **2** [kən'tækt] *verb* ponerse en contacto con *or* contactar *or* comunicar con *or* establecer contacto; **he tried to contact his office by phone** = trató de ponerse en contacto con su oficina por teléfono; **can you contact the solicitors representing the vendors?** = ¿puede ponerse en contacto con los abogados que representan a los vendedores?

contain [kən'teɪn] *verb* contener; **the contract contains some clauses which are open to misinterpretation** = el contrato contiene algunas cláusulas que pueden dar lugar a interpretaciones equívocas *or* erróneas; **some of the instructions contained in the will are quite impossible to carry out** = algunas de las instrucciones contenidas en el testamento son imposibles de llevar a cabo

contemnor [kən'temnə] *noun* rebelde *mf or* persona *f* que comete desacato a los tribunales

contempt [kən'tempt] *noun* desprecio *m or* desdén *m or* desacato *m or* contumacia *f;* **contempt of court** = desacato *m* a los tribunales; **constructive contempt** = contumacia indirecta; **direct contempt** = contumacia directa; **guilty of contempt** = contumaz; **to be in contempt** = haber mostrado desacato a un tribunal; **declared in contempt of court** = declarado, -da en rebeldía; **at common law, conduct tending to interfere with the course of** justice in particular legal proceedings constitutes criminal contempt = en el derecho común anglosajón, la conducta que tiende a interferir en el curso de la justicia en procesos legales concretos constituye delito de desacato criminal; **contempt of Parliament** *or* **contempt of the House** = conducta *f* que desprestigia al Parlamento; **to purge one's contempt** = purgar uno su desacato *or* falta de respeto mostrada

content ['kɒntent] *noun* contenido *m;* **the content of the letter** = el contenido de la carta

◊ **contents** ['kɒntents] *plural noun* contenido *m;* **the contents of the bottle poured out onto the floor** = el contenido de la botella se derramó en el suelo; **the customs officials inspected the contents of the box** = los aduaneros inspeccionaron el contenido de la caja; **the contents of the letter** = el contenido de la carta

contentious [kən'tenʃəs] *adjective & noun* contencioso, -sa

contest 1 ['kɒntest] *noun (competition)* competición *m or* prueba *f or* lucha *f* **2** [kən'test] *verb* **(a)** *(to argue against)* defender *or* refutar *or* rebatir; **I wish to contest the statement made by the witness** = deseo rebatir la declaración hecha por el testigo **(b)** *(to fight an election)* presentarse como candidato a *or* disputar; **the seat is being contested by five candidates** = el escaño es disputado por cinco candidatos *or* hay cinco candidatos en pugna para el escaño; **contested takeover** = oferta de adquisición disputada *or* rebatida

context ['kɒntekst] *noun* contexto *m;* **the words can only be understood in the context of the phrase in which they occur** = las palabras sólo pueden ser entendidas en el contexto de la frase en la que aparecen; **the action of the police has to be seen in the context of the riots against the government** = la actuación de la policía tiene que considerarse en el contexto de los disturbios en contra del gobierno; **the words were quoted out of context** = citaron las palabras fuera de su contexto (NOTE: an example of words being quoted out of context might be: 'the Minister has said that the government might review the case', when what the Minister actually said was: 'it is true that under certain circumstances the government might review such a case, but the present situation is quite different')

contingency [kən'tɪnʒəsni] *noun* contingencia *f or* imprevisto *m or* eventualidad *f;* **contingency fund** *or* **contingency reserve** = fondo *m or* reserva *f* para imprevistos *or* para contingencias; **contingency plan** = plan *m* de contingencia

◊ **contingent** [kən'tɪnʒənt] *adjective* contingente; **contingent expenses** = gastos *mpl* imprevistos *or* contingentes; *US* **contingent fee** = honorario *m* condicional; **contingent policy** = política *f* de contingencia; *US* **contingent interest** = interés *m* condicional

continue [kən'tɪnjuː] *verb* continuar *or* proseguir
◊ **continual** [kən'tɪnjul] *adjective* continuo, -nua
◊ **continually** [kən'tɪnjuli] *adverb* continuamente
◊ **continuation** [kəntɪnju'eɪʃn] *noun* continuación *f*
◊ **continuous** [kən'tɪnjuəs] *adjective* continuo, -nua *or* seguido, -da; **to be in continuous employment** = tener trabajo continuo *or* trabajar durante un periodo continuo sin interrupción; **continuous feed** = alimentación *f* continua; **continuous stationery** = papel *m* continuo
◊ **continuously** [kən'tɪnjuəsli] *adverb* continuadamente *or* sin interrupción; **the meeting discussed the problem of budgets continuously for five hours** = la junta debatió el problema de los presupuestos durante cinco horas sin interrupción

contra ['kɒntrə] **1** *preposition* contra **2** *noun (account which offsets another account)* **contra account** = cuenta *f* compensada; **contra entry** = contraasiento *m;* **per contra** *or* **as per contra** = palabras *fpl* que indican que se ha realizado un contraasiento **3** *verb* **to contra an entry** = introducir un contraasiento
◊ **contra proferentem** ['kɒntræ prɒfə'rentem] *Latin phrase* 'contra el que expone la cuestión' : principio que establece que cualquier ambigüedad en un documento es perjudicial para la parte que lo redactó

contraband ['kɒntrəbænd] *noun* contrabando *m;* **contraband (goods)** = (mercancías *fpl*) de contrabando

contract ['kɒntrækt] **1** *noun* **(a)** *(legal agreement)* contrato *m;* **to draw up a contract** = redactar un contrato; **to draft a contract** = hacer un borrador de un contrato; **to sign a contract** = firmar un contrato; **the contract is binding on both parties** = el contrato es vinculante *or* obliga a las dos partes; **under contract** = bajo contrato *or* según contrato; **the firm is under contract to deliver the goods by November** = según contrato, la empresa debe entregar las mercancías para noviembre; **outside the contract** = extracontractual; **to void a contract** = anular un contrato; **contract of employment** = contrato de trabajo; **service contract** *or* **contract of service** = contrato de servicio; **exchange of contracts** = intercambio *m* de contratos **(b)** **contract law** *or* **law of contract** = derecho *m* de contratos; **by private contract** = por contrato privado; **contract note** = contrato de Bolsa **(c)** *(agreement to supply)* contrato *or* contrata *f;* **contract work** = trabajo a contrata; **contract for services** = contrato de servicios; **contract for the supply of spare parts** = contrato de suministro de piezas de repuesto; **to enter into a contract to supply spare parts** = concertar un contrato para suministrar piezas de repuesto; **to sign a contract for £10,000 worth of spare parts** = firmar un contrato de suministro de repuestos por valor de

10.000 libras; **to put work out to contract** = contratar a otra empresa para que haga un trabajo; **to award a contract to a company** *or* **to place a contract with a company** = adjudicar un contrato a una empresa; **to tender for a contract** = licitar *or* presentar una oferta para un contrato; **conditions of contract** *or* **contract conditions** = condiciones de contrato; **breach of contract** = incumplimiento *m or* violación *f* de contrato; **the company is in breach of contract** = la empresa ha incumplido el contrato; **contract work** = trabajo por contrato **(d)** *(slang)* acuerdo *m* para matar a alguien por dinero; **there is a contract out for him** = han puesto precio a su cabeza *or* han contratado a un matón para que le asesine **2** *verb* contratar *or* comprometerse por contrato; **to contract to supply spare parts** *or* **to contract for the supply of spare parts** = comprometerse a suministrar piezas de repuesto por contrato; **the supply of spare parts was contracted out to Smith Ltd** = el suministro de piezas de repuesto fue adjudicado a Smith Ltd; **to contract out of an agreement** = retirarse de un acuerdo con el permiso escrito de la otra parte

COMMENT: a contract is an agreement between two or more parties to create legal obligations between them. Some contracts are made 'under seal', i.e. they are signed and sealed by the parties; most contracts are made orally or in writing. The essential elements of a contract are: (a) that an offer made by one party should be accepted by the other; (b) consideration; (c) the intention to create legal relations. The terms of a contract may be express or implied. A breach of contract by one party entitles the other party to sue for damages or in some cases to seek specific performance

contracting ['kɒntræktɪŋ] *adjective* contratante; **contracting party** = parte *f* contratante
◊ **contractor** [kən'træktə] *noun* contratista *mf*
◊ **contractual** [kən'træktʃuəl] *adjective* contractual *or* por contrato; **contractual liability** = responsabilidad *f* contractual; **to fulfil your contractual obligations** = cumplir las obligaciones contractuales; **he is under no contractual obligation to buy** = no está obligado por contrato a comprar
◊ **contractually** [kən'træktʃuəli] *adverb* contractualmente; **the company is contractually bound to pay his expenses** = la empresa está obligada por contrato a pagar sus gastos

contradict [kɒntrə'dɪkt] *verb* contradecir; **the statement contradicts the report in the newspapers** = la declaración contradice lo publicado en los periódicos; **the witness contradicted himself several times** = el testigo se contradijo varias veces
◊ **contradiction** [kɒntrə'dɪkʃn] *noun* contradicción *f;* **the witness' evidence was a mass of contradictions** = la declaración del testigo fue

una pura contradicción; **there is a contradiction between the Minister's statement in the House of Commons and the reports published in the newspapers** = existe una contradicción entre la declaración del ministro en la Cámara de los Comunes y las noticias publicadas en los periódicos

◊ **contradictory** [kɒntrə'dɪktri] *adjective* contradictorio, -ria; **a mass of contradictory evidence** = un montón de pruebas contradictorias

contrary ['kɒntrəri] *noun* contrario *m;* **failing instructions to the contrary** = a no ser que se den instrucciones diferentes *or* si no se dan instrucciones contrarias; **on the contrary** = al contrario *or* por el contrario; **counsel was not annoyed with the witness - on the contrary, he praised her** = el abogado no estaba enfadado con la testigo - al contrario, la elogió

contravene ['kɒntrə'viːn] *verb* contravenir *or* ir en contra de; **the workshop has contravened the employment regulations** = el taller ha contravenido el reglamento laboral; **the fire department can close a restaurant if it contravenes the safety regulations** = el cuerpo de bomberos puede cerrar un restaurante si no cumple con las normas de seguridad

◊ **contravention** ['kɒntrə'venʃn] *noun* contravención *f or* infracción *f;* **in contravention of** = que contraviene; **the restaurant is in contravention of the safety regulations** = el restaurante contraviene las normas de seguridad; **the management of the cinema locked the fire exits in contravention of the fire regulations** = la dirección del cine cerró las salidas de incendios con llave contraviniendo las normas de seguridad

contribute [kən'trɪbjuːt] *verb* **(a)** *(money)* contribuir *or* aportar; **to contribute 10% of the profits** = contribuyó con el 10% de los beneficios; **he contributed to the pension fund for ten years** = contribuyó al fondo de pensiones durante diez años **(b)** *(help)* **to contribute to** = contribuir a; **the public response to the request for information contributed to the capture of the gang** = la respuesta del público a la petición de información contribuyó a la captura de la banda

◊ **contribution** [kɒntrɪ'bjuːʃn] *noun* contribución *f;* **employer's contribution** = cuota *f* patronal; **National Insurance contributions** = cuotas de la Seguridad Social; **pension contributions** = cuotas de pensión

◊ **contributor** [kən'trɪbjutə] *noun* contribuyente *mf;* **contributor of capital** = contribuyente de capital

◊ **contributory** [kən'trɪbjutəri] **1** *adjective* contributivo, -va *or* que contribuye *or* contribuyente; **contributory pension plan** *or* **scheme** = plan *m* de pensiones con aportaciones del trabajador *or* cotizable; **contributory causes** = causas *fpl* contribuyentes; **contributory factor** = factor *m* contribuyente; **contributory negligence** =

negligencia *f* concurrente **2** *noun* accionista *mf* que está vinculado por acciones parcialmente pagadas a una compañía disuelta

con trick ['kɒn 'trɪk] *noun (informal)* = CONFIDENCE TRICK

contrition [kən'trɪʃn] *noun* arrepentimiento *m*

control [kən'trəʊl] **1** *noun* **(a)** *(domination)* control *m or* mando *m;* **the company is under the control of three shareholders** = la empresa está bajo el control de tres accionistas; **to gain control of a business** = conseguir el control de un negocio; **to lose control of a business** = perder el control de un negocio; **the family lost control of its business** = la familia perdió el control de su negocio; *(tax assessment)* **control test** = prueba *f* de control: prueba para decidir si una persona está empleada por cuenta propia o ajena **(b)** *(check)* control; **under control** = bajo control; **out of control** = fuera de control; **to get out of control** = desmandarse **(c)** **exchange control** = control de divisas; **the government imposed exchange controls to stop the rush to buy dollars** = el gobierno impuso un control de divisas para detener la afluencia de compra de dólares; **price control** = control de precios; **rent control** = control de alquileres **(d)** *(computer)* **control systems** = sistemas *mpl* de control **2** *verb* **(a)** *(to direct)* **to control a business** = dirigir *or* controlar un negocio; **the business is controlled by a company based in Luxembourg** = el negocio está dirigido por una empresa con base en Luxemburgo; **the company is controlled by the majority shareholder** = la empresa está dirigida *or* bajo el mando del accionista mayoritario **(b)** *(to keep in check)* controlar; **the government is fighting to control inflation** *or* **to control the rise in the cost of living** = el gobierno está luchando por controlar la inflación *or* para controlar el aumento del coste de vida

◊ **controlled** [kən'trəʊld] *adjective* **(a)** *(ruled)* controlado, -da *or* dirigido, -da; **government-controlled** = dirigido por el gobierno; **controlled economy** = economía *f* dirigida **(b)** **controlled drugs** *or* US **controlled substances** = estupefacientes *mpl; see comment at* DRUG

◊ **controller** [kən'trəʊlə] *noun* **(a)** director, -ra financiero, -ra *or* interventor, -ra **(b)** US contable jefe

◊ **controlling** [kən'trəʊlɪŋ] *adjective* que controla; **to have a controlling interest in a company** = tener un interés mayoritario en una empresa

convene [kən'viːn] *verb* convocar; **to convene a meeting of shareholders** = convocar una junta de accionistas

◊ **convener** *or* **convenor** [kən'viːnə] *noun (of a meeting)* organizador, -ra *or* presidente, -ta *(de comisión) or* responsable *mf* sindical

convenience [kən'vi:niəns] *noun* **at your earliest convenience** = en cuanto le sea posible; **ship sailing under a flag of convenience** = embarcación *f* que navega con pabellón de conveniencia
◊ **convenient** [kən'vi:niənt] *adjective* conveniente *or* cómodo, -da *or* práctico, -ca; **a bank draft is a convenient way of sending money abroad** = un giro bancario es una forma cómoda de enviar dinero al extranjero; **is 9.30 a.m. a convenient time for the meeting?** = ¿les parece las 9.30 de la mañana una hora conveniente para la reunión?

convention [kən'venʃn] *noun* **(a)** *(general way in which something is done)* convención *f or* costumbre *f;* **social conventions** = convenciones sociales; **it is the convention for American lawyers to designate themselves 'Esquire'** = es costumbre entre abogados americanos llamarse *Esquire* **(b)** *(international treaty)* convención *or* congreso *m;* **Geneva Convention(s) on Human Rights** = Convención de Ginebra sobre Derechos Humanos

conversion [kən'və:ʃn] *noun* *(crime)* apropiación *f* indebida *or* ilícita; **conversion of funds** = apropiación ilícita de fondos *or* malversación *f* de fondos
◊ **convert** [kən'və:t] *verb* **(a)** *(to change property into another form)* convertir *or* transformar **(b)** *(to change money)* cambiar; **we converted our pounds into Swiss francs** = cambiamos nuestras libras a francos suizos **(c)** *(crime)* **to convert funds to one's own use** = apropiarse ilícitamente de fondos
◊ **convertible** [kən'və:təbl] *adjective* convertible; **convertible loan stock** = obligaciones *fpl* convertibles

convey [kən'veɪ] *verb* transportar; **to convey a property to a purchaser** = traspasar una propiedad a un comprador
◊ **conveyance** [kən'veɪəns] *noun* traspaso *m* de dominio *or* transmisión *f* del título de propiedad; **fraudulent conveyance** = transmisión fraudulenta de propiedad
◊ **conveyancer** [kən'veɪənsə] *noun* notario *m* que hace escrituras de traspaso
◊ **conveyancing** [kən'veɪənsɪŋ] *noun* **(a)** *(document)* redacción *f* de una escritura de traspaso **(b)** *(procedure)* ley *f* y procedimiento *m* de un traspaso de propiedad; **do-it-yourself conveyancing** = redacción de una escritura de traspaso sin la ayuda de un abogado

convict 1 ['kɒnvɪkt] *noun* presidiario, -ria *or* convicto, -ta; **self-confessed convict** = convicto y confeso; **convict settlement** = campo *m* de prisión **2** [kən'vɪkt] *verb* **to convict someone of a crime** = condenar a alguien *or* declarar a alguien culpable de un delito; **he was convicted of manslaughter and sent to prison** = fue declarado culpable de

homicidio involuntario y enviado a prisión; **convicted criminal** = criminal *mf* condenado y sentenciado
◊ **conviction** [kən'vɪkʃn] *noun* **(a)** *(being sure that something is true)* convicción *f;* **it is his conviction that the plaintiff has brought the case maliciously** = está convencido de que el demandante ha entablado el pleito maliciosamente **(b)** *(finding guilty)* condena *f or* fallo condenatorio; **spent conviction** = culpa redimida; **he has had ten convictions for burglary** = lleva diez condenas por robo con allanamiento de morada; *compare* SENTENCE

convince [kən'vɪns] *verb* convencer *or* persuadir; **counsel tried to convince the jury that the accused was not guilty** = el abogado intentó convencer al jurado de que el acusado no era culpable; **he convinced the owner of the shop that the building needed painting** = convenció al propietario de la tienda de que el edificio necesitaba pintarse; **the two conmen convinced the woman that they were plainclothes policemen** = los dos timadores convencieron a la mujer de que eran policías vestidos de paisano

cooling off period *or* US **cooling time** ['ku:lɪŋ 'ɒf 'pi:riəd] *noun* **(a)** *(during an industrial dispute)* tregua *f* laboral **(b)** *(on hire-purchase)* periodo *m* permitido para pensar sobre una posible compra

co-operate [kəʊ'ɒpəreɪt] *verb* cooperar; **the governments are co-operating in the fight against piracy** = los gobiernos están cooperando en la lucha contra la piratería; **the two firms have co-operated on planning the computer system** = las dos firmas han cooperado en la planificación del sistema informático
◊ **co-operation** [kəʊɒpə'reɪʃn] *noun* cooperación *f;* **the work was completed ahead of schedule with the co-operation of the whole staff** = el trabajo se finalizó antes de lo previsto con la cooperación de todo el personal
◊ **co-operative** ['kəʊ'ɒpərətɪv] **1** *adjective* cooperativo, -va; **the staff have not been co-operative over the management's reorganization plan** = los empleados no han cooperado con el plan de reorganización de la dirección; **co-operative society** = sociedad *f* cooperativa **2** *noun* cooperativa *f;* **industrial co-operative** = cooperativa laboral; **to set up a workers' co-operative** = fundar una cooperativa de trabajadores

co-opt ['kəʊ'ɒpt] *verb* **to co-opt someone onto a committee** = nombrar por coopción *or* invitar a alguien a formar parte de una comisión

co-owner ['kəʊ'əʊnə] *noun* copropietario, -ria; **the two sisters are co-owners of the property** = las dos hermanas son copropietarias de los bienes

◊ **co-ownership** [ˈkəuˈəunəʃɪp] *noun* **(a)** *(property)* copropiedad *f* **(b)** *(shares in a company)* coparticipación *f or* consorcio *m*

cop [kɒp] **1** *noun* **(a)** *(policeman)* poli *mf* **(b)** *(slang)* arresto *m or* detención *f; it's a fair cop* = me has pillado **2** *verb (slang)* pescar *or* pillar *or* cargarse; **to cop a plea** = conformarse con los cargos *or* la pena

co-partner [ˈkəuˈpɑːtnə] *noun* copartícipe *mf or* consorcio *m*
◊ **co-partnership** [ˈkəuˈpɑːtnəʃɪp] *noun* coparticipación *f or* consorcio *m*

cope [kəup] *verb* arreglárselas *or* hacer frente *or* poder con; **the judges have difficulty in coping with all the divorce cases** = los jueces no pueden con todos los casos de divorcio; **how can the police cope with inner city violence when they do not have enough staff?** = ¿cómo puede la policía hacer frente a toda la violencia del centro de la ciudad sin tener personal suficiente?

copper [ˈkɒpə] *noun GB (informal)* poli *mf*
◊ **copper-bottomed** [ˈkɒpəˈbɒtəmd] *adjective* (garantía *f*) que no se puede romper

co-property [ˈkəuˈprɒpəti] *noun* copropiedad *f*
◊ **co-proprietor** [ˈkəuprəˈpraɪətə] *noun* copropietario, -ria

copy [ˈkɒpi] **1** *noun* **(a)** *(identical document)* copia *f or* duplicado *m;* **carbon copy** = copia carbón; **certified copy** = copia certificada; **file copy** = copia de archivo **(b)** *(document)* copia; **attested** *or* **true copy** = compulsa *f or* copia fiel; **fair copy** *or* **final copy** = copia en limpio; **hard copy** = texto *m* impreso; **rough copy** = borrador *m;* **top copy** = original *m* **(c)** *(book, newspaper)* ejemplar *m;* **have you kept yesterday's copy of 'The Times'?** = ¿has guardado el 'The Times' de ayer?; **I read it in the office copy of 'Fortune'** = lo leí en el ejemplar de 'Fortune' de la oficina; **where is my copy of the telephone directory?** = ¿dónde está mi ejemplar de la guía telefónica? **2** *verb* copiar; **he copied the company report at night and took it home** = copió el informe de la empresa por la noche y se lo llevó a casa
◊ **copier** *or* **copying machine** [ˈkɒpɪə *or* ˈkɒpɪɪŋ məˈʃiːn] *noun* copiadora *f*

copyright [ˈkɒpiraɪt] **1** *noun* derechos *mpl* de autor *or* propiedad *f* intelectual *or* propiedad literaria *or* 'copyright' *m;* **Copyright Act** = Ley *f* de los derechos de autor; **copyright law** = leyes sobre la propiedad intelectual; **work which is out of copyright** = obra *f* cuyos derechos de autor son del dominio público; **work still in copyright** = obra protegida por los derechos de autor; **infringement of copyright** *or* **copyright infringement** = violación *f* de la propiedad intelectual *or* de los derechos de autor; **copyright notice** = nota *f* de copyright; **copyright owner** = propietario, -ra de

los derechos de autor **2** *verb* registrar como propiedad literaria **3** *adjective* protegido, -da por los derechos de autor; **it is illegal to take copies of a copyright work** = es ilegal hacer copias de un libro protegido por los derechos de autor
◊ **copyrighted** [ˈkɒpiraɪtɪd] *adjective* registrado, -da como propiedad literaria *or* con derechos de autor

> COMMENT: copyright lasts for 50 years after the author's death according to the Berne Convention, and for 25 years according to the Universal Copyright Convention. In the USA, copyright is for 50 years after the death of an author for books published after January 1st, 1978. For books published before that date, the original copyright was for 28 years after the death of the author, and this can be extended for a further 28 year period up to a maximum of 75 years. In 1995, the European Union adopted a copyright term of 70 years after the death of the author. The copyright holder has the right to refuse or to grant permission to copy copyright material, though under the Paris agreement of 1971, the original publishers (representing the author or copyright holder) must, under certain circumstances, grant licences to reprint copyright material. The copyright notice has to include the symbol c the name of the copyright holder and the date of the copyright (which is usually the date of first publication). The notice must be printed in the book and usually appears on the reverse of the title page. A copyright notice is also printed on other forms of printed material such as posters. The change of the term of copyright in the European Union has created problems for publishers and copyright holders, in cases where the author died more than fifty years but less than seventy years ago; in effect, such authors have returned to copyright, and royalties, etc., are due to their estates until the seventy year term expires (this applies to well-known authors such as Beatrix Potter and James Joyce, as well as to composers, such as Elgar)

cordon [ˈkɔːdən] **1** *noun* cordón *m;* **a police cordon** = un cordón *m* policial **2** *verb* **to cordon off** = acordonar; **the street was cordoned off after the bomb was discovered** = la calle fue acordonada después de que se descubrió la bomba

co-respondent [ˈkəurɪsˈpɒndənt] *noun* **(a)** *(accomplice)* codemandado, -da *or* cómplice *mf* del demandado **(b)** *(in divorce cases)* demandado en una causa de adulterio; *see also* CORRESPONDENT

coroner [ˈkɒrənə] *noun* magistrado, -da público, -ca (médico, -ca *or* juez, -za de primera instancia) que investiga los casos de muerte accidental violenta o por causa desconocida; **coroner's court** = tribunal *m* presidido por un magistrado público;

coroner's inquest = investigación *f* llevada a cabo por un magistrado para determinar la causa de muerte no natural

COMMENT: coroners investigate deaths which are violent or unexpected, deaths which may be murder *or* manslaughter, deaths of prisoners and deaths involving the police

corporal punishment ['kɔːprəl 'pʌnɪʃmənt] *noun* castigo *m* corporal

corporate ['kɔːprət] *adjective* social *or* de una sociedad *or* constituido en sociedad; **corporate personality** = personalidad *f* jurídica; **corporate planning** = planificación *f* empresarial; **corporate profits** = beneficios *mpl* de una sociedad
◊ **corporation** [kɔːpə'reɪʃn] *noun* **(a)** *(legal body incorporated)* corporación *f or* sociedad *f* mercantil anónima *or* compañía *f* de capital; *US* empresa *f* que ha sido constituida en sociedad en los EE UU **(b)** *(large company)* sociedad *f* empresa *f or* compañía *f*; **finance corporation** = financiera *f or* sociedad financiera

corporeal hereditaments [kɔː'pɔːriəl herɪ'dɪtəmənts] *plural noun* derechos *mpl* de propiedad sobre bienes tangibles

corps [kɔː] *noun* cuerpo *m;* **diplomatic corps** = cuerpo diplomático

corpse [kɔːps] *noun GB* cadáver *m (NOTE: US English is* **cadaver)**

corpus ['kɔːpəs] *noun* cuerpo *m or* recopilación *f* (de leyes); *see also* HABEAS CORPUS (NOTE: plural is **corpora)**
◊ **corpus delicti** ['kɔːpəs dɪ'lɪktaɪ] *Latin phrase* cuerpo *m* del delito
◊ **corpus legis** ['kɔːpəs 'ledʒɪs] *Latin phrase* libros *mpl* del derecho civil romano

correct [kə'rekt] **1** *adjective* correcto, -ta *or* exacto, -ta; **the published accounts do not give a correct picture of the company's financial position** = el balance publicado no ofrece una visión correcta del estado financiero de la empresa **2** *verb* corregir *or* rectificar; **the secretary will have to correct all these errors before you send the contract** = la secretaria tendrá que corregir todos estos errores antes de que usted envíe el contrato
◊ **correction** [kə'rekʃn] *noun* corrección *f;* **he made some corrections to the draft contract** = dio algunos retoques al borrador del contrato
◊ **correctional institution** ['kə'rekʃənl ɪnstɪ'tjuːʃn] *noun US* correccional *m*
◊ **corrective** [kə'rektɪv] *adjective* correctivo, -va; **he was sent to the detention centre for corrective training** = se le envió a un centro de detención para delincuentes juveniles

correspond [kɒrə'spɒnd] *verb* **(a)** *(to write letters)* **to correspond with someone** = mantener correspondencia con alguien **(b)** *(to fit or match)* **to**

correspond with something = corresponder con *or* coincidir con
◊ **correspondence** [kɒrə'spɒndəns] *noun (letter writing)* correspondencia *f;* **business correspondence** = correspondencia comercial; **to be in correspondence with someone** = mantener correspondencia con alguien
◊ **correspondent** [kɒrə'spɒndənt] *noun* **(a)** *(person who writes letters)* persona *f* que escribe cartas *or* epistológrafo, -fa **(b)** *(journalist)* corresponsal *mf;* **a financial correspondent** = un corresponsal financiero; **'The Times' legal correspondent** = el corresponsal jurídico de 'The Times'; **he is the Paris correspondent of the 'Telegraph'** = es el corresponsal en París del 'Telegraph'; *see also* CO-RESPONDENT

corrigendum [kɒrɪ'dʒndəm] *noun* errata *f* (NOTE: plural is **corrigenda)**

corroborate [kə'rɒbəreɪt] *verb* corroborar; **the witness corroborated the accused's alibi, saying that at the time of the murder he had seen him in Brighton** = el testigo corroboró la coartada del acusado, diciendo que lo había visto en Brighton a la hora del asesinato
◊ **corroboration** [kərɒbə'reɪʃn] *noun* corroboración *f or* pruebas *fpl* confirmatorias; **the witness was unable to provide corroboration of what he had told the police** = el testigo fue incapaz de proporcionar pruebas que corroborasen lo que le había dicho a la policía
◊ **corroborative** [kə'rɒbərətɪv] *adjective* corroborativo, -va; **the letter provides corroborative evidence, showing that the accused did know that the victim lived alone** = la carta proporciona pruebas corroborativas, demostrando que el acusado sabía que la víctima vivía sola

corrupt [kə'rʌpt] **1** *adjective* corrompido, -da *or* corrupto, -ta *or* ímprobo; **to become corrupt** = enviciarse **2** *verb* corromper *or* enviciar; *(with money)* sobornar; **to corrupt someone's morals** = corromper a alguien
◊ **corruption** [kə'rʌpʃn] *noun* corrupción *f;* **the government is keen to stamp out corruption in the police force** = el gobierno está deseando erradicar la corrupción del cuerpo de policía; **bribery and corruption are difficult to control** = el soborno y la corrupción son difíciles de controlar
◊ **corruptly** [kə'rʌptli] *adverb* corruptamente; **he corruptly offered the officer money to get the charges dropped** = sobornó al oficial para que se retiraran los cargos

Cosa Nostra ['kəuzə 'nɒstrə] = MAFIA

cosh [kɒʃ] **1** *noun* porra *f or* cachiporra *f* **2** *verb* dar un porrazo a *or* aporrear; **the burglars coshed the shopkeeper and stole money from the till** = los ladrones aporrearon al tendero y robaron el dinero de la caja

cost [kɒst] **1** *noun* **(a)** *(price)* coste *m* gasto *m* precio *m;* **computer costs are falling each year** = los precios de los ordenadores bajan cada año; **we cannot afford the cost of two telephones** = no podemos permitirnos el gasto de dos teléfonos; **to cover costs** = cubrir gastos **(b)** *(expenses in a court case)* **costs** = costas *fpl;* **the judge awarded costs to the defendant** = el juez asignó las costas al demandado; **costs of the case will be borne by the prosecution** = las costas del caso correrán a cargo de la acusación; **the court awarded the plaintiff £2,000 in damages, with costs** = el tribunal concedió al demandante 2.000 libras por daños y perjuicios, además de las costas; **to pay costs** = pagar las costas; **costs order** = orden *m* judicial de pago de las costas; **fixed costs** = costas fijas (cantidad de dinero establecida a que tiene derecho un demandante en procedimientos legales); **taxed costs** = cantidad de dinero variable que se puede obtener en procedimientos legales **2** *verb* **(a)** *(to have a price)* costar; **how much does the machine cost?** = ¿cuánto cuesta la máquina?; **rent of the room will cost £50 a day** = el alquiler de la habitación cuesta 50 libras al día **(b)** *(to calculate a price)* **to cost a product** = calcular el coste de un producto

◊ **cost of living** [ˈkɒst əv ˈlɪvɪŋ] *noun* carestía *f* *or* coste de vida; **to allow for the cost of living in salaries** = incluir un plus de carestía de vida en los salarios; **cost-of-living allowance** = plus *m* de carestía de vida *or* subsidio *m* por aumento del coste de vida; **cost-of-living increase** = aumento *m* de salario por coste de vida; **cost-of-living index** = índice *m* del coste de vida

coterminous [ˌkəʊˈtɜːmɪnəs] *adjective* con la misma fecha de cierre; **the leases are coterminous** = los arrendamientos finalizan al mismo tiempo

council [ˈkaʊnsəl] *noun* **(a)** *(official group)* consejo *m;* **consumer council** = asociación *f* de consumidores; **borough council** *or* **town council** = ayuntamiento *m* *or* concejo *m* municipal *or* consistorio *m;* **executive council** = consejo ejecutivo; **family council** = consejo de familia; *(EU)* **Council of Ministers** = Consejo de Ministros; **Security Council** = Consejo de Seguridad **(b)** = PRIVY COUNCIL Consejo Privado de la Corona *or* Soberanía; **Order in Council** = decreto *m* ley *or* legislación *f* establecida por la Reina en Consejo que no necesita que el Parlamento la ratifique

◊ **councillor** [ˈkaʊnsələ] *noun* concejal, -la; *see also* PRIVY COUNCILLOR

counsel [ˈkaʊnsəl] *noun* abogado, -da; **defence counsel** = abogado defensor *or* defensa *f;* **prosecution counsel** = fiscal *mf* *or* acusación *f;* **the plaintiff appeared in court with his solicitor and two counsel** = el demandante compareció en juicio con su procurador y dos abogados; **counsel's advice** *or* **opinion** = informe *m* de un abogado sobre un caso; **leading counsel** = abogado principal;

Queen's Counsel = abogado de la Reina nombrado por el Presidente de la Cámara de los Lores y el Ministro de Justicia (NOTE: **Queen's Counsel** is usually abbreviated to **QC**. Note that there is no plural for counsel which is always used in the singular whether it refers to one barrister or several, and it is never used with the article. On the other hand the abbreviation QC can have a plural: **two QCs represented the defendant**)

◊ **counsellor** [ˈkaʊnsələ] *noun* US asesor, -ra jurídico, -ca

count [kaʊnt] **1** *noun* cargo *m;* **he was found guilty on all four counts** = se le declaró culpable de los cuatro cargos **2** *verb* **(a)** *(to add figures)* contar *or* sumar; **he counted up the sales for the six months to December** = sumó las ventas de los seis meses hasta diciembre **(b)** *(to include)* tener en cuenta *or* considerar *or* incluir; **did the defence count the accused's theft of money from the till as part of the total theft?** = ¿tuvo en cuenta *or* incluyó en la defensa que el dinero de la caja robado por el acusado formaba parte del robo total?

◊ **count on** [ˈkaʊnt ˈɒn] *verb* **(a)** *(to expect)* contar con *or* esperar; **the defence seems to be counting on winning the sympathy of the jury** = la defensa parece que cuenta con ganarse la compasión del jurado **(b)** *(to rely on)* confiar en; **you can count on Mr Jones, he is an excellent solicitor** = puede confiar en el Sr Jones, es un abogado excelente

counter [ˈkaʊntə] **1** *noun* mostrador *m* *or* ventanilla *f;* **over the counter** = de venta libre; **goods sold over the counter** = mercancías vendidas al por menor; **under the counter** = ilegalmente *or* bajo mano; **under-the-counter sales** = ventas *fpl* en el mercado negro; *(Stock Exchange)* **over-the-counter market (OTC)** = mercado *m* de acciones que no se cotizan en Bolsa *or* mercado de valores extrabursátil *or* segundo mercado **2** *adverb* **counter to** = en contra de *or* frente a; **the decision of the court runs counter to the advice of the clerk to the justices** = la decisión del tribunal va en contra del consejo del secretario del juzgado

counter- [ˈkaʊntə] *prefix* contra

◊ **counterclaim** [ˈkaʊntəkleɪm] **1** *noun* **(a)** *(in a court)* contradenuncia *f* *or* reclamación *f* interpuesta inmediatamente a otra anterior *or* reconvención *f* **(b)** *(reply to a previous claim)* reclamación recíproca por daños y perjuicios; **Jones claimed £25,000 in damages against Smith, and Smith entered a counterclaim of £50,000 for loss of office** = Jones reclamó 25.000 libras por daños y perjuicios a Smith, y Smith presentó, a su vez, una demanda de 50.000 libras por despido **2** *verb* reconvenir *or* presentar una reclamación como respuesta a otra interpuesta por otra persona; **Jones claimed £25,000 in damages and Smith counterclaimed £50,000 for loss of office** = Jones reclamó 25.000 libras por daños y perjuicios y

Smith, como contrapartida, reclamó 50.000 por despido

◊ **counterfeit** ['kaʊntəfɪt] **1** *adjective* falsificado, -da *or* falso, -sa *or* espurio, -ria; **counterfeit money** = dinero falso *or* moneda falsa; **he was charged with passing counterfeit notes in shops** = se le acusó de poner billetes falsos en circulación en tiendas **2** *verb* falsificar

◊ **counterfeiting** ['kaʊntəfɪtɪŋ] *noun* falsificación *f*

◊ **counter-intelligence** ['kaʊntəin'telɪdʒəns] *noun* contraespionaje *m;* **the offices were bugged by counter-intelligence agents** = los agentes de contraespionaje intervinieron las oficinas con micrófonos ocultos

◊ **countermand** ['kaʊntəmɑːnd] *verb* revocar *or* cancelar; **to countermand an order** = revocar una orden

◊ **counteroffer** ['kaʊntəɒfə] *noun* contraoferta *f*

◊ **counterpart** ['kaʊntəpɑːt] *noun* **(a)** *(copy of a lease)* copia *f* de un contrato de arrendamiento **(b)** *(person with a similar job in another company)* colega *mf or* homólogo, -ga; **John is my counterpart in Smith's** = John es mi homólogo en Smith's

◊ **counter-promise** ['kaʊntəprɒmɪs] *noun* promesa *f* hecha en respuesta a otra promesa

◊ **countersign** ['kaʊntəsaɪn] *verb* refrendar *or* confirmar; **the payment has to be countersigned by the mortgagor** = el pago tiene que ser refrendado por el deudor hipotecario

country ['kʌntri] *noun* país *m;* **the contract covers sales in the countries of the Common Market** = el contrato cubre las ventas en los países del Mercado Común; **some African countries export oil** = algunos países africanos exportan petróleo; **country of origin** = país de origen

county ['kaʊnti] *noun* condado *m;* **county council** = diputación *f or* consejo *m* del condado; **County Court** = juzgado *m* local *or* del condado; **County Court Rules** = reglamento *m* interno de los juzgados locales *or* del condado; *see also* GREEN BOOK

> COMMENT: the County Court hears most civil cases up to a value of £5,000

coup (d'état) ['kuː deɪ'tæ] *noun* golpe *m* de estado

coupon ['kuːpɒn] *noun* cupón *m*

course [kɔːs] *noun* **(a) in the course of** = en el transcurso de *or* durante; **in the course of duty** = en acto de servicio; **in the course of employment** = durante el trabajo; **in the course of the hearing, several new allegations were made by the defendant** = en el transcurso de la vista, el demandado hizo varias alegaciones nuevas **(b)** *(series of lessons)* curso *m;* **he is taking a management course** = está haciendo un curso de dirección; **she has finished her secretarial course** = ha finalizado su curso de secretariado; **the company has paid for her to attend a course for trainee sales managers** = la empresa le ha pagado un curso de formación de directores de ventas **(c) course of action** = línea *f* de acción *or* de conducta; **what is the best course of action the defendant should take?** = ¿cuál es la mejor línea de conducta que debe tomar el demandado? **(d) of course** = por supuesto *or* claro *or* naturalmente *or* desde luego; **of course the company is interested in profits** = por supuesto que la empresa está interesada en los beneficios; **are you willing to go on a sales trip to Australia? - of course!** = ¿quieres ir a Australia en viaje de negocios? - ¡desde luego!

court [kɔːt] *noun* **(a) court calendar** = lista *f* de causas *or* de pleitos; **court of law** *or* **law court** = juzgado *m;* **the law courts are in the centre of the town** = los juzgados están en el centro de la ciudad; **she works in the law courts as an usher** = trabaja en los juzgados como portero de estrados; **court action** *or* **court case** = proceso *m or* acción *f* judicial; **to take someone to court** = llevar a alguien *or* ante los tribunales; **in court** = presente en el juicio; **the defendant was in court for three hours** = el acusado estuvo presente en el juicio durante tres horas; **in open court** = en audiencia pública; **a settlement was reached out of court** *or* **the two parties reached an out-of-court settlement** = se llegó a un acuerdo amistoso *or* las dos partes llegaron a un arreglo amistoso *or* extrajudicialmente; **contempt of court** = desacato *m* a los tribunales; **court order** = orden *f* judicial; **the court made an order for maintenance** *or* **made a maintenance order** = el tribunal dictó una orden judicial de manutención; **he refused to obey the court order and was sent to prison for contempt** = se negó a obedecer la orden judicial y le enviaron a prisión por desacato **(b) Criminal Court** = tribunal *m* penal *or* sala *f* de lo criminal; **Civil Court** = tribunal civil *or* sala de lo civil; **Court of Appeal** *or* **Appeal Court** = Tribunal de Apelación *or* juzgado de segunda instancia; **court of first instance** = juzgado de primera instancia; **Court of Protection** = tribunal que administra los bienes de personas con alguna incapacidad; **High Court (of Justice)** = Tribunal Superior; **International Court of Justice** = Tribunal Internacional de Justicia; **magistrates' court** = tribunal de magistrados *or* juzgado de instrucción; **police court** *or* **duty magistrates' court** = juzgado de guardia; **Supreme Court (of Judicature)** = *GB* Tribunal Supremo *US* tribunal federal superior; *(in Scotland)* **Court of Session** = tribunal civil superior en Escocia **(c)** *(judges or magistrates in a court)* tribunal; **the court will retire for thirty minutes** = el tribunal se retirará durante treinta minutos

◊ **court-martial** ['kɔːt'mɑːʃl] **1** *noun* **(a)** *(court)* tribunal militar **(b)** *(trial)* consejo *m* de guerra; **the court-martial was held in the army** headquarters = el consejo de guerra tuvo lugar en el cuartel general del ejército; **he was found guilty by the court-martial and sentenced to imprisonment** = fue declarado culpable por el tribunal militar y sentenciado a prisión (NOTE: plural is **courts-martial**) **2** *verb* juzgar en consejo de guerra (NOTE: **court-martialled**)

◊ **courtroom** ['kɔːtruːm] *noun* sala *f* de un tribunal

COMMENT: in England and Wales the main courts are: **the Magistrates' Court:** petty crime; adoption; affiliation; maintenance and domestic violence; licensing; **the County Court:** most civil actions up to a value of £5,000; **the High Court:** most civil claims where the value exceeds £5,000; **the Crown Court:** major crime; **the Court of Appeal:** appeals from lower courts; **the House of Lords:** the highest court of appeal in the country; **the Privy Council:** appeals on certain matters from England and Wales, and appeals from certain Commonwealth countries; **the European Court of Justice:** appeals where EU legislation is involved. Other courts include **Industrial tribunals:** employment disputes; **courts-martial:** military matters

---

covenant ['kʌvnənt] **1** *noun* convenio *m* or pacto *m;* **he signed a covenant against underletting the premises** = firmó un convenio para no subarrendar el local; **deed of covenant** = escritura *f* de convenio or ejecución *f* de un pacto; **covenant to repair** = pacto or convenio para mantener en buen estado una propiedad alquilada; **restrictive covenant** = cláusula *f* restrictiva or de restricción de un contrato **2** *verb* convenir or pactar el pago de una cantidad de dinero al año; **to covenant to pay £10 per annum to a charity** = convenir el pago de 10 libras al año a obras de beneficiencia

---

COMMENT: examples of restrictive covenants could be a clause in a contract of employment which prevents the employee from going to work for a competitor, or a clause in a contract for the sale of a property which prevents the purchaser from altering the building. There is a tax advantage to the recipient of covenanted money; a charity pays no tax, so it can reclaim tax at the standard rate on the money covenanted

---

cover ['kʌvə] **1** *noun* **(a)** *(protection)* cobertura *f;* **insurance cover** = póliza *f* de seguros; **do you have cover against theft?** = ¿está asegurado or cubierto contra robo?; **to operate without adequate cover** = operar sin cobertura suficiente; **to ask for additional cover** = solicitar un seguro or cobertura adicional; **full cover** = seguro *m* a todo riesgo or cobertura total; **cover note** = nota *f* de cobertura or póliza *f* provisional **(b)** *(security to guarantee a loan)* garantía *f;* **do you have sufficient cover for**

this loan? = ¿tienes garantía suficiente para este préstamo? **(c) to send something under separate cover** = enviar algo por separado; **to send a document under plain cover** = enviar un documento en un sobre blanco **(d)** *(of a book)* cubierta *f* **2** *verb* **(a)** *(to deal with, to refer to)* cubrir or abarcar or informar sobre; **the agreement covers all agencies** = el acuerdo cubre todas las agencias; **the newspapers have covered the murder trial** = los periódicos han informado exhaustivamente sobre el juicio por asesinato; **the fraud case has been covered by the consumer protection legislation** = el caso de fraude está cubierto por la legislación de protección al consumidor **(b)** *(insurance)* **to cover a risk** = estar asegurado contra un riesgo; **to be fully covered** = estar asegurado a todo riesgo; **the insurance covers fire, theft and loss of work** = el seguro cubre incendios, robo y pérdida de trabajo **(c)** *(to have enough money to pay)* cubrir; **the damage was covered by the insurance** = el seguro cubrió los daños; **to cover a position** = tener respaldo económico **(d)** *(to make enough money to pay for something)* cubrir gastos; **we do not make enough sales to cover the expense of running the shop** = las ventas no son suficientes para cubrir los gastos de mantenimiento de la tienda; **we hope to reach the point soon when sales will cover all costs** = esperamos alcanzar pronto el momento en que las ventas cubran todos los gastos; **the dividend is covered four times** = el dividendo está cubierto cuatro veces or los beneficios cuadruplican el dividendo pagado

◊ **coverage** ['kʌvrɪdʒ] *noun* **(a) press coverage** or **media coverage** = cobertura *f* de prensa or de medios de comunicación; **the company had good media coverage for the launch of its new model** = la empresa dispuso de una amplia cobertura en los medios de comunicación para el lanzamiento de su nuevo modelo **(b)** *US* cobertura de un seguro; **do you have coverage against fire damage?** = ¿está asegurado contra posibles daños ocasionados por incendios?

◊ **covering** ['kʌvrɪŋ] *adjective;* **covering letter** or **covering note** = carta *f* explicatoria or de cobertura

◊ **cover-up** ['kʌvəˈʌp] *noun* encubrimiento *m*

covert ['kəuvəːt] *adjective* secreto, -ta or cubierto, -ta; **covert action** = acción *f* secreta; *see also* FEME COVERT

◊ **coverture** ['kʌvətʃuə] *noun* estado *m* legal de una mujer casada

CPS ['siː 'piː 'es] = CROWN PROSECUTION SERVICE

cracksman ['kræksmən] *noun (slang)* ladrón *m* de cajas fuertes

create [kriˈeɪt] *verb* crear; **by acquiring small unprofitable companies he soon created a large**

trading group = con la adquisición de pequeñas empresas poco rentables pronto creó un gran grupo comercial; **the government scheme aims at creating new jobs for young people** = el plan del gobierno tiene como fin crear nuevos puestos de trabajo para la gente joven

◊ **creation** [kri'eɪʃn] *noun* creación *f*; **job creation scheme** = plan *m* de creación de empleo

credere ['kreɪdəri] *see* DEL CREDERE

credibility [kredɪ'bɪlɪti] *noun* credibilidad *f*

credit ['kredɪt] **1** *noun* **(a)** *(time given to a debtor to pay)* crédito *m*; **to give someone six months' credit** = conceder seis meses de crédito a alguien; **to sell on good credit terms** = vender en buenas condiciones de crédito; **credit account** = cuenta *f* de crédito; **credit agency** *or* US **credit bureau** = agencia *f* de informes comerciales; **credit bank** = banco *m* comercial; **credit card** = tarjeta *f* de crédito; **credit facilities** = facilidades *fpl* de crédito; **letter of credit** = carta *f* de crédito; **irrevocable letter of credit** = carta de crédito irrevocable; **credit limit** = límite *m* de crédito; **credit rating** = clasificación *f* crediticia; **to buy on credit** = comprar a crédito **(b)** *(money received or recorded)* abono *m*; **to enter £100 to someone's credit** = anotar 100 libras en el haber de alguien; **to pay in £100 to the credit of Mr Smith** = abonar 100 libras en el haber del Sr Smith; **debit and credit** = debe *m* y haber; **credit side** = haber **2** *verb* ingresar *or* acreditar *or* abonar en cuenta *or* registrar *or* anotar en el haber; **to credit an account with £100** *or* **to credit £100 to an account** = ingresar 100 libras en una cuenta

◊ **creditor** ['kredɪtə] *noun* acreedor, -ra; **creditors' meeting** = junta *f* de acreedores; **judgment creditor** = acreedor por sentencia *or* judicial; **preferential creditor** = acreedor preferente; **secured** *or* **unsecured creditor** = acreedor asegurado *or* no asegurado; acreedor con *or* sin garantía

crime [kraɪm] *noun* **(a)** *(illegal act punishable by law)* delito *m* *or* crimen *m*; **attempted crime** = delito frustrado; **crimes against the person** = delitos contra las personas; **crimes against property** = delitos contra la propiedad; **deliberate crimes** = delitos dolosos; **there has been a 50% increase in crimes of violence** = los delitos violentos han experimentado un aumento del 50% **(b)** *(illegal acts generally)* criminalidad *f* *or* delincuencia *f*; **crime is on the increase** = la criminalidad va en aumento; **there has been an increase in violent crime** = los delitos violentos han experimentado un aumento; **crime rate** = índice *m* de criminalidad; **crime wave** = oleada *f* de crímenes *or* ola *f* de criminalidad (NOTE: no plural for this meaning)

COMMENT: a crime is an illegal act which may result in prosecution and punishment by the state if the accused is convicted. Generally, in order to be convicted of a crime, the accused must be shown to have committed an unlawful act **(actus reus)** with a criminal state of mind **(mens rea)**. The main types of crime are: **1. crimes against the person:** murder; manslaughter; assault, battery, wounding; grievous bodily harm; abduction; **2. crimes against property:** theft; robbery; burglary; obtaining property *or* services *or* pecuniary advantage by deception; blackmail; handling stolen goods; going equipped to steal; criminal damage; possessing something with intent to damage *or* destroy property; forgery; **3. sexual offences:** rape; buggery; bigamy; indecency; **4. political offences:** treason; terrorism; sedition; breach of the Official Secrets Act; **5. offences against justice:** assisting an offender; conspiracy; perjury; contempt of court; perverting the course of justice; **6. public order offences:** obstruction of the police; unlawful assembly; obscenity; possessing weapons; misuse of drugs; breach of the peace; **7. road traffic offences:** careless *or* reckless driving; drunken driving; driving without a licence *or* insurance. Most minor crime is tried before the Magistrates' Courts; more serious crime is tried at the Crown Court which has greater powers to sentence offenders. Most crimes are prosecuted by the police or the Crown Prosecutors, though private prosecutions brought by individuals are possible

criminal ['krɪmɪnl] **1** *adjective* **(a)** *(illegal)* delictivo, -va; **misappropriation of funds is a criminal act** = la apropiación indebida de fondos es un acto delictivo; **criminal offence** = delito *m* **(b)** *(referring to crime)* criminal *or* facineroso, -sa; **criminal action** = acción *f* penal; **criminal bankruptcy** = quiebra *f* criminal *or* fraudulenta; **criminal court** = tribunal *m* penal *or* juzgado *m* *or* sala *f* de lo penal; **criminal damage** = daño *m* criminal *or* penal; **criminal investigation department (CID)** = policía judicial *or* brigada de investigación criminal; **criminal law** = derecho *m* penal; **criminal lawyer** = criminalista *mf*; **criminal libel** = difamación *f*; **criminal negligence** = culpa *f* penal *or* imprudencia *f*; **the criminal population** = población *f* con antecedentes penales *or* población delincuente *or* criminal; **criminal record** = antecedentes *mpl* penales *or* historial *m* delictivo; **the accused had no criminal record** = el acusado no tenía antecedentes penales; **he has a criminal record going back to the time when he was still at school** = tiene un historial delictivo que se remonta a sus días de colegio; **age of criminal responsibility** = edad *f* de responsabilidad penal **2** *noun* criminal *mf* *or* delincuente *mf* *or* facineroso, -sa; **the police have contacted known criminals to get leads on the gangland murder** = la policía ha contactado con conocidos criminales para obtener pistas sobre el asesinato en el hampa; **a hardened criminal** = un criminal empedernido *or* incorregible *or* de difícil reinserción

COMMENT: in GB the age of criminal responsibility is ten years. Children under ten years old cannot be charged with a crime

Criminal Injuries Compensation Board
['krɪmɪnl 'ɪndʒərɪz kɒmpən'seɪʃn 'bɔːd] *noun* comité *m* de compensación a víctimas de delitos

criminology [krɪmɪ'nɒlədʒi] *noun* criminología *f*

criterion [kraɪ'tiəriən] *noun* criterio *m;* **using the criterion of the ratio of cases solved to cases reported, the police force is becoming more efficient** = si aplicamos el criterio de la proporción de casos resueltos sobre el total de casos denunciados, el cuerpo de policía está actuando con más eficacia (NOTE: plural is **criteria**)

criticize ['krɪtɪsaɪz] *verb* criticar; **the judge criticized the police for their handling of the rape case** = el juez criticó a la policía por la forma en que había llevado el caso de violación
◊ **criticism** ['krɪtɪsɪzm] *noun* crítica *f;* **the judge made some criticisms of the way in which the police handled the case** = el juez hizo algunas críticas sobre el modo en que la policía había llevado el caso

crook [krʊk] *noun (slang)* timador, -ra *or* ladrón, -ona *or* criminal *mf*

cross [krɒs] *verb* **(a) to cross a cheque** = cruzar un cheque; **crossed cheque** = cheque *m* cruzado **(b)** *GB (in the House of Commons)* **to cross the floor** = cambiar de partido
◊ **cross benches** ['krɒs 'bentʃɪz] *noun* escaños ocupados por diputados independientes
◊ **crossbencher** ['krɒs'bentʃə] *noun* diputado, -da independiente
◊ **cross off** ['krɒs 'ɒf] *verb* tachar; **he crossed my name off his list** = tachó mi nombre de su lista; **you can cross him off our mailing list** = puede tacharle de nuestra lista de direcciones
◊ **cross out** ['krɒs 'aʊt] *verb* tachar; **she crossed out £250 and put in £500** = tachó 250 libras y puso 500 libras

cross-examine
['krɒsɪg'zæmɪn] *verb* repreguntar *or* interrogar testigos (para tratar de desarmar sus argumentos)
◊ **cross-examination** ['krɒsɪgzæmɪ'neɪʃn] *noun* repregunta *f or* interrogatorio *m* hecho a testigos (para tratar de desarmar sus argumentos)

Crown [kraʊn] *noun GB* **(a) the Crown** = la Corona *or* el Estado; **Crown Prosecution Service (CPS)** = Fiscalía General del Estado; **Mr Smith is appearing for the Crown** = el Sr Smith representa

al Estado; **the Crown submitted that the maximum sentence should be applied in this case** = el Estado alegó que se debía aplicar la máxima pena a este caso; **the Crown case** *or* **the case for the Crown was that the defendants were guilty of espionage** = el Estado alegó que los acusados eran culpables de espionaje (NOTE: in legal reports, the Crown is referred to as **Rex** *or* **Regina** (abbreviated to **R.**) depending on whether there is a King or Queen reigning at the time: **the case of R.v. Smith Limited) (b)** **associate of the Crown Office** = secretario, -ria de juzgado; **Crown Lands** *or* **Crown property** = patrimonio *m* de la Corona *or* del Estado; **Crown copyright** = propiedad *f* intelectual del Estado
◊ **Crown Court** ['kraʊn 'kɔːt] *noun* Tribunal *m* de la Corona

COMMENT: a Crown Court is formed of a circuit judge and jury, and hears major criminal cases

◊ **Crown privilege** ['kraʊn 'prɪvɪlɪdʒ] *noun* privilegio *m* según el cual el gobierno no tiene que reproducir documentos ante un tribunal por razones de Estado
◊ **Crown prosecutor** ['kraʊn 'prɒsɪkjuːtə] *noun* fiscal *mf* del Estado

cruelty ['kruːəltɪ] *noun* crueldad *f; (against spouse)* malos tratos *mpl;* **extreme cruelty** = ensañamiento *m*

CTT ['siː 'tiː 'tiː] = CAPITAL TRANSFER TAX

culpable ['kʌlpəbl] *adjective* culpable; **culpable homicide** = homicidio *m or* asesinato *m;* **culpable negligence** = negligencia *f* delictiva *or* culpable
◊ **culpability** [kʌlpə'bɪlɪti] *noun* culpabilidad *f*

culprit ['kʌlprɪt] *noun* culpable *mf*

curiam ['kjuriəm] *see* PER CURIAM

currency ['kʌrənsi] *noun* moneda *f or* divisa *f;* **blocked currency** = divisa bloqueada; **foreign currency** = divisa *or* moneda extranjera; **free currency** = moneda de libre circulación *or* exenta de restricciones; **hard currency** = moneda fuerte *or* convertible; **legal currency** = moneda de curso legal; **soft currency** = moneda débil *or* no convertible

current ['kʌrənt] *adjective* actual *or* corriente; **current account** = cuenta *f* corriente; **current liabilities** = obligaciones *fpl* a corto plazo
◊ **currently** ['kʌrəntli] *adverb* actualmente *or* en la actualidad; **six murders which are currently being investigated** = seis asesinatos que están actualmente bajo investigación

curriculum vitae (CV) [kə'rɪkjʊləm 'viːtaɪ] *noun* currículum *m* vitae *or* historial *m* profesional; **candidates should send a letter of application with a curriculum vitae to the administrative office** = los candidatos deberán enviar una carta de solicitud con un currículum vitae al departamento de administración (NOTE: the US English is **résumé**)

curtilage ['kɜ:tɪlɪdʒ] *noun* tierras *fpl* de alrededor de una casa

custody ['kʌstədi] *noun* **(a)** *(kept in prison)* prisión *f or* detención *f;* **the young men were kept in police custody overnight** = los jóvenes permanecieron bajo custodia durante *or* toda la noche; **remanded in custody** = mantenido bajo custodia **(b)** *(care of children after divorce)* patria *f* potestad *or* custodia *f;* **legal custody** = custodia *or* protección *f* judicial; **protective custody** = custodia preventiva; **custody of the children was awarded to the mother** = se concedió a la madre la custodia de los hijos; **the court granted the mother custody of both children** = el tribunal concedió a la madre la custodia de ambos hijos
◊ **custodial** [kʌs'təʊdiəl] *adjective;* **custodial establishment** *or* **institution** = prisión *f or* cárcel *f;* **custodial sentence** = sentencia *f* de ingreso en prisión
◊ **custodian** [kʌs'təʊdiən] *noun* guardián, -ana

custom ['kʌstəm] *noun* **(a)** *(how things are done)* costumbre *f;* **it is the custom that everyone stands up when the magistrates enter the courtroom** = es costumbre que todo el mundo se levante cuando los magistrados entran en la sala; **local custom** = costumbre local *or* del lugar; **the customs of the trade** = los usos comerciales *or* de un comercio **(b)** *(regular clients)* clientela *f;* **to lose someone's custom** = perder la clientela
◊ **customary** ['kʌstəmri] *adjective* acostumbrado, -da
◊ **customs** *or* **Customs and Excise** ['kʌstəmz] *plural noun* aduana *f or* Departamento *m* de Derechos Arancelarios e Impuestos Indirectos; **to go through customs** = pasar por la aduana; **he**

was stopped by customs = se le detuvo en la aduana; **her car was searched by customs** = le registraron el coche en la aduana; **customs barrier** = barrera arancelaria; **customs clearance** = despacho *m* de aduanas; **customs declaration** = declaración *f* de aduana; **customs union** = unión aduanera

cut [kʌt] **1** *noun* **(a)** *(lowering of price or salary)* reducción *f or* recorte *m or* rebaja *f;* **price cuts** *or* **cuts in prices** = reducciones de precios; **salary cuts** *or* **cuts in salaries** = recortes salariales **(b)** *(share in payment)* parte *f;* **he introduces new customers and gets a cut of the salesman's commission** = introduce nuevos clientes y recibe una parte de la comisión del vendedor **2** *verb* **(a)** *(to lower suddenly)* bajar *or* reducir; **we are cutting prices on all our models** = hemos rebajado los precios de todos nuestros modelos; **to cut (back) production** = reducir la producción **(b)** *(to reduce numbers)* reducir *or* parar; **to cut jobs** = reducir el empleo *or* los puestos de trabajo
◊ **cut in on** ['kʌt 'ɪn 'ɒn] *verb* **to cut someone in on** = hacer partícipe a alguien en *or* incluir en

CV ['si: 'vi:] *noun* = *CURRICULUM VITAE;* **please apply in writing, enclosing a current CV** = se ruega presenten la solicitud por escrito, adjuntando un CV actualizado

cycle ['saɪkl] *noun* ciclo *m*
◊ **cyclical** ['sɪklɪkl] *adjective* cíclico, -ca; **cyclical factors** = factores *mpl* cíclicos

cy-près ['si: 'preɪ] *adjective & adverb* lo más cerca posible; **cy-près doctrine** = doctrina *f* que establece que cuando una institución benéfica no puede dirigir sus fondos a lo que pensaba inicialmente, un tribunal puede dirigirlos a un propósito lo más cercano posible a la intención original

Dd

D [diː] *fourth letter of the alphabet;* **category 'D' prisoners** = reclusos, -sas en régimen de prisión abierta; **Schedule D** = divisiones *fpl* de la tarifa del impuesto sobre la renta referentes al impuesto sobre oficios, profesiones, intereses y otras ganancias que no proceden del empleo; **Table D** = escritura *f* de constitución y estatutos *mpl* tipo de una compañía pública con aportación de capital limitado por garantía, expuesto en la Ley de Sociedades de 1985

DA ['diː 'eɪ] *US* = DISTRICT ATTORNEY

dabs [dæbz] *plural noun (slang)* huellas *fpl* dactilares

Dail (Éireann) ['dɔɪl 'eərən] *noun (Eire)* Cámara *f* de Representantes del Parlamento de la República de Irlanda; **the Foreign Minister reported on the meeting to the Dail** = el ministro de Asuntos Exteriores elevó un informe de la reunión a la Cámara de los Representantes; NOTE: the members of the Dail are called **Teachta Dala (TD)**

daily ['deɪli] *adverb* diariamente *or* a diario

damage ['dæmɪdʒ] **1** *noun* **(a)** *(harm)* daño *m or* perjuicio *m;* **brain damage** = lesión *f* cerebral; **fire damage** = daños por incendio; **malicious damage** = daño doloso; **reparable damages** = daños resarcibles; **storm damage** = daños causados por tormentas; **to suffer damage** = sufrir daños; **to cause damage** = causar daños o perjuicios; **causing criminal damage** = que causa daño criminal *or* penal; **damage feasant** = daño material producido por los animales de una persona en la propiedad de otra (NOTE: no plural in this meaning) **(b)** *(compensation)* **damages** = daños *mpl* y perjuicios *mpl;* **actual damages** = daños efectivos; **to claim £1,000 in damages** = exigir 1.000 libras por daños y perjuicios; **to pay £25,000 in damages** = pagar 25.000 libras por daños y perjuicios; **to be liable for *or* in damages** = estar obligado a indemnizar por daños; **to bring an action for damages against someone** = presentar una demanda por daños y perjuicios contra alguien; **aggravated damages** = daños con agravante *or* indemnización suplementaria; **compensatory damages** = indemnización por daños y perjuicios; **exemplary damages** = daños punitivos *or* ejemplares *or* indemnización que el acusado debe pagar por daños causados al demandante; **general damages** = daños generales o directos; **liquidated damages** = indemnización por daños y perjuicios cuantificada; **measure of damages** = medida *f or* evaluación *f* de los daños; **mitigation of damages** = atenuante *m or* minoración *f* de la indemnización por daños; **nominal damages** = daños no importantes *or* nominales; **special damages** = daños calculables (NOTE: damages are noted at the end of a report on a case as: *Special damages: £100; General damages: £2,500)* **2** *verb* dañar; **the storm damaged the cargo** = la tormenta dañó la carga; **stock which has been damaged by water** = existencias dañadas por el agua; **he alleged that the newspaper article was damaging to the company's reputation** = alegó que el artículo periodístico perjudicaba *or* dañaba la reputación de la compañía

◊ **damaged** ['dæmɪdʒd] *adjective* dañado, -da *or* perjudicado, -da; **fire-damaged goods** = artículos dañados por el incendio

danger ['deɪnʒə] *noun* **(a)** *(possibility of being harmed)* peligro *m or* riesgo *m;* **to be in danger** = estar en peligro; **out of danger** = fuera de peligro; **there is danger to the workers in using old machinery** = los trabajadores corren un riesgo al usar maquinaria antigua **(b)** *(likelihood)* **there is no danger of the case being heard early** = no hay peligro que la vista del caso sea a corto plazo; **in danger of** = en peligro de; **he is in danger to being in contempt of court** = corre el riesgo de caer en desacato a los tribunales

◊ **danger money** ['deɪnʒə 'mʌni] *noun* plus *m* de peligrosidad; **the workers have stopped work and asked for danger money** = los trabajadores han hecho un paro laboral en petición de un plus de peligrosidad

◊ **dangerous** ['deɪnʒrəs] *adjective* peligroso, -sa; **dangerous animals** = animales peligrosos; **dangerous driving** = conducción temeraria; **dangerous drugs** = drogas peligrosas; **dangerous job** = trabajo arriesgado *or* peligroso; **dangerous weapon** = arma peligrosa

data ['deɪtə] *noun* datos *mpl or* información *f;* **data bank** *or* **bank of data** = banco *m* de datos; **data processing** = proceso *m* de datos; **data protection** = protección *f* de datos (NOTE: **data** is usually singular: **the data is easily available)**

◊ **database** ['deɪtəbeɪs] *noun* base *f or* banco *m* de datos; **the police maintain a database of fingerprints** = la policía guarda un banco de huellas dactilares

date ['deɪt] **1** *noun* **(a)** fecha *f;* **date of commencement** = fecha de entrada en vigor de una ley parlamentaria; **date stamp** = fechador *m;* **date of receipt** = fecha de recepción; **due date** = fecha de vencimiento **(b) at an early date** = en fecha próxima; **up to date** = al día; **to bring something up to date** = poner algo al día; **to keep something up to date** = tener *or* mantener algo al día **(c) to date** = hasta la fecha; **interest to date** = intereses *mpl* hasta la fecha **2** *verb* fechar; **the cheque was dated March 24th** = el cheque tenía fecha del 24 de marzo; **he forgot to date the cheque** = olvidó fechar el cheque

◊ **dated** ['deɪtɪd] *adjective* fechado, -da *or* con fecha; **the murderer's letter was dated June 15th** = la carta del asesino tenía fecha del 15 de junio

day [deɪ] *noun* **(a)** *(period of 24 hours)* día *m;* **there are thirty days in June** = junio tiene treinta días; **the first day of the month is a public holiday** = el primer día del mes es festivo; **three clear days** = tres días laborables *or* hábiles; **to give ten clear days' notice** = avisar con diez días laborables de antelación; **allow four clear days for the cheque to be paid into the account** = cuente con cuatro días laborables para que el cheque sea abonado en cuenta; **early day motion** = moción *f* exploratoria a debatir en fecha próxima **(b)** *(period of work)* jornada *f* laboral; **pay-day** = día de pago; **working day** = día hábil *or* día laborable; **the trial lasted ten days** = el juicio duró diez días

◊ **day-to-day** ['deɪtə'deɪ] *adjective* cotidiano, -na *or* diario, -ria; **the clerk organizes the day-to-day running of the courts** = el secretario organiza el funcionamiento diario de los tribunales

◊ **day training centre** ['deɪ 'treɪnɪŋ 'sentə] *noun* centro *m* ocupacional para delincuentes

daybook ['deɪbʊk] *noun* diario *m*

DC ['di: 'si:] = DETECTIVE CONSTABLE

DCC ['di: 'si: 'si:] = DEPUTY CHIEF CONSTABLE

dead [ded] *adjective* **(a)** *(not alive)* muerto, -ta *or* fallecido, -da; **to consider dead** *or* **to give up for dead** = dar por muerto; **six people were dead as a result of the accident** = seis personas resultaron muertas como consecuencia del accidente; **we inherited the house from my dead grandfather** = heredamos la casa a la muerte de mi abuelo **(b)** *(not longer used)* inactivo, -va; **dead account** = cuenta *f* sin movimiento *or* inactiva; **dead letter** = reglamento *m* anticuado *or* en desuso *or* papel *m* mojado; **this law has become a dead letter** = esta ley ha caído en desuso; **dead loss** = pérdida *f or* siniestro *m* total; **the car was written off as a dead loss** = declararon el coche siniestro total

◊ **deadline** ['dedlaɪn] *noun* fecha *f* límite *or* plazo *m or* cierre *m;* **to meet a deadline** = cumplir un plazo establecido *or* acabar algo a tiempo *or* en el plazo previsto; **to miss a deadline** = no acabar algo en el plazo previsto

◊ **deadlock** ['dedlɒk] **1** *noun* punto *m* muerto; **to break a deadlock** = desbloquear las negociaciones *or* restablecer el diálogo **2** *verb* estar en punto muerto *or* bloquear *or* paralizar; **talks have been deadlocked for ten days** = las negociaciones están paralizadas desde hace diez días

deal [di:l] **1** *noun* **(a)** transacción *f* negocio *m or* trato *m or* acuerdo *m or* convenio *m;* **to arrange a deal** *or* **to set up a deal** *or* **to do a deal** = fijar un acuerdo *or* negociar un acuerdo *or* hacer un trato; **to sign a deal** = firmar un acuerdo; **to call off a deal** = cancelar *or* anular un acuerdo; **package deal** = acuerdo global; **it's a deal** = trato hecho **(b)** **a great deal** *or* **a good deal of something** = mucho, -cha *or* una gran cantidad de algo; **he has made a good deal of money on the stock market** = ha ganado mucho dinero en la bolsa; **counsel wasted a great deal of time cross-examining the dead man's father** = el abogado perdió mucho tiempo interrogando al padre del fallecido **2** *verb* **to deal with** = tratar con; **Crown Courts do not deal with civil cases** = los Tribunales de la Corona no tratan causas civiles

◊ **dealer** ['di:lə] *noun* comerciante *mf or* agente *mf;* **authorized dealer** = distribuidor, -ra autorizado, -da; **wine dealer** = comerciante de vinos; **foreign exchange dealer** = operador de cambios *or* cambista

◊ **dealing** ['di:lɪŋ] *noun* **(a)** *(Stock Exchange)* transacciones *fpl or* operaciones *fpl* en bolsa; **fair dealing** = operaciones comerciales correctas; *(copyright)* cita *f* legalmente autorizada; **foreign exchange dealing** = cambio *m or* operaciones de cambio; **forward dealings** = transacciones de futuros; **insider dealing** = operaciones de iniciado **(b)** *(goods)* comercio *m;* **to have dealings with someone** = hacer negocios con alguien *or* comerciar con alguien

death [deθ] *noun* muerte *f or* fallecimiento *m;* **death benefit** = indemnización *f* por fallecimiento; **death certificate** = certificado *m or* partida *f* de defunción; **death grant** = ayuda *f* de sepelio; **death in service** = indemnización *or* subsidio *m* por fallecimiento de un trabajador durante su trabajo en una empresa; **death penalty** = pena *f* de muerte; **death sentence** = condena *f* a muerte *or* sentencia *f* de muerte; *US* **death duty** *or* **death tax** = derechos *mpl* de sucesión *or* impuesto *m* de sucesión; **death toll** = índice *m* de mortalidad; **accidental death** *or* **death by misadventure** = muerte accidental; **sudden death** = muerte repentina; **violent death** = muerte violenta *or* muerte a mano armada; **presumption of death** = presunción *f* de muerte

debate [dɪ'beɪt] **1** *noun* debate *m;* **several MPs criticized the government in** *or* **during the debate on the Finance Bill** = varios diputados criticaron al gobierno durante el debate sobre la ley presupuestaria; **the Bill passed its Second Reading after a short debate** = tras un breve debate, el proyecto de ley pasó su segunda lectura; **the debate continued until 3 a.m.** = el debate se alargó hasta las 3 de la madrugada **2** *verb* debatir; **the MPs are still debating the Data Protection Bill** = los diputados continúan debatiendo el proyecto de ley de protección de datos

debenture [dɪ'bentʃə] *noun* bono *m or* pagaré *m or* obligación *f* de interés fijo; **mortgage debenture** = cédula *f* hipotecaria *or* título *m* garantizado por hipoteca; **debenture issue** *or* **issue of debentures** = emisión *f* de obligaciones garantizada por los activos de la compañía; **debenture bond** = obligación no hipotecaria; **debenture capital** *or* **debenture stock** = obligaciones garantizadas por los activos de la compañía; **debenture holder** = obligacionista *mf or* tenedor *m* de obligaciones; **debenture register** *or* **register of debentures** = registro *m* de obligacionistas

debit ['debɪt] **1** *noun* débito *m or* debe *m;* **debit and credit** = debe y haber *m;* **debit column** = columna *f* del debe; **debit entry** = asiento *m* del débito *or* adeudo *m;* **debit side** = debe *m;* **debit note** = nota *f* de adeudo *or* de cargo; **direct debit** = domiciliación *f* bancaria; *compare* STANDING ORDER **2** *verb* **to debit an account** = adeudar *or* cargar en cuenta; **his account was debited with the sum of £25** = cargaron 25 libras en su cuenta

◊ **debitable** ['debɪtəbl] *adjective* abonable *or* adeudable

debt [det] *noun* deuda *f;* **outstanding debt** = debido y no pagado; **public debt** = deuda pública; **the company stopped trading with debts of over £1 million** = la compañía dejó de operar con deudas superiores a un millón de libras; **to be in debt** = estar en deuda *or* deber dinero; **to get into debt** = endeudarse *or* contraer deudas; **to be out of debt** = estar libre de deudas; **to pay back a debt** = reembolsar *or* devolver una deuda; **to pay off a debt** = liquidar *or* terminar de pagar una deuda; **to service a debt** = pagar intereses sobre una deuda; **bad debt** = deuda incobrable *or* morosa; **debt collection** *or* **collecting** = cobro *m* de morosos; **debt collection agency** *or* **collecting agency** = agencia *f* de cobro de morosos; **debt collector** = agente cobrador de morosos; **debt factor** = agente comprador de deudas

◊ **debtor** ['detə] *noun* deudor, -ra *or* prestatario,-ria; **debtor side** = debe *m;* **debtor nation** = nación *f* deudora *or* país endeudado; **bad debtor** = cliente fallido; **judgment debtor** = deudor por sentencia judicial firme

decease [dɪ'siːs] *noun (formal)* fallecimiento *m or* defunción *f;* **on his decease all his property will go to his widow** = a su muerte, todas sus propiedades pasarán a su viuda

◊ **deceased** [dɪ'siːst] *adjective & noun* difunto, -ta *or* fallecido, -da *or* muerto, -ta; **the deceased left all his property to his widow** = el difunto dejó todas sus propiedades a su viuda; **she inherited the estate of a deceased aunt** = heredó la fortuna de una tía que murió

deceive [dɪ'siːv] *verb* engañar

◊ **deceit** *or* **deception** [dɪ'siːt *or* dɪ'sepʃn] *noun* fraude *m or* engaño *m or* falacia *f;* **she obtained £10,000 by deception** = obtuvo 10.000 libras por medio de estafas; **obtaining a pecuniary advantage by deception** = obtener ventajas económicas por estafa; **obtaining property by deception** = obtener propiedades por estafa *or* fraude

◊ **deceitful** [dɪ'siːtful] *adjective* falaz

◊ **deceiver** [dɪ'siːvə] *noun* impostor, -ra *or* embustero, -ra

◊ **deceptive** [dɪ'septɪv] *adjective* engañoso, -sa

decent ['diːsənt] *adjective* decente; **this book should be banned - it will shock any decent citizen** = este libro debería prohibirse - escandalizará a cualquier ciudadano decente

◊ **decency** ['diːsənsi] *noun* decencia *f;* **the film shocked public decency** = la película escandalizó a la decencia pública

decide [dɪ'saɪd] *verb* **(a)** *(to pass judgment)* sentenciar; **the judge decided in favour of the plaintiff** = el juez sentenció a favor del demandante **(b)** *(to make one's mind up)* decidir *or* optar; **we have decided to take our neighbours to court** = hemos decidido llevar a nuestros vecinos ante los tribunales; **the tribunal decided against awarding any damages** = el tribunal sentenció en contra de la concesión de daños y perjuicios

◊ **decided case** [dɪ'saɪdɪd 'keɪs] *noun* caso *m* resuelto *or* precedente *m*

◊ **decidendi** [desɪ'dendaɪ]*see* RATIO

◊ **deciding factor** [dɪ'saɪdɪŋ 'fæktə] *noun* factor *m* decisivo

◊ **decision** [dɪ'sɪʒn] *noun* **(a)** *(judgment in a civil court)* fallo *m;* **the decision of the House of Lords is final** = el fallo de la Cámara de los Lores es irrevocable **(b)** *(making up one's mind)* decisión *f;* **decision-making body** = órgano decisivo; **to come to a decision** *or* **to reach a decision** = llegar a una decisión *or* decidirse; **decision making** = toma *f* de decisiones; **the decision-making processes** = los procesos decisorios; **decision maker** = persona *f* que toma las decisiones

◊ **decisis** [dɪ'saɪsɪs] *see* STARE DECISIS

◊ **decisive** [dɪ'saɪsɪv] *adjective* decisorio, -ria

deck [dek] *noun* cubierta *f* (de un buque)

declare [dɪ'kleə] *verb* declarar *or* prestar declaración; **to declare a court in session** =

declarar abierta la sesión; **to declare someone bankrupt** = declarar a alguien en quiebra; **to declare a dividend of 10%** = declarar un dividendo del 10%; **to declare goods to the customs** = declarar mercancías en la aduana; **to declare an interest** = declarar un interés

◊ **declared** [dɪ'kleəd] *adjective* declarado, -da; **declared value** = valor *m* declarado

◊ **declaration** [deklə'reɪʃn] *noun* declaración *f;* **declaration of association** = declaración de asociación; **declaration of bankruptcy** = declaración de quiebra; **declaration of income** = declaración de la renta; **customs declaration** = declaración de aduana; **statutory declaration** = declaración jurada (ante testigos) *or* declaración estatutaria (ante el Registro Mercantil); **VAT declaration** = declaración del IVA

◊ **declaratory judgment** [dɪ'klærətri 'steɪtmənt] *noun* sentencia declarativa *or* interpretativa de una escritura *or* documento

declassify [di:'klæsɪfaɪ] *verb* levantar el secreto oficial; **the government papers relating to the war have recently been declassified** = los papeles del gobierno referentes a la guerra se han hecho públicos recientemente

◊ **declassification** [di:klæsɪfɪ'keɪʃn] *noun* levantamiento *m* del secreto oficial

decline [dɪ'klaɪn] **1** *noun* baja *f or* descenso *m or* disminución *f;* **the decline in the value of the peseta** = el descenso del valor de la peseta; **a decline in buying power** = una disminución del poder adquisitivo; **the last year has seen a decline in real wages** = durante el año pasado los salarios reales han experimentado una baja **2** *verb* negarse; **the witness declined to take the oath** = el testigo se negó a prestar juramento

decontrol [di:kən'trəʊl] *verb* liberalizar; **to decontrol the price of petrol** = liberalizar el precio de la gasolina (NOTE: **decontrolled - decontrolling**)

decrease ['di:kri:s] *verb* disminuir *or* bajar *or* reducir; **the government proposes to decrease the rate of VAT** = el gobierno propone disminuir la cotización del IVA

decree [dɪ'kri:] **1** *noun* **(a)** *(order made by a head of state)* decreto *m;* **decree law** = decreto-ley; **to govern by decree** = gobernar por decreto **(b)** *(divorce)* **decree nisi** = sentencia *f* provisional de divorcio; **decree absolute** = sentencia de divorcio definitiva **2** *verb* decretar; **the President decreed that June 1st should be a National Holiday** = el Presidente decretó que el día 1 de junio sería fiesta nacional

deduce [dɪ'dju:s] *verb* concluir *or* deducir; **from his clothes, we can deduce that the victim was a rich man** = por su atuendo, podemos deducir que la víctima era rica

◊ **deducing title** [dɪ'dju:sɪŋ 'taɪtl] *noun* título *m* de propiedad

deduct [dɪ'dʌkt] *verb* deducir *or* descontar; **to deduct £3 from the price** = descontar 3 libras del precio; **to deduct a sum for expenses** = deducir una cantidad para gastos; **to deduct 5% from salaries** = deducir un 5% de los salarios; **tax deducted at source** = impuestos deducidos en origen

◊ **deductible** [dɪ'dʌktəbl] *adjective* deducible; **tax-deductible** = desgravable *or* que desgrava; **these expenses are not tax-deductible** = estos gastos no son desgravables

◊ **deduction** [dɪ'dʌkʃn] *noun* **(a)** *(conclusion reached)* deducción *f or* inferencia *f;* **by deduction, the detective came to the conclusion that the dead person has not been murdered** = por deducción, el inspector concluyó que el muerto no ha sido asesinado **(b)** *(money removed from total)* deducción; **net salary is salary after deduction of tax and social security contributions** = el sueldo neto es el sueldo bruto después de deducir los impuestos y la contribución a la seguridad social; **deductions from salary** *or* **salary deductions** *or* **deductions at source** = deducciones *fpl* de salario *or* en origen; **tax deductions** = deducción fiscal impositiva *or US* gastos *mpl* deducibles

deed [di:d] *noun* escritura *f or* título *m;* **deed of arrangement** = escritura de acuerdo entre deudor y acreedor; **deed of assignment** = escritura de cesión; **deed of covenant** = escritura de garantía; **deed of conveyance** = escritura de traspaso; **deed of partnership** = escritura de sociedad; **deed of transfer** = escritura de transferencia *or* transmisión *f* de acciones; **title deeds** = escritura de propiedad *or* títulos de propiedad; **we have deposited the deeds of the house in the bank** = hemos depositado la escritura de propiedad de la casa en el banco

◊ **deed poll** ['di:d 'pəʊl] *noun* escritura *f* legal de declaración unilateral; **to change one's name by deed poll** = cambiarse el apellido de manera oficial *or* cambio de inscripción en el registro civil

deem [di:m] *verb* considerar *or* creer; **the judge deemed it necessary to order the court to be cleared** = el juez consideró necesario ordenar que se desalojara la sala; **if no payment is made, the party shall be deemed to have defaulted** = de no efectuarse ningún pago, el partido será considerado deudor moroso

de facto ['deɪ 'fæktəʊ] *Latin phrase* de facto *or* de hecho; **de facto powers** = poderes fácticos; **he is the de facto owner of the property** = él es el dueño real de la propiedad; *see also* DE JURE

defalcation [di:fæl'keɪʃn] *noun* desfalco *m*

defame [dɪ'feɪm] *verb* difamar

◊ **defamation** [defə'meɪʃn] *noun* difamación *f;* **defamation of character** = difamación de la reputación

COMMENT: defamation is a tort and may be libel (if it is in a permanent form, such as printed matter) or slander (if it is spoken)

◊ **defamatory** [dɪ'fæmətri] *adjective* difamatorio, -ria; **defamatory statement** = declaración *f* difamante *or* difamatoria

default [dɪ'fɔːlt] **1** *noun* incumplimiento *m or* omisión *f or* falta *f* de pago; **in default of payment** = por falta de pago *or* por incumplimiento de pago; **the company is in default** = la compañía es morosa *or* demora los pagos *or* no cubre sus deudas; **by default** = por falta de *or* por defecto *or* por ausencia; **he was elected by default** = fue elegido por ausencia de otros candidatos; **judgment by default** *or* **default judgment** = juicio *m* en rebeldía *or* por falta de comparecencia; **default action** = demanda *f* judicial por falta de pago; **default summons** = citación *f* judicial (realizada por un juzgado del Condado) por falta de pago **2** *verb* incumplir (un contrato *or* pago) *or* faltar *or* no pagar; **to default on payments** = no pagar los plazos *or* las deudas *or* incumplir *or* retrasar los pagos
◊ **defaulter** [dɪ'fɔːltə] *noun* moroso, -sa

defeasance [dɪ'fiːzəns] *noun* anulación *f or* abrogación *f or* revocación *f* de algún contrato *or* cláusula *f* resolutoria *or* de nulidad

defeat [dɪ'fiːt] **1** *noun* derrota *f;* **the minister offered to resign after the defeat of the motion in the House of Commons** = el Ministro ofreció su dimisión después de la derrota de la moción en la Cámara de los Comunes **2** *verb* derrotar *or* vencer *or* rechazar *or* anular; **the bill was defeated in the Lords by 52 to 64** = el proyecto de ley fue rechazado en la Cámara de los Lores por 52 votos a favor y 64 en contra; **the government was defeated in a vote on law and order** = el gobierno resultó derrotado en una votación sobre el orden público

defect 1 ['diːfekt] *noun* defecto *m or* fallo *m or* tara *f* **2** [dɪ'fekt] *verb* (*of a spy or agent or government employee*) desertar *or* huir
◊ **defective** [dɪ'fektɪv] *adjective* **(a)** *(not functioning)* defectuoso, -sa; **the machine broke down because of a defective cooling system** = la máquina se rompió debido a un sistema de enfriamiento defectuoso **(b)** *(not valid)* defectuoso, -sa *or* incompleto, -ta; **his title to the property was defective** = su título de la propiedad tiene vicios jurídicos

defector [dɪ'fektə] *noun* tránsfuga *mf*

defence *US* **defense** [dɪ'fens] *noun* **(a)** *(protection)* defensa *f;* **without a defence** = indefenso, -sa; **the merchant bank is organizing the company's defence against the takeover bid** = el banco mercantil está organizando la defensa de la compañía frente a la oferta de adquisición **(b)** *(in a lawsuit)* defensa *or* apología *f;* **defence counsel** =

abogado defensor *or* de la parte demandada **(c)** *(arguments used in a case)* defensa *or* eximente *m;* **special defence** = eximente especial; **his defence was that he did not know the property was stolen** = alegó en su defensa que no sabía que los bienes eran robados; **to file a defence** = presentar una defensa **(d)** *(document that sets out the defendant's case)* defensa; *compare* PROSECUTION

◊ **defenceless** [dɪ'fensləs] *adjective* indefenso, -sa
◊ **defend** [dɪ'fend] *verb* **(a)** *(to protect)* defender; **the company is defending itself against the takeover bid** = la compañía se está defendiendo frente a la oferta de adquisición **(b)** *(in a lawsuit)* defender; **he hired the best lawyers to defend him against the tax authorities** = contrató a los mejores abogados para que le defendieran contra las autoridades fiscales; **to defend an action** = defender una acción
◊ **defendant** [dɪ'fendənt] *noun* **(a)** *(civil case)* parte demandada *or* demandado, -da **(b)** *(criminal case)* acusado, -da; *compare* PLAINTIFF

defer [dɪ'fɜː] *verb* aplazar *or* diferir; **to defer judgment** = aplazar el juicio; **the decision has been deferred until the next meeting** = el fallo ha sido aplazado hasta la próxima reunión (NOTE: **deferring - deferred**)
◊ **deferment** [dɪ'fɜːmənt] *noun* aplazamiento *m or* prórroga *f or* moratoria *f;* **deferment of payment** = aplazamiento de pago; **deferment of a decision** = aplazamiento de un fallo; **deferment of sentence** = aplazamiento de sentencia
◊ **deferred** [dɪ'fɜːd] *adjective* aplazado, -da *or* diferido, -da; **deferred creditor** = acreedor *m* diferido; **deferred payment** = pago *m* aplazado; **deferred stock** *or* **shares** = acciones con derecho a dividendo después de haber abonado dividendo a las demás acciones

defiance [dɪ'faɪəns] *noun* desafío *m*

deficiency [dɪ'fɪʃənsi] *noun* deficiencia *f or* falta *f US* déficit *m;* **deficiencies** = escasez *f or* déficit; *see also* SUPPLEMENTAL APPROPRIATIONS

deficit ['defɪsɪt] *noun* déficit *m;* **the council is trying to agree on how to reduce its current deficit** = el ayuntamiento está intentando llegar a un acuerdo para reducir el déficit actual; **the President has promised to reduce the budget deficit** = el Presidente ha prometido reducir el déficit presupuestario; **trade deficit** = déficit de la balanza de pagos

define [dɪ'faɪn] *verb* definir *or* precisar; **immigrant persons as defined in Appendix 3** = las personas inmigrantes tal y como se definen en el apéndice 3; **the judge asked counsel to define what he meant by 'incapable'** = el juez pidió al acusado que precisase lo que quería decir con 'incapaz'

deforce [diː'fɔːs] *verb* detentar *or* usurpar la posesión de bienes a un tercero
◊ **deforcement** [diː'fɔːsmənt] *noun* detención *f or* usurpación *f*

defraud [dɪ'frɔːd] *verb* defraudar *or* estafar; **he defrauded the Inland Revenue of thousands of pounds** = defraudó miles de libras a Hacienda (NOTE: you defraud someone **of** something)

defray [dɪ'freɪ] *verb* pagar *or* costear *or* sufragar; **the company agreed to defray the costs of the prosecution** = la compañía accedió a sufragar las costas del juicio

defy [dɪ'faɪ] *verb* desafiar

degree [dɪ'griː] *noun* **(a)** *(measure of relationship)* grado *m;* **degree of kinship** = grado de parentesco; **prohibited degrees** = relaciones *fpl* ilegales por existir consanguinidad **(b)** *US* sistema *m* de clasificación de asesinatos; **first degree murder** = asesinato *m* en primer grado *or* con premeditación; **second degree murder** = homicidio *m* por imprudencia *or* no premeditado

COMMENT: in the US, the penalty for first degree murder can be death

de jure ['deɪ 'dʒʊəreɪ] *Latin phrase* de derecho; **he is the de jure owner of the property** = es el dueño de derecho de la propiedad; *see also* DE FACTO

delay [dɪ'leɪ] **1** *noun* retraso *m or* atraso *m or* demora *f or* mora *f;* **there was a delay of thirty minutes before the hearing started** *or* **the hearing started after a thirty minute delay** = la vista empezó con treinta minutos de retraso **2** *verb* tardar *or* atrasar *or* demorar *or* retrasar; **judgment was delayed while the magistrates asked for advice** = se demoró el juicio mientras los magistrados pedían peritaje

del credere agent ['del 'kreɪdəri 'eɪdʒənt] *noun* agente *mf* del crédere *or* agente comisionista que responde del crédito de los compradores

delegate 1 ['delɪgət] *noun* representante *mf or* delegado, -da; **the management refused to meet the trade union delegates** = la dirección se negó a reunirse con los representantes de los sindicatos **2** ['delɪgeɪt] *verb* delegar; **to delegate authority** = delegar la autoridad; **delegated legislation** = legislación *f* delegada
◊ **delegation** [delɪ'geɪʃn] *noun* **(a)** *(group of delegates)* delegación *f;* **a Chinese trade delegation** = una delegación china de comercio; **the management met a union delegation** = la dirección se reunió con una delegación sindical **(b)** *(passing responsibility to others)* delegación (NOTE: no plural for this meaning)
◊ **delegatus non potest delegare** [delɪ'gɑːtʌs nɒn pɒtest delɪ'gɑːreɪ] *Latin phrase* 'el delegado no puede delegar en otro'

delete [dɪ'liːt] *verb* suprimir; **the court ordered the newspaper to delete all references to the divorce case** = el tribunal ordenó al periódico que suprimiera toda referencia al caso de divorcio; **the lawyers have deleted clause two from the contract** = los abogados han suprimido la cláusula segunda del contrato

deliberate 1 [dɪ'lɪbrət] *adjective* deliberado, -da *or* premeditado, -da; **the police suggest that the letter was a deliberate attempt to encourage disorder** = la policía insinúa que la carta fue un intento deliberado para provocar disturbios **2** [dɪ'lɪbəreɪt] *verb* deliberar; **the committee deliberated for several hours before reaching a decision** = la comisión estuvo deliberando durante varias horas antes de llegar a una resolución
◊ **deliberately** [dɪ'lɪbrətli] *adverb* a propósito *or* deliberadamente *or* con intención; **he was accused of deliberately setting fire to the shop** = le acusaron de prender fuego a la tienda intencionadamente
◊ **deliberations** [dɪlɪbə'reɪʃnz] *plural noun* discusiones *fpl or* debate *m or* deliberaciones *fpl;* **the result of the committee's deliberations was passed to the newspapers** = se transmitió a los periódicos el resultado de las deliberaciones de la comisión

delicti [dɪ'lɪktaɪ] *see* CORPUS

delicto [dɪ'lɪktəʊ] *see* IN FLAGRANTE DELICTO

delinquency [dɪ'lɪŋkwənsi] *noun* delincuencia *f*
◊ **delinquent** [dɪ'lɪŋkwənt] **1** *adjective* delincuente *or* delictivo, -va *or* US debido y no pagado **2** *noun* delincuente *mf;* **a juvenile delinquent** *or* US **a delinquent** = un delincuente *m or* una delincuente *f* juvenil

deliver [dɪ'lɪvə] *verb* repartir *or* entregar; **goods delivered free** *or* **free delivered goods** = entrega gratuita de productos; **goods delivered on board** = entrega de mercancías a bordo; **to deliver a speech** = pronunciar un discurso; **to deliver a verdict** = dictar una sentencia
◊ **delivery** [dɪ'lɪvri] *noun* **(a)** *(transport of goods)* entrega *f;* **delivery of goods** = reparto *m* de productos; **delivery note** = albarán *m;* **delivery order** = orden *f* de expedición; **recorded delivery** = servicio *m* de entrega de cartas certificadas *or* con acuse de recibo; **cash on delivery** = pago *m* contra reembolso; **to take delivery of goods** = aceptar la entrega de mercancías **(b)** *(goods delivered)* entrega *f;* **we take in three deliveries a day** = recogemos tres entregas diarias; **there were four items missing in the last delivery** = faltaban cuatro artículos en la última entrega **(c)** *(transfer of a bill of exchange)* transferencia *f or* cesión *f* de una letra de cambio **(d)** *(of a deed)* expedición *f;* **deeds take effect only from the time of delivery** = las escrituras surten efecto únicamente desde el

momento de la expedición **(e)** *(speech)* exposición *f* oral

demagogue ['deməgɒg] *noun (usually as criticism)* demagogo, -ga
◊ **demagogy** *or* **demagoguery** ['deməgɒgi *or* 'deməgɒgri] *noun* demagogia *f*

demand [dɪ'mɑːnd] **1** *noun* **(a)** *(request for payment)* reclamación *f or* requerimiento *m* de pago; **payable on demand** = pagadero a la vista; **demand bill** = letra *f or* giro *m* a la vista; **final demand** = último requerimiento *or* requerimiento final; **letter of demand** = carta *f* de requerimiento **(b)** *(need for goods)* demanda *f*; **supply and demand** = oferta *f* y demanda; **law of supply and demand** = ley *f* de la oferta y la demanda **(c)** *(requirement)* exigencia *f* **2** *verb* reclamar *or* exigir *or* requerir; **they were accused of demanding payment with threats** = les acusaron de requerir el pago con amenazas
◊ **demanding with menaces** [dɪ'mɑːndɪŋ wɪθ 'menəsɪz] *noun* exigencia bajo amenazas

démarche ['deɪmɑːʃ] *noun* gestión *f* oficial

de minimis non curat lex [deɪ 'mɪnɪmɪs nɒn 'kjʊəræt 'leks] *Latin phrase* 'la ley no trata asuntos triviales'

demise [dɪ'maɪz] *noun* **(a)** *(death)* defunción *f or* fallecimiento *m or* muerte *f or* óbito *m*; **on his demise the estate passed to his daughter** = a su muerte, la fortuna pasó a su hija **(b)** *(on a lease)* cesión *f or* transmisión *f*; **demise charter** = fletamento *m* de un barco sin tripulación

democracy [dɪ'mɒkrəsi] *noun* **(a)** *(system)* democracia *f*; **after the coup, democracy was replaced by a military dictatorship** = tras el golpe de estado, la democracia se sustituyó por una dictadura militar **(b)** *(country)* democracia; **the pact was welcomed by western democracies** = las democracias occidentales recibieron muy bien el acuerdo
◊ **democrat** ['deməkræt] *noun* demócrata *mf*
◊ **democratic** [demə'krætɪk] *adjective* **(a)** *(referring to a democracy)* democrático, -ca; **after the coup the democratic processes of government were replaced by government by decree** = después del golpe, los procesos democráticos del Estado fueron sustituidos por un gobierno por decreto **(b)** *(reflecting the views of the majority)* democrático, -ca; **the resolution was passed by a democratic vote of the council** = la moción fue aprobada por un voto democrático del ayuntamiento; **the action of the leader is against the wishes of the party as expressed in a democratic vote at the party conference** = la acción del líder va en contra de los deseos del partido según la votación democrática que tuvo lugar en el congreso general

demonstrate ['demənstreɪt] *verb* **(a)** *(to show)* demostrar *or* probar; **the police demonstrated how** the bomb was planted = la policía demostró cómo fue colocada la bomba; **counsel was able to demonstrate how it was impossible for the accused to climb through the window** = el abogado pudo probar que al acusado le habría sido imposible subir por la ventana **(b)** *(to protest)* manifestarse *or* hacer una manifestación; **crowds of students were demonstrating against the government** = multitud de estudiantes se manifestaban en contra del gobierno
◊ **demonstration** [demən'streɪʃn] *noun* manifestación *f*; **police broke up the student demonstration** = la policía disolvió la manifestación estudiantil
◊ **demonstrative legacy** [dɪ'mɒnstrətɪv 'legəsi] *noun* legado *m* preferente con cargo a fondo particular
◊ **demonstrator** ['demənstreɪtə] *noun* manifestante *mf*

demur [dɪ'mɜː] **1** *noun* objeción *f or* protesta *f*; **counsel made no demur to the proposal** = el abogado no hizo ninguna objeción a la propuesta **2** *verb* **(a)** *(not to agree)* hacer objeciones *or* tener algo que objetar; **counsel stated that there was no case to answer, but the judge demurred** = el abogado expuso que no había motivos para continuar el juicio, pero el juez hizo objeciones **(b)** *(formal objection)* objetar *or* protestar (NOTE: **demurring - demurred)**
◊ **demurrage** [dɪ'mʌrɪdʒ] *noun* gastos *mpl* de demora
◊ **demurrer** [dɪ'mɜːrə] *noun* demora *f or* excepción *f* perentoria

den [den] *noun* cueva *f or* antro *m*

denomination [dɪnɒmɪ'neɪʃn] *noun* valor *m* nominal *or* denominación *f*; **small denomination banknotes** = billetes *mpl* de pequeño valor; **coins of all denominations** = monedas de todos los valores

de novo ['deɪ 'nəʊvəʊ] *Latin phrase* '(comenzar) de nuevo'

deny [dɪ'naɪ] *verb* **(a)** *(not to allow someone to do something)* denegar; **he was denied the right to see his lawyer** = se le denegó el derecho a ver a su abogado **(b)** *(to state that you have not done something)* negar algo *or* contradecir *or* desmentir; **to deny the facts** = negar los hechos; **he denied being in the house at the time of the murder** = negó haber estado en la casa a la hora del asesinato (NOTE: you deny someone something or deny doing or having done something)
◊ **denial** [dɪ'naɪəl] *noun* **(a)** *(not allowing)* denegación *f*; **denial of human rights** = denegación de derechos humanos; **denial of justice** = denegación de justicia **(b)** *(stating that you have not done something)* negación *f or* negativa *f*; **in spite of his denials he was found guilty** = a pesar de sus negativas le declararon culpable

depart [dɪ'pɑːt] *verb* **(a)** *(to leave)* marcharse *or* salir; **the plane departs at 11.15** = el avión sale a las 11.15 **(b)** *(to act differently)* **to depart from normal practice** = salirse de la norma

department [dɪ'pɑːtmənt] *noun* **(a)** *(office)* departamento *m or* sección *f*; **complaints department** = sección de reclamaciones; **legal department** = departamento jurídico; **accounts department** = departamento de contabilidad; **head of department** *or* **department head** *or* **department manager** = jefe, -fa del departamento **(b)** *(section of a large store)* sección; **furniture department** = sección de muebles **(c)** *(government department)* **Department of State** = Departamento *m* de Estado; **the Department of Trade and Industry** = el Ministerio de Industria y Comercio; **the Department of Education and Science** = el Ministerio de Educación y Ciencia
◊ **departmental** [diːpɑːt'mentl] *adjective* departamental; **if you want to complain, you should first talk to your departmental head** = si quieres quejarte, deberías hablar primero con el jefe del departamento

departure [dɪ'pɑːtʃə] *noun* **(a)** *(leaving)* salida *f*; **the plane's departure was delayed by two hours** = la salida del avión se retrasó dos horas **(b)** *(new venture)* novedad *f or* nueva orientación comercial; **selling records will be a departure for the local bookshop** = la venta de discos será una novedad para la librería local **(c)** *(different from before)* cambio *m*; **departure from** = desviación *f*; **this forms a departure from established practice** = esto constituye una desviación de la práctica establecida; **any departure from the terms and conditions of the contract must be advised in writing** = cualquier desviación de los términos y condiciones del contrato debe notificarse por escrito

depend [dɪ'pend] *verb* **(a)** **to depend on** = depender de; **the company depends on efficient service from its suppliers** = la compañía depende del buen servicio de sus proveedores; **we depend on government grants to pay the salary bill** = dependemos de las ayudas del Estado para pagar los salarios **(b)** *(to happen because of something)* depender; **the success of the anti-drug campaign will depend on the attitude of the public** = el éxito de la campaña anti-droga dependerá de la actitud del público; **depending on** = dependiendo de; **depending on the circumstances, the accused may receive a fine or be sent to prison** = según las circunstancias, el acusado puede recibir una multa o ser enviado a prisión
◊ **dependant** [dɪ'pendənt] *noun* persona *f* a cargo *or* derechohabiente *mf or* familiar *mf* dependiente; **he has to provide for his family and dependants out of a very small salary** = tiene que mantener a su familia y dependientes con un sueldo muy reducido

◊ **dependency** [dɪ'pendənsi] *noun* dependencia *f*
◊ **dependent** [dɪ'pendənt] *adjective* familiar dependiente; **tax relief is allowed for dependent relatives** = se autoriza la desgravación de impuestos por tener familiares a cargo

deponent [dɪ'pəunənt] *noun* declarante *mf or* deponente *mf*

deport [dɪ'pɔːt] *verb* deportar *or* expulsar; **the illegal immigrants were deported** = los inmigrantes ilegales fueron deportados
◊ **deportation** [diːpɔː'teɪʃn] *noun* expulsión *f or* deportación *f*; **the convicts were sentenced to deportation** = se condenó a los reos a ser deportados; **deportation order** = orden *f* de expulsión *or* de deportación; **the minister signed the deportation order** = el ministro firmó la orden de deportación

depose [dɪ'pəuz] *verb* **(a)** *(to state under oath)* declarar bajo juramento **(b)** *(to remove from the throne)* destronar
◊ **deposition** [depə'zɪʃn] *noun* declaración escrita *or* deposición *f*

deposit [dɪ'pɒzɪt] **1** *noun* **(a)** *(money placed in a bank)* depósito *m or* ingreso *m or* imposición *f*; **certificate of deposit** = certificado *m* de depósito; **deposit account** = cuenta *f* de depósito *or* cuenta a plazo; **licensed deposit-taker** = depositario, -ria financiero, -ra *or* entidad *f* financiera **(b)** *(bank safe)* **safe deposit** = depósito en caja fuerte *or* caja de custodia; **safe deposit box** = caja de seguridad **(c)** *(money paid in advance)* señal *f or* depósito; *(on property)* entrada *f*; **to leave £10 as deposit** = dejar una señal de 10 libras; **to forfeit a deposit** = perder una señal **(d)** *(in elections)* depósito desembolsado por los candidatos en las elecciones; **he polled only 25 votes and lost his deposit** = sólo obtuvo 25 votos y perdió su depósito **2** *verb* **(a)** *(for safe keeping)* depositar; **we have deposited the deeds of the house with the bank** = hemos depositado las escrituras de la casa en el banco; **he deposited his will with his solicitor** = confió el testamento a su abogado **(b)** *(bank account)* depositar *or* ingresar; **to deposit £100 in a current account** = depositar 100 libras en una cuenta corriente
◊ **depositary** [dɪ'pɒzɪtri] *noun US* depositario, -ria
◊ **depositor** [dɪ'pɒzɪtə] *noun* impositor, -ra *or* depositante *mf*
◊ **depository** [dɪ'pɒzɪtri] *noun* **(a)** *(place to leave something)* almacén *m*; **furniture depository** = guardamuebles *m* **(b)** *(person to leave something with)* depositario, -ria

deprave [dɪ'preɪv] *verb* depravar *or* corromper *or* pervertir; **TV programmes which may deprave the minds of children who watch them** = programas de televisión que pueden corromper las mentes infantiles

depreciation [dɪpriːʃiˈeɪʃn] *noun* amortización *f* or depreciación *f*

deprive [dɪˈpraɪv] *verb* privar; **to deprive someone of something** = privar a alguien de algo; **the prisoners were deprived of contact with their families** = se privó a los prisioneros del contacto con sus familias; **the new Bill deprives aliens of the right to appeal** = el nuevo proyecto de ley priva a los extranjeros del derecho de apelación

dept [dɪˈpaːtmənt] = DEPARTMENT

deputy [ˈdepjuti] *noun* **(a)** *(of a higher official)* delegado, -da *or* suplente *mf or* ayudante *mf;* **to act as deputy for someone** *or* **to act as someone's deputy** = hacer las funciones de otro, -tra *or* actuar como sustituto, -ta de alguien; **deputy chairman** = vicepresidente; **deputy attorney** = teniente *mf* fiscal **(b)** *US* ayudante del sheriff **(c)** *(in Canada)* **Deputy Minister** = alto funcionario (de un ministerio) **(d)** *(in some countries)* diputado, -da; **Chamber of Deputies** = congreso *m* de los diputados

◊ **deputize** [ˈdepjutaɪz] *verb* **to deputize for someone** = sustituir a alguien

derangement [dɪˈreɪnʒmənt] *noun* locura *f;* **mental derangement** = alienación *f*

deregulation [diːregjuˈleɪʃn] *noun* reducción *f* del control gubernamental sobre una industria; **the deregulation of the airlines** = la reducción del control de las líneas aéreas por parte del gobierno

derelict [ˈderɪlɪkt] **1** *adjective* abandonado, -da *or* marginado, -da **2** *noun (nautical)* buque derelicto ◊ **dereliction of duty** [derɪˈlɪkʃn əv ˈdjuːti] *noun* negligencia *f;* **he was found guilty of gross dereliction of duty** = le declararon culpable de gran negligencia

derive [dɪˈraɪv] *verb* **(a)** *(to come from)* proceder; **this law derives from** *or* **is derived from the former Roman law of property** = esta ley procede del antiguo derecho romano de propiedad **(b)** *(to obtain)* sacar *or* obtener; **he derived financial benefit from the transaction** = sacó beneficios económicos de la transacción ◊ **derivative action** [dɪˈrɪvətɪv ˈækʃn] *noun* demanada derivada (interpuesta por accionistas minoritarios de una empresa)

derogate [ˈderəgeɪt] *verb* **to derogate from something which has been agreed** = atentar contra *or* ir en contra de un acuerdo ◊ **derogation** [derəˈgeɪʃn] *noun* derogación *f* de una ley *or* menosprecio *m or* desestimación *f;* **derogation of responsibility** = eludiendo toda responsabilidad

descend [dɪˈsend] *verb* descender ◊ **descended from** [dɪˈsendɪd ˈfrɒm] *adjective* descendiente de; **he is descended from William I** = desciende de Guillermo I

◊ **descendant** [dɪˈsendənt] *noun* descendiente *mf;* **his wife is a descendant of King Charles I** = su mujer es una descendiente del rey Carlos I

descent [dɪˈsent] *noun* **(a)** *(family ties)* descendencia *f or* linaje *m;* **he is British by descent** *or* **he is of British descent** = es de ascendencia británica; **lineal descent** = descendencia en línea directa **(b)** *(inheritance)* **by descent** = por herencia *or* transmisión hereditaria

describe [dɪˈskraɪb] *verb* describir; **she described her attacker to the police** = describió a su atacante a la policía; **he described the judge as a silly old man** = describió al juez como un viejo ridículo ◊ **description** [dɪˈskrɪpʃn] *noun* descripción *f;* **the police circulated a description of the missing boy** *or* **of the wanted man** = la policía puso en circulación una descripción del niño desaparecido *or* del hombre buscado; **false description of contents** = descripción engañosa del contenido; **trade description** = descripción comercial; *GB* **Trade Descriptions Act** = Ley de Normativa para el Comercio (referente a la descripción del producto)

desecrate [ˈdesɪkreɪt] *verb* profanar ◊ **desecration** [desɪˈkreɪʃn] *noun* profanación *f*

desert [dɪˈzɜːt] *verb* **(a)** *(army)* desertar; **he deserted and went to live in South America** = desertó y se fue a vivir a Sudamérica **(b)** *(family)* abandonar; **the two children have been deserted by their father** = los dos niños han sido abandonados por su padre ◊ **deserter** [dɪˈzɜːtə] *noun* desertor, -ra *or* prófugo, -ga *or* tránsfuga *mf* ◊ **desertion** [dɪˈzɜːʃn] *noun* **(a)** *(army)* deserción *f* **(b)** *(spouse)* abandono *m* conyugal *or* de hogar; **he divorced his wife because of her desertion** = se divorció de su mujer porque ésta abandonó el hogar

desk [desk] *noun* escritorio *m*

designate 1 [ˈdezɪgnət] *adjective* designado, -da *or* nombrado, -da; **the chairman designate** = el Presidente designado (NOTE: always follows a noun) **2** [ˈdezɪgneɪt] *verb* designar *or* nombrar; **the area was designated a National Park** = la zona fue declarada Parque Nacional

despatch [dɪˈspætʃ] = DISPATCH

destitute [ˈdestɪtjuːt] *adjective* desamparado, -da *or* indigente

destruction [dɪˈstrʌkʃn] *noun* destrucción *f;* **the destruction of the evidence in the fire at the police station made it difficult to prosecute** = la destrucción de las pruebas al incendiarse en la comisaría hicieron difícil la acusación; **child destruction** = aborto *m or* interrupción *f* del embarazo

detail ['diːteɪl] **1** *noun* detalle *m or* pormenor *m;* **in detail** = con todo detalle *or* detalladamente; **the contract lists all the markets in detail** = el contrato enumera todos los mercados detalladamente **2** *verb* **(a)** *(describe)* enumerar detalladamente *or* detallar; **the document details the arrangements for maintenance payments** = el documento detalla los acuerdos sobre los pagos de manutención; **the terms of the licence are detailed in the contract** = los términos de la licencia se detallan en el contrato **(b)** *(to tell someone to do something)* destacar; **six officers were detailed to search the premises** = seis inspectores fueron destacados para registrar las instalaciones
◊ **detailed** ['diːteɪld] *adjective* detallado, -da; **detailed account** = cuenta *or* factura detallada

detain [dɪ'teɪn] *verb* detener; **the suspects were detained by the police for questioning** = los sospechosos fueron detenidos por la policía para ser interrogados *or* la policía detuvo a los sospechosos para interrogarles
◊ **detainee** [diːteɪ'niː] *noun* detenido, -da
◊ **detainer** [dɪ'teɪnə] *noun* detención *f*

detect [dɪ'tekt] *verb* detectar *or* descubrir; **the machine can detect explosives** = la máquina puede detectar explosivos
◊ **detection** [dɪ'tekʃn] *noun* descubrimiento *m or* detección *f;* **detection rate** = índice *m* de crímenes resueltos
◊ **detective** [dɪ'tektɪv] *noun* detective *mf;* **private detective** = detective privado; **detective agency** = agencia *f* de detectives

COMMENT: the ranks of detectives in the British Police Force are Detective Constable, Detective Sergeant, Detective Inspector, Detective Chief Inspector, Detective Superintendent, and Detective Chief Superintendent

detector [dɪ'tektə] *noun* **lie detector** = detector de mentiras

détente [deɪtɒnt] *noun* distensión *f*

detention [dɪ'tenʃn] *noun* **(a)** *(people)* detención *f or* arresto *m;* **the suspects were placed in detention** = los sospechosos fueron detenidos *or* detuvieron a los sospechosos; **detention centre** = centro *m* de rehabilitación *or* correccional *m;* **detention order** = orden *f* de detención **(b)** *(goods)* retención *f* ilegal de enseres ajenos

deter [dɪ'təː] *verb* disuadir; **it is hoped that long jail sentences will deter others from smuggling drugs** = se espera que las largas condenas disuadirán a otros del contrabando de droga (NOTE: **deterring - deterred.** Note also that you deter someone **from** doing something)
◊ **deterrence** [dɪ'terəns] *noun* disuasión *f*

◊ **deterrent** [dɪ'terənt] **1** *adjective* disuasivo, -va *or* disuasorio, ria; **deterrent sentence** = sentencia *f* disuasoria *or* ejemplar **2** *noun* freno *m or* fuerza *f* de disuasión; **a long prison sentence will act as a deterrent to other possible criminals** = una condena larga *or* pena larga de prisión actuará como freno para otros posibles criminales

determine [dɪ'təːmɪn] *verb* **(a)** *(to fix or to arrange or to decide)* determinar *or* fijar *or* decidir; **to determine prices** *or* **quantities** = fijar precios *or* cantidades; **the conditions of the contract are still to be determined** = las condiciones del contrato están todavía por determinar **(b)** *(to bring to an end)* resolver; **the tenancy was determined by a notice to quit** = el alquiler quedó rescindido por una notificación de desalojo

detinue ['detɪnjuː] *noun* retención *f* ilegal de bienes muebles; **action in detinue** = acción *f* para recobrar la posesión de bienes muebles

detriment ['detrɪmənt] *noun* detrimento *m or* perjuicio *m;* **to the detriment of** = en menoscabo de; **without detriment to his claim** = sin causar detrimento *or* perjuicio a su reclamación; **his action was to the detriment of the plaintiff** = su acción causó perjuicio al demandante
◊ **detrimental** [detrɪ'mentəl] *adjective* perjudicial; **action detrimental to the maintenance of public order** = acción *f* perjudicial para el mantenimiento del orden público

devaluation [diːvælju'eɪʃn] *noun* depreciación *f*

develop [dɪ'veləp] *verb* **(a)** *(plan and produce)* desarrollar *or* producir; **to develop a new product** = desarrollar un producto nuevo **(b)** *(plan and build)* urbanizar *or* desarrollar; **to develop an industrial estate** = desarrollar una zona industrial
◊ **developer** [dɪ'veləpə] *noun* **property developer** =; promotor de viviendas *or* promotor inmobiliario =
◊ **development** [dɪ'veləpmənt] *noun* **(a)** *(production)* desarrollo *m or* expansión *f or* avance *m;* **industrial development** = expansión industrial; **development area** *or* **development zone** = área *f* de desarrollo **(b)** *(change)* cambio *m or* giro *m;* **the case represents a new development in the law of libel** = el caso representa un nuevo giro en la Ley de Libelo

deviate ['diːvieɪt] *verb* **to deviate from a course of action** = desviarse

device [dɪ'vaɪs] *noun* **(a)** *(mechanism or tool)* aparato *m or* dispositivo *m;* **safety device** = dispositivo de seguridad **(b)** *(strategem)* ardid *m or* estratagema *f;* **a device to avoid paying tax** *or* **a tax-saving device** = una estratagema para evadir impuestos

devil ['devəl] **1** *noun* abogado,-da que lleva casos de otro abogado *or* pasante *mf* **2** *verb* actuar *or* llevar casos de otro abogado *or* servir como pasante; **to devil for someone** = llevar casos de otro abogado

devise [dɪˈvaɪz] **1** *noun* disposiciones *fpl* testamentarias *or* legado *m* **2** *verb* legar

> COMMENT: giving of other types of property is a **bequest**

devisee [diːvaɪˈziː] *noun* legatario, -ria *or* heredero, -ra

devolve [dɪˈvɒlv] *verb* traspasar competencias; **power is devolved to regional assemblies** = se han traspasado competencias a las asambleas regionales ◊ **devolution** [devəˈluːʃn] *noun* devolución *f or* traspaso *m* de competencias

> COMMENT: devolution involves passing more power than decentralization. In a devolved state, the regional authorities are almost autonomous

dial [ˈdaɪl] *verb (telephone)* marcar

diary [ˈdaɪəri] *noun* agenda *f or* diario *m*

dictate [dɪkˈteɪt] **1** *noun* dictamen *m or* documento *m or* mandato *m* **2** *verb* dictar

dictator [dɪkˈteɪtə] *noun* dictador, -ra; **the country has been ruled by a military dictator for six years** = el país ha sido gobernado por un dictador militar durante seis años; **the MPs accused the party leader of behaving like a dictator** = los diputados acusaron de dictador al líder del partido ◊ **dictatorial** [dɪktəˈtɔːrɪəl] *adjective* **(a)** *(referring to a dictator)* dictatorial; **a dictatorial form of government** = un gobierno dictatorial **(b)** *(behaving like a dictator)* dictatorio, -ria; **officials dislike the Minister's dictatorial way of working** = a los oficiales les desagradan los métodos dictatorios del ministro ◊ **dictatorship** [dɪkˈteɪtəʃɪp] *noun* **(a)** *(rule)* dictadura *f;* **under the dictatorship of Mussolini, personal freedom was restricted** = bajo la dictadura de Mussolini se limitó la libertad personal; **the dictatorship of the proletariat** = la dictadura del proletariado **(b)** *(country ruled by a dictator)* dictadura *f;* **a military dictatorship** = una dictadura militar

dictum [ˈdɪktəm] *noun* dictamen *m;* **obiter dicta** = opiniones accesorias *or* dictámenes accidentales; *see also* RATIO DECIDENDI (NOTE: plural is **dicta**)

die [daɪ] *verb* morir; **to die instantly** = morir en el acto

differ [ˈdɪfə] *verb* **(a)** *(not to agree)* disentir *or* discrepar *or* no estar de acuerdo; **one of the appeal judges differed from the others** = uno de los magistrados no estaba de acuerdo con el resto; **I beg to differ** = siento disentir *or* no estar de acuerdo **(b)** *(to be different)* diferir *or* ser distinto

◊ **difference** [ˈdɪfrəns] *noun* diferencia *f*
◊ **different** [ˈdɪfrənt] *adjective* diferente

digest [ˈdaɪdʒest] *noun* digesto *m or* resumen *m or* compendio *m;* **law digest** = recopilación *f* de leyes

dignity [ˈdɪgnəti] *noun* dignidad *f*

dilatory [ˈdɪlətri] *adjective* dilatorio, -ria; **dilatory motion** = moción dilatoria; **dilatory plea** = excepción dilatoria

dilemma [dɪˈlemə] *noun* dilema *m or* disyuntiva *f*

diminish [dɪˈmɪnɪʃ] *verb* disminuir; **diminished responsibility** *or* US **diminished capacity** = circunstancia *f* eximente por tener las facultades disminuidas *or* responsabilidad reducida

DInsp = DETECTIVE INSPECTOR

dip [dɪp] *noun (slang)* carterista *mf*

diplomat *or* **diplomatist** [ˈdɪpləmæt *or* dɪˈpləʊmətɪst] *noun* diplomático, -ca ◊ **diplomacy** [dɪˈpləʊməsi] *noun* **(a)** *(of government)* diplomacia *f;* **the art of diplomacy is to anticipate the next move by the other party** = el arte de la diplomacia consiste en anticipar la reacción de la otra parte; **gunboat diplomacy** = diplomacia de cañón; **quiet diplomacy** = diplomacia en privado; **secret diplomacy** = diplomacia en secreto; **he is a master of diplomacy** = es un experto en diplomacia **(b)** *(tact)* diplomacia *f* ◊ **diplomatic** [dɪpləˈmætɪk] *adjective* **(a)** *(referring to diplomats)* diplomático, -ca; **the diplomatic bag** = valija diplomática; **he was accused of shipping arms into the country in the diplomatic bag** = le acusaron de enviar armas al país en la valija diplomática; **diplomatic channels** = vía diplomática; **the message was delivered by diplomatic channels** = entregaron el mensaje por la vía diplomática; **they are working to restore diplomatic channels between the two countries** = están tratando de restablecer la vía diplomática entre los dos países; **diplomatic corps** = cuerpo diplomático; **his car had a diplomatic number plate** = su coche llevaba una matrícula del cuerpo diplomático; **she was using a diplomatic passport** = usaba un pasaporte del cuerpo diplomático; **diplomatic immunity** = inmunidad *f* diplomática; **he claimed diplomatic immunity to avoid being arrested** = invocó la inmunidad diplomática para evitar ser detenido; **to grant someone diplomatic status** = conceder categoría diplomática a alguien **(b)** *(tactful)* diplomático, -ca

direct [daɪˈrekt] **1** *verb* **(a)** *(to control)* dirigir **(b)** *(to order)* ordenar *or* mandar; **the judge directed the jury to acquit all the defendants** = el juez ordenó al jurado que absolviera a todos los acusados; **the Crown Court directed the justices to rehear the case** = el Tribunal de la Corona ordenó a los jueces la revisión del caso **2** *adjective* directo, -ta; **direct debit** = domiciliación bancaria; **direct evidence** = prueba *f* directa; **direct examination** = interrogatorio *m* directo; **direct mail** = venta *f* por correo; **direct selling** = venta directa; **direct taxation** = impuestos *mpl* directos *or* imposición *f* directa **3** *adverb* directamente; **we pay income tax direct to the government** = pagamos el impuesto sobre la renta directamente al gobierno; **the fine is paid direct to the court** = la multa se paga directamente al tribunal

◊ **direction** [dɪˈrekʃn] *noun* **(a)** *(path)* dirección *f or* rumbo *m;* **the new evidence changed the direction of the hearing** = la nueva prueba cambió el rumbo de la vista **(b)** *(managing)* dirección *f;* **he took over the direction of a large bank** = se hizo cargo de la dirección de un importante banco **(c)** *(instructions)* **directions** = instrucciones *fpl or* órdenes *fpl;* **the court is not able to give directions to the local authority** = el tribunal no está capacitado para dar órdenes a la autoridad local

◊ **directive** [daɪˈrektɪv] *noun* directriz *m or* directiva *f or* orden *f or* instrucción *f;* **the Commission issued a directive on food prices** = la Comisión publicó una directiva sobre los precios de los alimentos

◊ **directly** [dɪˈrektli] *adverb* **(a)** *(immediately)* inmediatamente; **the summons was served directly after the magistrate had signed the warrant** = la citación judicial fue entregada inmediatamente después que el juez firmara la orden judicial **(b)** *(straight)* de un modo directo *or* directamente; **the Metropolitan Police Commissioner is directly responsible to the Home Secretary** = el Comisario *or* Jefe de la Policía Metropolitana es directamente responsable ante el Ministro del Interior

◊ **director** [dɪˈrektə] *noun* **(a)** *(company)* director, -ra; **managing director** = director gerente; **chairman and managing director** = presidente y director gerente *or* consejero delegado; **board of directors** = consejo *m* de administración *or* junta *f* directiva; **directors' report** = informe *m or* memoria *f* anual del consejo de administración; **executive director** = director ejecutivo; **non-executive director** = director no ejecutivo *or* director de asesoramiento; **outside director** = director exterior *or* externo que trabaja fuera de la empresa **(b)** *(person in charge)* director, -ra; **he is the director of a government institute** = es director de un instituto de gestión estatal *or* oficial; **she was appointed director of the charity** = la nombraron directora de la sociedad benéfica *or* de los asuntos de beneficiencia; **Director-General of Fair Trading** = Director General del servicio oficial de protección al consumidor

◊ **directorate** [dəˈrektərət] *noun* directiva *f or* consejo *m* de administración *or* junta *f* directiva

◊ **Director of Public Prosecutions (DPP)** [dɪˈrektə əv ˈpʌblɪk prɒsɪˈkjuːʃnz] *noun* Director, -ra de la Acusación Pública; **the papers in the**

fraud case have been sent to the Director of Public Prosecutions = se ha enviado la documentación sobre el caso de fraude al Director de la Acusación Pública

◊ **directorship** [dɪˈrektəʃɪp] *noun* cargo *m* de director *or* dirección *f;* **he was offered a directorship with Smith Ltd** = le ofrecieron un cargo de director en Smith Ltd

directory [daɪˈrektri] *noun* directorio *m; (repertorio)* anuario *m;* **classified directory** = directorio comercial por secciones; **commercial directory** *or* **trade directory** = directorio comercial *or* páginas amarillas; **street directory** = guía urbana *or* callejero *m;* **telephone directory** = guía telefónica

dirty [ˈdəːti] *adjective* sucio, -cia

disability [dɪsəˈbɪlɪti] *noun* **(a)** *(unable to use one's body properly)* incapacidad *f* física *or* inhabilitación *f or* impedimento *m;* **partial disability** = incapacidad parcial; **temporary disability** = incapacidad laboral transitoria *or* temporal; **total disability** = inhabilitación total *or* incapacidad absoluta; **permanent total disability** = incapacidad absoluta permanente **(b)** *(lack of legal capacity)* incapacidad jurídica; **person under a disability** = persona incapacitada jurídicamente

◊ **disabled** [dɪsˈeɪbld] *adjective* incapacitado, -da; **mentally disabled** = incapacitado mental; **disabled person** = persona disminuida físicamente *or* disminuido *m* físico *or* disminuida *f* física

◊ **disabling statute** [dɪsˈeɪblɪŋ ˈstætjuːt] *noun* ley *f* que restringe el ejercicio de un derecho

disadvantage [dɪsədˈvɑːntɪdʒ] *noun* desventaja *f or* inconveniente *m;* **it is a disadvantage for a tax lawyer not to have studied to be an accountant** = para un abogado especializado en impuestos es un inconveniente no haber estudiado contabilidad; **to be at a disadvantage** = estar en desventaja *or* en situación desventajosa; **not having studied law puts him at a disadvantage** = el hecho de no haber estudiado derecho le sitúa en desventaja

◊ **disadvantageous** [dɪsædvənˈteɪdʒəs] *adjective* desventajoso, -sa

disagree [dɪsəˈgriː] *verb* discrepar *or* no estar de acuerdo; **the jury disagreed and were not able to return a verdict** = no hubo acuerdo entre los miembros del jurado y no pudieron dar un veredicto

◊ **disagreement** [dɪsəˈgriːmənt] *noun* desacuerdo *m or* disconformidad *f or* desavenencia *f;* **there was disagreement among the MPs about how the police should deal with terrorist attacks** = hubo desacuerdo entre los diputados sobre el modo en que la policía debía enfrentarse a los ataques terroristas

disallow [dɪsəˈlaʊ] *verb* rechazar *or* denegar; **the judge disallowed the defence evidence** = el juez rechazó la prueba de la defensa; **he claimed £2000 for fire damage, but the claim was disallowed** =

pidió 2.000 libras por daños de incendio pero la petición fue denegada

disappear [dɪsə'pɪə] *verb* desaparecer

disapprove [dɪsə'pruːv] *verb* desaprobar; **the Appeal Court disapproved the County Court decision** = el Tribunal de Apelación desaprobó la decisión del Juzgado del Condado; **to disapprove of something** = estar en contra de *or* desaprobar; **the judge openly disapproved of juries** = el juez se manifestó públicamente en contra de los jurados
◊ **disapproval** [dɪsə'pruːvl] *noun* desaprobación *f*

disbar [dɪs'bɑː] *verb (barristers)* expulsar del Colegio de Abogados *or* prohibir a un abogado que ejerza la profesión (NOTE: **disbarring - disbarred**)

disburse [dɪs'bɜːs] *verb* desembolsar
◊ **disbursement** [dɪs'bɜːsmənt] *noun* desembolso *m*

discharge 1 ['dɪstʃɑːdʒ] *noun* **(a)** *(ending a contract)* cese *m or* despido *m* (por vencimiento o por incumplimiento de contrato) *or* extinción *f* de un contrato *or* liberación *f* parcial de un contrato; **discharge by agreement** = finalización *f* de contrato por mutuo acuerdo *or* finiquito *m* por consenso; **discharge by performance** = cese por cumplimiento *or* finalización de un contrato; **discharge in *or* of bankruptcy** = rehabilitación *f* de quiebra **(b)** *(payment of debt)* pago *m or* reembolso *m*; **in full discharge of a debt** = en pago total de una deuda *or* totalmente libre de deudas; **final discharge** = pago *or* desembolso final *or* último pago **(c)** *(release)* exoneración *f*; *(from prison)* liberación *f* de un prisionero; *(from army)* exención *f* del servicio militar; **absolute discharge** = absolución *f* (incondicionada) *or* libre absolución; **conditional discharge** = libertad *f* condicional **(d)** **in discharge of his duties as director** = en el ejercicio de sus funciones como director **(e)** *US* **Discharge Calendar**; *see comment at* CALENDAR **2** [dɪs'tʃɑːdʒ] *verb* **(a)** *(to set someone free)* liberar *or* absolver *or* poner en libertad; **the prisoners were discharged by the judge** = los acusados fueron absueltos por el juez; **the judge discharged the jury** = el juez dispensó *or* despidió al jurado **(b)** *(to release from bankruptcy)* **to discharge a bankrupt** = rehabilitar al quebrado **(c)** *(to pay a debt)* **to discharge a debt** *or* **to discharge one's liabilities** = saldar una deuda *or* las deudas que uno tiene **(d)** *(to dismiss or to sack)* despedir; **to discharge an employee** = despedir a un empleado

discipline ['dɪsɪplɪn] **1** *noun* disciplina *f* **2** *verb* castigar *or* disciplinar; **the clerk was disciplined for leaking the report to the newspapers** = se castigó al empleado por pasar el informe a la prensa
◊ **disciplinary** [dɪsɪ'plɪnəri] *adjective* disciplinario, -ria; **disciplinary action** = expediente disciplinario; **disciplinary measure** = corrección disciplinaria; **disciplinary procedure** = procedimiento *m* disciplinario; **to take disciplinary action against someone** = emprender una acción disciplinaria contra alguien

disclaim [dɪs'kleɪm] *verb* negarse a admitir *or* renunciar; **he disclaimed all knowledge of the bomb** = dijo que no sabía nada sobre la bomba *or* se negó a admitir cualquier conocimiento sobre la bomba; **the management disclaims all responsibility for customers' property** = la dirección no admite responsabilidad por objetos personales de los clientes *or* la dirección elude toda responsabilidad sobre los objetos de valor de su clientela
◊ **disclaimer** [dɪs'kleɪmə] *noun* **(a)** *(legal refusal)* renuncia *f or* abandono *m or* negativa *f* a aceptar una responsabilidad *or* un derecho **(b)** *(clause in a contract)* cláusula *f* contractual de renuncia de responsabilidad

disclose [dɪs'kləuz] *verb* revelar; **the bank has no right to disclose details of my account to the tax office** = el banco no tiene derecho a revelar detalles de mi cuenta a la oficina de recaudación de impuestos
◊ **disclosure** [dɪs'kləuʒə] *noun* divulgación *f or* revelación *f*; **the disclosure of the takeover bid raised the price of the shares** = la divulgación de la oferta de adquisición elevó el precio de las acciones; **the defendant's case was made stronger by the disclosure that the plaintiff was an undischarged bankrupt** = la defensa del acusado se hizo más sólida al descubrirse que el demandante era un quebrado no rehabilitado; *see also* NON-DISCLOSURE

disconnect [dɪskə'nekt] *verb* desconectar

discord ['dɪskɔːd] *noun* discordia *f or* discordancia *f*

discount ['dɪskaunt] *noun* descuento *m;* **we give a 30% discount for large orders** = hacemos un 30% de descuento en pedidos grandes; **he buys stock at a discount and sells at full price to the public** = compra las existencias a precio de descuento y las vende al público a precio de mercado

discover [dɪs'kʌvə] *verb* descubrir *or* enterarse *or* averiguar; **the auditors discovered some errors in the accounts** = los auditores descubrieron algunos errores en las cuentas
◊ **discovery** [dɪs'kʌvri] *noun* descubrimiento *m* de las pruebas *or* exhibición *f* de documentos entre las partes antes del comienzo de la vista (de un proceso civil)

discredit [dɪs'kredɪt] *verb* desacreditar; **the prosecution counsel tried to discredit the defence witnesses** = la acusación intentó desacreditar a los testigos de la defensa

discrepancy [dɪs'krepənsi] *noun* diferencia *f or* discrepancia *f;* **there is a discrepancy between the crime figures released by the Home Office and those of the Metropolitan Police Force** = hay discrepancia entre el número de delitos publicado por el Ministerio del Interior y el del Cuerpo de Policía Metropolitana

discretion [dɪs'kreʃn] *noun* arbitrio *m or* albedrío *m or* discreción *f;* **magistrates have a discretion to allow an accused person to change his election from a summary trial to a jury trial** = los magistrados tienen arbitrio para permitir que un acusado cambie su elección de un juicio sumario a un juicio ante jurado; **the judge refused the application, on the ground that he had a judicial discretion to examine inadmissible evidence** = el juez rechazó la petición sobre la base de que tenía facultad discrecional para examinar pruebas improcedentes; **to exercise one's discretion** = obrar como mejor le parezca a uno; **the court exercised its discretion** = el tribunal ejerció su arbitrio; **I leave it to your discretion** = lo dejo a su parecer *or* a su discreción *or* a su juicio; **at the discretion of someone** = al arbitrio de alguien *or* depender de alguien; **membership is at the discretion of the committee** = la afiliación es a discreción del comité; **sentencing is at the discretion of the judge** = condenar es asunto del juez; **the granting of an injunction is at the discretion of the court** = la concesión de un requerimiento corre a cargo del tribunal
◊ **discretionary** [dɪs'kreʃənri] *adjective* discrecional; **the minister's discretionary powers** = los poderes discrecionales del ministro; **the tribunal has wide discretionary power** = el tribunal tiene amplio poder discrecional; **discretionary trust** = fideicomiso *m* discrecional *or* sociedad *f* general de inversiones

discriminate [dɪs'krɪmɪneɪt] *verb* discriminar *or* diferenciar; **the planning committee finds it difficult to discriminate between applications which improve the community, and those which are purely commercial** = a la comisión de planificación le resulta difícil diferenciar entre las peticiones para mejorar la comunidad y las que son puramente comerciales; **to discriminate against someone** = discriminar; **the council was accused of discriminating against women in its recruitment policy** = acusaron al ayuntamiento de discriminar a las mujeres en su política de reclutamiento; **he claimed he had been discriminated against because of his colour** = declaró que le habían discriminado por el color de su piel
◊ **discrimination** [dɪskrɪmɪ'neɪʃn] *noun* **(a)** *(noting differences)* discernimiento *m* **(b)** *(unfair treatment)* discriminación *f;* **sexual discrimination** *or* **sex discrimination** *or* **discrimination on grounds of sex** = discriminación sexual; **age**

discrimination = discriminación por razones de edad

discuss [dɪs'kʌs] *verb* discutir *or* hablar de *or* tratar; **they spent two hours discussing the details of the contract** = se pasaron dos horas discutiendo los detalles del contrato; **the lawyers discussed the possibility of an acquittal** = los abogados discutieron la posibilidad de una absolución
◊ **discussion** [dɪs'kʌʃn] *noun* discusión *f or* debate *m;* **after some discussion the magistrates agreed to an adjournment** = después de cierta discusión los magistrados acordaron un aplazamiento

disenfranchise *or* **disfranchise** [dɪsɪn'fræntʃaɪz] *verb* privar de los derechos civiles o del derecho de votación *or* inhabilitar; **the company has tried to disenfranchise the ordinary shareholders** = la compañía ha tratado de privar a los accionistas ordinarios del derecho de votación

disentitle [dɪsɪn'taɪtl] *verb* privar de un título o derecho

disguise [dɪs'gaɪz] **1** *noun* disfraz *m;* **the spy crossed the border in disguise** = el espía cruzó la frontera disfrazado **2** *verb* disimular *or* disfrazarse; **to disguise yourself as someone** = disfrazarse de alguien; **he entered the country disguised as a policeman** = entró en el país disfrazado de policía

dishonest [dɪs'ɒnɪst] *adjective* deshonesto, -ta *or* fraudulento, -ta *or* ímprobo, -ba; **the public has been warned to look out for dishonest shopkeepers** = se ha advertido al público que tenga cuidado con los comerciantes poco honrados; **he assisted the trustees to commit a dishonest breach of trust** = ayudó a los fideicomisarios a cometer un abuso de confianza deshonesto
◊ **dishonestly** [dɪs'ɒnɪstli] *adverb* de un modo engañoso *or* fraudulento; **he was accused of dishonestly acquiring the jewels** = se le acusó de adquirir las joyas fraudulentamente

dishonour [dɪs'ɒnə] **1** *noun* impago *m;* **the dishonour of the cheque brought her business to a stop** = el impago del cheque paralizó sus negocios; **notice of dishonour** = carta *f* de requerimiento de pago **2** *verb* deshonrar *or* negarse a pagar *or* rechazar por falta de fondos; **to dishonour a bill** = devolver una letra; **the bank dishonoured his cheque** = el banco se negó a pagar su cheque

disinherit [dɪsɪn'herɪt] *verb* desheredar; **he was disinherited by his father** = fue desheredado por su padre

disinterment [dɪsɪn'tɜːmənt] *noun* exhumación *f*

disk [dɪsk] *noun* disco *m;* **floppy disk** = disco flexible *or* diskette *m or* 'floppy' *m;* **hard disk** =

disco duro; **disk drive** = unidad *f* de disco *or* disquetera *f*

◊ **diskette** [dɪ'sket] *noun* diskette *m or* disquete *m*

disloyal [dɪs'lɔɪəl] *adjective* desleal
◊ **disloyalty** [dɪs'lɔɪəlti] *noun* deslealtad *f*

dismantle [dɪs'mæntl] *verb* desarticular; **to dismantle a criminal organisation** = desarticular una banda de criminales

dismember [dɪs'membə] *verb* descuartizar *or* desmembrar

dismiss [dɪs'mɪs] *verb* **(a)** *(to sack)* despedir; **to dismiss an employee** = despedir a un empleado; **he was dismissed for being late** = le despidieron por llegar tarde **(b)** *(to refuse to accept)* desestimar *or* descartar *or* rechazar; **case dismissed** = no ha lugar; **the court dismissed the appeal** *or* **the application** *or* **the action** = el tribunal desestimó el recurso *or* la petición *or* la demanda; **the justices dismissed the witness' evidence out of hand** = los magistrados descartaron la declaración del testigo inmediatamente
◊ **dismissal** [dɪs'mɪsl] *noun* **(a)** *(cancelling)* cese *m* **(b)** despido *m or* remoción *f;* **dismissal procedure** = procedimiento *m* de despido; **constructive dismissal** = despido analógico *or* dimisión *f* bajo presión de la dirección; **unfair dismissal** = despido injusto; **wrongful dismissal** = despido improcedente *or* injusto

> COMMENT: an employee can complain of unfair dismissal to an industrial tribunal, or of wrongful dismissal to the County Court

disobey [dɪsə'beɪ] *verb* desobedecer; **the husband disobeyed the court order to pay maintenance to his children** = el marido desobedeció el apremio de pagar la manutención a sus hijos
◊ **disobedience** [dɪsə'bi:dɪəns] *noun* desobediencia *f;* **the prisoners were put in solitary confinement as punishment for their disobedience of the governor's orders** = se dejó a los presos incomunicados como castigo por no haber obedecido las órdenes del director de la prisión; **civil disobedience** = resistencia *f* pasiva; **the group planned a campaign of civil disobedience as a protest against restrictions on immigrants** = el grupo planeó una campaña de resistencia pasiva en protesta contra las restricciones a los *or* de inmigrantes

disorder [dɪs'ɔːdə] *noun* desorden *m or* trastorno *m;* **civil disorder** *or* **public disorder** *or* **public disorders** = disturbios *mpl;* **mental disorder** = trastorno mental
◊ **disorderly** [dɪs'ɔːdəli] *adjective* escandaloso, -sa *or* alborotador, -ra; **he was charged with disorderly conduct** *or* **with being drunk and disorderly** = le acusaron de conducta escandalosa

or de borracho y alborotador; **keeping a disorderly house** = llevar una casa de lenocinio *or* prostitución

dispatch [dɪ'spætʃ] **1** *noun* despacho *m* **2** *verb* despachar *or* enviar; **the letters about the rates were dispatched yesterday** = las cartas de las contribuciones se enviaron ayer; **the Defence Minister was dispatched to take charge of the operation** = enviaron al ministro de Defensa para que dirigiera la operación
◊ **dispatch box** [dɪ'spætʃ 'bɒks] *noun* **(a)** *(for government papers)* valija *f or* cartera *f* ministerial **(b)** *(in the House of Commons)* tribuna *f;* **to be at the dispatch box** = dirigirse al parlamento

dispense [dɪs'pens] *verb* **(a)** *(to give out justice)* administrar justicia **(b)** *(to do without)* **to dispense with something** = prescindir de algo; **the chairman of the tribunal dispensed with the formality of taking minutes** = el presidente del tribunal prescindió de la formalidad de levantar actas; **the accused decided to dispense with the services of a lawyer** = el acusado decidió prescindir de los servicios de un abogado
◊ **dispensation** [dɪspən'seɪʃn] *noun* **(a)** *(giving out justice)* administración *f* de justicia **(b)** *(special permission)* dispensa *f or* exención *f*

display [dɪ'spleɪ] *verb* exhibir *or* exponer; **on display** = expuesto, -ta; **all cars must display a valid parking permit** = todos los vehículos deben exhibir un permiso de aparcamiento vigente

dispose [dɪ'spəʊz] *verb* **to dispose of** = deshacerse de *or* vender; **to dispose of excess stock** = deshacerse de *or* vender las existencias sobrantes; **to dispose of one's business** = vender el negocio propio
◊ **disposable** [dɪ'spəʊzəbl] *adjective* **(a)** *(that can be thrown away)* desechable *or* de usar y tirar **(b)** **disposable income** = renta *f* disponible
◊ **disposal** [dɪ'spəʊzl] *noun* **(a)** *(sale)* venta *f or* traspaso *m;* **disposal of securities** *or* **of property** = venta de valores *or* traspaso de propiedad; **lease** *or* **business for disposal** = arrendamiento *m or* negocio *m* en venta **(b)** *(available)* **to have at one's disposal** = disponer de
◊ **disposition** [dɪspə'zɪʃn] *noun* disposición *f or* traspaso *m;* **to make testamentary dispositions** = hacer disposiciones testamentarias *or* hacer testamento

dispossess [dɪspə'zes] *verb* desposeer *or* desahuciar *or* despojar
◊ **dispossession** [dɪspə'zeʃn] *noun* desahucio *m*

dispute [dɪ'spjuːt] **1** *noun* disputa *f or* litigio *m or* contienda *f or* querella *f;* **industrial disputes** *or* **labour disputes** = conflictos *mpl* laborales *or* colectivos; **international dispute** = litigio internacional; **pay dispute** = conflicto salarial; **in dispute** = en litigio; **to adjudicate** *or* **to mediate in a dispute** = servir de intermediario en un conflicto;

trade dispute = *(over trade matters)* conflicto comercial internacional; *(between management and workers)* conflicto laboral **2** *verb* poner en duda *or* discutir *or* cuestionar; **the defendant disputed the claim** = el acusado puso en duda la declaración; **she disputed the policeman's version of events** = puso en duda la versión de los hechos que dio el policía

disqualify [dɪsˈkwɒlɪfaɪ] *verb* incapacitar *or* inhabilitar; **being a judge disqualifies you from being a Member of Parliament** = ser juez es incompatible con ser diputado; **after the accident he was fined £1000 and disqualified from driving for two years** = después del accidente le impusieron una multa de 1.000 libras y le retiraron el carnet de conducir durante dos años; **he was convicted for driving a motor vehicle while disqualified** = le condenaron por conducir un vehículo en periodo de inhabilitación
◊ **disqualification** [dɪskwɒlɪfɪˈkeɪʃn] *noun* **(a)** *(from driving)* inhabilitación *f* para conducir *or* retirada *f* del permiso de conducir **(b)** **disqualification from office** = inhabilitación para el cargo

disrepute [dɪsrɪˈpjuːt] *noun* mala reputación; **to bring something into disrepute** = desprestigiar *or* desacreditar; **he was accused of bringing the club into disrepute by his bad behaviour** = le acusaron de desprestigiar el club con su mal comportamiento

disrespect [dɪsrɪsˈpekt] *noun* falta *f* de respeto; **he was accused of showing disrespect to the judge** = le acusaron de faltar al respeto al juez

disseisin [dɪsˈsiːzɪn] *noun* desposesión *f or* desposeimiento *m* ilegal

dissemination [dɪsemɪˈneɪʃn] *noun* difusión *f or* propagación *f*

dissent [dɪˈsent] **1** *noun* disensión *f or* disentimiento *m or* desacuerdo *m;* **the opposition showed its dissent by voting against the Bill** = la oposición mostró su disidencia votando en contra del proyecto de ley **2** *verb* disentir; **one of the appeal judges dissented** = uno de los jueces de la apelación disintió
◊ **dissenting** [dɪˈsentɪŋ] *adjective* disconforme *or* disidente; **dissenting judgment** = juicio *m or* sentencia *f* disidente

dissident [ˈdɪsɪdənt] **1** *adjective* disidente **2** *noun* disidente *mf*

dissolve [dɪˈzɒlv] *verb* disolver; **to dissolve a marriage** *or* **a partnership** *or* **a company** = disolver un matrimonio *or* una sociedad *or* una compañía; **to dissolve Parliament** = disolver el Parlamento
◊ **dissolution** [dɪsəˈluːʃn] *noun* disolución *f* de un matrimonio *or* una sociedad; **dissolution of Parliament** = disolución del Parlamento

distinction [dɪˈstɪŋkʃn] *noun* distinción *f;* **the judge made no distinction between the parties** = el juez no hizo distinción entre las dos partes; **I see no distinction between the two claims** = no veo diferencia entre las dos declaraciones
◊ **distinguish** [dɪˈstɪŋgwɪʃ] *verb* distinguir; **to distinguish a case** = distinguir un caso de su precedente (NOTE: you distinguish one thing **from** another, or you distinguish **between** two things)

distrain [dɪˈstreɪn] *verb* embargar
◊ **distress** [dɪˈstres] *noun* embargo *m;* **distress sale** = venta *f* de bienes embargados

distribute [dɪˈstrɪbjuːt] *verb* distribuir *or* repartir; **the money in the estate is to be distributed among the members of the deceased's family** = el dinero de la herencia se debe repartir entre los familiares del difunto
◊ **distribution** [dɪstrɪˈbjuːʃn] *noun* distribución *f or* reparto *m;* **distribution of assets** = reparto de bienes

district [ˈdɪstrɪkt] *noun* barrio *m or* región *f or* distrito *m*
◊ **district attorney (DA)** [ˈdɪstrɪkt əˈtɜːni] *noun* US fiscal *mf* de un distrito judicial *or* fiscal del estado
◊ **district court** [ˈdɪstrɪkt ˈkɔːt] *noun* US tribunal *mf* federal de primera instancia

disturb [dɪˈstɜːb] *verb* **to disturb the peace** = perturbar *or* alterar la paz
◊ **disturbance** [dɪˈstɜːbəns] *noun* alboroto *m or* disturbio *m or* alteración *f;* **street disturbances forced the government to resign** = los disturbios callejeros forzaron al gobierno a dimitir; **he was accused of making a disturbance in the public library** = le acusaron de armar alboroto en la biblioteca pública

divide [dɪˈvaɪd] *verb* **(a)** *(to split)* dividir *or* repartir; **England and Wales are divided into six court circuits** = Inglaterra y el País de Gales están divididos en seis distritos judiciales; **the two companies agreed to divide the market between them** = las dos compañías acordaron repartirse el mercado entre ellas **(b)** *(in the House of Commons)* votar; **the House divided at 10.30** = la Cámara votó a las 10.30

dividend [ˈdɪvɪdend] *noun* dividendo *m or* cupón *m;* **final dividend** = dividendo final; **interim dividend** = dividendo provisional *or* a cuenta

division [dɪˈvɪʒn] *noun* **(a)** *(section of something large)* cada una de las secciones pertenecientes al Tribunal Superior **(b)** *(part of a large group of companies)* sucursal *f;* **Smith's is now a division of the Brown group of companies** = Smith's es ahora una sucursal del grupo de compañías Brown **(c)** *(to disagree)* división *f;* **to have a division of opinion** = discrepar *or* haber división de opiniones **(d)** *(voting in the House of Commons)* votación *f;* **in the**

division on the Law and Order Bill, the government had a comfortable majority = en la votación sobre el proyecto de Ley del Orden Público el gobierno obtuvo una amplia mayoría

◊ **divisional** [dɪ'vɪʒnəl] *adjective* divisionario, -ria *or* divisional; **divisional court** = juzgado *m* de una sección del Tribunal Superior; **divisional judge** = juez, -za de una sección del Tribunal Superior

divorce [dɪ'vɔːs] **1** *noun* divorcio *m;* **divorce petition** = petición *f or* demanda *f* de divorcio; **uncontested divorce** *or* **divorce by consent** = divorcio con el consentimiento de las partes *or* de mutuo acuerdo; **she was granted a divorce on the grounds of unreasonable behaviour by her husband** = le concedieron el divorcio a causa del comportamiento irracional de su marido **2** *verb* divorciarse; **he divorced his wife and married his secretary** = se divorció de su mujer y se casó con su secretaria

◊ **Divorce Registry** [dɪ'vɔːs 'redʒɪstri] *noun* juzgado londinense especializado en divorcios

COMMENT: under English law, the only basis of divorce is the irretrievable breakdown of marriage. This is proved by one of five grounds: (a) adultery; (b) unreasonable behaviour; (c) one of the parties has deserted the other for a period of two years; (d) the parties have lived apart for two years and agree to a divorce; (e) the parties have lived apart for five years. In the context of divorce proceedings the court has wide powers to make orders regarding custody and care and control of children, and ancillary relief. Divorce proceedings are normally dealt with by the County Court, or in London at the Divorce Registry. Where divorce proceedings are defended, they are transferred to the High Court, but this is rare and most divorce cases are now conducted by what is called the 'special procedure'

divulge [daɪ'vʌldʒ] *verb* divulgar *or* revelar; **he refused to divulge any information about his bank account** = se negó a revelar información alguna sobre su cuenta bancaria; **she divulged that she had been with the accused on the evening of the murder** = reveló que había estado con el acusado la noche del asesinato

dock [dɒk] **1** *noun* **(a)** *(court)* banquillo *m* de los acusados; **the prisoner in the dock** = el acusado en el banquillo; **dock brief** = antiguo sistema según el cual un acusado podía escoger por una cantidad simbólica un abogado de entre los presentes en la sala, para que le representara **(b)** *(wharf)* muelle *m;* **the docks** = puerto *m;* **dock dues** = derechos *mpl* de dársena **2** *verb* **(a)** *(of ship)* atracar; **the ship docked at 17.00** = el barco atracó a las 17.00 **(b)** *(to remove money)* deducir *or* descontar del sueldo; **we will have to dock his pay if he is late for work again** = tendremos que descontarle algo del sueldo si vuelve a llegar tarde al trabajo; **he had £20**

docked from his pay for being late = le descontaron 20 libras de su sueldo por llegar tarde

docket ['dɒkɪt] *noun* **(a)** *(of a package)* lista *f* del contenido de un paquete **(b)** *(of a trial)* lista de causas *or* de pleitos; *US* registro de sumarios de causas

doctrine ['dɒktrɪn] *noun* doctrina *f US* **the Monroe Doctrine** = la doctrina Monroe *or* principio según el cual los EE UU tienen interés en prevenir interferencias exteriores en los asuntos internos de otros estados norteamericanos

document ['dɒkjumənt] *noun* documento *m;* **deeds, contracts and wills are all legal documents** = las escrituras, los contratos y los testamentos son todos ellos documentos legales; **list of documents** = lista de documentos relevantes para una acción procesal

◊ **documentary** [dɒkju'mentri] *adjective* documental; **documentary evidence** *or* **documentary proof** = prueba *f* documental

◊ **documentation** [dɒkjumen'teɪʃn] *noun* documentación *f;* **please send me the complete documentation concerning the sale** = le ruego me envíe toda la documentación referente a la venta

Dod's Parliamentary Companion ['dɒdz pɑːlə'mentri kəm'pænjən] *noun GB* libro de referencia que registra información sobre el parlamento británico

Doe [dəʊ] **John Doe** = nombre que se usa como ejemplo en casos ficticios

doli capax *or* **doli incapax** ['dəʊli 'kæpæks *or* 'ɪnkæpæks] *Latin phrases* 'capaz de intención criminal' *or* 'incapaz de intención criminal'

COMMENT: children under ten years of age are doli incapax and cannot be prosecuted for criminal offences; children aged between 10 and 14 are presumed to be doli incapax but the presumption can be reversed if there is evidence of malice or knowledge

domain [də'meɪn] *noun* dominio *m or* ámbito *m or* esfera *f;* **public domain** = dominio público; **work which is in the public domain** = obra *f* de dominio público

Domesday Book ['duːmzdeɪ 'bʊk] *noun* catastro *m* realizado por el rey Guillermo I en 1086 en el que se registraban todas las tierras feudales del reino con sus propietarios y habitantes

domestic [də'mestɪk] *adjective* **(a)** *(family)* doméstico, -ca; **domestic premises** = instalaciones *fpl* destinadas a viviendas; **domestic proceedings** = proceso *m* judicial doméstico *or* familiar **(b)** *(national)* nacional *or* interior; **domestic consumption** = consumo *m* interior; **domestic market** = mercado *m* interior *or* nacional; **domestic production** = producción *f* nacional

domicile ['dɒmɪsaɪl] **1** *noun* domicilio *m* permanente; **domicile of origin** = domicilio natural *or* de origen; **domicile of choice** = domicilio real *or* verdadero **2** *verb* **he is domiciled in Denmark** = está domiciliado en Dinamarca; **bills domiciled in France** = letras de cambio domiciliadas en Francia

dominant ['dɒmɪnənt] *adjective* dominante
◊ **dominant tenement** ['dɒmɪnənt 'tenəmənt] *noun* propiedad *f or* heredad *f* dominante (NOTE: also called 'dominant estate' in the USA)

> COMMENT: the grantor of the easement is the servient tenement

dominion [də'mɪnjən] *noun* **(a)** *(power of control)* dominio *m;* **to exercise dominion over a country** = mantener un país bajo dominio **(b)** *(an independent state, part of the British Commonwealth)* **a Dominion** = un dominio

donate [də'neɪt] *verb* donar
◊ **donatio mortis causa** [dənɑ:tiəʊ 'mɔ:tɪs 'kaʊzə] *Latin phrase* 'donación por muerte'
◊ **donation** [də'neɪʃn] *noun* donativo *m or* dádiva *f*
◊ **donee** [dəʊ'ni:] *noun* donatario, -ria
◊ **donor** ['dəʊnə] *noun* donante *mf*

dormant ['dɔ:mənt] *adjective* inactivo, -va; **dormant account** = cuenta *f* sin movimiento; **dormant partner** = SLEEPING PARTNER

double [dʌbl] **1** *adjective* **(a)** *(twice as large)* doble; **double taxation** = doble imposición; **double taxation agreement** *or* **treaty** = tratado *m* de doble imposición **(b)** *(which happens twice)* doble; **in double figures** = de dos cifras; **inflation is in double figures** = la inflación es de dos cifras; **we have had double-figure inflation for some years** = hemos tenido una inflación de dos cifras durante algunos años; **double jeopardy** = excepción *f* al principio según el cual ninguna persona puede ser juzgada dos veces por el mismo delito **2** *verb* duplicarse *or* doblarse

doubt [daʊt] *noun* duda *f;* **beyond reasonable doubt** *or* **US beyond a reasonable doubt** = fuera de toda duda (prueba necesaria para condenar a una persona en un caso criminal)
◊ **doubtful** ['daʊtfʊl] *adjective* dudoso, -sa

dove [dʌv] *noun (diplomatic person)* paloma *f*
◊ **doveish** ['dʌvɪʃ] *adjective* como una paloma; **he was accused of having doveish tendencies** = le acusaron de comportarse como las palomas

down [daʊn] *adverb & preposition* hacia abajo *or* abajo; **the crime rate is gradually coming down** = el índice de criminalidad está descendiendo poco a poco; **the price of petrol has gone down** = el precio del petróleo ha bajado; **to pay money down** = pagar una entrada
◊ **downgrade** ['daʊngreɪd] *verb* degradar; **his job was downgraded in the company**

reorganization = con la reorganización de la compañía redujeron la importancia de su cargo

Downing Street ['daʊnɪŋ 'stri:t] *noun GB* calle *f* de Londres en la cual residen el/la Primer Ministro y el/la Ministro de Hacienda *or* el gobierno británico; **10 Downing Street** = residencia *f* oficial del o de la Primer Ministro y sede del ejecutivo; **No. 11 Downing Street** = residencia oficial del o de la Ministro de Hacienda (NOTE: the words 'Downing Street' are often used to mean 'the Prime Minister' or even 'the British government': **a Downing Street spokesman revealed that the plan had still to be approved by the Treasury; Downing Street sources indicate that the Prime Minister has given the go-ahead for the change; Downing Street is angry at suggestions that the treaty will not be ratified**)

dowry ['daʊri] *noun* dote *f or* bienes dotales

doyen of the diplomatic corps ['dɔɪən əv ðə dɪplə'mætɪk 'kɔ:] *noun* el embajador que lleva más tiempo en un país

DPP ['di: 'pi: 'pi:] = DIRECTOR OF PUBLIC PROSECUTIONS

draft [drɑ:ft] **1** *noun* **(a)** *(payment)* giro *m* bancario; **to make a draft on a bank** = realizar un giro bancario; **bank draft** *or* **banker's draft** = giro bancario; **sight draft** = efecto *m or* letra *f* de cambio a la vista **(b)** *(rough plan)* borrador *m or* proyecto *m;* **draft of a contract** *or* **draft contract** = borrador de un contrato; **he drew up the draft agreement on the back of an envelope** = redactó el proyecto del acuerdo en el reverso de un sobre; **the first draft of the contract was corrected by the managing director** = el primer borrador del contrato lo corrigió el director gerente; **the draft Bill is with the House of Commons lawyers** = el anteproyecto de ley está en manos de los abogados de la Cámara de los Comunes; **rough draft** = bosquejo *m or* borrador *m* **2** *verb* hacer un proyecto *or* bosquejar *or* pergeñar; **to draft a contract** *or* **a document** *or* **a bill** = redactar un contrato *or* un documento *or* un escrito; **the contract is still being drafted** *or* **is still in the drafting stage** = todavía se está redactando el contrato
◊ **drafter** ['drɑ:ftə] *noun* redactor, -ra
◊ **drafting** ['drɑ:ftɪŋ] *noun* redacción *f or* elaboración *f or* preparación *f;* **the drafting of the contract took six weeks** = la redacción del contrato duró seis semanas; **the drafting stage of a parliamentary Bill** = el periodo de redacción de un proyecto de ley parlamentaria
◊ **draftsman** ['drɑ:ftsmən] *noun* redactor *m* de documentos; **costs draftsman** = redactor del estado de gastos para el sistema fiscal tributario; **parliamentary draftsman** = redactor de proyectos de ley

drain [dreɪn] *noun* **brain drain** = fuga *f* de cerebros

draw [drɔ:] *verb* **(a)** *(money)* sacar; **to draw money out of an account** = sacar dinero de una cuenta; **to draw a salary** = cobrar un sueldo **(b)** *(cheque)* girar *or* extender un cheque; **to draw a cheque on a bank** = extender un cheque bancario; **he paid the invoice with a cheque drawn on an Egyptian bank** = pagó la factura con un cheque librado contra un banco egipcio **(c) to draw a conclusion** = sacar una conclusión
◊ **drawee** [drɔ:'i:] *noun* librado, -da
◊ **drawer** ['drɔ:ə] *noun* librador, -ra; **the bank returned the cheque to drawer** = el banco devolvió el cheque al librador; *see also* RD
◊ **drawings** ['drɔ:ɪŋz] *plural noun* sueldo *m* que gana el socio de una sociedad
◊ **draw up** ['drɔ: 'ʌp] *verb* preparar *or* redactar; **to draw up a contract** *or* **an agreement** = redactar un contrato *or* un acuerdo; **to draw up a company's articles of association** = redactar los estatutos de una compañía

drive [draɪv] *verb* **(a)** *(vehicle)* conducir; **he was driving to work when he heard the news on the car radio** = iba conduciendo al trabajo cuando oyó la noticia en la radio; **she drives a company car** = conduce un coche de la empresa; **careless driving** *or* **driving without due care and attention** = conducción imprudente y temeraria *or* conducir peligrosamente *or* conducir sin el cuidado y la atención debidos; **drunken driving** *or* **US driving while intoxicated (DWI)** = conducir con imprudencia en estado de embriaguez *or* borracho *or* bajo los efectos del alcohol; **reckless driving** = conducir con imprudencia **(b) he drives a hard bargain** = es difícil cerrar un trato con él *or* es un duro negociador (NOTE: **driving - drove - driven**)

drop [drɒp] **1** *noun* **(a)** *(fall)* caída *f or* baja *f or* disminución *f;* **drop in sales** = disminución de ventas; **sales show a drop of 10%** = las ventas han bajado en un 10%; **a drop in prices** = una caída de los precios **(b) drop shipment** = envío *m or* embarque *m* directo **2** *verb* **(a)** *(to fall)* bajar *or* descender; **sales have dropped by 10%** *or* **have dropped 10%** = las ventas han disminuido un 10%; **the pound dropped three points against the dollar** = la libra ha descendido tres puntos frente al dólar **(b)** *(to stop a case)* detener un proceso *or* retirar los cargos; **the prosecution dropped all charges against the accused** = la acusación retiró todos los cargos contra el acusado; **the plaintiff decided to drop the case against his neighbour** = el demandante decidió detener el proceso contra su vecino (NOTE: **dropping - dropped**)
◊ **drop ship** ['drɒp 'ʃɪp] *verb* enviar un pedido directamente al cliente

drug [drʌg] *noun* droga *f or* narcótico *m or* medicamento *m;* **dangerous drugs** = drogas peligrosas; **drug addiction** = toxicomanía *f or* drogadicción *f;* **the Drug Squad** = la brigada antidroga; **drug dealer** = narcotraficante *mf;* **drug**

trafficking = tráfico *m* de drogas *or* de estupefacientes *or* narcotráfico *m;* **drug use** = consumo *m* de drogas; **controlled drugs** *or* *US* **controlled substances** = estupefacientes *mpl or* drogas controladas por la ley

COMMENT: there are three classes of controlled drugs: **Class 'A' drugs:** (cocaine, heroin, crack, LSD, etc.); **Class 'B' drugs:** (amphetamines, cannabis, codeine, etc.); and **Class 'C' drugs:** (drugs which are related to the amphetamines, such as benzphetamine). The drugs are covered by five schedules under the Misuse of Drugs Regulations: **Schedule 1:** drugs which are not used medicinally, such as cannabis and LSD, for which possession and supply are prohibited; **Schedule 2:** drugs which can be used medicinally, such as heroin, morphine, cocaine, and amphetamines: these are fully controlled as regards prescriptions by doctors, safe custody in pharmacies, registering of sales, etc. **Schedule 3:** barbiturates, which are controlled as regards prescriptions, but need not be kept in safe custody; **Schedule 4:** benzodiazepines, which are controlled as regards registers of purchasers; **Schedule 5:** other substances for which invoices showing purchase must be kept

drunk [drʌŋk] *adjective* borracho, -cha *or* ebrio, -a; **drunk and disorderly** = borracho y alborotador; **drunk driving** = conducción *f* en estado de embriaguez
◊ **drunkard** ['drʌŋkəd] *noun* borracho, -cha; *see also* HABITUAL

DSgt = DETECTIVE SERGEANT

dual [djuːəl] *adjective* doble *or* dual; **person of dual nationality** *or* **person who has dual nationality** = persona *f* con doble nacionalidad

dubious ['djuːbiəs] *adjective* dudoso, -sa

duchess ['dʌtʃɪs] *noun* duquesa *f*
◊ **duchy** ['dʌtʃi] *noun* ducado *m*

dud [dʌd] *adjective & noun (informal)* falso, -sa; **the £50 note was a dud** = el billete de 50 libras era falso; **dud cheque** = cheque *m* sin fondos

due [djuː] *adjective* **(a)** *(owed)* pagadero, -ra *or* vencido, -da *or* a pagar; **due and payable** = vencido y pagadero; **to fall due** *or* **to become due** = vencer (un plazo); **bill due on May 1st** = letra *f* con vencimiento el 1 de mayo; **balance due to us** = saldo *m* a nuestro favor; **due date** = fecha *f* de vencimiento **(b)** *(expected)* se espera que llegue *or* tener prevista la llegada; **the plane is due to arrive at 10.30** *or* **is due at 10.30** = el avión tiene prevista su llegada a las 10.30 **(c)** *(proper)* debido, -da; **due course** = como es debido; **due notice** = debida notificación; **in due form** = escrito en buena y debida forma *or* como es debido; **receipt in due form** = recibo *m or* factura *f* conforme; **contract**

drawn up in due form = contrato redactado en la forma debida; **driving without due care and attention** = conducir sin el cuidado y la atención debidos; **after due consideration of the problem** = después de considerar la cuestión debidamente; **the due process of the law** = el debido procedimiento legal **(d) due to** = debido a; **supplies have been delayed due to a strike at the warehouse** = los suministros se han retrasado debido a una huelga en el almacén; **the company continues to pay the wages of staff who are absent due to illness** = la empresa sigue pagando el sueldo de los empleados que están de baja por enfermedad

◊ **dues** [djuːz] *plural noun* **(a)** *(payment)* tributos *mpl or* derechos *mpl;* **dock dues** *or* **port dues** *or* **harbour dues** = derechos de dársena; **membership dues** = cuotas *fpl* de asociaciones **(b)** *(orders)* pedidos *mpl* por servir

duke [djuːk] *noun* duque *m; see also* DUCHY

duly [ˈdjuːli] *adverb* **(a)** *(properly)* debidamente; **duly authorized representative** = representante debidamente autorizado **(b)** *(as was expected)* a su debido tiempo; **we duly received his letter of 21st October** = acuso recibo de su carta de 21 de octubre *or* recibimos su carta del 21 de octubre a su debido tiempo

dummy [ˈdʌmi] **1** *adjective* ficticio, -cia; **dummy corporation** = empresa fantasma **2** *noun (House of Commons)* proyecto *m* de ley

dungeon [ˈdʌnʒən] *noun* calabozo *m or* mazmorra *f*

duplicate 1 [ˈdjuːplɪkət] *noun* copia *f or* duplicado *m;* **he sent me the duplicate of the contract** = me envió una copia del contrato; **duplicate receipt** *or* **duplicate of a receipt** = recibo duplicado; **in duplicate** = por duplicado; **receipt in duplicate** = recibo por duplicado; **to print an invoice in duplicate** = imprimir una factura por duplicado **2** [ˈdjuːplɪkeɪt] *verb* **(a)** *(bookkeeping)* **to duplicate with another entry** = duplicar con otra partida **(b)** *(copy)* **to duplicate a letter** = copiar una carta *or* escribir una carta por duplicado

◊ **duplicating** [ˈdjuːplɪkeɪtɪŋ] *noun* duplicación *f;* **duplicating machine** = multicopista *f;* **duplicating paper** = cliché *m* para multicopista

◊ **duplication** [djuːplɪˈkeɪʃn] *noun* duplicación *f;* **duplication of work** = duplicar el trabajo

◊ **duplicator** [ˈdjuːplɪkeɪtə] *noun* multicopista *f*

duress [djuˈres] *noun* coacción *f;* **duress provides no defence to a charge of murder** = la coacción no supone atenuante en una acusación de asesinato; **under duress** = bajo coacción *or* coaccionado; **they alleged they had committed the crime under duress from another defendant** = alegaron que habían cometido el crimen coaccionados por otro de los acusados; **he signed**

the confession under duress = le coaccionaron para que firmara la confesión

duty [ˈdjuːti] *noun* **(a)** *(responsibility)* deber *m or* obligación *f or* función *f;* **it is the duty of every citizen to serve on a jury if called** = todo ciudadano tiene la obligación de actuar como jurado en caso de ser convocado; **the government has a duty to protect the citizens from criminals** = el gobierno tiene la obligación de proteger a los ciudadanos de los criminales; **duty of care** = deber de todo ciudadano de actuar de una manera responsable **(b)** *(work)* **to be on duty** = estar de servicio *m or* de guardia *f;* **night duty** = turno *m* de noche *or* servicio de guardia nocturna; **PC Smith is on night duty this week** = el policía Smith hace las guardias de noche de esta semana; **official duty** = función pública; **point duty** = dirección *f* del tráfico *or* control *m* de la circulación *or* punto *m* de control del tráfico; **duty sergeant** = sargento *mf* de servicio *or* de guardia **(c)** *(tax)* impuesto *m;* **to take the duty off alcohol** = suprimir los impuestos sobre el alcohol; **to put a duty on cigarettes** = gravar el tabaco; **ad valorem duty** = derecho *m* ad valorem; **customs duty** *or* **import duty** = derechos *mpl* de aduana *or* de importación; **excise duty** = impuesto sobre el consumo; **goods which are liable to duty** = productos *mpl* sujetos a impuesto; **duty-paid goods** = productos con impuestos aduaneros pagados; **stamp duty** = derecho *or* impuesto de timbre; **estate duty** *or* US **death duty** = impuesto sobre herencias y donaciones

◊ **duty bound** [ˈdjuːti ˈbaʊnd] *adjective* obligado, -da; **witnesses under oath are duty bound to tell the truth** = los testigos bajo juramento están obligados a decir la verdad

◊ **duty-free** [ˈdjuːtiˈfriː] *adjective & adverb* libre de impuestos; **he bought a duty-free watch at the airport** *or* **he bought the watch duty-free** = compró un reloj, libre de impuestos, en el aeropuerto; **duty-free shop** = tienda *f* libre de impuestos (en aeropuertos y barcos)

◊ **dutiable** [ˈdjuːtiəbl] *adjective;* **dutiable goods** *or* **dutiable items** = artículos sujetos a derechos de aduana

dwelling [ˈdwelɪŋ] *noun* alojamiento *m or* vivienda *f;* **the tax on dwellings has been raised** = el impuesto sobre la vivienda ha aumentado

DWI [ˈdiː ˈdʌblju ˈaɪ] US = DRIVING WHILE INTOXICATED

dynasty [ˈdɪnəsti] *noun* **(a)** *(family of rulers)* dinastía *f;* **the Ming dynasty ruled China from 1368 to 1644** = la dinastía Ming gobernó China entre 1368 y 1644 **(b)** *(period of rule)* dinastía

◊ **dynastic** [dɪˈnæstɪk] *adjective* dinástico, -ca; **the rules of dynastic succession** = las leyes de la sucesión dinástica

Ee

E [iː] *fifth letter of the alphabet;* **Schedule E** = divisiones *fpl* de la tarifa del impuesto sobre la renta referente a sueldos y pensiones; **E list** = lista *f* de prisioneros que intentan evadirse de la prisión con frecuencia; **Table E** = escritura *f* de constitución y estatutos tipo de una sociedad no limitada con capital compartido, establecido en la Ley de Sociedades

e. & o.e. [iː ənd 'əʊ 'iː] = ERRORS AND OMISSIONS EXCEPTED

early ['əːli] *adjective & adverb* **(a)** *(before the usual time)* temprano, -na; **early closing day** = día *m* en que las tiendas cierran por la tarde; **at your earliest convenience** = a la mayor brevedad; **at an early date** = en fecha próxima *or* muy pronto; **early day motion** = moción *f* exploratoria **(b)** *(at the beginning of a period of time)* pronto *or* temprano; **he took an early flight to Paris** = se fue a París en un vuelo de madrugada; **we hope for an early resumption of negotiations** = esperamos una pronta reanudación de las negociaciones

earmark ['ɪəmaːk] *verb* afectar *or* asignar *or* destinar *or* reservar; **to earmark funds for a project** = asignar *or* afectar fondos a un proyecto; **the grant is earmarked for computer systems development** = la subvención *or* la beca está destinada al desarrollo de sistemas informáticos

earn [əːn] *verb* **(a)** *(money)* ganar *or* percibir; **to earn £150 a week** = ganar 150 libras a la semana; **our agent in Paris certainly does not earn his commission** = la verdad es que nuestro agente de París no se gana su comisión **(b)** *(interest)* devengar intereses *or* dividendos; **what level of dividend do these shares earn?** = ¿qué clase de dividendos devengan estas acciones?; **account which earns interest at 10%** = cuenta *f* que devenga intereses al 10%
◊ **earnings** ['əːnɪŋz] *plural noun* **(a)** *(of individual)* salario *m or* sueldo *m or* ingresos *mpl;* **attachment of earnings** = retención *f* del salario *or* salarial *or* de la paga; *see also* GARNISHEE ORDER **(b)** *(of a business)* rendimiento *m or* beneficio *m;* **earnings per share** = rendimiento por acción

earnest ['əːnɪst] *noun* prenda *f or* señal *f;* **he deposited £1,000 with the solicitor as earnest of** his intention to purchase = entregó 1.000 libras al abogado como señal de su intención de compra

easement ['iːzmənt] *noun* servidumbre *f or* derecho *m* de paso; **affirmative easement** = servidumbre positiva; **negative easement** = negatoria *f; see also* DOMINANT, SERVIENT, TENEMENT

Easter ['iːstə] *noun* uno de los cuatro periodos de sesiones de los Tribunales de Justicia

easy ['iːzi] *adjective* fácil; **easy terms** = facilidades *fpl* de pago; **the loan is repayable in easy payments** = el préstamo se devuelve en cómodos plazos
◊ **easily** ['iːzɪli] *adverb* **(a)** *(without difficulty)* fácilmente *or* tranquilamente *or* sin problemas; **the motion was passed by the Commons easily** = la moción fue aprobada por los Comunes fácilmente **(b)** *(a lot or much)* con mucho *or* con gran diferencia; **he is easily the most important international criminal to have been arrested this year** = él es, con mucho, el criminal internacional más importante al que han detenido este año; **the firm is easily the biggest in the market** = la firma es, con gran diferencia, la mayor del mercado; **this is easily the largest consignment of drugs we have seized** = éste es, con mucho, el mayor alijo de drogas que hemos aprehendido

EC ['iː 'siː] = EUROPEAN COMMUNITY; **EC ministers met today in Brussels** = los ministros de la CE se reunieron hoy en Bruselas; **the USA is increasing its trade with the EC** = los EE UU están incrementando el comercio con la CE

ecclesiastical [ɪkliːziˈæstɪkl] *adjective* eclesiástico, -ca; **ecclesiastical court** = Tribunal Eclesiástico

economy [ɪˈkɒnəmi] *noun* **(a)** *(saving)* economía *f or* ahorro *m;* **an economy measure** = una medida para reducir gastos; **economies of scale** = economías de escala **(b)** *(financial state of a country)* economía *or* sistema económico; **black economy** = economía sumergida; **free market economy** = economía de libre mercado
◊ **economic** [iːkəˈnɒmɪk] *adjective* económico, -ca; **economic sanctions** = sanciones *fpl* económicas

edict ['i:dɪkt] *noun* edicto *m*

edition [ɪ'dɪʃn] *noun* edición *f*

editor ['edɪtə] *noun (newspaper)* redactor, -ra jefe *or* jefe, -fa de redacción de un periódico; *(book)* director, -ra de una obra de consulta; *(proofreader)* corrector, -ra de estilo; **the city editor** = director financiero de un periódico británico
◊ **editorial** [edɪ'tɔ:rɪəl] **1** *adjective* editorial *or* de la dirección; **editorial board** = equipo *m* editorial *or* consejo *m* de redacción *or* grupo *m* de redactores **2** *noun* editorial *f or* artículo *m* de fondo

effect [ɪ'fekt] **1** *noun* **(a)** *(result)* efecto *m;* **terms of a contract which take effect** *or* **come into effect from January 1st** = términos de un contrato que entran en vigor el 1 de enero; **prices are increased 10% with effect from January 1st** = a partir del 1 de enero los precios aumentarán un 10%; **to remain in effect** = continuar en vigencia *or* seguir vigente **(b)** *(meaning)* sentido *m or* fin *m or* intención *f or* propósito *m;* **clause to the effect that** = cláusula que significa que; **we have made provision to this effect** = hemos hecho las disposiciones reglamentarias para este fin **(c) personal effects** = efectos *mpl* personales **2** *verb* efectuar *or* realizar *or* llevar a cabo; **to effect a payment** = efectuar *or* realizar un pago; **to effect customs clearance** = pasar algo por la aduana; **to effect a settlement between two parties** = realizar un acuerdo entre dos partes
◊ **effective** [ɪ'fektɪv] *adjective* efectivo, -va *or* eficaz; **the police are trying to find an effective means of dealing with young offenders** = la policía está intentando encontrar un medio efectivo de resolver el problema de la delincuencia juvenil; **effective date** = fecha *f* de entrada en vigor; **clause effective as from January 1st** = cláusula efectiva desde el 1 de enero

efficient [ɪ'fɪʃnt] *adjective* eficiente *or* eficaz *or* de buen rendimiento; **an efficient secretary** = una secretaria eficiente; **the efficient policing of city centres** = el buen mantenimiento del orden en el centro de las ciudades
◊ **efficiently** [ɪ'fɪʃntli] *adverb* eficazmente *or* eficientemente; **the police coped efficiently with the crowds of protesters** = la policía hizo frente a la multitud de manifestantes de una manera eficiente

e.g. ['i: 'dʒi:] ej., *or* por ejemplo; **the contract is valid in some countries (e.g. France and Belgium) but not in others** = el contrato es válido en algunos países (ej. Francia y Bélgica) pero no en otros

EGM [ɪ'dʒekt] = EXTRAORDINARY GENERAL MEETING

eject [ɪ'dʒekt] *verb* expulsar *or* desahuciar
◊ **ejection** [ɪ'dʒekʃn] *noun* expulsión *f or* desahucio *m*

◊ **ejectment** [ɪ'dʒekmənt] *noun* **action of ejectment** = acción *f or* demanda *f or* proceso *m* de desahucio

COMMENT: ejection of someone who is legally occupying a property is an **ouster,** while removing a tenant is **eviction**

ejusdem generis *or* eiusdem generis

[i:'dʒusdem *or* eɪ'ju:sdem 'dʒenərɪs] *Latin phrase* 'del mismo género' (regla de interpretación legal según la cual, se sobreentiende que el significado de una palabra o frase corresponde al de las palabras o frases que la preceden)

COMMENT: in the phrase **houses, flats and other buildings** other buildings can mean only other dwellings, and would not include, for example, a church

elapse [ɪ'læps] *verb (of time)* transcurrir; **six weeks elapsed before the court order was put into effect** = transcurrieron seis semanas hasta que la orden judicial entró en vigor; **we must allow sufficient time to elapse before making a complaint** = debemos dejar transcurrir el tiempo suficiente antes de presentar una queja

elect [ɪ'lekt] *verb* **(a)** *(to choose someone by vote)* elegir; **to elect the officers of an association** = elegir a los directivos de una asociación; **she was elected president** = fue elegida presidenta **(b)** *(to choose to do something)* elegir; **he elected to stand trial by jury** = eligió ser juzgado por un jurado
◊ **-elect** [ɪ'lekt] *suffix* electo, -ta; **she is the president-elect** = es la presidenta electa (NOTE: the plural is **presidents-elect**)
◊ **election** [ɪ'lekʃn] *noun* **(a)** *(choosing by vote)* elección *f;* **general election** = elecciones generales; **his election as president of the society** = su elección como presidente de la compañía; **local elections** *or* **municipal elections** = elecciones locales *or* municipales; **election agent** = agente *mf* electoral; *see also* BY-ELECTION **(b)** *(act of choosing a course of action)* **the accused made his election for jury trial** = el acusado se decantó por un juicio con jurado **(c)** *(under a will)* opción *f* (que tiene el heredero a aceptar o repudiar los beneficios y los cargos de una herencia)
◊ **elector** [ɪ'lektə] *noun* elector, -ra; **register of electors** = censo *m or* registro *m* electoral
◊ **electoral** [ɪ'lektərəl] *adjective* electoral; **electoral roll** = REGISTER OF ELECTORS; **electoral college** = colegio *m* electoral

COMMENT: the President of the USA is elected by an electoral college made up of people elected by the states of the USA

◊ **electorate** [ɪ'lektərət] *noun* electorado *m*

electric chair [ɪ'lektrɪk 'tʃeə] *noun* silla *f* eléctrica

eleemosynary [eli:'mɒzɪnəri] *adjective* caritativo, -va

element ['elɪmənt] *noun* elemento *m* or parte *f;* **the elements of a settlement** = las partes de un acuerdo

eligible ['elɪdʒɪbl] *adjective* elegible *or* con derecho a; **she is eligible for re-election** = tiene derecho a presentarse a reelección
◊ **eligibility** [elɪdʒɪ'bɪlɪti] *noun* elegibilidad *f;* **the chairman questioned her eligibility to stand for re-election** = el presidente cuestionó su elegibilidad para presentarse a reelección

emancipation [ɪmænsɪ'peɪʃn] *noun* emancipación *f*

embargo [ɪm'bɑːgəʊ] **1** *noun* embargo *m* or prohibición *f* or bloqueo *m* (económico); **to lay** or **put an embargo on trade with a country** = imponer un embargo comercial a un país or prohibir el comercio con un país; **to lift an embargo** = levantar un embargo; **to be under an embargo** = estar prohibido (NOTE: plural is **embargoes**) **2** *verb* embargar *or* prohibir; **the government has not embargoed trade with the Eastern countries** = el gobierno no ha prohibido el comercio con los países del Este

embark [ɪm'bɑːk] *verb* **(a)** *(ship)* embarcar; **the passengers embarked at Southampton** = los pasajeros embarcaron en Southampton **(b)** *(to start)* **to embark on** = emprender *or* embarcarse en; **the company has embarked on a development programme** = la compañía ha emprendido un programa de expansión
◊ **embarkation** [embɑː'keɪʃn] *noun* embarco *m* or embarque *m;* **port of embarkation** = puerto de embarque; **embarkation card** = tarjeta *f* de embarque

embassy ['embəsi] *noun* embajada *f*

embezzle [ɪm'bezl] *verb* malversar *or* desfalcar *or* distraer fondos; **he was sent to prison for six months for embezzling his clients' money** = le mandaron a la cárcel durante seis meses por malversar el dinero de sus clientes
◊ **embezzlement** [ɪm'bezlmənt] *noun* malversación *f* de fondos *or* desfalco *m;* **he was sent to prison for six months for embezzlement** = le mandaron a la cárcel durante seis meses por desfalco
◊ **embezzler** [ɪm'bezlə] *noun* malversador, -ra *or* desfalcador, -ra

emblements ['embəlmənts] *plural noun* frutos *mpl* de la tierra

embracery [ɪm'breɪsri] *noun* cohecho *m* or soborno *m* or corrupción *f* a un miembro del jurado

emergency [ɪ'məːdʒənsi] *noun* emergencia *f* or urgencia *f;* **the government declared a state of** emergency = el gobierno declaró el estado de excepción; **to take emergency measures** = tomar medidas de emergencia excepcionales; **emergency powers** = poderes *mpl* de emergencia; **emergency reserves** = dinero *m* para imprevistos

emigrate ['emɪgreɪt] *verb* emigrar
◊ **emigration** [emɪ'greɪʃn] *noun* emigración *f*
◊ **emigrant** ['emɪgrənt] *noun* emigrante *mf*

eminent domain ['emɪnənt də'meɪn] *noun* derecho *m* del Estado a la expropiación de propiedad privada para el uso público

emoluments [ɪ'mɒljumənts] *plural noun* *(wages, salaries, fees, etc.)* honorarios *mpl* or emolumentos *mpl*

empanel [ɪm'pænəl] *verb* **to empanel a jury** = seleccionar un jurado (NOTE: GB spelling is **empanelling - empanelled** but US spelling is **empaneling - empaneled)**

employ [ɪm'plɔɪ] *verb* emplear; **to employ twenty staff** = emplear a veinte personas; **to employ twenty new staff** = emplear a veinte personas más
◊ **employed** [ɪm'plɔɪd] **1** *adjective* **(a)** *(work)* empleado, -da *or* contratado, -da; **he is not gainfully employed** = no tiene un trabajo remunerado; **self-employed** = trabajador autónomo *or* por cuenta propia; **he worked in a bank for ten years but now is self-employed** = trabajó en un banco durante diez años pero ahora lo hace por cuenta propia **(b)** *(money)* en uso *or* utilizado, -da; **return against capital employed** = rendimiento *m* sobre el capital **2** *plural noun* personas *fpl* que tienen un trabajo *or* empleados, -das; **the employers and the employed** = los empresarios y los empleados; **the self-employed** = los trabajadores autónomos *or* independientes *or* por cuenta propia
◊ **employee** [ɪmplɔɪ'iː] *noun* empleado, -da *or* trabajador, -ra; **employees of the firm are eligible to join a profit-sharing scheme** = los empleados de la firma tienen derecho a entrar en un plan de participación en los beneficios; **relations between management and employees have improved** = las relaciones entre la dirección y los empleados han mejorado; **the company has decided to take on new employees** = la compañía ha decidido contratar nuevos empleados; **employee share ownership** = oferta *f* de acciones a los empleados
◊ **employer** [ɪm'plɔɪə] *noun* empresario, -ria *or* patrón *or* patrono, -na; **employers' organization** *or* **association** = asociación *f* de empresarios *or* organización *f* patronal *or* patronato *m;* **employer's contribution** = cuota *f* patronal; **employer's liability** = responsabilidad *f* patronal
◊ **employment** [ɪm'plɔɪmənt] *noun* empleo *m* or ocupación *f* or trabajo *m;* **permanent employment** = empleo fijo *or* permanente; **seasonal employment** = empleo estacional; **short term employment** = empleo precario; **conditions of**

employment = condiciones *fpl* de empleo *or* de trabajo; **contract of employment** *or* **employment contract** = contrato *m* de trabajo; **security of employment** = estabilidad *f* en el trabajo; **employment office** *or* **bureau** *or* **agency** = oficina *f* de empleo *or* agencia *f* de colocación; **Employment Appeal Tribunal** = Magistratura Central del Trabajo

empower [ɪmˈpaʊə] *verb* facultar *or* autorizar *or* dar poder; **the agent is empowered to sell the property** = el agente está autorizado a vender la propiedad; **she was empowered by the company to sign the contract** = la compañía le autorizó a firmar el contrato; **a constable is empowered to arrest a person whom he suspects of having committed an offence** = un policía está autorizado a detener a una persona sospechosa de haber cometido un delito

emptor [ˈemptə] *see* CAVEAT

EMS [ˈiː ˈem ˈes] = EUROPEAN MONETARY SYSTEM

enable [ɪˈneɪbl] *verb* permitir *or* autorizar *or* posibilitar; **enabling legislation** *or* **statute** = ley *f* de autorización

enact [ɪˈnækt] *verb* decretar; *(law)* promulgar
◊ **enactment** [ɪˈnæktmənt] *noun* promulgación *f*; *(Act of Parliament)* ley parlamentaria

enclose [ɪnˈkləʊz] *verb* adjuntar *or* remitir (adjunto) *or* acompañar; **to enclose an invoice with a letter** = adjuntar una factura a una carta; **I am enclosing a copy of the contract** = adjunto copia del contrato; **a letter enclosing two cheques** = una carta con dos cheques adjuntos; **please find the cheque enclosed herewith** = le envío adjunto el cheque
◊ **enclosure** [ɪnˈkləʊʒə] *noun* **(a)** *(documents)* documento adjunto *or* carta adjunta *or* anexo *m* **(b)** *(land)* cercado *m*

encourage [ɪnˈkʌrɪdʒ] *verb* animar *or* alentar *or* fomentar *or* incitar *or* estimular; **the probation service encourages ex-offenders to settle in new jobs** = la libertad condicional anima a los ex-delincuentes a asentarse en nuevos trabajos; **leaving windows open only encourages burglars** = con dejar las ventanas abiertas sólo se consigue animar a los ladrones; **some people believe that lenient sentences encourage crime** = algunas personas creen que las condenas indulgentes fomentan el crimen

encroach [ɪnˈkrəʊtʃ] *verb* usurpar

encroachment [ɪnˈkrəʊtʃmənt] *noun* usurpación *f or* intrusión *f*

encumber [ɪnˈkʌmbə] *verb* afectar

encumbrance [ɪnˈkʌmbrəns] *noun* carga *f or* hipoteca *f or* gravamen *m*

end [end] **1** *noun* fin *m or* final *m*; **year end** = fin de año; **in the end** = al final; **to meet a violent end** = tener un final violento **2** *verb* terminar *or* poner fin

endanger [ɪnˈdeɪndʒə] *verb* poner en peligro *or* arriesgar; **endangering railway passengers** = poner en peligro a los pasajeros de un tren; **endangering life at sea** = arriesgar la vida en el mar; **criminal damage endangering life** = daño criminal en el que se pone en peligro la vida

endorse [ɪnˈdɔːs] *verb* **(a)** *(to agree with)* aprobar *or* ratificar; **the court endorsed counsel's view** = el tribunal aprobó la opinión del abogado **(b)** *(to sign on the back)* endosar *or* anotar al dorso; **to endorse a bill** *or* **a cheque** = avalar una letra *or* endosar un cheque **(c)** *(traffic sanction)* escribir los detalles de una sanción en el carnet de conducir **(d)** *(in a legal document)* escribir un resumen del contenido de un acta legalizada en la parte exterior del acta plegada
◊ **endorsee** [endɔːˈsiː] *noun* endosatario, -ria
◊ **endorsement** [ɪnˈdɔːsmənt] *noun* **(a)** *(act of endorsing)* endoso *m or* aval *m or* resumen *m* de un acta legal anotado en la parte exterior del acta plegada **(b)** *(condition of insurance policy)* adición *f* a una póliza *or* ampliación *f* de póliza mediante endoso **(c)** *(note on driving licence)* anotación *f* en el carnet de conducir que muestra que el titular ha sido condenado por un delito de tráfico; *see also* TOTTING UP
◊ **endorser** [ɪnˈdɔːsə] *noun* endosante *mf*

endow [ɪnˈdaʊ] *verb* dotar

endowment [ɪnˈdaʊmənt] *noun* dotación *f*; **endowment assurance** *or* **endowment policy** = póliza *f* mixta *or* póliza dotal; **endowment mortgage** = hipoteca *f* avalada por una póliza de seguro dotal *or* 'endowment' *m*

enforce [ɪnˈfɔːs] *verb* hacer cumplir *or* imponer; **to enforce the terms of a contract** = ejecutar *or* hacer cumplir los términos de un contrato; **to enforce a debt** = exigir el pago de una deuda
◊ **enforceable** [ɪnˈfɔːsəbl] *adjective* ejecutable *or* ejecutorio, -ria *or* aplicable
◊ **enforcement** [ɪnˈfɔːsmənt] *noun* cumplimiento *m or* aplicación *f or* ejecución *f*; **enforcement of the terms of a contract** = cumplimiento de los términos de un contrato; **law enforcement** = aplicación *or* cumplimiento *or* ejecución de la ley; **law enforcement officers** = funcionarios encargados del cumplimiento de la ley

enfranchise [ɪnˈfræntʃaɪz] *verb* conceder el derecho de voto
◊ **enfranchisement** [ɪnˈfræntʃaɪzmənt] *noun* concesión *f* del derecho de voto; **leasehold enfranchisement** = arrendamiento *m or* alquiler *m* con derecho a compra

engage [ɪnˈɡeɪdʒ] *verb* **(a)** **to engage someone to do something** = comprometer *or* obligar a alguien a hacer algo por medio de un contrato; **the contract**

engages the company to purchase minimum annual quantities of goods = el contrato obliga a la compañía a realizar un mínimo de compras anuales *or* a comprar una cantidad mínima de productos anualmente (b) *(employ)* contratar; we have engaged the best commercial lawyer to represent us = hemos contratado al mejor abogado mercantil para que nos represente (c) to be engaged in = dedicarse *or* estar trabajando en; he is engaged in work on computers = se dedica a la informática; the company is engaged in trade with Africa = la compañía se dedica al comercio con África

◊ engaged [ɪnˈgeɪdʒd] *adjective; (telephone)* línea ocupada *or* comunicando; you cannot speak to the manager - his line is engaged = no puede hablar con el director - su teléfono comunica *or* está comunicando

◊ engagement [ɪnˈgeɪdʒmənt] *noun* (a) *(agreement)* compromiso *m or* obligación *f;* to break an engagement to do something = romper un compromiso (b) *(meetings)* engagements = compromisos *mpl or* citas *fpl;* I have no engagements for the rest of the day = no tengo más compromisos para el resto del día; she noted the appointment in her engagements diary = anotó la cita en su agenda

engross [ɪnˈgrəʊs] *verb* redactar de forma definitiva una escritura pública; *US* engrossed Bill = copia definitiva de un proyecto de ley

◊ engrossment [ɪnˈgrəʊsmənt] *noun* redacción definitiva de una escritura pública *or* acta *f* legal en su forma definitiva; engrossment paper = papel grueso en el que se redactan las escrituras legales en su forma definitiva

enjoin [ɪnˈdʒɔɪn] *verb* mandar

enjoy [ɪnˈdʒɔɪ] *verb* disfrutar *or* gozar

enjoyment [ɪnˈdʒɔɪmənt] *noun* disfrute *m;* quiet enjoyment of land = disfrute privado de la tierra

enlist [ɪnˈlɪst] *verb* (a) *(conscript)* reclutar (b) *(get help)* conseguir apoyo (c) *(join up)* alistarse

enmity [ˈenmətɪ] *noun* enemistad *f*

enquire *or* enquiry [ɪnˈkwæɪə *or* ɪnˈkwæɪrɪ] = INQUIRE, INQUIRY

enrolled bill [ɪnˈrəʊld ˈbɪl] *noun US* copia *f* final de un proyecto de ley

ensuing [ɪnˈsjuːɪŋ] *adjective* siguiente; in the ensuing argument, the defendant hit the plaintiff with a bottle = en la discusión que siguió el acusado golpeó al demandante con una botella

entail [ɪnˈteɪl] 1 *noun* vínculo *m* 2 *verb* suponer *or* implicar; itemizing the sales figures will entail about ten days' work = detallar las cifras de ventas supondrá unos diez días de trabajo; *see also* FEE TAIL

enter [entə] *verb* (a) *(to go in)* entrar en *or* penetrar; they all stood up when the judges entered the courtroom = todos se levantaron cuando los jueces entraron en la sala; the company has spent millions trying to enter the do-it-yourself market = la compañía ha gastado millones intentando penetrar *or* introducirse *or* entrar en el mercado del bricolaje (b) *(to write)* apuntar *or* inscribir *or* registrar *or* presentar; to enter a name on a list = inscribir *or* apuntar un nombre en una lista; the clerk entered the objection in the records = el empleado registró la objeción en las actas; the defendant entered defence of justification = el acusado presentó defensa en un juicio por difamación; to enter appearance = aceptar la comparecencia del acusado; to enter a bid for something = hacer una oferta de compra; to enter a caveat = hacer una advertencia; to enter judgment for someone = registrar la sentencia por alguien *or* en nombre de alguien; judgment was entered for the plaintiff = se registró la sentencia en nombre del demandante; the plaintiff entered judgment = el demandante registró la sentencia (c) to enter into = iniciar *or* establecer; *(to agree to do something)* concertar; to enter into relations with someone = entablar relaciones con alguien; to enter into negotiations with a foreign government = iniciar negociaciones con un gobierno extranjero; to enter into a partnership with a friend = asociarse con un amigo; to enter into an agreement *or* a contract = concertar un contrato *or* formalizar un acuerdo

◊ entering [ˈentrɪŋ] *noun* registro *m or* entrada *f or* inscripción *f*

enterprise [ˈentəpraɪz] *noun* (a) *(system of carrying on a business)* empresa *f;* free enterprise = libre empresa; enterprise zone = zona *f* empresarial (b) *(a business)* empresa *or* negocio *m;* she runs a mail order enterprise = dirige una empresa de ventas por correo

entertain [entəˈteɪn] *verb* (a) *(a guest)* entretener *or* convidar *or* recibir clientes (b) *(an idea)* considerar; the judge will not entertain any proposal from the prosecution to delay the start of the hearing = el juez no considerará ninguna propuesta de la acusación para retrasar el comienzo de la vista

entice [ɪnˈtaɪs] *verb* convencer; they tried to entice the managers to join the new company = trataron de convencer a los directores para que se unieran a la nueva compañía

◊ enticement [ɪnˈtaɪsmənt] *noun* tentación *f*

entitle [ɪnˈtaɪtl] *verb* dar derecho a *or* autorizar; he is entitled to four weeks' holiday = tiene derecho a cuatro semanas de vacaciones

◊ entitlement [ɪnˈtaɪtlmənt] *noun* derecho *m;* holiday entitlement = derecho a un periodo de vacaciones; **pension entitlement** = derecho a percibir una pensión

entity ['entɪtɪ] *noun* entidad *f or* ente *m;* **public entity** = ente público; **his private company is a separate entity** = su compañía privada es una entidad separada

entrapment [ɪn'træpmənt] *noun (done by someone in authority, such as a police officer)* inducción*f* dolosa *or* autoría *f* intelectual a la comisión de un delito para poder detener al delincuente (no se puede alegar por la defensa en el derecho británico pero sí en los EE UU)

entrenched [ɪn'trenʃt] *adjective* afianzado, -da; **the government's entrenched position on employees' rights** = la posición afianzada del gobierno sobre los derechos de los trabajadores; **entrenched clause** = artículo *m* inalterable

entrust [ɪn'trʌst] *verb* confiar *or* encomendar; **to entrust someone with something** *or* **to entrust something to someone** = confiar algo a alguien

entry ['entrɪ] *noun* **(a)** *(going in)* entrada *f or* acceso *m;* **forcible entry** = allanamiento *m* de morada; **there is no right of entry through this door** = no existe derecho de entrada por esta puerta **(b)** *(written information)* entrada *or* anotación *f or* asiento *m;* **cash entry** = asiento de caja; **the sergeant copied the entries into the report** = el sargento copió las entradas en el informe **(c)** *(court)* **entry of appearance** = aceptación *f* de comparecencia por causa de la defensa; **entry of judgment** = registro *m* de la sentencia
◊ **entryism** ['entriɪzm] *noun* infiltracionismo *m*
◊ **entryist** ['entriɪst] *adjective* de infiltración; **the party leader condemned entryist techniques** = el líder del partido condenó las técnicas de infiltración

envelope ['envələup] *noun* sobre *m*

environment [ɪn'vaɪrənmənt] *noun* medio ambiente *m;* **Department of the Environment** = ministerio del Medio Ambiente
◊ **environmental** [ɪnvaɪrən'mentl] *adjective* medioambiental; **the Opposition spokesman on environmental issues** = el portavoz de la oposición sobre cuestiones del medio ambiente; **environmental health** = protección *f* del medio ambiente; **Environmental Health Officer** = funcionario público responsable de la protección del medio ambiente

envoy ['envɔɪ] *noun* **(a)** *(person who is sent with a message)* enviado, -da; **the President's special envoy to the Middle East** = el enviado especial del Presidente al Medio Oriente **(b)** *(senior diplomat with a rank below that of ambassador)* jefe, -fa de delegación

equal ['iːkwəl] **1** *adjective* igual *or* equitativo, -va; **Equal Opportunities Commission** *or* **US Equal Employment Opportunity Commission** =

Comisión *f* de Igualdad de Oportunidades; **equal opportunities programme** = programa *m* de igualdad de oportunidades (NOTE: in US English this is **affirmative action program**); **equal pay** = igual salario; **male and female workers have equal pay** = los trabajadores del sexo masculino y femenino reciben igual salario **2** *verb* ser igual a *or* igualar; **production this month has equalled our best month ever** = la producción de este mes ha igualado a la del mejor mes que hemos tenido (NOTE: GB spelling is **equalling - equalled** but US spelling is **equaling - equaled**)
◊ **equality** [ɪ'kwɒlɪtɪ] *noun* igualdad *f;* **equality of opportunity** = igualdad de oportunidades
◊ **equalize** [iːkwəlaɪz] *verb* igualar *or* compensar *or* equilibrar; **to equalize dividends** = igualar dividendos
◊ **equalization** [iːkwəlaɪ'zeɪʃn] *noun* **GB Exchange Equalization Account** = cuenta *f* de compensación de cambios
◊ **equally** ['iːkwəlɪ] *adverb* igualmente *or* por igual *or* de la misma manera *or* equitativamente; **costs will be shared equally between the two parties** = las costas se compartirán equitativamente entre las dos partes

equitable ['ekwɪtəbl] *adjective* justo, -ta *or* equitativo, -va; **equitable jurisdiction** = jurisdicción *f* justa *or* de equidad; **equitable lien** = gravamen *m* equitativo; **equitable mortgage** = hipoteca *f* de equidad *or* no formalizada que nace con la entrega del dinero

equity ['ekwɪtɪ] *noun* **(a)** *(fair system of laws)* equidad *f or* justicia *f or* sistema legal justo; **equity of redemption** = derecho *m* de redimir una hipoteca *or* de rescate **(b)** *(profit)* beneficio *m* **(c)** *(capital)* participación *f* de capital en una sociedad; **shareholders' equity** *or* **equity capital** = capital *m* en acciones ordinarias *or* capital accionista *or* acciones *fpl or* capital propio *or* cuenta *f* de participación
◊ **equities** ['ekwɪtiːz] *plural noun* títulos *mpl* u obligaciones *fpl or* acciones ordinarias

equivalence [ɪ'kwɪvələns] *noun* equivalencia *f or* paridad *f*
◊ **equivalent** [ɪ'kwɪvələnt] *adjective* equivalente; **to be equivalent to** = equivaler a *or* ser equivalente a; **the total dividend paid is equivalent to one quarter of the total profits** = el dividendo total pagado es equivalente a un cuarto del beneficio total

equivocal [ɪ'kwɪvəkl] *adjective* equívoco, -ca *or* dudoso, -sa; **the court took the view that the defendant's plea was equivocal** = el tribunal decidió que el alegato del acusado era dudoso

error ['erə] *noun* error *m or* equivocación *f;* **he made an error in calculating the total** = cometió un error al calcular el total; **the secretary must have made a typing error** = la secretaria ha debido cometer un error de transcripción; **clerical error** = error de copia; **computer error** = error de ordenador; **errors and omissions excepted (e. & o.e.)** = salvo error u omisión (s.e.u.o)

Erskine May [ˈɜːskɪn ˈmeɪ] *noun GB* libro *m* de procedimiento parlamentario

> COMMENT: Erskine May's 'Treatise on the Law, Privileges, Proceedings and Usage of Parliament' was originally published in 1844. The author, Sir Thomas Erskine May, was clerk of the House of Commons. The book is updated frequently, and is the authority on questions of parliamentary procedure

escalate [ˈeskəleɪt] *verb* subir *or* escalar
◊ **escalation** [eskəˈleɪʃn] *noun* subida *f;* **escalation of prices** = subida *or* escalada *f* de precios; **escalation clause** = ESCALATOR CLAUSE
◊ **escalator clause** [ˈeskəleɪtə ˈklɔːz] *noun* cláusula de reajuste de precios *or* salarios

escape [ɪˈskeɪp] **1** *noun* fuga *f or* escapatoria *f or* evasión *f;* **escape clause** = cláusula *f* de excepción **2** *verb* evadir *or* fugarse *or* escaparse (de prisión) *or* darse a la fuga; **three prisoners escaped by climbing over the wall** = tres presos se fugaron saltando el muro

escrow [ˈeskrəʊ] *noun* plica *f;* **in escrow** = en depósito; **document held in escrow** = documento *m* en depósito; *US* **escrow account** = cuenta *f* de garantía bloqueada

espionage [ˈespiənɑːʒ] *noun* espionaje *m;* **industrial espionage** = espionaje *m* industrial

esquire [ɪˈskwaɪə] *noun* **(a)** *GB* Señor Don (SR.D.); **letter addressed to J. Smith, Esq.** = carta dirigida al Señor Don J.Smith (NOTE: you can use **Mr** before a name, or **Esq.** after it; both are titles, but **Esq.** is more formal and suggests that the man is more important. **Esq.** is used by lawyers, bank managers, etc., when writing to clients) **(b)** *US* título otorgado a abogados de los EE UU

essential [ɪˈsenʃl] *adjective* esencial *or* substancial *or* imprescindible; **it is essential that all the facts of the case should be presented as clearly as possible** = es imprescindible que todos los datos del caso se presenten lo más claramente posible; **mens rea is one of the essential elements of a crime** = la intención criminal es uno de los elementos esenciales de un crimen

establish [ɪˈstæblɪʃ] *verb* **(a)** *(to set up)* establecer *or* fundar *or* consolidar *or* implantar; **the company has established a branch in Australia** = la compañía ha establecido una sucursal en Australia; **the business was established in Scotland in 1823** = el negocio se fundó en Escocia en 1823; **established post** = puesto *m* de plantilla *or* puesto fijo como funcionario; **to establish oneself**

in business = establecerse en un negocio *or* crearse una reputación **(b)** *(land)* **established use** = uso establecido **(c)** *(to decide what is correct)* probar *or* demostrar *or* comprobar; **the police are trying to establish his movements on the night of the murder** = la policía está intentando comprobar sus movimientos en la noche del asesinato; **it is an established fact that the car could not have been used because it was out of petrol** = está demostrado que el coche no pudo haber sido utilizado porque no tenía gasolina
◊ **establishment** [ɪˈstæblɪʃmənt] *noun* **(a)** *(a business)* establecimiento *m;* **he runs an important printing establishment** = dirige un importante establecimiento tipográfico **(b)** *(in the EU)* **right of establishment** = derecho *m* de establecimiento *or* de fijación de residencia **(c)** *(number of people working in a company)* personal *m or* plantilla *f;* **establishment charges** = gastos *mpl* de plantilla *or* gastos de personal *or* gastos de establecimiento; **to be on the establishment** = formar parte del personal *or* estar en plantilla; **office with an establishment of fifteen** = oficina *f* con una plantilla de quince empleados

estate [ɪˈsteɪt] *noun* **(a)** *(right to hold and occupy land)* propiedad *f;* **life estate** = dominio *m* vitalicio **(b)** **real estate** = bienes *mpl* raíces *or* bienes inmuebles *or* propiedad inmobiliaria; **estate agency** = agencia inmobiliaria; **estate agent** = agente inmobiliario **(c)** **industrial estate** *or* **trading estate** = zona *f* comercial *or* polígono *m* industrial **(d)** *(inheritance)* herencia *f;* **to break up an estate** = dividir una herencia; **his estate was valued at £100,000** *or* **he left estate valued at £100,000** = su herencia se valoró en 100.000 libras *or* dejó una herencia valorada en 100.000 libras; *US* **estate tax** = impuesto *m* de sucesión *or* sobre transmisiones *or* impuesto sobre herencias y donaciones

estimate 1 [ˈestɪmət] *noun* **(a)** *(approximate calculation)* estimación *f or* aproximación *f or* cálculo *m or* valoración *f or* apreciación *f;* **rough estimate** = cálculo aproximado; **at a conservative estimate** = calculando por lo bajo *or* según una apreciación prudente *or* un cálculo moderado; **the crime rate has risen by at least 20% in the last year, and that is a conservative estimate** = el índice de criminalidad ha aumentado al menos un 20% durante el pasado año, y eso haciendo un cálculo moderado; **these figures are only an estimate** = estas cifras son sólo aproximadas; **estimates of expenditure** = estimación presupuestaria *or* cálculo del presupuesto **(b)** *(written calculation of cost)* presupuesto *m;* **before we can give the grant we must have an estimate of the total costs involved** = antes de conceder la subvención debemos tener un presupuesto de los costes totales en juego; **to ask a builder for an estimate for building the warehouse** = pedir a un constructor presupuesto para la construcción del almacén; **to put in an estimate** = presentar un presupuesto **2** [ˈestɪmeɪt] *verb* **(a)** *(calculate approximately)* apreciar *or* estimar *or* calcular aproximadamente; **to estimate that it will cost £1m** *or* **to estimate costs at £1m** = calcular los gastos en un millón de libras aproximadamente **(b)** *(to cost)* hacer un presupuesto; **to estimate for a job** = hacer un presupuesto de un trabajo

◊ **estimation** [estɪˈmeɪʃn] *noun* opinión *f or* estimación *f or* valoración *f or* juicio *m;* **in my estimation, he is the best commercial lawyer in town** = a mi juicio es el mejor abogado mercantil de la ciudad

◊ **estimator** [ˈestɪmeɪtə] *noun* tasador, -ra

estoppel [ɪˈstɒpəl] *noun* impedimento *m* legal *or* acción *f* innegable *or* desestimación *f* de una demanda por entrar en contradicción con algo anterior; **estoppel of** *or* **by record** = impedimento por registro público; **estoppel by deed** = desestimación *or* impedimento por escritura; **estoppel by conduct** *or* **in pais** = desestimación *or* impedimento por razón de conducta; **estoppel by silence** = impedimento por falta de declaración; *see also* PROMISSORY

estovers [ɪˈstəʊvəz] *plural noun* derecho *m* de hacer leña *or* derecho a cortar árboles en un predio arrendado

estreat [ɪˈstriːt] **1** *noun* extracto *m or* copia *f* de una orden judicial que impone una multa o decreta fianza **2** *verb* **(a)** *(get a copy of a record)* obtener copia de una orden judicial en la que se impone una multa o se decreta fianza **(b)** *(forfeit)* perder la fianza (por no comparecer ante los tribunales); **estreated recognizance** = fianza confiscada

et al. *or* **et alia** [ˈet ˈæl *or* ˈet ˈeɪliə] *Latin phrase* 'y otros' *or* 'y otras cosas'

etc. *or* **etcetera** [etˈsetrə] etcétera *or* etc.; **the import duty is to be paid on expensive items including cars, watches, etc.** = hay que pagar derechos de aduana por los artículos de lujo como coches, relojes, etc.

etiquette [etɪˈket] *noun* etiqueta *f or* protocolo *m or* normas *fpl* profesionales

et seq. *or* **et sequenter** [ˈet ˈsek] *Latin phrase* 'y lo siguiente'

EU [ˈiː ˈjuː] = EUROPEAN UNION; **EU ministers met today in Brussels** = los ministros de la UE se reunieron hoy en Bruselas; **the USA is increasing its trade with the EU** = los EE UU están incrementando el comercio con la UE

Euro- [ˈjʊərəʊ] *prefix* euro-
◊ **European** [jʊərəʊˈpiːən] *adjective* europeo, -ea; **the European Community (EC)** = la Comunidad Europea (CE); **European Community Law** = Ley *f* de la Comunidad Europea; **European Court of Justice** = Tribunal *m* de Justicia Europeo;

European Court of Human Rights = Tribunal Europeo de Derechos Humanos; **the European Monetary System (EMS)** = el Sistema Monetario Europeo (SME); **the European Parliament (EP)** = el Parlamento Europeo (PE); **the European Union (EU)** = la Unión Europea (UE)

euthanasia [juːθəˈneɪziə] *noun* eutanasia *f*

evade [ɪˈveɪd] *verb* evadir *or* eludir; **to evade tax** = evadir impuestos

evaluate [ɪˈvæljueɪt] *verb* valuar *or* valorar *or* evaluar *or* calcular; **to evaluate costs** = evaluar los costes
◊ **evaluation** [ɪvæljuˈeɪʃn] *noun* valoración *f or* evaluación *f;* **job evaluation** = valoración de puestos de trabajo

evasion [ɪˈveɪʒn] *noun* evasión *f;* **tax evasion** = evasión fiscal *or* fraude *m* fiscal *or* defraudación *f* fiscal; *see also* AVOIDANCE
◊ **evasive** [ɪˈveɪzɪv] *adjective* evasivo, -va; **to be evasive** *or* **to give evasive answers** = contestar con evasivas

event [ɪˈvent] *noun* suceso *m or* acontecimiento *m;* **the police are trying to piece together the events of the previous evening** = la policía está intentando reconstruir los sucesos de la noche anterior; **the newspaper reports covered the events following the football match** = los artículos periodísticos informaron de los sucesos ocurridos tras el partido de fútbol; **in the event of** *or* **in the event that** = en caso de *or* en caso de que; **in the event of a disagreement** *or* **in the event that the parties fail to agree, the case will be submitted to arbitration** = si las partes no llegan a un acuerdo *or* en caso de desacuerdo *or* en caso de que las partes no lleguen a un acuerdo, se someterá el caso a arbitraje

evict [ɪˈvɪkt] *verb* desahuciar *or* desalojar *or* expulsar; **all the tenants were evicted by the new landlords** = todos los inquilinos fueron desahuciados por los nuevos propietarios
◊ **eviction** [ɪˈvɪkʃn] *noun* desahucio *m;* **eviction order** = orden *f* de deshaucio; **eviction proceedings** = juicio *m* de deshaucio

evidence [ˈevɪdəns] **1** *noun* prueba *f or* evidencia *f or* hechos *mpl or* datos *mpl;* **all the evidence points to arson** = las pruebas parecen indicar que el incendio fue provocado; **evidence for the prosecution** *or* **for the defence** = prueba de cargo *or* de descargo; **admissible evidence** = prueba admisible; **circumstantial evidence** = prueba circunstancial; **conclusive evidence** = indicio claro *or* prueba contundente; **direct evidence** = prueba directa; **documentary evidence** = prueba documental; **extrinsic evidence** = prueba extrínseca; **false evidence** = prueba falsa *or* falsificada; **inconclusive evidence** = indicio dudoso; **irrefutable evidence** = prueba irrefutable;

strong evidence = indicios vehementes; **written evidence** = prueba escrita; **the secretary gave evidence against her former employer** = la secretaria prestó declaración en contra de su anterior jefe; **fabrication of evidence** = falsificación *f* de pruebas; **taking of evidence** = toma *f* de declaración; **to admit as evidence** = aceptar como prueba *or* recibir a prueba; **to give evidence** = testificar; **to plant evidence** = poner pruebas falsas con la intención de implicar a alguien; **rule of evidence** = principio *m* de admisión de pruebas; **to turn Queen's evidence** *or* *US* **to turn state's evidence** = delatar a un cómplice (con la esperanza de ver rebajada la condena propia) (NOTE: no plural; to refer to a single item say **a piece of evidence**) **2** *verb* evidenciar *or* probar; **the lack of good will, as evidenced by the defendant's behaviour in the witness stand** = la ausencia de buena voluntad tal y como se ha probado por el comportamiento del acusado en el estrado

ex [eks] *preposition & prefix* **(a)** *(out or from)* fuera de *or* sin; **price ex warehouse** = precio *m* en *or* de almacén; **price ex works** *or* **ex factory** = precio de fábrica **(b)** **share quoted ex dividend** = acción *f* cotizada sin dividendos **(c)** *(former)* antiguo, -gua *or* ex-; **Mr Smith, the ex-chairman of the company** = el Sr. Smith, el antiguo presidente de la compañía; **she claimed maintenance from her ex-husband** = reclamó la manutención a su ex-marido **(d)** **ex-directory number** = número *m* que no figura en la guía telefónica

examine [ɪɡ'zæmɪn] *verb* examinar *or* revisar *or* registrar; **the customs officials asked to examine the inside of the car** = los oficiales de aduanas quisieron registrar el interior del coche; **the police are examining the papers from the managing director's safe** = la policía está examinando los papeles de la caja fuerte del director gerente; **examining justice** *or* **magistrate** = juez, -za de instrucción
◊ **examination** [ɪɡzæmɪ'neɪʃn] *noun* **(a)** *(asking questions)* interrogatorio *m* **(b)** **examination in chief** *or* *US* **direct examination** = interrogatorio directo de los testigos **(c)** *(looking closely)* examen *m or* revisión *f or* registro *m;* **customs examination** = registro aduanero **(d)** *(test)* examen; **he passed his law examinations** = aprobó los exámenes de derecho; **she came first in the final examination for the course** = sacó la mejor nota en el examen de final de curso; **he failed his examination and so had to leave his job** = suspendió el examen y por eso tuvo que dejar el trabajo; *see also* CROSS-EXAMINE, CROSS-EXAMINATION
◊ **examiner** [ɪɡ'zæmɪnə] *noun* examinador, -ra

example [ɪɡ'zɑːmpl] *noun* ejemplo *m or* modelo *m;* **to set an example to someone** = dar ejemplo a alguien; **to make an example of someone** = imponer a alguien un castigo ejemplar; **these** sentences are a good example of the harshness of the military tribunals = estas sentencias son un buen ejemplo de la severidad de los tribunales militares; **new laws on computer copying provide an example of how the law changes to keep in step with new inventions** = las nuevas leyes sobre la piratería informática ofrecen un ejemplo de cómo la ley cambia para mantenerse al día con los nuevos inventos; **for example (e.g.)** = por ejemplo (ej.); **the government took steps to control drugs, and, for example, increased the numbers of policemen in the Drug Squad** = el gobierno tomó medidas para controlar la droga y, por ejemplo, aumentó el número de policías de la brigada antidroga *or* de estupefacientes; **the police ought to set an example to the community** = la policía debería dar ejemplo a la comunidad; **the rioters were sentenced to periods of imprisonment as an example to others** = se condenó a los alborotadores a prisión a modo de ejemplo para los demás

exceed [ɪk'siːd] *verb* exceder *or* superar *or* rebasar *or* sobrepasar; **to exceed one's powers** = excederse en sus funciones; **the judge exceeded his powers in criticizing the court of appeal** = el juez se excedió en sus funciones al criticar al tribunal de apelación; **he was arrested for exceeding the speed limit** = le arrestaron por sobrepasar el límite de velocidad; **he has exceeded his credit limit** = ha rebasado su límite de crédito

excellent ['ekslənt] *adjective* excelente; **the accused is a person of excellent character** = el acusado es una bellísima persona

except [ɪk'sept] *preposition & conjunction* excepto *or* salvo *or* con excepción de; **VAT is levied on all goods and services except books, newspapers and children's clothes** = se incluye el IVA en todos los artículos y servicios, con excepción de libros, periódicos y ropa infantil; **sales are rising in all markets except the Far East** = las ventas están aumentando en todos los mercados excepto en el Extremo Oriente; **the rule applies in all cases, except where otherwise stated** = la norma se aplica en todos los casos excepto en donde se indique lo contrario
◊ **excepted** [ɪk'septɪd] *adverb* excepto *or* salvo; **errors and omissions excepted (e. & o.e.)** = salvo error u omisión (s.e.u.o.); **excepted persons** = tipo de trabajadores excluidos de una póliza de seguros
◊ **exception** [ɪk'septʃn] *noun* **(a)** *(not included)* excepción *f;* **with the exception of** = excepto; **all the accused were acquitted with the exception of Jones who was sent to prison for three months** = todos los acusados fueron absueltos excepto Jones que fue condenado a tres meses de prisión **(b)** *(objection)* objeción *f;* **to take exception to something** = objetar *or* protestar; **counsel for the defence took exception to the witness'remarks** = el abogado defensor protestó por los comentarios del testigo; **he has taken exception to the reports**

of the trial in the newspapers = ha protestado por los artículos del juicio publicados en los periódicos

◊ **exceptional** [ɪk'sepʃənəl] *adjective* excepcional; **exceptional items** = registros *mpl or* partidas *fpl* excepcionales; **exceptional needs payment** = subvención *f* estatal a un individuo para asuntos urgentes de primera necesidad

excess [ɪk'ses] *noun* **(a)** *(over a limit)* exceso *m;* **excess alcohol in the blood** = exceso de alcohol en la sangre; **excess fare** = suplemento *m;* **excess of jurisdiction** = exceso de jurisdicción; **excess profits** = beneficios *mpl* extraordinarios; **in excess** = en exceso *or* superior a *or* por encima de; **quantities in excess of twenty-five kilos** = cantidades superiores a los veinticinco kilos **(b)** *(insurance claim)* excedente *m;* **he has to pay a £50 excess, and the damage amounted to over £1,000** = tiene que pagar un excedente de 50 libras y los daños ascendieron a más de 1.000 libras

◊ **excessive** [ɪk'sesɪv] *adjective* excesivo, -va; **we found the bill for costs excessive and applied to have it reduced** = encontramos la relación de gastos excesiva y pedimos un descuento; **the driver had an excessive amount of alcohol in his blood** = el conductor tenía una cantidad excesiva de alcohol en la sangre

exchange [ɪks'tʃeɪnʒ] **1** *noun* **(a)** *(swap)* cambio *m or* intercambio *m or* trueque *m or* canje *m or* permuta *f;* **part exchange** = canje parcial *or* entrega *f* de un producto como parte del pago por uno nuevo; **exchange of contracts** = intercambio de contratos **(b)** *(currency)* **foreign exchange** = divisas *fpl or* moneda *f* extranjera; **foreign exchange broker** = agente *mf* de cambio de divisas; **foreign exchange market** = mercado *m* de divisas *or* mercado cambiario; **rate of exchange** *or* **exchange rate** = tipo *m* de cambio; **exchange control** = control *m* de divisas *or* control de cambio; **the government had to impose exchange controls to stop the rush to buy dollars** = el gobierno tuvo que imponer controles de divisas para detener la compra masiva de dólares; *GB* **Exchange Equalization Account** = cuenta *f* de compensación de cambios **(c)** **bill of exchange** = letra *f* de cambio **(d)** **Stock Exchange** = la bolsa *or* bolsa de valores; **commodity exchange** = lonja *f* de contratación *or* bolsa de contratación **2** *verb* **(a)** *(swap)* canjear; **to exchange an article for another** = cambiar *or* intercambiar un artículo por otro **(b)** *(property)* **to exchange contracts** = intercambiar contratos **(c)** *(currency)* cambiar divisas *or* moneda extranjera

◊ **exchangeable** [ɪks'tʃeɪnʒəbl] *adjective* cambiable *or* canjeable *or* intercambiable

◊ **exchanger** [ɪks'tʃeɪnʒə] *noun* agente *mf* de cambio

Exchequer [ɪks'tʃekə] *see* CHANCELLOR

excise 1 ['eksaɪz] *noun* **(a)** **excise duty** *or* **tax** = impuesto *m* específico sobre el consumo *or* sobre la venta **(b)** *(British government department dealing with taxes on imports and VAT)* **Customs and Excise** *or* **Excise Department** = administración *f* de aduanas e impuestos sobre el consumo **2** [ɪk'saɪz] *verb* extirpar *or* suprimir; **the chairman ordered the remarks to be excised from the official record** = el presidente ordenó que se suprimieran los comentarios del informe oficial

◊ **exciseman** ['eksaɪzmən] *noun* recaudador *m* de impuestos

exclude [ɪks'kluːd] *verb* excluir *or* no admitir

◊ **excluding** [ɪks'kluːdɪŋ] *preposition* excepto *or* con exclusión de *or* exceptuando a; **the regulations apply to members of the public, excluding those serving in the emergency services** = las reglas se aplican a los miembros del público, exceptuando a aquéllos que están en los servicios de emergencia; **not excluding** = sin excluir *or* inclusive; **government servants, not excluding judges, are covered by the Bill** = los funcionarios del gobierno, inclusive los jueces, están protegidos *or* amparados por el proyecto de ley

◊ **exclusion** [ɪks'kluːʒn] *noun* exclusión *f;* **exclusion clause** = cláusula *f* de exclusión; **to the exclusion of** = con exclusión de; **exclusion order** = sentencia *f* , en procesos matrimoniales, que prohíbe al cónyuge acudir a la residencia matrimonial; **exclusion zone** = aguas *fpl* jurisdiccionales *or* terreno *m* jurisdiccional

◊ **exclusive** [ɪks'kluːzɪv] *adjective* exclusivo, -va **(a)** **exclusive agreement** = contrato *m* en exclusiva; **exclusive licence** = licencia *f* en exclusiva; **exclusive right to market a product** = derechos exclusivos de venta de un producto **(b)** **exclusive of** = excluyendo *or* sin tener en cuenta *or* no incluido

◊ **exclusivity** [eksklu:'zɪvɪti] *noun* exclusividad *f or* exclusiva *f*

excuse 1 [ɪk'skjuːs] *noun* excusa *f or* disculpa; **what was his excuse for arriving late in court?** = ¿qué excusa dio por llegar tarde a la audiencia?; **the judge refused to accept the defendant's excuse** = el juez se negó a aceptar *or* rechazó la excusa del acusado; *see also* IGNORANCE **2** [ɪk'skjuːz] *verb* **(a)** *(apologize)* disculpar *or* perdonar **(b)** *(exempt)* dispensar de *or* eximir de; **he was excused jury service because he was deaf** = le dispensaron de actuar como jurado a causa de su sordera

execute ['eksɪkjuːt] *verb* **(a)** *(order)* ejecutar; **executed consideration** = contraprestación *f* ejecutada *or* efectuada **(b)** *(terms of contract)* cumplir **(c)** *(death sentence)* fusilar *or* ejecutar; **he was executed by firing squad** = fue ejecutado por el pelotón de fusilamiento

◊ **execution** [eksɪ'kjuːʃn] *noun* **(a)** *(order)* ejecución *f* de una orden *or* cumplimiento *m* de los términos de un contrato **(b)** **stay of execution** = aplazamiento *m* de una sentencia; **the court granted the company a two-week stay of execution** = el tribunal concedió a la empresa dos semanas de prórroga; **warrant of execution** = mandamiento *m* de pago *or* orden *f* de ejecución de pago **(c)** *(death sentence)* ejecución *f or* fusilamiento *m*

◊ **executioner** [eksı'kju:ʃnə] *noun* verdugo *m*

◊ **executive** [ıg'zekjutıv] **1** *adjective* **(a)** *(managing)* ejecutivo, -va; **executive committee** = comisión *f* ejecutiva; **executive director** = director, -ra ejecutivo, -va; **executive powers** = poderes *mpl* ejecutivos; *US* **executive session** = sesión *f* ejecutiva *US* **executive clemency** = indulto *m* concedido por el Presidente; **executive document** = documento *m* oficial que el Presidente de los EE UU manda al Senado para que sea ratificado; **executive order** = decreto *m* del poder ejecutivo *or* decreto del Presidente de los EE UU; **executive privilege** = inmunidad *f* del ejecutivo **2** *noun* **(a)** *(manager)* ejecutivo, -va; **chief executive** = jefe, -fa ejecutivo, -va; **legal executive** = pasante *mf;* **top executive** = alto cargo **(b)** *(section of government)* **the Executive** = el poder ejecutivo *or US* el Presidente

executor [ıg'zekjutə] *noun* albacea *m or* ejecutor *m* testamentario; **general executor** = albacea universal; **he was named executor of his brother's will** = le nombraron albacea testamentario de su hermano

◊ **executory** [ıg'zekjutri] *adjective* ejecutorio, -ria; **executory bequest** = legado *m* diferido; **executory consideration** = contraprestación *f* por realizarse

◊ **executrix** [ıg'zekjutrıks] *noun* albacea *f or* ejecutora *f* testamentaria

exemplary [ıg'zemplərı] *adjective* ejemplar; **her conduct in the case was exemplary** = su conducta en el caso fue ejemplar; **exemplary damages** = daños *mpl* punitivos *or* ejemplares *or* indemnización *f* que el acusado debe pagar por daños causados al demandante; **exemplary sentence** = condena *f or* sentencia *f* ejemplar

exempt [ıg'zempt] **1** *adjective* exento, -ta *or* eximido, -da *or* dispensado, -da; **exempt from tax** *or* **tax-exempt** = exento de impuestos; **exempt supplies** = suministros exentos del IVA **2** *verb* eximir *or* dispensar *or* liberar; **to exempt from tax** = liberar de impuestos; **non profit-making organizations are exempt(ed) from tax** = las organizaciones no lucrativas están exentas de impuestos; **food is exempt(ed) from sales tax** = los alimentos están exentos del impuesto sobre las ventas; **the government exempted trusts from tax** = el gobierno eximió de impuestos a los fideicomisos

◊ **exemption** [ıg'zempʃn] *noun* exención *f;* **exemption clause** = cláusula *f* de exención; **exemption from tax** *or* **tax exemption** = exención fiscal; **as a non profit-making organization you can claim tax exemption** = como organización no lucrativa, puedes reclamar exención fiscal

exercise ['eksəsaız] **1** *noun* ejercicio *m;* **a court can give directions to a local authority as to the exercise of its powers in relation to children in care** = un tribunal puede dar instrucciones a una autoridad local en lo que se refiere al ejercicio de sus poderes en materia de tutela infantil; **exercise of an option** = ejercicio del derecho a opción **2** *verb* ejercitar *or* ejercer *or* usar de; **to exercise one's discretion** = ejercer el poder de decisión *or* hacer lo que a uno le parezca; **the magistrates exercised their discretion and let the accused off with a suspended sentence** = los magistrados ejercieron su poder de decisión y dieron al acusado una condena condicional; **to exercise an option** = realizar una opción *or* elección *or* ejercer el derecho a *or* de opción; **he exercised his option to acquire sole marketing rights for the product** = ejerció su derecho a opción para adquirir derechos exclusivos de comercialización del producto; **not many shareholders exercised their option to buy the new issue of shares** = no hubo muchos accionistas que ejercitaran su opción a compra de la nueva emisión de acciones

ex gratia ['eks 'greıʃə] *Latin phrase* 'como favor'; **an ex gratia payment** = pago *m* de una reclamación aunque no se esté obligado a ello

exhaust [ıg'zɔ:st] *verb* agotar; **the appellant has exhausted all channels of appeal** = el apelante ha agotado todas las vías de apelación; **the company has exhausted all its development budget** = la compañía ha agotado todo el presupuesto dedicado a la expansión

exhibit [ıg'zıbıt] *noun* objeto *m or* documento *m* expuesto como prueba ante un tribunal

exhort [ıg'zɔ:t] *noun* exhortar

exhume [eks'hju:m] *verb* exhumar

◊ **exhumation** [ekshju'meıʃn] *noun* exhumación *f*

exile ['egzaıl] **1** *noun* **(a)** *(punishment)* exilio *m;* **the ten members of the opposition party were sent into exile** = los diez miembros del partido de la oposición fueron enviados al exilio (NOTE: no plural in this meaning) **(b)** *(person)* exiliado, -da **2** *verb* exiliar *or* exilar; **he was exiled for life** = le exiliaron de por vida; **she was exiled to an island in the North Sea** = le exiliaron a una isla del Mar del Norte

exist [ıg'zıst] *verb* existir; **the right of way has existed since the early nineteenth century** = el derecho de paso ha existido desde comienzos del siglo XIX

◊ **existence** [ıg'zıstəns] *noun* existencia *f;* **to come into existence** = nacer *or* empezar a existir; **the custom came into existence during the eighteenth century** = la costumbre nació durante el siglo XVIII; **immemorial existence** = existencia inmemorial (antes de 1189 fecha desde la que se supone que recordamos los acontecimientos)

exit ['egzɪt] *noun* salida *f*

ex officio [eks ə'fɪʃiəʊ] *Latin phrase* 'de oficio' *or* nato; **the treasurer is ex officio a member** *or* **an ex officio member of the finance committee** = el tesorero es un miembro de oficio de la comisión financiera; **the judge is ex officio a member of the committee** = el juez es miembro nato de la comisión

exonerate [ɪg'zɒnəreɪt] *verb* exonerar de *or* dispensar de; **the judge exonerated the driver from all responsibility for the accident** = el juez exoneró al conductor de toda responsabilidad por el accidente
◊ **exoneration** [ɪgzɒnə'reɪʃn] *noun* exoneración *f or* dispensa *f*

ex parte ['eks 'pɑːteɪ] *Latin phrase* 'unilateral' *or* 'de una de las partes' *or* 'en nombre de' *or* 'de parte de'; **an ex parte application** = solicitud *f* unilateral *or* solicitud de una de las partes; **the wife applied ex parte for an ouster order against her husband** = la esposa solicitó una orden de desalojo contra su marido; *see also* INTER PARTES (NOTE: in legal reports, abbreviated to **ex p** as in: *Williams v. Smith*, *ex p White* showing that White was the party which applied for the hearing to take place)

expatriate 1 [eks'pætriət] *noun* expatriado, -da; **there is a large expatriate community** *or* **a large community of expatriates in Geneva** = hay una gran comunidad de expatriados en Ginebra **2** [eks'pætrieɪt] *verb* desterrar *or* expatriar
◊ **expatriation** [ekspætri'eɪʃn] *noun* expatriación *f*

expect [ɪk'spekt] *verb* esperar; **we are expecting him to arrive at 10.45** = esperamos que llegue a las 10.45; **they are expecting a cheque from their agent next week** = esperan un cheque de su agente la semana que viene; **the house was sold for more than the expected price** = la casa se vendió a un precio superior al que se esperaba
◊ **expectancy** *or* **expectation** [ɪks'pektənsi *or* ekspel'teɪʃn] *noun* expectación *f or* expectativa *f or* esperanza *f*; **expectation of life** *or* **life expectancy** = esperanza de vida *or* expectativa de vida
◊ **expected** [ɪk'spektɪd] *adjective* previsto, -ta

expenditure [ek'spendɪtʃə] *noun* gasto *m or* desembolso *m;* **capital expenditure** = gastos de capital *or* activo fijo *or* inversiones; **revenue expenditure** = gastos de operación (NOTE: no plural in GB English; US English uses **expenditures**)
◊ **expense** [ɪk'spens] *noun* **(a)** *(money spent)* gasto *m;* **at great expense** = con mucho gasto **(b)** **expense account** = cuenta *f* de gastos de representación
◊ **expenses** [ɪk'spensɪz] *plural noun* gastos *mpl;* **all expenses paid** = con todos los gastos pagados;

allowable expenses = gastos deducibles; **business expenses** = gastos de explotación; **entertainment expenses** = gastos de representación; **fixed expenses** = gastos fijos; **incidental expenses** = gastos imprevistos; **legal expenses** = costas *f* judiciales; **overhead expenses** *or* **general expenses** *or* **running expenses** = gastos generales *or* gastos corrientes; **travelling expenses** = gastos de desplazamiento

experience [ɪk'spɪəriəns] **1** *noun* **(a)** *(years of practice)* experiencia *f;* **he is a lawyer of considerable experience** = es un abogado con mucha experiencia; **she has a lot of experience of dealing with divorce cases** = tiene mucha experiencia en casos de divorcio; **he gained most of his legal experience in the Far East** = adquirió la mayor parte de su experiencia jurídica en el Extremo Oriente **(b)** *(something one has lived through)* experiencia; **the accident was a terrible experience for her** = el accidente fue una experiencia horrible para ella **2** *verb* experimentar *or* sufrir *or* vivir
◊ **experienced** [ɪk'spɪəriənst] *adjective* experimentado, -da *or* experto, -ta; **he is the most experienced negotiator I know** = es el negociador más experto que conozco; **we have appointed a very experienced woman as sales director** = hemos nombrado directora de ventas a una gran experta

expert ['ekspɜːt] *noun* experto, -ta *or* perito, -ta; **an expert in the field of fingerprints** *or* **a fingerprints expert** = un experto en huellas dactilares; **the company asked a financial expert for advice** *or* **asked for expert financial advice** = la compañía pidió consejo a un experto en finanzas; **expert's report** = informe *m* pericial; **expert witness** = perito *m* testigo *or* testigo *m* pericial *or* prueba *f* pericial
◊ **expertise** [ekspɜː'tiːz] *noun* pericia *f or* habilidad *f or* competencia *f;* **we hired Mr Smith because of his financial expertise** *or* **because of his expertise in the African market** = contratamos al Sr. Smith por su competencia financiera *or* por sus conocimientos del mercado africano

expiration [ekspɪ'reɪʃn] *noun* expiración *f or* terminación *f or* vencimiento *m;* **expiration of an insurance policy** = expiración de una póliza de seguros; **to repay before the expiration of the stated period** = pagar antes de que expire el plazo establecido; **on expiration of the lease** = al expirar el arriendo
◊ **expire** [ek'spaɪə] *verb* finalizar *or* expirar *or* terminar *or* caducar *or* vencer; **the lease expires in five years' time** = el arrendamiento expira en cinco años; **his passport has expired** = su pasaporte está caducado; **the deadline expired** = transcurrió el plazo
◊ **expiry** [ek'spaɪri] *noun* expiración *f or* vencimiento *m or* caducidad *f;* **expiry of an**

insurance policy = vencimiento de una póliza de seguros; **expiry date** = fecha *f* de caducidad *or* plazo *m* de vencimiento

explain [ɪk'spleɪn] *verb* explicar; **he explained to the customs officials that the two computers were presents from friends** = explicó a los oficiales de aduanas que los dos ordenadores eran regalos de amigos; **can you explain to the jury how you came to be in the house on Thursday 13th July?** = ¿puede explicar al jurado cómo es que estaba usted en la casa el jueves 13 de julio?
◊ **explanation** [eksplə'neɪʃn] *noun* explicación *f or* aclaración *f;* **the VAT inspector asked for an explanation of the invoices** = el inspector del IVA pidió una aclaración de las facturas; **he could give no explanation of how the drugs came to be in his suitcase** = no supo dar explicación de cómo las drogas habían llegado a su maleta
◊ **explanatory** [ɪk'splænətri] *noun* explicativo, -va *or* aclaratorio, -ria; **read the explanatory notes before filling in the form** = lea las notas aclaratorias antes de rellenar el formulario

explicit [ɪk'splɪsɪt] *adjective* explícito, -ta; **his explicit intention was to leave his house to his wife** = su intención explícita era dejar la casa a su mujer
◊ **explicitly** [ɪk'splɪsɪtli] *adverb* explícitamente; **the contract explicitly prohibits sale of the goods in Europe** = el contrato prohíbe explícitamente la venta de productos en Europa

exploit [ɪk'splɔɪt] *verb* explotar
◊ **exploitation** [eksplɔɪ'teɪʃn] *noun* explotación *f*

explore [ɪk'splɔ:] *verb* explorar *or* examinar *or* investigar; **we are exploring the possibility of opening an office in London** = estamos investigando la posibilidad de abrir una oficina en Londres

explosive [ɪk'spləʊzɪv] **1** *adjective* explosivo, -va; **an explosive device** = un artefacto explosivo **2** *noun* explosivo *m;* **the car was full of explosives** = el coche estaba lleno de explosivos

export 1 ['ekspɔ:t] *noun* exportación *f;* **export licence** = licencia *f* de exportación **2** [ɪk'spɔ:t] *verb* exportar; **most of the company's products are exported to the USA** = la mayoría de los productos de la compañía se exportan a los EE UU

expose [ɪk'spəʊz] *verb* descubrir *or* exponer *or* revelar *or* desenmascarar; **the police investigation exposed corruption in the government** = la investigación policial reveló que había corrupción dentro del gobierno; **he was exposed as the boss of the gang of forgers** = fue desenmascarado como el jefe de la banda de falsificadores
◊ **exposure** [ɪk'spəʊʒə] *noun* denuncia *f or* revelación *f or* descubrimiento *m;* **the report's exposure of corruption in the police force** = la denuncia en el informe sobre la existencia de

corrupción policial; **indecent exposure** = exhibicionismo *m*

ex post facto ['eks 'pəʊst 'fæktəʊ] *Latin phrase* 'con efecto retroactivo'

express [ɪk'spres] **1** *adjective* **(a)** *(fast)* rápido, -da *or* urgente; **express letter** = carta *f* urgente; **express delivery** = entrega *f* urgente *or* envío *m* urgente **(b)** *(clearly shown in words)* expreso, -sa *or* explícito, -ta *or* por escrito; **the contract has an express condition forbidding sale in Africa** = el contrato tiene una prohibición expresa que prohíbe la venta en África; **express term** = término (de un contrato) *m* expreso *or* explícito **2** *verb* **(a)** *(to put into words or diagrams)* expresar; **this chart shows crime in London expressed as a percentage of total crime in the UK** = este gráfico muestra el crimen en Londres expresado como porcentaje del crimen total del Reino Unido **(b)** *(to send very fast)* enviar por transporte *or* correo urgente; **we expressed the order to the customer's warehouse** = enviamos el pedido al almacén del cliente por transporte urgente
◊ **expressly** [ɪk'spresli] *adverb* expresamente *or* explícitamente; **the contract expressly forbids sales to the United States** = según el contrato queda terminantemente prohibido vender a los EE UU; **the franchisee is expressly forbidden to sell goods other than those supplied by the franchisor** = el franquiciado tiene terminantemente prohibida la venta de cualquier otro producto que no le sea directamente suministrado por el franquiciador

expressio unius est exclusio alterius [ɪk'spresiəʊ 'u:niəs est ɪks'klu:ziəʊ ɔ:l'teriəs] *Latin phrase* 'la mención de que algo se incluye implica que otra cosa está expresamente excluida'

expression [ɪk'spreʃn] *noun* expresión *f;* **legal expression** = expresión jurídica

expropriate [ɪk'sprəʊprɪeɪt] *verb* expropiar
◊ **expropriator** [ɪk'sprəʊprɪeɪtə] *noun* expropiador, -ra
◊ **expropriation** [ɪksprəʊprɪ'eɪʃn] *noun* **(a)** *GB* enajenación *f* forzosa *or* confiscación *f* sin indemnización **(b)** *US* expropiación *f (NOTE: the equivalent in the UK is* **compulsory purchase**)

expunge [ɪk'spʌnʒ] *verb* borrar *or* tachar *or* suprimir; **inadmissible hearsay evidence was expunged from the report** = se suprimieron del informe las pruebas basadas en rumores inadmisibles

extend [ɪk'stend] *verb* **(a)** *(to grant)* dar *or* conceder *or* otorgar *or* extender; **to extend credit to a customer** = conceder crédito a un cliente; **to extend a mortgage** = aplazar el vencimiento de una hipoteca **(b)** *(to make longer)* prolongar *or* ampliar *or* prorrogar; **to extend a contract for two years** = prorrogar un contrato por dos años; **the court**

extended the defendant's time for serving his defence by fourteen days = el tribunal concedió una prórroga de catorce días al acusado para ejercer su defensa; he was sentenced to five years imprisonment, extended = le ampliaron la condena a cinco años de prisión; extended credit = crédito a largo plazo; extended family = familia y amigos íntimos; extended sentence = condena ampliada

◊ extension [ɪk'stenʃn] noun (a) (of time, credit) prórroga f or extensión f or prolongación f or ampliación f; to get an extension of credit = conseguir una prórroga del plazo de pago; extension of a contract = prolongación de un contrato; extension of time = prórroga; the defendant applied for an extension of time in which to serve her defence = la acusada solicitó una prórroga para ejercer su defensa (b) (in an office) extensión f (telefónica); can you get me extension 21? - extension 21 is engaged = ¿me puede poner con la extensión 21? - la extensión 21 está comunicando; the legal department is on extension 53 = el departamento jurídico está en la extensión 53

◊ extensive [ɪk'stensɪv] adjective extenso, -sa or extensivo, -va; he has an extensive knowledge of drugs = posee un extenso conocimiento en materia de drogas; she has extensive contacts in the underworld = tiene múltiples contactos en el mundo del hampa

◊ extent [ɪk'stent] noun extensión f; they are assessing the extent of the damage after the fire = están evaluando la extensión de los daños tras el incendio; to a certain extent = hasta cierto punto; he was correct to a certain extent = tenía razón hasta cierto punto; the recommendations of the report were carried out to a certain extent = se llevaron a cabo las recomendaciones del informe hasta cierto punto

extenuating circumstances [ɪk'stenjueɪtɪŋ 'sə:kəmstænsɪz] plural noun circunstancias fpl atenuantes

◊ extenuation [ɪkstenju'eɪʃn] noun atenuante m; in extenuation of something = como atenuante de; counsel pleaded the accused's age in extenuation of his actions = el abogado alegó la edad del acusado como circunstancia atenuante de los hechos

extinction [ɪk'stɪŋkʃn] noun extinción f; the extinction of a legal right = la extinción de un derecho jurídico

extinguishment [ɪks'tɪŋgwɪʃmənt] noun extinción f or prescripción f

extort [ɪk'stɔ:t] verb extorsionar or arrancar or sacar por la fuerza; he extorted £20,000 from local shopkeepers = extorsionó 20.000 libras a los comerciantes locales

◊ extortion [ɪk'stɔ:ʃn] noun extorsión f or concusión f; extortion racket = negocio sucio dedicado a la extorsión

◊ extortionate [ɪk'stɔ:ʃənət] adjective exorbitante or desorbitado, -da; extortionate credit bargain = negocio dedicado al préstamo monetario a interés desorbitado

◊ extortionist [ɪk'stɔ:ʃənɪst] noun extorsionista mf or concusionario, -ria

extra- ['ekstrə] prefix extra-

◊ extra-territoriality ['ekstrəterɪtɔ:ri'ælɪti] noun extraterritorialidad f

extract ['ekstrækt] 1 noun extracto m; the solicitor sent an extract of the deeds = el abogado envió un extracto de las escrituras 2 [ɪk'strækt] verb obtener o sacar información de alguien; the confession was extracted under torture = sacaron la confesión mediante torturas or usaron torturas para sacar la confesión; the magistrate extracted an admission from the witness that he had not seen the accident = el juez consiguió que el testigo admitiera que no había visto el accidente

extradite ['ekstrədaɪt] verb extraditar; he was arrested in France and extradited to stand trial in Germany = le detuvieron en Francia y le extraditaron para ser juzgado en Alemania

◊ extradition [ekstrə'dɪʃn] noun extradición f; the USA requested the extradition of the leader of the drug gang = los EE UU pidieron la extradición del dirigente de la banda de narcotraficantes; extradition treaty = tratado m de extradición

extraordinary [ek'strɔ:dnəri] adjective extraordinario, ria; Extraordinary General Meeting (EGM) = Junta General Extraordinaria; extraordinary items = partidas fpl extraordinarias; the auditors noted several extraordinary items in the accounts = los auditores observaron varias partidas extraordinarias en las cuentas; extraordinary resolution = resolución extraordinaria

COMMENT: notice that an extraordinary resolution will be put to a meeting must be given, but no minimum period is specified by law, as opposed to a 'special resolution' for which 21 days' notice must be given. An extraordinary resolution could be a proposal to wind up a company voluntarily, but changes to the articles of association, such as a change of name, or of the objects of the company, need a special resolution

extremist [ɪk'stri:mɪst] 1 noun (as criticism) extremista mf; the party has been taken over by left-wing extremists = la izquierda extremista domina el partido; the meeting was broken up by extremists from the right of the party = los extremistas del ala derecha del partido interrumpieron la reunión 2 adjective extremista;

the electorate decisively rejected the extremist parties = el electorado rechazó de manera contundente a los partidos extremistas

◊ **extremism** [ɪkˈstriːmɪzm] *noun (as criticism)* extremismo *m*

extrinsic evidence [eksˈtrɪnsɪk ˈevɪdəns] *noun* prueba *f* extrínseca; *compare* INTRINSIC

ex turpi causa non oritur actio [ˈeks tʊəpiː ˈkaʊzə nɒn ˈɒrɪtə ˈæktiəʊ] *Latin phrase* es legalmente imposible hacer cumplir un contrato ilegal

eye witness [ˈaɪ ˈwɪtnəs] *noun* testigo *mf* ocular *or* presencial; **he gave an eye witness account of the bank hold-up** = contó su versión del atraco al banco, como testigo ocular

Ff

F [ef] *sixth letter of the alphabet;* **Class F charge** = adeudo sobre una propiedad registrada a nombre de un cónyuge que reclama el derecho a vivir en la propiedad no siendo dueño de ella; **Schedule F** = división de la tarifa del impuesto sobre la renta referente al impuesto que se debe pagar sobre el rendimiento del capital

face [feɪs] **1** *noun* cara *f or* parte *f* delantera; **face value** = valor *m* nominal **2** *verb* **to face a charge** = hacer frente a *or* afrontar una acusación *or* enfrentarse a unos cargos; **he faces three charges relating to firearms** = se enfrenta a tres cargos relacionados con armas de fuego

facie ['feɪʃi] *see* PRIMA FACIE

facilitate [fə'sɪlɪteɪt] *verb* facilitar

facsimile (copy) [fɒk'sɪmɒli] *noun* facsímil *m*

fact [fækt] *noun* hecho *m or* dato *m or* realidad *f or* información *f;* **the chairman of the tribunal asked to see all the facts on the income tax claim** = el presidente del tribunal quiso examinar con detalle los datos de la reclamación del impuesto sobre la renta; **in fact** *or* **in point of fact** = de hecho *or* en realidad; **matters of fact** = realidades *fpl or* hechos *mpl or* cosas *fpl* probadas; *see also* ACCESSORY
◊ **fact-finding** ['fækt'faɪndɪŋ] *adjective* determinación de los hechos; **a fact-finding delegation** = una delegación *or* misión de investigación

faction ['fækʃn] *noun* facción *f*

facto ['fæktəʊ] *see* DE FACTO, IPSO FACTO

factor ['fæktə] *noun* **(a)** *(thing which is important or relevant)* factor *m or* elemento *m or* coeficiente *m;* **the rise in unemployment is an important factor in the increased crime rate** = el aumento del paro es un factor importante en el reciente índice de criminalidad; **cyclical factors** = factores cíclicos; **contributory factor** = factor contribuyente; **deciding factor** = factor decisivo; **factors of production** = factores de producción **(b)** *(person or company)* agente de ventas; **debt factor** = factor *or* agente comprador de deudas
◊ **factoring** ['fæktrɪŋ] *noun* gestión *f* de deudas con descuento

factory ['fæktri] *noun* fábrica *f*

faculty ['fækʌlti] *noun* facultad *f or* autorización *f*
◊ **Faculty of Advocates** ['fækʌlti ɒv 'ædvɒkəts] *noun* Colegio de Abogados de Escocia

fail [feɪl] *verb* **(a)** *(not succeed)* fallar *or* fracasar; *(not to do something)* dejar de; **fail to fulfill** = incumplir; **he failed to appear at the probation office** = no se presentó en la oficina de control de personas en libertad condicional; **counsel failed to persuade the jury that his client was innocent** = el abogado no consiguió convencer al jurado de la inocencia de su cliente **(b)** *(to be unsuccessful in business)* quebrar; **the company failed** = la compañía quebró
◊ **failing** ['feɪlɪŋ] **1** *noun* defecto *m or* punto *m* flaco *or* debilidad *f;* **the chairman has one failing - he goes to sleep at boardmeetings** = el presidente tiene un defecto - se duerme en las reuniones del consejo de administración **2** *preposition* a falta de *or* salvo; **failing instructions to the contrary** = salvo instrucciones *or* órdenes al contrario; **failing prompt payment** = salvo pronto pago; **failing that** = en su defecto *or* si eso no funciona *or* no da resultado; **try the company secretary, and failing that the chairman** = prueba con la secretaria de la empresa y, si no da resultado, con el presidente
◊ **failure** ['feɪljə] *noun* **(a)** *(breaking down)* fracaso *m or* interrupción *f;* **the failure of the negotiations** = la interrupción de las negociaciones **(b)** *(not doing something which should be done)* fallo *m or* incumplimiento *m;* **his failure to comply with the court order** = su incumplimiento de la orden judicial; **their failure to meet the deadline** = su incumplimiento de respetar el plazo fijado; **her failure to pay a bill** = su incumplimiento en el pago de una factura **(c)** *(bankruptcy)* quiebra *f;* **commercial failure** = quiebra comercial; **he lost all his money in the bank failure** = perdió todo el dinero en la quiebra bancaria

fair [feə] **1** *noun* **trade fair** = feria *f* comercial **2** *adjective* **(a)** *(honest, correct)* justo, -ta *or* equitativo, -va *or* leal; **fair comment** = comentario *m* acertado *or* oportuno; **fair deal** = trato justo; **fair price** = precio *m* razonable *or* precio justo; **fair rent** = alquiler justo; **fair retribution** = castigo justo; **fair trade** = comercio justo *or* sistema de comercio con reciprocidad arancelaria; *US* = RESALE PRICE MAINTENANCE; **fair trading** *or* **fair**

dealing = prácticas comerciales leales *or* justas; *GB* **Office of Fair Trading** = Oficina *f* de Protección al Consumidor; **fair trial** = juicio imparcial; **fair use** = uso debido de citas; **fair value** *or US* **fair market value** = valor justo de venta *or* de mercado; **fair wear and tear** = desgaste natural; **the insurance policy covers most damage, but not fair wear and tear to the machine** = la póliza de seguros cubre la mayoría de los daños a excepción del desgaste natural de la máquina **(b)** *(clean)* **fair copy** = copia *f* en limpio; **fair play** = juego limpio

faith [feɪθ] *noun* fe *f or* confianza *f;* **to have faith in something** *or* **someone** = tener fe *or* confianza en algo *or* en alguien *or* fiarse de; **in good faith** = de buena fe; **he acted in good faith** *or* **in bad faith** = actuó de buena fe *or* de mala fe; **to buy something in good faith** = comprar algo de buena fe; **he bought the car in good faith, not knowing it had been stolen** = compró el coche de buena fe, sin saber que había sido robado

◊ **faithful** ['feɪθful] *adjective* leal

◊ **faithfully** ['feɪθfəli] *adverb (ending a letter)* **yours faithfully** = le saluda atentamente

fake [feɪk] **1** *noun* falsificación *f;* **the shipment came with fake documentation** = el envío llegó con documentación falsa **2** *verb* falsificar *or* simular; **they faked a break-in to make the police believe the documents had been stolen** = simularon una entrada forzada para que la policía creyera que habían robado los documentos

fall [fɔːl] **1** *noun* caída *f;* **sharp fall** = caída repentina **2** *verb* caer; **the national holiday falls on a Monday** = la fiesta nacional cae en lunes; **the bill fell due** = la letra venció; **to fall outside** = caer fuera *or* salirse de; **the case falls outside the jurisdiction of the court** = el caso se sale de la jurisdicción de la audiencia; **to fall within** = entrar dentro; **the newspaper report falls within the category of defamation** = el artículo periodístico entra dentro de la categoría de difamación

fallacious [fəˈleɪʃəs] *adjective* falaz

false [fɒls] *adjective* falso, -sa *or* falseado, -da *or* erróneo, -a; **to make a false entry in the record** = hacer una entrada falsa en el registro; **false accounting** = contabilidad *f* ficticia *or* falseada; **false imprisonment** = retención *f or* detención *f* ilegal o injustificada; **false information** = tergiversación *f* de los hechos; **to give false information** = tergiversar los hechos; **false pretence(s)** *or US* **false pretense** = estafa *f* por medios fraudulentos *or* con engaño; **he was sent to prison for obtaining money by false pretences** = fue encarcelado por estafar dinero; **false representation** = declaración *f* falsa; **false weight** = peso *m* trucado *or* peso falso *or* balanza *f* trucada

◊ **falsehood** ['fɒlshud] *noun* falsedad *f or* mentira *f;* **injurious falsehood** *or* **malicious falsehood** = mentira maliciosa *or* injuriosa

◊ **falsify** ['fɒlsɪfaɪ] *verb* falsificar *or* adulterar; **to falsify accounts** = falsificar cuentas; **to falsify evidence** = adulterar pruebas

◊ **falsification** [fɒlsɪfɪˈkeɪʃn] *noun* falsificación *f;* **falsification of accounts** = falsificación *f* de cuentas

family ['fæmli] *noun* **(a)** *(relations)* familia *f;* **extended family** = parientes lejanos y amigos íntimos; **family company** = empresa *f* familiar; **Family Division** = Sala del Tribunal Supremo encargada de Asuntos de la Familia; **family law** = derecho *m* de familia **(b)** *(slang)* la familia (nombre utilizado para designar a un grupo de gánsters pertenecientes a la Mafia y gobernados por un padrino)

fatal ['feɪtl] *adjective* mortal *or* fatal; **he took a fatal dose of drugs** = tomó una dosis mortal de drogas; **there were six fatal accidents in the first week of the year** = durante la primera semana del año hubo seis accidentes mortales

Father of the House ['fɑːðə əv ðə 'haus] *noun GB* el diputado más veterano de la Cámara de los Comunes

fault [fɔːlt] *noun* **(a)** *(blame)* culpa *f or* falta *f;* **the witness said the accident was the fault of defective machinery** = el testigo dijo que el accidente se debió al estado defectuoso de la maquinaria; **was it the fault of the police if the protest march developed into a riot?** = ¿Tuvo la culpa la policía de que la manifestación acabara en disturbios públicos? **(b)** *(defect)* defecto *m or* avería *f or* imperfección *f;* **the technical staff are trying to correct a fault in the computer** = el personal del servicio técnico está intentando corregir un defecto en el ordenador; **we think there is a basic fault in the construction of the product** = creemos que existe un defecto de base en la elaboración del producto

◊ **faulty** ['fɔːlti] *adjective* defectuoso, -sa *or* imperfecto, ta; **the accident was caused by faulty brakes** *or* **by faulty repairs to the brakes** = la causa del accidente fue un defecto en los frenos *or* una reparación defectuosa de los frenos

favour *or US* **favor** ['feɪvə] **1** *noun* favor *m* **(a)** **as a favour** = como favor *or* como un favor especial; **he asked the secretary for a loan as a favour** = le pidió a la secretaria un préstamo como favor especial **(b) in favour of** = a favor de; **most of the workers are in favour of shorter working hours** = la mayoría de los trabajadores está a favor de una jornada laboral más corta; **six members of the cabinet are in favour of the proposal, and three are against it** = seis miembros del gabinete están a favor de la propuesta y tres en contra **2** *verb* estar a favor de *or* apoyar; **judges favour deterrent sentences for hooligans** = los jueces están a favor de las sentencias disuasorias para los gamberros

◊ **favourable** ['feɪvrəbl] *adjective* favorable; **to buy on favourable terms** = comprar algo en condiciones favorables

FBI ['ef 'bi: 'eɪ] = FEDERAL BUREAU OF INVESTIGATION

fear ['fɪə] *noun* miedo *m or* temor *m;* **unconquerable fear** = miedo insuperable

feasant [fi:zənt] *see* DAMAGE FEASANT

feasible ['fi:zəbl] *adjective* factible
◊ **feasibility** [fi:zə'bɪlɪti] *noun* viabilidad *f;* **feasibility study** *or* **feasibility report** = estudio *m* de viabilidad; **the council asked the planning department to comment on the feasibility of the project** = el ayuntamiento pidió al departamento de urbanismo que hiciera comentarios sobre la viabilidad del proyecto; **the department has produced a feasibility report on the development project** = el departamento ha elaborado un estudio de viabilidad sobre el proyecto de desarrollo

federal ['fedrl] *adjective* federal; **federal court** *or* **federal laws** = tribunal federal *or* leyes federales
◊ **Federal Bureau of Investigation (FBI)** ['fedrl 'bjuərəu əv ɪnvestɪ'geɪʃn] *noun* Oficina Federal de Investigación (FBI)
◊ **federalism** ['fedrəlɪzm] *noun* federalismo *m*
◊ **federation** [fedə'reɪʃn] *noun* federación *f*

fee [fi:] *noun* **(a)** *(for services)* honorarios *mpl or* emolumentos *mpl or* comisión *f or* minuta *f;* **scale of fees** = arancel de honorarios; **we charge a small fee for our services** = cobramos unos pequeños honorarios por nuestros servicios; **a barrister's fees** = los honorarios de un abogado; *US* **contingent fee** = honorarios *mpl* condicionales **(b)** *(money paid for something)* tasa *f or* cuota *f;* **entrance fee** *or* **admission fee** = entrada *f;* **registration fee** = matrícula *f or* derechos *mpl* de matrícula *or* de inscripción **(c)** *(ownership of land)* **fee simple** = propiedad *f* absoluta de un inmueble *or* dominio *m* simple; **to hold an estate in fee simple** = tener la propiedad absoluta de un inmueble; **fee tail** = vínculo *m or* dominio limitado a herederos directos; *see also* ENTAIL

feed [fi:d] **1** *noun* alimentación *f;* **continuous feed** = alimentación de papel continuo; **sheet feed** = alimentación de hojas sueltas **2** *verb (computer)* introducir información en un ordenador *or* alimentar (NOTE: **feeding - fed - has fed**)

feel [fi:l] *verb* sentir *or* sentirse; **to feel uncomfortable** *or* **embarrased** = sentirse molesto

felony ['feləni] *noun (formerly)* delito grave *or* conducta criminal; **to commit a felony** = cometer un delito grave (NOTE: still used in **treason felony**)
◊ **felonious** [fə'ləuniəs] *adjective* criminal *or* delictivo, -va; **he carried out a felonious act** = llevó a cabo una acción criminal

feme covert ['fæm 'kəuvət] *French phrase meaning* 'mujer casada'
◊ **feme sole** ['fæm 'səul] *French phrase meaning* mujer no casada

fence [fens] **1** *noun (informal)* encubridor, -ra *or* receptor, -ra de objetos robados **2** *verb* traficar con objetos robados

feud [fju:d] *noun* enemistad *f* (entre familias)

fiat ['fi:æt] *noun* **(a)** fiat *m or* autorización *f* **(b)** **fiat money** = moneda *f* fiduciaria *or* de curso forzoso
◊ **fiat justicia** ['fi:æt dʒʌs'tɪsiə] *Latin phrase* 'que se haga justicia'

fiction ['fɪkʃn] *noun* ficción *f;* **fiction of law** *or* **legal fiction** = ficción *f* de derecho *or* legal
◊ **fictitious** [fɪk'tɪʃəs] *adjective* ficticio, -cia; **fictitious assets** = activo *m* ficticio

fiddle ['fɪdl] **1** *noun (informal)* trampa *f or* timo *m or* chanchullo *m;* **it's all a fiddle** = no es más que un timo; **he's on the fiddle** = hace trampa **2** *verb (informal)* embaucar *or* amañar *or* falsificar *or* falsear; **he tried to fiddle his tax returns** = intentó amañar su declaración de la renta; **the salesman was caught fiddling his expense account** = sorprendieron al vendedor amañando su cuenta de gastos

fide ['faɪdi:] *see* BONA FIDE

fiduciary [fɪ'dju:ʃiəri] *adjective* & *noun* fiduciario, -ria; **a company director owes a fiduciary duty to the company** = un director de empresa tiene una obligación fiduciaria para con la compañía; **he was acting in a fiduciary capacity** = actuaba de fideicomisario *or* de administrador

fieri facias ['faɪraɪ 'feɪʃiæs] *Latin phrase* 'haz que ocurra'; **writ of fieri facias** = auto *m* ordenando una ejecución (NOTE: often abbreviated to **fi. fa.**)

fi. fa. *see* FIERI FACIAS

FIFO = FIRST IN FIRST OUT

Fifth Amendment ['fɪfθ ə'mendmənt] *noun US* Quinta Enmienda *f* de la Constitución de los EE UU (según la cual nadie puede ser obligado a declarar en perjuicio propio); **to plead** *or* **to take the Fifth Amendment** = negarse a declarar para no ser inculpado

figure ['fɪgə] *noun* **(a)** *(number)* cifra *f or* cantidad *f;* **he put a very low figure on the value of the lease** = calculó muy por debajo *or* infravaloró el valor del arrendamiento **(b)** *(written numbers)* **figures** = cifras *fpl or* números *mpl;* **sales figures** = cifras de ventas; **to work out the figures** = calcular; **his income from protection rackets runs into five figures** *or* **he has a five-figure income from protection rackets** = recibe ingresos superiores a las 10.000 libras de chantajes; **in round figures** = en números redondos; **the number of prisoners in jail is 45,000 in round figures** = el número de presos encarcelados es de 45.000 en números redondos **(c)** *(results)* **figures** = cifras (de producción) *or* resultados *mpl;* **the figures for last year** *or* **last year's figures** = las cifras de producción del año pasado

file [faɪl] **1** *noun* **(a)** *(cardboard holder for documents)* carpeta *f or* fichero *m or* archivador *m;* **put these letters in the unsolved cases file** = coloca estas cartas en la carpeta de los casos sin resolver; **look in the file marked 'Scottish police forces'** = mire en la carpeta que dice 'fuerzas de policía escocesa'; **box file** = caja archivadora *or* archivo *m or* archivador **(b)** *(documents kept for reference)* expediente *m or* archivo; **police file** = ficha policial; **the police keep a file of missing vehicles** = la policía guarda un archivo de vehículos desaparecidos; **look up her description in the missing persons' file** = busca su descripción en el archivo de personas desaparecidas; **to place something on file** = archivar algo; **to keep someone's name on file** = archivar el nombre de alguien; **file copy** = copia *f* de archivo; **card file** = fichero *m or* ficha *f;* **computer file** = archivo *or* ficha de ordenador **(c)** *(data on computer)* archivo *or* fichero; **how can we protect our computer files?** = ¿Cómo podemos proteger nuestros archivos del ordenador? **(d)** **rank and file** = base *f or* militantes de un partido **2** *verb* **(a)** *(to put in order)* **to file documents** = archivar *or* clasificar documentos; **the correspondence is filed under 'complaints'** = la correspondencia se archiva en la carpeta de 'reclamaciones' **(b)** *(to make an official report)* elevar *or* interponer; **to file a petition** = presentar una demanda *or* una petición; **to file a petition in bankruptcy** = presentar una declaración de quiebra *or* declararse en quiebra; **to file a motion** *or* **a claim** = elevar un recurso *or* una reclamación; **to file an appeal** = interponer un recurso de apelación **(c)** *(to send a document to court)* presentar un documento en un juzgado; **to file for divorce** = entablar demanda de divorcio; **the defence must be filed and served in seven days** = la defensa debe presentarse en el juzgado y notificarse a la otra parte en un plazo de siete días **(d)** *(to register something officially)* cursar *or* hacer una petición oficial *or* presentar oficialmente; **to file an application for a patent** = presentar la solicitud de una patente; **to file a return to the tax office** = presentar una declaración a la Delegación de Hacienda

◊ **filing** ['faɪlɪŋ] *noun* **(a)** *(to court)* presentación *f* de un documento en un juzgado; **date of filing** = fecha de presentación **(b)** *(put in order)* documentos *mpl* por archivar; **there is a lot of filing to do at the end of the week** = al finalizar la semana hay que archivar un montón de documentos; **the manager looked through the week's filing to see what letters had been sent** = el director hojeó los documentos archivados

durante la semana para ver qué cartas se habían enviado; **filing basket** *or* **filing tray** = bandeja *f* para documentos; **filing cabinet** = archivador *m or* fichero *m;* **filing card** = ficha *f;* **filing clerk** = archivero, -ra; **filing system** = sistema *m* de archivo *or* clasificación

filibuster ['fɪlɪbʌstə] *noun* obstrucción *f* del trabajo parlamentario mediante intervenciones largas; **the Democrats organized a filibuster in the Senate** = los Demócratas intervinieron en el Senado con el fin de causar obstrucción

◊ **filibustering** ['fɪlɪbʌstərɪŋ] *noun* filibusterismo *m or* causar obstrucciones en una sesión parlamentaria

COMMENT: filibusters are possible in the US Senate, because the rules of the Senate allow unlimited debate. A filibuster may be ended by a cloture motion; the technique is also used in the UK (see also TALK OUT)

final ['faɪnl] *adjective* último, -ma *or* final *or* definitivo,-va; **to pay the final instalment** = pagar el último plazo; **to make the final payment** = efectuar el último pago; **to put the final details on a document** = dar los últimos toques a un documento; **final date for payment** = fecha *f* de vencimiento (de pago); **final demand** = última notificación de pago *or* demanda final; **final discharge** = reembolso *m* final; **final dividend** = dividendo *m* final; **final judgment** = sentencia definitiva *or* firme *or* final

◊ **finally** ['faɪnli] *adverb* finalmente *or* por último *or* por fin; **the contract was finally signed yesterday** = el contrato se firmó finalmente ayer; **after ten hours of discussions, the House of Commons finally rose at two o'clock in the morning** = tras diez horas de debate, la Cámara de los Comunes finalmente levantó la sesión a las dos en punto de la madrugada

finance 1 ['faɪnæns] *noun* **(a)** *(money used by a company)* finanzas *fpl or* fondos *mpl or* recursos *mpl;* **finance charge** = costes financieros; **financial intermediary** = agente de finanzas *or* sociedad financiera; **to make financial provision for someone** = asegurarse que alguien tenga suficientes medios económicos para vivir; **Financial Secretary to the Treasury** = ministro de Hacienda; *see also* CHIEF SECRETARY; **financial statement** = balance general *or* estado de cuentas; **where will the authority find the finance to pay the higher salaries?** = ¿Dónde conseguirán las autoridades fondos para pagar el aumento de salarios *or* los salarios más altos?; **he is the secretary of the local authority finance committee** = es el secretario de la comisión de finanzas del Ayuntamiento; **Finance Act** = Ley *f* de Finanzas **2** [faɪˈnæns] *verb* financiar; **the new building must be financed by the local authority** = el nuevo edificio debe ser financiado por el

Ayuntamiento; **a government-financed programme of prison construction** = un programa de construcción de prisiones financiado por el gobierno

◊ **financial** [faɪ'nænʃl] *adjective* financiero, -ra; **he has a financial interest in the company** = tiene un interés financiero por la compañía; **financial assistance** = ayuda financiera; **she receives financial assistance from the local authority** = recibe ayuda financiera del Ayuntamiento; **financial institution** = institución financiera; **to make financial provision for someone** = atender a las necesidades financieras de alguien; **financial rating** = categoría financiera; **financial resources** = medios económicos *or* medios de vida; **financial statement** = estado financiero

◊ **financially** [faɪ'nænʃli] *adverb* financieramente; **he is financially involved in the property company** = está metido financieramente en la empresa inmobiliaria; **the company is financially very strong** = financieramente, la empresa es muy fuerte *or* sólida

COMMENT: in most countries, the government department dealing with finance is called the Finance Ministry, with a Finance Minister in charge. Both in the UK and the USA, the department is called the Treasury, and the minister in charge is the Chancellor of the Exchequer in the UK, and the Treasury Secretary in the USA

find [faɪnd] *verb* **(a)** *(something which was not there before)* encontrar *or* hallar *or* dar con algo; **to find backing for a project** = encontrar apoyo para un proyecto; **to find guilty** = hallar culpable; **to find out** = averiguar *or* enterarse **(b)** *(reach a legal decision)* declarar *or* emitir un fallo jurídico *or* fallar; **the tribunal found that both parties were at fault** = el tribunal declaró culpables a las dos partes; **the court found the accused guilty on all charges** = el tribunal declaró al acusado culpable de todos los cargos; **the judge found for the defendant** = el juez falló a favor del acusado (NOTE: finding - found)

◊ **finder's fee** ['faɪndəz 'fiː] *noun* comisión *f*

◊ **findings** ['faɪndɪŋz] *plural noun* fallo *m or* decisión *f or* conclusiones *fpl;* **the findings of a commission of enquiry** = las conclusiones de una comisión investigadora

fine [faɪn] **1** *noun* multa *f;* **the court sentenced him to pay a £25,000 fine** = el tribunal le condenó a pagar 25.000 libras de multa; **we had to pay a £10 parking fine** = tuvimos que pagar una multa de 10 libras por aparcamiento indebido; **the sentence for dangerous driving is a £1,000 fine or two months in prison** = la condena por conducir con imprudencia temeraria consiste en una multa de 1.000 libras o dos meses de arresto **2** *verb* multar; **to fine someone £2,500 for obtaining money by**

false pretences = multar a alguien con 2.500 libras por estafar dinero

fingerprint ['fɪŋgəprɪnt] **1** *noun* huella *f* dactilar *or* impresión *f* digital; **they found his fingerprints on the murder weapon** = encontraron sus huellas dactilares en el arma homicida; **the court heard evidence from a fingerprint expert** = el tribunal oyó el testimonio presentado por un experto en huellas dactilares; **to take someone's fingerprints** = tomar las huellas dactilares a alguien **2** *verb* tomar las huellas dactilares; **the police fingerprinted the suspect after charging him** = la policía tomó las huellas dactilares al sospechoso después de haberle expuesto los cargos

finish ['fɪnɪʃ] *verb* terminar

fire ['faɪə] **1** *noun* **(a)** *(which burns)* fuego *m or* incendio *m;* **the shipment was damaged in the fire on board the cargo boat** = el envío resultó dañado en el incendio que se declaró a bordo del carguero; **half the stock was destroyed in the warehouse fire** = la mitad de las existencias quedaron destruidas en el incendio del almacén; **to catch fire** = incendiarse *or* prenderse; **the papers in the waste paper basket caught fire** = los papeles de la papelera se incendiaron; **to set fire** = prender fuego; **fire certificate** = certificación *f* municipal de que un edificio está debidamente protegido contra incendios; **fire damage** = daños *mpl* por incendio; **he claimed £250 for fire damage** = reclamó 250 libras en concepto de daños por incendio; **fire-damaged goods** = artículos dañados en un incendio; **fire door** = puerta *f* de incendios *or* de emergencia; **fire escape** = escalera *f* de incendios *or* salida *f* de emergencia; **fire hazard** *or* **fire risk** = peligro *m or* riesgo *m* de incendio; **that warehouse full of paper is a fire hazard** = ese almacén lleno de papel es un peligro en caso de incendio; **fire insurance** = seguro *m* contra incendios; **fire regulations** = regulaciones *fpl* en materia de incendios **(b)** *(act of shooting)* fuego *m or* disparo *m;* **cease-fire** = alto el fuego; **the police opened fire on the crowd** = la policía abrió fuego contra la multitud **2** *verb* **(a)** *(to shoot)* disparar; **he fired two shots at the crowd** = disparó dos tiros a la multitud **(b)** *(to dismiss)* **to fire someone** = despedir a alguien; **the new managing director fired half the sales force** = el nuevo director gerente despidió a la mitad del personal de ventas

◊ **firearm** ['faɪɑːm] *noun* arma *f* de fuego; **firearms certificate** = licencia *f* de armas

◊ **fireproof** ['faɪəpruːf] *adjective* ininflamable *or* incombustible *or* a prueba de incendios; **we packed the papers in a fireproof safe** = guardamos los papeles en una caja a prueba de incendios; **it is impossible to make the office completely fireproof** = es imposible conseguir que la oficina esté completamente a prueba de incendios

◊ **fire-raiser** ['faɪəreɪzə] *noun* incendiario, -ria

◊ **fire-raising** ['faɪəreɪzɪŋ] *noun* incendio *m* premeditado *or* intencionado; *see also* ARSON, ARSONIST

◊ **firing squad** ['faɪrɪŋ 'skwɒd] *noun* pelotón *m* de fusilamiento *or* de ejecución

firm [fəːm] **1** *noun* empresa *f or* firma *f or* compañía *f;* **he is a partner in a law firm** = es socio de un bufete de abogados; **a firm of accountants** = una firma de auditores *or* asesores contables; **an important publishing firm** = una empresa editorial importante (NOTE: firm is often used when referring to incorporated companies, but this is not correct) **2** *adjective* **(a)** *(definitive)* firme *or* en firme *or* sólido, -da; **to make a firm offer for something** = hacer una oferta en firme; **to place a firm offer for two aircraft** = hacer una oferta en firme por dos aviones; **they are quoting a firm price of £1.22 per case** = están cotizando un precio en firme de 1,22 libras por caja **(b)** *(with no tendency to fall in price)* estable *or* firme; **the pound was firmer on the foreign exchange markets** = la libra se mostró más firme en los mercados de divisa extranjera; **shares remained firm** = las acciones se mantuvieron firmes **3** *verb* afirmar(se) *or* consolidar(se); **the shares firmed at £1.50** = las acciones se consolidaron a 1,50 libras

◊ **firmness** ['fəːmnəs] *noun* firmeza *f or* estabilidad *f;* **the firmness of the pound** = la estabilidad de la libra

first [fəːst] *noun* primero, -ra; **our company was one of the first to sell into the European market** = nuestra empresa fue una de las primeras en introducirse en el mercado europeo; **first quarter** = primer trimestre del año; **first half** *or* **first half-year** = primer semestre; **case of first impression** = caso *m* sin precedentes; **first offence** = primer delito; **first offender** = delincuente *mf* sin antecedentes penales; **First Reading** = primera lectura de un proyecto de ley en el Parlamento

◊ **first-class** ['fəːst'klɑːs] *adjective & noun* **(a)** *(top quality)* de primera clase *or* excelente *or* sobresaliente; **he is a first-class accountant** = es un contable excelente; **to travel first-class** = viajar en primera clase; **first-class travel provides the best service** = los viajes en primera clase ofrecen el mejor servicio; **a first-class ticket** = un billete de primera clase; **to stay in first-class hotels** = alojarse en hoteles de primera categoría; **first-class mail** = *GB* correo de primera clase *or US* servicio de correos para cartas y postales; **a first-class letter should get to Scotland in a day** = una carta de primera clase debería llegar a Escocia en un día

◊ **first degree murder** ['fəːst d'griː 'məːdə] *noun US* homicidio *m* premeditado

◊ **first in first out (FIFO)** ['fəːst ɪn 'fəːst aut] *phrase* **(a)** *(accounting policy)* política contable según la cual las existencias se valoran al precio de las adquisiciones más antiguas *or* método de valoración de existencias apoyado en el principio

'primero en entrar, primero en salir' **(b)** *(redundancy policy)* política de despido según la cual las personas que llevan más tiempo trabajando son las primeras en ser despedidas

◊ **first instance** ['fəːst 'ɪnstəns] *noun* **court of first instance** = tribunal *m* de primera instancia

fiscal ['fɪskl] *adjective* fiscal; **the government's fiscal policies** = la política *f* fiscal del gobierno; **fiscal measures** = medidas *fpl* fiscales; **fiscal year** = año *m* fiscal *or* ejercicio *m* económico; **Procurator Fiscal** = Fiscal Procurador de Escocia que decide si un presunto criminal debe ser procesado

fit [fɪt] *adjective* apto, -ta *or* capacitado, -da; **the solicitor stated that his client was not fit to plead** = el abogado declaró que su cliente no estaba capacitado para declararse culpable *or* inocente

◊ **fitness** ['fɪtnəs] *noun* aptitud *f;* **fitness for purpose** = aptitud *or* adecuación *f* a la finalidad que poseen

◊ **fittings** ['fɪtɪŋz] *see* FIXTURE

fix [fɪks] *verb* **(a)** *(to arrange or to agree)* fijar; **to fix a budget** = fijar un presupuesto; **to fix a meeting for 3 p.m.** = fijar una reunión para las 3 de la tarde; **the date of the hearing has still to be fixed** = la fecha de la vista todavía está por fijar; **the price of gold was fixed at $300** = el precio del oro se fijó en 300 dólares; **the punishment for drug offences has been fixed by Parliament** = la pena por delitos relacionados con drogas ha sido fijada por el Parlamento **(b)** *(to mend)* arreglar *or* reparar; **the maintenance staff are coming to fix the telephone** = el servicio de mantenimiento vendrá a arreglar el teléfono; **can you fix the copying machine?** = ¿puedes arreglar la fotocopiadora?

◊ **fixed** [fɪkst] *adjective* **(a)** *(permanent)* fijo, -ja; **fixed assets** = activo *m* fijo; **fixed capital** = capital *m* fijo; **fixed charge** = precio *or* coste fijo; *see also* FLOATING CHARGE; **fixed costs** = costes fijos; *(court case)* cantidad establecida de dinero a que tiene derecho un demandante en procedimientos legales (opuesto a costes sujetos a impuesto); **fixed deposit** = depósito *m* a plazo fijo; **fixed expenses** = gastos *mpl* fijos; **fixed income** = renta *f* fija; **fixed-interest investments** = inversiones *mpl* de renta fija; **fixed-price agreement** = acuerdo *m or* contrato *m* a tanto alzado; **fixed scale of charges** = escala *f* fija de precios; **fixed term** = plazo *m* fijo **(b)** **no fixed abode** = paradero *m* desconocido *or* sin residencia *f* fija

◊ **fixing** ['fɪksɪŋ] *noun* **(a)** *(arranging)* fijación *f;* **fixing of charges** = fijación de precios *or* tarifas; **fixing of a mortgage rate** = fijación del interés de una hipoteca **(b)** **price fixing** = fijación *f or* ajuste *m* de los precios **(c)** **the London gold fixing** = precio del día en el mercado londinense del oro

◊ **fixture** ['fɪkstʃə] *noun* objeto *m* de instalación fija en una propiedad (p.ej. el lavabo); **fixtures and fittings** = instalaciones *fpl* fijas y accesorios;

furniture and fixtures = muebles y enseres; *see also* TRADE FIXTURES

flag [flæg] **1** *noun* bandera *f or* pabellón *m;* **flag of convenience** = pabellón de conveniencia *or* registro *m* de buques en naciones extranjeras; **to fly a flag** = enarbolar una bandera; **ship flying the British flag** = embarcación de bandera británica; **ship flying a flag of convenience** = embarcación que navega con pabellón de conveniencia **2** *verb* **(a) to flag a ship** = registrar un buque **(b)** *(in computing or documents)* remarcar *or* señalar; **the committee clerk flagged all the references to building repairs** = el funcionario del comité remarcó todas las referencias a las obras de reparación

flagrant ['fleigrənt] *adjective* flagrante *or* claro *or* evidente; **a flagrant case of contempt of court** = un caso flagrante de desacato a los tribunales; **a flagrant violation of human rights** = una violación flagrante de los derechos humanos
◊ **flagrante** [flə'grænti] *see* IN FLAGRANTE DELICTO

flat [flæt] **1** *adjective* **(a)** *(not moving because of low demand)* inactivo, -va *or* átono, -na; **the market was flat today** = la bolsa estuvo inactiva hoy **(b)** *(not changing)* uniforme *or* fijo, -ja; **flat rate** = porcentaje *m* fijo *or* cuota *f* fija *or* tanto *m* alzado; **we pay a flat rate for electricity each quarter** = pagamos una cantidad fija por la electricidad cada trimestre; **he is paid a flat rate of £2 per thousand** = le pagan un tanto alzado de 2 libras por mil **2** *noun* piso *m;* **he has a flat in the centre of town** = tiene un piso en el centro de la ciudad; **she is buying a flat close to her office** = va a comprar un piso cerca de su oficina; **company flat** = piso de la empresa (NOTE: US English is **apartment)**

floating charge ['fləutiŋ 'tʃɑːdʒ] *noun* costes *mpl* circulantes *or* flotantes

flotsam ['flɒtsəm] *noun* restos *mpl* flotantes de un naufragio

floating voter ['fləutiŋ 'vəutə] *noun* votante indeciso *or* volátil; **the floating vote** = voto de los votantes indecisos; **the Opposition is trying to capture the bulk of the floating vote** = la oposición está tratando de captar la mayor parte de los votos indecisos

floor [flɔː] *noun* **(a)** *(in a building)* suelo *m or* piso *m* **(b)** *(parliament)* **the floor of the House** = hemiciclo *m or* la sala *f* del congreso; **debates on the floor of the House are often lively** = los debates en la sala del congreso suelen ser animados; **floor manager** = presidente de la comisión responsable de que un proyecto de ley sea aprobado NOTE: in the UK, 'floor' is usually taken to refer to the backbenchers: **the feeling on the floor of the House was that the Minister should resign (c)** *(stock exchange)* corro *m or* parqué *m*

flout [flaut] *verb* quebrantar *or* incumplir; **by selling alcohol to minors, the shop is deliberately flouting the law** = la tienda está deliberadamente quebrantando la ley al vender alcohol a menores

f.o.b. ['ef 'əu 'biː] = FREE ON BOARD

Foggy Bottom ['fɒgi 'bɒtəm] *noun US (informal)* Departamento de Estado

follow ['fɒləu] *verb* seguir *or* actuar de acuerdo con; **the court has followed the precedent set in the 1972 case** = los tribunales han actuado de acuerdo con el precedente establecido en el caso de 1972
◊ **follow up** ['fɒləu 'ʌp] *verb* seguir *or* profundizar *or* estudiar; **the police are following up several leads** = la policía está siguiendo varias pistas; **to follow up an initiative** = desarrollar una iniciativa

foolscap ['fuːlzkæp] *noun* papel *m* tamaño folio; **the letter was on six sheets of foolscap** = la carta estaba escrita en seis folios; **a foolscap envelope** = sobre *m* tamaño folio

footprint ['futprint] *noun* huella *f* (de pisada)

forbear [fɔː'beə] *verb* abstenerse de algo; **to forbear from doing something** = abstenerse de hacer algo; **he forbore from taking any further action** = se abstuvo de emprender otra acción judicial (NOTE: **forbearing - forbore - has forborne)**
◊ **forbearance** [fɔː'beərəns] *noun* abstención *f*

forbid [fə'bid] *verb* prohibir; **the contract forbids sale of the goods to the USA** = el contrato prohíbe la venta de los productos a los EE UU; **the staff are forbidden to use the front entrance** = los empleados tienen prohibido el uso de la entrada principal; **the judge forbade any reference to the defendant in the media** = el juez prohibió cualquier alusión al acusado en los medios de comunicación (NOTE: **forbidding - forbade - has forbidden)**

force [fɔːs] **1** *noun* **(a)** *(strength)* fuerza *f or* vigor *m;* **force of law** = fuerza legal *or* de ley; **to be in force** = estar en vigor *or* estar vigente *or* regir; **the rules have been in force since 1946** = el reglamento está en vigor desde 1945; **to come into force** = entrar en vigor; **the new regulations will come into force on January 1st** = las nuevas normas entrarán en vigor el 1 de enero; **the new regulations have the force of law** = las nuevas normas tienen fuerza de ley **(b)** *(group of people)* cuerpo *m or* contingente *m;* **labour force** = mano *f* de obra *or* obreros *mpl;* **the management has made an increased offer to the labour force** = la dirección ha ofrecido un aumento al personal *or* a los obreros; **we are opening a new factory in the Far East because of the cheap local labour force** = abriremos una nueva fábrica en Extremo Oriente para aprovechar la mano de obra local barata; **police force** = policía *f or* fuerza *f* pública;

members of several local police forces have collaborated in searching for the murderer = miembros de varios cuerpos de policía local han colaborado en la búsqueda del asesino **(c) force majeure** = fuerza mayor **2** *verb* forzar *or* obligar; **competition has forced the company to lower its prices** = la competencia ha obligado a la empresa a bajar los precios

◊ **forced** [fɒːst] *adjective* forzado, -da; **forced sale** = venta *f* forzosa

◊ **forcible** ['fɔːsɪbl] *adjective* a la fuerza *or* por fuerza; **forcible entry** = allanamiento *m* de morada *or* violación *f* de domicilio; **forcible feeding** = alimentación *f* forzosa (en un caso de huelga de hambre)

foreclose [fɔːˈkləuz] *verb* entablar juicio hipotecario *or* ejecutar una hipoteca *or* privar del derecho de redimir una hipoteca; **to foreclose on a mortgaged property** = ejecutar la hipoteca de una propiedad *or* vender una propiedad hipotecada por orden judicial

◊ **foreclosure** [fɔːˈkləuʒə] *noun* ejecución forzosa de una hipoteca *or* juicio hipotecario; **foreclosure order nisi** = orden *f* judicial provisional de ejecución de una hipoteca; **foreclosure order absolute** = orden judicial firme de ejecución de una hipoteca

foreign ['fɒrən] *adjective* extranjero, -ra; **foreign cars have flooded our market** = los coches extranjeros han inundado nuestro mercado; **we are increasing our trade with foreign countries** = estamos incrementando el comercio con países extranjeros; **foreign currency** = moneda *f* extranjera *or* divisa *f;* **foreign goods** = productos *mpl* extranjeros; **foreign investments** = inversiones *fpl* exteriores *or* extranjeras; **foreign trade** = comercio *m* exterior

◊ **foreigner** ['fɒrənə] *noun* extranjero, -ra *or* forastero, -ra

◊ **foreign exchange** ['fɒrən ɪksˈtʃeɪndʒ] *noun* cambio *m* de moneda *or* de divisas; **foreign exchange broker** *or* **dealer** = cambista *mf or* operador, -ra de cambios; **foreign exchange dealing** = operaciones *fpl* de cambio *or* cambio; **the foreign exchange markets** = mercados *mpl* de divisas *or* cambiarios; **foreign exchange reserves** = reservas *fpl* de divisas; **foreign exchange transfer** = transferencia *f* de divisas

◊ **Foreign (and Commonwealth) Office** ['fɒrən ənd 'kɒmənwelθ 'ɒfɪs] *noun GB* Ministerio *m* de Asuntos Exteriores

◊ **Foreign Secretary** ['fɒrən 'sekrtri] *noun* Ministro *m* de Asuntos Exteriores

COMMENT: in most countries, the government department dealing with other countries is called the Foreign Ministry, with the Foreign Minister in charge. In the UK, these are the Foreign Office and Foreign Secretary; in the USA, they are the State Department and the Secretary of State

foreman of the jury ['fɔːmən əv ðə 'dʒuəri] *noun* presidente, -ta *or* portavoz *mf* del jurado

forensic [fəˈrenzɪk] *adjective* forense *or* legal; **forensic medicine** = medicina *f* legal *or* forense; **forensic science** = ciencia *f* legal *or* forense; **forensic surgeon** = médico forense

foresee [fɔːˈsiː] *verb* prever; **he did not foresee that his letter could be taken as a threat** = no previó que su carta podía entenderse como una amenaza; **the closure of the company was not foreseen by the staff** = el cierre de la compañía no fue previsto por los empleados (NOTE: **foreseeing -foresaw -has foreseen**)

◊ **foreseeability** [fɔːsiːəˈbɪlɪti] *noun* previsibilidad *f;* **foreseeability test** = prueba *f* de previsibilidad

◊ **foresight** ['fɔːsaɪt] *noun* previsión *f*

forfeit ['fɔːfɪt] **1** *noun* confiscación *f or* pérdida *f* legal de algún derecho como castigo *or* decomiso *m;* **forfeit clause** = cláusula *f* de confiscación *or* cláusula decomisoria; **the goods were declared forfeit** = la mercancía fue confiscada **2** *verb* decomisar *or* confiscar *or* perder el derecho a algo; **to forfeit a deposit** = perder una entrada *or* un depósito

◊ **forfeiture** ['fɔːfɪtʃə] *noun* decomiso *m or* confiscación *f* de una propiedad *or* pérdida *f* de un derecho; **forfeiture of shares** = pérdida del derecho a unas acciones por no haberlas reclamado

forge [fɔːdʒ] *verb* falsificar *or* falsear; **he tried to enter the country with forged documents** = trató de entrar en el país con documentación falsa; **she wanted to pay the bill with a forged £10 note** = quiso pagar la cuenta con un billete falso de 10 libras

◊ **forgery** ['fɔːdʒri] *noun* **(a)** *(crime)* falsificación *f;* **he was sent to prison for forgery** = le enviaron a la cárcel acusado de falsificación (NOTE: no plural in this meaning) **(b)** *(illegal copy)* documento *m or* billete *m* falso *or* moneda *f* falsa; **the signature was proved to be a forgery** = se probó que la firma era falsificada

forget [fəˈget] *verb* olvidar *or* olvidarse; **to forget to do something** = olvidarse de hacer algo

fori ['fɔːri] *see* LEX FORI

form [fɔːm] **1** *noun* **(a)** *(legal document)* **form of words** = términos *mpl* protocolarios *or* fórmulas *fpl* judiciales utilizadas en un documento legal; **receipt in due form** = recibo *m* expedido en la forma debida *or* como es debido **(b)** *(official printed paper)* hoja (impresa) *or* formulario *m or* impreso *m;* **admissions form** *or* **registration form** = impreso de inscripción *or* de matrícula; **you have to fill in form A20** = tiene que rellenar el impreso A20;

customs declaration form = formulario de declaración aduanera; **a pad of order forms** = un bloc de hojas de pedidos; **application form** = impreso *m* de solicitud *or* formulario de inscripción; **claim form** = hoja *or* formulario de reclamación **2** *verb* formar *or* crear *or* constituir; **the brothers have formed a new company** = los hermanos han creado una nueva empresa

◊ **formation** *or* **forming** [fɔːˈmeɪʃn *or* ˈfɔːmɪŋ] *noun* formación *f or* creación *f or* constitución *f;* **the formation of a new company** = la creación de una nueva empresa

forma [ˈfɔːmə] *see* PRO FORMA

formal [ˈfɔːməl] *adjective* formal; **to make a formal application** = hacer una solicitud formal; **to send a formal order** = enviar un pedido en firme

◊ **formality** [fɔːˈmælɪti] *noun* formalidad *f or* trámite *m;* **the chairman dispensed with the formality of reading the minutes** = el presidente prescindió del trámite de leer las actas; **customs formalities** = trámites *mpl* aduaneros

◊ **formalize** [ˈfɔːməlaɪz] *verb* formalizar

◊ **formally** [ˈfɔːməli] *adverb* formalmente; **we have formally applied for planning permission for the new shopping precinct** = hemos solicitado permiso oficial de construcción para el recinto de la nueva zona comercial

former [ˈfɔːmə] *adjective* anterior

formulate [ˈfɔːmjuleɪt] *verb* formular

forthwith [fɔːθˈwɪθ] *adverb* en seguida *or* en el acto *or* inmediatamente

fortiori [fɔːtiˈɔːraɪ] *see* A FORTIORI

forum [ˈfɔːrəm] *noun* foro *m;* **the magistrates' court is not the appropriate forum for this application** = el juzgado de instrucción no es el foro adecuado para esta petición

forward [ˈfɔːwəd] **1** *adjective* de futuros *or* adelantado, -da *or* a plazo *or* para el futuro *or* en fecha futura; **forward buying** *or* **buying forward** = especulación *f or* compras *fpl* por adelantado *or* para entrega futura; **forward contract** = contrato *m* a plazo fijo; **forward market** = mercado *m* a plazo fijo *or* mercado de futuros; **forward (exchange) rate** = tipos *mpl* de cambio futuros *or* divisas *fpl* a plazo; **forward sales** = ventas *fpl* futuras **2** *adverb* **(a) to date an invoice forward** = poner a una factura fecha posterior a la actual; **carriage forward** *or* **freight forward** = porte debido *or* a cargo del cliente; **charges forward** = gastos *mpl* a cargo del cliente *or* gastos a cobrar a la entrega **(b) to buy forward** = comprar divisas a futuros; **to sell forward** = vender divisas a futuros **(c) balance brought forward** *or* **carried forward** = saldo *m* a cuenta nueva **3** *verb* **(a)** *(to send)* **to forward something to someone** = expedir *or* enviar algo a alguien *or* proponer; **please forward** *or* **to be**

forwarded = remítase al destinatario *or* a las nuevas señas **(b)** *(to refer to)* elevar

foster [ˈfɒstə] *verb* adoptar *or* criar a un hijo adoptivo *or* acoger en una familia; **foster child** = hijo *m* adoptivo *or* hija *f* adoptiva; **foster home** = hogar *m* adoptivo *or* de adopción; **foster mother** *or* **foster father** *or* **foster parent** = madre *f* adoptiva *or* padre *m* adoptivo

foul [faul] *adjective* defectuoso, -sa; **foul bill of lading** = conocimiento *m* de embarque defectuoso

founder [ˈfaundə] *noun* fundador, -ra; **founder's shares** = acciones *fpl* de fundador

fours [fɔːz] *see* ALL

frais [freɪ] *see* SANS FRAIS

frame [freɪm] *verb* *(informal)* amañar una acusación contra alguien *or* incriminar a alguien; **he has been framed** = le han incriminado *or* han amañado las pruebas para que la culpa recaiga sobre él

franchise [ˈfræntʃaɪz] **1** *noun* **(a)** *(right to vote)* derecho *m* de voto *or* a votar; **universal franchise** = derecho universal de voto (NOTE: no plural in this meaning) **(b)** *(licence to trade under a brand name)* franquicia *f or* licencia; **he has bought a printing franchise** *or* **a hot dog franchise** = ha adquirido una franquicia de imprenta *or* una concesión de venta de perritos calientes **2** *verb* franquiciar *or* conceder una licencia de explotación; **his sandwich bar was so successful that he decided to franchise it** = su bocatería tuvo tanto éxito que decidió explotarlo en régimen de franquicia

◊ **franchisee** [fræntʃaɪˈziː] *noun* franquiciado, -da *or* licenciatario, -ria *or* concesionario, -ria

◊ **franchiser** [ˈfræntʃaɪzə] *noun* franquiciador, -ra *or* persona que concede franquicias

◊ **franchising** [ˈfræntʃaɪzɪŋ] *noun* concesión *f or* licencia *f;* **he runs his sandwich chain as a franchising operation** = lleva su cadena de bocaterías en régimen de franquicia

◊ **franchisor** [fræntʃaɪˈzɔː] *noun* = FRANCHISER

franco [ˈfræŋkəu] *adverb* franco, -ca *or* libre

frank [fræŋk] *verb* franquear; **franking machine** = máquina *f* franqueadora *or* de franquear

fraud [frɔːd] *noun* fraude *m or* estafa *f or* falacia *f;* **to obtain money by fraud** = obtener dinero por medio de fraude *or* engaños; **he got possession of the property by fraud** = se hizo con la propiedad estafando *or* por medio de la estafa; **he was accused of frauds relating to foreign currency** = se le acusó de fraude de divisas; **Fraud Squad** = brigada contra el fraude; **he was convicted of a series of frauds against insurance companies** = le condenaron por una serie de estafas a compañías aseguradoras; **computer fraud** = estafa informática

COMMENT: frauds are divided into **fraud by a director** and other fraud

◊ **fraudulent** ['frɔːdjʊlənt] *adjective* fraudulento, -ta; **fraudulent conveyance** = transmisión *f* fraudulenta de una sociedad; **fraudulent misrepresentation** = impostura *f or* representación falsa con ánimo de fraude *or* engaño para que alguien firme un contrato; **fraudulent preference** = pago realizado por una compañía insolvente a un acreedor particular con preferencia a otros acreedores; **fraudulent trading** = comercio *m* fraudulento

◊ **fraudulently**   ['frɔːdjʊləntli]   *adverb* fraudulentamente; **goods imported fraudulently** = mercancías importadas fraudulentamente

free [friː] **1** *adjective & adverb* **(a)** *(without payment)* gratis *or* gratuito, -ta; **he was given a free ticket to the exhibition** = le dieron una entrada gratuita para la exposición; **the price includes free delivery** = el transporte va incluido en el precio; **goods are delivered free** = el transporte de la mercancía es gratuito; **price list sent free on request** = solicite envío gratuito de lista de precios; **free gift** = regalo *m;* **free sample** = muestra *f* gratuita; **free trial** = prueba *f* gratuita y sin compromiso de compra; **to send a piece of equipment for two weeks' free trial** = enviar un aparato por un periodo de prueba de dos semanas; **free of charge** = gratis; **free on board (f.o.b.)** = franco a bordo; *US* contrato de venta por el que quedan incluidos en el precio todos los gastos del vendedor hasta que la mercancía llega a un lugar determinado **(b)** *(not in prison)* libre; **to set someone free** = liberar a alguien *or* poner en libertad; **the crowd attacked the police station and set the three prisoners free** = la multitud asaltó la comisaría de policía y liberó a los tres prisioneros **(c)** *(with no restrictions)* libre; **free circulation of goods** = libre circulación *f* de mercancías *or* bienes; **free collective bargaining** = convenio *m* colectivo libre; **free competition** = libre competencia *f;* **free currency** = moneda *f* de libre circulación *or* disponibilidad; **free enterprise** = libre empresa *f;* **free market economy** = economía *f* de (libre) mercado; **free movement of capital** = libre circulación de capital; **free port** *or* **free trade zone** = zona *f* franca; **free of tax** *or* **tax-free** = exento, -ta de impuestos *or* libre de impuestos; **interest-free credit** *or* **loan** = crédito *m or* préstamo *m* sin intereses; **free of duty** *or* **duty-free** = libre *or* exento de derechos de aduana; **free trade** = libre comercio *m or* libre cambio *m;* **free trade area** = zona *f* de libre cambio; **free will** = libre albedrío *f* **(d)** *(not busy or not occupied)* libre *or* sin ocupar; **are there any tables free in the restaurant?** = ¿Hay alguna mesa libre en el restaurante?; **the solicitor will be free in a few minutes** = el abogado terminará en unos minutos; **the hearing was delayed because there was no**

courtroom free = la vista se retrasó al no haber ninguna sala libre **2** *verb* liberar *or* poner en libertad; **to free someone of a duty** = liberar a alguien de un deber; **the new president freed all political prisoners** = el nuevo presidente liberó a todos los presos políticos

◊ **freelance** ['friːlɑːns] *adjective, noun & adverb* que trabaja por su cuenta *or* autónomo, -ma *or* independiente; **she is a freelance reporter for the local newspaper** = trabaja para el periódico local como reportera independiente; **he works freelance as an advertising agent** = trabaja independientemente *or* por libre como agente de publicidad

◊ **freely** ['friːli] *adverb* libremente *or* sin restricciones; **money should circulate freely within the European Union** = el dinero debería circular libremente dentro de la Unión Europea

◊ **free pardon** ['friː 'pɑːdən] *noun* indulto *m* medida de gracia *or* amnistía *f or* perdón *m*

freedom ['friːdəm] *noun* **(a)** *(not held in custody)* libertad *f;* **the president gave the accused man his freedom** = el presidente dio la libertad al acusado **(b)** *(without restriction)* libertad; **freedom of association** = libertad de asociación; **freedom of assembly** *or* **of meeting** = libertad de reunión; **freedom of information** = libertad de información; **freedom of the press** = libertad de prensa; **freedom of speech** = libertad de expresión; **testamentary freedom** = libertad testamentaria

freehold ['friːhəʊld] *noun* propiedad *f* absoluta; **freehold property** = dominio *m* absoluto de una propiedad

◊ **freeholder** ['friːhəʊldə] *noun* propietario, -ria absoluto, -ta *or* nudo propietario

freeze [friːz] *verb* congelar *or* bloquear; **the court ordered the company's bank account to be frozen** = el tribunal ordenó que se bloqueara la cuenta bancaria de la compañía; **frozen assets** = activo *m* congelado

freight [freɪt] *noun* **(a)** *(carriage)* flete *m or* porte *m or* transporte *m;* **freight charges** *or* **freight rates** = cuotas *or* tarifas de flete **(b)** *(goods carried)* carga *f or* mercancía *f*

French [frentʃ] *noun* francés *m*

COMMENT: French was used in England together with Latin as the language of the law courts for some centuries after the conquest by King William I. It still survives in some legal words and phrases, such as **chose, tort, oyez, puisne, autrefois convict, feme covert**

fresh pursuit ['freʃ pə'sjuːt] *noun* persecución *f* de un ladrón para recuperar lo que ha robado

friend [frend] *noun* amigo, -ga

◊ **friendly** ['frendli] *adjective* simpático, -ca *or* amistoso, -sa *or* amigable

◊ **friendly society** ['frendli sə'saɪəti] *noun* mutualidad *f or* sociedad de ayuda mutua (en caso de enfermedad o de dificultades financieras)

frisk [frɪsk] *verb* cachear *or* registrar

frivolous ['frɪvələs] *adjective;* **frivolous complaint** *or* **frivolous action** = demanda *f or* acción *f* de poco peso *or* de poca entidad *or* fútil

frolic ['frɒlɪk] *noun* **frolic of his own** = daño a sí mismo o a algo (causado por un trabajador fuera de su trabajo por el que su patrono no puede hacerse responsable)

frozen ['frəʊzn] *see* FREEZE

frustrate [frʌ'streɪt] *verb* frustrar *or* impedir que se cumplan los términos de un contrato
◊ **frustration** [frʌ'streɪʃn] *noun* impedimento *m or* frustración *f or* situación en la que no se pueden cumplir los términos de un contrato

fugitive ['fjuːdʒətɪv] *adjective & noun* fugitivo, -va; **fugitive offender** *or* *US* **fugitive from justice** = delincuente *m* fugitivo *or* prófugo de la justicia

fulfil *US* **fulfill** [fʊl'fɪl] *verb* cumplir *or* satisfacer; **to fulfill a contract** = cumplir un contrato; **to fulfill a promise** = cumplir una promesa; **the company has fulfilled all the terms of the agreement** = la empresa ha cumplido todos los términos del contrato

full [fʊl] *adjective* **(a)** *(with as much inside as possible)* lleno, -na; **prisoners have to share cells because the prisons are too full** = los presos tienen que compartir las celdas por estar las prisiones demasiado llenas *or* porque las prisiones están demasiado llenas; **the court has to deal with a full list of cases** = el juzgado tiene que hacerse cargo de una extensa lista de casos **(b)** *(complete or including everything)* completo, -ta *or* máximo, -ma *or* pleno, -na; **we are working at full capacity** = estamos trabajando a tope *or* a pleno rendimiento; **full costs** = costes *mpl* totales; **full cover** = cobertura *f* total; **full-time** = tiempo completo; **in full discharge of a debt** = totalmente libre de deudas; **the plaintiff accepted £500 in full and final settlement of his claim for £600, to avoid going to court** = el demandante aceptó 500 libras como pago íntegro y final de su reclamación de 600 libras para evitar ir a juicio; **full title** = título *m* íntegro (de una ley parlamentaria); **full trial** = juicio *m* íntegro organizado según el procedimiento correcto **(c)** **in full** = completamente *or* íntegramente; **give your full name and address** *or* **your name and address in full** = dé su nombre, apellidos y dirección; **he accepted all our conditions in full** = aceptó todas nuestras condiciones sin reservas; **full refund** *or* **refund paid in full** = reembolso total *or* devolución íntegra; **he got a full refund when he complained about the service** = le reembolsaron íntegramente cuando se quejó del servicio; **the clerk read out**

the charges in full = el secretario leyó las acusaciones sin omisiones; **full payment** *or* **payment in full** = pago *m* completo de una deuda
◊ **fully** ['fʊli] *adverb* completamente *or* totalmente *or* enteramente; **fully paid-up shares** = acciones *fpl* liberadas *or* cubiertas; **fully paid-up capital** = capital *m* totalmente desembolsado *or* cubierto

function ['fʌŋkʃn] *noun* función *f or* acto *m;* **public function** = acto público

functus officio ['fʌŋktəs ɒ'fɪʃiəʊ] *Latin phrase* 'exentos de poder *or* jurisdicción'; **the justices' clerk asserted that the justices were functi officio** = el secretario del juzgado afirmó que los jueces estaban exentos de jurisdicción (NOTE: plural is **functi officio**)

fund [fʌnd] *noun* **(a)** *(money collected for special purpose)* fondo *m or* reserva *f;* **pension fund** = fondo de pensiones; **reserve fund** = fondo de reserva; **slush fund** = fondo *or* dinero para sobornos; **European Development Fund** = Fondo Europeo de Desarrollo; **European Social Fund** = Fondo Social Europeo; **Interterritorial Compensation Fund** = Fondo de Compensación Territorial **(b)** *(money available for a purpose)* **funds** = fondos *mpl;* **conversion of funds** = apropiación *f* ilícita *or* indebida de fondos; **to convert funds to one's own use** = apropiarse de fondos ajenos en beneficio propio; **public funds** = fondos públicos

fundamental [fʌndə'mentl] *adjective* fundamental *or* básico *or* esencial; **fundamental breach** = incumplimiento *m* de un término fundamental de un contrato

fungible goods *or* **fungibles** ['fʌndʒɪbl 'gʊdz] *plural noun* bienes *mpl* fungibles *or* material *m* fungible

furandi [fʊ'rændi] *see* ANIMUS

furnish ['fɜːnɪʃ] *verb* **(a)** *(to supply or provide)* abastecer *or* suministrar *or* proveer *or* facilitar *or* proporcionar *or* dar; **he was asked to furnish the court with proof of his identity** = le pidieron que diera pruebas de su identidad al tribunal **(b)** *(to put furniture)* amueblar; **he furnished his office with secondhand chairs and desks** = amuebló la oficina con sillas y mesas de segunda mano; **the company spent £10,000 on furnishing the chairman's office** = la compañía gastó 10.000 libras en amueblar la oficina del presidente; **furnished accommodation** = piso *m* amueblado *or* casa amueblada

future ['fjuːtʃə] **1** *adjective* futuro, -ra; **future delivery** = entrega *f* futura *or* a plazo; **future estate** = término antiguo para designar la posesión y disfrute futuro de una propiedad; **future interests** = intereses futuros **2** *noun* futuro *m;* **try to be more**

careful in future = procura ser más cuidadoso en lo sucesivo; **in future all reports must be sent to Australia by air** = en el futuro todos los informes deberán enviarse a Australia por avión

◊ **futures** ['fju:tʃəz] *plural noun (shares or commodities bought for delivery at a later date)* futuros *mpl or* entregas *fpl* a plazo

fuzz [fʌz] *noun (slang)* la bofia *or* la palma

Gg

gain [geɪn] **1** *noun* **(a)** *(increase)* aumento *m;* **gain in profitability** = aumento de la rentabilidad **(b)** *(increase in profit or price or value)* ganancia *f or* beneficio *m;* **to deal in stolen goods for gain** = traficar con objetos robados para sacar un beneficio; **capital gains** = plusvalía *f;* **capital gains tax** = impuesto *m* sobre la plusvalía **2** *verb* conseguir *or* adquirir; **he gained some useful experience working in a bank** = adquirió una experiencia práctica trabajando en un banco; **to gain control of a business** = conseguir el control de un negocio *or* hacerse con el control de un negocio
◊ **gainful** ['geɪnfʊl] *adjective;* **gainful employment** = empleo *m* lucrativo *or* remunerado
◊ **gainfully** ['geɪnfli] *adverb* **he is not gainfully employed** = no ejerce un empleo remunerado

gallows ['gæləʊz] *plural noun* cadalso *m or* patíbulo *m or* horca *f*

game [geɪm] *noun* **(a)** *(hunting)* caza *f;* **game licence** = licencia *f or* permiso *m* de caza **(b)** **game of chance** = juego *m* de azar
◊ **gaming** ['geɪmɪŋ] *noun* juego *m;* **gaming licence** = licencia de juego

gang [gæŋ] *noun* pandilla *f or* banda *f* de criminales; **a drugs gang** = una banda de traficantes de droga; **a gang of jewel thieves** = una banda de ladrones de joyas; **gang of robbers** = cuadrilla *f* de ladrones
◊ **gangland** ['gæŋlænd] *noun* hampa *m;* **a gangland murder** = un asesinato *or* un ajuste de cuentas entre criminales
◊ **gangster** ['gæŋstə] *noun* gángster *mf or* miembro *m* de una banda de criminales; **the police shot two gangsters in the bank raid** = la policía mató a dos atracadores en el asalto al banco

gaol [dʒeɪl] **1** *noun* GB cárcel *f* **2** *verb* GB encarcelar
◊ **gaoler** ['dʒeɪlə] *noun* GB carcelero, -ra; *for examples see* JAIL, JAILER

garnish ['gɑːnɪʃ] *verb* embargar
◊ **garnishee** [gɑːnɪ'ʃiː] *noun* embargado, -da; **garnishee order** = orden *f* de embargo
◊ **garnisher** [gɑːnɪ'ʃɔː] *noun* embargante *mf*

gas chamber ['gæs 'tʃeɪmbə] *noun* cámara *f* de gas

COMMENT: used in some states in the USA

gather ['gæðə] *verb* **(a)** *(to put together)* juntar *or* reunir *or* recoger *or* recopilar; **to gather information** = recopilar datos; **he gathered his papers together before the meeting started** = recogió todos sus papeles antes de que empezara la reunión; **she has been gathering information on import controls from various sources** = ha estado recopilando información de varias fuentes sobre los controles a la importación **(b)** *(to find out)* tener entendido que *or* sacar la conclusión de que *or* averiguar; **I gather he has left the office** = tengo entendido que ha dejado la oficina; **did you gather who will be at the meeting?** = ¿averiguaste quién estará en la reunión?

GATT [gæt] = GENERAL AGREEMENT ON TARIFFS AND TRADE

gazump [gə'zʌmp] *verb* romper un acuerdo *or* retirar un contrato de venta de una propiedad para venderla a un precio más alto; **he was gazumped** = hubo un postor que ofreció más que él
◊ **gazumping** [gə'zʌmpɪŋ] *noun* **(a)** *(of a buyer)* ofrecer más dinero que otro comprador por una propiedad para asegurarse la compra **(b)** *(of a seller)* rechazo *m* de una oferta de compra de una propiedad cuando aparece una oferta mejor

GBH ['dʒiː 'biː 'eɪtʃ] = GRIEVOUS BODILY HARM

GDP ['dʒiː 'diː 'piː] = GROSS DOMESTIC PRODUCT

general ['dʒenrl] *adjective* **(a)** *(ordinary)* general *or* común; **general expenses** = gastos *mpl* generales; **general manager** = director, -ra general; **general office** = oficina *f* central **(b)** *(dealing with everything or everybody)* general; **general audit** = auditoría *f* general; **general average** = avería *f* gruesa; **general damages** = daños *mpl* generales *or* daños directos *or* daño emergente; **general election** = elecciones *fpl* generales; **general lien** = embargo *m* preventivo general; *compare also* PARTICULAR AVERAGE, PARTICULAR LIEN; **general meeting** = junta *f* general; **general strike** = huelga *f* general; **Annual General Meeting (AGM)** = junta general anual; **Extraordinary General Meeting (EGM)** = junta general extraordinaria **(c) General Agreement on Tariffs and Trade (GATT)** = Acuerdo *m* General sobre Aranceles Aduaneros y Comercio (NOTE: replaced by **World Trade Organization (WTO)**

◊ **generally** ['dʒenrli] *adverb* generalmente *or* por lo general *or* en general; **the office is generally closed between Christmas and the New Year** = la oficina cierra en general entre Navidad y Año Nuevo; **political crimes are generally dealt with more harshly in the military courts** = los crímenes políticos son, por lo general, tratados con más dureza en los tribunales militares

Geneva Convention(s) [dʒə'niːvə kən'venʃnz] *noun* Convención *f* de Ginebra; **the attacking army was accused of violating the Geneva Convention** = el ejército agresor fue acusado de violar la Convención de Ginebra; *see also* HAGUE

genocide ['dʒenəsaɪd] *noun* genocidio *m*

gentleman ['dʒentlmən] *noun* caballero *m*; **gentleman's agreement** *or* **US gentlemen's agreement** = acuerdo *m* entre caballeros

genuine ['dʒenjuɪn] *adjective* verdadero, -ra *or* auténtico, -ca *or* genuino, -na; **this old table is genuine** = esta mesa antigua es genuina; **a genuine Picasso** = un Picasso auténtico; **a genuine leather purse** = un monedero de cuero legítimo; **the genuine article** = el artículo auténtico *or* original; **genuine purchaser** = persona auténticamente interesada en comprar

◊ **genuineness** ['dʒenjuɪnnəs] *noun* autenticidad *f*

gerrymandering ['dʒerimændrɪŋ] *noun* tongo *m or* amañamiento *m* de resultados electorales

get [get] *verb* **(a)** *(to receive)* recibir *or* obtener *or* cobrar; **we got a letter from the solicitor this morning** = recibimos una carta del abogado esta mañana; **he got a £25 fine** *or* **a parking ticket** = le pusieron una multa de 25 libras *or* una multa de aparcamiento **(b)** *(to arrive)* llegar; **the shipment got to Canada six weeks late** = el cargamento llegó a Canadá seis semanas tarde; **she finally got to the courtroom at 10.30** = por fin llegó a la sala del tribunal a las 10.30 **(c) to get even** = ajustar cuentas (NOTE: **getting - got - has got** *or* **US gotten**)

◊ **get back** ['get 'bæk] *verb* recuperar *or* recobrar; **I got my money back after I had complained to the manager** = recuperé el dinero después de quejarme al director; **he got his initial investment back in two months** = recuperó su inversión inicial en dos meses

◊ **get off** ['get 'ɒf] *verb* escapar *or* librarse; **the boys got off with a reprimand from the magistrate** = los muchachos escaparon con una reprimenda del juez

◊ **get on** ['get 'ɒn] *verb* **(a)** *(to work or to manage)* desenvolverse *or* hacer progresos; **how is the new secretary getting on?** = ¿Cómo se

desenvuelve la nueva secretaria? **(b)** *(to succeed)* irle bien a uno *or* hacer progresos; **my son is getting on well - he has just been promoted** = a mi hijo le va muy bien - le acaban de ascender

◊ **get on with** ['get 'ɒn 'wɪð] *verb* **(a)** *(to be friendly)* llevarse bien con alguien; **she does not get on with her new boss** = no se lleva bien con su nuevo jefe **(b)** *(to go on doing work)* seguir trabajando *or* no interrumpir el trabajo; **the staff got on with the work and finished the order on time** = los empleados no interrumpieron su trabajo y terminaron el pedido a tiempo

◊ **get out** ['get 'aʊt] *verb* **(a)** *(to produce)* publicar *or* sacar *or* hacer *or* confeccionar; **the Royal Commission got out the report in time for the meeting** = la Comisión Real confeccionó el informe a tiempo para la reunión **(b)** *(to sell an investment)* vender *or* liquidar; **he didn't like the annual report, so he got out before the company became insolvent** = no le gustó el informe anual, por eso vendió sus acciones antes de que la compañía se declarara insolvente

◊ **get round** ['get 'raʊnd] *verb* soslayar *or* evitar; **we tried to get round the embargo by shipping from Canada** = intentamos soslayar el embargo enviando el cargamento desde Canadá; **can you advise me how we can get round the quota system?** = ¿puede aconsejarme sobre cómo podemos evitar el sistema de cuotas?

get *or* **gett** [get] *noun* divorcio *m* según la costumbre religiosa judía

gift [gɪft] **1** *noun* regalo *m or* dádiva *f or* donativo *m*; **gift inter vivos** = donación *f* entre vivos *or* inter vivos; **free gift** = prima *f* **2** *verb* dar *or* donar

COMMENT: a gift is irrevocable

gilt-edged securities *or* **gilts** ['gɪlt'edʒd sɪ'kjʊərɪtɪz] *plural noun* valores *mpl or* títulos *mpl* de máxima garantía

give [gɪv] *verb* **(a)** *(as a gift)* regalar *or* donar; **the office gave him a clock when he retired** = en la oficina le regalaron un reloj cuando se jubiló **(b)** *(to pass)* dar; **to give evidence** = testificar *or* deponer; **to give the go ahead** = dar el visto bueno; **she gave the documents to the accountant** = le dio los documentos al contable; **can you give me some information about the new computer system?** = ¿puede darme alguna información sobre el nuevo sistema informático?; **do not give any details to the police** = no le dé ningún detalle a la policía **(c)** *(organize)* dar *or* organizar; **the company gave a party after they won their appeal** = la compañía dio una fiesta después de ganar el recurso (NOTE: **giving - gave - given**)

◊ **give away** ['gɪv ə'weɪ] *verb* regalar; **we are giving away a pocket calculator with each £10 of purchases** = regalamos una calculadora de bolsillo por cada 10 libras de compra

◊ **giveaway** [ˈgɪvəweɪ] **1** *adjective* tirado, -da *or* de saldo; **to sell at giveaway prices** = vender a precio de saldo **2** *noun* regalo *m or* obsequio *m*

◊ **give in** *or* **give up** [ˈgɪv ˈɪn] *verb* darse por vencido

◊ **give rise to** [ˈgɪv ˈraɪz tʊ] *verb* causar *or* ocasionar; **the decision has given rise to complaints from the family of the defendant** = el fallo ha ocasionado quejas por parte de la familia del acusado

gloss [glɒs] *noun* glosa *f or* aclaración *f*

GNP [ˈdʒiː ˈen ˈpiː] = GROSS NATIONAL PRODUCT

go [gəʊ] *verb* **(a)** *(to move from one place to another)* ir *or* salir; **to go to the polls** = acudir a las urnas; **the cheque went to your bank yesterday** = el cheque fue enviado ayer a su banco; **the plane goes to Frankfurt, then to Rome** = el avión va a Francfort, luego a Roma; **he is going to our Lagos office** = va a nuestra oficina de Lagos **(b)** *(to be placed)* colocarse *or* ponerse *or* ir; **the date goes at the top of the letter** = la fecha se coloca en la parte superior de la carta **(c)** *(work)* **to go sick** = darse de baja (en el trabajo) (NOTE: **going - went - has gone**)

◊ **go back on** [ˈgəʊ ˈbæk ˈɒn] *verb* faltar a la palabra *or* faltar *or* retractarse; **two months later they went back on the agreement** = dos meses más tarde se retractaron del acuerdo

◊ **going concern** [ˈgəʊɪŋ kənˈsɜːn] *noun* empresa *f* en plena actividad *or* negocio *m* en marcha *or* que funciona bien

◊ **going equipped for stealing** [ˈgəʊɪŋ ɪˈkwɪpt fə ˈstiːlɪŋ] *noun* delito grave que consiste en llevar instrumentos de robo

◊ **go into** [ˈgəʊ ˈɪntʊ] *verb* **(a) to go into business** = meterse en negocios *or* abrir *or* emprender un negocio; **he went into business selling cars** = empezó el negocio vendiendo coches; **she went into business in partnership with her son** = emprendió un negocio a medias con su hijo **(b)** *(to examine carefully)* examinar a fondo *or* profundizar; **the bank wants to go into the details of the inter-company loans** = el banco quiere examinar a fondo los detalles de los préstamos entre compañías; **the fraud squad is going into the facts behind the property deals** = la brigada contra el fraude está investigando a fondo los datos sobre las transacciones de propiedad

◊ **go on** [ˈgəʊ ˈɒn] *verb* **(a)** *(to continue)* continuar *or* seguir; **the staff went on working in spite of the fire** = los empleados continuaron trabajando a pesar del incendio; **the chairman went on speaking for two hours** = el presidente siguió hablando durante dos horas **(b)** *(to work with)* partir de *or* basarse; **two fingerprints are all the police have to go on** = la policía sólo cuenta con dos huellas dactilares en las que basarse

◊ **go through** [ˈgəʊ ˈθruː] *verb* pasar *or* atravesar; **to go through customs** = pasar por la aduana; **you can't go through** = no se puede pasar

◊ **go to law** [ˈgəʊ tə ˈlɔː] *verb* ir a juicio; **we went to law to try to regain our property** = fuimos a juicio para tratar de recuperar nuestros bienes

◊ **go with** [ˈgəʊ ˈwɪθ] *verb* acompañar

godfather [ˈgɒdfɑːðə] *noun (slang)* padrino *m*

good [gʊd] *adjective* **(a)** *(not bad)* bueno, -na; **a good buy** = una buena compra *or* una ganga **(b)** *(plenty)* **a good deal of** = mucho, -cha; **we wasted a good deal of time discussing the arrangements for the AGM** = perdimos mucho tiempo discutiendo las disposiciones de la junta general anual; **the company had to pay a good deal of money for the building** = la compañía tuvo que pagar mucho dinero por el edificio; **a good many** = un buen número *or* muchos, -chas; **a good many staff members have joined the union** = un buen número de empleados se ha afiliado al sindicato

◊ **good behaviour** [ˈgʊd bɪˈheɪvjə] *noun* buen comportamiento *m;* **the magistrates bound him over to be of good behaviour** = los jueces le obligaron legalmente a tener buen comportamiento; **she was sentenced to four years in prison, but was released early for good behaviour** = la condenaron a cuatro años de prisión pero la pusieron en libertad pronto por buena conducta

◊ **good cause** [ˈgʊd ˈkɔːz] *noun* buena causa *or* buena razón *or* motivo *m* suficiente; **the court asked the accused to show good cause why he should not be sent to prison** = el tribunal pidió al acusado que justificara una causa suficiente para no ir a la cárcel (NOTE: not used with **the**)

◊ **good consideration** [ˈgʊd kənsɪdəˈreɪʃn] *noun* la consideración *f* debida *or* la debida consideración

◊ **good faith** [ˈgʊd ˈfeɪθ] *noun* buena fe *f;* **in good faith** = de buena fe; **he acted in good faith** = actuó de buena fe; **to buy something in good faith** = comprar algo de buena fe; **he bought the car in good faith, not knowing that it had been stolen** = compró el coche de buena fe, sin saber que había sido robado

◊ **goods** [gʊdz] *plural noun* **(a)** *(personal possessions)* **goods and chattels** = muebles *mpl* y enseres *mpl;* **household goods** = artículos *mpl* de uso doméstico **(b)** *(merchandise)* mercancía *f or* artículos *mpl or* género *m;* **goods and services** = bienes *mpl* y servicios *mpl;* **goods (held) in bond** = retención *f* de mercancías en la aduana; **capital goods** = bienes de capital *or* bienes de equipo; **consumer goods** = bienes de consumo; **goods train** = tren *m* de mercancías

◊ **good title** [ˈgʊd ˈtaɪtl] *noun* título *m* de propiedad (con plenos derechos)

◊ **goodwill** [gʊdˈwɪl] *noun* fondo *m* de comercio *or* clientela *m;* **he paid £10,000 for the goodwill of the shop and £4,000 for the stock** = pagó 10.000

libras por la clientela y 4.000 libras por las existencias

COMMENT: goodwill can include the trading reputation, the patents, the trade names used, the value of a 'good site', etc., and is very difficult to establish accurately. It is an intangible asset, and so is not shown as an asset in a company's accounts, unless it figures as part of the purchase price paid when acquiring another company

gossip ['gɒsɪp] *verb* murmurar

govern ['gʌvən] *verb* **(a)** *(to rule a country)* gobernar *or* dirigir; **the country is governed by a group of military leaders** = el país está gobernado por un grupo de dirigentes militares **(b)** *(to be in authority)* guiar *or* regir *or* dominar *or* regular; **the amount of damages is governed by the seriousness of the injuries suffered** = la cuantía de los daños viene regulada según la gravedad de las heridas sufridas

◊ **government** ['gʌvənmənt] *noun* **(a)** *(way of ruling)* gobierno *m or* administración *f* del Estado; **people want democratic government** = la gente quiere un gobierno democrático; **the leader of the Opposition is promising to provide effective government** = el líder de la oposición promete que conseguirá un gobierno eficaz **(b)** **central government** = el Estado *or* la Administración; **local government** = Administración local **(b)** *(from the government)* gubernamental *or* estatal *or* del estado; **government intervention** *or* **intervention by the government** = intervención *f* del estado *or* estatal; **a government ban on the import of arms** = una prohibición gubernamental sobre la importación de armamento; **a government investigation into organized crime** = una investigación oficial sobre el crimen organizado; **government officials prevented him leaving the country** = funcionarios del gobierno no le permitieron salir del país; **government policy is outlined in the book** = la política del gobierno está resumida en el libro; **government regulations state that import duty has to be paid on expensive items** = las normas estatales establecen que los artículos caros deben pagar derechos de aduana; **government contractor** = contratista *mf* del Estado; NOTE: **government** can take a singular or plural verb: **the government have decided to repeal the Act; the government feels it is not time to make a statement.** Note also that the word **government** is used, especially by officials, without the article: **Government has decided that the plan will be turned down; the plan is funded by central government**

◊ **governing** ['gʌvnɪŋ] *adjective* rector, ra

◊ **governmental** [gʌvən'mentl] *adjective* gubernamental *or* gubernativo, -va

◊ **governor** ['gʌvnə] *noun* **(a)** *(of a state)* gobernador, -ra; **Ronald Reagan was Governor of California before becoming President** = Ronald

Reagan fue gobernador de California antes de pasar a ser Presidente **(b)** *(of a prison)* director, -ra; **a prison governor** = director de una prisión; **the prisoners applied to the governor for parole** = los presos solicitaron la libertad condicional al director de la prisión **(c)** *(informal)* jefe, -fa **(d)** *(of public institution)* miembro del consejo

◊ **Governor-General** ['gʌvnə'dʒenrəl] *noun* GB Gobernador, -ra General (representante de la monarquía británica en países de la Commonwealth); *see also* LIEUTENANT-GOVERNOR

gown [gaʊn] *noun* toga *f; see also* SILK

grace [greɪs] *noun* gracia *f or* cortesía *f* prórroga *f;* **to give a creditor a period of grace** *or* **two weeks' grace** = conceder a un acreedor un periodo de gracia *or* de cortesía *or* dos semanas de prórroga (especial)

graft ['grɑːft] *noun* *(informal)* soborno *m or* corrupción *f* de funcionarios

grand [grænd] **1** *adjective* gran *or* importante; **grand plan** = proyecto *m* importante; **grand total** = total *m* general **2** *noun* *(informal)* mil libras *fpl or* mil dólares *mpl;* **they offered him fifty grand for the information** = le ofrecieron cincuenta mil libras *or* dólares por la información (NOTE: no plural in English)

◊ **grand jury** ['grænd 'dʒʊəri] *noun* US gran jurado *m or* jurado de acusación

◊ **grand larceny** ['grænd 'lɑːsni] *noun* US hurto *m* de gran cuantía

grant [grɑːnt] **1** *noun* **(a)** *(act of giving something to someone)* cesión *f or* donación *f or* concesión *f;* **he made a grant of land to his son** = hizo una concesión de tierras a su hijo; **grant of letters of administration** = concesión de nombramiento de administrador judicial; **grant of probate** = concesión *or* garantía *f* de legalidad de un testamento *or* documento *m* oficial que prueba la legalidad de un testamento **(b)** *(money given by a government to help pay for something)* subvención *f or* beca *f or* subsidio *m;* **the institute has a government grant to cover the cost of the development programme** = el instituto tiene una subvención estatal para cubrir el coste del programa de desarrollo; **the local authority has allocated grants towards the costs of the scheme** = el gobierno municipal ha asignado subvenciones para sufragar los gastos del proyecto; **grant-aided scheme** = proyecto *m* subvencionado; **death grant** = ayuda *f* de sepelio **2** *verb* conceder *or* otorgar *or* asentir; **to grant a delay** = acordar una moratoria; **to grant a licence** *or* **a patent** = otorgar una licencia *or* una patente; **to grant a request** = acceder a una petición; **to grant someone permission to build a house** *or* **to leave the country** = conceder permiso a alguien para construir una casa *or* para abandonar el país; **the local authority granted the company an**

interest-free loan to start up the new factory = el gobierno municipal concedió un préstamo sin intereses a la empresa para poner en funcionamiento la nueva fábrica; **he was granted parole** = le concedieron la libertad condicional *or* libertad bajo palabra; **the government granted an amnesty to all political prisoners** = el gobierno concedió una amnistía a todos los presos políticos **(c) to take for granted** = dar por hecho

◊ **grantee** [grɑːnˈtiː] *noun* cesionista *mf or* becado, -da

◊ **grantor** [grɑːnˈtɔː] *noun* otorgante *mf or* donante *mf*

graphology [grəˈfɒlədʒi] *noun* grafología *f*

grass [grɑːs] *(slang)* **1** *noun* **(a)** *(informer)* chivato, -ta *or* confidente *mf; see also* SUPERGRASS **(b)** *(drug)* marihuana *or* mariguana *or* marijuana *f* **2** *verb* cantar *or* chivarse; **to grass on someone** = dar el chivatazo *or* chivarse de alguien

◊ **grass-roots** [ˈgrɑːs ˈrʊts] *noun* base *f* popular *or* las bases; **the party has considerable support at grass-roots level** = el partido cuenta con el apoyo de las bases

grata [ˈgrɑːtə] *see* PERSONA

gratia [ˈgreɪʃə] *see* EX GRATIA

gratis [ˈgrɑːtɪs] *adverb* gratis *or* sin pagar; **we got into the exhibition gratis** = entramos en la exposición gratis

gratuitous [grəˈtjuːɪtəs] *adjective* gratuito, -ta; **gratuitous promise** = promesa *f* gratuita

gratuity [grəˈtjuːɪti] *noun* propina *f or* gratificación *f;* **the staff are instructed not to accept gratuities** = los empleados tienen órdenes de no aceptar propinas

Gray's Inn [ˈgreɪz ˈɪn] *noun* uno de los cuatro Colegios de Abogados de Londres

great [ˈgreɪt] *adjective* grande; **a great deal of** = mucho, -cha *or* una gran cantidad; **he made a great deal of money on the Stock Exchange** = ganó mucho dinero en la Bolsa; **there is a great deal of work to be done before the company can be made really profitable** = habrá que trabajar mucho para que la compañía sea verdaderamente rentable

◊ **Great Seal** [ˈgreɪt ˈsiːl] *noun* Sello *m* Real

green [ˈgriːn] *adjective* verde; **green belt** = zona verde

◊ **Green Book** [ˈgriːn ˈbʊk] *noun* libro *m* de reglas procedimentales de los juzgados locales

◊ **green card** [ˈgriːn ˈkɑːd] *noun* **(a)** *(car insurance certificate)* carta *f* verde **(b)** *(US work or residence permit)* tarjeta *f* verde *or* permiso *m* de residencia en EE UU

◊ **green form** [ˈgriːn ˈfɔːm] *GB noun* formulario *m* (de color verde) que debe rellenarse para obtener un abogado de oficio; **the green form scheme** = sistema *m or* programa *m* que permite recurrir a un abogado de oficio gratuitamente o por medio de subvención

◊ **Green Paper** [ˈgriːn ˈpeɪpə] *GB noun* libro *m* verde (informe del gobierno británico sobre un proyecto de ley presentado al Parlamento)

grievance [ˈgriːvəns] *noun* queja *f or* agravio *m;* **grievance procedure** = procedimiento *m* de tramitación de quejas; **list of grievances** = memorial *m* de agravios

grievous bodily harm (GBH) [ˈgriːvəs ˈbɒdɪli ˈhɑːm] *noun* lesión *f* física grave

gross [grəʊs] *adjective* **(a)** *(with no deductions)* total *or* bruto, -ta; **gross domestic product (GDP)** = producto *m* interior bruto (PIB); **gross earnings** *or* **gross income** *or* **gross salary** = ingresos brutos *or* renta bruta *or* sueldo bruto; **gross margin** = margen bruto *or* beneficio bruto; **gross national product (GNP)** = producto nacional bruto (PNB); **gross profit** = beneficio bruto; **gross receipts** = ingresos brutos; **gross weight** = peso *m* bruto **(b)** *(serious)* grande *or* grave; **gross indecency** = delito *m* de conducta sexual indecente; **gross negligence** = imprudencia temeraria

ground [graʊnd] *noun* **(a)** *(soil)* suelo *m or* tierra *f;* **ground landlord** = propietario *m* absoluto; **ground lease** = enfiteusis *f;* **ground rent** = renta *f* que paga el enfiteuta al propietario absoluto **(b)** *(basic reasons)* **grounds** = motivos *mpl or* razones *fpl or* causas *fpl or* fundamento *m or* base *f;* **grounds for divorce** = motivos de divorcio; **legal grounds** = fundamentos de derecho; **reasonable grounds** = motivo fundado *or* con motivo; **does he have good grounds for complaint?** = ¿tiene motivos fundados para quejarse?; **there are no grounds on which we can be sued** = no hay razones por las que nos puedan demandar; **what are the grounds for the claim for damages?** = ¿en base a qué se formula la reclamación por daños y perjuicios? (NOTE: in this meaning the word can be used in the singular if only one reason exists: **the judge refused the application on the ground that he had discretion to remove the hearsay evidence from the report**)

◊ **groundless** [ˈgraʊndləs] *adjective* sin fundamento

group [gruːp] **1** *noun* **(a)** *(of people)* grupo *m;* **steering group** = comité *m* de dirección; **a group of staff members has sent a memorandum to the chairman complaining about noise in the office** = un grupo de empleados ha enviado una nota al presidente quejándose del ruido que hay en la oficina **(b)** *(businesses)* grupo; **the group chairman** *or* **the chairman of the group** = el presidente del grupo; **group turnover** *or* **turnover for the group** = facturación *f or* producción *f or* volumen *m* de ventas del grupo; **group results** = resultados *mpl* del grupo de empresas **2** *verb* **to group together** = agrupar *or* agruparse; **civil**

wrongs against persons and their property are grouped together under the heading 'torts' = los daños civiles contra las personas y sus propiedades están agrupados bajo el título de 'agravios indemnizables en juicio civil'

grow [grəʊ] *verb* crecer

guarantee [gærənˈtiː] **1** *noun* **(a)** *(for goods)* garantía *f*; **certificate of guarantee** *or* **guarantee certificate** = certificado *m* de garantía; **the guarantee lasts for two years** = la garantía tiene una duración de dos años *or* tiene una garantía de dos años; **the computer is sold with a two-year guarantee** = el ordenador se vende con dos años de garantía; **the car is still under guarantee** = el coche todavía está en periodo de garantía **(b)** *(person)* garantía *or* aval *m* *or* afianzamiento *m* **(c)** *(thing given as security)* fianza *f* *or* garantía; **to leave share certificates as a guarantee** = dejar títulos de acciones como fianza *or* garantía **2** *verb* garantizar *or* avalar *or* asegurar; **to guarantee a debt** = avalar una deuda; **to guarantee an associated company** = avalar a una compañía asociada *or* empresa afiliada; **to guarantee a bill of exchange** = avalar una letra de cambio; **the product is guaranteed for twelve months** = el producto está garantizado por doce meses *or* tiene una garantía de doce meses

COMMENT: in English law, a guarantee must usually be in writing. The person making a guarantee is secondarily liable if the person who is primarily liable defaults. Compare INDEMNITY

◊ **guarantor** [gærənˈtɔː] *noun* garante *mf* *or* fiador, -ra; **to stand guarantor for someone** = avalar a alguien *or* ser garante de alguien
◊ **guaranty** [ˈgærəntiː] *US* = GUARANTEE

guard [gɑːd] **1** *noun* **(a)** *(person who protects property or people)* guardia *mf* *or* guarda *mf*; **there were three guards on duty at the door of the bank** *or* **three bank guards were on duty** = había tres guardias de servicio en la puerta del banco; **the prisoner was shot by the guards as he tried to escape** = el prisionero fue tiroteado por los guardias al intentar escapar; **security guard** = guardia jurado **(b)** *(being protected)* vigilancia *f* *or* custodia *f*; **the prisoners were brought into the courtroom under armed guard** = los acusados fueron llevados a la sala del tribunal bajo vigilancia armada **2** *verb* proteger *or* escoltar *or* custodiar *or* vigilar; **the building is guarded by a fence and ten guard dogs** = el edificio está protegido por una verja y diez perros guardianes; **the prisoners are guarded night and day** = los presos están vigilados día y noche
◊ **guardian** [ˈgɑːdiən] *noun* tutor, -ra; **guardian for the suit** = curador, -ra; **guardian ad litem** = curador nombrado para un proceso; *see also* NEXT FRIEND

◊ **guardianship** [ˈgɑːdiənʃip] *noun* tutela *f* *or* amparo *m* *or* protección *f*; **guardianship order** = orden *f* judicial de tutela *or* orden judicial que nombra a una autoridad local tutor de un menor

guerilla [gəˈrilə] *noun* guerrillero, -ra; **the train was attacked by guerillas** = el tren fue asaltado por guerrilleros; **the appeal was made by a guerilla radio station** = el llamamiento fue hecho por una emisora de radio perteneciente a guerrilleros

guidelines [ˈgaidlainz] *plural noun* líneas *fpl* directivas *or* pautas *fpl* *or* directrices *fpl*; **the government has issued guidelines on increases in wages and prices** = el gobierno ha dado directrices sobre aumentos de salarios y precios; **the Law Society has issued guidelines to its members on dealing with rape cases** = el Colegio de Abogados ha dado directrices a sus miembros sobre cómo resolver los casos de violación; **the Secretary of State can issue guidelines for expenditure** = el Secretario de Estado puede dar directrices sobre gastos; **the Lord Justice said he was not laying down guidelines for sentencing** = el Juez dijo que no estaba exponiendo directrices para formular sentencias

guillotine [ˈgilətiːn] **1** *noun* **(a)** *(form of execution)* guillotina *f* **(b)** *(motion in House of Commons)* moción *f* de la Cámara de los Comunes para finalizar un debate a una hora determinada **2** *verb* guillotinar

guilt [gilt] *noun* culpa *f* *or* culpabilidad *f*; **guilt by association** = presunción *f* de culpabilidad de una persona por su relación con otra que es culpable; **he admitted his guilt** = admitió su culpabilidad
◊ **guilty** [ˈgilti] *adjective* culpable; **not guilty** = inocente *or* inculpable; **guilty of contempt** = contumaz; **he was found guilty of libel** = le declararon culpable de difamación; **the company was guilty of evading the VAT regulations** = la compañía era culpable de evadir las disposiciones del IVA; **guilty knowledge** = MENS REA; *(of a judge or jury)* **to find someone guilty** *or* **to return a verdict of guilty** *or* **to return a guilty verdict** = declarar a alguien culpable; *(of an accused person)* **to plead guilty** *or* **not guilty** = declararse culpable *or* inocente; **the accused pleaded not guilty to the charge of murder, but pleaded guilty to the lesser charge of manslaughter** = el acusado se declaró inocente de la acusación de asesinato, pero culpable del cargo menor de homicidio involuntario

gun [gʌn] *noun* arma *f* *or* pistola *f* *or* fusil *m*; **the police are not allowed to carry guns** = la policía no tiene permitido llevar armas; **they shouted to the robbers to drop their guns** = gritaron a los atracadores que tiraran las armas
◊ **gunboat** [ˈgʌnbəʊt] *see* DIPLOMACY
◊ **gun down** [ˈgʌn ˈdaʊn] *verb* matar a tiros; **he was gunned down in the street outside his office**

= le mataron a tiros en la calle delante de su oficina (NOTE: **gunned - gunning**)

◊ **gunman** ['gʌnmən] *noun* pistolero *m* *or* hombre *m* armado; **the security van was held up by three gunmen** = la furgoneta de seguridad fue asaltada por tres hombres armados

◊ **gunpoint** ['gʌnpɔɪnt] *noun* **at gunpoint** = a punta de pistola; **he was forced at gunpoint to open the safe** = le obligaron a abrir la caja fuerte a punta de pistola

◊ **gunshot** ['gʌnʃɒt] *noun* disparo *m* *or* tiro *m;* **he died of gunshot wounds** = murió de heridas de bala

Hh

habeas corpus ['heɪbiəs 'kɔːpəs] *Latin phrase* ley básica de protección al ciudadano para evitar la retención ilegal; **writ of habeas corpus** = orden *f* de habeas corpus

habendum [hə'bendəm] *noun* sección de una escritura de traspaso que da detalles sobre cómo debe cederse la propiedad al comprador

habitual [hə'bɪtjuəl] *adjective* habitual; **habitual criminal** *or* **habitual offender** = delincuente *mf* habitual *or* reincidente; **habitual drunkard** = borracho, -cha empedernido, -da *or* ebrio, -bria habitual; **habitual residence** = residencia *f* *or* domicilio *m* habitual

Hague Convention(s) ['heɪg kən'venʃnz] *plural noun* Convención de la Haya; *see also* GENEVA

half [hɑːf] *adjective* mitad; **he is paid time and a half on Sundays** = los domingos cobra la mitad más
◊ **half-yearly** ['hɑːf'jɔːli] *adverb* cada seis meses *or* semestralmente

hall [hɔːl] *noun* **town hall** = ayuntamiento *m* *or* casa *f* consistorial

hallmark ['hɔːlmɑːk] **1** *noun* marca *f* de contraste *or* sello *m* **2** *verb* poner el contraste a una pieza de oro o plata; **a hallmarked spoon** = una cuchara con la marca de contraste

halt [hɒlt] *noun* alto *m*

hand [hænd] *noun* **(a)** *(part of the body)* mano *f*; **to shake hands** = dar la mano *or* estrechar la mano; **to shake hands on a deal** = darse la mano para sellar un trato *or* cerrar un trato con un apretón de manos **(b) by hand** = a mano; **to send a letter by hand** = entregar una carta en mano **(c) in hand** = en reserva; **balance in hand** *or* **cash in hand** = saldo líquido *or* dinero *m* en efectivo *or* disponible *or* en caja; **work in hand** = trabajo *m* actual *or* entre manos **(d) goods left on hand** = productos *mpl* sobrantes *or* mercancías *fpl* que no se han vendido **(e) out of hand** = en seguida *or* inmediatamente *or* sin pensarlo dos veces *or* sin miramientos; **the justices dismissed his evidence out of hand** = los jueces desestimaron la prueba inmediatamente **(f) to hand** = aquí *or* a mano; **I have the invoice to hand** = tengo la factura aquí **(g) show of hands** = a mano alzada; **the motion was carried on a show of hands** = la moción se llevó a cabo a mano alzada **(h) to change hands** = cambiar de dueño; **the shop changed hands for £100,000** = la tienda cambió de dueño por 100.000 libras **(i) note of hand** = letra *f* a cargo propio *or* pagaré *m;* **in witness whereof, I set my hand** = en fe de lo cual, firmo la presente *or* firmo de mi puño y letra

◊ **handcuffs** ['hændkʌfs] *plural noun* esposas *fpl*
◊ **handcuffed** ['hændkʌft] *adjective* esposado, -da; **the accused appeared in court handcuffed to two policemen** = el acusado compareció ante el tribunal esposado a dos policías
◊ **hand down** ['hænd 'daʊn] *verb* **(a)** transmitir *or* pasar; **the house has been handed down from father to son since the nineteenth century** = la casa ha ido pasando de padres a hijos desde el siglo XIX **(b) to hand down a verdict** = anunciar un veredicto
◊ **handgun** ['hændgʌn] *noun* pistola *f;* **the police found six handguns when they searched the car** = cuando la policía registró el coche encontró seis pistolas
◊ **hand over** ['hænd 'əʊvə] *verb* entregar *or* ceder *or* transmitir; **she handed over the documents to the lawyer** = entregó los documentos al abogado; **he handed over to his deputy** = cedió el puesto a su adjunto
◊ **hand up** ['hænd 'ʌp] *verb* elevar *or* presentar; **the exhibit was handed up to the judge** = el documento fue elevado al juez
◊ **handwriting** ['hændraɪtɪŋ] *noun* **(a)** *(written by hand)* letra *f* *or* escritura *f;* **send a letter of application in your own handwriting** = envíe carta de solicitud manuscrita *or* escrita a mano; **handwriting expert** = experto *or* perito en grafología *or* caligrafía; **he faked** *or* **forged his father's handwriting** = falsificó la letra de su padre **(b)** *(slang)* marca *f* *or* sello *m* personal de un delincuente
◊ **handwritten** ['hændrɪtən] *adjective* escrito, -ta a mano *or* manuscrito, -ta; **it is more professional to send in a typed rather than a handwritten letter of application** = es más profesional enviar una carta de solicitud a máquina que a mano

handicap ['hændɪkæp] *noun* *(disability)* impedimento *m* físico
◊ **handicapped** ['hændɪkæpt] *noun* impedido, -da; **mentally handicapped** = deficiente mental

handle ['hændl] *verb* **(a)** *(to deal with)* ocuparse de *or* organizar *or* tratar *or* despachar *or* encargarse de; **the courts had difficulty in handling all the cases** = los tribunales se encontraron con dificultades para ocuparse de todos los casos; **the fraud squad handles cases of business malpractice** = la brigada contra el fraude se ocupa de casos de negligencia empresarial **(b)** *(to trade in)* vender *or* comerciar; **we do not handle foreign cars** = no comerciamos en coches extranjeros; **they will not handle goods produced by other firms** = no venderán mercancía producida por otras firmas
◊ **handling** ['hændlɪŋ] *noun* manejo *m* *or* manipulación *f;* **handling charges** = gastos *mpl* de manipulación *or* de transporte interno; **handling stolen goods** = manipulación *or* manejo *or* tráfico *m* de objetos robados

---

COMMENT: handling stolen goods is a more serious crime than theft, and the penalty can be higher

---

hang [hæŋ] *verb* **(a)** *(clothes)* colgar; **hang your coat on the hook behind the door** = cuelga el abrigo en el perchero detrás de la puerta; **he hung his umbrella over the back of his chair** = colgó el paraguas en el respaldo de su silla **(b)** *(execution)* ahorcar; *see also* HUNG (NOTE: **hanging - hung** for meaning (a) and **hanging - hanged** for meaning (b)
◊ **hanging** ['hæŋɪŋ] *noun* ejecución *f* en la horca *or* ahorcamiento *m;* **the hangings took place in front of the prison** = les ahorcaron delante de la prisión
◊ **hangman** ['hæŋmən] *noun* verdugo *m* *or* ejecutor, -ra de la justicia

Hansard ['hænsɑːd] *noun* diario *m* de sesiones *or* actas *fpl* oficiales de los debates parlamentarios

happen ['hæpn] *verb* pasar; **what happened?** = ¿qué ha pasado? *or* ¿qué pasó?

harass ['hærəs *or* hə'ræs] *verb* acosar *or* hostigar
◊ **harassment** ['hærəsmənt *or* hə'ræsmənt] *noun* acoso *m* *or* hostigamiento *m;* **he complained of police harassment** *or* **of harassment by the police** = se quejó de acoso policial

harbour ['hɑːbə] **1** *noun* puerto *m* **2** *verb* encubrir a un criminal *or* cobijar a un delincuente
◊ **harbouring** ['hɑːbərɪŋ] *noun* dar cobijo a un delincuente

hard [hɑːd] *adjective* **(a)** *(strong)* duro, -ra *or* fuerte; **to take a hard line in trade union negotiations** = adoptar una postura intransigente en las negociaciones sindicales **(b)** *(difficult)* difícil; **a hard case** = un caso difícil **(c)** *(solid)* duro, -ra *or* sólido, -da *or* real; **hard cash** = dinero *m* en metálico *or* efectivo *or* contante y sonante; **he paid

out £100 in hard cash for the chair** = pagó 100 libras en metálico por la silla; **hard copy** = copia *f* dura *or* legible *or* impresa; **hard disk** = disco *m* duro **(d)** **hard bargain** = trato *m* poco ventajoso *or* negocio duro *or* difícil; **to drive** *or* **to strike a hard bargain** = cerrar un trato en condiciones favorables para uno *or* imponer duras condiciones *or* pedir mucho **(e)** **hard currency** = moneda *f* convertible *or* divisa *f* fuerte
◊ **hardened criminal** ['hɑːdənd 'krɪmɪnəl] *noun* criminal *mf* habitual *or* reincidente
◊ **hard labour** ['hɑːd 'leɪbə] *noun* trabajos *mpl* forzados *or* forzosos
◊ **hardship** ['hɑːdʃɪp] *noun* dificultades *fpl* económicas *or* apuros *mpl* económicos; **the court order may cause hardship to the family of the defendant** = la orden judicial puede causar dificultades económicas a la familia del acusado; **in hardship cases** *or* **in cases of hardship, the local authority may offer temporary accommodation** = en casos de dificultad económica, las autoridades locales pueden ofrecer alojamiento temporal

harm [hɑːm] **1** *noun* daño *m* *or* perjuicio *m;* **the newspaper report has done a lot of harm to the firm's reputation** = el artículo *or* el reportaje periodístico ha lesionado en gran medida la reputación de la firma **2** *verb* dañar *or* perjudicar *or* estropear; **to harm someone's reputation** = desacreditar *or* lacerar; **the news that the chairman has been arrested for fraud has harmed the company's reputation** = la noticia de que el presidente ha sido arrestado por fraude ha desacreditado la compañía
◊ **harmful** ['hɑːmfʊl] *adjective* nocivo, -va

harmonization [hɑːmənaɪ'zeɪʃn] *noun* *(in the EU)* armonización *f* de leyes

harmony ['hɑːməni] *noun* armonía *f*

harsh [hɑːʃ] *adjective* duro, -ra *or* severo, -ra *or* violento, -ta; **the magistrate gave harsh sentences to the rioters** = el magistrado impuso severas condenas a los alborotadores; **they complained of harsh treatment on the part of the warders** = se quejaron de tratamiento violento por parte de los carceleros
◊ **harshly** ['hɑːʃli] *adverb* severamente *or* de un modo violento; **the prisoners have complained that they are harshly treated in the military prisons** = los presos se han quejado de recibir trato violento en las prisiones militares
◊ **harshness** ['hɑːʃnəs] *noun* severidad *f;* **the newspapers commented on the harshness of the sentence** = la prensa comentó la severidad de la condena

haste [heɪst] *noun* precipitación *f*

hatred ['heɪtrəd] *noun* odio *m;* **his hatred of injustice** *or* **of inequality** = su odio por la injusticia y la desigualdad; **racial hatred** = odio racial

have [hæv] *verb* tener; **to have and to hold** = tener y poseer; **to have a right to** = tener derecho a

hazard ['hæzəd] *noun* peligro *m or* riesgo *m;* **fire hazard** = peligro *or* riesgo de incendio

H-block ['eɪtʃ 'blɒk] *noun (in a prison)* edificio *m or* pabellón *m* en forma de H

head [hed] **1** *noun* **(a)** *(most important person)* jefe, -fa *or* director, -ra; **head of department** *or* **department head** = jefe de sección *or* departamento; **head of state** = jefe de estado *or* primer mandatario **(b)** *(main)* principal *or* más importante; **head clerk** = jefe de oficina; **head porter** = conserje jefe; **head salesman** = vendedor en jefe *or* principal; **head waiter** = jefe de comedor *or* de camareros; **head office** = oficina *f* principal *or* central *or* sede *f* central *or* casa *f* matriz **(c)** *(top part)* parte *f* superior *or* cabecera *f;* **write the name of the company at the head of the list** = escriba el nombre de la compañía al principio de la lista **(d)** *(person)* persona *f or* cabeza *f;* **allow £10 per head for expenses** = calcula 10 libras para gastos por persona; **representatives cost on average £25,000 per head per annum** = los representantes cuestan por término medio 25.000 libras al año por persona **(e)** *(of document)* epígrafe *m or* título *m;* **heads of agreement** = epígrafes de un acuerdo; **head of damage** = sección *f or* capítulo *m* de daños **2** *verb* **(a)** *(to be the manager)* dirigir *or* conducir; **to head a department** = dirigir un departamento; **he is heading a government delegation to China** = conduce una delegación del gobierno a China **(b)** *(to be first)* encabezar; **the list of cases to be heard is headed by two murder cases** = la lista de casos por ver está encabezada por dos casos de asesinato; **the two largest oil companies head the list of stock market results** = las dos compañías petrolíferas más grandes encabezan la lista de resultados de la bolsa

COMMENT: a head of state may not have much political power, and may be restricted to ceremonial duties (meeting ambassadors, laying wreaths at national memorials, opening parliament, etc.) The head of government is usually the effective ruler of the country, except in countries where the President is the executive ruler, and the head of government is in charge of the administration. In the United Kingdom, the Queen is head of state, and the Prime Minister is head of government. In the United States, the President is both head of state and head of government

◊ **headed** ['hedɪd] *adjective;* **headed paper** = papel *m* con membrete

◊ **headhunt** ['hedhʌnt] *verb* cazar talentos; **he was headhunted** = lo enganchó un cazador de talentos

◊ **headhunter** ['hedhʌntə] *noun* cazatalentos *mf*

◊ **heading** ['hedɪŋ] *noun* **(a)** encabezamiento *m or* epígrafe *m or* título *m or* breve introducción *f;* items are listed under several headings = los artículos están clasificados por títulos; **look at the figure under the heading 'Costs 95-96'** = observen la cifra bajo el título 'Costes 95-96' **(b)** **letter heading** *or* **heading on notepaper** = membrete *m*

◊ **head lease** ['hed 'liːs] *noun* (primer) arrendamiento *m*

◊ **head licence** ['hed 'laɪsəns] *noun* primera licencia *f*

◊ **headnote** ['hednəʊt] *noun* nota *f* de cabecera al comienzo de un informe jurídico que ofrece un resumen del caso

◊ **headquarters** [hed'kwɔːtəz] *plural noun* sede *f* central *or* domicilio *m* social; **police headquarters** = cuartel *m* general de la policía *or* jefatura *f* de policía

health [helθ] *noun* salud *f or* sanidad *f;* **health inspector** = inspector, -ra de sanidad; **bill of health** = patente *f* de sanidad; **medical officer of health (MOH)** = jefe, -fa de sanidad municipal; **public health** = salud pública

◊ **healthy** ['helθi] *adjective* sano, -na

hear [hɪə] *verb* **(a)** *(a sound)* oír; **you can hear the printer in the next office** = se puede oír la impresora de la oficina contigua *or* de al lado; **the traffic makes so much noise that I cannot hear my phone ringing** = el tráfico hace tanto ruido que no puedo oír si el teléfono suena **(b)** *(from someone)* tener noticias de alguien *or* saber de alguien; **we have not heard from them for some time** = hace algún tiempo que no tenemos noticias de ellos; **we hope to hear from the lawyers within a few days** = esperamos tener noticias de los abogados dentro de pocos días *or* en breve **(c)** *(court case)* proceder a la vista de un caso *or* oír un caso *or* conocer de una causa; **the judge heard the case in chambers** = el juez realizó la vista del caso en privado; **the case will be heard next month** = la vista del caso tendrá lugar el mes próximo; **the court has heard the evidence for the defence** = el tribunal ha oído al testigo de descargo (NOTE: **hearing - heard**)

◊ **hearing** ['hɪərɪŋ] *noun* vista *f* de un caso judicial *or* juicio *m or* audiencia *f;* **private hearing** = audiencia a puerta cerrada; **public hearing** = vista pública; **the hearing lasted ten days** = la vista duró diez días; **hearing in camera** = vista a puerta cerrada; **preliminary hearing** = diligencias *fpl* previas *or* preliminares

◊ **hearsay** ['hɪəseɪ] *noun* rumor *m*

◊ **hearsay evidence** ['hɪəseɪ 'evɪdəns] *noun* testimonio *m or* prueba *f* testimonial por referencia

heavy ['hevi] **1** *adjective* grave *or* duro, -ra *or* grande *or* importante; **the looters were given heavy jail sentences** = impusieron duras condenas de prisión a los saqueadores; **he was sentenced to pay a heavy fine** = le condenaron a pagar una multa importante **2** *noun (slang)* matón *m*

◊ **heavily** ['hevɪli] *adverb* fuertemente; **he had to borrow heavily to pay the fine** = tuvo que empeñarse hasta la camisa para pagar la multa *or* tuvo que contraer grandes deudas para pagar la multa

heir [eə] *noun* heredero *m;* **heir unconditional** = heredero absoluto; **rightful heir** = heredero legítimo; **universal heir** *or* **sole heir** = único heredero; **his heirs split the estate between them** = sus herederos dividieron la propiedad entre ellos; **heirs and assigns** = herederos *mpl* y cesionarios *mpl;* **heir apparent** = heredero forzoso; **heir presumptive** = presunto heredero
◊ **heiress** ['eəres] *noun* heredera *f*
◊ **heirloom** ['eəlu:m] *noun* reliquia *f* or joya *f* familiar *or* de familia; **the burglars stole some family heirlooms** = los ladrones robaron algunas joyas de familia

heist [heɪst] *noun (slang)* atraco *m* a mano armada

help [help] **1** *noun* ayuda *f;* **she finds the computer a great help in writing letters** = el ordenador le resulta de gran ayuda para escribir cartas; **the company was set up with help from the government** = la compañía se estableció con ayuda estatal; **counsel did not get much help from the witness** = el abogado no obtuvo mucha ayuda del testigo **2** *verb* ayudar *or* asistir; **his evidence did not help the case for the defendant** = su declaración no ayudó la defensa del acusado; **his case was not helped by the evidence of the expert witness** = su caso no se vio ayudado por la declaración del testigo pericial; **to help police with their inquiries** = prestar declaración en comisaría *or* ser llevado a comisaría para declarar

henceforth [hens'fɔ:θ] *adverb* de ahora en adelante; **henceforth it will be more difficult to avoid customs examinations** = de ahora en adelante será más difícil evitar registros aduaneros

henchman ['henʃmən] *noun (bodyguard)* guardaespaldas *m* or gorila *m*

here- [hɪə] *prefix* en este momento *or* aquí
◊ **hereafter** [hɪər'ɑ:ftə] *adverb* de ahora en adelante *or* más adelante
◊ **hereby** [hɪə'baɪ] *adverb* por este medio *or* por la presente; **we hereby revoke the agreement of January 1st 1982** = por la presente revocamos el acuerdo del 1 de enero de 1982

hereditament [herɪ'dɪtəmənt] *noun* bienes *mpl* que pueden ser objeto de herencia *or* herencia *f;* **corporeal hereditaments** = derechos *mpl* de propiedad sobre bienes materiales *or* tangibles; **incorporeal hereditaments** = derechos de propiedad sobre bienes intangibles como patentes *or* derechos de autor

hereditary [hɪ'redɪtri] *adjective* hereditario, -ria; **hereditary office** = cargo *m* hereditario; **hereditary peer** = par *m* hereditario

herein [hɪə'ɪn] *adverb* en la presente *or* sobre este punto *or* en este documento; **the conditions stated herein** = las condiciones establecidas en este documento; **see the reference herein above** = véase la referencia sobre este punto más arriba
◊ **hereinafter** [hɪərɪn'ɑ:ftə] *adverb* más adelante *or* a continuación *or* más abajo; **the conditions hereinafter listed** = las condiciones enumeradas a continuación
◊ **hereof** [hɪə'rɒv] *adverb* de lo cual *or* de lo mismo; **in confirmation hereof we attach a bank statement** = en confirmación de lo cual adjuntamos un extracto de cuentas bancario
◊ **hereto** [hɪə'tu:] *adverb* a esto *or* de esto *or* hasta el momento; **according to the schedule of payments attached hereto** = de acuerdo con el sistema de pago adjunto; **as witness hereto** = como testigo de este hecho; **the parties hereto** = las partes de este acuerdo
◊ **heretofore** [hɪətu'fɔ:] *adverb* antes *or* anteriormente *or* hasta ahora; **the parties heretofore acting as trustees** = actuando como administradores las partes anteriores
◊ **hereunder** [hɪə'ʌndə] *adverb* más abajo *or* a continuación *or* más adelante; **see the documents listed hereunder** = véanse los documentos enumerados a continuación
◊ **herewith** [hɪə'wɪð] *adverb* adjunto, -ta *or* con la presente; **please find the cheque enclosed herewith** = adjunto le enviamos el cheque

heritage ['herɪtɪdʒ] *noun* patrimonio *m;* **cultural** *or* **national heritage** = patrimonio cultural *or* nacional

Her Majesty's pleasure ['hɜ: 'mædʒəstɪz 'pleʒə] *noun* **detention at** *or* **during Her Majesty's pleasure** = arresto *m* por tiempo indefinido *or* hasta que el Ministro del Interior decida la libertad del preso

COMMENT: used as a punishment for people under a disability and children who commit murder

heroin ['herəʊɪn] *noun* heroína *f, (slang)* caballo *m*

hesitate ['hezɪteɪt] *verb* dudar *or* no estar seguro; **the jury is hesitating about its verdict** = el jurado no está seguro del veredicto; **she hesitated for some time before answering the question** = dudó un momento antes de responder a la pregunta

hide [haɪd] *verb* esconder
◊ **hidden** ['hɪdn] *adjective* escondido, -da *or* oculto, -ta *or* encubierto, -ta; **hidden asset** = diferencia *f* entre valor contable y de mercado; **hidden reserves** = reservas *fpl* ocultas; **hidden defect in the program** = defecto *m* oculto en el programa
◊ **hiding** ['haɪdɪŋ] *noun* **to go into hiding** = pasar a la clandestinidad

high [haɪ] **1** *adjective* **(a)** *(tall)* alto, -ta; **the shelves are 30 cm high** = las estanterías miden 30 cm de alto; **the top of the table is 20 inches high** = la parte superior de la mesa mide alrededor de 51 cm; **the door is not high enough to let us get the machines into the building** = no podemos meter las máquinas en el edificio porque la puerta no es lo bastante alta; **they are planning a 30-storey high office block** = están diseñando un bloque de oficinas de 30 pisos de alto **(b)** *(large)* grande; **highest bidder** = mejor postor *m;* **high flier** = *(person)* persona ambiciosa *or* de gran talento *or* triunfador, -ra; *(share)* valor *m* cuyo precio aumenta muy rápidamente; **high sales** = grandes ingresos por ventas; **high taxation** = impuestos *mpl* altos; **high volume (of sales)** = gran volumen *m* de ventas **2** *adverb* **prices are running high** = los precios están muy altos **3** *noun* récord *m;* **sales volume has reached an all-time high** = el volumen de ventas ha alcanzado un récord nunca visto *or* la cifra más alta jamás registrada
◊ **High Commission** [ˈhaɪ kəˈmɪʃn] *noun* representación *f* diplomática *or* embajada *f* de un estado de la Commonwealth en otro estado de la Commonwealth
◊ **High Court (of Justice)** [ˈhaɪ ˈkɔːt] *noun* Tribunal Superior (de Justicia) en Inglaterra y Gales

> COMMENT: in England and Wales, the High Court is divided into three divisions: the Queen's Bench, the Chancery and the Family Divisions; the Court hears most civil claims where the value exceeds £5,000

◊ **High Court of Justiciary** [ˈhaɪ ˈkɔːt əv dʒʌˈstɪʃiəri] *noun* Tribunal Superior de Justicia criminal en Escocia
◊ **high seas** [ˈhaɪ ˈsiːz] *plural noun* alta mar (NOTE: usually used with 'the': **an accident on the high seas**)
◊ **High Sheriff** [ˈhaɪ ˈʃerɪf] *noun* gobernador civil (Inglaterra) *or* primer presidente del tribunal de un condado (Gales)
◊ **higher** [ˈhaɪə] *adjective* superior
◊ **highlight** [ˈhaɪlaɪt] *verb* destacar
◊ **highly** [ˈhaɪli] *adverb* sumamente; **they employed a team of highly qualified legal assistants** = contrataron a un equipo de asesores jurídicos sumamente cualificados
◊ **highway** [ˈhaɪweɪ] *noun* vía *f* pública *or* carretera *f;* **the Highway Code** = Código *m* de Circulación

> COMMENT: the Highway Code is not itself part of English law

hijack [ˈhaɪdʒæk] **1** *noun* secuestro *m* (aéreo); **the hijack was organized by a group of opponents to the government** = el secuestro fue organizado por un grupo de opositores al gobierno **2** *verb* secuestrar; **the plane was hijacked by six armed terrorists** = el avión fue secuestrado por seis terroristas armados; **the bandits hijacked the lorry and killed the driver** = los bandidos secuestraron el camión y mataron al conductor
◊ **hijacker** [ˈhaɪdʒækə] *noun* secuestrador, -ra *or* pirata *mf* del aire
◊ **hijacking** [ˈhaɪdʒækɪŋ] *noun* secuestro *m;* **the hijacking took place just after the plane took off** = el secuestro se produjo nada más despegar el avión; **there have been six hijackings so far this year** = en lo que va de año se han producido seis secuestros

Hilary [ˈhɪləri] *noun* una de las cuatro sesiones de los tribunales jurídicos *or* uno de los cuatro periodos de sesiones jurídicas

hire [ˈhaɪə] **1** *noun* **(a)** *(rent)* alquiler *m;* **car hire firm** *or* **equipment hire firm** = compañía *f* de alquiler de coches; **hire car** = coche *m* alquilado *or* de alquiler **(b)** *(sign on taxi)* **'for hire'** = 'libre' **2** *verb* **(a)** *(people)* contratar *or* emplear; **to hire staff** = contratar personal; **we have hired the best lawyers to represent us** = hemos contratado a los mejores abogados para que nos representen; **they hired a small company to paint the offices** = contratamos los servicios de una pequeña empresa para que pintara las oficinas **(b)** *(things)* alquilar; **to hire a car** *or* **a crane** = alquilar un coche *or* una grúa
◊ **hire out** [ˈhaɪə ˈaʊt] *verb* alquilar; **to hire out cars** *or* **equipment** = alquilar coches *or* herramientas
◊ **hired** [ˈhaɪəd] *adjective;* **a hired car** = coche *m* alquilado *or* de alquiler; **hired killer** = asesino, -na a sueldo
◊ **hire purchase (HP)** [ˈhaɪə ˈpɜːtʃəs] *noun* compra *f* a plazos; **to buy a refrigerator on hire purchase** = comprar un frigorífico a plazos; **to sign a hire-purchase agreement** = firmar un contrato de venta a plazos; **hire-purchase company** = compañía *f* financiera (que financia la compra a plazos) (NOTE: the US English is **installment plan**)
◊ **hirer** [ˈhaɪərə] *noun* arrendador, -ra

hit [hɪt] *verb (slang)* matar
◊ **hit and run** [ˈhɪt ən ˈrʌn] *noun (driving offence)* situación en la que el conductor se da a la fuga tras un accidente o un atropello
◊ **hit man** [ˈhɪt ˈmæn] *noun (slang)* asesino a sueldo

hoard [hɔːd] *verb* acumular *or* atesorar
◊ **hoarder** [ˈhɔːdə] *noun* acaparador, -ra
◊ **hoarding** [ˈhɔːdɪŋ] *noun* **(a)** *(accumulate)* acaparamiento *m or* atesoramiento *m;* **hoarding of supplies** = acumulación *f* de provisiones **(b)** *(billboard)* **advertisement hoarding** = valla *f* publicitaria *or* cartelera *f*

hoax [həʊks] **1** *noun* broma *f* pesada *or* burla *f;* **bomb hoax** = falsa alarma de bomba; **hoax phone call** = llamar a la policía o a los bomberos haciendo creer que hay peligro *f* **2** *verb* burlar

hoc [hɒk] *see* AD HOC

hold [həuld] *verb* **(a)** *(to keep)* tener *or* guardar *or* poseer; **to have and to hold** = tener y poseer; **to hold office** = ostentar un cargo público; **he holds 10% of the company's shares** = posee el 10% de las acciones de la compañía; **she holds the land under a lease from the property company** = tiene la tierra en arrendamiento de la compañía inmobiliaria **(b)** *(to contain)* contener; **the tin holds twenty packets** = la lata *or* el bote contiene veinte paquetes; **each box holds 250 sheets of paper** = cada caja contiene 250 hojas de papel; **a bag can hold twenty kilos of sugar** = en una bolsa caben veinte kilos de azúcar **(c)** *(land)* ocupar; **he holds fifty acres in South Scotland** = tiene ocupados cincuenta acres en el sur de Escocia (200.000 metros cuadrados) **(d)** *(make something happen)* celebrar *or* tener *or* hacer; **to hold a discussion** = tener una discusión *or* una charla; **to hold a meeting** *or* **a trial** *or* **a hearing** = celebrar una reunión *or* una vista *or* un juicio; **the hearings were held in camera** = las vistas se celebraron a puerta cerrada; **the receiver will hold an auction of the company's assets** = el recaudador judicial celebrará una subasta de los bienes de la compañía; **the inquiry will be held in London in June** = la investigación se llevará a cabo en Londres durante el mes de junio **(e)** *(to keep in custody)* detener *or* retener; **the prisoners are being held in the police station** = retienen a los presos en comisaría; **twenty people were held in the police raid** = detuvieron a veinte personas en la redada policial; **she was held for six days without being able to see her lawyer** = fue retenida durante seis días sin que pudiera ver a su abogado **(f)** *(to decide)* considerar *or* mantener *or* sostener *or* creer; **the court held that there was no case to answer** = el tribunal consideró que la defensa no tenía suficientes argumentos jurídicos; **the appeal judge held that the defendant was not in breach of his statutory duty** = el juez de apelación sostuvo que el acusado no incurría en incumplimiento de deber (NOTE: **holding - held**)

◊ **hold back** [ˈhəuld ˈbæk] *verb* abstenerse *or* contenerse *or* esperar; **he held back from signing the lease until he had checked the details** = se abstuvo de firmar el contrato de arrendamiento hasta que hubo comprobado los detalles; **payment will be held back until the contract has been signed** = no se realizará el pago hasta que se haya firmado el contrato

◊ **holder** [ˈhəuldə] *noun* **(a)** *(owner)* tenedor, -ra *or* titular *mf or* poseedor, -ra *or* portador, -ra; **holders of government bonds** *or* **bondholders** = tenedores de bonos del estado *or* obligacionistas *mfpl*; **holder of stock** *or* **of shares in a company** = tenedor de acciones *or* accionista *mf*; **holder of an insurance policy** *or* **policy holder** = titular de una póliza de seguros; **she is a British passport holder** *or* **she is the holder of a British passport** = tiene pasaporte británico; **credit card holder** = titular de una tarjeta de crédito; **debenture holder** = obligacionista **(b)**

(of a cheque) portador *or* titular de un cheque **(c)** *(of bill of exchange)* tenedor de una letra de cambio *or* de un pagaré; **holder in due course** = tenedor de buena fe *or* legal **(d)** *(thing that keeps or protects something)* receptáculo *m or* soporte *m or* funda *f*; **card holder** *or* **message holder** = funda protectora de tarjetas *or* de mensajes; **credit card holder** = billetera *f* para tarjetas de crédito *or* funda de la tarjeta de crédito

◊ **holding** [ˈhəuldɪŋ] *noun* valores *mpl* en cartera; **he has sold all his holdings in the Far East** = ha vendido toda su cartera del Extremo Oriente; **the company has holdings in German manufacturing companies** = la compañía tiene valores de sociedades manufactureras alemanas; **cross holdings** = propiedad de acciones recíproca; **the two companies have protected themselves from takeover by a system of cross holdings** = las dos compañías se han protegido mutuamente contra la absorción por un sistema de 'cross holdings' *or* mediante la tenencia recíproca de acciones

◊ **holding charge** [ˈhəuldɪŋ ˈtʃɑːdʒ] *noun* acusación *f* menor *or* cargo *m* menor

◊ **holding company** [ˈhəuldɪŋ ˈkʌmpni] *noun* 'holding' *m or* sociedad *f* de cartera

◊ **holding over** *US* **holdover** [ˈhəuldɪŋ ˈəuvə *or* ˈhəuldəuvə] *noun* situación en la que una persona que tenía un arrendamiento por un periodo determinado continúa ocupando la propiedad después de la finalización del mismo

◊ **hold out** [ˈhəuld ˈaut] *verb* **(a)** *(to mislead)* comportarse de un modo engañoso; **he held himself out as a director of the company** = se comportaba como si fuera el director de la compañía **(b)** **to hold out for** = insistir en; **he held out for a 50% discount** = insistió en que se le diera un 50% de descuento; **the union is holding out for a 10% wage increase** = el sindicato insiste en un aumento de los salarios del 10%

◊ **hold over** [ˈhəuld ˈəuvə] *verb* **(a)** *(to postpone)* aplazar *or* posponer; **discussion of item 4 was held over until the next meeting** = la discusión del punto 4 quedó aplazada para la próxima reunión **(b)** *(to extend or prolong)* prolongar el arrendamiento a alguien

◊ **hold to** [ˈhəuld ˈtu] *verb* atenerse a *or* mantenerse fiel a *or* ajustarse a *or* limitar; **we will try to hold him to the contract** = trataremos de que se ajuste al contrato; **the government hopes to hold wage increases to 5%** = el gobierno espera limitar el aumento de salarios a un 5%

◊ **hold up** [ˈhəuld ˈʌp] *verb* **(a)** *(to steal)* asaltar *or* atracar; **six gunmen held up the bank** *or* **the security van** = seis hombres armados atracaron el banco *or* asaltaron la furgoneta de seguridad **(b)** *(to stay high)* sostenerse *or* mantenerse; **share prices have held up well** = los precios de las acciones se han mantenido bien; **sales held up during the tourist season** = las ventas se mantuvieron durante la época turística **(c)** *(to delay)* retrasar *or* retener; **the shipment has been held up at the customs** =

el cargamento ha sido retenido en la aduana; **payment will be held up until the contract has been signed** = se retrasará el pago hasta la firma del contrato; **the strike will hold up delivery for some weeks** = la huelga retrasará el reparto algunas semanas

◊ **holdup** [ˈhəʊldʌp] *noun* atraco *m or* asalto *m;* **the gang committed three armed holdups on the same day** = la banda perpetró tres atracos a mano armada en el mismo día

◊ **hold-up** [ˈhəʊldʌp] *noun* retraso *m;* **the strike caused hold-ups in the shipment of goods** = la huelga causó retrasos en el envío de la mercancía

holiday [ˈhɒlɪdeɪ] *noun* (a) *(day)* día *m* festivo; **bank holiday** = fiesta *f* oficial *or* día festivo; **Easter Monday is a bank holiday** = el Lunes de Pascua es festivo; **legal holiday** = día inhábil *or* no laboral; **public holiday** = fiesta nacional; **statutory holiday** = fiesta oficial *or* legal (b) *(rest from work)* vacaciones *fpl;* **to take a holiday** *or* **to go on holiday** = tomarse unas vacaciones *or* irse de vacaciones; **when is the manager taking his holidays?** = ¿Cuándo se toma las vacaciones el director?; **my secretary is off on holiday tomorrow** = mi secretaria empieza sus vacaciones mañana; **he is away on holiday for two weeks** = estará de vacaciones durante dos semanas; **the job carries five weeks' holiday** = el trabajo ofrece cinco semanas de vacaciones; **the summer holidays** = las vacaciones de verano; **holiday entitlement** = periodo *m* de vacaciones pagadas a las que un trabajador tiene derecho; **holiday pay** = paga *f* correspondiente al periodo de vacaciones (c) **tax holiday** = franquicia *f* fiscal *or* tributaria *or* exoneración *f* parcial concedida a una nueva empresa

holograph [ˈhɒləɡrɑːf] *adjective and noun* ológrafo *or* documento ológrafo; **holograph will** *or* *US also* **holographic will** = testamento ológrafo; **he left a holograph will** = dejó un testamento ológrafo

home [həʊm] *noun* (a) *(place where one lives)* casa *f or* vivienda *f or* hogar *m;* **community home** = hogar tutelar de menores (b) *(country of origin)* país *m* (de origen); **home-produced products** = productos *mpl* nacionales *or* productos del país

◊ **Home Office** [ˈhəʊm ˈɒfɪs] *noun* Ministerio *m* del Interior

◊ **Home Secretary** [ˈhəʊm ˈsekrətri] *noun* Ministro, -tra del Interior

> COMMENT: in most countries the government department dealing with the internal order of the country is called the Ministry of the Interior, with a Minister of the Interior in charge

◊ **homeless** [ˈhəʊmləs] *adjective & noun* sin hogar *or* sin techo

◊ **homestead** [ˈhəʊmsted] *noun US* hacienda *f or* heredad *f*

> COMMENT: a homestead cannot be the subject of a sale by court order to satisfy creditors

homicide [ˈhɒmɪsaɪd] *noun* (a) *(killing of a person)* homicidio *m;* **he was found guilty of homicide** = le declararon culpable de homicidio; **the homicide rate has doubled in the last ten years** = el índice de homicidios se ha duplicado en los diez últimos años; **culpable homicide** = homicidio *or* asesinato *m;* **justifiable homicide** = homicidio justificado (b) *(murder)* asesinato *m;* **the Homicide Squad** = La Brigada de Homicidios

> COMMENT: homicide covers the crimes of murder, manslaughter and infanticide

◊ **homicidal** [hɒmɪˈsaɪdl] *adjective* homicida

honest [ˈɒnɪst] *adjective* sincero, -ra *or* honrado, -da *or* honesto, -ta; **to play the honest broker** = actuar de amigable componedor

◊ **honestly** [ˈɒnəstli] *adverb* sinceramente *or* honradamente

◊ **honesty** [ˈɒnəsti] *noun* rectitud *f or* honradez *f;* **the court praised the witness for her honesty in informing the police of the crime** = el tribunal alabó a la testigo por su rectitud al informar a la policía del crimen

honorarium [ɒnəˈreəriəm] *noun* honorarios *mpl or* emolumentos *mpl*

◊ **honorary** [ˈɒnəri] *adjective* honorario, -ria; **honorary secretary** = secretario honorario; **honorary president** = presidente honorario; **honorary member** = miembro honorario

honour *US* **honor** [ˈɒnə] **1** *noun* (a) *(reputation)* honor *m* (b) *(title)* **your honour** = vuestra merced **2** *verb* aceptar *or* pagar (un cheque *or* una letra de cambio); **to honour a debt** = pagar una deuda; **to honour a signature** = aceptar una firma *or* reconocer una firma

◊ **honourable** *US* **honorable** [ˈɒnərəbl] **1** *adjective* honorable *or* ilustre **2** *noun GB (title used amongst MPs)* honorable *mf or* ilustre *mf;* **Right Honourable** = título o tratamiento de protocolo a los miembros del Privy Council (NOTE: usually written **Hon.: the Hon. Member; the Rt.Hon. William Smith, M.P.**)

> COMMENT: various conventions are attached to the use of the word in Parliament. In general, MPs can refer to each other as 'the hon. Member for...'; the Speaker will refer to all MPs as 'hon. Members'. To distinguish MPs of one's own party from those on the other side of the House, an MP will say 'my hon. Friend'. To distinguish between women and men MPs, you can say 'the hon. Lady' or 'the hon. Gentleman'. Lawyers may be addressed as 'hon. and learned'

hoodlum ['huːdləm] *noun US* matón *m or* rufián *m or* gángster *m*

hooligan ['huːlɪgən] *noun* gamberro, -rra *or* alborotador, -ra; **the police put up barriers to prevent the football hooligans from damaging property** = la policía colocó barricadas para impedir que los hinchas más violentos del fútbol causaran destrozos
◊ **hooliganism** ['huːlɪgənɪzm] *noun* vandalismo *m or* gamberrismo *m*

hospital ['hɒspɪtəl] *noun* hospital *m;* **hospital order** = orden *f* de internamiento psiquiátrico de un delincuente

hostage ['hɒstɪdʒ] *noun* rehén *mf;* **he was taken hostage by the guerillas** = los guerrilleros le tomaron como rehén; **the bandits took away the bank manager and kept him hostage** = los bandidos se llevaron al director del banco y lo tuvieron de rehén; **the terrorists released three hostages** = los terroristas liberaron a tres rehenes

hostile ['hɒstaɪl] *adjective* hostil *or* enemigo, -ga; **hostile witness** = testigo *mf* desfavorable *or* hostil; **she was ruled a hostile witness by the judge** = el juez la calificó de testigo desfavorable

hostility [hɒ'stɪlɪti] *noun* enemistad *f*

hot [hɒt] *adjective* **(a)** *(not safe)* peligroso, -sa; **to make things hot for someone** = ponerle las cosas difíciles a alguien; **customs officials are making things hot for the drug smugglers** = los oficiales de aduanas están poniendo las cosas difíciles a los traficantes de droga; **hot money** = dinero *m* caliente *or* especulativo *or* dinero que pasa de un país a otro; **he is in the hot seat** = tiene un puesto de mucha responsabilidad **(b)** *(informal)* robado, -da; **hot jewels** = joyas robadas; **a hot car** = un coche robado
◊ **hot pursuit** [hɒt pə'sjuːt] *noun* persecución *f* de un barco en aguas internacionales *or* de un sospechoso en otro país

hotchpot ['hɒtʃpɒt] *noun* colación *f* (de bienes)

house [haus] *noun* **(a)** *(building)* casa *f or* vivienda *f;* **house property** = viviendas particulares *or* inmuebles *mpl* residenciales; **house agent** = agente *mf* inmobiliario **(b)** *(in Parliament)* cámara *f;* **the Houses of Parliament** = las Casas del Parlamento *or* el Parlamento Británico **(c)** *US* **the House** = la Cámara de Representantes
◊ **house arrest** ['haus ə'rest] *noun* arresto *m* domiciliario; **the opposition leader has been under house arrest for six years** = el líder de la oposición lleva seis años bajo arresto domiciliario
◊ **housebreaker** ['hausbreɪkə] *noun* ladrón, -ona de casas
◊ **housebreaking** ['hausbreɪkɪŋ] *noun* robo *m* en una casa *or* allanamiento *m* de morada

◊ **household** ['haushəuld] *noun* casa *f or* familia *f;* **household effects** = efectos *mpl* domésticos *or* enseres *mpl*
◊ **householder** ['haushəuldə] *noun* cabeza *m* de familia *or* dueño, -ña de una casa *or* inquilino, -na
◊ **House of Commons** ['haus əv 'kɒmənz] *noun* Cámara de los Comunes
◊ **House of Lords** ['haus əv 'lɔːdz] *noun* Cámara de los Lores; **Judicial Committee of the House of Lords** = Comité Judicial de la Cámara de los Lores

COMMENT: as a court, the decisions of the House of Lords are binding on all other courts, and the only appeal from the House of Lords is to the European Court of Justice

◊ **House of Representatives** ['haus əv reprɪ'zentətɪvz] *noun* Cámara de Representantes
◊ **house-to-house** ['haustə'haus] *adjective* de puerta en puerta *or* a domicilio; **the police carried out a house-to-house search for the escaped prisoners** = la policía llevó a cabo una búsqueda de los presos evadidos de puerta en puerta

human ['hjuːmən] *adjective* humano, -na; **human error** = error *m* humano; **human rights** = derechos *mpl* humanos

hung [hʌŋ] *adjective* sin mayoría; **hung jury** = jurado *m* que no puede llegar a un veredicto por unanimidad; **hung parliament** = parlamento *m* que carece de mayoría para gobernar; *see also* HANG

hunger strike ['hʌŋgə 'straɪk] *noun* huelga *f* de hambre; **he went on hunger strike until the prison authorities allowed him to receive mail** = se declaró en huelga de hambre hasta que las autoridades de prisiones le permitieron recibir el correo

hunt [hʌnt] **1** *noun* caza *f or* búsqueda *f or* busca *f;* **the police have organized a hunt for the stolen gold** *or* **for the escaped prisoners** *or* **for the murder weapon** = la policía ha organizado una búsqueda del oro robado *or* de los presos huidos *or* del arma homicida; **murder hunt** = búsqueda del asesino **2** *verb* buscar *or* cazar; **the police are hunting for clues to the murder** = la policía está buscando pistas del asesinato

hurdle ['hɜːdl] *noun* obstáculo *m;* **the defendant will have to overcome two hurdles if his appeal is to be successful** = el acusado tendrá que superar dos obstáculos si quiere que su recurso prospere

hurry ['hʌri] **1** *noun* prisa *f or* precipitación *f;* **there is no hurry for the figures, we do not need them until next week** = no tenemos prisa por conocer los resultados, no los necesitamos hasta la semana que viene; **in a hurry** = de prisa **2** *verb* darse prisa *or* apresurarse; **the government whips are trying to hurry the bill through the committee stages** = los líderes del grupo parlamentario están tratando de acelerar el proyecto de ley a su paso por la comisión; **the chairman does not want to be hurried into making a decision** = el presidente no quiere que le obliguen a tomar una decisión precipitadamente; **the directors hurried into the meeting** = los directores se apresuraron a la reunión

hurt [həːt] *verb* dañar *or* herir *or* afectar *or* perjudicar; **the criticism in the newspapers did not hurt our sales** = la crítica por parte de la prensa no afectó a nuestras ventas; **sales of summer clothes were hurt by the bad weather** = el mal tiempo perjudicó la venta de ropa de verano; **the company has not been hurt by the recession** = la compañía no se ha visto perjudicada por la recesión *or* la recesión no ha perjudicado a la compañía

husband ['hʌzbənd] *noun* marido *m or* esposo *m*

hush money ['hʌʃ 'mʌni] *noun (informal)* mamela *f or* guante *m or* soborno *m*

hybrid offence ['haɪbrɪd ə'fens] *noun* delito *m* que puede ser juzgado por magistrados *or* por un juez y un jurado

hypothecation [haɪpɒθɪ'keɪʃn] *noun (using property as collateral for a loan)* pignoración *f*

Ii

ibid *or* **ibidem** ['ɪbɪd] *adverb* ibídem

ID ['aɪ 'diː] = IDENTITY; **ID card** = IDENTITY CARD

id *or* **idem** ['ɪdem] *pronoun* ídem; **ad idem** = de acuerdo

identify [aɪ'dentɪfaɪ] *verb* identificar; **she was able to identify her attacker** = pudo identificar a su atacante; **passengers were asked to identify their suitcases** = se pidió a los pasajeros que identificaran sus maletas; **the dead man was identified by his fingerprints** = se identificó al fallecido por sus huellas dactilares
◊ **identification** [aɪdentɪfɪ'keɪʃn] *noun* identificación *f;* **positive identification** = identificación positiva; **proof of identification** = prueba *f* de identificación *or* documentos *mpl* de identidad; **the policeman asked him for proof of identification** = el policía le pidió que se identificara; **identification parade** = rueda *f* de identificación
◊ **identikit** [aɪ'dentɪkɪt] *noun* retrato *m* robot; **the police issued an identikit picture of the mugger** = la policía puso en circulación un retrato robot del atracador; *see also* PHOTOFIT
◊ **identity** [aɪ'dentɪtɪ] *noun* **(a)** *(who someone is)* identidad *f;* **he changed his identity** = cambió de identidad; **he was asked for proof of identity** = le pidieron que diera pruebas de su identidad; **identity card** *or* **ID card** = carnet *m or* documento *m or* tarjeta *f* de identidad; **identity disk; identity parade** = *or* placa *f* de identidad careo *m* (de sospechosos); *see also* IDENTIFICATION PARADE; **case of mistaken identity** = caso *m* de identificación errónea **(b)** *(being the same)* identidad; **identity of parties** = identidad de las partes

i.e. ['aɪ 'iː] es decir *or* o sea; **the largest companies, i.e. Smith's and Brown's, show very good profits** = las empresas más grandes, es decir, Smith's y Brown's, muestran importantes beneficios; **the import restrictions apply to expensive items, i.e. items costing more than $2,500** = las restricciones sobre importación se aplican a artículos caros, o sea artículos que cuestan más de 2.500 dólares

ignorance ['ɪgnərəns] *noun* ignorancia *f;* **to plead ignorance** = alegar ignorancia; **ignorance of the law is no excuse** = la ignorancia de la ley no exime su cumplimiento

ignorantia legis non *or* **neminem** *or* **haud excusat** [ɪgnə'ræntiə 'ledʒɪs nɒn eks'kjuːzæt] *Latin phrase* 'la ignorancia de la ley no exime su cumplimiento'

ignore [ɪg'nɔː] *verb* ignorar *or* hacer caso omiso *or* no hacer caso

ill [ɪl] *adjective* enfermo, -ma
◊ **ill fame** *or* **ill repute** ['ɪl 'feɪm *or* rɪ'pjuːt] *noun* mala fama *f or* mala reputación *f;* **of ill fame** = de mala fama
◊ **ill-gotten** ['ɪlgɒtən] *adjective* mal adquirido; **ill-gotten gains** = beneficios obtenidos de un negocio poco honrado
◊ **ill-treated** [ɪl'triːtɪd] *adjective* maltratado, -da
◊ **ill-treatment** [ɪl'triːtmənt] *adjective* maltrato *m or* malos tratos
◊ **ill-will** ['ɪl'wɪl] *noun* enemistad manifiesta
◊ **illness** ['ɪlnəs] *noun* enfermedad *f*

illegal [ɪ'liːgəl] *adjective* ilegal *or* ilícito, -ta; **the illegal carrying of arms** = tenencia ilícita de armas; **illegal immigrants are deported** = los inmigrantes ilegales son deportados; **illegal contract** = contrato *m* ilegal
◊ **illegality** [ɪlɪ'gælɪtɪ] *noun* ilegalidad *f*
◊ **illegally** [ɪ'liːgəli] *adverb* ilegalmente; **he was accused of illegally bringing firearms into the country** = le acusaron de introducir ilegalmente armas de fuego en el país

illegitimate [ɪlɪ'dʒɪtɪmət] *adjective* **(a)** *(against the law)* ilegítimo, -ma **(b)** *(person born to parents not married to each other)* ilegítimo, -ma
◊ **illegitimacy** [ɪlɪ'dʒɪtɪməsi] *noun* ilegitimidad *f*

COMMENT: children who are illegitimate can nevertheless inherit from their parents

illicit [ɪ'lɪsɪt] *adjective* ilícito, -ta; **illicit sale of alcohol** = venta ilícita de alcohol; **trade in illicit alcohol** = comercio ilícito de alcohol

ILO ['aɪ 'el 'əʊ] = INTERNATIONAL LABOUR ORGANIZATION

IMF ['aɪ 'em 'ef] = INTERNATIONAL MONETARY FUND

imitate ['ɪmɪteɪt] *verb* imitar; **this new gang is imitating all the tricks of the famous Chinese gang of the 1930s** = esta nueva banda está imitando todos los trucos de la famosa banda china de los años treinta
◊ **imitation** [ɪmɪ'teɪʃn] *noun* imitación *f;* **beware of imitations** = desconfíe de las imitaciones

immaterial [ɪmə'tɪərɪəl] *adjective* sin importancia *or* ajeno al caso

immediate [ɪ'miːdɪət] *adjective* inmediato, -ta; **he wrote an immediate letter of complaint** = escribió una carta de reclamación inmediatamente; **the magistrate ordered her immediate release** = el juez ordenó su liberación inmediata
◊ **immediately** [ɪ'miːdɪətli] *adverb* inmediatamente; **immediately afterwards** = acto seguido; **as soon as she arrived in the country, she was immediately arrested by the airport police** = nada más llegar al país, fue arrestada por la policía del aeropuerto; **as soon as he heard the news he immediately phoned his office** = en cuanto se enteró de la noticia llamó inmediatamente a su oficina; **can you phone immediately after you get the information?** = ¿Puede llamar por teléfono en cuanto consiga la información?

immemorial [ɪmə'mɔːrɪəl] *adjective* inmemorial; **immemorial existence** *or* **time immemorial** = existencia *f* inmemorial *or* tiempo *m* inmemorial; **from time immemorial** = desde tiempo inmemorial

immigrate ['ɪmɪgreɪt] *verb* inmigrar
◊ **immigration** [ɪmɪ'greɪʃn] *noun* inmigración *f;* **Immigration Laws** = leyes *fpl* de inmigración; **immigration officers** = oficiales *or* funcionarios de inmigración
◊ **immigrant** ['ɪmɪgrənt] *noun* inmigrante *mf;* **illegal immigrant** = inmigrante (en situación) ilegal; *see also* EMIGRATE, EMIGRANT

immoral earnings ['ɪ'mɒrəl 'əːnɪŋz] *plural noun* ingresos obtenidos ejerciendo la prostitución; **living off immoral earnings** = vivir de la prostitución

immovable [ɪ'muːvəbl] *adjective & noun* inmóvil *or* inmueble; **immovable property** *or* **immovables** = propiedad *f* inmobiliaria *or* bienes *mpl* raíces *or* inmuebles *mpl*

immune [ɪ'mjuːn] *adjective;* **immune from prosecution** = inimputable

immunity [ɪ'mjuːnɪti] *noun* inmunidad *f or* inviolabilidad *f;* **diplomatic immunity** = inmunidad diplomática; **when he offered to give information to the police, he was granted immunity from prosecution** = cuando se ofreció a dar información a la policía, le garantizaron la inmunidad judicial; **judicial immunity** = inmunidad judicial; **sovereign immunity** = inmunidad soberana

COMMENT: immunity from prosecution is also granted to magistrates, counsel and witnesses as regards their statements in judicial proceedings. Families and servants of diplomats may be covered by diplomatic immunity

impact ['ɪmpækt] *noun* incidencia *f;* **the warnings have had little impact** = los avisos han tenido poca incidencia

impanel [ɪm'pænəl] = EMPANEL

impartial [ɪm'pɑːʃl] *adjective* imparcial; **a judgment must be impartial** = un juicio debe ser imparcial; **to give someone a fair and impartial hearing** = ofrecer a alguien un juicio justo e imparcial
◊ **impartiality** [ɪmpɑːʃi'ælɪti] *noun* imparcialidad *f;* **the newspapers doubted the impartiality of the judge** = la prensa dudó de la imparcialidad del juez
◊ **impartially** [ɪm'pɑːʃəli] *adverb* imparcialmente; **the adjudicator has to decide impartially between the two parties** = el juez tiene que decidir imparcialmente entre las dos partes

impeach [ɪm'piːtʃ] *verb* **(a)** *(formerly)* acusar a una persona de traición ante el parlamento **(b)** acusar a un jefe de estado de traición *or* US acusar a altos funcionarios de traición u otros delitos graves **(c)** *US* recusar *or* poner en tela de juicio
◊ **impeachment** [ɪm'piːtʃmənt] *noun* proceso *m* de destitución *or* acusación *f* de traición *or* formulación *f* de cargos contra un jefe de estado o alto funcionario; *US* **articles of impeachment** = acusación formulada contra un alto cargo

impediment [ɪm'pedɪmənt] *noun (obstacle)* impedimento *m;* **prohibitive impediment** = impedimento impediente

impending [ɪm'pendɪŋ] *adjective* inminente; **the newspapers carried stories about the impending divorce case** = la prensa difundió rumores sobre el inminente caso de divorcio

imperfect [ɪm'pəːfɪkt] *adjective* imperfecto, -ta *or* defectuoso, -sa; **sale of imperfect items** = venta *f* de artículos defectuosos; **to check a shipment for imperfect products** = comprobar los productos defectuosos de un cargamento
◊ **imperfection** [ɪmpə'fekʃn] *noun* defecto *m or* imperfección *f;* **to check a shipment for imperfections** = comprobar los defectos de un cargamento

impersonal [ɪm'pəːsənl] *adjective* impersonal; **an impersonal style of management** = un estilo de dirección impersonal

impersonate [ɪm'pəːsəneɪt] *verb* hacerse pasar por otra persona *or* suplantar la personalidad; **he gained entrance to the house by impersonating a local authority inspector** = consiguió entrar en la casa haciéndose pasar por un inspector de las autoridades locales

◊ **impersonation** [ɪmpɜːsəˈneɪʃn] *noun* personificación *f or* suplantación *f* de la personalidad *or* uso *m* de nombre supuesto; **impersonation of a public officer** = usurpación *f* de funciones; **he was charged with impersonation of a police officer** = le acusaron de haberse hecho pasar por un oficial de policía

implement 1 [ˈɪmplɪmənt] *noun* herramienta *f or* instrumento *m;* **he was hit on the head with a heavy implement** = le golpearon la cabeza con una herramienta pesada **2** [ˈɪmplɪment] *verb* poner en práctica *or* llevar a cabo *or* ejecutar; **to implement an agreement** *or* **a decision** = poner en práctica un acuerdo *or* una decisión

◊ **implementation** [ɪmplɪmenˈteɪʃn] *noun* aplicación *f or* realización *f or* ejecución *f or* puesta *f* en práctica *or* implementación *f;* **the implementation of new rules** = la puesta en práctica de las nuevas normas *or* la aplicación de nuevas reglas

implicit [ɪmˈplɪsɪt] *adjective* implícito, -ta

imply [ɪmˈplaɪ] *verb* suponer *or* dar a entender; **counsel implied that the witness had not in fact seen the accident take place** = el abogado dio a entender que el testigo no había visto en realidad cómo ocurrió el accidente; **do you wish to imply that the police acted improperly?** = ¿Quiere usted dar a entender que la policía actuó incorrectamente?

◊ **implied** [ɪmˈplaɪd] *adjective* implícito, -ta *or* tácito, ta; **implied contract** = contrato *m* tácito *or* sobreentendido *or* cuasicontrato *m;* **implied malice** = intención *f* delictuosa; **implied terms and conditions** = condiciones *fpl* implícitas; **implied trust** = fideicomiso *m* implícito *or* tácito

import 1 [ˈɪmpɔːt] *noun* importación *f;* **the import of firearms is forbidden** = la importación de armas de fuego está prohibida; **import levy** = gravamen *or* sobre las importaciones; **import licence** = permiso *m or* licencia *f* de importación **2** [ɪmˈpɔːt] *verb* importar

◊ **imports** [ˈɪmpɔːts] *plural noun* importaciones *fpl;* **all imports must be declared to the customs** = todas las importaciones deben declararse en la aduana

importance [ɪmˈpɔːtəns] *noun* importancia *f;* **the bank attaches great importance to the deal** = el banco da mucha importancia al acuerdo *or* a la transacción

◊ **important** [ɪmˈpɔːtənt] *adjective* importante; **he left a pile of important papers in the taxi** = se dejó un montón de papeles importantes en el taxi; **she has an important meeting at 10.30** = tiene una reunión muy importante a las 10.30; **he was promoted to a more important position** = le ascendieron a un puesto más importante

importune [ɪmpɔːˈtjuːn] *verb* importunar *or* abordar con fines deshonestos

◊ **importuning** [ɪmpəˈtjuːnɪŋ] *noun* hacer proposiciones deshonestas

impose [ɪmˈpəʊz] *verb* imponer *or* gravar; **to impose a tax** = establecer impuestos; **the court imposed a fine of £100** = el tribunal impuso una multa de 100 libras; **to impose a tax on bicycles** = gravar las bicicletas con un impuesto; **they tried to impose a ban on smoking** = trataron de imponer una prohibición sobre el consumo del tabaco; **the government imposed a special duty on oil** = el gobierno impuso un impuesto especial sobre el petróleo; **the customs have imposed a 10% tax increase on electrical items** = la aduana ha aumentado en un 10% los aranceles sobre artículos eléctricos; **the unions have asked the government to impose trade barriers on foreign cars** = los sindicatos han pedido al gobierno que imponga barreras comerciales a los coches extranjeros

◊ **imposition** [ɪmpəˈzɪʃn] *noun* imposición *f or* impuesto *m*

impossible [ɪmˈpɒsbl] *adjective* imposible; **it is impossible for the police force to work harder than they are working already** = a la policía le resulta imposible trabajar más de lo que lo hace ya *or* la policía trabaja más de lo que puede; **getting skilled staff is becoming impossible** = se está haciendo imposible conseguir personal cualificado; **government regulations make it impossible for us to sell our computer parts** = la reglamentación oficial hace imposible la venta de nuestras piezas de ordenadores

◊ **impossibility** [ɪmpɒsɪˈbɪlɪti] *noun* imposibilidad *f;* **impossibility of performance** = imposibilidad de cumplimiento; **physical impossibility** = imposibilidad material

impostor [ɪmˈpɒstə] *noun* impostor, -ra

impound [ɪmˈpaʊnd] *verb* confiscar *or* embargar *or* incautarse; **the customs impounded the whole cargo** = los oficiales de aduana confiscaron todo el cargamento

◊ **impounding** [ɪmˈpaʊndɪŋ] *noun* embargo *m or* confiscación *f*

impression [ɪmˈpreʃn] *noun* impresión *f;* **counsel's speech made a strong impression on the jury** = el discurso del abogado causó una fuerte impresión en el jurado; **the judge got the impression that the witness worked in a bank** = el juez tuvo la impresión de que el testigo trabajaba en un banco; **case of first impression** = caso *m* sin precedentes

imprison [ɪmˈprɪzən] *verb* encarcelar *or* arrestar; **he was imprisoned by the secret police for six months** = estuvo encarcelado por la policía secreta durante seis meses

◊ **imprisonment** [ɪmˈprɪzənmənt] *noun* encarcelamiento *m or* cárcel *m or* privación *f* de libertad; **the penalty for the first offence is a fine of £200 or six weeks' imprisonment** = el castigo por el primer delito consiste en una multa de 200 libras o seis semanas de cárcel; **a term of imprisonment** = un periodo de cárcel; **he was sentenced to the maximum term of imprisonment** = le condenaron a la máxima pena de prisión; **false imprisonment** = retención *f or* detención *f or* encarcelamiento *m* ilegal; **life imprisonment** = cadena perpetua

COMMENT: life imprisonment is a term of many years, but not necessarily for the rest of the prisoner's life

improper [ɪmˈprɒpə] *adjective* impropio, -pia *or* incorrecto, -ta *or* inadecuado, -da *or* deshonesto, -ta
◊ **improperly** [ɪmˈprɒpəli] *adverb* impropiamente *or* incorrectamente *or* indebidamente; **the police constable's report was improperly made out** = el informe del policía estaba redactado incorrectamente; **he was accused of acting improperly in going to see the prisoner's father** = le acusaron de actuar indebidamente al ir a ver al padre del acusado

impulse [ˈɪmpʌls] *noun* impulso *m;* **irresistible impulse** = impulso irresistible

impunity [ɪmˈpjuːnɪti] *noun* impunidad *f;* **with impunity** = impunemente; **no one can flout the law with impunity** = nadie puede burlarse de la ley impunemente

impute [ɪmˈpjuːt] *verb* imputar *or* atribuir *or* achacar; **to impute a motive to someone** = atribuir un móvil a alguien
◊ **imputation** [ɪmpjuˈteɪʃn] *noun* imputación *f or* acusación *f;* **imputation of malice** = acusación de malicia *or* existencia *f* de malicia

in absentia [ɪn əbˈsentiə] *adverb* en ausencia de alguien; **she was tried and sentenced to death in absentia** = fue juzgada y condenada a muerte en rebeldía

inadmissible [ɪnədˈmɪsəbl] *adjective* (prueba) improcedente *or* inadmisible

inalienable [ɪnˈeɪliənəbl] *adjective* (derecho) inalienable

Inc = INCORPORATED

in camera [ˈɪn ˈkæmərə] *adverb* a puerta cerrada; **the case was heard in camera** = la vista del caso se realizó a puerta cerrada

incapable [ɪnˈkeɪpəbl] *adjective* incapaz *or* incapacitado, -da; **he was incapable of fulfilling the terms of the contract** = fue incapaz de cumplir los términos del contrato; **a child is considered legally incapable of committing a crime** = un menor es considerado legalmente incapaz de cometer un delito; **drunk and incapable** = borracho e incapacitado

◊ **incapacity** [ɪnkəˈpæsɪti] *noun* incapacidad *f;* **the court had to act because of the incapacity of the trustees** = el juzgado tuvo que actuar *or* tomar cartas en el asunto a causa de la incapacidad de los administradores

incapax [ˈɪnkæpæks] *see* DOLI INCAPAX

incarcerate [ɪnˈkɑːsəreɪt] *verb* encarcelar; **he was incarcerated in a stone tower** = fue encarcelado en una torre de piedra
◊ **incarceration** [ɪnkɑːsəˈreɪʃn] *noun* encarcelamiento *m or* encarcelación *f*

incest [ˈɪnsest] *noun* incesto *m*

in chambers [ˈɪn ˈtʃeɪmbəz] *adverb* en privado; **the judge heard the application in chambers** = el juez oyó la petición en privado

inchoate [ɪnˈkəʊeɪt] *adjective* incompleto, -ta; **inchoate instrument** = documento *m* incompleto *or* no registrado; **inchoate offences** = delitos *mpl* incompletos

incidence [ˈɪnsɪdəns] *noun* incidencia *f or* frecuencia *f;* **the incidence of cases of rape has increased over the last years** = la frecuencia de casos de violación ha aumentado durante los últimos años; **a high incidence of accidents relating to drunken drivers** = una alta incidencia de accidentes relacionados con conductores en estado de embriaguez

incident [ˈɪnsɪdənt] *noun* **1** incidente *m;* **three incidents were reported when police vehicles were attacked by a crowd** = se dio parte de tres incidentes cuando los vehículos policiales fueron atacados por una multitud; *(police)* **incident room** = centro *m* de coordinación *or* sala *f* de incidencias de una comisaría **2** *adjective;* **incident to something** = inherente a *or* propio de
◊ **incidental** [ɪnsɪˈdentl] *adjective* imprevisto, -ta *or* incidental *or* secundario, -ria *or* accesorio, ria; **incidental expenses** = gastos *mpl* imprevistos

incite [ɪnˈsaɪt] *verb* incitar *or* instigar
◊ **incitement** [ɪnˈsaɪtmənt] *noun* incitación *f;* **incitement to racial hatred** = incitación al odio racial
◊ **inciter** [ɪnˈsaɪtə] *noun* incitador, -ra

COMMENT: it is not necessary for a crime to have been committed for incitement to be proved

include [ɪnˈkluːd] *verb* incluir; **the charge includes VAT** = el IVA está incluido en el precio; **the total comes to £1,000 including freight** = el total asciende a 1.000 libras incluido el flete *or* transporte; **the total is £140 not including insurance and freight** = el total es de 140 libras sin incluir ni seguro ni flete; **the account covers services up to and including the month of June** = la cuenta cubre los servicios hasta el mes de junio inclusive; **including, but not limited to** = incluyendo este artículo pero sin excluir a otros

◊ **inclusive** [ɪnˈkluːsɪv] *adjective* inclusive *or* inclusivo, -va *or* incluido, -da; **inclusive of tax** *or* **not inclusive of VAT** = impuestos incluidos *or* IVA no incluido; **inclusive sum** *or* **inclusive charge** = precio *m* que incluye todos los gastos; **the meeting runs from the 12th to the 16th inclusive** = la reunión durará desde el 12 al 16 ambos inclusive

income [ˈɪŋkʌm] *noun* ingresos *mpl or* renta *f;* **income tax** = impuesto *m* sobre la renta; **income support** = subsidio *m* complementario (de bajos ingresos)

incoming [ˈɪnkʌmɪŋ] *adjective* **(a)** *(from outside)* que se recibe de fuera; **incoming call** = llamada *f* de fuera; **incoming mail** = correo *m* entrante **(b)** *(recently elected or appointed)* nuevo, -va; **the incoming government** *or* **Minister** = el nuevo gobierno *or* el nuevo ministro; **the chairman welcomed the incoming committee** = el presidente dio la bienvenida a la nueva comisión

incompetent [ɪnˈkɒmpɪtənt] *adjective* **(a)** *(who cannot do something)* incapaz *or* incompetente; **the sales manager is quite incompetent** = el director de ventas es bastante incompetente; **the company has an incompetent sales director** = la empresa tiene un director de ventas incompetente **(b)** *(who is not legally able to do something)* incapacitado, -da; **he is incompetent to sign the contract** = no está capacitado para firmar el contrato
◊ **incompetency** [ɪnˈkɒmpɪtənsi] *noun* incompetencia *f*

inconvenience [ɪnkənˈviːniəns] **1** *noun* inconvenientes *mpl;* **the protest march caused some inconvenience to the local shopkeepers** = la manifestación de protesta causó algunos inconvenientes a los comerciantes de la zona **2** *verb* molestar *or* causar molestias

incorporate [ɪnˈkɔːpəreɪt] *verb* **(a)** *(to form part)* incorporar *or* incluir; **income from the 1984 acquisition is incorporated into the accounts** = la renta procedente de la adquisición de 1984 está incluida en las cuentas; **the list of markets is incorporated into the main contract** = la lista de mercados está incluida en el contrato principal **(b)** *(registered company)* constituirse en sociedad *or* formar una sociedad; **a company incorporated in the USA** = una empresa constituida en EE UU; **an incorporated company** = una sociedad constituida legalmente; **J. Doe Incorporated** = J. Doe, sociedad anónima
◊ **incorporation** [ɪnkɔːpəˈreɪʃn] *noun* constitución *f* de una sociedad; **articles of incorporation** = estatutos *mpl;* **certificate of incorporation** = autorización *f* para convertirse en sociedad anónima

incorporeal [ɪnkɔːˈpɔːriəl] *adjective* intangible *or* incorpóreo, -rea; **incorporeal chattels** = bienes *mpl* intangibles (patentes *fpl or* derechos *mpl* de autor); **incorporeal hereditaments** = derechos de propiedad sobre bienes intangibles que pueden heredarse

incorrect [ɪnkʌˈrekt] *adjective* incorrecto, -ta; **the minutes of the meeting were incorrect and had to be changed** = las actas de la reunión no eran correctas y tuvieron que modificarse
◊ **incorrectly** [ɪnkəˈrektli] *adverb* incorrectamente *or* erróneamente; **the indictment was incorrectly worded** = la acusación estaba redactada incorrectamente

incorrigible [ɪnˈkɒrɪdʒəbl] *adjective* incorregible

incorrupt [ɪnkəˈrʌpt] *adjective* incorrupto, -ta

increase 1 [ˈɪŋkriːs] *noun* **(a)** *(growth, becoming larger)* aumento *m or* subida *f or* incremento *m;* **increase in tax** *or* **tax increase** = aumento *or* subida de los impuestos; **increase in price** *or* **price increase** = aumento *or* subida de los precios; **profits showed a 10% increase** *or* **an increase of 10% on last year** = los beneficios registraron un aumento del 10% sobre el año pasado; **increase in the cost of living** = incremento del coste de vida **(b)** *(higher salary)* aumento *or* subida de sueldo; **increase in pay** *or* **pay increase** = subida de sueldo; **increase in salary** *or* **salary increase** = aumento de sueldo; **the government hopes to hold salary increases to 3%** = el gobierno espera ajustar el aumento de sueldos en un 3%; **cost-of-living increase** = aumento del coste de vida; **merit increase** = aumento salarial por mérito **(c)** **on the increase** = en aumento; **stealing from shops is on the increase** = el robo cometido en comercios va en aumento **2** [ɪnˈkriːs] *verb* **(a)** *(to grow bigger)* aumentar *or* incrementar *or* subir *or* ampliar; **to increase in price** = aumentar de precio; **to increase in size** = crecer *or* aumentar de tamaño; **to increase in value** = aumentar de valor *or* apreciarse **(b)** *(pay rise)* **his salary was increased to £20,000** = le subieron el sueldo a 20.000 libras
◊ **increasing** [ɪnˈkriːsɪŋ] *adjective* creciente *or* en aumento; **increasing profits** = beneficios *mpl* crecientes *or* en aumento; **the company has an increasing share of the market** = la empresa tiene una participación creciente en el mercado
◊ **increasingly** [ɪnˈkriːsɪŋli] *adverb* cada vez más; **the company has to depend increasingly on the home consumer market** = la empresa tiene que depender cada vez más del mercado de consumo interior

incriminate [ɪnˈkrɪmɪneɪt] *verb* incriminar *or* inculpar; **he was incriminated by the recorded message he sent to the victim** = le incriminaron por el mensaje grabado que envió a la víctima

◊ **incriminating** [ɪnˈkrɪmɪneɪtɪŋ] *adjective* que evidencia la culpabilidad de alguien; **incriminating evidence was found in his car** = encontraron en su coche pruebas evidentes de su culpabilidad

incumbent [ɪnˈkʌmbənt] **1** *adjective;* **it is incumbent upon him** = le incumbe a él *or* es de su incumbencia; **it is incumbent upon justices to give some warning of their doubts about a case** = es incumbencia de los jueces advertir de sus dudas sobre un caso **2** *noun* titular *mf* (de un cargo oficial)

incumbrance [ɪnˈkʌmbrəns] = ENCUMBRANCE

incur [ɪnˈkəː] *verb* incurrir en; **to incur the risk of a penalty** = incurrir en el riesgo de una multa; **to incur debts** *or* **costs** = contraer deudas *or* incurrir en gastos; **the company has incurred heavy costs to implement the development programme** = la empresa ha incurrido en gastos elevados para llevar a cabo el programa de desarrollo (NOTE: **incurring - incurred**)

incuriam [ɪnˈkjuːriæm] *see* PER INCURIAM

indebted [ɪnˈdetɪd] *adjective* endeudado, -da; **to be indebted to a property company** = estar endeudado con una empresa inmobiliaria
◊ **indebtedness** [ɪnˈdetɪdnəs] *noun* deuda *f;* **state of indebtedness** = situación *f* de deuda

indecent [ɪnˈdiːsənt] *adjective* indecente *or* indecoroso, -sa; **indecent assault** = atentado *m* contra el pudor *or* abusos *mpl* deshonestos; **indecent exposure** = exhibicionismo *m*
◊ **indecency** [ɪnˈdiːsənsi] *noun* indecencia *f;* **to commit an act of gross indecency** = tener contactos sexuales con otro hombre *or* con un menor de 14 años

indefeasible right [ɪndɪˈfiːzəbl ˈraɪt] *noun* derecho *m* irrevocable

indefinite [ɪnˈdefənət] *adjective* indefinido, -da; **for an indefinite period of time** = por un periodo indefinido de tiempo

indemnification [ɪndemnɪfɪˈkeɪʃn] *noun* indemnización *f*
◊ **indemnify** [ɪnˈdemnɪfaɪ] *verb* indemnizar; **to indemnify someone for a loss** = indemnizar a alguien por una pérdida
◊ **indemnity** [ɪnˈdemnɪti] *noun* **(a)** *(liability to pay compensation)* indemnidad *f* **(b)** *(compensation)* indemnización *f;* **he had to pay an indemnity of £100** = tuvo que pagar una indemnización de 100 libras; **letter of indemnity** = garantía *f* de indemnización

COMMENT: the person making an indemnity is primarily liable and can be sued by the person with whom he makes the transaction. Compare GUARANTEE

indent 1 [ˈindent] *noun* **(a)** *(order)* pedido *m or* orden *f* de compra de un importador; **he put in an indent for a new stock of spare parts** = presentó una orden de compra para importar una nueva partida de piezas de repuesto **(b)** *(paragraph)* sangrado *m* **2** [ɪnˈdent] *verb* **(a)** **to indent for something** = hacer un pedido; **the department has indented for a new computer** = el departamento ha cursado un pedido para comprar un nuevo ordenador **(b)** *(paragraph)* sangrar; **indent the first line three spaces** = sangra tres espacios en la primera línea

indenture [ɪnˈdentʃə] **1** *noun* contrato *m* entre dos *or* más partes; **indentures** *or* **articles of indenture** = contrato de aprendizaje **2** *verb* realizar un contrato de aprendizaje; **he was indentured to a builder** = se le hizo un contrato de aprendizaje con un maestro de obras

independence [ɪndɪˈpendəns] *noun* **(a)** *(freedom)* independencia *f;* **the colony struggled to achieve independence** = la colonia luchó para conseguir la independencia; **Britain granted her colonies independence in the years after the Second World War** = Gran Bretaña concedió la independencia a sus colonias tras la Segunda Guerra Mundial; **the American War of Independence** = la Guerra de Independencia (de los EE.UU); **Declaration of Independence; Unilateral Declaration of Independence (UDI)** = Declaración Unilateral de Independencia **(b)** *(time when a country became independent)* independencia; **the ten years since independence have seen many changes** = se han producido muchos cambios en los últimos diez años tras la independencia
◊ **Independence Day** [ɪndɪˈpendəns ˈdeɪ] *noun* día *m* de la Independencia

independent [ɪndɪˈpendənt] *adjective* independiente; **independent company** = empresa *f* independiente; **independent contractor** = contratista *mf* independiente; **independent trader** *or* **independent shop** = comerciante *mf* independiente *or* comercio *m* independiente
◊ **independently** [ɪndɪˈpendəntli] *adverb* independientemente; **the two detectives reached the same conclusion independently of each other** = los dos detectives llegaron a la misma conclusión independientemente del otro

index [ˈɪndeks] **1** *noun* **(a)** *(list of items)* índice *m or* repertorio *m;* **we keep a card index of clients** = llevamos un fichero de clientes **(b)** *(regular report)* índice *or* relación *f;* **cost-of-living index** = índice del coste de la vida **2** catalogar *or* clasificar

indicate [ˈɪndɪkeɪt] *verb* indicar *or* mostrar; **the latest figures indicate a fall in the crime rate** = las últimas cifras muestran un descenso del índice de criminalidad

◊ **indication** [ɪndɪ'keɪʃn] *noun* indicación *f or* señal *f or muestra f;* **he gave no indication that he was lying** = no dio muestras de estar mintiendo
◊ **indicator** ['ɪndɪkeɪtə] *noun* indicador *m;* **government economic indicators** = índices económicos oficiales

indict [ɪn'daɪt] *verb* acusar; **he was indicted for murder** = fue acusado de asesinato
◊ **indictable offence** [ɪn'daɪtəbl ə'fens] *noun* antiguamente, delito grave que podía ser juzgado por el Tribunal de la Corona (NOTE: now called **notifiable offence**)
◊ **indictment** [ɪn'daɪtmənt] *noun* acusación *f or* auto *m* de procesamiento; **the clerk to the justices read out the indictment** = el secretario del juzgado leyó en voz alta la acusación; **bill of indictment** = acta *f* de acusación *or US* lista *f* de cargos que se da a un gran jurado para que formule la acusación; **to prefer an indictment** = levantar acta de acusación

indiscretion [ɪndɪ'skreʃn] *noun* desliz *m*

individual [ɪndɪ'vɪdʒuəl] **1** *adjective* individual; **the prisoners are kept in individual cells** = se tiene a los presos en celdas individuales **2** *noun* individuo *m or* sujeto, -ta; **he was approached by two individuals in white coats** = se le acercaron dos individuos que vestían abrigos blancos

indorse [ɪn'dɔːs] *verb* endosar; **the writ was indorsed with details of the plaintiff's claim** = la escritura tenía, en la parte de atrás, los detalles de la reclamación formulada por el demandante; **he indorsed the cheque over to his solicitor** = endosó el cheque para que se lo pudieran pagar a su abogado
◊ **indorsement** [ɪn'dɔːsmənt] *noun* endoso *m or* anotaciones *fpl* en un documento, especialmente aquellas que se refieren a los detalles de la reclamación de un demandante en su demanda; **special indorsement** = endoso completo; *see also* ENDORSE, ENDORSEMENT

induce [ɪn'djuːs] *verb* inducir *or* persuadir *or* inclinar a; **he was induced to steal the plans by an offer of a large amount of money** = le persuadieron a que robara los planos ofreciéndole una gran suma de dinero; **the lack of money induced him to steal** = la falta de dinero le inclinó a robar
◊ **inducement** [ɪn'djuːsmənt] *noun* incentivo *m or* estímulo *m or* inducción *f;* **they offered him a company car as an inducement to stay** = le ofrecieron un coche de la empresa como incentivo para que se quedara; **inducement to break contract** = inducción al quebrantamiento de un contrato

industrial [ɪn'dʌstriəl] *adjective* industrial *or* profesional *or* laboral; **industrial dispute** = conflicto *m* colectivo; **industrial property** = propiedad *f* industrial; **industrial tribunal** = Magistratura *f* del Trabajo *or* juzgado *m* de lo social

inept [ɪn'ept] *adjective* inepto, -ta

in esse ['ɪn 'eseɪ] *Latin phrase* 'siendo'

inevitable [ɪn'evɪtəbl] *adjective* (accidente) inevitable

infamous ['ɪnfəməs] *adjective* infame

infant ['ɪnfənt] *noun* menor *mf (NOTE: this is an old term, now replaced by **minor**)*
◊ **infanticide** [ɪn'fæntɪsaɪd] *noun* infanticidio *m*

infer [ɪn'fəː] *verb* inferir *or* deducir *or* sobreentender; **he inferred from the letter that the accused knew the murder victim** = por la carta dedujo que el acusado conocía a la víctima del asesinato; **counsel inferred that the witness had not been present at the time of the accident** = el abogado dedujo que el testigo no había estado presente en el momento del accidente

inferior [ɪn'fɪəriə] *adjective* inferior *or* de poca calidad; **inferior products** *or* **products of inferior quality** = productos *mpl* de poca calidad; **inferior court** = tribunal *m* inferior

in flagrante delicto [ɪn flə'grænti dɪ'lɪktəʊ] *Latin phrase* '(sorprendido) en el acto *or* momento de cometer un delito'

inflation [ɪn'fleɪʃn] *noun* inflación *f;* **rate of inflation** *or* **inflation rate** = índice *m* de inflación

inflict [ɪn'flɪkt] *verb* infligir; **to inflict harm** *or* **a punishment** = infligir daño *or* un castigo

influence ['ɪnfluəns] **1** *noun* influencia *f;* **he was charged with driving under the influence of alcohol** = le acusaron de conducir bajo los efectos del alcohol; **the decision of the court was not influenced by the speech of the Prime Minister** = la decisión del tribunal no se vio influenciada por el discurso del Primer Ministro; **we are suffering from the influence of a high exchange rate** = sufrimos los efectos de un tipo de cambio elevado; **undue influence** = influencia desmedida *or* indebida **2** *verb* influenciar *or* influir; **the court was influenced in its decision by the youth of the accused** = el fallo del tribunal se vio influenciado por la juventud del acusado; **the price of oil has influenced the price of industrial goods** = el precio del petróleo ha influido en el precio de los productos industriales; **he was accused of trying to influence the magistrates** = le acusaron de tratar de influir sobre los magistrados

influential [ɪnflu'enʃl] *adjective* influyente

inform [ɪn'fɔːm] *verb* informar *or* comunicar; **I regret to inform you that your tender was not acceptable** = lamento comunicarle que su oferta no ha sido aceptada; **we are pleased to inform you that your offer has been accepted** = tenemos el placer de *or* nos es grato comunicarle que su oferta ha sido aceptada; **we have been informed by the Department of Trade that new tariffs are coming**

into force = el Ministerio de Comercio nos ha comunicado que van a entrar en vigor nuevos aranceles; **to inform on someone** = denunciar *or* delatar a alguien

◊ **informant** [ɪn'fɔːmənt] *noun* informante *mf or* fuente *f* de información; **is your informant reliable?** = ¿Su informante es de confianza?

◊ **information** [ɪnfə'meɪʃn] *noun* **(a)** *(details which explain something)* información *f;* **background information** = elementos *mpl* de juicio; **confidential information** = información confidencial; **false information** = información falsa; **have you any information on** *or* **about deposit accounts?** = ¿Tiene usted información sobre las cuentas de depósito?; **I enclose this leaflet for your information** = adjunto remito este folleto para su información; **to disclose a piece of information** = revelar información; **to answer a request for information** = responder a una petición de información; **for further information, please write to Department 27** = para mayor información, sírvase escribir a la sección 27; **disclosure of confidential information** = revelación *f* de información confidencial **(b)** *(details of a crime given to a magistrate)* denuncia *f or* acusación *f;* **laying (an) information** = presentar *or* hacer una denuncia *or* acusación; **the justices were ordered to rehear the information** = se ordenó a los jueces que volvieran a oír la denuncia *or* la acusación **(c) information technology** = informática *f;* **information retrieval** = recuperación *f* de datos **(d) information bureau** *or* **information office** = oficina *f* de información; **information officer** = empleado, -da del servicio de información (NOTE: no plural: to indicate one item use **a piece of information)**

◊ **informer** [ɪn'fɔːmə] *noun* delator, -ra *or* confidente *mf or* denunciante *mf*

informal [ɪn'fɔːml] *adjective* informal; **the head of the CID had an informal meeting with officers from Interpol** = el jefe de la Brigada Criminal se reunió de una manera informal con oficiales de la Interpol

◊ **informally** [ɪn'fɔːməli] *adverb* informalmente

in forma pauperis ['ɪn 'fɔːmə 'pɔːpərɪs] *Latin phrase* 'como persona indigente'

> COMMENT: a term formerly used to allow a person who could prove that he had little money to bring an action even if he could not pay the costs of the case; now replaced by Legal Aid

infringe [ɪn'frɪnʒ] *verb* infringir *or* violar; **to infringe a copyright** = infringir los derechos de autor; **to infringe a patent** = violar una patente

◊ **infringement** [ɪn'frɪnʒmənt] *noun* infracción *f or* violación *f;* **infringement of copyright** *or* **copyright infringement** = infracción de los

derechos de autor; **infringement of patent** *or* **patent infringement** = violación de patente

inhabitant [ɪn'hæbɪtənt] *noun* habitante *mf*

inherit [ɪn'herɪt] *verb* heredar; **when her father died she inherited the shop** = heredó la tienda a la muerte de su padre; **he inherited £10,000 from his grandfather** = heredó 10.000 libras de su abuelo

◊ **inheritance** [ɪn'herɪtəns] *noun* herencia *f*

◊ **inheritor** [ɪn'herɪtə] *noun* heredero, -ra

initial [ɪ'nɪʃəl] **1** *adjective* inicial *or* primero, -ra; **initial capital** = capital *m* inicial; **he started the business with an initial expenditure** *or* **initial investment of £500** = comenzó el negocio con un gasto inicial *or* con una inversión inicial de 500 libras **2** *noun* **initials** = iniciales *fpl;* **what do the initials QC stand for?** = ¿Qué significan las iniciales QC?; **the chairman wrote his initials by each alteration in the contract he was signing** = el presidente marcó con sus iniciales todas las modificaciones efectuadas en el contrato que estaba firmando **3** *verb* poner *or* marcar *or* firmar con las iniciales *or* rubricar; **to initial an amendment to a contract** = rubricar una enmienda de un contrato; **please initial the agreement at the place marked with an X** = por favor rubrique el acuerdo en el lugar marcado con una X

initio [ɪ'nɪʃiəʊ] *see* AB INITIO

injunction [ɪn'dʒʌŋkʃn] *noun* requerimiento *m or* mandato *m* judicial *or* interdicto *m;* **he got an injunction preventing the company from selling his car** = recibió un requerimiento impidiendo que la empresa vendiera su coche; **the company applied for an injunction to stop their competitor from marketing a similar product** = la empresa solicitó un requerimiento que impidiera a la competencia comercializar un producto parecido; **interim injunction** = requerimiento provisional; **interlocutory** *or* **temporary injunction** = requerimiento interlocutorio *or* cautelar; **prohibitory injunction** = requerimiento prohibitorio *or* interdicto prohibitivo *or* embargo *m* provisorio; *see also* MAREVA INJUNCTION

injure ['ɪndʒə] *verb* herir *or* perjudicar *or* dañar; **two workers were injured in the fire** = dos trabajadores resultaron heridos en el incendio; **nobody was injured in the accident** = no hubo heridos en el accidente

◊ **injured party** ['ɪndʒəd 'pɑːti] *noun* parte *f* perjudicada *or* agraviada

◊ **injurious** [ɪn'dʒʊəriəs] *adjective* injurioso, -sa *or* ofensivo, -va *or* perjudicial; **injurious falsehood** = mentira *f* injuriosa

◊ **injury** ['ɪndʒəri] *noun* herida *f or* lesión *f or* perjuicio *m or* daño *m;* **injury benefit** = subsidio *m or* indemnización *f* por lesiones; **industrial injuries** = daños causados en accidente laboral; **personal injury** = daños personales; **real injury** = perjuicio material; **no visible injuries** = sin lesiones apreciables; **to cause fatal injuries** = herir de muerte

injustice [ɪn'dʒʌstɪs] *noun* injusticia *f or* ignomia *f;* **manifest injustice** = injusticia notoria

inland ['ɪnlænd] *adjective* **(a)** *(inside a country)* interior *or* nacional; **inland postage** = correo *m* interior; **inland freight charges** = costes *mpl* del flete interior **(b) the Inland Revenue** = Hacienda *f or* Fisco *m*

in loco parentis ['ɪn 'ləʊkəʊ pə'rentɪs] *Latin phrase* 'en lugar del padre'; **the court is acting in loco parentis** = el tribunal actúa en lugar del padre

inmate ['ɪnmeɪt] *noun* recluso, -sa

Inn [ɪn] *noun (barristers)* **the Inns of Court** = los cuatro colegios de abogados de Londres

COMMENT: the four societies are **Gray's Inn, Lincoln's Inn, Inner Temple and Middle Temple**

Inner Temple ['ɪnə 'templ] *see* INN

innocent ['ɪnəsənt] *adjective* inocente *or* inculpable; **the accused was found to be innocent** = el acusado fue declarado inocente; **in English law, the accused is presumed to be innocent until he is proved to be guilty** = según la ley inglesa, el acusado es considerado inocente hasta que no se demuestre lo contrario
◊ **innocence** ['ɪnəsəns] *noun* inocencia *f;* **he tried to establish his innocence** = trató de demostrar su inocencia

innuendo [ɪnju'endəʊ] *noun* insinuación *f;* **an apparently innocent statement may be defamatory if it contains an innuendo** = una declaración en apariencia inocente puede ser difamatoria si contiene una insinuación

in personam ['ɪn pɜː'səʊnæm] *Latin phrase* 'contra una persona'; **action in personam** = acción *f* contra una persona; *see* IN REM

input ['ɪnpʊt] **1** *noun* entrada *f or* input *m;* **input tax** = IVA *m* **2** *verb* introducir datos en un ordenador (NOTE: **inputting - inputted**)

inquest ['ɪŋkwest] *noun* investigación *f* en caso de muerte violenta *or* ante el hallazgo de un tesoro; **coroner's inquest** = indagatoria *f* del forense

COMMENT: an inquest has to take place where death is violent or unexpected, where death could be murder *or* manslaughter, where a prisoner dies and when police are involved

inquisitorial procedure *noun* procedimiento *m* inquisitorial; *compare* ACCUSATORIAL

inquire [ɪŋ'kwaɪə] *verb* pedir información *or* informarse de *or* preguntar *or* hacer investigaciones *or* indagar; **he inquired if anything was wrong** =

preguntó si pasaba algo; **she inquired about the rate of crimes solved** = solicitó información sobre el número de crímenes resueltos; **the commission is inquiring into corruption in the police force** = la comisión está haciendo investigaciones sobre la corrupción dentro del cuerpo de policía
◊ **inquiry** [ɪŋ'kwaɪəri] *noun* investigación *f* (oficial) *or* indagación *f;* **preparatory inquiries** = diligencias *fpl* de instrucción; **there has been a government inquiry into the loss of the secret documents** = se ha realizado una investigación gubernamental sobre la pérdida de documentos secretos

inquorate [ɪn'kwɔːreɪt] *adjective* sin quórum; **the meeting was declared inquorate and had to be abandoned** = no hubo quórum para la reunión y tuvo que ser suspendida *or* la reunión se suspendió por falta de quórum

in re ['ɪn 'reɪ] *Latin phrase* 'concerniente' *or* 'en el caso de'

in rem ['ɪn 'rem] *Latin phrase* 'contra una cosa'; **action in rem** = acción *f* contra una propiedad, no contra una persona; *see* IN PERSONAM

insane [ɪn'seɪn] *adjective* loco, -ca *or* demente
◊ **insanity** [ɪn'sænɪti] *noun* locura *f or* enajenación *f* mental *or* demencia *f*

COMMENT: where an accused is found to be insane, a verdict of 'not guilty by reason of insanity' is returned and the accused is ordered to be detained at Her Majesty's pleasure

inside [ɪn'saɪd] **1** *adjective & adverb* **(a)** *(in)* en la propia empresa *or* casa *or* interior *or* dentro; **inside job** = delito *m* llevado a cabo por un empleado de la casa; **inside worker** = empleado, -da de oficina *or* fábrica **(b)** *(slang)* en prisión **2** *preposition* dentro de *or* en; **there was nothing inside the container** = no había nada dentro del contenedor; **we have a contact inside our main competitor's production department who gives us very useful information** = tenemos un contacto dentro del departamento de producción de nuestro principal competidor que nos da información muy útil
◊ **insider** [ɪn'saɪdə] *noun* iniciado, -da; **insider dealing** *or* **insider trading** = información *f* privilegiada (transacciones bursátiles realizadas por un iniciado)

insist [ɪn'sɪst] *verb* insistir *or* empeñarse; **he insisted on something being done** *or* **he insisted that something should be done to help the family of the plaintiff** = insistió en que se debía hacer algo para ayudar a la familia del demandante

insolvent [ɪn'sɒlvənt] *adjective* insolvente; **the company was declared insolvent** = la empresa fue declarada insolvente

◊ **insolvency** [ɪnˈsɒlvənsi] *noun* insolvencia *f;* **the company was in a state of insolvency** = la empresa se encontraba en un estado de insolvencia (NOTE: **insolvent** and **insolvency** are general terms, but are usually applied to companies; individuals are usually described as **bankrupt** once they have been declared so by a court)

inspect [ɪnˈspekt] *verb* inspeccionar *or* revisar *or* examinar *or* registrar; **to inspect a machine** *or* **a prison** = revisar una máquina *or* inspeccionar una cárcel; **to inspect the accounts of a company** = revisar las cuentas de una empresa; **to inspect products for defects** = realizar un control de calidad

◊ **inspection** [ɪnˈspekʃn] *noun* **(a)** *(close examination of something)* inspección *f or* registro *m;* **to make an inspection** *or* **to carry out an inspection of a machine** *or* **a new prison** = efectuar una inspección *or* llevar a cabo la revisión de una máquina *or* una inspección de una nueva cárcel; **inspection of a product for defects** = control *m* de calidad de un producto; **to carry out a tour of inspection** = realizar una visita de inspección; **to issue an inspection order** = dar una orden de inspección; **inspection stamp** = sello *m* de la inspección **(b)** *(examination of documents after discovery)* examen *m;* **inspection was ordered to take place seven days after discovery** = se ordenó que el examen de documentos tuviera lugar siete días después de su presentación

◊ **inspector** [ɪnˈspektə] *noun* **(a)** *(official who inspects)* inspector, -ra; **inspector of factories** *or* **factory inspector** = inspector de fábricas; **inspector of taxes** *or* **tax inspector** = inspector de Hacienda; **inspector of weights and measures** = inspector de pesos y medidas **(b)** *(police rank)* inspector de policía

◊ **inspectorate** [ɪnˈspektərət] *noun* cuerpo *m* de inspectores; **the factory inspectorate** = el cuerpo de inspectores de fábricas

inst [ɪnst] = INSTANT; **your letter of the 6th inst** = su carta del seis del corriente *or* del actual *or* de los corrientes

instalment *US* **installment** [ɪnˈstɔːlmənt] *noun* plazo *m;* **he paid off his creditors in twelve instalments** = pagó a sus acreedores en doce plazos; **you pay £25 down and twelve monthly instalments of £20** = se paga una entrada de 25 libras y el resto en doce plazos mensuales de 20 libras

◊ **installment plan** [ɪnˈstɔːlmənt ˈplæn] *noun US* venta *f or* compra *f* a plazos (NOTE: British English is **hire purchase**)

instance [ˈɪnstəns] *noun* ejemplo *m or* caso *m;* **in this instance we will overlook the delay** = en este caso pasaremos por alto el retraso; **court of the first instance** = tribunal *m* de primera instancia

instant [ˈɪnstənt] *adjective* **(a)** *(at this point)* del actual *or* del presente mes *or* de los corrientes; **our letter of the 6th instant** = nuestra carta del seis del actual *or* del corriente; **the instant case** = el caso que nos ocupa **(b)** *(immediately available)* inmediato, -ta *or* instantáneo, -nea; **instant credit** = crédito *m* instantáneo

in statu quo *Latin phrase* en la situación actual

instigate [ˈɪnstɪgeɪt] *verb* instigar

◊ **instigation** [ɪnstɪˈgeɪʃn] *noun* instigación *f or* incitación *f*

institute [ˈɪnstɪtjuːt] **1** *noun* instituto *m;* **research institute** = instituto de investigación **2** *verb* iniciar *or* entablar *or* incoar; **to institute proceedings against someone** = entablar un proceso contra alguien *or* incoar un proceso

◊ **institution** [ɪnstɪˈtjuːʃn] *noun* **(a)** *(organization)* institución *f or* ente *m;* **financial institution** = institución financiera **(b)** *(building for a special purpose)* establecimiento *m or* centro *m;* **mental institution** = manicomio *m or* centro de salud mental *or* centro psiquiátrico; **penal institution** = institución penitenciaria; **Young Offender Institution** = reformatorio *m* de menores (NOTE: formerly these were called **Borstals**)

◊ **institutional** [ɪnstɪˈtjuːʃnl] *adjective* institucional; **institutional buying** *or* **selling** = compra *f or* venta *f* institucional; **institutional investors** = inversores *mpl* institucionales

instruct [ɪnˈstrʌkt] *verb* **(a)** *(to give an order)* dar instrucciones *or* ordenar *or* mandar; **to instruct someone to do something** = ordenar a alguien que haga algo; **he instructed the credit controller to take action** = ordenó al inspector de préstamos que tomara cartas en el asunto **(b)** *(of a person)* **to instruct a solicitor** = contratar a un abogado *or* dar instrucciones a un abogado para que proceda judicialmente **(c)** *(of a solicitor)* **to instruct a barrister** = proporcionar a un abogado el expediente de la causa para que prepare la defensa ante un tribunal

◊ **instructions** [ɪnˈstrʌkʃnz] *plural noun* instrucciones *fpl;* **he gave instructions to his stockbroker to sell the shares immediately** = dio instrucciones a su corredor de bolsa para que vendiera las acciones inmediatamente; **to await instructions** = esperar instrucciones; **to issue instructions** = dar instrucciones; **in accordance with** *or* **according to instructions** = de acuerdo con *or* conforme a *or* según las instrucciones; **failing instructions to the contrary** = salvo instrucciones contrarias; **forwarding instructions** *or* **shipping instructions** = instrucciones de envío *or* transporte; *US* **instructions to the jury** = discurso *m* de un juez al término de un juicio (NOTE: British English is **summing up**)

◊ **instructor** [ɪnˈstrʌktə] *noun* instructor, -ra *or* monitor, -ra

instrument ['ɪnstrəmənt] *noun* **(a)** *(device)* instrumento *m or* herramienta *f;* **sharp instrument** = arma *f* blanca; **the technical staff have instruments to measure the output of electricity** = los empleados del servicio técnico poseen instrumentos para medir la potencia eléctrica **(b)** *(document)* instrumento *or* documento *m or* escrito *m* legal; **inchoate instrument** = documento incompleto *or* no registrado; **negotiable instrument** = instrumento negociable; **statutory instrument** = orden *f* reglamentaria *or* disposiciones *fpl* legislativas

insult 1 ['ɪnsʌlt] *noun* insulto *m or* afrenta *f or* injuria *f or* ultraje *m* **2** [ɪn'sʌlt] *verb* insultar; **insulting behaviour** = comportamiento *m* ofensivo *or* conducta *f* insultante

insure [ɪn'ʃʊə] *verb* asegurar; **to insure a house against fire** = asegurar una casa contra incendios; **to insure someone's life** = hacer un seguro de vida a alguien; **he was insured for £100,000** = estaba asegurado por valor de 100.000 libras; **to insure baggage against loss** = asegurar el equipaje (contra robos y pérdidas); **to insure against bad weather** = asegurarse contra el mal tiempo; **to insure against loss of earnings** = asegurarse contra la pérdida de ingresos
◊ **insurable** [ɪn'ʃʊrəbl] *adjective* asegurable; **insurable interest** = interés *m* asegurable
◊ **insurance** [ɪn'ʃʊərəns] *noun* **(a)** *(premium)* seguro *m;* **to take out insurance** = asegurarse; **to take out an insurance against fire** = hacerse un seguro contra incendios **(b) accident insurance** = seguro de accidentes; **car insurance** *or* **motor insurance** = seguro de automóviles; **fully comprehensive insurance** = seguro a todo riesgo; **legal expenses insurance** = seguro que cubre los gastos de un juicio; **life insurance** = seguro de vida; **medical insurance** = seguro médico; **National Insurance** = seguridad *f* social; **term insurance** = seguro temporal *or* seguro de vida por un periodo determinado; **third-party insurance** = seguro contra terceros; **whole-life insurance** = seguro corriente de vida (en oposición al seguro temporal)
◊ **insured** [ɪn'ʃʊəd] *adjective* asegurado, -da; **the life insured** = la persona asegurada; **the sum insured** = la suma asegurada
◊ **insurer** [ɪn'ʃʊərə] *noun* asegurador, -ra (NOTE: for life insurance, British English prefers to use **assurance, assure, assurer**)

intangible [ɪn'tændʒəbl] *adjective* intangible; **intangible assets** = activo *m* intangible

intellectual [ɪntə'lektʃuəl] *adjective* intelectual; **intellectual property** = propiedad *f* intelectual

intend [ɪn'tend] *verb* tener la intención *or* el propósito de hacer algo; **the company intends to sue for damages** = la empresa tiene la intención de ir a juicio por daños; **we intend to offer jobs to 250 unemployed young people** = tenemos la intención de ofrecer trabajo a 250 jóvenes parados; **intended murder** = asesinato *m* premeditado

◊ **intent** [ɪn'tent] *noun* intención *f or* propósito *m;* **with intent** = con ánimo de; **letter of intent** = carta *f* de intención; *see also* LOITERING, WOUNDING

◊ **intention** [ɪn'tenʃn] *noun (planning to do something)* intención *f or* propósito *m;* **he was accused of perjury with the intention of incriminating his employer** = le acusaron de perjurio con la intención de incriminar a su patrono; **intention to create a legal relationship is one of the essential elements of a contract** = la intención de crear una relación legal es uno de los elementos esenciales de un contrato

◊ **intentional** [ɪn'tenʃnl] *adjective* deliberado, -da *or* intencionado, -da; **an act of intentional cruelty** = un acto de deliberada crueldad

◊ **intentionally** [ɪn'tenʃnəli] *adverb* intencionadamente *or* a propósito; **he intentionally altered the date on the contract** = cambió la fecha en el contrato intencionadamente

inter- ['ɪntə] *prefix* inter- *or* entre; **inter-bank loan** = préstamo *m* interbancario; **the inter-city rail services are good** = los servicios ferroviarios interurbanos son buenos; **inter-company dealings** = operaciones *fpl* entre compañías; **inter-company comparisons** = estudios *mpl* comparativos entre compañías

inter alia ['ɪntə 'eɪliə] *Latin phrase* 'entre otras cosas'

intercede [ɪntə'siːd] *verb* intervenir *or* interceder; **intercede for** *or* **against somebody** = interceder a favor *or* en contra de alguien

intercourse ['ɪntəkɔːs] *noun* **sexual intercourse** = relaciones *fpl* sexuales; **sexual intercourse with a girl under sixteen is an offence** = mantener relaciones sexuales con una menor de dieciséis años es constitutivo de delito

interdict ['ɪntədɪkt] *noun (in Scotland)* interdicto *m or* prohibición *f*

interest ['ɪntrəst] **1** *noun* **(a)** *(special attention)* interés *m;* **of public interest** = de interés público; **the managing director takes no interest in the staff club** = el director gerente no tiene ningún interés por el club de los empleados; **the police showed a lot of interest in the abandoned car** = la policía mostró un gran interés por el coche abandonado **(b)** *(payment by a borrower)* interés; **simple interest** = interés simple; **compound interest** = interés compuesto; **accrual of interest** = acumulación *f* de interés; **accrued interest** = interés acumulado *or* devengado (pero no pagado o cobrado); **back interest** = interés atrasado; **fixed interest** = interés fijo; **high** *or* **low interest** = interés elevado *or* bajo interés **(c)** *(money paid as income on investments)* interés; **life interest** = usufructo *m*

vitalicio; **the bank pays 10% interest on deposits**
= el banco paga un 10% de interés sobre las
imposiciones a plazo fijo; **to receive interest at 5%**
= recibir un interés del 5%; **the loan pays 5%
interest** = el préstamo paga un 5% de interés;
deposit which yields or **gives** or **produces** or **bears
5% interest** = imposición f que da un interés del
5%; **account which earns interest at 10%** or
which earns 10% interest = cuenta f que devenga
un 10% de interés; **interest-bearing deposits** =
imposiciones *fpl* con interés or que producen
intereses **(d)** *(percentage paid for borrowing
money)* interés; **interest charges** = cargos *mpl* en
concepto de interés; **interest rate** or **rate of interest**
= tipo *m* or tasa f de interés; **interest-free credit** or
loan = préstamo *m* sin intereses; **the company
gives its staff interest-free loans** = la empresa
concede a sus empleados préstamos sin intereses
(e) *(money invested, financial share in a company)*
participación f; **beneficial interest** = derecho *m* de
usufructo; **conflict of interest(s)** = conflicto *m* de
intereses; **he has a controlling interest in the
company** = posee la mayor parte de las acciones de
la empresa or tiene un interés mayoritario or una
participación mayoritaria en la compañía; **life
interest** = renta f vitalicia; **majority interest** or
minority interest = participación mayoritaria or
participación minoritaria; **he has a majority
interest in a supermarket chain** = tiene una
participación mayoritaria en una cadena de
supermercados; **to acquire a substantial interest
in the company** = adquirir una participación
substancial en una empresa; **to declare** or **disclose
an interest** = declarar una participación en una
compañía **2** *verb* interesar; **he tried to interest
several companies in his new invention** = trató de
que varias empresas se interesaran por su nuevo
invento; **interested in** = interesado, -da en; **the
managing director is interested only in
increasing profitability** = el director gerente está
únicamente interesado en aumentar la rentabilidad;
interested party = parte f interesada
◊ **interesting** ['ıntrəstıŋ] *adjective* interesante;
**they made us a very interesting offer for the
factory** = nos hicieron una oferta muy interesante
por la fábrica

interfere [ıntə'fıə] *verb* entrometerse or interferir;
to interfere with witnesses = tratar de influir sobre
los testigos
◊ **interference** [ıntə'fıəns] *noun* intromisión f or
injerencia f; **the local authority complained of
continual interference from the central
government** = la autoridad local se quejó de
continua injerencia por parte del gobierno central
◊ **interference with vehicles** [ıntə'fıəns wıθ
'viːkəlz] *noun* intento *m* de robo de coches

interim ['ıntrım] *adjective* provisional or temporal
or a cuenta; **interim dividend** = dividendo *m*
provisional or a cuenta; **interim injunction** =

requerimiento *m* or intimación f temporal; **interim
order** = orden f provisional; **interim payment** =
pago *m* a cuenta; **interim report** = informe *m*
provisional; **in the interim** = en el ínterin or
entretanto

interior [ın'tıərıə] *noun* interior *m;* **Ministry of
the Interior** or **Interior Ministry** = Ministerio *m*
del Interior

COMMENT: in the UK, this ministry is called
the Home Office

interlocutory [ıntə'lɒkjutrı] *adjective*
interlocutorio, -ria; **interlocutory injunction** =
requerimiento interlocutorio or cautelar;
interlocutory judgment = juicio *m* interlocutorio;
interlocutory matter = asunto *m* interlocutorio;
interlocutory proceedings = acciones *fpl* or
reuniones *fpl* interlocutorias or autos *mpl*
incidentales

intermediary [ıntə'miːdıərı] *noun*
intermediario, -ria or agente *mf* mediador, -ra; **he
refused to act as an intermediary between the
two directors** = se negó a actuar de intermediario
entre los dos directores

intern [ın'tɜːn] *verb* internar
◊ **internal** [ın'tɜːnəl] *adjective* interno, -na; **an
internal call** = una llamada interna; **internal
affairs of a country** = asuntos *mpl* interiores; *US*
Internal Revenue Service (IRS) = Hacienda
pública de los EE UU (NOTE: in the UK, this is the
Inland Revenue)
◊ **internally** [ın'tɜːnəlı] *adverb (of a company)*
dentro de la empresa
◊ **internee** [ıntɜː'niː] *noun* internado, -da or
interno, -na
◊ **internment** [ın'tɜːnmənt] *noun*
encarcelamiento *m* sin juicio previo

international [ıntə'næʃnl] *adjective*
internacional; **International Bar Association** =
Asociación f Internacional de Abogados;
international call = llamada f internacional;
International Court of Justice = Tribunal *m*
Internacional de Justicia; **International Labour
Organization (ILO)** = Organización f
Internacional del Trabajo (OIT); **international law**
= derecho *m* internacional; **International
Monetary Fund (IMF)** = Fondo Monetario
Internacional (FMI)

inter partes ['ıntə 'pɑːtız] *Latin phrase* 'entre
las partes': vista de un caso en el que las dos partes
están representadas; **the court's opinion was that
the case should be heard inter partes as soon as
possible** = según el tribunal el caso debería verse
entre las partes lo antes posible; *see also* EX
PARTE

interpleader [ıntə'pliːdə] *noun* acción f legal
emprendida por el tenedor accidental de una

propiedad para que dos o más pretendientes a ella se sometan a la decisión de un tribunal

Interpol ['ɪntəpɒl] *noun* Interpol *f*; **they warned Interpol that the criminals might be disguised as women** = avisaron a la Interpol de que los criminales podían estar disfrazados de mujeres (NOTE: used without the in English)

interpose [ɪntə'pəʊz] *verb* interponer

interpret [ɪn'tɜːprət] *verb* **(a)** *(say what you think something means)* interpretar una ley *or* un precedente **(b)** *(to translate into another language)* interpretar; **my assistant knows Greek, so he will interpret for us** = mi ayudante sabe griego, así que actuará de intérprete para nosotros
◊ **interpretation** [ɪntɜːprə'teɪʃn] *noun* interpretación *f* de una ley *or* de un precedente; **to put an interpretation on something** = dar *or* hacer una interpretación de algo; **his ruling puts quite a different interpretation on the responsibility of trustees** = su decisión da una interpretación bastante diferente de la responsabilidad de los administradores; **Interpretation Act** = ley *f* que regula la interpretación de otras leyes parlamentarias; **interpretation clause** = cláusula *f* de interpretación
◊ **interpreter** [ɪn'tɜːprɪtə] *noun* intérprete *mf*; **my secretary will act as interpreter** = mi secretaria actuará de intérprete; **the witness could not speak English and the court had to appoint an interpreter** = el testigo no sabía hablar inglés y el tribunal tuvo que contratar a un intérprete

interregnum [ɪntə'regnəm] *noun* interregno *m*

interrogate [ɪn'terəgeɪt] *verb* interrogar; **the prisoners were interrogated for three hours** = interrogaron a los acusados por espacio de tres horas
◊ **interrogation** [ɪnterə'geɪʃn] *noun* interrogatorio *m*; **he confessed to the crime during his interrogation** = confesó el crimen durante el interrogatorio; **under interrogation, she gave the names of her accomplices** = sometida a interrogatorio, dio los nombres de sus cómplices
◊ **interrogator** [ɪn'terəgeɪtə] *noun* interrogador, -ra
◊ **interrogatories** [ɪntə'rɒgətriz] *plural noun* interrogatorios *mpl*

in terrorem [ɪn tə'rɔːrəm] *Latin phrase* con intención de aterrorizar

interrupt [ɪntə'rʌpt] *verb* interrumpir

COMMENT: in the House of Commons, an MP is allowed to interrupt another MP only if he wants to ask the member who is speaking to explain something or to raise a point of order

intervene [ɪntə'viːn] *verb* **(a)** *(to come between to make a change)* intervenir *or* mediar; **to intervene in a dispute** = mediar en una disputa *or*

conflicto **(b)** *(to become a party to an action)* intervenir
◊ **intervener** [ɪntə'viːnə] *noun* mediador, -ra
◊ **intervention** [ɪntə'venʃn] *noun* intervención *f*; **the government's intervention in the foreign exchange markets** = la intervención estatal en el mercado de divisas; **the central bank's intervention in the banking crisis** = la intervención del banco central en la crisis bancaria; **the association's intervention in the labour dispute** = la intervención de la asociación en el conflicto laboral; *(in the EU)* **intervention price** = precio *m* de intervención

interview ['ɪntəvjuː] *verb* entrevistar; **we interviewed ten candidates for the post of Chief Constable** = entrevistamos a diez candidatos para el puesto de Jefe de Policía; **the police want to interview a man in connection with the burglary** = la policía quiere entrevistar a un hombre en relación con el robo; **interview room** = sala *f* de entrevistas

inter vivos [ɪntə 'vaɪvəʊs] *Latin phrase* inter vivos: 'entre vivos'; **gift inter vivos** = donación *f* inter vivos

intestate [ɪn'testeɪt] *adjective*; **to die intestate** = morir sin haber testado *or* intestado *or* ab intestato; **intestate succession** = sucesión *f* ab intestato

COMMENT: when someone dies intestate, the property automatically goes to the surviving partner, unless there are children

◊ **intestacy** [ɪn'testəsi] *noun* hecho *m* de morir intestado

intimidate [ɪn'tɪmɪdeɪt] *verb* intimidar; **the accused was said to have intimidated the witnesses** = se dijo que el acusado había intimidado a los testigos
◊ **intimidation** [ɪntɪmɪ'deɪʃn] *noun* intimidación *f*

intoxicated [ɪn'tɒksɪkeɪtɪd] *adjective* embriagado, -da
◊ **intoxication** [ɪntɒksɪ'keɪʃn] *noun* embriaguez *f* *or* borrachera *f*

in transit ['ɪn 'trænzɪt] *adverb* **goods in transit** = mercancías en tránsito

intra vires ['ɪntrə 'vaɪriːz] *Latin phrase* 'dentro de lo permitido'; **the minister's action was ruled to be intra vires** = la acción del ministro fue calificada como dentro de la autoridad conferida; *see* ULTRA VIRES

intrinsic evidence [ɪn'trɪnzɪk 'evɪdəns] *noun* prueba *f* intrínseca; *see also* EXTRINSIC

introduce [ɪntrə'djuːs] *verb* presentar *or* introducir *or* implantar; **he is introducing a Bill in Parliament to prevent the sale of drugs** = está presentando un proyecto de ley ante el Parlamento para prevenir la venta de drogas; **the prosecution has introduced some new evidence** = la acusación ha presentado nuevas pruebas; **they introduced a new timetable** = implantaron un nuevo horario

◊ **introduction** [ɪntrə'dʌkʃn] *noun* presentación *f or* introducción *f;* **the introduction of new evidence into the case** = la presentación de nuevas pruebas para el caso; **introduction of a Bill** = presentación de un proyecto de ley ante el Parlamento

intruder [ɪn'truːdə] *noun* intruso, -sa

invalid [ɪn'vælɪd] *adjective* nulo, -la *or* inválido, -da; **permit that is invalid** = permiso nulo; **claim which has been declared invalid** = reclamación *f* que ha sido declarada nula
◊ **invalidate** [ɪn'vælɪdeɪt] *verb* invalidar *or* anular; **because the company has been taken over, the contract has been invalidated** = a causa de la absorción de la empresa, el contrato ha sido anulado
◊ **invalidation** [ɪnvælɪ'deɪʃn] *noun* invalidación *f or* anulación *f*
◊ **invalidity** [ɪnvə'lɪdɪti] *noun* invalidez *f or* nulidad *f;* **the invalidity of the contract** = la nulidad del contrato

invasion of privacy [ɪn'veɪʒn əv 'prɪvəsi] *noun* intromisión *f* en la vida privada *or* atentado *m* a la intimidad

invent [ɪn'vent] *verb* inventar; **she invented a new type of computer keyboard** = inventó un nuevo tipo de teclado de ordenador; **who invented shorthand?** = ¿Quién inventó la taquigrafía?; **the chief accountant has invented a new system of customer filing** = el jefe de contabilidad ha inventado un nuevo sistema de clasificación de clientes
◊ **invention** [ɪn'venʃn] *noun* invento *m or* invención *f;* **she filed a patent application for her invention** = presentó una solicitud de patente para su invento; **he tried to sell his latest invention to a US car company** = intentó vender su último invento a una empresa automovilística norteamericana
◊ **inventor** [ɪn'ventə] *noun* inventor, -ra; **he is the inventor of the all-plastic car** = es el inventor del coche fabricado enteramente de plástico
◊ **inventory** ['ɪnvəntri] **1** *noun* inventario *m* **2** *verb* inventariar

invest [ɪn'vest] *verb* invertir; **he invested all his money in a shop** = invirtió todo su dinero en una tienda; **she was advised to invest in real estate** = le aconsejaron que invirtiera en bienes raíces *or* propiedad inmobiliaria
◊ **investment** [ɪn'vestmənt] *noun* inversión *f;* **he lost all his money in risky investments on the Stock Exchange** = perdió todo su dinero en inversiones arriesgadas en la Bolsa; *US* **investment bank** = banco *m* de inversiones; **investment**

company *or* **investment trust** = compañía *f* de inversiones
◊ **investor** [ɪn'vestə] *noun* inversor, -ra *or* inversionista *mf*

investigate [ɪn'vestɪgeɪt] *verb* investigar *or* estudiar *or* indagar
◊ **investigation** [ɪnvestɪ'geɪʃn] *noun* investigación *f or* estudio *m;* **to conduct an investigation into irregularities in share dealings** = realizar una investigación sobre posibles irregularidades en operaciones con valores; **preliminary investigation** = indagatoria *f or* investigación preliminar
◊ **investigator** [ɪn'vestɪgeɪtə] *noun* investigador, -ra; **a government investigator** = un investigador oficial *or* estatal *or* del gobierno

invite [ɪn'vaɪt] *verb* invitar; **to invite someone to a meeting** = invitar a alguien a una reunión; **to invite someone to join the board** = invitar a alguien a formar parte del consejo; **to invite shareholders to subscribe to a new issue** = invitar a los accionistas a que suscriban una nueva emisión; **to invite tenders for a contract** = hacer una contrata *or* licitación
◊ **invitation** [ɪnvɪ'teɪʃn] *noun* invitación *f or* petición *f;* **to issue an invitation to someone to join the board** = extender una invitación a alguien para que forme parte del consejo; **invitation to tender for a contract** = concurso *m* público; **invitation to subscribe to a new issue** = oferta *f* para suscribir nuevas acciones; **invitation to treat** = solicitud *f* de ofertas de compra
◊ **invitee** [ɪnvaɪ'tiː] *noun* invitado, -da

invoice ['ɪnvɔɪs] *noun* factura *f or* albarán *m*

involuntary [ɪn'vɒləntri] *adjective* involuntario, -ria *or* sin premeditación; **involuntary conduct** = comportamiento *m* involuntario; **involuntary manslaughter** = homicidio *m* involuntario *or* sin premeditación
◊ **involuntarily** [ɪn'vɒləntrəli] *adverb* involuntariamente; **the accused's defence was that he acted involuntarily** = la defensa del acusado consistía en que había actuado involuntariamente

involve [ɪn'vɒlv] *verb* implicar *or* involucrar *or* concernir *or* afectar; **to get involved** = comprometerse; **there is an increase of crimes involving young girls** = hay un aumento de delitos que afectan a chicas jóvenes; **his claim involves money spent on trips abroad** = su reclamación concierne dinero gastado en viajes al extranjero; **deaths involving policemen** *or* **deaths where policemen are involved are always the subject of an inquest** = las muertes en las que policías están implicados son siempre motivo de investigación

IOU ['aɪ 'əu 'juː] *noun* = I OWE YOU vale *m or* pagaré *m;* **to pay a pile of IOUs** = hacer efectivos un montón de pagarés

ipso facto ['ɪpsəʊ 'fæktəʊ] *Latin phrase* ipso facto: 'por este mismo hecho' *or* 'el hecho mismo nos muestra'; **the writing of the letter was ipso facto an admission of guilt** = el hecho de haber escrito la carta fue ya de por sí una admisión de culpabilidad; **he was found in the vehicle at the time of the accident and ipso facto was deemed to be in charge of it** = le encontraron en el vehículo en el momento del accidente y por este mismo hecho le creyeron culpable del mismo

IRA ['aɪ 'ɑː 'eɪ] *US* = INDIVIDUAL RETIREMENT ACCOUNT

irreconcilable [ɪrekən'saɪləbl] *adjective* **(a)** *(differences between husband and wife)* irreconciliable **(b)** *(opinion)* incompatible; **to be irreconcilable with** = ser incompatible con

irrecoverable [ɪrɪ'kʌvrəbl] *adjective* irrecuperable *or* incobrable; **irrecoverable debt** = deuda *f* incobrable

irredeemable [ɪrɪ'diːməbl] *adjective* irredimible *or* inconvertible *or* no amortizable; **irredeemable bond** = obligación *f* perpetua *or* deuda *f* incobrable

irregular [ɪ'regjʊlə] *adjective* irregular *or* desigual; **irregular documentation** = documentación *f* irregular; **this procedure is highly irregular** = este procedimiento es muy irregular
◊ **irregularity** [ɪregjʊ'lærɪti] *noun* **(a)** *(not on time)* irregularidad *f*; **the irregularity of the postal deliveries** = la irregularidad del reparto del correo **(b)** *(not legal)* **irregularities** = irregularidades *fpl*; **to investigate irregularities in the share dealings** = investigar irregularidades en operaciones de valores

irrelevant [ɪ'reləvənt] *adjective; (evidence)* irrelevante *or* impertinente

irresistible [ɪrɪ'zɪstəbl] *adjective* irresistible; **irresistible impulse** = impulso *m* irresistible; **his irresistible impulse to set fire to shoe shops** = su impulso irresistible de prender fuego a las zapaterías

irresponsible [ɪrɪ'spɒnsɪbl] *adjective* irresponsable
◊ **irresponsibility** [ɪrɪspɒnsɪ'bɪlɪti] *noun* irresponsabilidad *f*

irretrievable [ɪrɪ'triːvəbl] *adjective* irreparable *or* irrecuperable; **irretrievable breakdown of a marriage** = ruptura *f* matrimonial irreconciliable
◊ **irretrievably** [ɪrɪ'triːvəbli] *adverb* de un modo irreparable *or* sin remedio; **it was agreed that the marriage had broken down irretrievably** = acordaron que el matrimonio se había deshecho de un modo irreparable

irrevocable [ɪ'revəkəbl] *adjective* irrevocable; **irrevocable acceptance** = aceptación *f* irrevocable;

irrevocable letter of credit = carta *f* de crédito irrevocable

IRS ['aɪ 'ɑː 'es] *US* = INTERNAL REVENUE SERVICE

Islam ['ɪzlɑːm] *noun* Islam *m*
◊ **Islamic** [ɪz'læmɪk] *adjective* islámico, -ca; **Islamic Law** = Derecho *m* Islámico

isolation [aɪsə'leɪʃn] *noun* **(a)** *(being alone)* aislamiento *m*; **splendid isolation** = política *f* de aislamiento **(b)** **in isolation** = sin nadie más *or* aisladamente
◊ **isolationism** [aɪsə'leɪʃnɪzm] *noun* aislacionismo *m*
◊ **isolationist** [aɪsə'leɪʃnɪst] *noun* aislacionista *mf*

issue ['ɪʃuː] **1** *noun* **(a)** *(child or children of a parent)* descendencia *f*; **he had issue two sons and one daughter** = tuvo tres descendientes: dos hijos y una hija; **she died without issue** = murió sin descendencia; **they have no issue** = no tienen descendencia (NOTE: in this meaning **issue** is either singular or plural and is not used with **the**) **(b)** *(subject of a dispute)* asunto *m or* cuestión *f or* tema *m*; **collateral issue** = cuestión *or* tema adicional; **point at issue** = el tema en discusión; **the point at issue is the ownership of the property** = el tema en discusión es la posesión de los bienes **(c)** *(giving out of new shares)* emisión *f*; **bonus issue** *or* **scrip issue** = emisión gratuita; **issue of debentures** *or* **debenture issue** = emisión de obligaciones; **issue of new shares** *or* **share issue** = emisión de acciones nuevas; **rights issue** = emisión de derechos **2** *verb* emitir *or* poner en circulación *or* expedir *or* publicar; **to issue a letter of credit** = expedir una carta de crédito; **to issue shares in a new company** = emitir acciones de una empresa nueva; **to issue statement** = evacuar un informe; **to issue a writ against someone** = demandar a alguien en juicio *or* emplazar a alguien ante el juez; **the government issued a report on London's traffic** = el gobierno publicó un informe sobre el tráfico de Londres; **the Secretary of State issued guidelines for expenditure** = el Secretario de Estado anunció las directrices sobre gastos; **he issued writs for libel in connection with allegations made in a Sunday newspaper** = hizo una serie de demandas por difamación relacionadas con declaraciones realizadas a un periódico dominical
◊ **issuance** ['ɪʃuəns] *noun* emisión *f or* expedición *f*; **upon issuance of the order, the bailiffs seized the property** = tras la expedición del mandato, los alguaciles embargaron la propiedad
◊ **issued** ['ɪʃuːd] *adjective* **issued capital** = capital *m* en cartera *or* emitido; **issued price** = precio *m* de salida de emisión
◊ **issuing** ['ɪʃuːɪŋ] *noun* emisión *f or* emisor, -ra; **issuing bank** *or* **issuing house** = banco emisor *or* casa emisora

item ['aɪtəm] *noun* **(a)** *(thing for sale)* artículo *m;* **cash items** = artículos de venta al contado **(b)** *(piece of information)* noticia *f;* **extraordinary items** = gastos extraordinarios *or* partidas extraordinarias; **item of expenditure** = partida de gasto **(c)** *(point on a list)* punto *m;* **items in the**

agenda = puntos a tratar en el orden del día; **we will now take item four on the agenda** = discutiremos ahora el punto cuatro del orden del día

◊ **itemize** ['aɪtəmaɪz] *verb* detallar *or* especificar; **itemizing the sales figures will take about two days** = detallar las cifras de ventas nos llevará unos dos días; **itemized account** = cuenta *f* detallada

Jj

J [dʒeɪ] *abbreviation* juez, -za *or* magistrado, -da; **Smith J said he was not laying down guidelines for sentencing** = el magistrado Smith dijo que no dictaba *or* establecía directrices para formular sentencia (NOTE: **Smith J** is spoken as 'Mr Justice Smith')

jactitation [dʒæktɪ'teɪʃn] *noun* jactancia *f or* impostura *f;* **jactitation of marriage** = falsa pretensión *f* al estado de matrimonio

jail *or* **gaol** [dʒeɪl] **1** *noun* cárcel *f or* prisión *f;* **he spent ten years in jail** = pasó diez años en la cárcel **2** *verb* encarcelar; **she was jailed for three years** = fue encarcelada tres años; **he was jailed for manslaughter** = le encarcelaron por homicidio involuntario
◊ **jailbird** ['dʒeɪlbɔːd] *noun* recluso, -sa *or* preso *m* reincidente
◊ **jailbreak** ['dʒeɪlbreɪk] *noun* evasión *f or* fuga *f;* **mass jailbreak** = fuga múltiple
◊ **jailer** ['dʒeɪlə] *noun* carcelero *m*

jargon ['dʒɑːgən] *noun* jerga *f;* **legal jargon** = jerga jurídica

jaywalker ['dʒeɪwɔːkə] *noun* peatón *mf* imprudente
◊ **jaywalking** ['dʒeɪwɔːkɪŋ] *noun* cruzar la calle imprudentemente

jeopardy ['dʒepədi] *noun* **to be in jeopardy** = estar en peligro; **his driving licence is in jeopardy** = se arriesga a perder su permiso de conducir; *see also* DOUBLE JEOPARDY
◊ **jeopardize** ['dʒepədaɪz] *verb* arriesgar *or* poner en peligro; **her arrest for drunken driving may jeopardize her work as a doctor specializing in child care** = su arresto por conducir en estado de embriaguez puede poner en peligro su trabajo como médico especialista en puericultura

jetsam ['dʒetsəm] *noun* echazón *f or* carga *f* arrojada al mar; **flotsam and jetsam** = pecios *mpl* y echazón

jettison ['dʒetɪzən] *verb* echar la carga al mar

jewel ['dʒuːəl] *noun* joya *f*
◊ **jewellery** ['dʒuːəlri] *noun* joyería *f*
◊ **jeweller** ['dʒuːələ] *noun* joyero, -ra
◊ **jewellers** ['dʒuːələz] *noun* joyería *f*

jobber [dʒɒbə] *noun (formerly on the Stock Exchange)* **(stock) jobber** = corredor intermediario en Bolsa *or* agente *mf* de bolsa especializado *or* agiotista *mf*

join [dʒɔɪn] *verb* **(a)** *(put things together)* juntar *or* unir; **the offices were joined together by making a door in the wall** = abrieron una puerta en la pared para juntar las oficinas; **the appendix is joined to the contract** = el apéndice se añade al contrato; **to join someone to an action** = incluir a alguien en una acción **(b)** *(to become part of)* afiliarse *or* unirse a *or* darse de alta; **to join a firm of solicitors** = entrar en *or* incorporarse a un despacho de abogados; **he joined on January 1st** = se incorporó el 1 de enero; **to join an association** *or* **a group** = hacerse socio de una asociación *or* de un grupo; **all the staff have joined the company pension plan** = todo el personal se ha acogido al plan de pensiones de la empresa; **he was asked to join the board** = le pidieron que entrara en la junta directiva; **Smith Ltd has applied to join the trade association** = Smith S.A. ha solicitado incorporarse a la asociación comercial
◊ **joinder** ['dʒɔɪndə] *noun* acumulación *f* de acciones *or* unión *f or* reunión *f or* fusión *f; see also* MISJOINDER, NONJOINDER

joint [dʒɔɪnt] **1** *adjective* **(a)** *(two or more organizations or people together)* unido, -da *or* colectivo, -va *or* conjunto, -ta; **joint account** = cuenta *f* conjunta *or* en participación; **joint commission of inquiry** *or* **joint committee** = comisión *f* mixta de investigación; **joint discussions** = negociaciones *fpl* conjuntas (entre patronal y trabajadores); **joint management** = dirección *f* conjunta *or* codirección *f;* **joint ownership** = copropiedad *f or* propiedad *f* mancomunada *or* condominio *m;* **US joint resolution** = proyecto *m* de ley aprobado por las dos cámaras; **joint-stock bank** = banco *m* por acciones *or* banco privado constituido en sociedad anónima; **joint-stock company** = sociedad *f* por acciones; **joint venture** *or* **US joint adventure** = negocio *m* en participación *or* empresa conjunta; **to assume joint responsibility** = mancomunar **(b)** *(two or more people who work together)* conjunto, -ta *or* colectivo, -va; **joint beneficiary** = cobeneficiario, -ria *or* beneficiario proindiviso;

joint managing director = codirector, -ra; joint owner = copropietario, -ria; joint signatory = signatario mancomunado *or* conjunto *or* firmante *m* conjunto; joint heir = coheredero, -ra; joint tortfeasors = responsables *mfpl* conjuntos de un agravio 2 *noun (slang)* antro *m;* to case a joint = investigar a fondo un edificio antes de entrar en él a la fuerza

◊ joint and several ['dʒɔɪnt ən 'sevrəl] *adjective* mancomunada y solidariamente; joint and several liability = responsabilidad *f* conjunta y solidaria

◊ jointly ['dʒɔɪntli] *adverb* conjuntamente *or* en común; to own a property jointly = poseer una propiedad en común; to manage a company jointly = dirigir una empresa conjuntamente; they are jointly liable for damages = son responsables de los daños en común; jointly and severally liable = responsable conjunta y solidariamente

◊ joint tenancy ['dʒɔɪnt 'tenənsi] *noun* coarriendo *m; see also* TENANCY IN COMMON

joke [dʒəuk] *noun* broma *f*

joy riding ['dʒɔɪ 'raɪdɪŋ] *noun* paseo *m* en coche sin autorización del dueño

JP ['dʒeɪ 'piː] *noun* = JUSTICE OF THE PEACE (NOTE: the plural is JPs)

judge [dʒʌdʒ] 1 *noun* juez, -za *or* magistrado, -da; County Court judge = juez de un juzgado municipal; judge in the Divorce Court = juez del tribunal de divorcios; the judge sent him to prison for embezzlement = la jueza le condenó a prisión por malversación de fondos *or* desfalco; judge in chambers = juez que ve un caso en privado; senior judge = magistrado de término; acting judge = magistrado en funciones; circuit judge *or* district judge = juez de distrito *or* juez comarcal *or* juez titular; prison judge = juez de vigilancia penitenciaria; Judges' Rules = reglamento *m* concerniente al interrogatorio de sospechosos por parte de la policía 2 *verb* juzgar *or* considerar; he judged it was time to call an end to the discussions = juzgó que era hora de poner fin a las discusiones

◊ Judge Advocate-General ['dʒʌdʒ 'ædvəkət 'dʒenrəl] *noun* Auditor Militar General

◊ Judge Advocate of the Fleet ['dʒʌdʒ 'ædvəkət əv ðə 'fliːt] *noun* Auditor Militar para la Marina

COMMENT: In England, judges are appointed by the Lord Chancellor. The minimum requirement is that one should be a barrister or solicitor of ten years' standing. The majority of judges are barristers, but they cannot practise as barristers. Recorders are practising barristers who act as judges on a part-time basis. The appointment of judges is not a political appointment, and judges remain in office unless they are found guilty of gross

misconduct. In the USA, state judges can be appointed by the state governor or can be elected; in the federal courts and the Supreme Court, judges are appointed by the President, but the appointment has to be approved by Congress

judgment *or* judgement ['dʒʌdʒmənt] *noun* juicio *m* *or* sentencia *f* *or* fallo *m;* certificate of judgment = testimonio *m* de sentencia; judgment by default *or* default judgment = sentencia en rebeldía *or* fallo por falta de comparecencia; final judgment = sentencia definitiva *or* citación *f* para sentencia; interlocutory judgment = juicio *m* interlocutorio; to pronounce judgment *or* to give one's judgment on something = pronunciar *or* dictar sentencia *or* emitir un juicio sobre algo; to enter judgement *or* to take judgment = registrar la sentencia; to enter judgment for *or* against the plaintiff = registrar la sentencia de aceptación o no aceptación de una demanda; the plaintiff entered judgment in default = se registró la aceptación de la demanda por falta de comparecencia del demandado; entry of judgment = registro *m* de la sentencia; judgment creditor = acreedor, -ra judicial *or* por sentencia firme; judgment debtor = deudor, -ra judicial *or* por sentencia firme; judgment summons = requerimiento *m* judicial de pago o en su defecto de ingreso en prisión; to overturn a judgment = casar una sentencia (NOTE: the spelling judgment is used by lawyers)

judicata [dʒuːdɪˈkɑːtə] *see* RES

judicature ['dʒuːdɪkətʃə] *noun* judicatura *f;* judicature paper = papel *m* grueso de los documentos judiciales; *see also* SUPREME COURT

judice ['dʒuːdəsi] *see* SUB JUDICE

judicial [dʒuˈdɪʃəl] *adjective* judicial *or* legal; the Judicial Committee of the House of Lords = el Tribunal Superior de Apelación para Inglaterra y Gales; the Judicial Committee of the Privy Council = el Tribunal de Apelación para países y colonias de la Commonwealth; judicial immunity = inmunidad *f* judicial; judicial notice = conocimiento *m* judicial; judicial precedent = precedente *m* judicial; judicial processes = procedimientos *mpl* judiciales; judicial review = revisión *f* *or* análisis *m* *or* examen *m* judicial; judicial separation = separación *f* legal; judicial trustee = fideicomisario, -ria judicial

judiciary [dʒuˈdɪʃəri] *noun* judicatura *f;* the judiciary = la magistratura *f* *or* el poder *m* judicial

junior ['dʒuːniə] 1 *adjective* menor *or* más joven *or* subalterno, -na *or* inferior; junior clerk = administrativo, -va de primera *or* pasante *mf;* junior executive *or* junior manager = ejecutivo, -va auxiliar *or* director, -ra más reciente; junior partner = socio, -cia subalterno, -na *or* de menor

antigüedad; **John Smith, Junior** = John Smith, hijo
2 *noun* **(a)** *(barrister who is not a Queen's Counsel)*
abogado, -da **(b)** *(barrister appearing with a
leader)* abogado, -da auxiliar **(c) office junior** =
auxiliar *mf* administrativo, -va *or* subalterno, -na

junta ['dʒʌntə] *noun (militar)* Junta *f*

jurat ['dʒuəræt] *noun* acta *f* notarial

juridical [dʒu'rɪdɪkl] *adjective* jurídico, -ca

jurisdiction [dʒuərɪs'dɪkʃn] *noun* jurisdicción *f*
or competencia *f*; **civil jurisdiction** = jurisdicción
civil; **criminal jurisdiction** = jurisdicción criminal;
within the jurisdiction of the court = dentro de la
competencia del tribunal; **outside the jurisdiction
of the court** = fuera de la competencia del tribunal;
**the prisoner refused to recognize the jurisdiction
of the court** = el prisionero se negó a reconocer la
competencia del tribunal; **equitable jurisdiction** =
jurisdicción justa *or* de equidad

jurisprudence   [dʒuərɪs'pruːdəns]   *noun*
jurisprudencia *f*

jurist ['dʒuərɪst] *noun* jurista *mf*
◊ **juristic** [dʒuə'rɪstɪk] *adjective* jurídico, -ca;
juristic person = ARTIFICIAL PERSON

juror ['dʒuərə] *noun* jurado, -da

> COMMENT: jurors can be selected from
> registered electors who are between eighteen
> and sixty-five years old and who have been
> resident in the UK for five years. Barristers,
> solicitors, judges, priests, doctors, Members of
> Parliament, people who are insane are among
> the categories of people disqualified from
> being jurors

jury ['dʒuəri] *noun* jurado *m;* **trial by jury** *or* **jury
trial** = juicio *m* con jurado; **he has been called for
jury service** *or* *US* **for jury duty** = le han llamado
para actuar como jurado; **'Members of the Jury'** =
'Miembros del Jurado'; **the foreman of the jury** =
el presidente del jurado; **jury vetting** = selección *f*
de los miembros del jurado; *US* **grand jury** = gran
jurado *or* jurado de acusación (NOTE: the word **jury**
can take a plural verb)
◊ **jury box** ['dʒuəri bɒks] *noun* panel *m* *or*
tribuna *f* *or* estrado *m* del jurado
◊ **juryman** ['dʒuərimæn] *noun* (miembro del)
jurado, -da (NOTE: plural is **jurymen**)
◊ **jury room** ['dʒuəri 'ruːm] *noun* sala *f* del
jurado

jus [dʒʌs] *Latin word* derecho justo

just [dʒʌst] *adjective* justo, -ta *or* imparcial; **to
show just cause** = mostrar causa justa

justice ['dʒʌstɪs] *noun* **(a)** *(fair treatment)*
justicia *f*; **to administer justice** = administrar
justicia; **to bring a criminal to justice** = llevar a un
criminal ante la justicia *or* ante los tribunales;
natural justice = justicia natural; *US* **Department
of Justice** *or* **Justice Department** = Ministerio *m*
de Justicia; *see also note at* MINISTRY;
perverting the course of justice = manipulación *f*
de la justicia **(b)** *(magistrate)* magistrado, -da *or*
juez, -za; **chairman of the justices** = presidente *m*
de un tribunal de magistrados; **justices' clerk** *or*
clerk to the justices = secretario, -ria de juzgado;
Lord Chief Justice = presidente del Tribunal
Supremo y miembro del Tribunal de Apelación; *US*
Chief Justice = presidente de la Sala **(c)** *(title given
to a High Court judge)* **Mr Justice Adams** = el
magistrado Sr Adams; **Lord Justice** = juez
miembro del Tribunal de Apelación (NOTE: usually
written as **J** or **LJ** after the name: **Adams J; Smith LJ**)
◊ **justice of the peace (JP)** ['dʒʌstɪs əv ðə
'piːs] *noun* juez de paz

justiciary [dʒʌ'stɪʃəri] *noun* magistratura *f*; *(in
Scotland)* **High Court of Justiciary** = Tribunal *m*
Superior de lo Penal

justify ['dʒʌstɪfaɪ] *verb* justificar; **the end
justifies the means** = el fin justifica los medios
◊ **justifiable** [dʒʌstɪ'faɪəbl] *adjective*
justificable; **justifiable homicide** = homicidio *m*
justificable
◊ **justification** [dʒʌstɪfɪ'keɪʃn] *noun*
justificación *f*; **in justification** = como
justificación; **in justification, the accused claimed
that the burglar had attacked him with an axe** =
el acusado declaró, como justificación, que el
ladrón le había atacado con un hacha; **defense of
justification** = defensa de una causa de difamación
alegando que las palabras en cuestión no son
difamatorias ya que representan la verdad; **the
defendant entered defence of justification** = la
parte demandada alegó, en su defensa, que las
palabras motivo de causa no eran difamatorias al ser
verdaderas

justitia [dʒʌs'tɪsɪə] *see* FIAT

juvenile ['dʒuːvənaɪl] *noun & adjective* joven *or*
juvenil; **juvenile court** = tribunal *m* de menores;
**the appeal court quashed the care order made by
the juvenile court** = el tribunal de apelación anuló
la orden de retirada de la patria potestad dictada por
el tribunal de menores; **juvenile delinquent** =
delincuente *mf* juvenil; **juvenile offender** =
delincuente juvenil que es juzgado en un tribunal de
menores

Kk

kangaroo court [kæŋgə'ru: 'kɔ:t] *noun* tribunal *m* desautorizado

KC ['keɪ 'si:] = KING'S COUNSEL

keep [ki:p] *verb* **(a)** *(to go on doing something)* seguir *or* continuar; **they kept working, even when the boss told them to stop** = continuaron trabajando, aun cuando el jefe les dijo que pararan; **the other secretaries complain that she keeps singing when she is typing** = las otras secretarias se quejan de que canta cuando escribe a máquina **(b)** *(to do what is necessary)* cumplir *or* mantener; **to keep a promise** = cumplir una promesa; **to keep an appointment** = acudir a una cita; **to keep the books of a company** *or* **to keep a company's books** = llevar la contabilidad *or* los libros de una empresa; **to keep the law** = mantener la ley; **to keep the peace** = mantener la paz; **he was bound over to keep the peace** = se le obligó a mantener la paz **(c)** *(to hold items)* guardar *or* mantener; **to keep someone's name on file** = tener el nombre de alguien en archivo; **we always keep this item in stock** = siempre disponemos de este producto; **to keep someone's name on file** = tener el nombre de alguien archivado *or* en archivo **(d)** *(to hold things at a certain level)* mantener; **we must keep our mailing list up to date** = debemos mantener nuestra lista de direcciones al día *or* actualizada; **to keep spending to a minimum** = reducir los gastos al mínimo; **the price of oil has kept the pound at a high level** = el precio del petróleo ha mantenido la libra alta; **the government is encouraging firms to keep prices low** = el gobierno está alentando a las empresas a mantener los precios bajos; **lack of demand for typewriters has kept prices down** = la escasa demanda de máquinas de escribir ha mantenido los precios bajos (NOTE: **keeping - kept**)
◊ **keeper** ['ki:pə] *noun* guarda *mf or* conservador, -ra; **Keeper of the Great Seal** = el presidente de la Cámara de los Lores y Ministro de Justicia
◊ **keeping** ['ki:pɪŋ] *noun* **safe keeping** = lugar *m* seguro *or* buen recaudo *m or* custodia *f;* **we put the documents into the bank for safe keeping** = guardamos los documentos en el banco para mayor seguridad; **keeping a disorderly house** = delito *m* de ser propietario de *or* dirigir un prostíbulo

Keogh plan ['ki:oʊ 'plæn] *noun US* plan *m* Keogh *or* plan privado de jubilación

kerb crawling ['kɔ:b 'krɑ:lɪŋ] *noun* incitación *f* a la prostitución desde un coche

key [ki:] **1** *noun* **(a)** *(lock)* llave *f;* **he has taken the office keys home with him, so no one can get in** = se ha llevado las llaves de la oficina, así que nadie puede entrar; **we have lost the keys to the computer room** = hemos perdido las llaves de la sala de ordenadores **(b)** *(premium)* **key money** = traspaso *m* **(c)** *(on computer, typewriter)* tecla *f;* **there are sixty-four keys on the keyboard** = hay sesenta y cuatro teclas en el teclado; **control key** = tecla de control; **shift key** = tecla de mayúsculas **2** *adjective (important)* clave; **a key witness has disappeared** = ha desaparecido un testigo clave
◊ **keyboard** ['ki:bɔ:d] *noun* teclado *m*

kickback ['kɪkbæk] *noun* comisión *f* ilegal *or* soborno *m*

kidnap ['kɪdnæp] *verb* secuestrar *or* raptar
◊ **kidnapper** ['kɪdnæpə] *noun* secuestrador, -ra *or* raptor, -ra
◊ **kidnapping** ['kɪdnæpɪŋ] *noun* secuestro *m or* rapto *m; (of children)* sustracción *f* de menores

kill [kɪl] *verb* matar; **he was accused of killing his girlfriend with a knife** = fue acusado de matar a su novia con un cuchillo
◊ **killer** ['kɪlə] *noun* asesino, -na; **child killer** = infanticida *mf;* **the police are searching for the girl's killer** = la policía está buscando al asesino de la chica

kin [kɪn] *plural noun* parientes *mfpl or* familia *f; see also* NEXT OF KIN
◊ **kinship** ['kɪnʃɪp] *noun* parentesco *m;* **degree of kinship** = grado *m* de parentesco

kind [kaɪnd] *noun* tipo *m or* clase *f;* **the printer produces two kinds of printout** = la impresora produce dos clases de impresión; **the law distinguishes several kinds of crime against the person** = la ley distingue varios tipos de delito contra la persona; **payment in kind** = pago *m* en especie

king [kɪŋ] *noun* rey; **Juan Carlos the First is the King of Spain** = Juan Carlos I es el rey de España; *see also* QUEEN (NOTE: often used with a name as a title: **King Juan Carlos)**

kingdom ['kɪŋdəm] *noun* reino *m;* **the United Kingdom of Great Britain and Northern Ireland** = el Reino Unido de Gran Bretaña e Irlanda del Norte; **the kingdom of Saudi Arabia** = el reino de Arabia Saudí

kitchen cabinet ['kɪtʃən 'kæbɪnət] *noun* consejo *m* informal y privado que asesora al Primer Ministro

kite mark ['kaɪt 'maːk] *noun* marca *f* de calidad en las mercancías británicas

kleptomania [kleptə'meɪnɪə] *noun* cleptomanía *f*

◊ **kleptomaniac** [kleptə'meɪnɪæk] *noun* cleptómano, -na *f*

knife [naɪf] *noun* cuchillo *m* **2** *verb* acuchillar

knock [nɒk] **1** *noun* golpe *m* **2** *verb* **(a)** *(to hit)* golpear *or* pegar; **he knocked on the door and went in** = llamó a la puerta y entró; **she knocked her head on the filing cabinet** = se golpeó la cabeza contra el archivo **(b) to knock the competition** = atacar a la competencia por medio de ventas masivas; **knocking copy** = publicidad *f* que critica los productos competidores *or* publicidad agresiva

◊ **knock down** ['nɒk 'daʊn] *verb* **(a)** *(run over)* atropellar **(b)** *(at an auction)* **to knock something down to a bidder** = adjudicar algo en una subasta; **the stock was knocked down to him for £10,000** = se le adjudicó la mercancía por 10.000 libras

◊ **knockdown** ['nɒkdaʊn] *noun* **knockdown prices** = precios *mpl* mínimos *or* precios de saldo *or* precios por los suelos; **he sold me the car at a knockdown price** = me vendió el coche a un precio de saldo

◊ **knock-for-knock agreement** ['nɒkfə'nɒk ə'griːmənt] *noun* acuerdo *m* entre dos compañías de seguros por el que no iniciarán acciones judiciales una contra la otra, y pagarán las indemnizaciones de sus propios clientes

◊ **knock off** ['nɒk 'ɒf] *verb* **(a)** *(stop working)* terminar (de trabajar) **(b)** *(sales)* rebajar; **he knocked £10 off the price for cash** = rebajó 10

libras el precio por pago en efectivo **(c)** *(slang)* birlar *or* mangar

◊ **knock-on effect** ['nɒk'ɒn ɪ'fekt] *noun* repercusión *f* efecto *m* secundario *or* efecto producido por una acción; **the strike by customs officers has had a knock-on effect on car production by slowing down exports of cars** = la huelga de los oficiales de aduana ha repercutido en la producción de coches al ralentizar las exportaciones

know [nəʊ] *verb* **(a)** *(to learn)* saber; **I do not know how a computer works** = no sé cómo funciona un ordenador; **does he know how long it takes to get to the airport?** ¿sabe cuánto se tarda en llegar al aeropuerto?; **the senior partner's secretary does not know where he is** = la secretaria no sabe dónde está el socio principal **(b)** *(to meet)* conocer; **not to know** = desconocer; **do you know Mr Jones, our new sales director?** = ¿conoce al Sr Jones, nuestro nuevo director de ventas? (NOTE: **knowing - known**)

◊ **know-how** ['nəʊ'haʊ] *noun* conocimientos *mpl* científicos *or* técnicos especializados; **you need some legal know-how to do this job** = se necesitan ciertos conocimientos jurídicos para hacer este trabajo; **he needs to acquire computer know-how** = necesita adquirir conocimientos de informática

◊ **knowingly** ['nəʊɪŋli] *adverb* deliberadamente *or* a sabiendas *or* a propósito; **it was charged that he knowingly broke the Official Secrets Act by publishing the document in his newspaper** = se le acusó de haber infringido deliberadamente la ley de Secretos Oficiales al publicar el documento en su periódico

◊ **knowledge** ['nɒlɪdʒ] *noun* conocimiento *m or* saber *m;* **he had no knowledge of the contract** = no sabía que el contrato existía *or* no tenía conocimiento de la existencia del contrato; **to the best of my knowledge** = casi con toda seguridad *or* por lo que yo sé *or* que yo sepa; **the witness said that to the best of his knowledge the accused had never left the room** = el testigo dijo que, según su leal saber y entender, el acusado no había salido en ningún momento de la habitación; **constructive knowledge** = conocimiento de causa *or* conocimiento implícito *or* por deducción

Ll

labour *or US* **labor** ['leibɔ] *noun* **(a)** *(work)* trabajo *m;* **labour exchange** = bolsa *f* de trabajo; **manual labour** = trabajo manual; **to charge for materials and labour** = cobrar los materiales y la mano de obra; **hard labour** = trabajos forzados *or* forzosos **(b)** *(workforce)* mano *f* de obra *or* trabajadores, -ras *or* obreros, -ras; **casual labour** = trabajadores eventuales; **cheap labour** = mano de obra barata; **local labour** = mano de obra local; **organized labour** = trabajadores sindicados *or* organizados; **skilled labour** = mano de obra especializada; **labour-intensive industry** = industria *f* que utiliza mucha mano de obra *or* con un alto coeficiente de mano de obra **(c)** **labour disputes** = conflictos *mpl* laborales; **labour law** *or* **labour laws** *or* **labour legislation** = derecho *m* del trabajo *or* derecho laboral *or* legislación *f* laboral; **labour relations** = relaciones *fpl* laborales; *US* **labor union** = sindicato *m* de trabajadores **(d)** **International Labour Organization (ILO)** = Organización *f* Internacional del Trabajo (OIT)

◊ **labourer** ['leibɔrɔ] *noun* peón *m or* obrero, -ra *or* trabajador, -ra; **casual labourer** = trabajador eventual; **manual labourer** = trabajador manual

laches ['lætʃiz] *noun* negligencia *f or* retraso *m* en reclamar un derecho *or* prescripción *f* negativa; *see also* STATUTE OF LIMITATIONS

lack [læk] **1** *noun* falta *f or* carencia *f or* escasez *f;* **the investigation has been held up by lack of information** = la investigación ha sido suspendida por falta de información; **charges cannot be brought for lack of evidence** = no se pueden formular acusaciones por falta de pruebas; **lack of data** *or* **lack of information** = falta de información; **the decision has been put back for lack of up-to-date information** = la decisión ha sido aplazada por falta de información actualizada; **lack of funds** = falta de fondos; **the project was cancelled because of lack of funds** = el proyecto fue suspendido por falta de fondos **2** *verb* carecer de *or* faltarle a uno *or* no tener; **the police lack any clues to the murder** = la policía carece de pistas sobre el asesinato *or* no tiene ninguna pista para resolver el asesinato; **the fraud squad lacks the necessary staff to undertake the investigation** = la brigada contra el fraude no posee el personal necesario para llevar a cabo la investigación

lading ['leidiŋ] *see* BILL

Lady Day ['leidi 'dei] *noun* 25 de marzo, día de pago del alquiler de tierras correspondiente al primer trimestre del año; *see also* QUARTER DAY

lag [læg] *noun* **old lag** = presidiario, -ria *or* ex-presidiario, -ria reincidente *or* sin posibilidades de enmendarse

laissez-faire *or* **laisser-faire** ['lesei'feɔ] *noun* liberalismo *m* (económico); **laissez-faire policies resulted in increased economic activity, but contributed to a rise in imports** = la política liberalista tuvo como resultado un crecimiento de la actividad económica pero contribuyó al aumento de las importaciones

lame duck president ['leim 'dʌk 'prezidɔnt] *noun* presidente, -ta cesante; **no foreign policy decisions can be made because of the lame duck presidency** = el presidente cesante no tiene poder para decidir sobre asuntos de política exterior

land [lænd] **1** *noun* **(a)** *(earth)* tierra *f;* **land agent** = administrador, -ra (de tierras); **land certificate** = certificado *m* de tierras; **land charges** = cargas *fpl or* deudas *fpl* territoriales; **land register** = catastro *m or* registro *m* de la propiedad; **land registration** = catastro *or* registro de tierras; **Land Registry** = Registro catastral *or* de la Propiedad; **land taxes** = impuestos *mpl* territoriales **(b)** *(estate)* **lands** = tierras; **Crown Lands** = patrimonio *m* del Estado *or* de la Corona **2** *verb* **(a)** *(from ship)* desembarcar *or* descargar; **landed costs** = coste *m* descargado **(b)** *(of plane)* aterrizar *or* hacer aterrizar; **the plane landed ten minutes late** = el avión aterrizó diez minutos tarde

COMMENT: under English law, the ownership of all land is vested in the Crown; individuals or other legal persons may however hold estates in land, the most important of which are freehold estates (which amount to absolute ownership) and leasehold estates (which last for a fixed period of time). Ownership of land usually confers ownership of everything above and below the land. The process of buying and selling land is 'conveyancing'. Any contract transferring land or any interest in land must be in writing. Interests in land can be disposed of by a will

◊ **landing** ['lændɪŋ] *noun* **landing card** = tarjeta *f* de desembarque; **landing charges** = gastos *mpl* de descarga; **landing order** = permiso *m* de descarga

◊ **landlady** ['lænleɪdi] *noun* propietaria *f or* casera *f or* ama *f*

◊ **landlord** ['lænlɔːd] *noun* propietario *m or* casero *m or* amo *m*; **ground landlord** = nudo propietario *or* propietario absoluto; **our ground landlord is an insurance company** = nuestro arrendador es una compañía de seguros; **the Landlord and Tenant Act** = Ley *f* de Arrendamiento de Propiedad

◊ **landmark** ['lænmaːk] *noun* mojón *m* hito *m*

◊ **landmark decision** ['lænmaːk dɪ'sɪʒn] *noun* fallo *m* que establece un importante precedente

◊ **landowner** ['lændəʊnə] *noun* propietario, -ria rural *or* terrateniente *mf*

◊ **Lands Tribunal** ['lændz traɪ'bjuːnəl] *noun* tribunal *m* que se ocupa de demandas de compensación o indemnización relacionadas con tierras

language ['læŋgwɪdʒ] *noun* lengua *f or* lenguaje *m or* idioma *m;* **he was accused of using offensive language to a policeman** = fue acusado de utilizar un lenguaje ofensivo con un policía; **computer language** *or* **programming language** = lenguaje informático *or* de programación; **native language** = lengua materna

lapse [læps] **1** *noun* **(a) a lapse of time** = un lapso *m or* intervalo *m* de tiempo **(b)** *(ending of a right or offer)* derogación *f or* caducidad *f or* prescripción *f* **(c)** *(failure of a legacy)* anulación *f* de legado **2** *verb* caducar; **to let an offer lapse** = dejar que una oferta expire; **lapsed legacy** = legado *m* anulado por fallecimiento del legatario; **lapsed passport** = pasaporte *m* caducado; **lapsed (insurance) policy** = suspensión *f* de una póliza de seguros por falta de pago de las cuotas

larceny ['laːsni] *noun* hurto *m or* robo *m or* latrocinio *m;* **he was convicted of larceny** = fue condenado por hurto; **petty larceny** *or* **grand larceny** = hurto *or* robo de menor cuantía *or* robo de cuantía mayor

COMMENT: larceny no longer exists in English law, having been replaced by the crime of theft

large [laːdʒ] *adjective* **(a)** grande *or* importante; **our company is one of the largest suppliers of computers to the government** = nuestra empresa es una de las mayores proveedoras de ordenadores del gobierno; **he is our largest customer** = es nuestro cliente más importante; **why has she got an office which is larger than mine?** = ¿por qué tiene ella un despacho más grande que el mío? **(b) at large** = en libertad *or* libre *or* suelto, -ta; **three prisoners escaped - two were recaptured, but one is still at large** = tres prisioneros escaparon - dos fueron capturados, pero uno está todavía en libertad

◊ **largely** ['laːdʒli] *adverb* en gran parte *or* sobre todo *or* considerablemente; **our sales are largely in the home market** = nuestras ventas se dirigen sobre todo al mercado nacional; **they have largely pulled out of the American market** = se han retirado prácticamente del mercado americano

last [laːst] **1** *adjective & adverb* **(a)** *(coming at the end of a series)* último, -ma *or* en último lugar *or* por último; **out of a queue of twenty people, I was served last** = de una cola de veinte personas, me sirvieron el último; **this is our last board meeting before we move to our new offices** = ésta es la última reunión de la junta antes de mudarnos a las nuevas oficinas; **this is the last case which the magistrates will hear before lunch** = éste es el último caso que los magistrados verán antes de la comida; **last quarter** = último trimestre; **court of last resort** = tribunal *m* de última instancia; **lender of the last resort** = prestamista *mf* en última instancia *or* de último recurso **(b)** *(most recent)* último, -ma *or* pasado, -da; **the last case was one of attempted murder, this one is for theft** = el último caso fue de intento de asesinato, éste es de robo; **last week** *or* **last month** *or* **last year** = la semana pasada *or* el mes pasado *or* el año pasado; **last year's accounts have to be ready by the AGM** = la contabilidad del año pasado tiene que estar lista para la Junta General Ordinaria; **last will and testament** = última voluntad y testamento **(c) the week** *or* **month** *or* **year before last** = la semana antepasada *or* el mes antepasado *or* el año antepasado **2** *verb* durar; **the hearing started in December and lasted until the second week of January** = la vista empezó en diciembre y duró hasta la segunda semana de enero

◊ **last in first out (LIFO)** ['laːst 'ɪn 'fɜːst 'aʊt] *phrase* **(a)** *(redundancy)* política *f* de reducción de plantilla por la que los últimos contratados son los primeros en ser despedidos **(b)** *(accounting)* método *m* contable según el cual las existencias se valoran al precio de las últimas compras; *see also* WILL

late [leɪt] **1** *adjective* **(a)** *(after the time stated)* tarde *or* tardío, -día; **we apologize for the late arrival of the plane from Amsterdam** = rogamos disculpen el retraso en la llegada del avión procedente de Amsterdam; **there is a penalty for late delivery** = hay un recargo por retraso en la entrega **(b)** *(last)* último, -ma; **latest date for signature of the contract** = última fecha para la firma del contrato **(c)** *(most recent)* **latest** = último, -ma *or* más reciente; **he always drives the latest model of car** = siempre lleva el último modelo de coche; **here are the latest accident figures** = aquí están las cifras de accidentes más recientes **(d)** *(dead)* difunto, -ta *or* fallecido, -da; **her late husband** = su difunto marido **2** *adverb* tarde *or* con retraso; **to be late** = atrasarse *or* retrasarse; **the hearing started late** = la vista comenzó tarde; **the**

shipment was landed late = el cargamento fue desembarcado tarde; **the plane was two hours late** = el avión se retrasó dos horas

◊ **late-night** ['leɪt 'naɪt] *adjective* nocturno,-na *or* a última hora de la noche; **they had a late-night meeting at the airport** = tuvieron una reunión a última hora de la noche en el aeropuerto; **their late-night negotiations ended in an agreement which was signed at 3 a.m.** = sus negociaciones nocturnas finalizaron con un acuerdo firmado a las 3 de la madrugada

latent ['leɪtənt] *adjective* latente *or* oculto, -ta; **latent ambiguity** = ambigüedad *f* latente en un contrato; **latent defect** = defecto *m or* vicio *m* oculto

Latin ['lætɪn] *noun* latín *m*

COMMENT: Latin was used as the language of the law courts for centuries, and its use still exists in many common legal phrases, such as **habeas corpus, in flagrante delicto, de jure** and **de facto**

launch [lɔːnʃ] *verb* emprender *or* lanzar; **the police have launched a campaign against drunken drivers** = la policía ha emprendido una campaña contra los conductores en estado de embriaguez

launder ['lɔːndə] *verb (slang)* blanquear dinero negro; **the proceeds of the robbery were laundered through a bank in the Caribbean** = las ganancias del robo fueron blanqueadas a través de un banco en el Caribe

law [lɔː] *noun* **(a)** *(rule)* ley *f or* fuero *m;* **law in force** = ley vigente; **decree law** = decreto-ley *m;* **law practitioner** = profesional *mf* de la abogacía; **a law has to be passed by Parliament** = una ley ha de ser aprobada por el Parlamento; **the government has proposed a new law to regulate the sale of goods on Sundays** = el gobierno ha propuesto una nueva ley para regular la venta de mercancías los domingos; **conflict of laws** = conflicto *m* de leyes; *(section in a country's statute)* Derecho Internacional Privado; **labour laws** = leyes laborales **(b)** *(all the statutes of a country taken together)* **law** = derecho *m;* **case law** = precedentes *mpl or* jurisprudencia *f;* **civil law** = derecho civil; **commercial law** = derecho mercantil; **company law** = derecho de empresa; **constitutional law** = derecho político; **contract law** *or* **the law of contract** = derecho de contratos; **copyright law** = derecho de autor *or* ley de propiedad intelectual; **criminal law** = derecho penal; **international law** = derecho internacional; **maritime law** *or* **the law of the sea** = derecho marítimo; **mercantile law** *or* **law merchant** = derecho mercantil; **private law** = derecho privado; **public law** = derecho público; **law and order** = orden *m* público; **there was a breakdown of law and order following the assassination of the president** = se alteró el orden

público después del asesinato del presidente; **law reform** = reforma *f* de la ley; **to take someone to law** = citar a alguien ante la justicia *or* llevar a alguien ante los tribunales; **inside the law** *or* **within the law** = dentro de la ley *or* según la ley; **against the law** *or* **outside the law** = contra la ley *or* fuera de la ley; **dismissing a worker without reason is against the law** = despedir a un trabajador sin razón va contra la ley *or* es ilegal despedir a un trabajador sin ninguna razón; **the company is operating outside the law** = la empresa está actuando fuera de la ley; **in law** = según la ley; **what are the duties in law of a guardian?** = ¿cuáles son las obligaciones de un tutor según la ley?; **to break the law** = violar *or* infringir *or* quebrantar la ley; **he is breaking the law by selling goods on Sunday** = está quebrantando la ley vendiendo mercancías el domingo; **you will be breaking the law if you try to take that computer out of the country without an export licence** = infringirás la ley si intentas sacar ese ordenador del país sin una licencia de exportación **(c)** *(general rule)* ley *or* regla *f or* norma *f;* **law of supply and demand** = ley de la oferta y la demanda **(d)** *(informal)* **the law** = la ley; **the law will catch up with him in the end** = tarde o temprano tendrá que vérselas con la ley; **if you don't stop making that noise I'll have the law on you** = si no deja de armar ruido le denunciaré; **the strong** *or* **long arm of the law** = el brazo fuerte de la ley

◊ **law-abiding** ['lɔːə'baɪdɪŋ] *noun* **to be law-abiding** = observar la ley

◊ **lawbreaker** ['lɔːbreɪkə] *noun* infractor, -ra de la ley

◊ **law-breaking** ['lɔːbreɪkɪŋ] *noun* violación *f* de la ley *or* transgresión *f* de la ley

◊ **Law Centre** ['lɔː 'sentə] *noun* cuerpo *m* de abogados de oficio

◊ **Law Commission** ['lɔː kə'mɪʃn] *noun* Comisión *f* de Derecho: organismo permanente que revisa el derecho inglés

◊ **law court** ['lɔː 'kɔːt] *noun* juzgado *m or* tribunal *m* de justicia

COMMENT: in civil cases the judge decides which party is right legally; in criminal cases the decision is made by a jury

◊ **lawful** ['lɔːfl] *adjective* legal *or* legítimo, -ma *or* lícito, -ta; **lawful practice** = práctica *f* lícita *or* legítima; **lawful trade** = comercio *m* legítimo

◊ **lawfully** ['lɔːfli] *adverb* legalmente *or* legítimamente

◊ **lawless** ['lɔːləs] *adjective* **(a)** *(not controlled by the law)* ilegal *or* ilícito, -ta *or* descontrolado, -da *or* anárquico, -ca; **the magistrates criticized the lawless behaviour of the football crowd** = los magistrados criticaron el comportamiento descontrolado de los hinchas del fútbol

◊ **lawlessness** ['lɔːləsnəs] *noun* desorden *m or* anarquía *f or* delincuencia *f;* **the government is** trying to fight lawlessness in large cities = el gobierno está tratando de luchar contra la delincuencia en las grandes ciudades

◊ **Law List** ['lɔː 'lɪst] *noun* lista *f* anual de abogados

◊ **Law Lords** ['lɔː 'lɔːdz] *plural noun* Jueces Lores *mpl*

◊ **law-making** ['lɔː'meɪkɪŋ] *noun* elaboración *f* de las leyes; **Parliament is the law-making body in Great Britain** = el Parlamento es el órgano legislativo en Gran Bretaña

◊ **lawman** ['lɔːmən] *noun US* policía *m* (NOTE: plural is **lawmen**)

◊ **Law Officers** ['lɔː 'ɒfɪsəz] *plural noun* magistrados generales británicos que son también diputados parlamentarios: el Fiscal General de la Corona y Procurador General de la Corona en Inglaterra y Gales y el Fiscal General y Fiscal-Jefe en Escocia

◊ **Law Reports** ['lɔː rɪ'pɔːts] *plural noun* casos *mpl* que representan precedentes jurídicos *or* repertorio *m* de jurisprudencia

◊ **law school** ['lɔː 'skuːl] *noun* facultad *f* de derecho

◊ **Law Society** ['lɔː sə'saɪətɪ] *noun (solicitors)* Colegio *m* de Abogados británico

◊ **Laws of Oleron** ['lɔːz əv 'ɒlərɒn] *plural noun* leyes *fpl* de Oleron: primeras leyes marítimas (de 1216), utilizadas como base para posteriores leyes internacionales

◊ **lawsuit** ['lɔːsuːt] *noun* pleito *m or* juicio *m or* proceso *m or* acción *f* procesal; **to bring a lawsuit against someone** = entablar un pleito contra alguien *or* demandar a alguien; **to defend a lawsuit** = defender una causa ante un tribunal

◊ **lawyer** ['lɔːjə] *noun* abogado, -da; **commercial lawyer** *or* **company lawyer** = abogado especialista en derecho mercantil *or* de empresa; **constitutional lawyer** = abogado especializado en derecho político; **criminal lawyer** = criminalista *mf*; **international lawyer** = abogado especialista en derecho internacional; **maritime lawyer** = abogado especialista en derecho marítimo

lay [leɪ] **1** *verb* **(a)** *(to put or to place)* poner *or* colocar; **to lay an embargo on trade with a country** = prohibir el comercio con un país *or* imponer un embargo comercial a un país; **to lay (an) information** = presentar una denuncia *or* hacer una denuncia *or* una acusación; **to lay a proposal before the House** = presentar un proyecto de ley ante el Parlamento; **to lay the blame** = achacar la culpa **(b) to lay down** = establecer *or* dictar *or* formular; **the conditions are laid down in the document** = las condiciones se establecen en el documento; **the guidelines lay down rules for dealing with traffic offences** = las directrices establecen normas para hacer frente a los delitos de tráfico (NOTE: **laying - laid - has laid**) **2** *adjective* profano, -na *or* lego, -ga; **lay assessor** = asesor, -ra de un tribunal en materias especializadas (no

jurídicas); **lay magistrate** = magistrado que no es un abogado cualificado

◊ **layman** ['leɪmən] *noun* lego *m or* profano *m* en derecho (NOTE: plural is **laymen**)

LC ['el 'siː] = LORD CHANCELLOR

L/C ['el 'siː] = LETTER OF CREDIT

LCJ ['el 'siː 'dʒeɪ] = LORD CHIEF JUSTICE

lead [liːd] **1** *noun* pista *f or* indicación *f*; **the police are following up several leads in the murder investigation** = la policía está siguiendo diversas pistas en la investigación del asesinato **2** *verb* **(a)** *(to be first)* encabezar *or* estar a la cabeza de *or* ir en primer lugar; **the company leads the market in cheap computers** = la empresa encabeza el mercado de ordenadores a precio económico **(b)** *(to be the main person in a group)* dirigir *or* ser el abogado principal; **the prosecution is led by J.M. Jones, QC** = la acusación está dirigida por J.M. Jones, QC; **Mr Smith is leading for the Crown** = el Sr Smith es el abogado principal de la Corona **(c)** *(to start to do something)* empezar *or* iniciar un caso; **Mr Jones led for the prosecution** = el Sr Jones inició la acusación; **the Home Secretary will lead for the Government in the emergency debate** = el Ministro del Interior iniciará el debate extraordinario en nombre del Gobierno **(d)** *(to bring evidence before a court)* presentar pruebas ante un tribunal **(e)** *(to induce an answer from a witness)* inducir a *or* guiar; **counsel must not lead the witness** = el abogado no debe inducir al testigo (NOTE: **leading - led - has led**)

◊ **leader** ['liːdə] *noun* **(a)** *(person)* líder *mf or* dirigente *mf or* jefe, -fa; **corporate leader** = dirigente empresarial; **the leader of the construction workers' union** *or* **the construction workers' leader** = el dirigente del sindicato de trabajadores de la construcción; **an employers' leader** = un dirigente de la patronal; **she is the leader of the trade delegation to Nigeria** = es la jefa de la delegación comercial para Nigeria; **the minister was the leader of the party of lawyers on a tour of American courts** = el ministro era el jefe del grupo de abogados en una visita a los juzgados americanos **(b)** *(main barrister)* abogado, -da principal **(c)** *(product which sells best)* artículo *m* que más vende; **a market leader** = artículo de mayor venta *or* empresa *f* líder de un sector del mercado; **loss-leader** = artículo de reclamo *or* de lanzamiento **(d)** *(important share)* acción *f* favorita *or* valor *m* principal de los cotizados en la bolsa

◊ **Leader of the House** ['liːdə əv ðə 'haʊs] *noun GB* portavoz *mf* del gobierno (y responsable de las relaciones con el Parlamento) ante una de las dos Cámaras

◊ **Leader of the Opposition** ['liːdə əv ðə ɒpə'zɪʃn] *noun* líder *mf* de la oposición

◊ **leading** ['liːdɪŋ] *adjective* **(a)** *(most important)* principal *or* dirigente *or* más importante; **leading** businessmen feel the end of the recession is near = varios empresarios destacados opinan que el final de la recesión está cerca; **leading shares rose on the Stock Exchange** = las acciones favoritas subieron en la Bolsa; **leading shareholders in the company forced a change in management policy** = los principales accionistas de la compañía impusieron un cambio en la dirección; **they are the leading company in the field** = es la empresa líder del sector; **leading cases** = casos *mpl* determinantes *or* que sientan jurisprudencia; **leading counsel** = abogado, -da principal **(b) leading question** = pregunta *f* capciosa *or* hecha de tal manera que sugiere la respuesta deseada

---
COMMENT: leading questions may be asked during cross-examination or during examination in chief

---

◊ **lead time** [ˈliːd ˈtaɪm] *noun* plazo *m* de espera *or* plazo de entrega; **the lead time on this item is more than six weeks** = el plazo de entrega de este artículo es de más de seis semanas

◊ **lead (up) to** [ˈliːd ʌp tʊ] *verb* llevar a *or* conducir a *or* desembocar en; **the discussions led to a big argument between the management and the union** = las negociaciones desembocaron en una gran discusión entre la patronal y el sindicato; **we received a series of approaches leading up to the takeover bid** = recibimos una serie de propuestas conducentes a la oferta de adquisición

leaflet [ˈliːflət] *noun* folleto *m* *or* hoja *f* suelta

leak [liːk] **1** *noun* **(a)** *(of information)* filtración *f*; **the government is investigating the latest leak of documents relating to the spy trial** = el gobierno está investigando la última filtración de documentos relacionada con el juicio por espionaje **(b)** *(of liquid)* fuga *f* *or* escape *m* **2** *verb* filtrar(se); **information about the government plans has been leaked to the Sunday papers** = la información sobre los planes del gobierno se ha filtrado a los periódicos dominicales

lease [ˈliːs] **1** *noun* **(a)** arrendamiento *m* *or* arriendo *m* *or* contrato *m* de arrendamiento; **long lease** *or* **short lease** = arrendamiento a largo plazo *or* a corto plazo; **to take an office building on a long lease** = tomar en arrendamiento un edificio de oficinas a largo plazo; **we have a short lease on our current premises** = el arriendo de nuestros locales actuales es a corto plazo; **to rent office space on a twenty-year lease** = alquilar un espacio para oficinas con un arriendo de veinte años; **full repairing lease** = arrendamiento en el que todas las reparaciones corren por cuenta del arrendatario; **head lease** = arrendamiento del propietario absoluto al inquilino; **sublease** *or* **underlease** = subarriendo *m;* **the lease expires** *or* **runs out in 1999** = el arrendamiento finaliza en 1999; **on expiration of the lease** = al finalizar el arriendo *or* al término del arrendamiento; *see also* DEMISE

(b) to hold a lease in the North Sea = arrendar una zona del mar del Norte **2** *verb* **(a)** *(of landlord or owner)* dar *or* ceder en arriendo *or* arrendar *or* alquilar; **to lease offices to small firms** = ceder oficinas en arriendo para pequeñas empresas; **to lease equipment** = arrendar equipo *or* alquilar material **(b)** *(of tenant)* alquilar *or* arrendar *or* ceder en arriendo; **to lease an office from an insurance company** = alquilar una oficina a una compañía de seguros; **all our company cars are leased** = todos los coches de nuestra empresa son alquilados

◊ **lease back** [ˈliːs ˈbæk] *verb* realizar una operación de cesión-arrendamiento *or* alquilar de nuevo lo que se ha vendido; **they sold the office building to raise cash, and then leased it back for twenty-five years** = vendieron el edificio de oficinas para obtener dinero, y luego lo arrendaron por veinticinco años

◊ **lease-back** [ˈliːsbæk] *noun* cesión-arrendamiento *f;* **they sold the office building and then took it back under a lease-back arrangement** = vendieron el edificio de oficinas y luego lo recuperaron otra vez por medio de un contrato de arriendo al vendedor

◊ **leasehold** [ˈliːshəʊld] *noun & adjective & adverb* arrendamiento *m* *or* propiedad *f* arrendada *or* en arriendo; **leasehold property** = propiedad arrendada; **the company has some valuable leaseholds** = la empresa tiene arrendamientos valiosos *or* de valor; **to purchase a property leasehold** = comprar una propiedad en arriendo; **leasehold enfranchisement** = arrendamiento *or* alquiler *m* con derecho a compra

◊ **leaseholder** [ˈliːshəʊldə] *noun* arrendatario, -ria

◊ **leasing** [ˈliːsɪŋ] *noun* arriendo *m* con opción a compra *or* arrendamiento *m* financiero *or* 'leasing' *m;* **the company has branched out into car leasing** = la empresa se ha pasado al campo del alquiler de coches; **a computer-leasing company** = una empresa de alquiler de ordenadores con opción de compra; **to run a copier under a leasing arrangement** = utilizar una multicopista en virtud de un contrato de arrendamiento financiero

leave [liːv] **1** *noun* **(a)** *(permission)* permiso *m;* **counsel asked leave of the court to show a film taken of the accident** = el abogado solicitó permiso del tribunal para mostrar una película que se tomó del accidente; **'by your leave'** = con su permiso; **leave to defend** = autorización *f* para defenderse **(b)** *(being away from work)* permiso *or* baja *f* *or* ausencia *f* del trabajo; **leave of absence** = excedencia *f;* **maternity leave** = permiso *or* licencia *f* por maternidad; **sick leave** = permiso por enfermedad *or* baja por enfermedad; **to go on leave** *or* **to be on leave** = estar de permiso; **she is away on sick leave** *or* **on maternity leave** = está de baja por enfermedad *or* por maternidad **2** *verb* **(a)** *(to go away)* irse *or* marcharse *or* salir; **he left his office early to go to the meeting** = salió de su despacho temprano para ir a la reunión; **the next plane leaves at 10.20** = el próximo avión sale a las 10.20 **(b)** *(to give property to someone when you die)* dejar *or* legar; **he left his house to his wife** = legó la casa a su mujer; **I was left £5,000 by my grandmother in her will** = mi abuela me dejó 5.000 libras en su testamento **(c)** *(to resign)* dejar *or* abandonar; **he left his job and bought a farm** = dejó su trabajo y se compró una granja (NOTE: **leaving - left - has left**)

◊ **leave out** ['liːv 'aʊt] *verb* omitir *or* saltarse; **she left out the date on the letter** = omitió poner la fecha en la carta; **the contract leaves out all details of marketing arrangements** = el contrato omite cualquier detalle sobre acuerdos de marketing

left [left] *noun* **(a)** *(politics)* **the left** = la izquierda; **the left have demanded political reform** = la izquierda ha exigido una reforma política; **many members of the left have been arrested** = muchos miembros de la izquierda han sido detenidos; **swing to the left** = viraje *m or* giro *m* a la izquierda **(b)** *(wing of party)* **the left** = el ala izquierda (de un partido); **he is on the left of the Conservative Party** = pertenece al ala izquierda del partido conservador; **the activists on the Labour left** = los extremistas del ala izquierda del partido laborista; NOTE: usually used with the article **the,** and takes a singular or plural verb

legacy ['legəsi] *noun* legado *m;* **trust legacy** = legado en fideicomiso; **she received a small legacy in her uncle's will** = recibió un pequeño legado en el testamento de su tío

COMMENT: freehold land left to someone in a will is a **devise**

legal ['liːgəl] *adjective* **(a)** *(according to the law)* legal *or* lícito, -ta; **the company's action was completely legal** = la acción de la empresa fue totalmente legal **(b)** *(referring to the law)* jurídico, -ca *or* judicial; **legal action** = acción *f* procesal; **to take legal action** *or* **to start legal proceedings** = entablar un pleito *or* iniciar un proceso; **to take legal advice** = asesorarse jurídicamente; **legal adviser** = asesor, -ra jurídico, -ca; *US* **legal age** = mayoría *f* de edad; **Legal Aid scheme** = programa *m* de asistencia jurídica gratuita *or* turno de oficio (NOTE: the US equivalent is the **Legal Aid Society**); **Legal Aid Centre** = centro *m* de Asistencia Jurídica Gratuita *or* turno de oficio; **legal aid lawyer** = abogado, -da de turno; **counsel appointed by the Legal Aid Board** = defensor, -ra de oficio; **legal capacity** = capacidad *f* legal *or* procesal; **legal capacity to sue** = facultad *f* procesal; **legal charge** = cargo *m* territorial que existe sobre una propiedad por hipoteca legal *or* deuda *f* territorial legal; **legal claim** = reivindicación *f* legal *or* derecho *m or* reclamación *f* legal; **he has no legal claim to the property** = no tiene derecho legítimo alguno sobre la propiedad; **legal costs** *or* **legal charges** *or* **legal expenses** = costas *fpl* judiciales; **legal currency** =

moneda *f* de curso legal; **legal department** *or* **legal section** = asesoría *f* jurídica *or* departamento *m* jurídico; **legal executive** = pasante *mf* (perteneciente al Instituto de Ejecutivos Jurídicos); **legal expert** = jurista *mf or* experto, -ta en derecho *or* experto jurídico; **legal fiction** = ficción *f* de derecho *or* ficción legal; **legal holiday** = fiesta *f* oficial; **legal matter** = cuestión *f* jurídica; **legal personality** = persona *f* jurídica; **legal separation** = separación *f* legal; **legal subtleties** = argucias *fpl* jurídicas; **legal tender** = moneda *f* de curso legal; **legal writer** = escritor, -ra jurídico, -ca *or* especializado, -da en derecho

◊ **legality** [lɪ'gælɪti] *noun* legalidad *f;* **there is doubt about the legality of the company's action in dismissing him** = puede que la empresa no haya actuado dentro de la legalidad al despedirle

◊ **legalize** ['liːgə'laɪz] *verb* legalizar *or* legitimar; **to legalize a marriage** = legalizar un matrimonio

◊ **legalization** [liːgəlaɪ'zeɪʃn] *noun* legalización *f or* legitimación *f;* **the campaign for the legalization of abortion** = la campaña para la legalización del aborto

◊ **legally** ['liːgəli] *adverb* legalmente *or* de forma legal; **the contract is legally binding** = este contrato es legalmente vinculante *or* compromete legalmente *or* tiene fuerza jurídica; **the directors are legally responsible** = los directores son responsables ante la ley

◊ **legal memory** ['liːgəl 'memri] *noun* tiempo *m* a partir del cual se supone que se recuerdan las cosas en derecho (considerándose el año 1189 como tal); **this practice has existed from before the time of legal memory** = esta práctica ha existido desde tiempo inmemorial; *see also* IMMEMORIAL

legatee [legə'tiː] *noun* legatario, -ria *or* acreedor, -ra testamentario, -ria; **residuary legatee** = heredero, -ra del remanente

legis ['ledʒɪs] *see* CORPUS

legislate ['ledʒɪsleɪt] *verb* legislar; **Parliament has legislated against the sale of drugs** = el Parlamento ha legislado en contra de la venta de drogas

◊ **legislation** [ledʒɪ'sleɪʃn] *noun* legislación *f;* **labour legislation** = legislación laboral

◊ **legislative** ['ledʒɪslətɪv] *adjective* legislativo, -va; **legislative power** *or* **capacity** = facultad *f* legislativa; **the legislative processes** = los procesos legislativos; **Parliament has a legislative function** = el Parlamento tiene una función legislativa

◊ **legislator** ['ledʒɪsleɪtə] *noun* legislador, -ra

◊ **legislature** ['ledʒɪslətʃə] *noun* legislatura *f or* cuerpo *m* legislativo

legitimate 1 [lɪ'dʒɪtɪmət] *adjective* **(a)** *(allowed by law)* legítimo, -ma; **he has a legitimate claim to the property** = tiene derecho legítimo a la propiedad **(b)** *(born to parents who are married to each other)* legítimo, -ma; **he left his property to**

his **legitimate offspring** = legó su propiedad a su hijo legítimo; *see also* ILLEGITIMATE **2** [lɪˈdʒɪtɪmeɪt] *verb* legitimar

◊ **legitimacy** [lɪˈdʒɪtɪməsi] *noun* **(a)** *(act)* legitimidad *f;* **the court doubted the legitimacy of his claim** = el tribunal dudó de la legitimidad de su demanda **(b)** *(court case)* juicio *m* para legitimar a alguien

◊ **legitimation** *or* **legitimization** [lɪdʒɪtɪˈmeɪʃn or lɪdʒɪtɪmaɪˈzeɪʃn] *noun* legitimación *f*

lend [lend] *verb* prestar; **to lend something to someone** *or* **to lend someone something** = prestar algo a alguien; **he lent the company money** *or* **he lent money to the company** = prestó dinero a la empresa; **she lent the company car to her daughter** = le prestó el coche de la empresa a su hija; **to lend money against security** = prestar dinero con garantía; **the bank lent him £50,000 to start his business** = el banco le prestó 50.000 libras para iniciar su negocio

◊ **lender** [ˈlendə] *noun* prestamista *mf;* **lender of the last resort** = prestamista en última instancia *or* de último recurso

◊ **lending** [ˈlendɪŋ] *noun* (concesión de un) préstamo *m;* **lending limit** = límite *m* de crédito

leniency [ˈliːniənsi] *noun* lenidad *f or* indulgencia *f*

lenient [ˈliːniənt] *adjective* clemente *or* poco severo, -ra *or* indulgente; **the judge took a lenient view of the offence** = el juez fue poco severo ante el delito; **because of the accused's age, the court passed a lenient sentence** = dada la edad del acusado, el tribunal dictó una sentencia poco severa

◊ **leniently** [ˈliːniəntli] *adverb* de forma poco severa *or* indulgentemente; **the accused were treated leniently by the military tribunal** = los acusados fueron tratados indulgentemente por el tribunal militar

lessee [leˈsiː] *noun* arrendatario, -ria *or* inquilino, -na

lessen [ˈlesn] *verb* disminuir *or* reducir; **the government is taking steps to lessen the overcrowding in prisons** = el gobierno está tomando medidas para disminuir la superpoblación *or* el congestionamiento en las cárceles

lesser [ˈlesə] *adjective* menor *or* más pequeño, -ña; **he pleaded guilty to the lesser charge of manslaughter** = se declaró culpable del cargo menor de homicidio involuntario

lessor [leˈsɔː] *noun* arrendador, -ra

let [let] **1** *verb* **(a)** *(to allow someone to do something)* permitir *or* dejar; **the magistrate let the prisoner speak to his wife** = el juez permitió que el detenido hablase con su mujer **(b)** *(to lend property for payment)* alquilar *or* arrendar; **to let an office** = alquilar una oficina; **offices to let** = oficinas en alquiler (NOTE: **letting - let - has let**) **2** *noun* **(a)** (periodo *m* de) alquiler *m or* arrendamiento *m;* **they took the office on a short let** = alquilaron la oficina por un breve periodo de tiempo **(b) without let or hindrance** = sin estorbo ni obstáculo

◊ **let off** [ˈlet ˈɒf] *verb* dispensar de *or* perdonar; **the magistrate let the boys off with a warning** = el juez dejó a los chicos en libertad con una amonestación

◊ **let-out clause** [ˈletaʊt ˈklɔːz] *noun* cláusula *f* de excepción; **he added a let-out clause to the effect that the payments would be revised if the exchange rate fell by more than 5%** = añadió una cláusula de excepción al efecto de que los pagos se revisarían si el tipo de cambio bajaba más de un 5%

letter [ˈletə] *noun* **(a)** carta *f;* **business letter** = carta comercial; **circular letter** = circular *f;* **covering letter** = carta adjunta *or* explicatoria *or* de cobertura; **follow-up letter** = carta de contestación *or* de reiteración a otra; **private letter** = carta personal; **standard (form) letter** = carta modelo **(b) letter before action** = carta previa a una actuación judicial; **letter of acknowledgement** = carta de acuse de recibo; **letters of administration** = nombramiento *m* de administrador judicial; **letter of allotment** *or* **allotment letter** = notificación *f* de adjudicación (de acciones); **letter of application** = carta de solicitud *or* de suscripción (de acciones); **letter of appointment** = notificación *f* del nombramiento para un puesto *or* carta de nombramiento; **letter of attorney** = poder *m* (notarial); **letter of comfort** *or* **comfort letter** = aval *m or* informe *m* a favor *or* carta de apoyo; **letter of complaint** = carta de reclamación; **letter of credence** = carta credencial; **letter of credit (L/C)** = carta de crédito; **letter of demand** = carta de requerimiento; **letter of indemnity** = garantía *f* de indemnización; **letter of intent** = carta de intención; **letters patent** = cédula *f or* patente *f* de privilegio *or* de invención; **letter of reference** = carta de recomendación; **threatening letter** = carta amenazadora; **letter of request** *or* **rogatory letter** = carta suplicatoria *or* comisión rogatoria **(c) air letter** = aerograma *m;* **airmail letter** = carta por avión; **registered letter** = carta certificada **(d) to acknowledge receipt by letter** = acusar recibo de algo por carta **(e)** *(written or printed sign)* letra *f;* **write your name and address in block letters** *or* **in capital letters** = escriba su nombre y dirección en letras de molde *or* mayúsculas

◊ **letterhead** [ˈletəhed] *noun* membrete *m*

letting [ˈletɪŋ] *noun* **letting agency** = agencia *f* de alquiler de la propiedad *or* de viviendas; **furnished lettings** = propiedad *f* amueblada *or* local *m* amueblado para alquilar; *see also* LET

levy [ˈlevi] **1** *noun* recaudación *f or* exacción *f* (de impuestos); **capital levy** = impuesto *m* sobre el capital; **import levy** = gravamen *m* sobre las importaciones; **training levy** = contribución *f* para formación profesional **2** *verb* exigir *or* recaudar *or* gravar *or* imponer; **the government has decided to levy a tax on imported cars** = el gobierno ha decidido gravar los coches importados con un impuesto; **to levy a duty on the import of computer parts** = imponer un arancel a las importaciones de piezas informáticas

lex [lɛks] *Latin word* ley *f;* **lex fori** = ley del foro *or* del tribunal; **lex loci actus** = ley del lugar del acto; **lex loci contractus** = ley del lugar del contrato; **lex loci delicti** = ley del lugar del delito

liability [laɪə'bɪlɪti] *noun* **(a)** *(legal responsibility)* responsabilidad *f;* **to accept** *or* **to admit liability for something** = aceptar *or* admitir la responsabilidad de algo; **his insurers have admitted liability but the amount of damages has not yet been agreed** = sus aseguradores han admitido la responsabilidad pero la cantidad de los daños aún no ha sido acordada; **to refuse liability for something** = rechazar *or* no admitir la responsabilidad de algo; **contractual liability** = responsabilidad contractual; **limited liability** = responsabilidad limitada; **limited liability company** = sociedad de responsabilidad limitada; **liability clause** = cláusula de responsabilidad limitada de los socios; **tax liability** = cuota *f* tributaria; **vicarious liability** = responsabilidad civil subsidiaria **(b)** *(business)* **liabilities** = pasivo *m or* deudas *fpl or* obligaciones fpl; **the balance sheet shows the company's assets and liabilities** = el balance general muestra el activo y el pasivo de la empresa; **current liabilities** = pasivo circulante; **long-term liabilities** = pasivo a largo plazo; **he was not able to meet his liabilities** = no pudo pagar sus deudas *or* no pudo hacer frente a sus deudas; **to discharge one's liabilities in full** = pagar todas las deudas propias
◊ **liable** ['laɪəbl] *adjective* **(a)** **liable (for)** = responsable de; **the customer is liable for breakages** = el cliente es responsable de los desperfectos; **the chairman was personally liable for the company's debts** = el presidente era personalmente responsable de las deudas de la empresa; **he was found by the judge to be liable for the accident** = el juez le declaró culpable del accidente; **he will be found liable if he assists a trustee to commit a dishonest breach of trust** = será declarado culpable si asiste a un fideicomisario en un acto deshonesto de abuso de confianza **(b)** **liable to** = obligado, -da *or* sujeto, -ta a *or* expuesto, -ta a; **sales which are liable to stamp duty** = ventas que están sujetas a impuesto del timbre; **such an act renders him liable to a fine** = un acto así *or* tal acto le expone a una multa *or* a pagar una multa

liar ['laɪə] *noun* embustero, -ra

libel ['laɪbl] **1** *noun* difamación *f* escrita *or* libelo *m;* **action for libel** *or* **libel action** *or* **libel suit** = pleito *m or* demanda *f* por difamación *or* por libelo

(NOTE: no plural in this meaning); **he claimed that the newspaper report was a libel** = declaró que la noticia era un libelo; **criminal libel** = difamación *or* calumnia *f* criminal; *see also* DEFAMATION, SLANDER **2** *verb* calumniar *or* difamar por escrito a alguien (NOTE: GB spelling is **libelling - libelled** but US spelling is **libeling - libeled**)
◊ **libeller** ['laɪblə] *noun* libelista *mf or* difamador, -ra
◊ **libellous** ['laɪbləs] *adjective* difamatorio, -ria; **he said that the report was libellous** = dijo que la noticia era difamatoria

liberate ['lɪbəreɪt] *verb* libertar *or* liberar *or* poner en libertad; **three prisoners were liberated** = tres presos fueron puestos en libertad

liberty ['lɪbəti] *noun* libertad *f;* **at liberty** = en libertad *or* libre; **they are still at liberty while waiting for charges to be brought** = están todavía en libertad mientras esperan a que se formulen las acusaciones; **civil liberties** = libertades civiles; **liberty of the individual** = libertad del individuo *or* de la persona (de actuar según la ley); **liberty of the press** = libertad de prensa; **liberty of the subject** = libertad del ciudadano *or* libertad individual *or* del individuo

licence *or US* **license** ['laɪsəns] *noun* **(a)** *(permission)* licencia *f or* permiso *m;* **he granted his neighbour a licence to use his field** = dio permiso a su vecino para utilizar su campo; **driving licence** = carnet *m or* permiso de conducir; **applicants for the police force should hold a valid driving licence** = los aspirantes al cuerpo de policía deben poseer un carnet de conducir válido *or* vigente; **gaming licence** = licencia de juego; **import licence** *or* **export licence** = licencia de importación *or* exportación; **licence to sell liquor** *or* **liquor licence** = licencia para vender alcohol; *GB* **off licence** = licencia de venta de bebidas alcohólicas para ser consumidas fuera del establecimiento; **on licence** = licencia para vender alcohol para ser consumido en el establecimiento; **occasional licence** = licencia eventual (para vender alcohol sólo en un lugar determinado y a una cierta hora) **(b)** *(prison)* condonación *f* de la pena *or* remisión *f* de la pena; **release on licence** = libertad *f* condicional *or* bajo palabra; **the appellant will be released on licence after eight months** = el apelante será puesto en libertad condicional después de ocho meses **(c)** **goods manufactured under licence** = productos *mpl* fabricados con licencia
◊ **license** ['laɪsəns] **1** *noun US* = LICENCE **2** *verb* conceder una licencia *or* un permiso; **licensed to sell beers, wines and spirits** = con licencia *or* autorizado para vender cervezas, vinos y licores; **to license a company to produce spare parts** = conceder una licencia a una empresa para fabricar piezas de repuesto; **he is licensed to drive a lorry** = tiene carnet para conducir un camión; **she is**

licensed to run an employment agency = tiene licencia para dirigir una oficina de empleo *or* una agencia de colocación; **licensed premises** = establecimiento autorizado para vender bebidas alcohólicas; **licensed trader** = comerciante autorizado

◊ **licensee** [laɪsən'siː] *noun* concesionario, -ria *or* persona *f* autorizada

◊ **licensing** ['laɪsənsɪŋ] *noun (referring to licences)* licencia *f or* autorización *f;* **licensing agreement** = acuerdo *m or* contrato *m* de concesión de licencia; *GB* **licensing hours** = horas *fpl* de licencia para la venta de bebidas alcohólicas; **licensing magistrates** = magistrados, -das que conceden licencias para la venta de alcohol

licit ['lɪsɪt] *adjective* lícito, -ta

lie [laɪ] *noun* mentira *f;* **white lie** = mentira piadosa; **lie detector** = detector *m* de mentiras; *see also* POLYGRAPH

lien [liːn] *noun* gravamen *m or* derecho *m* de retención *or* derecho prendario; **the garage had a lien on her car until she paid the repair bill** = el taller tenía derecho de retención sobre su coche hasta que pagara la factura de reparación; **lien on shares** = derecho de venta de acciones no pagadas en su totalidad; **carrier's lien** = derecho de retención del transportista; **equitable lien** = gravamen equitativo; **general lien** = embargo *m* preventivo general; **maritime lien** = derecho de retención de un barco; *US* **mechanic's lien** = embargo de constructor; **particular lien** = embargo preventivo llevado a cabo por una persona sobre la propiedad de otra; **repairer's lien** = derecho de retención del trabajador (NOTE: you have a lien **on** an item)

lieu [luː] *noun* **in lieu of** = en vez de *or* en lugar de; **to give someone two months' salary in lieu of notice** = dar a alguien dos meses de sueldo en lugar del aviso de despido

life [laɪf] *noun* **(a)** *(time when a person is alive)* vida *f;* **for life** = de por vida *or* para toda la vida *or* con carácter vitalicio; **his pension gives him a comfortable income for life** = su pensión le da unos cómodos ingresos de por vida; **life annuity** *or* **annuity for life** = pensión *f* vitalicia *or* vitalicio *m or* anualidad *f or* renta *f* vitalicia; **life assurance** *or* **life insurance** = seguro *m* de vida; **the life assured** *or* **the life insured** = la persona asegurada; **life expectancy** = esperanza *f* de vida; **life imprisonment** *or* **life sentence** = cadena *f* perpetua; **life interest** = usufructo *m* vitalicio; **life peer** = miembro *m* vitalicio de la Cámara de los Lores; *(slang)* **life preserver** = porra *f or* vergajo *m;* **to spare someone's life** = perdonar la vida a alguien **(b)** *(period of time something exists)* duración *f or* vida *f or* vigencia *f;* **the life of a loan** = plazo *m or* duración *or* vigencia de un préstamo; **during the life of the agreement** = mientras exista el acuerdo;

shelf life of a product = periodo *m* de conservación de un producto

◊ **lifer** ['laɪfə] *noun (slang)* condenado, -da a cadena perpetua

> COMMENT: life imprisonment lasts on average ten years

LIFO ['laɪfəʊ] = LAST IN FIRST OUT

lift [lɪft] *verb* **(a)** *(to remove)* levantar *or* suprimir; **the government has lifted the ban on imports of technical equipment** = el gobierno ha suprimido la prohibición a las importaciones de equipo técnico; **the minister has lifted the embargo on the export of firearms** = el ministro ha levantado el embargo a la exportación de armas de fuego **(b)** *(informal) (to steal)* robar *or* mangar *or* hurtar

light [laɪt] *noun* **ancient lights** = servidumbre *f* de luces *or* reclamación *f* del derecho a disfrutar de luz natural en una propiedad sin que los edificios vecinos la obstruyan; **green light** = luz verde

likelihood ['laɪklihʊd] *noun* posibilidad *f or* probabilidad *f;* **likelihood of bias** = posibilidad de que un juicio no sea imparcial a causa de la conexión entre un miembro del tribunal y una de las partes

likewise ['laɪkwaɪz] *adverb* así mismo *or* del mismo modo *or* lo mismo *or* igualmente; **the principal agrees to reimburse the agent, and likewise the agent agrees to reimburse his principal** = el mandante está de acuerdo en reembolsar el dinero al mandatario e igualmente el mandatario está de acuerdo en reembolsarlo al mandante

limit ['lɪmɪt] **1** *noun* límite *m or* acotación *f or* tope *m;* **to set limits to imports** *or* **to impose limits on imports** = imponer límites a *or* limitar las importaciones; **age limit** = edad *f* máxima; **credit limit** = límite de crédito; **he has exceeded his credit limit** = ha excedido su límite de crédito; **legal limit** = límite legal; **lending limit** = límite de crédito; **prescribed limits** = límite máximo de alcohol permitido a los conductores; **speed limit** = límite de velocidad; **time limit** = plazo *m or* término *m;* **weight limit** = límite de peso *or* peso *m* máximo; **within the limit** = dentro del ámbito; **to set a limit to** = poner límite a **2** *verb* limitar; **the court limited damages to £100** = el tribunal limitó los daños y perjuicios a 100 libras; **the banks have limited their credit** = los bancos han limitado su crédito

◊ **limitation** [lɪmɪ'teɪʃn] *noun* **(a)** *(act of allowing only a certain amount)* limitación *f or* restricción *f;* **the contract imposes limitations on the number of cars which can be imported** = el contrato impone restricciones sobre el número de coches que se pueden importar; **limitation of liability** = limitación de la responsabilidad (por daños o pérdidas); *(in a company)* limitación de la responsabilidad de los accionistas de una sociedad;

time limitation = plazo *m* de tiempo límite **(b)**
limitation of actions *or* **statute of limitations** =
normas *fpl* sobre prescripción para ejercer acciones
legales
◊ **limited** ['lɪmɪtɪd] *adjective* limitado, -da;
limited liability = responsabilidad *f* limitada;
limited market = mercado *m* limitado *or* con
escaso movimiento; **limited partnership** =
sociedad *f* en comandita; **limited liability company**
= sociedad de responsabilidad limitada; **private
limited company (Ltd)** = sociedad limitada (SL);
Public Limited Company (Plc) = sociedad
anónima (SA) (NOTE: a private limited company is
called **Ltd** or **Limited**; a Public Limited Company is called
Plc or **PLC** or **plc**)
◊ **limiting** ['lɪmɪtɪŋ] *adjective* restrictivo, -va *or*
limitativo, -va; **a limiting clause in a contract** =
una cláusula restrictiva de un contrato; **the short
holiday season is a limiting factor on the hotel
trade** = la corta temporada de vacaciones es un
factor restrictivo en la industria hotelera

Lincoln's Inn ['lɪŋkənz 'ɪn] *noun (barristers)*
uno de los cuatro Colegios de Abogados de Londres

lineal descent ['lɪnɪəl dɪ'sent] *noun*
(descendencia *f*) en línea directa

link [lɪŋk] *noun* enlace *m* *or* nexo *m*

liquid assets ['lɪkwɪd 'æsɪts] *noun* activo *m*
líquido *or* disponible
◊ **liquidate** ['lɪkwɪdeɪt] *verb* liquidar; **to
liquidate a company** = liquidar *or* disolver una
compañía; **to liquidate a debt** = saldar una deuda;
to liquidate assets *or* **stock** = liquidar activo *or* las
existencias; **liquidated damages** = estimación *f* de
daños y perjuicios
◊ **liquidation** [lɪkwɪ'deɪʃn] *noun* **(a)** liquidación
f; **liquidation of a debt** = liquidación *or* saldo *m* de
una deuda **(b)** *(winding up of a company)*
disolución *f*; **the company went into liquidation** =
la compañía fue disuelta *or* entró en periodo de
liquidación; **compulsory liquidation** = disolución
forzosa; **voluntary liquidation** = disolución
voluntaria
◊ **liquidator** [lɪkwɪ'deɪtə] *noun* depositario, -ria
or síndico *m*
◊ **liquidity** [lɪ'kwɪdɪti] *noun* liquidez *f*

lis [liːs] *Latin word* litis *m* *or* litigio *m*; **lis alibi
pendens** = proceso *m* judicial iniciado en otro lugar
or litigio pendiente en otro lugar; **lis pendens** = litis
pendencia *or* litigio pendiente; *see also* AD LITEM

list [lɪst] **1** *noun* **(a)** *(items written one after the
other)* lista *f* *or* relación *f*; **list of debtors** = lista de
deudores; **list of products** *or* **product list** = lista de
productos; **to add an item to a list** = añadir un
artículo a una lista; **to cross someone's name off a
list** = tachar el nombre de alguien de una lista; **list
of cases to be heard** = lista de casos para ver; **list of
members** = lista de socios; **address list** *or* **mailing
list** = lista de direcciones *or* destinarios; **black list** =

lista negra *or* lista de particulares, empresas y países
con los que se hallan prohibidas las relaciones
comerciales; **Law List** = lista anual de abogados
(b) *(catalogue)* catálogo *m;* **list price** = precio *m* de
catálogo **2** *verb* **(a)** hacer una lista *or* enumerar; **the
catalogue lists products by category** = el catálogo
enumera los productos por categorías; **the case is
listed to be heard next week** = el caso figura para
ser visto la semana próxima **(b)** **listed building** =
edificio *m* declarado de interés artístico o histórico;
listed company = sociedad *f* cotizada en bolsa;
listed securities = valores *mpl* registrados *or*
efectos *mpl* cotizables
◊ **listing** ['lɪstɪŋ] *noun* listado *m*

litem ['laɪtəm] *see* AD LITEM

literally ['lɪtrəli] *adverb* literalmente *or* al pie de
la letra

litigate ['lɪtɪgeɪt] *verb* litigar *or* pleitar
◊ **litigant** ['lɪtɪgənt] *noun* litigante *mf;* **litigant in
person** = litigante en persona, que inicia un proceso
judicial y defiende personalmente su causa ante el
tribunal; **vexatious litigant** = litigante oneroso *or*
vejatorio
◊ **litigation** [lɪtɪ'geɪʃn] *noun* litigio *m* *or* pleito *m*
or contienda *f;* **he has got into litigation with the
county council** = se ha metido en un pleito con el
gobierno municipal
◊ **litigious** [lɪ'tɪdʒəs] *adjective* litigioso, -sa;
litigious person = picapleitos *mf*

LJ = LORD JUSTICE (NOTE: written after the
surname of the judge in legal reports: **Smith LJ said he
was not laying down any guidelines for sentencing**
but **Smith LJ** is spoken as 'Lord Justice Smith')
◊ **LJJ** = LORD JUSTICES

LL.B. *or* **LL.M.** *or* **LL.D.** ['el 'el 'biː or 'el 'el 'em
or 'el 'el 'diː] letras *fpl* escritas detrás del nombre de
una persona que tiene el título de Licenciado en
Derecho, Máster en Derecho o Doctor en Derecho

Lloyd's [lɔɪdz] *noun* Compañía *f* de Seguros
Lloyd; **Lloyd's Register** = Registro *m* Marítimo de
Lloyd; **ship which is A1 at Lloyd's** = buque *m* en
perfectas condiciones *or* clasificado como A1 por
Lloyd

loan [ləun] **1** *noun* préstamo *m* *or* prestación *f;*
loan capital = empréstito *m;* **loan stock** =
obligaciones *fpl;* **convertible loan stock** =
empréstito *or* obligaciones convertibles; **bank loan**
= préstamo bancario; **bridging loan** = crédito *m*
puente; **mortgage loan** = préstamo hipotecario;
short-term loan *or* **long-term loan** = préstamo a
corto plazo *or* préstamo a largo plazo; **soft loan** =
préstamo sin interés; **unsecured loan** = préstamo
sin garantía **2** *verb* prestar

lobby ['lɒbi] **1** *noun* **(a)** *(House of Commons
chamber)* antesala *f* *or* antecámara *f;* **division lobby**
or **voting lobby** = sala *f* donde votan los diputados;
lobby fodder = diputados, -das que votan según la

indicación del partido **(b)** *(pressure group)* camarilla *f or* grupo *m* de presión; **the environmentalist lobby** = el grupo de presión ecologista **2** *verb* ejercer presión *or* presionar *or* cabildear; **a group of local businessmen has gone to London to lobby their MPs on the problems of unemployment in the area** = un grupo de empresarios de la ciudad ha ido a Londres para ejercer presión sobre los diputados acerca de los problemas del desempleo en la región

◊ **lobbyist** ['lɒbiɪst] *noun* cabildero, -ra que representa a un grupo de presión

local ['ləʊkəl] *adjective* local; **local authority** = autoridad *f* local *or* gobierno *m* municipal; **local court** = juzgado *m* local; **local government** = administración local; **a court can give instructions to a local authority as to the exercise of its powers in relation to children in care** = un tribunal puede dar instrucciones a una autoridad local en lo que se refiere al ejercicio de sus poderes en materia de tutela infantil; **a decision of the local authority pursuant to the powers and duties imposed on it by the Act** = una decisión del gobierno municipal conforme a los poderes y deberes impuestos sobre él por decreto

loc. cit. ['lɒk 'sɪt] *Latin phrase* en el lugar citado (NOTE: used when referring to a point in a legal text: **'see also Smith J in *Jones v. Associated Steel Ltd* loc. cit. line 26')**

lock [lɒk] **1** *noun* cerradura *f or* cerrojo *m;* **the lock is broken on the petty cash box** = la cerradura de la caja para gastos menores está rota; **I have forgotten the combination of the lock of the safe** = he olvidado la combinación de la cerradura de la caja fuerte; **time lock** = cerradura de apertura controlada **2** *verb* cerrar con llave; **the manager forgot to lock the door of the computer room** = el director olvidó cerrar con llave la puerta de la sala de ordenadores; **the petty cash box was not locked** = la caja para gastos menores no estaba cerrada con llave

◊ **lock out** ['lɒk 'aʊt] *verb* **to lock out workers** = declarar el cierre patronal

◊ **lockout** ['lɒkaʊt] *noun* cierre *m* patronal *or* 'lockout' *m*

◊ **lock up** ['lɒk 'ʌp] *verb* **(a)** *(to put someone in prison or mental hospital)* encarcelar *or* encerrar **(b) to lock up a shop or an office** = cerrar una tienda *or* una oficina (al finalizar la jornada laboral); **to lock up capital** = inmovilizar *or* bloquear capital

◊ **locking up** ['lɒkɪŋ 'ʌp] *noun* **the locking up of money in stock** = la inmovilización de dinero en acciones

◊ **lock-up** ['lɒkʌp] **1** *adjective;* **lock-up shop** = tienda *f* sin vivienda incorporada **2** *noun (informal)* cárcel *f or* chirona *f;* **police station lock-up** = dependencias *fpl* policiales *or* depósito *m* policial

loco ['ləʊkəʊ] *see* IN LOCO PARENTIS

locum (tenens) ['ləʊkəm] *noun* interino, -na *or* suplente *mf;* **locums wanted in South London** = se necesitan interinos *or* se requieren suplentes en el Sur de Londres

locus ['ləʊkəs] *Latin word* situación *f or* lugar *m*

lU us sigilli [['ləʊkəs sɪ'dʒɪlaɪ] *Latin phrase* lugar del sello

◊ **locus standi** ['ləʊkəs 'stændaɪ] *Latin phrase* derecho de audiencia ante un tribunal; **the taxpayer does not have locus standi in this court** = el contribuyente no tiene derecho de audiencia en este tribunal

lodge [lɒdʒ] *verb* depositar *or* colocar; **to lodge caution** = depositar una garantía en el Registro de la Propiedad para asegurar una propiedad; **to lodge a complaint against someone** = presentar *or* entablar una demanda contra alguien; **to lodge money with someone** = dar dinero en custodia a alguien; **to lodge securities as collateral** = depositar valores en un banco como garantía para un préstamo

◊ **lodger** ['lɒdʒə] *noun* inquilino, -na

logrolling ['lɒgrəʊlɪŋ] *noun* US intercambio *m* de favores políticos

loitering ['lɔɪtrɪŋ] *noun* **loitering (with intent)** = merodear con fines delictivos *or* con intenciones criminales

long [lɒŋ] **1** *adjective* largo, -ga; *(of time)* por mucho tiempo; **long credit** = crédito *m* de larga duración; **in the long term** = a la larga; **to take the long view** = planificar a largo plazo **2** *noun* **longs** = títulos *mpl* del estado a largo plazo

◊ **long-dated** ['lɒŋ'deɪtɪd] *adjective;* **long-dated bills or paper** = letras *fpl or* valores *mpl* con vencimiento a largo plazo

◊ **longhand** ['lɒŋhænd] *noun* escritura *f or* letra *f* a mano; **applications should be written in longhand and sent to the recruitment officer** = las solicitudes deberán ser manuscritas *or* escritas a mano y enviarse al jefe de contratación

◊ **long-standing** ['lɒŋ'stændɪŋ] *adjective; (agreement)* de hace tiempo *or* de muchos años *or* antiguo, -gua

◊ **long-term** ['lɒŋ'təːm] *adjective;* **on a long-term basis** = a largo plazo *or* para un periodo de tiempo largo; **long-term debts** = deudas *fpl* a largo plazo; **long-term forecast** = previsión *f* a largo plazo; **long-term loan** = préstamo *m* a largo plazo; **long-term objectives** = objetivos *mpl* a largo plazo

◊ **Long Vacation** ['lɒŋ və'keɪʃn] *noun* vacaciones *fpl* de verano de los tribunales de justicia y universidades

look [lʊk] *verb* **to look at** = mirar; **to look after** = cuidar

loophole ['luːphəʊl] *noun* escapatoria *f or* laguna *f;* **to find a loophole in the law** = encontrar una escapatoria *or* una laguna legal; **to find a tax loophole** = encontrar una laguna fiscal

loot [luːt] **1** *noun* botín *m or* presa *f or* pillaje *m* **2** *verb* saquear *or* llevar como botín *or* pillar *or* cometer pillaje; **the stores were looted by a mob of hooligans** = las tiendas fueron saqueadas por una pandilla de gamberros
◊ **looter** [ˈluːtə] *noun* saqueador, -ra
◊ **looting** [ˈluːtɪŋ] *noun* saqueo *m;* **the police cordoned off the area to prevent looting** = la policía acordonó la zona para evitar el saqueo

lord [lɔːd] *noun* lord *m;* **Lord of Appeal** = lord que actúa como tal en la Cámara de los Lores cuando ésta funciona como tribunal de apelación; **Lord of Appeal in Ordinary** = uno de los once lores que actúa como tal en la Cámara de los Lores cuando ésta funciona como tribunal de apelación; **Lord Justice** = título que ostenta un juez miembro del tribunal de apelación; **Lord Justice General** = Presidente del Tribunal Supremo de Escocia; **Lord Justice Clerk** = segunda autoridad judicial de Escocia (NOTE: Lord Justice is written **LJ** after the name: **Smith LJ** = Lord Justice Smith)
◊ **Lords** [lɔːdz] *plural noun* **(a)** *(The House)* la Cámara de los Lores; **the Lords voted to amend the Bill** = la Cámara de los Lores votó para enmendar el proyecto de ley **(b)** *(the members)* lores; **Lords Spiritual** = arzobispos *mpl* y obispos *mpl* de la Cámara de los Lores; **Lords Temporal** = miembros *mpl* de la Cámara de los Lores que no son obispos; **the Law Lords** = lores que son también jueces
◊ **Lord Advocate** [ˈlɔːd ˈædvəkət] *noun* miembro del gobierno y uno de los dos magistrados generales en Escocia (Fiscal y Procurador General)
◊ **Lord Chancellor** [ˈlɔːd ˈtʃɑːnsələ] *noun* Lord Canciller (presidente de la Cámara de los Lores)

> COMMENT: the Lord Chancellor is a member of the Cabinet; he presides over debates in the House of Lords; he is the head of the judicial system and advises on the appointment of judges

◊ **Lord Chief Justice** [ˈlɔːd ˈtʃiːf ˈdʒʌstɪs] *noun* *GB* Presidente del Tribunal Supremo
◊ **Lord Ordinary** [ˈlɔːd ˈɔːdɪnri] *noun* juez de primera instancia de la sección civil del Tribunal Supremo de Escocia
◊ **Lord President** [ˈlɔːd ˈprezɪdənt] *noun* juez del Tribunal Supremo de Escocia
◊ **Lord President of the Council** [ˈlɔːd ˈprezɪdənt əv ðə ˈkaunsəl] *noun* ministro sin cartera del gobierno, miembro de la Cámara de los Lores, Presidente del Consejo Privado (del monarca)

lose [luːz] *verb* **(a)** *(not to win in legal proceedings)* perder; **he lost his appeal to the House of Lords** = perdió la apelación presentada a la Cámara de los Lores; **she lost her case for compensation** = perdió el juicio por indemnización

(b) *(not to have something any more)* perder; **to lose an order** = perder un pedido; **during the strike, the company lost six orders to American competitors** = durante la huelga, la empresa perdió seis pedidos frente a competidores americanos; **to lose control of a company** = perder la dirección *or* la participación mayoritaria *or* el control de una empresa; **she lost her job when the factory closed** = perdió su empleo cuando la fábrica cerró; **lost profits** = lucro *m* cesante *or* pérdida *f* de beneficios **(c)** *(to have less money)* perder; **he lost £25,000 in his father's computer company** = perdió 25.000 libras en la empresa de ordenadores de su padre; **the pound has lost value** = la libra ha perdido valor; **(d)** *(to drop to a lower price)* bajar; **the dollar lost two cents against the pound** = el dólar bajó dos centavos con respecto a la libra; **gold shares lost 5% on the market yesterday** = las acciones del oro bajaron ayer un 5% en el mercado (NOTE: **losing - lost - has lost**)
◊ **lose out** [ˈluːz ˈaut] *verb* salir perdiendo *or* perder; **the company has lost out in the rush to make cheap computers** = la empresa ha salido perdiendo al precipitarse a fabricar ordenadores a bajo precio

loss [lɒs] *noun* **(a)** *(not having something which was had before)* pérdida *f;* **compensation for loss of earnings** = compensación *f* por pérdida de ganancias; **compensation for loss of office** = indemnización *f* por pérdida de empleo *or* por cese en el cargo; **loss incurred** = siniestro *m* pendiente; **loss of nationality** = pérdida de nacionalidad; **accidental loss** = pérdida por siniestro **(b)** *(not making a profit)* pérdida; **the company suffered a loss** = la empresa sufrió pérdidas; **to report a loss** = anunciar un déficit; *(accounts)* hacer constar una pérdida en el balance de resultados; **capital loss** = pérdidas de capital *or* minusvalías; **the car was written off as a dead loss** *or* **a total loss** = el coche fue declarado siniestro total; **trading loss** = pérdida del ejercicio; **at a loss** = con pérdidas *or* sin beneficios; **the company is trading at a loss** = la empresa opera con pérdidas; **he sold the shop at a loss** = vendió la tienda con pérdida; **to cut one's losses** = frenar las pérdidas **(c)** *(insurance)* **partial loss** = pérdida parcial; **actual total loss** = siniestro total; **constructive total loss** = pérdida total constructiva **(d)** **loss in weight** = pérdida de peso; **loss in transport** = pérdidas durante el transporte
◊ **loss-leader** [ˈlɒsˈliːdə] *noun* artículo *m* de reclamo *or* artículo de lanzamiento

lot [lɒt] *noun* **(a)** *(large quantity)* mucho, -cha *or* gran cantidad *f;* **a lot of people** *or* **lots of people are out of work** = hay mucha gente desempleada *or* en el paro *or* sin trabajo **(b)** *(group of items)* lote *m;* **he put in a bid for lot 23** = hizo una oferta por el lote 23; **at the end of the auction half the lots had not been sold** = al final de la subasta la mitad de los lotes no se habían vendido **(c)** *(group of shares)* paquete *m or* lote; **to sell shares in small lots =** vender acciones en pequeños lotes **(d)** *(piece of land) US* parcela *f or* terreno *m*

lottery ['lɒtri] *noun* lotería *f*

lower ['ləʊə] *adjective* inferior; **lower chamber** *or* **lower house =** cámara *f* baja (NOTE: the opposite is **upper**)

> COMMENT: In a bicameral system, the upper chamber is normally a revising chamber, with some limited powers to delay passing of legislation. Bills normally have to be passed by both houses before they can become law. The lower house of the British legislature is the House of Commons, and in many ways it has more power, especially over financial matters, than the House of Lords, which is the upper house

loyal ['lɔɪəl] *adjective* fiel
◊ **loyalty** ['lɔɪəlti] *noun* lealtad *f*

luck [lʌk] *noun* suerte *f;* **good luck** *or* **bad luck =** buena *or* mala suerte

lucrative ['luːkrətɪv] *adjective* lucrativo, -va *or* provechoso, -sa; **there is a lucrative black market in car spare parts =** existe un lucrativo mercado negro de piezas de repuesto de coche; **he signed a lucrative contract with a TV company =** firmó un contrato lucrativo con una compañía de televisión

lump sum ['lʌmp 'sʌm] *noun* pago *m* único *or* tanto *m* alzado *or* suma *f* global; **he received a lump sum payment of £500 =** recibió un pago total de 500 libras; **the company offered a lump sum of £1,000 as an out-of-court settlement =** la empresa ofreció una suma total de 1.000 libras si se acordaba no llevar el caso a los tribunales

lynch [lɪnʃ] *verb* linchar
◊ **lynch law** ['lɪnʃ 'lɔː] *noun* linchamiento *m or* ley *f* de lynch

Mm

mace [meɪs] *noun* maza *f*

◊ **mace-bearer** *noun* macero *m*

> COMMENT: the significance of the mace in the House of Commons is so great that if it is not on the table, no business can be done. The mace is carried by the Serjeant at Arms in official processions; it is kept under the table in the House of Commons and placed on the table at the beginning of each sitting; it is taken off the table when the House goes into Committee. In the House of Lords, the mace is placed on the Woolsack. Local authorities usually also have maces which are carried in front of the mayor on ceremonial occasions by the mace-bearer, and often placed on the table at full council meetings. In the US House of Representatives, the mace is placed beside the Speaker's chair when the House is in session. There is no mace in the Senate, but a ceremonial gavel is placed on the vice-president's desk when the Senate is in session

machine [məˈʃiːn] *noun* **(a)** máquina *f;* **copying machine** *or* **duplicating machine** = copiadora *f;* **dictating machine** = dictáfono *m* **(b) machine code** *or* **machine language** = lenguaje *m or* código *m* de máquina; **machine-readable codes** = códigos en lenguaje de máquina *or* códigos usados por un ordenador

◊ **machinery** [məˈʃiːnri] *noun* **(a)** *(machine)* maquinaria *f;* **the inspector found that the machinery in the factory was dangerous** = el inspector consideró que la maquinaria de la fábrica era peligrosa **(b)** *(system)* mecanismo *m or* organización *f or* aparato *m;* **the local government machinery** *or* **the machinery of local government** = la organización del gobierno local; **administrative machinery** = aparato administrativo; **the machinery for awarding government contracts** = los trámites para conceder los contratos del gobierno

Madam [ˈmædəm] *noun* Señora *f;* **Dear Madam** = Muy Sra. Mía; **Madam Chairman** = Señora Presidenta; **Madam Speaker** = Presidenta de la Cámara de los Comunes

Mafia [ˈmæfiə] *noun* **the Mafia** = la Mafia

magistrate [ˈmædʒɪstreɪt] *noun* magistrado, -da *or* juez, -za; **magistrates' clerk** = secretario, -ria de un tribunal de magistrados *or* oficial *mf* de juzgado que asesora a los magistrados; **magistrates' court** = juzgado *m* de paz *or* tribunal *m* de magistrados; **duty magistrate** = juez de guardia; **examining magistrate** = juez de primera instancia; **lay magistrate** = juez de paz; **stipendiary magistrate** = juez *or* juez letrado (NOTE: unpaid magistrates are also called **Justices of the Peace** or **JPs**)

> COMMENT: the Magistrates' Court hears cases of petty crime, adoption, affiliation, maintenance and violence in the home; it can commit someone for trial or for sentence in the Crown Court. A stipendiary magistrate is a qualified lawyer who usually sits alone; lay magistrates usually sit as a bench of three

Magna Carta [ˈmægnə ˈkɑːtə] *noun* Carta *f* Magna

magnetic tape *or (informal)* **mag tape** [mægˈnetɪk ˈteɪp *or* ˈmæg ˈteɪp] *noun* cinta *f* magnética

maiden speech [ˈmeɪdən ˈspiːtʃ] *noun* primera intervención parlamentaria de un nuevo diputado

mail [meɪl] *noun* correo *m;* **by mail** = por correo; **e-mail** = correo electrónico; **ordinary mail** = correo ordinario; **registered mail** = correo certificado; **snail mail** = correo postal

maintain [meɪnˈteɪn] *verb* **(a)** *(keep going)* mantener *or* sostener; **to maintain good relations with one's customers** = mantener buenas relaciones con los clientes; **to maintain contact with an overseas market** = mantener contacto con un mercado exterior; **mounted police were brought in to maintain law and order** = se trajo a la policía montada para mantener la ley y el orden **(b)** *(to keep something working at the same level)* mantener *or* conservar; **the company has maintained the same volume of business in spite of the recession** = la empresa ha mantenido el mismo volumen de negocios a pesar de la recesión; **to maintain an interest rate at 5%** = mantener un tipo de interés al 5%; **to maintain a dividend** = mantener un dividendo **(c)** *(to pay for the food and clothing for a child or adult)* mantener *or* sustentar;

the ex-husband was ordered to maintain his wife and three children = se ordenó al ex-marido a que mantuviera a su mujer y tres hijos

◊ **maintenance** ['meɪntnəns] *noun* **(a)** *(keeping things going or working)* mantenimiento *m;* **the maintenance of law and order is in the hands of the local police force** = el mantenimiento de la ley y el orden está en manos del cuerpo de policía local **(b)** *(keeping a machine in good working order)* mantenimiento *or* conservación *f;* **maintenance contract** = contrato *m* de mantenimiento **(c)** *(payment made to a former spouse to help pay for living expenses and the cost of bringing up the children)* manutención *f or* mantenimiento *or* pensión *f;* **maintenance agreement** = acuerdo *m* de manutención; **maintenance order** = orden de manutención; **maintenance pending suit** = manutención pendiente de litigio (NOTE: US English is **alimony**) **(d)** *(formerly)* intermediación *f* ilegal en pleito de alguien no interesado (mediante pago a una de las partes)

Majesty ['mædʒəsti] *noun* majestad *f;* GB **Her Majesty's Government** = el gobierno británico; **On Her Majesty's Service (OHMS)** = 'al servicio de su majestad' (palabras impresas en los documentos oficiales del gobierno británico); **Her Majesty's Stationery Office (HMSO)** = organismo editor e impresor de las publicaciones oficiales del Estado; *see also* HER MAJESTY'S PLEASURE

majeure [mæ'dʒɜːr] *see* FORCE MAJEURE

major ['meɪdʒə] *adjective* importante *or* prioritario, -ria; **major shareholder** = accionista *mf* importante

◊ **majority** [mə'dʒɒriti] *noun* **(a)** *(larger group)* mayoría *f;* **majority of the shareholders** = mayoría de los accionistas; **the board accepted the proposal by a majority of three to two** = la junta aceptó la propuesta por una mayoría de tres sobre dos; **majority vote** *or* **majority decision** = voto *m* mayoritario *or* decisión *f* mayoritaria; **majority shareholding** *or* **majority interest** = mayoría de acciones *or* participación *f* mayoritaria *or* interés *m* mayoritario; **a majority shareholder** = un accionista mayoritario; **majority verdict** = veredicto *m* por mayoría (al menos diez miembros del jurado) **(b)** *(age)* mayoría *f* (de edad)

COMMENT: the age of majority in the UK and US is eighteen

make [meɪk] *verb* hacer; **to make allowances** = hacer concesiones; **to make a will** = otorgar un testamento; **to make available** = poner a disposición

makeshift ['meɪkʃɪft] *noun* arreglo *m* improvisado

maladministration [mælədmɪnɪ'streɪʃn] *noun* mala administración *f*

mala in se ['mælə 'ɪn 'seɪ] *Latin phrase* malo, -la per se: actos *mpl* (como el asesinato) que constituyen delitos por sí mismos

◊ **mala prohibita** ['mælə prəʊ'hɪbɪtə] *Latin phrase* malo, -la por razón de ley: actos (como pisar el césped de un parque) prohibidos aunque no constituyen delitos por sí mismos

malefactor ['mælɪfæktə] *noun* malhechor, -ra

malfeasance [mæl'fiːzəns] *noun* acto *m* ilegal *or* conducta *f* ilegal

malice ['mælɪs] *noun* intención *f* delictuosa *or* malicia *f or* maldad *f;* **with malice aforethought** = con premeditación; **without malice** = sin premeditación; **express malice** = malicia expresa *or* intención de matar a alguien; **implied malice** = intención de causar daños físicos graves a alguien

◊ **malicious** [mə'lɪʃəs] *adjective* malicioso, -sa; **malicious damage** = daño *m* doloso; **malicious falsehood** = mentira *f* maliciosa; **malicious prosecution** = denuncia *f* maliciosa *or* demanda *f* de mala fe; **malicious wounding** = causar daño intencional

◊ **maliciously** [mə'lɪʃəsli] *adverb* maliciosamente *or* con alevosía; **he claimed that he had been prosecuted maliciously** = declaró que había sido denunciado maliciosamente

◊ **maliciousness** [mə'lɪʃəsnəs] *noun* mala intención *f*

malpractice [mæl'præktɪs] *noun* negligencia *f or* incuria *f*

man [mæn] *noun* hombre *m;* **front man** = hombre de paja *or* testaferro *m;* **right-hand man** = hombre de confianza

manage ['mænɪdʒ] *verb* **(a)** *(to be in charge of)* dirigir *or* llevar *or* administrar *or* gestionar; **to manage a department** = dirigir un departamento; **to manage a branch office** = llevar una sucursal **(b) to manage property** = administrar propiedad **(c) to manage to** = conseguir (hacer algo) *or* arreglárselas; **did you manage to see the solicitor?** = ¿conseguiste ver al abogado?; **counsel managed to have the hearing adjourned** = el abogado consiguió que la vista se aplazara; **she managed to write six orders and take three phone calls all in two minutes** = se las arregló para anotar seis pedidos y atender tres llamadas telefónicas en dos minutos

◊ **manageable** ['mænɪdʒəbl] *adjective* manejable *or* que puede resolverse

◊ **management** ['mænɪdʒmənt] *noun* **(a)** *(running a business)* dirección *f or* administración *f or* gestión *f or* gerencia *f;* **to study management** = estudiar dirección de empresas *or* ciencias empresariales; **good management** *or* **efficient management** = buena gestión *or* gestión eficiente; **financial management** = gestión financiera; **line management** = gerencia lineal; **management accountant** = contable *mf* de gestión; **management** accounts = cuentas *fpl* de gestión; **management consultant** = asesor, -ra de empresa; **management course** = curso *m* de dirección *or* de gestión empresarial; **management by objectives** = dirección por objetivos; **management team** = equipo *m* directivo; **management training** = formación *f* de mandos; **management trainee** = ejecutivo,-va en formación **(b)** *(group of managers or directors)* dirección *or* consejo *m* de administración *or* patronato *m;* **top management** = alta dirección; **middle management** = mandos *mpl* intermedios; **junior management** = directores adjuntos *or* directores de departamentos

◊ **manager** ['mænɪdʒə] *noun* **(a)** *(head of a department in a company)* director *m or* jefe *m;* **accounts manager** = jefe de contabilidad; **area manager** = director regional; **general manager** = director general **(b)** *(person in charge of a branch or shop)* director *or* gerente *m or* encargado *m;* **bank manager** = director de banco *or* de sucursal bancaria; **branch manager** = director de sucursal

◊ **manageress** [mænɪdʒə'res] *noun* directora *f or* gerente *f or* encargada *f or* jefa *f*

◊ **managerial** [mænə'dʒɪərɪəl] *adjective* directivo, -va *or* gerencial *or* administrativo, -va *or* empresarial; **to be appointed to a managerial position** = ser nombrado para un puesto directivo; **decisions taken at managerial level** = decisiones tomadas por la dirección

◊ **managing** ['mænɪdʒɪŋ] *adjective;* **managing clerk** = (antiguo término para designar) un ejecutivo jurídico; **managing director** = director, -ra gerente *or* consejero, -ra delegado, -da; **chairman and managing director** = presidente y director gerente

mandamus [mæn'deɪməs] *Latin word* mandamiento *m* judicial; **the Chief Constable applied for an order of mandamus directing the justices to rehear the case** = el jefe de policía solicitó un mandamiento judicial para que los magistrados revisaran el caso

Mandarin ['mændərɪn] *noun (informal)* mandarín *m; GB* **Whitehall Mandarin** = alto funcionario público

mandate ['mændeɪt] *noun* mandato *m;* **bank mandate** = orden *f* de pago

mandatory ['mændətrɪ] *adjective* obligatorio, -ria *or* imperativo, -va; **mandatory injunction** = requerimiento *m* imperativo *or* mandamiento *m* preceptivo; **mandatory meeting** = reunión *f or* junta *f* obligatoria

manendi [mæ'nendaɪ] *see* ANIMUS

maniac ['meɪnɪæk] *noun* maníaco, -ca; **sex maniac** = maníaco sexual

manifest ['mænɪfest] **1** *adjective* manifiesto, -ta *or* evidente; **a manifest injustice** = una injusticia

manifiesta **2** *noun* manifiesto *m;* **passenger manifest** = lista *f* de pasajeros de un barco *or* avión

manipulate [mə'nɪpjuːleɪt] *verb* manipular *or* manejar; **to manipulate the accounts** = falsear *or* amañar el estado de cuentas de una empresa; **to manipulate the market** = manipular el mercado de la Bolsa

◊ **manipulation** [mənɪpju'leɪʃn] *noun* manipulación *f;* **stock market manipulation** = maniobra *f* de Bolsa

◊ **manipulator** [mə'nɪpjuleɪtə] *noun* **stock market manipulator** = manipulador, -ra de Bolsa

manslaughter ['mænslɔːtə] *noun* homicidio *m* culposo *or* imprudente *or* por imprudencia *or* no premeditado *or* sin premeditación; **involuntary manslaughter** = homicidio involuntario; **he was accused of manslaughter** = fue acusado de homicidio culposo; **she was convicted of the manslaughter of her husband** = se le declaró culpable del homicidio involuntario de su marido; **voluntary manslaughter** = homicidio intencionado con circunstancias atenuantes

Mareva injunction [mə'reɪvə ɪn'dʒʌŋkʃn] *noun* requerimiento *m or* interdicto *m* para congelar los activos de una persona que ha marchado al extranjero o de una empresa con base en el extranjero

COMMENT: called after the case of *Mareva Compañía Naviera SA v. International Bulk-Carriers SA*

margin ['mɑːdʒɪn] *noun (profit per unit)* margen *m* (de beneficio); **gross margin** = beneficio *m* bruto *or* margen bruto

Maria [mə'raɪə] *see* BLACK

marine [mə'riːn] **1** *adjective* marino, -na *or* marítimo, -ma; **marine insurance** = seguro *m* marítimo; **marine underwriter** = asegurador, -ra marítimo, -ma **2** *noun* **the merchant marine** = la marina mercante

◊ **maritime** ['mærɪtaɪm] *adjective* marítimo, -ma; **maritime law** = derecho *m* marítimo; **maritime lawyer** = abogado, -da especializado, -da en derecho marítimo; **maritime lien** = derecho de retención de un barco; **maritime perils** = PERILS OF THE SEA; **maritime trade** = comercio *m* marítimo

marital ['mærɪtl] *adjective* marital *or* matrimonial; **marital privileges** = privilegios *mpl* matrimoniales (de no testimoniar en contra del cónyuge en ciertos procesos)

mark [mɑːk] **1** *noun* **(a)** *(sign)* marca *f or* señal *f;* **assay mark** = sello *m* de contraste *or* marca de ensaye; **kite mark** = marca de garantía en las mercancías británicas; **to leave a mark** = dejar huella **(b)** *(cross 'X' in place of a signature)* cruz *f or* signo *m* **(c)** *(target)* **to hit the mark** = dar en el blanco (d) *(limit)* to overstep the mark = pasar de la raya 2 *verb (to put a sign on something)* señalar *or* marcar *or* indicar; to mark a product 'for export only' = indicar en un producto 'sólo para la exportación'; article marked at £1.50 = artículo marcado con (un precio de) 1,50 libras; to mark the price on something = poner el precio a algo; because he could not write he marked an 'X' in place of his signature = puesto que no sabía escribir, puso una 'X' en lugar de su firma

◊ marksman ['mɑːksmən] *noun* (a) *(person who can shoot a gun accurately)* tirador *m* (b) *(person who cannot write)* persona *f* que firma con una cruz *or* analfabeto,-ta

◊ mark up ['mɑːk 'ʌp] *verb US* enmendar; to mark up a bill = enmendar un proyecto de ley en comisión

market ['mɑːkɪt] 1 *noun* (a) *(place)* mercado *m;* market day = día *f* de mercado *or* día en que hay mercado; market dues = cuota *f* por un puesto en el mercado (b) *(formerly)* the Common Market = el Mercado Común; the Common Market policy on trade restrictions = la política del Mercado Común sobre restricciones en el comercio; the Common Market ministers = los ministros del Mercado Común (c) *(area where a product might be sold, people who might buy a product)* mercado; home *or* domestic market = mercado interior *or* nacional; market share = cuota de mercado (d) *(possible sales of a product)* mercado; a growth market = un mercado en expansión *or* en crecimiento (e) black market = estraperlo *m or* mercado negro; to pay black market prices = pagar precios de mercado negro; there is a lucrative black market in spare parts for cars = hay un lucrativo mercado negro de piezas de recambio de coches; he bought gold coins on the black market = compró monedas de oro en el mercado negro (f) a buyer's market = un mercado favorable al comprador; a seller's market = un mercado favorable al vendedor (g) closed market = mercado controlado *or* cautivo; free market economy = economía *f* de libre mercado; open market = mercado libre; market overt = mercado abierto *or* público; market value = valor de mercado (h) capital market = mercado de capitales; the foreign exchange markets = los mercados de divisas *or* mercados cambiarios; forward markets = mercados de futuros (i) stock market = bolsa *f or* mercado de valores; to buy shares in the open market = comprar acciones en el mercado libre; over-the-counter market = mercado de valores sin cotización oficial; market capitalization = valor *m* de mercado del capital emitido; market maker = persona que compra y vende acciones en Bolsa *or* que comercia en Bolsa; market price = precio *m* de mercado 2 *verb* poner en venta *or* a la venta *or* lanzar al mercado; this product is being marketed in all European countries = este producto se vende en todos los países europeos

◊ marketable ['mɑːkɪtəbl] *adjective* vendible *or* comercial; marketable title = título *m* vendible (sin gravámenes)

marriage ['mærɪdʒ] *noun* matrimonio *m;* by marriage = por matrimonio; she became a British citizen by marriage = pasó a ser ciudadana británica por matrimonio; civil marriage = matrimonio civil; unconsummated marriage = matrimonio rato *or* no consumado; marriage settlement = capitulaciones *fpl* matrimoniales; sham marriage *or* marriage of convenience = matrimonio de conveniencia *or* de interés

marry ['mæri] *verb* casar; to get married = casarse

marshal ['mɑːʃl] *noun* (a) Marshal of the Admiralty Court = oficial *mf* a cargo del Tribunal del Almirantazgo (b) *US* oficial de justicia

martial ['mɑːʃl] *adjective* marcial; martial law = ley *f* marcial; the president imposed *or* declared martial law in two provinces = el presidente declaró la ley marcial en dos provincias; the government lifted martial law = el gobierno suprimió la ley marcial; *see also* COURT-MARTIAL

master ['mɑːstə] *noun* (a) *(High Court)* oficial *mf* del Tribunal Supremo que examina y decide sobre cuestiones preliminares a un juicio; Practice Master = oficial del Tribunal Supremo que asesora a los abogados sobre cómo llevar a cabo las actuaciones judiciales; Taxing Master = oficial del Tribunal Supremo que valora las costas de una acción judicial (b) Masters of the Bench = miembros de la Junta del Gobierno de cada uno de los Colegios de Abogados británicos (c) *(employer)* master and servant = patrono *m* y empleado *m;* the law of master and servant = ley *f* de empleo (d) *(main or original)* original; master copy of a file = copia *f* original de un archivo informático ◊ Master of the Rolls ['mɑːstə əv ðə 'rəʊlz] *noun* presidente *m* del Tribunal de Apelación y responsable de admitir abogados al mismo

material [mə'tɪərɪəl] 1 *noun* (a) *(physical)* material *m;* building materials = materiales de construcción; raw materials = materias *fpl* primas (b) display material = material de exposición (NOTE: no plural for this meaning) 2 *adjective* esencial *or* fundamental *or* pertinente; material alteration = alteración *f* fundamental hecha en un documento legal; material evidence = prueba *f* pertinente *or* substancial; material witness = testigo fundamental

matricide ['mætrɪsaɪd] *noun* matricidio *m*

matrimony ['mætrɪmʌni] *noun* matrimonio *m* ◊ matrimonial [mætrɪ'məʊnɪəl] *adjective* matrimonial *or* conyugal *or* marital; matrimonial causes = pleitos *mpl or* juicios *mpl* matrimoniales;

matrimonial home = domicilio *m* matrimonial *or* conyugal

matter ['mætə] **1** *noun* **(a)** *(problem)* asunto *m or* cuestión *f or* problema *m;* **it is a matter of concern to the members of the committee** = es un asunto que preocupa a los miembros del comité **(b) printed matter** = impresos *mpl or* material *m* impreso (NOTE: no plural in this meaning) **(c)** *(problem to be discussed)* tema *f or* asunto *or* cuestión; **the most important matter on the agenda** = el asunto más importante del orden del día; **we shall consider first the matter of last month's fall in prices** = veremos primero el tema de la baja de precios del mes pasado; **interlocutory matter** = tema de disputa secundario que se trata antes de un juicio *or* asunto interlocutorio; **matter of fact** = cuestión de hecho; **matters of fact** = cuestiones de hecho (referentes a un caso); **matters of law** = cuestiones de derecho (referentes a un caso); **it is a matter of fact whether the parties entered into the contract, but it is a matter of law whether or not the contract is legal** = es una cuestión de hecho si las partes firmaron el contrato, pero es una cuestión de derecho si el contrato es legal o no **2** *verb* importar; **does it matter if one month's sales are down?** = ¿importa si las ventas de un mes son bajas?

mature [mə'tʃʊə] *verb* vencer; **bill which will mature in three months** = letra *f* que vencerá en tres meses
◊ **maturity** [mə'tʃʊərɪti] *noun* vencimiento *m*

maxim ['mæksɪm] *noun* máxima *f*

maximum ['mæksɪməm] **1** *noun* máximo *m;* **up to a maximum of £10** = hasta un máximo de 10 libras (NOTE: plural is **maxima**) **2** *adjective* máximo, -ma; **maximum income tax rate** *or* **maximum rate of tax** = tarifa *f* máxima del impuesto sobre la renta *or* tarifa máxima del impuesto; **he was sentenced to the maximum sentence of imprisonment** = fue sentenciado a la máxima pena de cárcel; **to increase production to the maximum level** = aumentar la producción al máximo

mayhem ['meɪhem] *noun (riot)* disturbio *m or* alboroto *m US* mutilación *f* criminal de una de las extremidades del cuerpo

mayor ['meə] *noun* alcalde *m; GB* **Lord Mayor** = alcalde de una gran ciudad
◊ **mayoral** ['meərəl] *adjective* de alcalde *or* relativo al alcalde
◊ **mayorality** *or* **mayor's office** ['meərlti *or* 'meəz 'ɒfɪs] *noun* alcaldía *f*
◊ **mayoress** [meə'res] *noun* alcaldesa *f*

COMMENT: previously, a mayor was the head of the elected government of a town, and the head of the majority party. His governmental responsibilities have now been taken over by the Leader of the Council, and the office of mayor is largely ceremonial. It is an honour often given to a long-serving or distinguished councillor. In Scotland, a mayor is called a Provost. Note also that 'Mayor' is used in English to apply to persons holding similar positions in other countries: **the Mayor of Berlin**

McNaghten [mək'nɔːtən] *see* M'NAGHTEN

mean [miːn] *verb* significar
◊ **meaning** ['miːnɪŋ] *noun* significado *m*

means [miːnz] *plural noun* medios *mpl or* recursos *mpl;* **statement of means** = declaración *f* de recursos económicos; **means of transport** = medios de transporte; **legal means** = medios legales; **economic means** = medios de vida *or* medios económicos

measure ['meʒə] **1** *noun* **(a)** *(way of calculating size or quantity)* medida *f;* **cubic measure** = medida de volumen; **dry measure** = medida de áridos; **square measure** = medida de superficie; **inspector of weights and measures** = inspector, -ra de pesas y medidas; **measure of damages** = evaluación *f* de los daños **(b)** *(type of action)* medida *or* proyecto *m* de ley *or* ley *f;* **a government measure to reduce crime in the inner cities** = un proyecto de ley del gobierno para reducir la criminalidad en el centro de las ciudades; **to take measures to prevent something happening** = tomar medidas preventivas; **to take emergency measures** = tomar medidas de emergencia; **an economy measure** = una medida de ahorro; **fiscal measures** = medidas fiscales; **as a precautionary measure** = como medida preventiva *or* de precaución; **safety measures** = medidas de seguridad **2** *verb* **(a)** *(to find out the size or quantity)* tomar las medidas *or* medir *or* calibrar; **to measure the size of a package** = medir el tamaño de un paquete; **a package which measures 10cm by 25cm** *or* **a package measuring 10cm by 25cm** = un paquete que mide 10cm por 25cm **(b)** *(to judge how well something is working)* **to measure the government's performance** = sopesar *or* juzgar la actuación del gobierno
◊ **measurement** ['meʒəmənt] *noun* **(a)** *(size)* measurements = medidas *fpl or* dimensiones *fpl;* **to write down the measurements of a package** = anotar las medidas de un paquete **(b)** *(way of judging something)* medición *f or* medida; **performance measurement** *or* **measurement of performance** = evaluación *f* de rendimiento; **measurement of profitability** = medición de la rentabilidad

mechanical reproduction rights [mɪ'kænɪkl rɪprə'dʌkʃn 'raɪts] *plural noun* derechos *mpl* de reproducción

mechanic's lien [mɪ'kænɪks 'liːn] *see* LIEN

mediate ['miːdɪeɪt] *verb* ser mediador en *or* servir de intermediario en *or* mediar *or* conciliar; **to**

mediate between the manager and his staff = servir de intermediario entre el director y sus empleados; **the government offered to mediate in the dispute** = el gobierno se ofreció a mediar en el conflicto

◊ **mediation** [miːdiˈeɪʃn] *noun* mediación *f;* **the employers refused an offer of government mediation** = los empresarios rehusaron una oferta de mediación del gobierno; **the dispute was ended through the mediation of union officials** = la disputa se resolvió a través de la mediación de los cargos sindicales

◊ **mediator** [ˈmiːdieɪtə] *noun* mediador,-ra *or* intermediario,-ria; **official mediator** = mediador del gobierno (en una disputa laboral)

medical [ˈmedɪkl] **1** *noun* reconocimiento *m* médico *or* revisión *f* médica **2** *adjective* médico, -ca; **medical certificate** = certificado *m* médico; **medical inspection** = inspección *f* médica (de un lugar de trabajo); **medical insurance** = seguro *m* médico; **medical officer of health (MOH)** = jefe, -fa de sanidad municipal; **he resigned for medical reasons** = dimitió por razones de salud

◊ **medicine** [ˈmedsɪn] *noun* medicina *f;* **forensic medicine** = medicina forense *or* legal

meet [miːt] *verb* **(a)** *(with someone)* encontrarse (con) *or* reunirse (con) *or* dar con alguien; **to meet a negotiating committee** = reunirse con un comité negociador; **to meet an agent at his hotel** = reunirse con un representante en su hotel; **the two sides met in the lawyer's office** = las dos partes se encontraron en el despacho del abogado **(b)** *(to be satisfactory for)* satisfacer *or* cumplir; **to meet a customer's requirements** = satisfacer los requisitos de un cliente; **he failed to meet the conditions of the court order** = no pudo cumplir las condiciones de la orden judicial; **to meet the demand for a new product** = satisfacer la demanda de un nuevo producto; **we will try to meet your price** = trataremos de acordar un precio que sea satisfactorio para usted; **they failed to meet the deadline** = no pudieron cumplir el plazo fijado **(c)** *(to pay for)* costear *or* cubrir *or* correr con *or* hacer frente a; **to meet someone's expenses** = cubrir los gastos de alguien; **the company will meet your expenses** = la empresa correrá con sus gastos; **he was unable to meet his mortgage repayments** = no pudo hacer frente a los pagos de la hipoteca; **to meet your obligations** = saldar las deudas de uno mismo (NOTE: **meeting - met - has met**)

◊ **meeting** [ˈmiːtɪŋ] *noun* **(a)** *(group of people)* reunión *f or* junta *f or* asamblea *f;* **management meeting** = junta de dirección; **staff meeting** = reunión del personal; **board meeting** = reunión del consejo de dirección *or* junta de directores; **general meeting** *or* **meeting of shareholders** *or* **shareholders' meeting** = asamblea general *or* junta de accionistas; **Annual General Meeting** = junta general ordinaria; **Extraordinary General Meeting** = junta general extraordinaria **(b)**

freedom of meeting = libertad *f* de reunión; **to hold a meeting** = celebrar una reunión; **the meeting will be held in the committee room** = la reunión se celebrará en la sala de juntas; **to open a meeting** = abrir una sesión; **to conduct a meeting** = dirigir una junta *or* reunión; **to close a meeting** = levantar una sesión; **to put a resolution to a meeting** = presentar una propuesta a voto en una reunión

member [ˈmembə] *noun* **(a)** *(person belonging to a group)* miembro *mf or* socio, -cia; **ordinary member** = miembro ordinario; **honorary member** = miembro honorario; **founding member** = socio fundador **(b)** *(shareholder)* socio, -cia **(c)** *(organization which belongs to a society)* miembro; **the member countries** *or* **the member states of the EU** = los países miembros *or* los estados miembros de la UE; **the members of the United Nations** = los miembros de las Naciones Unidas; **the member companies of a trade association** = las compañías afiliadas a una asociación comercial

◊ **Member of Parliament** [ˈmembə əv ˈpɑːləmənt] *noun* diputado, -da (NOTE: often abbreviated to **MP**. The plural is **MPs**)

◊ **Member of the European Parliament (MEP)** [ˈmembə əv ðə juːrəˈpiːən ˈpɑːləmənt] *noun* eurodiputado, -da *or* diputado,-da del Parlamento Europeo

◊ **membership** [ˈmembəʃɪp] *noun* **(a)** *(being a member)* calidad *f* de socio *or* miembro *or* afiliación *f;* **membership qualifications** = requisitos *mpl* para hacerse socio; **conditions of membership** = condiciones *fpl* de ingreso; **to pay your membership** *or* **your membership fees** = pagar la cuota de socio; **Turkey has applied for membership of the EU** = Turquía ha solicitado el ingreso en la UE **(b)** *(all the members of a group)* miembros *or* socios; **union membership** = afiliación sindical; **the membership was asked to vote for the new president** = se pidió a los socios que votaran a un nuevo presidente; **the club's membership secretary** = el secretario de la asociación; **the club has a membership of five hundred** = el club tiene quinientos socios

memorandum [meməˈrændəm] *noun* memorándum *m or* informe *m or* nota *f;* **memorandum of association** = escritura *f* de constitución de una sociedad mercantil *or* acta *f* constitutiva de sociedad; **memorandum of satisfaction** = documento *m* de levantamiento de una hipoteca *or* de liquidación de un pago (NOTE: plural is **memoranda**)

menace [ˈmenəs] *noun* amenaza *f;* **demanding money with menaces** = pedir dinero bajo amenazas

mens rea [ˈmens ˈreɪə] *Latin phrase* intención *f* criminal *or* dolo *m; see note at* CRIME; *and compare* ACTUS REUS

mental ['mentl] *adjective* mental; **mental cruelty** = crueldad *f* mental; **mental disorder** = trastorno *m* mental
◊ **mentally** ['mentli] *adverb* mentalmente; **mentally ill criminals are committed to special establishments** = los criminales con trastornos mentales son internados en instituciones especializadas

mention ['menʃn] **1** *noun* vista *f* de corta duración *or* vista rápida *f* **2** *verb* mencionar *or* aludir a *or* decir; **the judge mentioned the need for the jury to examine all the documents** = el juez mencionó la necesidad de que el jurado examinara todos los documentos; **can you mention to them that the date of the next meeting has been changed?** = ¿puede decirles que se ha cambiado la fecha de la próxima reunión?

mentis ['mentɪs] *see* COMPOS MENTIS

MEP ['em 'iː 'piː] = MEMBER OF THE EUROPEAN PARLIAMENT

mercantile law *or* **law merchant** ['məːkəntaɪl 'lɔː *or* lɔː 'mertʃənt] *noun* derecho *m* mercantil

merchantable quality ['məːtʃəntəbl 'kwɒlɪti] *noun* calidad *f* comerciable

mercy ['məːsi] *noun* clemencia *f or* compasión *f*; **prerogative of mercy** = privilegio *m* de conmutación *or* remisión de una sentencia; **to be at the mercy of** = estar a la merced de
◊ **mercy killing** ['məːsi 'kɪlɪŋ] *noun* eutanasia *f*

merge [məːdʒ] *verb* fusionar(se) *or* unir(se); **the two companies have merged** = las dos empresas se han fusionado; **the firm merged with its main competitor** = la firma se fusionó con su principal competidor
◊ **merger** ['məːdʒə] *noun* fusión *f*; **as a result of the merger, the company is the largest in the field** = como resultado de la fusión, la empresa es la más grande del sector

meridiem [mə'rɪdiəm] *see* A.M., P.M.

merit ['merɪt] *noun* mérito *m*; **merit award** *or* **merit bonus** = prima *f or* bonificación *f* por méritos; **merit increase** = aumento *m* salarial por méritos; **merit rating** = valoración *f* de méritos
◊ **merits of the case** ['merɪts əv ðə 'keɪs] *plural noun* fondo *m* del caso *or* méritos *mpl* de la causa

mesne [miːn] *adjective* intermedio, -dia; **mesne process** = emplazamiento *m or* auto *m* interlocutorio; **action for mesne profits** = acción *f* judicial para recuperar los beneficios obtenidos mediante posesión ilegal

Messrs ['mesəz] *noun* Sres *mpl*; **Messrs White, White & Smith** = los Sres White, White y Smith

messuage ['meswɪdʒ] *noun* casa *f* con sus dependencias y tierras

Met [met] *noun (informal)* **the Met** = la policía metropolitana

metropolitan [metrə'pɒlɪtən] *adjective* metropolitano, -na; **the Metropolitan Police** = la policía metropolitana de Londres; **the Metropolitan Police Commissioner** = el comisario de la policía metropolitana; **solicitor for the Metropolitan Police** = el abogado de la policía metropolitana

COMMENT: the higher ranks in the Metropolitan Police are Deputy Assistant Commissioner, Assistant Commissioner, and Commissioner. See also DETECTIVE, POLICE

Michaelmas ['mɪklməs] *noun* **(a)** *(rent)* 29 de septiembre, día de pago del alquiler de tierras correspondiente al tercer trimestre del año; *see also* QUARTER DAY **(b)** *(one of the law terms)* uno de los cuatro periodos de sesiones de los tribunales *or* uno de los cuatro trimestres del año jurídico

microfiche ['maɪkrəufiːʃ] *noun* microficha *f*; **we hold our records on microfiche** = guardamos nuestros informes en microficha
◊ **microfilm** ['maɪkrəufɪlm] **1** *noun* microfilm *m*; **we hold our records on microfilm** = guardamos nuestros informes en microfilm **2** *verb* microfilmar; **send the 1997 correspondence to be microfilmed** *or* **for microfilming** = mande la correspondencia de 1997 a que sea microfilmada

middle ['mɪdl] *adjective* medio, -dia *or* central *or* de en medio; **middle management** = mandos *mpl* intermedios *or* intermediados
◊ **middleman** ['mɪdlmæn] *noun* intermediario, -ria *or* agente *mf* de negocios; **we sell direct from the factory to the customer and cut out the middleman** = vendemos directamente de la fábrica al cliente y así suprimimos al intermediario (NOTE: plural is **middlemen**)
◊ **Middle Temple** ['mɪdl 'templ] *noun* uno de los cuatro Colegios de Abogados de Londres

Midland and Oxford Circuit ['mɪdlənd ənd 'ɒksfəd 'səːkɪt] *noun* uno de los seis circuitos del tribunal de la Corona al que pertenecen los abogados, con su centro en Birmingham

Midsummer day ['mɪdsʌmə 'deɪ] *noun* el día de San Juan: uno de los días del trimestre en el que se paga la renta de la tierra

militant ['mɪlɪtənt] *adjective & noun* activista *mf or* extremista *mf or* militante *mf*; **the speaker was shouted down by militant union members** = activistas del sindicato hicieron callar a la persona que hablaba

mind [maɪnd] *noun* **of unsound mind** = privado, -da de razón; **to be out of one's mind** = no estar en sus cabales

minder ['maɪndə] *noun (slang)* guardaespaldas *mf*

minimal ['mɪnɪməl] *adjective* mínimo, -ma; **there was a minimal quantity of imperfections in the new stock** = la cantidad de defectos del nuevo surtido de mercancías era mínima; **the head office exercises minimal control over the branch offices** = la oficina central ejerce un control mínimo sobre las sucursales

◊ **minimis** ['mɪnɪmi:s] *see* DE MINIMIS

◊ **minimize** ['mɪnɪmaɪz] *verb* minimizar *or* reducir al mínimo *or* menospreciar *or* subestimar; **do not minimize the risks involved** = no menosprecie los posibles riesgos; **he always minimizes the difficulty of the project** = siempre minimiza la dificultad del proyecto

◊ **minimum** ['mɪnɪməm] **1** *noun* mínimo *m;* **to keep expenses to a minimum** = gastar lo menos posible *or* gastar lo mínimo; **to reduce the risk of a loss to a minimum** = reducir el riesgo de pérdidas al mínimo **2** *adjective* mínimo, -ma; **minimum dividend** = dividendo *m* mínimo; **minimum payment** = pago *m* mínimo; **minimum sentence** = condena *f* mínima; **minimum wage** = salario *m* mínimo

minister ['mɪnɪstə] *noun* ministro, -tra; **a government minister** = un ministro del gobierno; **the Minister of Information** *or* **the Information Minister** = el ministro de Información; **the Minister of Foreign Affairs** *or* **the Foreign Minister** = el ministro de Asuntos Exteriores; **the Minister of Justice** *or* **the Justice Minister** = el ministro de Justicia; **Minister of State** = secretario, -ria de Estado

COMMENT: in the USA, heads of government departments are called **secretary: the Secretary for Commerce;** in the UK, heads of government departments (see below) are called **Secretary of State: the Secretary of State for Defence**

ministerial ['mɪnɪ'stɪrɪəl] *adjective* ministerial; **ministerial tribunal** = tribunal *m* ministerial

◊ **ministry** ['mɪnɪstri] *noun* **(a)** *(department in the government)* ministerio *m;* **he works in the Ministry of Finance** *or* **the Finance Ministry** = trabaja en el ministerio de Hacienda; **he is in charge of the Ministry of Information** *or* **of the Information Ministry** = está al cargo del ministerio de Información; **a ministry official** *or* **an official from the ministry** = un funcionario del ministerio **(b)** *(government)* gobierno *m;* **during the Wilson ministry** = durante el gobierno de Wilson

COMMENT: in Britain and the USA, important ministries are called **departments: the Department of Trade and Industry; the Commerce Department.** Note also that the UK does not have a government department called the 'Ministry of Justice', and the duties of supervising the administration of justice fall to the Lord Chancellor's office and the Home Office

minor ['maɪnə] **1** *adjective* menor *or* pequeño, -ña *or* de poca importancia *or* secundario, -ria; **minor expenditure** = gastos menores; **minor shareholders** = accionistas pequeños; **a loss of minor importance** = una pérdida de poca importancia **2** *noun* menor *mf* de edad

◊ **minority** [mɪ'nɒrəti] *noun* **(a)** *(being under age)* minoría *f* de edad; **a person is not liable for debts contracted during his minority** = una persona no está obligada a pagar las deudas contraídas cuando era menor de edad **(b)** *(less than half the total)* minoría; **a minority of board members opposed the chairman** = una minoría de miembros de la junta se opuso al presidente; **minority shareholding** *or* **minority interest** = interés *m* minoritario *or* participación *f* minoritaria en las acciones; **minority shareholder** = accionista *mf* minoritario, -ria; **in the minority** = en la minoría; **the small parties are in the minority on the local council** = los pequeños partidos son una minoría en el concejo municipal

mint [mɪnt] *noun* casa *f* de la moneda

minute ['mɪnɪt] **1** *noun* **(a)** *(time)* minuto *m;* **counsel cross-examined the witness for fifty minutes** = el abogado interrogó a los testigos durante cincuenta minutos **(b)** *(in a meeting)* **minutes** = actas *fpl;* **to take the minutes** = redactar las actas *or* levantar acta; **the chairman signed the minutes of the last meeting** = el presidente firmó las actas de la última junta; **this will not appear in the minutes of the meeting** = esto no constará en las actas de la junta **(c)** *(court)* **minutes of order** = borrador *m* de una orden judicial **2** *verb* anotar *or* tomar nota de *or* levantar acta de; **the chairman's remarks about the auditors were minuted** = los comentarios del presidente sobre los auditores quedaron reflejados en el acta; **I do not want that to be minuted** *or* **I want that not to be minuted** = no quiero que esto conste en acta

◊ **minutebook** ['mɪnɪtbʊk] *noun* libro *m* de actas

misadventure [mɪsəd'ventʃə] *noun* accidente *m;* **death by misadventure** = muerte *f* accidental; **the coroner's verdict was death by misadventure** = el forense dictaminó muerte accidental

misappropriate [mɪsə'prəʊprɪeɪt] *verb* malversar *or* apropiarse indebidamente de *or* distraer fondos

◊ **misappropriation** [mɪsəprəʊpri'eɪʃn] *noun* malversación *f or* apropiación *f* indebida

misbehaviour [mɪsbɪ'heɪvjə] *noun* mala conducta *f or* mal comportamiento *m*

miscalculate [mɪs'kælkjuleɪt] *verb* calcular mal; **the salesman miscalculated the discount, so we hardly broke even on the deal** = el vendedor calculó mal el descuento, así que apenas cubrimos los gastos en la operación
◊ **miscalculation** [mɪskælkju'leɪʃn] *noun* error *m* de cálculo *or* cálculo *m* erróneo

miscarriage ['mɪskærɪdʒ] *noun* aborto *m* no provocado
◊ **miscarriage of justice** ['mɪskærɪdʒ əv 'dʒʌstɪs] *noun* error *m* judicial *or* perjuicio *m* de derechos

miscellaneous [mɪsə'leɪnɪəs] *adjective* misceláneo,-nea *or* vario, -ria *or* variado, -da *or* diverso, -sa; **miscellaneous items** = artículos varios; **a box of miscellaneous pieces of equipment** = una caja de piezas variadas; **miscellaneous expenditure** = gastos varios

misconduct [mɪs'kɒndʌkt] *noun* mala conducta *f or* conducta indebida *or* negligencia *f or* falta *f* de ética; **gross misconduct** = falta grave; **professional misconduct** = negligencia profesional; **wilful misconduct** = negligencia malintencionada *or* conducta malintencionada

miscount 1 ['mɪskaʊnt] *noun* error *m* de cálculo *or* de suma *or* cálculo *m* erróneo **2** [mɪs'kaʊnt] *verb* equivocarse en la cuenta *or* calcular mal; **the votes were miscounted, so the ballot had to be taken again** = se equivocaron al contar los votos, así que la votación tuvo que repetirse

misdeed [mɪs'diːd] *noun* delito *m*

misdemeanour [mɪsdɪ'miːnə] *noun* infracción *f or* delito *m* menor; **he was charged with several misdemeanours, including driving without a valid licence and creating a disturbance** = fue acusado de varias infracciones, entre ellas la de conducir sin permiso vigente y la de provocar disturbios

misdescription [mɪsdɪ'skrɪpʃn] *noun* falsa descripción *f*

misdirect [mɪsdaɪ'rekt] *verb* instruir mal (al jurado) *or* informar erróneamente
◊ **misdirection** [mɪsdɪ'rekʃn] *noun* malas instrucciones *fpl* (al jurado)

misfeasance [mɪs'fiːzəns] *noun* infidencia *f or* acto *m* legal realizado con un fin ilegal

misfortune [mɪs'fɔːtjuːn] *noun* desgracia *f*

misinterpret [mɪsɪn'təːprət] *verb* interpretar mal; **the rioters misinterpreted the instructions of the police** = los alborotadores interpretaron mal las instrucciones de la policía
◊ **misinterpretation** [mɪsɪntəːprɪ'teɪʃn] *noun* mala interpretación *f or* interpretación errónea;

clause which is open to misinterpretation = cláusula que se presta a una interpretación errónea

misjoinder [mɪs'dʒɔɪndə] *noun* unión *f* errónea *or* indebida

mislead [mɪs'liːd] *verb* equivocar *or* desorientar *or* engañar; **the instructions in the document are quite misleading** = las instrucciones del documento engañan; **the wording of the will is misleading and needs to be clarified** = el texto del testamento es desorientador y debe ser aclarado; **the judge misled the jury in his summing up** = el juez desorientó al jurado en su discurso final (NOTE: **misleading - misled**)

mismanage [mɪs'mænɪdʒ] *verb* administrar mal *or* dirigir mal
◊ **mismanagement** [mɪs'mænɪdʒmənt] *noun* mala administración *f or* mala dirección *f*; **the company failed because of the chairman's mismanagement** = la empresa fracasó a causa de la mala administración de su presidente

misprision [mɪs'prɪʒn] *noun* ocultación *f or* encubrimiento *m* (de un delito); **misprision of treason** = ocultación *or* encubrimiento de traición

misrepresent [mɪsreprɪ'zent] *verb* tergiversar *or* falsear *or* deformar los hechos
◊ **misrepresentation** [mɪsreprɪzen'teɪʃn] *noun* tergiversación *f or* desfiguración *f or* desnaturalización *f* con el fin de que alguien firme un contrato; **fraudulent misrepresentation** = falseamiento *m* con ánimo de fraude *or* tergiversación fraudulenta *or* engaño *m* para que alguien firme un contrato

mission ['mɪʃn] *noun* **(a)** *(special purpose)* misión *f*; **his mission was to try to persuade the rebels to accept the government's terms** = su misión era tratar de convencer a los rebeldes que aceptaran las condiciones del gobierno **(b)** *(group of people)* delegación *f*; **a trade mission to Japan** = una delegación comercial a Japón; **the members of the government mission are staying in the embassy** = los miembros de la delegación del gobierno se quedan en la embajada **(c)** *(embassy)* embajada *f*; **the crowd gathered outside the gates of the British Mission** = la multitud se concentró delante de la puerta de la embajada

mistake [mɪ'steɪk] *noun* error *m or* equivocación *f or* falta *f*; **to make a mistake** = cometer un error *or* equivocarse; **by mistake** = por equivocación *or* por error; **mistake in venue** = error de jurisdicción
◊ **mistaken identity** [mɪs'teɪkn aɪ'dentɪtɪ] *noun* identificación *f* errónea; **he was arrested for burglary, but released after it had been established that it was a case of mistaken identity** = fue arrestado por robo con allanamiento de morada y liberado después de establecerse que era un caso de identificación errónea

mistrial [mɪs'traɪəl] *noun* juicio *m* declarado nulo

misunderstanding [mɪsʌndə'stændɪŋ] *noun* desavenencia *f or* desacuerdo *m or* malentendido *m or* equívoco *m;* **there was a misunderstanding over my tickets** = hubo un malentendido con mis billetes *or* entradas

misuse ['mɪs'juːs] *noun* uso *m* indebido *or* abuso *m or* mal uso; **misuse of funds** *or* **of assets** = uso indebido de fondos *or* de activos *or* de bienes

mitigate ['mɪtɪgeɪt] *verb* mitigar *or* atenuar *or* aliviar *or* paliar; **mitigating circumstances** *or* **factors** = circunstancias *fpl or* factores *mpl* atenuantes; **to mitigate damages** *or* **loses** = mitigar los daños *or* las pérdidas
◊ **mitigation** [mɪtɪ'geɪʃn] *noun* atenuación *f or* mitigación *f;* **in mitigation, counsel submitted evidence of his client's work for charity** = para atenuar la pena, el abogado presentó pruebas del trabajo de su cliente para la beneficiencia; **defence counsel made a speech in mitigation** = el abogado defensor hizo un discurso para atenuar la pena; **plea in mitigation** = alegato *m* para atenuar la pena; **mitigation of damages** = mitigación de daños *or* minoración *f* de la indemnización de perjuicios (NOTE: used in the construction **in mitigation of**)

M'Naghten Rules [mək'nɔːtən 'ruːlz] *noun* reglamento *m* que aplica un juez al decidir si una persona acusada de un crimen está en su sano juicio o no

COMMENT: to prove insanity, it has to be shown that because of a diseased mind, the accused did not know what he was doing *or* did not know that his action was wrong. Based on the case of *R v. M'Naghten* (1843) in which the House of Lords considered and ruled on the defence of insanity

mob [mɒb] *noun US* la Mafia
◊ **mobster** ['mɒbstə] *noun US* miembro *mf* de la Mafia

modify ['mɒdɪfaɪ] *verb* modificar; **the chairman modified the reporting system** = el presidente modificó el sistema de elaboración de informes; **this is the new modified agreement** = éste es el nuevo acuerdo modificado; **the car will have to be modified to pass the government tests** = el coche tendrá que ser modificado para pasar las pruebas oficiales
◊ **modification** [mɒdɪfɪ'keɪʃn] *noun* modificación *f;* **to make** *or* **to carry out modifications to the plan** = realizar *or* llevar a cabo modificaciones del plan; **we asked for modifications to the contract** = pedimos que se modificara el contrato

modus operandi ['məʊdəs ɒpə'rændiː] *Latin phrase* procedimiento *m or* modo *m* de actuar de un criminal por el que se le puede identificar

modus vivendi ['məʊdəs vɪ'vendi] *Latin phrase* arreglo *m or* modo *m* de vivir; **after years of**

confrontation, they finally have achieved a modus vivendi = después de años de confrontación, finalmente llegaron a un acuerdo

MOH ['em 'əʊ 'eɪtʃ] = MEDICAL OFFICER OF HEALTH

moiety ['mɔɪəti] *noun* mitad *f*

molest [mə'lest] *verb* importunar sexualmente a alguien bajo amenazas *or* cometer abusos deshonestos; **he was accused of molesting children in the park** = se le acusó de cometer abusos deshonestos con niños en el parque
◊ **molestation** [məʊle'steɪʃn] *noun* abusos *mpl* deshonestos; **non-molestation order** = orden *f* judicial que prohíbe importunar sexualmente al cónyuge bajo amenazas
◊ **molester** [mə'lestə] *noun* persona *f* que comete abusos deshonestos con otra persona *or* que importuna sexualmente a otra persona; **a convicted child molester** = condenado por abusos deshonestos a niños

monetary ['mʌnɪtri] *adjective* monetario, -ria; **International Monetary Fund (IMF)** = Fondo Monetario Internacional (FMI); **European Monetary System (EMS)** = Sistema Monetario Europeo (SME); **monetary unit** = unidad monetaria

money ['mʌni] *noun* **(a)** *(coins and notes)* dinero *m or* moneda *f;* **cheap money** = dinero *or* crédito *m* barato; **danger money** = plus *m* de peligrosidad; **dear money** = dinero *or* crédito caro; **hot money** = dinero caliente; *(strong currency)* divisas *fpl* movidas para evitar una depreciación; *(from corruption)* dinero ilegal *or* dinero procedente de la corrupción; **paper money** = papel *m* moneda; **ready money** = efectivo *m or* dinero líquido; **money had and received** = objeto *m* de litigio por dinero encubierto *or* objeto de litigio en el que una de las partes tenía dinero que no le pertenecía **(b)** **money supply** = circulante *m or* oferta *f* monetaria; **money markets** = mercados *mpl* monetarios; **money rates** = tipos *mpl* de interés del dinero **(c)** **money order** = giro *m* postal; **foreign money order** *or* **international money order** *or* **overseas money order** = giro internacional **(d)** *(capital)* **monies** = sumas *fpl or* fondos *mpl or* capitales *mpl;* **monies owing to the company** = capital que se debe a la empresa; **to collect monies due** = recaudar fondos a nuestro favor
◊ **moneylender** ['mʌnilendə] *noun* prestamista *mf*

monitor ['mɒnɪtə] **1** *noun* monitor *m;* *(TV or computer screen)* pantalla *f* **2** *verb* controlar *or* comprobar; **they are monitoring the new system of dealing with young offenders** = están comprobando el nuevo sistema para resolver el problema de la delincuencia juvenil

monogamy [mə'nɒgəmi] *noun* monogamia *f*

monopoly [mə'nɒpəli] *noun* monopolio *m;* **to have the monopoly of alcohol sales** *or* **to have the alcohol monopoly** = tener el monopolio de las ventas de alcohol *or* el monopolio del alcohol; **the company has the absolute monopoly of imports of French wine** = la empresa tiene el monopolio absoluto de las importaciones de vino francés; **public monopoly** *or* **state monopoly** = monopolio estatal; **the Monopolies (and Mergers) Commission** = comisión *f* británica que evita la creación de monopolios por medio de adquisiciones o fusiones de empresas (NOTE: American English uses **trust** more often)
◊ **monopolist** [mə'nɒpəlɪst] *noun* acaparador, -ra
◊ **monopolize** [mə'nɒpəlaɪz] *verb* monopolizar *or* acaparar
◊ **monopolization** [mənɒpəlaɪ'zeɪʃn] *noun* monopolización *f*
◊ **monopolizing** [mə'nɒpəlaɪzɪŋ] *noun* acaparamiento *m*

monopsony [mə'nɒpsəni] *noun* monopsonio *m or* monopolio *m* de demanda

Monroe doctrine [mʌn'rəʊ 'dɒktrɪn] *noun US* doctrina *f* Monroe: principio por el cual a los EE UU les interesa evitar las intervenciones exteriores en los asuntos internos de otros estados americanos

COMMENT: so called because it was first proposed by President Monroe in 1823

monthly ['mʌnθli] *adjective* mensual; **she paid off the debt in monthly instalments** = pagó la deuda en plazos mensuales; **he was ordered to pay a sum of money to his wife monthly** = se le ordenó que pagara mensualmente un suma de dinero a su mujer

moonlight ['muːnlaɪt] *verb (informal)* practicar *or* ejercer el pluriempleo (en la economía sumergida)
◊ **moonlighter** ['muːnlaɪtə] *noun* pluriempleado, -da
◊ **moonlighting** ['muːnlaɪtɪŋ] *noun* pluriempleo *m;* **he makes thousands a year from moonlighting** = gana miles al año por medio del pluriempleo

mooring ['mʊərɪŋ] *noun* amarradero *m or* atracadero *m*

moot case ['muːt 'keɪs] *noun* causa *f* determinante *or* caso *m* práctico *or* discusión *f* académica

moral ['mɒrl] *adjective* moral; **the high moral standard which should be set by judges** = el alto nivel moral que debería ser fijado por los jueces
◊ **morals** ['mɒrlz] *plural noun* moral *f or* ética *f or* moralidad *f;* **to corrupt someone's morals** = corromper a alguien

moratorium [mɒrə'tɔːriəm] *noun* moratoria *f;* **the banks called for a moratorium on payments** = los bancos pidieron una moratoria en los pagos (NOTE: plural is **moratoria**)

morning hour ['mɔːnɪŋ 'haʊə] *noun US* periodo al inicio de cada sesión del Congreso dedicado a asuntos de trámite

mortality [mɔː'tælɪti] *noun* mortalidad *f;* **mortality tables** = tabla *f* de mortalidad

mortgage ['mɔːgɪdʒ] **1** *noun* hipoteca *f;* **to take out a mortgage on a house** = obtener una hipoteca sobre una casa *or* hipotecar una casa; **to buy a house with a £20,000 mortgage** = comprar una casa con una hipoteca de 20.000 libras; **mortgage (re)payments** = pagos *mpl* de una hipoteca; **endowment mortgage** = hipoteca avalada por una póliza de seguro total; **equitable mortgage** = hipoteca de equidad *or* no formalizada que nace con la entrega del dinero; **first mortgage** = primera hipoteca; **puisne mortgage** = hipoteca secundaria en la que la escritura de propiedad no se ha entregado al prestamista; **second mortgage** = segunda hipoteca; **to foreclose on a mortgaged property** = ejecutar la hipoteca de una propiedad; **to pay off a mortgage** = redimir una hipoteca; **mortgage bond** = cédula *f* hipotecaria; **mortgage debenture** = título *m* garantizado por hipoteca **2** *verb* hipotecar; **the house is mortgaged to the bank** = la casa está hipotecada al banco; **he mortgaged his house to set up in business** = hipotecó su casa para establecerse por cuenta propia
◊ **mortgagee** [mɔːgɪ'dʒiː] *noun* acreedor hipotecario *or* acreedora hipotecaria
◊ **mortgagor** [mɔːgɪ'dʒɔː] *noun* deudor hipotecario *or* deudora hipotecaria

mortem ['mɔːtəm] *see* POST MORTEM

mortis ['mɔːtɪs] *see* DONATIO, RIGOR

mortuary ['mɔːtjʊəri] *noun* depósito *m* de cadáveres *or* tanatorio *m*

most favoured nation ['məʊst 'feɪvəd 'neɪʃn] *noun* nación *f* más favorecida; **most-favoured-nation clause** = cláusula *f* de nación más favorecida

mother ['mʌðə] *noun* madre *f;* **mother-in-law** = suegra *f or* madre política; **surrogate mother** = madre portadora

motion ['məʊʃn] *noun* **(a)** *(moving about)* movimiento *m;* **time and motion study** = estudio *m* de desplazamientos y tiempos **(b)** *(proposal put to a meeting)* moción *f;* **to propose** *or* **to move a motion** = proponer una moción; **the meeting voted on the motion** = la junta votó la moción; **to speak against a motion** = criticar *or* hablar en contra de una moción; **to speak for a motion** = apoyar una moción; **the motion was carried** *or* **was defeated by 220 votes to 196** = la moción fue aprobada *or* rechazada por 220 votos contra 196; **to table a motion** = presentar una moción **(c)** *(application to a judge in court)* petición *f* de orden judicial; **notice of motion** = aviso *m* de petición *or* solicitud *f* al tribunal; **motion to vacate** = recurso *m* de casación; **motion for a new trial** = petición de nuevo juicio

motive ['məʊtɪv] *noun* motivo *m or* móvil *m;* **with a motive** = con motivo

mounted ['maʊntɪd] *adjective* montado, -da *or* a caballo; **mounted police were brought in to control the crowd** = se mandó llamar a la policía montada para controlar a la multitud
◊ **mounting** ['maʊntɪŋ] *adjective* creciente *or* que aumenta; **there is mounting pressure on the police to solve the murder *or* to combat inner city crime** = existe una presión creciente en la policía para resolver el crimen *or* para combatir la delincuencia en el centro de la ciudad

move [muːv] *verb* **(a)** *(from one place to another)* cambiar(se) *or* trasladar(se); **the company is moving from London Road to the centre of town** = la empresa se traslada de London Road al centro de la ciudad; **we have decided to move our factory to a site near the airport** = hemos decidido trasladar nuestra fábrica a un solar cerca del aeropuerto **(b)** *(a motion)* proponer; **he moved that the accounts be agreed** = propuso que se acordase el estado de cuentas; **I move that the meeting should adjourn for ten minutes** = propongo que se suspenda la reunión durante diez minutos **(c)** *(to make an application to the court)* solicitar (al tribunal)
◊ **movable** *or* **moveable** ['muːvəbl] **1** *adjective* movible *or* móvil *or* mueble; **movable property** = bienes *mpl* muebles **2** *plural noun* **movables** = bienes *mpl* muebles
◊ **movement** ['muːvmənt] *noun* **(a)** *(motion)* movimiento *m or* variación *f;* **movements in the money markets** = movimientos en los mercados monetarios; **cyclical movements of trade** = movimientos cíclicos del comercio; **movements of capital** = movimientos de capital; **free movement of capital** = libre circulación *f* de capital; **stock movements** = traslado *m* de mercancías **(b)** *(group of people working towards an aim)* movimiento
◊ **mover** ['muːvə] *noun* autor, -ra de una moción

MP ['em 'piː] = MEMBER OF PARLIAMENT, MILITARY POLICE

MR = MASTER OF THE ROLLS (NOTE: usually written after the surname: **Lord Smith, MR** but spoken as 'the Master of the Rolls, Lord Smith')

Mr Big ['mɪstə 'bɪg] *noun (informal)* delincuente *m* anónimo que supuestamente organiza una gran operación criminal

muddle ['mʌdl] *noun* lío *m;* **the witness got into a muddle** = el testigo se hizo un lío

mug [mʌg] **1** *noun (slang)* **(a)** *(person easily cheated)* primo, -ma **(b)** *(face)* cara *f or* jeta *f;* **mug shot** = fotografía *f* para los archivos policiales *or* fotografía de archivo para la ficha policial **2** *verb* asaltar *or* atracar; **the tourists were mugged in the station** = los turistas fueron atracados en la estación; **he was accused of mugging an old lady in the street** = se le acusó de atracar a una anciana en la calle (NOTE: **mugging - mugged**)
◊ **mugger** ['mʌgə] *noun* asaltador, -ra *or* atracador, -ra
◊ **mugging** ['mʌgɪŋ] *noun* asalto *m or* ataque *m* con robo; **the number of muggings has increased sharply over the last few years** = el número de asaltos ha aumentado bruscamente en los últimos años

multiple ['mʌltɪpl] *adjective* múltiple; **multiple entry visa** = visado *m* de entradas múltiples; **multiple ownership** = propiedad *f* conjunta

municipal [mjuːˈnɪsɪpl] *adjective* **(a)** *(town)* municipal; **municipal area** = término *m* municipal; **municipal taxes** = impuestos *mpl* municipales; **municipal offices** = oficinas *fpl* municipales *or* locales **(b) municipal law** = derecho *m* local
◊ **municipality** [mjuːnɪsɪˈpælɪti] *noun* municipio *m or* municipalidad *m*

muniments ['mjuːnɪmənts] *noun* escrituras *fpl* de propiedad

murder ['məːdə] **1** *noun* **(a)** *(offence)* asesinato *m or* homicidio *m;* **attempted murder** = homicidio frustrado; **he was charged with murder *or* he was found guilty of murder** = fue acusado de asesinato *or* se le declaró culpable de asesinato; **the murder rate has fallen over the last year** = el índice de homicidios ha bajado en el último año (NOTE: no plural in this meaning) **(b)** *(act of killing)* asesinato; **three murders have been committed during the last week** = se han cometido tres asesinatos durante la última semana; *see also* FIRST DEGREE, THIRD DEGREE **2** *verb* asesinar
◊ **murderer** ['məːdrə] *noun* asesino *m or* homicida *m*
◊ **murderess** ['məːdrəs] *noun* asesina *f* homicida *f*

Muslim ['mʌzləm] *adjective* musulmán, -ana

mutiny ['mjuːtɪni] **1** *noun* motín *m or* rebelión *f* **2** *verb* amotinarse *or* sublevarse *or* rebelarse
◊ **mutineer** [mjuːtɪˈnɪə] *noun* amotinador, -ra *or* amotinado, -da *or* rebelde *mf*

mutual ['mjuːtʃul] *adjective* mutuo, -tua; **mutual (insurance) company** = mutua *f* de seguros; *US* **mutual fund** = fondos *mpl* mutuos *or* mutualistas *mfpl* de inversión *or* sociedades *fpl* de inversión *or* mutualidad *f;* **mutual wills** = testamentos *mpl* mutuos *or* recíprocos
◊ **mutuality** [mjuːtʃuˈælɪti] *noun* mutualidad *f or* reciprocidad *f*

Nn

name [neim] **1** *noun* nombre *m;* **brand name** = marca *f* comercial *or* marca conocida; **corporate name** = razón *f* social *or* nombre comercial; **under the name of** = con el nombre de; **trading under the name of 'Best Foods'** = sus productos se venden con el nombre de 'Best Foods' **2** *verb* llamar *or* nombrar *or* mencionar; **the Chief Constable was named in the divorce case** = el jefe de policía fue mencionado en el caso de divorcio; **to name a Member of Parliament** = acusar a un diputado de prevaricación
◊ **named** [neimd] *adjective;* **person named in the policy** = beneficiario, -ria de la póliza

nark [nɑːk] *noun (slang)* soplón, -ona

nation [ˈneiʃn] *noun* nación *f*
◊ **national** [ˈnæʃnəl] **1** *adjective; (referring to a particular country)* nacional; **National Anthem** = Himno *m* Nacional; *GB* **National Audit Office** = Tribunal *m* de Cuentas; *GB* **National Insurance** = seguridad *f* social; *GB* **National Insurance contributions (NIC)** = cotizaciones *fpl* a la seguridad social; **gross national product (GNP)** = producto *m* nacional bruto (PNB); **net national product (NNP)** = producto nacional neto (PNN); **National Savings** = Caja *f* Postal de Ahorros **2** *noun (citizen of a state)* súbdito, -ta *or* ciudadano, -na; **foreign nationals** = súbditos extranjeros; **the government ordered the deportation of all foreign nationals** = el gobierno ordenó la deportación de todos los ciudadanos extranjeros
◊ **nationalism** [ˈnæʃnlɪzm] *noun* nacionalismo *m*
◊ **nationalist** [ˈnæʃnlɪst] *noun & adjective* nacionalista *mf*
◊ **nationality** [næʃəˈnæləti] *noun* nacionalidad *f;* **he is of British nationality** = es de nacionalidad británica; **he has dual nationality** = tiene doble nacionalidad
◊ **nationalize** [ˈnæʃnəlaɪz] *verb* nacionalizar
◊ **nationalized** [ˈnæʃnəlaɪzd] *adjective* nacionalizado, -da; **nationalized industry** = industria nacionalizada
◊ **nationalization** [næʃnəlaɪˈzeiʃn] *noun* nacionalización *f; compare* NATURALIZATION
◊ **nationwide** [ˈneiʃnwaɪd] *adjective* de ámbito nacional; **the union called for a nationwide strike** = el sindicato convocó una huelga a escala nacional

nature [ˈneitʃə] *noun* índole *f or* género *m or* clase *f or* tipo *m;* **what is the nature of the contents of the parcel?** = ¿qué clase de género contiene el paquete?; **the nature of his business is not known** = se desconoce el tipo de negocios a los que se dedica
◊ **natural** [ˈnætʃrl] *adjective* **(a)** *(found in the earth)* natural; **natural resources** = recursos *mpl* naturales **(b)** *(not man-made)* natural; **natural fibre** = fibra *f* natural **(c)** *(normal)* natural *or* normal; **natural child** = hijo, -ja natural; **natural justice** = justicia *f or* derecho *m* natural; **natural law** = ley *f or* derecho natural; **natural parents** = padres *mpl* naturales; **natural person** = persona *f* física; **natural right** = derecho natural; **natural wastage** = reducción *f* del número de trabajadores por jubilación o baja voluntaria
◊ **natural-born subject** [ˈnætʃrlˈbɔːn ˈsʌbdʒckt] *noun* (antiguamente) súbdito, -ta británico, -ca de nacimiento
◊ **naturalization** [nætʃrlaɪˈzeiʃn] *noun* naturalización *f or* (concesión *f* de la) ciudadanía *f;* **naturalization papers** = carta *f* de naturaleza; **she has applied for naturalization** = ha solicitado la ciudadanía; **you must fill in the naturalization papers** = debe rellenar la carta de ciudadanía *or* de naturaleza; *compare* NATIONALIZATION
◊ **naturalized** [ˈnætʃrlaɪzd] *adjective* naturalizado, -da *or* nacionalizado, -da; **he is a naturalized British citizen** = es un ciudadano británico nacionalizado

necessary [ˈnesəsri] *adjective* necesario, -ria; **where necessary** = en caso necesario; **it is necessary to fill in the form correctly** = es preciso rellenar el formulario debidamente; **you must have all the necessary documentation before you apply for a subsidy** = debe reunir la documentación necesaria antes de solicitar una ayuda
◊ **necessaries** [ˈnesəsriz] *plural noun* lo esencial *or* lo indispensable (para un niño o persona incapacitada)
◊ **necessarily** [ˈnesəsrəli] *adverb* necesariamente; **the imposition of a fine is not necessarily the only course open to the court** = la imposición de una multa no es necesariamente el único camino abierto al tribunal

◊ **necessity** [nəˈsesəti] *noun* **(a)** *(absolutely important)* requisito *m* indispensable; **the necessities of life** = los bienes de primera necesidad **(b)** *(state of need)* necesidad *f;* **of necessity** = por necesidad *or* forzosamente; **a judge must of necessity be impartial** = un juez debe ser forzosamente imparcial

negative [ˈnegətɪv] *adjective* negativo, -va; **the answer was in the negative** = la respuesta fue negativa; **the breathalyser test was negative** = la prueba del alcoholímetro dio negativa

neglect [nɪˈglekt] **1** *noun* **(a)** *(not doing a duty)* incumplimiento *m or* negligencia *f* **(b)** *(lack of care)* descuido *m or* abandono *m or* desatención *f;* **the children had suffered from neglect** = los niños habían sufrido abandono; **wilful neglect** = negligencia deliberada **2** *verb* **(a)** *(to fail to take care)* descuidar *or* desatender *or* abandonar; **he neglected his three children** = desatendió a sus tres hijos **(b)** *(to omit to do something)* **to neglect to do something** = olvidar hacer algo *or* dejar de hacer algo *or* no cumplir con algo; **he neglected to return his income tax form** = no envió el impreso de declaración de la renta
◊ **neglected** [nɪˈglektɪd] *adjective* descuidado, -da *or* abandonado, -da; **the local authority applied for a care order for the family of neglected children** = las autoridades locales solicitaron una orden de retirada de la patria potestad para la familia de los niños abandonados

negligence [ˈneglɪdʒəns] *noun* negligencia *f or* descuido *m or* imprevisión *f;* **contributory negligence** = negligencia concurrente; **criminal negligence** = culpa *f* penal *or* imprudencia *f;* **culpable negligence** = negligencia delictiva *or* culpable; **gross negligence** = imprudencia temeraria *or* culpa lata; **ordinary negligence** = culpa leve
◊ **negligent** [ˈneglɪdʒənt] *adjective* negligente *or* descuidado, -da; **negligent act** = omisión *f* dolosa; **the defendant was negligent in carrying out his duties as a trustee** = el demandado incurrió en conducta negligente al llevar a cabo sus obligaciones como fideicomisario
◊ **negligently** [ˈneglɪdʒəntli] *adverb* negligentemente *or* con descuido *or* descuidadamente; **the guardian acted negligently towards his ward** = el tutor actuó negligentemente *or* con negligencia hacia su pupilo
◊ **negligible** [ˈneglɪdʒəbl] *adjective* insignificante *or* despreciable *or* desdeñable; **not negligible** = nada despreciable

negotiable [nɪˈgəʊʃəbl] *adjective* negociable; *(words written on a cheque to show that it can be paid only to a certain person)* **'not negotiable'** = 'no negociable'; **negotiable cheque** = cheque *m* negociable; **negotiable instrument** = documento *m* negociable

◊ **negotiability** [nɪgəʊʃəˈbɪliti] *noun* negociabilidad *f or* posibilidad *f* de ser negociado
◊ **negotiate** [nɪˈgəʊʃieit] *verb* negociar *or* gestionar; **to negotiate with someone** = negociar con alguien; **the management refused to negotiate with the union** = la patronal se negó a negociar con el sindicato; **to negotiate terms and conditions** *or* **to negotiate a contract** = negociar los términos y las condiciones de un contrato *or* negociar un contrato; **negotiating committee** = comité *m* negociador *or* comisión *f* negociadora
◊ **negotiation** [nɪgəʊʃiˈeiʃn] *noun* negociación *f;* **contract under negotiation** = contrato *m* en negociación; **a matter for negotiation** = una cuestión *f* para ser negociada; **to enter into negotiations** *or* **to start negotiations** = entablar negociaciones; **to resume negotiations** = reanudar las negociaciones; **to break off negotiations** = interrumpir las negociaciones; **to conduct negotiations** = mantener *or* llevar a cabo negociaciones
◊ **negotiator** [nɪˈgəʊʃieitə] *noun* negociador, -ra

neighbour [ˈneibə] *noun* vecino, -na; **he was accused of setting fire to his neighbour's car** = se le acusó de incendiar el coche de su vecino; **she sued her next door neighbour for damages** = demandó al vecino de al lado por daños y perjuicios
◊ **neighbourhood** [ˈneibəhud] *noun* vecindad *f or* vecindario *m or* barrio *m;* **we live in a very quiet neighbourhood** = vivimos en un barrio muy tranquilo; **in the neighbourhood of** = cerca de *or* alrededor de; **the factory is in the neighbourhood of the prison** = la fábrica está cerca de la prisión; **neighbourhood watch** = sistema *m* de patrullas callejeras formadas por los propios vecinos
◊ **neighbouring** [ˈneibərɪŋ] *adjective* vecino, -na *or* cercano, -na; **he lives in the neighbouring street** = vive en la calle vecina; **the factory is in the neighbouring town** = la fábrica está en la ciudad vecina

nemine contradicente *or* **nem con** [ˈnemineɪ ˌpʊntrædiˈsenteɪ *or* ˈnem ˈkɒn] *Latin phrase meaning* 'por unanimidad' *or* 'unánimemente'; **the motion was adopted nem con** = la moción fue aprobada por unanimidad

nemo dat quod non habet [ˈneiməu dæt kwɒd nɒn ˈhæbet] *Latin phrase meaning* 'nadie puede dar lo que no tiene': reglamento *m* por el que ninguna persona puede dar o vender a otra persona una cosa a la que no tiene derecho (como objetos robados)

neo- [ˈniəu] *prefix* neo; **a neo-fascist movement** = un movimiento neofascista; **a neo-Nazi organization** = una organización neonazi *or* neonazista; **neocolonialism** = neocolonialismo *m*

net *or* **nett** [net] *adjective & adverb* neto, -ta; **the company's net profit was £10,000** = la compañía obtuvo un beneficio neto de 10.000 libras; **net**

earnings *or* net income = ganancias netas *or* ingresos netos; **net salary** = salario *or* sueldo neto; **net estate** = activo neto relicto; **net gain** = ganancia neta; **the government lost twenty seats and gained thirty one, making a net gain of eleven** = el gobierno perdió veinte escaños y ganó treinta y uno, lo cual supuso una ganancia neta de once escaños NOTE: opposite is **gross**

neutral ['njutrəl] 1 *adjective* **(a)** *(not taking sides)* neutral; **the conference agreed to refer the dispute to a neutral power** = el congreso acordó someter la disputa a un poder neutral; **the UN sent in neutral observers to observe the elections** = la ONU envió a observadores neutrales para que observaran las elecciones **(b)** *(country)* neutral; **during the Second World War, Switzerland and Sweden remained neutral** = Suiza y Suecia permanecieron neutrales durante la Segunda Guerra Mundial; **the navy was accused of having attacked neutral shipping** = acusaron a la marina de atacar embarcaciones neutrales; **neutral states in the area have tried to bring an end to the war** = los estados neutrales de la zona han intentado poner fin a la guerra 2 *noun* país neutral
◊ **neutralism** *noun* neutralismo *m*
◊ **neutrality** [nju'træliti] *noun* neutralidad *f*; **armed neutrality** = neutralidad armada

new [nju:] *adjective* nuevo, -va; **under new management** = cambio *m* de dirección *or* de dueño; **new for old policy** = póliza *f* de seguros que permite reemplazar con artículos nuevos los usados; **new issue** = nueva emisión; **new trial** = nuevo juicio *m*
◊ **news** [nju:z] *noun* noticia *f or* noticias *fpl*; **news agency** = agencia *f* de información *or* de prensa; **news release** = comunicado *m* de prensa

next ['nekst] *adjective & adverb* **(a)** *(order)* próximo, -ma *or* siguiente; **on Wednesday he arrived in London and the next day tried to assassinate the Prime Minister** = llegó a Londres el miércoles y el día siguiente intentó asesinar al Primer Ministro; **the first case this morning was one of murder, the next of attempted murder** = el primer caso de esta mañana fue de asesinato, el siguiente de intento de asesinato; **the court's next decision was judged to be unconstitutional** = la siguiente decisión del tribunal se consideró inconstitucional **(b)** *(neighbouring)* vecino, -na *or* (de) al lado (de); **the trial was adjourned to the next courtroom** = el juicio fue trasladado a la sala vecina; **the plaintiff sat next to his solicitor** = el demandante se sentó al lado de su abogado
◊ **next friend** ['nekst 'frend] *noun* persona *f* que entabla una demanda en favor de un menor
◊ **next of kin** ['nekst əv 'kin] *noun* pariente *mf* más cercano *or* vínculo *m* de consanguinidad; **his only next of kin is an aunt living in Scotland** = su único pariente es una tía que vive en Escocia; **the police have informed the next of kin of the**

people killed in the accident = la policía ha informado a los parientes más cercanos de las personas muertas en el accidente (NOTE: can be singular or plural)

nick [nik] *(slang)* 1 *noun* chirona *f or* trena *f* 2 *verb* **(a)** *(steal)* birlar **(b)** *(arrest)* pillar *or* pescar *or* coger

nil [nil] *noun* cero *m or* nada *f*; **to make a nil return** = declarar un rendimiento nulo

nisi ['naisai] *see* DECREE, FORECLOSURE

NNP = NET NATIONAL PRODUCT

nobble ['nɒbl] *verb (slang)* sobornar *or* ejercer presión sobre; **he tried to nobble one of the jurors** = intentó sobornar a uno de los miembros del jurado

nobody ['nəubədi] *pronoun* nadie; **there was nobody** = no había nadie

no-claims bonus ['nəu'kleimz 'bəunəs] *noun* bonificación *f* por ausencia de indemnizaciones en una póliza de seguros

nod [nɒd] *verb* asentir con la cabeza; **when the chairman asked him if he would head the subcommittee, the treasurer nodded** = cuando el presidente le pidió si podía dirigir el subcomité, el tesorero asintió con la cabeza; **the proposal went through on the nod** = la propuesta fue aprobada sin debate ni votación; *(Houses of Parliament)* **to nod through** = registrar el voto de un diputado

nolle prosequi ['nɒli 'prɒsikwai] *Latin phrase meaning* 'no prosiga': suspensión *f* de causa a petición del Fiscal de la Corona

nominal ['nɒminl] *adjective* **(a)** *(very small payment)* simbólico, -ca *or* nominal; **we make a nominal charge for our services** = cobramos un precio simbólico por nuestros servicios; **they are paying a nominal rent** = pagan un alquiler nominal *or* una renta simbólica; **nominal damages** = daños *mpl* poco importantes *or* no relevantes **(b)** **nominal capital** = capital *m* nominal; **nominal value** = valor *m* nominal

nominate ['nɒmineit] *verb* nombrar *or* designar *or* proponer la candidatura de; **to nominate a candidate** *or* **to nominate someone to a post** = proponer a un candidato *or* nombrar a alguien para un puesto; **to nominate someone as proxy** = dar poderes a alguien *or* nombrar a alguien apoderado *or* representante
◊ **nomination** [nɒmi'neiʃn] *noun* designación *f or* nombramiento *m*
◊ **nominee** [nɒmi'ni:] *noun* candidato, -ta *or* nominatario, -ria; **nominee account** = cuenta *f* administrada por un apoderado; **nominee shareholder** = accionista *mf* tenedor de acciones pero no propietario real de las mismas

COMMENT: in the UK, a person who is nominated as a candidate for local or national elections, has to have the signatures of local residents as his sponsors, and (in the case of national elections) has to deposit a sum of money which he forfeits if he does not poll enough votes. In the United States, the executive (i.e. the President) nominates people to federal offices such as members of the Supreme Court or the cabinet, but these nominations are subject to confirmation by the Senate. Most nominations are accepted without discussion, but some are debated, and some are not confirmed. If the executive nominates someone to a federal post in one of the states without consulting the senators for that state, they can object to the nominee by saying that he is 'personally obnoxious' to them

non- [nɒn] *prefix* no

◊ **non-acceptance** [ˈnɒnəkˈseptəns] *noun* no aceptación ƒ *or* rechazo *m* de una letra de cambio

◊ **non-arrestable offence** [ˈnɒnəˈrestəbl əˈfens] *noun* delito *m* sin prisión preventiva (con una pena de hasta 5 años de prisión)

◊ **non-bailable** [ˈnɒnˈbeɪləbl] *adjective* no caucionable

◊ **non-capital crime** *or* **offence** [ˈnɒnˈkæpɪtl ˈkraɪm *or* əˈfens] *noun* delito *m* no capital

◊ **non compos mentis** [ˈnɒn ˈkɒmpəs ˈmentɪs] *Latin phrase* demente *mf*

◊ **non-conformance** [ˈnɒnkənˈfɔːməns] *noun* disconformidad ƒ *or* no conformidad ƒ; **he was criticized for non-conformance with the regulations** = fue criticado por falta de conformidad a la normativa

◊ **non-consummation** [ˈnɒnkɒnsəˈmeɪʃn] *noun* **non-consummation of marriage** = matrimonio *m* sin consumar *or* no consumado

◊ **non-contributory** [ˈnɒnkənˈtrɪbjutri] *adjective;* **non-contributory pension scheme** = plan *m* de pensiones sin aportación del trabajador

◊ **non-direction** [ˈnɒndaɪˈrekʃn] *noun (of a judge)* no dar suficientes instrucciones a un jurado

◊ **non-disclosure** [ˈnɒndɪsˈkləʊʒə] *noun* omisión ƒ del deber de revelar datos o información

◊ **non-executive director** [ˈnɒnɪgˈzekjutɪv dɪˈrektə] *noun* director, -ra sin poderes ejecutivos

◊ **nonfeasance** [nɒnˈfiːzəns] *noun* delito *m* por omisión *or* incumplimiento *m*

◊ **non-intervention** [ˈnɒnɪntəˈvenʃn] *adjective;* **non-intervention policy** = política ƒ de no intervención

◊ **nonjoinder** [nɒnˈdʒɔɪndə] *noun* falta ƒ de unión *or* de asociación entre las partes necesarias para la causa del demandante

◊ **non-molestation order** [ˈnɒnmɒləsˈteɪʃn ˈɔːdə] *noun* orden ƒ judicial que prohíbe importunar sexualmente al cónyuge bajo amenazas

◊ **non-negotiable instrument** [ˈnɒnnɪˈgəʊʃəbl ˈɪnstrəmənt] *noun* documento *m* no negociable

◊ **non-payment** [ˈnɒnˈpeɪmənt] *noun* **non-payment of a debt** = impago *m* de una deuda *or* deuda ƒ impagada

◊ **non profit-making organization** *or US* **non-profit corporation** [ˈnɒnˈprɒfitmeɪkɪŋ ɔːgənaɪˈzeɪʃn] *noun* organización ƒ no lucrativa *or* sin fines de lucro

◊ **non-recurring items** [ˈnɒnrɪˈkʌrɪŋ ˈaɪtəmz] *noun* partidas ƒpl extraordinarias

◊ **non-refundable** [ˈnɒnrɪˈfʌndəbl] *adjective* no reembolsable

◊ **non-resident** [ˈnɒnˈrezɪdənt] *noun* no residente *mf*

◊ **non-returnable** [ˈnɒnrɪˈtɜːnəbl] *adjective* sin devolución ƒ *or* de usar y tirar; **non-returnable packing** = envase *m* no retornable *or* desechable

◊ **non-stop** [nɒnˈstɒp] *adverb* sin parar

◊ **nonsufficient funds** [ˈnɒnsəˈfɪʃənt ˈfʌndz] *noun US* falta ƒ de fondos

◊ **nonsuit** *or* **nonsuited** [ˈnɒnsuːt *or* nɒnˈsuːtɪd] *adjective; (in civil proceedings)* **to be nonsuit** *or* **nonsuited** = desestimación ƒ *or* denegación ƒ *or* sobreseimiento *m or; (in criminal proceedings)* situación ƒ en un proceso penal en la que el juez instruye al jurado para que absuelva al acusado

◊ **non-taxable** [ˈnɒnˈtæksəbl] *adjective* libre *or* exento, -ta de impuestos *or* no imponible

◊ **non-voting shares** [ˈnɒnˈvəʊtɪŋ ˈʃeəz] *plural noun* acciones ƒpl sin derecho a voto

North-Eastern Circuit, Northern Circuit [ˈnɔːθˈiːstən *or* ˈnɔːðən ˈsɜːkɪt] *noun* distrito *m* del Noroeste, distrito del Norte: dos de los distritos (*or* jurisdicciones) del tribunal de la Corona al que pertenecen los abogados, con sedes en Leeds y Manchester

noscitur a sociis [ˈnɒskɪtə ɑː ˈsəʊsiis] *Latin phrase meaning* el significado de palabras *or* frases ambiguas se puede aclarar por referencia al contexto en el que éstas son utilizadas

notary public [ˈnəʊtəri ˈpʌblɪk] *noun* notario *mf* *(NOTE: plural is* notaries public)

◊ **notarial** [nəʊˈteəriəl] *adjective* notarial; **notarial act** = acta ƒ notarial

◊ **notarization** [nəʊtəraɪˈzeɪʃn] *noun* atestación ƒ por notario público

note [nəʊt] **1** *noun* **(a)** *(short document)* nota ƒ *or* aviso *m;* **advice note** = aviso de expedición *or* de envío; **contract note** = nota de compraventa de acciones; **cover note** = póliza ƒ provisional *or* nota de cobertura; **covering note** = carta ƒ adjunta *or* explicatoria; **credit note** = aviso *or* nota de abono *or* de crédito; **debit note** = nota de cargo *or* débito; **note of costs** = nota *or* factura ƒ; **note of hand** *or* **promissory note** = pagaré *m* *or* letra ƒ al propio cargo **(b)** *(short letter)* nota; **the foreman of the jury passed a note to the judge** = el presidente del jurado le pasó una nota al juez; **to make a note of something** = tomar nota de *or* apuntar algo; **to take notes of a meeting** = tomar notas *or* apuntes de una reunión **(c) to take note of something** = tomar nota de algo *or* tener muy en cuenta; **the jury was asked to take note of the evidence given by the**

pathologist = se pidió al jurado que tomara nota de las pruebas aportadas por el patólogo **(d) bank note** *or* **currency note** = billete *m* de banco **2** *verb* **(a)** *(to pay attention to something)* fijarse en *or* observar *or* tener en cuenta; **members of the jury will note that the defendant does not say he was at home on the night of the crime** = los miembros del jurado tendrán en cuenta que el acusado no dice que estaba en casa la noche del crimen **(b)** *(to write down details)* anotar *or* apuntar *or* tomar nota de *or* hacer constar; **the policeman noted the number of the car in his notebook** = el policía apuntó el número del coche en su libreta; **your complaint has been noted** = se ha tomado nota de su reclamación **(c) to note a bill** = protestar una letra (de cambio)

◊ **notebook** ['nəʊtbʊk] *noun* cuaderno *m or* libreta *f*

◊ **notepad** ['nəʊtpæd] *noun* bloc *m* de notas

not-for-profit corporation ['nɒtfə'prɒfɪt kɔːpə'reɪʃn] *US* = NON-PROFIT CORPORATION

nothing ['nʌθɪŋ] *pronoun* nada; **she said nothing** = no dijo nada

notice ['nəʊtɪs] **1** *noun* **(a)** *(piece of written information)* anuncio *m or* letrero *m or* cartel *m;* **the company secretary pinned up a notice about the pension scheme** = la secretaria de la empresa puso un anuncio sobre el plan de pensiones en el tablón; **copyright notice** = nota *f* sobre los derechos de autor **(b)** *(official passing of information to someone)* aviso *m or* notificación *f;* **to give someone notice** *or* **to serve notice on someone** = entregar *or* dar un aviso a alguien; **to give a tenant notice to quit** *or* **to serve a tenant with notice to quit** = darle a un inquilino el aviso de que se marche *or* darle la notificación de desahucio *or* desalojo; **she has handed in** *or* **given her notice** = presentó su dimisión; **period of notice** = periodo *m* de notificación (de despido *or* de dimisión) *or* periodo de previso; **notice of motion** = notificación *f* de petición o de solicitud al tribunal (dirigida a la parte demandada); **to give notice of appeal** = notificar una apelación *or* iniciar los trámites oficiales para la presentación de una apelación; **notice of opposition** = no aceptación de una solicitud de patente; **strike notice** = aviso de huelga; **without notice** = sin previo aviso **(c)** *(time allowed before something takes place)* **until further notice** = hasta nuevo aviso; **at short notice** = con poco tiempo de antelación *or* con poca anticipación; **you must give seven days' notice of withdrawal** = tiene que dar un plazo de siete días para sacar dinero **(d)** *(knowledge of a fact)* conocimiento *m;* **actual notice** = conocimiento real; **constructive notice** = conocimiento sobre un hecho que la ley da por sentado que una persona posee *or* puede poseer; **judicial notice** = conocimiento judicial **2** *verb* fijarse

◊ **noticeboard** ['nəʊtɪsbɔːd] *noun* tablón *m* de anuncios; **the list of electors is put up on the noticeboard in the local offices** = la lista de electores se coloca en el tablón de anuncios de las oficinas municipales

notify ['nəʊtɪfaɪ] *verb* notificar *or* avisar; **to notify someone of something** = comunicar algo a alguien; **they were notified of the impending court action** = se les notificó el inminente proceso judicial

◊ **notifiable** [nəʊtɪ'faɪəbl] *adjective* de declaración obligatoria *or* que hay que declarar a las autoridades; **notifiable offence** = delito *m* grave (que puede ser juzgado en el tribunal de la Corona)

◊ **notification** [nəʊtɪfɪ'keɪʃn] *noun* notificación *f or* aviso *m*

not proven ['nɒt 'pruːvn] *adjective; (in Scotland)* (veredicto *m*) sin probar *or* de absolución por falta de pruebas

notwithstanding [nɒtwɪθ'stændɪŋ] *adverb & preposition* sin embargo *or* no obstante *or* a pesar de; **the case proceeded notwithstanding the objections of the defendant** *or* **the defendant's objections notwithstanding** = el juicio prosiguió a pesar de las objeciones del acusado (NOTE: can be used before or after the phrase)

novation [nəʊ'veɪʃn] *noun* novación *f*

now [naʊ] *adverb* ahora

noxious ['nɒkʃəs] *adjective* nocivo, -va *or* perjudicial *or* dañino, -na; **noxious substance** = sustancia nociva; **noxious smell** = olor *m* perjudicial

NSF ['en 'es 'ef] *US* = NONSUFFICIENT FUNDS

nuisance ['njuːsəns] *noun* perjuicio *m or* daño *m;* **public nuisance** *or* **common nuisance** = daño *or* perjuicio público *or* molestia *f* pública; **private nuisance** = daño particular *or* perjuicio privado

null [nʌl] *adjective* nulo, -la; **the contract was declared null and void** = el contrato fue declarado nulo y sin valor; **to render a decision null** = anular un fallo *or* una decisión

◊ **nullification** [nʌlɪfɪ'keɪʃn] *noun* anulación *f*

◊ **nullify** ['nʌlɪfaɪ] *verb* anular

◊ **nullity** ['nʌlɪti] *noun* nulidad *f*

Number Ten ['nʌmbə 'ten] *noun GB* Núm.10 de Downing Street, la residencia oficial del Primer Ministro; **he is hoping to move into Number 10 after the election** = espera trasladarse al Núm.10 de Downing Street tras las elecciones; **the plan was turned down by Number Ten** = el proyecto fue rechazado por el gobierno; **sources close to Number Ten say that the cabinet is close to agreement on the draft legislation** = según fuentes oficiales, el gobierno está a punto de llegar a un acuerdo sobre el proyecto de legislación; **it is rumoured that Number Ten was annoyed at the**

story = se rumorea que la historia irritó al gobierno (NOTE: used to refer to the Prime Minister or the government in general)

numeric *or* **numerical** [nju'merɪkl] *adjective* numérico, -ca; **numerical order** = orden numérico;

the documents are filed in numerical order = los documentos están archivados por orden numérico

nuncio ['nʌnsiəʊ] *noun* nuncio *m;* **Papal Nuncio** = nuncio apostólico

nuncupative will ['nʌnkjupətɪv 'wɪl] *noun* testamento abierto *or* última voluntad ante testigos (formalizada posteriormente)

Oo

OAP ['ɔʊ 'cɪ 'piː] = OLD AGE PENSIONER

oath [ɔʊθ] *noun* juramento *m;* **taking an oath** = prestación *f* de juramento; **he was on oath** *or* **under oath** = estaba bajo juramento *or* había prestado juramento; **to administer an oath to someone** = tomar juramento a alguien; **commissioner for oaths** = notario público

obey [ɔ'beɪ] *verb* obedecer *or* cumplir; **the crowd refused to obey the police instructions** = la multitud se negó a obedecer las órdenes de la policía; **he was asked to give an undertaking that he would obey the court order** = se le pidió que diera su promesa de que cumpliría la orden judicial
◊ **obedience** [ɔ'biːdɪəns] *noun* obediencia *f;* **the army swore obedience to the president** = el ejército juró obediencia al presidente; **every citizen should show obedience to the laws of the state** = todo ciudadano debería mostrar obediencia a las leyes del estado

obiter dicta ['ɒbɪtə 'dɪktə] *Latin phrase* juicio *m or* opinión *f* no vinculante; *see also* RATIO DECIDENDI (NOTE: the singular is **obiter dictum**)

object 1 ['ɒbdʒɪkt] *noun* propósito *m or* objeto *m or* fin *m;* **objects clause** = cláusula *f* sobre el propósito de una empresa **2** [ɔb'dʒɛkt] *verb* oponerse *or* objetar; **to object to a clause in a contract** = oponerse a una cláusula de un contrato; **to object to a juror** = objetar a un jurado (NOTE: you object **to** something or someone)
◊ **objection** [ɔb'dʒɛkʃn] *noun* impugnación *f;* **objection to a judge** *or* **to a jury** = impugnación de un juez *or* de un jurado; **to raise an objection to something** = poner reparos a algo *or* hacer objeciones a algo; **the union delegates raised an objection to the wording of the agreement** = los delegados del sindicato pusieron reparos al texto del acuerdo

objective [ɔb'dʒɛktɪv] **1** *noun* objetivo *m;* **long-term objective** *or* **short-term objective** = objetivo a largo plazo *or* a corto plazo; **management by objectives** = dirección *f* por objetivos **2** *adjective* objetivo, -va; **the judge asked the jury to be objective in considering the evidence put before them** = el juez pidió al jurado que fuera objetivo al considerar las pruebas que se le presentaban; **you must be objective in assessing the performance of the staff** = debe ser objetivo al evaluar la actuación del personal; **to carry out an objective review of current legislation** = llevar a cabo una revisión objetiva de la legislación actual

obligate ['ɒblɪgɪt] *verb especially US* **to be obligated to do something** = estar obligado a hacer algo
◊ **obligation** [ɒblɪ'geɪʃn] *noun* **(a)** *(duty)* obligación *f or* compromiso *m;* **legal obligation** = obligación legal; **to be under an obligation to do something** = tener la obligación de hacer algo *or* verse en la obligación de hacer algo; **he is under no contractual obligation to buy** = no tiene obligación contractual de comprar; **to fulfil one's contractual obligations** = cumplir sus obligaciones contractuales *or* cumplir con las obligaciones contractuales; **two weeks' free trial without obligation** = periodo *m* de prueba de dos semanas sin compromiso de compra **(b)** *(debt)* deuda *f;* **to meet one's obligations** = saldar las deudas
◊ **obligatory** [ɔ'blɪgətri] *adjective* obligatorio, -ria; **each person has to pass an obligatory medical examination** = todas las personas deben pasar un examen médico obligatorio
◊ **oblige** [ɒb'laɪdʒ] *verb* obligar *or* forzar *or* apremiar; **to oblige someone to do something** = obligar a alguien a hacer algo; **he felt obliged to cancel the contract** = se vio *or* se sintió obligado a anular el contrato
◊ **obligee** [ɒblɪ'dʒiː] *noun* acreedor, -ra
◊ **obligor** [ɒblɪ'gɔː] *noun* deudor, -ra

obscene [ɔb'siːn] *adjective* obsceno, -na *or* indecente *or* pornográfico, -ca; **the magazine was classed as an obscene publication** = la revista fue clasificada como publicación obscena; **the police seized a number of obscene films** = la policía se incautó de una serie de películas pornográficas
◊ **obscenity** [ɔb'sɛnɪti] *noun* obscenidad *f or* indecencia *f;* **the magistrate commented on the obscenity of some parts of the film** = el magistrado comentó la obscenidad de algunas partes de la película; **obscenity laws** = leyes *fpl* referentes a publicaciones *or* películas pornográficas

observe [ɔb'zɔːv] *verb* **(a)** *(to obey a rule or law)* cumplir *or* observar; **failure to observe the correct

procedure = incumplimiento *m* del procedimiento correcto; **all members of the association should observe the code of practice** = todos los miembros de la asociación deben cumplir el reglamento de régimen interno **(b)** *(to watch or to notice)* observar *or* notar; **officials have been instructed to observe the conduct of the election** = se les ha pedido a los funcionarios que observen cómo se desarrollan las elecciones
◊ **observance** [əb'zɔːvəns] *noun* observancia *f or* cumplimiento *m or* acatamiento *m;* **the government's observance of international agreements** = el cumplimiento por parte del gobierno de los acuerdos internacionales
◊ **observation** [ɒbzə'veɪʃn] *noun* **(a)** *(noticing what is happening)* observación *f* **(b)** *(remark)* observación *or* comentario *m;* **the judge made some observations about the conduct of the accused during the trial** = el juez hizo algunas observaciones sobre la conducta del acusado durante el juicio
◊ **observer** [əb'zɔːvə] *noun* observador, -ra; **two official observers attended the meeting** = a la reunión asistieron dos observadores oficiales

obsolete ['ɒbsəliːt] *adjective* anticuado, -da *or* obsoleto, -ta; **the law has been made obsolete by new developments in forensic science** = la ley ha quedado anticuada a causa de los nuevos adelantos en la ciencia forense

obstruct [əb'strʌkt] *verb* obstruir *or* estorbar *or* obstaculizar *or* poner trabas; **the parked cars are obstructing the traffic** = los coches aparcados obstruyen el tráfico; **obstructing the police** = obstaculizar la labor de la policía
◊ **obstruction** [əb'strʌkʃn] *noun* **(a)** *(thing which gets in the way)* obstáculo *m or* estorbo *m or* obstrucción *f;* **the car caused an obstruction to the traffic** = el coche causó una obstrucción del tráfico **(b)** *(act of obstructing)* obstrucción; **obstruction of the police** = obstaculizar la labor de la policía

obtain [əb'teɪn] *verb* **(a)** *(to get)* conseguir *or* obtener *or* lograr; **to obtain supplies from abroad** = obtener suministros del extranjero; **we find these items very difficult to obtain** = nos resulta muy difícil conseguir estos artículos; **to obtain an injunction against a company** = obtener un requerimiento contra una compañía; **he obtained control by buying the family shareholding** = consiguió el control comprando las acciones pertenecientes a la familia; **obtaining by deception** = obtener (dinero *or* propiedades) por estafa; **obtaining credit** = delito *m* por el que un quebrado no rehabilitado consigue un crédito de más de 50 libras; **to obtain a property by fraud** *or* **by deception** = conseguir una propiedad por medio del fraude *or* de la estafa; **obtaining a pecuniary advantage by deception** = obtener ventajas económicas por estafa **(b)** *(to have legal status)* regir; **this right does not obtain in judicial proceedings** = este derecho no rige en procesos judiciales; **a rule obtaining in international law** = una norma que rige en el derecho internacional
◊ **obtainable** [əb'teɪnəbl] *adjective* obtenible *or* que se puede conseguir *or* obtener; **prices fall when raw materials are easily obtainable** = los precios bajan cuando las materias primas son fáciles de conseguir; **our products are obtainable in all computer shops** = nuestros productos se pueden adquirir en todas las tiendas de material informático

occasion [ə'keɪʒn] **1** *noun* ocasión *f or* momento *m;* **the opening of the trial was the occasion of protests by the family of the accused** = el comienzo del juicio provocó protestas por parte de la familia del acusado **2** *verb* ocasionar *or* causar *or* provocar; **he pleaded guilty to assault occasioning actual bodily harm** = se declaró culpable de agresión ocasionando lesiones a la persona
◊ **occasional** [ə'keɪʒnl] *adjective* ocasional *or* que ocurre de vez en cuando; **occasional licence** = licencia *f* eventual (para vender alcohol en determinado lugar y a determinada hora)
◊ **occasionally** [ə'keɪʒnli] *adverb* de vez en cuando *or* ocasionalmente; **he admitted that he occasionally visited the house** = admitió que de vez en cuando visitaba la casa

occupancy ['ɒkjupənsi] *noun* **(a)** *(of building)* ocupación *f or* tenencia *f;* **with immediate occupancy** = de ocupación inmediata **(b)** *(of property)* ocupación de una propiedad sin dueño para adquirir derecho sobre ella
◊ **occupant** ['ɒkjupənt] *noun* ocupante *mf; (of a house)* inquilino, -na *or* habitante *mf*
◊ **occupation** [ɒkju'peɪʃn] *noun* **(a)** occupation of a building = ocupación de un edificio **(b)** *(job or work)* ocupación *f or* profesión *f;* **what is her occupation?** = ¿cuál es su profesión?; **his main occupation is house building** = su principal ocupación es la construcción de casas; **occupations** = tareas *fpl or* trabajos *mpl;* **people in professional occupations** = profesionales *mfpl*
◊ **occupational** [ɒkju'peɪʃnl] *adjective* profesional *or* laboral; **occupational accident** = accidente *m* laboral *or* de trabajo; **occupational disease** = enfermedad *f* profesional; **occupational hazards** = riesgos *mpl* laborales *or* gajes *mpl* del oficio; **occupational pension scheme** = plan *m* de pensiones de la empresa
◊ **occupier** ['ɒkjupaɪə] *noun* ocupante *mf or* inquilino, -na; **beneficial occupier** = usufructuario, -ria; **occupier's liability** = responsabilidad *f* del inquilino de que los visitantes no sufran daños; **owner-occupier** = ocupante y dueño *m* de una propiedad

COMMENT: the occupier has the right to stay in or on a property, but is not necessarily an owner

◊ **occupy** [ˈɒkjupaɪ] *verb* **(a)** *(to live in a property)* ocupar *or* vivir en; **all the rooms in the hotel are occupied** = todas las habitaciones del hotel están ocupadas; **the company occupies three floors of an office block** = la empresa ocupa tres pisos de un edificio de oficinas **(b)** *(to enter and stay in a property illegally)* ocupar (ilegalmente *or* por la fuerza); **the rebels occupied the Post Office** = los rebeldes ocuparon la oficina de Correos; **squatters are occupying the building** = el edificio está siendo ocupado ilegalmente por okupas **(c) to occupy a post** = ocupar un puesto

occur [əˈkɜː] *verb* ocurrir *or* producirse *or* tener lugar; **the witness described how the argument occurred** = el testigo narró cómo se produjo la discusión; **no infringements have occurred since the court order was made** = no se han producido infracciones desde que se dictó la orden judicial

off [ɒf] **1** *adverb* **(a)** *(cancelled)* suspendido, -da *or* cancelado, -da *or* desconectado, -da; **the agreement is off** = el acuerdo ha sido cancelado; **they called the strike off** = suspendieron la huelga **(b)** *(reduced by)* con descuento *or* descontado, -da; **these carpets are sold at £25 off the marked price** = estas alfombras se venden con un descuento de 25 libras sobre el precio marcado; **we give 5% off for quick settlement** = descontamos un 5% por pronto pago **2** *preposition* **(a)** *(discount)* (de) descuento del precio; **to take £25 off the price** = descontar 25 libras del precio; **we give 10% off our normal prices** = ofrecemos un descuento del 10% sobre nuestros precios normales **(b)** *(away from work)* ausente *or* fuera del trabajo; **to take time off work** = tomarse tiempo libre durante el trabajo; **to take three days off** = tomarse tres días libres; **we give the staff four days off at Christmas** = damos al personal cuatro días de vacaciones por Navidad; **it is the secretary's day off tomorrow** = mañana es el día libre de la secretaria **(c)** *(at a meeting)* **off the record** = fuera de actas

offence *or US* **offense** [əˈfens] *noun* delito *m or* infracción *f or* acto *m* delictivo; **he was charged with three serious offences** = se le acusó de tres delitos graves; **the minister was arrested and charged with offences against the Official Secrets Act** = el ministro fue arrestado y acusado de cometer delitos contra la Ley de Secretos Oficiales; **offences against justice** = delitos contra la administración de justicia; **offence against the person** = delito contra las personas; **offence against property** = delito contra la propiedad; **offence against public order** = delito contra el orden público; **offence against the state** = delito contra el Estado; **first offence** = primer delito *or* primera infracción; **second offence** = delito reincidente; **ordinary offence** = delito común; **offences against justice** = delitos contra la justicia; **as it was a first offence, he was fined and not sent to prison** = como era el primer delito, le pusieron

una multa y no tuvo que ir a prisión; **inchoate offences** = delitos incompletos; **notifiable offence** = delito grave (que puede ser juzgado en el Tribunal de la Corona); **political offence** = delito político; **public order offence** = delito contra el orden público; **road traffic offences** = delitos contra el código de circulación; **sexual offences** = delitos contra la libertad sexual; **offence triable either way** = delito que puede ser juzgado en el tribunal de magistrados *or* de la Corona

◊ **offend** [əˈfend] *verb* cometer un delito *or* infringir *or* violar la ley

◊ **offender** [əˈfendə] *noun* delincuente *mf or* infractor, -ra; **first offender** = delincuente sin antecedentes penales; **fugitive offender** = delincuente fugitivo; **persistent offender** = reincidente *mf;* **young offenders** = delincuentes juveniles; **Young Offender Institution** = reformatorio *m* de menores (NOTE: formerly these were called **Borstals**)

◊ **offensive weapon** [əˈfensɪv ˈwepn] *noun* arma *f* ofensiva *or* peligrosa; **carrying offensive weapons** = tenencia *f* ilícita de armas *or* posesión *f* de objetos contundentes

> COMMENT: many things can be considered as offensive weapons if they are used as such: a brick *or* a bottle *or* a piece of wire

offer [ˈɒfə] **1** *noun* **(a)** *(statement by one party to a contract that he proposes to do something)* oferta *f or* propuesta *f* **(b) offer to buy** = oferta de compra; **to make an offer for a company** = hacer una oferta por una empresa; **he made an offer of £10 a share** = ofreció 10 libras por acción; **we made a written offer for the house** = hicimos una oferta por la casa por escrito; **£1,000 is the best offer I can make** = 1.000 libras es lo máximo que puedo ofrecer; **to accept an offer of £1,000 for the car** = aceptar una oferta de 1.000 libras por el coche; **the house is under offer** = se ha hecho una oferta por la casa; **we are open to offers** = admitimos toda clase de ofertas; **cash offer** = oferta de pago en efectivo; **or near offer (o.n.o.)** = precio *m* a discutir; **asking price: £200 o.n.o.** = precio pedido: 200 libras u oferta menor aproximada *or* 200 libras discutibles **(c) offer to sell** = oferta de venta; **offer for sale** = oferta pública de acciones; **offer price** = precio de oferta de acciones; **bargain offer** = venta *f* de ocasión; **special offer** = oferta especial **(d)** *(work)* **he received six offers of jobs** *or* **six job offers** = recibió seis ofertas de trabajo **2** *verb* **(a) to offer someone a job** = ofrecer a alguien un trabajo **(b)** *(to buy)* ofrecer(se) *or* proponer; **he offered to buy the house** = propuso comprar la casa; **to offer someone £100,000 for his house** = ofrecer a alguien 100.000 por su casa; **he offered £10 a share** = ofreció 10 libras por acción **(c)** *(to sell)* ofrecer (en venta) *or* vender; **we offered the house for sale** = pusimos la casa en venta

COMMENT: the offer (and acceptance by the other party) is one of the essential elements of a contract

◊ **offeree** [ɒfə'riː] *noun* receptor, -ra de la oferta
◊ **offeror** [ɒfə'rɔː] *noun* oferente *mf*

office ['ɒfɪs] *noun* **(a)** *(place of work)* oficina *f;* **branch office** = sucursal *f or* filial *f;* **head office** *or* **main office** = sede *f* central *or* oficina principal; **registered office** = domicilio *m* social; **lawyer's office** = bufete *m* de abogados **(b) office block** *or* **a block of offices** = un bloque *m* de oficinas; **office hours** = horario *m* de oficina; **office junior** = auxiliar administrativo, -va; **office space** *or* **office accommodation** = espacio *m* para oficinas *or* espacio ocupado por oficinas; **office staff** = personal *m* administrativo *or* de oficina **(c)** *(room)* despacho *m or* oficina; **come into my office** = entre en mi despacho; **she has a pleasant office which looks out over the park** = tiene un despacho agradable que da al parque; **the senior partner's office is on the third floor** = el despacho del socio principal está en el tercer piso **(d)** *(theatre, cinema)* **booking office** = taquilla *f or* despacho *m* de billetes; **box office** = taquilla; **general office** = oficina principal; **information office** *or* **inquiry office** = oficina de información; **ticket office** = taquilla **(e)** *(government department)* ministerio *m;* **GB the Foreign Office** = el Ministerio de Asuntos Exteriores; **the Home Office** = el Ministerio del Interior; **Office of Fair Trading** = departamento de control de prácticas comerciales **(f)** *(post or position)* cargo *m;* **he holds** *or* **performs the office of treasurer** = tiene *or* desempeña el cargo de tesorero; **high office** = alto cargo; **office of profit (under the Crown)** = puesto *m* gubernamental incompatible con el de diputado; *see also* CHILTERN HUNDREDS; **compensation for loss of office** = indemnización *f* por despido

officer ['ɒfɪsə] *noun* **(a)** *(police)* agente *mf or* oficial *mf;* **duty officer** = inspector, -ra de guardia *or* policía *mf* de servicio; **police officer** = agente de policía (NOTE: used in US English with a name: **Officers Smith and Jones went to the scene of the accident**; GB English is **constable) (b)** *(person in an official position)* funcionario, -ria *or* oficial *mf;* **customs officer** = aduanero, -ra *or* oficial de aduanas; **fire safety officer** = responsable *mf* del sistema contra incendios; **information officer** = jefe, -fa de información; **personnel officer** = director, -ra de personal *or* jefe, -fa de personal; **training officer** = jefe de formación *or* responsable de la capacitación; **the company officers** *or* **the officers of a company** = los ejecutivos *mpl or* los directores *mpl* de una empresa **(c)** *(official of a club or a society)* dirigente *mf;* **the election of officers of an association** = la elección de los dirigentes de una asociación

◊ **Law Officers** ['lɔː 'ɒfɪsəz] *plural noun GB* magistrados que son también miembros del gobierno: el Fiscal General y el Procurador General de la Corona en Inglaterra y Gales y el Fiscal General y Fiscal-Jefe en Escocia

official [ə'fɪʃl] **1** *adjective* **(a)** *(authorized by a government department)* oficial; **on official business** = en asuntos oficiales; **he left official documents in his car** = se dejó documentos oficiales en el coche; **she received an official letter of explanation** = recibió una carta oficial explicatoria; **official secret** = secreto *m* de estado; **Official Secrets Act** = Ley *f* parlamentaria sobre Secretos Oficiales; **speaking in an official capacity** = hablando oficialmente; **to go through official channels** = seguir el conducto reglamentario **(b)** *(approved by a person in authority)* oficial; **official letter** = oficio judicial; **for official use only** = reservado para uso oficial; **this must be an official order - it is written on the company's notepaper** = ésta debe de ser una orden oficial - está escrita en papel de la empresa; **the strike was made official** = la huelga se hizo oficial *or* fue aprobada por el sindicato **(c) Official Journal** = Boletín *m* Oficial de la UE; *Spain* Boletín Oficial del Estado (BOE); **the Official Receiver** = interventor *or* administrador judicial; **official referee** = juez especialista en casos técnicos de gran complejidad; **Official Solicitor** = abogado que actúa en el Tribunal Supremo en representación de personas que se encuentran incapacitadas oficialmente **2** *noun* funcionario, -ria *or* oficial *mf;* **public official** = burócrata *mf;* **airport officials inspected the shipment** = los funcionarios del aeropuerto inspeccionaron el envío; **government officials stopped the import licence** = los funcionarios del gobierno suspendieron la licencia de importación; **customs official** = aduanero, -ra *or* oficial de aduanas; **high official** = alto funcionario; **minor official** = funcionario subalterno *or* de poca categoría
◊ **officialese** [əfɪʃə'liːz] *noun* lenguaje *m* administrativo *or* burocrático
◊ **officially** [ə'fɪʃli] *adverb* oficialmente; **officially he knows nothing about the problem, but unofficially he has given us a lot of advice about it** = oficialmente no sabe nada acerca del problema, pero extraoficialmente nos ha dado buenos consejos

officio [ə'fɪʃiəu] *see* EX OFFICIO, FUNCTUS OFFICIO

off-licence ['ɒf'laɪsns] *noun* **(a)** *(licence)* licencia *f* de venta de bebidas alcohólicas para consumo fuera del establecimiento **(b)** *(shop)* bodega *f or* establecimiento *m* que vende bebidas alcohólicas para consumo externo

offspring ['ɒfsprɪŋ] *noun* hijo, -ja *or* hijos *or* descendencia *f or* vástago *m;* **his offspring**

inherited the estate = sus hijos heredaron sus bienes *or* propiedades; **they had two offspring** = tuvieron dos hijos (NOTE: offspring is both singular and plural)

old ['əʊld] *adjective* viejo, -ja *or* antiguo, -gua; **the company is 125 years old next year** = la empresa cumple 125 años el año que viene; **we have decided to get rid of our old computer system and put in a new one** = hemos decidido deshacernos del viejo sistema de ordenadores e instalar uno nuevo

◊ **old age** ['əʊld 'eɪdʒ] *noun* vejez *f;* **old age pension** = pensión *f* de vejez *or* jubilación *f or* pensión de retiro; **old age pensioner** = pensionista *mf or* jubilado, -da *or* retirado, -da

◊ **Old Bailey** ['əʊld 'beɪli] *noun* sede *f* del Tribunal de lo Penal en Londres

Oleron ['ɒlərɒn] *noun* **Laws of Oleron** = Leyes *fpl* de Oleron: primeras leyes marítimas (de 1216), utilizadas como base para posteriores leyes internacionales

ombudsman ['ɒmbʌdzmən] *noun* defensor *m* del pueblo

COMMENT: there are in fact several ombudsmen: the main one is the Parliamentary Commissioner, but there are also others, such as the Health Service Commissioner, who investigates complaints against the Health Service, and the Local Ombudsman who investigates complaints against local authorities, the Banking Ombudsman, who investigates complains against banks, etc. Although an ombudsman will make his recommendations to the department concerned, and may make his recommendations public, he has no power to enforce them. The Parliamentary Commissioner may only investigate complaints which are addressed to him through an MP; the member of the public first brings his complaint to his MP, and if the MP cannot get satisfaction from the department against which the complaint is made, then the matter is passed to the Ombudsman

omit [ə'mɪt] *verb* **(a)** *(to leave something out)* omitir *or* suprimir *or* olvidar; **the secretary omitted the date when typing the contract** = la secretaria omitió la fecha al pasar a máquina el contrato **(b)** *(not to do something)* dejar de *or* olvidar(se de); **he omitted to tell the managing director that he had lost the documents** = no le dijo al director gerente que había perdido los documentos (NOTE: **omitting - omitted**)

◊ **omission** [ə'mɪʃn] *noun* omisión *f or* olvido *m;* **errors and omissions excepted** = salvo error u omisión (s.e.u.o.)

one minute speech ['wʌn 'mɪnɪt 'spiːtʃ] *noun* US discurso *m* que se pronuncia en la Cámara de Representantes al comienzo de la sesión

one-party state ['wʌn 'pɑːti 'steɪt] *noun* estado *m* de partido único

one-party system ['wʌn 'pɑːti 'sɪstəm] *noun* sistema *m* de partido único

onerous ['ɒnərəs] *adjective* oneroso, -sa *or* pesado, -da; **the repayment terms are particularly onerous** = las condiciones de pago son especialmente onerosas

o.n.o. ['əʊ 'en 'əʊ] = OR NEAR OFFER

onus ['əʊnəs] *noun* responsabilidad *f;* **onus of proof** *or* **onus probandi** = obligación *f* de probar lo alegado *or* carga *f* de la prueba; **the onus of proof is on the plaintiff** = la carga de la prueba recae sobre el demandante *or* el demandante es quien debe probar que lo que alega es cierto; **if there is a prosecution the onus will normally be on the prosecutor to prove the case** = si hay acusación, el acusador tendrá que probar la veracidad de las alegaciones en juicio; *see also* BURDEN

op. cit. ['ɒp 'sɪt] *Latin phrase* op. cit. *or* obra *f* citada (NOTE: used when referring to a legal text: **'see Smith LJ in** *Jones v. Amalgamated Steel Ltd* **op. cit. p. 260')**

open ['əʊpn] **1** *adjective* **(a)** *(not closed)* abierto, -ta; **the store is open on Sunday mornings** = la tienda abre los domingos por la mañana; **our offices are open from 9 to 6** = nuestras oficinas abren de 9 a 6; **they are open for business every day of the week** = abren al público todos los días de la semana **(b)** *(available)* abierto, -ta; **the job is open to all applicants** = todos los interesados pueden solicitar el trabajo; **open to offers** = se admiten ofertas; **the company is open to offers for the empty factory** = la empresa admite ofertas por la fábrica vacía **(c)** **open account** = cuenta *f* abierta; **open cheque** = cheque *m* no cruzado *or* abierto; **open court** = juicio *m* público; **in open court** = en audiencia pública; **open credit** = crédito *m* abierto; **open market** = mercado *m* libre *or* abierto; **open policy** = póliza *f* flotante *or* no valorada; **open prison** = prisión *f* abierta; **open ticket** = billete *m* abierto; **open verdict** = veredicto *m* de muerte por causa desconocida; **the court recorded an open verdict on the two policemen** = el tribunal consignó un veredicto que no especificaba las circunstancias de la muerte de los dos policías **2** *verb* **(a)** *(to start a new business)* abrir *or* poner un negocio; **she has opened a shop in the High Street** = ha puesto una tienda en la calle Mayor; **we have opened an office in London** = hemos abierto una oficina en Londres **(b)** *(to start work or to be at work)* abrir; **the office opens at 9 a.m.** = la oficina abre a las 9 de la mañana; **we open for business on Sundays** = abrimos al público los domingos **(c)** *(to begin)* entablar (una conversación) *or* iniciar *or* empezar (a hablar) *or* comenzar; **counsel for the prosecution opened with a description of the accused's family**

background = el abogado de la acusación comenzó con una descripción del entorno familiar del acusado; **to open negotiations** = entablar conversaciones *or* iniciar negociaciones; **he opened the discussions with a description of the product** = inició las discusiones con una descripción del producto; **the chairman opened the meeting at 10.30** = el presidente inició la reunión a las 10.30 **(d)** *(to start something working)* abrir; **to open a bank account** = abrir una cuenta bancaria; **to open a line of credit** = abrir una línea de crédito; **to open a loan** = conceder un préstamo **(e)** *(start disciplinary proceedings)* **to open a file** = abrir un expediente

◊ **open-ended** *or US* **open-end** ['əupn'endɪd] *adjective* abierto, -ta *or* sin límites fijos *or* no limitado, -da de antemano; **an open-ended agreement** = un acuerdo no limitado de antemano *or* acuerdo modificable

◊ **opening** ['əupnɪŋ] **1** *noun* **(a)** *(act of starting a new business)* apertura *f or* inauguración *f;* **the opening of a new branch** *or* **of a new market** *or* **of a new office** = la inauguración de una nueva sucursal *or* de un nuevo mercado *or* de una nueva oficina **(b) opening hours** = horas *fpl* de apertura **(c)** *(opportunity)* **job openings** = puestos *mpl* vacantes *or* vacantes *fpl;* **a market opening** = apertura de nuevos mercados **2** *adjective* inaugural *or* de apertura *or* inicial; **opening statement** = declaración *f* inaugural; **the judge's opening remarks** = los comentarios iniciales del juez; **the opening speech from the defence counsel** *or* **from the Home Secretary** = el discurso de apertura del abogado defensor *or* del ministro del Interior; **opening balance** = saldo *m* inicial; **opening bid** = oferta *f or* puja *f* inicial; **opening entry** = asiento *m* de apertura *or* inicial

◊ **openly** ['əupnli] *adverb* abiertamente; **he openly admitted that he had sold drugs** = admitió abiertamente que había vendido drogas

operandi [ɒpəˈrændiː] *see* MODUS

operate ['ɒpəreɪt] *verb* **(a)** *(work)* operar *or* funcionar *or* entrar en vigor; **the new terms of service will operate from January 1st** = las nuevas condiciones del servicio funcionarán a partir del 1 de enero; **the rules operate on inland postal services** = el reglamento opera en los servicios postales del territorio nacional **(b) to operate a machine** = manejar *or* hacer funcionar una máquina

◊ **operating** ['ɒpəreɪtɪŋ] *noun* funcionamiento *m or* explotación *f or* operación *f;* **operating budget** = presupuesto *m* de explotación *or* de funcionamiento; **operating costs** *or* **operating expenses** = costes *mpl or* gastos *mpl* de explotación; **operating profit** *or* **operating loss** = beneficio *m or* pérdida *f* de explotación; **operating system** = sistema *m* operativo

◊ **operation** [ɒpəˈreɪʃn] *noun* **(a)** *(business organization)* operación *f;* **the company's**

operations in West Africa = las operaciones de la compañía en Africa occidental; **he heads up the operations in Northern Europe** = dirige las operaciones en el Norte de Europa; **operations review** = análisis *m or* investigación *f* de operaciones; **franchising operation** = explotación en régimen de franquicia **(b) Stock Exchange operation** = operación de Bolsa *or* bursátil **(c) in operation** = en vigor *or* vigente *or* en funcionamiento; **the system will be in operation by June** = el sistema entrará en funcionamiento en junio; **the new system came into operation on June 1st** = el nuevo sistema entró en vigor el 1 de junio

◊ **operational** [ɒpəˈreɪʃnl] *adjective* **(a)** *(how somethin works)* operativo, -va *or* operacional; **operational budget** = presupuesto *m* de explotación; **operational costs** = costes *mpl* de funcionamiento; **operational planning** = planificación *f* operativa; **operational research** = investigación *f* operativa **(b) the system became operational on June 1st** = el sistema empezó a funcionar el 1 de junio

◊ **operative** ['ɒprətɪv] **1** *adjective* operativo, -va *or* operante; **to become operative** = entrar en vigor *or* empezar a funcionar; **operative words** = palabras *fpl* clave de una escritura **2** *noun* operario, -ria *or* maquinista *mf*

opinion [əˈpɪnjən] *noun* **(a) public opinion** = opinión *f* pública; **opinion poll** *or* **opinion research** = sondeo *m* de opinión *or* encuesta *f;* **to be of the opinion** = ser de la opinión *or* ser del parecer *or* opinar; **the judge was of the opinion that if the evidence was doubtful the claim should be dismissed** = el juez opinaba que si las pruebas eran dudosas la demanda se debía desestimar **(b)** *(piece of expert advice)* opinión *or* dictamen *m;* **advisory opinion** = dictamen consultivo; **legal opinion** = dictamen jurídico; **expert opinion** = dictamen pericial; **the lawyers gave their opinion** = los abogados dieron su opinión; **to ask an adviser for his opinion on a case** = pedir a un asesor su opinión sobre un caso; **counsel prepared a written opinion** = el abogado preparó un dictamen escrito; **counsel's opinion** = informe *m or* dictamen de un abogado sobre un caso **(c)** *(judgment delivered by a court)* decisión *f or* resolución *f or* fallo *m*

opponent [əˈpəunənt] *noun* adversario, -ria *or* contrario, -ria *or* oponente *mf;* **the prosecution tried to discredit their opponents in the case** = la acusación intentó desacreditar a sus contrarios en el caso

oppose [əˈpəuz] *verb* oponerse a *or* ir en contra de; **a minority of board members opposed the motion** = una minoría de los miembros del consejo se opuso a la moción; **we are all opposed to the takeover** = estamos todos en contra de la adquisición; **counsel for the plaintiff opposed the defendant's application for an adjournment** = el abogado del demandante se opuso a la petición de aplazamiento por parte del demandado; **the police opposed bail** *or* **opposed the granting of bail** = la policía se opuso a la libertad bajo fianza

◊ **opposite** ['ɒpəzɪt] *adjective* contrario, -ria *or* opuesto, -ta

◊ **opposition** [ɒpə'zɪʃn] *noun* **(a)** *(antagonism)* oposición *f or* desacuerdo *m;* **there was considerable opposition to the plan for reorganizing the divorce courts** = hubo una oposición considerable al proyecto para reorganizar los tribunales de divorcio; **the voters showed their opposition to the government by voting against the proposal in the referendum** = los votantes mostraron su desacuerdo con el gobierno votando contra la propuesta en el referéndum; **notice of opposition** = no aceptación *f* de una solicitud de patente **(b)** *(political party)* partido *m* de la oposición; *(group of parties)* la oposición; **the opposition tried to propose a vote of censure on the Prime Minister** = la oposición intentó proponer un voto de censura contra el Primer Ministro; **Leader of the Opposition** = líder *mf* de la oposición

optimal ['ɒptɪməl] *adjective* óptimo, -ma

◊ **optimum** ['ɒptɪməm] *adjective* óptimo, -ma; **the market offers optimum conditions for sales** = el mercado ofrece condiciones óptimas para las ventas

option ['ɒpʃn] *noun* **(a)** *(choice)* opción *f or* posibilidad *f* de firmar un contrato en fecha posterior; **option to purchase** *or* **to sell** = opción de compra *or* de venta; **first option** = primera opción; **to grant someone a six-month option on a product** = conceder a alguien una opción de seis meses para ser el agente *or* para fabricar un producto; **to take up an option** *or* **to exercise an option** = ejercer el derecho a opción *or* consolidar el mercado de opción; **he exercised his option** *or* **he took up his option to acquire sole marketing rights to the product** = ejerció su derecho a opción para adquirir derechos exclusivos de comercialización del producto; **I want to leave my options open** = quiero tener la posibilidad de elección *or* quiero poder ejercer el derecho a opción *or* no quiero comprometerme; **to take the soft option** = escoger el camino más fácil **(b)** *(Stock Exchange)* **call option** = opción de compra (de acciones); **put option** = opción de venta (de acciones); **share option** = opción de compra *or* venta de acciones a cierto precio para el futuro; **stock option** = prima *f* de opción para compra de acciones (ofrecida a los empleados de una compañía); **option contract** = derecho *m* de opción de compra *or* de venta de acciones a precio fijo; **option dealing** *or* **option trading** = operación *f* de opción

◊ **optional** ['ɒpʃnl] *adjective* optativo, -va *or* facultativo, -va; **the insurance cover is optional** = la póliza de seguros es optativa

oral ['ɔːrl] *adjective* oral *or* verbal; **oral evidence** = declaración *f* verbal *or* testimonio *m* oral

◊ **orally** ['ɔːrəli] *adverb* oralmente *or* de palabra

order ['ɔːdə] **1** *noun* **(a)** *(general state of peace)* orden *m;* **there was a serious breakdown of law and order** = hubo una seria alteración del orden público; **public order** = orden público; **offence against public order** *or* **public order offence** = delito *m* contra el orden público **(b)** *(command)* orden *f or* resolución *f or* aviso *m;* **court order** = orden judicial *or* apremio *m;* **the prisoner was removed by order of the court** = el preso fue trasladado por orden judicial; **the factory was sold by order of the receiver** = la fábrica fue vendida por orden del administrador judicial; **committal order** = orden de ingreso en prisión por desacato; **compensation order** = orden de indemnización; **delivery order** = orden de expedición; **order of discharge** = orden de rehabilitación de la quiebra; **interim order** = orden *or* apremio provisional; **preservation order** = orden de conservación **(c)** *(legislation)* **orders** = órdenes *fpl* ministeriales; **Order in Council** = Real Orden **(d)** *(arrangement of records)* orden *m;* **alphabetical order** = orden alfabético; **chronological order** = orden cronológico; **numerical order** = orden numérico **(e)** *(House of Commons)* orden *m* de asuntos tratados en la Cámara de los Comunes; **order book** = libro *m* de asuntos a tratar en la Cámara de los Comunes durante el periodo parlamentario; **order paper** = orden del día de asuntos a tratar en la Cámara de los Comunes **(f)** *(Parliament)* **standing orders** = reglamento *m* general *or* estatuto *m;* **to call a meeting to order** = abrir la sesión; **to bring a meeting to order** = llamar al orden en una reunión; **order! order!** = ¡orden! ¡orden!; **point of order** = cuestión *f* de orden *or* de procedimiento; **he raised a point of order** = planteó una cuestión de orden; **on a point of order, Mr Chairman, can this committee approve its own accounts?** = según las reglas de procedimiento, Sr Presidente, ¿puede este comité aprobar sus propias cuentas?; **the meeting was adjourned on a point of order** = se aplazó la reunión por una cuestión de procedimiento **(g)** *(working arrangement)* regla *f or* funcionamiento *m;* **machine in full working order** = máquina *f* que funciona perfectamente; **the telephone is out of order** = el teléfono no funciona; **is all the documentation in order?** = ¿está toda la documentación en regla? **(h)** **pay to Mr Smith or order** = páguese al Sr Smith o según indique éste; **pay to the order of Mr Smith** = páguese directamente a la cuenta del Sr Smith **(i)** *(official request for goods to be supplied)* pedido *m;* **to give someone an order** *or* **to place an order with someone for twenty filing cabinets** = encargar veinte archivos *or* hacer un pedido de veinte archivos; **to fill** *or* **to fulfil an order** = servir *or* entregar un pedido; **purchase order** = orden *f* de compra; **items available to order only** = artículos *mpl* disponibles sólo según encargo; **on order** = pedido, -da *or* en camino *or* encargado, -da; **back orders** *or* **outstanding orders** = pedidos pendientes; **order book** = libro *m* de pedidos; **telephone orders** = pedidos por teléfono **(j)** *(document which allows money to be sent to someone)* giro *m;* **he sent us an order on the Chartered Bank** = nos envió un giro a través del Banco Comercial; **banker's order** *or* **standing order** = orden *f* de pago regular *or* domiciliación *f* bancaria; **money order** = giro postal **2** *verb* **(a)** *(to tell someone to do something)* ordenar *or* mandar; **he ordered the police to search the premises** = ordenó a la policía que registrara el local; **the government ordered the army to occupy the radio station** = el gobierno ordenó al ejército que ocupara la estación de radio **(b)** *(to ask for goods to be supplied)* pedir *or* hacer un pedido *or* encargar; **to order twenty filing cabinets to be delivered to the warehouse** = encargar veinte archivos para su entrega en el almacén; **they ordered a new Rolls Royce for the managing director** = encargaron un nuevo Rolls Royce para el director gerente **(c)** *(to put in a certain way)* ordenar *or* clasificar; **the address list is ordered by country** = la lista de direcciones está ordenada por países; **that filing cabinet contains invoices ordered by date** = ese archivo contiene facturas clasificadas según la fecha

ordinance ['ɔːdɪnəns] *noun* **(a)** ordenanza *f* **(b)** *US* reglamento *m* municipal efectivo sólo en esa jurisdicción

ordinary ['ɔːdnri] *adjective* corriente *or* ordinario, -ria *or* habitual; **ordinary member** = miembro *mf* ordinario; **ordinary offence** = delito *m* común; **ordinary proceedings** = vía *f* ordinaria; **ordinary resolution** = resolución *f* ordinaria; **ordinary shares** = acciones *fpl* ordinarias; **ordinary shareholder** = accionista *mf* ordinario, -ria
◊ **ordinarily** ['ɔːdnrli] *adverb* generalmente *or* en general *or* habitualmente; **ordinarily resident** = con residencia habitual

organization [ɔːgnaɪ'zeɪʃn] *noun* **(a)** *(way of arranging something)* organización *f;* **the organization of a protest meeting** = la organización de un mitin de protesta; **the organization of an appeal to the House of Lords** = la preparación de una apelación interpuesta en la Cámara de los Lores **(b)** *(institution)* organización *or* asociación *f;* **he runs an organization for the rehabilitation of criminals** = dirige una organización para la rehabilitación de delincuentes
◊ **organize** ['ɔːgnaɪz] *verb* organizar; **organized crime** = crimen *m* organizado; **organized labour** = trabajadores, -ras sindicados, -das

origin ['ɒrɪdʒɪn] *noun* origen *m or* procedencia *f;* **spare parts of European origin** = piezas *fpl* de recambio de procedencia europea; **certificate of origin** = certificado *m* de origen; **country of origin** = país *m* de origen *or* de procedencia
◊ **original** [ə'rɪdʒnl] **1** *adjective* original *or* primero, -ra; **they sent a copy of the original invoice** = enviaron una copia de la factura original; **original evidence** = testimonio *m* basado en hechos que el testigo sabe que son verdaderos **2** *noun* original *m;* **send the original and file two copies** = envíe el original y archive dos copias
◊ **originally** [ə'rɪdʒnli] *adverb* al principio *or* originariamente
◊ **originate** [ə'rɪdʒəneɪt] *verb* comenzar *or* empezar *or* originar; **originating application** = comienzo *m* de ciertos casos en un juzgado municipal; **originating summons** = primera citación para ciertos casos en el Tribunal Supremo

orphan ['ɔːfən] *noun* huérfano, -na

ostensible [ɒ'stensəbl] *adjective* aparente; **ostensible partner** = socio, -cia aparente

OTC ['əʊ 'tiː 'siː] = OVER-THE-COUNTER

otherwise ['ʌðəwaɪz] *adverb* de otra manera *or* de otro modo *or* si no *or* de lo contrario; **John Smith, otherwise known as 'the Butcher'** = John Smith, también conocido como 'el Carnicero'; **except as otherwise stated** = excepto cuando se afirme lo contrario; **unless otherwise agreed** = salvo que se acuerde lo contrario *or* salvo pacto en contrario

oust [aʊst] *verb* despojar de

ouster ['aʊstə] *noun* despojo *m or* desposeimiento *m;* **he had to apply for an ouster order** = tuvo que solicitar una orden de desposeimiento; **the judge made an ouster order** = el juez dictó una orden de desposeimiento; *compare* EJECT

outcome ['aʊtkʌm] *noun* resultado *m;* **we are waiting for the outcome of the enquiry** = estamos esperando el resultado de la investigación; **the outcome of the trial was in doubt** = el resultado del juicio era dudoso

outlaw ['aʊtlɔː] **1** *noun* proscrito, -ta *or* persona fuera de la ley *or* fugitivo , -va **2** *verb* prohibir *or* declarar ilegal; **the government has proposed a bill to outlaw drinking in public** = el gobierno ha propuesto un proyecto de ley para prohibir el consumo de bebidas en público

outline ['aʊtlaɪn] **1** *noun* resumen *m or* esquema *m or* líneas *fpl* generales; **they drew up the outline of a plan** *or* **an outline plan** = trazaron las líneas generales de un proyecto; **outline planning permission** = permiso *m* provisional de un proyecto de planeamiento urbanístico *or* permiso provisional para edificar **2** *verb* perfilar *or* explicar en términos generales *or* dar una idea general de; **the chairman**

outlined the company's plans for the coming year = el presidente perfiló los planes de la empresa para el próximo año

out of court ['aʊt əv 'kɔːt] *adverb & adjective;* **a settlement was reached out of court** = se llegó a un acuerdo amistoso entre las partes *or* se llegó a un acuerdo para no ir a juicio; **they are hoping to reach an out-of-court settlement** = confían en llegar a un acuerdo amistoso *or* a un acuerdo para no ir a juicio

out of pocket ['aʊt əv 'pɒkɪt] *adjective & adverb* con pérdidas; **out-of-pocket expenses** = gastos *mpl* reemborsables

output ['aʊtpʊt] **1** *noun* **(a)** *(amount produced)* producción *f or* rendimiento *m;* **output has increased by 10%** = la producción ha aumentado en un 10%; **25% of our output is exported** = el 25% de nuestra producción se exporta; **output tax** = impuesto *m* sobre las ventas de bienes *or* de servicios **(b)** *(information which is produced by a computer)* datos *mpl* de salida **2** *verb* producir (por ordenador) *or* dar salida; **the printer will output colour charts** = la impresora hará gráficos en color; **that is the information outputted from the computer** = ésa es la información de salida del ordenador (NOTE: **outputting - outputted**)

outrage ['aʊtreɪdʒ] **1** *noun* atropello *m or* escándalo *m or* ultraje *m* **2** *verb* atropellar *or* ultrajar

outright ['aʊtraɪt] *adverb & adjective* completo, -ta *or* total *or* en su totalidad; **to purchase something outright** *or* **to make an outright purchase** = comprar algo con todos los derechos inherentes

outside [aʊt'saɪd] *adjective & adverb* externo, -na *or* exterior *or* fuera (de la empresa); **to send work to be done outside** = enviar trabajo para que se realice fuera de la empresa; **outside office hours** = fuera de horas de oficina; **outside dealer** = corredor, -ra libre *or* no perteneciente a la Bolsa oficial; **outside director** = director, -ra no empleado, -da por la compañía; **outside line** = línea *f* externa; **outside worker** = trabajador, -ra exterior *or* que trabaja fuera de la empresa; **outside the contract** = extracontractual

outstanding [aʊt'stændɪŋ] *adjective* **(a)** *(unpaid)* sin pagar *or* pendiente; *(unresolved)* sin resolver; **outstanding debts** = deudas *fpl* sin pagar *or* pendientes; **outstanding offences** = delitos *mpl* pendientes; **outstanding orders** = pedidos *mpl* pendientes de servirse en parte; **matters outstanding from the previous meeting** = cuestiones *fpl* pendientes de la reunión anterior **(b)** *(notable)* destacado, -da

outvote [aʊt'vəʊt] *verb* vencer en una votación; **the chairman was outvoted** = el presidente perdió en la votación

overbooking [əʊvə'bʊkɪŋ] *noun* 'overbooking' *m or* exceso *m* de contratación

overcharge 1 ['əʊvətʃɑːdʒ] *noun* precio *m or* cobro *m* excesivo *or* recargo *m;* **to pay back an overcharge** = devolver el importe pagado en exceso *or* lo que se se ha cobrado de más **2** [əʊvə'tʃɑːdʒ] *verb* cobrar más de lo debido *or* cobrar de más; **the hotel overcharged us for meals** = el hotel nos cobró de más por las comidas; **we asked for a refund because we had been overcharged** = pedimos un reembolso porque se nos había cobrado más de lo debido

overcome [əʊvə'kʌm] *verb* vencer *or* superar; **the defendant will have to overcome two hurdles if his appeal is to succeed** = el acusado tendrá que vencer dos obstáculos si quiere que su apelación prospere (NOTE: **overcame - has overcome**)

overdue [əʊvə'djuː] *adjective* vencido, -da *or* atrasado, da; **overdue payment** = pago *m* retrasado; **interest payments are three weeks overdue** = el pago de los intereses venció hace tres semanas

overestimate [əʊvə'estɪmeɪt] *verb* sobrestimar *or* sobrevalorar; **he overestimated the amount of time needed to prepare his case** = sobrestimó la cantidad de tiempo necesaria para preparar su caso

overlook [əʊvə'lʊk] *verb* **(a)** *(to look out over)* dar a *or* tener vista a; **his chambers overlook the garden of the Middle Temple** = su despacho da al jardín de Middle Temple **(b)** *(not to pay attention)* pasar por alto *or* dejar pasar; **in this instance we will overlook the delay** = en este caso pasaremos por alto el retraso; **the court overlooked the fact that the defendant's car was not insured** = el tribunal pasó por alto el hecho de que el coche del demandado no estaba asegurado

overreaching [əʊvə'riːtʃɪŋ] *noun* principio *m* legal por el que un interés sobre la tierra se reemplaza por un derecho directo al dinero resultante de su venta

override [əʊvə'raɪd] *verb* no hacer caso de *or* no tener en cuenta *or* dominar *or* invalidar; **the appeal court overrode the decision of the lower court** = el tribunal de apelación invalidó la decisión del tribunal inferior; **overriding interest** = interés *m* predominante *or* absoluto; **his wife established an overriding interest in the property against the bank's charge on it** = su mujer estableció un interés sobre la propiedad que predominaba sobre la hipoteca del banco en la misma (NOTE: **overriding - overrode - has overridden**)

◊ **overrider** *or* **overriding commission** [əʊvə'raɪdə *or* əʊvə'raɪdɪŋ kə'mɪʃn] *noun* compensación *f* extra

overrule [əʊvə'ruːl] *verb* **objection overruled** = no ha lugar; *(of a higher court)* establecer un nuevo precedente que se opone a la decisión de un tribunal inferior

overrun [əʊvə'rʌn] *noun* rebasar *or* exceder; **the construction company overran the time limit set to complete the factory** = la empresa de construcción excedió el límite de tiempo establecido para terminar la fábrica (NOTE: overrunning - overran - has overrun)

overseas [əʊvə'siːz] *adjective & adverb* en el extranjero

oversight ['əʊvəsaɪt] *noun* olvido *m*

overt ['əʊvəːt] *adjective* abierto, -ta *or* evidente *or* manifiesto, -ta; **overt act** = acto *m* con intención delictiva manifiesta; *see also* MARKET OVERT

overtake [əʊvə'teɪk] *verb* adelantar a un vehículo

over-the-counter (OTC) ['əʊvəðə'kaʊntə] *adjective;* **over-the-counter market** = mercado *m* no oficial de valores *or* mercado de valores sin cotización oficial; **over-the-counter sales** = venta *f* de valores sin cotización oficial

overtime ['əʊvətaɪm] **1** *noun* horas *fpl* extraordinarias *or* horas extra; **to work six hours' overtime** = hacer seis horas extraordinarias; **the overtime rate is one and a half times normal pay** = la tarifa por horas extraordinarias es una vez y media la tarifa del salario normal; **overtime ban** = prohibición *f* de hacer horas extraordinarias; **overtime pay** = paga *f* por horas extra **2** *adverb* **to work overtime** = hacer horas extraordinarias

overturn [əʊvə'təːn] *verb* anular; **to overturn a judgment** = casar una sentencia

owe [əʊ] *verb* deber; **he owes the company for the stock he purchased** = debe a la empresa la mercancía que compró

◊ **owing** ['əʊɪŋ] *adjective* **(a)** *(not paid back)* debido, -da *or* que se debe; **money owing to the directors** = dinero que se debe a los directores; **how much is still owing to the company?** = ¿cuánto dinero más hay que pagarle a la empresa? **(b)** *(because of)* **owing to** = debido a *or* a causa de; **the plane was late owing to fog** = el avión llegó tarde a causa de la niebla; **I am sorry that owing to pressure of work, we cannot supply your order on time** = me temo que debido a un exceso de trabajo, no podemos hacerle entrega de su pedido a tiempo

own [əʊn] *verb* poseer *or* tener; **a wholly-owned subsidiary** = una filial propiedad de la empresa; **a state-owned industry** = una industria estatal *or* de propiedad estatal

◊ **owner** ['əʊnə] *noun* dueño, -ña *or* propietario, -ria; **beneficial owner** = usufructuario, -ria *or* propietario beneficiario; **lawful owner** = tenedor legal; **legal owner** = nudo propietario; **sole owner** = propietario único *or* único dueño; **rightful owner** = propietario legítimo; **owner-occupier** = explotador directo *or* ocupante y dueño de una propiedad; **goods sent at owner's risk** = mercancías *fpl* enviadas por cuenta y riesgo del propietario

◊ **ownership** ['əʊnəʃɪp] *noun* propiedad *f or* posesión *f;* **collective ownership** = propiedad colectiva; **common ownership** *or* **ownership in common** = propiedad en común; **joint ownership** = copropiedad *f;* **legal ownership** = nuda propiedad; **full legal ownership** = título *m* absoluto; **public ownership** *or* **state ownership** = propiedad pública; **the company has been put into state ownership** = la empresa ha pasado a ser propiedad del estado; **private ownership** = propiedad privada; **the ownership of the company has passed to the banks** = la propiedad de la empresa ha pasado a los bancos

oyez [əʊ'jez] *French word meaning* ¡atención! *or* ¡oíd! (expresión usada al principio de algunos juicios)

Pp

pack [pæk] *verb* formar un jurado tendencioso (con partidarios y simpatizantes); **the left-wing group packed the committee with activists** = el grupo izquierdista llenó la comisión de activistas

pact [pækt] *noun* pacto *m;* **the countries in the region signed a non-aggression pact** = los países de la zona firmaron un pacto de no-agresión; **the two minority parties signed an electoral pact not to oppose each other in certain constituencies** = los dos partidos de la oposición firmaron un pacto para no enfrentarse en ciertos distritos electorales

pair [pɛə] **1** *noun (House of Commons)* dos diputados de opiniones distintas que se abstienen de votar durante cierto tiempo por mutuo acuerdo para que los votos sean compensados; **he was not able to find a pair, so had to come back from Paris to attend the debate** = como no encontró a nadie de la oposición que también pudiera abstenerse en la votación, tuvo que regresar de París para asistir al debate **2** *verb* organizar que dos diputados de partidos opuestos se abstengan de votar al mismo tiempo para que los votos sean compensados

pais [pɛɪ] *see* ESTOPPEL

palimony ['pælɪmɔnɪ] *noun* pensión *f* alimenticia pagadera al compañero, -ra *or* ex-cónyuge tras la separación *or* divorcio

pamphlet ['pæmflət] *noun* panfleto *m or* folleto *m*

pan- [pæn] *prefix* pan; **pan-African** *or* **pan-American** = panafricano, -na *or* panamericano, -na

panel ['pænl] *noun* **(a)** *(flat surface)* panel *m;* **display panel** = panel de exposición; **advertisement panel** = espacio *m* para publicidad en un periódico o revista **(b)** *(group of people)* **panel of experts** = comisión *f or* grupo *m* tribunal *m* de expertos; *see also* EMPANEL

paper ['pɛɪpə] *noun* **(a)** *(writing, wrapping)* papel *m;* **carbon paper** = papel carbón; **copier paper** = papel de impresora; **duplicating paper** = papel para multicopista; **headed paper** = papel con membrete; **engrossment paper** *or* **judicature paper** = papel grueso de los documentos judiciales; **lined paper** = papel rayado; **typing paper** = papel

para máquina de escribir; **paper feed** = alimentador *m* del papel (NOTE: no plural in this meaning); **(b)** *(outline report)* informe *m or* documento *m;* **the treasurer asked his deputy to write a paper on new funding** = el director de finanzas pidió a su delegado que preparara un informe sobre nuevos métodos de financiación; **the planning department prepared a paper for the committee on the possible uses of the site** = el departamento de planificación urbana preparó un documento para la comisión sobre los posibles usos del solar; *see also* GREEN PAPER, WHITE PAPER **(c)** *(House of Commons)* **order paper** = orden *m* del día **(d)** *(documents)* **papers** = documentos *mpl or* papeles *mpl or* documentación *f;* **the solicitor sent me the relevant papers on the case** = el abogado me envió los documentos pertinentes al caso; **the police have sent the papers on the fraud to the Director of Public Prosecutions** = la policía ha enviado los documentos sobre el fraude al Director de la Acusación Pública; **he has lost the customs papers** = ha perdido los papeles de la aduana; **the office is asking for the VAT papers** = la oficina requiere los papeles del IVA **(e)** **on paper** = sobre el papel *or* en teoría; **on paper the system is ideal, but we have to see it working before we will sign the contract** = en teoría el sistema es perfecto, pero tenemos que verlo en funcionamiento antes de firmar el contrato; **paper loss** = pérdida *f* ficticia *or* sobre el papel; **paper profit** = beneficio *m* ficticio *or* sobre el papel **(f)** *(documents which can represent money)* valores *mpl or* títulos *mpl;* **bankable paper** = valores aceptados por un banco en garantía de un préstamo; **negotiable paper** = título negociable **(g)** *(banknotes)* **paper money** *or* **paper currency** = billete *m* de banco *or* papel moneda **(h)** *(newspaper)* periódico *m or* diario *m;* **trade paper** = revista *f* comercial; **free paper** *or* **giveaway paper** = periódico gratuito

◊ **paperwork** ['pɛɪpəwɔːk] *noun* papeleo *m or* trabajo *m* administrativo

parade [pə'rɛɪd] *noun* **identification** *or* **identity parade** = rueda *f* de identificación *or* chequeo *m* de sospechosos

paragraph ['pærəgrɑːf] *noun* **(a)** *(in a written text)* párrafo *m or* parágrafo *m;* **the first paragraph of your letter** *or* **paragraph one of your letter** = el primer párrafo de su carta **(b)** *(in a legal document)* párrafo *or* sección *f* de una disposición legal; **please refer to the paragraph in the contract on 'shipping instructions'** = le rogamos se remita al párrafo del contrato sobre 'instrucciones de envío'

paralegal [pærə'li:gl] **1** *adjective* relacionado con la ley pero sin formar parte de la misma **2** *noun* persona *f* que trabaja en un bufete de abogados sin tener el título

paramount ['pærəmaunt] *adjective* superior *or* supremo, -ma; **paramount title** = título *m* de propiedad indiscutible

parcel ['pɑ:sl] *noun* parcela *f;* **for sale: a parcel of land in the Borough of Richmond** = se vende una parcela en el municipio de Richmond

pardon ['pɑ:dn] **1** *noun* indulto *m or* medida *f* de gracia; **free pardon** = indulto en caso de sentencia y condena nulas; **full pardon** = absolución *f* incondicionada; **conditional pardon** = absolución condicional; **unconditional pardon** = amnistía *f* total e incondicional **2** *verb* indultar; **the political prisoners were pardoned by the president** = los presos políticos fueron indultados por el presidente

COMMENT: not the same as 'quashing' a conviction, which means that the conviction has been made void; both 'pardoning' and 'quashing' have the same effect

parent ['peərənt] *noun* **parents** = padres *mpl;* **parent company** = sociedad *f* matriz *or* central

parentis [pə'rentis] *see* IN LOCO PARENTIS

pari passu ['pæri 'pæsu:] *Latin phrase* igualdad *f* de tratamiento en igualdad de condiciones *or* sin distinciones *or* al mismo nivel; **the new shares will rank pari passu with the existing ones** = las nuevas acciones se situarán al mismo nivel que las ya existentes

parish ['pærɪʃ] *noun* parroquia *f;* **parish council** = consejo *m* del distrito; **parish meeting** = junta *f* local; **parish pump politics** = política *f* local

parity ['pærəti] *noun* igualdad *f or* paridad *f;* **the female staff want parity with the men** = el personal femenino quiere igualdad de condiciones con los hombres; **the pound fell to parity with the dollar** = la libra bajó hasta alcanzar la paridad con el dólar

parking offences ['pɑ:kɪŋ ə'fensɪz] *noun* infracciones *fpl* por estacionamiento indebido

parliament ['pɑ:ləmənt] *noun* parlamento *m;* **Act of Parliament** = Ley *f* parlamentaria; **contempt of Parliament** = conducta *f* que desprestigia al Parlamento; **Member of Parliament (MP)** = diputado, -da *or* miembro *mf* del Parlamento; **Mother of Parliaments** = el Parlamento británico en Westminster; **the**

European Parliament = el Parlamento Europeo (NOTE: often used without **'the': Parliament voted to abolish the death penalty; this is one of the Bills which will shortly be coming before Parliament)**

◊ **parliamentarian** [pɑ:ləmən'teəriən] *noun* **(a)** *GB* parlamentario, -ria (miembro de una de las dos cámaras del Parlamento); **a delegation of British parliamentarians was invited to visit Canada** = invitaron a una delegación de parlamentarios británicos para visitar Canadá **(b)** *US* parlamentario, -ria (funcionario del Congreso, por el Senado o por la Cámara de Representantes, que asesora la mesa sobre cuestiones de derecho parlamentario)

◊ **parliamentary** [pɑ:lə'mentri] *adjective* parlamentario, -ria; **parliamentary agents** = agentes *mfpl* que asesoran sobre cómo presentar un proyecto de ley en el Parlamento; **Parliamentary Commissioner** = defensor, -ra del pueblo (que investiga las quejas del público contra los ministerios); **parliamentary draftsman** = redactor, -ra de proyectos de ley; **Parliamentary Labour Party (PLP)** = diputados, -das del Partido Laborista; **parliamentary privilege** = inmunidad *f* parlamentaria

◊ **Parliamentary Secretary** *or* **Parliamentary Under-Secretary** [pɑ:lə'mentri 'setrətri] *noun* miembro del gobierno que trabaja en un departamento bajo la dirección de un ministro (NOTE: to avoid confusion, they are called Parliamentary Under-Secretaries in departments where the head of the department is a Secretary of State)

parol [pə'rəul] *adjective* verbal *or* oral *or* (de) palabra; **parol agreement** *or* **contract** = acuerdo *m or* contrato *m* verbal; **parol evidence** = testimonio *m* oral

parole [pə'rəul] **1** *noun* libertad *f* condicional; *(for a short time)* libertad vigilada *or* permiso *m* carcelario; **he was given a week's parole to visit his mother in hospital** = le concedieron un permiso carcelario de una semana para visitar a su madre en el hospital; **after six month's good conduct in prison she is eligible for parole** = después de seis meses de buena conducta en la cárcel, puede concedérsele la libertad condicional; **on parole** = bajo palabra (de honor); **he was let out on parole and immediately burgled a house** = le concedieron la libertad condicional e inmediatamente entró a robar en una casa; **parole board** = junta *f* de régimen y administración del centro penitenciario que regula la concesión de la libertad condicional **2** *verb* conceder la libertad condicional *or* libertad vigilada *or* dar un permiso carcelario; **if you're lucky you will be paroled before Christmas** = si tienes suerte te concederán la libertad condicional antes de Navidad

part [pɑ:t] **1** *noun* **(a)** *(piece or section)* parte *f;* **part of the shipment was damaged** = se estropeó una parte del envío; **part of the staff is on overtime**

= parte del personal hace horas extraordinarias; **part of the expenses will be refunded** = se reembolsará una parte de los gastos **(b) in part** = en parte; **to contribute in part to the costs** = contribuir a parte de las costas; **to pay the costs in part** = pagar una parte de las costas **(c) spare part** = pieza *f* de recambio *or* de repuesto **(d) part-owner** = copropietario, -ria; **part-ownership** = copropiedad *f* **(e) part exchange** = canje *m* parcial; **part payment** = pago *m* parcial; **part performance** = cumplimiento *m* parcial de contrato **2** *verb* **to part with something** = entregar *or* ceder *or* deshacerse de algo; **he was tricked into parting with the keys to the safe** = le engañaron para que soltara las llaves de la caja fuerte

parte ['pɑːteɪ] *see* EX PARTE, INTER PARTES, AUDI ALTERNAM PARTEM

partial ['pɑːʃl] *adjective* **(a)** *(not complete)* parcial; **partial loss** = pérdida *f* parcial; **he was awarded partial compensation for the damage to his house** = le concedieron una indemnización parcial por los daños sufridos en su casa **(b)** *(biased)* parcial; **the defendant complained that the judge was partial** = el demandado se quejó de que el juez era parcial

particular [pəˈtɪkjʊlə] **1** *adjective* particular *or* especial *or* concreto, -ta; **particular average** =; *(maritime law)* avería *f* simple; **particular lien** = embargo *m* preventivo llevado a cabo por una persona sobre la propiedad de otra; *compare* GENERAL AVERAGE, GENERAL LIEN **2** *noun* **(a)** **particulars** = detalles *mpl or* pormenores *mpl*; *(of a person)* datos personales; **sheet which gives particulars of the items for sale** = hoja que da información detallada sobre los artículos en venta; **the inspector asked for particulars of the missing car** = el inspector pidió detalles sobre el coche desaparecido; **to give full particulars of something** = dar información completa sobre algo; **request for further and better particulars** = petición de los pormenores de la demanda *or* defensa de la parte contraria en un procedimiento civil; **particulars of claim** = fundamentos *mpl* fácticos *or* relato *m* de los hechos **(b) in particular** = particularmente *or* especialmente; **goods which are easily damaged, in particular glasses, need special packing** = la mercancía frágil, especialmente la cristalería, precisa un embalaje especial

partition [pɑːˈtɪʃn] *noun* partición *f or* reparto *m* de tierra; **partition of chattles** = reparto de bienes muebles

partly ['pɑːtli] *adverb* parcialmente; **partly-paid capital** = capital *m* parcialmente desembolsado; **partly-paid up shares** = acciones *fpl* no liberadas totalmente; **partly-secured creditors** = acreedores *mpl* con garantía parcial *or* parcialmente asegurados

partner ['pɑːtnə] *noun* socio, -cia *or* asociado, -da *or* partícipe *mf*; **he became a partner in a firm of solicitors** = pasó a ser socio de una firma de abogados; **active partner** *or* **working partner** = socio activo; **junior partner** *or* **senior partner** = socio minoritario *or* socio principal; **limited partner** = socio comanditario; **sleeping partner** *or* **dormant partner** = socio comanditario *or* en comandita; **partner in crime** = cómplice *mf or* consorte *mf*

◊ **partnership** ['pɑːtnəʃɪp] *noun* **(a)** sociedad *f or* sociedad personal *or* consorcio *m;* **to go into partnership with someone** = asociarse con alguien; **to join with someone to form a partnership** = unirse con alguien para formar una sociedad; **articles of partnership** = escritura *f* de sociedad *or* escritura de constitución de sociedad *or* estatutos *mpl;* **to offer someone a partnership** *or* **to take someone into partnership with you** = tomar a alguien como socio; **to dissolve a partnership** = disolver una sociedad; **partnership at will** = sociedad sin límite de tiempo establecido **(b) limited partnership** = sociedad en comandita *or* sociedad personal de responsabilidad limitada); **sleeping partnership** = sociedad en comandita

party ['pɑːti] *noun* **(a)** *(company or person)* parte *f or* persona *f or* interesado, -da; **aggrieved party** = parte perjudicada; **party to a crime** = cómplice *mf;* **interested party** = parte interesada; **one of the parties to the suit has died** = una de las partes litigantes ha fallecido; **the company is not a party to the agreement** = la empresa no ha firmado el acuerdo; **identity of parties** = identidad *f* de las partes; **party and party costs** = sistema *m* normal de tasación de las costas que incluye todos los gastos incurridos por una de las partes en el proceso **(b) third party** = tercero *m;* **third party insurance** *or* **third party policy** = seguro *m* contra terceros *or* contra tercera persona **(c) working party** = grupo *m or* comisión *f* de trabajo; **the government has set up a working party to study the problems of industrial waste** = el gobierno ha formado una comisión para estudiar los problemas de los residuos industriales; **Professor Smith is the chairman of the working party on drug abuse** = el catedrático Smith es el presidente del grupo de trabajo sobre drogodependencia; **search party** = equipo *m* de rescate **(d) political party** = partido *m* político; **party politics** = política *f* de partido *or* partidismo *m; (in a two-party system)* **third party** = tercer partido; **a third party candidate** = candidato, -ta de un tercer partido

◊ **party list system** ['pɑːti 'lɪst 'sɪstəm] *noun* sistema *m* electoral europeo en el que cada uno de los partidos presenta una lista de candidatos que son elegidos según el número de votos obtenidos por el partido; *see also* ADDITIONAL MEMBER

◊ **party wall** ['pɑːti 'wɔːl] *noun* pared *f* medianera

pass [pɑːs] **1** *noun (permit)* pase *m;* **you need a pass to enter the ministry offices** = necesita un pase para entrar en las oficinas del ministerio; **all members of staff must show a pass** = todos los miembros del personal deben mostrar su pase **2** *verb* **(a)** *(to approve)* aprobar *or* dar el visto bueno a *or* adoptar; **Parliament passed the Bill which has now become law** = el Parlamento aprobó el proyecto de ley que ahora se ha convertido en ley; **the finance director has to pass an invoice before it is sent out** = el director financiero tiene que aprobar las facturas antes de su pago; **the loan has been passed by the board** = el préstamo ha sido aprobado por la junta; **to pass a resolution** = aprobar una moción *or* adoptar un acuerdo; **to pass an examination** *or* **an exam** = aprobar un examen *or* pasar una prueba; **the meeting passed a proposal that salaries should be frozen** = la junta aprobó una propuesta para congelar los salarios **(b) to pass sentence on someone** = sentenciar a alguien *or* dictar sentencia *or* dictaminar *or* anunciar una condena; **the jury returned a verdict of guilty, and the judge will pass sentence next week** = el jurado pronunció un veredicto de culpabilidad y el juez dictará sentencia la semana próxima **(c) to pass a dividend** = no declarar un dividendo **(d)** *(to be successful)* aprobar; **he passed his typing test** = aprobó el examen de mecanografía; **she has passed all her exams and now is a qualified solicitor** = ha aprobado todos los exámenes y ya es abogada titulada

◊ **pass off** [ˈpɑːs ˈɒf] *verb* **to pass something off as something else** = hacer pasar una cosa por otra

◊ **passing off** [ˈpɑːsɪŋ ˈɒf] *noun* acto *m* ilícito civil consistente en hacer creer que un producto es de otra persona, aprovechando la reputación de ésta, para venderlo

◊ **passer-by** [ˈpɑːsəˈbaɪ] *noun* transeúnte *mf*

passport [ˈpɑːspɔːt] *noun* pasaporte *m;* **we had to show our passports at the customs post** = tuvimos que mostrar los pasaportes en el puesto de aduana; **his passport is out of date** = su pasaporte ha expirado; **the passport officer stamped my passport** = el oficial selló mi pasaporte; **passport holder** = titular *mf* de un pasaporte; **she is a British passport holder** = tiene pasaporte británico

password [ˈpɑːswɜːd] *noun* contraseña *f*

patent [ˈpæt ənt *or* peɪt ənt] **1** *noun* **(a)** *(invention)* patente *f;* **to take out a patent for a new type of light bulb** = sacar una patente para un nuevo tipo de bombilla; **to apply for a patent for a new invention** = solicitar la patente de un nuevo invento; **he has received a grant of patent for his invention** = se le ha concedido la patente de su invento; **patent applied for** *or* **patent pending** = pendiente de patente *or* patente solicitada; **to forfeit a patent** = pérdida *f* legal de una patente (por falta de pago); **to infringe a patent** = violar una patente; **patent agent** = agente *mf* de patentes y marcas; **to**

file a patent application = solicitar una patente; **patent examiner** = encargado, -da de examinar patentes; **patent holder** = titular *mf* de una patente; **infringement of patent** *or* **patent infringement** = violación *f* de patente; **patent number** = número *m* de patente; **patent office** = oficina *f or* registro *m* de patentes y marcas; **patent rights** = derechos *mpl* de patente; **patent specification** = descripción *f* de una patente **(b) letters patent** = cédula *f or* patente de invención *or* título *m* de privilegio **2** *verb* **to patent an invention** = patentar un invento **3** *adjective* patente *or* evidente *or* manifiesto, -ta; **the prisoner's statement is a patent lie** = la declaración del acusado es una mentira evidente; **patent defect** = defecto *m or* imperfección *f* evidente

◊ **patented** [ˈpætntɪd *or* ˈpeɪtntɪd] *adjective* patentado, -da

◊ **patentee** [peɪtnˈtiː] *noun* poseedor, -ra de una patente

◊ **patently** [ˈpeɪtnli] *adverb* evidentemente *or* manifiestamente; **he made a patently false statement to the court** = hizo una declaración al tribunal que era manifiestamente incierta

paternity [əˈtɜːntɪti] *noun* paternidad *f;* **paternity leave** = permiso *m or* licencia *f* por paternidad

◊ **paternity action** *or* **suit** [əˈtɜːntɪti ˈækʃn *or* suːt] *noun* litigo *m* de paternidad

pathology [pəˈθɒlədʒi] *noun* patología *f*

◊ **pathologist** [pəˈθɒlədʒɪst] *noun* patólogo, -ga; *(especialmente)* médico, -ca forense; **Home Office pathologist** = médico forense del Ministerio del Interior

patrial [ˈpeɪtrɪəl] *noun* persona *f* con derecho a vivir en el Reino Unido al tener familia en el país

patricide [ˈpætrɪsaɪd] *noun* parricidio *m*

patrol [pəˈtrəul] **1** *noun* patrulla *f;* **a police patrol** = una patrulla de policía; **on patrol** = de patrulla *or* patrullando; **we have six squad cars on patrol in the centre of the town** = tenemos seis coches patrullando en el centro de la ciudad; **on foot patrol** = patrullando a pie **2** *verb* patrullar por; **groups of riot police were patrolling the centre of the town** = grupos de policía antidisturbios patrullaban por el centro de la ciudad

◊ **patrol car** [pəˈtrəul ˈkɑː] *noun* coche *m* patrulla

◊ **patrolman** [pəˈtrəulmən] *noun US* policía *m or* guardia *m;* **Patrolman Jones was at the scene of the accident** = el policía Jones se encontraba en el lugar del accidente

patronage [ˈpætrənɪdʒ] *noun* derecho *m* del gobierno a conceder cargos, honores o condecoraciones *or* influencia *f;* **the Prime Minister has considerable patronage** = el primer ministro tiene una influencia considerable; **patronage secretary** = funcionario, -ria del ministerio responsable del nombramiento de cargos

pattern ['pætən] *noun* **(a)** *(sample)* **pattern book** = libro *m* de muestras **(b)** *(model)* pauta *f or* modelo *m or* norma *f;* **the pattern of crime in the inner cities is different from the pattern in the country** = la pauta general del crimen en el centro de las ciudades es diferente de la del campo

pauperis ['pɔːpəris] *see* IN FORMA PAUPERIS

pause [pɔːz] *noun* alto *m or* pausa *f*

pawn [pɔːn] **1** *noun* prenda *f;* **to put something in pawn** = dejar algo en prenda *or* empeñar algo; **to take something out of pawn** = desempeñar algo; **pawn ticket** = recibo *m* del objeto empeñado *or* papeleta *f* de empeño **2** *verb* empeñar; **to pawn a watch** = empeñar un reloj

◊ **pawnbroker** ['pɔːnbrəukə] *noun* prestamista *mf*

◊ **pawnshop** ['pɔːnʃɒp] *noun* casa *f* de empeños *or* monte *m* de piedad

pay [peɪ] **1** *noun* **(a)** *(salary)* paga *f or* sueldo *m or* salario *m;* **back pay** = atrasos *mpl or* salario atrasado; **basic pay** = sueldo base; **take-home pay** = salario *or* sueldo neto; **unemployment pay** = subsidio *m* de desempleo *or* de paro **(b)** **pay cheque** = cheque *m* de sueldo *or* salario; **pay day** = día *m* de pago *or* de cobro; **pay negotiations** *or* **pay talks** = negociaciones *fpl* salariales **2** *verb* **(a)** *(give money)* pagar *or* abonar; **to pay in advance** = pagar por adelantado; **to pay in instalments** = pagar a plazos; **to pay cash** = pagar al contado *or* en efectivo; **to be paid** = cobrar; *(written on cheque)* **'pay cash'** = 'pago al contado'; **to pay on demand** = pagar a la vista; **to pay a dividend** = distribuir un dividendo; **to pay interest** = pagar un interés; **building societies pay interest of 10%** = las empresas constructoras pagan un interés del 10%; **pay as you earn (PAYE)** *or US* **pay-as-you-go** = sistema *m* fiscal de retención directa **(b)** *(to give a worker money for work done)* pagar; **the workers have not been paid for three weeks** = no se ha pagado a los trabajadores durante tres semanas; **we pay good wages for skilled workers** = pagamos buenos salarios a los trabajadores especializados; **how much do they pay you per hour?** = ¿cuánto te pagan por hora?; **to be paid by the hour** = cobrar por horas; **to be paid at piece-work rates** = cobrar a destajo (NOTE: **paying - paid - has paid**)

◊ **payable** ['peɪəbl] *adjective* pagadero, -ra; **payable in advance** = pagadero por adelantado; **payable on delivery** = pagadero a la entrega; **payable on demand** = pagadero a la vista; **payable at sixty days** = pagadero a sesenta días; **cheque made payable to bearer** = cheque *m* pagadero al portador; **shares payable on application** = acciones *fpl* pagaderas en el momento de la suscripción; **accounts payable** = cuentas *fpl* a pagar; **bills payable** = cuentas *or* efectos *mpl* a pagar; **electricity charges are payable by the**

tenant = los gastos de electricidad corren a cuenta del inquilino

◊ **pay back** ['peɪ 'bæk] *verb* devolver *or* reembolsar; **to pay back a loan** = devolver un préstamo; **I lent him £50 and he promised to pay me back in a month** = le presté 50 libras y prometió devolvérmelas en un mes; **he has never paid me back the money he borrowed** = nunca me ha devuelto el dinero que le presté

◊ **payback** ['peɪbæk] *noun* devolución *f or* reembolso *m;* **payback clause** = cláusula *f* de reembolso de un préstamo; **payback period** = plazo *m* de reembolso *or* plazo de amortización

◊ **pay cheque** *or* **paycheck** ['peɪ 'tʃek] *noun* cheque *m* del sueldo

◊ **pay down** ['peɪ 'daun] *verb* **to pay money down** = dejar una señal *or* hacer un desembolso inicial *or* dar una entrada; **he paid £50 down and the rest in monthly instalments** = dejó una señal de 50 libras y el resto lo pagó en plazos mensuales

◊ **PAYE** ['piː 'eɪ 'waɪ 'iː] = PAY AS YOU EARN

◊ **payee** [peɪ'iː] *noun* beneficiario, -ria *or* tenedor, -ra *or* portador, ra *m*

◊ **payer** ['peɪə] *noun* pagador, -ra; **slow payer** = moroso, -sa

◊ **pay in** *or* **into** ['peɪ 'ɪn] *verb (of a defendant)* consignar; **to pay in** *or* **to pay money into court** = prestar fianza *or* pagar dinero al principio de un juicio para que, si el caso se pierde, el demandado no tenga que cargar con las costas del demandante

COMMENT: if at trial the plaintiff fails to recover more than the amount the defendant has paid in, he will have to pay the defendant's costs from the date of the payment in

◊ **payment** ['peɪmənt] *noun* **(a)** *(transfer of money)* pago *m or* retribución *f;* **payment by results** = pago *or* cobro *m* a destajo; **payment in cash** *or* **cash payment** = pago al contado; **payment by cheque** = pago mediante cheque *or* talón; **payment of interest** *or* **interest payment** = pago de intereses; **payment on account** = pago a cuenta *or* pago parcial; **the solicitor asked for a payment of £100 on account** = el abogado pidió 100 libras a cuenta; **full payment** *or* **payment in full** = pago total *or* pago íntegro *or* pago de liberación; **payment on invoice** = pago al recibo de la factura; **payment in** *or* **payment into court** = pago hecho al principio de un juicio para que, si éste se pierde, el demandado no tenga que cargar con las costas del demandante **(b)** *(money paid)* pago; **back payment** = pago atrasado; **deferred payments** = pagos aplazados; **down payment** = depósito *m or* pago inicial *or* entrada *f* a cuenta; **monthly payment** = mensualidad *f;* **interim payment** = pago a cuenta; **part payment** = pago parcial

◊ **pay off** ['peɪ 'ɒf] *verb* **(a)** *(debt)* saldar *or* liquidar *or* reembolsar; **to pay off a mortgage** = redimir una hipoteca; **to pay off a loan** = amortizar un préstamo **(b)** *(employment)* despedir; **when the company was taken over the factory was closed** and all the workers were paid off = cuando la empresa fue absorbida, cerraron la fábrica y despidieron a todos los trabajadores

◊ **payoff** ['peɪɒf] *noun* pago *m* de liquidación *or* de saldo

◊ **payroll** ['peɪrəʊl] *noun* nómina *f or* plantilla *f*

◊ **pay up** ['peɪ 'ʌp] *verb* pagar *or* saldar una deuda; **the company paid up only when we sent them a letter from our solicitor** = la empresa no pagó la deuda hasta que nuestro abogado no les envió una carta; **he finally paid up six months late** = pagó finalmente con seis meses de retraso

PC ['piː 'siː] = PERSONAL COMPUTER, POLICE CONSTABLE, PRIVY COUNCIL, PRIVY COUNCILLOR (NOTE: the plural is **PCs**)

peace [piːs] *noun* **(a)** *(calm existence)* tranquilidad *f;* paz *f;* **breach of the peace** = perturbación *f* del orden público *or* alteración *f* del orden público **(b)** *(not being at war)* paz; **after six years of civil war, the country is now at peace** = tras seis años de guerra civil, el país está ahora en paz; **the peace treaty was signed yesterday** = ayer se firmó el tratado de paz; **both sides claimed the other side broke the peace agreement** = ambos lados afirman que la otra parte rompió el acuerdo de paz

pecuniary [pɪ'kjuːnɪəri] *adjective* pecuniario, -ria; **obtaining a pecuniary advantage by deception** = obtener ventajas económicas por estafa; *(made no profit)* **he gained no pecuniary advantage** = no sacó ninguna ventaja pecuniaria

pedlar ['pedlə] *noun* buhonero, -ra; *(drugs)* **drug pedlar** = narcotraficante *mf; (slang)* camello *m or* narcotraficante

peer [pɪə] *noun* **(a)** *(House of Lords)* par *m;* **hereditary peer** = par hereditario; **life peer** = par vitalicio *or* miembro vitalicio de la Cámara de los Lores **(b)** *(same group or rank)* igual *mf;* **peer group** = grupo *m* de personas del mismo rango

◊ **peeress** [pɪər'es] *noun* paresa *f or* par *f* vitalicia de la Cámara de los Lores

penal ['piːnəl] *adjective* penal *or* castigable *or* punible; **penal code** = código *m* penal; **penal colony** = penal *m;* **penal institution** = institución *f* penal; **penal laws** *or* **the penal system** = las leyes penales *or* el sistema penal; **penal servitude** = trabajos *mpl* forzosos *or* forzados

◊ **penalize** ['piːnəlaɪz] *verb* penalizar *or* penar *or* castigar *or* sancionar; **to penalize a supplier for late deliveries** = penalizar a un proveedor por entregas tardías; **they were penalized for bad service** = se les penalizó por un servicio deficiente

penalty ['penəlti] *noun* pena *f or* multa *f or* castigo *m;* **the penalty for carrying an offensive weapon is a fine of £2,000 and three months in prison** = el castigo por llevar un arma ofensiva es una multa de 2.000 libras y tres meses de arresto; **death penalty**

= pena de muerte; **the president has introduced the death penalty for certain crimes against the state** = el presidente ha introducido la pena de muerte por determinados delitos contra el estado; **penalty clause** = cláusula *f* penal *or* de penalización; **the contract contains a penalty clause which fines the company 1% for every week the completion date is late** = el contrato contiene una cláusula de penalización que multa a la empresa en un 1% por cada semana que se retrasa la fecha de cumplimiento

COMMENT: penalty clauses in a contract are sometimes unenforceable

pendens ['pendenz] *see* LIS

◊ **pendente lite** [pen'denteɪ 'laɪteɪ] *Latin phrase* durante el juicio; *see also* ALIMONY

pending ['pendɪŋ] **1** *adjective* pendiente *or* sin resolver; **pending action** = pendiente de juicio *or* en espera de juicio; **pending decision** = pendiente de resolución; **pending suit** = mientras el juicio continúa; **maintenance pending suit** = manutención *f* pendiente de litigio *or* pensión *f* de manutención provisional hasta la celebración del juicio; **patent pending** = patente *f* solicitada *or* en trámite **2** *adverb* **pending advice from our lawyers** = hasta recibir asesoramiento de nuestros abogados

penitentiary [penɪ'tenʃəri] *noun* US penitenciaría *f or* penal *m or* centro *m* penitenciario; **the Pennsylvania State Penitentiary** = la penitenciaría del estado de Pensilvania

penology [piː'nɒlədʒi] *noun* penología *f*

pension ['penʃn] **1** *noun* **(a)** pensión *f;* **retirement pension** *or* **old age pension** = jubilación *f or* pensión de retiro *or* pensión de vejez; **occupational pension** = plan *m* de pensiones de la empresa *or* pensión laboral **(b)** **pension contributions** = cuotas *fpl* de pensión *or* contribuciones *fpl* al fondo de pensiones; **pension entitlement** = derecho *m* a percibir una pensión; **pension fund** = fondo *m* de pensiones *or* de jubilaciones; **pension plan** *or* **pension scheme** = plan *m* de pensiones *or* de previsión social; **contributory pension scheme** = plan de pensiones con contribución del empleado *or* plan de pensiones contributivo; **graduated pension scheme** = plan de pensiones proporcional; **non-contributory pension scheme** = plan de pensiones gratuito; **personal pension plan** = plan de pensiones personal **2** *verb* **to pension someone off** = jubilar a alguien (NOTE: the US equivalent is **Individual Retirement Account**)

◊ **pensionable** ['penʃnəbl] *adjective* con derecho a jubilación; **pensionable age** = edad *f* de jubilación *or* de retiro

◊ **pensioner** ['penʃnə] *noun* pensionista *mf;* **old age pensioner** = pensionista *or* retirado, -da *or* jubilado, -da

peppercorn rent ['pepəkɔːn 'rent] *noun* alquiler *m* nominal *or* simbólico; **to pay a peppercorn rent** = pagar un alquiler simbólico; **to lease a property for** *or* **at a peppercorn rent** = arrendar una propiedad por un alquiler mínimo

per [pɔː *or* pə] *preposition* **(a)** as per = según *or* de acuerdo con; **as per invoice** = según factura; **as per sample** = según muestra; **as per previous order** = según pedido anterior **(b)** por *or* a; **per hour** *or* **per day** *or* **per week** *or* **per year** = por hora *or* a la hora *or* por día *or* al día *or* por semana *or* a la semana *or* por año *or* al año; **the rate is £5 per hour** = la tarifa es de 5 libras por hora; **he makes about £2,500 per month** = gana cerca de 2.500 libras al mes; **we pay £10 per hour** = pagamos 10 libras por hora *or* pagamos 10 libras la hora; **the earnings per share** = los dividendos por acción; **per head** = por cabeza *or* por persona; **allow £15 per head for expenses** = calcula unas 15 libras para gastos por persona; **the rate of imperfect items is about twenty-five per thousand** = la proporción de artículos defectuosos es de aproximadamente veinticinco por mil; **the birth rate has fallen to twelve per hundred** = el índice de natalidad ha descendido al doce por ciento

◊ **per annum** ['pə 'ænəm] *adverb* al año *or* anual; **the rent is £2,500 per annum** = la renta es de 2.500 libras al año; **what is their turnover per annum?** = ¿cuál es su volumen de ventas anual?; **reliable staff cost on average £15,000 per head per annum** = el personal de confianza cuesta una media de 15.000 libras por persona y año

◊ **per autre vie** ['pə 'əutrə 'viː] *French phrase meaning* 'para la vida de otra persona'

◊ **per capita** ['pə 'kæptɪə] *adjective & adverb* **(a)** *(in a will)* por persona *or* per cápita **(b)** *(for each person)* por cabeza *or* por persona *or* per cápita; **average income per capita** *or* **per capita income** = ingresos *mpl* medios per cápita; **per capita expenditure** = gastos *mpl* per cápita

◊ **per curiam** ['pə 'kjuːriəm] *Latin phrase* por el tribunal en pleno: decisión *f* de un tribunal que puede ser utilizada como precedente

◊ **per diem** ['pə 'diːəm] *Latin phrase* por día *or* al día *or* diariamente

◊ **per incuriam** ['pə ɪn'kjuːriəm] *Latin phrase* 'por falta de cuidado': decisión errónea de un tribunal que no puede ser utilizada como precedente

◊ **per my et per tout** ['pə mi: eɪ pə 'tuː] *French phrase meaning* modo *m* de descripción de la propiedad conjunta

per pro ['pə: 'prəu] = PER PROCURATIONEM por poder *or* con la autoridad de; **the secretary signed per pro the manager** = el secretario firmó por poderes del director

◊ **per procurationem** ['pə prɒkjuræsi'əunəm] *Latin phrase* por poder *or* con la autoridad de

◊ **per quod** ['pə 'kwɒd] *Latin phrase* por lo que *or* por lo cual

◊ **per se** ['pə 'seɪ] *Latin phrase* por sí mismo, -ma *or* en sí mismo, -ma; **actionable per se** = procesable por sí mismo *or* per se

◊ **per stirpes** ['pə: 'stəːpiːz] *Latin phrase* por estirpes *or* por ramas (en testamentos)

per cent ['pə 'sent] *adjective & adverb* por cien *or* por ciento; **eighty per cent (80%) of crimes are solved** = el ochenta por ciento (80%) de los delitos son resueltos (NOTE: usually written % after figures)

◊ **percentage** [pə'sentɪdʒ] *noun* porcentaje *m* or tanto *m* por ciento; **percentage increase** = aumento *m* or incremento *m* porcentual *or* porcentaje de aumento; **a percentage point** = un punto *m* porcentual; **what is the percentage of crimes committed at night?** = ¿cuál es el porcentaje de delitos cometidos por la noche?; **the number of crimes of violence has fallen by two percentage points over the last three years** = el número de delitos con violencia ha caído en dos puntos porcentuales en los tres últimos años

perceive [pə'siːv] *verb* percibir

peremptory challenge [pə'remptri 'tʃælɪndʒ] *noun* recusación *f* sin causa *or* objeción *f* a un miembro del jurado sin especificar las razones por las que se realiza

perfect ['pəːfɪkt] **1** *adjective* perfecto, -ta; **we check each shipment to make sure it is perfect** = comprobamos cada envío para asegurarnos de que está en perfecto estado *or* de que es correcto; **she did a perfect typing test** = hizo una prueba de mecanografía perfecta; **perfect right** = justo *or* perfecto derecho **2** *verb* perfeccionar; **he perfected the process for making high quality steel** = perfeccionó el proceso para fabricar acero de alta calidad

◊ **perfectly** ['pəːfɪktli] *adverb* perfectamente; **she typed the letter perfectly** = mecanografió la carta perfectamente

perform [pə'fɔːm] *verb* **(a)** *(to do well or badly)* funcionar *or* actuar *or* comportarse *or* rendir; **the company** *or* **the shares performed badly** = la compañía tuvo una mala actuación *or* la cotización de las acciones de la empresa descendió *or* las acciones de la empresa se cotizaron por debajo de lo normal **(b)** *(to do a duty)* cumplir (con un deber) *or* ejecutar *or* desempeñar

◊ **performance** [pə'fɔːməns] *noun* **(a)** *(way in which something or someone acts)* actuación *f* or funcionamiento *m* or rendimiento *m;* **the poor performance of the shares on the stock market** = la baja cotización de las acciones en el mercado de valores; **as a measure of the company's performance** = como medida del rendimiento de la empresa; **performance of personnel against objectives** = rendimiento del personal en relación a los objetivos marcados; **performance review** =

entrevista *f* anual entre empleado y director para revisar el rendimiento del primero **(b)** *(carrying out of something)* cumplimiento *m* or ejecución *f;* **they were asked to put up a £1m performance bond** = se les pidió que depositaran 1 millón de libras como fianza de cumplimiento del contrato; **discharge by performance** = cumplimiento de un contrato; **impossibility of performance** = imposibilidad *f* de cumplimiento de contrato; **part performance** = cumplimiento parcial de contrato; **specific performance** = orden *f* judicial de ejecución de contrato según sus términos

◊ **performing right** [pə'fɔːmɪŋ 'raɪt] *noun* derecho *m* de interpretación de una pieza musical protegida por propiedad intelectual

peril ['perɪl] *noun* peligro *m* or riesgo *m;* **perils of the sea** or **maritime perils** = peligros del mar

period ['pɪəriəd] *noun* **(a)** *(length of time)* periodo *m* or plazo *m;* **period of grace** = periodo de gracia; **training period** = periodo de aprendizaje; **for a period of time** or **for a period of months** or **for a six-year period** = por un periodo de tiempo or por un periodo de meses or por un plazo de seis años; **to deposit money for a fixed period** = depositar dinero a plazo fijo **(b) accounting period** = periodo contable **(c)** *(duration)* **period of appointment** = duración *f* de las funciones

◊ **periodic** or **periodical** [pɪəri'ɒdɪkl] **1** *adjective* periódico, -ca; **periodical payments** = pagos *mpl* periódicos or plazos *mpl;* **periodic tenancy** = arrendamiento *m* periódico or alquiler *m* periódico **2** *noun* **periodical** = periódico *m* or revista *f* periódica or publicación *f* periódica

perjure ['pɜːdʒə] *verb* **to perjure yourself** = prestar falso testimonio or jurar en falso

◊ **perjury** ['pɜːdʒəri] *noun* perjurio *m* or falso testimonio *m* or juramento *m* falso; **to commit perjury** = hacer juramento en falso; **he was sent to prison for perjury** = se le condenó a prisión por perjurio; **she appeared in court on a charge of perjury** or **on a perjury charge** = compareció ante el tribunal por una acusación de perjurio

permanent ['pɜːmənənt] *adjective* permanente or definitivo, -va or fijo, -ja or estable; **he has found a permanent job** = ha encontrado un trabajo fijo; **she is in permanent employment** = tiene trabajo fijo; **the permanent staff work a thirty-five hour week** = el personal de plantilla trabaja treinta y cinco horas a la semana

◊ **Permanent Secretary** ['pɜːmənənt 'sekrətri] *noun* secretario, -ria permanente (NOTE: in Canada, called **Deputy Minister)**

COMMENT: Permanent Secretaries are appointed by the Prime Minister but are responsible to the Secretary of State in charge of the relevant department

◊ **permanency** ['pɜːmənənsi] *noun* permanencia *f* or puesto *m* fijo

◊ **permanently** ['pɜːmənəntli] *adverb* permanentemente or definitivamente; **he was permanently disabled by the accident** = el accidente le dejó inválido para toda la vida

permission [pə'mɪʃn] *noun* permiso *m* or autorización *f* or licencia *f;* **written permission** = permiso escrito or autorización escrita; **verbal permission** = autorización verbal; **to give someone permission to do something** = dar permiso a alguien para hacer algo or autorizar a alguien a hacer algo

permissive waste [pə'mɪsɪv 'weɪst] *noun* deterioro *m* de una vivienda por negligencia del inquilino

permit 1 ['pɜːmɪt] *noun* permiso *m* or licencia *f;* **building permit** = licencia de obras or permiso de construcción; **entry permit** = permiso de entrada or visado *m;* **export permit** or **import permit** = licencia de exportación or de importación; **work permit** = permiso de trabajo **2** [pə'mɪt] *verb* permitir; **this document permits the export of twenty-five computer systems** = este documento permite la exportación de veinticinco sistemas informáticos; **the ticket permits three people to go into the exhibition** = el billete permite la entrada de tres personas a la exposición

perpetrate ['pɜːpɪtreɪt] *verb* perpetrar or cometer

◊ **perpetrator** ['pɜːpɪtreɪtə] *noun* autor, -ra or perpetrador, -ra

perpetuity [pɜːpə'tjuːəti] *noun* perpetuidad *f;* **in perpetuity** = a perpetuidad; **rule against perpetuities** = principio *m* que limita la inalienabilidad de bienes

persistent offender [pə'sɪstənt ə'fendə] *noun* reincidente *mf*

person ['pɜːsən] *noun* **(a)** *(someone)* persona *f;* **insurance policy which covers a named person** = póliza de seguros nominativa; **the persons named in the contract** = las personas que figuran en el contrato; **the document should be witnessed by a third person** = un tercero debería dar fe del documento; **person concerned** = persona interesada; **in person** = en persona or personalmente; **this important package is to be delivered to the chairman in person** = este importante paquete debe ser entregado al presidente en mano or en persona; **he came to see me in person** = vino a verme personalmente; **litigant in person** = litigante *mf* en persona, que inicia un proceso judicial y defiende personalmente su causa ante el tribunal **(b) legal person** or **artificial person** = persona jurídica

◊ **persona** [pə'səunə] *noun* **(a)** *(which has personality)* persona *f* **(b) persona non grata** = persona non grata

◊ **personal** ['pɜːsnl] *adjective* **(a)** *(referring to one person)* personal; **personal action** = acción *f* personal; *(against someone)* acción contra una persona = ACTION IN PERSONAM; **personal allowances** = deducciones *fpl* personales; **personal assets** = bienes *mpl* muebles personales; **personal chattels** *or* **chattels personal** = bienes muebles; **personal computer** = ordenador *m* personal; **personal estate** *or* **personal property** = propiedad *f* mobiliaria (que se puede transmitir por herencia) *or* bienes muebles; **personal income** = renta *f* personal *or* ingresos *mpl* personales; **personal injury** = daños *mpl* personales *or* corporales; **personal representative** = albacea *mf* *or* representante *mf* testamentario; **personal service** = entrega *f* de una notificación en persona *or* en mano **(b)** *(private)* personal *or* privado, -da; **I want to see the director on a personal matter** = quiero ver al director para un asunto personal; **personal assistant** = secretario, -ria personal

◊ **personally** ['pɜːsnli] *adverb* personalmente *or* en persona *or* uno mismo; **he personally opened the envelope** = él mismo abrió el sobre; **she wrote to me personally** = me escribió personalmente

◊ **personality** [pɜːsə'nælɪti] *noun* personalidad *f*; **legal personality** = personalidad jurídica; **corporate personality** = personalidad jurídica de una sociedad anónima

◊ **personalty** ['pɜːsnlti] *noun* bienes *mpl* muebles *or* propiedad *f* mobiliaria

◊ **personam** [pə'səʊnəm] *see* ACTION

◊ **personate** ['pɜːsneɪt] *verb* suplantar la personalidad

◊ **personation** [pɜːsə'neɪʃn] *noun* usurpación *f* de personalidad

personnel [pɜːsə'nel] *noun* personal *m* *or* empleados *mpl*; **all the personnel have to sign the Official Secrets Act** = todo el personal tiene que firmar la Ley relativa a los Secretos Oficiales; **personnel officer** = director, -ra de personal *or* jefe, -fa de personal (NOTE: no plural; **personnel** usually takes a plural verb)

persuade [pə'sweɪd] *verb* persuadir *or* convencer; **after ten hours of discussion, they persuaded the plaintiff to accept an out-of-court settlement** = tras diez horas de debate, persuadieron al demandante para que aceptara un acuerdo amistoso; **we could not persuade the French company to sign the contract** = no pudimos persuadir a la empresa francesa para que firmara el contrato

◊ **persuasive precedent** *or* **authority** [pə'sweɪzɪv 'presɪdənt] *noun* precedente *m* a tener en cuenta (no vinculante pero importante para dictar sentencia)

pertain [pə'teɪn] *verb* **to pertain to** = referirse a *or* relacionarse con; **the law pertaining to public order** = la ley referente al orden público

perverse [pə'vɜːs] *adjective* adverso, -sa *or* contrario, -ria; **perverse verdict** = veredicto *m* contrario (a lo que se considera la decisión correcta *or* a la opinión del juez)

pervert 1 ['pɜːvɜːt] *noun* pervertido, -da **2** [pə'vɜːt] *verb* desvirtuar *or* desnaturalizar *or* interferir *or* pervertir; **to attempt to pervert the course of justice** = tratar de interferir el curso de la justicia

> COMMENT: perverting the course of justice is a notifiable offence

petition [pə'tɪʃn] **1** *noun* **(a)** *(written application to a court)* petición *f* *or* solicitud *f* *or* recurso *m*; **bankruptcy petition** = declaración *f* de quiebra *or* petición de quiebra; **to file a petition in bankruptcy** = presentar una petición de quiebra *or* declararse en quiebra; **divorce petition** = demanda *f* de divorcio; **winding up petition** = solicitud de liquidación; **to file a petition** = cursar una demanda *or* una petición **(b)** *(written request supported by a list of signatures)* escrito *m*; **they presented a petition with a million signatures to Parliament, asking for the law to be repealed** = presentaron un escrito con un millón de firmas al Parlamento, pidiendo que la ley fuera revocada **2** *verb* dirigir una petición *or* solicitar *or* presentar una solicitud; **he petitioned the government for a special pension** = solicitó una pensión especial al gobierno; **the marriage had broken down and the wife petitioned for divorce** = el matrimonio se había venido abajo y la esposa presentó una demanda de divorcio

◊ **petitioner** [pə'tɪʃnə] *noun* solicitante *mf* peticionario, -ria

petty ['peti] *adjective* pequeño, -ña *or* sin importancia *or* insignificante; **petty cash** = fondo *m* *or* dinero *m* para gastos menores; **petty crime** = delitos *mpl* menores; **petty offence** = falta *f* leve; **petty sessions** = tribunal *m* de primera instancia *or* de magistrados; **petty theft** = hurto *m* menor *or* ratería *f*

◊ **petty-sessional division** ['peti'seʃnl dɪ'vɪʒn] *noun* sección *f* del país que cubre un tribunal de magistrados

photofit ['fəʊtəufɪt] *noun* retrato *m* robot; **the police issued a photofit picture of the mugger** = la policía puso en circulación un retrato robot del atracador; *see also* IDENTIKIT

physical ['fɪzɪkl] *adjective* físico, -ca; **the court was told of acts of physical violence committed against the police** = se informó al tribunal de actos de violencia física contra la policía

◊ **physically** ['fɪsɪkli] *adverb* físicamente; **the testator was physically fit, but mentally incapable of understanding the terms of the will** = el testador gozaba de buena salud física, pero era mentalmente incapaz de comprender los términos del testamento

pick [pɪk] 1 *noun* elección *f or* selección *f;* **take your pick** = escoja el que quiera *or* elija a su gusto; **the pick of the group** = el mejor del grupo *or* lo más selecto *or* lo más escogido 2 *verb* **(a)** *(choice)* elegir *or* escoger *or* seleccionar; **the government has picked a leading QC to be the new chairman of the tribunal** = el gobierno ha elegido a un importante abogado para que sea el nuevo presidente del tribunal; **the board picked the finance director to succeed the retiring managing director** = la junta escogió al director financiero para suceder al director gerente que se retiraba; **the Association has picked Paris for its next meeting** = la Asociación ha escogido París para su próxima reunión **(b) to pick someone's pocket** = robar algo del bolsillo de alguien; **to pick a lock** = forzar una cerradura *or* abrir una cerradura con ganzúa
◊ **picklock** ['pɪklɒk] *noun* ganzúa *f*
◊ **pickpocket** ['pɪkpɒkɪt] *noun* ratero, -ra *or* carterista *mf or* caco *m*
◊ **picker** ['pɪkə] *noun (slang)* en una banda de rateros, el que actúa como carterista; *compare* RUNNER
◊ **pick up** ['pɪk 'ʌp] *verb* **(a)** *(to improve)* recuperarse *or* mejorar; **business *or* trade is picking up** = los negocios se recuperan *or* el comercio está mejorando **(b)** *(informal)* coger *or* detener; **he was picked up by the police at the airport** = fue detenido por la policía en el aeropuerto

picket ['pɪkɪt] 1 *noun* piquete *m* de huelga; **picket line** = piquete de vigilancia 2 *verb* **to picket a factory** = organizar piquetes a la entrada de una fábrica
◊ **picketing** ['pɪkɪtɪŋ] *noun* formación *f* de piquetes laborales a la entrada de una fábrica; **lawful *or* peaceful picketing** = formación *f* de piquetes laborales en una huelga legal *or* piquetes pacíficos; **mass picketing** = formación de piquetes múltiples *or* en masa; **secondary picketing** = formación de piquetes secundarios

pilfer ['pɪlfə] *verb* hurtar *or* sisar *or* ratear
◊ **pilferage *or* pilfering** ['pɪlfrɪdʒ or 'pɪlfrɪŋ] *noun* hurto *m or* sisa *f or* ratería *f*
◊ **pilferer** ['pɪlfrə] *noun* ladronzuelo, -la *or* ratero, -ra

pillage ['pɪlɪdʒ] *noun* expolio *m*

pimp [pɪmp] *noun* proxeneta *m or* chulo *m or* alcahuete *m*

pinch [pɪntʃ] *verb (informal)* **(a)** *(to steal)* mangar *or* birlar **(b)** *(to arrest)* agarrar *or* pescar

pirate ['paɪrət] 1 *noun* **(a)** *(person who attacks ships at sea)* pirata *m* **(b)** *(person who copies and sells a patented invention or copyright)* pirata *or* pirateador, -ra 2 *adjective* pirata; **a pirate copy of a**

book = una copia pirata de un libro; **pirate radio station** = emisora *f* de radio pirata 3 *verb* piratear *or* hacer una edición pirata de; **a pirated book *or* a pirated design** = una edición pirata de un libro *or* un diseño pirata; **the drawings for the new dress collection were pirated in the Far East** = los dibujos para la nueva colección de vestidos fueron pirateados en Extremo Oriente
◊ **piracy** ['paɪrəsi] *noun* **(a)** *(at sea)* piratería *f* **(b)** *(copyright)* edición *f* pirata; **laws to ban book piracy** = leyes *fpl* para prohibir la piratería editorial

place [pleɪs] 1 *noun* **(a)** *(where something is or something happens)* lugar *m or* sitio *m;* **hiding place** = escondite *m;* **to take place** = tener lugar *or* suceder *or* celebrarse; **the meeting will take place in our offices** = la reunión se celebrará en nuestras oficinas; **meeting place** = lugar de encuentro *or* de reunión; **place of performance** = lugar de ejecución; **place of work** = puesto *m* de trabajo *or* lugar de trabajo; **public place** = lugar público; *(in the House of Commons)* **the other place *or* another place** = la Cámara de los Lores (NOTE: the convention is that MPs never refer to the House of Lords in debates, but can only talk of 'the other place': 'following a decision in another place'; 'will my hon. Friend confirm that that opinion was expressed not only in the other place but also in this House?') **(b)** *(job)* puesto *m or* empleo *m or* colocación *f;* **he was offered a place with an insurance company** = le ofrecieron un puesto en una agencia de seguros; **she turned down three places before accepting the one we offered** = rechazó tres empleos antes de aceptar el que le ofrecimos **(c)** *(position in text)* lugar (en un texto) *m or* punto *m or* página *f;* **she marked her place in the text with a red pen** = señaló en rojo el punto del texto en donde se había quedado; **I have lost my place and cannot remember where I have reached in my filing** = he perdido el lugar en el que estaba y no puedo recordar hasta dónde había archivado 2 *verb* **(a)** colocar *or* poner; **to place money in an account** = depositar dinero en una cuenta; **to place a block of shares** = colocar un paquete de acciones; **to place a contract with a company** = adjudicar un contrato a una empresa; **to place an order** = hacer un pedido; **to place something on file** = archivar algo; **to place in custody** = poner a disposición de; **to place under surveillance** = mantener vigilado, -da **(b)** *(work)* **to place staff** = emplear *or* colocar a los empleados
◊ **placement** ['pleɪsmənt] *noun* colocación *f*
◊ **placing** ['pleɪsɪŋ] *noun* **the placing of a line of shares** = la colocación de una emisión de acciones

plagiarism ['pleɪdʒərɪzm] *noun* plagio *m*
◊ **plagiarize** ['pleɪdʒəraɪz] *verb* plagiar

plainclothes ['pleɪnkləʊðz] *adjective; (not in uniform)* de paisano *or* de incógnito; **a group of plainclothes police went into the house** = un grupo de policías sin uniforme entró en la casa; **a**

plainclothes detective travelled on the train = en el tren viajaba un detective de incógnito

plain cover ['pleɪn 'kʌvə] *noun* **to send something under plain cover** = enviar algo en un sobre blanco

plaint [pleɪnt] *noun* demanda *f or* querella *f;* **plaint note** = nota *f* puesta en circulación por un juzgado municipal al principio de una acción judicial
◊ **plaintiff** ['pleɪntɪf] *noun* demandante *mf or* querellante *mf;* **plaintiff's answer** = tríplica *f; compare* DEFENDANT

plan [plæn] **1** *noun* **(a)** *(project)* plan *m or* proyecto *m;* **contingency plan** = plan de emergencia *or* medidas *fpl* de prevención; **the government's economic plans** = los planes económicos del gobierno; **a Five-Year Plan** = un plan quinquenal; **open-plan** = régimen abierto **(b)** *(drawing)* plano *m or* mapa *m;* **floor plan** = plano de la planta; **street plan** *or* **town plan** = plano de la ciudad **2** *verb* planear *or* planificar; **the bank robbery was carefully planned in advance** = el atraco al banco fue minuciosamente planeado *or* preparado con antelación; **he plans to disguise himself as a policeman** = tiene la intención de disfrazarse de policía; **to plan for an increase in bank interest charges** = tener en cuenta *or* prever un aumento de los gastos en concepto de intereses bancarios; **to plan investments** = planificar las inversiones
◊ **planned** [plænd] *adjective* planeado, -da *or* planificado, -da; **planned economy** = economía *f* planificada
◊ **planner** ['plænə] *noun* **(a)** planificador, -ra; **the government's economic planners** = los planificadores económicos del gobierno; **town planner** = urbanista *mf* **(b)** **desk planner** *or* **wall planner** = calendario *m* de trabajo
◊ **planning** ['plænɪŋ] *noun* **(a)** *(organizing how something should be done)* planificación *f or* proyecto *m;* **economic planning** = planificación económica; **family planning** = planificación familiar **(b)** *(organizing how land and buildings should be used)* planeamiento *m* urbanístico *or* ordenación *f or* planificación urbana; **planning authority** = organismo *m* local que regula el planeamiento urbanístico; **planning department** = departamento *m* de planificación urbana; **planning inquiry** = solicitud *f or* tramitación *f* de un proyecto de planeamiento urbanístico; **planning permission** = permiso *m* de construcción; **outline planning permission** = aprobación *f* provisional de un proyecto de construcción; **to be refused planning permission** = denegarle a alguien la licencia de construcción; **we are waiting for planning permission before we can start building** = estamos esperando el permiso de construcción para empezar a construir; **the land is to be sold with outline planning permission for four houses** = el

solar se vende con la aprobación provisional para la construcción de cuatro casas

plant [plɑːnt] **1** *noun* maquinaria *f or* instalaciones *fpl* y bienes *mpl* de equipo **2** *verb* **to plant evidence** = falsear las pruebas *or* colocar pruebas falsas con la intención de implicar a alguien en un crimen

plc *or* **PLC** *or* **Plc** ['piː 'el 'siː] = PUBLIC LIMITED COMPANY

plea [pliː] **1** *noun* alegato *m;* **plea of guilty** *or* **of not guilty** = alegación *f* de culpabilidad *or* declaración *f* de inocencia; **to enter a plea of not guilty** = declararse inocente de los cargos; **plea of defence** = pliego *m* de defensa; **plea in mitigation** = alegato en favor del acusado para atenuar la pena; **tender a plea** = contestar a la demanda; **dilatory plea** = excepción *f* dilatoria **2** *verb* interpelar
◊ **plea bargaining** ['pliː 'bɑːgnɪŋ] *noun* sentencia *f* acordada *or* de conformidad *or* negociación *f* entre la defensa y la acusación con respecto a los cargos; *see also* DILATORY

plead [pliːd] *verb* **(a)** *(to answer an allegation or a charge)* alegar *or* hacer un alegato *or* declararse; **fit** *or* **unfit to plead** = capacitado *or* incapacitado para ser juzgado *or* para declararse culpable o inocente; **to plead guilty** *or* **not guilty** = declararse culpable *or* inocente **(b)** *(to speak on behalf of a client in court)* abogar *or* defender
◊ **pleading** ['pliːdɪŋ] *noun* **(a)** *(documents)* **pleadings** = alegaciones *fpl or* alegatos *mpl;* **the damage is itemized in the pleading** = los daños se especifican en las alegaciones; **the judge found that the plaintiff's pleadings disclosed no cause of action** = el juez consideró que las alegaciones del demandado no revelaban objeto de litigio; **pleadings must be submitted to the court when the action is set down for trial** = las alegaciones se deben presentar ante el tribunal cuando la acción esté fijada para juicio **(b)** *(speaking on someone's behalf)* defensa *f (NOTE: no plural in this meaning)*

pleasure ['pleʒə] *see* HER MAJESTY'S PLEASURE

pledge [pledʒ] **1** *noun* **(a)** *(collateral)* pignoración *f or* empeño *m* **(b)** *(pawned object)* prenda *f or* garantía *f;* **to redeem a pledge** = rescatar una prenda; **unredeemed pledge** = prenda *or* garantía sin rescatar **2** *verb* pignorar *or* dar en prenda; **to pledge share certificates** = pignorar acciones
◊ **pledgee** [ple'dʒiː] *noun* depositario, -ria
◊ **pledger** ['pledʒə] *noun* pignorador, -ra

plenary ['pliːnəri] *adjective* plenario, -ria; **plenary session** = sesión plenaria *or* completa

plenipotentiary [plenɪpə'tenʃəri] *noun* plenipotenciario, -ria

plot [plɒt] **1** *noun* intriga *f or* trama *f* **2** *verb* intrigar *or* maquinar

plunder ['plʌndə] **1** *noun* botín *m or* pillaje *m* **2** *verb* saquear *or* cometer pillaje *or* robar

p.m. *or* **post meridiem** ['piː 'em] *Latin phrase* después de las 12 del mediodía; **the train leaves at 6.50 p.m.** = el tren sale a las 6.50 de la tarde; **if you phone New York after 6 p.m. the calls are at a cheaper rate** = las llamadas a Nueva York después de las seis de la tarde son más baratas

PM ['piː 'em] = POST MORTEM, PRIME MINISTER

PO ['piː 'əʊ] = POST OFFICE

poaching ['pəʊtʃɪŋ] *noun* **(a)** *(hunting or stealing game)* caza *f or* pesca *f* furtiva **(b)** *(enticing workers)* atraer la mano de obra de la competencia *or* convencer a los trabajadores de un sindicato de que se asocien a otro

pocket ['pɒkɪt] **1** *noun* bolsillo *m* **2** *verb* embolsar
◊ **pocket borough** ['pɒkɪt 'bʌrə] *noun (formerly)* distrito *m* municipal donde una persona influyente ejercía control sobre los votos durante las elecciones
◊ **pocket veto** ['pɒkɪt 'viːtəʊ] *noun US* veto *m* que el presidente aplica indirectamente al no firmar un proyecto dentro del plazo establecido

COMMENT: normally the President has ten days to object to a bill which has been passed to him by Congress; if Congress adjourns during that period, the President's veto kills the bill

point [pɔɪnt] *noun* punto *m or* cuestión *f;* **point of fact** = cuestión de hecho; **in point of fact** = en realidad; **point of law** = cuestión de derecho; **counsel raised a point of law** = el abogado planteó una cuestión de derecho; **the case illustrates an interesting point of legal principle** = el caso ilustra una interesante cuestión de principio legal; **point of order** = cuestión de orden *or* de procedimiento; **he raised an interesting point of order** = planteó una interesante cuestión de orden; **on a point of order, Mr Smith asked the chairman to give a ruling on whether the committee could approve its own accounts** = según las reglas de procedimiento, el Sr Smith pidió al presidente que estableciera una norma sobre si el comité podía aprobar sus propias cuentas

poison ['pɔɪzn] **1** *noun* veneno *m;* **she killed the old lady by putting poison in her tea** = mató a la anciana poniéndole veneno en el té **2** *verb* envenenar; **he was not shot, he was poisoned** = no le dispararon, le envenenaron

police [pə'liːs] **1** *noun* policía *f;* **police file** *or* **record** = ficha *f* policial; **suspect with a police record** = delincuente fichado por la policía; **police evidence** = pruebas aportadas por la policía; **police patrol** = ronda *f* policial; **the police have cordoned off the town centre** = la policía ha acordonado el

centro de la ciudad; **the government is relying on the police to keep law and order during the elections** = el gobierno confía en la policía para mantener el orden público durante las elecciones; **the bank robbers were picked up by the police at the railway station** = los atracadores del banco fueron detenidos por la policía en la estación de ferrocarril; **military police** = policía militar; **secret police** = policía secreta; **police cordon** = cordón *m* policial; **police court** = tribunal *m* de policia *or* juzgado *m* de guardia (NOTE: no plural. **Police** is usually followed by a plural verb) **2** *verb* **(a)** *(to keep law and order)* vigilar *or* mantener el orden en; **the meeting was policed by plainclothes men** = la reunión fue vigilada por policías sin uniforme; **the council is debating the Chief Constable's policing policy** = el consejo está debatiendo el sistema de mantenimiento del orden propuesto por el jefe de policía **(b)** *(to make sure that regulations are carried out)* supervisar *or* vigilar

COMMENT: under English law, a policeman is primarily an ordinary citizen who has certain powers at common law and by statute. The police are organized by area, each area functioning independently with its own police force. London, and the area round London, is policed by the Metropolitan Police Force under the direct supervision of the Home Secretary. Outside London, each police force is answerable to a local police authority, although day-to-day control of operations is vested entirely in the Chief Constable

◊ **police authority** [pə'liːs ɔː'θɒrɪti] *noun* autoridad *f* que supervisa la labor de un cuerpo de policía local
◊ **Police Commissioner** [pə'liːs kə'mɪʃənə] *noun* comisario *m* de policía; **Metropolitan Police Commissioner** = comisario de la policía metropolitana
◊ **Police Complaints Board** [pə'liːs kɒm'pleɪnts 'bɔːd] *noun* comité *m* de quejas a la policía
◊ **police constable** [pə'liːs 'kʌnstəbl] *noun* agente *mf* de policía; **Police Constables Smith and Jones are on patrol** = los policías Smith y Jones están de patrulla; **Woman Police Constable MacIntosh was at the scene of the accident** = la mujer policía MacIntosh estaba en el lugar del accidente (NOTE: usually abbreviated to **PC** and **WPC**)
◊ **police force** [pə'liːs 'fɔːs] *noun* cuerpo *m* de policía *or* policía *f or* fuerza *f* pública; **the members of several local police forces have collaborated in the murder hunt** = los miembros de varios cuerpos de policía local han colaborado en la búsqueda del asesino; **the London police force is looking for more recruits** = la policía de Londres está buscando nuevos agentes; *see also* DETECTIVE, METROPOLITAN

COMMENT: the ranks in a British police force

are: **Police Constable, Police Sergeant, Inspector, Chief Inspector, Superintendent, Chief Superintendent, Assistant Chief Constable, Deputy Chief Constable and Chief Constable**

police headquarters [pə'liːs hed'kwɔːtəz] *noun* jefatura *f* de policía
◊ **police inspector** [pə'liːs ɪn'spektə] *noun* inspector, -ra de policía
◊ **policeman** [pə'liːsmən] *noun* policía *m* or guardia *m;* **plain clothes policeman** = policía vestido de paisano (NOTE: the plural is **policemen**)
◊ **police officer** [pə'liːs 'ɒfɪsə] *noun* agente *mf* de policía or policía *mf*
◊ **police precinct** [pə'liːs 'priːsɪŋkt] *noun US* distrito *m* policial
◊ **police sergeant** [pə'liːs 'saːdʒənt] *noun* sargento *mf* de policía
◊ **police station** [pə'liːs 'steɪʃn] *noun* comisaría *f* de policía
◊ **police van** [pə'liːs 'væn] *noun* coche *m* celular
◊ **policewoman** ['pə'liːswʊmən] *noun* mujer *f* policía (NOTE: the plural is **policewomen**)
◊ **policing** [pə'liːsɪŋ] *noun* vigilancia *f* or mantenimiento *m* del orden; **community policing** = acción *f* conjunta de la policía y los miembros de una comunidad para el mantenimiento de la ley y el orden

policy ['pɒlɪsi] *noun* **(a)** *(agreed plan of action)* política *f* or norma *f* or principio *m* or línea *f* programática; **government policy on wages** or **government wages policy** = la política del gobierno sobre salarios; **the government's prices policy** = la política de precios del gobierno; **the country's economic policy** = la política económica del gobierno; **our policy is to submit all contracts to the legal department** = tenemos por norma que la asesoría jurídica examine todos los contratos; **the government made a policy statement** or **made a statement of policy** = el gobierno hizo una declaración pública sobre su política; **budgetary policy** = política presupuestaria; **foreign policy** = política exterior; *see also* PUBLIC POLICY **(b)** *(insurance)* póliza *f* or seguro *m;* **insurance policy** = póliza de seguros; **accident policy** = seguro de accidentes or contra accidentes; **comprehensive** or **all-risks policy** = póliza de seguro a todo riesgo; **contingent policy** = póliza para imprevistos; **endowment policy** = póliza de seguro dotal; **open policy** = póliza flotante or no valorada; **policy holder** = tenedor, -ra de una póliza de seguros

politeness [pə'laɪtnəs] *noun* cortesía *f* or educación *f*

politics ['pɒlɪtɪks] *noun* política *f* or arte *m* de gobernar; **local politics** = política local; **national** or **international politics** = política nacional or internacional; **power politics** = política de

agresión; **party politics** = política de partido or partidismo *m*
◊ **political** [pə'lɪtɪkl] *adjective* político, -ca; **political asylum** = asilo *m* político; **to ask for political asylum** = pedir asilo político; **political crime** = crimen *m* político; **political funds** = fondos *mpl* que un sindicato destina a fines políticos; **political levy** = parte *f* de la cuota pagada por un miembro de un sindicato destinada a ayudar económicamente a un partido político; **political party** = partido *m* político; **political prisoner** = preso *m* político
◊ **politician** [pɒlɪ'tɪʃn] *noun* político, -ca; **a full-time politician** = diputado, -da que se dedica exclusivamente a la política

poll [pəʊl] **1** *noun* **(a)** *(voting)* votación *f* or elecciones *fpl* or escrutinio *m;* **to go to the polls** = ir a las urnas or a votar; **the polls opened an hour ago** = se puede votar desde hace una hora; **the polls close at 10 o'clock** = las mesas electorales cierran a las 10 en punto **(b)** **opinion poll** = encuesta *f* or sondeo *m* de opinión; **exit poll** = encuesta que se lleva a cabo a la salida de los colegios o mesas electorales para pronosticar el resultado de las elecciones; **straw poll** = sondeo informal; **a straw poll among members of staff shows the government is in the lead** = según los votos de tanteo del personal, el gobierno sigue en cabeza **(c)** **deed poll** = escritura *f* legal; **she changed her name by deed poll** = cambió su nombre por escritura legal **2** *verb* **(a)** *(to receive votes)* obtener (votos en unas elecciones); **he polled only 123 votes in the general election** = obtuvo sólo 123 votos en las elecciones generales **(b)** *(to sample a group of people)* sondear; **to poll a sample of the population** = sondear a una muestra de la población; **to poll the members of the club on an issue** = sondear la opinión de los socios del club sobre un asunto
◊ **polling booth** ['pəʊlɪŋ 'buːð] *noun* cabina *f* electoral
◊ **polling day** ['pəʊlɪŋ 'deɪ] *noun* día *m* de las elecciones
◊ **polling station** ['pəʊlɪŋ 'steɪʃn] *noun* colegio *m* or mesa *f* electoral
◊ **pollster** ['pəʊlstə] *noun* analista *mf* profesional *mf* de opinión pública
◊ **poll tax** ['pəʊl 'tæks] *noun* impuesto *m* de capitación or per cápita

pollute [pə'luːt] *verb* contaminar
◊ **pollutant** [pə'luːtənt] *noun* agente *m* contaminante or contaminador; **discharge pipes take pollutants away from the coastal area into the sea** = los agentes contaminantes se transportan de la zona costera al mar a través de conductos de vertidos; **air pollutant** or **atmospheric pollutant** = polución *f* or contaminación *f* atmosférica
◊ **polluter** [pə'luːtə] *noun* persona *f* or compañía *f* que contamina; **certain industries are major polluters of the environment** = ciertas industrias

son las mayores responsables de la contaminación del medio ambiente; **polluter pays principle** = principio *m* según el cual una persona *or* una compañía debe hacerse responsable de los daños causados por la contaminación y de introducir medidas preventivas

◊ **pollution** [pə'lu:ʃn] *noun* contaminación *f;* **air pollution** *or* **atmospheric pollution** = polución *f or* contaminación atmosférica; **environmental pollution** = contaminación del medio ambiente; **noise pollution** = contaminación acústica; **water pollution** = contaminación del agua; **pollution charges** = impuesto *m* ecológico; **pollution control** = medidas *fpl* de control para reducir la contaminación

> COMMENT: pollution is caused by natural sources or by human action. Pollution can be caused by a volcanic eruption or by a nuclear power station. Pollutants are not only chemical substances, but can be a noise or an unpleasant smell (as from a grinding works or from a sewage farm)

polygamy [pə'lɪgəmi] *noun* poligamia *f*
◊ **polygamous** [pə'lɪgəməs] *adjective* polígamo, -ma; **a polygamous society** = una sociedad polígama

polygraph ['pɒlɪgrɑ:f] *noun* detector *m* de mentiras

popular ['pɒpjulə] *adjective* popular *or* de moda *or* que gusta a mucha gente; **this is our most popular model** = éste es el modelo que más gusta; **the South Coast is the most popular area for holidays** = la costa del Sur es la zona de moda para las vacaciones; **popular prices** = precios *mpl* populares; **popular vote** = votación *f* popular *or* democrática; **the president is elected by popular vote** = el presidente es elegido por votación popular

pornography [pɔ:'nɒgrəfi] *noun* pornografía *f*

porridge ['pɒrɪdʒ] *noun (slang)* chirona *f;* **to do porridge** = estar en chirona

port [pɔ:t] *noun* puerto *m;* **port of embarkation** = puerto de embarque; **port of registry** *or* **registry port** = puerto de registro de un buque

portfolio ['pɔ:t'fəuliəu] *noun* **(a)** *(shares)* cartera *f* (de valores); **his portfolio contains shares in the major oil companies** = su cartera contiene valores en las principales empresas petroleras **(b)** *(office of a minister)* cartera; **Minister without Portfolio** = ministro sin cartera

portion ['pɔ:ʃn] *noun* parte *f* que recibe una persona joven de los bienes del patrimonio familiar (ya sea en dinero *or* propiedad)

position [pə'zɪʃn] *noun* **(a)** *(state of affairs)* situación *f or* posición *f or* postura *f;* **bargaining position** = postura negociadora; **to cover a position** = tener respaldo económico **(b)** *(job)* puesto *m or*

cargo *m or* empleo *m;* **to apply for a position as manager** = solicitar un puesto de director; **we have several positions vacant** = tenemos varios puestos vacantes; **all the vacant positions have been filled** = todos los puestos vacantes han sido cubiertos; **she retired from her position in the accounts department** = se retiró de su cargo en el departamento de contabilidad; **position of trust** = puesto de confianza

positive ['pɒzɪtɪv] *adjective* positivo, -va *or* afirmativo,-va; **positive identification** = identificación positiva; **the board gave a positive reply** = la junta dio una respuesta afirmativa; **the breath test was positive** = la prueba de alcoholemia dio positiva; **positive vetting** = investigación *f* que da como resultado la poca fiabilidad de una persona

possess [pə'zes] *verb* poseer *or* tener; **the company possesses property in the centre of the town** = la empresa posee propiedades en el centro de la ciudad; **he lost all he possessed when his company was put into liquidation** = perdió todo lo que tenía cuando su empresa fue disuelta
◊ **possession** [pə'zeʃn] *noun* **(a)** *(control over property)* posesión *f;* **actual possession** = posesión real *or* efectiva; **chose in possession** = objeto *m* en posesión; **possession in law** = posesión legal *or* de jure; **adverse possession** = prescripción *f* adquisitiva *or* posesión ilegítima; **unlawful possession of weapons** = tenencia *f* ilícita de armas; **vacant possession** = propiedad *f or* casa *f* desocupada *or* libre de inquilinos; **the property is to be sold with vacant possession** = la propiedad debe venderse libre de inquilinos **(b)** *(physically holding something)* poder *m or* tenencia *f;* **the documents are in his possession** = los documentos están en su poder; **how did it come into his possession** *or* **how did he get possession of it?** = ¿cómo lo adquirió? *or* ¿cómo llegó a sus manos?; **possession of drugs** = tenencia de drogas; **unlawful possession of drugs** = posesión ilícita de drogas **(c)** **possessions** = posesiones *or* bienes *mpl;* **they lost all their possessions in the fire** = perdieron todo lo que poseían en el incendio (NOTE: no plural for (a) and (b))
◊ **possessive action** [pə'zesɪv 'ækʃn] *noun* acción *f* para recuperar una propiedad
◊ **possessory** [pə'zesəri] *adjective* posesorio, -ria; **possessory title** = título *m* de propiedad

post [pəust] **1** *noun* **(a)** *(system of sending letters)* correo *m;* **to send an invoice by post** = enviar una factura por correo; **he put the letter in the post** = echó la carta al correo; **the cheque was lost in the post** = el cheque se perdió en el correo; **to send a reply by return of post** = enviar una respuesta *or* responder a vuelta de correo; **letter post** *or* **parcel post** = servicio *m* de cartas postales *or* paquetes postales; **post room** = sala *f* de reparto de correo **(b)** *(letters sent or received)* correo *or* cartas *fpl;* **has the post arrived yet?** = ¿ha llegado ya el correo?; **my**

secretary opens the post as soon as it arrives = mi secretaria abre las cartas en cuanto llegan; **the receipt was in this morning's post** = el recibo estaba en el correo de esta mañana; **the letter did not arrive by first post this morning** = la carta no llegó en el primer reparto de esta mañana **(c)** *(job)* puesto *m or* empleo *m or* cargo *m;* **to apply for a post as legal executive** = solicitar un puesto de pasante; **we have three posts vacant** = tenemos tres puestos vacantes; **all our posts have been filled** = todos nuestros puestos han sido cubiertos; **we advertised three posts in 'The Times'** = anunciamos tres puestos de trabajo en 'The Times' **2** *verb* **(a)** *(to send something by post)* enviar por correo *or* echar al correo; **to post a letter** *or* **to post a parcel** = enviar una carta *or* enviar un paquete **(b)** *(banking)* **to post an entry** = pasar un asiento a una cuenta **(c)** *(to announce)* **to post up a notice** = poner un anuncio; **to post an increase** = anunciar un aumento

post- [pəust] *prefix* post *or* después; **post-obit** = después de la muerte

postage ['pəustidʒ] *noun* franqueo *m or* tarifa *f* postal

postal ['pəustl] *adjective* postal; **postal packet** = paquete *m* postal; **postal service** = servicio *m* postal *or* entrega *f* de notificación por correo

post code ['pəust 'kəud] *noun* código *m* postal (NOTE: US English is **zip code**)

postdate [pəust'deit] *verb* posfechar *or* poner fecha posterior a la del día; **he sent us a postdated cheque** = nos mandó un cheque con una fecha futura; **his cheque was postdated to June** = su cheque llevaba fecha del próximo mes de junio

poste restante ['pəust 'restɒnt] *noun* lista *f* de correos; **send any messages to 'Poste Restante, Athens'** = envíe cualquier mensaje a 'Lista de Correos, Atenas'

posteriori [pɒsteri'ɔːrai] *see* A POSTERIORI

post free ['pəust 'friː] *adverb* con porte pagado *or* con franqueo pagado; **the leaflet is obtainable post free from the Law Society** = el folleto se puede obtener con franqueo pagado del colegio de abogados

posthumous ['pɒstʃuməs] *adjective* póstumo, -ma

post mortem ['pəust 'mɔːtəm] *noun* autopsia *f or* necropsia *f or* necroscopia *f;* **the post mortem was carried out** *or* **was conducted by the police pathologist** = la autopsia fue llevada a cabo por el médico forense de la policía

post obit bond ['pəust 'əubit 'bɒnd] *noun* obligación *f* de devolver un préstamo cuando el prestatario reciba un legado

post office ['pəust 'ɒfis] *noun* **(a)** correos *m or* oficina *f* de correos; **sub-post office** = estafeta *f* de

correos **(b) the Post Office** = Administración *f* de Correos *or* Correos; **Post Office officials** *or* **officials of the Post Office** = funcionarios, -rias de Correos *or* de la Administración de Correos; **Post Office box number** = número *m* del apartado de correos

postpone [pəs'pəun] *verb* aplazar *or* posponer; **he postponed the meeting until tomorrow** = aplazó la reunión hasta mañana; **they asked if they could postpone payment until the cash situation was better** = preguntaron si podían aplazar el pago hasta que la situación de caja fuera mejor; **which cannot be postponed** = inaplazable

◊ **postponement** [pəs'pəunmənt] *noun* aplazamiento *m;* **I had to change my appointments because of the postponement of the board meeting** = tuve que cambiar mis compromisos a causa del aplazamiento de la reunión del consejo

post scriptum ['pəust 'skriptəm] *see* P.S.

pound [paund] *noun* depósito *m* de objetos incautados

power ['pauə] *noun* **(a)** *(strength)* poder *m or* capacidad *f or* posibilidad *f or* fuerza *f;* **bargaining power** = poder *or* fuerza de negociación *or* capacidad negociadora; **borrowing power** = capacidad de préstamo *or* de endeudamiento; **earning power** = rentabilidad *f* económica *or* poder adquisitivo **(b)** *(legal right)* poder *or* autoridad *f or* facultad *f;* **the powers of a local authority in relation to children in care** = las facultades de una autoridad local en relación a la custodia de menores; **the powers and duties conferred on the tribunal by the statutory code** = los poderes y deberes conferidos al tribunal por ley; **the president was granted wide powers under the constitution** = concedieron al presidente amplios poderes según la constitución; **executive power** = poder ejecutivo; **power of attorney** = poder notarial *or* poderes *mpl;* **power of appointment** = facultad que permite nombrar a un beneficiario para disponer de una propiedad; **power of election** = facultad que permite a la demanda elegir sus recursos; **the full power of the law** = toda la fuerza de la ley; **we will apply the full power of the law to regain possession of our property** = aplicaremos toda la fuerza de la ley para recuperar la posesión de nuestra propiedad; **power of search** = autorización para registrar el domicilio

p.p. ['piː 'piː] *verb* = PER PROCURATIONEM; **to p.p. a receipt** *or* **a letter** = firmar un recibo *or* una carta en nombre de alguien; **the secretary p.p.'d the letter while the manager was at lunch** = la secretaria firmó la carta en nombre del director, mientras éste estaba comiendo

PR ['piː 'ɑː] = PROPORTIONAL REPRESENTATION, PUBLIC RELATIONS

practice ['præktɪs] *noun* **(a)** *(way of doing things)* práctica *f or* procedimiento *m or* costumbre *f;* **standard practice** = prácticas establecidas; **his practice was to arrive at work at 7.30 and start counting the cash** = tenía la costumbre de llegar al trabajo a las 7.30 y empezar a hacer el recuento de caja; **business practices** *or* **industrial practices** *or* **trade practices** = prácticas empresariales *or* industriales *or* comerciales; **restrictive practices** = prácticas restrictivas; **sharp practice** = mañas *fpl;* **code of practice** = código *m* de conducta *or* ética profesional; **practice direction** = instrucciones *fpl* de los jueces sobre el correcto procedimiento en la aplicación de las leyes **(b) in practice** = en la práctica *or* en la realidad; **the scheme for dealing with young offenders seems very interesting, but what will it cost in practice?** = el proyecto para acabar con la delicuencia juvenil parece muy interesante, pero ¿qué costará en la práctica? **(c)** *(office and clients)* bufete *m or* despacho *m or* clientela *f or* clientes *mfpl;* **he has set up in practice as a solicitor** *or* **a patent agent** = ha puesto un bufete de abogados *or* se ha establecido como agente de patentes; **he is a partner in a country solicitor's practice** = es socio de un bufete de abogados del país **(d)** *(carrying on a profession)* ejercicio *m;* **he has been in practice for twenty years** = ha ejercido durante veinte años

◊ **Practice Master** ['præktɪs 'mɑːstə] *noun* oficial *mf* del Tribunal Supremo que asesora a los abogados sobre el procedimiento general de las actuaciones judiciales

practise ['præktɪs] *verb* ejercer; **he is a practising solicitor** = es un abogado en ejercicio; **practising certificate** = certificado *m* de ejercicio de la abogacía

praecipe ['priːsɪpi] *noun* petición *f* escrita a un tribunal para que redacte y ponga en circulación un documento legal

pray [preɪ] *verb* pedir *or* rogar; **to pray in aid** = acogerse a; **I pray in aid the Statute of Frauds** = me acojo al estatuto de fraudes

◊ **prayer** [preə] *noun* súplica *f* (que resume lo que pide el litigante al tribunal)

pre- [priː] *prefix* antes *or* previo, -via; **pre-contract discussion** = discusión previa al contrato; **pre-trial** = anterior a la causa; **pre-trial proceedings** = instrucción de una causa; **a pre-stocktaking sale** = una venta previa al recuento de existencias; **there will be a pre-AGM board meeting** = habrá una reunión del consejo previa a la junta general ordinaria

preamble [priˈæmbl] *noun* preámbulo *m*

precatory ['prekətri] *adjective* suplicante; **precatory words** = súplica *f or* palabras *fpl* de súplica

precaution [prɪˈkɔːʃn] *noun* precaución *f or* medida *f* cautelar; **safety precautions** = medidas de seguridad; **to take precautions to prevent thefts in the office** = tomar precauciones para evitar robos en la oficina; **the company did not take proper fire precautions** = la empresa no tomó las debidas precauciones contra incendios

◊ **precautionary** [prɪˈkɔːʃnri] *adjective;* **as a precautionary measure** = como medida preventiva

precede [prɪˈsiːd] *verb* preceder; **see the preceding paragraph of my letter** = vea el párrafo anterior de mi carta; **the preceding clause gives details of the agency arrangements** = la cláusula precedente da detalles de los acuerdos de representación

precedent ['presɪdənt] **1** *noun* precedente *m or* antecedente *m;* **to set a precedent** = sentar un precedente; **to follow a precedent** = seguir un precedente *or* basarse en un precedente; **the judge's decision sets a precedent for future cases of contempt of court** = la decisión del juez sienta un precedente para futuros casos de desacato a los tribunales; **the tribunal's ruling has established a precedent** = el fallo del tribunal sienta precedente; **the court followed the precedent set in 1926** = el tribunal se basó en el precedente establecido en 1926; **binding precedent** = precedente vinculante; **judicial precedent** = precedente que sólo puede ser revocado por un tribunal superior; **persuasive precedent** = precedente a tener en cuenta (no vinculante pero importante para dictar sentencia) **2** *adjective;* **condition precedent** = condición *f* suspensiva

COMMENT: although English law is increasingly governed by statute, the doctrine of precedent still plays a major role. The decisions of higher courts bind lower courts, except in the case of the Court of Appeal, where the court has power to change a previous decision reached per incuriam. Cases can be distinguished by the courts where the facts seem to be sufficiently different

precept ['priːsept] *noun* orden *f* de recaudar *or* mandato *m* judicial para el pago de los impuestos locales; **precepting body** = organismo *m* oficial que cursa una orden de recaudar

precinct ['priːsɪŋkt] *noun* **(a)** *(closed to traffic)* recinto *m;* **pedestrian precinct** *or* **shopping precinct** = zona *f* reservada para peatones *or* zona peatonal *or* zona comercial **(b)** *US* distrito *m* electoral; **police precinct** = distrito policial

precise [prɪˈsaɪs] *adjective* preciso, -sa *or* exacto, -ta; **the will gives precise instructions about the settlement of the estate** = el testamento da instrucciones precisas sobre el acuerdo de traspaso de la propiedad; **the pathologist was unable to**

give a precise time for the murder = el médico forense fue incapaz de precisar la hora del asesinato

preclude [prɪ'kluːd] *verb* impedir *or* imposibilitar *or* excluir; **the High Court is precluded by statute from reviewing such a decision** = el Tribunal Superior está imposibilitado por ley para revisar dicho fallo; **this agreement does not preclude a further agreement between the parties in the future** = este acuerdo no excluye un acuerdo entre las partes en el futuro

predecease [priːdɪ'siːs] *verb* morir antes que; **he predeceased his father** = murió antes que su padre; **his estate is left to his daughter, but should she predecease him, it will be held in trust for her children** = su herencia es donada a su hija, pero en el caso de que ésta muera antes, se dejará en depósito para los hijos de la misma
◊ **predecessor** ['priːdɪsesə] *noun* predecesor, -ra *or* antecesor, ra; **he took over from his predecessor last May** = sustituyó a su predecesor el pasado mes de mayo; **she acquired her predecessor's list of clients** = adquirió la lista de clientes de su predecesor

pre-empt ['priː'empt] *verb* adelantarse a alguien *or* adelantarse a los acontecimientos para impedir *or* prevenir algo
◊ **pre-emption** ['priː'empʃn] *noun* derecho *m* preferente de compra; **pre-emption clause** = cláusula *f* de prioridad

prefer [prɪ'fəː] *verb* **(a)** *(to like better or best)* preferir; **he prefers to deal directly with his clients himself** = prefiere tratar él mismo directamente con sus clientes; **most people prefer to avoid taking their neighbours to court** = la mayoría de la gente prefiere evitar llevar a sus vecinos a juicio **(b)** *(creditors)* dar prioridad a (un acreedor) **(c)** *(to bring charges against someone)* presentar (una demanda) *or* entablar (un pleito); **to prefer charges** = acusar de un delito *or* presentar cargos (NOTE: **preferring - preferred**)
◊ **preference** ['prefrəns] *noun* preferencia *f or* prioridad *f;* **fraudulent preference** = pago *m* preferencial de una empresa insolvente a un acreedor; **preference shares** = acciones *fpl* preferentes; **preference shareholders** = accionistas *mfpl* preferentes; **cumulative preference shares** = acciones preferentes acumulativas
◊ **preferential** [prefə'renʃl] *adjective* preferente *or* preferencial; **preferential creditor** = acreedor, -ra preferente; **preferential debt** = deuda *f* privilegiada; **preferential duty** *or* **preferential tariff** = arancel *m* preferencial *or* tarifa *f* preferencial; **preferential payment** = pago *m* preferencial; **preferential terms** *or* **preferential treatment** = condiciones *fpl* preferenciales *or* trato *m* preferencial
◊ **preferment** [prɪ'fəːmənt] *noun* **preferment of charges** = acusación *f* por delito penal

◊ **preferred** [prɪ'fəːd] *adjective* preferente; **preferred creditor** = acreedor, -ra preferente; **preferred shares** *or* *US* **preferred stock** = acciones *fpl* preferentes; *US* **cumulative preferred stock** = acciones preferentes acumulativas

pregnancy ['pregnənsi] *noun* embarazo *m;* **to terminate a pregnancy** = interrumpir un embarazo *or* abortar
◊ **pregnant** ['pregnənt] *adjective* embarazada *or* en estado *or* encinta; *(colloquial)* preñada

prejudge [priː'dʒʌdʒ] *verb* prejuzgar *or* juzgar de antemano; **do not prejudge the issue - hear what defence counsel has to say** = no prejuzgue la cuestión - escuche lo que el abogado defensor tiene que decir

prejudice ['predʒədɪs] **1** *noun* **(a)** *(bias)* prejuicio *m or* parcialidad *f;* **racial prejudice** = prejuicio racial **(b)** *(harm)* perjuicio *m or* daño *m;* **forgery is the copying of a real document, so that it is accepted as genuine to someone's prejudice** = la falsificación es la copia de un documento verdadero, de manera que es aceptado como auténtico en perjuicio de alguien; **without prejudice** = sin perjuicio; **to act to the prejudice of a claim** = actuar en detrimento *or* perjuicio de una demanda **2** *verb* perjudicar; **to prejudice someone's claim** = perjudicar la demanda de alguien
◊ **prejudiced** ['predʒədɪst] *adjective* parcial *or* predispuesto, -ta *or* con prejuicio; **the judge seemed to be prejudiced against foreigners** = el juez parecía predispuesto contra los extranjeros

preliminary [prɪ'lɪmɪnri] *adjective* preliminar; **preliminary discussion** *or* **preliminary meeting** = discusión *f* preliminar *or* reunión *f* preliminar; **preliminary hearing** = vista *f* preliminar; **preliminary inquiries** = investigación *f* preliminar relativa a una compraventa de propiedad llevada a cabo por el abogado del futuro comprador; **preliminary enquiry** *or* **investigation** = investigación *f* preliminar de un caso; **preliminary ruling** = fallo *m* provisional del Tribunal Europeo

premeditated [priː'medɪteɪtɪd] *adjective* premeditado, -da; **the crime was premeditated** = el crimen fue premeditado; **a premeditated murder** = un asesinato premeditado *or* con premeditación
◊ **premeditation** [priːmedɪ'teɪʃn] *noun* premeditación *f*

Premier ['premiə] *noun* Primer Ministro *or* Primera Ministra *or* premier *mf*

premises ['premɪsɪz] *plural noun* **(a)** *(building)* local *m or* edificio *m or* establecimiento *m;* **business premises** *or* **commercial premises** = local comercial; **office premises** *or* **shop premises** = oficinas *fpl or* establecimiento comercial; **lock-up premises** = local sin vivienda incorporada; **licensed**

premises = establecimiento autorizado para vender bebidas alcohólicas; **on the premises** = en el local *or* en el edificio; **there is a doctor on the premises at all times** = hay un doctor en el local *or* en el edificio a todas horas **(b)** *(in an argument)* parte *f* inicial *or* premisas *fpl* (NOTE: *used at the end of a* *pleading:* **in the premises the defendant denies that he is indebted to the plaintiff as alleged or at all)**

premium ['priːmiəm] *noun* **(a)** *(sum of money)* prima *f;* **insurance premium** = prima de seguros; **additional premium** = prima adicional; **the annual premium is £150** = la prima anual es de 150 libras; **you pay either an annual premium of £360 or twelve monthly premiums of £32** = usted paga una prima anual de 360 libras o doce primas mensuales de 32 libras **(b)** *(amount paid for the right to take over a lease)* traspaso *m;* **flat to let with a premium of £10,000** = piso *m* para alquilar con traspaso de 10.000 libras; **annual rent: £8,500 - premium: £25,000** = renta anual: 8.500 libras - prima: 25.000 libras **(c)** *(extra charge)* prima; **exchange premium** = prima cambiaria; **the dollar is at a premium** = el dólar está sobre la par; **shares sold at a premium** = acciones *fpl* vendidas sobre la par *or* con prima de emisión **(d) premium bonds** = bonos *mpl* del estado que participan en un sorteo nacional *or* bonos de ahorro con prima

prerogative [prɪ'rɒgətɪv] *noun* prerrogativa *f;* **royal prerogative** = prerrogativa real; **prerogative order** *or* **writ** = auto *m* de prerrogativa *or* mandamiento *m* de prerrogativa

prescribe [prɪ'skraɪb] *verb* prescribir; **prescribed limit** = límite *m* máximo permitido
◊ **prescription** [prɪ'skrɪpʃn] *noun* prescripción *f or* precepto *m*

presence ['prezəns] *noun* presencia *f;* **in the presence of the court** = ante la sala; **the will was signed in the presence of two witnesses** = el testamento fue firmado en presencia de dos testigos

present ['preznt] **1** *noun* **(a)** *(gift)* regalo *m or* obsequio *m;* **these calculators make good presents** = estas calculadoras son un buen regalo; **the office gave her a present when she got married** = la oficina le hizo un regalo cuando se casó **(b)** *(document, letter)* **these presents** = la presente *or* el presente documento; **know all men by these presents** = comuníquese por la presente *or* sépase por el presente documento **2** *adjective* **(a)** *(happening now)* actual *or* presente; **the shares are too expensive at their present price** = las acciones son demasiado caras al precio actual; **what is the present address of the company?** = ¿cuál es la dirección actual de la empresa? **(b)** *(being there when something happens)* presente; **to be present** = hacer acto de presencia; **two police officers were present when the bailiffs seized the property** = dos policías estaban presentes cuando los agentes

judiciales embargaron los bienes; **only six directors were present at the board meeting** = solamente seis directores estuvieron presentes en la reunión del consejo **3** *verb* **(a)** *(to give someone something)* regalar; **he was presented with a watch on completing twenty-five years' service with the company** = le regalaron un reloj al cumplir los veinticinco años de servicio a la empresa **(b)** *(to show a document)* presentar; **to present a bill for acceptance** = presentar una letra a aceptación; **to present a bill for payment** = presentar una letra al pago **4** *adverb* **at present** = actualmente *or* en la actualidad
◊ **presentation** [prezən'teɪʃn] *noun* **(a)** *(showing a document)* presentación *f;* **presentation of a bill of exchange** = presentación de una letra de cambio; **cheque payable on presentation** = cheque *m* pagadero a su presentación; **free admission on presentation of this card** = entrada *f* gratuita al presentar esta tarjeta **(b)** *(exhibition)* presentación; **the marketing company made a presentation of the services they could offer** = la empresa de márketing hizo una presentación de los servicios que ofrecía; **we have asked two PR firms to make presentations of proposed advertising campaigns** = hemos pedido a dos empresas de relaciones públicas que hagan presentaciones de las campañas de publicidad propuestas
◊ **presentment** [prɪ'zentmənt] *noun* presentación *f;* **presentment of a bill of exchange** = presentación de una letra de cambio
◊ **present value** ['prezənt 'væljuː] *noun (value now)* valor *m* actual; **in 1974 the pound was worth five times its present value** = en 1974 la libra estaba cinco veces por encima de su valor actual

preservation order [prezə'veɪʃn 'ɔːdə] *noun* orden *m* de conservación *or* preservación

preside [prɪ'zaɪd] *verb* presidir; **to preside over a meeting** = presidir una reunión; **the meeting was held in the committee room, Mr Smith presiding** = la reunión se celebró en la sala de juntas y fue presidida por el Sr Smith; **presiding judge** = juez presidente de la sala

president ['prezɪdənt] *noun* **(a)** *(head of a republic)* Presidente, -ta; **the President of the United States** = el Presidente de los Estados Unidos (NOTE: *as a title of a head of state, President can be used with a surname:* **President Ford, President Wilson**) **(b)** *(head of a company or a department)* presidente *m or* presidenta *f;* **he was elected president of the sports club** = fue elegido presidente del club deportivo; **A.B.Smith has been appointed president of the company** = A. B. Smith ha sido nombrado presidente de la compañía; **President of the Family Division** = presidente de la sección del Tribunal Supremo relativa al derecho de familia; **President of the European Commission** = presidente de la Comisión Europea

COMMENT: a president is the head of state of a republic; this may be a ceremonial title, with some executive powers, as in India, while the real power resides in the Prime Minister. In other states (such as the USA), the President is both head of state and head of government. The President of the USA is elected by an electoral college, and holds the executive power under the United States constitution. The legislative power lies with Congress, and the President cannot force Congress to enact legislation, although he can veto legislation which has been passed by Congress.
In Britain 'president' is a title sometimes given to a non-executive former chairman of a company; in the USA, the president is the main executive director of a company. The President of the United States is both head of state and head of government. He is elected by an electoral college, and holds the executive power under the United States constitution. The legislative power lies with Congress, and the President cannot force Congress to enact legislation, although he can veto legislation which has been passed by Congress

◊ **presidential** [prezɪ'denʃl] *adjective* presidencial; **the US presidential elections** = las elecciones presidenciales de los EE UU; **three presidential candidates have appeared on television** = tres candidatos presidenciales aparecieron en televisión; **the National Guard has surrounded the Presidential Palace** = la Guardia Nacional ha rodeado el palacio presidencial; **presidential government** = gobierno *m* presidencial
◊ **presidency** ['prezɪdənsi] *noun* **(a)** *(position of president)* presidencia *f;* **the presidency of the European Union passes from country to country every six months** = la presidencia de la Unión Europea pasa de un país a otro cada seis meses **(b)** *(period when a president is governing)* presidencia *f* mandato *m* (presidencial); **during Kennedy's presidency** *or* **during the Kennedy presidency** = durante el mandato del presidente Kennnedy

press [pres] **1** *noun* prensa *f;* **the local press** = la prensa local; **the national press** = la prensa nacional; **press conference** = rueda *f* de prensa; **Press Council** = cuerpo *m* regulador de la prensa; **Press Complaints Committee** = comisión *f* reguladora de prensa; **press coverage** = cobertura *f* de prensa; **press gallery** = tribuna *f* de prensa; **press release** = comunicado *m* de prensa; **press secretary** = secretario, -ria de prensa; **freedom of the press** = libertad *f* de prensa **2** *verb* **(a)** *(to put pressure on)* presionar *or* apremiar **(b) to press charges against someone** = formular acusaciones contra alguien; **he was very angry when his neighbour's son set fire to his car, but decided not to press charges** = se enfadó mucho cuando el hijo de su vecino incendió su coche, pero decidió no formular acusaciones

◊ **pressing** ['presɪŋ] *adjective* urgente; **pressing engagements** = compromisos *mpl* urgentes; **pressing bills** = facturas *fpl* urgentes

pressure ['preʃə] *noun* presión *f;* **pressure group** = grupo *m* de presión *or* camarilla *f;* **pressure politics** = política *f* de presión; **the army exerts strong political pressure on the President** = el ejército ejerce fuerte presión política sobre el presidente; **the Prime Minister gave in to pressure from the backbenchers** = el primer ministro cedió frente a la presión de los diputados sin cargo; **the Whips applied pressure on the rebel MPs to vote with the government** = los jefes de los grupos parlamentarios pusieron presión sobre los diputados rebeldes para que votaran a favor del gobierno

presume [prɪ'zjuːm] *verb* presumir *or* suponer; **the court presumes the maintenance payments are being paid on time** = el tribunal presume que los pagos de la manutención se están efectuando puntualmente; **the company is presumed to be still solvent** = se supone que la empresa es todavía solvente; **we presume the shipment has been stolen** = suponemos que el envío ha sido robado; **two sailors are missing, presumed drowned** = dos marineros han desaparecido, presuntamente ahogados

COMMENT: in English law, the accused is presumed to be innocent until he is proved to be guilty, and presumed to be sane until he is proved to be insane

◊ **presumption** [prɪ'zʌmpʃn] *noun* presunción *f or* suposición *f;* **presumption of death** = presunción de fallecimiento; **presumption of innocence** = presunción de inocencia; **absolute presumption** = sospecha *f* fundada
◊ **presumptive** [prɪ'zʌmptɪv] *adjective* presunto, -ta; **presumptive evidence** = pruebas *fpl* presuntivas *or* por indicio; **heir presumptive** = presunto heredero

pretence [prɪ'tens] *noun* pretensión *f or* pretexto *m; false pretence(s)* *or* *US* **false pretense** = fraude *m; under false pretences* = con dolo *or* por medios fraudulentos; **he was sent to prison for obtaining money by false pretences** = fue encarcelado por obtener dinero por fraude *or* fraudulentamente

pretend [prɪ'tend] *verb* fingir *or* aparentar *or* simular; **he got in by pretending to be a telephone engineer** = consiguió entrar fingiendo ser un ingeniero de teléfonos; **she pretended she had 'flu and asked to have the day off** = fingió que tenía gripe y pidió el día libre

pretrial review ['priːtraɪəl rɪ'vjuː] *noun* revisión *f* de los detalles antes de un proceso civil *or* vista *f* preliminar

prevail [prɪ'veɪl] *verb* imponerse *or* prevalecer; **to prevail upon someone to do something** = persuadir a alguien para hacer algo *or* convencer a alguien de que haga algo; **counsel prevailed upon the judge to grant an adjournment** = el abogado convenció al juez para que concediera un aplazamiento
◊ **prevailing** [prɪ'veɪlɪŋ] *adjective* dominante

prevaricate [prɪ'værɪkeɪt] *verb* andar con rodeos *or* tergiversar *or* contestar con evasivas

prevent [prɪ'vent] *verb* impedir *or* evitar *or* prevenir; **we must try to prevent the takeover bid** = debemos intentar impedir la oferta de absorción; **the police prevented anyone from leaving the building** = la policía impidió que nadie saliera del edificio; **we have changed the locks on the doors to prevent the former managing director from getting into the building** = hemos cambiado las cerraduras de las puertas para evitar que el anterior director gerente entre en el edificio
◊ **prevention** [prɪ'ventʃn] *noun* prevención *f or* impedimento *m;* **prevention of corruption** = medidas *fpl* preventivas contra la corrupción; **prevention of terrorism** = la prevención del terrorismo
◊ **preventive** [prɪ'ventɪv] *adjective* preventivo, -va; **preventive action** = proceso *m* cautelar; **preventive measure** = medida preventiva; **to take preventive measures against theft** = tomar medidas preventivas contra el robo; **preventive detention** = (antiguamente) detención *f* para la prevención de actos criminales *or* arresto *m* preventivo

> COMMENT: now replaced by **extended sentence**

previous ['priːvɪəs] *adjective* anterior *or* previo, -via; **he could not accept the invitation because he had a previous engagement** = no pudo aceptar la invitación porque ya se había comprometido anteriormente; **to ask for six previous convictions to be taken into consideration** = pedir al tribunal que considere las seis condenas anteriores del acusado; **a person of previous good character** = una persona sin antecedentes penales
◊ **previously** ['priːvɪəsli] *adverb* anteriormente *or* previamente

price [praɪs] **1** *noun* precio *m;* **agreed price** = precio convenido *or* acordado; **all-in price** = precio total *or* todo incluido; **asking price** = precio ofrecido; **fair price** = precio justo *or* razonable; **firm price** = precio fijo *or* definitivo; **net price** = precio neto; **retail price** = precio al por menor; **spot price** = precio de entrega inmediata; **price controls** = controles *mpl* de precios; **price fixing** = estabilización *f* de precios *or* fijación *f* de precios (entre competidores) **(b)** *(on the Stock Exchange)* **asking price** = precio solicitado; **closing price** = cotización *f* al cierre; **opening price** = cotización de

apertura *or* primer curso *m;* **price/earnings ratio** = relación *f* precio-ganancias *or* relación entre la cotización de una acción y sus beneficios **2** *verb* poner precio a *or* tasar *or* valorar; **car priced at £5,000** = coche valorado en 5.000 libras
◊ **pricing** ['praɪsɪŋ] *noun* tasación *f or* valoración *f or* fijación *f* de los precios; **pricing policy** = política *f* de precios; **common pricing** = estabilización *f* de precios *or* fijación de precios (entre competidores)

prima facie ['praɪmə 'feɪʃi] *Latin phrase* a primera vista; **prima facie evidence** = indicios *mpl* razonables (pero no concluyentes); **there is a prima facie case to answer** = a primera vista, existe motivo de demanda

primary ['praɪmri] *adjective* primario, -ria *or* principal *or* fundamental; **primary evidence** = pruebas *fpl* primarias *or* prueba instrumental *or* testifical
◊ **primarily** ['praɪmrli] *adverb* ante todo *or* en primer lugar *or* principalmente; **he is primarily liable for his debts** = él es el primer responsable de sus deudas; *see also* SECONDARY, SECONDARILY

prime [praɪm] *adjective* **(a)** *(most important)* primordial *or* principal *or* fundamental; **prime time** = horas *fpl* de mayor índice de audiencia **(b)** *(basic)* básico, ca- *or* esencial; **prime bills** = efectos *mpl* de primera clase *or* primeras *fpl* de cambio; **prime cost** = coste *m* de producción *or* coste básico; **prime rate** = tipo *m* de interés preferente
◊ **Prime Minister** ['praɪm 'mɪnɪstə] *noun* Primer Ministro *or* Primera Ministra; **the Australian Prime Minister** *or* **the Prime Minister of Australia** = el Primer Ministro australiano *or* el Primer Ministro de Australia

> COMMENT: the British Prime Minister is not the head of state, but the head of government. The Prime Minister is usually the leader of the party which has the majority of the seats in the House of Commons, and forms a cabinet of executive ministers who are either MPs or members of the House of Lords

primogeniture [praɪmə'dʒenɪtʃə] *noun* primogenitura *f or* derechos *mpl* del primogénito

principal ['prɪnsəpl] **1** *noun* **(a)** *(person in charge)* director, -ra *or* jefe, -fa *or* autor, -ra (de un crimen) **(b)** *(represented by an agent)* mandante *mf or* poderdante *mf;* **the agent has come to London to see his principals** = el mandatario ha venido a Londres a ver a sus mandantes **(c)** *(money)* capital *m* de una deuda *or* de un préstamo *or* principal *m* de un capital; **to repay principal and interest** = pagar capital e intereses **2** *adjective; (most important)* principal; **the principal shareholders asked for a meeting** = los accionistas principales pidieron una reunión; **the country's principal products are paper and wood** = los productos principales del país son el papel y la madera; *compare* PRINCIPLE

◊ **principality** [prɪnsə'pælətі] *noun* principado *m;* **the Principality of Monaco** = el principado de Mónaco NOTE: in Britain, 'the Principality' is the name given to Wales

principle ['prɪnsəpl] *noun* principio *m;* **basic principle** = principio fundamental; **legal principles** = principios jurídicos; **in principle** = en principio; **agreement in principle** = acuerdo *m* en lo principal; **it is against his principles** = va en contra de sus principios; *compare* PRINCIPAL

print [prɪnt] *verb* imprimir
◊ **printed** ['prɪntɪd] *adjective* impreso, -sa; **printed form** = hoja impresa

printout ['prɪntaʊt] *noun* copia *f* impresa *or* impresión *f* de salida

prior ['praɪə] *adjective* anterior *or* previo, -via; **prior agreement** = acuerdo *m* previo; **prior charge** = derechos *mpl* preferentes *or* cargo *m* principal; **prior notice** = previo aviso; **without prior knowledge** = sin conocimiento previo
◊ **priori** [praɪ'ɔːraɪ] *see* A PRIORI
◊ **priority** [praɪ'ɒrɪti] *noun* prioridad *f;* **to have priority** = tener prioridad; **to have priority over** *or* **to take priority over something** = tener prioridad sobre algo; **debenture holders have priority over ordinary shareholders** = los tenedores de obligaciones tienen prioridad sobre los accionistas ordinarios; **to give priority** = dar preferencia; **top priority** = asunto *m* prioritario; **to give something top priority** = dar prioridad absoluta a algo; **the government has given the maintenance of law and order top priority** = el gobierno ha dado prioridad absoluta al mantenimiento del orden público

prison ['prɪzn] *noun* cárcel *f or* prisión *f or* presidio *m;* **prison wing** = galería *f* (de una cárcel); **the government has ordered the construction of six new prisons** = el gobierno ha ordenado la construcción de seis nuevas cárceles; **the prison was built 150 years ago** = la cárcel fue construida hace 150 años; **prison officer** *or* **prison governor** = funcionario, -ria de prisiones *or* director, -ra de un centro penitenciario; **open prison** = prisión abierta; **top security prison** = prisión de alta seguridad; **he was sent to prison for six years** = fue encarcelado durante seis años; **they have spent the last six months in prison** = han pasado los últimos seis meses en prisión; **he escaped from prison by climbing over the wall** = se escapó de la prisión escalando el muro (NOTE: no plural for (b), which is also usually written without the article: **in prison; out of prison; sent to prison**)
◊ **prisoner** ['prɪznə] *noun* preso, -sa *or* recluso, -sa; **prisoner of war** = prisionero, -ra de guerra; **prisoner at the bar** = acusado, -ra ante un tribunal;

prisoner under death sentence = reo, rea de muerte
◊ **prison visitor** ['prɪzn 'vɪzɪtə] *noun see* VISITOR

privacy ['prɪvəsi] *noun* intimidad *f;* **invasion of privacy** = privación *f or* violación *f* del derecho a la intimidad

private ['praɪvət] *adjective* **(a)** *(of one person)* privado, -da *or* personal *or* particular; **letter marked 'private and confidential'** = carta *f* privada y confidencial; **Private Bill** *or* **Private Act of Parliament** = proyecto *m* de ley de interés local; *see below* PRIVATE MEMBER'S BILL; **private business** = asunto *m* privado; **the committee held a special meeting to discuss some private business** = el comité celebró una reunión especial para discutir unos asuntos privados; **private client** *or* **private customer** = cliente *mf* personal; **private effects** = efectos *mpl* personales; **private detective** *(informal)* **private eye** = detective *mf* privado, -da; **private law** = derecho *m* privado; **Private Member's Bill** = proposición *f* de ley presentada por un diputado; **private nuisance** = daño *m or* perjuicio *m* a un particular; **private property** = propiedad *f* privada *or* propiedad particular; **private prosecution** = acusación *f* particular **(b)** **in private** = en privado; **he asked to see the managing director in private** = pidió ver al director gerente en privado **(c)** **private limited company** = sociedad *f* limitada (cuyas acciones no se comercian en Bolsa); **private enterprise** = empresa *f* privada; **the private sector** = el sector privado
◊ **privately** ['praɪvətli] *adverb* en privado *or* privadamente; **the deal was negotiated privately** = el trato fue negociado en privado
◊ **privatize** ['praɪvətaɪz] *verb* privatizar

privilege ['prɪvlɪdʒ] *noun* **(a)** *(protection from the law)* privilegio *m or* prerrogativa *f or* inmunidad *f;* **absolute privilege** = inmunidad (por ostentar cargo público); **breach of parliamentary privilege** = violación *f* de la inmunidad parlamentaria; **Committee of Privileges** = comité de la Cámara de los Comunes que examina casos de violación de inmunidad; **Crown privilege** = privilegio según el cual el gobierno no tiene que presentar documentos ante un tribunal por razones de Estado; **qualified privilege** = inmunidad condicionada a la ausencia de malicia; **question of privilege** = asunto que atañe al parlamento o a uno de los diputados; *US* **question of personal privilege** = asunto que atañe a uno de los miembros del Congreso y que tiene prioridad sobre otros asuntos **(b)** *US* orden de prioridad; **motion of the highest privilege** = moción *f* prioritaria
◊ **privileged** ['prɪvlɪdʒd] *adjective* privilegiado, -da *or* que goza de inmunidad; **privileged communication** = carta privilegiada *or* carta que goza de inmunidad; **privileged meeting** = reunión *f*

de confianza *or* secreta; **privileged person** = persona *f* aforada

privity of contract ['prɪvəti əv 'kɒntrækt] *noun* relación *f* contractual *or* relación particular de las partes contratantes

Privy Council ['prɪvi 'kaʊnsəl] *noun* Consejo *m* de Estado *or GB* Consejo Privado de la Corona; **Judicial Committee of the Privy Council** = Tribunal *m* de Apelación para países de la Commonwealth y colonias

◊ **Privy Councillor** ['prɪvi 'kaʊnslə] *noun* miembro *mf* del Consejo Privado de la Corona

prize [praɪz] *noun* **(a)** *(competition)* premio *m;* **prize court** = tribunal *m* que regula la adjudicación de premios **(b)** *(in war)* presa *f or* botín *m* de guerra

pro [prəʊ] *preposition & noun* pro *or* en pro de; **per pro** = por poder *or* con la autoridad de; **pros and cons** = (argumentos) a favor y en contra

probable ['prɒbəbl] *adjective* probable *or* verosímil; **he is trying to prevent the probable takeover of the company** = está intentando evitar la probable absorción de la empresa; **a heart attack was the probable cause of death** = un ataque al corazón fue la causa probable de la muerte *or* es probable que muriera a causa de un ataque al corazón

◊ **probably** ['prɒbəbli] *adverb* probablemente; **the judge is probably going to retire next year** = el juez se va a retirar probablemente el próximo año; **his death was probably caused by a heart attack** = su muerte fue causada probablemente por un ataque al corazón

probate ['prəʊbeɪt] *noun* legalización *f* de un documento *or* legalización de un testamento; **grant of probate** = garantía *f* de legalidad de un testamento *or* concesión *f* de legalidad de un testamento; **the executor was granted probate *or* obtained a grant of probate** = se comunicó al albacea la legalidad del testamento; **Probate Registry** = Registro *m* General de Actos de Última Voluntad

probation [prə'beɪʃn] *noun* **(a)** *(workers)* periodo *m* de prueba **(b)** *(criminals)* libertad *f* vigilada *or* condicional a prueba; **she was sentenced to probation for one year** = le concedieron la libertad vigilada durante un año; **probation officer** = oficial *mf* a cargo de los que están bajo libertad vigilada; **probation order** = orden *f* judicial de libertad vigilada *or* condicional **(c) on probation** = *(being tested)* a prueba; *(order from a court)* en *or* bajo libertad vigilada *or* condicional a prueba; **he is on three months' probation** = está a prueba durante un periodo de tres meses; **to take someone on probation** = contratar a alguien a prueba

◊ **probationary** [prə'beɪʃnri] *adjective* de prueba *or* probatorio, -ria; **a probationary period of three months** = un periodo de prueba de tres meses; **after the probationary period the company decided to offer him a full-time contract** = después del periodo de prueba la empresa decidió ofrecerle un contrato a jornada completa

◊ **probationer** [prə'beɪʃnə] *noun* persona *f* que está en libertad vigilada *or* empleado, -da a prueba

probative *adjective* probatorio, -ria; *US* **probative value** = valor probatorio

problem ['prɒbləm] *noun* problema *m;* **the company suffers from cash flow problems *or* staff problems** = la empresa tiene problemas de flujo de caja *or* problemas laborales; **to solve a problem** = resolver un problema; **problem area** = área *f* problemática *or* asunto *m* problemático; **drug-related crime is a problem area in large cities** = los delitos relacionados con las drogas son un asunto problemático en las grandes ciudades

procedure [prə'siːdʒə] *noun* procedimiento *m;* **to follow the proper procedure** = seguir el procedimiento adecuado; **this procedure is very irregular** = este procedimiento es muy irregular; **civil procedure** = procedimiento civil; **criminal procedure** = procedimiento criminal; **disciplinary procedure** = procedimiento disciplinario; **dismissal procedures** = trámites *mpl* de despido; **complaints procedure *or* grievance procedure** = procedimiento de resolución de conflictos *or* juicio *m* de faltas *or* tramitación *f* de quejas; **legal procedure** = tramitación legal; **ordinary *or* special procedure** = procedimiento ordinario *or* especial; **dismissal procedures** = procedimientos de despido

◊ **procedural** [prə'siːdʒərl] *adjective* procesal *or* de procedimiento; **procedural law** = derecho *m* procesal; **procedural problem *or* question** = problema *m or* cuestión *f* de procedimiento; **the hearing was held up while counsel argued over procedural problems** = la vista se interrumpió mientras el abogado discutía sobre problemas de procedimiento

proceed [prə'siːd] *verb* continuar *or* seguir *or* avanzar; **the negotiations are proceeding slowly** = las negociaciones avanzan con lentitud; **to proceed against someone** = proceder contra alguien *or* iniciar una causa contra alguien; **to proceed with something** = seguir con algo *or* proseguir algo; **the hearing proceeded after the protesters were removed from the courtroom** = la vista prosiguió después de que los grupos de protesta fueran expulsados de la sala

◊ **proceedings** [prə'siːdɪŋz] *plural noun* **(a)** **conference proceedings** = actas *fpl* de un congreso **(b) legal proceedings** = procedimiento *m* legal *or* acción *f or* proceso *m* judicial; **bankruptcy proceedings** = procedimiento de quiebra; **court proceedings** = autos *mpl or* trámites *mpl* judiciales; **disciplinary proceedings** = proceso disciplinario;

interlocutory proceedings = autos incidentales; **oral proceedings** = juicio *m* oral *or* procedimiento verbal; **probate proceedings** = juicio testamentario *or* proceso testamentario; **review proceedings** = procedimiento de revisión; **to take proceedings against someone** = entablar un proceso contra alguien; **the court proceedings were adjourned** = el proceso fue suspendido; **to institute** *or* **to start proceedings against someone** = entablar un proceso *or* iniciar un procedimiento legal contra alguien; **committal proceedings** = vista *f* preliminar de un caso; **interlocutory proceedings** = vista interlocutoria

◊ **proceeds** ['prəusiːdz] *plural noun* ganancias *fpl or* ingresos *mpl;* **the proceeds of a sale** = el producto de una venta

process ['prəuses] **1** *noun* **(a)** decision-making processes = procedimiento *m* de toma de decisiones; **industrial processes** = procedimientos laborales *or* proceso *m* de fabricación **(b)** *(way in which a court acts)* procedimiento legal *(legal procedure)* proceso; **summary process** = proceso sumario; **the due process of the law** = el curso formal de la ley *or* el debido proceso legal; **abuse of process** = abuso *m* de derecho **(c)** *(writs issued by a court)* citación *f* **(d)** **in process** = en curso **2** *verb* **(a)** *(computer)* **to process figures** = procesar las cifras; **the sales figures are being processed by our accounts department** = las cifras de ventas se están procesando en nuestro departamento de contabilidad; **data is being processed in our computer** = los datos están siendo procesados en nuestro ordenador **(b)** *(to deal with)* tramitar *or* preparar *or* elaborar; **to process an insurance claim** = tramitar una reclamación al seguro; **the incident room is processing information received from the public** = la sala de incidencias está tramitando la información recibida del público

◊ **processing** ['prəusesɪŋ] *noun* **(a)** *(computer)* procesamiento *m or* tratamiento *m;* **processing of information** *or* **of figures** = tratamiento de información *or* de cifras; **data processing** *or* **information processing** = proceso *m* procesamiento de datos *or* de información; **word processing** *or* **text processing** = tratamiento *or* procesamiento de textos **(b)** **the processing of a claim for insurance** = la tramitación de una indemnización por daños *or* reclamación al seguro

◊ **process-server** ['prəuses'səːvə] *noun* agente *mf* judicial *or* notificador, -ra de la citación *or* persona *f* que entrega la citación

proctor ['prɒktə] *noun (in a university)* oficial *mf* encargado, -da de la disciplina *or* vigilante *mf;* **Queen's Proctor** = procurador, -ra que actúa para la Corona en casos matrimoniales y de legalización de testamentos

procurationem [prɒkjuræsi'əunəm] *see* PER PROCURATIONEM

Procurator Fiscal ['prɒkjureɪtə 'fɪskl] *noun (in Scotland)* procurador, -ra fiscal que decide si un presunto criminal debe ser procesado

procure [prə'kjuə] *verb* **(a)** *(obtain)* conseguir *or* lograr algo **(b)** *(sexual offence)* llevar a la prostitución *or* dedicarse al proxenetismo
◊ **procuring** *or* **procurement** [prə'kjuərɪŋ *or* prə'kjuəmənt] *noun* lenocinio *m or* proxenetismo *m*
◊ **procurer** [prə'kjuərə] *noun* proxeneta *m or* alcahuete *m*
◊ **procuress** [prə'kjuəres] *noun* alcahueta *f*

produce [prə'djuːs] *verb* **(a)** *(to bring out)* mostrar *or* presentar *or* sacar; **the police produced a number of weapons seized during the riot** = la policía mostró una serie de armas incautadas durante los disturbios; **the summons required him to produce a certain document before the court** = la citación le exigía presentar cierto documento ante el tribunal **(b)** *(to make)* elaborar **(c)** *(yield)* rendir

product ['prɒdʌkt] *noun* **(a)** *(thing which is made)* producto *m;* **basic product** = producto básico; **end product** *or* **final product** *or* **finished product** = producto final *or* producto acabado; **product liability** = responsabilidad *f* legal por un producto **(b)** **gross domestic product** = producto interior bruto (PIB); **gross national product** = producto nacional bruto (PNB)

production [prə'dʌkʃn] *noun* **(a)** *(action of showing)* presentación *f;* **on production of** = al presentar; **the case will be released by the customs on production of the relevant documents** = la aduana devolverá la maleta al presentarse los documentos pertinentes; **goods can be exchanged only on production of the sales slip** = la mercancía se puede intercambiar solamente al presentar el recibo de venta **(b)** *(making of goods)* producción *f;* **production will probably be held up by industrial action** = la producción probablemente se interrumpirá por la huelga; **we are hoping to speed up production by putting in new machinery** = esperamos acelerar la producción con la instalación de nueva maquinaria; **domestic production** = producción nacional; **mass production** = producción en serie *or* producción a gran escala; **rate of production** *or* **production rate** = ritmo *m* de producción
◊ **productive** [prə'dʌktɪv] *adjective* productivo, -va; **productive capital** = capital *f* productivo; **productive discussions** = discusiones *fpl* fructíferas
◊ **productively** [prə'dʌktɪvli] *adverb* productivamente

proferentem [prɒfə'rentem] *see* CONTRA

profession [prə'feʃn] *noun* **(a)** *(occupation)* profesión *f;* **the managing director is a lawyer by profession** = el director gerente es abogado de profesión **(b)** *(group of specialized workers)* profesión *or* miembros *mpl* de la profesión; **the**

legal profession = el cuerpo de abogados; **the medical profession** = la profesión médica

◊ **professional** [prə'feʃnl] **1** *adjective* **(a)** *(referring to one of the professions)* profesional *or* de profesión *or* facultativo, -va; **the accountant sent in his bill for professional services** = el contable mandó la factura por los servicios prestados; **we had to ask our lawyer for professional advice on the contract** = tuvimos que pedirle a nuestro abogado asesoramiento profesional sobre el contrato; **a professional man** = un profesional; **professional misconduct** = negligencia *f* profesional; **professional qualifications** = títulos *mpl* profesionales **(b)** *(expert or skilled)* experto, -ta; **professional witness** = testigo *mf* pericial **2** *noun* profesional *mf*

profit ['prɒfɪt] *noun* beneficio *m or* ganancia *f;* **clear profit** = beneficio neto *or* líquido; **gross profit** = beneficio bruto; **net profit** = beneficio neto; **non-profit making** = sin ánimo de lucro; **operating profit** = beneficio de explotación; **trading profit** = resultado *m* de la explotación *or* beneficio de explotación *or* beneficio comercial; **profit and loss account** = cuenta *f* de pérdidas y ganancias; **profit before tax** *or* **pretax profit** = beneficio sin deducir los impuestos *or* utilidad *f* antes de impuesto; **profit-sharing** = distribución *f* de beneficios; **profit after tax** = beneficio después de impuestos *or* utilidad después de impuesto; **share in the profits** = participación *f* en los beneficios

◊ **profitability** [prɒfɪtə'bɪlɪti] *noun* **(a)** *(ability to make profit)* rentabilidad *f* **(b)** *(amount of profit made)* rentabilidad; **measurement of profitability** = valoración *f* de la rentabilidad

◊ **profitable** ['prɒfɪtəbl] *adjective* rentable *or* productivo, -va *or* lucrativo, -va *or* fructífero, -ra

◊ **profitably** ['prɒfɪtəbli] *adverb* productivamente *or* lucrativamente

◊ **profit à prendre** ['prɒfi æ 'prɒndr] *French phrase meaning* derecho *m* de explotación de la tierra (comunal)

◊ **profiteer** [prɒfɪ'tɪə] *noun* aprovechado, -da *or* acaparador, -ra *or* estraperlista *mf or* agiotista *mf*

◊ **profiteering** [prɒfɪ'tɪərɪŋ] *noun* usura *f or* realización *f* de ganancias *or* beneficios excesivos

pro forma ['prəu 'fɔːmə] *Latin phrase* pro forma; **pro forma (invoice)** = (factura *f*) pro forma; **pro forma letter** = carta *f* pro forma *or* informe *m* proforma

program ['prəugræm] **1** *noun* programa *m;* **computer program** = programa de ordenador *or* programa informático **2** *verb* programar; **the computer is programmed to search the police records for a certain type of fingerprint** = el ordenador está programado para buscar cierto tipo de huella dactilar en los archivos policiales; **programming language** = lenguaje *m* de programación

◊ **programmer** ['prəugræmə] *noun* **computer programmer** = programador, -ra

progress 1 ['prəugres] *noun* progreso *m or* marcha *f or* avance *m;* **in progress** = en curso; **the superintendent briefed the press on the progress of the investigation** = el comisario informó a la prensa sobre la marcha de la investigación; **the fraud squad is making progress in the false insurance case** = la brigada contra el fraude está haciendo progresos en el caso de la falsificación de la póliza de seguros **2** [prə'gres] *verb* progresar *or* avanzar; **the investigation progressed rapidly once the details were put onto the police computer** = la investigación avanzó rápidamente una vez que se introdujeron los detalles en el ordenador de la policía

prohibit [prə'hɪbɪt] *verb* prohibir; **parking is prohibited in front of the garage** = se prohíbe aparcar frente al garaje; **the law prohibits the sale of alcohol to minors** = la legislación prohíbe la venta de alcohol a menores de edad; **prohibited degrees** = relaciones *fpl* de consanguinidad que impiden el matrimonio; **prohibited goods** = bienes *mpl* que tienen prohibida la importación

◊ **prohibition** [prəuhɪ'bɪʃn] *noun* **(a)** *(act of forbidding)* prohibición *f* **(b)** *(High Court order)* auto *m* de un tribunal superior ordenando la suspensión de actuaciones a otro inferior *f*

◊ **prohibitive** [prəu'hɪbɪtɪv] *adjective* prohibitivo, -va

◊ **prohibitory injunction** [prə'hɪbɪtri ɪn'dʒʌkʃn] *noun* requerimiento *m* prohibitorio

promise ['prɒmɪs] **1** *noun* promesa *f;* **to keep a promise** = cumplir una promesa; **to go back on a promise** = faltar a una promesa; **a promise to pay** = un pagaré; **breach of promise** = (antiguamente) incumplimiento *m* de palabra (*or* promesa) de matrimonio; **gratuitous promise** = promesa gratuita **2** *verb* prometer; **they promised to pay the last instalment next week** = prometieron pagar el último plazo la semana próxima; **the personnel manager promised to look into the grievances of the office staff** = el director de personal prometió examinar las quejas de los empleados de la oficina

◊ **promisee** [prɒmɪ'siː] *noun* tenedor, -ra de una promesa

◊ **promisor** [prɒmɪ'sɔː] *noun* prometedor, -ra

◊ **promissory** [prə'mɪsri] *adjective* promisorio, -ria; **promissory estoppel** = impedimento *m* promisorio; **promissory note** = pagaré *m or* letra *f* a cargo propio

promote [prə'məut] *verb* **(a)** *(to introduce a new Bill into Parliament)* presentar **(b)** *(to give someone a more important job)* ascender *or* promover; **he was promoted from salesman to sales manager** = fue ascendido de vendedor a director de ventas **(c)** *(to advertise)* anunciar *or* promocionar; **to promote a new product** = promocionar un nuevo producto **(d)** *(to encourage something to grow)* fomentar *or* estimular; **to promote a new company** = fundar una empresa

◊ **promoter** [prə'məutə] *noun* **(a)** *(in Parliament)* persona f que presenta una proposición de ley **(b)** *(of company)* gestor, -ra *or* promotor, -ra; **company promoter** = fundador, -ra *or* promotor, -ra (de una compañía) *or* empresario, -ria

◊ **promotion** [prə'məuʃn] *noun* **(a)** *(moving to a more important job)* ascenso *m or* promoción f; **to earn promotion** = ganarse el ascenso **(b)** **promotion of a company** = fundación f de una empresa **(c)** *(publicity)* **promotion of a product** = promoción *or* lanzamiento *m* de un producto

◊ **promotional** [prə'məuʃnl] *adjective* de promoción *or* en promoción; **promotional budget** = presupuesto *m* de promoción *or* gastos *mpl* de lanzamiento

prompt [prɒmt] **1** *adjective* pronto, -ta *or* rápido, -da *or* inmediato, -ta; **the minister issued a prompt denial of the allegations against him** = el ministro negó inmediatamente las alegaciones contra él; **failing prompt payment** = a falta de pronto pago **2** *verb* apuntar *or* incitar a alguien a decir algo; **the judge warned counsel not to prompt the witness** = el juez advirtió al abogado que no apuntara al testigo *or* que no incitara al testigo a decir ciertas cosas

◊ **promptly** [prɒmtli] *adverb* pronto *or* con prontitud *or* rápidamente *or* inmediatamente; **the defendant promptly counterclaimed against the plaintiff** = el demandado presentó inmediatamente una demanda en respuesta a la del demandante

proof [pruːf] *noun* **(a)** *(evidence that something is true)* prueba f *or* pruebas fpl; **documentary proof** = prueba documentada; **burden of proof** *or* **onus of proof** = obligación f de probar lo alegado *or* carga f de la prueba; **the onus of proof is on the plaintiff** = el demandante es quien debe probar que lo que alega es cierto; **proof beyond reasonable doubt** = prueba suficiente sin que quede duda razonable **(b)** *(evidence that a creditor is owed money by a bankrupt company)* comprobante *m* de deuda; **proof of debt** = solicitud f de inclusión de un crédito en la masa de la quiebra; **proof of evidence** = declaración f escrita de un testigo (de su testimonio en juicio); **proof of identity** = prueba de la identidad; **proof of service** = prueba de entrega de notificación

◊ **-proof** [pruːf] *suffix* resistente *or* a prueba de; **burglarproof door** = puerta f a prueba de robos *or* puerta blindada; **inflation-proof pension** = pensión f que resiste la inflación; **escape-proof prison** = cárcel de máxima seguridad

◊ **proofreader** ['pruːfriːdə] *noun* corrector, -ra de pruebas

proper ['prɒpə] *adjective* propio, -pia *or* apropiado, -da *or* adecuado, -da *or* razonable; **proper law of the contract** = ley f por la que se debe regir un contrato

property ['prɒpəti] *noun* **(a)** *(ownership)* propiedad f; **law of property** = derecho *m* de la propiedad **(b)** *(anything which can be owned)* propiedad *or* bienes *mpl;* **community property** = bien *m* ganancial; **industrial property** = propiedad industrial; **intellectual property** = propiedad intelectual; **personal property** = bienes muebles *or* propiedad mobiliaria (que se puede trasmitir por herencia); **the storm caused considerable damage to personal property** = la tormenta causó importantes daños materiales; **the management is not responsible for property left in the hotel rooms** = la dirección no se hace responsable de los objetos de valor que el cliente deje en las habitaciones del hotel; **separate property** = bien propio; **unattended property** = objeto *m* abandonado **(c)** *(land and buildings)* **(real) property** = bienes inmuebles *or* bienes raíces *or* propiedad inmobiliaria; **freehold property** = propiedad de dominio absoluto; **property tax** *or* **tax on property** = impuesto *m* sobre los bienes *or* impuesto sobre la propiedad *or* impuesto sobre el patrimonio; **damage to property** *or* **property damage** = daños *mpl* materiales; **the commercial property market is declining** = el mercado de los bienes comerciales está en decadencia *or* en crisis; **common** *or* **public property** = bien comunal; **inherited property** = bienes heredados; **property company** = sociedad f inmobiliaria *or* promotora f; **property developer** = promotor, -ra de viviendas *or* de industrias; **private property** = propiedad privada *or* particular **(d)** *(building)* edificio *m;* **we have several properties for sale in the centre of the town** = tenemos varios edificios en venta en el centro de la ciudad

proportion [prə'pɔːʃn] *noun* proporción f *or* parte f; **a proportion of the pretax profit is set aside for contingencies** = una parte de los beneficios brutos se reserva para imprevistos; **only a small proportion of our sales comes from retail shops** = sólo una pequeña parte de nuestras ventas procede de tiendas al por menor; **in proportion to** = en proporción con

◊ **proportional** [prə'pɔːʃnl] *adjective* proporcional; **proportional representation (PR)** = representación f proporcional

◊ **proportionately** [prə'pɔːʃnətli] *adverb* proporcionalmente

proposal [prə'pəuzl] *noun* **(a)** *(suggestion)* propuesta f *or* proposición f; **to make a proposal** *or* **to put forward a proposal** = presentar *or* hacer una propuesta; **to lay a proposal before the House** = presentar un proyecto de ley ante el Parlamento; **the committee turned down the proposal** = el comité rechazó la propuesta **(b)** **proposal form** = propuesta de seguro

◊ **propose** [prə'pəuz] *verb* **(a)** *(to put forward)* proponer; **the Bill proposes that any party to the proceedings may appeal** = el proyecto de ley propone que cualquier parte en el proceso pueda apelar; **to propose a motion** = proponer una moción; **to propose someone as president** = proponer a alguien para presidente **(b) to propose to** = tener intención de *or* proponerse; **I propose to repay the loan at £20 a month** = tengo intención de pagar el préstamo a 20 libras al mes

proprietary [prə'praɪətri] *adjective* **(a)** *(product)* de marca registrada *or* patentado, -da; **proprietary drug** = especialidad *f* farmacéutica *or* medicamento *m* de marca registrada; **proprietary right** = derecho *m* de propiedad **(b)** *(in South Africa and Australia)* **proprietary company (Pty)** = sociedad *f* limitada
◊ **proprietor** [prə'praɪətə] *noun* propietario *m* or amo *m* or dueño *m;* **the proprietor of a hotel** *or* **a hotel proprietor** = el propietario de un hotel
◊ **proprietorship** [prə'praɪətəʃɪp] *noun* propiedad *f* or derecho *m* de propiedad; **proprietorship register** = registro *m* de propietarios
◊ **proprietress** [prə'praɪətrəs] *noun* propietaria *f* or ama *f* or dueña *f;* **the proprietress of an advertising consultancy** = la propietaria de una empresa asesora en publicidad

pro rata ['prəu 'rɑːtə] *adjective & adverb* **(a)** prorrata *or* proporcionalmente; **a pro rata payment** = un pago a prorrata; **to pay someone pro rata** = pagar a alguien a prorrata

prorogation [prəurə'geɪʃn] *noun* clausura *f* del periodo de sesiones en el Parlamento
◊ **prorogue** [prə'rəug] *verb* clausurar el periodo de sesiones del Parlamento; **Parliament was prorogued for the summer recess** = el Parlamento fue clausurado por el periodo veraniego

proscribe [prəskraɪb] *verb* proscribir; **a proscribed organization** *or* **political party** = una organización proscrita *or* un partido político proscrito

prosecute ['prɒsɪkjuːt] *verb* **(a)** *(to bring someone to court to answer a criminal charge)* procesar *or* enjuiciar *or* entablar una acción judicial; **he was prosecuted for embezzlement** = fue procesado por malversación de fondos **(b)** *(to speak against the accused in court)* actuar para la acusación; **Mr Smith is prosecuting, and Mr Jones is appearing for the defence** = el Sr Smith actúa para la acusación y el Sr Jones para la defensa
◊ **prosecution** [prɒsɪ'kjuːʃn] *noun* **(a)** *(legal action)* procesamiento *m* or enjuiciamiento *m;* **criminal prosecution** = proceso *m* criminal; **prosecution for embezzlement** = procesamiento por malversación de fondos **(b)** *(prosecuting side)* acusación *f* or parte *f* demandante; *(lawyers representing the prosecuting side)* ministerio *m* fiscal; **Director of Public Prosecutions** = Director, -ra de la Acusación Pública; **Crown Prosecution Service (CPS)** = fiscalía *f* general del estado; **the**

costs of the case will be borne by the prosecution = las costas del caso correrán a cargo de la acusación; **prosecution counsel** *or* **counsel for the prosecution** = fiscal *mf* or abogado, -da de la acusación *or* abogado acusador; *see also* DEFENCE
◊ **prosecutor** ['prɒsɪkjuːtə] *noun* demandante *mf* or querellante *mf;* **Crown prosecutor** = fiscal de la Corona; **public prosecutor** = fiscal *or* acusador público; **public prosecutor's office** = fiscalía *f;* **private prosecutor** = acusador particular

prosequi ['prɒsɪkwaɪ] *see* NOLLE

prospectus [prə'spektəs] *noun* **(a)** *(leaflet)* prospecto *m* or folleto *m* informativo *or* de propaganda; **the restaurant has girls handing out prospectuses in the street** = el restaurante tiene chicas contratadas para repartir propaganda en la calle **(b)** *(for a new company)* presupuesto *m* sobre emisión de acciones (NOTE: plural is **prospectuses**)

prostitution [prɒstɪ'tjuːʃn] *noun* prostitución *f*
◊ **prostitute** ['prɒstɪtjuːt] *noun* prostituta *f* or ramera *f;* **male prostitute** = prostituto *m*

protect [prə'tekt] *verb* proteger *or* amparar; **the workers are protected from unfair dismissal by government legislation** = la legislación estatal protege a los trabajadores contra el despido injusto; **the computer is protected by a plastic cover** = el ordenador está protegido por una funda de plástico; **the cover protects the machine from dust** = la funda protege la máquina del polvo; **to protect an industry by imposing tariff barriers** = proteger una industria por medio de la imposición de barreras arancelarias; **protected person** = persona con derecho a protección oficial; **protected tenancy** = arrendamiento *m* protegido contra desahucio (NOTE: you protect someone **from** something or **from having** something done to him)
◊ **protection** [prə'tekʃn] *noun* protección *f* or amparo *m* or tutela *f;* **consumer protection** = protección del consumidor; **Court of Protection** = tribunal *m* que administra los bienes de personas con alguna incapacidad; **data protection** = protección de datos; **police protection** = protección policial; **the minister was given police protection** = le dieron protección policial al ministro; **protection racket** = chantaje *m* or organización *m* de gángsteres que demanda dinero a cambio de 'protección'; **legal protection** = amparo legal *or* jurídico; **appeal for legal protection** = recurso *m* de amparo; **under court protection** = al amparo de los tribunales
◊ **protective** [prə'tektɪv] *adjective* **(a)** *(action)* proteccionista; **protective measure** = medida de protección; **protective tariff** = arancel *m* proteccionista **(b)** *(cover)* protector, -ra; **protective cover** = funda protectora

pro tem *or* **pro tempore** ['prəu 'tem] *Latin phrase* provisionalmente *or* por el momento

protest 1 ['prəʊtest] *noun* **(a)** *(statement or action)* protesta *f or* queja *f;* **protest for non-payment** = protesto *m* por falta de pago; **to make a protest against high prices** = hacer una protesta contra los precios altos; **sit-down protest** = huelga de brazos caídos *or* sentada *f;* **protest march** = manifestación *f or* marcha *f* de protesta; **in protest at** = en protesta por; **the staff occupied the offices in protest at the low pay offer** = los empleados ocuparon las oficinas en protesta por los bajos salarios ofrecidos; **to do something under protest** = hacer algo forzado *or* actuar bajo protesta **(b)** *(official document)* protesto *m* **2** [prə'test] *verb* **(a) to protest against something** = protestar contra algo; **the retailers are protesting against the ban on imported goods** = los minoristas protestan contra la prohibición de importar mercancías (NOTE: in this meaning GB English is **to protest against something,** but US English is **to protest something**); **(b) to protest a bill** = protestar una letra
◊ **protester** [prə'testə] *noun* protestador, -ra; *(in a demonstration)* manifestante *mf*

protocol ['prəʊtəkɒl] *noun* **(a)** *(draft memorandum)* protocolo *m or* conjunto *m* de puntos que han sido acordados **(b)** *(correct diplomatic behaviour)* protocolo; **protocol requires that the president sits at the head of the table** = el protocolo exige que el presidente presida la mesa

prove ['prəʊtəkɒl] *verb* demostrar *or* comprobar *or* probar *or* verificar; **the tickets proved that he was lying** = las entradas demostraron que estaba mintiendo; **dispatch of the packet was proved by the Post Office receipt** = se pudo verificar el envío del paquete mediante el recibo de la oficina de Correos; **the claim was proved to be false** = la demanda resultó ser falsa; **to prove a debt** = comprobar una deuda; **to prove a will** = homologar un testamento
◊ **provable** ['pruːvəbl] *adjective* demostrable; **provable debts** = deudas *fpl* comprobables
◊ **proven** ['pruːvn] *adjective; (in Scotland)* **not proven** = veredicto *m* de absuelto por falta de pruebas

provide [prə'vaɪd] *verb* **(a) to provide for something** = prever algo *or* estipular algo; **the contract provides for an annual increase in charges** = el contrato prevé un incremento anual de los gastos; **£10,000 has been provided for in the budget** = se han previsto 10.000 libras en el presupuesto; **these expenses have not been provided for** = estos gastos no han sido previstos; **payments as provided in schedule 6 attached** = pagos estipulados en el apéndice 6 adjunto; **to provide for someone** = mantener a alguien *or* dar a alguien lo suficiente para vivir; **he provided for his daughter in his will** = aseguró el porvenir de su hija en su testamento **(b)** *(to put money aside as a precaution)* reservar dinero para imprevistos *or* tomar precauciones *or* precaverse; **£25,000 is**

provided against bad debts = se reservan 25.000 libras para deudas incobrables **(c) to provide someone with something** = facilitar *or* proporcionar algo a alguien *or* proveer a alguien de algo; **the defendant provided the court with a detailed account of his movements** = el demandado proporcionó al tribunal un informe detallado de sus movimientos; **to provide information** = facilitar información; **duress provides no defence to a charge of murder** = la coacción no supone atenuante en una acusación de asesinato

◊ **provided that** *or* **providing** [prə'vaɪdɪd *or* prə'vaɪdɪŋ] *conjunction* a condición de que *or* con tal que *or* siempre que; **the judge will sentence the convicted man next week provided (that)** *or* **providing the psychiatrist's report is received in time** = el juez sentenciará al reo la próxima semana siempre que el informe del psiquiatra se reciba a tiempo (NOTE: in deeds, the form **provided always that** is often used)

province ['prɒvɪns] *noun* **(a)** *(administrative division of a country)* provincia *f;* **the ten provinces of Canada** = las diez provincias de Canadá; **the premier of the Province of Alberta** = el premier de la provincia de Alberta **(b)** *(area away from the capital)* **in the provinces** = en las provincias **(c) the Province** = Northern Ireland

provision [prə'vɪʒn] *noun* **(a) to make provision for** = prever *or* atender a las necesidades de *or* asegurar el porvenir de; **to make financial provision for someone** = atender a las necesidades económicas de alguien; **there is no provision for** *or* **no provision has been made for car parking in the plans for the office block** = no está previsto un aparcamiento de coches en los planos del bloque de oficinas **(b)** *(money put aside)* reserva *f or* aprovisionamiento *m or* provisión *f;* **the company has made a £2m provision for bad debts** = la empresa ha reservado 2 millones de libras para deudas incobrables **(c)** *(legal condition)* disposición *f or* estipulación *f;* **the provisions of a Bill** = las disposiciones de un proyecto de ley; **we have made provision to this effect** = ha sido estipulado en el contrato con este fin
◊ **provisional** [prə'vɪʒnl] *adjective* provisional; **provisional budget** = presupuesto *m* provisional; **they wrote to give their provisional acceptance of the contract** = escribieron para dar su aceptación provisional del contrato; **provisional liquidator** = depositario *m or* síndico *m* nombrado por un tribunal; **provisional injunction** = requerimiento *m* provisional *or* interlocutorio
◊ **provisionally** [prə'vɪʒnli] *adverb* provisionalmente; **the contract has been accepted provisionally** = el contrato ha sido aceptado provisionalmente; **he was provisionally appointed director** = fue nombrado director provisionalmente

proviso [prə'vaizəu] *noun* condición *f or* estipulación *f or* salvedad *f;* **we are signing the contract with the proviso that the terms can be discussed again in six months' time** = firmamos el contrato con la condición de que los términos puedan ser discutidos de nuevo dentro de seis meses (NOTE: the proviso usually begins with the phrase 'provided always that')

provocation [prɒvə'keiʃn] *noun* provocación *f;* **he acted under provocation** = actuó por provocación *or* porque se le provocó
◊ **provoke** [prə'vəuk] *verb* provocar *or* incitar *or* mover; **the strikers provoked the police to retaliate** = los huelguistas incitaron a la policía a tomar represalias; **the murders provoked a campaign to increase police protection for politicians** = los asesinatos provocaron una campaña para aumentar la protección policial de los políticos (NOTE: you provoke someone to do something)
◊ **provocateur** [prəvɒkə'tə:] *see* AGENT PROVOCATEUR

proxy ['prɒksi] *noun* **(a)** *(document)* procuración *f or* poder *m or* poderes *mpl or* delegación *f;* **to sign by proxy** = firmar por poderes; **proxy vote** = voto *m* por poderes **(b)** *(person who acts on behalf of someone else)* apoderado, -da *or* mandatario, -ria *or* poderhabiente *mf;* **to act as proxy for someone** = actuar como apoderado de alguien

P.S. ['pi: 'es] = POST SCRIPTUM P.D. *or* posdata *f;* **did you read the P.S. at the end of the letter?** = ¿Leyó la posdata al final de la carta?

PSBR ['pi: 'es 'bi: 'ɑ:] = PUBLIC SECTOR BORROWING REQUIREMENT

psephology [sə'fɒlədʒi] *noun* análisis *m* electoral
◊ **psephologist** [sə'fɒlədʒɪst] *noun* analista *mf* electoral

psychiatry [saɪ'kaɪətri] *noun* psiquiatría *f*
◊ **psychiatric** [saɪki'ætrɪk] *adjective* psiquiátrico, -ca; **psychiatric hospital** = hospital *m* psiquiátrico; **he was sent to hospital for psychiatric treatment** = le enviaron al hospital para que recibiera tratamiento psiquiátrico; **the court was shown a psychiatric report** = se enseñó al tribunal un informe psiquiátrico
◊ **psychiatrist** [saɪ'kaɪətrɪst] *noun* psiquiatra *mf*

Pty [prə'praɪətri] = PROPRIETARY COMPANY

public ['pʌblɪk] **1** *adjective* **(a)** *(referring to all the people in general)* público, -ca; **Public Bill** = proyecto *m* de ley ordinario, presentado por un ministro y referente a un asunto de interés para el público en general; **public domain** = dominio público; **work in the public domain** = obra *f* de dominio público; **public holiday** = fiesta *f* nacional;

public house = taberna *f or* bar *m;* **public image** = imagen pública; **the police are trying to improve their public image** = la policía está intentando mejorar su imagen pública; **public law** = derecho público; **public notice** = declaración *f or* proclama *f;* **public nuisance** = perjuicio *or* daño público; **public order** = orden público; **offence against the public order** *or* **public order offence** = delito *m* contra el orden público; **public place** = lugar público; **public policy** = bien público; **public transport** = transporte público; **Public Trustee** = administrador público **(b)** *(referring to the state)* público; **Public Accounts Committee** = Tribunal *m* de Cuentas del Reino; **public administration** = administración pública; **public expenditure** = gasto público; **public finance** = hacienda pública; **public funds** = fondos públicos; **public ownership** = propiedad pública; **public records office** = archivo público **(c)** **public limited company (plc)** = sociedad *f* anónima; **the company is going public** = la empresa va a hacer públicas algunas de sus acciones **2** *noun* **the public** *or* **the general public** = el público en general; **in public** = en público
◊ **publication** [pʌblɪ'keɪʃn] *noun* **(a)** *(action)* publicación *f;* **publication of Cabinet papers takes place after thirty years** = la publicación de los documentos del Consejo de Ministros tiene lugar transcurridos treinta años **(b)** *(printed document)* publicación; **obscene publication** = publicación obscena; **the magazine was classed as an obscene publication and seized by the customs** = la revista fue clasificada como publicación obscena y retirada de la circulación por los oficiales de aduanas
◊ **public relations (PR)** ['pʌblɪk rɪ'leɪʃnz] *plural noun* relaciones *fpl* públicas; **public relations department** = departamento *m* de relaciones públicas; **public relations officer** = funcionario encargado de las relaciones públicas
◊ **public sector** ['pʌblɪk 'sektə] *noun* sector *m* público; **a report on wage rises in the public sector** *or* **on public sector wage settlements** = un informe sobre aumento de salarios en el sector público; **public sector borrowing requirement** = necesidad *f* de endeudamiento del sector público

publish ['pʌblɪʃ] *verb* publicar *or* editar; **the society publishes its list of members annually** = la sociedad publica una lista de sus miembros anualmente; **the government has not published the figures on which its proposals are based** = el gobierno no ha publicado las cifras en las que se basan sus propuestas; **the company publishes six magazines for the business market** = la empresa publica seis revistas para el mercado financiero
◊ **publisher** ['pʌblɪʃə] *noun* **(a)** *(person)* editor, -ra **(b)** *(company)* editorial *f*

puisne ['pju:ni] *adjective; (less important)* inferior *or* menor; **puisne judge** = magistrado, -da de término; **puisne mortgage** = hipoteca *f* secundaria sobre una propiedad no inscrita en el registro

punish ['pʌnɪʃ] *verb* castigar; **you will be punished for hitting the policeman** = te castigarán por golpear al policía
◊ **punishable** ['pʌnɪʃəbl] *adjective* delictivo, -va *or* castigable *or* que merece castigo *or* merecedor, -ra de castigo; **crimes punishable by imprisonment** = delitos *mpl* castigados con penas de prisión
◊ **punishment** ['pʌnɪʃmənt] *noun* **(a)** *(act of punishing)* castigo *m or* pena *f*; **corporal punishment** = castigo corporal; **capital punishment** = pena capital *or* pena de muerte **(b)** *(for a crime)* castigo; **the punishment for treason is death** = el castigo por traición es la muerte *or* la traición se castiga con la muerte

punitive damages ['pjuːnɪtɪv 'dæmɪdʒɪz] *noun* daños *mpl* punitivos *or* ejemplares

pupillage ['pjuːpɪlɪdʒ] *noun* pupilaje *m or* pasantía *f*

pur autre vie ['puːə 'əutrə 'viː] *see* PER AUTRE VIE

purchase ['pɜːtʃəs] **1** *noun* compra *f or* adquisición; **purchase order** = orden *f* de compra; **purchase price** = precio *m* de compra; **purchase tax** = impuesto *m* sobre compras; **compulsory purchase** = expropiación *f* forzosa (NOTE: the US English for this is **expropriation**); **compulsory purchase order** = orden de expropiación; **hire purchase** = venta *f* a plazos; **hire purchase agreement** = contrato *m* de venta a plazos **2** *verb* comprar; **to purchase something for cash** = comprar al contado
◊ **purchaser** ['pɜːtʃəsə] *noun* comprador, -ra *or* adquiriente *mf*
◊ **purchasing** ['pɜːtʃəsɪŋ] *adjective;* **purchasing power** = poder *m* adquisitivo

purge ['pɜːdʒ] *verb* purgar *or* depurar; **to purge one's contempt** *or* **to purge a contempt of court** = retractarse de una acción de desacato a los tribunales *or* expiar una acción de desacato a los tribunales

purpose ['pɜːpəs] *noun* objetivo *m or* propósito *m or* intención *f*; **on purpose** = intencionadamente *or* a propósito; **she hid the knife on purpose** = escondió el cuchillo a propósito; **we need the invoice for tax purposes** *or* **for the purpose of declaration to the tax authorities** = necesitamos la factura para la declaración de la renta; **fitness for purpose** = aptitud *f or* adecuación *f* a la finalidad que poseen

pursue [pə'sjuː] *verb* proseguir *or* continuar
◊ **pursuant to** [pə'sjuːənt 'tu] *adverb* según *or* conforme a *or* de conformidad con; **matters pursuant to Article 124 of the EU treaty** =

asuntos de conformidad con el artículo 124 del tratado de la UE; **pursuant to the powers conferred on the local authority** = según los poderes conferidos a las autoridades locales

pursuit [pə'sjuːt] *noun* **in pursuit** = en persecución *or* en busca; **the bank robbers escaped in a car with the police in pursuit** = los atracadores del banco escaparon en un coche con la policía en su busca; *see also* FRESH, HOT

purview ['pɜːvjuː] *noun* alcance *m or* competencia *f* de una ley parlamentaria

put [put] **1** *noun* **put option** = derecho *m* de venta *or* prima *f* de opción de venta de acciones en una fecha determinada **2** *verb* poner *or* fijar *or* someter *or* llevar; **to put aside** = poner aparte; **to put on bail** = poner bajo fianza; **to put behind bars** = poner entre rejas; **to put to a vote** = someter a votación; **to put right** = subsanar; **to put a proposal to the vote** = someter una propuesta a voto; **to put a proposal to the board** = llevar una propuesta al consejo de dirección (NOTE: **putting - put - has put**)
◊ **put away** ['put ə'weɪ] *verb* enviar a prisión; **he was put away for ten years** = le pusieron entre rejas durante diez años
◊ **put down** ['put 'daun] *verb* **(a)** *(deposit)* hacer un desembolso inicial; **to put money on a house** = dar una entrada para la compra de una casa **(b)** *(to write an item in a ledger)* apuntar en el libro de cuentas; **to put down a figure for expenses** = apuntar una cifra en la columna de gastos
◊ **put in** ['put 'ɪn] *verb* presentar *or* cursar; **to put an ad in a paper** = poner un anuncio en un periódico; **to put in an appearance** = hacer acto de presencia; **to put in a bid for something** = hacer una oferta por algo; **to put in an estimate for something** = presentar un presupuesto; **to put in a claim for damage** *or* **loss** = pedir una indemnización *or* presentar una reclamación por daños *or* pérdida
◊ **put into** ['put 'ɪntu] *verb* **to put money into a business** = invertir en un negocio
◊ **put off** ['put 'ɒf] *verb* aplazar; **the hearing was put off for two weeks** = la vista se aplazó dos semanas; **he asked if we could put the visit off until tomorrow** = preguntó si podíamos aplazar la visita hasta mañana
◊ **put on** ['put 'ɒn] *verb* **to put an item on the agenda** = poner en el orden del día un asunto a tratar; **to put an embargo on trade** = prohibir el comercio; **to put on record** = dejar constancia
◊ **put out** ['put 'aut] *verb* encargar; **to put work out to freelance workers** = encargar trabajo a trabajadores independientes *or* autónomos; **we put all our typing out to a bureau** = encargamos todo el trabajo de mecanografía a una agencia; **to put work out to contract** = subcontratar trabajo

putative ['pjuːtətɪv] *adjective* putativo, -va; **putative father** = padre putativo

pyramid selling ['pɪrəmɪd 'selɪŋ] *noun* venta *f* piramidal

◊ **pyramiding** ['pɪrəmɪdɪŋ] *noun* uso *m* ilegal de nuevas inversiones para pagar intereses debidos

pyromaniac [paɪrəʊ'meɪniæk] *noun* pirómano, -na *or* incendiario, -ria

Qq

QB *or* **QBD** ['kju: 'bi: 'di:] = QUEEN'S BENCH DIVISION

QC ['kju: 'si:] = QUEEN'S COUNSEL (NOTE: written after the surname of the lawyer: **W. Smith QC.** Note also that the plural is written **QCs**)

qua [kwɑ:] *conjunction* como; **a decision of the Lord Chancellor qua head of the judiciary** = una decisión del Presidente de la Cámara de los Lores como jefe supremo del poder judicial

quadruplicate [kwɒ'dru:plɪkət] *noun* cuadruplicado, -da; **in quadruplicate** = por cuadruplicado; **the invoices are printed in quadruplicate** = las facturas están impresas por cuadruplicado

qualification [kwɒlɪfɪ'keɪʃn] *noun* **(a)** *(professional title)* título *m or* cualificación *f or* aptitud *f;* **to have the right qualifications for the job** = tener la titulación adecuada para el trabajo; **professional qualifications** = títulos profesionales **(b)** **period of qualification** = periodo de prueba *or* de formación; *(financial assistance)* periodo de cotización necesario para tener derecho a una ayuda o subsidio; **qualification shares** = acciones *fpl* necesarias para ser director de una empresa

◊ **qualify** ['kwɒlɪfaɪ] *verb* **(a) to qualify for** = tener derecho a; **he does not qualify for Legal Aid** = no tiene derecho a la asistencia jurídica gratuita; **she qualifies for unemployment pay** = tiene derecho al subsidio de desempleo **(b) to qualify as** = sacar *or* obtener el título de; **she has qualified as an accountant** = ha sacado el título de contable; **he will qualify as a solicitor next year** = terminará la carrera de abogado *or* obtendrá el título de abogado el año que viene **(c)** *(to change or to amend)* cambiar *or* modificar; **the auditors have qualified the accounts** = los auditores han aprobado las cuentas con reservas

◊ **qualified** ['kwɒlɪfaɪd] *adjective* **(a)** *(in a subject)* cualificado, -da *or* calificado, -da *or* titulado, -da; **she is a qualified solicitor** = es una abogada titulada *or* tiene el título de abogado; **highly qualified** = altamente cualificado *or* muy cualificado *or* idóneo; **all our staff are highly qualified** = todos nuestros empleados están altamente cualificados; **they employ twenty-six highly qualified legal assistants** = contratan a veintiséis asesores jurídicos sumamente cualificados **(b)** *(with reservations)* con reservas *or* condicionado, -da; **qualified acceptance of a bill of exchange** = aceptación *f* condicionada de una letra de cambio; **the plan received qualified approval from the board** = el plan recibió la aprobación del consejo con reservas; **qualified privilege** = inmunidad *f* condicionada a la ausencia de malicia; **qualified title** = título *m* imperfecto *or* limitado de una propiedad *or* título no absoluto **(c)** **qualified accounts** = cuentas *fpl* aceptadas *or* aprobadas con reservas

◊ **qualifying** ['kwɒlɪfaɪɪŋ] *adjective* **(a)** **qualifying period** = periodo *m* de prueba *or* de formación; *(financial assistance)* periodo de cotización necesario para tener derecho a una ayuda o subsidio; **there is a six month qualifying period before you can get a grant from the local authority** = hay que cotizar durante seis meses para poder recibir una ayuda de las autoridades locales **(b) qualifying shares** = acciones *fpl* con garantía *or* número *m* de acciones necesarias para obtener determinados derechos

quango ['kwæŋgəʊ] *noun* organismo *m* paraestatal (NOTE: plural is **quangos**)

quantify ['kwɒntɪfaɪ] *verb* cuantificar; **to quantify the effect of something** = cuantificar el efecto de algo; **it is impossible to quantify the effect of the new legislation on the crime rate** = es imposible cuantificar el efecto de la nueva legislación sobre el índice de criminalidad

◊ **quantifiable** [kwɒntɪ'faɪəbl] *adjective* cuantificable; **the effect of the change on the prison population is not quantifiable** = el efecto del cambio en el número de presos no es cuantificable

quantity ['kwɒntɪtɪ] *adjective* **(a)** *(amount)* cantidad *f or* cuantía *f;* **a small quantity of illegal drugs** = una pequeña cantidad de drogas ilegales; **he bought a large quantity of spare parts** = compró una gran cantidad de piezas de repuesto **(b)** *(bulk)* gran cantidad; **the company offers a discount for quantity purchase** = la empresa hace un descuento cuando se compra en grandes cantidades

quantum ['kwæntəm] *noun* parte *f or* cuantificación *f;* **liability was admitted by the defendants, but the case went to trial because they could not agree the quantum of damages** = los demandados admitieron su responsabilidad pero el caso se llevó a juicio al no poder llegar a un acuerdo sobre la cuantificación de los daños

◊ **quantum meruit** ['kwɒntəm 'meruːit] *Latin phrase* 'lo que se merece': regla según la cual una de las partes tiene derecho al cobro por trabajo realizado, cuando existe incumplimiento de contrato

quarantine ['kwɒrəntiːn] **1** *noun* cuarentena *f;* **the animals were put in quarantine on arrival at the port** = los animales fueron puestos en cuarentena a su llegada al puerto; **quarantine restrictions have been lifted on imported animals from that country** = se han levantado las restricciones de cuarentena con animales importados de aquel país (NOTE: used without **the**: **the dog was put in quarantine** or **was held in quarantine** or **was released from quarantine**) **2** *verb* poner en cuarentena; **the ship was searched and all the animals on it were quarantined** = se hizo un registro en el barco y todos los animales a bordo fueron puestos en cuarentena

quarter ['kwɔːtə] *noun* **(a)** *(period of three months)* trimestre *m;* **first quarter** or **second quarter** or **third quarter** or **fourth quarter** or **last quarter** = primer trimestre or segundo trimestre or tercer trimestre or cuarto trimestre or último trimestre; **the instalments are payable at the end of each quarter** = los plazos se pagan a últimos de cada trimestre; **the first quarter's rent is payable in advance** = el alquiler correspondiente al primer trimestre se paga por adelantado; **quarter day** = día *m* de ajuste or día final del trimestre para el pago de la renta **(b)** **Quarter Sessions** = audiencia *f* trimestral or término antiguo para designar al tribunal de lo penal sustituido por el Tribunal de la Corona

COMMENT: in England the quarter days are 25th March (Lady Day), 24th June (Midsummer Day), 29th September (Michaelmas Day) and 25th December (Christmas Day)

quarterly ['kwɔːtəli] *adjective & adverb* trimestral or trimestralmente; **there is a quarterly charge for electricity** = los gastos de electricidad se pagan por trimestres; **the bank sends us a quarterly statement** = el banco nos manda un extracto de cuenta trimestralmente; **we agreed to pay the rent quarterly** or **on a quarterly basis** = acordamos pagar el alquiler trimestralmente or cada tres meses

quash [kwɒʃ] *verb* anular; **the appeal court quashed the verdict** = el tribunal de apelación

anuló la sentencia; **he applied for judicial review to quash the order** = solicitó una revisión del caso para anular la orden judicial; **a conviction obtained by fraud or perjury by a witness will be quashed** = toda declaración de culpabilidad obtenida por medio del fraude o del perjurio de un testigo será anulada

quasi- ['kweizai] *prefix* semi- or cuasi or casi; **a quasi-official body** = un organismo semioficial; **a quasi-judicial investigation** = una investigación semijudicial

◊ **quasi-contract** ['kweizai'kɒntrækt] *noun* = *IMPLIED CONTRACT*

Queen's Bench Division (QBD) ['kwiːnz 'bentʃ di'viʒn] *noun* una de las principales divisiones del Tribunal Supremo

Queen's Counsel ['kwiːnz 'kaunsl] *noun GB* abogado de prestigio (que ha sido elevado a la máxima categoría profesional por el Presidente de la Cámara de los Lores) (NOTE: abbreviated to **QC**)

Queen's evidence ['kwiːnz 'evidəns] *noun* **to turn Queen's evidence** = delatar a un cómplice

Queen's Proctor ['kwiːnz 'prɒtə] *noun* procurador que actúa para la Corona en casos matrimoniales y de legalización de testamentos

Queen's Speech ['kwiːnz 'spiːtʃ] *noun* discurso *m* de apertura de una sesión parlamentaria realizado por la Reina

query ['kwiəri] **1** *noun* pregunta *f;* **the chief accountant had to answer a mass of queries from the auditors** = el contable jefe tuvo que responder a un montón de preguntas de los auditores **2** *verb* **(a)** *(ask)* preguntar **(b)** *(doubt)* poner en duda; **counsel queried the statements of the police witnesses** = el abogado puso en duda las declaraciones de los testigos de la policía

question ['kwestʃn] **1** *noun* **(a)** *(which needs an answer)* pregunta *f;* **counsel asked the witness questions about his bank accounts** = el abogado hizo preguntas al testigo sobre sus cuentas bancarias; **counsel for the prosecution put three questions to the police inspector** = el fiscal hizo tres preguntas al inspector de policía; **the managing director refused to answer questions about redundancies** = el director gerente se negó a responder preguntas sobre despidos; **the market research team prepared a series of questions to test the public's attitude to problems of law and order** = el equipo de investigación de mercado preparó una serie de preguntas destinadas a analizar las reacciones del público hacia problemas de orden público; **Question Time** = ruegos *mpl* y preguntas *fpl* **(b)** *(problem)* problema *m* or cuestión *f* or asunto *m;* **he raised the question of the cost of the lawsuit** = planteó el problema del coste del proceso judicial; **the main question is that of time** = el principal problema es el tiempo; **the tribunal discussed the question of redundancy payments** = el tribunal discutió el problema de las indemnizaciones por despido **(c) question of fact** = cuestión de hecho; **question of law** = cuestión de derecho **2** *verb* **(a)** *(to ask questions)* preguntar; *(to a suspect)* interrogar; **the police questioned the accounts staff for four hours** = la policía interrogó a los contables durante cuatro horas; **she questioned the chairman about the company's investment policy** = interrogó al presidente sobre la política de inversiones de la empresa **(b)** *(to query)* poner en duda *or* cuestionar *or* poner en entredicho; **counsel questioned the reliability of the witness' evidence** = el abogado puso en duda la fiabilidad de la declaración del testigo; **the accused questioned the result of the breathalyser test** = el acusado puso en duda el resultado de la prueba de alcoholemia

◊ **questioning** ['kwestʃnɪŋ] *noun* interrogatorio *m or* preguntas *fpl;* **the man was taken to the police station for questioning** = llevaron al hombre a la comisaría de policía para ser interrogado; **during questioning by the police, she confessed to the crime** = durante el interrogatorio de la policía, confesó el crimen; **the witness became confused during questioning by counsel for the prosecution** = el testigo se desconcertó durante el interrogatorio del fiscal

◊ **questionnaire** [kwestʃə'neə] *noun* cuestionario *m;* **to send out a questionnaire to test the opinions of users of the system** = enviar un cuestionario para averiguar las opiniones de los usuarios del sistema; **to answer** *or* **to fill in a questionnaire about problems of inner city violence** = responder *or* rellenar un cuestionario sobre problemas de violencia en el centro de las ciudades

queue [kjuː] **1** *noun* **(a)** *(line of people)* cola *f;* **to form a queue** *or* **to join a queue** = hacer cola *or* ponerse en la cola; **queues formed at the doors of the Crown Court on the morning of the murder trial** = se formaron colas a la puerta de la Audiencia la mañana del juicio por asesinato **(b)** *(documents)* serie *f* de documentos que se tratan por orden; **mortgage queue** = lista *f* de personas que esperan obtener una hipoteca **2** *verb* hacer cola; **when food was in short supply, people had to queue for bread** = cuando había escasez de alimentos, la gente tenía que hacer cola para conseguir pan; **we queued for hours to get into the courtroom** = hicimos cola durante horas para entrar en la sala

quick [kwɪk] *adjective* rápido, -da; **the company made a quick recovery** = la empresa tuvo una recuperación rápida; **he is hoping for a quick trial** = espera que el juicio sea rápido

◊ **quickie (divorce)** ['kwɪki] *noun* divorcio *m* rápido

◊ **quickly** ['kwɪkli] *adverb* rápidamente; **the divorce case went through the courts quickly** = el caso de divorcio pasó por los tribunales rápidamente; **the accountant quickly looked through the pile of invoices** = el contable echó una rápida ojeada al montón de facturas

quid pro quo ['kwɪd prəu 'kwəu] *Latin phrase* 'una cosa por otra': acción a cambio de algo hecho *or* prometido

quiet ['kwaɪət] *adjective* tranquilo, -la; **the prisoner seemed very quiet when the clerk read out the charges** = el acusado parecía muy tranquilo cuando el secretario le leyó los cargos; **on the quiet** = a escondidas *or* en secreto *or* sigilosamente; **he transferred his bank account to Switzerland on the quiet** = transfirió su cuenta bancaria a Suiza en secreto; **quiet enjoyment** = disfrute *m* en privado *or* derecho *m* de ocupación de un alquiler sin interferencias

◊ **quietly** ['kwaɪətli] *adverb* tranquilamente

quit [kwɪt] *verb* dimitir *or* dejar un empleo *or* desocupar una vivienda; **he quit after an argument with the managing director** = dejó el puesto tras una discusión con el director gerente; **several of the managers are quitting to set up their own company** = varios de los directores dejan sus puestos para establecer su propia empresa; **notice to quit** = notificación *f or* aviso *m* de desahucio; **to serve a tenant with notice to quit** = entregar a un inquilino notificación de desahucio (NOTE: **quitting - quit - has quit**)

quo [kwəu] *see* STATUS QUO

quorum ['kwɔːrəm] *noun* quórum *m;* **to have a quorum** = haber quórum; **do we have a quorum?** = ¿hay quórum?; **the meeting was adjourned since there was no quorum** = la reunión se pospuso al no haber quórum

◊ **quorate** ['kwɔːreɪt] *adjective* con quórum; **the resolution was invalid because the shareholders' meeting was not quorate** = la decisión no tuvo validez porque la reunión de los accionistas no tenía quórum; *see also* INQUORATE

quota ['kwəutə] *noun* cuota *f or* cupo *m;* **import** *or* **export quota** = cuota de importación *or* de exportación *or* contingente *m;* **the government has imposed a quota on the import of cars** = el gobierno ha impuesto un cupo de importación de coches; **the quota on imported cars has been lifted** = se ha aumentado el cupo de coches importados; **quota system** = sistema *m* de cupos

quote [kwəut] *verb* **(a)** *(words)* citar *or* leer textualmente; **counsel quoted from the statement made by the witness at the police station** = el abogado citó textualmente de la declaración realizada por el testigo en la comisaría de policía **(b)** *(reference number)* dar una cifra *or* hacer referencia a un número; **she quoted figures from**

the annual report = dio las cifras del informe anual; **in reply please quote this number: PC 1234** = en su contestación le rogamos haga referencia a este número: PC 1234 **(c)** *(to estimate costs)* cotizar *or* calcular *or* ofrecer un precio; **to quote a price for supplying stationery** = dar un precio para el suministro de material de oficina; **to quote a price in dollars** = calcular un precio en dólares; **their prices are always quoted in dollars** = sus precios siempre se cotizan en dólares; **he quoted me a price of £1,026** = me calculó un precio de 1.026 libras; **can you quote for supplying 20,000 envelopes?** = ¿Puede darnos el precio para el suministro de 20.000 sobres?; **quoted company** = empresa *f* que cotiza en bolsa

◊ **quotation** [kwəʊ'teɪʃn] *noun* **(a)** *(estimate of how much something will cost)* cotización *f* or cálculo *m* estimativo *or* presupuesto *m;* **they sent in their quotation for the job** = presentaron su presupuesto para el trabajo; **to ask for quotations for building a new courtroom** = pedir presupuestos para la construcción de una nueva sala de vistas; **his quotation was much lower than all the others** = su oferta fue mucho más baja que las demás; **we accepted the lowest quotation** = aceptamos el presupuesto más bajo **(b)** quotation on the Stock Exchange *or* Stock Exchange quotation = cotización *f* oficial en la Bolsa; **the company is going for a quotation on the Stock Exchange** = la empresa ha solicitado entrar en la cotización oficial de la Bolsa

quo warranto ['kwəʊ 'wærəntəʊ] *Latin phrase* 'por autoridad': juicio *m* or acción *f* llevada a cabo para probar la autoridad de una persona

q.v. *or* **quod vide** ['kjuː 'viː] *Latin phrase* 'que ve'

Rr

R [rɪ'dʒaɪnə] = REGINA, REX (NOTE: used in reports of cases where the Crown is a party: *R. v. Smith Ltd)*

race [reɪs] *noun* raza *f;* **race relations** = relaciones *fpl* raciales
◊ **racial** ['reɪʃl] *adjective* racial; **racial hatred** = odio *m* racial; **incitement to racial hatred** = incitación *f* al odio racial; **racial prejudice** *or* **racial discrimination** = prejuicio *m* racial *or* discriminación *f* racial
◊ **racism** *or* **racialism** ['reɪsɪzm *or* 'reɪʃlɪzm] *noun* racismo *m*
◊ **racist** *or* **racialist** ['reɪsɪst *or* 'reɪʃlɪst] *adjective* & *noun* racista *mf*

rack rent ['ræk 'rent] *noun* **(a)** *(yearly rent)* alquiler *m* anual de una propiedad **(b)** *(very high rent)* alquiler exagerado *or* exorbitante

racket ['rækɪt] *noun* chantaje *m or* negocio *m* sucio que utiliza la estafa *or* la extorsión; **he runs a cheap ticket racket** = lleva un negocio sucio de reventa de entradas; *see also* PROTECTION
◊ **racketeer** [rækɪ'tɪə] *noun* chantajista *mf or* timador, -ra *or* estafador, -ra *or* extorsionador,-ra
◊ **racketeering** [rækɪ'tɪərɪŋ] *noun* chantaje *m or* crimen *m* organizado *or* negocio *m* ilícito *or* deshonesto

rage [reɪdʒ] *noun* arrebato *m;* **road rage** = cólera *f* en la carretera *or* violencia *f* vial

raid [reɪd] **1** *noun* ataque *m; (police)* redada *f* (por sorpresa); **six people were arrested in the police raid on the club** = seis personas fueron arrestadas durante la redada policial en el club **2** *verb* realizar un ataque *or* hacer una redada (por sorpresa); **the police have raided several houses in the town** = la policía ha realizado redadas en varias casas de la ciudad; **drugs were found when the police raided the club** = se encontraron drogas durante la redada policial en el club

raise [reɪz] **1** *noun* US aumento *m* de sueldo; **he asked the boss for a raise** = le pidió al jefe un aumento de sueldo; **she is pleased - she has had her raise** = está satisfecha; le han aumentado el sueldo (NOTE: British English is **rise**) **2** *verb* **(a)** to **raise a question** *or* **a point at a meeting** = plantear una cuestión *or* un asunto en una reunión; **in answer to the point of order raised by Mr Smith** = en relación a las cuestiones planteadas por el Sr.Smith; **to raise an objection** = formular una protesta *or* hacer objeciones; **the union representatives raised a series of objections to the wording of the agreement** = los representantes del sindicato hicieron una serie de objeciones sobre la redacción del acuerdo **(b)** *(to increase)* aumentar; **the government has raised the penalties for drug smuggling** = el gobierno ha aumentado la pena por tráfico de drogas; **the company raised its dividend by 10%** = la empresa aumentó su dividendo en un 10% **(c)** *(to obtain money or a loan)* conseguir *or* obtener; **the company is trying to raise the capital to fund its expansion programme** = la empresa está tratando de conseguir el capital necesario para invertir en su programa de expansión; **the government raises money by taxation** = el gobierno consigue dinero por medio de los impuestos; **where will he raise the money from to start up his business?** = ¿de dónde conseguirá el dinero para empezar su negocio? **(d)** *children)* criar

rank [ræŋk] **1** *noun* **(a)** *(class)* graduación *f or* categoría *f or* grado *m or* rango *m* **(b)** **rank and file** = base *f or* militantes *mfpl* de un partido; **he was promoted to the rank of Chief Superintendent** = le ascendieron a la graduación de superintendente jefe; **to reduce someone to the ranks** = degradar a un oficial **2** *verb (to be in a certain position)* situar *or* colocar *or* poner; **the new shares will rank pari passu with the existing ones** = las nuevas acciones se situarán al mismo ritmo que las ya existentes
◊ **ranking** ['ræŋkɪŋ] *noun* orden *m* de importancia

raison d'état ['reɪzɒŋ deɪ'tæ] *French phrase* razón *f* de estado

> COMMENT: raison d'état is open to criticism because it can be used to justify acts such as the abolition of individual rights, if the general good of the people may seem to require it at the time

ransom ['rænsəm] **1** *noun* rescate *m or* redención *f;* **the daughter of the banker was held by kidnappers who asked for a ransom of £1m** = la hija del banquero fue retenida por los secuestradores que pedían un rescate de un millón de libras; **to hold someone to ransom** = pedir *or* exigir rescate por alguien; **ransom note** = nota *f* de rescate **2** *verb* pagar un rescate; **she was ransomed by her family** = su familia pagó el rescate por su liberación

rape [reɪp] **1** *noun* violación *f;* **he was brought to court and charged with rape** = fue llevado ante los tribunales y acusado de violación; **the incidence of cases of rape has increased over the last years** = la incidencia de casos de violación ha aumentado durante los últimos años **2** *verb* violar *or* forzar

rapprochement [ræ'prɒʃmɒŋ] *French word* acercamiento *m;* **political commentators have noted the rapprochement which has been taking place since the old president died** = los comentaristas políticos han observado el acercamiento que ha venido teniendo lugar desde la muerte del antiguo presidente

rata ['rɑːtə] *see* PRO RATA

rate [reɪt] **1** *noun* **(a)** *(price)* tasa *f or* precio *m or* tarifa *f;* **all-in rate** = precio todo incluido *or* total; **fixed rate** = tarifa fija; **flat rate** = tanto *m* alzado *or* tarifa uniforme; **full rate** = precio íntegro *or* sin descuento; **reduced rate** = tarifa reducida **(b)** **insurance rates** = tarifas *fpl* de seguros; **interest rate** *or* **rate of interest** = tipo *m* de interés; **rate of return** = tasa de rendimiento **(c)** **exchange rate** *or* **rate of exchange** = tipo de cambio *or* tasa de cambio; **forward rate** = cambio *m* a plazo; **freight rates** = tarifas de carga *or* de flete; **letter rate** *or* **parcel rate** = franqueo *m* de cartas *or* de paquetes; **night rate** = tarifa telefónica de noche *or* nocturna **(d)** *(index)* índice *m or* ritmo *m; (ratio)* coeficiente *m;* **birth rate** = índice de natalidad; **error rate** = índice de errores **(e)** *GB (formerly British local taxes on property)* **the rates** = impuestos *mpl* locales *or* municipales sobre la propiedad; **the local authority has fixed** *or* **has set the rate for next year** = las autoridades locales han fijado los impuestos para el año que viene; **our rates have gone up by 25% this year** = nuestros impuestos locales han subido un 25% este año; **to set a legal rate** = establecer un impuesto legal; **uniform business rate (UBR)** = impuesto municipal abonado por comerciantes o empresas **2** *verb* **(a) to rate someone highly** = estimar mucho a alguien **(b) highly-rated part of London** = distrito de Londres con impuestos municipales elevados
◊ **rateable** ['reɪtəbl] *adjective;* **rateable value** = valor *m* imponible de la propiedad
◊ **ratepayer** ['reɪpeɪə] *noun* **domestic ratepayer** = contribuyente *mf* municipal *or* individual; **business ratepayer** = contribuyente comercial

ratify ['rætɪfaɪ] *verb* ratificar *or* sancionar; **the treaty was ratified by Congress** = el tratado fue ratificado por el congreso; **the agreement has to be ratified by the board** = el acuerdo tiene que ser ratificado por el consejo de dirección; **although the directors had acted without due authority, the company ratified their actions** = aunque los directores habían actuado sin la debida autoridad, la empresa ratificó sus acciones
◊ **ratification** [rætɪfɪ'keɪʃn] *noun* ratificación *f*

ratio ['reɪʃiəʊ] *noun* coeficiente *m*

ratio decidendi ['rætiəʊ desɪ'dendaɪ] *Latin phrase* 'razón para decidir': parte principal de un juicio que establece los principios legales aplicables al caso; *see also* OBITER DICTA

RD = REFER TO DRAWER

re [riː or reɪ] *preposition* respecto a *or* con referencia a *or* relativo a; **re your inquiry of May 29th** = respecto a su petición del 29 de mayo; **re: Smith's memorandum of yesterday** = referencia: informe de Smith de ayer; **re: the agenda for the AGM** = relativo a: el orden del día de la Junta General Ordinaria; **in re** = concerniente a; **in re Jones & Co Ltd** = concerniente a *Jones & Co. Ltd; see also* IN RE, RES

re- [riː] *prefix* de nuevo

rea ['reɪə] *see* MENS REA

reach [riːtʃ] *verb (to arrive at a place or at a point)* llegar a *or* alcanzar; **to reach an agreement** = llegar a un acuerdo; **the jury was unable to reach a unanimous decision** = el jurado no pudo llegar a una decisión unánime

read [riːd] *verb* leer; **to read between the lines** = leer entre líneas
◊ **reading** ['riːdɪŋ] *noun* lectura *f;* **First Reading** *or* **Second Reading** *or* **Third Reading** = primera lectura *or* segunda lectura *or* tercera lectura: las tres etapas de discusión de un proyecto de ley en el parlamento

COMMENT: First Reading is the formal presentation of the Bill; Second Reading is the stage when the Bill is explained by the Minister proposing it and a vote is taken; the Bill is then discussed in Committee and at the Report Stage; Third Reading is the final discussion of the Bill in the whole House of Commons

ready ['redi] *adjective* listo, -ta *or* preparado, -da; **to be always ready** = estar siempre listo; **to get ready** = prepararse

real ['rɪəl] *adjective* **(a)** *(true)* real *or* genuino, -na *or* verdadero, -ra *or* auténtico, -ca *or* fáctico, -ca; **his case is made of real leather** *or* **he has a real leather case** = su maleta es de cuero auténtico *or* tiene una maleta de cuero auténtico; **that car is a real bargain at £300** = al precio de 300 libras, ese coche es una verdadera ganga; **real income** *or* **real wages** = renta *f* real *or* neta *or* salario *m* neto *or* real; **in real terms** = realmente *or* en realidad *or* en términos reales; **sales have gone up by 3% but**

with inflation running at 5% that is a fall in real terms = las ventas han subido un 3% pero con una inflación del 5% supone un descenso en términos reales **(b)** *(computer)* **real time** = tiempo *m* real (de ordenador); **real-time system** = sistema *m* (de ordenador) a tiempo real **(c)** **chattels real** = propiedades *fpl* que se disfrutan en calidad de arrendamiento *or* derechos *mpl* sobre bienes raíces que no constituyen derechos de dominio absoluto **(d)** *(property)* **real estate** *or* **real property** = bienes *mpl* inmuebles *or* bienes raíces *or* propiedad *f* inmobiliaria

realize ['rɪəlaɪz] *verb* **(a)** *(to understand clearly)* darse cuenta *or* comprender; **counsel realized the defendant was making a bad impression on the jury** = el abogado se dio cuenta de que el acusado estaba causando una mala impresión en el jurado; **the small shopkeepers realized that the supermarket would take away some of their trade** = los pequeños comerciantes se dieron cuenta de que el supermercado les quitaría una parte de su clientela; **when he went into the police station he did not realize he was going to be arrested** = cuando entró en la comisaría no se dio cuenta de que le iban a detener **(b)** *(to make something become real)* realizar; **to realize a project** *or* **a plan** = realizar un proyecto *or* un plan **(c)** *(to sell for money)* convertir en efectivo; **to realize property** *or* **assets** = convertir bienes *or* activos en efectivo; **the sale realized £100,000** = la venta produjo 100.000 libras
◊ **realizable** [rɪə'laɪzəbl] *adjective;* **realizable assets** = activos *mpl* convertibles *or* realizables
◊ **realization** [rɪəlaɪ'zeɪʃn] *noun* **(a)** *(gradual understanding)* comprensión *f;* **the chairman's realization that he was going to be outvoted** = el presidente comprendió que iba a ser derrotado en la elección **(b)** *(making real)* realización *f;* **the realization of a project** = la realización de un proyecto; **the plan moved a stage nearer realization when the contracts were signed** = el plan avanzó hacia su realización al firmarse los contratos **(c)** **realization of assets** = liquidación *f* de activos *or* valor *m* en liquidación

realty ['rɪəlti] *noun* bienes *mpl* raíces

reapply [riːə'plaɪ] *verb* volver a solicitar; **the company reapplied for an injunction against the union** = la empresa volvió a solicitar un requerimiento en contra de los sindicatos; **she reapplied for a maintenance order** = volvió a solicitar la pensión alimenticia; **when he saw that the job had still not been filled, he reapplied for it** = al ver que el puesto seguía vacante, volvió a solicitarlo
◊ **reapplication** [riːæplɪ'keɪʃn] *noun* segunda solicitud *f*

reason ['riːzn] *noun* razón *f or* explicación *f or* causa *f or* motivo *m;* **unknown reason** = causa desconocida; **for health reasons** = por motivo de salud; **the defence gave no reason for their objections to the juror** = la defensa no dio explicación de sus objeciones al jurado; **the chairman of the magistrates asked him for the reason why he was late again** = el presidente de los magistrados le preguntó el porqué *or* motivo de su nuevo retraso *or* le pidió explicaciones por su nuevo retraso; **the witness was asked for his reasons for returning to the fire** = le preguntaron al testigo las razones por las que volvió al lugar del incendio
◊ **reasonable** ['riːznəbl] *adjective* **(a)** *(sensible or not annoyed)* razonable *or* sensato, -ta *or* comprensivo, -va; **the magistrates were very reasonable when she explained that the driving licence was necessary for her work** = los jueces se mostraron muy razonables cuando ella explicó que necesitaba el permiso de conducir para su trabajo; **beyond reasonable doubt** = sin que quepa la menor duda *or* duda alguna *or* la más mínima duda (prueba necesaria para condenar a una persona en un caso criminal); **the prosecution in a criminal case has to establish beyond reasonable doubt that the accused committed the crime** = en un caso criminal, la acusación tiene que demostrar sin que quepa duda alguna que el acusado cometió el crimen; **reasonable force** = fuerza *f* necesaria; **the police were instructed to use reasonable force in dealing with the riot** = la policía recibió instrucciones de utilizar la fuerza necesaria para controlar los disturbios; **reasonable man** = persona *f* razonable; **no reasonable offer refused** = no se rechazará ninguna oferta que sea razonable **(b)** *(not expensive)* módico, -ca *or* moderado, -da; **the restaurant offers good food at reasonable prices** = el restaurante ofrece buena comida a precios módicos *or* a precios moderados
◊ **reasoned** ['riːznd] *adjective* razonado, -da *or* motivado,-da; **after three months, the judge delivered a reasoned judgment** = después de tres meses, el juez emitió un juicio razonado
◊ **reasoning** ['riːznɪŋ] *noun* razonamiento *m;* **it is difficult to understand the reasoning behind the judge's decision** = es difícil de entender el razonamiento que llevó a la decisión del juez

rebate ['riːbeɪt] *noun* reembolso *m or* bonificación *f;* **rent rebate** = ayuda *f* estatal destinada a pagar el alquiler de viviendas; **tax rebate** = desgravación *f* fiscal *or* bonificación tributaria

rebel 1 ['rebəl] *noun* rebelde *mf or* amotinado, -da; **anti-government rebels have taken six towns** = los rebeldes opuestos al gobierno han tomado seis ciudades; **rebel ratepayers have occupied the town hall** = los contribuyentes rebeldes han ocupado el ayuntamiento **2** [rɪ'bel] *verb* rebelarse *or* sublevarse (NOTE: **rebelling - rebelled**)
◊ **rebellion** [rɪ'beljən] *noun* rebelión *f or* sublevación *f or* acto *m* de rebeldía; **the army has**

crushed the rebellion in the southern province = el ejército ha aplastado la rebelión en el sur

rebut [rɪ'bʌt] *verb* rebatir *or* refutar *or* impugnar; **he attempted to rebut the assertions made by the prosecution witness** = intentó rebatir las afirmaciones realizadas por el testigo de la acusación (NOTE: **rebutting - rebutted)**
◊ **rebuttal** [rɪ'bʌtl] *noun* refutación *f or* impugnación *f*

recall [rɪ'kɔːl] **1** *noun* **(a)** *(asking someone to come back)* retirada *f or* convocatoria *f*; **MPs are asking for the recall of Parliament to debate the crisis** = los diputados piden una convocatoria del parlamento para debatir la crisis; **after his recall, the Ambassador was interviewed at the airport** = tras su retirada, el embajador fue entrevistado en el aeropuerto **(b)** *US* destitución *f* **2** *verb* **(a)** *(to ask someone to come back)* llamar *or* hacer volver; **the witness was recalled to the witness box** = el testigo fue llamado a declarar de nuevo; **to recall an ambassador** = retirar a un embajador **(b)** *(to remember)* recordar; **the witness could not recall having seen the accused** = el testigo no podía recordar si había visto al acusado

recapture [rɪ'kæptʃə] *verb* volver a capturar; **six prisoners escaped, but they were all quickly recaptured** = se fugaron seis presos, pero pronto volvieron a ser capturados

recd = RECEIVED

receipt [rɪ'siːt] **1** *noun* **(a)** *(paper showing money has been paid)* recibo *m or* justificante *m or* resguardo *m or* comprobante *m;* **customs receipt** = recibo de aduana; **rent receipt** = recibo del alquiler; **receipt for items purchased** = recibo de compra (de artículos); **please produce your receipt if you want to exchange items** = en caso de que quiera cambiar los artículos comprados se ruega presentar el recibo; **receipt book** *or* **book of receipts** = talonario *m* de recibos **(b)** *(receiving)* recibo *or* recepción *f*; **goods will be supplied within thirty days of receipt of order** = la mercancía se suministrará dentro de los treinta días siguientes al recibo del pedido; **invoices are payable within thirty days of receipt** = las facturas deberán abonarse dentro de los treinta días siguientes a su recepción; **on receipt of the notification, the company lodged an appeal** = al recibir la notificación, la empresa interpuso una apelación; **to acknowledge receipt of a letter** = acusar recibo de una carta; **we acknowledge receipt of your letter of the 15th** = acusamos recibo de su carta del 15 del corriente; **in receipt of** = habiendo recibido *or* he recibido *or* obra en mi poder; **we are in receipt of a letter of complaint** = obra en nuestro poder una carta de reclamación; **he was accused of being in receipt of stolen cheques** = le acusaron de receptación de cheques robados **(c)** *(sales)* **receipts** = entradas *fpl or* ingresos *mpl;* **to itemize receipts**

and expenditure = detallar los ingresos y los gastos; **receipts are down against the same period of last year** = los ingresos han bajado en comparación con el mismo periodo del año pasado (NOTE: no plural for (b)) **2** *verb* acusar recibo de *or* dar un recibo por

receive [rɪ'siːv] *verb* **(a)** *(payment, goods)* recibir *or* cobrar; **we received the payment ten days ago** = recibimos el pago hace diez días; **the workers have not received any salary for six months** = hace seis meses que los obreros no cobran *or* los obreros no cobran desde hace seis meses; **the goods were received in good condition** = la mercancía se recibió en buen estado; **'received with thanks'** = recibí *m* **(b)** *(crime)* **to receive stolen goods** = encubrir *or* ocultar objetos robados
◊ **receivable** [rɪ'siːvəbl] *adjective* por cobrar; **accounts receivable** = cuentas *fpl* por cobrar *or* activo *m* exigible
◊ **receivables** [rɪ'siːvəblz] *plural noun* efectos *mpl or* deudas *fpl* por cobrar
◊ **receiver** [rɪ'siːvə] *noun* **(a)** *(person who receives something)* destinatario , -ria *or* depositario, -ria *or* receptor, -ra; **receiver of wrecks** = funcionario del Ministerio de Comercio encargado de los problemas legales derivados de los naufragios ocurridos dentro de su jurisdicción **(b)** **Official Receiver** = *(government official)* Administrador, -ra Judicial *or* interventor, -ra *or* síndico *m* de quiebra; *(administrator in a company)* receptor, -ra oficial de una empresa *or* por delegación o nombramiento; **the court appointed a receiver for the company** = el tribunal nombró un receptor para la empresa; **the company is in the hands of the receiver** = la empresa está en quiebra *or* en manos del receptor; **the Court of Protection appointed a receiver to administer the client's affairs** = el Tribunal de Protección nombró un interventor para que administrara los asuntos del cliente **(c)** *(stolen goods)* receptador, -ra *or* encubridor,-ra de objetos robados
◊ **receivership** [rɪ'siːvəʃɪp] *noun* administración *f or* intervención *f* judicial; **the company went into receivership** = la empresa entró en liquidación *or* pasó a administrarse judicialmente
◊ **receiving** [rɪ'siːvɪŋ] *noun* **(a)** *(getting something which has been delivered)* recepción *f*; **receiving clerk** = recepcionista *mf*; **receiving department** = servicio *m* de recepción; **receiving office** = oficina *f* de recepción; **receiving stolen property** = encubrimiento *m or* receptación *f* de objetos robados **(b)** *(bankruptcy)* **receiving order** = mandato *m* por el que se designa un administrador judicial a una empresa *or* orden *f* judicial por la que se nombra a un administrador judicial a cargo de los bienes de una persona antes de realizar una orden de quiebra

recess [rɪ'ses] *noun* descanso *m or* suspensión *f* de sesiones *or* vacaciones *fpl* parlamentarias

recession [rɪ'seʃn] *noun* recesión *f;* **the recession has put many people out of work** = la recesión ha dejado a mucha gente sin trabajo; **he lost all his money in the recession** = perdió todo su dinero durante la recesión

recidivist [rɪ'sɪdəvɪst] *noun* reincidente *mf*

recipient [rɪ'sɪpiənt] *noun* destinatario, -ria *or* receptor, -ra *or* beneficiario, -ria; **the recipient of an allowance from the company** = el receptor de una ayuda procedente de la empresa

reciprocal [rɪ'sɪprəkl] *adjective* recíproco, -ca *or* mutuo, -tua *or* bilateral; **reciprocal holdings** = tenencia recíproca de acciones; **reciprocal trade** = comercio *m* recíproco; **reciprocal wills** = testamentos *mpl* recíprocos
◊ **reciprocate** [rɪ'sɪprəkeɪt] *verb* corresponder a; **they offered us an exclusive agency for their cars and we reciprocated with an offer of the agency for our buses** = nos ofrecieron un concesionario en exclusiva de sus coches y nosotros correspondimos ofreciéndoles un concesionario de nuestros autocares
◊ **reciprocity** [resɪ'prɒsɪti] *noun* reciprocidad *f*

recitals [rɪ'saɪtlz] *plural noun* introducción *f* de una escritura en la que se establece una relación de las partes así como su principal finalidad

reckless ['rekləs] *adjective* imprudente *or* inconsciente; **reckless driving** = conducción *f* imprudente *or* temeraria
◊ **recklessly** ['rekləsli] *adverb* imprudentemente; **the company recklessly spent millions of pounds on a new factory** = la empresa gastó imprudentemente millones de libras en una nueva fábrica; **he was accused of driving recklessly** = le acusaron de conducción temeraria
◊ **recklessness** ['rekləsnəs] *noun* imprudencia *f* temeraria *or* temeridad *f*

reclaim [rɪ'kleɪm] *verb* reclamar

recognize ['rekəgnaɪz] *verb* **(a)** *(to know)* reconocer; **she recognized the man who attacked her** = reconoció al hombre que la atacó; **I recognized his voice before he said who he was** = reconocí su voz antes de que dijera quién era; **do you recognize the handwriting on the letter?** = ¿Reconoce la letra de la carta? **(b)** *(to approve)* reconocer *or* admitir; **to recognize a government** = reconocer un gobierno; **the prisoner refused to recognize the jurisdiction of the court** = el acusado se negó a admitir la jurisdicción del tribunal; **to recognize a union** = reconocer un sindicato; **although all the staff had joined the union, the management refused to recognize it** = aunque todos los empleados pertenecían al sindicato, la dirección se negó a reconocerlo; **recognized agent** = representante reconocido *or* agente acreditado **(c) to recognize the speaker** = conceder la palabra

◊ **recognition** [rekəg'nɪʃn] *noun* reconocimiento *m;* **to grant a government** *or* **a trade union recognition** = reconocer un gobierno *or* un sindicato

◊ **recognizance** [rɪ'kɒgnɪzns] *noun* caución *f* judicial *or* compromiso *m* de comparecencia ante la ley para responder de las acusaciones imputadas, personalmente o por delegación, so pena del pago de una multa; **he was remanded on his own recognizance of £4,000** = fue puesto en libertad a condición de pagar una multa de 4.000 libras si no comparecía ante los tribunales; **estreated recognizance** = pérdida del derecho al compromiso de comparecencia ante los tribunales *or* pérdida del derecho a la libertad por falta de comparecencia ante los tribunales; *US* **release on recognizance (ROR)** = libertad provisional bajo promesa de comparecer ante un tribunal en caso necesario

recommend [rekə'mend] *verb* **(a)** *(suggest action)* aconsejar *or* recomendar; **the legal adviser recommended applying for an injunction against the directors of the company** = el asesor jurídico aconsejó solicitar un requerimiento contra los directores de la empresa; **we do not recommend bank shares as a safe investment** = no creemos que los valores bancarios sean una inversión segura; **the Parole Board recommended him for parole** = el comité *or* la junta recomendó al preso para la libertad condicional; **he was sentenced to life imprisonment, the judge recommending that he should serve a minimum of twenty years** = fue condenado a cadena perpetua y el juez recomendó que, como mínimo, debería cumplir veinte años **(b)** *(to say that someone or something is good)* recomendar; **I certainly would not recommend Miss Smith for the job** = yo nunca recomendaría a la Srta. Smith para el trabajo; **the board meeting recommended a dividend of 10p a share** = la reunión del consejo recomendó un dividendo de 10 peniques por acción; **can you recommend a good hotel in Amsterdam?** = ¿me puede recomendar un buen hotel en Amsterdam? (NOTE: you recommend someone **for** a job or you recommend something **to** someone or that someone **should do something**)

◊ **recommendation** [rekəmen'deɪʃn] *noun* **(a)** *(advice)* recomendación *f;* **he was sentenced to life imprisonment, with a recommendation that he should serve at least twenty years** = fue condenado a cadena perpetua, con la recomendación de que debería cumplir, al menos, veinte años; **he was released on the recommendation of the Parole Board** *or* **on the Parole Board's recommendation** = fue puesto en libertad por recomendación del comité encargado de la libertad condicional **(b)** *(praise)* recomendación; **we appointed him on the recommendation of his former employer** = lo nombramos por recomendación de su anterior jefe

reconcile ['rekənsaɪl] *verb* **(a)** *(people)* reconciliar **(b)** *(accounts)* cuadrar una cuenta *or* comprobar declaraciones; **to reconcile one account with another** = cuadrar una cuenta con otra; **to reconcile the accounts** = cuadrar las cuentas
◊ **reconciliation** [rekənsɪli'eɪʃn] *noun* reconciliación *f* contable *or* concertación *f* de las partes *or* comparación *f* de declaraciones; **reconciliation statement** = estado *m* de reconciliación

reconsider [riːkən'sɪdə] *verb* reconsiderar *or* recapacitar; **the applicant asked the committee to reconsider its decision to refuse the application** = el candidato pidió a la comisión que reconsiderara su decisión de rechazar la solicitud; *US* **motion to reconsider a vote** = moción *f* al final de un debate para que se vuelva a considerar el resultado de la votación

reconstruction [riːkən'strʌkʃn] *noun* reconstrucción *f*; *(of a crime)* reconstrucción de los hechos; **the reconstruction of a company** = la reestructuración de una empresa

re-convict [riːkən'vɪkt] *verb* volver a condenar
◊ **re-conviction** ['riːkən'vɪkʃn] *noun* reincidencia *f* or condena *f* a un reincidente; **the re-conviction rate is rising** = el índice de condenas a reincidentes está aumentando

record ['rekɔːd] **1** *adjective* máximo *or* más alto; **record crime figures** *or* **record losses** *or* **record profits** = índice de criminalidad máximo *or* pérdidas máximas *or* beneficios máximos; **1994 was a record year for bankruptcies** = el año 1994 fue el año que registró más bancarrotas **2** *noun* **(a)** *(report of something which has happened)* informe *m* or actas *fpl* de un tribunal; **record of the proceedings** = actas del proceso; **the chairman signed the minutes as a true record of the last meeting** = el presidente firmó el acta como expresión fiel de la última reunión; **a matter of record** = hecho *m* establecido; **for the record** *or* **to keep the record straight** = para que conste *or* para dejar las cosas en claro *or* anotar algo detalladamente; **on record** = oficialmente *or* que consta; **the chairman is on record as saying that profits are set to rise** = el presidente ha dicho oficialmente que los beneficios van a aumentar; **off the record** = extraoficialmente *or* oficiosamente *or* confidencialmente *or* en privado; **he made some remarks off the record about the rising crime figures** = hizo algunos comentarios extraoficialmente sobre el aumento de la criminalidad **(b)** *(documents)* **records** = archivos *mpl*; **records held at the public registry office** = libros *mpl* del registro civil; **the names of customers are kept in the company's records** = los nombres de los clientes están en los archivos de la empresa; **we find from our records that our invoice number 1234 has not been paid** = según

nuestros libros la factura número 1234 no ha sido pagada **(c)** *(description of what has happened)* historial *m* or hoja *f* de servicios *or* expediente *m*; **the clerk's record of service** *or* **service record** = la hoja de servicios del empleado; **the company's record in industrial relations** = el historial de la empresa en cuanto a relaciones laborales; **criminal record** = historial delictivo *or* antecedentes *mpl* penales; **he has a criminal record stretching back twenty years** = tiene un historial delictivo que se remonta a los últimos veinte años; **the court was told she had no previous criminal record** = el tribunal fue informado de que no poseía antecedentes penales; **track record** = historial *or* experiencia *f* or antecedentes *mpl*; **he has a good track record as a detective** = tiene un buen historial como detective; **the company has no track record in the computer market** = la empresa no tiene experiencia en el mercado de la informática **(d)** *(better than anything before)* récord *m*; **road accidents in 1993 equalled the record of 1990** = el número de accidentes de tráfico ocurridos en 1993 igualó al récord de 1990; **the figure for muggings has set a new record** *or* **has broken all previous records** = el número de asaltos ha establecido un nuevo récord **3** [rɪ'kɔːd] *verb* consignar *or* tomar nota de *or* hacer constar *or* registrar; **the company has recorded another year of increased sales** = la empresa ha registrado un año más de aumento de ventas; **your complaint has been recorded and will be investigated** = hemos tomado nota de su reclamación y será investigada; **the court recorded a plea of not guilty** = el tribunal consignó una declaración de inocencia; **the coroner recorded a verdict of death by misadventure** = el juez de primera instancia consignó un veredicto de muerte accidental; **recorded delivery** = correo *m* certificado *or* servicio *m* de correos con acuse de recibo
◊ **recorder** [rɪ'kɔːdə] *noun* magistrado, -da municipal; **Recorder of London** = magistrado principal del Tribunal Central de lo Penal; *see comment at* JUDGE
◊ **recording** [rɪ'kɔːdɪŋ] *noun* consignación *f* or registro *m*; **the recording of an order** *or* **of a complaint** = la consignación de una orden judicial *or* el registro de una reclamación

recours [rɪ'kɔːs] *see* SANS

recourse [rɪ'kɔːs] *noun* **to decide to have recourse to the courts** = decidir recurrir a los tribunales

recover [rɪ'kʌvə] *verb* **(a)** *(to get back)* obtener *or* recuperar; **he never recovered his money** = nunca recuperó su dinero; **the initial investment was never recovered** = nunca se recuperó el desembolso inicial; **to recover damages from the driver of the car** = obtener daños y perjuicios del conductor del coche; **to start a court action to recover property** = iniciar acciones legales para

recuperar bienes **(b)** *(to get better or to rise)* mejorar *or* recuperarse; **the market has not recovered from the rise in oil prices** = el mercado no se ha recuperado de la subida de los precios del petróleo; **the stock market fell in the morning, but recovered during the afternoon** = la bolsa bajó por la mañana , pero se recuperó en el transcurso de la tarde
◊ **recoverable** [rɪˈkʌvrəbl] *adjective* recuperable
◊ **recovery** [rɪˈkʌvri] *noun* **(a)** *(getting back something which has been lost)* recuperación *f;* **we are aiming for the complete recovery of the money invested** = nuestro propósito es la recuperación total del dinero invertido; **to start an action for recovery of property** = iniciar una acción judicial para recuperar bienes **(b)** *(movement upwards)* recuperación *or* reactivación *f;* **the economy showed signs of a recovery** = la economía mostró síntomas de recuperación; **the recovery of the economy after a recession** = la recuperación de la economía tras la recesión

recruit [rɪˈkruːt] **1** *noun* **(a)** *(member)* nuevo miembro *or* socio, -cia; **new recruits have to take a special training course** = los nuevos miembros tienen que realizar un curso especial de entrenamiento *or* de formación **(b)** *(army)* recluta *mf* **2** *verb* reclutar *or* contratar nuevo personal; **twenty-five women were recruited into the local police force** = veinticinco mujeres fueron reclutadas en el cuerpo de policía local
◊ **recruitment** [rɪˈkruːtmənt] *noun* reclutamiento *m or* contratación *f or* alistamiento *m;* **the recruitment rate is rising** = el índice de reclutamiento está subiendo

rectify [ˈrektɪfaɪ] *verb* rectificar *or* corregir; **the court rectified its mistake** = el tribunal rectificó su error
◊ **rectification** [rektɪfɪˈkeɪʃn] *noun* rectificación *f*

recur [rɪˈkəː] *verb* repetirse; **I hope it will never recur** = espero que nunca vuelva a repetirse

recusal [rɪˈkjuːzl] *noun* recusación *f*

red bag [ˈred ˈbæg] *noun* bolsa *f* de color rojo en la que un abogado lleva su toga; *see also* BLUE BAG

redeem [rɪˈdiːm] *verb* **(a)** *(pay back)* amortizar *or* pagar *or* cancelar *or* rescatar **(b) to redeem a bond** = vender un bono
◊ **redeemable** [rɪˈdiːməbl] *adjective* amortizable *or* rescatable; **redeemable preference shares** = acciones *fpl* de pago preferente

redemption [rɪˈdempʃn] *noun* **(a)** *(repayment of a loan)* amortización *f* de una deuda *or* rescate *m* de un empréstito; **redemption date** = fecha *f* de rescate; **redemption before due date** = amortización anticipada *or* rescate anticipado; **redemption value** = valor *m* de rescate **(b)**

(repayment of debt) reembolso *m or* cancelación *f* de una deuda *or* redención *f;* **equity of redemption** = derecho *m* del propietario al rescate de un bien hipotecado mediante el pago de la deuda (incluso una vez iniciada la ejecución)

red-handed [ˈredˈhændɪd] *adjective* en flagrante *or* con las manos en la masa; **he was caught red-handed** = le sorprendieron en flagrante *or* le cogieron con las manos en la masa

red tape [ˈred ˈteɪp] *noun* **(a)** *(ribbon)* cinta *f* roja utilizada para atar documentos jurídicos **(b)** *(administrative work)* papeleo *m or* burocracia *f;* **the application has been held up by red tape** = la solicitud se ha retrasado por el papeleo

reduce [rɪˈdjuːs] *verb* reducir *or* rebajar *or* recortar; **to reduce expenditure on prisons** *or* **on crime detection** = reducir el gasto en prisiones *or* en investigaciones criminales; **the Appeal Court reduced the fine imposed by the magistrates** *or* **reduced the sentence to seven years' imprisonment** = el Tribunal de Apelación redujo la multa impuesta por los jueces *or* redujo la condena a siete años de prisión; **we have made some staff redundant to reduce costs** = hemos despedido a algunos empleados para reducir gastos; **the government's policy is to reduce inflation to 5%** = la política del gobierno es reducir la inflación al 5%
◊ **reduced** [rɪˈdjuːst] *adjective* reducido, -da *or* rebajado, -da; **he received a reduced sentence on appeal** = recurrió y le redujeron la condena; **prices have fallen due to a reduced demand for the goods** = los precios han bajado debido a una menor demanda de la mercancía
◊ **reduction** [rɪˈdʌkʃn] *noun* reducción *f or* rebaja *f;* **price reductions** = rebaja de precios; **tax reductions** = reducción de impuestos; **staff reductions** = reducción de personal; **reduction of expenditure** = reducción de gastos; **reduction in demand** = reducción de la demanda; **a reduction in the nominal capital of a limited company requires the leave of the court** = una reducción en el capital nominal de una sociedad limitada requiere la autorización del tribunal

redundancy [rɪˈdʌndənsi] *noun* **(a)** *(work)* excedente *m* de plantilla *or* despido *m or* pérdida *f* del puesto de trabajo; **redundancy payment** = indemnización *f or* compensación *f* por despido; **voluntary redundancy** = baja *f* incentivada *or* baja voluntaria con derecho a indemnización **(b)** *(person who has lost a job)* parado, -da *or* desempleado, -da; **the takeover caused 250 redundancies** = la adquisición resultó en 250 despidos *or* en 250 empleados sin trabajo
◊ **redundant** [rɪˈdʌndənt] *adjective* **(a)** *(more than is needed)* excesivo, -va *or* superfluo, -flua *or* innecesario, -ria; **this law is now redundant** = esta ley es superflua; **a redundant clause in a contract**

= una cláusula innecesaria en un contrato; **the new legislation has made clause 6 redundant** = la nueva legislación ha convertido la cláusula 6 en superflua **(b)** *(work)* **to make someone redundant** = despedir a alguien; **redundant staff** = empleados despedidos

re-entry [riːˈentri] *noun (to country)* reingreso *m*; *(to society)* reintegración *f*; *(to property)* recuperación *f* de una propiedad; **right of re-entry** = derecho de recuperación de una propiedad *or* derecho que tiene un residente a volver a entrar en un país, después de haber estado ausente durante algún tiempo

re-examine [ˈriːɪgˈzæmɪn] *verb (of counsel)* volver a interrogar

◊ **re-examination** [riːɪgzæmɪˈneɪʃn] *noun* nuevo interrogatorio *m*

refer [rɪˈfɔː] *verb* **(a)** *(mention)* mencionar *or* referirse *or* remitirse; **we refer to your letter of May 26th** = nos remitimos a su carta del 26 de mayo; **he referred to an article which he had seen in 'The Times'** = se refirió a un artículo que había visto en 'The Times'; **referring to the court order dated June 4th** = referente a la orden judicial del 4 de junio; **the schedule before referred to** = el programa mencionado con anterioridad **(b)** *(to hand on to someone)* remitir *or* elevar; **to refer to a higher court** = elevar a un tribunal superior; **to refer a question to a committee** = remitir un problema a un comité; **we have referred your complaint to the tribunal** = hemos remitido su queja al tribunal **(c)** *(to return)* **the bank referred the cheque to drawer** = el banco remitió el cheque al librador; **'refer to drawer'** = 'remitir al librador' (NOTE: **referring - referred**)

◊ **referee** [refəˈriː] *noun* **(a)** *(for a job)* persona que da referencias *or* informes de otra *or* referencia *f*; **to give someone's name as referee** = dar el nombre de alguien como referencia; **she gave the name of her boss as a referee** = dio el nombre de su jefe como referencia; **when applying please give the names of three referees** = al hacer la solicitud se ruega incluir el nombre de tres personas como referencia **(b)** *(in a dispute)* árbitro *m*; **the question of maintenance payments is with a court-appointed referee** = el asunto de la manutención lo lleva un árbitro nombrado por el tribunal; **official refereee** = árbitro *or* juez especialista en casos técnicos de gran complejidad

◊ **reference** [ˈrefrəns] *noun* **(a)** *(passing a problem to a referee)* referencia *f or* consulta *f*; **terms of reference** = mandato *m or* (áreas de) competencia; **under the terms of reference of the committee, it cannot investigate complaints from the public** = conforme a su mandato, el comité no puede investigar quejas del público; **the tribunal's terms of reference do not cover traffic offences** = las áreas de competencia del tribunal no cubren

delitos de tráfico **(b)** *(dealing with)* referencia; **with reference to** = en lo que afecta a; *(in letter)* **with reference to your letter of May 25th** = con referencia a *or* con respecto a *or* en cuanto a su carta del 25 de mayo **(c)** *(numbers or letters which identify a document)* referencia; **our reference: PC/MS 1234** = nuestra referencia es: PC/MS 1234; **thank you for your letter (reference 1234)** = gracias por su carta (referencia 1234); **please quote this reference in all correspondence** = sírvanse indicar esta referencia en su correspondencia; **when replying please quote reference 1234** = cuando conteste le rogamos mencione la referencia 1234 **(d)** *(written report on someone's character or ability)* informe *m or* referencias *fpl*; **to write someone a reference** *or* **to give someone a reference** = dar referencias de alguien; **to ask applicants to supply references** = pedir a los candidatos que proporcionen sus referencias; **to ask a company for trade references** *or* **for bank references** = pedir a una empresa referencias comerciales *or* referencias bancarias; **letter of reference** = carta *f* de recomendación **(e)** *(person who reports on someone's character or ability)* persona que da referencias *or* informes de otra *or* referencia *f*; **to give someone's name as reference** = dar el nombre de alguien que pueda proporcionar una referencia; **please use me as a reference if you wish** = puedes dar mi nombre como referencia si lo deseas

referendum [refəˈrendəm] *noun* referéndum *m*; **the government decided to hold a referendum on the abolition of capital punishment** = el gobierno decidió hacer un referéndum sobre la abolición de la pena de muerte (NOTE: plural is **referenda**)

reform [rɪˈfɔːm] **1** *noun* reforma *f*; **they have signed an appeal for the reform of the remand system** = han firmado un recurso para la reforma del sistema de detención preventiva; **the reform in the legislation was intended to make the court procedure more straightforward** = la reforma de la legislación se hizo con la intención de simplificar los procedimientos judiciales; **law reform** = reforma judicial **2** *verb* reformar; **the group is pressing for the prison system to be reformed** = el grupo está presionando para que se reforme el régimen penitenciario; **the prisoner has committed so many crimes of violence that he will never be reformed** = el recluso ha cometido tantos delitos violentos que no podrán reformarle nunca

◊ **reformatory** [rɪˈfɔːmətri] *noun* reformatorio *m or* presidio *m* correccional

refrain [rɪˈfreɪn] *verb* abstenerse; **to refrain from something** = abstenerse de algo; **he was asked to give an undertaking to refrain from political activity** = le pidieron que prometiera abstenerse de toda actividad política

refresher [rɪ'freʃə] *noun* honorarios *mpl* suplementarios; **counsel's brief fee was £1,000 with refreshers of £250** = los honorarios del abogado por la preparación del expediente consistían en 1.000 libras, con una cantidad suplementaria de 250 libras por día

refuge ['refjuːdʒ] *noun* asilo *m;* **to take refuge** = refugiarse
◊ **refugee** [refjuː'dʒiː] *noun* refugiado, -da *or* asilado, -da; **political refugee** = refugiado político

refund 1 ['rɪfʌnd] *noun* devolución *f or* reembolso *m;* **full refund** *or* **refund in full** = reembolso íntegro *or* total **2** [rɪ'fʌnd] *verb* reembolsar *or* devolver *or* reintegrar; **to refund the cost of postage** = reembolsar los gastos de franqueo; **travelling expenses will be refunded to witnesses giving evidence to the tribunal** = se reintegrarán los gastos de desplazamiento a los testigos que presten declaración ante el tribunal; **all money will be refunded if the goods are not satisfactory** = si los artículos no son de su total satisfacción, le devolveremos el dinero

refuse [rɪ'fjuːz] *verb* negarse a *or* rechazar *or* rehusar; **the court refused to allow the witness to speak** = el tribunal se negó a permitir que el testigo hiciera uso de la palabra; **the accused refused to take the oath** = el acusado se negó a prestar juramento; **the bank refused to lend the company any more money** = el banco se negó a prestar más dinero a la empresa; **he asked for a rise but it was refused** = pidió un aumento pero se lo denegaron; **the loan was refused by the bank** = el préstamo fue denegado por el banco; **the customer refused the goods** *or* **refused to accept the goods** = el cliente rechazó los artículos *or* se negó a aceptar los artículos (NOTE: you **refuse to do something** or **refuse something**)
◊ **refusal** [rɪ'fjuːzl] *noun* denegación *f or* negativa *f or* opción *f or* rechazo *m;* **his request met with a refusal** = su petición fue denegada; **to give someone first refusal of something** = dar a alguien primera opción de compra; **blanket refusal** = rechazo *or* negativa global

regard [rɪ'gɑːd] *noun* **having regard to** *or* **as regards** *or* **regarding** = teniendo en cuenta *or* por lo que concierne a; **having regard to the opinion of the European Parliament** = teniendo en cuenta la opinión del Parlamento Europeo; **as regards** *or* **regarding the second of the accused, the jury was unable to reach a majority verdict** = por lo que concierne al segundo de los acusados, el jurado no pudo llegar a un veredicto mayoritario
◊ **regardless** [rɪ'gɑːdləs] *adverb* **regardless of** = sin tener en cuenta; **such conduct constitutes contempt of court regardless of intent** = un comportamiento tal constituye desacato a los tribunales sin tener en cuenta la intención; **the court takes a serious view of such crimes,**

regardless of the age of the accused = el tribunal considera graves los delitos de ese tipo, sin tener en cuenta la edad del acusado

regent ['riːdʒənt] *noun* regente, -ta
◊ **regency** ['riːdʒənsi] *noun* regencia *f*

regime *noun* régimen *m;* **under a military regime, civil liberties may be severely curtailed** = los derechos individuales suelen ser duramente restringidos bajo un régimen militar; **life was better under the previous regime** = se vivía mejor con el régimen anterior

Regina [rɪ'dʒaɪnə] *Latin word* 'la Reina': la Corona *or* el estado como una de las partes en procedimientos legales (NOTE: in written reports, usually abbreviated to R: **the case of R. v. Smith**)

region ['riːdʒən] *noun* región *f*
◊ **regional** ['riːdʒənl] *adjective* regional; *(in Scotland)* **Regional Council** = Consejo *m* Regional; **Regional Development Plan** = plan *m* de desarrollo regional

register ['redʒɪstə] **1** *noun (official list)* registro *m or* libro *m* registro; **to enter something in a register** = apuntar algo en un registro; **to keep a register up to date** = mantener un registro al día; **companies' register** *or* **register of companies** = registro de empresas; **register of charges** = registro de cargas *or* registro de gravámenes; **register of debentures** *or* **debenture register** = registro de obligaciones; **register of directors** = relación *f* de directivos de una empresa; **register of electors** = censo *m* electoral; **land register** = catastro *m or* registro de la propiedad; **Lloyd's register** = el registro de Lloyds; **register of members** *or* **of shareholders** *or* **share register** = relación de accionistas; **official register** = diario *m* oficial **2** *verb* **(a)** *(in an official list)* registrar *or* inscribir en un registro; **to register a company** = inscribir a una empresa en el registro; **to register a sale** = registrar una venta; **to register a property** = registrar una propiedad *or* dar una propiedad de alta; **to register a trademark** = registrar una marca comercial; **to register a marriage** *or* **a death** = inscribir un matrimonio en el registro civil *or* declarar una defunción en el registro civil **(b)** *(on voting list)* empadronar **(c)** *(sign on arrival at a hotel or conference)* inscribirse *or* registrarse; **they registered at the hotel under the name of MacDonald** = se registraron en el hotel con el nombre de MacDonald **(d)** *(post)* certificar *or* enviar una carta certificada; **I registered the letter, because it contained some money** = envié la carta certificada porque contenía dinero
◊ **registered** ['redʒɪstəd] *adjective* **(a)** *(noted on an official list)* registrado, -da oficialmente; **registered company** = sociedad *f* legalmente constituida *or* inscrita en el registro mercantil; **registered land** = propiedad registrada; **a company's registered office** = domicilio *m* social

de una empresa; **registered trademark** = marca registrada; **registered user** = persona *or* empresa autorizada a usar una marca registrada **(b)** **registered letter** *or* **registered parcel** = carta certificada *or* paquete certificado; **to send documents by registered mail** *or* **registered post** = enviar documentos por correo certificado

◊ **Register Office** ['redʒɪstə 'ɒfɪs] *noun* Oficina *f* del Registro Civil

◊ **registrar** [redʒɪ'strɑ:] *noun* **(a)** *(person who keeps official records)* registrador, -ra; **Registrar of Companies** = secretario, -ria del registro mercantil; **registrar of trademarks** = encargado, -da del registro de marcas **(b)** *(official of a court)* oficial *mf* del juzgado que asiste a discusiones preliminares de juicios civiles **(c)** **district registrar** = encargado, -da del registro civil de un distrito

◊ **Registrar-General** [redʒɪ'strɑ: 'dʒenrl] *noun* secretario, -ria general *or* funcionario, -ria jefe del registro civil

◊ **registration** [redʒɪ'streɪʃn] *noun* **(a)** *(act of having something noted)* inscripción *f or* registro *m or* matrícula *f*; **registration of a trademark** *or* **of a share transaction** = inscripción de una marca en el registro *or* registro de una transferencia de acciones; **certificate of registration** *or* **registration certificate** = certificado *m* de inscripción; **registration fee** = derecho *m* de registro *or* derechos *mpl* de inscripción *or* matrícula; **registration number** = número *m* de matrícula *or* de inscripción *or* de registro **(b)** **land registration** = registro de la propiedad

◊ **registry** ['redʒɪstri] *noun* **(a)** *(place where official records are kept)* registro *m;* **Land Registry** = registro de la propiedad *or* registro catastral; **Probate Registry** = Registro General de Actos de Última Voluntad; **district registry** *or* **registry office** = registro civil **(b)** *(ship)* registro de un buque; **certificate of registry** = certificado de registro de un buque; **port of registry** *or* **registry port** = puerto *m* de registro de un buque

regret [rɪ'gret] **1** *noun* pena *f* **2** *verb* lamentar; **we regret to inform you that** = lamentamos informarles que

regulate ['regjuleɪt] *verb* **(a)** *(to adjust)* regular *or* ajustar **(b)** *(by law)* reglamentar; **prices are regulated by supply and demand** = los precios se regulan por la oferta y la demanda; **government-regulated price** = precio *m* regulado por el gobierno; **regulated tenancy** = PROTECTED TENANCY

◊ **regulation** [regju'leɪʃn] *noun* *(action)* regulación *f or* reglamentación *f;* **the regulation of trading practices** = la regulación de las prácticas comerciales

◊ **regulations** [regju'leɪʃnz] *plural noun* **(a)** *(law submitted to Parliament)* disposiciones *fpl or* normas *fpl or* reglamentación *f;* **the new government regulations on standards for electrical goods** = las nuevas disposiciones

gubernamentales sobre normas de producción de artículos eléctricos; **safety regulations which apply to places of work** = normas de seguridad en el lugar de trabajo; **regulations concerning imports and exports** = reglamentación en materia de importación y exportación; **fire regulations** = reglamentación en materia de incendios **(b)** *(rules laid down by the Comission of the European Communities)* reglamento *m*

regulatory ['regjələtri] *adjective* regulador, -ra *or* reglamentario, -ria; **the independent radio and television companies are supervised by a regulatory body** = las compañías de radio y televisión independientes son controladas por un cuerpo regulador; **complaints are referred to several regulatory bodies** = las quejas se dirigen a varios cuerpos reguladores

rehabilitate [ri:hə'bɪlɪteɪt] *verb* rehabilitar

◊ **rehabilitation** [ri:həbɪlɪ'teɪʃn] *noun* rehabilitación *f;* **rehabilitation centre** = centro *m* de rehabilitación; **rehabilitation of offenders** = rehabilitación de delincuentes

COMMENT: by the Rehabilitation of Offenders Act, 1974, a person who is convicted of an offence, and then spends a period of time without committing any other offence, is not required to reveal that he has a previous conviction

rehear [ri:'hɪə] *verb* revisar un caso

◊ **rehearing** [ri:'hɪərɪŋ] *noun* revisión *f* de un caso

reign [reɪn] **1** *noun* reinado *m;* **an Act dating back to the reign of Queen Victoria** = una ley que se remonta al reinado de la reina Victoria **2** *verb* **(a)** *(to be king or queen)* reinar **(b)** *(to exist)* reinar; **chaos reigned in the centre of town until the police arrived** = el caos reinaba en el centro de la ciudad hasta que llegó la policía

reimburse [ri:ɪm'bɜ:s] *verb* reembolsar; **witnesses' travelling expenses will be reimbursed** = los gastos de desplazamiento de los testigos serán reembolsados

reinstate [ri:ɪn'steɪt] *verb* restituir

reinsurance [ri:ɪn'ʃʊərəns] *noun* reaseguro *m*

reject 1 ['ri:dʒekt] *noun* desecho *m or* pieza *f* defectuosa *or* producto defectuoso; **sale of rejects** *or* **of reject items** = venta de piezas defectuosas; **to sell off reject stock** = vender existencias defectuosas **2** [rɪ'dʒekt] *verb* rechazar; **the appeal was rejected by the House of Lords** = la apelación fue rechazada por la Cámara de los Lores; **the union rejected the management's proposals** = el sindicato rechazó las propuestas de la patronal; **the magistrate rejected a request from the defendant** = el juez rechazó una petición del acusado; **the**

company rejected the takeover bid = la empresa rechazó la oferta de adquisición

◊ **rejection** [rɪ'dʒektʃn] *noun* rechazo *m;* **the rejection of the defendant's request** = el rechazo de la petición del acusado; **the rejection of the appeal by the tribunal** = el rechazo de la apelación por parte del tribunal

rejoinder [rɪ'dʒɔɪndə] *noun* contestación *f or* dúplica *f or* contrarréplica *f*

relapse [rɪ'læps] *noun* reincidencia *f*

relate [rɪ'leɪt] *verb* **to relate to** = relacionarse con *or* tener alguna relación con
◊ **related** [rɪ'leɪtɪd] *adjective* relacionado, -da *or* afín; **offences related to drugs** *or* **drug-related offences** = delitos relacionados con drogas; **the law which relates to drunken driving** = la legislación relativa a la conducción en estado de embriaguez; **related company** = compañía *f* afiliada; **earnings-related pension** = pensión *f* calculada en función del salario
◊ **relating to** [rɪ'leɪtɪŋ 'tʊ] *adverb* relativo, -va *or* relacionado, -da con; **documents relating to the case** = documentos relacionados con el caso

relation [rɪ'leɪʃn] *noun* **(a)** *(referring to)* acerca de *or* referente a; **in relation to** = con referencia a *or* con relación a *or* relativo, -va a; **documents in relation to the case** = documentos relativos al caso; **the court's powers in relation to children in care** = los poderes judiciales relativos a la custodia de los hijos **(b)** *(links)* **relations** = relaciones *fpl;* **blood relations** = parientes consanguíneos; **to enter into relations with someone** = entablar relaciones comerciales con alguien; **to break off relations with someone** = interrumpir las relaciones comerciales con alguien; **industrial relations** *or* **labour relations** = relaciones *fpl* laborales; **public relations** = relaciones públicas; **public relations department** = departamento *m* de relaciones públicas; **public relations officer** = responsable *mf* de relaciones públicas
◊ **relationship** [rɪ'leɪʃnʃɪp] *noun* relación *f or* parentesco *m;* **what is the relationship between the accused and witness?** = ¿qué relación existe entre el acusado y el testigo?; **there is no relationship between the two crimes** = no hay relación alguna entre los dos delitos
◊ **relations** *or* **relatives** [rɪ'leɪnz or 'relətɪvz] *plural noun* parientes *mfpl*
◊ **relator** ['rɪ'leɪtə] *noun* particular *m* que sugiere al Fiscal de la Corona que debe iniciarse un proceso judicial (normalmente contra un estamento público)
◊ **relative** ['relətɪv] **1** *adjective* relativo, -va **2** *noun* pariente *mf;* **close** *or* **distant relative** = pariente cercano *or* lejano

release [rɪ'liːs] **1** *noun* **(a)** *(setting free)* liberación *f or* puesta *f* en libertad; *(discharge)* exoneración *f;* **release on licence** = libertad *f* condicional; **release on-trial** = libertad provisional;

release without bail = libertad provisional sin fianza; **day release** = acuerdo *m* según el cual una empresa permite a un trabajador acudir a una facultad o escuela un día a la semana **(b)** *(abandoning of rights)* cesión *f or* renuncia *f* de un derecho **(c)** *(news)* **press release** = comunicado *m* de prensa; **the company sent out** *or* **issued a press release about the launch of the new car** = la empresa emitió un comunicado de prensa sobre el lanzamiento del nuevo coche **2** *verb* **(a)** *(to free)* liberar *or* poner en libertad *or* soltar; **to release on parole** = conceder libertad condicional; **to release from prison** = excarcelar; **the president released the opposition leader from prison** = el presidente puso en libertad al líder de la oposición; **to release goods from customs** = recuperar los artículos retenidos en la aduana; **the customs released the goods against payment of a fine** = los oficiales de aduanas nos devolvieron los artículos tras el pago de una multa; **to release someone from a debt** *or* **from a contract** = liberar a alguien de una deuda *or* de un contrato **(b)** *(to make something public)* publicar *or* divulgar; **the company released information about the new mine in Australia** = la empresa publicó información sobre la nueva mina de Australia; **the government has refused to release figures for the number of unemployed women** = el gobierno se ha negado a revelar las cifras referentes al número de mujeres en paro

relevance ['reləvəns] *noun* pertinencia *f;* **counsel argued with the judge over the relevance of the documents to the case** = el abogado discutió con el juez si los documentos tenían alguna relación con el caso
◊ **relevant** ['reləvənt] *adjective* pertinente *or* relacionado, -da *or* apropiado, -da; **the question is not relevant to the case** = la pregunta no es pertinente *or* no está relacionada con el caso; **which is the relevant government department?** = ¿a qué ministerio concierne?; **can you give me the relevant papers?** = ¿puede darme los documentos pertinentes?

reliable [rɪ'laɪəbl] *adjective* fiable *or* de fiar *or* de confianza *or* seguro, -ra *or* fidedigno, -na *or* fehaciente; **reliable source** = fuente *f* fidedigna *or* solvente; **he is a reliable witness** *or* **the witness is completely reliable** = es un testigo de confianza; **the police have reliable information about the gang's movements** = la policía tiene información fidedigna sobre los movimientos de la banda
◊ **reliability** [rɪlaɪə'bɪlɪti] *noun* fiabilidad *f;* **the court has to decide on the reliability of the witnesses** = el tribunal tiene que decidir sobre la fiabilidad de los testigos

relief [rɪ'liːf] *noun* **(a)** *(legal action)* indemnización *f or* reparación *f* presentada ante los tribunales *or* desagravio *m or* compensación *f;* **the relief the plaintiff sought was an injunction and damages** = la indemnización que el demandante solicitaba consistía en una intimación y daños **(b)** *(help)* socorro *m or* auxilio *m or* ayuda *f;* **ancillary relief** = estipulación *f* financiera *or* ajuste *m* de derechos de propiedad que un tribunal dispone para un cónyuge o hijo en trámites de divorcio *or* ayuda *f* económica ordenada por un tribunal para el cónyuge *or* para los hijos en casos de divorcio; **mortgage (interest) relief** = deducción *f* de impuestos sobre los intereses de una hipoteca; **tax relief** = deducción impositiva **(c)** *(comfort)* alivio *m* **(d)** *(take-over)* relevo *m;* **the relief was delayed** = se retrasó el relevo

rem [rem] *see* ACTION, IN REM

remain [rɪ'meɪn] *verb* **(a)** *(to be left)* quedar *or* sobrar; **half the stock remained on the shelves** = la mitad de las existencias quedó sin vender; **we will sell off the old stock at half price and anything remaining will be thrown away** = pondremos a la venta las existencias antiguas a mitad de precio y lo que sobre lo tiraremos **(b)** *(to stay)* quedarse *or* permanecer; **she remained behind at the office after 6.30 to finish her work** = se quedó en la oficina pasadas las 6.30 para terminar su trabajo
◊ **remainder** [rɪ'meɪndə] **1** *noun* **(a)** *(things left behind)* sobrante *m or* resto *m;* **the remainder of the stock will be sold off at half price** = el resto de las existencias se liquidará a mitad de precio; **remainders** = restos *mpl* de edición **(b)** *(lease)* nudo, -da propietario, -ria; **contingent remainder** = derecho *m* expectante *or* interino; **interest in remainder** = interés *m* residual en una propiedad *or* derecho relativo a una propiedad que se podrá ejercitar una vez expiren los derechos posesorios de un tercero; **vested remainder** = nuda propiedad *f* efectiva; *see also* REVERSION **2** *verb* **to remainder books** = saldar libros

remand [rɪ'mɑ:nd] **1** *noun* libertad *f* condicional *or* custodia *f* por aplazamiento de caso; **in remand** = prisión *f* preventiva; **prisoner on remand** *or* **remand prisoner** = preso en prisión preventiva; **remand centre** = reformatorio *m or* prisión preventiva **2** *verb* **(a)** *(prisoner)* mantener bajo custodia *or* liberar *or* poner en libertad bajo fianza; **he was remanded in custody** *or* **remanded on bail for two weeks** = se le mantuvo bajo custodia *or* fue puesto en libertad bajo fianza por dos semanas **(b)** *US* remitir un caso a un tribunal inferior

remedy ['remədi] **1** *noun* **(a)** *(solution)* remedio *m or* solución *f* jurídica; **without remedy** = irremediable(mente); **the plaintiff is seeking remedy through the courts** = el demandante está buscando remedio a través de los tribunales **(b)** *(illness)* cura *f* **2** *verb* remediar *or* curar

remember [rɪ'membə] *verb* recordar *or* acordarse de; **do you remember seeing the defendant in the house?** = ¿recuerda si vio al acusado en la casa?; **she cannot remember where**

she left the jewels = no puede recordar dónde dejó las joyas; **he remembered the registration number of the car** = recordó la matrícula del coche; **the last thing he remembered was the sound of the police siren** = lo último que recordaba era el sonido de la sirena de la policía; **I remember locking the door of the safe** = recuerdo que cerré con llave la caja de seguridad; **did you remember to sign the statement?** = ¿se acordó de firmar la declaración? (NOTE: you **remember doing something** which you did in the past; you **remember to do something** in the future)

remind [rɪ'maɪnd] *verb* recordar; **I must remind the court of the details of the defendant's relationship with the plaintiff** = debo recordar al tribunal los detalles de la relación del acusado con el demandante; **can you remind me to lock the safe?** = ¿me puedes recordar que cierre con llave la caja de seguridad?
◊ **reminder** [rɪ'maɪndə] *noun* notificación *f or* aviso *m* de pago *or* recordatorio *m;* **he paid the maintenance after several reminders** = pagó la pensión alimenticia tras varias notificaciones

remission [rɪ'mɪʃn] *noun* remisión *f or* reducción *f* de una condena; **he was sentenced to five years, but should serve only three with remission** = le condenaron a cinco años, pero con la remisión sólo cumplirá tres; **she got six months' remission for good behaviour** = le remitieron seis meses de pena por buena conducta

remit 1 ['ri:mɪt] *noun* responsabilidad *f or* mandato *m;* **this department can do nothing on the case as it is no part of** *or* **beyond our remit** = el departamento no puede actuar sobre el caso ya que queda fuera de nuestra área de responsabilidad **2** [rɪ'mɪt] *verb* **(a)** *(sentence)* reducir **(b)** *(debt)* perdonar **(c)** *(to send)* remitir **(d)** *(to send money)* enviar dinero; **to remit by cheque** = enviar dinero por medio de un cheque (NOTE: **remitting - remitted**)
◊ **remittance** [rɪ'mɪtəns] *noun* envío *m or* giro *m or* remesa *f;* **please send remittances to the treasurer** = se ruega enviar los pagos al tesorero; **the family lives on a weekly remittance from their father in the USA** = la familia vive de los giros que semanalmente les envía el padre desde los EE UU

remote [rɪ'məʊt] *adjective* remoto, -ta; **the court decided that the damage was too remote to be recoverable by the plaintiff** = el tribunal decidió que los daños no estaban lo suficientemente relacionados con el caso como para que el demandante pudiera tener derecho a reparación
◊ **remoteness** [rɪ'məʊtnəs] *noun* improbabilidad *f;* **remoteness of damage** = daños que no están suficientemente relacionados con un caso *or* principio legal según el cual los daños que no están suficientemente relacionados con un caso no obligan al acusado

remove [rɪ'muːv] *verb* quitar *or* levantar *or* borrar *or* relevar *or* destituir *or* eliminar; **we can remove his name from the mailing list** = podemos borrar su nombre de la lista de direcciones; **the government has removed the ban on imports from Japan** = el gobierno ha levantado el embargo sobre las importaciones de Japón; **the minister has removed the embargo on the sale of computer equipment** = el ministro ha levantado el embargo sobre la venta de material informático; **two directors were removed from the board at the AGM** = dos directores del consejo de administración fueron destituidos en la Junta General Ordinaria

◊ **removal** [rɪ'muːvl] *noun* (a) *(moving to a new house or office)* mudanza *f or* traslado *m;* **removal company** = compañía *f* de mudanzas *or* empresa *f* de transportes (b) *(sacking someone)* despido *m or* destitución *f;* **the removal of the managing director is going to be very difficult** = el despido del director gerente va a ser muy difícil

remuneration [rɪmjuːnə'reɪʃn] *noun* remuneración *f;* **he receives no remuneration for his work as honorary secretary of the football club** = no recibe remuneración por su trabajo como secretario honorario del club de fútbol

render ['rendə] *verb* hacer; **failure to observe the conditions of bail renders the accused liable to arrest** = de no cumplirse las condiciones de la fianza el acusado se hace susceptible de arresto; **the state of health of the witness renders his appearance in court impossible** = el estado de salud del testigo hace imposible su aparición ante los tribunales

renew [rɪ'njuː] *verb* renovar *or* prorrogar; **to renew a bill of exchange** *or* **to renew a lease** = renovar una letra de cambio *or* un contrato de arrendamiento; **to renew a subscription** = renovar una subscripción *or* un abono; **to renew an insurance policy** = renovar una póliza de seguros

◊ **renewal** [rɪ'njuːəl] *noun* renovación *f or* prórroga *f;* **renewal of a lease** *or* **of a subscription** *or* **of a bill** = renovación de un contrato de arrendamiento *or* de una subscripción *or* de una letra; **the lease is up for renewal next month** = habrá que renovar el contrato de arrendamiento el mes que viene; **when is the renewal date of the bill?** = ¿cuándo es la fecha de renovación de la letra?; **renewal notice** = aviso *m* de renovación de un seguro; **renewal premium** = prima *f* sucesiva *or* de renovación

renounce [rɪ'naʊns] *verb* renunciar; **the government has renounced the use of force in dealing with international terrorists** = el gobierno ha renunciado al uso de la fuerza en el trato con terroristas internacionales

rent [rent] **1** *noun* renta *f or* alquiler *m or* arriendo *m;* **high** *or* **low rent** = alquiler elevado *or* barato; **to pay three months' rent in advance** = pagar tres meses de alquiler por adelantado; **back rent** = alquiler atrasado; **ground rent** = renta de la tierra *or* del terreno; **nominal rent** *or* **peppercorn rent** = renta nominal *or* alquiler nominal; **rack rent** = arriendo exhorbitante; **rent action** = acción judicial encaminada a obtener alquileres atrasados; **rent controls** = control gubernamental sobre precios de alquiler; **income from rents** *or* **rent income** = renta por arrendamiento *or* por alquiler; **rent allowance** *or* **rent rebate** = subsidio estatal destinado a pagar el alquiler; **rent tribunal** = tribunal *m* que decide en litigios sobre alquileres y adjudica alquileres justos **2** *verb* (a) *(pay money to hire something from someone)* alquilar; **to rent an office** *or* **a car** = alquilar una oficina *or* un coche; **he rents an office in the centre of town** = tiene alquilada una oficina en el centro de la ciudad; **they were driving a rented car when they were stopped by the police** = conducían un coche alquilado cuando la policía les detuvo (b) *(receive money by hiring something to someone)* **to rent (out)** = alquilar; **we rented part of the building to an American company** = alquilamos parte del edificio a una empresa americana

◊ **rental** ['rentl] *noun* alquiler *m or* arrendamiento *m;* **the telephone rental bill comes to over £500 a quarter** = la cuenta de alquiler del teléfono asciende a más de 500 libras al trimestre; **rental income** *or* **income from rentals** = renta *f* por arrendamiento *or* ingresos *mpl* por alquiler

◊ **rentcharge** ['rentʃɑːdʒ] *noun* pago *m* del alquiler de una propiedad en dominio absoluto (prácticamente inexistente excepto en relación a terrenos)

renunciation [rɪnʌnsi'eɪʃn] *noun* renuncia *f;* **letter of renunciation** = carta *f* de renuncia

reopen [riː'əʊpn] *verb* reabrir *or* volver a abrir; **after receiving new evidence, the police have reopened the murder inquiry** = después de recibir nuevas pruebas, la policía ha vuelto a abrir la investigación sobre el asesinato; **the hearing reopened on Monday afternoon** = la vista se volvió a abrir el lunes por la tarde

reorganize [riː'ɔːgənaɪz] *verb* reorganizar
◊ **reorganization** [riːɔːgənaɪ'zeɪʃn] *noun* reorganización *f;* **the reorganization of a company** *or* **a company reorganization** = la reorganización de una empresa

repair [rɪ'peə] **1** *noun* (a) *(mending)* arreglo *m or* reparación *f;* **the landlord carried out repairs to the roof** = el propietario efectuó reparaciones en el tejado; **the bill for repairs to the car came to £250** = la cuenta por la reparación del coche ascendía a 250 libras (b) *(physical condition of something)* **state of repair** = estado *m* de conservación; **the**

house was in a bad state of repair when he bought it = la casa estaba en mal estado de conservación cuando la compramos **2** *verb* arreglar *or* reparar *or* componer; **to repair an injustice** = reparar una injusticia; **full repairing lease** = arrendamiento en el que las reparaciones corren por cuenta del arrendatario

◊ **repairer** [rɪ'peərə] *noun* reparador, -ra; **repairer's lien** = derecho de retención de un reparador sobre el artículo reparado hasta no haber cobrado por ello

repatriate [riː'pætrieɪt] *verb* repatriar
◊ **repatriation** [riːpætri'eɪʃn] *noun* repatriación *f*

repay [rɪ'peɪ] *verb* devolver *or* pagar *or* reembolsar *or* resarcir; **the loan is to be repaid at the rate of £50 a month** = tenemos que devolver el préstamo pagando la cantidad de 50 libras al mes
◊ **repayable** [rɪ'peɪəbl] *adjective* reembolsable *or* a devolver; **the loan is repayable over five years** = el préstamo es a cinco años *or* es reembolsable en cinco años
◊ **repayment** [rɪ'peɪmənt] *noun* devolución *f or* pago *m or* reembolso *m;* **he was unable to meet** *or* **to keep up with his mortgage repayments** = no pudo hacer frente a los pagos de la hipoteca

repeal [rɪ'piːl] **1** *noun* abrogación *f or* revocación *f;* **MPs are pressing for the repeal of the Immigration Act** = los diputados están presionando para que se abrogue la Ley de Extranjería **2** *verb* abolir *or* abrogar *or* revocar; **the Bill seeks to repeal the existing legislation** = el proyecto de ley está encaminado a revocar la legislación existente

repeat [rɪ'piːt] *verb* **(a)** *(to say again)* repetir; **he repeated his evidence slowly so that the police officer could write it down** = repitió su declaración más despacio para que el oficial de policía pudiera tomar nota; **when asked what he planned to do, the chairman of the magistrates repeated 'Nothing'** = cuando se le preguntó qué pensaba hacer, el presidente de los magistrados repitió 'Nada' **(b)** *(to do again)* **to repeat an offence** = reincidir
◊ **repetition** [repɪ'tɪʃn] *noun* repetición *f or* reiteración *f;* **repetition of a libel is an offence** = la repetición de una difamación es un delito

repent [rɪ'pent] *verb* arrepentirse
◊ **repentance** [rɪ'pentəns] *noun* arrepentimiento *m*

replevin [rɪ'plevɪn] *noun* desembargo *m or* recuperación *f* de bienes muebles bajo fianza

reply [rɪ'plaɪ] **1** *noun* **(a)** *(answer)* contestación *f or* respuesta *f;* **there was no reply to my letter** *or* **to my phone call** = no contestaron a mi carta *or* a mi llamada de teléfono; **in reply to your letter of the 24th** = en contestación a su carta del 24; **the company's reply to the takeover bid** = la

respuesta de la empresa a la oferta de adquisición; **international postal reply coupon** = cupón *m* de respuesta internacional; **reply paid card** *or* **letter** = carta *f or* tarjeta *f* a franquear en destino **(b)** *(statement by prosecution counsel)* alegación *f or* réplica *f or* discurso *m* (en respuesta a las quejas realizadas por la defensa); **written reply to charges** = pliego *m* de descargo; **right of reply** = derecho *m* de réplica; **he demanded the right of reply to the newspaper allegations** = exigió el derecho de réplica a las alegaciones realizadas por el periódico **2** *verb* **(a)** *(to answer)* responder *or* contestar; **to reply to a letter** = contestar a una carta; **the company has replied to the takeover bid by offering the shareholders higher dividends** = la empresa ha contestado a la oferta de adquisición ofreciendo a los accionistas dividendos mayores **(b)** *(to give an opposing view)* contestar *or* replicar

report [rɪ'pɔːt] **1** *noun* **(a)** *(document)* informe *m or* memoria *f or* atestado *m or* parte *m;* **police report** = atestado policial *or* parte de la policía; **accident report** = parte de un accidente; **medical report** = parte médico; **to make a report** *or* **to present a report** *or* **to send in a report** = hacer *or* presentar *or* enviar un informe; **the court heard a report from the probation officer** = el tribunal oyó un informe del oficial encargado de la libertad condicional; **the chairman has received a report from the insurance company** = el presidente ha recibido un informe de la compañía aseguradora; **the company's annual report** *or* **the chairman's report** *or* **the directors' report** = el informe anual de la empresa *or* del presidente *or* del director; **confidential report** = informe *m* confidencial; **Law Reports** = precedentes *mpl or* casos *mpl* que representan precedentes jurídicos; **progress report** = informe sobre la marcha de los trabajos; **the treasurer's report** = informe del tesorero **(b)** *(news item)* **a report in a newspaper** *or* **a newspaper report** = un artículo *m* de un periódico *or* una noticia *f;* **can you confirm the report that charges are likely to be brought?** = ¿puede confirmar el rumor sobre la posible acusación? **(c)** *(from a government committee)* informe; **the government has issued a report on the problems of inner city violence** = el gobierno ha publicado un informe sobre los problemas de la violencia en el centro de las ciudades **2** *verb* **(a)** *(to make a statement)* informar *or* presentar un informe *or* dar parte de *or* declarar; **the probation officer reported on the progress of the two young criminals** = el oficial encargado de la custodia presentó un informe sobre el progreso de los dos delincuentes juveniles; **he reported the damage to the insurance company** = dio parte de los daños a la compañía aseguradora; **we asked the bank to report on his financial status** = pedimos al banco un informe sobre su estado financiero; **reporting restrictions** = restricciones *fpl* informativas (sobre un caso en la prensa); **reporting restrictions were**

lifted = se levantaron las restricciones informativas **(b) to report to someone** = ser responsable ante alguien *or* estar a las órdenes de alguien *or* rendir cuentas a alguien; **he reports direct to the managing director** = está a las órdenes del director gerente **(c)** *(go to a place)* presentarse *or* asistir; **to report for an interview** = presentarse a una entrevista; **please report to our London office for training** = le rogamos se presente en nuestra oficina de Londres para los cursos de formación; **a condition of bail is that he has to report to the police station once a week** = libertad bajo fianza significa que tiene que presentarse en la comisaría de policía una vez a la semana

◊ **reported case** [rɪ'pɔːtɪd 'keɪs] *noun* precedente *m or* caso *m* que sienta un precedente *or* que puede ser utilizado como precedente legal

◊ **Report Stage** [rɪ'pɔːt 'steɪdʒ] *noun* etapa *f* en la discusión de un proyecto de ley en la Cámara de los Comunes, en la que las enmiendas propuestas por el Comité son debatidas por la Cámara en pleno

repossess [riːpə'zes] *verb* recuperar *or* recobrar un objeto comprado a plazos por falta de pago de los mismos

◊ **repossession** [riːpə'zeʃn] *noun* ejecución *f* forzosa de una hipoteca

reprehend [reprɪ'hend] *verb* reprender

◊ **reprehensible** [reprɪ'hensəbl] *adjective* reprensible

represent [reprɪ'zent] *verb* **(a)** *(to show or state)* mostrar *or* mostrarse; **he was represented as a man of great honour** = se le mostró como hombre de gran honor **(b)** *(to act on behalf of someone)* representar *or* actuar de parte de alguien; **the defendant is represented by his solicitor** = el acusado está representado por su abogado **(c)** *(to be elected representative)* representar; **he represents one of the Northern industrial constituencies** = representa a una de las circunscripciones industriales del norte

◊ **representation** [reprɪzen'teɪʃn] *noun* **(a)** *(statement)* planteamiento *m or* informe *m* encaminado a convencer a alguien de la firma de un contrato; **false representation** = planteamiento *or* informe engañoso **(b)** *(to complain)* **to make representations** = formular *or* elevar una protesta a **(c)** *(by a lawyer)* representación *f* a cargo de un abogado; **the applicant had no legal representation** = el solicitante carecía de representante legal **(d)** *(Parliament)* sistema *m* de elección de representantes en el parlamento; *GB* **the Representation of the People Act** = ley electoral; **proportional representation** = representación proporcional

◊ **representative** [reprɪ'zentətɪv] *noun* **(a)** *(person who represents another person)* representante *mf*; **the court heard the representative of the insurance company** = el tribunal oyó al representante de la compañía de seguros; **personal representative** = albacea *mf or* representante testamentario **(b)** *US* representante en la cámara baja del Congreso; **House of Representatives** = Cámara de Representantes (NOTE: a Representative is also referred to as **Congressman**)

reprieve [rɪ'priːv] **1** *noun* suspensión *f* temporal de una pena *or* orden *f* judicial **2** *verb* indultar *or* conmutar *or* suspender la pena de; **he was sentenced to death but was reprieved by the president** = le condenaron a muerte pero fue indultado por el presidente

reprimand ['reprɪmɑːnd] **1** *noun* reprimenda *f*; **the police officer received an official reprimand after the inquiry into the accident** = el oficial de policía recibió una reprimenda oficial tras la investigación del accidente **2** *verb* reprender *or* reconvenir; **he was reprimanded by the magistrate** = fue reprendido por el juez

reproduce [riːprə'djuːs] *verb* reproducir; **the documents relating to the hearings are reproduced in the back of the report** = los documentos relacionados con las vistas están reproducidos en el reverso del informe

◊ **reproduction** [riːprə'dʌkʃn] *noun* reproducción *f*; **the reproduction of copyright material without the permission of the copyright holder is banned by law** = la ley prohíbe la reproducción de material sujeto a derechos de autor sin el permiso de éste *or* del mismo; **mechanical reproduction rights** = derechos *mpl* de reproducción (de una pieza musical *or* documento impreso)

repudiate [rɪ'pjuːdieɪt] *verb* negarse a cumplir *or* repudiar *or* cancelar; **to repudiate an agreement** *or* **a contract** = negarse a cumplir un acuerdo *or* un contrato

◊ **repudiation** [rɪpjuːdi'eɪʃn] *noun* rechazo *m or* repudio *m*

reputable ['repjutəbl] *adjective* acreditado, -da *or* reputado, -da *or* de confianza; **we use only reputable carriers** = únicamente utilizamos transportistas acreditados; **a reputable firm of accountants** = una firma acreditada de asesores contables

◊ **reputation** [repju'teɪʃn] *noun* reputación *f or* fama *f*; **to harm someone's reputation** = desacreditar *or* lacerar a alguien; **company with a reputation for quality** = una empresa que se distingue por la calidad de sus productos; **he has a reputation for being difficult to negotiate with** = tiene fama de ser una persona con la que es difícil negociar

request [rɪ'kwest] **1** *noun* petición *f or* solicitud *f or* ruego *m*; **request for payment** = intimación *f* de pago; **they put in a request for a government subsidy** = presentaron una solicitud para una ayuda estatal; **his request for an adjournment was turned down by the coroner** = su solicitud de aplazamiento fue rechazada por el juez de primera instancia; **on request** = a petición; **we will send samples on request** *or* **'samples available on request'** = solicite envío de muestras *or* muestras disponibles a petición del interesado; **letter of request** = ROGATORY LETTER **2** *verb* pedir *or* solicitar; **to request assistance from the government** = solicitar ayuda del gobierno *or* pedir ayuda al Estado; **the witness requested permission to give evidence sitting down** = el testigo pidió permiso para prestar declaración sentado

require [rɪˈkwaɪə] *verb* (a) *(demand something)* pedir *or* exigir *or* intimar; **to require a full explanation of expenditure** = exigir una aclaración total de los gastos; **the law requires you to submit all income to the tax authorities** = la ley exige declarar todos los ingresos a las autoridades fiscales; **the Bill requires social workers to seek the permission of the juvenile court before taking action** = el proyecto de ley exige que los asistentes sociales busquen permiso del tribunal de menores antes de entrar en acción (b) *(to need)* necesitar *or* requerir; **the document requires careful study** = el documento requiere un estudio en profundidad *or* un examen cuidadoso; **to write the program requires a computer specialist** = para escribir el programa se requiere un especialista en informática

◊ **requirement** [rɪˈkwaɪəmənt] *noun* requisito *m or* necesidad *f;* **legal requirement** = imperativo *m* legal; **public sector borrowing requirement** = necesidad de endeudamiento del sector público

requisition [rekwɪˈzɪʃn] **1** *noun* **requisition on title** = requisitoria *f* del título de propiedad *or* solicitud *f* del título de propiedad **2** *verb* requisar; **the army requisitioned all the trucks to carry supplies** = el ejército requisó todos los camiones para llevar provisiones

res [reɪz] *Latin word* 'cosa' *f or* 'asunto' *m*
◊ **res gestae** [ˈreɪz ˈdʒestaɪ] *Latin phrase* circunstancias esenciales
◊ **res ipsa loquitur** [reɪz ˈɪpsə ˈlɒkwɪtə] *Latin phrase* 'el hecho habla por sí solo': situación en la que los hechos son tan obvios que es el acusado el que tiene que demostrar que no fue negligente y no el demandante probar su reclamación
◊ **res judicata** [ˈreɪz dʒuːdɪˈkætə] *Latin phrase* 'cosa juzgada'

resale *noun* reventa *f*
◊ **resale price maintenance (RPM)** [ˈriːseɪl ˈpraɪs ˈmeɪntns] *noun* sistema *m* de fijación de precios para asegurar un precio mínimo

COMMENT: this system applies in the UK to certain products only, such as books and newspapers

rescind [rɪˈsɪnd] *verb* rescindir *or* anular; **to rescind a contract** *or* **an agreement** = rescindir un contrato *or* un acuerdo
◊ **rescinding** *or* **rescission** [rɪˈsɪndɪŋ *or* rɪˈsɪʃn] *noun* rescisión *f*

rescue [ˈreskjuː] **1** *noun* rescate *m;* **rescue operation** = operación *f* de rescate **2** *verb* rescatar

COMMENT: if a rescuer is injured while rescuing someone from danger caused by the defendant's negligence, the defendant is liable for damages to the rescuer as well as to the person rescued

reserve [rɪˈzəːv] **1** *noun* (a) *(money from profits)* reserva *f or* provisión *f;* **bank reserves** = reservas bancarias *or* activo *m* de caja; **cash reserves** = reservas en metálico *or* reservas de capital; **contingency reserve** *or* **emergency reserve** = reserva para imprevistos; **reserve for bad debts** = reserva para deudas incobrables; **hidden reserves** = reservas ocultas; **reserve fund** = fondos *mpl* de reserva (b) *(strong currency)* **reserve currency** = divisas *fpl* de reserva *or* divisas fuertes; **currency reserves** = reservas de divisas; **a country's foreign currency reserves** = las reservas de divisas de un país (c) *(to be used at a later date)* **in reserve** = en reserva *or* de reserva (d) *(at an auction)* **reserve (price)** = precio mínimo aceptable; **the painting was withdrawn when it did not reach its reserve** = el cuadro fue retirado al no alcanzar el precio mínimo **2** *verb* (a) *(to book)* reservar; **to reserve a room** *or* **a table** *or* **a seat** = reservar una habitación *or* una mesa *or* un billete; **I want to reserve a table for four people** = quiero reservar una mesa para cuatro personas; **can your secretary reserve a seat for me on the train to Glasgow?** = ¿puede su secretaria reservarme un billete de tren para Glasgow? (b) *(to keep back)* reservar *or* reservarse; **to reserve one's defence** = reservarse la defensa en espera del juicio definitivo; **to reserve judgment** = reservarse el juicio; **to reserve the right to do something** = reservarse el derecho de hacer algo; **he reserved the right to cross-examine witnesses** = se reservó el derecho de interrogar a los testigos; **we reserve the right to appeal against the tribunal's decision** = nos reservamos el derecho de apelar contra el fallo del tribunal
◊ **reservation** [rezəˈveɪʃn] *noun* (a) *(booking)* reserva *f;* **he phoned reservations and asked to book a room for four nights** = llamó a la sección de reservas *or* a recepción y pidió una habitación para cuatro noches (b) *(doubt)* reserva; **mental reservation** = restricción *f* mental; **he expressed reservations about the legality of the action** = manifestó sus reservas con respecto a la legalidad de la acción; **the plan was accepted by the committee with some reservations** = el plan fue aceptado por el comité con ciertas reservas (c) *(keeping something back)* reserva; **reservation of**

title clause = cláusula *f* de reserva de dominio; *see also* ROMALPA CLAUSE

residence ['rezidəns] *noun* **(a)** *(place where someone lives)* residencia *f or* casa *f or* domicilio *m;* **he has a country residence where he spends his weekends** = tiene una casa de campo donde pasa los fines de semana **(b)** *(act of living in a country)* residencia; **residence permit** = permiso *m* de residencia; **he has applied for a residence permit** = ha solicitado un permiso de residencia; **she was granted a residence permit for one year** = le concedieron un permiso de residencia de un año
◊ **resident** ['rezidənt] **1** *adjective* residente; **resident alien** = extranjero, -ra con permiso de residencia **2** *noun* residente *mf or* habitante *mf;* **the company is resident in Spain** = la empresa tiene su residencia en España; **person ordinarily resident in the UK** = persona con residencia habitual en el Reino Unido; **non-resident** = no residente *or* transeúnte *mf;* **he has a non-resident account with a Spanish bank** = tiene una cuenta de no residente en un banco español; **she was granted a non-resident visa** = le concedieron un visado de no residente

residue ['rezidju:] *noun* residuo *m or* resto *m or* bienes *mpl* residuales; **after paying various bequests the residue of his estate was split between his children** = después de pagar varios legados, los bienes residuales de su fortuna se dividieron entre sus hijos
◊ **residual** [rɪ'zɪdjuəl] *adjective* residual
◊ **residuary** [rɪ'zɪdjuəri] *adjective* residual; **residuary devisee** = legatario, -ria residual *or* remanente; **residuary estate** = bienes *mpl* intestados; *(after debts have been paid)* patrimonio *m* hereditario residual; **residuary legatee** = legatario, -ria del remanente *or* heredero, -ra universal

resign [rɪ'zaɪn] *verb* dimitir *or* darse de baja; **he resigned from his post as treasurer** = dimitió de su cargo de tesorero; **he has resigned with effect from July 1st** = ha presentado su dimisión con efectos desde el 1 de julio; **she resigned as finance director** = dimitió como directora financiera
◊ **resignation** [rezɪg'neɪʃn] *noun* dimisión *f or* renuncia *f;* **he wrote his letter of resignation to the chairman** = escribió su carta de dimisión al presidente; **to hand in** *or* **to give in** *or* **to send in one's resignation** = presentar la dimisión

COMMENT: MPs are not allowed to resign their seats in the House of Commons. If an MP wants to leave the House, he has to apply for an office of profit under the Crown, such as the Stewardship of the Chiltern Hundreds, which will disqualify him from membership of the House of Commons

resist [rɪ'zɪst] *verb* resistir *or* oponer resistencia; **the accused resisted all attempts to make him confess** = el acusado resistió todas las presiones para obligarle a confesar; **the company is resisting the takeover bid** = la empresa se resiste a la oferta de adquisición; **resisting arrest** = resistencia *f* a la autoridad
◊ **resistance** [rɪ'zɪstəns] *noun* resistencia *f;* **there was a lot of resistance from the prison officers to the new plan** = había mucha resistencia al nuevo plan por parte de los funcionarios de prisiones; **the Home Secretary's proposal met with strong resistance from the probation service** = la propuesta del ministro del interior provocó una gran resistencia por parte del servicio encargado de la libertad condicional

resolution [rezə'lu:ʃn] *noun* resolución *f or* moción *f;* **to put a resolution to a meeting** = presentar una resolución en una reunión *or* someter una moción a votación; **ordinary resolution** = resolución ordinaria; **extraordinary** *or* **special resolution** = resolución extraordinaria *or* especial; *US* **joint resolution** = proyecto *m* de ley aprobado por las dos cámaras

resort [rɪ'zɔ:t] **1** *noun* recurso *m;* **court of last resort** = tribunal *m* de última instancia; **lender of the last resort** = prestamista *mf* en última instancia *or* de último recurso **2** *verb* **to resort to** = recurrir a; **he had to resort to threats of court action to get repayment of the money owing** = tuvo que recurrir a la amenaza de emprender una acción judicial para conseguir la devolución del dinero que le debían; **workers must not resort to violence in industrial disputes** = los trabajadores no deben recurrir a la violencia en los conflictos laborales

respect [rɪ'spekt] **1** *noun* **(a)** *(consideration)* acatamiento *m or* respeto *m* **(b)** *(concerning)* respecto *m;* **with respect to** *or* **in respect of** = con respecto a; **his right to an indemnity in respect of earlier disbursements** = su derecho a indemnización con respecto a desembolsos anteriores; **the defendant counterclaimed for loss and damage in respect of a machine sold to him by the plaintiff** = el acusado reclamó por su parte los daños debidos a rotura y extravío con respecto a una máquina que el acusado le había vendido **2** *verb* respetar; **to respect a clause in an agreement** = respetar una cláusula de un acuerdo; **the company has not respected the terms of the contract** = la empresa no ha respetado los términos del contrato
◊ **respectively** [rɪ'spektɪvli] *adverb* respectivamente

respondeat superior [rɪ'spɒndeɪæt su'perɪɔ:] *Latin phrase* 'que el superior sea responsable': norma según la cual el mandante es responsable de los actos del mandatario *or* el patrón de las acciones del empleado

respondent [rɪ'spɒndənt] *noun* demandado, -da; *(in a divorce case)* demandado, -da en un caso de divorcio; *(in an appeal)* apelado, da; *see also* CO-RESPONDENT

responsibility [rɪspɒnsə'bɪlɪti] *noun* **(a)** *(duty or thing which you are responsible for doing)* responsabilidad *f;* **he finds the responsibilities of being managing director too heavy** = las responsabilidades de su cargo como director gerente le resultan demasiado pesadas; **keeping the interior of the building in good order is the responsibility of the tenant** = el inquilino tiene la responsabilidad de mantener el interior del edificio en buen estado **(b)** *(being responsible)* responsabilidad; **there is no responsibility on the company's part for loss of customers' property** = la empresa no se hace responsable de la pérdida de objetos pertenecientes a los clientes; **the management accepts full responsibility for loss of goods in storage** = la dirección se hace responsable total de la pérdida de artículos en depósito; **collective responsibility** = responsabilidad colectiva; **age of criminal responsibility** = edad *f* de responsabilidad penal; **diminished responsibility** = circunstancia *f* eximente por tener las facultades disminuidas
◊ **responsible** [rɪ'spɒnsɪbl] *adjective* **(a)** *(being in charge)* **responsible for** = responsable de *or* culpable de *or* autor, -ra de; **to be responsible for one's actions** = obrar con conocimiento de causa; **the tenant is responsible for all repairs to the building** = las reparaciones del edificio corren a cargo del inquilino; **the consignee is held responsible for the goods he has received on consignment** = el consignatario se hace responsable de los artículos recibidos; **she was responsible for a series of thefts from offices** = era la autora de una serie de robos en oficinas **(b)** *(being under someone's authority)* **responsible to someone** = responsable ante alguien; **magistrates are responsible to the Lord Chancellor** = los jueces son responsables ante el presidente de la Cámara de los Lores **(c)** *(important)* **a responsible job** = un trabajo *or* un puesto *m* de responsabilidad
◊ **responsibly** [rɪ'spɒnsɪbli] *adverb* con seriedad *or* con formalidad; **the judge congratulated the jury on acting responsibly** = el juez felicitó al jurado por haber actuado con seriedad

rest [rest] **1** *noun* descanso *m* **2** *verb* descansar

restante ['restɒnt] *see* POSTE RESTANTE

restitutio in integrum [restɪ'tuːtiəʊ ɪn ɪn'tegrəm] *Latin phrase* 'devolver todo al estado anterior' *or* restitutio in integrum: cumplimiento de una obligación cuya prestación consiste en la reparación del agravio como si la infracción no hubiera tenido lugar

restitution [restɪ'tjuːʃn] *noun* **(a)** *(giving back)* restitución *f;* **the court ordered the restitution of**

assets to the company = el tribunal ordenó la restitución de los bienes a la empresa; **restitution order** = orden *f* de restitución **(b)** *(compensation)* indemnización *f* por daños y perjuicios **(c)** *US* **export restitution** = ayudas *fpl* a exportadores europeos de alimentos *or* a la exportación de alimentos procedentes de la UE

restore [rɪ'stɔː] *verb* restablecer; **to restore order** = restablecer el orden

restrain [rɪ'streɪn] *verb* **(a)** *(to control)* reducir *or* frenar *or* restringir; **the prisoner fought and had to be restrained by two policemen** = el detenido opuso resistencia y tuvo que ser reducido por dos policías; **to restrain oneself** = dominarse *or* controlarse **(b)** *(to tell someone not to do something)* impedir; **the court granted the plaintiff an injunction restraining the defendant from breaching copyright** = el tribunal garantizó al demandante un requerimiento que impidiera al acusado la infracción en materia de derechos de autor
◊ **restraining order** [rɪ'streɪnɪŋ 'ɔːdə] *noun* juicio *m* de amparo *or* orden *f* judicial que impide la acción al acusado mientras el tribunal esté decidiendo
◊ **restraint** [rɪ'streɪnt] *noun* restricción *f;* **pay restraint** *or* **wage restraint** = moderación salarial; **restraint of liberty** = restricción de libertad
◊ **restraint of trade** [rɪ'streɪnt əv 'treɪd] *noun* **(a)** *(worker)* restricción *f* laboral *or* profesional *or* prohibición *f* de utilizar información confidencial al cambiar de trabajo **(b)** *(price fixing)* restricción comercial *or* limitación *f* al libre comercio

restrict [rɪ'strɪkt] *verb* restringir *or* limitar; **the agreement restricts the company's ability to sell its products** = el acuerdo limita la capacidad de ventas de la empresa; **we are restricted to twenty staff by the size of our offices** = el tamaño de nuestras oficinas hace que el número de empleados quede reducido a veinte; **to restrict the flow of trade** *or* **to restrict imports** = limitar las importaciones *or* restringir el flujo comercial
◊ **restriction** [rɪ'strɪkʃn] *noun* restricción *f;* **import restrictions** *or* **restrictions on imports** = restricciones a la importación; **to impose restrictions on imports** *or* **on credit** = imponer restricciones a la importación *or* de crédito; **to lift credit restrictions** = levantar las restricciones crediticias *or* suavizar las restricciones de crédito; **reporting restrictions** = restricciones sobre la publicación de información; **reporting restrictions were lifted** = se levantaron las restricciones sobre la publicación de información
◊ **restrictive** [rɪ'strɪktɪv] *adjective* restrictivo, -va; **restrictive covenant** = convenio *m* de restricción (del comercio); **restrictive practices** = prácticas *fpl* restrictivas; **Restrictive Practices Court** = Tribunal *m* de Defensa de la Competencia

restructuring [riːˈstrʌtʃərɪŋ] *noun* **(a)** *(of company)* reestructuración *f* **(b)** *(of loan)* consolidación *f*

resume [rɪˈzjuːm] *verb (to start again)* reanudar *or* comenzar de nuevo; **the discussions resumed after a two hour break** = las discusiones se reanudaron tras un descanso de dos horas

résumé [ˈreɪzumeɪ] *noun US* currículum *m* vitae *or* currículo *m (NOTE: British English is* **curriculum vitae)**

resumption [rɪˈzʌmpʃn] *noun* reanudación *f;* **we expect an early resumption of negotiations** = esperamos una pronta reanudación de las negociaciones

retail [ˈriːteɪl] *noun* venta *f* al por menor *or* al detall; **retail price** = precio *m* al por menor
◊ **retailer** [ˈriːteɪlə] *noun* minorista *mf; see also* WHOLESALE

retain [rɪˈteɪn] *verb* **(a)** *(to keep)* retener *or* preservar *or* apartar *or* quedarse con; **out of the profits, the company has retained £50,000 as provision against bad debts** = la empresa ha apartado 50.000 libras de los beneficios como provisión frente a deudas incobrables; **retained income** = beneficios no distribuidos **(b)** *(lawyer)* **to retain a lawyer to act for you** = contratar a un abogado para que actúe en el nombre de uno
◊ **retainer** [rɪˈteɪnə] *noun (fee paid in advance)* iguala *f or* minuta *f; (to a barrister)* anticipo *m* sobre los honorarios (de un abogado); **we pay him a retainer of £1,000 per annum** = reservamos el derecho a sus servicios por un pago de 1.000 libras al año

retaliate [rɪˈtælieɪt] *verb* vengarse *or* tomar represalias *or* desquitarse; **the court granted an injunction to the workers, and the management retaliated by locking the office doors** = el tribunal concedió un requerimiento a los trabajadores y la dirección tomó represalias cerrando las puertas de la oficina
◊ **retaliation** [rɪtæliˈeɪʃn] *noun* represalias *fpl or* desquite *m;* **the robbers fired at the bank staff, and the police fired back in retaliation** = los atracadores dispararon a los empleados del banco y la policía respondió del mismo modo como represalia

retire [rɪˈtaɪə] *verb* **(a)** *(to stop work and take a pension)* jubilarse; **she retired with a £6,000 pension** = se jubiló con una pensión de 6.000 libras; **the chairman of the company retired at the age of 65** = el presidente de la empresa se retiró a la edad de 65 años; **the shop is owned by a retired policeman** = la tienda pertenece a un policía retirado; **retiring age** = edad *f* de jubilación **(b)** *(to make a worker stop work and take a pension)* retirar *or* jubilar *or* dar la jubilación; **they decided to retire all staff over 50 years of age** = decidieron jubilar a

todos los empleados mayores de 50 años **(c)** *(to come to the end of a term of elected office)* retirarse *or* terminar un mandato; **the treasurer retires after six years** = el tesorero se retira después de seis años; **two retiring directors offer themselves for re-election** = dos directores salientes se presentan para la reelección **(d)** *(to go away from a court for a period of time)* retirarse *or* abandonar un juzgado por un tiempo; **the magistrates retired to consider their verdict** = los jueces se retiraron a considerar su veredicto; **the jury retired for four hours** = el jurado se retiró durante cuatro horas
◊ **retiral** [rɪˈtaɪrəl] *noun US & Scottish* = RETIREMENT
◊ **retirement** [rɪˈtaɪəmənt] *noun* **(a)** *(from work)* retiro *m or* jubilación *f;* **to take early retirement** = acogerse a la jubilación anticipada; **retirement age** = edad *f* de jubilación; **retirement pension** = jubilación *f or* pensión *f* de retiro; **retirement plan** = plan *m* de pensiones *or* de jubilación; *US* **individual retirement account (IRA)** = plan de pensiones particular **(b)** *(of a jury)* deliberación *f*

retrial [riːˈtraɪəl] *noun* nuevo juicio *m or* revisión *f* de un caso; **the Court of Appeal ordered a retrial** = el tribunal de apelación ordenó la revisión del caso

retroactive [retrəʊˈæktɪv] *adjective* retroactivo, -va; **they received a pay rise retroactive to last January** = recibieron un aumento de sueldo con efecto retroactivo desde el pasado enero
◊ **retroactively** [retrəʊˈæktɪvli] *adverb* retroactivamente

retrospective [retrəˈspektɪv] *adjective* retrospectivo, -va; **retrospective legislation** = legislación *f* retrospectiva *or* con efecto retroactivo; **with retrospective effect** = con efecto retroactivo; **the tax ruling has retrospective effect** = las disposiciones sobre impuestos tienen efecto retroactivo
◊ **retrospectively** [retrəˈspektɪvli] *adverb* retrospectivamente; **the ruling is applied retrospectively** las disposiciones se aplican con efecto retroactivo

retry [riːˈtraɪ] *verb* revisar *or* volver a examinar un caso; **the court ordered the case to be retried** = el tribunal ordenó la revisión del caso

return [rɪˈtɜːn] **1** *noun* **(a)** *(going back)* vuelta *f or* regreso *m;* **return journey** = viaje *m* de regreso; **return fare** = tarifa *f* de ida y vuelta **(b)** *(sending back)* reexpedición *f or* devolución *f;* **he replied by return of post** = contestó a vuelta de correo; **return address** = remite *m or* remitente *mf;* **these goods are all on sale or return** = todos estos artículos pueden ser devueltos en caso de no venderse **(c)** *(profit from investment)* beneficio *m or* rendimiento *m or* rédito *m;* **return on investment** *or* **on capital** = rendimiento de la inversión *or* del capital; **rate of return** = tasa *f* de rendimiento **(d)** *(tax)* official

return = declaración *f* oficial; **joint tax return** = declaración conjunta; **to make a return to the tax office** *or* **to make an income tax return** = hacer una declaración a Hacienda *or* hacer una declaración de renta; **to fill in a VAT return** = rellenar una declaración del IVA; **annual return** = rendimiento anual; **nil return** = rendimiento nulo **(e)** *(election of MP)* elección *f* **2** *verb* **(a)** *(to go back)* volver; **to return to work** = darse de alta (en el trabajo) **(b)** *(to send back)* devolver; **to return damaged stock to the wholesaler** = devolver existencias defectuosas al mayorista; **to return a letter to sender** = devolver una carta al remitente **(c)** *(to make a statement)* declarar; **to return income of £15,000 to the tax authorities** = declarar unos ingresos de 15.000 libras a Hacienda *or* al fisco **(d)** *(of a jury)* **to return a verdict** = pronunciar un veredicto; **the jury returned a verdict of not guilty** = el jurado pronunció un veredicto de inocencia **(e)** *(to elect an MP)* elegir; **he was returned with an increased majority** = fue elegido por una amplia mayoría

◊ **returning officer** [rɪ'tɜːnɪŋ 'ɒfɪsə] escrutador, -ra

reus ['reɪəs] *see* ACTUS REUS

reveal [rɪ'viːl] *verb* revelar; **examination of the bank account revealed that large sums had been drawn out in August** = un estudio de la cuenta bancaria reveló que en agosto habían sido retiradas grandes sumas de dinero; **the garden revealed several clues to the murder** = el jardín reveló varias pistas del asesinato

revenge [rɪ'vendʒ] *noun* venganza *f*

revenue [revənjuː] *noun (money received by a government in tax)* ingresos *mpl or* renta *f;* **Inland Revenue** *or US* **Internal Revenue Service (IRS)** = Hacienda *f or* fisco *m;* **to make a declaration to the Inland Revenue** = hacer una declaración a Hacienda; **revenue officer** = delegado, -da de Hacienda *or* oficial *mf* de aduanas

reversal [rɪ'vɜːsl] *noun* **(a)** *(of a decision)* revocación *f;* **the reversal of the High Court ruling by the Court of Appeal** = la revocación del fallo del Tribunal Superior por el Tribunal de Apelación **(b)** *(of profit)* cambio *m* completo *or* revés *m;* **the company suffered a reversal in the Far East** = la empresa sufrió un revés en Extremo Oriente

reverse [rɪ'vɜːs] **1** *adjective* opuesto, -ta *or* contrario, -ria; **reverse takeover** = contra OPA *or* adquisición *f* inversa; **reverse charge call** = llamada *f* a cobro revertido **2** *verb* **(a)** *(a decision)* cambiar completamente *or* revocar; **to reverse a judgment on appeal** = anular un juicio en la instancia de apelación; **the Appeal Court reversed the decision of the High Court** = el Tribunal de Apelación revocó el fallo del Tribunal Superior **(b)**

(payment) **to reverse the charges** = llamar a cobro revertido

revert [rɪ'vɜːt] *verb* volver a *or* revertir; **the property reverts to its original owner in 1998** = los bienes revierten a su propietario inicial en 1998

◊ **reversion** [rɪ'vɜːʃn] *noun* reversión *f or* devolución *f;* **he has the reversion of the estate** = recuperará la propiedad al terminar el arrendamiento actual

◊ **reversionary** [rɪ'vɜːʃnri] *adjective* (bienes) de reversión; **reversionary annuity** = anualidad *f* revertible *or* que se paga a alguien a la muerte de otra persona; **reversionary right** = derecho *m* de los herederos de un escritor a los derechos de autor tras su muerte *or* derechos de autor revertibles a los herederos de un escritor a su muerte; *see also* REMAINDER

review [rɪ'vjuː] **1** *noun* **(a)** *(close examination)* revisión *f or* análisis *m or* examen *m* general; **to conduct a review of sentencing policy** = hacer un análisis del sistema empleado para dictar sentencias; **the coroner asked for a review of police procedures** = el juez de primera instancia solicitó un análisis de los procedimientos policiales; **financial review** = análisis financiero; **judicial review** = revisión judicial; **wage review** *or* **salary review** = revisión salarial **(b)** *(magazine)* revista *f or* publicación *f* periódica no diaria **2** *verb* revisar; **a committee has been appointed to review judicial salaries** = se ha nombrado una comisión para revisar los salarios del estamento judicial; **the High Court has reviewed the decision** = el Tribunal Superior ha revisado el fallo

revise [rɪ'vaɪz] *verb* modificar *or* revisar *or* corregir; **the revised examination procedures have been published** = se ha publicado la modificación de los procedimientos de instrucción; **the judge revised his earlier decision not to consider a submission from defence counsel** = el juez modificó su anterior decisión de no tener en cuenta una alegación del abogado defensor

◊ **revision** [rɪ'vɪʒn] *noun* modificación *f;* **the Lord Chancellor has proposed a revision of the divorce procedures** = el presidente de la Cámara de los Lores ha propuesto una modificación de los procedimientos de divorcio

revocandi [revə'kændi] *see* ANIMUS

revoke [rɪ'vəuk] *verb* revocar *or* cancelar *or* anular; **to revoke a clause in an agreement** = anular una cláusula de un acuerdo; **the treaty on fishing rights has been revoked** = el tratado sobre derechos de pesca ha sido cancelado; **to revoke a will** = quebrantar *or* revocar un testamento

◊ **revocable** ['revəkbl] *adjective* revocable

◊ **revocation** [revə'keɪʃn] *noun* cancelación *f or* anulación *f;* **revocation of probate** = anulación de un testamento

revolution [revə'lu:ʃn] *noun* revolución *f*; **the government was overthrown by a revolution led by the head of the army** = el gobierno fue derrocado por una revolución encabezada por el jefe del ejército

reward [rɪ'wɔ:d] **1** *noun* recompensa *f or* premio *m or* gratificación *f*; **she offered a £50 reward to anyone who found her watch** = ofreció una recompensa de 50 libras a quien encontrara su reloj; **the police have offered a reward for information about the man seen at the bank** = la policía ha ofrecido una recompensa a cambio de información sobre el hombre visto en el banco **2** *verb* recompensar *or* gratificar

Rex [reks] *Latin word* 'el Rey': la Corona *or* el estado como una de las partes en procedimientos judiciales (NOTE: in written reports, usually abbreviated to R: **the case of** *R. v. Smith*)

rider ['raɪdə] *noun* cláusula *f* suplementaria *or* adicional; **to add a rider to a contract** = añadir una cláusula adicional a un contrato

right [raɪt] *noun* **(a)** *(legal title to something)* derecho *m*; **right of renewal of a contract** = derecho de renovación de un contrato; **she has a right to the property** = tiene derecho a los bienes; **he has no right to the patent** = no tiene derechos sobre la patente; **the staff have a right to know what the company is doing** = los empleados tienen derecho a saber lo que está haciendo la empresa; **civil rights** = derechos *mpl* civiles; **conjugal rights** = derechos conyugales; **constitutional right** = derecho constitucional; **foreign rights** = derechos de venta en un país extranjero; **human rights** = derechos humanos; **water rights** = servidumbre *f* de aguas; **right of action** = derecho a interponer una demanda *or* derecho a acudir a la vía judicial; **right of benefit** = derecho a prestaciones sociales; **right of sanctuary** = derecho de asilo; **right of way** = derecho de paso *or* servidumbre de paso; **right to legal representation** = derecho a asistencia letrada; **right to privacy** = derecho a la intimidad; **right to strike** = derecho a la huelga; *see also* BILL OF RIGHTS **(b)** *(shares)* **rights issue** = emisión *f* de derechos (para comprar acciones a un precio inferior) *or* emisión de acciones con derecho preferente por parte de los accionistas
◊ **rightful** ['raɪtful] *adjective* legítimo, -ma; **rightful claimant** = derecho habiente; **rightful owner** = propietario legítimo

rigor mortis ['rɪgə 'mɔ:tɪs] *Latin phrase* 'rigidez cadavérica': estado de rigidez al que se llega después de la muerte y que, en algunos casos, puede permitir a un patólogo calcular la hora de la muerte

ring [rɪŋ] **1** *noun* **(a)** *(price fixing)* coalición *f or* cartel *m* de empresas que se ponen de acuerdo para fijar precios **(b)** *(lobby)* camarilla *f* **2** *verb (car fraud)* manipular los números que aparecen en el motor o chasis de un coche para que no pueda descubrirse el origen

riot ['raɪət] **1** *noun* motín *m or* disturbio *m* **2** *verb* amotinarse *or* provocar disturbios
◊ **rioter** ['raɪətə] *noun* alborotador, -ra *or* manifestante *mf or* amotinado, -da; **rioters attacked the banks and post offices** = los alborotadores destrozaron bancos y oficinas de correos
◊ **riotous assembly** ['raɪətəs ə'sembli] *noun* reunión *f* sediciosa

riparian [rɪ'peərɪən] *adjective* ribereño, -ña; **riparian rights** = derechos ribereños

rise [raɪz] **1** *noun* **(a)** *(increase)* aumento *m or* subida *f*; **a rise in the crime rate** *or* **in interest rates** = un aumento del índice de criminalidad *or* una subida del tipo de interés **(b)** *(increase in salary)* aumento de sueldo (NOTE: US English is **raise**); **2** *verb* **(a)** *(to increase)* aumentar *or* subir; **prices are rising faster than inflation** = los precios suben más deprisa que la inflación; **the clear-up rate for crimes of violence has risen by 15%** = el índice neto de delitos violentos ha aumentado en un 15% **(b)** *(to stand up)* ponerse en *or* de pie (NOTE: **rising - rose - has risen**)

risk [rɪsk] **1** *noun* **(a)** *(danger)* riesgo *m*; **to run a risk** = correr un riesgo; **in allowing him to retain his passport, the court runs the risk that the accused may try to escape to the USA** = al permitirle conservar su pasaporte, el tribunal corre el riesgo de que el acusado intente huir a los EE UU; **at owner's risk** = por cuenta y riesgo del propietario **(b)** *(insurance)* riesgo *or* peligro *m*; **fire risk** = peligro de incendio; **he is a bad risk** = él es un gran riesgo; **he is likely to die soon, so is a bad risk for an insurance company** = es probable que muera pronto, por eso es un gran riesgo para una compañía de seguros **2** *verb* arriesgar *or* arriesgarse *or* poner en peligro *or* exponerse; **he is risking his job by complaining to the police** = está poniendo en peligro su trabajo al quejarse a la policía; **he risked being arrested** *or* **he risked arrest by throwing an egg at the Prime Minister** = se arriesgó a que le detuvieran por lanzarle un huevo al Primer Ministro
◊ **risky** ['rɪski] *adjective* arriesgado, -da *or* peligroso, -sa; **risky business** = negocio arriesgado

road tax ['rəud 'tæks] *noun* impuesto *m* de vehículos rodados

rob [rɒb] *verb* robar *or* atracar; **they robbed a bank in London and stole a car to make their getaway** = atracaron un banco en Londres y robaron un coche para poder huir; **the gang robbed shopkeepers in the centre of the town** = la banda se dedicaba a atracar tiendas del centro de la ciudad (NOTE: **robbing - robbed**. Note also that you rob someone **of** something)

◊ **robber** ['rɒbə] *noun* atracador, -ra *or* ladrón, -ona
◊ **robbery** ['rɒbri] *noun* robo *m; (act of stealing with violence)* atraco *m;* **he committed three petrol station robberies in two days** = atracó tres gasolineras en dos días; **armed robbery** = robo *or* asalto *m* a mano armada; **robbery with violence** = robo a mano armada *or* con intimidación; **attempted robbery** = intento *m* de robo (NOTE: no plural for this meaning)

robe [rəub] *noun* toga *f*

rogatory letter ['rɒgətri 'letə] *noun* exhorto *m*

roll [rəul] *noun* (a) *(paper)* rollo *m;* **the desk calculator uses a roll of paper** = la calculadora de mesa lleva un rollo de papel (b) *(list of names)* censo *m or* lista *f;* **Roll of Solicitors** = censo *or* escalafón *m* de abogados; **he was struck off the roll** = fue apartado de la práctica de la abogacía; **Master of the Rolls** = Presidente, -ta del Tribunal de Apelación; **electoral roll** = lista electoral; **judgment roll** = legajo *m* de sentencia
◊ **roll over** ['rəul 'əuvə] *verb* **to roll over credit** = ofrecer crédito por un periodo continuado

Romalpa clause [rə'mælpæ 'klɔːz] *noun* cláusula *f* de un contrato por la que el vendedor estipula que la propiedad de los artículos no pasa al comprador hasta que éste no haya efectuado el pago total de ellos: el nombre procede del caso *Aluminium Industrie Vaassen BV v. Romalpa Ltd)*

Roman law ['rəumən 'lɔː] *noun* derecho *m* Romano

COMMENT: Roman law is the basis of the laws of many European countries but has had only negligible and indirect influence on the development of English law

room [rum] *noun* sala *f;* **detention room** = sala de interrogatorios

root of title ['ruːt əv 'taitl] *noun* escritura *f* de propiedad

ROR ['ɑː 'əu 'ɑː] = RELEASE ON RECOGNIZANCE

rotation [rəu'teiʃn] *noun* turno *m or* rotación *f;* **to fill the post of chairman by rotation** = ocupar la presidencia por turno; **two directors retire by rotation** = dos directores se retiran por haber concluido su turno

rough [rʌf] *adjective* (a) *(approximate)* aproximado, -da; **rough calculation** *or* **rough estimate** = cálculo aproximado (b) *(hard)* severo, -ra; **rough justice** = justicia *f* severa *or* aplicada al pie de la letra (c) *(not finished)* preliminar *or* sin terminar; **rough copy** = borrador *m or* copia *f* preliminar
◊ **roughly** ['rʌfli] *adverb* aproximadamente *or* más o menos; **the turnover is roughly twice last**

year's = el volumen de ventas es aproximadamente el doble que el del año pasado; **the development cost of the project will be roughly £25,000** = el coste del desarrollo del proyecto será de unas 25.000 libras
◊ **rough out** ['rʌf 'aut] *verb* esbozar *or* hacer un borrador; **the finance director roughed out a plan of investment** = el director financiero esbozó un plan de inversión

rout [raut] *noun* delito *m* de reunión para llevar a cabo un acto ilegal *or* disturbio *m or* tumulto *m*

royal ['rɔiəl] *adjective* real; **Royal Assent** = sanción *f* real; **by Royal Command** = por orden del rey *or* de la reina; **Royal Commission** = comisión *f* real; **Royal pardon** = indulto *m* real

royalty ['rɔilti] *noun* derecho *m* de autor *or* de inventor *or* de propietario de tierras; **oil royalties make up a large proportion of the country's revenue** = los cánones del petróleo suponen una gran parte de los ingresos del país; **he is receiving royalties from his invention** = recibe regalías por su invención

RSVP ['ɑː 'es 'viː 'piː] = REPONDEZ S'IL VOUS PLAIT *French expression* se ruega contestación

ruin ['ruːin] *noun* ruina *f*

RPM ['ɑː 'piː 'em] = RESALE PRICE MAINTENANCE

rule [ruːl] **1** *noun* (a) *(general order of conduct)* regla *f or* norma *f;* **company rules (and regulations)** = reglamento *m or* normas *fpl* de la empresa; **work to rule** = paro *m* técnico *or* huelga *f* de celo; **to work to rule** = ceñirse al reglamento *or* negarse a hacer horas extraordinarias *or* hacer huelga de celo *or* estar en paro técnico; **to stick to the rules** = ajustarse a la letra del reglamento; **Judges' Rules** = reglamento concerniente al interrogatorio de sospechosos por parte de la policía; **Rules of the Supreme Court** = reglamento del Tribunal Supremo; *see also* WHITE BOOK (b) *(way in which a country is governed)* dominio *m or* mandato *m;* **the country has had ten years of military rule** = el país ha soportado diez años de dominio castrense; **the rule of law** = el imperio de la ley (c) *(decision made by a court)* fallo *m or* decisión *f;* **rule of law** = principio *m* de derecho; **Rule in Rylands v. Fletcher** = normativa según la cual cuando alguien trae a su tierra algo peligroso (substancia *or* animal) si llegase a producir daños, esa persona es absolutamente responsable de los daños causados **2** *verb* (a) *(to give an official decision)* fallar *or* pronunciarse *or* decidir *or* sentenciar *or* dictaminar; **we are waiting for the judge to rule on the admissibility of the defence evidence** = estamos esperando que el juez se pronuncie sobre la admisibilidad de las pruebas de la defensa; **the commission of inquiry ruled that**

the company was in breach of contract = la comisión de investigación decidió que la empresa estaba incurriendo en incumplimiento de contrato **(b)** *(to be in force)* regir; **prices which are ruling at the moment** = los precios que rigen en el momento actual **(c)** *(to govern)* gobernar *or* mandar; **the country is ruled by a group of army officers** = el país está gobernado por un grupo de oficiales del ejército

◊ **rule out** *verb* descartar

◊ **ruling** ['ru:lıŋ] **1** *adjective* actual *or* vigente *or* que rige; **we will invoice at ruling prices** = extenderemos la factura a los precios actuales **2** *noun* fallo *m or* decisión *f or* providencia *f;* **preliminary ruling** = cuestión *f* prejudicial; **to issue a ruling** = dictar una providencia; **the inquiry gave a ruling on the case** = la investigación pronunció un fallo sobre el caso; **according to the ruling of the court, the contract was illegal** = según el fallo del tribunal, el contrato era ilegal

rumour ['ru:mə] *noun* rumor

run [rʌn] **1** *noun* **(a)** *(machine)* funcionamiento *m or* ciclo *m* de trabajo (especialmente de una máquina); **a cheque run** = una serie de cheques emitidos por ordenador; **a computer run** = periodo *m* de funcionamiento de un ordenador; **test run** = prueba *f* **(b)** *(rush to buy something)* gran demanda *f;* **a run on the bank** = retirada masiva de fondos de un banco; **a run on the pound** = venta apresurada de la libra **2** *verb* **(a)** *(to be in force)* ser válido, -da *or* estar vigente; **the lease runs for twenty years** = el alquiler tiene una validez de veinte años; **the**

lease has only six months to run = el alquiler tiene una validez de seis meses solamente; **a covenant which runs with the land** = un convenio que va asociado a la posesión de la tierra **(b)** *(to amount to)* ascender a; **the costs ran into thousands of pounds** = los costes ascendieron a miles de libras **(c)** *(to manage or to organize)* dirigir *or* llevar; **to run a business** = llevar un negocio; **she runs a mail-order business from home** = lleva un negocio de pedidos por correo desde su casa; **they run a staff sports club** = llevan un club deportivo para los empleados; **he is running a multimillion-pound company** = lleva una empresa multimillonaria **(d)** *(to work on a machine)* usar *or* hacer funcionar; **do not run the copying machine for more than four hours at a time** = no utilice la fotocopiadora más de cuatro horas seguidas; **the computer was running invoices all night** = el ordenador estuvo haciendo facturas toda la noche **(e)** *(of buses, trains etc.)* circular *or* cubrir el servicio *or* salir; **there is an evening plane running between London and Madrid** = hay un avión nocturno entre Londres y Madrid; **this train runs on weekdays** = este tren sale los días laborables (NOTE: **running - ran - has run**)

◊ **run over** ['rʌn 'əpvə] *verb* atropellar

◊ **runner** ['rʌnə] *noun (slang)* enlace *m or* miembro de una banda de carteristas encargado de recoger el botín y ponerlo a buen recaudo

rustle [rʌsl] *verb* robar ganado

◊ **rustler** ['rʌslə] *noun* ladrón, -ona de ganado *or* abigeo *m;* **a cattle rustler** = un ladrón de ganado

◊ **rustling** ['rʌslıŋ] *noun* robo *m* de ganado *or* abigeato *m*

Ss

sabotage ['sæbətɑːʒ] *noun* sabotaje *m or* daño *m* premeditado; **several acts of sabotage were committed against radio stations** = se cometieron diversas acciones de sabotaje contra emisoras de radio

sack [sæk] **1** *noun* **(a)** *(large bag)* saco *m;* **the burglars carried a sack of clocks from the shop** = los ladrones se llevaron un saco lleno de relojes de la tienda **(b)** *(work)* **to get the sack** = ser despedido **2** *verb* **to sack someone** = despedir a alguien; **he was sacked after being late for work** = le despidieron por llegar tarde al trabajo
◊ **sacking** ['sækɪŋ] *noun* despido *m;* **the union protested against the sackings** = el sindicato manifestó su protesta por los despidos

safe [seɪf] **1** *noun* caja *f* fuerte *or* de caudales; **put the documents in the safe** = pon los documentos en la caja fuerte; **we keep the petty cash in the safe** = guardamos el dinero para gastos menores en la caja fuerte; **fire-proof safe** = caja fuerte a prueba de incendios; **night safe** = caja nocturna; **wall safe** = caja fuerte empotrada **2** *adjective* **(a)** *(out of danger)* seguro, -ra; **keep the documents in a safe place** = guarda los documentos en lugar seguro; **safe keeping** = custodia *f;* **we put the documents into the bank for safe keeping** = guardamos los documentos en el banco para mayor seguridad **(b)** *(without risk)* **safe investments** = inversiones *fpl* seguras
◊ **safe-conduct** ['seɪf'kɒndʌkt] *noun* salvoconducto *m*
◊ **safe deposit** ['seɪf dɪ'pɒzɪt] *noun* caja *f* de seguridad
◊ **safe deposit box** ['seɪf dɪ'pɒzɪt 'bɒks] *noun* caja *f* de seguridad
◊ **safeguard** ['seɪfgɑːd] **1** *noun* protección *f;* **the proposed legislation will provide a safeguard against illegal traders** = la legislación propuesta ofrecerá protección contra comerciantes ilegales **2** *verb* proteger; **the court acted to safeguard the interests of the shareholders** = el tribunal intervino para proteger los intereses de los accionistas
◊ **safely** ['seɪfli] *adverb* sin peligro *or* sin sufrir daño alguno; **the cargo was unloaded safely from the sinking ship** = la mercancía fue descargada del barco que se hundía sin sufrir daño alguno

◊ **safety** ['seɪfti] *noun* **(a)** *(free from danger or risk)* seguridad *f;* **Health and Safety at Work Act** = Ordenanza *f* General de Seguridad e Higiene en el Trabajo; **safety margin** = margen *m* de seguridad; **to take safety precautions** *or* **safety measures** = tomar precauciones *or* medidas de seguridad; **safety regulations** = normas *fpl* de seguridad **(b)** **fire safety** = prevención *f* de incendios; **fire safety officer** = encargado, -da de la prevención de incendios **(c)** **for safety** = para mayor seguridad; **put the documents in the cupboard for safety** = coloca los documentos en el armario para mayor seguridad; **to take a copy of the disk for safety** = hacer una copia del disco *or* disquete para mayor seguridad

sale [seɪl] *noun* **(a)** *(act of selling)* venta *f;* **forced sale** = venta forzosa; **sale and lease-back** = venta y posterior arrendamiento de una propiedad al comprador; **sale or return** = compra *f* con derecho a devolución; **bill of sale** = *(to a buyer)* contrato *m* de compraventa *or* factura *f* de venta; *(to a borrower)* documento *m* que el prestatario da al prestamista en el que se muestra que éste posee bienes que respaldan un préstamo; **conditions of sale** *or* **terms of sale** = condiciones *fpl* de venta; **Sale of Goods Act** = ley *f* de venta de mercancías; **the law relating to the sale of goods is governed by the Sale of Goods Act 1979** = la ley de 1979 rige el derecho relativo a la venta de mercancías **(b)** *(ready to be sold)* **for sale** = en venta; *(sign)* 'se vende'; **to offer something for sale** *or* **to put something up for sale** = poner algo en venta; **they put the factory up for sale** = pusieron la fábrica en venta; **his shop is for sale** = su tienda está en venta; **these items are not for sale to the general public** = estos artículos no están a la venta al gran público **(c)** *(selling at specially low prices)* liquidación *f* *or* rebajas *fpl or* saldo *m;* **clearance sale** = liquidación de existencias; **the shop is having a sale to clear old stock** = la tienda ha organizado unas rebajas para liquidar las existencias antiguas; **the sale price is 50% of the normal price** = el precio rebajado es el 50% del precio normal; **half-price sale** = rebajas a mitad de precio; **the sales** = las rebajas *fpl*
◊ **sales** [seɪlz] *noun* ventas *fpl;* **sales conference** *or* **sales meeting** = reunión *f* de profesionales de ventas; **sales department** = departamento *m* de

ventas; **domestic sales** *or* **home sales** = ventas nacionales; **sales figures** = cifra *f* de ventas; **forward sales** = ventas a plazos *or* futuras *or* para entrega futura; **sales tax** = impuesto *m* sobre la venta

salvage ['sælvɪdʒ] **1** *noun* **(a)** *(act)* salvamento *m* *or* rescate *m;* **salvage agreement** = acuerdo *m* de salvamento de un barco en peligro de naufragio; **salvage (money)** = premio *m* de salvamento; **salvage vessel** = buque *m* de salvamento **(b)** *(goods or objects)* objetos *mpl* *or* mercancías *fpl* salvadas de un naufragio *or* de un incendio, etc; **a sale of flood salvage items** = liquidación *f* de objetos salvados de una inundación (NOTE: no plural in English) **2** *verb* **(a)** *(contents of a ship)* salvar; **we are selling off a warehouse full of salvaged goods** = ponemos a la venta un almacén lleno de objetos procedentes de un salvamento **(b)** *(save from loss)* salvar; **the company is trying to salvage its reputation after the managing director was sent to prison for fraud** = la empresa está tratando de salvar su reputación tras el envío a prisión del director gerente por fraude; **the receiver managed to salvage something from the failure of the company** = el administrador judicial consiguió salvar algo de la ruina de la empresa

sample ['sɑːmpl] **1** *noun* muestra *f* *or* muestreo *m;* **they polled a sample group of voters** = hicieron un sondeo de opinión entre un grupo de votantes; **blood sample** *or* **urine sample** = muestra de sangre *or* muestra de orina **2** *verb* analizar una muestra *or* tomar una muestra para examen; **the suspect's breath was sampled and the test proved positive** = se analizó el aliento del sospechoso y la prueba dio positiva

sanction ['sæŋkʃn] **1** *noun* **(a)** *(official permission)* autorización *f* *or* permiso *m;* **you will need the sanction of the local authorities before you can knock down the office block** = necesitará la autorización de las autoridades locales para poder derribar el bloque de oficinas; **the payment was made without official sanction** = el pago se realizó sin autorización oficial **(b)** *(punishment)* sanción *f;* **(economic) sanctions** = sanciones económicas; **to impose sanctions on a country** *or* **to lift sanctions** = imponer sanciones a un país *or* levantar las sanciones impuestas **2** *verb* autorizar *or* permitir *or* aprobar; **the board sanctioned the expenditure of £1.2m on the development plan** = la dirección autorizó el gasto de 1,2 millones de libras en el plan de desarrollo

sane [seɪn] *adjective* cuerdo, -da *or* en su sano juicio; **was he sane when he made the will?** = ¿estaba en su sano juicio al hacer el testamento? ◊ **sanity** ['sænɪti] *noun* cordura *f* *or* juicio *m*

sans recours ['sænz rə'kuːə] *French phrase* 'sin recurso': utilizado para mostrar que el endosador de una letra no es responsable de su pago

satisfaction [sætɪs'fækʃn] *noun* **(a)** *(payment)* liquidación *f* *or* cumplimiento *m* *or* aceptación *f* de dinero *or* de bienes; **accord and satisfaction** = oferta y aceptación de modificación; **memorandum of satisfaction** = documento de cancelación de una hipoteca *or* de liquidación de un pago **(b)** *(good feeling)* satisfacción *f;* **job satisfaction** = satisfacción en el trabajo ◊ **satisfy** ['sætɪsfaɪ] *verb* **(a)** *(to convince that something is correct)* convencer; **when opposing bail the police had to satisfy the court that the prisoner was likely to try to leave the country** = la policía, al oponerse a la libertad bajo fianza, tuvo que convencer al tribunal de que era probable que el acusado tratara de abandonar el país **(b)** *(to please)* satisfacer; **to satisfy a client** = satisfacer a un cliente; **a satisfied customer** = un cliente satisfecho **(c)** *(to fulfil)* cumplir con *or* satisfacer; **has he satisfied all the conditions for parole?** = ¿cumple todas las condiciones para que se le conceda la libertad condicional?; **the company has not satisfied all the conditions laid down in the agreement** = la empresa no ha cumplido con todas las condiciones establecidas en el acuerdo; **we cannot produce enough to satisfy the demand for the product** = no podemos producir lo suficiente para satisfacer la demanda del producto

save [seɪv] *verb* **(a)** *(to keep money)* ahorrar; **he is trying to save money by walking to work** = intenta ahorrar dinero y va al trabajo a pie; **she is saving to buy a house** = está ahorrando para comprar una casa **(b)** *(not to waste)* ahorrar *or* economizar; **to save time, let us continue the discussion in the taxi to the airport** = para ahorrar tiempo, sigamos con la discusión en el taxi mientras nos lleva al aeropuerto; **the government is encouraging companies to save energy** = el gobierno está alentando a las empresas a ahorrar energía **(c)** *(on a computer)* archivar *or* guardar; **do not forget to save your files when you have finished correcting them** = no te olvides de salvar los archivos cuando hayas terminado de corregirlos ◊ **savings** ['seɪvɪŋz] *noun* ahorro *m* *or* economía *f;* **savings book** = cartilla *f* de ahorros; **National Savings** = Caja Postal de Ahorros

scaffold ['skæfəʊld] *noun* cadalso *m* *or* patíbulo *m*

scale [skeɪl] **1** *noun* **(a)** *(system graded into levels)* escala *f* *or* baremo *m;* **scale of charges** *or* **scale of prices** = escala de precios; **scale of fees** = arancel *m* de honorarios; **fixed scale of charges** = escala fija de precios; **scale of salaries** *or* **salary scale** = escala de salarios; **sliding scale** = escala móvil **(b)** **large scale** *or* **small scale** = gran escala *or* pequeña escala; **to start in business on a small scale** = empezar un negocio a pequeña escala; **economies of scale** = economías de escala **2** *verb* **to scale down** *or* **to scale up** = reducir *or* aumentar proporcionalmente *or* a escala

scam [skæm] *noun US (informal)* caso *m* de fraude

scapegoat ['skeɪpgəʊt] *noun* chivo *m* expiatorio

scene [siːn] *noun* escenario *m;* **the scene of the crime** = el escenario del crimen *or* el lugar del crimen

schedule ['ʃedjuːl *US* 'skedʒuːl] **1** *noun* **(a)** *(timetable)* horario *m or* programa *m;* **to be ahead of schedule** = ir adelantado *or* llegar antes de lo previsto; **to be on schedule** = ir al ritmo previsto; **to be behind schedule** = ir retrasado; **the Bill is on schedule** = el proyecto de ley se desarrolla al ritmo previsto; **the Second Reading was completed ahead of schedule** = el proyecto de ley se debatió por segunda vez antes de lo previsto; **I am sorry to say that we are three months behind schedule** = siento comunicarle que llevamos tres meses de retraso; **the managing director has a busy schedule of appointments** = el director gerente tiene un programa de entrevistas muy apretado; **his secretary tried to fit me into his schedule** = su secretaria intentó hacerme un hueco en su horario **(b)** *(legal document)* apéndice *m;* **schedule of markets to which a contract applies** = apéndice relativo a mercados en los que un contrato es de aplicación *or* en los que se aplica un contrato; **see the attached schedule** *or* **as per the attached schedule** = véase el apéndice correspondiente; **the schedule before referred to** = el apéndice al que nos hemos referido anteriormente **(c)** *(list)* lista *f;* **schedule of charges** = lista de precios; **schedule of court costs** = arancel *m* judicial **(d)** *GB* **tax schedules** = escalas impositivas; **Schedule A** = escalas impositivas referentes a los impuestos sobre las rentas de los bienes inmobiliarios; **Schedule B** = escalas impositivas referentes a los impuestos sobre las rentas de los bosques; **Schedule C** = escalas impositivas referentes a los impuestos sobre los beneficios del capital del gobierno; **Schedule D** = escalas impositivas referentes a los impuestos sobre oficios, profesiones, intereses y otras ganancias que no proceden del empleo; **Schedule E** = escalas impositivas referentes a ingresos procedentes de salarios y pensiones; **Schedule F** = escalas impositivas referentes a los impuestos sobre dividendos **2** *verb* **(a)** *(to list)* catalogar *or* registrar *or* notificar oficialmente; **scheduled prices** *or* **scheduled charges** = precios *mpl or* tarifas *fpl* oficiales *or* precios según tarifa **(b)** *(to plan)* programar *or* fijar *or* proyectar *or* prever; **the building is scheduled for completion in May** = está previsto que el edificio se termine en mayo

scheme [skiːm] *noun* esquema *m*

◊ **scheme of arrangement** ['skiːm əv əˈreɪnʒmənt] *noun* disposición *f or* transacción *f* previa a la quiebra *or* propuesta *f* de concordato

scope [skəʊp] *noun* ámbito *m or* alcance *m or* competencia *f;* **within the scope** = dentro del ámbito; **the question does not come within the scope of the authority's powers** = la cuestión no entra en el ámbito de los poderes de la autoridad; **the Bill plans to increase the scope of the tribunal's authority** = el proyecto de ley propone aumentar la autoridad del tribunal

screen [skriːn] **1** *noun* pantalla *f* **2** *verb* **to screen candidates** = seleccionar candidatos *or* pasar los candidatos por el tamiz *or* la criba
◊ **screening** ['skriːnɪŋ] *noun* criba *f;* **the screening of candidates** = la selección de candidatos

screw [skruː] *noun (slang)* carcelero, -ra

scrip [skrɪp] *noun* certificado *m* provisional de posesión de acciones en una empresa; **scrip issue** = emisión *f* gratuita de acciones distribuidas entre los accionistas

scuttle ['skʌtl] *verb* hundir

seal [siːl] **1** *noun* **(a)** *(stamp)* sello *m* (de lacre); **common seal** *or* **company's seal** = sello de la compañía; **to attach the company's seal to a document** = poner el sello de la compañía a un documento; **contract under seal** = contrato *m* sellado **(b)** *(piece of paper or metal or wax attached to close something)* sello *or* precinto *m;* **the seals on the ballot box had been tampered with** = han forzado los precintos de la urna; **customs seal** = precinto aduanero *or* de aduana **2** *verb* **(a)** *(to close tightly)* cerrar herméticamente *or* precintar; **the computer disks were sent in a sealed container** = los discos del ordenador fueron enviados en un paquete precintado; **sealed envelope** = sobre *m* cerrado; **the information was sent in a sealed envelope** = se envió la información en sobre cerrado; **the company has asked for sealed bids for the warehouse** = la empresa ha pedido ofertas lacradas para el almacén; **sealed tenders** = ofertas *fpl* lacradas *or* licitaciones *fpl* en pliego cerrado **(b)** *(to attach a seal)* sellar *or* precintar; **the customs sealed the shipment** = la aduana precintó el envío; **sealed instrument** = documento *m* firmado y sellado
◊ **seal off** ['siːl 'ɒf] *verb* acordonar *or* aislar; **police sealed off all roads leading to the town** = la policía aisló todas las carreteras que conducían a la ciudad

search [səːtʃ] **1** *noun* **(a)** *(inspection)* búsqueda *f or* registro *m or* inspección *f;* **search party** = equipo *m* de rescate; **search warrant** = orden *f* de registro; **body search** = cacheo *m* **(b)** *(examination of documents regarding a property for sale)* **searches** = examen *m* del registro de la propiedad para ver las cargas que pesan sobre un inmueble *or* comprobación *f* del catastro por parte de un abogado para asegurarse de que el vendedor de una propiedad tiene derecho a venderla **2** *verb* **(a)** *(place)* registrar *or* examinar; **the agent searched his files for a record of the sale** = el representante buscó en sus archivos un justificante de la venta; **all drivers and their cars are searched at the customs post** = todos los conductores y sus vehículos son registrados en el puesto de aduanas; **the police searched the area round the house for clues** = la policía registró la zona de alrededor de la casa en busca de pistas **(b)** *(body)* cachear

seat *noun* **(a)** *(chair)* silla *f*; **seats have been placed on the platform for the members of the council** = se han colocado sillas en la tribuna para los miembros del consejo; **seat belt** = cinturón *m* de seguridad **(b)** *(in parliament)* escaño *m*; **he lost his seat in the general election** = perdió su escaño en las elecciones generales; **Opposition MPs left their seats and walked out of the chamber in protest** = los diputados de la oposición abandonaron sus escaños y salieron de la cámara en señal de protesta; *see also* EURO-SEAT, UNSEAT

COMMENT: in the British House of Commons, the seats are arranged in rows facing each other across the chamber, with the table in between the front benches and the Speaker's chair at the end. In other legislative chambers (as in the French National Assembly), the seats are arranged in a semi-circle facing the rostrum with the seat of the President of the Assembly behind it

secede *verb* separarse *or* escindirse; **the American colonies seceded from Great Britain in 1776 and formed the USA** = las colonias norteamericanas se separaron de Gran Bretaña en 1776 y formaron los EE.UU de América
◊ **secession** *noun* secesión *f*

second ['sekənd] **1** *adjective* segundo, -da; **second quarter** = segundo trimestre; **second mortgage** = segunda hipoteca **2** *verb* **to second a motion** = apoyar una moción
◊ **secondary** ['sekəndri] *adjective* secundario, -ria; **secondary banks** = bancos *mpl* subsidiarios; **secondary action** *or* **secondary picketing** = piquete *m* subsidiario; **secondary evidence** = pruebas derivadas, como copias en ausencia de originales, a las que se recurre si no hay medios de prueba directos

COMMENT: secondary evidence can be admitted if there is no primary evidence available

◊ **secondarily** ['sekəndrəli] *adverb* en segundo lugar; **the person making a guarantee is secondarily liable if the person who is primarily liable defaults** = la persona que realiza un aval es responsable en segundo lugar si la persona

responsable en primer lugar deja de cumplir el pago; *see also* PRIMARY, PRIMARILY
◊ **seconder** ['sekəndə] *noun* persona que secunda o apoya una propuesta o moción; **Mr Brown has been proposed by Mr Jones, and Miss Smith is his seconder** = el Sr. Brown ha sido propuesto por el Sr. Jones y la propuesta ha sido secundada por la Srta. Smith
◊ **second ballot** ['sekənd 'bælət] *noun* votación *f* en segunda vuelta
◊ **second degree murder** ['sekənd dɪ'griː 'məːdə] *noun* US homicidio *m* por imprudencia
◊ **Second Reading** ['sekənd 'riːdɪŋ] *noun* GB segunda lectura de un proyecto de ley en el parlamento *or* último debate y votación de un proyecto de ley en el parlamento; *US* examen detallado de un proyecto de ley en la Cámara de Representantes antes de su paso por el Senado

secret ['siːkrət] **1** *adjective* secreto, -ta; **the Chief Constable kept the report secret from the rest of the force** = el jefe de policía no reveló el informe al resto de la plantilla; **they signed a secret deal with their main competitor** = firmaron un acuerdo secreto con su principal competidor; **secret ballot** = voto *m* secreto; **in secret session** = en reunión privada **2** *noun* secreto *m*; **official secret** = secreto de estado; **Official Secrets Act** = Ley *f* de Secretos Oficiales; **trade secret** = secreto profesional; **to keep a secret** = guardar un secreto; **in secret** = en secreto; **he photographed the plans of the new missile in secret** = fotografió los planes del nuevo misil en secreto; **the gang leader met the detective inspector in secret** = el jefe de la banda se reunió con el inspector detective en secreto; **he photographed the plan of the bank vault in secret** = fotografió el plano de la cámara acorazada del banco en secreto
◊ **secretly** ['siːkrətli] *adverb* en secreto; **the treaty was signed secretly by the Prime Minister and the President** = el tratado fue firmado en secreto por el Primer Ministro y el Presidente; **he offered to copy the plans secretly and sell them to another firm** = se ofreció a copiar los planos en secreto y venderlos a otra firma

secretary ['sekrətri] *noun* **(a)** *(person who helps someone with office work)* secretario, -ria; **secretary and personal assistant** = secretaria y ayudante personal; **my secretary deals with visitors** = mi secretario se ocupa de las visitas; **her secretary phoned to say she would be late** = su secretario telefoneó para decir que llegaría tarde; **legal secretary** = secretario, -ria de una firma de abogados *or* del departamento jurídico de una empresa **(b)** *(official of a company or society)* **company secretary** = secretario, -ria de la compañía; **honorary secretary** = secretario honorario **(c)** *(member of the government in charge of a department)* GB ministro, -tra del gobierno; **Education Secretary** = ministro de Educación;

Foreign Secretary = ministro de Asuntos Exteriores; *US* **Secretary of the Treasury** = ministro de Hacienda **(d)** *(senior civil servant)* **Permanent Secretary** = secretario, -ria permanente (NOTE: in Canada called **Deputy Minister.** Permanent Secretaries are appointed by the Prime Minister and are responsible to the Secretary of State in charge of the relevant department); **Cabinet Secretary** *or* **Secretary to the Cabinet** = Secretario, -ria del Gabinete; **Private Secretary** = secretario, -ria personal

◊ **Secretary-General** ['skrətri'dʒenrəl] *noun* secretario, -ria general

◊ **Secretary of State** ['sekrətri əv 'steɪt] *noun* **(a)** *GB* ministro, -tra (con cartera) **(b)** *US* Secretario, -ria de Estado *or* ministro, -tra de Asuntos Exteriores; *see also notes at* FOREIGN, MINISTER

COMMENT: the uses of the words **Secretary** and **Secretary of State** are confusing: **1.** In the UK, a Secretary of State is the head of a government department, usually a Cabinet Minister. Other members of the government, though not in the Cabinet, are Parliamentary Secretaries or Parliamentary Under-Secretaries of State, who are junior ministers in a department. Finally the Parliamentary Private Secretary is a minister's main junior assistant in Parliament **2.** In the USA, the Secretary of State is the person in charge of the Department of State, which is concerned with foreign policy. The equivalent in most other countries is the Foreign Minister (Foreign Secretary in the UK). Other heads of department in the US government are called simply Secretary: Secretary for Defense or Defense Secretary **3.** In the British civil service, a government department is headed by a Permanent Secretary, with several Deputy Secretaries and Under-Secretaries. They are all government employees and are not MPs. Also a civil servant is a minister's Private Secretary, who is attached to the minister personally, and acts as his link with the department. The British Civil Service formerly used the titles Permanent Secretary, Deputy Secretary, Assistant Secretary and Principal Secretary as grades, but these have now been replaced by a system of numbers (G1, G2, G3, etc.) **4.** Both in the UK and USA, the word Secretary is used in short forms of titles with the name of the department. So, the Secretary of State for Education and Science in the UK, and the Secretary for Education in the USA are both called Education Secretary for short. In the USA, the word Secretary can be used as a person's title: Secretary Smith

secretarial [sekrə'teəriəl] *adjective* de secretario, -ria; **she is taking a secretarial course** = está haciendo un curso de secretariado; **he is looking for secretarial work** = está buscando un trabajo de secretario; **we need extra secretarial**

help to deal with the mailings = necesitamos más secretarios, para que se ocupen de los envíos por correo; **secretarial college** = escuela *f* de secretariado

secretariat [sekrə'teəriət] *noun* secretaría *f or* secretariado *m;* **the United Nations secretariat** = la secretaría de las Naciones Unidas

section ['sekʃn] *noun* **(a)** *(department)* departamento *m;* **legal section** = asesoría jurídica *or* departamento jurídico; **visa section** = departamento de visados **(b)** *(bylaw)* artículo *m or* apartado *m or* sección *f* de un texto legal; **he does not qualify for a grant under section 2 of the Act** = según el artículo 2 de la Ley, no satisface los requisitos para la subvención

sector ['sektə] *noun* sector *m;* **private sector** = sector privado; **public sector** = sector público; **public sector borrowing requirement (PSBR)** = necesidad de endeudamiento del sector público

secure [sɪ'kjuːə] **1** *adjective* **(a)** *(safe or which cannot be changed)* seguro, -ra; **secure job** = empleo *m* seguro *or* fijo; **secure investment** = inversión *f* segura; **secure tenant** = arrendatario, -ria con derecho a comprar la propiedad alquilada a un precio ventajoso **(b)** *(safe or not likely to be opened)* seguro, -ra; **the documents should be kept in a secure place** = los documentos deben guardarse en lugar seguro; **the police and army have made the border secure** = la policía y el ejército han asegurado la frontera **2** *verb* **(a)** *to secure a loan* = garantizar un préstamo **(b)** *(to get into your control)* conseguir *or* asegurar; **they secured the release of the hostages** = consiguieron la liberación de los rehenes

◊ **secured** [sɪ'kjuːəd] *adjective;* **secured loan** = préstamo con garantía; **secured creditor** = acreedor con garantía *or* asegurado *or* pignoraticio; **secured debts** = deudas *fpl* garantizadas

◊ **securities** [sɪ'kjuːrɪtiz] *plural noun* valores *mpl or* títulos *mpl;* **gilt-edged securities** *or* **government securities** = títulos del Estado *or* valores de máxima garantía *or* títulos de crédito de primerísima clase; **listed securities** = efectos *mpl* cotizables; **the securities market** = mercado *m or* bolsa *f* de valores; **securities trader** = comerciante *mf* en valores *or* títulos

◊ **security** [sɪ'kjuːrɪti] *noun* **(a)** *(being safe)* seguridad *f or* garantía *f;* **security of employment** = seguridad de permanencia en el empleo; **security for costs** = caución *f* de arraigo *or* caución respecto de costas procesales; **the master ordered that the plaintiff should deposit £2,000 as security for the defendant's costs** = el funcionario encargado de examinar el caso ordenó que el demandante depositara 2.000 libras como garantía del pago de las costas del demandado; **security of tenure** = derecho *m* a conservar un puesto de trabajo *or* una vivienda alquilada **(b)** *(being protected)* seguridad;

airport security = medidas de seguridad en aeropuertos; **security guard** = guardia jurado; **office security** = medidas de seguridad en oficinas; **top security prison** = prisión *f* de máxima seguridad **(c)** *(being secret)* secreto *m;* **security in this office is nil** = la seguridad en esta oficina es nula; **security printer** = impresor, -ra de títulos *or* de documentos de valor **(d) social security** = seguridad social; **he lives on social security payments** = vive de la paga que recibe de la seguridad social **(e)** *(guarantee that someone will repay money borrowed)* garantía *f or* fianza *f or* aval *m;* **mortgage security** = garantía hipotecaria; **to stand security for someone** = avalar a alguien; **to give something as security for a debt** = garantizar una deuda; **to use a house as security for a loan** = utilizar una casa como garantía de un préstamo; **the bank lent him £20,000 without security** = el banco le prestó 20.000 libras sin necesidad de aval *or* sin fianza

COMMENT: where a foreign plaintiff or a company which may become insolvent brings proceedings against a defendant, the defendant is entitled to apply to the court for an order that the proceedings be stayed unless the plaintiff deposits money to secure the defendant's costs if the plaintiff fails in his action

◊ **Security Council** [sɪ'kjuːrɪti 'kaʊnsəl] *noun* Consejo *m* de Seguridad (Naciones Unidas)

COMMENT: the Security Council has fifteen members, five of which (USA, Russia, UK, France and China) are permanent members, the other ten being elected by the General Assembly for periods of two years. The five permanent members each have a veto over the decisions of the Security Council

sedition [sɪ'dɪʃn] *noun* sedición *f*

COMMENT: sedition is a lesser crime than treason

◊ **seditious** [sɪ'dɪʃəs] *adjective* sedicioso, -sa; **seditious libel** = difamación *f* escrita *or* comunicación *f* escrita de carácter sedicioso

seek [siːk] *verb* **(a)** *(to ask for)* pedir *or* solicitar; **they are seeking damages for loss of revenue** = piden una indemnización por la pérdida de ingresos; **the applicant sought judicial review to quash the order** = el solicitante pidió una revisión judicial para anular la orden; **the Bill requires a social worker to seek permission of the Juvenile Court** = el proyecto de ley exige que un asistente social pida permiso al tribunal de menores; **a creditor seeking a receiving order under the Bankruptcy Act** = acreedor que pide una orden de intervención judicial según la legislación sobre quiebras; **to seek an interview** = solicitar una entrevista; **she sought an interview with the**

minister = solicitó una entrevista con el ministro **(b)** *(to look for)* buscar (algo *or* a alguien); **to seek employment** = buscar trabajo; **the police are seeking a tall man who was seen near the scene of the crime** = la policía busca a un hombre alto que fue visto cerca del lugar del crimen; **two men are being sought by the police** = la policía está buscando a dos hombres **(c)** *(to try)* tratar *or* procurar; **the local authority is seeking to place the ward of court in accommodation** = las autoridades locales están buscando alojamiento para un menor bajo la tutela del tribunal (NOTE: seeking - sought - has sought)

segregate ['segrəgeit] *verb* segregar *or* separar
◊ **segregation** [segrə'geɪʃn] *noun* segregación *f;* **racial segregation** = segregación racial

seised [siːzd] *adjective;* **seised of a property** = en posesión legal de una propiedad en dominio absoluto
◊ **seisin** ['siːzɪn] *noun* posesión *f* de tierra

seize [siːz] *verb* confiscar *or* secuestrar *or* embargar *or* incautarse de; **the customs seized the shipment of books** = los oficiales de aduanas se incautaron del cargamento de libros; **his case was seized at the airport** = su maleta fue confiscada en el aeropuerto; **the court ordered the company's funds to be seized** = el tribunal ordenó la incautación de los fondos de la compañía
◊ **seizure** ['siːʒə] *noun* incautación *f or* embargo *m;* **the court ordered the seizure of the shipment** *or* **of the company's funds** = el tribunal ordenó la incautación del envío *or* de los fondos de la compañía

select [sɪ'lekt] **1** *adjective* **(a)** *(class)* de primera calidad *or* selecto, -ta; **our customers are very select** = nuestros clientes son muy selectos; **a select group of clients** = un selecto grupo de clientes **(b)** *(in the House of Commons)* **select committee** = comisión *f* especial; **the Select Committee on Defence** *or* **the Defence Select Committee** = la Comisión especial de Defensa **2** *verb* escoger *or* elegir; **three members of the committee have been selected to speak at the AGM** = se han escogido tres miembros de la comisión para que hablen en la Junta General Anual; **he has been selected as a candidate for a Northern constituency** = ha sido escogido como candidato de uno de los distritos electorales del norte

COMMENT: the main sessional Select Committees in the house of Commons are: **the Committee of Privileges** which considers breaches of parliamentary privilege; **the Committee of the Parliamentary Commissioner** which considers the reports of the Ombudsman; **the Public Accounts Committee** which examines government expenditure. The departmental select committees are: **Agriculture, Defence,**

Education, Employment, Energy, Environment, Foreign Affairs, Home Affairs, Scottish Affairs, Social Services, Trade and Industry, Transport, Treasury, Welsh Affairs

selection [sɪ'lekʃn] *noun* **(a)** *(choice)* elección *f* **(b)** *(thing chosen)* selección *f*; **selection board** *or* **selection committee** = comisión de selección; **selection procedure** = procedimiento *m* de selección

self-defence ['selfdɪ'fens] *noun* legítima defensa *f or* defensa propia; **he pleaded that he had acted in self-defence when he had hit the mugger** = alegó que había actuado en legítima defensa al golpear al asaltante

COMMENT: this can be used as a defence to a charge of a crime of violence, where the defendant pleads that his actions were attributable to defending himself rather than to a desire to commit violence

self-determination ['selfdɪtɜːmɪ'neɪʃn] *noun* autodeterminación *f*
◊ **self-government** *or* **self-rule** ['self'gʌvənmənt *or* 'self'ruːl] *noun* autonomía *f*
◊ **self-incrimination** ['selfɪnkrɪmɪ'neɪʃn] *noun* autoincriminación *f*; **right against self-incrimination** = derecho según el cual nadie puede ser obligado a declarar en perjuicio propio

self-enforcing ['selfɪn'fɔːsɪŋ] *noun* de aplicación inmediata

self-incrimination ['selfɪnkrɪmɪ'neɪʃn] *noun* autoinculpación *f*; **right against self-incrimination** = derecho *m* a permanecer en silencio

sell [sel] *verb* vender; **to sell cars** *or* **refrigerators** = vender coches *or* frigoríficos; **they have decided to sell their house** = han decidido vender su casa; **they tried to sell their house for £100,000** = intentaron vender su casa por 100.000 libras; **to sell something on credit** = vender algo a crédito; **her house is difficult to sell** = su casa es difícil de vender; **their products are easy to sell** = sus productos son fáciles de vender; **to sell forward** = vender a término *or* a futuros *or* para entrega futura (NOTE: **selling - sold - has sold**)
◊ **seller** ['selə] *noun* **(a)** *(person who sells)* vendedor, -ra; **there were few sellers in the market, so prices remained high** = había pocos vendedores en el mercado, por eso los precios se mantuvieron altos; **seller's market** = mercado *m* favorable al vendedor **(b)** *(thing which sells)* producto *m* que se vende bien; **this book is a good seller** = este libro se vende bien; **best-seller** = 'best-seller' *m or* artículo *m* de mayor venta
◊ **selling** ['selɪŋ] *noun* venta *f*; **direct selling** = venta *f* directa; **mail-order selling** = venta por correo; **selling price** = precio *m* de venta

semble ['sembl] *French word* 'parece': palabra utilizada para discutir una sentencia judicial en la que hay cierta incertidumbre sobre la intención del tribunal *or* la validez de la misma

senate ['senət] *noun* **(a)** *(government)* senado *m*; **the Senate of the USA** = el Senado de los EE UU; **the Senate Foreign Relations Committee** = la comisión de relaciones exteriores del Senado **(b)** *(of a university, college, etc.)* rectorado *m*
◊ **senator** ['senətə] *noun* senador, -ra (NOTE: written with a capital letter when used as a title: **Senator Jackson)**

COMMENT: the US Senate has 100 members, each state electing two senators by popular vote. Bills may be introduced in the Senate, with the exception of bills relating to finance. The Senate has the power to ratify treaties and to confirm presidential appointments to federal posts

sender ['sendə] *noun* remitente *mf*

senior ['siːnjə] *adjective* mayor *or* superior *or* más antiguo, -gua; **senior manager** *or* **senior executive** = gerente *mf or* director, -ra principal; **senior partner** = socio, -cia mayoritario, -ria *or* principal; **John Smith, Senior** = John Smith padre
◊ **seniority** [siːni'ɒrɪti] *noun* superioridad *f* en rango *or* edad; antigüedad *f*; **the managers were listed in order of seniority** = se hizo una lista de los directores por orden de antigüedad en la empresa *or* por orden de superioridad en el cargo desempeñado

sentence ['sentəns] **1** *noun* sentencia *f or* condena *f*; **death sentence** = condena a *or* sentencia de muerte; **extended sentence** = pena *f* ampliada; **maximum sentence** = pena máxima; **he received a three-year jail sentence** = le condenaron a tres años de prisión; **the two men accused of rape face sentences of up to six years in prison** = los dos hombres acusados de violación se enfrentan a condenas de hasta seis años de prisión; **to pass sentence on someone** = sentenciar *or* condenar a alguien *or* dictar sentencia *or* imponer una pena; **the jury returned a verdict of manslaughter and the judge will pass sentence next week** = el jurado emitió un veredicto de homicidio involuntario y el juez dictará sentencia la semana que viene; **to pronounce sentence** = decretar una pena; **concurrent sentence** = sentencia coincidente; **consecutive sentences** = sentencias sucesivas; **custodial sentence** = orden *f* de prisión; **death sentence** = sentencia *or* pena de muerte; **serving of sentence** = cumplimiento *m* de sentencia; **to carry out a sentence** = ejecutar una sentencia; **suspended sentence** = sentencia *f* condicional **2** *verb* sentenciar *or* condenarverb **the judge sentenced him to six months in prison** *or* **he was sentenced to six months' imprisonment** = el juez le condenó a seis meses de prisión *or* le condenaron a seis meses de arresto; **the accused was convicted of murder and will be sentenced next week** = el acusado fue declarado culpable de asesinato y será sentenciado la semana que viene; *compare* CONVICT

◊ **sentencer** ['sentənsə] *noun* juez, -za *or* persona que dicta sentencia

separate ['seprət] **1** *adjective* separado, -da *or* aparte; **to send something under separate cover** = mandar algo por separado **2** *verb* dividir *or* separar; **the personnel are separated into part-timers and full-time staff** = el personal se divide entre los que trabajan a tiempo parcial y los que lo hacen con dedicación exclusiva

◊ **separately** ['seprətli] *adverb* por separado *or* separadamente; **the two brothers were charged separately** = se cobró a los dos hermanos por separado

◊ **separation** [sepə'reɪʃn] *noun* **(a)** *(of marriage)* separación *f* matrimonial; **judicial** *or* **legal separation** = separación legal **(b)** US dimisión *f or* retiro *m or* despido *m* de un trabajo **(c)** *(keeping separate)* **separation of powers** = separación de poderes

> COMMENT: in the USA, the three parts of the power of the state are kept separate and independent: the President does not sit in Congress; Congress cannot influence the decisions of the Supreme Court, etc. In the UK, the powers are not separated, because Parliament has both legislative powers (it makes laws) and judicial powers (the House of Lords acts as a court of appeal); the government (the executive) is not independent and is responsible to Parliament which can outvote it and so cause a general election. In the USA, members of government are not members of Congress, though their appointment has to be approved by Senate; in the UK, members of government are usually Members of Parliament, although some are members of the House of Lords

seq [sek] *see* ET SEQ

sequester *or* **sequestrate** [sɪ'kwestə *or* 'si:kwəstreɪt] *verb* embargar *or* confiscar *or* secuestrar

◊ **sequestration** [si:kwə'streɪʃn] *noun* secuestro *m* embargo *m or* confiscación *f;* **his property has been kept under sequestration** = se le ha retenido la propiedad bajo orden de embargo

◊ **sequestrator** ['si:kwəstreɪtə] *noun* embargador, -ra

sergeant ['sɑ:dʒənt] *noun* **(police) sergeant** = sargento *mf* (de policía); US **Sergeant at Arms** = funcionario, -ria que mantiene el orden; *see* SERJEANT AT ARMS

seriatim [sɪəri'eɪtɪm] *Latin word* 'sucesivamente' *or* 'por separado'

serious ['sɪəriəs] *adjective* grave *or* serio, -ria; **he faces six serious charges** = se enfrenta a seis acusaciones graves *or* tiene que hacer frente a seis acusaciones graves; **she claims there has been a serious miscarriage of justice** = reclama que ha habido un grave error judicial

◊ **Serious Fraud Office (SFO)** ['sɪəriəs 'frɔ:d 'ɒfɪs] *noun* juzgado *m* especial de delitos monetarios *or* brigada *f* anti-fraude

◊ **seriousness** ['sɪəriəsnəs] *noun* gravedad *f or* seriedad *f;* **the length of the prison sentence depends on the seriousness of the crime** = la duración de la pena de prisión depende de la gravedad del delito; **the Police Commissioner asked for a report on the seriousness of the situation in the centre of town** = el jefe superior de Comisionado de la policía solicitó un informe sobre la gravedad de la situación en el centro de la ciudad

Serjeant ['sɑ:dʒənt] *see* COMMON SERJEANT

servant ['sə:vənt] *noun* **(a)** *(employee)* empleado, -da; **civil servant** = funcionario, -ria del estado; **master and servant** = patrono *m* y obrero *m;* **the law of master and servant** = ley *f* del patrono y del obrero *or* ley de empleo **(b)** *(worker in someone's house)* criado, -da *or* sirviente, -ta

serve [sə:v] *verb* **(a)** *(to spend time in prison)* **to serve a sentence** = cumplir una condena *or* una sentencia; **he served six months in a local jail** = cumplió seis meses en una prisión provincial; **she still has half her sentence to serve** = le queda todavía la mitad de la sentencia por cumplir **(b)** *(to do a type of work)* desempeñar un trabajo; **to serve articles** = trabajar como pasante *or* servir bajo contrato a un abogado para aprender derecho; **to serve a customer** = abastecer *or* atender a un cliente; **to serve in a shop** *or* **in a restaurant** = despachar en una tienda *or* servir mesas en un restaurante; **to serve on a jury** = prestar sevicio como jurado **(c) to serve a pleading** = presentar un alegato; **to serve proceedings** = iniciar acciones judiciales; **to serve a warrant** = ejecutar una orden de detención; **to serve someone with a writ** *or* **to serve a writ on someone** = entregar *or* notificar a alguien un mandamiento *or* una orden judicial

◊ **server** ['sə:və] *noun* **process-server** = notificador, -ra *or* persona que entrega la notificación

service ['sə:vɪs] *noun* **(a) service (of process)** *or* **personal service** = entrega *f* de una notificación en persona; **address for service** = dirección *f* oficial de un litigante *or* de un interesado en un proceso; **to acknowledge service** = acusar recibo de una entrega; **acknowledgement of service** = acuse *m* de recibo de entrega *or* acta *f* de reconocimiento de una entrega de notificación; *see also* SUBSTITUTED **(b)** *(duty to do work for someone)* servicio *m;* **contract of service** *or* **service contract** = contrato *m* de servicio; **community service order** = orden *f* de servicio a la comunidad; **jury service** = prestación *f* de servicio como jurado; **service charge** = *(by a landlord)* cuota *f* de servicios (en una comunidad de vecinos); *(in restaurant)* propina *f or* porcentaje *m* por el servicio **(c) civil service** = administración *f* pública *or* funcionariado *m*

servient tenement ['sə:viənt 'tenɪmənt] *noun* predio *m* sirviente

> COMMENT: the grantee of the easement is the 'dominant tenement'

servitude ['sə:vɪtjuːd] *noun* **penal servitude** = trabajos *mpl* forzados

session ['seʃn] *noun* **(a)** *(meeting)* sesión *f*; **full session** *or* **plenary session** = plenario, -ria; **the morning session** *or* **the afternoon session will be held in the conference room** = la sesión de la mañana *or* de la tarde tendrá lugar en la sala de conferencias; **opening session** *or* **closing session** = sesión de apertura *or* sesión de clausura; **closed session** = sesión a puerta cerrada **(b)** *(Parliament)* sesión parlamentaria; **the government is planning to introduce the Bill at the next session of Parliament** = el gobierno piensa introducir el proyecto de ley en la próxima sesión parlamentaria **(c)** *(in Scotland)* **Court of Session** = Tribunal Supremo de Escocia

◊ **sessions** ['seʃnz] *plural noun* juzgado *m or* tribunal *m;* **petty sessions** = tribunal de magistrados *or* jueces de paz encargados de causas menores; **special sessions** = tribunal de magistrados formado en un distrito para casos especiales

> COMMENT: the Parliamentary session starts in October with the Opening of Parliament and the Queen's Speech. It usually lasts until August. In the USA, a new congressional session starts on the 3rd of January each year

set [set] *verb* poner *or* establecer *or* fijar; **to set a date** = fijar una fecha; **to set free** = excarcelar; **to set a date for the trial** = señalar el día de la vista

◊ **set aside** ['set ə'saɪd] *verb* abandonar *or* anular *or* dejar de lado; **the arbitrator's award was set aside on appeal** = el fallo del árbitro fue anulado en la apelación

◊ **set down** ['set 'daʊn] *verb* **(a)** *(to record)* poner por escrito *or* registrar **(b)** *(to arrange for a trial to take place)* fijar (la fecha de un juicio); **pleadings must be submitted to the court when the action is set down for trial** = las alegaciones deben presentarse ante el tribunal cuando esté fijada la fecha del juicio

◊ **set forth** ['set 'fɔːθ] *verb* exponer por escrito; **the argument is set forth in the document from the European Court** = el argumento está expuesto en el documento del Tribunal Europeo

◊ **set-off** ['setɒf] *noun* derecho *m* del demandado a deducir cualquier reclamación contra el demandante

◊ **set out** ['set 'aʊt] *verb* **(a)** *(to put down in writing)* exponer (por escrito); **the claim is set out in the enclosed document** = la demanda está expuesta en el documento adjunto; **the figures are set out in the tables at the back of the book** = las cifras están expuestas en las tablas de la parte posterior del libro **(b)** *(to try to do something)* proponerse; **counsel for the prosecution has set out to discredit the defence witness** = la acusación se ha propuesto desacreditar al testigo de la defensa

◊ **set up** ['set 'ʌp] *verb* montar; **to set up house** = montar una casa; **to set up a stolen car business** = montar un negocio de coches robados

settle ['setl] *verb* **(a)** *(payment)* **to settle an account** = saldar *or* liquidar una cuenta; **to settle a claim** = pagar una reclamación; **the insurance company refused to settle his claim for storm damage** = la compañía aseguradora se negó a indemnizar los daños causados por el temporal; **to settle out of court** = llegar a un acuerdo extrajudicial; **the two parties settled out of court** = las dos partes llegaron a un acuerdo al margen de los tribunales *or* llegaron a un acuerdo amistoso **(b)** *(land)* **to settle property on someone** = asignar una propiedad en fideicomiso a futuros propietarios **(c)** *(to write out in final form)* transcribir *or* dar la forma final; **counsel is instructed to settle the defence** = el abogado tiene instrucciones de dar la forma final a la defensa

◊ **settled land** ['setld 'lænd] *noun* propiedad *f* objeto de fideicomiso

◊ **settlement** ['setlmənt] *noun* **(a)** *(payment of an account)* finiquito *m or* pago *m;* **settlement day** = día *m* de liquidación; **our basic discount is 20% but we offer an extra 5% for rapid settlement** = nuestro descuento normal es de un 20% pero ofrecemos un 5% más por pronto pago; **settlement in cash** *or* **cash settlement** = pago en efectivo; **settlement of a mortgage** = redención *f* de una hipoteca; **pay settlement** = acuerdo *m* salarial **(b)** *(agreement after an argument)* acuerdo *m or* acomodamiento *m or* acomodo *m or* arreglo *m or* componenda *f;* **amicable settlement** = acuerdo amistoso *or* transacción amistosa; **out-of-court settlement** = arreglo extrajudicial; **to effect a settlement between two parties** = llevar a un acuerdo a las dos partes; **to accept something in full settlement** = aceptar algo como pago íntegro **(c)** *(land, property)* **settlement of an estate** = disposición sucesoria (de fincas en fideicomiso mediante administradores o fiduciarios); **marriage settlement** = capitulaciones *fpl* matrimoniales **(d)** *(prison camp)* **convict settlement** = penal *m*

◊ **settle on** ['setl 'ɒn] *verb* legar *or* asignar; **he settled his property on his children** = legó sus bienes a sus hijos

◊ **settlor** ['setlə] *noun* fideicomitente *mf*

several ['sevrl] *adjective* **(a)** *(some)* varios, -rias *or* algunos, -nas; **several judges are retiring this year** = este año se retiran varios jueces **(b)** *(separate)* individual; **joint and several liability** = responsabilidad conjunta y solidaria
◊ **severally** ['sevrli] *adverb* separadamente *or* respectivamente *or* por separado; **they are jointly and severally liable** = son responsables solidariamente *or* en grupo y por separado *or* individualmente

severance ['svrəns] *noun* **(a)** *(of tenancy)* finalización *f* de un arrendamiento colectivo *or* coarriendo; *see* TENANCY **(b)** *(of employment)* finalización de un contrato de trabajo; **severance pay** = indemnización *f* por despido *or* cesantía *f*

severe [sə'viə] *adjective* severo, -ra *or* grave; **the judge passed severe sentences on the rapists** = el juez dictó severas condenas contra los violadores
◊ **severely** [sı'viəli] *adverb* severamente *or* con severidad *or* fuertemente *or* gravemente *or* de gravedad; **the police has asked for the gang to be treated severely** = la policía ha pedido que se trate a la banda con severidad; **he was severely wounded in the battle with the rebel army** = le hirieron gravemente en la batalla contra el ejército rebelde
◊ **severity** [sı'verəti] *noun* severidad *f or* gravedad *f;* **the law treats convicted rapists with great severity** = la ley trata a los culpables de violación con gran severidad; **the press commented on the severity of the sentences** = la prensa comentó la severidad de las penas

sexual ['sekʃuəl] *adjective* sexual; **sexual discrimination** *or* **sex discrimination** *or* **discrimination on grounds of sex** = discriminación *f* sexual; **sexual intercourse** = relaciones *fpl* sexuales; **it is an offence to have sexual intercourse with a girl under sixteen years of age** = es un delito tener relaciones sexuales con una chica menor de dieciséis años; **sexual offences** = delitos *mpl* contra la libertad sexual

SFO ['es 'ef'əu] = SERIOUS FRAUD OFFICE

shadow ['ʃædəu] *adjective* sombra *f;* **the Shadow Cabinet** = consejo *m* de gobierno en la sombra

shady ['ʃeidi] *adjective* turbio, -bia *or* dudoso, -sa *or* sospechoso, -sa; **shady deal** = negocio *m* sucio

sham [ʃæm] *adjective* falso, -sa *or* fingido, -da; **sham marriage** = matrimonio *m* de conveniencia

share [ʃeə] **1** *noun* **(a)** *(part of a company's capital)* acción *f;* **he bought a block of shares in Marks and Spencer** = compró una serie de acciones de Marks and Spencer; **shares fell on the London market** = las acciones bajaron en la bolsa londinense; **the company offered 1.8m shares on the market** = la empresa ofreció 1,8 millones de acciones en la bolsa; **'A' shares** = acciones de clase

A con derecho a voto limitado; **'B' shares** = acciones ordinarias con derechos especiales de voto (normalmente propiedad del fundador y su familia); **deferred shares** = capital *m* en acciones diferidas; **ordinary shares** = acciones ordinarias; **preference shares** = acciones preferentes; **share capital** = capital social *or* en acciones *or* accionario; **share certificate** = certificado *m or* título *m* de acciones; **share issue** = emisión *f* de acciones **(b)** *(portion)* participación *f;* **market share** *or* **share in the market** = cuota *f* de mercado *or* participación en el mercado; **share in the profits** = participación en los beneficios **2** *verb* **(a)** *(to own or use something with someone else)* compartir; **to share a telephone** = compartir un teléfono; **to share an office** = compartir una oficina **(b)** *(to divide among several people)* dividir *or* repartir; **three companies share the market** = el mercado está repartido entre tres empresas; **to share computer time** = compartir *or* dividir el tiempo que se utiliza el ordenador; **to share the profits among the senior executives** = dividir los beneficios entre los directivos; **to share information** *or* **to share data** = compartir información *or* datos
◊ **shareholder** ['ʃeəhəuldə] *noun* accionista *mf or* tenedor, -ra; **shareholders' equity** = capital *m* de los accionistas; **majority** *or* **minority shareholder** = accionista mayoritario *or* minoritario; **the solicitor acting on behalf of the minority shareholders** = el abogado que actúa en nombre de los accionistas minoritarios
◊ **shareholding** ['ʃeəhəuldıŋ] *noun* tenencia *f* de acciones; **a majority shareholding** *or* **a minority shareholding** = una tenencia de acciones mayoritaria *or* una tenencia de acciones minoritaria

sharp [ʃɑːp] *adjective* **(a)** *(sudden)* fuerte *or* repentino, -na *or* rápido, -da *or* brusco, -ca *or* acusado, -da; **sharp rise in crimes of violence** = aumento brusco de delitos violentos; **sharp drop in prices** = baja repentina de precios *or* caída acusada de los precios **(b)** *(not honest)* **sharp practice** = negocio *m* deshonesto (pero no ilegal) *or* mañas *fpl or* chanchullo *m*
◊ **sharper** *noun* **card sharper** = estafador, -ra *or* fullero, -ra
◊ **sharply** ['ʃɑːpli] *adverb* bruscamente *or* repentinamente *or* fuertemente; **the number of mugging cases has risen sharply over the last few years** = el número de atracos ha aumentado bruscamente durante los últimos años

sheet [ʃiːt] *noun* hoja *f;* **fact sheet** = hoja de datos

shelter ['ʃeltə] **1** *noun* cobijo *m or* albergue *m or* refugio *m* **2** *verb* cobijar *or* albergar *or* dar cobijo *or* refugiarse

shelve [ʃelv] *verb* dar carpetazo

sheriff ['ʃerıf] *noun* **(a)** *US* 'sheriff' *mf or* jefe, -fa de la policía del condado **(b)** *GB* **(High) Sheriff** = funcionario nombrado como representante del gobierno en un condado, responsable de llevar a cabo decisiones judiciales tales como el envío de alguaciles para embargar bienes y que a su vez actúa de escrutador en elecciones parlamentarias **(c)** *(in Scotland)* juez presidente del tribunal de un condado; **Sheriff Court** = tribunal *m* presidido por un 'sheriff'

shield [ʃiːld] *noun* **tax shield** = amparo *m* fiscal

ship [ʃip] **1** *noun* barco *m or* buque *m; to jump ship* = desertar del barco en el que se está enrolado **2** *verb* expedir *or* enviar (no necesariamente por barco); **to ship goods to the USA** = enviar mercancía a los EE UU; **we ship all our goods by rail** = enviamos toda la mercancía por ferrocarril; **the consignment of cars was shipped abroad last week** = la expedición de coches fue enviada al extranjero la semana pasada
◊ **shipment** [ˈʃipmənt] *noun* envío *m or* carga *f;* **consolidated shipment** = envío agrupado de mercancías (procedentes de diferentes empresas); **drop shipment** = entrega *f* directa de un pedido a tienda *or* a almacén sin intermediarios
◊ **shipper** [ˈʃipə] *noun* expedidor, -ra *or* transportista *mf or* remitente *mf*
◊ **shipping** [ˈʃipiŋ] *noun* envío *m or* transporte *m or* expedición *f;* **shipping agent** = agente *mf or* agencia *f* de transporte; **shipping company** *or* **shipping line** = compañía *f* naviera *or* línea *f* marítima; **shipping instructions** = instrucciones *fpl* de embarque *or* de envío; **shipping note** = nota *f* de envío
◊ **shipwreck** [ˈʃiprek] *noun* naufragio *m*

shire [ˈʃaɪə] *noun (formerly)* **the shires** = condados *mpl* rurales de Inglaterra

shoot [ʃuːt] *verb* **(a)** *(weapon)* disparar *or* fusilar **(b)** *(drugs)* picarse *or* pincharse

shop [ʃop] **1** *noun* **(a)** *(place where goods are sold)* tienda *f;* **a bookshop** = una librería; **a computer shop** = una tienda de informática; **an electrical goods shop** = una tienda de artículos de electricidad; **he has bought a shoe shop in the centre of town** = ha comprado una zapatería en el centro de la ciudad; **she opened a women's wear shop** = abrió una tienda de moda femenina; **all the shops in the centre of town close on Sundays** = todas las tiendas del centro de la ciudad cierran los domingos; **bucket shop** = agencia *f* paralela; **retail shop** = tienda al por menor **(b)** *(workshop)* taller *m or* fábrica *f;* **machine shop** = taller mecánico; **repair shop** = taller de reparaciones **(c)** **closed shop** *or* US **union shop** = sistema *m* de contratación exclusiva de trabajadores sindicados **2** *verb* **(a) to shop (for) something** = ir a buscar *or* ir a comprar algo **(b)** *(to give information to the police)* denunciar *or* delatar *or* cantar; **he was shopped to the police by the leader of the other gang** = fue denunciado a la policía por el cabecilla de la otra banda (NOTE: **shopping - shopped**)

◊ **shoplifter** [ˈʃopliftə] *noun* ladrón, -ona que roba en las tiendas *or* ratero, -ra de tiendas *or* mechera *mf*
◊ **shoplifting** [ˈʃopliftiŋ] *noun* hurto *m or* robo *m* en las tiendas
◊ **shop steward** [ˈʃop ˈstjuːəd] *noun* enlace *mf* sindical

Short Cause List [ˈʃoːt ˈkoːz ˈlist] *noun* número de casos cuya vista en el *Queen's Bench Division* se prevé de corta duración

shorthand [ˈʃoːthænd] *noun* taquigrafía *f;* **the court proceedings were taken down in shorthand** = se tomó nota taquigráficamente de las actas del tribunal; **the reporters could take notes in shorthand** = los periodistas sabían escribir en taquigrafía; **shorthand writer** = taquígrafo, -fa

shorthold tenancy [ˈʃoːthəuld ˈtenənsi] *noun* arrendamiento *m* protegido por un tiempo limitado de menos de cinco años

short sharp shock [ˈʃoːt ˈʃɑːp ˈʃok] *noun* tipo de tratamiento aplicado a delincuentes juveniles consistente en someterlos durante un breve periodo de tiempo a una severa disciplina en un centro de detención de menores

short title [ˈʃoːt ˈtaitl] *noun* título *m* abreviado de una ley

show [ʃəu] **1** *noun* **(a)** *(exhibition)* exposición *f or* feria *f;* **motor show** = salón *m* del automóvil; **computer show** = salón de la informática **(b)** *(casting votes)* **show of hands** = votación *f* a mano alzada; **the motion was carried on a show of hands** = la moción se aprobó a mano alzada **2** *verb* enseñar *or* mostrar *or* indicar; **to show a gain** *or* **a fall** = indicar un aumento *or* un descenso; **to show a profit** *or* **a loss** = mostrar un beneficio *or* una pérdida; **to show cause** = presentar motivos justificantes de que un decreto condicional no debe hacerse definitivo; **to show preference** = decantarse
◊ **show up** [ˈʃəu ˈʌp] *verb* aparecer

SI [ˈes ˈai] = STATUTORY INSTRUMENT

sic [sik] *noun* sic; **the letter stated : 'my legal adviser intends to apply for attack (sic) of earnings'** = la carta decía : 'mi asesor jurídico tiene la intención de solicitar incautación (sic) de salarios'

sick [sik] *noun* enfermo, -ma; **sick leave** = permiso *m or* baja *f* por enfermedad
◊ **sickness** [ˈsiknəs] *noun* enfermedad *f*

sign [sain] **1** *noun* letrero *m or* señal *f or* rótulo *m* **2** *verb* firmar; **to sign a letter** *or* **a contract** *or* **a document** *or* **a cheque** = firmar una carta *or* un contrato *or* un documento *or* un cheque; **the letter is signed by the managing director** = la carta está firmada por el director gerente; **the cheque is not valid if it has not been signed by the finance**

director = el cheque carece de validez si no está firmado por el director financiero

◊ **signatory** ['sɪgnətri] *noun* signatario, -ria *or* firmante *mf;* **you have to get the permission of all the signatories to the agreement if you want to change the terms** = si desea cambiar los términos del acuerdo tiene que conseguir el permiso de todos los firmantes

◊ **signature** ['sɪgnətʃə] *noun* firma *f;* **the contract has been engrossed ready for signature** = se ha pasado a limpio el contrato listo para la firma; **a pile of letters waiting for the managing director's signature** = un montón de cartas a la espera de la firma del director gerente; **a will needs the signature of the testator and two witnesses** = un testamento necesita la firma del testador y dos testigos; **all the company's cheques need two signatures** = todos los cheques de la empresa necesitan dos firmas

silence ['saɪləns] *noun* silencio *m;* **the accused maintained silence throughout the trial** = el acusado se mantuvo en silencio durante todo el juicio; **right of silence** = derecho *m* a guardar silencio *or* a no prestar declaración

silk [sɪlk] *noun* **(a) to take silk** = tomar la toga *or* hacerse abogado, -da **(b)** *(informal)* **a silk** = abogado elevado a la categoría de Queen's Counsel

similiter [sɪ'mɪlɪtə] *Latin word* 'de un modo similar'

simple ['sɪmpl] *adjective* sencillo, -lla *or* simple; **the case appears to be a simple one** = el caso parece sencillo; **it was a simple misunderstanding of the government regulations** = fue una simple malinterpretación de las normas gubernamentales; **simple interest** = interés *m* simple; **simple contract** = contrato *m* simple *or* verbal; *see also* FEE

sincerely [sɪn'sɪəli] *adverb (on letters)* **yours sincerely** *or US* **sincerely yours** = le saluda atentamente

sine die ['saɪni: 'di:eɪ] *Latin phrase* 'sin día' *or* aplazar indefinidamente; **the hearing was adjourned sine die** = la vista se pospuso sine die

sine qua non ['sɪni kwa: 'nɒn] *Latin phrase* 'sin lo que nada': requisito indispensable; **agreement by the management is a sine qua non of all employment contracts** = el acuerdo por parte de la dirección es un requisito indispensable de todos los contratos de trabajo

single ['sɪŋgl] *adjective* **(a)** *(only one)* único, -ca; **single currency** = moneda única; **Single European Act** = Acta Unica Europea; **Single European Market** = Mercado Unico Europeo **(b)** *(not married)* soltero, -ra

◊ **single chamber** ['sɪŋgl 'tʃeɪmbə] **1** *adjective* unicameral **2** *noun* cámara *f* única

sit [sɪt] *verb* **(a)** *(to meet)* reunirse *or* celebrar sesión; **the court sat from eleven to five o'clock** = el tribunal estuvo reunido desde las once hasta las cinco **(b) to sit on the bench** = ser magistrado *or* juez

◊ **sitting** ['sɪtɪŋ] *noun* **(a)** *(meeting)* sesión *f* **(b)** *(periods when courts sit)* **sittings** = sesiones *fpl* (jurídicas) *or GB* periodo *m* de sesiones en el que se reúnen los tribunales *or* el parlamento

COMMENT: a Parliamentary sitting usually starts at 2.30 p.m. (11 a.m. on Fridays) and lasts until about midnight. All-night sittings happen occasionally, usually when Parliament is discussing very important or controversial matters. There are four sittings in the legal year: **Michaelmas, Hilary, Easter** and **Trinity**

site [saɪt] *noun* sitio *m or* lugar *m or* local *m or* escenario *m;* **the judge and jury visited the site of the crime** = el juez y el jurado visitaron el lugar del crimen; **the planning application includes a photograph of the site** = la solicitud de planificación incluye una fotografía del lugar

situation [sɪtju'eɪʃn] *noun* **(a)** *(state of affairs)* situación *f or* estado *m;* **financial situation of a company** = la situación financiera de una empresa; **the general situation of the economy** = el estado general de la economía **(b)** *(job)* empleo *m or* trabajo *m or* colocación *f;* **situations vacant** = ofertas *fpl* de trabajo; **situations wanted** = solicitudes *fpl* de trabajo **(c)** *(place where something is)* localización *f or* situación *f or* ubicación *f;* **the factory is in a very pleasant situation by the sea** = la fábrica tiene una situación muy agradable al lado del mar

◊ **situate** *or* **situated** ['sɪtʃueɪt] *adjective* situado, -da; **a freehold property situate in the borough of Richmond** = una propiedad (absoluta) situada en el distrito de Richmond

skilful ['skɪlful] *adjective* hábil

slander ['slɑːndə] **1** *noun* difamación *f or* calumnia *f* oral *or* acusación *f* falsa; **action for slander** *or* **slander action** = demanda *f* por difamación **2** *verb* calumniar *or* difamar; **to slander someone** = difamar; *compare* LIBEL

◊ **slanderer** ['slɑːndrə] *noun* calumniador, -ra

◊ **slanderous** ['slɑːndrəs] *adjective* difamatorio, -ria; **he made slanderous statements about the Prime Minister on television** = hizo declaraciones difamatorias sobre el Primer Ministro por televisión

slaughter ['slɔːtə] *noun* matanza *f or* carnicería *f or* mortandad *f*

sleeping partner ['sliːpɪŋ 'pɑːtnə] *noun* socio, -cia comanditario, -ria

slip [slɪp] *noun* **(a)** *(small piece of paper)* nota *f or* ficha *f* (en especial nota de los detalles de una póliza marítima de seguros) *or* recibo *m or* resguardo *m;* **compliments slip** = saluda *m* **(b)** *(mistake)* error *m* *or* desliz *m; ***slip of the tongue** = lapsus *m* linguae; **he made a couple of slips in calculating the discount** = cometió un par de errores al calcular el descuento; **slip rule** = reglamento *m* del Tribunal Supremo que permite la corrección de errores en alegaciones

◊ **slip up** [ˈslɪp ˈʌp] *verb* cometer un error *or* equivocarse; **we slipped up badly in not signing the agreement with the Chinese company** = cometimos un grave error al no firmar el acuerdo con la compañía china

◊ **slip-up** [ˈslɪpʌp] *noun* error

small [smɔːl] *adjective* pequeño, -ña; **small ads** = anuncios *mpl* por palabras; **small claim** = demanda *f* por un valor inferior a 500 libras en un juzgado municipal; **small claims court** = tribunal *m* de instancia (que se ocupa de demandas de menor cuantía)

◊ **small-scale** [ˈsmɔːlˈskeɪl] *adjective* a pequeña escala

smuggle [ˈsmʌgl] *verb* pasar *or* hacer contrabando; **to smuggle in** = introducir mercancías de contrabando; **they had to smuggle the spare parts into the country** = tuvieron que pasar las piezas de recambio de contrabando

◊ **smuggled** [ˈsmʌgld] *adjective;* **smuggled goods** = alijo *m;* **consignment of smuggled arms** = alijo de armas

◊ **smuggler** [ˈsmʌglə] *noun* contrabandista *mf*

◊ **smuggling** [ˈsmʌglɪŋ] *noun* contrabando *m;* **he made his money in arms smuggling** = hizo su fortuna con el contrabando de armas

snatch [snætʃ] *verb* arrebatar

social [ˈsəuʃl] *adjective* social; **social health worker** = ayudante técnico sanitario (ATS); **social outcast** = marginado, -da social; **social security** = seguridad *f* social; **social services** = servicios *mpl* sociales; **social worker** = asistente, -ta social

sodomy [ˈsɒdəmi] = BUGGERY

soft [sɒft] *adjective* blando, -da *or* flojo, -ja; **soft currency** = moneda *f* blanda *or* débil *or* no convertible; **soft loan** = préstamo *m* sin interés *or* crédito en condiciones muy favorables

sole [səul] *adjective* único, -ca *or* exclusivo, -va; **sole owner** *or* **sole proprietor** = propietario único *or* único dueño; **sole trader** = comerciante *mf* exclusivo; *see also* FEME

solemn [ˈsɒləm] *adjective* solemne; **solemn and binding agreement** = acuerdo *m* solemne y obligatorio

solicit [səˈlɪsɪt] *verb* **(a)** *(goods)* pedir *or* solicitar; **to solicit orders** = solicitar pedidos *or* ofrecer servicios **(b)** *(prostitution)* abordar *or* importunar *or* ofrecerse a realizar el acto sexual a cambio de dinero

◊ **soliciting** [səˈlɪsɪtɪŋ] *noun* abordamiento *m or* abordaje *m or* delito *m* de ofrecerse a realizar el acto sexual a cambio de dinero

◊ **solicitor** [səˈlɪsɪtə] *noun (in England and Wales)* abogado, -da (que acumula las funciones de procurador, notario, asesor y, en algunos casos, de abogado defensor); **to instruct a solicitor** = contratar *or* dar instrucciones a un abogado; **duty solicitor** = abogado, -da de guardia *or* de servicio; **the Official Solicitor** = abogado, -da que actúa en el Tribunal Supremo en representación de personas que se encuentran incapacitadas oficialmente; **the Treasury Solicitor** = Procurador General de su Majestad; *see* BARRISTER

◊ **Solicitor-General** [səˈlɪsɪtəˈdʒenrl] *noun* procurador general *or* de la Corona; **Solicitor-General for Scotland** = (en Escocia) subfiscal jefe

solitary confinement [ˈsɒlɪtri kənˈfaɪnmənt] *noun* incomunicación *f;* **he was kept in solitary confinement for six months** = le mantuvieron incomunicado durante seis meses

solus agreement [ˈsəuləs əˈgriːmənt] *noun* acuerdo *m* en el que una de las partes está unida únicamente a la otra parte, especialmente un acuerdo en el que un minorista compra toda la mercancía a un único proveedor

solution [səˈluːʃn] *noun* solución *f;* **a compromise solution was reached after some discussion** = después de una larga discusión, se llegó a una solución que beneficiaba a todos

solve [sɒlv] *verb* resolver *or* solucionar; **to solve a crime** = resolver un crimen; **to solve a problem** = solucionar un problema; **the loan will solve some of our short-term problems** = el préstamo solucionará algunos de nuestros problemas a corto plazo

solvent [ˈsɒlvənt] **1** *adjective* solvente; **when he bought the company it was barely solvent** = la empresa apenas era solvente cuando la compró **2** *noun* disolvente *m or* solvente *m;* **solvent abuse** = inhalación *f* de disolventes

◊ **solvency** [ˈsɒlvənsi] *noun* solvencia *f*

sought [sɔːt] *see* SEEK

sound [saund] *adjective* razonable *or* prudente *or* sólido, -da *or* seguro, -ra *or* cabal; **the company's financial situation is very sound** = la situación financiera de la empresa es muy sólida; **the solicitor gave us some very sound advice** = el abogado nos dio muy buenos consejos; **the evidence brought forward by the police is not very sound** = las pruebas presentadas por la policía no son muy seguras; **of sound mind** = en su sano juicio; **he was of sound mind when he wrote the will** = se encontraba en su sano juicio cuando escribió el testamento

◊ **soundness** [ˈsaundnəs] *noun* sensatez *f*

soundbite ['saʊndbaɪt] *noun (short phrase used by politicians in the media)* **she is a master of the soundbite** = es una experta en el uso de los titulares

source ['sɔːs] *noun* fuente *f or* origen *m;* **source of income** = fuente de ingresos; **you must declare income from all sources to the Inland Revenue** = se tienen que declarar todas las fuentes de ingresos al fisco; **income which is taxed at source** = ingresos *mpl* sujetos a retención en el origen

South-Eastern Circuit ['saʊθ'iːstən 'sɜːkɪt] *noun* distrito *m or* jurisdicción *f* del sudeste *or* uno de los seis distritos *or* jurisdicciones del Tribunal de lo Penal al que pertenecen los abogados, con sede en Londres

sovereign ['sɒvrɪn] *noun* soberano, -na
◊ **sovereign state** ['sɒvrɪn 'steɪt] *noun* estado *m* soberano
◊ **sovereignty** ['sɒvrɪnti] *noun* soberanía *f;* **to have sovereignty over a territory** = tener soberanía sobre un territorio

Speaker ['spiːkə] *noun (in Parliament)* presidente *m* (NOTE: *MPs address the Speaker as* **Mr Speaker** *or* **Madam Speaker**)

COMMENT: in the House of Commons, the speaker is an ordinary Member of Parliament chosen by the other members; the equivalent in the House of Lords is the Lord Chancellor. In the US Congress, the speaker of the House of Representatives is an ordinary congressman, elected by the other congressmen; the person presiding over meetings of the Senate is the Vice-President

special ['speʃl] *adjective* especial; **he offered us special terms** = nos ofreció condiciones especiales; **the car is being offered at a special price** = el coche se ofrece a un precio especial; **special agent** = representante *mf* especial; *(for a government)* agente *mf* secreto; **special constable** = guardia *mf* auxiliar; **special damages** = daños *mpl* indirectos; **special deposits** = depósitos *mpl* especiales; **special procedure** = procedimiento *m* especial utilizado en casos de divorcio por el que las partes interesadas pueden obtenerlo sin necesidad de juicio; **special resolution** = resolución *f* especial; **special sessions** = sesiones *fpl* especiales
◊ **specialism** ['speʃlɪzm] *noun* especialidad *f*
◊ **specialist** ['speʃlɪst] *noun* especialista *mf;* **you should go to a specialist in divorce cases** *or* **to a divorce specialist for advice** = deberías consultar a un especialista en casos de divorcio *or* en divorcios
◊ **speciality** [speʃi'ælɪti] *noun* especialidad *f*
◊ **specialize** ['speʃlaɪz] *verb* especializarse; **to specialize in something** = especializarse en algo; **this firm of solicitors specializes in divorce cases** = esta firma de abogados está especializada en casos de divorcio; **a QC who specializes in international contract cases** = un abogado especializado en casos de contratos internacionales

◊ **specialty contract** ['speʃlti 'kɒntrækt] *noun* contrato *m* formal

specific [spə'sɪfɪk] *adjective* específico, -ca; **specific performance** = ejecución *f* de un contrato según sus términos
◊ **specifically** [spə'sɪfɪkli] *adverb* específicamente *or* explícitamente; **the contract specifically excludes the USA** = el contrato excluye explícitamente a los Estados Unidos; **he drafted the will specifically to benefit his grandchildren** = redactó el testamento específicamente en beneficio de sus nietos

specify ['spesɪfaɪ] *verb* especificar *or* precisar *or* indicar; **to specify full details of the grounds for complaint** = especificar con detalle los motivos de una reclamación; **the contract specifies that the goods have to be delivered to London** = el contrato especifica que la mercancía debe ser entregada en Londres
◊ **specification** [spesɪfɪ'keɪʃn] *noun* descripción *f* detallada *or* especificación *f* *or* pliego *m* de condiciones; **patent specification** = descripción de una patente

specimen ['spesɪmən] *noun* muestra *f or* modelo *m or* espécimen *m;* **to give specimen signatures on a bank mandate** = dar espécimen de firmas de una orden bancaria

speculation [spekju'leɪʃn] *noun* agio *m*

speculator ['spekjuleɪtə] *noun* agiotista *mf*

speech [spiːtʃ] *noun* **(a)** *(ability to speak)* habla *f or* palabra *f;* **freedom of speech** = libertad *f* de expresión **(b)** *(talk in public)* conferencia *f or* discurso *m;* **opening speech** = discurso inaugural; **to make a speech in Parliament** = pronunciar un discurso en el parlamento; **counsel's closing speech to the jury** = conclusiones *fpl* finales; *GB* **Queen's Speech** = discurso de apertura del parlamento pronunciado por la Reina

speed [spiːd] *verb* **speed up** = acelerar
◊ **speeding** ['spiːdɪŋ] *noun* exceso *m* de velocidad

spend [spend] *verb* **(a)** *(money)* gastar (dinero); **they spent all their savings on buying the shop** = se gastaron todos sus ahorros en la compra de la tienda; **the company spends thousands of pounds on research** = la empresa se gasta miles de libras en investigación **(b)** *(time)* pasar *or* dedicar *or* emplear tiempo; **the tribunal spent weeks on hearing evidence** = el tribunal empleó semanas en tomar declaraciones; **the chairman spent yesterday afternoon with the auditors** = el presidente se pasó la tarde de ayer con los auditores; **spent conviction** = condena *f* anterior (NOTE: **spending - spent - has spent**)

sphere of influence [sfɪə əv 'ɪnfluəns] *noun* esfera *f* de influencia; **some Latin American states**

fall within the USA's sphere of influence = algunos países latinoamericanos caen bajo la esfera de influencia de los EEUU

spin doctor ['spɪn 'dɒktə] *noun (media)* asesor de imagen vinculado a un partido político; **government spin doctors have been having some difficulty in dealing with the news items about the minister's family** = los asesores de imagen del gobierno no han sabido cómo reaccionar ante las noticias sobre la familia del ministro

spinster ['spɪnstə] *noun* mujer *f* soltera *or* solterona *f*

spiritual ['spɪrɪtʃuəl] *adjective;* **Lords Spiritual** = arzobispos y obispos anglicanos de la Cámara de los Lores

split [splɪt] *verb* partir; **his skull was split open** = le partieron el cráneo

spoil [spɔɪl] *verb* estropear *or* deteriorar *or* echar a perder; **half the shipment was spoiled by water** = la mitad del cargamento quedó deteriorada a causa del agua; **the company's results were spoiled by the last quarter** = los resultados de la empresa se echaron a perder por el último trimestre; **spoilt ballot paper** = voto *m* nulo *or* invalidado (NOTE: **spoiling - spoiled** *or* **spoilt**)
◊ **spoils of war** ['spɔɪlz əv 'wɑː] *plural noun* botín *m* de guerra

spokesman ['spəʊksmən] *noun* portavoz *m;* **a White House spokesman denied the news report** = un portavoz de la Casa Blanca negó la noticia; **a government spokesman in the House of Lords revealed that discussions had been concluded on the treaty** = un portavoz del gobierno en la Cámara de los Lores reveló que había concluido el debate sobre el tratado

spokesperson ['spəʊkspɜːsən] *noun* portavoz *mf*

spokeswoman ['spəʊkswʊmən] *noun* portavoz *f*

sponsor ['spɒnsə] **1** *noun* **(a)** *(which sponsors an MP)* patrocinador, -ra *or* padrino *m or* madrina *f* **(b)** *(MP who proposes a Bill in the House of Commons)* proponente *mf* **2** *verb* **(a)** **to sponsor an MP** = patrocinar **(b)** *(to propose a Bill in the House of Commons)* proponer
◊ **sponsorship** [s'pɒnsəʃɪp] *noun* patrocinio *m;* **sponsorship of two MPs cost the union several thousand pounds** = el sindicato pagó varias miles de libras por el patrocinio de dos diputados

spouse [spaʊz] *noun* esposo, -sa *or* cónyuge *mf or* consorte *mf*

spy [spaɪ] **1** *noun* espía *mf;* **he spent many years as a spy for the enemy** = trabajó muchos años de espía para el enemigo; **he was arrested as a spy** = le arrestaron acusado de espionaje **2** *verb* trabajar de espía; **she was accused of spying for the enemy** = le acusaron de trabajar de espía para el enemigo

squad [kwɒd] *noun* **(a)** *(police)* brigada *f* especial; **the Fraud Squad** = la brigada contra el fraude *or* contra la estafa *or* brigada anticorrupción; **flying squad** = brigada móvil; **the Homicide Squad** *or* **Murder Squad** = la brigada de homicidios **(b)** *(soldiers)* pelotón *m;* **firing squad** = pelotón de ejecución
◊ **squad car** ['skwɒd 'kɑː] *noun* coche *m* patrulla

squat [skwɒt] *verb* ocupar ilegalmente una vivienda *or* okupar (NOTE: **squatting - squatted**)
◊ **squatter** ['skwɒtə] *noun* ocupa *mf or* okupa *mf or* persona que ocupa ilegalmente una vivienda; **squatter's rights** = derecho *m* de la persona que ocupa ilegalmente una vivienda a permanecer en ella hasta que se le ordene judicialmente desalojarla
◊ **squatting** ['skwɒtɪŋ] *noun* ocupación *f* ilegal de un edificio

squeal [skwiːl] *verb (slang)* denunciar *or* delatar

squire ['skwaɪə] *noun US* funcionario jurídico municipal como, por ejemplo, un magistrado

staff [stɑːf] *noun* personal *m;* **member of staff** = empleado, -da; **to be on the staff** = pertenecer a la plantilla

stakeholder ['steɪkhəʊldə] *noun* tenedor, -ra de apuestas

stamp [stæmp] **1** *noun* **(a)** *(device for making marks on documents)* sello *m or* tampón *m or* estampilla *f or* cuño *m;* **the invoice has the stamp 'Received with thanks' on it** = la factura tiene el sello del recibí; **the customs officer looked at the stamps in his passport** = el oficial de aduanas le miró los sellos del pasaporte; **date stamp** = fechador *m;* **rubber stamp** = tampón *or* sello de goma **(b)** *(postage)* **a (postage) stamp** = un sello de correos; **a £1 stamp** = un sello de 1 libra **(c)** **stamp duty** = impuesto *m* del timbre **2** *verb* **(a)** *(to put a mark on)* sellar; **to stamp an invoice 'Paid'** = ponerle a una factura el sello de 'pagado' *or* 'recibí'; **the documents were stamped by the customs officials** = los funcionarios de aduana sellaron los documentos **(b)** *(postage)* poner sellos *or* franquear; **stamped addressed envelope (s.a.e.)** = sobre *m* con dirección y franqueo

stand [stænd] **1** *noun* **(a)** *(active campaign against something)* postura *f;* **the government's stand against racial prejudice** = la postura del gobierno contra el perjuicio racial; **the police chief criticized the council's stand on law and order** = el jefe de policía criticó al consejo por su postura en cuanto al orden público **(b)** *(position of a member of Congress on a question)* posición *f* **(c)** *(at a trial)* banquillo *m;* **witness stand** = estrado *m;* **to take the stand** = dirigirse al banquillo *or* al estrado **2** *verb* **(a)** *(in an election)* presentarse como candidato; **he stood as a Liberal candidate in the**

General Election = se presentó como candidato del partido liberal en las elecciones generales; **she was persuaded to stand for parliament** = la persuadieron para que se presentara como candidata al parlamento; **he has stood for office several times, but has never been elected** = ha presentado su canditatura varias veces pero nunca ha sido elegido **(b)** *(to exist or to be in a state)* permanecer *or* seguir vigente; **to stand mute** = permanecer callado *or* en silencio; **the report stood referred to the Finance Committee** = se remitió el informe a la comisión de finanzas NOTE: **stands - stood (c) to stand trial** = someterse a juicio; **to stand by someone** = apoyar (a alguien); **the House stands adjourned** = se levanta la sesión

◊ **stand down** ['stænd 'daʊn] *verb* retirarse; **the wife of one of the candidates is ill and he has stood down** = la mujer de uno de los candidatos está enferma y él se ha retirado

◊ **stand in for** ['stænd 'ɪn fə] *verb* sustituir; **Mr Smith is standing in for the chairman who is away on holiday** = el Sr. Smith sustituye al presidente que se encuentra de vacaciones

◊ **stand over** ['stænd 'əʊvə] *verb* posponer; **the case has been stood over to next month** = el caso se ha pospuesto hasta el mes próximo

◊ **stand up** ['stænd 'ʌp] *verb* ponerse en *or* de pie

standard ['stændəd] **1** *noun* patrón *m or* modelo *m or* norma *f or* nivel *m;* **standard of living** *or* **living standards** = nivel de vida; **production standards** = normas de producción; **up to standard** = que satisface los requisitos *or* conforme a la norma; **gold standard** = patrón oro **2** *adjective* normal *or* corriente *or* general *or* estándar; **the standard charge for consultation is £50** = el precio normal por consulta es de 50 libras; **we have a standard charge of £25 for a thirty minute session** = tenemos un precio general de 25 libras por cada sesión de treinta minutos; **standard agreement** *or* **standard contract** = contrato-tipo *m;* **standard form contract** = contrato-tipo formal *or* contrato de adhesión; **standard letter** = carta *f* tipo *or* estándar; **standard rate** = tipo *m* de interés vigente *or* tasa *f* de impuesto normal

standi ['stændaɪ] *see* LOCUS

standing ['stændɪŋ] **1** *adjective* **(a)** *(permanent)* permanente; **standing committee** = comisión *f* permanente; *(Parliament)* comisión parlamentaria permanente; *see also* AD HOC **(b) long-standing customer** *or* **customer of long standing** = cliente *mf* de toda la vida **2** *noun* reputación *f or* situación *f;* **the financial standing of a company** = la situación financiera de una empresa; **company of good standing** = empresa de muy buena reputación

◊ **standing order** ['stændɪŋ 'ɔːdə] *noun* **(a)** *(bank account)* domiciliación *f* bancaria; **I pay my subscription by standing order** = pago mi suscripción por domiciliación bancaria *or* a través

del banco; *compare* DIRECT DEBIT **(b)** *(rules)* **standing orders** = reglamento *m*

Star Chamber ['stɑː 'tʃeɪmbə] *noun* **(a)** *(formerly)* antiguo tribunal *m* inglés de Inquisición **(b)** *(recently)* comisión *f* delegada del Consejo de Ministros que estudia las propuestas de gasto de los diferentes departamentos gubernamentales

stare decisis ['stɑːreɪ dɪ'saɪsɪs] *Latin phrase* decisiones *fpl* precedentes *or* 'a lo decidido'

start [stɑːt] *verb* empezar; **to start disciplinary proceedings** = abrir un expediente

state [steɪt] **1** *noun* **(a)** *(country or part of federation)* estado *m;* **to turn state's evidence** = delatar a un cómplice (con la esperanza de ver rebajada la condena propia); *see also* SECRETARY OF STATE **(b)** *(government of a country)* gobierno *m or* estado *m;* **offence against the state** = delito *m* contra el estado; **state enterprise** = empresa *f* estatal; **the bosses of state industries are appointed by the government** = los directores de industrias estatales son nombrados por el gobierno *or* los puestos de directores de industrias estatales son de libre designación; **state ownership** = propiedad *f* pública **(c) state of emergency** = estado de emergencia; **state of mind** = estado de ánimo **2** *verb* declarar *or* afirmar; **the document states that all revenue has to be declared to the tax office** = el documento indica que todo ingreso tiene que ser declarado al fisco; **case stated** = hechos *mpl* probados

◊ **state-controlled** [steɪtkən'trəʊld] *adjective* sujeto, -ta a control estatal; **state-controlled television** = televisión estatal *or* sujeta a control estatal

◊ **State Department** ['steɪt dɪ'pɑːtmənt] *noun* ministerio *m* estadounidense de Asuntos Exteriores; *see note at* FOREIGN

◊ **stateless person** ['steɪtləs 'pɜːsən] *noun* apátrida *mf or* sin patria

◊ **state-owned** ['steɪt'əʊnd] *adjective* estatal *or* de propiedad pública

statement ['steɪtmənt] *noun* **(a)** *(saying something clearly)* declaración *f or* afirmación *f;* **to make a statement** = deponer *or* hacer una declaración a la prensa *or* a la policía; **false statement** = aseveración *f or* declaración falsa; **to make a false statement** = hacer una declaración falsa; **taking of statement** = toma *f* de declaración; **opening statement** = declaración inaugural; **statement of claim** = exposición *f* de la demanda *or* alegato *m* que contiene los detalles del caso de un demandante y el desagravio buscado contra el acusado; **statement in support of a criminal act** = apología *f* del delito; **sworn statement** = juramento *m* asertorio *or* atestado *m;* **Statement of Means** = declaración de haberes presentada junto a la solicitud de asistencia jurídica gratuita **(b) bank statement** = extracto *m* de cuenta; **monthly** *or*

quarterly statement = balance *m* bancario mensual *or* trimestral **(c)** *(balance)* **financial statement** = balance general; **statement of affairs** = balance de liquidación; **profit and loss statement** = balance de resultados; **the accounts department have prepared a financial statement for the shareholders** = el departamento de cuentas ha preparado un balance general para los accionistas **(d)** *(from supplier to customer)* **statement of account** = estado *m* de cuenta

statesman ['steɪtsmən] *noun* estadista *m or* hombre *m* de estado; **several statesmen from Western countries are meeting to discuss defence problems** = varios estadistas de los países occidentales se han reunido para discutir sobre los problemas de la defensa

◊ **statesmanlike** ['steɪtsmənlaɪk] *adjective* de estadista

◊ **statesmanship** ['steɪtsmənʃɪp] *noun* arte *m* de gobernar *or* habilidad *f* política

station [steɪʃn] **1** *noun* **(a) police station** = comisaría *f* de policía; **six demonstrators were arrested and taken to the police station** = seis manifestantes fueron arrestados y llevados a la comisaría; **he spent the night in the station cells** = pasó la noche en las celdas de la comisaría **(b)** *(transport)* estación *f;* **coach** *or* **bus station** = estación de autobuses; **the train leaves the Central Station at 14.15** = el tren sale de la estación central a las 14.15 **(c)** *(media)* **TV station** *or* **radio station** = estudios *mpl or* canal *m* de televisión *or* emisora *f* de radio **2** *verb* apostar *or* estacionar; **six police officers were stationed at the door of the courtroom** = seis oficiales de policía fueron estacionados a la puerta de la sala del Tribunal

stationer ['steɪʃnə] *noun* librero, -ra *or* papelero, -ra; **law stationer** = proveedor, -ra de papelería especializado en firmas jurídicas

◊ **stationery** ['steɪʃnri] *noun* objetos *mpl* de escritorio *or* papel *m* de escribir y sobres; **legal stationery supplier** = proveedor especializado en material de papelería utilizado en asuntos jurídicos; **shop selling office stationery** = tienda *f* que vende material de oficina; **continuous stationery** = papel continuo; **Her Majesty's Stationery Office (HMSO)** = organismo *m* que imprime y publica documentos, folletos y libros oficiales

status [steɪtəs] *noun* **(a)** *(importance or position in society)* estatus *m or* categoría *f or* posición *f* social; **loss of status** = pérdida *f* de categoría; **status inquiry** = petición *f* de informes sobre crédito **(b) legal status** = personalidad *f* jurídica; **marital status** = estado civil

◊ **status quo** ['steɪtəs 'kwəʊ] *noun* estatus *m or* statu quo *m;* **the contract does not alter the status quo** = el contrato no altera el statu quo; **status quo ante** = situación *f* anterior *or* statu quo anterior; *see also* IN STATU QUO

statute ['stætjuːt] *noun* **(a)** *(law made by Parliament)* ley *f* parlamentaria **(b)** *(ordinance or byelaw)* estatuto *m;* **statute book** = código *m* de leyes; **statute of limitations** = ley de prescripción *or* exención *f* de derechos

◊ **statute-barred** ['stætjuːtbɑːd] *adjective* prescrito, -ta

◊ **statutorily** ['stætʃʊtrɪli] *adverb* reglamentariamente *or* por (la) ley; **a statutorily protected tenant** = un inquilino protegido por la ley

◊ **statutory** ['stætʃʊtri] *adjective; (fixed by law)* estatutario, -ria *or* reglamentario, -ria *or* legal; **against statutory rights** = antiestatutario, -ria; **there is a statutory period of probation of thirteen weeks** = existe *or* hay un periodo reglamentario de prueba de trece semanas; **the authority has a statutory obligation to provide free education to all children** = las autoridades tienen una obligación establecida por ley de ofrecer educación gratuita a todos los niños; **powers conferred on an authority by the statutory code** = poderes conferidos a una autoridad por el código reglamentario; **statutory books** = libros *mpl* reglamentarios; **statutory declaration** = declaración reglamentaria ante el encargado del Registro Mercantil *or* declaración ante el juez; **statutory duty** = obligación *f* reglamentaria; **statutory holiday** = vacaciones *fpl* reglamentarias *or* establecidas por ley; **statutory instrument** = orden *f* reglamentaria *or* disposiciones legislativas; **statutory sick pay** = indemnización *f* por enfermedad *or* baja laboral; **statutory undertakers** = proveedores reglamentarios del agua, gas, electricidad, etc

stay [steɪ] **1** *noun* **(a)** *(time spent in one place)* estancia *f or* permanencia *f;* **the tourists were in town only for a short stay** = los turistas estuvieron en la ciudad únicamente durante una breve estancia **(b)** *(temporary stopping of a legal order)* aplazamiento *m or* sobreseimiento *m;* **stay of execution** = aplazamiento *or* suspensión *f* de la ejecución de una sentencia; **the court granted the company a two-week stay of execution** = el tribunal garantizó a la empresa un plazo de dos semanas de prórroga; **stay of proceedings** = sobreseimiento **2** *verb* **(a)** *(to stop at a place)* hospedarse *or* permanecer *or* quedarse *or* alojarse; **the chairman is staying at the Hotel London** = el presidente se hospeda en el Hotel London; **inflation has stayed high in spite of the government's efforts to bring it down** = la inflación sigue siendo alta a pesar de los esfuerzos del gobierno por reducirla **(b)** *(to stop temporarily)* aplazar; **the defendant made an application to stay the proceedings until the plaintiff gave security for costs** = el acusado solicitó un aplazamiento del proceso hasta que el demandante se hiciera cargo de las costas

steal [stiːl] *verb* robar *or* llevarse; **two burglars broke into the office and stole the petty cash** = dos ladrones asaltaron la oficina y robaron el dinero suelto que había en aquel momento; **one of our managers left to form his own company and stole the list of our clients' addresses** = uno de nuestros directores se fue para formar su propia empresa y se llevó la lista de direcciones de nuestros clientes; **one of our biggest problems is stealing in the wine department** = uno de nuestros mayores problemas es el robo en el departamento de vinos; **stolen goods** = mercancía *f* robada *or* objetos *mpl* robados; **handling** *or* **receiving stolen goods** = manipulación *f* *or* receptación *f* de objetos robados (NOTE: **stealing - stole - has stolen.** Note also that you steal things **from** a person *or* company)
◊ **stealing** ['stiːlɪŋ] *noun* robo *m;* **going equipped for stealing** = ir con las herramientas necesarias para robar

stenographer [stə'nɒgrəfə] *noun (official person who writes shorthand)* taquígrafo, -fa

step- [step] *prefix* prefijo que se utiliza para nombrar una relación adquirida a través del nuevo casamiento de un cónyuge
◊ **step-mother** ['stepmʌðə] *noun* madrastra *f*
◊ **step-father** ['stepfɑːðə] *noun* padrastro *m*

step [step] *noun* paso *m;* **step by step** = paso a paso; **to take a false step** = dar un paso en falso

stiff [stɪf] *adjective* rígido, -da *or* duro, -ra *or* difícil; **he received a stiff prison sentence** = recibió una dura condena de prisión; **he had to take a stiff test before he qualified** = tuvo que realizar un examen muy duro para sacar el título

stipendiary magistrate [staɪ'pendiəri 'mædʒɪstreɪt] *noun* magistrado, -da remunerado, -da

COMMENT: a stipendiary magistrate usually sits alone

stipulate ['stɪpjuleɪt] *verb (to demand that a condition be put into a contract)* estipular; **to stipulate that the contract should run for five years** = estipular que el contrato tenga una validez de cinco años; **to pay the stipulated charges** = pagar el precio estipulado; **the company failed to pay on the stipulated date** *or* **on the date stipulated in the contract** = la empresa no hizo efectivo el pago en la fecha estipulada *or* en la fecha estipulada en el contrato; **the contract stipulates that the seller pays the buyer's legal costs** = el contrato estipula que el vendedor pagará los costes legales del comprador
◊ **stipulation** [stɪpju'leɪʃn] *noun (condition in a contract)* cláusula *f or* estipulación *f*

stirpes ['stɜːpiːz] *see* PER STIRPES

stir up ['stɜː 'ʌp] *verb* agitar

stock [stɒk] **1** *noun* **(a)** *(quantity of raw materials)* reservas *fpl;* **we have large stocks of oil** *or* **coal** = tenemos grandes reservas de petróleo *or* carbón; **the country's stocks of butter** *or* **sugar** = las reservas del país de mantequilla *or* azúcar **(b)** *(quantity of goods for sale)* existencias *fpl or* surtido *m;* **opening stock** = existencias al comienzo de un periodo contable; **closing stock** = existencias al cierre de un periodo contable; **stock control** = control *m* de existencias; **stock valuation** = valoración *f or* tasación *f* de existencias; **to buy a shop with stock at valuation** = comprar una tienda con las existencias según valoración **(c)** *(available in a warehouse or store)* **in stock** *or* **out of stock** = en existencia *or* en almacén *or* agotado, -da **(d)** **stocks and shares** = acciones *fpl or* valores *mpl* mobiliarios; **stock certificate** = certificado *m or* título *m* de acciones; **debenture stock** = obligaciones *fpl* de renta fija *or* acciones no redimibles; **dollar stocks** = acciones en empresas americanas; **government stocks** = títulos del estado *or* valores públicos; **loan stock** = obligaciones de interés fijo; *US* **common stock** = acciones ordinarias **2** *verb (to hold goods for sale)* tener existencias *or* almacenar
◊ **stockbroker** ['stɒkbrəukə] *noun* corredor, -ra de bolsa *or* agente *mf* de bolsa; **stockbroker's commission** = comisión *f* que recibe un corredor de bolsa al terminar una operación
◊ **stockbroking** ['stɒkbrəukɪŋ] *noun* corretaje *m or* correduría *f* de bolsa; **a stockbroking firm** = una firma de corretaje de bolsa
◊ **Stock Exchange** ['stɒk 'ɪkstʃeɪndʒ] *noun* Bolsa *f;* **he works on the Stock Exchange** = trabaja en la Bolsa; **shares in the company are traded on the Stock Exchange** = las acciones de la empresa se negocian en la Bolsa; **Stock Exchange listing** = cotizaciones *fpl* de la Bolsa *or* boletín *m* de Bolsa
◊ **stockholder** ['stɒkhəuldə] *noun* accionista *mf or* tenedor, -ra de acciones
◊ **stockholding** ['stɒkhəuldɪŋ] *noun* número *m* de acciones en propiedad
◊ **stock market** ['stɒk 'mɑːkɪt] *noun* bolsa *f or* mercado *m* de valores; **stock market price** *or* **price on the stock market** = precio *m* en el mercado de valores; **stock market valuation** = tasación *f* de acciones basada en su valor actual en bolsa

stop [stɒp] *noun* alto *m or* parada *f*
◊ **stop and search** *or US* **stop and frisk** ['stɒp ən 'sɜːtʃ *or* 'frɪsk] *noun* poder *m* que tiene la policía para registrar; *(of body)* cachear a un sospechoso aunque no existan pruebas

straight [streɪt] *adjective* recto, -ta *or* honesto, -ta *or* honrado, -da; **to play straight** *or* **to act straight with someone** = actuar honestamente con alguien; **to go straight** = enmendarse

strict [strɪkt] *adjective* riguroso, -sa *or* estricto, -ta *or* exacto, -ta; **in strict order of seniority** = por riguroso orden de antigüedad; **to follow a strict**

interpretation of the rules = hacer una interpretación estricta de las normas; **strict liability** = responsabilidad *f* rigurosa *or* total

◊ **strictly** ['strɪktli] *adverb* rigurosamente *or* estrictamente; **the police ask all drivers to follow strictly the new highway code** = la policía pide a todos los conductores que sigan estrictamente el nuevo código de circulación

strife [straɪf] *noun* lucha *f or* conflicto *m;* **civil strife** = conflictos civiles

strike [straɪk] **1** *noun* **(a)** *(stopping of work by workers)* huelga *f;* **general strike** = huelga general; **official strike** = huelga oficial *or* aprobada por los sindicatos; **protest strike** = huelga de protesta; **token strike** = huelga simbólica *or* paro *m* breve; **unofficial strike** = huelga ilegal *or* no aprobada por el sindicato **(b) to take strike action** = declararse en huelga; **strike ballot** *or* **strike vote** = voto *m* de huelga; **strike call** = llamada *f* a la huelga *or* convocatoria *f* de huelga; **no-strike agreement** *or* **no-strike clause** = cláusula *f* antihuelga; **strike fund** = fondo *m* de huelga; **strike pay** = subsidio *m* de huelga **(c) to come out on strike** *or* **to go on strike** = declararse en huelga; **the office workers are on strike for higher pay** = los oficinistas están en huelga en petición de un aumento de salario; **to call the workers out on strike** = llamar a los trabajadores a la huelga *or* convocar una huelga de trabajadores **2** *verb* **(a)** *(to stop working)* declararse en huelga *or* ir a la huelga; **to strike for higher wages** *or* **for shorter working hours** = declararse en huelga para conseguir aumentos salariales *or* una reducción de la jornada laboral; **to strike in protest against bad working conditions** = declararse en huelga en protesta por malas condiciones laborales; **to strike in sympathy with the postal workers** = declararse en huelga de solidaridad con los trabajadores de correos **(b)** *(to hit)* pegar *or* golpear; **two policemen were struck by bottles** = dos policías fueron golpeados con botellas; **he was struck on the head by a cosh** = le golpearon en la cabeza con una porra (NOTE: **striking - struck**) **(c)** *(borrar)* **to strike from the record** = borrar del acta

◊ **strike off** ['straɪk 'ɒf] *verb* tachar (un nombre de una lista); **to strike someone off the rolls** = excluir a alguien de la lista de abogados

◊ **strike out** ['straɪk 'aʊt] *verb* cancelar una acción legal por incomparecencia del demandante *or* otra razón; **the statement of claim was struck out because it disclosed no cause of action** = la demanda fue cancelada porque revelaba ausencia de causa para la acción

stroke [strəʊk] *noun* golpe *m or* ataque *m* fulminante

strong [strɒŋ] *adjective* fuerte *or* vigoroso, -sa *or* firme; **a strong demand for the abolition of capital punishment** = peticiones enérgicas a favor de la abolición de la pena de muerte; **the country**

needs a strong police force = el país necesita un cuerpo de policía firme

◊ **strongbox** ['strɒŋbɒks] *noun* caja *f* fuerte *or* de caudales

◊ **strongroom** ['strɒŋruːm] *noun* cámara *f* acorazada

struggle ['strʌgl] **1** *noun* forcejeo *m* **2** *verb* forcejear

study ['stʌdi] **1** *noun (examining something carefully)* estudio *m;* **the government has asked the commission to prepare a study of prison systems in other countries** = el gobierno ha pedido a la comisión que prepare un estudio sobre los sistemas carcelarios de otros países; **he has read the government study on inner city crime** = ha leído el estudio del gobierno sobre delincuencia urbana; **to carry out a feasibility study on a project** = llevar a cabo un estudio de viabilidad de un proyecto **2** *verb (to examine carefully)* estudiar; **we are studying the possibility of setting up an office in New York** = estamos estudiando la posibilidad de abrir una oficina en Nueva York; **the government studied the committee's proposals for two months** = el gobierno estudió las propuestas del comité durante dos meses

sub- [sʌb] *prefix* menos importante *or* sub-; **sub-agency** = subagencia *f;* **sub-agent** = subagente *mf or* encargado, -da de una sucursal; **sub-committee** = subcomisión *f or* subcomité *m;* **he is chairman of the Finance Sub-Committee** = es el presidente de la subcomisión de finanzas; **sub-post office** = sucursal *f* de correos

subcontract 1 [sʌb'kɒntrækt] *noun* subcontrato *m;* **they have been awarded the subcontract for all the electrical work in the new building** = les han concedido el subcontrato para toda la instalación eléctrica del nuevo edificio; **we will put the electrical work out to subcontract** = solicitaremos ofertas a subcontratistas para la instalación eléctrica **2** [sʌbkən'trækt] *verb* ceder en subcontrato *or* subcontratar; **the electrical work has been subcontracted to Smith Ltd** = la instalación eléctrica ha sido subcontratada a Smith Ltd

◊ **subcontractor** [sʌbkən'træktə] *noun* subcontratista *mf*

subject ['sʌbdʒɪkt] *noun* **(a)** *(what something is concerned with)* motivo *m;* **the subject of the action was the liability of the defendant for the plaintiff's injuries** = el motivo de la acción era la responsabilidad del acusado frente a los daños del demandante **(b)** *(of a country)* súbdito, -ta; **he is a British subject** = es un súbdito británico; **British subjects do not need visas to visit EU countries** = los súbditos británicos no necesitan visado para visitar los países de la UE; **liberty of the subject** = libertad *f* individual *or* del individuo

◊ **subject to 1** ['sʌbdʒɪkt tʊ] *adjective* **(a)** *(depending on)* dependiente de *or* sujeto, -ta a *or* afecto, -ta a; **the contract is subject to government approval** = el contrato depende de la aprobación del gobierno; **agreement** *or* **sale subject to contract** = acuerdo *or* venta sujeta a contrato; **offer subject to availability** = oferta *f* según disponibilidad **(b)** *(which can receive)* sujeto, -ta a; **these articles are subject to import tax** = estos artículos están sujetos a tasas de importación **2** [sʌb'dʒekt tʊ] *verb* sojuzgar *or* someter; **he was subjected to torture** = le sometieron a tortura; **she subjected her husband to bad treatment** = sometió a su marido a malos tratos

sub judice [sʌb 'dʒuːdəsi] *Latin phrase* 'bajo la ley': sub judice *or* pendiente de resolución; **the papers cannot report the case because it is still sub judice** = la prensa no puede informar sobre el caso porque todavía está sub judice

sublease 1 ['sʌbliːs] *noun (lease from a tenant to another tenant)* subarriendo *m* **2** [sʌb'liːs] *verb* subarrendar *or* realquilar; **they subleased a small office in the centre of town** = subarrendaron una pequeña oficina en el centro de la ciudad
◊ **sublessee** [sʌble'siː] *noun* subarrendatario, -ria
◊ **sublessor** [sʌble'sɔː] *noun* subarrendador, -ra
◊ **sublet** [sʌb'let] *verb* subarrendar *or* realquilar; **we have sublet part of our office to a financial consultancy** = hemos subarrendado parte de nuestra oficina a una asesoría financiera (NOTE: **subletting - sublet - has sublet)**

submit [səb'mɪt] *verb* **(a)** *(to put forward)* presentar *or* someter; **to submit a proposal to the committee** = presentar una propuesta al comité; **he submitted a claim to the insurers** = presentó una reclamación a los aseguradores **(b)** *(to plead an argument in court)* alegar; **to submit evidence** = alegar pruebas; **counsel submitted that the defendant had no case to answer** = el abogado alegó que el acusado no tenía argumentos para defenderse; **it was submitted that the right of self-defence can be available only against unlawful attack** = se alegó que el derecho a la legítima defensa sólo puede ser posible contra un acto de agresión delictiva **(c)** *(to agree to be ruled)* rendirse *or* someterse; **he refused to submit to the jurisdiction of the court** = se negó a someterse a la jurisdicción del tribunal (NOTE: **submitting - submitted)**
◊ **submission** [səb'mɪʃn] *noun* alegato *m;* **the court heard the submission of defence counsel that there was no case to answer** *or* **in the submission of defence counsel there was no case to answer** = el tribunal oyó el alegato de la defensa que no había acusación a la que responder

subordinate [sʌ'bɔːdɪnət] **1** *adjective; (less important)* subordinado, -da; **subordinate to** = subordinado a *or* dependiente de **2** *noun (member of*

staff) subordinado, -da; **his subordinates find him difficult to work with** = a sus subordinados les resultaba difícil trabajar con él

subornation of perjury [səbɔː'neɪʃn əv 'pɜːdʒri] *noun* soborno *m* con el fin de que otro cometa perjurio

subpoena [sə'piːnə] **1** *noun* citación *f* judicial *or* apercibimiento *m;* **subpoena ad testificandum** = citación de un testigo; **subpoena duces tecum** = citación de un testigo para comparecer con determinadas pruebas **2** *verb (to order someone to appear in court)* citar *or* mandar comparecer *or* emplazar; **the finance director was subpoenaed by the prosecution** = el director financiero fue citado por la acusación

subrogation [sʌbrəʊ'geɪʃn] *noun* subrogación *f*

subscribe [səb'skraɪb] *verb* **(a)** *(to a journal)* suscribirse *or* abonarse; **to subscribe to a magazine** = suscribirse a una revista **(b)** *(to apply for shares in a new company)* **to subscribe for shares** = suscribir acciones
◊ **subscriber** [səb'skraɪbə] *noun* suscriptor, -ra *or* abonado, -da; **subscriber shares** = primeras acciones *fpl* que emite una empresa nueva

sub-section ['sʌbsekʃn] *noun* artículo *m;* **you will find the information in sub-section 3 of Section 47** = encontrarás la información en el artículo 3 de la sección 47

subsequent ['sʌbsɪkwənt] *adjective* subsiguiente *or* resolutorio, -ra; **condition subsequent** = condición *f* resolutoria

subsidiary [sʌb'sɪdiəri] *adjective; (less important)* secundario, -ria *or* de menor importancia *or* subsidiario, -ria; **he faces one serious charge and several subsidiary charges arising out of the main charge** = se enfrenta a una acusación grave y a varias de menor importancia derivadas de la acusación principal; **subsidiary company** = filial *f* *or* empresa *f* subsidiaria

subsidiarity [səbsɪdi'ærɪti] *noun (in the EU)* subsidiariedad *f*

subsidize ['sʌbsɪdaɪz] *verb (to help by giving money)* subvencionar; **the government has refused to subsidize the car industry** = el gobierno se ha negado a subvencionar la industria automovilística; **subsidized accommodation** = alojamiento subvencionado *or* vivienda subvencionada
◊ **subsidy** ['sʌbsɪdi] *noun* **(a)** *(money given to help)* subsidio *m* *or* subvención *f* *or* ayuda *f* estatal; **the industry exists on government subsidies** = la industria depende de las subvenciones estatales; **the government has increased its subsidy to the car industry** = el gobierno ha aumentado la subvención a la industria automovilística **(b)** *(money given to make a product cheaper)* subvención

substance ['sʌbstəns] *noun* **(a)** *(material)* material *m;* **dangerous substance** = material peligroso **(b)** *(basis of a report or argument)* fundamento *m;* **there is no substance to the stories about his resignation** = las historias sobre su dimisión no tienen ningún fundamento

substandard [sʌb'stændəd] *adjective* inferior

substantial [sʌb'stænʃl] *adjective; (large or important)* abundante *or* importante *or* sustancial *or* considerable; **she was awarded substantial damages** = le concedieron una importante cantidad por daños y perjuicios; **to acquire a substantial interest in a company** = adquirir un importante número de acciones de una empresa *or* una participación sustancial en una compañía

substantive [səb'stæntɪv] *adjective* real *or* positivo; **substantive law** = derecho *m* positivo; **substantive offence** = delito *m* cometido *or* realizado

substitute ['sʌbstɪtjuːt] **1** *noun* sustituto, -ta *or* suplente *mf* **2** *verb (to take the place of someone else)* sustituir; **substituted service** = hacer llegar un documento legal a alguien por método distinto al prescrito por la ley

subtenancy [sʌb'tenənsi] *noun (agreement to sublet a property)* subarriendo *m*
◊ **subtenant** [sʌb'tenənt] *noun* subarrendatario, -ria

suburb ['sʌbəːb] *noun* barrio *m* residencial

subversive [səb'vəːsɪv] *adjective* subversivo, -va; **the police are keeping subversive elements under surveillance** = la policía vigila *or* mantiene bajo control elementos subversivos

succeed [sək'siːd] *verb* **(a)** *(to follow someone)* seguir *or* suceder; **to succeed to a property** = heredar una propiedad **(b)** *(success)* tener éxito
◊ **succession** [sək'seʃn] *noun* sucesión *f;* **law of succession** = ley *f* de sucesión; **intestate succession** = sucesión ab intestato; **testamentary succession** = sucesión testada
◊ **successor** [sək'sesə] *noun (person who takes over from someone else)* sucesor, -ra; **Mr Smith's successor as chairman will be Mr Jones** = el sucesor del Sr. Smith como presidente será el Sr. Jones

suddenly ['sʌdnli] *adverb* de golpe *or* de repente

sue [suː] *verb* demandar *or* entablar juicio *or* interponer una querella; **to sue someone for damages** = demandar a alguien por daños y perjuicios; **he is suing the company for £50,000 compensation** = ha presentado una demanda de 50,000 libras contra la compañía

sufferance ['sʌfrəns] *noun* consentimiento *m* tácito *or* tolerancia *f;* **he has been allowed to live in the house on sufferance** = se le ha tolerado que

viva en la casa; **tenancy at sufferance** = alquiler *m* tácitamente prorrogado

sufficient [sə'fɪʃnt] *adjective* suficiente; **the company has sufficient funds to pay for its expansion programme** = la empresa tiene fondos suficientes para pagar su programa de expansión

suffrage ['sʌfrɪdʒ] *noun* sufragio *m or* derecho *m* al voto; **universal suffrage** = sufragio universal

suggest [sə'dʒest] *verb* sugerir *or* proponer; **the chairman suggested (that) the next meeting should be held in October** = el presidente sugirió que la siguiente reunión se celebrara en octubre; **we suggested Mr Smith for the post of treasurer** = propusimos al Sr Smith para el puesto de tesorero
◊ **suggestion** [sə'dʒestʃn] *noun* sugerencia *f or* propuesta *f;* **suggestion box** = buzón *m* de sugerencias

suicide ['suːɪsaɪd] *noun* **(a)** *(act of killing yourself)* suicidio *m;* **after shooting his wife, he committed suicide in the bedroom** = después de disparar a su mujer, se suicidó en la habitación; **police are treating the death as suicide, not murder** = la policía considera la muerte como suicidio, no como asesinato; **to commit suicide** = suicidarse; **suicide pact** = pacto *m* de suicidio **(b)** *(person who has committed suicide)* suicida *mf*

> COMMENT: aiding suicide is a notifiable offence

◊ **suicidal** [suːɪ'saɪdl] *adjective* suicida; **the warders should keep close watch on that prisoner - we think he may be suicidal** = los carceleros deberían vigilar estrechamente a ese prisionero; puede tener intenciones suicidas

sui generis ['suːaɪ 'dʒenrɪs] *Latin phrase* 'de su propia clase': sui generis

sui juris ['suːaɪ 'dʒʊərɪs] *Latin phrase* 'con capacidad legal'

suit [suːt] *noun* pleito *m or* litigio *m;* **US class suit** = pleito *or* acción *f* legal en beneficio de un grupo de personas *or* acción popular

suitability [suːtə'bɪlɪti] *noun* conveniencia *f*

suitable ['suːtəbl] *adjective* conveniente *or* adecuado, -da *or* apropiado, -da; **Wednesday is the most suitable day for the hearing** = el miércoles es el día más apropiado para la celebración de la vista; **we had to advertise the job again because there were no suitable candidates** = tuvimos que poner de nuevo el anuncio del trabajo porque no se presentó ningún candidato idóneo

sum [sʌm] **1** *noun* **(a)** *(of money)* suma *f or* cantidad *f;* **a sum of money was stolen from the personnel office** = robaron dinero de la oficina de personal; **he lost large sums on the Stock Exchange** = perdió grandes sumas de dinero en la bolsa; **she received the sum of £500 in compensation** = recibió la cantidad de 500 libras de indemnización **(b)** *(insurance)* **the sum insured** = la cantidad asegurada; **lump sum** = cantidad *or* suma global **(c)** *(total)* suma *or* total *m* **2** *verb (of a judge)* **to sum up** = pronunciar un discurso el juez al término de un juicio para instruir al jurado (NOTE: **summing - summed**)

◊ **summing up** ['sʌmɪŋ 'ʌp] *noun* resumen *m or* discurso *m* final del juez al término de un juicio (NOTE: US English is **instructions**)

summary ['sʌmri] **1** *adjective* sumario, -ria; **summary arrest** = arresto *m* sin orden de detención; **summary conviction** = condena *f* por juez sin jurado; **summary dismissal** = despido *m* sumario; **summary judgment** = juicio *m* sumario; **summary jurisdiction** = jurisdicción *f* sumaria; **summary offence** = delito *m* menor; **summary trial** = juicio de faltas **2** *noun* resumen *m or* sumario *m or* recopilación *f*; **the chairman gave a summary of his discussions with the German delegation** = el presidente dio un resumen de sus conversaciones con la delegación alemana; **the police inspector gave a summary of events leading to the raid on the house** = el inspector de policía dio un resumen de los acontecimientos que desembocaron en el asalto a la casa

◊ **summarily** ['sʌmrəli] *adverb* sumariamente; **magistrates can try a case summarily or refer it to the Crown Court** = los magistrados pueden someter a juicio un caso sumariamente o remitirlo al Tribunal de la Corona

◊ **summarize** ['sʌməraɪz] *verb* resumir; **the case was summarized in the evening papers** = el caso se resumió en los periódicos de la tarde

summit ['sʌmɪt] *noun* cumbre *f*; **the summit conference** *or* **summit meeting was held in Geneva** = la cumbre se celebró en Ginebra; **the matter will be discussed at next week's summit of the EU leaders** = el tema se discutirá la próxima semana en la conferencia cumbre de los líderes de los países de la UE

◊ **summitry** ['sʌmɪtri] *noun* diplomacia *f* propia de una cumbre

summon ['sʌmən] *verb* citar *or* emplazar; **he was summoned to appear before the committee** = le emplazaron para que compareciera ante la comisión

summons ['sʌmənz] *noun (official order to appear in court)* apercibimiento *m or* citación *f* judicial *or* emplazamiento *m or* requerimiento *m* judicial *or* auto *m* de comparecencia; **he tore up the summons and went on holiday to Spain** = rompió la citación judicial y se marchó de vacaciones a España; **judgment summons** = requerimiento judicial de pago *or* en su defecto de ingreso en prisión; **originating summons** = primera citación (normalmente ante el tribunal de justicia del Tribunal Supremo en casos relativos a la tierra o a la

administración de una propiedad); **writ of summons** = documento *m* de emplazamiento *or* citación judicial

sundry ['sʌndri] *adjective & noun* diversos, -sas *or* varios , -rias; **sundry items** *or* **sundries** = miscelánea *f or* artículos *mpl* diversos

supergrass ['su:pəgrɑːs] *noun (slang)* soplón,-na *or* delator,-ra *or* confidente *mf* de la policía que informa sobre las actividades de otros delincuentes

superintend [su:pən'tend] *verb* supervisar; **he superintends the company's overseas sales** = supervisa las ventas de la empresa en el extranjero

◊ **superintendent** [su:pən'tendənt] *noun* supervisor, -ra; **(police) superintendent** = Comisario jefe *or* superintendente (de policía)

superior [su'pɪərɪə] **1** *adjective* **(a)** *(of better quality)* superior; **our product is superior to all competing products** = nuestro producto es superior a todos los productos de la competencia; **their sales are higher because of their superior service** = sus ventas son más elevadas porque ofrecen un servicio superior **(b)** *(more important)* superior *or* más importante; **the case will be heard in a superior court** = su caso se verá en un tribunal superior; **he tried to blackmail a superior officer** = trató de chantajear a un oficial superior **2** *noun (more important person)* superior *mf or* jefe, -fa; **each manager is responsible to his superior for accurate reporting of sales** = cada encargado es responsable ante su superior de informar con exactitud de las ventas

supersede [su:pə'si:d] *verb* reemplazar *or* sustituir; **the government has published a Bill to supersede the current legislation** = el gobierno ha publicado un proyecto de ley que reemplaza la legislación actual

supervise ['su:pəvaɪz] *verb* supervisar; **the move to the new offices was supervised by the administrative manager** = el traslado a las nuevas oficinas fue supervisado por el director administrativo; **she supervises six girls in the legal department** = supervisa a seis chicas en el departamento jurídico

◊ **supervision** [su:pə'vɪʒn] *noun* supervisión *f or* vigilancia *f*; **new staff work under supervision for the first three months** = el personal de nueva contratación trabaja bajo supervisión durante los tres primeros meses; **she is very experienced and can be left to work without any supervision** = tiene mucha experiencia y se le puede dejar trabajar sin necesidad de supervisión; **the cash was counted under the supervision of the finance director** = el recuento del dinero se hizo bajo la supervisión del director financiero; **supervision order** = orden *f* de supervisión referente a la libertad vigilada de un delincuente juvenil

◊ **supervisor** [ˈsuːpəvaɪzə] *noun* supervisor, -ra
◊ **supervisory** [suːpəˈvaɪzəri] *adjective* de supervisión *or* de control; **supervisory staff** = personal *m* de supervisión; **he works in a supervisory capacity** = realiza un trabajo de supervisión *or* trabaja en calidad de supervisor

supplemental [sʌplɪˈmentl] *adjective* suplementario, -ria *or* adicional; *US* **supplemental appropriations** = provisión *f* de fondos adicionales

supplementary [sʌplɪˈmentri] *adjective* suplementario, -ria *or* secundario, -ria; **supplementary questions** *or* **supplementaries** = preguntas secundarias

supply [səˈplaɪ] **1** *noun* **(a)** *(providing something which is needed)* oferta *f or* abastecimiento *m or* suministro *m or* aprovisionamiento *m;* **money supply** = oferta monetaria; **Supply Bill** = proyecto *m* de ley de Presupuestos del Estado; **supply price** = precio *m* de oferta; **supply and demand** = oferta *f* y demanda *f;* **the law of supply and demand** = la ley de la oferta y la demanda **(b) in short supply** = escaso, -sa; **spare parts are in short supply because of the strike** = las piezas de repuesto escasean a causa de la huelga **(c)** *(stock of something which is needed)* suministro *m or* material *m or* reserva *f;* **the factory is running short of supplies of coal** = la fábrica se está quedando sin suministro de carbón; **supplies of coal have been reduced** = se han reducido las provisiones de carbón; **office supplies** = material *or* artículos de oficina **(d) supplies** = suministros *mpl or* provisiones *fpl;* **exempt supplies** = artículos *mpl* exentos del pago del IVA **2** *verb (provide something which is needed)* proveer *or* suministrar *or* proporcionar *or* abastecer; **to supply a factory with spare parts** = suministrar piezas de repuesto a una fábrica; **the prosecution supplied the court with a detailed map of the area where the crime took place** = la acusación proporcionó al tribunal un mapa detallado de la zona en la que ocurrió el crimen; **details of staff addresses and phone numbers can be supplied by the personnel department** = el departamento de personal puede proporcionar detalles sobre la dirección y el número de teléfono de los empleados
◊ **supplier** [səˈplaɪə] *noun* proveedor, -ra *or* suministrador, -ra *or* abastecedor, -ra

support [səˈpɔːt] **1** *noun* **(a)** *(giving money to help)* ayuda *f* económica *or* apoyo *m* económico; **the government has provided support to the computer industry** = el gobierno ha proporcionado ayuda económica a la industria informática; **we have no financial support from the banks** = no tenemos apoyo económico de los bancos **(b)** *(agreement or encouragement)* apoyo *m;* **the chairman has the support of the committee** = el presidente tiene el apoyo del comité; **support price** = precio *m* de subvención **2** *verb* **(a)** *(to give money*

to help) subvencionar *or* prestar ayuda económica; **the government is supporting the computer industry to the tune of $2m per annum** = el gobierno subvenciona la industria informática a razón de 2 millones de dólares al año; **we hope the banks will support us during the expansion period** = esperamos que los bancos nos ayuden durante el periodo de expansión **(b)** *(to encourage or to agree with)* apoyar *or* respaldar *or* aguantar; **she hopes the other members of the committee will support her** = confía en que el resto de los miembros del comité la apoyarán; **the market will not support another price increase** = el mercado no aguantará otra subida de precios

suppress [səˈpres] *verb* ocultar *or* callar; **the government tried to suppress the news about the prison riot** = el gobierno trató de ocultar la noticia sobre el motín de la prisión
◊ **suppression** [səˈpreʃn] *noun* ocultación *f;* **the suppression of the truth about the case** = la ocultación de la verdad sobre un caso

suppressio veri [səˈpresiəu ˈveraɪ] *Latin phrase* 'ocultar la verdad'

supra [ˈsuːprə] *adverb* arriba *or* véase más arriba

supreme court [səˈpriːm ˈkɔːt] *noun* **(a) Supreme Court (of Judicature)** = Tribunal *m* Supremo de Justicia en Inglaterra y Gales **(b)** *US* Tribunal Supremo Federal

surcharge [ˈsɜːtʃɑːdʒ] *noun* recargo *m;* **import surcharge** = sobretasa *f* de importación

surety [ˈʃɔːrəti] *noun* **(a)** *(person who guarantees)* garante *mf or* fiador, -ra; **bankruptcy surety** = fiador en bancarrota; **to stand surety for someone** = salir fiador *or* garante de alguien **(b)** *(sum guaranteed)* fianza *f or* garantía *f*

surname [ˈsɜːneɪm] *noun* apellido *m;* **a woman usually takes the surname of her husband when she marries** = las mujeres normalmente adoptan el apellido del marido al casarse

surplus [ˈsɜːpləs] *noun* excedente *m*

surrender [səˈrendə] **1** *noun* abandono *m or* renuncia *f or* entrega *f or* rescate *m or* capitulación *f;* **the contract becomes null and void when these documents are surrendered** = el contrato se anula y pierde su valor al producirse la devolución de estos documentos; **surrender value** = valor *m* de rescate **2** *verb* **(a)** *(to give in or give up)* entregar un documento *or* renunciar a un derecho; **the court ordered him to surrender his passport** = el tribunal le ordenó que entregara su pasaporte; **to surrender a policy** = rescatar una póliza de seguros **(b)** *(to give oneself up)* rendirse *or* entregarse; **the hijackers surrendered to the airport security guards** = los secuestradores del avión se entregaron a los guardias de seguridad del aeropuerto

surrogate ['sʌrəgeɪt] *noun* sustituto, -ta *or* suplente *mf*

surveillance [sə'veɪləns] *noun* vigilancia *f*; **the diplomats were placed under police surveillance** = los diplomáticos fueron puestos bajo vigilancia policial; **surveillance at international airports has been increased** = se ha incrementado la vigilancia en los aeropuertos internacionales; **surveillance device** = mecanismo *m* de control *or* vigilancia; **electronic surveillance** = vigilancia controlada por medio de aparatos electrónicos

survive [sə'vaɪv] *verb* sobrevivir; **he survived his wife** = sobrevivió a su mujer; **she is survived by her husband and three children** = deja marido y tres hijos *or* le sobreviven el marido y tres hijos; **he left his estate to his surviving relatives** = dejó sus bienes a los parientes con vida
◊ **survivor** [sə'vaɪvə] *noun* superviviente *mf*
◊ **survivorship** [sə'vaɪvəʃɪp] *noun* derecho *m* del superviviente de un coarriendo a la propiedad, antes que los herederos del arrendatario fallecido

SUS law ['sʌs 'lɔː] *noun* ley *f* que permite a la policía detener a una persona de la que sospecha ha cometido un delito

suspect 1 ['sʌspekt] *noun* sospechoso, -sa; **suspect who does not confess** *or* **who denies the charges** = inconfeso, -sa; **the police have taken six suspects into custody** = la policía tiene a seis sospechosos bajo custodia; **the police are questioning the suspect about his movements at the time the crime was committed** = la policía está interrogando al sospechoso sobre sus movimientos a la hora en que se cometió el crimen **2** [sə'spekt] *verb* sospechar; **he was arrested as a suspected spy** = lo arrestaron bajo sospecha de espionaje; **the police suspect that the thefts were committed by a member of the shop's staff** = la policía sospecha que los robos fueron cometidos por uno de los empleados de la tienda (NOTE: you suspect someone of committing a crime)

suspend [sʌ'spend] *verb* **(a)** *(to stop for a time)* suspender *or* interrumpir; **we have suspended payments while we are waiting for news from our agent** = hemos suspendido los pagos en espera de noticias de nuestro agente; **the hearings have been suspended for two weeks** = se han suspendido las vistas durante dos semanas; **work on the preparation of the case has been suspended** = se ha suspendido el trabajo sobre la preparación del caso; **the management decided to suspend negotiations** = la dirección decidió suspender las negociaciones; **suspended sentence** = remisión *f* de condena *or* sentencia *f* condicional **(b)** *(to stop someone working for a time)* suspender *or* privar temporalmente de sus funciones; **he was suspended on full pay while the police investigations were proceeding** = le suspendieron

de empleo y sueldo mientras tenían lugar las investigaciones policiales
◊ **suspension** [sʌ'spenʃn] *noun* **(a)** *(stopping something for a time)* suspensión *f*; **suspension of payments** = suspensión de pagos; **suspension of deliveries** = suspensión de entregas **(b)** *(stopping from attending meetings)* expulsión *f or* suspensión temporal; **suspension of a sitting** = expulsión de una sesión; **the suspension of an MP** = suspender temporalmente a un diputado

COMMENT: when an MP is 'named' by the Speaker, the House will vote to suspend him. Suspension is normally for five days, though it may be for longer if the MP is suspended twice in the same session of Parliament

suspicion [sə'spɪʃn] *noun* sospecha *f or* temor *m*; **on suspicion** = bajo sospecha; **he was arrested on suspicion of being an accessory to the crime** = le arrestaron bajo sospecha de encubrimiento *or* complicidad
◊ **suspicious** [sə'spɪʃəs] *adjective* sospechoso, -sa; **to be suspicious of** = sospechar de; **the police are dealing with the suspicious package found in the car** = la policía está investigando el paquete sospechoso encontrado en el coche; **suspicious substances were found in the man's pocket** = encontraron substancias sospechosas en el bolsillo del hombre

swear [sweə] *verb* jurar *or* prestar juramento; **the witness has been duly sworn** = el testigo ha prestado juramento; **he swore to tell the truth** = juró decir la verdad; **'I swear to tell the truth, the whole truth and nothing but the truth'** = 'juro decir la verdad, toda la verdad y nada más que la verdad' (NOTE: **swearing - swore - has sworn**)
◊ **swear in** ['sweə 'ɪn] *verb* tomar juramento a alguien; **he was sworn in as a Privy Councillor** = le tomaron juramento como Consejero Privado; **swearing-in** = juramento *m* de un cargo
◊ **swearword** ['sweəwɔːd] *noun* palabrota *f or* taco *m*

swindle ['swɪndl] **1** *noun* estafa *f or* timo *m* **2** *verb* estafar *or* timar *or* embaucar; **he made £50,000 by swindling small shopkeepers** = ganó 50.000 libras estafando a pequeños comerciantes; **the gang swindled the bank out of £1.5m** = la banda estafó al banco un millón y medio de dólares
◊ **swindler** ['swɪndlə] *noun* estafador, -ra *or* timador, -ra *or* embaucador, ra

syllabus ['sɪləbəs] *noun US* titular que resume un caso

syndicalism ['sɪndɪkəlɪzm] *noun* sindicalismo *m*

system ['sɪstəm] *noun* **(a)** *(arrangement or organization)* sistema *m*; **legal system** = régimen jurídico; **the British legal system has been taken as the standard for many other legal systems** = el sistema jurídico británico ha servido de modelo para muchos otros sistemas jurídicos; **filing system** = sistema de archivo; **to operate a quota system** = utilizar un sistema de cupos **(b) computer system** = sistema informático; **control system** = sistema de control para verificar que un ordenador funciona

debidamente **(c) systems analysis** = análisis *m* de sistemas; **systems analyst** = analista *mf* de sistemas

◊ **systematic** [sɪstə'mætɪk] *adjective* sistemático, -ca; **he ordered a systematic report on the probation service** = pidió un informe sistemático del servicio de libertad condicional

Tt

tabs [tæbz] *plural noun GB* banda *f* de tela blanca que llevan los abogados en vez de corbata cuando actúan ante los tribunales

table ['teɪbl] **1** *noun* **(a)** *(list of figures or facts)* lista *f or* tabla *f or* cuadro *m;* **table of contents** = índice *m* de materias; **actuarial tables** = tabla de mortalidad; **Table A, B, C, D, E** = escritura y estatutos modelo para la constitución de una sociedad descritos en la Ley de Sociedades; *see* A, B, C, D, E **(b)** *(piece of furniture)* mesa *f; (conference)* **round table** = mesa redonda **2** *verb* **(a)** *(put items before a meeting)* presentar la información necesaria antes del comienzo de una reunión; **the report of the finance committee was tabled** = se presentó el informe del comité financiero; **to table a motion** = presentar una moción **(b)** *US (to shelve an item indefinitely)* aplazar el examen de una moción

tacit ['tæsɪt] *adjective* tácito, -ta; **he gave the proposal his tacit approval** = dio su aprobación tácita a la propuesta; **the committee gave its tacit agreement to the proposal** = el comité dio su tácito consentimiento a la propuesta

tack [tæk] **1** *noun (in Scotland)* arrendamiento *m* **2** *verb (mortgage)* añadir una segunda hipoteca a la primera

tackle ['tækl] *verb* abordar

tail [teɪl] *see* FEE

take [teɪk] **1** *noun (money received in a shop)* ingresos *mpl* (de una tienda) **2** *verb* **(a)** *(to receive or to get)* recibir; *(of a lawyer)* **to take instructions** = recibir instrucciones de un cliente; **when the defence offered £1,000, the plaintiff's solicitor said he would take his client's instructions** = cuando la defensa ofreció 1.000 libras, el abogado del demandante dijo que tendría que recibir instrucciones de su cliente **(b)** *(do a certain action)* tomar; **to take action** = tomar medidas; **you must take immediate action if you want to stop thefts** = debe tomar medidas de inmediato si quiere frenar los robos; **to take effect** = tomar efecto; **to take into account** = tomar en cuenta; **to take office** = tomar posesión de un cargo; **to take sides** = tomar partido; **to take bribes** = aceptar sobornos; **to take notice** = hacer caso; **to take possession** =

apropiarse; **to take refuge** = acogerse; **to take steps** = hacer gestiones *or* tomar medidas; **to take someone to court** *or* **to take proceedings against someone** = mover pleito a una persona; **to take the chair** = asumir la presidencia de una reunión; **in the absence of the chairman his deputy took the chair** = en ausencia del presidente presidió su adjunto; **to take someone to court** = llevar a alguien a juicio **(c)** *(to need time or quantity)* tardar tiempo *or* necesitar *or* llevar *or* hacer falta; **it took the jury six hours to reach a verdict** *or* **the jury took six hours to reach a verdict** = el jurado tardó seis horas en llegar a un veredicto; **it will take her all morning to type my letters** = le llevará toda la mañana pasar mis cartas a máquina; **it took six policemen to hold the burglar** = fueron necesarios seis policías para atrapar al ladrón (NOTE: **taking - took - has taken**)

◊ **take in** ['teɪk 'ɪn] *verb* engañar *or* estafar a alguien; **we were taken in by his promise of quick profits** = nos dejamos engañar por su promesa de unos beneficios rápidos

◊ **take out** ['teɪk 'aʊt] *verb (to remove)* sacar; **to take out a patent for an invention** = sacar la patente de un invento *or* patentar un invento; **to take out insurance against theft** = hacerse un seguro contra robo

◊ **take over** ['teɪk 'əʊvə] *verb* **(a)** *(start doing something in place of someone else)* hacerse cargo de *or* sustituir *or* tomar posesión; **Miss Black took over from Mr Jones on May 1st** = la Srta. Black sustituyó al Sr. Jones el 1 de mayo; **the new chairman takes over on July 1st** = el nuevo presidente toma posesión el 1 de julio; **the take-over period is always difficult** = el periodo de relevo siempre es difícil **(b)** **to take over a company** = adquirir una compañía; **the buyer takes over the company's liabilities** = el comprador se hace cargo de las obligaciones de la empresa; **the company was taken over by a large international corporation** = la empresa fue absorbida por una gran multinacional

◊ **takeover** ['teɪkəʊvə] *noun (buying a business)* adquisición *f;* **takeover bid** *or* **offer** = oferta *f* pública de adquisición (OPA); **to make a takeover bid for a company** = hacer una oferta de adquisición de una empresa; **to withdraw a takeover bid** = retirar una oferta de adquisición;

the company rejected the takeover bid = la empresa rechazó la oferta de adquisición; **the disclosure of the takeover bid raised share prices** = la revelación de la oferta de adquisición hizo subir el precio de las acciones; **Takeover Panel** = cuerpo *m* regulador y supervisor de las operaciones de adquisición; **contested takeover** = adquisición no aceptada por la junta directiva de la empresa

talaq ['tælæk] *noun* costumbre *f* islámica según la cual el marido puede divorciarse de su mujer de un modo unilateral y por medio de una declaración oral realizada tres veces

tamper ['tæmpə] *verb* **(a) to tamper with something** = amañar *or* estropear *or* manipular *or* falsificar (algo); **the police were accused of tampering with the evidence** = la policía fue acusada de falsificar las pruebas; **the charges state that he tampered with the wheels of the victim's car** = se le acusa de manipular las ruedas del coche de la víctima **(b)** *(interfere with a person)* sobornar

tangible ['tændʒɪbl] *adjective* tangible *or* concreto, -ta; **tangible assets** *or* **property** = activo *m* tangible *or* bienes *mpl* tangibles

tap [tæp] *verb* escuchar; *(slang)* pinchar; **telephone tapping** = escucha *f* telefónica

target ['tɑːgət] *noun* blanco *m;* **to hit the target** = dar en el blanco

tariff ['tærɪf] *noun* **(a)** *(tax)* arancel *m;* **customs tariffs** = aranceles aduaneros *or* de aduanas; **tariff barriers** = barreras *fpl* arancelarias; **to impose tariff barriers on** *or* **to lift tariff barriers from a product** = imponer barreras arancelarias *or* levantar barreras arancelarias a un producto; **General Agreement on Tariffs and Trade (GATT)** = Acuerdo *m* General sobre Tarifas y Comercio (GATT); **protective tariff** = arancel proteccionista **(b)** *(price)* tarifa *f or* lista *f* de precios

tax [tæks] **1** *noun* **(a)** *(money taken by government)* impuesto *m;* **tax deducted at source** = retención *f* impositiva en origen; **capital gains tax (CGT)** = impuesto sobre las plusvalías; **capital transfer tax (CTT)** = impuesto sobre las transferencias de capital; **death tax** = impuesto de sucesión; **excess profits tax** = impuesto sobre beneficios extraordinarios; **income tax** = impuesto sobre la renta; **land tax** = contribución *f* territorial rústica; **road tax** = impuesto de carretera *or* impuesto de vehículos rodados; **sales tax** = impuesto sobre las ventas; **Value Added Tax (VAT)** = impuesto sobre el valor añadido (IVA); **double tax treaty** = tratado *m* de doble imposición; *US* **tax court** = tribunal *m* de apelación fiscal **(b)** **ad valorem tax** = impuesto ad valorem, por porcentaje fijo del valor *or* impuesto sobre el precio; **back tax** = impuesto atrasado; **basic rate tax** = impuesto básico; **to levy a tax** *or* **to impose a tax** = establecer un impuesto; **the government has**

imposed a 15% tax on petrol = el gobierno ha establecido un impuesto del 15% sobre la gasolina; **to lift a tax** = suprimir un impuesto **2** *verb* **(a)** *(to make someone pay)* imponer contribuciones a *or* gravar con un impuesto; **to tax businesses at 50%** = gravar las empresas con un impuesto del 50%; **income is taxed at 29%** = la renta está sujeta a un impuesto del 29%; **these items are heavily taxed** = estos artículos están sujetos a un impuesto elevado **(b)** *(to assess charges)* tasar; **the court ordered the costs to be taxed if not agreed** = el tribunal ordenó que se tasaran las costas si no se llegaba a un acuerdo; **taxed costs** = costas *fpl* procesales fijadas por el tasador del Tribunal Supremo

◊ **tax adviser** *or* **tax consultant** ['tæks əd'vaɪzə *or* kən'sʌltənt] *noun* asesor, -ra fiscal

◊ **tax allowances** *or* **allowances against tax** ['tæks ə'lauənsɪz] *noun* exenciones *fpl or* desgravaciones *fpl* fiscales

◊ **tax avoidance** ['tæks ə'vɔɪdəns] *noun* elusión *f* de impuestos

◊ **tax code** ['tæks 'kəud] *noun* código *m* impositivo *or* fiscal

◊ **tax concession** ['tæks kən'seʃn] *noun* desgravación *f* impositiva *or* privilegio *m* tributario

◊ **tax credit** ['tæks 'kredɪt] *noun* crédito *m* por impuestos pagados

◊ **tax-deductible** ['tæksdɪ'dʌktɪbl] *adjective* desgravable *or* deducible de impuestos; **these expenses are not tax-deductible** = estos gastos no son deducibles

◊ **tax deduction** ['tæks dɪ'dʌkʃnz] *noun* deducción *f* del salario en concepto de impuesto; *US* desgravación *f* impositiva por gastos

◊ **tax evasion** ['tæks ɪ'veɪʒn] *noun* evasión *f* fiscal

◊ **tax-exempt** ['tæksɪg'zempt] *adjective* exento, -ta de impuestos

◊ **tax exemption** ['tæks ɪg'zempʃn] *noun* exención *f* fiscal *or* tributaria *or US* desgravación *f* impositiva

◊ **tax-free** ['tæks'friː] *adjective* libre de impuestos

◊ **tax haven** ['tæks 'heɪvn] *noun* paraíso *m* fiscal *or* tributario

◊ **tax holiday** ['tæks 'hɒlɪdeɪ] *noun* franquicia *f* fiscal *or* tributaria

◊ **tax inspector** *or* **inspector of taxes** ['tæks ɪn'spektə] *noun* inspector, -ra fiscal *or* de Hacienda

◊ **tax liability** ['tæks laɪə'bɪlɪti] *noun* cuota *f* tributaria

◊ **tax loophole** ['tæks 'luːphəul] *noun* laguna fiscal

◊ **tax planning** ['tæks 'plænɪŋ] *noun* planificación *f* fiscal

◊ **tax point** ['tæks 'pɔɪnt] *noun* momento en el que se empieza a aplicar un impuesto; *(VAT)* momento en el que se suministran los artículos y se paga el IVA

◊ **tax relief** ['tæks rɪ'liːf] *noun* reducción *f* impositiva

◊ **tax return** or **tax declaration** ['tæks rɪ'tɔːn or deklə'reɪʃn] *noun* declaración f de la renta

◊ **tax system** ['tæks 'sɪstəm] *noun* sistema m tributario

◊ **tax year** ['tæks 'jɪə] *noun* año m or ejercicio m fiscal

taxable ['tæksəbl] *adjective* imponible or sujeto, -ta a impuesto; **taxable items** = artículos mpl sujetos a impuesto; **taxable income** = renta f imponible; **taxable base** = base f imponible

taxation [tæk'seɪʃn] *noun* (a) imposición f or impuestos mpl; **direct taxation** = impuestos directos; **double taxation** = doble imposición; **double taxation treaty** = tratado m sobre la doble imposición (b) **taxation of costs** = tasación f de costas procesales

Taxing Master ['tæksɪŋ 'mɑːstə] *noun* tasador, -ra or funcionario, -ria del Tribunal Supremo que valora las costas procesales

taxpayer ['tækspeɪə] *noun* contribuyente mf; **basic taxpayer** or **taxpayer at the basic rate** = contribuyente de a pie or contribuyente base or contribuyente que paga el tipo de impuesto base; **corporate taxpayers** = sociedad sujeta al pago de impuestos

TD ['tiː 'diː or 'tiæχtə 'dælə] = TEACHTA DALA miembro de la Cámara de Representantes del Parlamento de la República de Irlanda

technical ['teknɪkl] *adjective* técnico, -ca; **nominal damages were awarded as the harm was judged to be technical rather than actual** = se concedieron daños no relevantes al juzgarse que el daño era más técnico que real

◊ **technicality** [teknɪ'kælɪti] *noun (special interpretation of a legal point)* interpretación f or formalidad f; **the Appeal Court rejected the appeal on a technicality** = el Tribunal de Apelación rechazó la apelación en base a una interpretación tecnicista or estricta

teller ['telə] *noun* (a) *(House of Commons)* escrutador, -ra de la Cámara de los Comunes (b) *(bank)* cajero, -ra

COMMENT: when a division is called in the House of Commons, the Speaker appoints four MPs as tellers, two for the motion and two against. They do not vote, but check the other MPs as they pass through the division lobbies

tem [tem] *see* PRO TEM

Temple ['templ] *see* INNER TEMPLE, MIDDLE TEMPLE

temporary ['tempri] *adjective* temporal or provisional or eventual or interino, -na or transitorio, -ria; **the police took temporary measures to close the street to traffic** = la policía cerró la calle al tráfico como medida provisional; **temporary**

injunction = interdicto m temporal or requerimiento m provisional or interlocutorio; **he was granted a temporary injunction** = le concedieron un requerimiento provisional; **temporary employment** = empleo m provisional or trabajo m temporal or eventual; **she has a temporary job** or **temporary post with a firm of solicitors** = es interina en un bufete de abogados; **he has a temporary job as a filing clerk** or **he has a job as a temporary filing clerk** = tiene trabajo eventual como archivero; **temporary staff** = personal m eventual; **on a temporary basis** = con carácter transitorio

◊ **temporarily** ['tempərəli] *adverb* temporalmente or provisionalmente

tenancy ['tenənsi] *noun* arrendamiento m or alquiler m; *(period of agreement)* periodo m de arrendamiento or alquiler; **joint tenancy** = coarriendo m; **several tenancy** = tenencia f de una propiedad por varias personas; **protected tenancy** = arrendamiento protegido contra desahucio; **tenancy in common** = copropiedad f or comunidad f de bienes or condominio m propiedad f indivisa; **tenancy at will** = arrendamiento a voluntad or cancelable sin plazo fijo

◊ **tenant** ['tenənt] *noun* arrendatario, -ria or inquilino, -na; **the tenant is liable for repairs** = las reparaciones corren por cuenta del arrendatario or el inquilino es responsable de las reparaciones; **tenant at will** = inquilino a voluntad (cuyo arrendamiento está sujeto a la voluntad del propietario); **tenant for life** = inquilino vitalicio or que ocupa una propiedad de por vida; **tenant for years** = inquilino a término; **secure tenant** = arrendatario de una autoridad local con derecho a la compra de la propiedad que ocupa a un precio especial; **sitting tenant** = inquilino de una propiedad or que continúa ocupando una vivienda que se ha vendido

tendency ['tendənsi] *noun* inclinación f; **to have criminal tendencies** = tener inclinaciones criminales; **he has a tendency to steal** = tiene tendencia a robar

tender ['tendə] **1** *noun* (a) *(work)* oferta f or licitación f; **to put a project out to tender** or **to ask for** or **to invite tenders for a project** = sacar una obra a contrata or a licitación; **to put in a tender** or **to submit a tender** = hacer una oferta para realizar una obra; **to sell shares by tender** = ofertar acciones or hacer una oferta pública de acciones or sacar acciones a oferta escrita; **sealed tenders** = ofertas fpl cerradas (b) *(currency)* **legal tender** = moneda f de curso legal (NOTE: no plural in this meaning) **2** *verb* (a) **to tender for a contract** = hacer una oferta de contratación or presentar una oferta de licitación or licitar para un contrato; **to tender for the construction of a hospital** = hacer una oferta para la construcción de un hospital or licitar para la construcción de un hospital (b) **to tender one's resignation** = presentar la dimisión

◊ **tenderer** ['tendərə] *noun* postor, -ra *or* licitador, -ra; **the company was the successful tenderer for the project** = la empresa consiguió la contrata del proyecto

tenement ['tenəmənt] *noun* propiedad *f* alquilada; *(in Scotland)* edificio *m* de apartamentos en alquiler; **dominant tenement** = predio *m* dominante; **servient tenement** = predio sirviente

tenens ['tenenz] *see* LOCUM

tentative ['tentətɪv] *adjective* provisional; **they reached a tentative agreement over the proposal** = llegaron a un acuerdo provisional sobre la propuesta; **we suggested Wednesday May 10th as a tentative date for the next meeting** = sugerimos el miércoles 10 de mayo como fecha provisional para la próxima reunión
◊ **tentatively** ['tentətɪvli] *adverb* provisionalmente *or* a modo de prueba *or* de tanteo; **we tentatively suggested Wednesday as the date for our next meeting** = sugerimos provisionalmente el miércoles como fecha de nuestra próxima reunión

tenure ['tenjə] *noun* (a) *(right to hold property or position)* tenencia *f or* ocupación *f or* posesión *f* de un cargo; **security of tenure** = derecho a conservar un puesto de trabajo *or* una vivienda alquilada; **land tenure** = tenencia de tierras (b) *(time when a position is held)* mandato *m;* **during his tenure of the office of chairman** = durante su mandato como presidente

term [tə:m] *noun* (a) *(period when something is legally valid)* periodo *m or* plazo *or* duración *f or* vigencia *f;* **the term of a lease** = el periodo de arrendamiento; **the term of the loan is fifteen years** = el plazo de amortización del préstamo es de quince años; **to have a loan for a term of fifteen years** = obtener un préstamo por un plazo de quince años; **during his term of office as chairman** = durante su mandato como presidente; **term deposit** = depósito *m* a plazo; **term insurance** = seguro *m* temporal; **term loan** = préstamo *m* a plazo fijo; **term of years** = periodo fijo de tiempo (de un arrendamiento); **term shares** = depósito a plazo fijo de una sociedad de préstamo inmobiliario; **fixed term** = plazo *m* fijo (de un contrato); **short-term** = a corto plazo; **long-term** = a largo plazo; **medium-term** = a plazo medio (b) *(conditions or duties)* **term** *or* **terms** = condiciones *fpl or* términos *mpl;* **terms and conditions** = plazos y condiciones; **he refused to agree to some of the terms of the contract** = se negó a aceptar algunas de las condiciones del contrato; **by** *or* **under the terms of the contract, the company is responsible for all damage to the property** = según los términos del contrato, la empresa es responsable de todos los daños contra la propiedad; **terms of payment** *or* **payment terms** = condiciones de pago; **terms of sale** = condiciones de venta; **cash terms** = pago *m* al contado; **implied terms and conditions** = términos y condiciones implícitos de un contrato; **trade terms** = descuento para comerciantes del sector (c) *(part of a legal or university year)* trimestre *m;* **the autumn** *or* **winter term starts in September** = el trimestre de otoño *or* de invierno comienza en septiembre (d) **terms of employment** = condiciones de servicio; **terms of reference** = mandato *m or* campo *m* de aplicación *or* puntos *mpl* de consulta; **under the terms of reference of the committee it can only investigate complaints from the public** = conforme a su mandato, el comité sólo puede investigar quejas del público; **the tribunal's terms of reference do not cover traffic offences** = las competencias del tribunal no cubren delitos de tráfico

COMMENT: the four law terms are Easter, Hilary, Michaelmas and Trinity

terminate ['tə:mɪneɪt] *verb* terminar *or* finalizar *or* concluir; **to terminate an agreement** = finalizar un acuerdo; **his employment was terminated** = concluyó su periodo de empleo; **an offer terminates on the death of the offeror** = la oferta finaliza al morir el oferente
◊ **terminable** ['tə:mɪnəbl] *adjective* terminable *or* que puede finalizar
◊ **termination** [tə:mɪ'neɪʃn] *noun* (a) *(bringing to an end)* terminación *f or* expiración *f or* extinción *f or* rescisión *f;* **the termination of an offer** *or* **of a lease** = la rescisión de una oferta *or* la terminación de un arrendamiento; **to appeal against the termination of a foster order** = apelar contra la terminación de una orden judicial de adopción; **termination clause** = cláusula *f* resolutoria (b) *US (leaving a job)* cese *m* de un puesto de trabajo (por dimisión, retiro, o despido)

territory ['terɪtri] *noun* territorio *m or* zona *f;* **their government has laid claim to part of our territory** = su gobierno ha formulado una reivindicación sobre parte de nuestro territorio
◊ **territorial** [terɪ'tɔːriəl] *adjective* territorial; **territorial claims** = reivindicaciones *fpl* territoriales; **territorial waters** = aguas *fpl* territoriales *or* jurisdiccionales; **outside territorial waters** = en aguas internacionales
◊ **territoriality** [terɪtɔːri'ælɪti] *noun* territorialidad *f; see also* EXTRA-

terrorism ['terərɪzm] *noun* terrorismo *m;* **the act of terrorism was condemned by the Minister of Justice** = el acto terrorista fue condenado por el Ministro de Justicia
◊ **terrorist** ['terərɪst] *noun* terrorista *mf;* **the bomb was planted by a terrorist group** *or* **by a group of terrorists** = la bomba fue puesta por un grupo terrorista *or* por un grupo de terroristas; **six people were killed in the terrorist attack on the airport** = seis personas resultaron muertas en el atentado terrorista ocurrido en el aeropuerto

test [test] **1** *noun* **(a)** *(examination)* prueba *f or* examen *m;* **test certificate** = certificado *m* de aptitud; **control test** = prueba de control (para comprobar si alguien trabaja por cuenta propia *or* ajena con vistas a la valoración del impuesto); **feasibility test** = examen *or* prueba de viabilidad **(b) test case** = juicio *m* que hace jurisprudencia *or* sienta precedente para posibles casos posteriores **2** *verb* probar *or* tantear; **to test a computer system** = probar un sistema informático *or* de ordenador

testament ['testəmənt] *noun* testamento *m;* **last will and testament** = testamento *or* última voluntad *f*
◊ **testamentary** [testə'mentəri] *adjective* testamentario, -ria; **testamentary capacity** = capacidad *f* de testar; **testamentary disposition** = disposición *f* testamentaria; **testamentary freedom** = libertad *f* testamentaria

testate ['testeɪt] *adjective* testado, -da; **did he die testate?** = ¿murió habiendo testado?; *see also* INTESTATE
◊ **testator** [te'steɪtə] *noun* testador *m*
◊ **testatrix** [te'steɪtrɪks] *noun* testadora *f*

testify ['testɪfaɪ] *verb* testificar *or* atestar *or* dar testimonio *or* declarar

testimonium clause [testɪ'məʊniəm 'klɔ:z] *noun* cláusula *f* final de un testamento que prueba que éste se ha realizado ante testigos *or* cláusula testimonial

> COMMENT: the testimonium clause usually begins with the words: 'in witness whereof I have set my hand'

testimony ['testɪməni] *noun* declaración *f or* testimonio *m or* prueba *f* testifical; **she gave her testimony in a low voice** = pronunció su declaración en voz baja

text [tekst] *noun* texto *m;* **he wrote notes at the side of the text of the agreement** = escribió anotaciones en el margen del texto del acuerdo; **text processing** = procesamiento *m* de textos
◊ **textbook** ['tekstbʊk] *noun* libro *m* de texto

theft [θeft] *noun* robo *m or* hurto *m or* sustracción *f;* **we have brought in security guards to protect the store against theft** = hemos puesto guardias de seguridad para proteger la tienda contra robos; **the company is trying to reduce losses caused by theft** = la empresa está tratando de reducir las pérdidas causadas por robos; **to take out insurance against theft** = hacerse un seguro contra robo; **petty theft** = hurto menor *or* ratería *f;* **there has been a wave of thefts from newsagents** = ha habido una ola de robos contra quioscos de prensa

> COMMENT: types of theft which are notifiable offences are: theft from the person of another; theft in a dwelling; theft by an employee; theft of mail *or* pedal cycle *or* motor vehicle; theft

from vehicles *or* from a shop *or* from an automatic machine or meter

there- [ðeə] *prefix* aquello *or* eso (NOTE: the following words formed from **there-** are frequently used in legal documents)
◊ **thereafter** [ðeə'ɑ:ftə] *adverb* después *or* más tarde
◊ **thereby** [ðeə'baɪ] *adverb* por eso *or* por ello
◊ **therefor** [ðeə'fɔ:] *adverb* por lo tanto *or* por consiguiente
◊ **therefrom** [ðeə'frɒm] *adverb* de allí *or* de ahí
◊ **therein** [ðeə'ɪn] *adverb* allí dentro
◊ **thereinafter** [ðeəɪn'ɑ:ftə] *adverb* más abajo *or* más adelante
◊ **thereinbefore** [ðeəɪnbɪ'fɔ:] *adverb* más arriba
◊ **thereinunder** [ðeəɪn'ʌndə] *adverb* bajo el encabezamiento
◊ **thereof** [ðeə'ɒv] *adverb* de eso; **in respect thereof** = con respecto a eso
◊ **thereto** [ðeə'tu:] *adverb* a eso *or* a ello
◊ **theretofore** [ðeətu'fɔ:] *adverb* antes de aquel tiempo
◊ **therewith** [ðeə'wɪð] *adverb* con eso

thief [θi:f] *noun* ladrón, -ona; **thieves broke into the office and stole the petty cash** = entraron ladrones en la oficina y robaron *or* se llevaron el dinero para gastos menores; **petty thief** = ratero *m* (NOTE: plural is **thieves**)

think [θɪŋk] *verb* pensar; **without thinking** = sin pensar

third [θɜ:d] *noun* tercero, -ra *or* tercio; **to sell everything at one third off** = vender todo por la tercera parte de su valor
◊ **third party** ['θɜ:d 'pɑ:ti] *noun (any person other than the two main parties involved in a contract)* tercero *m;* **third party claim to ownership** = tercería *f* de dominio; **third-party insurance** = seguro *m* contra terceros; **third party notice** = notificación *f* de inclusión de un tercero; **third party proceedings** = tercería *or* proceso en el que se incluye un tercero; **the case is in the hands of a third party** = el caso está en manos de un tercero; *see also* PARTY
◊ **Third Reading** ['θɜ:d 'ri:dɪŋ] *noun* GB tercera lectura de un proyecto de ley en el parlamento *or* último debate y votación de un proyecto de ley en el parlamento

thrash [θræʃ] *verb* azotar

threat [θret] *noun (written or spoken)* amenaza *f*
◊ **threaten** ['θretn] *verb* amenazar; **he threatened to take the tenant to court** *or* **to have the tenant evicted** = amenazó con llevar al inquilino ante los tribunales *or* con deshauciar al inquilino; **she complained that her husband threatened her with a knife** = alegó que su marido la había amenazado con un cuchillo; **threatening behaviour** = comportamiento *m* ofensivo *or* conducta *f* amenazante

throne [θrəun] *noun* trono *m;* **speech from the throne** = QUEEN'S SPEECH

throw out ['θrəu 'aut] *verb* **(a)** *(to reject or to refuse to accept)* rechazar; **the proposal was thrown out by the planning committee** = el comité de planificación rechazó la propuesta; **the board threw out the draft contract submitted by the union** = el consejo de administración rechazó el borrador del contrato propuesto por el sindicato **(b)** *(to get rid of something which is not wanted)* echar *or* tirar *or* deshacerse de; **we threw out the old telephones and put in a computerized system** = tiramos todos los teléfonos antiguos e instalamos un sistema informático; **the AGM threw out the old board of directors** = la Junta General Ordinaria se deshizo del antiguo Consejo de Administración (NOTE: **throwing - threw - has thrown**)

thug [θʌg] *noun* gamberro, -rra *or* bruto, -ta; **a group of teenage thugs attacked the couple as they left the shop** = un grupo de gamberros adolescentes atacó a la pareja cuando salía de la tienda

◊ **thuggery** ['θʌgri] *noun* gamberrismo *m*

ticket ['tɪkɪt] *noun US* lista *f* electoral; **he ran for governor on the Republican ticket** = se presentó como candidato a Gobernador en la lista de los republicanos

tied cottage ['taɪd 'kɒtɪdʒ] *noun* vivienda *f* destinada a un empleado mientras ocupa un puesto determinado

tight [taɪt] *adjective* apretado, -da

time [taɪm] *noun* **(a)** *(period when something takes place)* tiempo *m;* **computer time** = tiempo de utilización de un ordenador (pagado a horas); **real time** = tiempo real; **time charter** = fletamento *m* por tiempo determinado; **time policy** = póliza *f* marítima con vencimiento fijo; **time immemorial** = (desde) tiempo inmemorial; **time share** = multipropiedad *f;* **time summons** = requerimiento *m* de ampliación de plazo; **extension of time** = ampliación *f or* prórroga *f* de plazo; **wrong time** = mal momento **(b)** *(time of the day)* hora *f;* **the time of arrival** *or* **the arrival time is indicated on the screen** = la hora de llegada viene indicada en la pantalla; **departure times are delayed by up to fifteen minutes because of the volume of traffic** = el horario de salida lleva un retraso de hasta quince minutos debido a la cantidad de tráfico; **on time** = puntualmente *or* a tiempo; **the plane was on time** = el avión fue puntual; **you will have to hurry if you want to get to the hearing on time** *or* **if you want to be on time for the hearing** = tendrás que apresurarte si quieres llegar a tiempo a la vista **(c)** *(system of hours)* horario *m or* hora *f;* **Summer Time** *or* **Daylight Saving Time** = horario de verano; **Standard Time** = hora normal **(d)** *(hours worked)* **he is paid time and a half on Sundays** = los domingos cobra paga y media *or* la mitad más **(e)** *(period before something happens)* **time limit** = plazo *or* término; **time limit for legal action** = plazo de prescripción; **to keep within the time limits** *or* **within the time schedule** = cumplir el plazo estipulado; **time lock** = cerradura *f* de seguridad *or* temporizador *m*

◊ **timetable** ['taɪmteɪbl] **1** *noun* **(a)** *(trains or planes or buses)* horario *m;* **according to the timetable, there should be a train to London at 10.22** = según el horario, debería haber un tren a Londres a las 10.22; **the bus company has brought out its new timetable for the next twelve months** = la empresa de autobuses ha publicado su nuevo horario para los próximos doce meses **(b)** *(list of appointments or events)* horario *m or* programa *m;* **Mr Smith has a very full timetable, so I doubt if he will be able to see you today** = el Sr. Smith tiene un programa muy apretado, dudo que pueda recibirle a usted hoy; **conference timetable** = programa de un congreso **2** *verb (make a list of time)* realizar un horario *or* preparar un horario

tip [tɪp] *noun (stock exchange)* información *f* confidencial

◊ **tip-off** ['tɪpɒf] *noun (police)* chivatazo *m*

tipstaff ['tɪpstɑːf] *noun* funcionario del Tribunal Supremo encargado del arresto de las personas que incurren en desacato a los tribunales

title ['taɪtl] *noun* **(a)** *(right)* derecho *m;* **title to property** = derecho *m* a la propiedad; **she has no title to the property** = no tiene derecho a la propiedad; **he has a good title to the property** = tiene justo derecho a la propiedad **(b)** *(document)* título *m;* **title deeds** = título de propiedad *or* escritura *f;* **absolute title** = título absoluto *or* de plena propiedad; **to have a clear title to something** = tener un título de propiedad de algo saneado y sin cargas; **good title** = título válido; **possessory title** = título de una propiedad adquirido por la ocupación continua de ésta (por lo general un periodo de doce años); **qualified title** = título imperfecto *or* limitado de una propiedad *or* título no absoluto **(c)** *(in a job)* cargo *m;* **he has the title 'Chief Executive'** = tiene el cargo de 'Director Ejecutivo' **(d)** *(rank)* título nobiliario **(e)** *(label)* título de una ley parlamentaria; **full title** *or* **long title** = título completo de una ley parlamentaria; **short title** = título abreviado

token ['təukn] *noun (sign or symbol)* muestra *f or* prueba *f or* señal *f or* símbolo *m;* **token charge** = precio *m* simbólico; **a token charge is made for heating** = se cobra un precio simbólico por la calefacción; **token payment** = pago *m* simbólico *or* señal *or* pago de una pequeña parte de la deuda; **token rent** = renta *f* simbólica; **token strike** = huelga *f* simbólica

toll [təʊl] **1** *noun (payment for using a service)* peaje *m* **2** *verb US* suspender una ley temporalmente

tort [tɔːt] *noun (lawsuit)* agravio *m* indemnizable en juicio civil *or* daño *m* legal *or* injusticia *f or* acto ilícito civil; **action in tort** = acción *f* legal por daños *or* agravios *or* acción de agravio *or* de trasgresión; **proceedings in tort** = proceso *m* judicial por daños *or* por agravio

◊ **tortfeasor** [tɔːtˈfiːzə] *noun* agresor, -ra *or* persona *f* que comete una agresión o un daño; **joint tortfeasors** = agresores que cometen un daño conjuntamente *or* responsables conjuntos de un agravio

◊ **tortious** [ˈtɔːʃəs] *adjective* referente a un agravio *or* daño; **tortious act** = agravio *m or* daño *m;* **tortious liability** = responsabilidad *f* por negligencia profesional

torture [ˈtɔːtʃə] **1** *noun* tortura *f* **2** *verb* torturar

◊ **torturer** [ˈtɔːtʃərə] *noun* verdugo *m*

tot up [ˈtɒt ˈʌp] *verb* sumar

◊ **totting up** [ˈtɒtɪŋ ˈʌp] *noun (traffic offences)* suma *f* de previos delitos de tráfico a una nueva sentencia

total [ˈtəʊtl] **1** *adjective* total; **total amount** = cantidad *f* total; **total assets** = activos *mpl* totales; **total cost** = coste *m* total; **total expenditure** = gastos *mpl* totales; **total income** = renta *f* total; **total output** = producción *f* total; **total revenue** = ingresos *mpl* totales **2** *noun (amount)* total *m or* totalidad *f;* **the total of the charges comes to more than £1,000** = el total de los gastos asciende a más de 1.000 libras; **he was sentenced to a total of twelve years' imprisonment** = le condenaron a un total de doce años de prisión; **grand total** = total general *or* global *or* suma *f* total **3** *verb* ascender a *or* totalizar; **costs totalling more than £25,000** = costes que suman más de 25.000 libras (NOTE: **totalling - totalled** but American spelling **totaling - totaled**)

◊ **total loss** [ˈtəʊtl ˈlɒs] *noun (insurance)* **actual total loss** = siniestro *m* total; **the cargo was written off as a total loss** = el cargamento fue declarado siniestro total

◊ **totally** [ˈtəʊtli] *adverb* totalmente; **the factory was totally destroyed in the fire** = la fábrica quedó totalmente destruida en el incendio; **the cargo was totally ruined by water** = la mercancía quedó totalmente estropeada por el agua

totalitarian [təʊtælɪˈteəriən] *adjective; (often as criticism)* totalitario, -ria; **a totalitarian state** = un estado totalitario; **the totalitarian regime of the junta** = el régimen totalitario de la junta

◊ **totalitarianism** [təʊtælɪˈteəriənɪzm] *noun (usually as criticism)* totalitarismo *m;* **many extreme right-wing or left-wing governments have been accused of practising totalitarianism** = se ha acusado a muchos gobiernos de extrema derecha o extrema izquierda de totalitarismo

toties quoties [ˈtəʊʃiːz ˈkwəʊʃiːz] *Latin phrase* 'con la frecuencia necesaria'

town [taʊn] *noun* ciudad *f;* **Town Clerk** = (antiguamente) secretario, -ria del ayuntamiento; **Town Council** = Corporación *f or* Consejo *m* Municipal; **Town Hall** = ayuntamiento *m or* casa *f* consistorial; **town planner** = urbanista *mf;* **town planning** = urbanismo *m*

trace [treɪs] **1** *noun* huella *f or* rastro *m;* **they disappeared leaving no trace** = desaparecieron sin dejar rastro **2** *verb* **(a)** *(to follow or to look for someone or something)* seguir *or* buscar *or* rastrear; **the police traced the two men to a hotel in London** = la policía siguió a los dos hombres hasta un hotel de Londres **(b)** *(to find)* encontrar *or* localizar; **we have traced the missing documents** = hemos localizado los documentos que faltaban **(c)** **tracing action** = proceso *m or* acción *f* judicial en búsqueda de un dinero o de las ganancias de una venta

trade [treɪd] **1** *noun* **(a)** *(business of buying or selling)* comercio *m;* **export trade** *or* **import trade** = comercio de exportación *or* comercio de importación; **home trade** = comercio interior **(b)** **fair trade** = convenio *m* internacional de reciprocidad arancelaria; **free trade** = libre comercio *or* libre cambio; **free trade area** = zona *f* de libre cambio *or* zona franca; **trade agreement** = acuerdo *m or* convenio *m or* tratado *m* comercial; **trade description** = descripción *f* comercial; **Trade Descriptions Act** = Ley *f* de Normativa para el Comercio (ley que regula la descripción comercial de productos); **trade directory** = repertorio *m or* guía *f* comercial; **to ask a company to supply trade references** = pedir referencias comerciales a una empresa; **trade dispute** = conflicto *m* comercial; **trade fixtures** = instalaciones *fpl* comerciales **(c)** *(companies dealing in the same line of product)* industria *f or* ramo *m or* gremio *m;* **he is in the secondhand car trade** = se dedica a la compra-venta de coches de segunda mano; **she is very well known in the clothing trade** = es muy conocida dentro del ramo de la confección; **trade association** = asociación *f* comercial *or* agrupación *f* sectorial *or* de comerciantes y empresarios **2** *verb (to carry on a business)* comerciar *or* negociar; **to trade with another country** = comerciar con otro país; **to trade on the Stock Exchange** = negociar en la Bolsa; **the company has stopped trading** = la empresa ha cerrado *or* cesado; **he trades under the name or as 'Eeziphitt'** = la compañía opera bajo el nombre de 'Eeziphitt'

◊ **trademark** *or* **trade mark** *or* **trade name** [ˈtreɪdmɑːk *or* ˈtreɪd ˈneɪm] *noun* marca *f* registrada *or* nombre *m* comercial; **you cannot call your beds 'Softn'kumfi' - it is a registered trademark** = no puede llamar a sus camas 'Softn'kumfi' - es una marca registrada

◊ **trader** ['treɪdə] *noun* comerciante *mf or* negociante *mf;* **commodity trader** = comerciante de artículos de consumo; **free trader** = librecambista *mf;* **sole trader** = comerciante individual

◊ **trade union** *or* **trades union** ['treɪd 'juːnɪən] *noun* sindicato *m;* **they are members of a trade union** *or* **they are trade union members** = están afiliados a un sindicato; **he has applied for trade union membership** *or* **he has applied to join a trade union** = ha solicitado la afiliación a un sindicato; **Trades Union Congress** = Confederación *f* de Sindicatos en G.B. (NOTE: although **Trades Union Congress** is the official name for the organization, **trade union** is commoner than **trades union**)

◊ **trading** ['treɪdɪŋ] *noun* comercio *m;* **fair trading** = comercio justo *or* prácticas comerciales justas; **Office of Fair Trading** = departamento *m* de control de prácticas comerciales; **fraudulent trading** = comercio fraudulento

traffic [træfik] **1** *noun* tráfico *m or* circulación *f;* **traffic offences** = delitos *mpl* de tráfico *or* contra el código de la circulación; **traffic police** = policía *f* de tráfico; **traffic warden** = agente *mf* de circulación **2** *verb* **to traffic in something** = traficar en algo; **he was charged with trafficking in drugs** *or* **with drug trafficking** = le acusaron de tráfico de estupefacientes *or* tráfico de drogas

trail [treɪl] *noun* rastro *m;* **they followed his trail** = le siguieron el rastro

train [treɪn] **1** *noun* tren *m;* **commuter train** = tren de cercanías **2** *verb* **(a)** *(to teach)* formar *or* capacitar *or* preparar **(b)** *(to learn)* estudiar; **he is a trained accountant** = es contable cualificado; **the director is American-trained** = el director tiene una formación americana; **day training centre** = centro *m* de educación especial para delincuentes juveniles *or* centro ocupacional para delincuentes

◊ **trainee** [treɪ'niː] *noun* aprendiz, -za; *(trainee lawyer)* pasante *mf*

◊ **training** ['treɪnɪŋ] *noun* adiestramiento *m or* educación *f;* **day training centre** = centro de educación especial para delincuentes juveniles

transact [træn'zækt] *verb* **to transact business** = llevar a cabo un negocio *or* hacer negocios

◊ **transaction** [træn'zækʃn] *noun* gestión *f;* **business transaction** = transacción *f or* trámite *m or* operación *f* comercial; **cash transaction** = operación *f* al contado; **a transaction on the Stock Exchange** = operación de Bolsa *or* bursátil; **the paper publishes a daily list of Stock Exchange transactions** = el periódico publica una lista diaria de operaciones bursátiles; **exchange transaction** = operación en divisas; **fraudulent transaction** = operación fraudulenta

transcript ['trænskrɪpt] *noun* transcripción *f or* texto *m* íntegro; **the judge asked for a full transcript of the evidence** = el juez pidió una transcripción completa de la declaración; **transcripts of cases are available in the Supreme Court Library** = las transcripciones de los casos se pueden consultar en la biblioteca del Tribunal Supremo

transfer 1 ['trænsfə] **1** *noun* traslado *m; (sale)* traspaso *m;* **transfer of property** = transferencia *f or* transmisión *f* de propiedad; **transfer of shares** = cesión *f* de acciones; **bank transfer** = transferencia bancaria; **capital transfer tax** = impuesto *m* sobre las transferencias de capital; **credit transfer** *or* **transfer of funds** = transferencia bancaria *or* transferencia de fondos; **deed of transfer** = escritura *f* de cesión de acciones; **stock transfer form** = formulario *m* de transacciones bursátiles **2** [træns'fə:] *verb* **(a)** *(to move someone or something to a new place)* trasladar *or* transferir; **to transfer a business** = traspasar un negocio; **the accountant was transferred to our Scottish branch** = el contable fue trasladado a nuestra sucursal de Escocia; **he transferred his shares to a family trust** = cedió sus acciones a un fideicomiso familiar; **she transferred her money to a deposit account** = transfirió su dinero a una cuenta de depósito; **transferred charge call** = llamada *f* a cobro revertido **(b)** *(to change from one type of travel to another)* transbordar *or* hacer transbordo *or* cambiar; **when you get to London airport, you have to transfer onto an internal flight** = cuando llegue al aeropuerto de Londres, tiene que hacer transbordo *or* cambiar a un vuelo nacional (NOTE: transferring - transferred)

◊ **transferable** [træns'fə:rəbl] *adjective* transferible; **the season ticket is not transferable** = el billete de abono no es transferible; **single transferable vote** = votación *f* única transferible *or* sistema *m* de votación con representación proporcional (en la que cada votante vota por los candidatos por orden de preferencia y su voto es transferido al candidato siguiente si su primera elección no resulta elegida)

◊ **transferee** [trænzfə'ri:] *noun* beneficiario, -ria *or* cesionario, -ria

◊ **transferor** [trænzfə'rɔ:] *noun* cedente *mf*

transit ['trænzɪt] *see* IN TRANSIT

transport ['trænspɔ:t] *noun* transporte *m;* **private** *or* **public transport** = transporte particular *or* público; **means of transport** = medio *m* de transporte

traverse [trə'və:s] *noun* negación *f or* denegación *f*

tray [treɪ] *noun* bandeja *f;* **filing tray** = bandeja para documentos

treason ['tri:zn] *noun* traición *f;* **he was accused of treason** = se le acusó de traición; **three men**

were executed for treason = ejecutaron a tres hombres por traición; **the treason trial lasted three weeks** = el juicio por traición duró tres semanas; **high treason** = alta traición; **misprision of treason** = ocultación *f or* encubrimiento *m* de traición; **treason felony** = delito *m* grave de traición

◊ **treasonable** ['triːznəbl] *adjective* traidor, -ra *or* desleal; **he was accused of making treasonable remarks** = le acusaron de hacer comentarios que podían incurrir en delito de traición

treasure ['treʒə] *noun* tesoro *m;* **thieves broke into the palace and stole the king's treasure** = entraron ladrones en el palacio y robaron el tesoro del rey; **treasure trove** = tesoro descubierto

> COMMENT: treasure which has been found is declared to the coroner, who decides if it is treasure trove. If it is declared treasure trove, it belongs to the state, though the person who finds it will usually get a reward equal to its market value

◊ **treasurer** ['treʒərə] *noun* **(a)** *(financial officer of a club or society)* tesorero, -ra; **honorary treasurer** = tesorero honorario **(b)** *US (main financial officer of a company)* director, -ra de finanzas de una compañía

◊ **treasury** ['treʒəri] *noun (government department)* erario *m;* **public treasury** = erario público; **the Treasury** = el Ministerio de Hacienda *or* el Tesoro *or* la Hacienda Pública; **the Treasury Benches** = los bancos azules *or* primera fila de escaños en la Cámara de los Comunes ocupada por los ministros del gobierno; **Treasury Bill** = bono *m* del tesoro *or* pagaré *m* del Tesoro; **treasury bonds** = bonos del tesoro (a largo plazo) de los EE UU; **Treasury counsel** = abogado, -da del Estado; **the Treasury Solicitor** = en Inglaterra, el abogado jefe del departamento jurídico del gobierno *or* Procurador General; *US* **Secretary to the Treasury** *or* **Treasury Secretary** = Secretario *or* Ministro de Hacienda

> COMMENT: in most countries, the government's finances are the responsibility of the Ministry of Finance, headed by the Finance Minister. In the UK, the Treasury is headed by the Chancellor of the Exchequer

treatment ['triːtmənt] *noun* trato *m;* **special treatment** = trato preferente

treaty ['triːti] *noun* **(a)** *(agreement between countries)* tratado *m;* **commercial treaty** = tratado comercial; **cultural treaty** = tratado cultural; **Treaty of Accession** = Tratado de Adhesión a la UE; **Treaty of Rome (EU)** = Tratado de Roma (UE) **(b)** *(agreement between individuals)* acuerdo *m;* **to sell (a house) by private treaty** = vender (una casa) por acuerdo privado

treble [trebl] *verb* triplicar; **the company's borrowings have trebled** = los préstamos de la empresa se han triplicado

trend [trend] *noun* tendencia *f;* **there is a trend away from old-style policing methods** = hay una tendencia en contra de los métodos de supervisión tradicionales; **a downward trend in investment** = una tendencia a la baja en las inversiones; **we notice a general trend to sell to the student market** = observamos una tendencia general a vender al mercado estudiantil; **the report points to upwards trends in reported crimes of violence** = según el informe, el número de delitos de violencia denunciados está en aumento; **economic trends** = tendencias económicas

trespass ['trespəs] **1** *noun* intrusión *f or* entrada *f* ilegal *or* transgresión *f or* violación *f* de la propiedad; **trespass to goods** = transgresión *or* usurpación *f* de bienes; **trespass to land** = entrada ilegal en la propiedad de alguien; **trespass to the person** = trangresión de los derechos de la persona **2** *verb* entrar ilegalmente en la propiedad de alguien
◊ **trespasser** ['trespəsə] *noun* intruso, -sa *or* infractor, -ra

> COMMENT: trespass on someone's property is not a criminal offence

triable ['traɪəbl] *adjective* (delito) que se puede enjuiciar *or* que puede ser objeto de enjuiciamiento; **offence triable either way** = delito que puede ser juzgado en el tribunal de magistrados *or* de la Corona

trial ['traɪəl] *noun* **(a)** *(court case)* juicio *m or* proceso *m or* procedimiento *m* penal; **fair trial** = juicio imparcial; **the trial lasted six days** = el proceso duró seis días; **the judge ordered a new trial when one of the jurors was found to be the accused's brother** = el juez ordenó la celebración de un nuevo juicio cuando se supo que uno de los miembros del jurado era el hermano del acusado; **he is on trial** *or* **is standing trial for embezzlement** = se le juzga por desfalco; **to commit someone for trial** = citar a alguien ante los tribunales; **trial judge** = juez encargado de un caso **(b)** *(test of a product)* prueba *f or* ensayo *m;* **on trial** = a prueba; *(court case)* procesado, -da; **the product is on trial in our laboratories** = el producto está siendo sometido a prueba en nuestros laboratorios; **trial period** = periodo *m* de prueba; **trial sample** = muestra *f* de prueba *or* de ensayo; **free trial** = prueba sin compromiso de compra *or* prueba gratuita **(c)** *(draft adding of debits and credits)* **trial balance** = balance *m* de comprobación

tribunal [traɪˈbjuːnl] *noun* tribunal *m or* juzgado *m;* **industrial tribunal** = Magistratura *f* de Trabajo *or* tribunal laboral; **Lands Tribunal** = tribunal que se ocupa de demandas de compensación o indemnización relacionadas con tierras; **military**

tribunal = tribunal militar; **rent tribunal** = tribunal que decide en disputas sobre alquileres y es capaz de fijar una renta justa; **to sit on a tribunal** = formar parte de un tribunal

trick [trɪk] **1** *noun* engaño *m or* estafa *f or* truco *m;* **confidence trick** = engaño o estafa basado en el abuso de confianza **2** *verb* engañar *or* embaucar a alguien para conseguir algo; **the gang tricked the bank manager into giving them the keys of the vault** = la banda embaucó al director del banco para sacarle las llaves de la cámara acorazada; **they tricked the old lady out of £25,000** = timaron a la anciana 25.000 libras
◊ **trickster** [ˈtrɪkstə] *noun* **confidence trickster** = persona que estafa a otra con abuso de confianza *or* estafador, -ra

trier of fact [ˈtraɪə əv ˈfækt] *noun US* juez *m or* jueza *f or* miembro de un jurado que decide sobre los hechos

Trinity [ˈtrɪnɪti] *noun* una de las cuatro sesiones de los tribunales *or* uno de los cuatro trimestres del año jurídico
◊ **Trinity House** [ˈtrɪnɪti ˈhaʊs] *noun* estamento *m* que supervisa los faros y a los prácticos en algunas zonas de la costa británica

trip [trɪp] *noun* viaje *m;* **business trip** = viaje de negocios

triplicate [ˈtrɪplɪkət] *noun* triplicado *m;* **in triplicate** = por triplicado; **to print an invoice in triplicate** = hacer una factura por triplicado; **invoicing in triplicate** = facturación *f* por triplicado

trouble [ˈtrʌbl] *noun* problema *m or* dificultad *f;* **the police are expecting trouble at the football match** = la policía teme que haya problemas durante el partido de fútbol; **there was some trouble in the courtroom after the verdict was announced** = hubo algunos problemas en la sala de audiencias tras el anuncio del veredicto
◊ **troublemaker** [ˈtrʌblmeɪkə] *noun* alborotador, -ra *or* faccioso, -sa
◊ **troubleshooter** [ˈtrʌblʃuːtə] *noun (person whose job is to solve problems)* mediador, -ra

trough [trɒf] *noun (low point in economic cycle)* mínimo *m* de actividad económica *or* punto *m* más bajo

trove [trəʊv] *see* TREASURE

trover [ˈtrəʊvə] *noun* acción *f* de daños por ocupación indebida de una propiedad mueble

truce [truːs] *noun* tregua *f*

true [truː] *adjective* verdadero, -ra *or* exacto, -ta; **true bill** = veredicto *m* cierto; **true copy** = compulsa *f or* copia *f* fiel *or* exacta; **I certify that this is a true copy** = certifico que ésta es una copia fiel; **certified as a true copy** = compulsado, -da

truly [ˈtruːli] *adverb* **Yours truly** *or US* **Truly yours** = atentamente *or* le saluda atentamente

trust [trʌst] **1** *noun* **(a)** *(confidence)* confianza *f;* **we took his statement on trust** = nos fiamos de sus afirmaciones; **breach of trust** = abuso *m* de confianza *or* prevaricación *f;* **position of trust** = puesto *m or* cargo *m* de confianza; **constructive trust** = confianza personal *or* que nace del comportamiento de una persona; **implied trust** = confianza implícita (NOTE: no plural in this meaning) **(b)** *(passing something to someone to look after)* fideicomiso *m or* albaceazgo *m or* patronato *m;* **family trust** = fideicomiso familiar; **in trust** = en fideicomiso; **they set up a family trust for their grandchildren** = establecieron un albaceazgo familiar para sus nietos; **he left his property in trust for his grandchildren** = dejó sus bienes en fideicomiso para sus nietos; **trust for sale** = bienes *mpl or* propiedad *f* en depósito que el depositario o fideicomisario puede vender; *US* **trust company** = trust *m or* asociación *f* de empresas *or* fideicomiso; **trust deed** *or* **instrument** = contrato *m* de fideicomiso *or* acto *m* de constitución de un fideicomiso; **trust fund** = fondo *m* de fideicomiso *or* fondo fiduciario; **discretionary trust** = sociedad *f* general de inversiones; **investment trust** = sociedad de inversión; **unit trust** = sociedad inversora por obligaciones **(c)** *US* grupo pequeño de empresas que controla el abastecimiento de un producto; **trust territory** = territorio *m* bajo tutela *or* fideicomisado **2** *verb* **to trust someone with something** = encomendar *or* confiar algo a alguien; **can he be trusted with all that cash?** = ¿puede confiársele todo ese dinero?
◊ **trustee** [trʌˈstiː] *noun* fideicomisario, -ria *or* administrador, -ra de una empresa *or* agente *mf* fiduciario; **board of trustees** = patronato *m;* **the trustees of the pension fund** = los administradores del fondo de pensiones; **trustee in bankruptcy** = síndico *m* de una quiebra; **Public Trustee** = administrador público; **Trustee Savings Bank** = caja *f* de ahorros
◊ **trusteeship** [trʌˈstiːʃɪp] *noun* administración *f* fiduciaria *or* síndico *m*
◊ **trustworthy** [ˈtrʌstwɜːði] *adjective* digno, -na de confianza *or* de fiar *or* cumplidor, -ra *or* fiel; **the staff who deal with cash are completely trustworthy** = los empleados que se ocupan del dinero son de total confianza
◊ **trusty** [ˈtrʌsti] *noun (slang)* preso, -sa que goza de ciertos privilegios por su buena conducta

truth [truːθ] *noun* verdad *f;* **the court is trying to find out the truth about the payments** = el tribunal está tratando de averiguar la verdad sobre los pagos; **counsel for the defence said that the plaintiff was not telling the truth** = el abogado defensor dijo que el demandante no estaba diciendo la verdad; **witnesses have to swear to tell the truth** = los testigos tienen que jurar decir la verdad; *US*

Truth in Lending Act = Ley *f* de 1969 que obliga al prestamista a dar a conocer las condiciones del préstamo al prestatario

◊ **truthful** [ˈtruːθfʊl] *adjective* (declaración) veraz

try [traɪ] *verb* juzgar *or* procesar *or* someter a juicio; **he was tried for murder and sentenced to life imprisonment** = fue juzgado por asesinato y condenado a cadena perpetua; **the court is not competent to try the case** = el tribunal carece de competencia para juzgar el caso

TUC [ˈtiː ˈjuː ˈsiː] = TRADES UNION CONGRESS

turn [təːn] **1** *noun* (a) *(movement)* vuelta *f or* giro *m* (b) *(profit or commission)* ganancia *f or* comisión *f*; **jobber's turn** = ganancia del intermediario *or* corredor de Bolsa **2** *verb* girar *or* dar vueltas; **to turn Queen's evidence** *or* *US* **to turn state's evidence** = delatar a un cómplice para conseguir una condena más leve

◊ **turn down** [ˈtəːn ˈdaʊn] *verb (to refuse)* rechazar; **the court turned down his petition** = el tribunal rechazó su petición; **the bank turned down their request for a loan** = el banco rechazó su petición de préstamo; **the application for a licence was turned down** = la solicitud de licencia fue rechazada

◊ **turnkey operation** [ˈtəːnkiː ɒpəˈreɪʃn] *noun* operación *f* llaves en mano

◊ **turn over** [ˈtəːn ˈəʊvə] *verb (to have a certain amount of sales)* tener un volumen de ventas de; **we turn over £2,000 a week** = tenemos un volumen de ventas de 2.000 libras a la semana

◊ **turnover** [ˈtəːnəʊvə] *noun* (a) *GB (amount of sales)* volumen *m* de ventas *or* de negocios *or* facturación *f*; **the company's turnover has increased by 23.5%** = el volumen de ventas de la empresa ha aumentado en un 23,5%; **we based our calculations on last year's turnover** = basamos nuestros cálculos en el volumen de ventas del año pasado (b) *(changes in staff)* **staff turnover** *or* **turnover of staff** = cambio *m* de plantilla *or* rotación *f* de personal (c) *US (number of times something is sold in a period)* porcentaje *m* de venta anual

turncoat [ˈtəːnkəʊt] *noun* tránsfuga *mf*

twin [twɪn] *verb* hermanar; **to twin a town with another town** = hermanar una ciudad con otra similar de un país distinto; **the town is twinned with Richmond** = la ciudad está hermanada con Richmond

◊ **twinning** [ˈtwɪnɪŋ] *noun* hermanamiento *m* (entre ciudades de distintos países); **the district council's town-twinning committee** = comisión *f* del ayuntamiento que organiza el hermanamiento de dos ciudades

two-party system [ˈtuːˈpɑːti ˈsɪstəm] *noun* sistema *m* de dos partidos

type [taɪp] **1** *noun* (a) *(sort)* tipo *m or* clase *f*; **a new type of drug** = un nuevo tipo de droga; **several types of murder** = varias clases de asesinato (b) *(print)* carácter *m* **2** *verb* mecanografiar *or* escribir a máquina; **he can type quite fast** = sabe escribir a máquina a mucha velocidad; **all his reports are typed on his typewriter** = todos sus informes están mecanografiados en su máquina de escribir

◊ **typeface** [ˈtaɪpfeɪs] *noun* carácter *m* de imprenta

tyrant [ˈtaɪrənt] *noun* déspota *mf or* tirano, -na

Uu

uberrimae fidei [u:'berɪmi: 'faɪdeɪ] *Latin phrase* 'de total buena fe'; **an insurance contract is uberrimae fidei** = un contrato de seguros es de total buena fe

UDI ['ju: 'di: 'aɪ] = UNILATERAL DECLARATION OF INDEPENDENCE

ulterior motive [ʌl'tɪərɪə 'məʊtɪv] *noun* segunda intención *f*

ultimate ['ʌltɪmət] *adjective* último, -ma *or* final; **ultimate consumer** = consumidor, -ra final; **ultimate owner** = dueño, -ña verdadero, -ra *or* final ◊ **ultimatum** [ʌltɪ'meɪtəm] *noun* ultimátum *m;* **the union officials argued among themselves over the best way to deal with the ultimatum from the management** = los cargos sindicales discutieron entre ellos sobre la mejor manera de hacer frente al ultimátum de la dirección (NOTE: plural is **ultimatums** or **ultimata**)

ultra vires ['ʌltrə 'vaɪri:z] *Latin phrase* 'más allá de los poderes'; **their action was ultra vires** = su acción fue antiestatutaria *or* se excedía de sus poderes legales *or* de su capacidad legal; *see* INTRA VIRES

umpire ['ʌmpaɪə] **1** *noun* árbitro *m* **2** *verb* arbitrar

UN *or* **UNO** ['ju: 'en *or* 'ju:nəʊ] = UNITED NATIONS ORGANIZATION

unable [ʌn'eɪbl] *adjective* incapaz; **to be unable to do something** = no poder hacer algo; **the court was unable to adjudicate because one side had not finished presenting its evidence** = el tribunal no tenía capacidad para pronunciar sentencia ya que una de las partes no había terminado de presentar sus pruebas

unanimous [ju:'nænɪməs] *adjective* unánime; **there was a unanimous vote against the proposal** = hubo un voto unánime contra la propuesta; **they reached unanimous agreement** = alcanzaron *or* llegaron a un acuerdo unánime; **unanimous verdict** = veredicto *m* unánime; **the jury reached a unanimous verdict of not guilty** = el jurado pronunció un veredicto unánime de inocencia ◊ **unanimously** [ju:'nænɪməsli] *adverb* por unanimidad *or* unánimemente; **the proposals were adopted unanimously** = las propuestas fueron

adoptadas por unanimidad; **the Appeal Court decided unanimously in favour of the defendant** = el Tribunal de Apelación pronunció su sentencia a favor del acusado por unanimidad

unappealable [ʌnə'pi:ləbl] *adjective* inapelable *or* irrecurrible

unascertained [ʌnæsə'teɪnd] *adjective* sin identificar; **title to unascertained goods cannot pass to the buyer until the goods have been ascertained** = el comprador no puede obtener el título de propiedad de bienes hasta que no hayan sido identificados

unavoidable [ʌnə'vɔɪdəbl] *adjective* inevitable; **planes are subject to unavoidable delays** = los vuelos están sujetos a retrasos inevitables ◊ **unavoidably** [ʌnə'vɔɪdəbli] *adverb* inevitablemente; **the hearing was unavoidably delayed** = la vista se retrasó inevitablemente

unbecoming [ʌnbɪ'kʌmɪŋ] *adjective* impropio, -pia *or* indecoroso, -sa

unborn [ʌn'bɔːn] *adjective* nonato, -ta

unchallengeable [ʌn'tʃæləndʒəbl] *adjective* irrecusable

unchallenged [ʌn'tʃæləndʒd] *adjective* incontestado, -da *or* indisputable *or* (pruebas) no recusadas

unclean [ʌn'kli:n] *see* CLEAN HANDS

unconditional [ʌnkən'dɪʃnl] *adjective* incondicional *or* sin condiciones *or* terminante; **unconditional acceptance of the offer by the board** = aceptación *f* incondicional de la oferta por parte del Consejo de Administración; **on the plaintiff's application for summary judgment the master gave the defendant unconditional leave to defend** = ante la solicitud por parte del demandante de un juicio sumarísimo, el ayudante del juez dio al acusado permiso incondicional para defenderse; **the offer went unconditional last Thursday** = la oferta se hizo terminante *or* perdió su carácter condicional el pasado jueves ◊ **unconditionally** [ʌnkən'dɪʃnli] *adverb* incondicionalmente; **the offer was accepted unconditionally** = la oferta se aceptó incondicionalmente *or* sin condiciones

unconfirmed [ʌnkən'fəːmd] *adjective* sin confirmar *or* no confirmado, -da; **there are unconfirmed reports that our agent has been arrested** = hay noticias sin confirmar de que nuestro representante ha sido detenido

unconscious [ʌn'kɒnʃəs] *adjective* inconsciente

unconstitutional [ʌnkɒnstɪ'tjuːʃnl] *adjective* inconstitucional *or* anticonstitucional *or* antiestatutario, -ria; **the chairman ruled that the meeting was unconstitutional** = el presidente decidió que la reunión era inconstitucional; **the Appeal Court ruled that the action of the Attorney-General was unconstitutional** = el Tribunal de Apelación decidió que la acción del fiscal general era inconstitucional

uncontested [ʌnkən'testɪd] *adjective* incontestado, -da *or* sin oposición *or* indisputable; **an uncontested divorce case** = un caso de divorcio incontestado *or* no disputado; **an uncontested election** = elecciones *fpl* incontestadas *or* sin oposición *or* con una única candidatura

uncontrollable [ʌnkən'trəuləbl] *adjective* incontrolable; **uncontrollable inflation** = inflación *f* incontrolable; **he had an uncontrollable impulse to steal** = tenía impulsos incontrolables que le inducían al robo

uncrossed cheque ['ʌnkrɒst 'tʃek] *noun* cheque *m* sin cruzar *or* no cruzado

undefended [ʌndɪ'fendɪd] *adjective* (caso) sin defensa; **an undefended divorce case** = caso de divorcio sin defensa *or* de mutuo acuerdo

undeniable [ʌndɪ'naɪəbl] *adjective* incontestable

under ['ʌndə] *preposition* **(a)** *(below)* debajo de *or* por debajo de *or* menos de; **the interest rate is under 10%** = el tipo de interés está por debajo del 10%; **under 50% of reported crimes are solved** = el número de delitos denunciados que se resuelven está por debajo del 50% **(b)** *(according to)* según *or* conforme a *or* de conformidad con; **regulations under the Police Act** = normativa *f* conforme a la Ley Policial; **under the terms of the agreement, the goods should be delivered in October** = según los términos del acuerdo, la mercancía debe ser entregada en octubre; **he is acting under rule 23 of the union constitution** = actúa conforme a la regla 23 del estatuto del sindicato; **she does not qualify under section 2 of the 1979 Act** = según la sección 2ª de la ley de 1979, no reúne las condiciones necesarias; **a creditor seeking a receiving order under the Bankruptcy Act 1974** = un acreedor que solicita una orden de intervención judicial según la ley de quiebra de 1974 **(c)** *(subject to)* bajo; **under care** = bajo custodia; **under duress** = bajo coacción; **under oath** = bajo juramento;

under the influence of alcohol = bajo los efectos del alcohol

◊ **undercover agent** [ʌndəkʌvə 'eɪdʒənt] *noun* agente *mf* secreto

◊ **underestimate** **1** [ʌndə'estɪmət] *noun* infravaloración *f or* estimación *f* baja; **the figure of £50,000 in legal costs was a considerable underestimate** = la cifra de 50.000 libras por las costas legales fue una infravaloración considerable *or* fue calculada muy por lo bajo **2** [ʌndə'estɪmeɪt] *verb* subestimar *or* infravalorar *or* calcular por lo bajo; **they underestimated the effects of the sanctions on their sales** = subestimaron los efectos de las sanciones en las ventas; **he underestimated the amount of time needed to finish the work** = calculó por lo bajo el tiempo necesario para terminar el trabajo

◊ **undergo** [ʌndə'gəu] *verb* atravesar

◊ **underlease** ['ʌndəliːs] *noun* subarriendo *m or* subarrendamiento *m*

◊ **underlet** ['ʌndəlet] *verb* subarrendar *or* realquilar

◊ **undermentioned** [ʌndə'menʃnd] *adjective* mencionado, -da más abajo *or* citado, -da a continuación

◊ **undersheriff** ['ʌndəʃerɪf] *noun* GB subgobernador, -ra civil

◊ **undersigned** [ʌndə'saɪnd] *noun* el *or* la abajo firmante *mf or* quien esto suscribe; **we, the undersigned** = nosotros, los abajo firmantes (NOTE: can be singular or plural)

◊ **understand** [ʌndə'stænd] *verb* comprender *or* entender

◊ **understanding** [ʌndə'stændɪŋ] *noun* acuerdo *m* privado; **the two parties came to an understanding about the division of the estate** = las dos partes llegaron a un acuerdo sobre la partición de la propiedad; **on the understanding that** = a condición de que *or* con tal que *or* siempre que; **we accept the terms of the contract, on the understanding that it has to be ratified by the full board** = aceptamos los términos del contrato, a condición de que sea ratificado por el Consejo de Administración en pleno

◊ **undertake** [ʌndə'teɪk] *verb* prometer *or* emprender *or* encargarse de *or* comprometerse; **to undertake an investigation of the fraud** = emprender una investigación del fraude; **the members of the jury have undertaken not to read the newspapers** = los miembros del jurado han prometido no leer los periódicos; **he undertook to report to the probation office once a month** = prometió presentarse en la oficina de control de libertad condicional una vez al mes (NOTE: **undertaking - undertook - has undertaken**)

◊ **undertaking** [ʌndə'teɪkɪŋ] *noun* **(a)** *(company)* empresa *f*; **a commercial undertaking** = una empresa comercial **(b)** *(promise)* promesa *f or* compromiso *m* que hay que cumplir; **they have given us a written undertaking that they will not infringe our patent** = nos han dado promesa escrita de que no violarán nuestra patente; **the judge accepted the defendant's undertaking not to harass the plaintiff** = el juez aceptó la promesa del acusado de no acosar al demandante **(c)** *(task)* tarea *f*

◊ **undertenant** [ʌndə'tenənt] *noun* subarrendatario, -ria

◊ **underworld** ['ʌndəwɔːld] *noun* hampa *f or* gente *f* maleante; **the police has informers in the London underworld** = la policía tiene confidentes en el hampa londinense; **the indications are that it is an underworld killing** = todos los indicios apuntan a que se trata de una matanza del hampa *or* de un ajuste de cuentas

◊ **underwrite** [ʌndə'raɪt] *verb* **(a)** *(to accept responsibility for)* garantizar; **to underwrite a share issue** = asegurar *or* garantizar una emisión de acciones (comprometiéndose a adquirir las que no hayan sido vendidas); **the issue was underwritten by three underwriting companies** = la emisión fue garantizada por tres sociedades; **to underwrite an insurance policy** = garantizar una póliza de seguros **(b)** *(to agree to pay)* garantizar el pago; **the government has underwritten the development costs of the building** = el gobierno ha garantizado el pago de los costes de ampliación del edificio (NOTE: **underwriting - underwrote - has underwritten**)

◊ **underwriter** ['ʌndəraɪtə] *noun* suscriptor, -ra *or* asegurador, -ra; **Lloyd's underwriter** = asegurador de Lloyd *or* compañía aseguradora de riesgos marinos Lloyd; **marine underwriter** = asegurador marítimo *or* asegurador contra riesgos marítimos

undischarged bankrupt [ʌndɪs'tʃɑːdʒd 'bæŋkrʌpt] *noun* quebrado no rehabilitado

undisclosed [ʌndɪs'kləuzd] *adjective* sin revelar; **undisclosed principal** = mandante *mf* sin revelar *or* encubierto, -ta

COMMENT: the doctrine of the undisclosed principal means that the agent may be sued as well as the principal if his identity is discovered

undisputable [ʌndɪ'spjuːtəbl] *adjective* incontestable *or* incontrovertible

undivided [ʌndɪ'vaɪdɪd] *adjective* proindiviso, -sa

undue influence [ʌn'djuː 'ɪnfluəns] *noun* influencia *f or* intimidación *f* desmedida

unemployed [ʌnɪm'plɔɪd] *adjective & noun* en paro *or* parado, -da *or* desempleado, -da; **the unemployed** = los parados

◊ **unemployment** [ʌnɪm'plɔɪmənt] *noun* paro *m or* desempleo *m;* **the unemployment figures** *or* **the figures for unemployment are rising** = las cifras del desempleo están subiendo; **unemployment benefit** = subsidio *m* de paro *or* de desempleo; **seasonal unemployment** = paro *or* desempleo estacional

unenforceable [ʌnɪn'fɔːsəbl] *adjective* (contrato) que no se puede imponer *or* (derecho) que no se puede hacer respetar *or* cumplir *or* ejecutar

unequal [ʌn'iːkwəl] *adjective* desigual

unequivocal [ʌnɪ'kwɪvəkl] *adjective* inequívoco, -ca *or* claro, -ra

unfair [ʌn'feə] *adjective* injusto, -ta; **unfair competition** = competencia *f* desleal; **unfair contract term** = término injusto de un contrato; **unfair dismissal** = despido injusto *or* improcedente

◊ **unfairness** [ʌn'feənəs] *noun* ignominia *f*

COMMENT: an employee can complain of unfair dismissal to an industrial tribunal

unfit [ʌn'fɪt] *adjective;* **unfit to plead** = incapacitado, -da *or* no apto, -ta para ser procesado

unforgivable [ʌnfə'gɪvəbl] *adjective* inexcusable

unharmed [ʌn'hɑːmd] *adjective* ileso, -sa; **to come out unharmed** = salir ileso

unilateral [juːni'lætərl] *adjective* unilateral; **they took the unilateral decision to cancel the contract** = tomaron la decisión unilateral de anular el contrato

◊ **unilaterally** [juːni'lætərli] *adverb* unilateralmente; **they cancelled the contract unilaterally** = anularon el contrato unilateralmente

unincorporated association [ʌnɪn'kɔːpəreɪtɪd əsəusi'eɪʃn] *noun* asociación *f* no constituida como sociedad anónima *or* no inscrita en registro

uninsured [ʌnɪn'ʃuəd] *adjective* sin asegurar *or* no asegurado, -da *or* sin seguro; **the driver of the car was uninsured** = el conductor del vehículo no estaba asegurado

union ['juːniən] *noun* **(a)** *(federation)* unión *f or* confederación *f;* **European Union** = Unión Europea; **the States of the Union** = los Estados miembros de los EE UU; **State of the Union message** = discurso *m* anual del Presidente de los EE UU que resume la situación política del país **(b)** *(organization which represents workers)* sindicato *m;* **trade union** *or* **trades union** *or US* **labor union** = sindicato; **union agreement** = acuerdo *m* sindical; **union dues** *or* **union subscription** = cuota *f* de inscripción sindical; **union recognition** = reconocimiento *m* sindical *or* reconocimiento de un sindicato **(c)** *(agreement between several countries)* **customs union** = unión aduanera

◊ **unionist** ['juːniənɪst] *noun* sindicalista *mf*

◊ **unionized** ['juːniənaɪzd] *adjective* sindicado, -da

United Kingdom (UK) [juː'naɪtɪd 'kɪŋdəm] *noun* (el) Reino Unido; **he came to the UK to study** = vino a estudiar al Reino Unido; **does she**

have a UK passport? = ¿tiene pasaporte
británico?; is he a UK citizen? = ¿es ciudadano
británico?; *see also* BRITISH ISLES, GREAT
BRITAIN

◊ **United Nations** *or* **United Nations
Organization (UNO** *or* **UN)** [juːˈnaɪtɪd ˈneɪʃnz]
noun Organización *f* de las Naciones Unidas
(ONU); *see also* GENERAL ASSEMBLY,
SECURITY COUNCIL

◊ **United States of America (USA)** [juːˈnaɪtɪd
ˈsteɪts əv əˈmerɪkə] *noun* (los) Estados Unidos de
América (EE UU); **the United States Code** =
recopilación *f* de las leyes vigentes en los Estados
Unidos de América

> COMMENT: the federal government (based in
> Washington D.C.) is formed of a legislature
> (the Congress) with two chambers (the Senate
> and House of Representatives), an executive
> (the President) and a judiciary (the Supreme
> Court). Each of the fifty states making up the
> USA has its own legislature and executive (the
> Governor) as well as its own legal system and
> constitution

universal [juːniˈvɜːsəl] *adjective* universal;
universal franchise *or* **suffrage** = sufragio *m*
universal

unjust [ʌnˈdʒʌst] *adjective* injusto, -ta
◊ **unjustly** [ʌnˈdʒʌstli] *adverb* injustamente; **she
was unjustly accused of wasting police time** = se
le acusó injustamente de malgastar el tiempo de la
policía
◊ **unjustified** [ʌnˈdʒʌstɪfaɪd] *adjective* sin
fundamento *or* injustificado, -da

unlawful [ʌnˈlɔːfəl] *adjective* ilegal *or* ilegítimo,
-ma *or* ilícito, -ta *or* antijurídico, -ca; **unlawful
entry** = allanamiento *m* de morada; **unlawful
trespass on property** = violación *f* ilegal de una
propiedad; **unlawful sexual intercourse** = acto *m*
sexual ilegal; **unlawful assembly** = asociación *f*
ilegal
◊ **unlawfully** [ʌnˈlɔːfəli] *adverb* ilegalmente; **he
was charged with unlawfully carrying firearms**
= le acusaron de tenencia ilícita de armas de fuego

unlikely [ʌnˈlaɪkli] *adjective* inverosímil

unlimited [ʌnˈlɪmɪtɪd] *adjective* ilimitado, -da;
the bank offered him unlimited credit = el banco
le ofreció crédito ilimitado; **unlimited company** =
empresa *f* cuyos accionistas tienen responsabilidad
ilimitada; **unlimited liability** = responsabilidad *f*
ilimitada

unliquidated claim [ʌnˈlɪkwɪdeɪtɪd ˈkleɪm]
noun reclamación *f* pendiente de pago
◊ **unliquidated damages** [ʌnˈlɪkwɪdeɪtɪd
ˈdæmɪdʒɪz] *plural noun* daños *mpl* no determinados

> COMMENT: torts give rise to claims for
> unliquidated damages

unmarried [ʌnˈmærɪd] *adjective* soltero, -ra

unofficial [ʌnəˈfɪʃl] *adjective* extraoficial *or* no
oficial *or* oficioso, -sa; **unofficial strike** = huelga *f*
ilegal *or* no autorizada *or* no aprobada por los
sindicatos
◊ **unofficially** [ʌnəˈfɪʃli] *adverb*
extraoficialmente *or* oficiosamente; **the tax office
told the company, unofficially, that it would be
prosecuted** = la delegación de Hacienda le dijo
extraoficialmente a la compañía que sería
procesada

unopposed [ʌnəˈpəʊzd] *adjective* **(a)** *(motion)*
sin votos en contra; **the Bill had an unopposed
second reading in the House** = el proyecto de ley
pasó su segunda lectura en la Cámara, sin ningún
voto en contra **(b)** *(proceedings)* aprobado, -da

unpaid [ʌnˈpeɪd] *adjective* sin pagar *or* por pagar;
(person) no retribuido, -da

unparliamentary [ʌnpɑːləˈmentri] *adjective*
impropio, -pia de un parlamento; **unparliamentary
language** = lenguaje impropio de un parlamento

> COMMENT: various terms of abuse are
> considered unparliamentary, in particular
> words which suggest that an MP has not told
> the truth. In a recent exchange in the House of
> Commons, a Member called others 'clowns'
> and 'drunks'; the Deputy Speaker said: 'Order.
> That is unparliamentary language, and I must
> ask the hon. Member to withdraw'. Another
> recent example occurred when an MP said: 'if
> the hon. Member were honest, I suspect that
> he would have to do the same'. *Mr. Speaker:*
> 'Order. All hon. Members are honest.'

unprecedented [ʌnˈpresɪdəntɪd] *adjective* sin
precedentes; **in an unprecedented move, the
tribunal asked the witness to sing a song** = en una
maniobra sin precedentes, el tribunal pidió al
acusado que cantara una canción

unprejudiced [ʌnˈpredʒʊdɪst] *adjective* sin
prejuicio

unprofessional conduct [ʌnprəˈfeʃnl
ˈkɒndʌkt] *noun* conducta *f* impropia *or* contraria a la
ética profesional

unpunished [ʌnˈpʌnɪʃt] *adjective* impune

unquantifiable [ʌnkwɒntɪˈfaɪəbl] *adjective;*
(damage or loss) incalculable *or* sin cuantificar *or*
que no se pueden calcular

unreasonable [ʌnˈriːznəbl] *adjective;*
(behaviour) irracional *or* poco razonable;
unreasonable conduct = conducta *f* poco
razonable; **his answer to our letter consisted of a
number of unreasonable demands for money** =
respondió a nuestra carta con peticiones
exorbitantes de dinero
◊ **unreasonably** [ʌnˈriːznəbli] *adverb*
irracionalmente; **approval shall not unreasonably**

be withheld = la aprobación no será negada irracionalmente

unredeemed pledge [ʌnrɪ'diːmd 'pledʒ] *noun* prenda *f or* garantía *f* no rescatada *or* sin desempeñar

unregistered [ʌn'redʒɪstəd] *adjective; (land)* sin registrar *or* no registrado, -da

unreliable [ʌnrɪ'laɪəbl] *adjective* de poca confianza *or* poco seguro, -ra *or* que no es de fiar; **the prosecution tried to show that the driver's evidence was unreliable** = la acusación trató de demostrar que la declaración del conductor no era de fiar; **the defence called two witnesses and both were unreliable** = la defensa llamó a dos testigos y ninguno era de fiar

unreported [ʌnrɪ'pɔːtɪd] *adjective* **(a)** *(to the police)* sin denunciar; **there are thousands of unreported cases of theft** = hay miles de casos de robo sin denunciar **(b)** *(in the Law Reports)* que no constituyen precedentes jurídicos; **counsel referred the judge to a number of relevant unreported cases** = el abogado remitió al juez a una serie de casos relevantes que no constituían precedentes jurídicos

unsafe [ʌn'seɪf] *adjective* **(a)** *(dangerous)* peligroso, -sa *or* arriesgado, -da **(b)** *(judgement)* no firme *or* recurrible

unsecured [ʌnsɪ'kjuəd] *adjective* sin fianza; **unsecured creditor** = acreedor, -ra común *or* sin garantía; **unsecured debt** = deuda *f* no garantizada; **unsecured loan** = préstamo *m* sin garantía

unsolicited [ʌnsə'lɪsɪtɪd] *adjective* no solicitado, -da; **an unsolicited gift** = un regalo no solicitado; **unsolicited goods** = mercancía no solicitada; **unsolicited testimonial** = testimonio no solicitado

unsolved [ʌn'sɒlvd] *adjective; (crime)* sin resolver *or* pendiente

unsound [ʌn'saund] *adjective* **(a)** *(not sane)* perturbado, -da; **persons of unsound mind** = personas dementes *or* mentalmente inestables **(b)** *(opinion)* erróneo, -nea

unsuccessful [ʌnsək'sesfl] *adjective* sin éxito *or* infructuoso, -sa; **the police carried out an unsuccessful search for the suspect** = la policía llevó a cabo una búsqueda infructuosa del sospechoso

unsworn [ʌn'swɔːn] *adjective* no jurado, -da *or* sin juramento; **an unsworn statement** = una declaración no jurada *or* sin juramento

untrue [ʌn'truː] *adjective* falso, -sa; **he made an untrue statement in court** = realizó una declaración falsa en el juzgado

unwarranted [ʌn'wɒrəntɪd] *adjective* injustificado, -da

unwritten [ʌn'rɪtn] *adjective;* **unwritten agreement** = acuerdo *m* no escrito *or* acuerdo verbal; **unwritten law** = derecho *m* consuetudinario

update [ʌp'deɪt] *verb* poner al día

uphold [ʌp'həuld] *verb* confirmar *or* sostener *or* apoyar *or* mantener; **to uphold the law** = hacer respetar la ley; **to uphold a sentence** = confirmar una condena *or* ratificar una sentencia *or* rechazar una apelación; **the Appeal Court upheld the sentence** = el Tribunal de Apelación ratificó *or* confirmó la sentencia *or* rechazó la apelación (NOTE: **upholding - upheld**)

upper house ['ʌpə 'haus] *noun* cámara *f* superior de un parlamento bicameral; **after being passed by the legislative assembly, a bill goes to the upper house for further discussion** = un proyecto de ley pasa a la cámara superior para ser debatido una vez ha sido aprobado por la asamblea legislativa (NOTE: opposite is **lower**)

uprising ['ʌpraɪzɪŋ] *noun* alzamiento *m* (militar)

urgent ['əːdʒənt] *adjective* urgente
◊ **urgently** ['əːdʒəntli] *adverb* urgentemente *or* inmediatamente

urine ['juərɪn] *noun* orina *f*; **urine test** = análisis *m* de orina

usage ['juːzɪdʒ] *noun* **(a)** *(custom)* costumbre *f or* uso *m* **(b)** *(treatment)* trato *m or* tratamiento *m*; **rough treatment** = malos tratos

use 1 [juːs] *noun* **(a)** *(way in which something can be used)* uso *m*; **directions for use** = instrucciones *fpl* de uso; **to make use of something** = utilizar algo; **items for personal use** = artículos *mpl* de uso personal; **he has the use of a company car** = disfruta de un coche de la empresa **(b)** *(land held in trust)* usufructo *m or* disfrute *m*; **change of use** = cambio *m* de actividad; **land zoned for industrial use** = tierra *f* planificada para uso industrial **2** [juːz] *verb* emplear *or* utilizar *or* usar; **he used the courts to evict his tenants** = utilizaba los tribunales para desahuciar a sus inquilinos; **we use second-class mail for all our correspondence** = utilizamos la tarifa barata de correos para toda la correspondencia; **the office computer is being used all the time** = el ordenador de la oficina se utiliza continuamente; **they use temporary staff for most of their work** = emplean personal temporal para la mayor parte de su trabajo
◊ **usefulness** ['juːsfəlnəs] *noun* utilidad *f*
◊ **user** ['juːzə] *noun* usuario, -ria; **end user** = usuario final; **user's guide** *or* **handbook** = guía *f* del usuario; **registered user** = usuario con permiso oficial de una marca registrada
◊ **user-friendly** ['juːzə'frenli] *adjective* fácil de manejar *or* de fácil manejo *or* fácil para el usuario;

these programs are really user-friendly = estos programas son realmente fáciles de manejar

usher ['ʌʃə] *noun* ujier *mf or* portero, -ra de estrados *or* guardia *mf* de sala

usual ['juːzuəl] *adjective* normal *or* corriente *or* usual *or* habitual; **our usual terms** *or* **usual conditions are thirty days' credit** = nuestras condiciones normales consisten en un crédito de treinta días; **the usual practice is to have the contract signed by a director of the company** = lo normal es que el contrato sea firmado por un director de la empresa; **the usual hours of work** are from **9.30 to 5.30** = el horario normal de trabajo es de 9.30 a 5.30

usufruct ['juːzufrʌkt] *noun* usufructo *m*

usurp [juˈzɔːp] *verb* usurpar
◊ **usurpation** [juːzɔːˈpeɪʃn] *noun* usurpación *f*

usury ['juːʒri] *noun* usura *f*

utter ['ʌtə] *verb* **(a)** *(to say)* pronunciar *or* decir; **the prisoner did not utter a word when the sentence was read out** = el acusado no pronunció palabra alguna cuando se leyó la sentencia **(b)** *(to use forged documents)* poner en circulación documentación falsa; **forgery and uttering** = falsificación *f* y utilización *f* de documentación falsa

Vv

v. ['vɜːsəs] = VERSUS contra (NOTE: titles of cases are quoted as *Hills v. The Amalgamated Company Ltd; R. v. Smith*)

vacancy ['veɪkənsi] *noun* vacante *f or* puesto *m* vacante; **to fill a vacancy** = cubrir una vacante

vacant ['veɪkənt] *adjective* **(a)** *(not occupied)* desocupado, -da *or* disponible *or* libre *or* vacante; **vacant possession** = propiedad *f* desocupada *or* libre de inquilinos *or* de ocupación inmediata; **the house is for sale with vacant possession** = la casa está en venta y libre de inquilinos **(b)** *(in a newspaper)* **situations vacant** *or* **appointments vacant** = ofertas *fpl* de trabajo

vacantia [və'kæntiə] *see* BONA VACANTIA

vacate [və'keɪt] *verb* desocupar *or* evacuar; **to vacate the premises** = desalojar los locales
◊ **vacation** [və'keɪʃn] *noun* **(a)** *GB* periodo *m* en el que los tribunales se cierran *or* vacaciones *fpl* universitarias; **judicial vacation** = feria *f* judicial **(b)** *US (holiday)* vacaciones

vagrant ['veɪgrənt] *noun* vagabundo, -da *or* vago, -ga
◊ **vagrancy** ['veɪgrənsi] *noun* vagancia *f or* vagabundeo *m;* **he was charged with vagrancy** = le acusaron de ser un vagabundo *or* de ser un maleante

valid ['vælɪd] *adjective* **(a)** *(acceptable because true)* válido, -da; **that is not a valid argument** *or* **excuse** = ése no es un argumento válido *or* ésa no es una excusa válida **(b)** *(which can be used lawfully)* válido, -da *or* valedero, -ra *or* vigente *or* en regla; **the contract is not valid if it has not been witnessed** = el contrato no es válido si no ha sido firmado por un testigo; **ticket which is valid for three months** = billete valedero para tres meses; **he was carrying a valid passport** = llevaba un pasaporte vigente *or* en regla
◊ **validate** ['vælɪdeɪt] *verb* **(a)** *(to check if something is correct)* validar *or* convalidar *or* comprobar la validez de; **the document was validated by the bank** = la validez del documento fue comprobada por el banco **(b)** *(to make something valid)* validar *or* dar validez a; **the import documents have to be validated by the**

customs officials = los documentos de importación tienen que ser validados por los oficiales de aduana
◊ **validation** [vælɪ'deɪʃn] *noun* validación *f or* convalidación *f*
◊ **validity** [və'lɪdɪti] *noun* validez *f or* vigencia *f or* fuerza *f* legal; **period of validity** = periodo *m* de validez

valorem [və'lɔːrəm] *see* AD VALOREM

valuable ['væljʊbl] *adjective* valioso, -sa; **valuable consideration** = transmisión onerosa *or* título oneroso; **valuable property** *or* **valuables** = objetos *mpl* de valor
◊ **valuation** [vælju'eɪʃn] *noun* valoración *f or* estimación *f or* evaluación *f or* tasación *f;* **to ask for a valuation of a property before making an offer for it** = solicitar la valoración de una propiedad antes de hacer una oferta; **stock valuation** = valoración *or* tasación de existencias
◊ **value** ['væljuː] **1** *noun* valor *m;* **he imported goods to the value of £250** = importó mercancías por valor de 250 libras; **the fall in the value of the dollar** = la caída *or* la depreciación del dólar; **the valuer put the value of the stock at £25,000** = el tasador fijó el valor de las existencias en 25.000 libras; **asset value** = valor de activo; **book value** = valor contable *or* en los libros; **declared value** = valor declarado; **face value** *or* **nominal value** = valor nominal; **market value** = valor de mercado; **surrender value** = valor de rescate **2** *verb* valorar *or* tasar *or* apreciar; **goods valued at £250** = artículos valorados en £250; **he valued the stock at £25,000** = valoró las existencias en £25.000; **we are having the jewellery valued for insurance** = nos están tasando las joyas para el seguro; **valued policy** = póliza *f* marítima de seguros de valor prefijado
◊ **Value Added Tax (VAT)** ['væljuː 'ædɪd 'tæks] *noun* impuesto *m* sobre el valor añadido (IVA)
◊ **valuer** ['væljuə] *noun* tasador, -ra

van [væn] *noun* furgón *m;* **police van** = furgón policial

vandal ['vændəl] *noun* vándalo *m;* **vandals have pulled the telephones out of the call boxes** = unos vándalos han arrancado los teléfonos de las cabinas
◊ **vandalism** ['vændəlɪzm] *noun* vandalismo *m*

◊ **vandalize** ['vændəlaız] *verb* destruir *or* destrozar; **none of the call boxes work because they have all been vandalized** = no funciona ninguna de las cabinas telefónicas porque las han destrozado todas

vary ['veəri] *verb* variar *or* cambiar
◊ **variation** [veəri'eıʃn] *noun* variación *f;* **the petitioner asked for a variation in her maintenance order** = la demandante solicitó un cambio en su orden de manutención

VAT [væt] = VALUE ADDED TAX

vault [vɒlt] *noun* cámara *f* acorazada de un banco

VC ['vi: 'si:] = VICE CHANCELLOR

vendee [ven'di:] *noun* comprador, -ra

vendor [vendə] *noun* **(a)** *(person who sells)* vendedor, -ra; **the solicitor acting on behalf of the vendor** = el abogado que actúa en nombre del vendedor **(b) street vendor** = vendedor, -ra ambulante *or* buhonero, -ra

venue ['venju:] *noun (place where a meeting is to be held)* punto *m* de reunión *US* lugar donde un caso se puede llevar a juicio; **mistake in venue** = error *m* de jurisdicción

verbal ['və:bl] *adjective* verbal; **verbal agreement** = acuerdo *m* verbal; **to make a verbal agreement** = apalabrar; **verbal warning** = amonestación *f* verbal *or* de palabra
◊ **verbally** ['və:bli] *adverb* verbalmente; **they agreed to the terms verbally, and then started to draft the contract** = llegaron a un acuerdo verbal sobre las condiciones y seguidamente comenzaron a redactar el contrato
◊ **verbals** ['və:blz] *noun (informal)* palabras dirigidas a un policía por un sospechoso

verbatim [və:'beıtım] *adjective & adverb* palabra por palabra *or* literalmente *or* al pie de la letra; **a verbatim transcript of the trial** = una transcripción literal del juicio *or* una transcripción del juicio palabra por palabra

verdict ['və:dıkt] *noun* **(a)** *(jury)* veredicto *m or* fallo *m;* **to bring in** *or* **to return a verdict** = pronunciar un veredicto; **verdict of not guilty** *or* **not guilty verdict** = fallo absolutorio *or* veredicto absolutorio; **the jury brought in** *or* **returned a verdict of not guilty** = el jurado pronunció un fallo absolutorio; **to come to a verdict** *or* **to reach a verdict** = llegar a un veredicto; **the jury took two hours to reach their verdict** = el jurado tardó dos horas en llegar a un veredicto; **majority verdict** = veredicto por mayoría (al menos diez miembros del jurado) **(b)** *(coroner's court)* juicio *m or* veredicto; **the court returned a verdict of death by misadventure** = el tribunal pronunció un veredicto de muerte accidental; **open verdict** = veredicto de muerte por causa desconocida; **the court recorded an open verdict on the dead policeman** = el

tribunal dio un veredicto que no especificaba las circunstancias de la muerte del policía

verify ['verıfaı] *verb* verificar
◊ **verifiable** [verı'faıəbl] *adjective* comprobable
◊ **verification** [verıfı'keıʃn] *noun* verificación *f or* comprobación *f or* confirmación *f;* **the shipment was allowed into the country after verification of the documents by the customs** = se permitió la entrada del cargamento en el país después de que la aduana verificara los documentos

versa ['və:sə] *see* VICE VERSA

version ['və:ʃn] *noun* versión *f;* **she disputed the policeman's version of events** = puso en duda la versión de los hechos que dio el policía

versus ['və:səs] *preposition* contra (NOTE: usually abbreviated to **v.** as in **the case of** *Smith v. Williams*)

vest [vest] *verb* conceder *or* dar a *or* ceder a *or* recaer en; **the property was vested in the trustees** = los derechos sobre la propiedad fueron concedidos a los administradores (NOTE: you vest something **in** *or* **on** someone)
◊ **vested interest** ['vestid 'ıntrəst] *noun* **(a)** *(interest in a property)* interés *m* adquirido *or* intereses creados **(b)** *(special interest in keeping an existing state of affairs)* interés personal; **she has a vested interest in keeping the business working** = tiene un interés personal en hacer que el negocio siga funcionando
◊ **vested remainder** ['vestid rı'meındə] *noun* nuda propiedad *f* efectiva
◊ **vesting assent** ['vestıŋ ə'sent] *noun* sanción *f* que concede a un arrendatario la tierra que ocupa de por vida
◊ **vesting order** ['vestıŋ 'ɔ:də] *noun* orden *f* de transmisión de propiedad

vet [vet] *verb (to examine carefully)* someter a un examen riguroso *or* examinar rigurosamente *or* investigar; **all applications are vetted by the Home Office** = todas las solicitudes son rigurosamente inspeccionadas por el Ministerio del Interior; **positive vetting** = investigación *f* que da como resultado de la poca fiabilidad de una persona (NOTE: **vetting - vetted**)

veto ['vi:təu] **1** *noun* veto *m;* **the President has the power of veto over Bills passed by Congress** = el Presidente tiene derecho de veto sobre los proyectos de ley aprobados por el Congreso; **the UK used its veto in the Security Council** = el Reino Unido hizo uso de su veto en el Consejo de Seguridad **2** *verb* vetar *or* prohibir; **the resolution was vetoed by the president** = la resolución fue vetada por el presidente; **the council has vetoed all plans to hold protest marches in the centre of town** = el ayuntamiento ha prohibido (todos los planes encaminados a) hacer manifestaciones de protesta en el centro de la ciudad

COMMENT: in the United Nations Security Council, each of the five permanent members has a veto. In the USA, the President may veto a bill sent to him by Congress, provided he does so within ten days of receiving it. The bill then returns to Congress for further discussion, and the President's veto can be overridden by a two-thirds majority in both House of Representatives and Senate

vexatious [vek'seɪʃəs] *adjective* vejatorio, -ria *or* molesto, -ta; **vexatious action** *or* **litigation** = litigio *m or* pleito *vejatorio or juicio m* entablado para molestar al demandado; **vexatious litigant** = litigante *mf* oneroso *or* vejatorio

viable ['vaɪəbl] *adjective; (which can work in practice)* viable; *(not likely to make a profit)* **not commercially viable** = no viable comercialmente; **viable alternative** = alternativa *f* viable

vicarious [vɪ'keərɪəs] *adjective* indirecto, -ta; **vicarious performance** = ejecución *f* de un contrato de un modo indirecto; **vicarious liability** = responsabilidad *f* subsidiaria *or* indirecta

COMMENT: if the employee is on a frolic of his own, the employer may not be liable

◊ **vicariously** [vɪ'keərɪəsli] *adverb* indirectamente *or* por otro

vice- [vaɪs] *prefix* delegado, -da *or* suplente; **vice-chairman** = vicepresidente; **vice-chairwoman** = vicepresidenta; **vice-chairperson** = vicepresidente, -ta; **he is the vice-chairman of an industrial group** = es el vicepresidente de un grupo industrial; **she was appointed to the vice-chairmanship of the committee** = fue designada para que ocupara la vicepresidencia del comité
◊ **Vice Chancellor** ['vaɪs 'tʃɑːnsələ] *noun* Vicecanciller *mf or* GB magistrado presidente de la Chancery Division del Tribunal Superior; *(university)* rector, -ra de Universidad
◊ **Vice-President** ['vaɪs'prezɪdənt] *noun* US Vicepresidente, -ta

COMMENT: in the USA, the Vice-President is the president (i.e. the chairman) of the Senate. He also succeeds a president if the president dies in office (as Vice-President Johnson succeeded President Kennedy) or leaves

vice versa ['vaɪsə 'vɜːsə] *Latin phrase* 'posición contraria': viceversa; **the responsibilities of the employer towards the employee and vice versa** = las responsabilidades del contratante para con la persona contratada y viceversa

victim ['vɪktɪm] *noun* víctima *f;* **the victims** = los damnificados; **the mugger left his victim lying in the road** = el asaltante dejó a su víctima tirada en la carretera; **he was the victim of a con trick** = fue

víctima de una estafa; **the accident victims** *or* **victims of the accident were taken to hospital** = las víctimas del accidente fueron trasladadas al hospital

vide ['vɪdi] *Latin word* 'véase'

videlicet [vɪ'diːlɪset] *Latin word* 'es decir' (NOTE: usually abbreviated to **viz**)

view [vjuː] **1** *noun* opinión *f or* parecer *m;* **to take a view on something** = tener una opinión sobre algo; **to take the view that** = pensar que *or* tener la impresión de que; **the court takes the view that the defendant did not publish the defamation maliciously** = el tribunal es de la opinión que el acusado no publicó la difamación maliciosamente; **to take the long view** = planificar a largo plazo; **in view of** = en vista de; **in view of the age of the accused the magistrates gave him a suspended sentence** = en vista de la edad del acusado, los jueces le concedieron una remisión de condena **2** *verb* mirar *or* ver; **viewing the scene** = inspección *f* judicial de la escena del crimen
◊ **viewpoint** ['vjuːpɔɪnt] *noun* punto *m* de vista

villain ['vɪlən] *noun* GB *(informal)* ladrón, -ona *or* criminal *mf;* **the job of the policeman is to catch villains** = el trabajo de un policía consiste en detener criminales
◊ **villainy** ['vɪləni] *noun* villanía *f or* maldad *f*

violate ['vaɪəleɪt] *verb* violar *or* infringir *or* quebrantar; **the council has violated the planning regulations** = el ayuntamiento ha infringido las normas de planificación urbanística; **the action of the government violates the international treaty on commercial shipping** = la acción del gobierno quebranta el tratado internacional sobre transporte comercial
◊ **violation** [vaɪə'leɪʃn] *noun* infracción *f or* violación *f;* **the number of traffic violations has increased** = ha aumentado el número de infracciones de tráfico; **the court criticized the violations of the treaty on human rights** = el tribunal criticó las violaciones del tratado sobre los derechos humanos; **in violation of a rule** *or* **of a law** = quebrantando una norma *or* violando una ley; **the government has acted in violation of its agreement** = el gobierno ha actuado quebrantando el acuerdo

violent ['vaɪələnt] *adjective* violento, -ta *or* agresivo, -va; **a violent attack on the police** = un ataque violento a la policía; **the prisoner became violent** = el prisionero se mostró violento
◊ **violence** ['vaɪələns] *noun* violencia *f;* **robbery with violence** = robo *m* con violencia; **violence against the person** = violencia contra la persona
◊ **violently** ['vaɪələntli] *adverb* violentamente

virement ['vaɪəmənt] *noun* transferencia *f* de dinero de una cuenta a otra *or* de una sección del presupuesto a otra; **the council may use the**

virement procedure to transfer money from one area of expenditure to another = el consejo puede hacer transferencias de una sección del presupuesto a otra

vires ['vaɪriːz] *see* INTRA VIRES, ULTRA VIRES

virtute officii [vəˈtuːti ɒˈfɪsɪi] *Latin phrase* 'en virtud de su cargo'

vis major ['vɪs 'meɪdʒə] *Latin phrase* 'fuerza mayor'

visa ['viːzə] *noun* visado *m;* **you will need a visa before you go to the USA** = necesitarás un visado para poder entrar en los EE UU; **he filled in his visa application form** = rellenó el formulario de solicitud de visado; **entry visa** = visado de entrada; **multiple entry visa** = visado de entrada múltiple; **tourist visa** = visado turista; **transit visa** = visado de tránsito

visit ['vɪzɪt] **1** *noun* visita *f* **2** *verb* visitar
◊ **visiting hours** ['vɪzɪtɪŋ 'aʊəz] *noun* horas *fpl* de visita
◊ **visiting room** ['vɪzɪtɪŋ 'ruːm] *noun* locutorio *m* (de una cárcel)
◊ **visitor** ['vɪzɪtə] *noun* visitante *mf;* **prison visitor** = visitador, -ra de prisiones

viva voce ['vaɪvə 'vəʊtʃi] *Latin phrase* 'oral *or* de viva voz'

vivos ['vaɪvəʊs] *Latin word* 'los que viven'; **gift inter vivos** = donación *f* inter vivos

viz [viz *or* 'neɪmli] *see* VIDELICET

void [vɔɪd] **1** *adjective;* *(not legally valid)* nulo, -la *or* inválido, -da; **void marriage** = nulidad *f* matrimonial *or* matrimonio *m* nulo; **the contract was declared null and void** = el contrato fue declarado nulo y sin valor **2** *verb* **to void a contract** = anular *or* invalidar *or* rescindir un contrato
◊ **voidable** ['vɔɪdəbl] *adjective* rescindible *or* anulable

> COMMENT: a contract is void where it never had legal effect, but is voidable if it is apparently of legal effect and remains of legal effect until one or both parties take steps to rescind it

volenti non fit injuria [vəˈlenti nɒn fit ɪnˈdʒʊərɪə] *Latin phrase* 'si hay voluntad no existe injuria': norma según la cual si alguien accede a aceptar el riesgo de resultar herido no puede interponer una demanda por ello (como por ejemplo puede ocurrir en el boxeo)

volume ['vɒləntri] *noun* volumen *m* *or* tomo *m;* **Volume 13 of the Law Reports** = volumen 13 de la Compilación de Decisiones Judiciales *or* de la Jurisprudencia; **look in the 1985 volume of the regulations** = mira el tomo del reglamento correspondiente al año 1985

voluntary ['vɒləntri] *adjective* **(a)** *(done without being forced)* voluntario, -ria *or* espontáneo, -nea; **voluntary confession** = confesión *f* voluntaria; **voluntary disposition** = traspaso *m* de propiedad voluntario *or* donación *f* voluntaria; **voluntary liquidation** *or* **winding up** = liquidación *f* *or* disolución *f* voluntaria **(b)** *(where a worker asks to be made redundant)* **voluntary redundancy** = baja incentivada *or* baja voluntaria con derecho a indemnización **(c)** *(done without being paid)* a título gratuito *or* voluntario, -ria; **voluntary organization** = organización *f* a título gratuito *or* organización voluntaria
◊ **voluntarily** ['vɒləntrli] *adverb* **(a)** *(without being forced)* voluntariamente; **he voluntarily gave himself up to the police** = se entregó a la policía voluntariamente **(b)** *(without being paid)* sin percibir sueldo

volunteer [vɒlənˈtɪə] **1** *noun* **(a)** *(person who gives property without consideration)* bienhechor, -ra *or* benefactor, -ra **(b)** *(person who receives property without consideration)* beneficiario, -ria **(c)** *(person who does something without being forced)* voluntario, -ria **2** *verb* **(a)** *(to offer information)* ofrecer *or* dar información; **he volunteered the information that the defendant was not in fact a British subject** = informó que el acusado no era en realidad un súbdito británico **(b)** *(to do something without being forced)* ofrecerse voluntariamente; **six men volunteered to go into the burning house** = seis hombres se ofrecieron para entrar en la casa en llamas *or* incendiada

vote [vəʊt] **1** *noun* voto *m* *or* votación *f;* **to take a vote on a proposal** *or* **to put a proposal to the vote** = someter una propuesta a votación; **block vote** = voto por delegación *or* representación; **casting vote** = voto de calidad; **the chairman has the casting vote** = el presidente tiene el voto de calidad; **he used his casting vote to block the motion** = utilizó su voto de calidad para bloquear la moción; **popular vote** = votación popular; **the president is elected by popular vote** = el presidente es elegido por votación popular; **postal vote** = voto por correo; **vote of censure** *or* **censure vote** *or* **vote of no confidence** = voto de censura *or* voto de castigo *or* voto de no confianza; **the chairman resigned after the vote of no confidence in him was passed by the AGM** = el presidente dimitió cuando la Junta General Anual emitió el voto de no confianza *or* el voto de castigo *or* tras ser aprobado el voto de castigo *or* de no confianza en él por la Junta General Anual; **vote of thanks** = voto de gracias *or* voto de agradecimiento **2** *verb* votar; **to vote by proxy** = delegar el voto; **the meeting voted to close the factory** = la junta votó a favor del cierre de la fábrica; **52% of the members voted for Mr Smith as chairman** = el 52% de los socios votaron al Sr. Smith como presidente; **to vote for a proposal** *or* **to vote against a proposal** = votar a favor de una propuesta *or* votar en contra de una propuesta; **two directors were voted off the board at the AGM** = en la Junta General Anual se votó a favor del cese de dos directores; **she was voted on to the committee** = fue elegida (por votación) miembro del comité

◊ **vote down** ['vəut 'daun] *verb* rechazar una moción; **the proposal was voted down** = se rechazó la propuesta

◊ **vote in** ['vəut 'ɪn] *verb* elegir a alguien; **the Tory candidate was voted in** = el candidato conservador resultó elegido

◊ **vote out** ['vəut 'aut] *verb* hacer perder a alguien; **the government was voted out of office within a year** = el gobierno perdió las elecciones al cabo de un año

◊ **voter** ['vəutə] *noun* votante *mf*

◊ **voting** ['vəutɪŋ] *noun* votación *f;* **voting paper** = papeleta *f;* **voting rights** = derecho *m* a voto; **non-voting shares** = acciones *fpl* sin derecho a voto

vouch for ['vautʃ 'fɔː] *verb* responder de *or* garantizar; **I cannot vouch for the correctness of the transcript of proceedings** = no puedo responder de la exactitud de la transcripción de las actas

voucher [vautʃə] *noun (paper given instead of money)* vale *m or* bono *m*

Ww

wager ['weɪdʒə] **1** *noun* apuesta *f or* cantidad apostada **2** *verb* apostar; **he wagered £100 on the result of the election** = apostó 100 libras sobre el resultado de las elecciones

> COMMENT: a wager will not normally be enforced by a court under English law

wait [weɪt] **1** *noun* espera *f* **2** *verb* esperar *or* esperarse
◊ **waiting** ['weɪtɪŋ] *noun* a la espera

waive [weɪv] *verb* renunciar *or* desistir *or* eximir *or* dispensar; **to waive one's right** = abdicar de un derecho; **he waived his claim to the estate** = renunció a su derecho a la herencia; **to waive a payment** = eximir de un pago
◊ **waiver** ['weɪvə] *noun* renuncia *f or* desistimiento *m;* **if you want to work without a permit, you will have to apply for a waiver** = si quiere trabajar sin permiso, tendrá que solicitar una excepción; **waiver clause** = cláusula *f* de renuncia; **waiver of jury** = renuncia al derecho de juicio con jurado; **waiver of notice** = renuncia de citación

Wales and Chester Circuit ['weɪlz ən 'tʃestə 'sɜːkɪt] *noun* distrito *m* de Gales y Chester: uno de los seis distritos *or* jurisdicciones del tribunal de la Corona al que pertenecen los abogados, con sede en Cardiff

walking possession ['wɔːkɪŋ prə'seʃn] *noun* posesión *f* temporal de los bienes de un deudor por parte de un agente judicial

wallet ['wɒlɪt] *noun* cartera *f or* billetero *m or* billetera *f*

war [wɔː] *noun* guerra *f;* **the two countries are at war** = los dos países están en guerra; **to declare war on a country** = declarar la guerra a un país; **civil war** = guerra civil; **prisoner of war** = prisionero, -ra de guerra; **war crimes** = crímenes *mpl* de guerra

ward [wɔːd] **1** *noun* **(a)** *(minor protected by a guardian)* pupilo, -la; **Mr Jones acting on behalf of his ward, Miss Smith** = el Sr. Jones actuando en representación de su pupila, la Srta. Smith **(b)** *(minor protected by a court)* menor *mf* tutelado; **ward of court** = menor bajo la protección de un Tribunal; **the High Court declared the girl ward** of court, to protect her from her uncle who wanted to take her out of the country = el Tribunal Superior tomó a la niña bajo su tutela, para protegerla de su tío que quería sacarla del país **(c)** *(territorial division)* división *f* de un municipio a efectos administrativos o electorales **2** *verb* guardar *or* proteger *or* tutelar; **the court warded the girl** = el tribunal tomó a la niña bajo su tutela
◊ **wardship** ['wɔːdʃɪp] *noun* tutela *f or* pupilaje *m;* **the judge has discretion to exercise the wardship jurisdiction** = el juez tiene poder para ejercer la jurisdicción de tutela

warden ['wɔːdən] *noun* **(a)** *US* director,-ra de prisión (NOTE: the British equivalent is **prison governor**) **(b)** *(guard)* vigilante *mf;* **traffic warden** = guardia *mf* de tráfico

warder ['wɔːdə] *noun* carcelero, -ra *or* funcionario, -ria de prisiones

warehouse ['weəhaus] **1** *noun* almacén *m;* **bonded warehouse** = depósito *m* de aduana **2** *verb* almacenar
◊ **warehousing** ['weəhauzɪŋ] *noun* almacenaje *m;* **warehousing costs are rising rapidly** = los costes de almacenaje están subiendo rápidamente; **warehousing in bond** = almacenaje en depósito aduanero

warn [wɔːn] *verb* advertir *or* prevenir de *or* avisar de *or* anunciar; **the judge warned the jury that the trial would be long and complicated** = el juez advirtió al jurado que el juicio sería largo y complicado; **the policeman warned the motorist not to exceed the speed limit** = el policía advirtió al conductor que no excediese el límite de velocidad; **he warned the shareholders that the dividend might be cut** = advirtió a los accionistas que los dividendos podían verse reducidos; **the government warned of possible import duties** = el gobierno advirtió que podrían aplicarse aranceles a la importación (NOTE: you warn someone **of** something, or **that** something may happen)
◊ **warning** ['wɔːnɪŋ] *noun* advertencia *f or* aviso *m;* **written** *or* **verbal warning** = amonestación *f* escrita *or* verbal; **to issue a warning about pickpockets** = advertir al público de la existencia de carteristas; **warning notices were put up around the construction site** = se colocaron

carteles *or* letreros de advertencia por toda la obra; **he received a warning from the magistrate that for the next offence he might be sent to prison** = recibió un apercibimiento del juez diciendo que si cometía otro delito podía ser encarcelado; **drivers paid no attention to the warning signs** = los conductores ignoraron las señales de peligro

warrant ['wɒrənt] **1** *noun (official document)* autorización *f* legal *or* orden *f or* auto *m or* mandamiento *m;* **bench warrant** = requisitoria *f* judicial *or* orden de arresto por incomparecencia; **death warrant** = orden de ejecución de la pena de muerte; **general warrant** *or* **warrant for arrest** = auto de detención; **search warrant** = orden de registro; **warrant of committal** *or* **committal warrant** = orden de ingreso en prisión *or* auto de prisión; **warrant of execution** = auto de ejecución de embargo; **warrant for the arrest of a wanted person** = requisitoria *f;* **to issue a warrant for the arrest of someone** *or* **to issue an arrest warrant for someone** = extender una orden de detención de alguien; **to serve a warrant** = ejecutar una orden de detención **2** *verb* garantizar; **all the spare parts are warranted** = todas las piezas de repuesto están garantizadas; **the car is warranted in perfect condition** = el coche tiene garantía de estar en perfectas condiciones
◊ **warrantee** [wɒrən'tiː] *noun* afianzado, -da *or* persona *f* que recibe una garantía
◊ **warrantor** [wɒrən'tɔː] *noun* fiador, -ra *or* garante *mf*
◊ **warranty** ['wɒrənti] *noun* **(a)** *(guarantee)* garantía *f;* **the car is sold with a twelve-month warranty** = el coche se vende con doce meses de garantía; **the warranty covers spare parts but not labour costs** = la garantía cubre las piezas de repuesto pero no la mano de obra **(b)** *(contractual term)* término *m* contractual secundario (a la finalidad principal del contrato); **breach of warranty** = violación *f* de una garantía tácita *or* expresa **(c)** *(statement)* reafirmación *f* de un asegurado sobre la veracidad de los hechos relatados por él *or* justificación *f or* condición *f* de seguro

wash sale ['wɒʃ 'seɪl] *noun* compraventa *f* de existencias

wastage ['weɪstɪdʒ] *noun* pérdidas *fpl;* **natural wastage** = amortización *f* de vacantes de una plantilla *or* reducción *f* natural de la mano de obra por jubilación o baja voluntaria

waste [weɪst] **1** *noun* pérdida *f* de valor de un terreno por deterioro *or* desgaste **2** *verb* desperdiciar *or* malgastar *or* echar a perder; **to waste time** = perder el tiempo; **he was accused of wasting the court's time** *or* **of wasting police time** = le acusaron de hacer perder el tiempo al tribunal *or* a la policía

watch [wɒtʃ] *noun* ronda *f or* vigilancia *f;* **watch committee** = comisión de vigilancia; **neighbourhood watch** = sistema *m* de protección ciudadana en el cual los vecinos ayudan a la policía mediante patrullas callejeras
◊ **watchdog body** ['wɒtʃdɒg 'bɒdi] *noun* cuerpo *m or* órgano *m* de vigilancia (en especial de departamentos gubernamentales *or* firmas comerciales para que no se transgredan las normas)
◊ **watchman** ['wɒtʃmən] *noun* vigilante *m;* **night watchman** = guarda de noche *or* vigilante nocturno

way [weɪ] *noun* **(a)** *(act of going)* paso *m;* **public way** = vía publica; **right of way** = servidumbre *f or* derecho *m* de paso (NOTE: no plural) **(b)** *(manner of doing)* modo *m or* manera *f;* **no way** = de ninguna manera; **Committee of Ways and Means** = comisión *f* parlamentaria de ley presupuestaria

weak [wiːk] *adjective* débil; **weak case** = caso *m* criminal con poco fundamento *or* con pruebas poco sólidas
◊ **weakening** ['wiːknɪŋ] *noun* debilitamiento *m*
◊ **weakness** ['wiːknəs] *noun* falta *f* de pruebas; **the hearing was abandoned because of the weakness of the prosecution case** = se suspendió la vista por falta de pruebas de la acusación *or* contra el acusado

wealth [welθ] *noun* caudal *m or* riqueza *f*

weapon ['wepn] *noun* arma *f;* **dangerous** *or* **offensive weapon** = arma *f* ofensiva *or* peligrosa; **carrying offensive weapons** = tenencia *f* ilícita de armas *or* estar en posesión de objetos contundentes; **deadly** *or* **murder weapon** = arma homicida

wear and tear ['weə ən 'teə] *noun (acceptable damage caused by normal use)* **fair wear and tear** = desgaste *m* natural *or* normal; **the insurance policy covers most damage but not fair wear and tear to the machine** = la póliza de seguros cubre la mayoría de los daños, pero no el desgaste natural de la máquina

Weekly Law Reports (WLR) ['wiːkli 'lɔː rɪ'pɔːts] *plural noun* compilación *f* de decisiones judiciales publicada semanalmente por el Council of Law Reporting *or* compilación semanal de informes de casos que constituyen precedentes jurídicos

weigh [weɪ] *verb* **to weigh evidence** = ponderar pruebas

welfare ['welfeə] *noun (looking after people)* bienestar *m or* asistencia *f* social; **it is the duty of the juvenile court to see to the welfare of children in care** = es obligación del tribunal de menores velar por el bienestar de los menores tutelados; **welfare state** = estado *m* de bienestar

Western Circuit ['westən 'sɜːkɪt] *noun* distrito *m* del Oeste: uno de los seis distritos *or*

jurisdicciones del Tribunal de lo Penal al que pertenecen los abogados, con sede en Bristol

Westminster ['wesmɪnstə] *noun* distrito *m* de Londres en el cual se encuentra la sede del Parlamento (NOTE: often used to mean Parliament in general: **the news was greeted with surprise at Westminster; MPs returned to Westminster after the summer recess; rumours are current in Westminster that the plan will be defeated**)

whatsoever [wɒtsəʊ'evə] *adjective; (affirmative)* cualquier; *(negative)* de ninguna clase *or* de ningún tipo; **there is no substance whatsoever in the report** = no hay solidez de ninguna clase en el informe; **the police found no suspicious documents whatsoever** = la policía no encontró documentos sospechosos de ninguna clase (NOTE: always used after a noun and after a negative)

where- [weə] *prefix* el cual *or* la cual (NOTE: the following words formed from **where-** are frequently used in legal documents)
◊ **whereabouts** ['weərəbaʊts] *noun* paradero *m*; **of unknown whereabouts** = ilocalizable *or* paradero desconocido
◊ **whereas** [weər'æz] *conjunction* considerando que *or* visto que; **whereas the property is held in trust for the appellant** = considerando que la propiedad se mantiene en fideicomiso *or* en depósito para el demandante; **whereas the contract between the two parties stipulated that either party may withdraw at six months' notice** = visto que el contrato entre las dos partes estipulaba que cualquiera de las dos partes puede retirarse con previo aviso de seis meses
◊ **whereas clause** [weər'æz 'klɔːz] *noun* considerando *m*
◊ **whereby** [weə'baɪ] *adverb* por el que *or* por la que *or* por medio del cual *or* por medio de la cual; **a deed whereby ownership of the property is transferred** = una escritura por medio de la que se traspasa la posesión de la propiedad
◊ **wherein** [weə'ɪn] *adverb* en donde *or* en que *or* en el cual *or* en la cual; **a document wherein the regulations are listed** = un documento en el que se enumeran las normas
◊ **whereof** [weə'ɒv] *adverb* del que *or* de la que *or* de lo que; **in witness whereof I sign my hand** = en fe de lo cual firmo
◊ **whereon** [weə'ɒn] *adverb* en el que *or* en la que; **land whereon a dwelling is constructed** = terreno en el que *or* finca en la que se construye una vivienda
◊ **wheresoever** [weəsəʊ'evə] *adverb* dondequiera que; **the insurance covering jewels wheresoever they may be kept** = el seguro que cubre las joyas dondequiera que se tengan guardadas
◊ **whereupon** [weərə'pɒn] *adverb* acto seguido

whip [wɪp] **1** *noun* **(a)** *(weapon)* látigo *m* **(b)** *(MP)* diputado, -da responsable de un grupo parlamentario que controla la asistencia de los diputados, pertenecientes a su partido, a la Cámara de los Comunes y se asegura de que todos los parlamentarios voten **(c)** *(instruction given to MPs)* instrucción *f or* llamada *f* que da un miembro del Parlamento al resto de los diputados de su grupo parlamentario; **three line whip** = instrucción *or* llamada para que los diputados acaten la disciplina de voto **2** *verb* azotar

White Book ['waɪt 'bʊk] *noun* libro *m* blanco *or* libro que contiene las normas de derecho procesal civil del Tribunal Supremo y un comentario sobre ellas
◊ **white collar crime** ['waɪt 'kɒlə 'kraɪm] *noun* delincuencia *f* de guante blanco *or* delitos económicos

Whitehall ['waɪthɔːl] *noun* calle *f* de Londres en la que se encuentran varios ministerios (NOTE: used to refer to the Government or more particularly to the civil service: **Whitehall sources suggest that the plan will be adopted; there is a great deal of resistance to the idea in Whitehall**)

White House ['waɪt 'haʊs] *noun* Casa Blanca (NOTE: also used to mean the President himself, or the US government: **White House officials disclaimed any knowledge of the letter; the White House press secretary has issued a statement**)

White Paper ['waɪt 'peɪpə] *noun GB (report from the government)* libro *m* blanco *or* informe *m* del gobierno sobre un asunto determinado

whole [həʊl] *adjective* entero, -ra *or* todo, -da; **of the whole blood** = carnal; **Committee of the Whole House** = Cámara *f* de los Comunes actuando como comisión para examinar las cláusulas de un proyecto de ley *US* **Committee of the Whole** = comisión *f* constituida por un mínimo de cien miembros de la Cámara de Representantes para debatir un proyecto de ley que ha sido debatido anteriormente

COMMENT: in both the House of Commons and House of Representatives, when the House becomes a Committee of the Whole the speaker leaves the chair and his place is taken by a chairman

whole-life insurance *or* **whole-life policy** ['həʊl'laɪf] *noun* seguro *m* corriente de vida

wholesale ['həʊlseɪl] **1** *noun* venta *f* al por mayor **2** *adjective;* **wholesale dealer** = mayorista *mf or* comerciante *mf* al por mayor **3** *adverb* **he buys wholesale and sells retail** = compra al por mayor y vende al por menor
◊ **wholesaler** ['həʊlseɪlə] *noun* mayorista *mf or* comerciante *mf* al por mayor

wholly-owned subsidiary ['həʊli'əʊnd sʌb'sɪdiəri] *noun* filial *f* en propiedad absoluta

whore [hɔː] *noun* prostituta *f or* ramera *f*

widow [ˈwɪdəʊ] *noun* viuda *f*
◊ **widower** [ˈwɪdəʊə] *noun* viudo *m*

wife [waɪf] *noun* mujer *f or* esposa *f*; **common-law wife** = esposa por convivencia; **deserted wife** = esposa abandonada

wilful *US* **willful** [ˈwɪlfʊl] *adjective* (persona) obstinada *or* (acto) deliberado *or* intencionado; **wilful misconduct** = conducta *f* malintencionada *or* negligencia malintencionada; **wilful murder** = asesinato *m* con premeditación; **wilful neglect** = negligencia *f* deliberada
◊ **wilfully** [ˈwɪlfəli] *adverb* intencionadamente; **he wilfully set fire to the building** = prendió fuego al edificio intencionadamente

will [wɪl] *noun* **(a)** *(legal document)* testamento *m*; *(formal)* **last will and testament** = última voluntad *f*; **to make** *or* **to write a will** = hacer testamento; **he wrote his will in 1964** = escribió *or* hizo testamento en 1964; **according to her will, all her property is left to her children** = según el testamento, todos los bienes pasan a sus hijos; **holograph will** = testamento ológrafo; **nuncupative will** = testamento abierto *or* última voluntad ante testigos, formalizada posteriormente; **sealed will** = testamento cerrado; *see also* BEQUEST, DEVISE, LEGACY **(b)** *(wishing or wanting to do something)* voluntad *f*; **tenancy at will** = arrendamiento *m* a voluntad; **against the will** = sin el consentimiento

> COMMENT: to make a valid will, a person must be of age and of sound mind; normally a will must be signed and witnessed in the presence of two witnesses who are not interested in the will. In English law there is complete freedom to dispose of one's property after death as one wishes. However, any dependant may apply for provision to be made out of the estate of a deceased under the Inheritance (Provision for Family and Dependants) Act

win [wɪn] *verb* ganar; **to win a case** = ganar un pleito

wind up [ˈwaind ˈʌp] *verb* **(a)** *(to end a meeting)* concluir *or* terminar *or* clausurar; **he wound up the meeting with a vote of thanks to the committee** = concluyó la reunión dando las gracias al comité **(b)** *(liquidation)* **to wind up a company** = liquidar una empresa; **the court ordered the company to be wound up** = el tribunal ordenó que se liquidara la empresa (NOTE: **winding - wound - has wound**)
◊ **winding up** [ˈwaindɪŋ ˈʌp] *noun* liquidación *f or* disolución *f*; **compulsory winding up order** = orden *f* de liquidación forzosa; **voluntary winding up** = liquidación voluntaria; **winding up petition** = solicitud *f* de liquidación judicial de una empresa

winner takes all [ˈwinə ˈteiks ˈɔːl] sistema de votación en el que el candidato con mayor número de votos gana; *see also* FIRST-PAST-THE-POST

wiretapping [ˈwaiətæpiŋ] *noun* escuchas *fpl* telefónicas

with costs [ˈwið ˈkɒsts] *adverb* con costas; **judgment for someone with costs** = sentencia *f* que obliga a pagar las costas del juicio a la parte culpable *or* que estima correcto el alegato de una de las partes y obliga a pagar las costas del juicio a la otra parte

withdraw [wiðˈdrɔː] *verb* **(a)** *(money)* retirar *or* sacar; **to withdraw money from the bank** *or* **from your account** = sacar dinero del banco *or* de la cuenta propia; **you can withdraw up to £50 from any bank on presentation of a banker's card** = se pueden sacar hasta 50 libras de cualquier banco sólo con presentar la tarjeta de crédito **(b)** *(an offer)* retirar una oferta; **one of the company's backers has withdrawn** = uno de los capitalistas de la sociedad ha retirado su apoyo; **to withdraw a takeover bid** = retirar una oferta de absorción **(c)** *(charge or accusation)* retirar un cargo *or* una acusación *or* retractarse; **to withdraw from a suit** = apartarse *or* desistir de una demanda; **the prosecution has withdrawn the charges against him** = la acusación ha retirado los cargos contra él; **the opposition MPs forced the minister to withdraw his statement** = los diputados de la oposición obligaron al ministro a retractarse de su declaración; **the chairman asked him to withdraw the remarks he had made about the finance director** = el presidente le pidió que retirara las observaciones que había hecho sobre el director financiero (NOTE: **withdrawing - withdrew - has withdrawn**)
◊ **withdrawal** [wiðˈdrɔːl] *noun* *(removing money from an account)* retirada *f or* retiro *m or* reintegro *m*; **withdrawal without penalty at seven days' notice** = retirada de fondos de una cuenta a plazo fijo sin recargo, siempre que se avise con siete días de antelación

withhold [wiθˈhəʊld] *verb* ocultar *or* negarse a dar información; **he was charged with withholding information from the police** = le acusaron de negarse a dar información a la policía *or* de negarse a colaborar con la policía; **approval of any loan will not be unreasonably withheld** = la concesión de cualquier préstamo no será negada irracionalmente

within [wiðˈin] *preposition* dentro de; **the case falls within the jurisdiction of the court** = el caso entra dentro de la jurisdicción del tribunal *or* es de la competencia del tribunal; **he was within his rights when he challenged the statement made by the police officer** = estaba en su derecho al poner en duda la declaración realizada por el oficial de policía

without [wɪˈðaʊt] *preposition* sin; **without interruption** = seguido, -da *or* sin interrupción; **without prejudice** = sin menoscabo *or* sin perjuicio; **without reserve** = sin fijación de precio mínimo

witness [ˈwɪtnəs] **1** *noun* **(a)** *(at the time when something happens)* testimonio *m or* testigo *mf*; **witness to a will** = testigo testamentario; **to act as a witness to a document** *or* **a signature** = actuar de testigo *or* como testigo en la veracidad de un documento *or* firma; **the contract has to be signed in the presence of two witnesses** = el contrato tiene que firmarse en presencia de *or* ante dos testigos; **in witness whereof** = en fe de lo cual **(b)** *(in court)* testigo; **attesting witness** = testigo instrumental; **defence witness** *or* **witness for the defence** = testigo de descargo *or* de la defensa; **friendly witness** = testigo favorable; **prosecution witness** *or* **witness for the prosecution** = testigo de cargo *or* de la acusación; **adverse witness** = testigo desfavorable *or* hostil; **expert** *or* **professional** *or* **skilled witness** = perito testigo *or* testigo pericial; **evidence of a witness** = prueba *f* testifical **2** *verb* firmar como testigo *or* atestiguar; **to witness an agreement** *or* **a signature** = firmar como testigo de un acuerdo *or* ser testigo de una firma; **'now this deed witnesseth'** = 'ahora que la escritura ha sido presenciada por testigos'
◊ **witness box** [ˈwɪtnəs bɒks] *noun* estrado *m* (de testigos)

WLR [ˈdʌblju: ˈel ˈɑ:] = WEEKLY LAW REPORTS

Woolsack [ˈwʊlsæk] *noun* asiento *m* del 'Lord Chancellor' en la Cámara de los Lores

woman [ˈwʊmən] *noun* mujer *f*; **married** *or* **unmarried woman** = mujer casada *or* soltera

word [wɜːd] **1** *noun* palabra *f*; **word processing** = tratamiento *m* de textos; **to give one's word** = prometer *or* dar la palabra; **he gave his word that the matter would remain confidential** = prometió que el asunto permanecería confidencial; **words of art** = términos *mpl* jurídicos de uso establecido **2** *verb* expresar *or* redactar; **the contract was incorrectly worded** = el contrato estaba mal redactado
◊ **wording** [ˈwɜːdɪŋ] *noun* términos *mpl or* texto *m*; **did you understand the wording of the contract?** = ¿entendiste los términos del contrato?

work [wɜːk] **1** *noun* trabajo *m* **2** trabajar
◊ **workaholic** [wɜːkəˈhɒlɪk] *adjective* adicto, -ta al trabajo

worker [ˈwɜːkə] *noun* trabajador, -ra *or* empleado, -da

◊ **works** [wɜːks] *noun (building)* obras *fpl*; **clerk of works** = funcionario encargado de supervisar obras

workshop [ˈwɜːkʃɒp] *noun* taller *m*
◊ **work-to-rule** [ˈwɜːktəˈruːl] *noun* paro técnico

worse [wɜːs] *adjective* peor; **to get worse** = empeorar(se); **to make worse** = empeorar

wound [wuːnd] **1** *noun* herida *f*; **she has a knife wound in her leg** = tiene una herida de arma blanca en la pierna **2** *verb* herir; **he was wounded in the fight** = resultó herido en la pelea; **she was fatally wounded** = le causaron heridas de muerte; **wounding with intent** = causar heridas graves con intención

WPC [ˈdʌblju: ˈpi: ˈsi:] = WOMAN POLICE CONSTABLE

wreck [rek] **1** *noun* **(a)** *(sinking)* naufragio *m or* restos *mpl* de un naufragio *or* de una colisión; **they saved the cargo from the wreck** = salvaron la carga del naufragio **(b)** *(ship)* barco *m* hundido *or* naufragado; **oil poured out of the wreck of the ship** = el petróleo salía a raudales de los restos del barco **(c)** *(company which has collapsed)* empresa *f* en ruinas *or* insolvente; **he managed to save some of his investment from the wreck of the company** = consiguió salvar de la ruina de la empresa algo de lo que había invertido; **investors lost thousands of pounds in the wreck of the investment company** = los inversores perdieron miles de libras en el hundimiento de la sociedad inversora **2** *verb (to damage badly)* naufragar *or* hundirse *or* fracasar; **they are trying to salvage the wrecked ship** = están tratando de salvar el barco naufragado; **the defence case was wrecked by the defendant's behaviour in court** = el argumento de la defensa quedó hecho trizas por el comportamiento del acusado ante el tribunal

writ [rɪt] *noun* **(a)** *(legal document)* auto *m* judicial; **writ (of summons)** = orden *f or* emplazamiento *m or* mandamiento *m* judicial; **writ of execution** = auto *m or* providencia *f* de ejecución; **the company issued a writ to prevent the trade union from going on strike** = la empresa presentó un mandamiento judicial para impedir que el sindicato fuera a la huelga; **he issued writs for libel in connection with allegations made in a Sunday newspaper** = presentó demandas por difamación en relación con declaraciones publicadas en un periódico dominical; **to serve someone with a writ** = notificar un mandato judicial a alguien; **writ of habeas corpus** = auto *m* de hábeas corpus **(b)** *(legal action)* acción *f* judicial para celebrar una elección parcial; **to move a writ** = proponer una elección parcial en la Cámara de los Comunes

writing [ˈraɪtɪŋ] *noun* **in writing** = por escrito

wrong [rɒŋ] **1** *adjective* **(a)** *(not right or not correct)* equivocado, -da *or* incorrecto, -ta *or* erróneo, -nea; **the total in the last column is wrong** = el total de la última columna es incorrecto; **the driver gave the wrong address to the policeman** = el conductor dio la dirección equivocada al policía; **I tried to phone you, but I got the wrong number** = intenté telefonearte, pero me equivoqué de número *or* llamé a un número equivocado **(b)** *(illegal)* ilegal; **copying computer data is wrong** = la copia de datos informáticos es ilegal **2** *noun* daño *m or* perjuicio *m or* acto ílicito civil; **civil wrongs against persons or property are called 'torts'** = los daños civiles contra las personas o contra la propiedad se denominan 'agravios'

◊ **wrongdoer** ['rɒŋduːə] *noun* delincuente *mf or* autor, -ra de un daño

◊ **wrongdoing** ['rɒŋduːɪŋ] *noun* infracción *f or* delito *m (NOTE: no plural)*

◊ **wrongful** ['rɒŋfʊl] *adjective* ilegal; **wrongful dismissal** = despido *m* injusto

COMMENT: an employee can complain of wrongful dismissal to the County Court

◊ **wrongfully** ['rɒŋfəli] *adverb* ilegalmente; **he claimed he was wrongfully dismissed** = reclamó que fue injustamente despedido; **she was accused of wrongfully holding her clients' money** = la acusaron de retener el dinero de sus clientes ilegalmente

◊ **wrongly** ['rɒŋli] *adverb* erróneamente *or* equivocadamente; **he wrongly invoiced Smith Ltd for £250, when he should have credited them with the same amount** = facturó erróneamente a Smith Ltd la cantidad de 250 libras, cuando debería haberle abonado esa misma cantidad

Xx Yy Zz

Yard [jɑːd] *noun* **Scotland yard** *or* **the Yard** = sede *f* de la policía metropolitana de Londres

year [jəː] *noun* año *m;* **calendar year** = año civil *or* ejercicio *m* financiero; **financial year** = año *or* ejercicio económico; *(twelve month period on which taxes are calculated: in the UK April 6th to April 5th of the following year)* **fiscal year** *or* **tax year** = año fiscal *or* ejercicio económico; **year end** = cierre *m* de ejercicio; **the accounts department has started work on the year-end accounts** = el departamento de contabilidad ha comenzado a trabajar en la contabilidad de cierre *or* en las cuentas de cierre del ejercicio; **year-end adjustment** = ajuste *m* por cierre de ejercicio
◊ **yearbook** [ˈjəːbʊk] *noun* anuario *m*

yellow dog contract [ˈjeləʊ ˈdɒg ˈkɒntrækt] *noun US* contrato *m* laboral en el que se prohíbe al trabajador sindicarse

yield [jiːld] **1** *noun* rendimiento *m or* rentabilidad *f or* producción *f* **2** *verb* devengar *or* dar *or* producir *or* rendir; **the bonds yield 8%** = las obligaciones devengan un interés del 8%

young offender *or US* **youthful offender** [ˈjʌŋ əˈfendə] *noun* delincuente *mf* juvenil; **Young Offender Institution** = reformatorio *m* de menores (NOTE: formerly these were called **Borstals**)
◊ **young person** [ˈjʌŋ ˈpəːsən] *noun* persona *f* joven *or* joven *mf* (mayor de catorce años y menor de diecisiete)

youth [juːθ] *noun* joven *mf;* **youth custody order** = orden *f* de ingreso de un joven en un centro de acogida para menores tutelados

zeal [ziːl] *noun* celo *m*
◊ **zealous** [ˈzeləs] *adjective* exceso *m* de celo

zebra crossing [zebrə ˈkrɒsɪŋ] *noun* paso *m* de cebra

zero [ˈzɪərəʊ] *noun* cero *m;* **the code for international calls is zero zero (00)** = el código para llamadas internacionales es cero cero; **zero inflation** = inflación *f* cero *or* nula
◊ **zero-rated** [ˈzɪərəʊˈreɪtɪd] *adjective; (with a VAT rate of 0%)* con un IVA de 0%
◊ **zero-rating** [ˈzɪərəʊˈreɪtɪŋ] *noun (rating of an item at 0%)* imposición *f* del 0% de IVA

zip code [ˈzɪp ˈkəʊd] *noun US* código *m* postal (NOTE: GB English is **post code**)

zipper clause [ˈzɪpə ˈklɔːz] *noun US* cláusula *f* estándar en un contrato laboral que impide cualquier discusión sobre las condiciones de trabajo durante la vigencia del contrato

zone [zəʊn] **1** *noun* distrito *m or* zona *f* **2** *verb (to divide land for planning purposes)* dividir en zonas; **the land is zoned for industrial use** = el terreno está asignado para la industria ligera
◊ **zoning** [ˈzəʊnɪŋ] *noun* ordenación *f or* planificación *f* urbana

SPECIALIST SPANISH DICTIONARIES

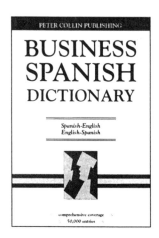

BUSINESS SPANISH DICTIONARY
SPANISH-ENGLISH/ENGLISH-SPANISH

The second edition of this respected dictionary. The dictionary is a fully bilingual edition that has been revised and updated to provide one of the most comprehensive and up-to-date dictionaries available. The dictionary includes accurate translation for over 50,000 terms that cover all aspects of business usage. Each entry includes example sentences, part of speech, grammar notes and comments.

ISBN 0-948549-90-4 hardback   680pages
ISBN 1-901659-23-2 paperback 680pages

BUSINESS GLOSSARY SERIES

A range of bilingual business glossaries that provide accurate translations for over 5,000 business terms. Each glossary is in a convenient paperback format with 196 pages.

Spanish-English/English-Spanish   ISBN 0-948549-54-8
Spanish-German/German-Spanish   ISBN 0-948549-98-X
Catalan-English/English-Catalan   ISBN 0-948549-57-2

For full details of all our English and bilingual titles, please request a catalogue or visit our web site.
tel: +44 181 943 3386 fax: +44 181 943 1673 email: info@pcp.co.uk
www.pcp.co.uk